The First-Time Trainer

*A Step-by-Step Quick Guide
for Managers, Supervisors,
and New Training Professionals*

Tom W. Goad

AMACOM

American Management Association

New York • Atlanta • Boston • Chicago • Kansas City • San Francisco
• Washington, D.C. • Brussels • Mexico City • Tokyo • Toronto

Library of Congress Cataloging-in-Publication Data

Goad, Tom W.
    The first-time trainer : a step-by-step quick guide for managers,
  supervisors, and new training professionals / Tom W. Goad.
        p.   cm.
    Includes bibliographical references and index.
    ISBN 0-8144-7942-1 (pbk.)
    1. Employees—Training of.   I. Title.
  HF5549.5.T7G535   1997
  658.3'124—dc21   97-3890
                                                                              CIP

Printing number

10   9   8   7   6   5   4   3   2   1

Table of Contents

List of Exhibits

A Word for the First-Time Trainer

Managers face challenges daily. One of the biggest is keeping employee skills updated. When skills are rendered obsolete with each new technological breakthrough—or the competition beats you to the punch—the challenge is magnified. This is true for both the profit sector and the nonprofit sector, large and small. The task of training employees is something facing more and more managers, professional people, and others in the workplace. It's often the only way to achieve desired results. Yet with tight budgets and flattened organizations, and especially small organizations with scarce resources, training is more easily talked about than done. So how do you get people trained? The easiest way is to turn them over to a competent, well-funded training department. But in the many organizations that do not have this option, training falls into the lap of managers or relatively inexperienced professional trainers.

When that happens, you have a critical job to do and perhaps little experience to call upon. Therefore, this book will serve as your guide. Every effort has been made to provide just the right amount of information and guidance—clearly and concisely, with no extra frills—to turn you into an effective trainer.

We all want to do our best, regardless of what the job is. Accordingly, this book represents best practice. It describes a process that has been boiled down to precisely what a manager or new trainer needs to know to get the job done: the eight steps to effective training.

Not every training session you may be called upon to deliver will require that all eight steps be used to their fullest; your task is relatively simple and straightforward for a short training presentation, for example. At the other extreme, some training can take months and large numbers of qualified persons to develop. Consider, for example, the training that must accompany a new multi-million-dollar military weapons system, or a new management information system installed for the first time in a company. The eight steps are summarized below and explained more fully at the end of Step One.

Eight Steps to Effective Training

Step One	**Facilitate learning**—The key to trainer success, which includes how to implement the other seven steps
Step Two	**Focus on performance**—Establishing the objective of the training and making sure you're on track—before you start
Step Three	**Focus on learning**—Making sure the training provides the maximum possibility for participant learning, with emphasis on how adults and organizations learn
Step Four	**Be prepared**—Developing the materials you'll need, bringing them together in the most effective order, and making sure everything is ready to go
Step Five	**Deliver effectively**—Learning the communication skills you'll need to present your training session successfully
Step Six	**Get learners involved**—Learning how to develop the best in all partiicpants and different ways to deliver the training
Step Seven	**Get feedback**—Developing ways to determine training success
Step Eight	**Improve continuously**—Keeping your trainer's portfolio up-to-date and strengthening your skills as a trainer

Numerous exhibits throughout the book facilitate your use of it. Many of them summarize ideas explained in detail in the text; you may find it helpful to scan through the exhibits to get a quick overview of the book or refresh your memory later.

Training is best approached as a system, so you'll notice some overlap between steps. For example, questioning techniques are applicable to both getting people involved (Step Six) and evaluation (Step Seven). You'll find cross-references to provide integration of the steps. A summary at the beginning of each step will help you quickly determine where you are, what is useful, and where to go next. You can come back and read the rest of the book another time, and you're encouraged to do so. Another approach you might want to take is to scan Steps One through Eight to get an idea of what functions and tools are available, and then use the eight steps as needed. Either way, read, enjoy—and prosper! And remember, common sense and good management skills will take you a long way as a trainer.

The First-Time Trainer

Introduction

Training and development is increasingly recognized as a most important organizational activity. The need for continuous training effort is constantly increasing.

—Robert Craig and Lester Bittel, eds.
Training and Development Handbook (1967)

Today, training has grown into one of the most critical success requirements in a highly competitive global marketplace. The reasons are clear. Increased emphasis on human resources effectiveness, including such concepts as human capital and human resources as an investment, is one. Worker skills must be continually updated. Diversity, workplace laws, skilled-worker shortages, rampant functional illiteracy, and intensive competition continue to influence, and often redefine, the way people work. When you add the fact that technology alone causes constant workplace change, the spotlight falls brighter than ever on the trainer. As more and more managers, team leaders, professionals, and others are finding out, there comes a time when we must all function as trainers. Customers demand it. Employees need it to survive. All the while, there's greater need for training.

Sometimes there's no formal training department, or the workload is too great even if there is one, or the requirement is so technical that the training department has no one who is qualified. The result is that many people are called upon to train. This ranges anywhere from a person who has never trained before to a professional trainer who finds his or her workload and levels of competence stretched by the increased demand and highly technical subject matter.

The Purpose of This Book

Since you are either new to training or have had little opportunity to train, you'll appreciate the singular purpose of this book: to serve as a simple, clearly stated set of proven guidelines to use when you conduct training. These are the functions you'll perform—no more or no less—to be a successful trainer. They're the same whether they're used for a once-in-a-lifetime performance or become something you'll need for the rest of your career. (It's more likely to be the latter, the way training is catching on.) The session you're called on to do may range across a wide spectrum of training—for example:

- Giving your boss a fifteen-minute overview and demonstration of a work project
- Offering a one-week training program that will allow your company to provide faster customer service
- Presenting a half-day session on implementing a new method of conducting performance appraisals
- Conducting a long-term program of converting your company from a traditional divisional organization with multiple layers to a matrix organization emphasizing a team approach to projects
- Appearing briefly on the agenda of a planning committee to explain how you're preparing to comply with new labor legislation
- Conducting a three-day workshop designed to bring in 200 people who have never worked together to form a team to implement a new government contract

These represent but a few of the possible combinations. A common situation for some managers is that they must deal with all the above. Whatever the nature of the training—from brief presentations to full-blown, formal training courses—the principles are the same. It's these principles that lead to success that are laid down in this book in the form of eight steps—the eight steps to effective training.

About Training

Let's look at the purpose of training in today's business organizations and why it has become so important.

The Purpose of Training

Training exists to facilitate the process of making organizations, and the people within them, more effective. For organizations to thrive, the function of training must be implemented to its fullest. Training must move and flow. It works best when it becomes an integral part of the organizational process, from strategic planning (e.g., including training as a fundamental part of ongoing organizational development) to reviewing the profit and loss statement (e.g., measuring training's effectiveness). Take the first example mentioned earlier of giving your boss a fifteen-minute overview and demonstration of a work project. Suppose the marketing team needs the input in order to start promoting the product, thus making the session, even if for but fifteen minutes, of utmost importance. (And sometimes you're lucky to get that much time, making it all the more critical to do a good job.)

Why Training Has Become So Important

Information and knowledge drive most businesses, and often training is the only way the information and knowledge, and attendant skills, can be provided. It has become clearer than ever that those organizations succeeding in today's marketplace will be the ones that help their employees perform to their fullest potential.

Tributes to the importance of training abound in the business news. Studies of successful organizations emphasize this fact by regularly showing how training has been key to companies' making it to the top in their industries. Its reason for being is to make people more effective, and therefore more valuable. The more knowledge and skills employees have, the more effective the company is. The relationship is direct and clear. Check your own information sources and the latest business news, and you'll realize that successful organizations most likely view training as an important part of the success equation. Some of the more important reasons for that include:

- *Technology that virtually upgrades itself.* The people who implement it must upgrade their skills to keep up with it. This is one of the greatest challenges facing everyone today, from the top to the bottom of organizations.
- *Organizations that have become so-called learning organizations.* That means that the people in them must use training as one method of continuing the learning process. Things move so fast that we must constantly be on the alert to learn how to keep up and, for the few, to stay ahead.
- *Team orientation.* Members of the work group must be cross-trained to perform one another's jobs. Teams have always been

around, but in the past decade or so, they have become wide-spread.

- *Participatory management.* More responsibility has been passed down the line to the worker.
- *Fewer workers to pass things down to because of massive downsizing.* Unfortunately, the work itself doesn't get downsized, just the people available to do it, which adds a further workplace load on the survivors. Downsizing turmoil continues as the process keeps rolling along.
- *Workplaces that have become more complex.* This isn't so true in fast-growing job areas like fast foods and service industries but is definitely so in professions offering the best rewards. All indications are that this situation will continue.
- *Government intervention in the workplace,* particularly with respect to far-reaching laws that have an impact on work and workers. This is true from the federal level down through the local community. Occasionally a law specifies that training be conducted.
- *Functional illiteracy and the need to train people in job basics, particularly entry-level ones.* Estimates are that one in five adults in the United States is functionally illiterate; they lack basic reading, writing, speaking, computing, or decision-making skills.

Many of these represent areas where you may be called upon as a trainer.

The training process can be highly formalized and long term, or quite informal and brief. The key is that learners come out of the process with new or stronger skills. Whereas the purpose of developing an organization is to make it more effective, the act of developing its people through training is to make individuals more effective in achieving organization goals.

Now let's find out more about the first step toward effective training: facilitation.

Step One

Facilitate Learning

Five principles of the learning organization:
1. *Everyone is a learner.*
2. *People learn from each other.*
3. *Learning enables change.*
4. *Learning is continuous.*
5. *Learning is an investment, not an expense.*

— Daniel Tobin, *Re-Educating the Corporation* (1993)

The trainer is a facilitator who assists an adult in acquiring the skills and knowledge required by the workplace. These skills may range from work rules a new employee needs to know, to how to operate a computer-aided design software system for an engineer, to how a manager can motivate employees to increase production in the wake of massive layoffs. One of the key growth areas has been for training to delve into such softer issues as motivation, interpersonal communication, self-esteem, achieving maximum potential, preventing sexual harassment, and managing stress. Clearly there is no limit to what topics may need to be covered at some time or another. The principles and techniques explained in this book work for all training needs and applications. See Exhibit 1-1 for a representative list of major training applications.

Filling the Gap

Training is the facilitation of learning. It focuses on identifying, ensuring, and helping to develop, through a carefully planned process,

Exhibit 1-1. Major Application Categories of Training

- **Executive development.** Includes leadership training, advanced executive degree programs, mentoring programs, rotating through various divisions of the organization, special assignments; deals with highest-level management leadership skills such as managing change and strategic decision making; aimed at corporate-level management.

- **Management development.** Includes strategic planning skills, leadership, networking with other managers, degree programs, management of change, time management, project management, coaching, goal setting, and mentoring.

- **Supervisory development.** Includes basic interpersonal communication skills, how to make decisions, how to give orders, coaching employees, setting objectives, time management, and other basic skills that newly promoted supervisors might need.

- **Professional development.** Covers a wide variety of training, such as interpersonal communication skills, stress management, computer literacy, and specific discipline-related skills (e.g., finance, purchasing, engineering, scientific, health care); a broad area of training covering both basic skills and refresher training.

- **Technical skills.** One of the largest growth areas in recent years. Training associated with getting work accomplished; includes computer skills, manufacturing processes, using particular systems and equipment, carrying out policies and procedures, and flight training; some overlap with professional development.

- **Literacy skills.** Includes the fundamental skills needed to be able to read, write, speak, compute, and make decisions at the entry level of jobs within an organization; process of making employees functionally literate, as well as training those already literate to move to higher levels.

- **Marketing and sales.** Ranges from training new sales representatives, to providing information on new products, to planning and resreach skills for marketing managers; involves the motivational aspects of marketing and interpersonal communication skills required.

- **Safety and health.** To ensure a safe, healthy workplace while reducing costs related to safety and health; increasingly includes aspects of job stress and wellness training for a healthier lifestyle; includes drug and substance abuse training.

- **Orientation.** For new employees to ensure they get off to a good start; formality varies from a few minutes to several weeks; ranges from basics about the workplace such as where the cafeteria is located, to a detailed indoctrination on the company's culture.

- **Organization development.** Training conducted in relation to interventions to manage organization change, such as total quality management programs, customer service, and team building.

the key competencies that enable individuals to perform jobs. Although our concern here is workplace learning, the concept extends to training in such areas as learning how to plant an organic garden or to throw a clay pot; how to do your own plumbing or plan your vacation; or how to be a Scout leader.

You might think that a trainer is a person who may fill a number of roles, but the number-one role is to facilitate learning. When you've completed a training session, you should expect that participants will have gained knowledge or acquired skills they didn't previously have. Think of it as the process of filling a gap—the difference between what participants know or can do and what they need to know or do—called *gap analysis* (see Step Two). The best way to ensure that this happens is to consider yourself the facilitator of the process. Sometimes, particularly if their jobs depend on it, participants will learn even if the process is improperly or ineffectively done (more on this in Step Three). If you think back to the teachers and trainers you've had, you'll likely agree that the best ones were those who allowed learning to take place, as opposed to those who considered themselves the experts and didn't let you forget it (and sometimes got in the way).

Step One Summary

This step, facilitation, provides the background needed to acquire skills. Since the primary role of a trainer is to facilitate learning, it is essential that every trainer approach any project from the perspective of helping learning to happen rather than attempting to force it. Key materials are:

- A more detailed definition of training
- Skills trainers need for success
- Diversity
- Continuous learning concept
- Newly emerging skills critical to today's workplace, providing the knowledge framework needed to successfully facilitate training
- Overview of the remaining seven steps and how to apply them

Skills Trainers Need

To be effective facilitators of learning, trainers must have a number of skills. They include, but certainly are not limited to:

- *Managerial ability.* The entire training process requires effective management to ensure success, especially within tight budgets. A trainer manages time (including the time of learners who are away from their jobs for training), resources, and funds, as well as staff members.
- *Communications skills.* A complete repertoire of these skills includes the ability to motivate and the use of electronic methods.
- *Analytical and problem-solving skills.* Analysis is an ongoing requirement.
- *Information literacy.* Workers need to find information and implement solutions to problems.
- *Computer literacy.* Because so much information is digitized, communications rely on automation and digital technology, and computers deliver more and more training for us.

Take a brief personal inventory of your own skills, and you'll likely see you're already in good shape for your new training role.

The Impact of Diversity

Diversity is one of the most commonly used words to describe today's workplace, and for good reason. Many companies are discovering that if they make the most of diversity and manage it to a purposeful end, productivity and effectiveness go up. It's a good return on investment. Diversity is more than cultural and racial. It has grown to encompass as well:

- People with disabilities
- People who speak different languages
- Women continuing to enter the workplace in large numbers
- Disadvantaged people
- Older people
- People who are functionally illiterate
- People of various sexual orientations
- People with various religious beliefs

Undoubtedly the list will grow longer as we become yet more diverse as a nation. Accordingly, your training approach needs to accommodate everyone. This is one of the exciting challenges of training, and there's plenty you can do to help deal with diversity. (This aspect of your training challenge is addressed in Step Five.)

Continuous Learning

Continuous learning is at the heart of the learning organization (see Step Three) and thus must be foremost in the mind of all managers and trainers. Like organizations, people must continually learn if they are to be successful and remain competitive. Technology, which seems to move at the speed of light, is a primary driver of the need to keep learning.

The explosion of information keeps us well supplied with material to learn from. What this means is that the trainer and manager need to create an environment of continuous learning. Formal training sessions are necessary. So are opportunities to learn and grow, such as taking classes outside work, learning by watching others, or providing an information base people can use to learn on their own. Purchasing built-in training with new software packages and communication systems is another example of how to ensure continuous learning. This is where the creative trainer can greatly enhance learning on the part of all people on the job.

Newly Emerging Skills

The skills needed for the future workplace are quite different, and probably more complex, than the ones that got us to this point in our organizational lives. These new skills are some of the most important ones trainers are involved with. Indeed, there are skills we'll need down the road that haven't even been identified yet! A key question emerges: "If we must continually learn, what skills must we acquire?" Fortunately, there's plenty of guidance here. These key skills are shown in Exhibit 1-2. It's not a long list, but each is vital.

Information Literacy

Much has already been said about the knowledge- or information-driven economy, which in turns means a knowledge-driven workplace.

Exhibit 1-2. Key Workplace Skills

- *Information literacy.* The ability to find, access, evaluate, and use information—possibly the most important skill in today's knowledge-driven workplace.
- *Interpersonal communiation skills.* Includes all aspects of how people communicate. This is often stated as good people skills and applies at all levels, particularly the management level.
- *Problem solving and decision making.* More and more people, at all levels, are being called on to solve problems and make decisions.
- *Creativity and innovation.* The ability to generate fresh ideas and new ways of doing things.
- *Computer literacy.* The ability to obtain information from a variety of sources.

Virtually everything we do involves acquiring and applying information in a knowledgeable way. First we have data, which the computer has given us in enormous quantities (often too much). Next we turn the data into information or glean the potentially useful information. From the information, we gain knowledge that allows us to be competitive and succeed on the job. This is where training comes in. From knowledge comes (we hope) the wisdom that sustains us, propelling us to succeed. Keep this thought in mind when developing and implementing training. For short-term operations, it may not mean much. But for the long haul, it can help keep us on track to develop meaningful long-term training and development for all workers— full-time employees, contract workers, part-timers, and all the others.

Information literacy has been defined as the ability to access, evaluate, and use information from a variety of sources. It sounds simple—but think for a moment about each segment of this sentence. To access information means you know how to get your hands on potentially relevant information, which in turn means you must know where to find it. Evaluating the mountains of information showered upon us can be an enormous task in itself. To use the information, once selected, is the mark of the truly successful manager and trainer. An information-literate person has the following characteristics:

- Recognizes the *need* for information before taking action.
- Recognizes that *accurate and complete* information is essential in order to make intelligent decisions.

- Formulates *questions,* based on information needs, that will lead to desired information.
- Develops successful, possibly diverse, *search strategies,* based on all potential sources.
- Accesses information *sources*—digitally based (e.g., computer, Internet, World Wide Web, individuals, data banks), analog, human, and other sources.
- *Evaluates* information to discern its relevance, setting aside anything that is irrelevant (which could easily be the bulk of it).
- *Organizes* information for practical application.
- *Integrates* new information into the existing body of knowledge (so that it fits in and potentially enhances it).
- *Applies* the information to critical thinking and problem solving (not hesitating to reenter the process at any step when the need arises).

Interpersonal Communication Skills

This skill set, which includes the full spectrum of how humans communicate with each other, has always been vital to workplace success, but if anything, it is more important today because of such practices as empowerment and working at home. The skills include:

- *The ability to read and comprehend,* sometimes as a rapid response to a particular work situation.
- *The ability to write.* This encompasses memos, e-mail messages that are well thought out yet written quickly, letters, reports, documents, and all those other communications, written and digital, that are common in the workplace. (This includes training materials, discussed in Step Four.)
- *Speaking* (addressed in depth in Step Five).
- *Listening.* This is an absolute necessity in the age of empowerment and team orientation.
- *Using nonverbal skills.* This means the ability to sense how you are perceived as a total person when communicating and being able to perceive someone else's total person and fully comprehend what he or she has to say.

There is a direct relationship between success and having good "people" skills. Yet another consideration, one we're still learning to deal with adequately, is how to accommodate the fact that many of the people we communicate with speak English as a second language, if at all. This is one of the challenges of diversity.

Problem Solving and Decision Making

One consequence of flattening in organizations is that more people than ever need good problem-solving and decision-making skills. The process is continually being pushed down to the lowest levels of the organization. If people are to become empowered in the workplace, they must have appropriate skills—that is, the ability to solve problems and make decisions. Managers want to hear solutions, not requests for advice on how to solve problems. Although it's a responsibility of managers to help develop others, the business environment today doesn't allow much time to pay a lot of attention to others.

Successful problem solvers have a proven problem-solving technique or model that they have mastered for solving challenges; many of these techniques contain most of the ones listed in Exhibit 1-3 (maybe all of them). The similarity of these actions to the eight steps to effective training isn't a coincidence.

Exhibit 1-3. A Problem-Solving Model

1. **Analysis.** Assess the problem to determine its causes (see Step Two for a detailed discussion of analysis).
2. **Solutions.** Identify alternatives to solve the problem.
3. **Selection.** Select one of the alternatives after weighing the pros and cons of how well the problem will be solved (prioritize and know there is no perfect solution).
4. **Action.** Implement the selected solution (which could require the ability to overcome procrastination).
5. **Evaluation.** Assess how well the solution is working and do not hesitate to make any needed corrections.

Creativity and Innovation

Successful companies have the ability to motivate employees to be creative and innovative. Risk taking and an environment where failure is okay are fundamental elements of creative organizations. A number of approaches have successfully been taken here, including mind mapping (placing the main topic in the center and branching off in different directions with subtopics), and thinking styles (thinking, using different, unconventional patterns), and special courses designed to take advantage of brain theories and strategies (e.g., left brain, right brain) have been developed. With carefully planned and executed training, people can learn on the job how to expand their creative horizons.

High-technology companies need creative employees if they are to stay on the cutting edge of competition—and so do all other organizations if they are to survive in the marketplace. Sometimes it is the person who can be creative in determining how to reduce the time that inventory stays on the shelf, for example, or figuring out how to take care of customer questions faster who can make the difference in the organization's success.

Computer Literacy

Computer literacy is more than knowing how to boot a computer and generate a document with a word processor application package. For instance, it now includes knowing at least the rudiments of an operating system such as Macintosh or Windows, or perhaps several systems. Some people find they must move between systems for a variety of reasons. Computer literacy assumes proficiency (even if one is a two-fingered typist) in word processing and means knowing the principles involved so that it isn't difficult to switch to a different word processor when the need arises. It could also mean knowing other applications such as spreadsheets, database management packages, and the company's customized software. (Games aren't on the list, although some people believe they should be.)

Proficiency in electronic mail, from local networks to worldwide ones, comes in here. Computer literacy has expanded to include the ability to use the Internet, intranets (exclusive organizational networks), and the World Wide Web as the world in general and companies in particular become more digital. This is where the concept of computer literacy takes on a broader dimension: that of being truly digital. Communication skills have reached into the digital world and all it brings with it, including telecommunications.

The Eight Steps

This book is built around eight simple, interrelated steps. Your particular need could be simply to prepare or deliver training, and nothing more. However, most training requires that some degree of attention be paid to all eight steps.

Step One: Facilitate Learning

Step One largely entails being able to integrate adult learning principles into training from start to finish. It means recognizing that people learn best if given the room to do so and are properly motivated. Training used to refer to an instructor standing before a captive audience while intoning the word according to the experts and expecting the audience to absorb every word. That has become a thing of the past. Step One also includes adeptness at implementing the other seven steps.

Step Two: Focus on Performance

Establishing training objectives and making sure you're on track *before starting* is essential for effective training. Front-end analysis—anything from looking at dwindling sales receipts to a full-scale analysis of major organization functions—must be conducted before objectives can be developed. Needs assessment helps identify performance deficiencies or perhaps areas where performance is adequate but improvement is desired. An understanding of the identified needs is used to develop precise, measurable objectives, which drive training.

These first two steps make the remainder of the process much easier, as well as provide a road map for success.

Step Three: Focus on Learning

This step serves the purpose of making sure that training maximizes participant learning. It emphasizes how adults and organizations learn. Two key concepts—core competency and mastery of the organization and its employees—set successful organizations apart, and the most successful of these have people who have mastered the core skills the organization needs to succeed. Both concepts must be factored into any training. In addition, we need to focus on new developments in learning and performance: the concept of the learning organization, learning how to learn, and new ways people learn and function, including multimodality (playing to all the senses and using as many ways to present the materials as possible, a concept you'll read more about in Step Three).

Step Four: Be Prepared

If you were ever a Scout, you know exactly what this means. It's what the Olympian does for months, possibly years, before the event. It's what the chief executive of a corporation does before standing in front of a room full of financial analysts to report the company's latest developments and chances for the future. It's also what trainers must do if training is to be highly successful. It involves developing the materials, bringing them together in the most effective order, and making sure everything is ready to go. This ranges from such simple things as making sure there's an electrical outlet for a projector, to creating a four-day workshop for two thousand people tuned in via satellite from around the world.

Step Five: Deliver Effectively

This is where communication skills used to present a training session come into play and where learning principles and knowledge of training technology are manifested. It also entails accommodating diversity. Group behavior is important to the trainer as well. How a group performs and interacts during training can make a difference in how successful the outcome is. Finally, the trainer must know how to deal with individual behavior, particularly when behavioral challenges arise in a classroom situation.

Step Six: Get Learners Involved

One of the keys to adult learning is to get the participants involved on their own terms. It includes knowing how to bring out the best in them, as well as using different ways to deliver training. Unless you have a background in group behavior and exposure to the specifics of how to do this successfully, you'll have to acquire the necessary skills. Fortunately, there are plenty of ways to get people intimately involved in learning. This is where the concept of multimodality can help you improve training.

Step Seven: Get Feedback

Only through feedback can we determine if the desired new performance has been achieved through training. This step works best when feedback is sought and applied throughout the process, not just when training is over. Feedback during the design and development phases contributes to a better end product.

Feedback is more than giving tests. There are many ways to determine training success by referring to the carefully developed objectives identified in Step Two.

Step Eight: Improve Continuously

Continuous learning applies to everyone in today's workforce, including trainers. In some ways, it applies even more because of the need for training to be relevant and up to date on the latest information on how people learn and perform on the job. This is the process of keeping your trainer's portfolio up-to-date and strengthening your skills as a trainer.

These are the eight steps that successful trainers have used to ply their trade for five decades, when training came into its own as a profession. (Actually, our ancestors used the same principles long before the word *training* came into being.) The key consideration is that they are proven steps; they will get the job done.

Using the Eight Steps for Various Situations

The examples shown in Exhibit 1-4 are based on two different possibilities—one from each end of the possible spectrum of requirements you may face. Extrapolate for situations that fall in between. The time available and the size of your budget will have a lot to say about how extensive each step along the way must be.

You'll soon find that each step includes one or more tools designed to help you quickly and professionally prepare and deliver training. But don't hesitate to use your own ideas; being creative and spontaneous can push good training over the top to become great training

Exhibit 1-4. How to Apply the Eight Steps to Training Situations

	Short Presentation	*Major Training Event*
Step One—Facilitate learning.	Brief review of eight steps to refresh the concept of facilitator and review the steps you'll be using.	Review the eight steps to lock in the concept of facilitator and ensure that you deal thoroughly with all eight.
Step Two—Focus on performance.	Take time to identify the objective of the session: to provide specific information to a well-defined audience.	This is an important step; training for an extended length of time, highly technical subject matter, or a large number of participants indicates a high level of need. There's a direct

relationship between the length of the session and having multiple learning objectives, so it is critical to have objectives to keep you on track. Front-end time here will save time later.

Step Three— Focus on learning.	Give some thought to ways you can get participants to relate the presentation to their own experiences.	Building adult and other learning theory into the training will contribute to ultimate success. Use the sixteen learning principles (see Exhibit 3-1) as a final checklist when the training is ready to be delivered. Think always of involvement and variety.
Step Four— Be prepared.	In a way, this is more important for a short session because there is no extra time to fall back and regroup. Never underestimate the need to be overprepared. Every second must be accounted for.	The nature of a longer session will dicate that you pay much attention to this step. Keep in mind the idea that variety will likely contribute positively to your training. You may find yourself using most, if not all, of the tools provided in this step. As a checklist, identify everything you think you may need before you begin.
Step Five— Deliver effectively.	This step is equally important regardless of the length of training. For shorter sessions, look through the guidelines in the step to determine which ones best fit your needs and the needs of your participants.	In a longer session, you will use more of the techniques. Of particular interest might be the use of a variety of methods while addressing the concept of multimodality. Here you'll have more opportunity to appeal to all learning styles. The length dictates that it be delivered effectively all the way through.

Exhibit 1-4 *(continued)*

	Short Presentation	*Major Training Event*
Step Six— Get learners involved.	There may be little chance to get participants involved in the session, although it's worth spending a little time to make sure that if there is a way, you use it. You can certainly get them mentally involved with a little forethought.	Fully exploit this step, because the end result will reflect positively for your having done so. In fact, the more time spent with participants, the more vital it is that they become involved. Just think how long you can sit still and listen to someone else speak, no matter how fascinating the person is. Completion of previous steps will pay dividends here.
Step Seven— Get feedback.	You want to get at least a word or two from participants on how things went. It may be possible to hand out a feedback form, but only if relevant. Certainly you can do a self-check.	It's essential to evaluate the training. Do self-assessment, and be sure to get feedback from participants and their managers. Only through feedback can you make improvements to training. Build evaluation into the training.
Step Eight— Improve continuously.	If this is the only training you'll ever conduct, you can ignore this step. However, if there's a chance you may do it again, try to improve the presentation or other pertinent skills.	Here is where you must practice what you preach to participants: to continually improve. There are plenty of ways, so pay attention to the advice and direction in this step. Continued professional development will be obvious to participants and contribute to your continued success as a trainer.

Step Two

Focus on Performance

The goal of this learning is improved performance, *never anything else.*

— Clay Carr, *Smart Training* (1992)

Effective training starts by determining what the needs are and— just as important—whether training is the answer. Many experienced trainers say unequivocally that you should never train without having first conducted needs analysis. This advice is sound, though the assessment might well be merely to confirm, for example, that the accidents occurring on the production line are the result of workers' not having been trained in the proper use of a new machine. As the situation becomes more complex, such as determining how to increase productivity in order to compete in a marketplace dominated by stiff international competition, needs analysis becomes key. Where major change is targeted and stakes are high, as when an organization is adopting a totally new approach to customer service or a quality improvement program, training needs assessment can make the difference between success and failure.

The front-end analysis preceding any important management action asks a number of important questions—for example: What are the issues? What are the problems? What is going wrong that needs fixing—or what needs to be done to keep things going well? After the assessment comes the process of determining exactly what action to take.

Some people have a knack for getting in the car, heading in the general direction they want to go, and arriving there a reasonable time later, all without a map and without a hitch. Most of us, however, need the map—and not just any map. It must be one that can get us where we want to be, with the least fuss and in the shortest time. In developing training, the way to be successful is to stay focused on performance, asking, What should the person be able to do when training is completed?

Step Two Summary

Needs assessment is one of two training tools we can use to lay out our training road map. The other is performance objectives. Both are successfully applied by managers every day to the critical things they have to do. Important management decisions of any kind are generally not made without assessing the situation and potential outcomes beforehand. Needs assessment determines where we want to go; learning objectives act as the road map showing how to get there. Included in this step are:

- Needs assessment tools
- Built-in analysis gauges
- Methods of gathering information
- Procedures for identifying learning objectives (with plenty of samples of how to develop good ones)

Needs Assessment

The needs assessment tools and examples you'll find here will likely be familiar to you because their principles are broadly applicable. One way to picture assessment is to use the analogy of paying a visit to your family physician. The doctor will ask you specific questions regarding your symptoms in order to determine what is the cause of the ailment and what can be done to provide relief and, ultimately, a cure. If your lifestyle is contributing to the problem or if the work you do is not conducive to your good health, the doctor may suggest you do something about it—perhaps take medication, begin therapy, undergo surgery, or change the way you eat. The trainer does the same thing: looking at the symptoms—for example, low productivity, lack of work skills, or unhappy customers—and assessing which problems and conditions training can help turn around.

Purpose of Needs Assessment

The purpose of needs assessment is to identify training needs. The ultimate goal is to be able to determine if employee performance, and thus organization performance, meets established standards.

A vital consideration is to ensure that the process sorts out the problems and concerns for which training offers a solution. Let's say a particular work crew has low productivity. Needs assessment may discover that the problem stems from a recent change in time-off policies that has affected several senior employees who stand to lose from it. In this situation, no amount of training will overcome the problem, unless it can be determined that an orientation session might pay off by helping to explain why the new policy was put into effect. Even so, the reason would have to be quite strong to have an impact on performance through training.

It's up to the trainer to do the detective work of uncovering the information needed to make a sound decision for improving performance through training. If someone has already done it, so much the better, but make sure you agree with the established need.

Bear in mind when conducting training needs analysis that you're not likely to have enough resources, time, and funding to solve all problems (let alone conduct an exhaustive assessment). This means you must become adept at prioritizing and identify situations where the most good—that is, the most effective improvement in overall performance—will be done. Realities of time and money have an impact on even the most well-staffed, dedicated, and successful training departments.

Here's a final important idea: Needs assessment is closely related to evaluation of training, the assessment done after the fact (Step Seven). When the analysis is done properly and thoroughly, it will be relatively easy to determine how well the training went: You compare what the training achieved to what you wanted it to achieve. This leads us to the next key concept of needs assessment.

Gap Analysis

If you've had the opportunity to ride the London Underground, chances are you've heard the message "Mind the gap" broadcast over the public address system just as the train pulls to a stop at the platform. It serves as a warning to boarding and leaving passengers that there's a gap between the platform and the deck of the car, so be careful. It's a message well worth heeding; a few train car models leave a gap large enough that a person's foot could get caught between car and platform.

This analogy serves well for what we want to achieve with training: We want to close the gap between current skills and desired skills. The gap may be easy to see; for example, giving word processing staff keyboard lessons will speed up data entry. It could be a larger divergence, such as that a major corporate employer must move from a local market to a global one. Needs assessment is the process by which we measure how wide the gap is, which tells us how much training is needed (and, indeed, if training can contribute to closing the gap). Exhibit 2-1 illustrates the gap analysis process and includes several examples.

Exhibit 2-1. Gap Analysis

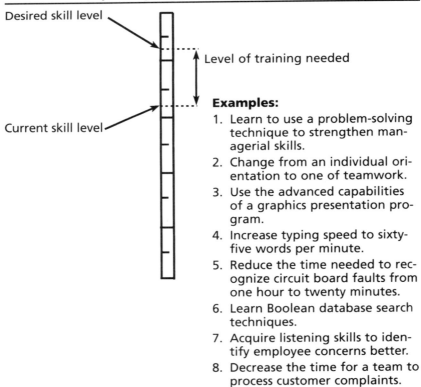

Desired skill level

Level of training needed

Current skill level

Examples:

1. Learn to use a problem-solving technique to strengthen managerial skills.
2. Change from an individual orientation to one of teamwork.
3. Use the advanced capabilities of a graphics presentation program.
4. Increase typing speed to sixty-five words per minute.
5. Reduce the time needed to recognize circuit board faults from one hour to twenty minutes.
6. Learn Boolean database search techniques.
7. Acquire listening skills to identify employee concerns better.
8. Decrease the time for a team to process customer complaints.

Four Ways to Keep Focused on Purpose

Determining training needs is a vital front-end process, and it takes time to accomplish. We must quickly get to the business of why training is needed in order to complete the front-end steps and get down to conducting the training. Staying focused on the issue at hand is crucial to effective and efficient needs analysis. Here are four important reminders for you to keep in front of you as you determine needs and verify the purpose of the training you are to conduct. They're summarized in Exhibit 2-2.

1. *Focus on problems that training can solve.* Everything else is a waste of your time, a problem for someone else to solve, or requires techniques and actions other than training. For example, if the circumstances point to conflicting policies within an organization that contribute to an identified business problem, training will not solve it, no matter how much is conducted. What's needed is a change of policy. If a breakdown in production stems from the fact that employees don't know the details of the policy, training might help—or perhaps merely restating the policy in clear terms and effectively communicating it might work. Another possibility is to develop a new policy and conduct a short training session to indoctrinate staff on how to implement it. The point to keep in mind is this: Training must be a prime candidate to resolve the issue under scrutiny.

Exhibit 2-2. Four Ways to Keep Focused on the Purpose of Training

1. ***Focus on problems that training can solve.*** There's nothing more frustrating than wasting time applying training to a lost cause. It also wastes two important commodities: time and money.

2. ***Focus on what is and what should be; then figure out how training can close the gap.*** Here you use a simple tool: gap analysis. This is nothing more than common sense—the sort of thing people do all the time to improve situations.

3. ***Focus on how to improve performance.*** This will keep you on track and help comply with the first two ways. This is what separates successful trainers from the pack.

4. ***Focus on simplicity.*** This is the stuff that keeps people out of trouble, holds costs down, makes bosses and folks receiving the training happy, and makes you, the trainer, successful.

2. *Focus on what is and what should be; then figure out how training can close the gap.* It's not enough to determine what the problem is—for example, that supervisors aren't doing a good job of listening to their subordinates. You must also determine such matters as how important listening is, how much attention you want the supervisors to pay to their workers, and so on. Your aim is to provide the amount of training—neither too much nor too little—that achieves the level of improvement and change desired.

   You might not be able to close the entire gap at once. In that case, implement a phased training approach, solving part of the problem and then taking another look. Let's say you are installing a completely new information system in your company. Trying to get employees up to speed on all aspects of it at once could easily be overwhelming to them.

3. *Focus on how to improve performance.* Performance is the name of the game. Needs assessment must determine whether you are challenged with making an improvement to solve a problem or, if there is no problem, then determine if productivity can be increased in order to meet competitive demands. Perhaps you need to do both. The point is that needs assessment must first establish the level of performance being achieved now and then define, as precisely as possible, how much improvement is to be made. We hear a lot about performance these days—performance management, pay for performance, team performance, and performance systems, to name a few—and for good reason. This is no mere buzzword or hot-ticket item. It's real and has a direct impact on the bottom line. Effective performance is what separates success from failure. In this era of corporate downsizing, this is particularly true when you have fewer people performing.

4. *Focus on simplicity.* When a problem is bearing down on an organization, taking time to conduct a needs assessment is a luxury that is *not* an option. This is true even if there's a generous budget. Simplicity provides the guiding light in the continuing challenge of balancing such factors as time and resources against needs assessment. Simplicity in this context means:

   - Making note of any problems that have turned up that you cannot solve through training and moving on to those that training can resolve.
   - Resisting the temptation to solve too many problems at once.
   - Determining if there's a reasonable training solution. In other words, don't try to take on a major training challenge

you know you won't get funding for, even if training is the obvious answer.
- Refraining from making the needs you identify fit predetermined solutions (e.g., training packages you've heard about from a colleague or read about in a professional journal).
- Reducing identified needs to their lowest common denominator (e.g., it isn't enough to determine that there's a drop in productivity; dig enough to find out why).
- Making sure that all needs you identify are clear to everyone who will need to deal with them.

Common sense and a solid grounding in problem-solving techniques—the sort of thing managers do every day—will stand the needs analyst in good stead (see Step One).

Organizational Factors Leading to Need for Training

Much of the detective work of trying to figure out whether training is needed can be met by taking a look at what is occurring within the organization. Some workplace issues and events automatically require that training be conducted (e.g., installation of a new computer system). Following are several common situations and events where training is often required: performance improvement, safety, promotions and advancement, new markets, new people, problems to solve, adding new technology, new laws, and organizational change. It's an extensive list, one that can assist you in anticipating future training needs.

- *Performance improvement.* There are many ways to determine if performance can be improved through training. One way to look at it is that there's always a need to improve, the question being whether training investment will yield an adequate return. Improved performance, as we know, keeps organizations competitive and ultimately successful, and it's what many of us must do to advance—possibly even to keep our job. But there are also indicators, both quantitative and qualitative, such as quarterly production figures and weekly sales reports. Common sense prevails here, since it's the manager's job to know if performance is where it should be.
- *Safety issues.* The best way to think of training for safety is in the positive sense: heading off problems before they occur by keeping a close eye on areas where safety is paramount and deter-

mining if the safety level is where it should be. For example, periodic safety review sessions might help keep workers alert to potential problems. The other side of this coin is to look at safety
numbers to determine if they're unacceptable. If the accident rate
for drivers is going up, a refresher training session might be in
order. There's a close correlation between safety and training, so
this is one area to review continually for possible training needs.

- *Promotions and advancement.* Executive succession planning is a
  serious organization concern. Also, where skills are in short supply, being ready to replace key workers may receive a lot of executive attention. One of the main things employees look for on
  the job is the ability to be upwardly mobile. Training is relevant
  to these situations. New responsibilities often require new skills
  that training can provide.

- *New markets and new lines of business.* Many companies are finding that they need to do more than enter new markets; they may
  have to undertake completely new lines of business. This is a fact
  of today's competitive marketplace and affects the nonprofit sector as well. Sometimes the solution is to redefine what the business is, such as from computers to information or trucking to
  transportation. Whatever the nature of the change, training may
  be essential for a number of reasons—for example, to learn about
  the new marketplace or product, prepare marketing staff on how
  to market in a new environment, or train production and service
  staff to produce and maintain the new product or service.

- *New employees.* Anytime new staff members come on board, there's
  need for training. They may need particular skills, or perhaps new
  supervisors must be trained to handle the expanded staff. Even if
  the new staff members have the desired skills (which could be the
  reason they were hired) they need orientation to your place of business. Most companies claim they conduct orientation training, but
  often this is little more than a brief session to show new staff where
  the coffee machine and rest rooms are located. Orientation is more;
  it means acquainting people with what your organization is all
  about—its mission, culture, and expectations, including performance expectations.

- *Problem solving.* Problem solving has made its way from the
  boardroom down to the lowest levels of organizations as downsizing, flattening, and empowering are put into place. Training is
  the best way to prepare people to deal with new problems and
  new challenges. If teams are involved, the need for training could
  be critical so the teams can function effectively. Firsthand experi-

ence is good, but made much better when put into a training context. In fact, problem-solving training—training people how to use tried-and-true problem-solving techniques—is a much-used and successful training application.

- *New technology, systems, or procedures.* Technology has a way of providing solutions to one set of problems (e.g., decreasing time spent in responding to customer queries), while creating new ones (e.g., causing people to scramble to learn how to use the new technology). A common tendency is to install new technology, different systems, or new procedures for getting work done but neglecting to train people how to use it to its best advantage. A simple rule to follow is this: When acquiring new technology, provide the training that people need to be able to use it in the most effective way. Sometimes this can be a simple matter of including a video training package with the purchase of a new piece of software or a few hours of training provided by the vendor. Similarly, when implementing new ways of doing things— whether converting to a team and customer-oriented workplace (a major change) or simply changing the way purchases are to be made—make sure the employees who will be affected by the change can properly use the new system or procedure—*before* it has to be used. More often than not, this means that training needs to be conducted. Front-end training costs will likely be less than lost productivity or effectiveness due to lack of skills.

- *New laws.* Anytime a new workplace-related law is enacted, it's not a bad idea to assume that you need to conduct training up front on how to comply with it—for example, by bringing in an expert to explain to everyone affected by it how to avoid problems. It may be necessary to weigh the cost of training against the potential cost of operating without knowledge of how to comply. Considering the amount of human resources, civil rights, safety, and other laws affecting the workplace, this is an area worth paying attention to.

- *Organization change.* This is closely related to the category of new technology, systems, and procedures. When a company seeks to change the way it goes about conducting its business, employees must be ready to conduct business in the new way immediately. Usually training is needed, possibly before the change takes place. The success of such massive organization changes as quality programs, customer service orientation, and implementing teams or other new organization forms is heavily dependent on training.

Types of Needs Assessment

There are a number of ways to conduct needs analysis. Using the same steps learned in engineering school or in a problem-solving or decision-making course will serve quite well. Common sense used in making important personal decisions will also work. Your intuition and experience may lead you quickly to what will work best for your situation. Commonly used types are task and skill analysis, focus groups, critical incidents, and performance reviews. (Exhibit 2-3 gives some examples of when to use these types of needs assessment.)

Task and Skill Analysis

This process is useful when a new system, such as converting a manufacturing process to a fully automated one, is being installed, and operator functions are now different, possibly even totally new. In this case, there would likely be no workers who can operate the new system. Task and skill analysis can also be used for processes such as planning or budgeting that can be broken down into discrete actions.

Exhibit 2-3. When to Use Selected Types of Needs Assessment

Type of Needs Assessment	Potential Applications
Task and skill analysis	Adding new technology (e.g., a new management information system) Creating new positions Redefining jobs Cross-training for teams
Focus groups	Solving organization problems Implementing new projects, contracts, or products
Critical incidents	Reviewing processes and activities for potential training needs Observing after changes have been made
Performance review	Checking performance Checking for training needs
Anticipating need for training	Reviewing processes and activities Monitoring for safety

To illustrate how to perform a task and skill analysis, consider a company that is upgrading its data-based management system to a customized version with considerably more capabilities than the old one. To perform the analysis, you will need to work with technical experts, including designers and programmers, on how to operate the new system. Instructional information, including manuals, online help, and job aids, will be a big help.

There are six steps to follow in conducting task and skills analysis:

1. *Identify a job(s) or process* (e.g., word processor operator, maintenance technician, planner).
2. *Break the job (or process) into its major tasks* (e.g., initializing the computer and word processing software package, typing and editing documents, file management, printing, and so on).
3. *Break each task into subtasks* (e.g., formatting with the word processor might include lines, pages, documents, and other capabilities and such steps as turning systems on and off, down to the step-by-step requirements for using the system).
4. *Identify all tasks and subtasks,* using appropriate terminology from the package and listing them on worksheets, with a separate one for each task, with subtasks listed.
5. *Identify skills required to perform each task and subtask* (e.g., typing, initializing the computer, initializing the word processing program).
6. *Determine which tasks and skills are subject to training* (e.g., if workers already know how to use the computer, it isn't necessary to provide training on initializing the system).

Exhibit 2-4 shows a sample breakdown for a task and skill analysis and illustrates a format that can be used.

This process is time-consuming and potentially expensive, so there must be a definite need to use it. When the need arises, though, it's a method that will ensure obtaining the desired results.

Focus Groups

Focus groups (also called task forces and tiger teams) have been used with great success to deal with a variety of situations.The scenario could be as exciting as taking on a major new project or solving a critical workplace problem. By calling together a small

Exhibit 2-4. Sample Task and Skill Analysis Worksheet

Job/Function: Word Processor_____ Analyst:_____ Date:_____

Task/Description	Steps	Equipment/Systems/ Resources
Formatting a document:	1. Margins 2. Line spacing 3. Font selection 4. Tabulation 5. Graphics 6. Columns 7. Headers/footers 8. Justification	PC Word processing application User's manual
Skills required:	• Touch typing • Windows operating program • Familiarity with icons and formatting commands • Adeptness at using mouse • Knowledge of business correspondence	

team of people who have the knowledge, skills, and motivation to resolve the issue, their ability to analyze and identify needs, and possibly solutions, pays dividends on the time spent together. The old saying about two heads being better than one is confirmed by focus groups.

For training needs analysis, there's no better way to determine precisely what the problem is and what might be done than by getting the right people together with the collective purpose of improving the situation. Identify people in the organization who are known for their analytical ability and include them. People from outside the organization who are affected, such as customers or suppliers, can join the group too. Outside expertise may be cost-effective, particularly if technology and complex systems are involved.

The process starts with the person who has called the group together describing the situation in a clearly defined problem statement and providing the available information. The group then focuses on the causes of the problem and, after deliberation, identifies potential solutions. A focus group's purpose can just as easily be to deal with proactive situations—maybe analyzing how to improve a situation, such as worker productivity, or implementing new processes and procedures for doing business, or simplifying processes and procedures. The ideal, we know, is to be so effective that serious problems never arise in the first place.

Brainstorming and consensus-building techniques may prove worthwhile for some problems, particularly complex ones.

Brainstorming is the process of having members of the group identify potential solutions without making judgments about them. It has been used extensively, and successfully, to identify workable ideas as well as solutions. Here is the process:

1. Identify the problem or issue at hand for which ideas and solutions are needed.
2. Ask each member of a group to quickly generate as many ideas or solutions as possible.
3. Record all ideas. Judgment is completely suspended.
4. Go through the list upon completion to select potentially useful items.

In *consensus building* a group of experts is assembled to go through a process that will result in consensus regarding a solution to a problem, action, or position to take on an issue or other appropriate topic that needs agreement. Here is the process:

1. Present a list of ideas or solutions (or have the group generate its own).
2. Discuss the pros and cons of each item.
3. Have members express their choices (e.g., by voting or applying predetermined weighting factors).
4. Review the results, eliminating items agreed on as not offering best practice.
5. Have members repeat their selection based on the resulting list, and generate the next version of the list.
6. Repeat the process until there is agreement on the solution.

Note that the group of experts does not need to be assembled in one place for this process.

Critical Incidents

Critical incidents—those that contribute, positively or negatively, toward achieving goals and objectives—provide a convenient and meaningful source of training analysis information. The principle is that specific events that occur on the job have a major impact on determining organization effectiveness. System breakdowns, urgent customer requests, and major milestones (such as a product delivery date or hitting too high a number of accidents) are examples of critical incidents.

Prior to implementing this method, identify critical incidents so they can be readily filtered from everyday incidents. Other incidents can be added at the time they happen. The incidents can be at departmental, team, process, or individual levels. Once this is done, the remaining steps are relatively easy to complete:

1. Establish the record-keeping guidelines and media where critical incidents are to be kept (e.g., work log, supervisor notes, online).
2. Assign responsibility for maintaining the records.
3. From time to time, analyze the records to determine which incidents detracted from organization effectiveness and which did not (or possibly which ones contributed positively, the reasons for their occurring, and what can be done to resolve the negative ones and what can be learned from the positive ones to improve performance.

At this point a focus group could take over.

Performance Reviews

Since the goal of training is to improve performance, reviewing the performance of individuals or a group is a potential method of needs analysis. The exact method of reviewing performance depends on the circumstances and objectives desired. For instance, reviewing the results of a department's annual performance appraisals and looking for shortfalls that could be resolved through training. Obviously pertinent information must be available, such as a record of productivity over a period of time or a log of customer complaints. The important point is to make sure the performance review looks at the desired improvement.

A highly desirable way to conduct performance reviews is to use the existing performance management and appraisal system, simply identifying needed training based on poor performance and areas where growth will lead to advancement. Several key points are worth keeping in mind when reviewing performance:

1. Use clear, agreed-on standards as the baseline.
2. Focus on desired performance.

3. Accurately note actual performance.
4. Determine the causes of the lack of desired performance levels.
5. Decide if training can facilitate achieving the desired performance.

Anticipating the Need for Training

The best way to avoid problems is to head them off. In other words, stop them before they start. A quick review of the factors leading to a need for training earlier in this step will make it evident that many of these factors, and maybe all of them, could be anticipated and dealt with before problems occur—for example:

1. Continually scan performance to identify potential improvement areas, and continually train to keep raising the levels of output.
2. Identify areas where safety or other issues are causing problems in similar businesses, and institute training to keep it from happening to you.
3. Have a standing program to train people for advancement and provide orientation for newcomers.
4. Make training a built-in part of any new acquisition of technology or any new policy, procedures, or other changes that are implemented.

A strong inclination for training, as identified in the concept of the learning organization (see Step Three), can go a long way toward reducing the amount of new needs assessment that must be done.

Sources of Needs Assessment Information

When deciding how to gather information for a needs analysis, keep three thoughts in mind:

1. Chances are that you won't get too much information, if for no other reason than time constraints. Be selective, but remember that you'll be better off having too much than too little. It's much easier to filter or ignore data than it is to have to search for more.
2. Two sources are usually better than one. The second validates the first and might turn up new, useful information. (Of course, you might not have enough time to go to more than one source.)

3. The closer to the source, the better. If customers are unhappy, meet with them; if production quality is lacking, go to the people who manufacture the products.

Though you can be innovative in seeking out information, there are five traditionally established information-gathering methods and sources: observation, data analysis, interviews, questionnaires and surveys, and instruments. As you implement one or more of these information-gathering methods, keep some questions in mind:

- What is the job?
- How is the job accomplished?
- How can job performance be improved?
- How can the skills, knowledge, and motivations required for the job be learned in the shortest time?

(For problematic situations, substitute the word *incident* or *problem* for *job*.)

Observation

The best way to find out how well someone is performing is to observe. You can see for yourself how many steps an employee uses to perform the computer-aided design of a circuit board and how well she uses the software package. Any problems in the way work is performed should become readily apparent by watching what goes on.

The first step in using observation techniques is to determine precisely what information is needed, then decide whom to observe in order to obtain it. You may need the help of a technical or functional expert at times. If there's a quality problem, for instance, observe two or three workers considered to be at the lower end of the performance spectrum and two or three deemed to be at the upper end. A comparison of the two sets of observations will help identify potential solutions.

Answering the question of what to observe is an important one. When in doubt, expand the desired range of data points. Integral to the observation method of data gathering is a way to record the data. Visions of old-fashioned time-and-motion studies, complete with clipboards and stopwatches, come to mind, and in fact, this may be what's needed. Direct entry of information into laptop computers may simplify and speed up the process. Videotape and audiotape recorders can capture information and relevant thoughts.

One of the greatest drawbacks to observation is that people being observed are conscious of it. Thus, it's possible they'll perform differently knowing that someone is watching each movement. This close scrutiny could produce better or worse performance than usual and significantly skew the results. Being as unobtrusive as possible and conducting more than one observation will help alleviate this situation. Again, all this must be weighed against the time available.

Data Analysis

Along with the explosion of computers as everyday workplace tools has come a close companion: an explosion of data. More-powerful computers generate considerably greater amounts of data—even an incomprehensible amount of data. Fortunately, powerful software analysis packages provide the means of easily manipulating the data. This technique is applicable when there are enormous amounts of data to work with, such as productivity records. A computer workstation is capable of keeping tabs on virtually everything the employee on the other end of the keyboard does during a workday. The fact that so many processes have been automated—manufacturing, communications, information, and paper handling—makes this a potentially lucrative source of information.

Interviews

Interviews can be either *formal*—the same questions are asked of all interviewees, using a standard format—or *informal*—open-ended with wide discretion for the interviewer to decide what information to obtain. Even informal interviews need to be at least partially structured to achieve consistency of data.

Here are steps to follow in conducting interviews as a needs analysis information-gathering technique:

1. Identify exactly what information is desired (but don't rule out the possibility of discovering additional, revealing facts—a potential of open-ended interviews).
2. Identify who is to be interviewed and how many people you'll need to talk to.
3. Prepare interview guidelines and, if necessary, interview work-

sheets, which contribute to consistency of data, even for informal interviews.

4. Brief the interviewers; train them if they're new to the process of interviewing.

5. Conduct the interviews (conduct practice ones first if necessary).

6. Compile and analyze the results.

Records Review

This may be one of the easiest methods of data gathering. Workplace records, schedules, work logs, purchase orders, progress reports, statistical analyses, manufacturing job travelers, injury reports, recorded telephone information logs (written logbooks, voice mail, electronic mail, and others), numerical records, and any other recorded information—both digital and the hard-copy variety—may provide insight needed for analysis. Information from these sources also may be subject to data analysis. Scanners and related software provide a way to capture handwritten and other information and digitize it.

Questionnaires and Surveys

When it's necessary to gather information from numerous sources (e.g., all word processor operators in a large organization with multiple locations), surveying them, by mail, fax, e-mail, telephone, or in person, will yield the necessary information. Having a carefully prepared worksheet for respondents to fill out or for the surveyor to complete when interviews are done in person or by telephone will facilitate the process and ensure that replies are consistent. This could work the same as an interview, where the interviewer fills in the questionnaire as a result of the interview.

As with the other data-gathering methods, it's mandatory to identify what information is needed before constructing the survey form. Once this is done, the questions must be stated in terms everyone will clearly comprehend. Here is the process for how to build an effective questionnaire:

1. Make a *list* of things you want to find out—perhaps the issues that created the need for the analysis or a list generated from brainstorming.

2. Turn the list of things, or items, into *questions*. (See Steps Six and Seven on questioning techniques for additional information.)

3. *Lay out* the questionnaire. If you can obtain everything you need by having respondents merely check a yes or no box, then do it this way. The simpler and easier to complete, the better. Other formats, such as where the respondent chooses one of five choices along a range (e.g., strongly agree to strongly disagree), ranked questions, or open-ended questions also work well in particular circumstances. It's a good idea, regardless of format, to allow people the option of adding their own comments. You never know what you might find out this way, and, too, people like having this option.

4. *Edit* the questionnaire with the audience in mind, and put it into final form. By keeping in mind the viewpoint of the potential respondents, including consideration for terminology they are familiar with, there's more assurance it will work well.

5. Have others *review* the questionnaire and make comments. The reviewers could include someone who is an expert in such matters and definitely should include someone from the intended responding audience.

6. Conduct a *pilot* run with the questionnaire using a small number of respondents, and evaluate the results. Choose the sample respondents from the same group to be surveyed on a broad scale so that the responses will be valid (unless there's extensive revision).

7. *Revise* the form as needed.

8. *Conduct* the survey.

It may be possible to find existing survey forms for standard purposes, such as evaluation forms. However, it's likely a questionnaire will have to be developed for your specific purpose, or else combined with an existing one.

Instruments

Instruments can be thought of as highly specialized questionnaires. Whereas questionnaires are designed to obtain straightforward data, instruments are more sophisticated, perhaps designed to determine how ready a group is for a training program or how resistant (or susceptible) a group is to organization change that's being planned. Other examples include instruments for assessing individual leadership styles, learning styles, and personality types. There are numerous commercially available instruments. It's important to realize that a great deal of expertise is needed to select the proper instrument and implement it effectively, so great care must be used when selecting and executing them. (See Step Six for further discussion on instruments as a tool for delivering training.)

Performance Objectives

Successful businesspeople long ago learned that having a plan—a clear goal or objective—is the only way to ensure success. That same principle holds for training. Learning objectives, also called *performance* or *behavioral objectives,* provide the road map to success in training. For the case of giving a project update to your manager, you have a clear-cut objective: to make sure he goes away with the information needed to make an intelligent decision regarding your project. It's easy to see how important objectives are for a three-day training workshop, which could eat up hundreds of labor hours and thousands of dollars to prepare and deliver. Objectives provide the insurance that people's time will be well spent. Since people and organizations tend to be goal oriented (we like to have something to shoot for), learning objectives fit in well with our work ethic.

Your Road Map to Success

The concept of learning objectives as the trainer's road map is uncomplicated: Achieve the objectives, and training is successful. It's that basic. Of course, there's a catch: You have to have a proper set of learning objectives. The secret is to write them as soon as you've completed the needs assessment and before you start designing the training. They thus serve a dual purpose: as a road map to designing, developing, and delivering effective training and as the learner's road map to completing the training course successfully. A third purpose is that of showing the training evaluator what to look for.

Here are some rules to follow in developing learning objectives:

1. *Be precise.* The learner is the ultimate person who must meet the objective and must understand what's intended.
2. *Use action words.* Performance is action.
3. *Keep the objectives simple.* This story will never be told enough times.
4. *Use measurable objectives.* Performance on the job must be measurable in order to determine the degree of success for the person and organization.

5. *Ensure that the measurements fit the situation.*

6. *Keep objectives to a minimum.* For each module or lesson of train-ing (e.g., a one-hour session), have a reasonably small number of objectives.

7. *Turn the desired skills into objectives.* There's a direct relationship between the skills desired and learning objectives.

8. *Understand the direct relationship between the items identified as need-ing training during the needs assessment and the learning objectives.* (This is virtually the same as skills desired.)

The Parts of a Learning Objective

Learning specialists tell us that a learning objective must have three parts in order to be complete and usable: performance, condition, and standard. And ideally, each objective should consist of all three parts. Nevertheless, it's possible initially to identify the perfor-mance only, then later add standards and conditions. The danger of doing this is that it could turn out to be difficult to identify condi-tions or standards that fit, making the performance less useful.

We will examine all three parts here, but keep in mind that some situations, particularly ones where time is of the essence, may dictate stopping with the performance. Also, conditions and stan-dards may be uniform for all parts of the learning process, and thus all the objectives. Use your judgment here, but at least develop sound performances for your objectives.

Performance

What skills, knowledge, or attitudes do you want the learner to go home with? What's expected? What behavior is to be changed? Is it to operate a bulldozer, plan a team meeting, generate a message over e-mail to selected parties, or provide the rules to follow for safe disposal of hazardous waste? If the training has been well thought out, meaning that a careful needs assessment was conducted, the objectives will literally leap out at you. This is the key part of the ob-jective, the one that must *always* be present.

Condition

This part of the objective deals with the condition under which the learner must perform the objective. It could be a simulated en-vironment (flight simulator), for example, or the actual workplace circumstance (actual aircraft). For knowledge objectives, it could be that references can be used, or perhaps must be achieved from memory. It could be an extreme situation such as an emergency, or a routine one that could be performed under any conditions. For a pilot undergoing emergency landing training in a flight simulator, the conditions are those generated by the simulator (which can be exceptionally realistic). For knowledge-related objectives, such as retrieving a particular piece of information for a planning decision, the conditions will be related to the resources that are available, such as planning tools and databases. Often the training environment itself is the condition, such as a classroom, simulator, or role play. The condition includes any tools, equipment, documents, aids, and systems that may be required.

Exhibit 2-5. Sample Learning Objectives

1. State Deming's fourteen steps for quality improvement *(performance)* verbatim *(standard)*, from memory *(condition)*.

2. After reading a case study *(condition)* illustrating Deming's fourteen steps, identify which of the steps were applied in the case *(performance)*, without leaving out any steps *(standard)*.

3. Demonstrate the correct technique for performing CPR *(performance)*, using "Annie" *(condition)* for five minutes *(standard)*.

4. Type sixty-five words per minute *(performance)* without any mistakes *(standard)*, using a standard keyboard *(condition)*.

5. Develop three satisfactory learning objectives for the introductory module of a stress management training course *(performance)*, using *The First Time Trainer (condition)*, in thirty minutes *(standard)*.

6. Parallel-park a four-door sedan within the lines of a parking space *(performance)* on a public street during peak traffic *(condition)*, within three minutes and without having to back up more than three times *(standard)*.

7. Demonstrate the proper response to an improper sexual advance *(performance)* during a role play *(condition)* in the manner that fits within stated company policy *(standard)*.

8. Shut down the assembly line *(performance)* during a simulated equipment malfunction *(condition)* within five seconds after the alarm goes off *(standard)*.

9. Generate a budget for the planning department *(performance)* that meets the company's standard budget submission requirements *(standard)*, using a spreadsheet application program *(condition)*.

10. After viewing a video clip *(condition)*, diagnose potential sexual harassment situations *(performance)* and categorize the level of severity of each using the company policy guidelines *(standard)*.

Standard

How well do you want the learner to perform the objective? The standard can be anywhere from performing a task a little bit better to achieving perfection. Is perfection the goal, or is plus or minus 10 percent accuracy sufficient? Think in terms of quantifiable items, such as percentages and time, or quality-related ones, such as perfection or something less. It's the standard that ultimately provides the "grade" for the learner's performance. Representative samples of learning objectives are shown in Exhibit 2-5.

Writing the Objectives

Remember that one of the key rules for writing good objectives is to use action words. A good way to apply this rule is to ask yourself how you would measure the objective if a particular word is used. For example, the word *understand* is commonly used in training and education. Does a student *understand* why the company is adopting a team approach to production? Does a manager *understand* why key people must be included in certain strategic decision-making situations? But how do you measure *understand*? When you think about it, *understand* might better be stated as being able to identify certain facts and conditions or stating reasons that an act was committed. By contrast, to be able to compute a solution to a statistical problem or identify and write the company's long-range goals is definitely measurable.

Here are examples of action words that are acceptable and unacceptable in writing learning objectives.

Acceptable Action Words

mark	name	install
state	fix	decide
identify	move	check
fill out	place	say
label	draw	ask
perform	operate	list
compare	load	fabricate
locate	quote	prepare
maneuver	repair	demonstrate
diagnose	run	build

Unacceptable Action Words

understand	conclude	know
discover	grasp	become
enjoy	infer	believe
think	solve	improve
develop	determine	appreciate
analyze	test	

Note that some of these could be on either side. *Test* might be a perfectly good word for an objective in a training session on how to administer training tests. *Analyze* might be just fine for a course in strategic planning. Obviously, there would have to be more explanation of what's required, such as "analyze using a prescribed technique." Generally, though, the clearer and easier to measure, the better. Some of these words, such as *understand*, can never be measured.

Step Three

Focus on Learning

What one knows is, in youth, of little moment; they know enough who know how to learn.

—Henry Brooks Adams
The Education of Henry Adams (1907)

Knowing how people learn is critical to effective training delivery. Since we're dealing with adults, this means applying adult learning theory. It's not difficult, because adults have a good idea of how they learn best. Just follow a few principles and practices, and learners will be enthusiastic about the process—and they'll learn more too.

Step Three Summary

This step deals with how people learn. A newly emerging aspect is how organizations learn. This step is closely related to learning objectives, which are directly tied to performance. It includes these elements:

- The relationship between learning and motivation
- Identification of the types of learning
- Principles of learning centered around adult learning theory
- Building learning principles into training
- Key concepts of core competency and mastery
- Learning how to learn
- Multiple ways of acquiring skills and knowledge
- The learning organization

- Building success factors into the training during design
- Reasons why the phase is so critical to training success

This step begins with a discussion of the critical relationship between learning and motivation. It identifies types of learning, then presents sixteen principles of learning that center around adult learning theory. Learning principles go hand in hand with learning objectives. Many of the learning principles addressed in this step are directly tied to objectives, which are tied to performance. Clearly the training-learning process is a closed-loop system.

Several aspects of learning must be considered to ensure that the process is properly built into training. These include core competency and mastery, learning how to learn, multiple ways of acquiring skills and knowledge, and one of the newest and most important developments in organizations, the learning organization. These factors are discussed following learning principles. Another consideration during this early design phase is addressed: the technique of building success factors into the training during design. The step concludes with a reminder of why the phase is so critical to training success.

The Learning Process

Learning and Motivation

People learn for a reason. It could be positive or negative, pleasure or survival. To say it another way, people are motivated to learn, and motivation plays a major role in the training and learning process. People are motivated to do the things they do because they feel the need to do so. Acquiring new skills through training could well be the way to meet personal needs. At a basic level, the motivation to work may be to pay the rent and food bills. At a higher level, people may become fully engrossed in work so they can move to the highest levels of the organization, fulfilling their dreams of making it to the top.

There's a direct relationship between motivation and two major trainer concerns. One is that the more motivated trainers are, the more successful training will be. The other is that adult learning theory is founded on concepts of motivation. In summary, learners must be motivated if training is to be successful, and trainers must be motivated to perform well as facilitators and to continually improve performance.

Motivation to perform after training by applying the newly acquired skills could well be the most important manifestation of motivation. For example, there could be opportunities for promotion or increased rewards based on increased skills, increased productivity, or overall improved organization performance. It isn't necessary to delve into motivational theories, but it's important to recognize that such concepts as the desire most people have to better themselves and get involved with meaningful work certainly apply to training. These are the same motivational principles managers apply to improve organization effectiveness.

Types of Learning

Learning psychologists have provided a straightforward, easily understood classification of learning types: knowledge, skills, and attitude. They've become widely accepted in education and training and provide a convenient means of organizing training.

Knowledge Learning

Also called *cognitive learning*, knowledge learning entails using knowledge and mental skills—for example, identifying key steps in the decision-making process, identifying marketing challenges based on market analysis data, or stating the rules of the nautical road for a sailboat overtaking a steamship. It ranges, for example, from being able to state the three parts of a learning objective to describing in detail the underlying reasons that expert systems can be used to corporate advantage. You may have heard the term *cognition*, or *cognitive domain*, as referring to memory and reasoning objectives. This form of learning goes together with such concepts as the knowledge-driven workplace, the learning organization, and other aspects of learning (all discussed in this step). Knowledge learning examples include learning and applying rules, identifying symbols and patterns, making decisions, recalling bodies of knowledge, and applying knowledge.

Skills Learning

Also called *kinesthetic* or *psychomotor skills learning*, this is the skill type that comes to mind when we think about teaching a person the physical skills needed to perform a task: performing gross and fine motor skills, exercising eye-hand coordination, steering and maneuvering, operating, manipulating, and communicating, among others. Learning to use a keyboard to do word processing is skills learning, as is learning to use a keyboard to play music, to operate an entertainment system, or to install a new muffler in an automobile. Many physical skills are straightforward and easy to categorize—for example, operating a lathe or driving a car. Because of the growing reliance on knowledge, however, more and more skills require both physical dexterity and knowledge skills.

Attitude Learning

Also called *affective learning*, it's related to values and interests; examples are taking a wallet full of money to the lost and found, being ethical in dealing with customers, adopting the *Semper Fi* attitude of a U.S. marine, or working overtime with no regrets in order to meet a deadline. This is where our deep concern for corporate ethics comes into play. A person's emotional capacity and individual objectives related to personal feeling and values also play an important role in attitude learning.

It isn't always possible to separate these three in actual practice, even though it may be possible for training purposes. For example, a word processor operator must have certain knowledge before he can apply physical skills in manipulating the keyboard. The pianist must have knowledge of notes and chords before she can play the melody from memory in front of a concert audience. And having the desire to perform the various skills to the absolute best of one's ability, which is attitude, can make a world of difference to the person and the organization—and the audience in the case of the pianist.

Learning Principles

Learning theory is a major field of study, with an extensive body of knowledge. Learning psychologists continue to supply research on how to facilitate the learning process. The theory is based on sound, field-tested principles. Because of this immense body of work, trainers don't have to worry about research and theory. We can feel quite safe in simply applying the principles. It helps that most are already familiar to most of us. All we're required to do is follow them, which over the long term will help guarantee successful training. It will also build in the motivational aspects that are so essential.

Here we look at sixteen learning principles—seven from adult learning theory, with the remaining nine being basic principles of how people learn. Chances are you're familiar with most, if not all, of them. When applied, they'll keep you on track toward effective training. (They are summarized in Exhibit 3-1.)

Exhibit 3-1. Sixteen Learning Principles for Effective Training

1. *Adults learn by doing.*
2. *Use realistic examples.*
3. *Adults relate their learning to what they already know.*
4. *Conduct the training in an informal environment.*
5. *Variety is the spice of life.*
6. *Remove the fear factor.*
7. *Serve as the facilitator of the learning process.*
8. *Inform learners of the learning objectives.*
9. *Practice makes perfect.*
10. *Guide and prompt; do not tell.*
11. *Give feedback.*
12. *Understand transfer of training.*
13. *Relate all activities to the learning objectives.*
14. *Make a good first impression.*
15. *Show enthusiasm.*
16. *Use repetition.*

1. *Adults learn by doing.* Adults want to be involved in whatever it is they do, particularly when learning something new. Don't demonstrate; let the adult learner do it. There's really nothing new here, because we know that getting our hands on the task—learning by doing—is what constitutes ultimate learning. Why talk about key learning points when you can let adult learners do as much of the work as possible? Be a facilitator. Not only are you more likely to succeed, but adult learners will appreciate the process more.

2. *Use realistic examples.* Use plenty of examples, and keep them realistic and relevant to learners. If you don't, the examples will be meaningless. For one reason why, look at the next item, about how adults use familiar frames of reference to enhance their learning. Along these lines, make sure the examples are interesting and attention getting so everyone enjoys the training.

3. *Adults relate their learning to what they already know.* Sometimes they do so in a pronounced way. Knowing their backgrounds and experiences will help immensely. Adults have plenty of experiences, with some being more prevalent than others. The result is that they compare the new with what they've already done and know, focusing on what they know best. The more ab-

stract you are, the less likely it is that the learner will relate to the learning. This concept is one good reason that icebreakers (see Step Six) serve more than one purpose, including allowing the facilitator to learn more about who is being facilitated. If the information can be obtained prior to the training sessions, so much the better.

4. *Conduct the training in an informal environment.* No one wants to sit through a rigid, by-the-numbers training session. Your best bet is to make it a user-friendly learning situation. This doesn't mean sloppy. It could range anywhere from specifying informal attire, to including low-key social events with the training, to simply making everyone feel at ease at the beginning of the session.

5. *Variety is the spice of life.* Change the pace and technique in training from time to time. Use different delivery methods and audiovisuals. Bring in other people, or change the setting. This concept of multimodality is another excellent example of variety that pays dividends. (Media and delivery methods, where you can accomplish this, are discussed in Steps Five and Seven.) Exhibit 3-2 provides examples of how to use multimodality approaches in training.

6. *Remove the fear factor.* People have memories, not always good, about cramming for tests and anxiously awaiting report cards and grade postings. Avoid this environment in adult training situations. (There may be times when this is impossible, as when personal safety is a critical factor.) Feedback is essential, but obtain it in informal ways—and often. Praise is the best form of reward. Provide the guidance needed in a win-win situation. Note how frequently performance and performance objectives are mentioned throughout the eight steps. If a person can meet the prescribed performance laid out in training, then there probably is no need for grading. Everyone will gain more if the fear factor is removed, or reduced as much as possible.

7. *Serve as the facilitator of the learning process.* Be a trainer, not a teacher. Granted, the learners probably will expect you to do some teaching. For example, if they come to the session to learn how to use a computer, some old-fashioned teaching is in order. Remember that the learners are most likely to be as accomplished in whatever it is they do as you are in what you do, so be sure to treat everyone respectfully. This principle also means that you must be flexible, quick to adapt to the situation if it means a greater chance for success.

8. *Inform the learners of the learning objectives.* It's up to you to provide the road map the learners need, checking frequently to determine if everyone is on track to achieve the objectives. Remember from Step Two that you need a well-defined set of objectives before designing and developing training, let alone delivering it.

Exhibit 3-2. Multimodality Approaches in Training

1. ***Show a video on ethics, followed by an open discussion.*** Have learners summarize by writing out the key points they learned. Substitute any number of topics for ethics, and the process still works to stimulate many learning styles.

2. ***Give a minilecture on a three-step planned change model.*** Have learners read a case study; then, have them form groups and discuss how the model could be used to deal with the problem situation. Following this, have each group present its solutions.

3. ***Have learners read a manual on how to set up an accounting form on a spreadsheet.*** Demonstrate how to set it up properly (a variation is to show a video of someone doing the process). Give learners an assignment, to work on in pairs, to set up an assigned form. Have each group demonstrate its results.

4. ***Have learners develop their personal definition of the topic under study*** (e.g., what constitutes good speaking skills). Show a video clip demonstrating a good presentation (or have someone else do it). Have small groups compare observed skills with the ones they developed. Summarize by writing their findings on a board or transparency.

5. ***Deliver a classroom presentation on a topic,*** such as the company's mission statement, for a new employee orientation class. Have learners look up competitor mission statements on the World Wide Web, and compare the statements in small discussion groups. Finally, ask learners to write a paragraph on what the mission statement means to them.

6. ***Show a video depicting a company where teams are used successfully.*** Next, have learners participate in an exercise where they must engage in teamwork to be successful. Finally, have them discuss (or write) what they see as being the keys to successful teams.

7. ***Use other ideas to stimulate learner senses:***
   - Add appropriate music (e.g., to announce transitions from one segment to another).
   - Incorporate storytelling and drama.
   - Move outdoors for exercises or go to different locations, such as actual workplaces, customers, or suppliers.
   - Have people experience unique situations, such as simulating other cultures or having a disability.

9. *Practice makes perfect.* Practice can bring the learner much closer to being able to achieve the desired objectives. It's a vital consideration, tied to one of the most popular, and potentially beneficial, ideas of today's workplace: competency and mastery. Multimodality and repetition (the last principle in this list) provide the means of applying and reinforcing this principle.

10. *Guide and prompt; do not tell.* Learning lasts much longer when the learner has to fully enter into the learning process. Provide all the help you can by citing references, giving examples, asking questions, and offering all the encouragement you can to learners so that they will provide the answers and demonstrate the desired performance.

11. *Give feedback.* This is essential, and must be done continually so everyone knows exactly what progress has been made and how much more needs to be done.

12. *Apply transfer of training.* The principle that one aspect of learning builds on another applies to most basic skills. For example, basic arithmetic skills can be transferred to learning how to balance a checkbook, then to learning simple accounting systems. Basic computer skills can be transferred to learning how to use a spreadsheet. Day-to-day decision-making skills for supervisors can be transferred into skills for making vital management decisions. One aspect of training builds on another, a principle that can be invaluable to trainers. This is a fundamental part of learning how to learn.

13. *Relate all activities to the learning objectives.* When you conduct an exercise, for example, make sure the purpose is tied to the objectives and that the learners are aware of it. Use learning objectives to keep all training on track. The only training events that don't deal directly with learning objectives are breaks, and even these serve the purpose of keeping learners refreshed for maximum learning.

14. *Make a good first impression.* This should go without saying and is closely related to the principle of being thoroughly prepared for every training event. We form quick opinions, usually negative ones, when things get off to a bad, slow, or boring start. There's heavy competition for people's attention, and you sometimes must vie for your share.

15. *Show enthusiasm.* Consider what must be going on in the learners' minds if you're dragging through a session. If you are the least bit bored, uncertain, or unenthusiastic, learners will be even more so.

Unless you are a seasoned performer, showing enthusiasm may take a bit of extra effort. Also, make sure your body language matches your voice and expression. (At times, acting as a stand-up comedian might save the day.)

16. *Use repetition.* This is the old principle of repetition, reiteration, and rote. Repeat things three times at least, preferably in slightly different ways. Here's where the concept of multi-modality comes in handy, by making repetition more interesting and exciting by doing it in different ways (e.g., telling how to manage conflict, demonstrating it, then having learners practice it in role plays).

Teaching or Training?

Is there a difference between teaching and training? At first glance, you might not think so, and, in fact, the words are often used interchangeably. Certainly there are similarities, and many people have moved successfully from education to training and development by applying the same principles. However, there are distinct differences, and no doubt those who have made the transition successfully know what they are. One of the primary differences is taking an adult approach to learning theory, recognizing the differences in the traditional way children learn and how adults learn. There are other differences as well:

- *Knowledge* This is largely *discover*ed in training rather than passed on, as in teaching. Rather than have the teacher tell learners what the "truth" is, the trainer facilitates learners' discovery of the truth.
- *Improvement* Teaching emphasizes making technical advancement within the organization, such as installing advanced computer systems and teaching people how to use them. Training emphasizes making improvement through developing the people—the human resources of the organization.
- *Orientation* The teaching approach is oriented toward the teacher; the training approach is oriented toward the learner.
- *Behavior* Teaching is concerned with measurable behavior. So is training, but it also cares about attitudes. Positive reinforcement is a boon to trainers.
- *Objectives* Teaching focuses on precise behavioral objectives, emphasizing the acquisition of information. Training also is con-

cerned with preciseness, but adds emphasis on interpersonal skills competencies (learning how to learn).

- *Content* Teaching relates content to technical skills. Training adds personal skills, such as decision making and critical thinking, and some of the softer skills required in interpersonal relations, management, and leadership.
- *Methodology* Teaching is subject oriented, perhaps emphasizing the principles toward the end of the list of sixteen learning principles, and employs the lecture approach. Training, more personalized and geared to the situation, stresses more involvement on the part of the learner.

As you can see, the trainer focuses more on the concept of the learner as a key resource of the organization. In addition, the trainer goes beyond basics.

Other Aspects of Learning

Several new concepts have emerged that are beginning to have a positive impact on training and learning: core competency and mastery, new ways of learning, and the learning organization. Each can be applied to the entire process of improving individual and organization performance through training and learning, and each adds an exciting, positive dimension to training.

Core Competency and Mastery

Intense competition for markets or resources, or both, has forced organizations worldwide to pay close attention to everything they do. One of the exciting outcomes as far as trainers are concerned is the increased focus on levels of workplace competence. How competent a person is at performing a particular job is important. Put all the employees of the organization together—everyone from the newest entry-level worker to the chief executive—and you can see why the idea is so vital. Greater competence leads to greater results, and training is a viable way to reach competency.

Mastery is the highest level of competence. It's essentially the process of a person being the best that is humanly possible to be at a particular job. It means more than being good at using a spreadsheet or developing a proposal for new business. The greatest success will be achieved by those who can use the spreadsheet or write proposals better than anyone else in the organization—perhaps anywhere else. Here are the characteristics of a master:

- *Continually improving.* Masters are never satisfied with their achievements and fully believe they can do better. They improve through all the ways identified in Step Eight, and more.
- *Always learning.* Masters recognize that there's always more to learn about a job. They use every way possible to learn and improve.
- *Willing to take risks.* Masters are willing to stick their necks out; they have full confidence that in most cases they'll succeed. Even when they fail, which is seldom, they know they'll improve from having tried.
- *Setting high goals.* The goals are high enough to cause a stretch to meet them, and once achieved, masters immediately set new ones. Restlessness is a distinct characteristic of masters.
- *Willing to try new ways of doing things.* Masters recognize that this can lead to better, more effective ways of doing the job. This characteristic goes hand in hand with risk taking and separates masters from those who may know one right way to accomplish a task and never deviate from it.

The organization where mastery is part of the culture has a much greater chance of succeeding in the world of learning and performance.

Competence and mastery form the first part of the equation for organization success. The second part is identifying both individual and organization core competencies. Whereas a company might have a core competency of providing high-quality financial protection services to families, a company employee's core competency might be the ability to discern a customer's needs and make recommendations that fit those needs. A scientist's core competency might be in applying innovative research techniques in drug research; the drug company employer's core competency might be in discovering cures for disease. The significance of core competency can be illustrated by noting that organizations that have identified their core competencies and stick to them are the ones most likely to succeed.

Learning principles can be integrated with competency to enhance the mastery of those skills needed to make the organization most effective. The key is to use core competencies to guide all training. Here is a four-step program:

1. Identify organization and individual core competencies (based on mission).
2. Place these competencies at the heart of all employee training.
3. Make mastery a fundamental concept of the organization.
4. Continually review organization objectives, core competencies, and ongoing training to ensure their alignment.

New Ways of Learning

If you stop to think about all the different things you're capable of doing, it will likely turn out that many of them you learned on your own, without a teacher and without attending an intensive workshop. The reason is that you've learned how to learn. In fact, successful, well-trained, and well-adjusted people often, without suggestion and completely on their own, learn what they need to know to progress in a job or task.

People who have learned how to learn have two general characteristics: they have taken control of their own learning, and they have developed several key learning skills.

Self-Control of Learning

People who have learned how to learn will learn even if their employer does absolutely nothing to help prepare them. They have a personal plan for learning and improvement laid out, and they follow it religiously. They are also likely to be quite familiar with how they learn best. For example, someone who learns best by reading makes sure there is always plenty of appropriate reading matter on the subject at hand. A hands-on learner learns from everything she comes in contact with, most certainly from others around her. She's the person who sits in the front row during a workshop and asks plenty of insightful questions, and the first to volunteer to perform a demonstration or give an example.

Learning to Learn Skills

For all practical purposes, the key skills learners need if they are to continue learning (i.e., learning how to learn) are the same ones a student needs in moving into college and graduate programs, further emphasizing the continuing integration of learning in all aspects of life and work. The skills include these:

- Strong study habits
- Self-motivation
- Ability to use information sources
- Excellent communication skills (reading, writing, speaking, listening)
- Problem-solving ability
- Abstract thinking
- Plan for learning, with specific goals
- Knowledge of how they learn best (research shows multiple types of human intelligence)

Note how closely these skills track the key skills needed in the workplace identified in Step One, particularly that of information literacy. The higher level of these skills that learners acquire, the more successful they'll be in achieving learning objectives.

New Strategies in Training and Developing People

Breakthroughs in how to acquire knowledge are keeping up with new ways to apply knowledge. The result is a challenge to trainers to keep up, but well worth the effort because of the potential for improved training results. We look briefly at several of these newer concepts. You're encouraged to keep these concepts, and any new ones you are aware of, in mind as you develop your own training. They worked for others and may be what you need to put your training over the top.

Participatory Learning

If participatory forms of managing (e.g., self-directed teams, quality circles) are being successfully implemented, it stands to reason that participatory forms of training are being tried out too—and successfully. The two go hand in hand. If the people closest to the work know best how to do it, then certainly they know best what kinds of training they need. This is empowerment at its fullest application. In the team format, for instance, it means that each team is its own training manager. Members make their own decisions about training. The concept works well when the people held responsible are given the resources and knowledge to implement it.

This also follows closely with the concept that people are responsible for their own destinies; that is, the individual, not the organization, is responsible for his or her career management. In work environments where individuals, not the organization, must take control of their own development, participatory learning is the norm, with the organization providing the climate and resources for this to work well.

Practical Training

Practical training is the process of focusing on the fastest and least expensive way to get training done. Actually, it's what good trainers and managers do all the time: They combine efficiency with effectiveness. Sometimes merely developing a job aid is just as good as training, and possibly better. Safety signs around equipment and instructions built into copy machines are two simple, effective examples. Combining an ongoing training program with actual work—on-the-job training—is another excellent example of practical training that works (see self-paced training in Step Four). It could be the act of having someone else do certain portions of a job if it doesn't seem reasonable to have a person learn to do something that will be done only occasionally. Primarily it's an attitude that borders on taking the position that training should be done only when absolutely necessary. Carefully followed, it can eliminate wasted training and wasted expense by focusing on what works best and most quickly. (Just be careful not to be too miserly.)

Action Learning

Many organizations are finding that learners who accomplish actual tasks rather than hypothetical ones during training get far more out of the process. This action learning often works well with teams. Companies that have tried this approach find that the more diverse the people on the team, the better it works.

How training results are measured varies when real business issues are used as the basis of training. Measurement can range from a discussion of the outcome to assessing results. Either way, accountability and risk are built into the process—one of the main reasons this training can be so effective. As you can see, this follows closely with much of what we've learned about how adults learn. (See Step Four on designing training and Step Six on getting learners involved for related discussion.)

Technology

Technology adds depth and versatility to training, and its application is increasing. It should not be used simply for the sake of using it or because someone you know has used it. But where it fits and can be cost justified, use it. It contributes to realism, cuts costs in the right situations, and more. (Specific technologies are addressed in Step Five.)

Lifelong Learning

We never stop learning. Anyone who has stopped learning is totally retired (and has made the decision to acquire no more new gadgets, computers, and the like). Here's where we bring together the concepts of learning how to learn, acquiring information-gathering skills, and continually updating skills to excel (sometimes to merely keep up), which are required in the knowledge-driven economy and workplace. Continuous learning is essential to success in virtually any field.

The Learning Organization

New management buzzwords pop up all the time. One that has come into its own in the last decade is the so-called *learning organization*—the concept that organizations, like individuals, can learn, and that to do so on an ongoing basis can lead to continuing organization success. A learning organization has the following characteristics:

- Learning continually is not only encouraged but expected.
- The organization's culture provides opportunities to learn and advance.
- The organization strives to perform at the highest levels.
- Creativity and innovation are common.
- People are allowed to fail.
- New ideas are always welcome.
- Organization mission and goals are clear and made known to all. They drive daily business affairs and outside relationships.
- Teams are the norm, and people are team players.
- New skills are acquired often before they are needed.
- The organization is viewed as a system.

Obviously the organization is learning through its people, which means that there must be an environment for learning and growing. Formal training may or may not be a fundamental element of a true learning organization, but training of some sort, albeit on the job, must be present. Chances are that training is built into the process. Review of long-term success in companies that have survived in the world arena shows that they've been learning and growing for a long time, without bothering to name the process. Creativity, empowerment, teamwork, mastery, and adapting to rapid change are core traits of a learning organization. When the organization is conscious of the need for continued learning, overall training will have an even greater impact on effectiveness.

Building In Success Factors

A smart trainer builds success factors into the training itself. Following tested procedures and practices, such as conducting a needs assessment and then developing carefully defined learning objectives, automatically builds in key success factors. Following are some other ways you can help to ensure that the training achieves appropriate results.

Evaluation

Results must be evaluated. Can the learner perform as desired after the training is completed? Making sure objectives are clearly measurable is one way to do this. Asking questions (see Step Six) at appropriate times during the session is another. Formulate questions to have ready to ask at any time. Be sure to have exercises (short, simple ones often suffice) to conduct. They both break up the training and give learners a chance to show they are improving. Building evaluation into the entire training process will provide continuous feedback and help ensure that training focuses on objectives.

Motivation

Be conscious of motivation at all times. When you're designing a training segment, for instance, think of ways to generate learner interest. A game or challenge pitting one team against the other works well, the challenge often bringing out the best in participants and taking advantage of adult learners' desire to increase applicable knowledge. It also keeps the learning process flowing smoothly and energetically. Another highly recommended technique is to have alternatives to move to when you see that learners are losing interest or that what you're doing isn't working. Always bear in mind that your action—and inaction—can greatly influence learner motivation.

Criteria for Success

Performance-based learning is clearly meaningful to adult learners, and it's the route to successful training. What better built-in feature could there be? Building in evaluation and motivation also leads to successful training. It's not enough to focus on performance and write solid learning objectives that measure desired performance. These objectives, and learner's achievement of them, must be kept posted for people to see at all times. Thus, feedback becomes one of the most productive ways of building in success. If nothing else, add frequent notes in the margins of your trainer's guide (described in Step Four) reminding you to provide feedback. Perhaps a lapel button saying "I love feedback" or a sign taped on the wall saying "Have you provided feedback lately?" would be worth considering.

Conclusion

You've now completed the design phase, although it's virtually impossible to delineate when one part of the training process stops and another begins. Nor does it matter. What does matter is that the right things get done before actually delivering training. Now you're ready to build the training.

Step Four

Be Prepared

Lead the way into the new workplace. Make it your mission to equip people with the survival skills they will need: vertical teamwork skills, skills for new kinds of affinity and communication, comfort with new ways of working, and consummate flexibility.

—*Training and Development* (May 1994)

Step Three identified training needs. Now it's time to determine how to deliver the training. Getting into the preparation stage, you'll quickly learn a poorly kept trainer's secret: There's never enough time to be fully prepared. The solution: Use your time judiciously—and always bear in mind that the payoff from preparing comes in doing a better job of delivering.

Fully customized classroom training can take as much as one to three days of development for every hour of delivered training. Even off-the-shelf packages require time to become familiar with them. Computer-based training can run into the hundreds of hours of development time per hour of delivered training. And that's not all. It takes time to prepare to deliver training once it's developed. A rule of thumb given to us by educators is that it takes three hours of preparation time for every one hour of class taught. The key is to make the most of valuable time in preparing the program.

Step Four blends together the disciplines of training and management. One ingredient is enough technical knowledge to select all the components that compose good training. The other ingredient is management skill to make intelligent decisions about which components will work best, within a reasonable budget, to get the job done. Guidelines and tools laid out in this critical step of preparing training will help you cut through the technical expertise and decision making you'll need to be prepared for successful training. It would be an easy step if all you needed to do was order a video from a catalog and show it. However, most training requires more than that, and demands extensive preparation.

Step Four Summary

Preparation is required in any training situation, whether it's a lengthy customized training program or a brief one that has been repeated frequently. The reason is that professionalism and performance, together powerful incentives, are at work to keep the trainer working hard to be well prepared. Included within this step are:

- Key principles of preparation
- Selecting delivery methods
- Selecting media
- Selecting evaluation methods
- Selecting facilitators
- Selecting learners
- Tools that help decide whether to make or to buy
- Methods for developing experiential exercises
- Methods for developing various types of training materials
- Tools that help choose locations and ensure full preparation

Preparation is a big step, made easier if assessment has led to well-defined learning objectives. Done well, the delivery and evaluation steps will be far easier to do. Exhibit 4-1 lists the many activities that may be required to one degree or another to be prepared. As you can see, this step is a big one. It covers a broad spectrum of what trainers do in plying their trade.

Key Principles of Preparation

Before delving deeper into this phase, it will be helpful to keep in mind a few key principles while developing training:

1. Proceed as if *you* are going to deliver the training, even if someone else is to do it. There's no surer way to make certain it's complete and will work well. (If this doesn't work, approach it as if your boss were going to deliver it.)

2. Keep the eight steps to effective training in mind at all times.
3. Always think in terms of variety (multimodality), and implement the concept wherever possible.
4. From time to time, review the adult learning principles outlined in Step Two.
5. Make the training the best you can the first time through; then keep reviewing as time permits to make it better.

Within this chapter, you'll find examples, lists, and checklists to help you. Start by determining what you need to provide in your training session. If you're making a short presentation where all you have to do is show up and speak, then most of the requirements identified in this step are unnecessary. On the other hand, if you're developing a training session from scratch, you may find yourself

Exhibit 4-1. Activities of Step Four: Preparation

1. **Training materials identification and selection**
   - Trainer guides
     Handouts
     Audiovisual media
   - Developing materials
     Make-or-buy decisions
     Organizing the flow of the session(s)
     Timing sessions
     Developing experiential exercises

2. **Delivery method selection**
   - Classroom
   - Self-paced
   - Audiovisual equipment (projectors, screens, etc.)
   - Computer-based systems
   - Teleconferencing, teletraining

3. **Training participants selection**

4. **Training facilitator selection**

5. **Evaluation methods selection**

6. **Logistics**
   - Location
   - Arrangement of room and seating
   - Refreshments and meals (as necessary)
   - Travel
   - Participant needs
   - Audiovisual and other equipment

7. **Pilot training**

applying most of the information. Examples are used freely with each of the discussions and tools to help you determine the applicability of the elements and to be fully prepared for your training.

Making Selections

Training course development can be thought of as a process of making selections about delivery method, media, exercises, learners, and trainers. The first three must be selected at this time, as should an evaluation method. It's also a good idea to select who is to receive the training and who is to deliver it now, too, because these decisions could affect the final product.

Selecting Delivery Method

Training has come a long way since the day when people first started learning from others. Formalized training has evolved from traditional forms similar to old-fashioned schoolhouse learning to exotic electronic gadgetry. Suffice it to say that there are more ways to deliver training than you'll likely ever use. The key is to choose the one that works well, which means within your means and time frame.

Types of Delivery Methods

In actual practice, many of the ways to deliver training are combined, providing perhaps the most effective approach. For our discussion, three primary categories have been selected: classroom, self-paced, and media driven. Among them, the delivery methods you might find useful can be identified.

Classroom

This category is the most commonly used method of training delivery. It's effective, and most organizations have suitable rooms in which to hold training classes. If not, commercial spaces are readily available. One of the main reasons this method is still used is that it's comfortable, it's the way most of us have conducted training, and has a lot going for it, including cost. When we think of training, in fact, many people immediately picture an instructor standing on a platform in front of the room, chalk in hand, overhead projector nearby, and students paying attention as training is presented. Actually, this is only part of the process of classroom training. It can also encompass some of the following activities:

- *Lecture*, with the instructor presenting detailed information—for example, the company accounting manager telling managers about a new twist in tax law that requires them to keep travel records differently.
- *Demonstration*, with someone demonstrating the proper way to do something for the attendees to observe and learn—for example, a technician showing administrative staff how to make computer system backups with a newly installed high-speed tape system.
- *Discussion*, as the total training effort or part of an overall training program (see Step Six). Because of how adults learn, discussion should be a natural part of all training.
- *Seminars*, with pertinent topics discussed by learners, possibly in small groups, in order to attain maximum participation of all in attendance. This could range from discussing a lengthy case study to a short newspaper article related to the topic at hand.
- *Exercises*, usually done in small groups to maximize participation. Using a class on business writing as an example, exercises can range from simple events (e.g., having learners pair off and discuss how they will use their new writing skills on their jobs) to major events (e.g., having them write several types of business correspondence at the end of the class).
- *Laboratory sessions*, exercises associated with systems and equipment. Most computer-related training falls into this category. The lab sessions are essential for learning how to use the system or equipment. For example, training on any type of software package would require hands-on lab time, as would training on how to use fax machines or copiers.

Self-Paced

Self-paced training has the potential of being extremely valuable because it can be conducted at times convenient to the learner—commuting to work, whiling away time when television fare is unexciting, or doing the morning jog or walk. It works well when learners are at remote locations, when the training isn't conducted often, and when there's motivation to learn on one's own. Of prime concern to the trainer is that it allows learning to take place without a facilitator. For persons eager to learn, this could mean a considerable amount of learning going on outside the workplace.

There are a number of ways to deliver self-paced training, ranging from simple paper-and-pencil assignments to sophisticated media approaches:

- *Workbooks.* This could be a combination of textual material with exercises and questions for the reader to complete at intervals. Programmed learning texts, where learners follow instructions and progress according to whether they have answered questions correctly, fit this category. The purpose is to guide the learner through material needed to achieve desired objectives. Usually these media are designed so that learners achieve success 90 percent of the time, keeping learning on a positive basis. Instead of a workbook, it could be a checklist used while learning on the job, where a supervisor initials items that have been demonstrated. This is also called on-the-job training, and is more than just turning people loose to learn on their own.

- *Mentoring and coaching.* Assigning qualified staff members as mentor or coach of a learner is a widely used form of self-paced learning. A *mentor* gives advice on career moves and workplace-related situations. A *coach* helps the learner through skills learning, possibly using checklists or workbooks, as well as demonstrating and critiquing.

- *Audio.* These are the cassette tapes to listen to during times when your mind is not fully engaged (e.g., while riding an exercise bicycle). They've become big business. Leadership and motivational programs, where the person speaking seeks to spur the listener on to greater performance, are widely used. Role plays can be presented, so the listener can learn about various situations critical to performance. Audiotapes are readily available from numerous sources.

- *Video.* Much like audiotapes, they can be viewed at leisure. Videos have become the number one training medium, in fact, so it stands to reason that you can find just about any topic you want to learn on your own with videos.

- *CD-ROM.* This medium is taking its place alongside videos as a means of not only training but entertainment as well. Most personal computers come equipped with them now, and retrofits are easy to add on. They can add a greater dimension than straight video because they can include learning-specific segments in addition to video (i.e., they can incorporate video), graphics, sound, and means of interaction.

- *Computerized.* This category includes a wide variety of approaches, among them the help capability of computer systems and software.

Media-Driven

More and more training programs use technology to deliver them. Media are highly interesting to learners, and they take advantage of the latest technology—but they are expensive. Another characteristic is that there are plenty of combinations to choose from, as you'll see from the following descriptions. One of the significant developments of personal computers, multimedia (CD-ROM, sound, video), can be fully exploited through computer-driven training. (A word of caution: There are as many terms as there are people who have been involved in the evolution of computers applied to training.) Here are some choices:

- *Computer-based training.* A computer controls all the functions. One of the more typical ways computers are used to deliver training is to implement a configuration specifically for training: the personal computer (PC), either laser disc or CD-ROM, and a special language to program the lessons and deliver them for learner interaction. Maintenance activities lend themselves well to this form, as does any subject where graphics are necessary. Computer-based training offers alphanumeric, graphics, animation, sound, and full-motion video capabilities. The learner interacts by answering queries given by the program, perhaps by touching the screen, and solving problems presented by the combination alphanumerics and graphic material.
- *Simulation.* This has been used for some time by the military and aviation industry to train pilots. Highly realistic flight simulators, with full-motion cockpits and actual cockpit controls, have taught thousands of pilots to land on aircraft carriers, handle emergency situations, and in general learn to fly aircraft they've never set foot in. Driver training simulators are also widely used.
- *Teleconferencing.* This can refer to anything from a conference call, where a small group of individuals are conducting a seminar, to a worldwide hookup via satellite, where several hundred people are on-line at the same time, fully visible and interactive with one another. The options selected—audio, video, or computer

based—depend on need and availability. Teleconferencing has these advantages:

- Brings a large number of participants together at the same time.
- Can be completely interactive, much the same as if everyone were in the same room.
- Eliminates expensive travel and related costs.
- Takes less time away from workplace.
- Can reach remote locations.
- Can get urgent topics on-line quickly.

- *Combinations.* By putting together various methods to meet your needs, a number of advantages can be gained: rapid delivery, ease of preparation, and a lively format, for example. For instance, you might use a commercially available video for initial training to meet fast turnaround demand, while developing your own workbooks and CD-ROMs for ongoing training.

Selection Criteria

Great care must be taken when selecting media to ensure a positive return on investment. In times when every dollar spent must be fully accounted for, it's imperative for the trainer to make bottom-line-related decisions. Factors to consider in selecting delivery methods are cost, ease of modifying, and degree of use.

Cost

A number of factors are related to cost, starting with possibly the biggest consideration: your budget. Unless you've had plenty of lead time to factor in cost elements, the budget often sets the level of spending before you embark on your training endeavor. Obviously you can't spend more than has been allotted, unless special circumstances arise.

The next consideration, and the most important in the long run, is whether you can justify the expense based on a return on investment (ROI) calculation. This is just another business decision, the same as for buying capital equipment, acquiring facilities, and purchasing raw materials and supplies. There must be a return on investment to allow expenditure. This is made easier if you've been thorough in determining how much you believe performance, productivity, or other critical measurements will be improved through training. You must be able to show how faster processing turnaround times will reduce costs and more than pay for training or be able to show how reduced stress, which you can do through training, will result in less sick time, fewer errors, lower medical costs, and so on.

If new resources are required, a prime consideration is whether they're reusable. If you decided that computer-based training using CD-ROMs is justified, consideration must be given to what use the systems will be put to after training is completed. If the training will be ongoing or the systems can be used for multiple purposes, the choice becomes easier.

Another consideration is the applicability of the delivery system to your requirements. If the staff being trained primarily uses computers and communications systems, does it make sense to give them a training package that's paper and pencil oriented? If they're accustomed to working on their own, does it make sense to do anything other than using a self-paced approach? Related to these considerations is whether the equipment and resources are already available. If PCs already sit on everyone's desk, it makes sense to consider using them for training. If facilities for recording and updating CD-ROMs are in place, then consider using them for training. If technology and resources are available (e.g., operational systems like computers and networks), then these move to the top of the list of possible delivery methods. And, finally, will you be able to use the equipment for other training? If so, then you have added reasons to consider a particular delivery method seriously.

Ease of Modification

How often will training require modification? It's one thing to issue change pages to written material, particularly when it can be shipped to remote sites electronically. It's quite another to update training programs that have been recorded on CD-ROM or video. If it's to be a highly used training program, modification costs can be justified on that basis.

Degree of Usage

Three quantitative considerations need to be made for this selection factor:

1. How many people are to be trained
2. How often the training will be conducted
3. How long the training program is to be in use

Exhibit 4-2. Selecting Delivery Methods and Media

Type	Use and Selection Factors
Classroom	• Knowledge-based learning • Need to work in groups • Need to train in a hurry • Little follow-on needed • Requires frequent updating • Technology can easily be brought in • Video can be used easily • Interactivity is easy to facilitate
Self-paced	• Wide geographic separation of learners • On-the-job training is the primary method of delivering training for the organization • Multimodality isn't critical • Supervisors can coach and track progress • Any technology required has built-in help
Media-driven	• Large numbers of learners • Ongoing requirement for repeated training • Available equipment, systems, and software • Heavy use of technology in the workplace • Technology and training systems readily available • Large numbers of participants geographically separated (for teleconferencing)

The first factor has related subfactors as well. One is where the people are located, and another is who they are. The larger the number, the easier it is to justify large initial investments, such as for expert training developers and technology. How far away the learners must travel or the ease of taking training to them will help you choose a method.

Rules of Thumb

Exhibit 4-2 summarizes the factors to consider when choosing delivery method. In addition, here are a few general rules to follow when making a decision:

- Classroom training is quickest and easiest to develop.
- Use existing equipment wherever possible (including word processing, reproduction, graphics, and audiovisual equipment).
- For training on using equipment and systems, practice on the actual systems as training devices whenever possible.

- Get help when using high-technology approaches (e.g., computer-based training, interactive video, teleconferencing).
- Think multimodality when choosing what to do, and use as many different methods as feasible, remembering that simple variations work well too.

If you need more analysis and information to make a decision, consult your training department or a qualified outside provider.

Selecting Media

Selecting media runs hand in hand with selecting delivery method since media have become primary delivery methods. Certainly the distinction between media and delivery methods is becoming blurred. Computer-based training is a case in point. It can be a medium used in the classroom, as well as the primary (possibly stand-alone) method of delivering.

Types of Media

For this discussion, media are divided into the general categories of *basic*—what has traditionally been used and is likely to be readily available (e.g., classroom and written media)—and *advanced*—associated more with evolving technology (e.g., virtual reality and expert systems).

Basic Media

This category includes everything we usually think about when the words *education* and *training* arise, because they're associated with classroom usage. They're heavily used and will likely be so for some time to come. Until the day when we are totally wired and digitized, the old-fashioned tools of chalkboards and overhead projectors will continue to serve, and serve well. Tips on how to use media are found in Step Five, and will be helpful in making decisions about which ones to choose, as ease of use is a prime reason for selection. Following are the media classified under this category.

- *Dryboards and chalkboards.* They're almost always available and require no technical expertise other than to be able to write (hopefully legibly).

- *Flip charts.* Readily available and portable, they offer many advantages, particularly for capturing participant thoughts for later review, update, and application.
- *Overhead projectors.* They're inexpensive, and it's easy to make transparencies (all you need is a copy machine or laser printer, items most organizations have). Color is becoming more common. Graphics and word processing capabilities of PCs make graphics and color for transparencies readily available.
- *Off-the-shelf video.* Monitors and video players (VCRs) are plentiful, and there are tens of thousands of training videos available on a seemingly endless number of topics.
- *Audio.* This requires inexpensive, simple equipment and is portable. Off-the-shelf topics are plentiful, and it's easy to generate customized tapes quickly.

Advanced Media

Thanks to technology, there are many choices of media to use in delivering training. Most of these are directly related to the PC and powerful peripherals associated with them. Following are the ones to consider when developing training:

- *Video.* Video can be customized for your use (e.g., to demonstrate a technique covered in the training or deliver a motivational message to learners). It requires the proper equipment and expertise to develop the videos, although small, stabilized camcorders have made great breakthroughs. Regular training sessions can be videotaped, but best results come from carefully rehearsed and staged presentations.
- *Projection methods.* This includes the ability to make hard copy from handwritten material on special boards and systems that make a variety of media through computers (35-mm slides, posters, charts, transparencies). Media service bureaus can produce the projected media from programs.
- *Computer-based training.* This requires authoring system software, appropriate hardware (including laser disc or CD-ROM), and a qualified person to develop the lessons. It can take advantage of color, graphics, and a host of other technology that improves the learning process.
- *Interactive video.* This requires all the above media plus multimedia equipment that can provide a wide array of capabilities.

- *Film.* Film is still around because so many 16-mm projectors re-main in use, and the quality is so good. Many films that are still relevant to training have been converted to video.
- *Slide-sound programs.* They combine 35-mm color slides (which can be generated from computer graphics programs) and audio-tape for a canned program.
- *Graphics and presentation software.* These systems for making computer-generated presentations for output to various devices and media, as well as directly projecting from computer onto a large screen, take full advantage of presentation system capabili-ties to produce powerful programs.
- *Liquid crystal displays.* These projection devices fit onto an over-head projector and project images from computer to a large screen. Large-screen video displays and projectors can also be used.
- *Simulators.* These can be specially built; they are expensive. PCs have made great strides here because of powerful simulation software that can emulate other systems. Simulation generated by virtual reality is the most advanced form.
- *Expert systems.* These programs capture human decision-making and diagnosis methods and are made available to end users to as-sist in a variety of functions and professions. Such programs can easily be added to training sessions.

Selection Criteria

Selection criteria for media are closely related to those for se-lecting delivery methods. This has become more the case as training and education have adopted the concept of using multimodality to deliver training that appeals to all learning styles. The ultimate con-cern is to deliver the most effective training, with effectiveness tak-ing into consideration return on training investment.

Make-or-Buy Decisions

No question about it—it's cheaper to buy ready-made training than to develop it from scratch. Custom-made is for organizations that can afford it—but there's a catch. Organizations are different, along with the people in them. Needs arise that are unique, and off-the-shelf training programs don't always meet the need. The result is that it may become necessary to initiate a make-or-buy decision-making process. The bottom-line secret is still quite simple: Does the training achieve the performance objectives you need to meet?

We have a number of choices when it comes to procuring training:

1. *Develop in-house from scratch*—if you have the staff, time, and other resources available or can contract out the work.

2. *Purchase complete packages from others*—if the packages fulfill most of your needs.

3. *Send learners off to let someone else train them*—if you have the time and resources to do this, and the other person's training fills the bill.

4. *Modify or adapt existing packages*—if you have the staff, time, and resources and if the training comes reasonably close to being what you need.

Other combinations could be developed, but these take care of most situations.

Several factors apply to determine whether to make or buy, starting with the budget:

- *Budget.* Even if there is justification for making large expenditures, if the funds aren't available, then developing a unique, customized program may be out of the question. Cash flow is always a consideration.

- *Criticality of training.* If company performance against growing competition is at issue, then the best available is probably justified.

- *Number of people to be trained.* If it's just a few, it may be more sensible to send them away; if it's hundreds, customizing may be well worth the effort.

- *Frequency of training.* How often will training be conducted? If not often, then find the best you can commercially.

- *Location of training.* Will you use multiple locations or only the home office? For multiple locations, geographic separation can be a central factor.

- *Applicability of off-the-shelf materials.* The materials need to be mostly, if not 100 percent, applicable (although it could be cost justified to use only that which is applicable and ignore the rest).

- *Need for customizing.* How close does the material come to filling your need? To what extent must it be altered?

- *Format.* Do the format and delivery method fit your need? For example, if it's video, do you have VCRs and monitors available?
- *Availability of trainers.* You need both instructors and developers.
- *Availability of resources* (computers, equipment, spaces, material).

Some of these factors will be more important than others. Weight the factors based on your needs and available resources to help you see if one method clearly outweighs the others (see Exhibit 4-3). You can select the key ones and assign values to them, then develop a decision matrix. In evaluating a particular training package, values ranging from 1 to 10 can be assigned to such factors as cost, number of people to be trained, frequency, applicability, format, and availability of trainers qualified to use the package. In this example, the highest value possible is 60. You may determine that a value as high as 45 would make the package a viable choice.

Selecting and Developing Experiential Exercises

Interaction is one of the secrets to success in training. Learning theory, new and old, and brain-related research on what makes people successful add to our knowledge on how best to interact. Interaction can be between the learner and subject material or equipment, between the facilitator and learners, and between learners. "All the above" is the best way. Any way it can be stimulated will help you succeed as a training facilitator. In short, experiential exercises are perhaps the best way people learn. (This concept is expanded in Step Five.)

Exhibit 4-3. Sample Weighting Factors for Making Selection Decisions

Factor	High Degree/ Weight	Low Degree/ Weight
• Criticality of training	• Urgent	• Not urgent
• Number of participants	• Large	• Small
• Frequency of delivering	• Often	• Once or infrequently
• Location of learners	• Many locations	• All or most at home office
• Training materials	• Must be customized	• Available off-the-shelf

Varieties of Exercises

There are many exercises to use with learners. Here are some common ones:

- *Icebreakers*, to get training sessions off to a good start. They can range from being as simple as having people introduce themselves, perhaps having them answer a specific question about themselves, all the way to definitive exercises, such as bingo games and solving puzzles. (You'll find some samples in Step Six.)
- *Climate setting*, to get into the subject early on. These are topic specific. For example, if the session is to be on listening skills, the exercise could be one that demonstrates how difficult it is to be a good listener.
- *Perception*, because this concept affects much of what we do and who we are. They do an excellent job of illustrating the concept of multiple, and sometimes contradictory, viewpoints. These often require a visual aid, with figures that can be interpreted in more than one way.
- *Team building*, to get teams up and running. These exercises are popular because learners usually enjoy participating. Often learners are broken into small groups and given problems to solve or tasks to perform. These exercises are designed to promote teamwork and illustrate the importance of teams. They might also combine other subject matter, such as group communication or problem-solving skills.
- *Problem solving*, to help develop this important skill. This can be used for team building or to have learners solve problems using a specific problem-solving method they're learning. Or it could be an exercise to solve a particular type of problem, such as return on investment for a management training course.
- *Leadership*, possibly designed to show how the absence of leadership leads to problems or to demonstrate specific leadership traits.
- *Determining roles*, to help people determine what their roles are. This could be part of team building, where the task is for learners to choose which role they want in a given exercise situation, which directly parallels what happens in real-life situations.
- *Self-concepts*, which lie at the bottom of skills acquisition. These are designed to help determine what people's views are on certain issues, such as prejudice for a diversity training session. These might

also be part of personality or leadership-related exercises or to help participants determine their learning styles.

These are representative of how exercises are used in training settings, and there are many others. As you can see, some are closely related, and it's easy to add to the list.

Forms of Exercises

Exercises come in many forms, ranging from the exchange of a few words, to paper-and-pencil challenges, to corporate cases using advanced computer technology. The ones described here provide a widely varied set from which to choose for training. Keep in mind that using a variety of exercise types will usually contribute positively to training. Remember also that for classroom training, exercises break up presentations and keep learners on their toes and motivated. Here are some of the more commonly used types:

- *Instruments*, which are often used to identify personality or learning traits or to measure attitudes and climates (as noted in Step Two regarding needs assessment). They can be for individual or group use. Examples of instruments for individual determinations include those to identify personal needs and motivational traits (e.g., participant, power, or affiliation orientation), teaching styles, learning styles, or personality types. Group-related instruments are used to determine group perceptions of management practices, readiness to change, and so forth. It's important that the correct instrument be selected (ready made, customized, or combination) and that the facilitator be thoroughly familiar with it. Some instruments (e.g., Meyers Briggs) require certification to be able to use them.
- *Case studies*, similar to the ones used in business schools. They have achieved wide use as training tools, largely because they represent the actual business world. They can be procured off the shelf or custom made for specific training situations and organizations. In fact, the case could well be a current management challenge that must be resolved. Numerous cases are available daily in the business news. Case studies apply equally to nonprofit organizations.
- *Role plays*, to add to the reality of behavioral training (e.g., diversity, customer relations). Long used in marketing and sales training, role plays require some expertise to facilitate, and not all

learners are comfortable role playing. However, they can be the next best thing to actual situations. There's much to be gained when a participant can feel the pain of being on the other end of an irate customer's tirade or someone who has just been discriminated against.

- *Games*, manual or automated, simple or quite involved. An example of a simple game would be one where participants are placed in the hypothetical situation of having been shipwrecked and must choose from a list of items those they believe would help them survive. More complex games might be computer based and involve giant corporations where a variety of financial, legal, and other management decisions must be made while competing with other learners in competitive companies. Good games can get learners heavily involved in the learning process, while taking advantage of one of the keys to adult learning.

- *Simulations*, which usually bring to mind flight simulators but are used in other areas. For example, there are sophisticated games using computer simulation that simulate highly articulated business situations. Games and simulations are closely related.

- *Group discussion and seminars*, which could be a simple exercise of giving small groups readings and instructions to discuss them, possibly answering a predetermined set of questions. Variations could be to have one group represent management, another labor, or perhaps governmental or competitive interests in the topic. The key is to get the learners involved in the subject matter and issues presented in the material. Debates on key issues within the training context provide a challenging option that can get participants fully and enthusiastically involved.

- *Practical work*, which refers to actual work situations for learners to perform. Computer training lends itself to this, as does learning any type of equipment or system. Learners could prepare a purchase order using the new system that was the subject of the training session, for example.

- *Demonstrations*, for complex situations or ones where there are not enough systems for everyone to have one. For example, a training session on how to program and use a new assembly-line robot might be started with a demonstration by an expert user. Learners could then take turns. Behavioral training also fits well, where both proper and improper behaviors (e.g., dealing with customers) can be demonstrated. Computer-related demonstrations can be projected using media.

- *Outdoor programs*, including survival situations and fitness, where learners become completely involved while acquiring teamwork, problem-solving, and creativity skills. These programs usually require some physical prowess, ranging anywhere from desert survival for pilots to tug-of-war for team members.
- *Assessment centers*, where actual work situations are set up and participants must deal with them. For example, in-basket exercises (where participants must make decisions based on action items in their in baskets) are often used with new management trainees, who must make decisions in dealing with priorities.

When to Use Exercises

Exercises can be used at virtually any time during a training session for a wide variety of purposes.

- *To get every one started on the right track and acquainted with one another*. It's one sure way for learners to become involved from the beginning.
- *For team building*. Given the importance of teams to the workplace, this training ranks among the top in terms of need.
- *To introduce new material*. This takes the mystery out of learning, particularly when people must learn something they have never been faced with before. First-time computer users fare much better when they get their feet wet at the outset of training, and the way to do it is to sit them down at the computer.
- *To reinforce material presented during a training session*.
- *To provide a multimodality approach*, particularly if the training is of the classroom type stressing lecture presentation. Exercises are relatively easy ways to add variety.
- *To illustrate actual situations*. This is becoming increasingly important in a work environment where lack of understanding of situations, and skills to deal with them, can be costly. Let the mistakes be made—and learning take place—through exercises in the training setting.
- *To demonstrate how things work*. This is especially helpful when the things in question are complex.
- *To model behavior*—both the right and the wrong approaches.
- *To measure performance or progress*. For performance-based learning, an exercise is a much better test of whether a learning objec-

tive has been achieved to a satisfactory level than a paper-and-pencil test.

- *To measure current skills and knowledge*. This is similar to measuring learning objectives, except that it may be done before the training.

Key Considerations for Exercise Selection

Keep these key considerations in mind when selecting or developing exercises:

- Be creative.
- Use what is available as much as possible.
- Use short exercises during training to break up material.
- Remember that variety is the spice of life.
- Keep the exercises as realistic as possible. This is what adults prefer.

Resources for Exercises

Fortunately, there are plenty of resources available. Because exercises and games are so widely used, numerous books and related materials are on the market, available from a variety of sources (see Step Eight and the Resources section for a further discussion).

Selecting Evaluation Methods

The reason for selecting the evaluation method at this time is to make sure it's tied into the learning objectives. Also, this decision can be made more easily at this point in the process, and it may be necessary to develop tests or evaluation exercises, which need to be prepared in advance.

The necessary balance for evaluating training is that it be as simple as possible while ensuring that training results are measured. The more formal the training, the greater the possibility for highly developed evaluation methods.

There are three primary evaluation methods: Verbal, written, and performance tests (e.g., to demonstrate that the learner can generate a spreadsheet, operate the piece of machinery, or use the desired technique for dealing with customer queries). Step Seven, Get Feedback, includes detailed information.

Selecting Participants

With few exceptions, resources for training are limited, so the key is to make sure the people being trained absolutely need it. If a person doesn't need a particular training course (say, it's a supervisory management session and a person isn't due to be promoted for several months), then don't include him or her; newly acquired skills that aren't applied right away are soon forgotten. Training should be performance based, so participants should be the ones who will perform the skills in question. Here are some selection criteria to use when determining who should attend training:

- The learners were identified during needs analysis.
- Training is directly pertinent to learners' jobs.
- Learners will be able to use the skills soon after they return to work.
- Learners meet prerequisites and need the skills.
- Learners are almost certain to be able to achieve the learning objectives. If not, preliminary or remedial training may be justified. (Training can be designed and used to screen people, but it's the exception.)
- Funding is available.
- The increased productivity when attendees return from training will considerably outweigh the lost work time caused by their absence.
- Learners are motivated to attend.
- When necessary and appropriate, prioritize who should attend. Keep a waiting list in case primary attendees cancel at the last moment.

Selecting Facilitators

As the workplace becomes more complex, so does training. For this reason, training facilitators often are subject matter experts. The challenge is to find facilitators—trainers—who are both expert in the subject and good trainers. Perhaps this is the reason you were chosen, so these eight steps will lead you to become a successful facilitator. Whatever the situation, it's imperative that both elements—subject matter expertise and facilitation—be present in the chosen facilitator. As a summary, here are the considerations, in addition to subject matter expertise and facilitation skills, to be made when selecting the person to be facilitator:

- Availability.
- Preparation time versus lost productivity (will the lost productivity of the expert be offset by his or her contribution to the training effort?).
- Previous experience.
- How many of the eight steps must be accomplished (e.g., is it only for delivering the training that a person is being chosen?)?
- Funding (e.g., if needs indicate that an outsider be brought in, are there funds to pay?).
- Skills (e.g., does the person have them?).
- Credibility (e.g., will learners accept the person as expert?).
- Motivation (e.g., will facilitator be motivated and motivate learners?).

Organizing Training

Organizing training lessons or modules is a process of sequencing learning events. Most training is job- and performance-oriented, meaning it follows a logical sequence of events. Organizing training into workable modules starts with the learning objectives. The terms *lesson* and *module* are often used interchangeably by trainers. For a large-scale training course, you may need to form modules that, in turn, have a certain number of lessons in them, but for our purposes, I'll keep the discussion simple.

Modularity is a vital consideration when turning training materials into a finished product ready for delivery. Keep the result as modular as possible, for two reasons. One is that it follows the logical process of laying out training. It will most likely fall into modules—groupings of materials and learning objectives that make sense. The other reason is that it will be more amenable to updating. Simply pull out those modules needing a change, make them, and put the package back together again.

How to Sequence

When subject matter is presented—a political speech, college lecture, sermon, planning report, or major training session—it must be presented in an orderly, logical manner if it is to make sense to the recipient. This means the presenter must have properly organized it in the first place. Fortunately, this isn't difficult to do. Exhibit 4-4 lays out a process to help you make sure training sessions are logi-

Exhibit 4-4. How to Organize a Training Session

1. *Start with learning objectives.*
   - Organize objectives into a logical sequence of lessons.
   - Each group will form a preliminary set of training modules. Note: Some training courses may be but one module, while others may be several modules covering several hours or days of training.
   - These groupings will form modules, or lessons, of your training.
   - Don't have too many objectives in one lesson (e.g., six objectives in a one-hour presentation with an exercise is probably too many).

2. *Analyze and sort each given grouping of objectives.*
   - Form the objectives into a lesson.
   - Treat each objective as a major element of the lesson.
   - Put the objectives of each module into logical order. (You may decide to move a few objectives around later, so this can still be a preliminary module.)
   - Identify elements to be included with each objective. These are the learning elements that may be needed to address the objective (e.g., an objective to parallel-park a car might include elements of backing up, using rearview mirrors, and spatial judgment).

3. *Organize the lesson.*
   - Sequence the objectives and elements into the order you want them.
   - Add detail as necessary for the presentation.

4. *Determine times.*
   - Determine the approximate time it will take to present each objective.
   - Add up times to determine the length of the module.

5. *Review the lesson, making any adjustments necessary.*

6. *Follow this process for each remaining grouping of objectives.*

cal and orderly—and successfully presented. Make sure the learning objectives can be achieved in the time you estimate you need to complete a session.

Another way to think of this is *chunking,* which means just what it says: Break the material into chunks. Each chunk should make sense, though it doesn't have to stand alone. Suppose the topic is how to overcome prospective customer objections to purchasing a maintenance contract when buying a new copy machine. The chunks might be:

- A review of the standard options for maintenance, including payment methods
- A list of reasons that maintenance contracts save the customer money over the long haul
- A list of potential customer objections
- A step-by-step process of how to deal with each objection
- How to ask for the order once objections are overcome

There's nothing scientific about chunking. In fact, it's the way many people learn. They absorb one chunk at a time until they have learned the whole lesson or skill. Using the developed learning objectives and common sense, particularly when the session is of a technical, subject matter orientation, will make sure your training flows smoothly.

Storyboarding

Another approach is to *storyboard* the module: identify the most important elements of the module (learning objectives) and present the message accordingly. This is the process media people use to develop television commercials. When you think how hard hitting and quick reacting an ad must be, you can see how applicable this could be to developing training.

Here are the steps to follow for storyboarding (a sample storyboard worksheet is shown in Exhibit 4-5):

1. Identify the key elements (objectives) of the module. Each of these becomes a frame.
2. On the top of a separate sheet of paper, write the frame number, subject, and learning objective or theme sentence.
3. Organize the elements into a logical sequence, adjusting frame numbers as appropriate.
4. Add subtopics to each key element to amplify the information.
5. Organize the subtopics into a logical sequence by numbering them in desired order.
6. Add visuals and exercises to the storyboard (these go on the right-hand side). Also include references, related stories, or anything else that will illustrate the frame.
7. Add times to each element to compute the estimated time for each module.

Exhibit 4-5. Sample Storyboard Worksheet

Frame No.: ___1___   Lesson/Presentation Title: Listening Skills   Date: _____

Subject/Learning Objective of This Frame: _____ Identify speaker concerns. _____

Theme Sentence/Learning Objective: Success in being a good listener starts with being able to determine why the

speaker needs to be listened to.

Amplifying Information	Illustration/Action/Reference
Reasons to be heard	
• Personal problem	Video showing failure of supervisor to pick up on a subordinate's concern
• Workplace-related problem	Discussion group
• Lack of knowledge about a	
work matter	Brainstorm session to identify reasons that people need to be listened to
• Simply lonely	
• Concerns about goals and	
objectives	Brainstorm to identify ways to find out what is causing the problem

Time required to complete: __20 minutes__

Using a Trainer's Guide

The sequencing process results in the input to the outline section of the trainer's guide. Even if key information is written down on the back of an envelope for a hastily put together management presentation, some representation of the guide is a must. (The exception is if the trainer has a photographic mind.) Keeping these on-line and available to those who might need them (including learners who can learn a lot simply by reviewing them) will make this and all other materials more valuable to everyone. Exhibit 4-6 shows the contents of a trainer's guide.

Other Materials

Trainers use a wide variety of materials, much of it in paper form, to present training. With word processing and readily available networks and printers, it's easy to generate materials quickly and easily. Learners who have computers available can access training materials on-line.

Handouts

Handouts can range from a single piece of paper summarizing the entire training session (usually the approach taken for busy executives who attend training and briefing sessions) to an outline for learners to fill in as the session progresses, perhaps in the form of a thick notebook. In between could be charts, books, actual work material—in fact, anything to augment the learning process. A word of caution: Do not overload the learners with too much information. This is where electronics, with the learner able to access information randomly and not have to carry around an armload of materials, comes in handy.

The advantage of a complete handout is that learners can concentrate on the task of learning, particularly if the subject is highly technical. On the other hand, use outlines to be filled in when there is a great deal of knowledge learning involved—for example, when employees are being trained to implement a new quality control program. The outline could include major topics, and the learner would take notes of key points as the session progresses. The combination of paying close attention to the presentation and taking notes can contribute to the learning process, particularly when there's an exercise or other activity to reinforce the material.

Exhibit 4-6. Trainer's Guide Contents

Part One

- Title of course/module and other pertinent information
- Date of latest revision and responsible person
- Learning objectives
- Target audience
- Prerequisites and learner participation
- Learner materials (e.g., handouts, exercises)
- Instructor materials (e.g., visual aids, tests)
- Audiovisual requirements
- Room setup requirements
- References
- Length of session/module

Part Two: The Session

Time	Topic/Event	Activity, Visual, and Handout
Estimated time for each major segment	• Main topics in outline form • Introduction to session —Introductions/icebreakers —Topics to be covered • First major topic (learning objective) As much detail in outline as needed to ensure that facilitator thoroughly covers material • Second major topic • Additional major topics • Summary Questions Evaluation Preparation for next session	Visual aid, exercise, handout

For a session on listening skills, the guide might look like this:

Time	Topic/Event	Activity, Visual, and Handout
5 min.	Introduction of participants • Discuss reasons for answers • Review what is to be covered	Think of a person you know who is not a good listener.
10 min.	Why listening is important • From supervisor's viewpoint	• Visual 1 • Visual 2

	• From workers' viewpoint	• Visual 3
	• From management viewpoint	• Visual 4
10 min.	Good listening techniques	Video depicting how to listen
10 min.	Detail the step used in video • Discuss with learners	Visual 5
20 min.	Exercise to demonstrate good skills • Divide into groups and give instructions	Exercise, using handouts
10 min.	Wrap-up and review of exercise	

Another type of handout is for a session where visual aids play a large role. Providing copies of the visuals (e.g., transparencies or computer-generated graphics) helps participants follow the presentation while making notes on the handout, and usually they can more readily recall it later.

Visual Aids

Visual aids, like handouts,must be prepared in advance. These are specialized materials to be used on the media selected. (See the discussion in Step Five on how to use media.) The key point to remember is that these must be designed and produced with all other materials.

Miscellaneous Materials

As with most other subjects, training has its miscellaneous material category. This is because just about anything can be classified as a training aid as long as it contributes to learning. Some of the items included in this category follow:

- A comprehensive workbook, which provides complete details of the training session. These can have places for the learner to fill in or else be complete and stand alone. These can be in digital form (e.g., on diskette).
- Job aids, usually taken from the workplace (e.g., a safety sign placed on a piece of equipment or a flight checklist or computer help menu).

Exhibit 4-7. Training Preparation Checklist

Training Session: _____

Date: _____ Location: _____

Number of Participants: _____ In Charge: _____

Item	Required	Completed	Comments
Facilities			
• Room(s) reserved	_____	_____	Note if third party.
• Layout specified/ arranged	_____	_____	Send copy to provider.
Materials			
• Trainer guides	_____	_____	
• Other materials (list)	_____	_____	
• Facilitator materials	_____	_____	
Equipment			
• Video monitor and VCR	_____	_____	
• Overhead projector	_____	_____	
• PC(s)	_____	_____	
• Liquid crystal display	_____	_____	
• Other projector	_____	_____	
• Screen	_____	_____	
• Sound system	_____	_____	
• Miscellaneous (extension cords, outlets, etc.)	_____	_____	
• Boards, markers, etc.	_____	_____	
• Chalkboard or dry board	_____	_____	
• Flip chart and tripod	_____	_____	
• Materials for equipment	_____	_____	
Food service (including special requirements)			
• Breaks (coffee, refreshments)	_____	_____	Note how many and when.
• Meals	_____	_____	Note how many and when.
Personal arrangements			
• Travel (learners, facilitator)	_____	_____	
• Lodging	_____	_____	
• Local travel	_____	_____	
• Social events	_____	_____	
• Recreation	_____	_____	

- Posters and signs.
- Mockups of equipment, including cutaways or pieces for training purposes.
- Equipment and systems user manuals.
- Actual equipment.

Preparation for Training

As a trainer, you must be prepared. This could easily require as much effort as developing or delivering the training. If the preparation is not adequate and complete, all your other efforts could quickly be erased. A good rule to use is that any problem that crops up in the training caused by lack of preparation will be fatal.

Use a checklist such as the one in Exhibit 4-7 to help you make sure everything is done, and done properly. Checklists will help you select appropriate persons for training, make advanced notification to all concerned (learners, trainers, bosses of both, resource persons), determine adequacy and amount of budget, then plan so there's a budget reserve (you never know when you might run out of coffee or pencils—little things like this can do serious damage), and more.

Having a contingency plan to cover a number of situations that could occur (cancellation, less time to conduct training, loss of media, having to move to a different location, etc.) is always a good idea.

Site Selection

Make reservations for space, equipment, travel, lodging, food, and everything else not directly under your control. Include plans for resources to be delivered or a person designated to be responsible for them. Also make all special accommodations required (particularly those regarding sites and equipment or persons with disabilities or special transportation needs).

Select a site of the appropriate size (too large or too small can cause problems) well in advance, and have backups. From this point come the details: electrical and telephone outlets, a storage room for lengthy sessions (to avoid having to move equipment and materials), accessibility for people with disabilities, location of rest rooms, and so on.

When considering outside facilities, ask, Is it worth the expense? As for the accommodations mentioned above, make sure you can rely on the third-party space provider to be able to provide accommodations for those who need them. If this means you must go to the facility in advance, do not hesitate; the trip may pay off in the long run.

Room Layout

Training rooms can be laid out in a number of ways as Exhibit 4-8 shows; the critical element is that the layout fit the situation and be comfortable for participants. The more flexible the room, the better. Bear in mind that some rooms don't lend themselves to certain layouts. For a half-hour session, this might not be a problem, but if learners get sore necks from viewing an inadequately mounted screen for three days running, the amount of learning will be directly affected—negatively.

Room layout needs must be clearly communicated to the outside facility in advance, with follow-up a must.

There are several things to keep in mind when you select the room (or rooms) for training, although some decisions may be made for you (e.g., if it's to be a computer-generated training, you'll need a space where enough workstations are available):

1. Make sure it's big enough—but too big can cause problems too (too big, however, is always better than too small).
2. Have working areas for writing and placing materials if needed.
3. Determine whether ventilation is available, comfortable, and controllable.
4. Consider whether the instructor work area is large enough for materials, media, projectors, and so on.
5. Be sure people in the back can see the screen.
6. Look for interference from other nearby spaces (other training sessions, working crews, and so on). Noise and other distractions tend to ruin a trainer's day, not to mention that of learners.
7. Check on the availability of personal comfort items (rest rooms, drinking water, refreshments, etc.).
8. See that lighting is adequate, with control over brightness if needed.

Exhibit 4-8. Sample Room Layouts

Circle or U-shape use for small groups; informal sessions; to encourage interaction

Screen / (Place to side if convenient)

Rows of tables (where workspace is needed) or theater seating (for large groups)

Tables can be slanted toward one another to encourage more interaction.

Logistics

This means just what it says. Perhaps you'll only need to have a glass of water available for the facilitator, but it must be there. Or you could need to plan for transportation, food (including special meals), lodging (including special accommodations), refreshments, supplies, equipment, shipping training materials, and more. Logistics are included on the preparation checklist (see Exhibit 4-7). These will be identified as you carefully plan the details of the training you've laid out, and outside providers must know what they are.

Pilot Training

Time permitting, do a practice run of your training. It can do you a lot of good—for example:

1. Get the rough edges off.
2. Help you adjust times.

3. Identify problem or weak areas, including what needs to be eliminated, redone, or rearranged.
4. Give you some experience delivering it.
5. Show you how learners might react.

If you can have some training experts and representatives from the group scheduled to receive the training, so much the better.

Right away you can see the potential problem with pilot training: It takes time and resources, including valuable people time. However, there are things you can do to go through a dress rehearsal of the session.

At least walk through it in your head, or discuss it with someone whose opinion you respect. You can actually walk through it, even if by yourself—certainly through the key parts and those segments you feel least confident about (e.g., using a piece of equipment you're unfamiliar with).

For a longer session, do as much of a full-blown walk-through as you can, because there's a lot at stake. If you have custom-designed a program that will be delivered to a large audience over a long period of time, conducting a pilot course becomes essential. Discovery of a flaw in the program in the middle of the session attended by 250 people is costly, embarrassing, and unprofessional.

Step Five

Deliver Effectively

> *A key need will be for managers who know how to make the best use of human resources. Workers without the skills and education to adapt to this evolving economy face a constrained and grim future.*
>
> —Arthur Wirth
> *Education and Work for the Year 2000* (1992)

Now that you've selected the methods and media for delivering training, it's time to implement the program. How trainers deliver training is changing dramatically. Not so long ago, the trainer was the focus of the process. Learning occurred only when the trainer acted. Today the trainer is a facilitator of a continuing learning process. This and the fact that diversity demands different approaches make delivery not only different but more important than ever.

Step Five Summary

How well the trainer communicates is the key to ultimate success. The best-written, most precise, and most measurable learning objective will be wasted if it isn't communicated properly. Accommodating diversity is a major part of this step. It includes:

- Discussion of trainer as communicator
- Proven communication tips
- Instructions on how to use media
- Instructions on good delivery
- Tips on how to accommodate diversity in training

Exhibit 5-1. Ways a Trainer Communicates

	Implementation	When Used
Verbal	Speaking and listening	• During front-end needs assessment (e.g., interviews and networking with others for ideas and information) • During selection processes to speak to experts • Making verbal training presentations and speaking to learners during other training activities • Obtaining feedback after training
Written	In many formats	• Capturing needs assessment information • Writing objectives • Writing materials • Communication with providers and participants • Evaluation
Nonverbal	Body language, expression	• During all verbal communication, as well as quiet training times • During teleconferences when the spotlight is on others
Electronic	E-mail, discussion groups	• Communicating with learners • During training exercises

The Trainer as Communicator

The most obvious form of communication by a trainer is speaking—presenting material to learners in a classroom environment. Yet verbal communication is but one way a trainer communicates. Written, nonverbal, and electronic means enter the picture too. Exhibit 5-1 lists some of the ways these forms of communication are used.

To be successful, the trainer must be able to communicate with others during the steps leading up to delivery and later, again through communication, determine if training has met desired objectives. This means communicating with others during needs assessment and working with subject-matter experts during the design and development phases of training. Because communication is such a vital part of training, we look first at the process of communicating, before addressing how to present training effectively.

Think of communication as it occurs at any point in the training process as a system. Exhibit 5-2 shows it as a closed-loop system; when something is put into it (e.g., a message delivered to a learner), something must come out (e.g., an acknowledgment that the message was received, and, you hope, some indication that the information or skill transmitted in the message will be put to good use). Until this loop is closed, communication hasn't occurred. Note from the exhibit the many pitfalls that can interfere with successful communication. Use this system to keep a clear picture of how to communicate effectively as you deliver training. In fact, it's a good idea to pause occasionally to consider whether what you just said (or the exercise just completed, the problem just solved, the role play enacted) communicated what was intended.

Trainer communication skills can be classified into three key types: verbal, listening, and motivating participants. All three must

Exhibit 5-2. The Communication Process: A Closed-Loop System

be effective to achieve maximum results. (Writing skills are also important, and are fundamental to preparation for training, as discussed in Step Four.)

Verbal Skills

Humans have communicated all their lives in some manner, mostly through a symbolic, or written, language. It's this characteristic that sets us apart from other creatures on earth. The fact that we speak to one another as the primary means of communication is usually taken for granted. However, the trainer as presenter can't afford to make assumptions about communicating with learners other than that it must always be done well. Several general principles apply to being a good presenter:

1. *Keep it simple.* For an audience you may have never met before, keep your presentation simple so everyone has a maximum opportunity to achieve the learning objectives by being able to understand what you are saying. Think also about diversity. More and more learners—valuable members of the workforce—speak English as a second language.

2. *Be clear.* Avoid using words with double meanings. This is where you apply the adult learning principle that learners use their own experiences, which means that the language must be that which they speak and use regularly. This is particularly true when learners from other cultures are present.

3. *Consider how your audience will perceive you.* Adults use their own perceptions to add meaning to the words they hear. This means that the stories, analogies, humor, and the like must be perceived by the recipients within the context of the training in general and learning objectives in particular.

4. *Use imagery.* People have pictures in their heads that have accumulated over their lifetimes. Don't rely on words alone when you can evoke mind pictures that will reinforce learning. This is where multimodality and exercises assist the trainer dramatically.

Listening Skills

All aspects of training, from needs assessment to after-the-fact evaluation, require you to listen carefully. You must be able to truly hear what people have to say about needs, assess who is not grasping the material, and understand what learners have to say about the completed training.

Following a few simple rules will help you hone your listening skills:

1. Recognize that the person has something to say and needs to talk it out.
2. Genuinely show interest in what the other person has to say.
3. Stop whatever it is you're doing to emphasize the previous rule.
4. Encourage continued communication on the other person's part. Sometimes all it takes is a nod of your head or a brief word.
5. Let the person talk it out, saying everything he or she needs to say.
6. Refrain from making judgments.
7. Give appropriate feedback.
8. Give honest recognition of the other person's feelings, whether it is anger or enthusiasm, disappointment or elation.

Motivating Participants

Motivation was discussed in Step Three, along with various aspects of adult learning theory. Refer to this step for a refresher on motivation and how important it is in communicating during training.

One of your prime responsibilities as facilitator is to go all out to motivate learners. Motivation provides the infrastructure for the communication and training facilitation processes.

As a review, here are selected ways to motivate learners:

1. Give them feedback. Rarely will you be found guilty of giving too much.
2. Always look for positive signs (e.g., a person has part of the answer or is on the right track), and call attention to them.
3. Present all aspects of training in a challenging manner.
4. Encourage participants to stretch their limits during learning.
5. Give simple prizes (e.g., pens, candy) to encourage competition.

How to Give an Effective Presentation

Much has been written and said about how to do a great job in making presentations. It generally follows the same principles found in the eight steps to effective training, starting with preparation, knowing the audience, and being highly motivated to present. The points identified in Exhibit 5-3 are based on best practice and experience; follow this outline when making any kind of presentation.

Exhibit 5-3. How to Be a Successful Presenter

1. Before the presentation
- Learn everything you can about the participants.
- Have well-stated objectives.
- Think through the questions and reactions participants might have, realizing that to deal effectively with them will take away any doubts and misunderstandings they might have. Having developed your own questions and responses in advance will be a big help.
- Prepare and practice. There's no substitute for going through every moment of the presentation or session. Use audio, video, and other people to give you advice on how to make improvements.
- Make one last walk-through to make sure all details are attended to, such as room arrangements and logistics. Use a checklist if appropriate, paying attention to any special needs required (e.g., a person with a disability).

2. During the presentation
- Be ready to make adjustments as needed, including having standby plans and exercises to use.
- Keep the proper pace. Do not let your presentation flag or move too fast.
- Stay with topic by focusing on the objectives established before you started.
- Be aware of your body language and tone of voice. Slumping or speaking in a monotone can contradict every good thing you have to say.
- Sometimes you'll have to pick up the presentation, for example, after a long, hearty lunch, so be prepared to step it up a notch to keep things moving, even if it means having a stand-up exercise or hilarious joke.
- Through your preparation, enthusiasm, and professional actions, let the audience know that your singular purpose is to make the presentation worth their while.

3. After the presentation
- Get feedback, using formal critique forms and face-to-face questioning of participants. Get feedback from observers too.
- Critique your own performance for future improvement (and to pat yourself on the back too).
- Make it clear that you value feedback and particularly want theirs.

One of the exciting elements of delivering training is that there's so much variety available, much of it due to innovations in technology and learning theory, to enhance the process. The challenge is that you must use them well. Included here are tips on using media, icebreakers, and humor and implementing multimodality approaches.

How to Use Media

Most of us have been around VCRs and television monitors for years. What could be so complicated about showing a video during a training session? Writing on a flip chart should be no different than scribbling on a chalkboard, right? These aren't trick questions. Video showings that go wrong and flip charts that are unreadable and ripped into shreds are commonplace for the trainer who doesn't pay attention to them, so pay attention to the general rules in Exhibit 5-4 when using media.

Each medium has its own unique requirements for best usage. Following are tips on how to use the commonly available training media.

Exhibit 5-4. General Rules for Using Media

1. **Walk through the usage in your mind beforehand** so you know exactly when and how the media are to be used.
2. **Practice using the media as many times as necessary** to make sure there will be no glitches. No two systems are alike, and the system you used yesterday may not be the one in the room today.
3. **Don't use a visual aid unless it's readable, concise, and makes sense to the viewers.** This includes eliminating the so-called eye chart visuals like those copied from pages of textbooks, visuals with errors on them, and ones that are blemished, faded, or otherwise have parts that are unreadable.
4. **Never make an excuse for a visual aid.** If you need to, it shouldn't have been used in the first place. To do so will detract from your credibility. The more excuses and apologies you make, the less credible you are.
5. **When a glitch does occur, don't try to cover it up;** rather, move right along, and don't dwell on it. When an apology is necessary, make it (say, "Sorry about that") and move along. Everyone makes mistakes, but keep in mind your role of the expert and the issue of credibility.
6. **The key to never having to worry about such things as apologies is preparation.** Make sure you are fully ready to begin.

Exhibit 5-4 (*continued*)

7. ***Have spare support materials available*** (lamps for projectors, markers, paper, extension cords, etc.).

8. ***When a simple medium will do, use it.***

9. ***Don't be afraid to skip use of some media,*** particularly visual aids, when you sense it's time to move along. When the audience starts drooping after the first ten of your twenty prepared transparencies, simply stop and move on to something else. Maybe there'll be some other use for the unused ten pieces, but if not, it's better to waste them than to force them onto learners who don't want them. It's better to have too much material than not enough.

10. Despite your best efforts, problems can occur at any time, and backup systems can fail. ***Be prepared by having an alternate plan for delivery***—possibly a couple of alternate plans. For example, use transparencies as notes to deliver a manual presentation without visuals if necessary. Use boards to sketch notes and diagrams in lieu of flip charts. The point is that sooner or later, the odds will catch up with you, no matter how hard you try, so be ready. The mark of a good trainer is to make the transition from planned, automated media presentation to backup as seamless as possible, as though you had planned it. The less distraction to the audience, the better, and by no means should you complain or make an issue of the situation. Even if it was of no fault of yours, you're the person standing in front of the room, so call as little attention to the problem as possible.

Videos

Videos are common—tens of thousands of them are available commercially—and people are accustomed to seeing them. When you want to use them in training, be sure they are appropriate. Your audience will watch whatever you set before them, being addicted to rectangular shapes and full color as they are, but your choice needs to contribute positively to achieving the learning objectives. Exhibit 5-5 contains tips on making the most of video in your presentation.

Exhibit 5-5. Using Videos

1. ***Never assume anything***—that the equipment works, that the tape has been rewound, that the sound is at proper level, that you know where all the controls are, that you know where the light switch or dimmer is located, that the right videotape is in the container you brought, that the remote has a good battery, and so on.

2. ***Room lights will probably have to be at least dimmed or partially turned off.***

3. ***Always preview any video you use.*** This follows the same principle as having read any written material assigned. If there are any surprises, with context, applicability, or quality, the learners will hold you fully responsible.

4. ***If at any time it looks as if there's a problem (e.g., inappropriate material, quality), stop immediately.*** It's better to stop than continue with the problem.

5. ***Have the tape positioned at the starting point and ready to run.*** If there's a several-second delay while awaiting the exact starting point, participants may drift away from the material at hand.

6. ***Use video clips where appropriate.*** If a three-minute segment of a video (e.g., one scene or event) will suffice, show just that. Determine at what time you want to start and stop, check it out before the start of the session, and show the small piece. (Caution: If it's a really great video, participants might want to see it all.)

7. ***Don't show videos immediately following a meal or at other times when learners might be tired.*** There are some hard-hitting ones available that might be okay, but the later in the day a video is shown (especially at night), the higher the probability is that some folks will nod off. (On the other hand, a good, dull video might serve well as a deep relaxation technique for a stress management class.)

8. Videos add variety to training, so ***use them to add insight, to reinforce previously presented material, or to introduce new concepts and ideas.***

9. ***Use videos as an excellent means of presenting cases and examples.*** Behavioral-related training uses video effectively to demonstrate proper and improper behaviors (a sort of before-and-after version of desired behaviors).

10. ***Make sure the screen is large enough for everyone to see.*** Check it out in advance by viewing it from the remotest part of the room.

11. ***Tune the picture in advance.***

12. ***Adjust sound by getting visual signals from the audience as you turn it up.*** Be careful not to have it come on and blast eardrums. Look toward the people in the back of the room to ensure that they can hear.

13. ***Don't stand in front of the monitor.***

14. ***Use a remote control, after first making sure it works.*** There's nothing more frustrating than trying to make an on-line adjustment by squatting down in front of the set and finding tiny buttons to push. A remote gives you far more control; you can stay in a position to see exactly what's going on. Anytime there's a problem or any doubt, stop the video immediately.

15. ***Don't push any buttons you aren't sure of.*** If in doubt, follow the previous instruction, even if it means pulling the power cord out of the socket. Expensive videos have been ruined by a facilitator's inadvertently hitting the wrong control.

Exhibit 5-6. Using Flip Charts

1. ***Make sure the tripod or other resting place for the newsprint is sturdy.*** If in doubt, try writing in a hurry, pressing down hard as you might do during a busy training session, to make sure the rig is steady. Be careful about using chairs and chalk racks on boards, because they aren't made to hold large pads of paper and can easily give up their contents during crucial times—falling on the floor or on your head.)

2. ***Use more than one color,*** which may take careful thought beforehand and a little practice. For example, ideas might be in blue, with red bullets to set them apart. Special notes might appear in purple or some other contrasting color. Studies have provided information about which colors work best, so if you care to, dig into this element further.

3. ***Be consistent with colors when you do use them.*** Otherwise your efforts might look like a preschool art class.

4. ***Practice tearing off pages and taping them to the wall.*** This is the key to flip chart use: that you can save thoughts and brilliant ideas for later review. You might even want to start the tear before the session begins, as well as have strips of masking tape fixed to the wall nearby, ready to use. This will speed things up, as well as keep you from looking foolish while ripping sheets in half and dropping things while attempting to tape sheets to the wall. Walk through this ahead of time.

5. ***Decide in advance where you want to put up the sheets.***

6. ***Have plenty of paper, markers, and tape.*** Never go in with only one marker and one roll of tape. One pad of newsprint is okay if it's reasonably full.

7. ***Have more than one pad and tripod for large rooms or for situations where a variety of thoughts and processes will take place.*** This way, people in the back of the room won't have to make their way to the front to write on the flip chart.

8. ***Place tripods and pads of paper (or possibly blank sheets taped on a wall) with markers for participants to jot down their comments or thoughts.*** For example, individual learners might be asked to write their expectations of the session when they arrive and set them aside for later review. There are many ways learners can use flip charts to enhance their involvement and learning.

9. ***Print legibly and large enough for everyone to be able to read.*** Some trainers who don't print neatly or are too busy to stop and write may need to recruit a participant to do the writing. (Careful here; some people don't like to do this.)
10. ***Prepare charts in advance where appropriate,*** including those where you want learners to fill in blanks, to keep things moving at a livelier pace.
11. ***Make sure everyone can see the flip charts,*** from both the tripods and the places where they're taped to walls.

Flip Charts

Flip charts lend themselves nicely to numerous training situations by capturing on-the-spot ideas and thoughts. Tips to follow when you use them are listed in Exhibit 5-6.

35mm Slides

When we think of 35mm slides, images of cameras with zoom lenses and exotic settings come to mind. Computer graphics has the potential of overriding many other media, though slides have received new life. This is because it's possible to use computer-generated imagery, including photography digitized via scanners and conversion software, to generate a wide assortment of slides. This, and the fact that there are still plenty of resources available in the field, keep them useful for training. Their quality alone makes them a versatile product. They provide the next best thing to color video and add variety. Tips to keep in mind when using slides are shown in Exhibit 5-7.

Exhibit 5-7. Using 35mm Slides

1. ***Make sure the room is dark,*** so work this out beforehand. Don't make it any darker than absolutely necessary. It should be light enough so people can take notes if desired.
2. ***Add sound through audiotape where appropriate.*** This provides the system known as sound-on-slide. There are special devices available for presentations.
3. ***Consider automating slide showing by playing through a computer program to control the slides.*** This allows random use as well, so it's easy to go back to a particular slide to clear up a point.
4. ***Make sure there's a spare lamp that fits the projector,*** and make sure you know how to replace it in a hurry.
5. ***Make sure the screen is the right distance for the best, clearest picture.***

Exhibit 5-7 (*continued*)

6. ***Use the right screen.*** Screens made for slides have a matte finish. Movie screens are beaded and don't portray slides as clearly. Sometimes a clean, light-colored or white wall will do quite nicely.

7. ***For large rooms, use a special lens (step-down)*** that will project the image properly from a distance.

Overhead Transparencies

Transparencies are widely used in training and education. Plenty of advantages come with transparencies: equipment is usually readily available, transparencies are inexpensive and can be quickly generated (both alphanumeric and graphic) from a word processor or graphics package, and even a novice can make them.

The transparencies can be generated using hard copy and a copy machine or by printing directly from a computer onto the transparency material using a laser printer. There are also machines available for making them. When changes need to be made, throw away the old transparency and make a new one. Color can also be used if there's a graphics package and color printer. Also, it isn't necessary to dim the lights in the presentation room. Lettering can be made with large fonts, making it easier for people with the weakest eyesight sitting in the back of a large room to see. Some tips for use are shown in Exhibit 5-8.

Exhibit 5-8. Using Overhead Transparencies

1. ***Use a large font.*** The standard is 24-point type, but don't hesitate to use larger, especially for large audiences. Even people with 20-20 vision don't like to squint to read. In fact, no one will make much effort to see things that are difficult to see (making these people nonparticipants).

2. ***Don't put too much information on any given piece.*** A good rule to follow is no more than four or five lines of text per visual, using phrases rather than complete sentences. For graphics, use a simplified version of complex diagrams, then additional pieces to show blow-ups of various segments. When in doubt, make up the visual, then sit and look at it as if you were the participant. The brain can take in only so much at a time, and by simplifying, learning will occur faster.

3. ***Turn the machine off when you aren't directly addressing a visual aid,*** even if you'll use it again in a minute or so. People will keep staring at the bright light projected onto the screen (or wall). When

you want them to focus on you or someone else or an object in the room, turn the machine off, even if there's a transparency on it.

4. **Use special markers to write on transparencies,** including using them as fill-in-the-blanks or as a chalkboard, generating information from scratch. The advantage is that the transparency can be saved for later use, even for subsequent classes.

5. **Have learners make transparencies of their solutions to group problems.** They can project them onto the screen for discussion and comparison to other group solutions.

6. **Use a pointer or pen as a marker by pointing directly to the desired position on the transparency.** There are also laser and other types of pointers available that can be directed to the appropriate place on the projected image.

7. **Cover all but the item under discussion with a piece of paper,** revealing each subsequent item on the list as you come to it. Otherwise, people will start reading ahead and taking notes while you're still discussing the first item on the list.

8. **Don't stand in front of the screen.**

9. **Don't make excuses for poor visuals.** Don't use them in the first place.

10. **Protect transparencies between uses.** The ink will come off eventually, but the transparency will last longer with care. There are covers available, as well as frames to both protect and make them easier to handle. At least place a clean piece of paper between them when not in use.

11. **Use washable ink markers designed for transparencies.**

Boards

Most of us remember attending school classrooms with the everpresent blackboard. They've changed the colors to brown and green, and many of these have given way to dry boards, but both are still prevalent today. They offer the opportunity for spontaneous reaction to learning situations and are invaluable to training and learning sessions. A few rules to keep in mind when using this old standby are identified in Exhibit 5-9.

Computer-Based Presentation Systems

You need a great deal of experience when delivering training using computer-based media. Whether you are using a liquid crystal display to project computer-generated images onto the screen or conducting full-blown computer-based training, you must do it

Exhibit 5-9. Using Boards

1. *Have spare markers or chalk and erasers on hand.* Never assume they'll be available unless you have visited the site recently and know they are there.

2. *Don't stand in front of information you've written or drawn on the board.* This is more critical than when using screens, because the board is often located directly behind the presenter. Always keep in mind the people in front of you. If you wrote something down (or a learner did), all others present will want to see it, and possibly take it down as notes.

3. *Practice penmanship before standing before the group.* Readability is important. When in doubt, spell it out verbally in order to make sure everyone knows what was said.

4. *Consider using electronic boards.* They can generate a hard copy of what is written on them. They work the same as dry marker boards and offer the advantage of capturing what is written.

5. *Don't erase until you're sure everyone has had a chance to see what has been written and record as needed.*

properly. Sometimes you merely need to be familiar with the equipment. At the other end of the spectrum, you might need to use a totally different method of facilitating training, and one that requires a good deal of expertise. Tips on using this training medium are shown in Exhibit 5-10.

Exhibit 5-10. Using Computer-Based Presentation Systems

1. *Make sure you know how to use the system* (be thoroughly familiar with it), or else have assistance.

2. *Try it out first* to determine the degree of darkness needed and also to see how much light you'll need to operate the system. Great graphics and color soon dissolve on the screen if there's a glare.

3. *Check out the peripheral equipment too* (e.g., the overhead projector if you are using one).

4. *Use a large font and figures.* Remember, some people may need a little extra help seeing. In other words, unless you have a large screen projector that will magnify the presentation many times, it will turn out to be the same as projecting a page of text in 12-point type onto the screen—which few people can read.

5. *Have backup systems or a manual presentation ready to go—* and be ready to change with little delay, as if you planned it that way.

6. **Rehearse as many times as necessary to ensure a smooth flow.** A pause while you fiddle with a mouse or click on the wrong icon can lose your audience.

Using Icebreakers

Exercises known as icebreakers are to do just that: break the ice at the beginning of a session. Because getting sessions started positively is vital to good training, this important exercise form is addressed here. The discussion is equally valid for Step Six, regarding getting learners involved. Reasons for a trainer to use an icebreaker in a training session include getting learners acquainted, setting the tone or theme for the session, and simply getting people involved immediately.

Getting Learners Acquainted

Get learners acquainted with one another as soon as you can, particularly if they've never met before. For a two-hour presentation, introductions should be quick, if done at all. If the learners are to be together several hours or days, the overall process will be more successful if they meet one another at the outset. They'll either ignore one another if you don't make sure they meet, which could be detrimental to the group process, or else take time to get acquainted anyway, which also would detract from the mission at hand.

Icebreakers can get the job done immediately so you can move on with the training. This is particularly crucial for group activities. Members need to know what their colleagues have to offer and what roles they'll be willing to play. From the facilitator's viewpoint, each person brings something to learning (occasionally the opposite), and here's where you can find out what it is. It's also a way to identify potential challenges (see Step Six on difficult behaviors).

Setting the Tone or Theme of the Training

This is a process of letting participants quickly learn the purpose of the training or to get started on a lively pace. For example, a session on diversity could use an icebreaker designed not only to get people acquainted but to show an element of diversity. Here are some other topics amenable to the use of icebreakers:

- Communication (all types)
- Motivation

- Perception
- Leadership
- Self-concepts
- Problem solving
- Transfer of training
- Making changes
- Team building
- Thinking in different ways

After participating in an icebreaker exercise, learners will be tuned in to the topic and purpose of the session, and quickly. While doing so, they will have implemented the basic learning premise that adults want to get heavily involved in the process.

Getting People Involved Immediately

Since a key to successful adult learning is active involvement in the process, it's a good idea to get people involved in the training session as soon as possible. Staging an icebreaker is an excellent way to do this. It also sends a positive message that you, as facilitator, expect them to take an active part in the session.

Icebreaker Resources

Experienced trainers have dozens of icebreakers in their bag of learning lore, gathered over the years from numerous sources. Fortunately, there are plenty of resources; their popularity has made it lucrative for many publishers and training materials providers to market them. For example, *Games Trainers Play* (1980) is a four-book series by Edward Scannel and John Newstrom. Many are made up on the spot, and you don't have to be clever. Having people go around the room and introduce themselves works well, and you can add such subtle steps as having them tell a little about themselves (e.g., what book they have read recently that they liked or their favorite subject in school). Some representative icebreakers are listed in Exhibit 5-11.

Exhibit 5-11. Sample Icebreakers

- *Bingo,* for getting acquainted. Make up a bingo sheet that has a variety of items on it, including several that are easy and several related to participants (e.g., was born in India, has red hair). Participants go around and get the person who fits the box to initial it (limiting the number of times any single person can sign). The first one to get a bingo (up, down, diagonal) wins. The more personalized the form is, the better. Prizes can be awarded if desired.

- **Two Facts and a Lie,** for getting acquainted. Each person states three things about himself or herself (e.g., was born in Japan, had six children, and once owned an ice cream store). Two of the facts are to be true and one false, but all three are to be stated as if all were true. The rest of the group guesses which one is incorrect. This game is fun and helps get things off to a good start, while accomplishing the goal of getting people acquainted with one another.

- **Story Time,** for listening skills. Participants are arranged in a circle. The person chosen to lead off is given a slip of paper with a brief statement printed on it and reads the statement to the second person, whispering in the person's ear. The second must whisper what he or she heard to person number three, and so on down the line. The last person in the circle (next to the originator) states what he or she heard out loud, and person number one compares what is said to what is on the sheet of paper. The result is often considerably different, and sometimes hilarious. It proves how difficult it is to listen to another human being.

- **Building a Team.** Participants are put in groups of three to five people and given a task to perform. No instructions are given on how to organize, who is to lead, or anything else. Participants are given a set amount of time to perform the task, such as to write a mission statement for a global electronics firm or determine how to deal with a problem employee. If necessary, provide a short synopsis of the situation they are to deal with on a piece of paper. The ensuing discussion will uncover the problems with establishing a team, determining who is to be the leader, and possibly to note the difficulties in obtaining consensus. The subject matter could also be a significant part of learning.

- **Drawing.** A person is selected to describe a drawing (or picture) on a piece of paper. The drawing can be a grouping of shapes (or anything else not easily perceived). The participants draw what they perceive the person is saying. The participants may not see the drawing and may ask no questions; the presenter can use only words—no hand motions or drawing on board. Compare and discuss the versions afterward.

- **Perception.** Show a picture that can be viewed in more than one way or have more than one meaning. A widely used one is a picture that is both an old and a young woman within the same drawing. Another is a drawing of two pedestals or glasses side by side, where the stems form faces. Use this as the lead-in to show how different people have different perceptions.

- **Random video clip.** Show a random video clip, say, from an old TV show or training video, and have people in groups brainstorm how to

Exhibit 5-11 (*continued*)

relate it to the topic at hand. This exercise illustrates thinking ability and could lead to some humorous interpretations.

- ***Tube of Toothpaste.*** Hold up an empty tube of toothpaste. Have participants work in pairs to come up with as many different ways as they can think of in a short time (e.g., four minutes) to squeeze the last glob of toothpaste out of the tube. Acknowledge the more creative ways, possibly giving a prize for the longest list. Add a twist of having people stand up while developing their responses, which would get them moving if they've been sitting a long time.

Using Humor

There's nothing like a good joke to loosen things up—that is, if it's an acceptable joke. The problem is that a lot of humor is unacceptable in the workplace, for a number of good reasons. When used properly, though, a bit of lightheartedness can go a long way toward making a training session fun, or at least more tolerable, for learners. It's both a good way to start off on the right track (with the audience loosened up after a laugh) and an excellent tonic after a tedious session or large lunch.

Skills training is directly related to workplace success, and the workplace, with all the competition for jobs and sources, can be a highly stressful place. Humor is a good way to help reduce stress anywhere, including in the training environment.

Representative ways to use humor in a training setting are listed in Exhibit 5-12.

Exhibit 5-12. Using Humor in Training

- To start off a training session, tell a joke (politically correct, of course) or lead an exercise that is humorous (see some of the games listed in Exhibit 5-11).
- During exercises, it helps people see that the facilitator (and they, where appropriate) is only human.
- Several nationally syndicated cartoon strips are directly related to the workplace and often provide grist for the trainer's humor mill. Get permission to use some of these. If you read the funny papers long enough, you'll find such subjects as diversity, sexual harassment, public speaking, quality management, training, motivation, and more presented through cartoon characters with truly human characteristics.

- Humor resources are readily available off the shelf on the topic of humor, such as jokes to use in speaking. Popular publications also have good materials.
- Humorous speakers can make guest appearances during longer training sessions.
- Training programs have taken advantage of the vast supply of old television comedy programs, and it's likely you can find one relevant to your need.

Incorporating Multimodality Approaches

This is a reminder about the importance of this concept. Review Exhibit 3-2.

Accommodating Diversity

This means learning how to accommodate all learners. It's an idea that pays off in increased performance. Theory and practice show that people have multiple learning styles (e.g., visual, tactile, musical, numeric, and so on), and your job as trainer is to make the most of this fact, which will go a long way to ensuring that learners acquire the new skills they need to be more effective in the workplace.

The approach to take is that everyone is different, and if an accommodation of any kind can be made to mesh better with an individual's learning, make it. In fact, one of the keys to success for a facilitator is to find ways to accommodate people's needs. We saw in Step One how broad the concept of diversity has become. As the workplace expands to accept a fully diverse workforce and it becomes more globally oriented, training must also expand. This means doing different things and training in different ways. If you've been in a meeting or attended a presentation where many attendees were from another culture, you have firsthand experience of what some of these differences are. Analogies are different, not to mention the language used. A story that may be hilarious or thought provoking to one person may be baffling or even shocking to someone from a different background.

Accommodations for adult learners have already been addressed in Step Two. In the remainder of this step, we will examine accommodations for persons with disabilities and older workers. For a quick review on accommodations, refer to Exhibit 5-13.

Exhibit 5-13. How to Accommodate Diversity in the Training Environment

- *Diversity definition.* Develop a clear, complete picture and understanding of true diversity. You must do this first.
- *Biases.* Keep personal biases on the shelf.
- *Ability and performance.* Focus on individual ability and performance. Nothing else matters.
- *Individual needs.* Always think in terms of accommodations to the greatest extent possible, remembering that many people need to be accommodated to maximize learning.
- *Accommodations.* Make accommodations accordingly. A major accommodation is to adopt a facilitation model that is flexible enough to deal with a diverse group of people. It is described in Step Six.
- *People orientation.* Transcend age, sex, race, and anything else, and train for performance through people, period.

Accommodating Learners With Disabilities

The first point to remember when training learners with disabilities is to be sensitive to their needs. This doesn't mean rushing around trying to move furniture and taking them by the arm every time they start to move; nor does it mean feeling sorry for them and calling attention to their disabilities. Simply treat them like any another participant, and make them feel just as at home as everyone else. The difference is that you may need to do something to accommodate their disability in the training setting—for example, having large-print materials for visually impaired persons and those who may have reading difficulties, or a special workstation and computer peripherals for a person with a physical disability.

People often provide their own accommodations; a blind person may bring her own Brailler for taking notes, or a person with a learning disability may bring a tape recorder. When in doubt, always ask the learner what works best.

People with disabilities are a growing presence in the workplace. Your job as trainer is to make the most of the situation and provide everyone the opportunity to come away with new skills and knowledge. To assist you in this endeavor, following is a discussion of sensitivity and types of disabilities to assist you in making accommodations. Exhibit 5-14 shows a checklist for accommodating learners with disabilities.

Exhibit 5-14. Checklist for Accommodating Learners With Disabilities

The following questions are geared to all aspects of the employee development program.

☐ Are instructors sensitive to the needs of persons with disabilities?

☐ Do instructors know how to make accommodations for trainees who have disabilities (by type of disability, such as hearing or visually impaired)?

☐ Do training materials, delivery methods, and audiovisual devices accommodate disabilities (e.g., open-captioned videos, interpreters for deaf persons, braille for blind persons, large print)?

☐ Are training facilities accessible (including travel, residential, food, transportation, and recreational facilities)?

☐ Do tests and other methods of measuring performance and training make appropriate accommodations?

☐ Do outside training providers comply with antidiscrimination and accommodation requirements in all aspects of training?

☐ Is language in all documentation nondiscriminatory?

☐ Are any forms used accessible to all persons with disabilities (instructors as well as trainees)?

☐ Are records kept for training treated confidentially for medical information for persons with disabilities?

☐ Is a multimodality approach used in delivering training?

Training sessions

☐ Use multimedia presentations.

☐ Provide written materials in large print and braille.

☐ Describe any video, film, filmstrips, transparencies, or slides.

☐ Read all still-projected material (e.g., transparencies).

☐ Describe any demonstrations or role plays.

☐ Have participants actively participate in "hands on" training activities in groups.

☐ Gear testing formats to the learning style of the person with a disability (e.g., braille version, given orally, demonstrated, and so on).

Sensitivity

The starting place for dealing with learners with disabilities is before training begins. When the training is being planned and announced, ask if any attendees need any sort of an accommodation.

(Don't ask if anyone has a disability.) It's up to the learner to let you know, so you will be prepared. Make it clear that you will provide reasonable accommodations for those who need them and that they must let you know so you can make them.

Being sensitive to persons with disabilities is easy to do if you follow a few simple rules:

1. Always put the person first and the disability second.
2. Don't automatically give assistance. If someone asks for it, willingly give it. When in doubt, you can ask if you might be of assistance, and the person will tell you.
3. Don't lean on a person's wheelchair.
4. Don't pet guide and assistance dogs. They're working and are not to be distracted.
5. Don't set persons with disabilities aside where they are conspicuous. They should be as much a part of the activities as anyone else.
6. Use terms such as *person with a disability, wheelchair user, blind person, deaf person, person with multiple sclerosis,* and so on. Don't use such demeaning terms as *handicapped, crippled, confined to a wheelchair, mute, hard of hearing,* and so on.

Types of Disabilities

A wheelchair is the symbol for disabilities. You see it on rest room doors, buses, and telephone kiosks. Disabilities, however, cover many more types than those requiring use of wheelchairs. General categories include physical disabilities, deaf and hearing impairment, blind and visual impairment, and nonapparent disabilities (e.g., learning disabilities, mental disabilities, persons with AIDS or who are HIV positive, and persons with cancer, diabetes, or epilepsy). The point is that for every one wheelchair user you might have in a training class, you're likely to have many others with a variety of disabilities to be accommodated. People with learning disabilities and lower-back ailments, neither being visible to the facilitator, provide a case in point. Estimates are that 10 percent of our population has a learning disability, and lower back ailments are one of the main types of workplace disabilities. The responsibility for making accommodations is mutual: You must offer, and it's up to the person with a disability to let you know what's needed. Exhibit 5-15 and the following discussion provide guidance for making accommodations for people with various disabilities.

Physical Disabilities

Wheelchair users may require a lower workstation. Make sure aisles are wide enough (usually 42 inches) for maneuverability. Most facilities accommodate wheelchairs, but never make the assumption; check it out to be sure. Disability support groups and rehabilitation programs can offer expert advice on how accessible your space is. Computers and related equipment may need assistive devices (e.g., alternative input devices such as voice-activated ones).

Exhibit 5-15. Training Tips for Accommodating People With Disabilities

1. ***Physical disabilities***
   - Wheelchair users may require a lower workstation.
   - Aisles should be wide enough (usually 42 inches) for maneuverability.
   - Most facilities accommodate wheelchairs, but you should never assume they do. Check them out to be sure.
   - Disability support groups and rehabilitation programs can offer expert advice on how accessible your space is.
   - Computers and related equipment may need assistive devices (alternative input, e.g., voice-activated, devices).

2. ***Deaf and hearing-impaired***
   - Deaf and hearing-impaired persons may require an interpreter who's qualified in American Sign Language.
   - The facilitator should always face the audience when speaking.
   - Don't speak to the interpreter when conversing with a deaf person. Rather, speak directly to the one who's deaf.
   - Many deaf and hearing-impaired people are adept at lipreading.
   - Be conscious of lighting, and avoid having bright lights behind a speaker.
   - Videos must have captioning.
   - Sound amplification devices are helpful for those who are hearing-impaired.

3. ***Blind and visually-impaired***
   - One of the main accommodations for a blind person is to explain what is happening in videos and to read every word on every visual aid.
   - If there's a role play, describe what the participants are doing.
   - Braille or recordings may be appropriate for training materials. So would tape recorders for recording presentations.
   - For visually impaired persons, large print and terminals that enlarge printed type and project it onto the screen are two common accommodations.

Exhibit 5-15 (*continued*)

4. ***Nonapparent disabilities***
   - These disabilities cover a wide spectrum, but can be accommodated in a number of ways.
   - For people who have medical conditions such as cancer or lower-back conditions, flexibility in scheduling and attendance may be in order (e.g., so that the person can rest for brief periods or take prescribed treatment).
   - Learning disabilities cover difficulties in reading, writing, spelling, computing, attention span, and organizing abilities—alternative formats may be needed, such as using tape recorders for training sessions, providing alternative methods of taking tests, allowing additional time to complete portions of training, prerecording materials, providing note takers, and other assistance in the learning process.

Deaf and Hearing-Impaired

Deaf and hearing-impaired people may require an interpreter who is qualified in American Sign Language. The facilitator should always face the audience when speaking. Don't speak to the interpreter when conversing with a deaf person. Rather, speak directly to the one who's deaf. Many deaf and hearing-impaired people are adept at lip-reading. Also be conscious of lighting, and avoid having bright lights behind a speaker. Videos must have captioning. Sound amplification devices are helpful for those who are hearing-impaired.

Blind and Visually-Impaired

One of the main accommodations for a blind person is to explain what is happening in videos and to read every word on every visual aid. If there is a role play, describe what the participants are doing. Braille or recordings may be appropriate for training materials, as well as tape recorders for recording presentations. For visually-impaired persons, large print and terminals that enlarge printed type and project it onto the screen are two common accommodations.

Nonapparent Disabilities

These disabilities cover a wide spectrum, but can be accommodated in a number of ways. For people who have medical conditions, such as cancer or lower back pain, flexibility in scheduling and attendance may be in order (e.g., so the person can rest for brief periods or take prescribed treatment). For people with learning disabilities—difficulties in reading, writing, spelling, computing, attention span, and organizing abilities—alternative formats may be needed, such as using tape recorders for training sessions, providing alternative methods of taking tests, allowing additional time to complete portions of training, prerecording materials, and providing note takers.

Dealing With Older Participants

There are a number of myths about older adults; *all* of them are untrue. Learning ability doesn't drop as people get older; older people want to continue working (many because they have to), and they show up on time, produce as much, and stay at work just as well as younger workers. Most important, older people are proving to be adaptable; they're willing to learn the new skills mandatory to workplace—and organization—success. It's important that trainers recognize that the number of older learners participating in training will continue to grow, so it's important to avoid stereotyping them. Treat older learners the same as everyone else; in fact, take advantage of their in-depth work experiences in training.

One of the ways you can take advantage of having older learners in the group is to call on them often during training so they can share their experiences and knowledge. Even before training starts, consult with them on how to develop meaningful exercises and other activities during the training. Also, be conscious that older adults may need accommodations because of visual and hearing losses.

Conclusion

Trainers are blessed with an enormous amount of material—checklists, books, journals, workshops, and more—to help them ply their trade. Some may think *overblessed* is a better word because there's so much information inundating them, with more each day. One of the keys to success in filtering through so much information is to look ahead at the training you'll be doing, and identify a few significant areas for review. For example, if you know older workers will be attending the training session, read up on some of the tips in this step and possibly do a World Wide Web search or make a telephone call to someone who has had similar experiences. If you'll be doing a lot of classroom presentation, review the material regarding speaking and presenting in this step, and possibly get a book on humor and exercises to conduct in order to make it as interesting as possible. For one last reminder before going on to the next step, Exhibit 5-16 lists a number of do's and don'ts for trainers. Use this as a last-minute check before stepping onto the platform to start your session.

Exhibit 5-16. Do's and Don'ts for Trainers

Do
- Speak clearly.
- Make eye contact.
- Get learners involved.
- Use learners' names.
- Keep interest up through changing your tone of voice.
- Get, and give, constant feedback.
- Be enthusiastic. If this is tough, take acting lessons.
- Be prepared.
- Use specific questions to determine if learning is taking place.
- Observe breakout groups. They miss you when you don't and may do something else.
- Be alert for those needing a little extra help—and give it to them.
- Move around.
- Accommodate each individual to the greatest extent possible.
- Use equipment and aids as if you've been doing this all your life—even if it's the first time.
- Set and observe time periods. The only acceptable time change is to end early.
- Dress appropriately.

Don't
- Mumble.
- Waste words ("you know," "uh").
- Read from notes.
- Take part in private conversations during sessions.
- Talk to visual aids.
- Lecture or preach.
- Ignore questions.
- Pace up and down.
- Turn your back to the audience while speaking.
- Stand in front of visual aids.
- Forget to make eye contact.
- Forget that there are people on both sides and in back of the room.
- Chew gum or food during a session.
- Give people busy-work in order to fill up the allotted time.
- Stay in one position for long periods (including being glued to the podium).
- Put your hands in your pockets or behind you, or use them excessively.
- Wear distracting attire.

Step Six

Get Learners Involved

The companies that train best deliver instruction when the employee needs it, sometimes in the classroom, sometimes by satellite TV, sometimes on a personal computer. Effective training is concise and interactive, interspersed with group projects, role-playing, and hands-on experiments.

—Ronald Hentoff
"Companies That Train Best," *Fortune* (March 23, 1993)

Involving learners in the learning process is the key to successful training. When an adult learner is mentally and physically dedicated to learning, learning will take place—and learning will go up in proportion to the degree of involvement.

You have already read a number of ideas for getting learners involved. This step now lays out a wide range of specific techniques and tools for you. Where appropriate, techniques have been associated with types of learning situations to help you choose. For this reason, this step goes hand in hand with Step Four, on selecting delivery methods and media. Sometimes experimentation is okay. Think of a way to get learners involved, and try it out. You'll be able to tell right away if it's working. If it's not, move on to something else. Also, it's always a good idea—perhaps make it mandatory with all your training—to have backup exercises, questions, techniques, and so on ready to go just in case.

Step Six Summary

A vital part of involvement is group dynamics and actions. Much training is done in groups, particularly in teams, to replicate actual workplace environments. To deliver training most effectively, the trainer must have a good grasp of group dynamics and be adept at facilitating group learning. Included within this step are:

- Discussion of group activities
- Tips for dealing with a variety of group situations
- Techniques for working with groups
- Action learning

Working With Groups

The training facilitator must be adept at working successfully with groups of all sizes. Knowledge of group dynamics and the ability to deal with problem behaviors within groups are essential facilitator skills. Fortunately, applying a few proven tips will lead you to success in working with groups.

Group Dynamics

Groups provide an excellent, efficient means to get things done— but they're also likely to present their share of challenges. Knowing how to deal with groups is essential to ultimate learning objective achievement. What you must remember is that groups, like individuals, have minds of their own, with motivations, likes, dislikes, objectives, standards, and desires. This holds true even if members have never seen one another before coming to the training session.

Groups are formed for specific purposes, formal or informal, and you must work successfully with them. Here are a few key items to keep in mind:

- Groups have goals, and in a training situation, the goals must coincide with those of the training at hand for maximum learning to take place.
- Groups have norms. You've probably been in a group when you wanted to speak up, but had the feeling that the group didn't want you to. Perhaps the norm was to make the leader work hard for results, or perhaps it was for the newcomer to keep silent and in the background until proper dues were paid.
- Groups have some sort of structure; it can be informal if a random group has drawn together for training purposes.

- Individual group members have specific roles to fill. Perhaps one person has been chosen as the unofficial leader, and everything must go through him or her. Or perhaps there are role conflicts that must be resolved before accomplishing your objectives, such as when two learners want to be leader.
- People within a group exhibit certain behaviors depending on what they expect to get out of the group. For example, people who want to establish themselves as experts may try to dominate training sessions.

Keep these rules in mind for a high success rate and to forestall problems when dealing with training groups in general. There'll be less concern when the session is short, or the group is ad hoc and not a cohesive work team brought in for training. Nevertheless, group behavior will play a strong role in everything that goes on during training.

Using Small Groups

Sometimes referred to as *breakout groups*, these comprise the people who are chosen to be with one another during a training session. Small groups can be used for case studies, exercises, problem solving, icebreakers, debates, and games. You can have all groups deal with the same problem or exercise, or use different exercises for each group. In longer sessions, you might want to re-form groups, so participants will have the experience of working with different people. This can add much needed freshness when there's a lot of group activity.

To form groups, have participants count off up to the number of groups desired (e.g., one to five), with the number ones meeting together, the twos together, and so on. Or you can divide people into groups before the training begins.

Dealing With Difficult Behaviors

There's always somebody in a training group who finds a way to go against the grain. When it comes to training, this person usually can't be ignored. Interruptions to a tightly scheduled training session detract from achieving objectives. Every time there's a delay, there's added lost time in trying to recover the momentum.

Among the skills you need are those for dealing with these individuals. They come in all types and can find ways to cause grief in a number of ways. Fortunately, they're usually in the minority, and there are ways to deal with them. Before getting into special situations, there are three cardinal rules to follow:

1. Never put anybody down (i.e., call attention to their behavior or chastise them in any way). It's okay to be firm, but always be polite and understanding.
2. However people act and whatever they do, remember that they have their reasons. You're not in a position to make judgments. You therefore need to respect that there's a reason for the behavior.
3. Treat learners with dignity and respect at all times.

Monopolizers, quiet ones, digressers, chatterboxes, and disruptive people are common. By assuming any and all could be present in any training session—and being prepared to deal with them—your training sessions will suffer little from them. Also, realize that these people may not be aware that their behavior is causing a problem. Anticipation will allow you to deal faster and more positively with these behaviors and promote learning. Exhibit 6-1 gives tips for handling them.

Exhibit 6-1. Tips for Handling Difficult Behaviors in Groups

1. **_Monopolizers_**
   - Recognize the person's contribution; then call on someone else.
   - Intervene, thank the person for the answer; then say you want to give someone else a chance.
   - Institute a practice of having people hold up their hands to respond; then ignore the monopolizer's hand most of the time.
   - Call on specific individuals.
2. **_Quiet Ones_**
   - Let it be known at the beginning that you appreciate and expect responses from everyone present.
   - Call on the quiet ones, giving advance warning that you will do so.
   - Start with easy questions, and work into more-difficult ones.
   - Ask a controversial question or take a controversial position (but be careful).
3. **_Digressers_**
   - Say the question or comment is beyond the scope of the session, but you'll be happy to discuss it during a break or when the session is over.

- Keep reminding participants of the main topic so they won't lose sight of it.
- When uncertain, make a note and tell the person that you'll give it some thought (or research it, call an expert, or whatever else is appropriate) and get back to him or her. In this case, you may have to say that you're unprepared to deal with the question or comment at the time, but will respond later.

4. *Chatterboxes*
   - Stop the presentation and wait for the people engaged in a private conversation to realize they're disrupting the class. Often this is all it takes, particularly if they don't realize they are causing a problem for others.
   - If it persists, politely interrupt and ask what it was the person said, as if you thought he or she was speaking to the group. Hopefully, the person will apologize.
   - Interrupt and politely ask them to put off the conversation until the break; then state when the break will be.
   - It could become necessary to confront them (politely, of course) at a break and ask them to stop. If it's something they must talk about, suggest they go outside and carry on the conversation, but remind them of the importance of being present at the training.

5. *Disrupters*
   - Stop and tell the person you understand his or her concern (or whatever other comment fits the situation) and will gladly discuss the matter after the session.
   - Break into a new activity to cut off further disruptive action.
   - Ask the person to participate in an exercise or assist in a training task (i.e., put this person in charge of some phase of the learning process).
   - Sometimes direct confrontation is necessary, despite your best efforts to avoid it. Tell the person that it's imperative that the session continue and that you would like to discuss the problem later. If it becomes necessary, suspend the training session temporarily and deal with the problem, even if it means contacting someone who can take action for you. Fortunately, being assertive and insisting, in a positive, tactful way, usually get things on track.

The Monopolizers

There's an excellent possibility that in any group of people, one or more individuals present will be exceptionally knowledgeable about the session topic. This person will have much to say and can easily take too much time saying it. Some people simply like to talk a lot, and a training session gives them a captive audience.

These two examples anchor the ends of a spectrum of people

who tend to monopolize meetings and conversations, as well as training classes. Either way, they detract from your mission to achieve specified learning objectives. Considering how tight schedules and budgets are, every minute must count. In other words, you must do something to prevent monopolizers from taking over a session.

Sometimes the other members of the group let the monopolizer know, in subtle or not-so-subtle ways, to be quiet. You shouldn't sit back and wait for this to happen, but it's usually okay to let it happen—without encouraging it. In other words, let the group tend to its own business, and intervene only if it looks as if there might be a disruptive conflict.

The Quiet Ones

One of the most frustrating moments for a teacher or trainer is a silent response to a challenging, well-developed question. There are plenty of reasons for lack of response: No one knows the answer, they didn't understand the question or request, they're bored, they believe the question or response is beneath them or perhaps insignificant, or there may be a monopolizer in the group and they've been intimidated to the point of not bothering to respond. Or it could be they just don't want to say anything (e.g., they're ready to go home and don't want to prolong the session)—or they simply don't care.

The Digressers

The digresser is the person who takes the meeting down side roads and gets off onto topics that have little, if anything, to do with the learning objectives. It isn't always deliberate, either. In fact, it's quite easy to go off on tangents and get sidetracked from the original purpose. People bring their own agendas to the training session. The ability to keep things on track is one of the many talents of good meeting leaders and trainers. It's of little matter whether the digression is intentional; it must be dealt with immediately. Wasted time adds up quickly, especially in the minds of participants.

The Kibitzers

Every group has these people—those who, usually from vantage points toward the back or side of the room, whisper into one another's ears during a presentation. There's a more severe version of this: those who don't whisper as they talk about everything from what they think of the training (which is probably not very much) to where they will go for lunch at the break (if it will ever get to that time). The behavior can be anywhere from innocent, such as two people who had work business to attend to and didn't know when there would be time later to exchange information, to ones who don't care if they disrupt. Either way, it's distracting to the others.

The Disrupters

This is a general category of people who interfere in one way or another with the learning process during a training evolution. The behaviors include such diverse actions as questioning everything you say or propose, challenging your credibility, making comments that the training is a waste, asking questions about material that was covered earlier in the session, refusing to participate or do what has been asked, and more. They may disrupt only briefly, or their mission may be to disrupt the entire proceedings. Perhaps the person is a skeptic about training in general or the new skills being offered in the training. Maybe he didn't want to be part of the session in the first place (and this could be for good reason, so don't be too quick to judge). Possibly the person has a personal problem and can't fully enter into the training. And it could be that the person is naturally cantankerous and disruptive by nature. Whatever the reason for the behavior, too much of it will ruin the process for everyone.

Dealing with disrupters is a challenge under any circumstances. Though it might seem okay simply to put them in their place, to do so would likely cause others to doubt your ability to work well under pressure and jeopardize your credibility as a trainer. Yet letting it go on is unthinkable, so you must take action.

There's a lot of overlap between these behaviors. A digresser could turn out to be a disrupter, just as could a monopolizer. There's also some overlap in the ways to deal with them. Whichever type that occurs in a session—and chances are that sooner or later you'll have one or more of them—deal with it immediately, in as positive a way as you can.

Techniques for Getting Learners Involved

Trainers, teachers, and researchers have given us many ways to get learners involved. They work well, they're fun, and they help deliver training that stresses all the senses and motivations of learners. Together they provide quite a powerful set of techniques for the facilitator. (These techniques are summarized in Exhibit 6-2.) You'll note that there's some overlap with material in other steps, which reflects the integrative, systems aspect of training.

Exhibit 6-2. Techniques for Interacting With Learners: A Summary

1. **Ask questions.**
   - Review questions prepared in advance.
2. **Conduct experiential exercises.**
   - Use all types.
   - It's possible to accomplish many learning objectives entirely through exercises where learners can experiment, practice, then demonstrate proficiency.
3. **Conduct role plays.**
   - Use for a variety of situations.
   - Follow rules.
4. **Learn each learner's name and use it.**
   - Spend time at the beginning of the training session working on names.
   - Repeat each person's name.
   - Spell the names.
   - Use name tags or name tents on tables.
   - Practice names at the beginning of subsequent sessions.
   - Let learners know you care about them and want to get their names right.
5. **Provide feedback during class.**
   - Make sure learners always have plenty of time to raise questions.
   - Be available before and after sessions, as well as during breaks and outside class hours.
   - Conduct formal surveys to find out problems, questions, and expectations. Do this in writing, so learners must respond, but make these surveys anonymous.
   - Learners may respond to this tack even if they have questions they won't ask in class.
6. **Turn instruction over to learners.**
   - Let them prepare and deliver parts or all of sessions.
   - When a learner asks a question, have another learner answer it.
7. **Let learners perform demonstrations.**
   - Do this even if they've never seen the equipment before. Help them out if necessary.
   - Turn demonstrations into exercises, and give learners time to prepare.

8. **Incorporate writing exercises.**
   - Writing reinforces learning.
   - Use a variety of exercise types.
9. **Make learning contracts.**
   - People respect contracts.
   - Make contracts in writing, even informal ones.
   - Meet individually with each learner and determine what his or her expectations are from training and from you.
10. **Use instruments to learn more about learners.**
   - Learning, trainer, and involvement styles help identify important information about individuals.
   - Instruction can be altered to accommodate these styles where appropriate.
   - Learning is made more interesting if learners learn something new, or confirm something about themselves.
11. **Hold individual meetings.**
   - Discuss progress and expectations.
   - Provide counseling to those learners needing it (e.g., regarding the training or personal situations that affect the training).
   - Establish learning contracts.
   - Get acquainted.
12. **Make training real time and action oriented.**
   - Add realism.
   - Use action learning, with actual workplace situations.
   - Use a team approach, emphasizing diversity.

Asking Questions

Thanks to the Greek philosopher Socrates, asking questions is one of the oldest and most effective ways to learn and grow. With modern technology and enormous strides made into learning how people learn, this technique remains one of the trainer's greatest tools. The ability to ask probing questions that cause learners to open their minds and focus on the topic under discussion is one of the best assets you can have. It's the same essential skill managers use to probe deeply into organization issues. By asking questions, you will know at all times if learning is taking place.

You can use questions in a number of ways. The most direct way is to ask questions at intervals throughout the training session, even if it's primarily an experiential session rather than a presentation format. Ask questions about everything. Rather than provide information, present it as a question. Written questions also can be used, such as in a test. Also, provide a list of specific questions to be answered for cases and similar exercises. It'll keep learning on target and keep discussion groups focused. Questions prepared in advance will always serve you well.

Open-Ended and Closed Questions

A *closed question* most likely has only one answer (e.g., true or false, yes or no, or a direct fact answer). It works well during a training session to find out if learners are paying attention and the facilitator is getting the job done. *Open-ended questions* require more thought, and the learner can answer in his or her own words. They probe more deeply into how well learning objectives were met, though they are more difficult to critique.

The better kind of questions, as any successful sales representative will tell you, are open-ended ones. These are ones that begin with the proverbial "who, what, when, why, where, how and if," the so-called five W's, H, and I. They require thought to answer.

Direct and Indirect Questions

This is a matter of either asking a specific person to answer a question (*direct*) or presenting it to the entire group (*indirect*) for anyone to answer. Sometimes both are required. For example, if learners seem reluctant to respond to indirect questions, first ask the question in general, then turn to a particular learner and ask for an answer. You are giving advance warning, and the person can start formulating an answer. Sometimes indirect questions can be used to introduce a topic and nudge the learners to start thinking, though no answer is expected.

How to Ask Questions

Here is a list of things you should know about asking questions:

1. Let learners know up front that you will ask lots of questions, that you expect them to provide answers, and that it is okay if the answers are sometimes wrong.
2. Open-ended questions work best (who, what, where, when, why, how, and if).
3. Questions should make people think, which is what open-ended ones will do.
4. The greater the chance a learner has of answering a question, the more effective it will be. A rule is to ensure a 90 percent chance the learner will get the correct answer.

5. Give credit for partial answers.

6. Never make fun of an answer, unless the person providing the answer laughs first.

7. Ask questions at the beginning of the session. The answers will help you determine where learners stand and show how much knowledge they already have.

8. Ask questions regularly during the session to determine if learning is occurring, as well as to give you a sense if it's time to change the pace.

9. Use questions at the end of a session segment as a way to summarize the material and determine if it has been successful.

10. Use a variety of types of questions, including direct and indirect ones. (It's okay to ask simple ones that have yes or no or specific pieces of information as answers to provide variety. These simpler questions also help decrease anxiety when the material is difficult.)

11. First address a question to the entire group, so everyone can start thinking of the answer. Then single out an individual to provide the answer.

12. Give plenty of time for the person to respond.

13. Give hints if they will help. This communicates that you sincerely want the person to learn and that it is okay to not always have the answers.

14. Give everyone a chance to answer. Calling on specific people is a way to make it fair and equal for everyone. You can go down the row sometimes to ensure uniformity.

15. Try to find something positive about every answer that is given.

16. Do your best not to answer the question yourself. This can be a challenge if the group is quiet.

17. Deal with an irrelevant question by politely stating it isn't pertinent.

18. When you make a mistake in answering (and human nature being what it is, it will certainly happen sooner or later—hopefully later), admit it.

19. If the asker is asking a question to achieve something else, try to rephrase the question to a more legitimate one.

20. If the question indicates a person is lost, find a way to help that person out (e.g., during a break).

21. Keep questions and the process of asking them as simple as possible (i.e., never use trick questions).

Learners may ask questions. When they do:

1. Get someone else to answer.
2. Solicit comments.
3. Don't evade the question.
4. Don't engage in put-downs.

Conducting Experiential Exercises

This topic was covered at length in Step Four. Refer to the examples given in that step and never hesitate to implement exercises freely during training. Here are some more things to keep in mind when using exercises:

1. Be familiar with the exercise. If you've never done it before, try to find someone who has used it and discuss it with that person. Carefully walk through the exercise in your head, possibly even in the training room, to make sure you know how to conduct it.
2. Make sure the exercise fits the situation.
3. Always discuss the results of the exercise. You will get valuable feedback, including finding out whether learners liked doing it. If they didn't, determine why.
4. Think of variations of exercises, particularly if it's one you've found in a resource document. Customize it as much as possible for your group—much as you would alter the characters in a story you are telling to fit the group you're presenting to.
5. Time exercises to make sure you've allowed enough time. Also be careful about exercises that could become too lengthy.
6. Make sure you have all the resources that the exercise calls for. Realizing you need newsprint and markets halfway through the exercise is equivalent to telling a joke and forgetting the punch line.

Role-Playing

Drama has a way of getting people absorbed in the situation. You can add it to your training session in a number of ways, including through video and exercises, or more directly through role plays.

You'll need time to prepare and participants who are willing to do their best to take on the assigned roles.

Role plays are excellent for demonstrating behaviors and having learners gain firsthand experience in what it feels like to be on the receiving end. They can be used to show both positive and negative situations, and sometimes both for comparison purposes. Role plays are useful for training in a number of areas:

- Sales training, to illustrate prospective client behaviors and how to turn them to advantage
- Diversity training, in which learners take on roles of various groups
- Communications training, to demonstrate any number of situations, ranging from listening skills training to body language
- Management development, to demonstrate desired managerial situations and how to deal with them (e.g., how to be a coach or mentor)
- Interview training, so that interviewers learn how to conduct interviews according to legal and other guidelines
- Conflict management, for dealing with customer complaints and internal conflicts

When you conduct role plays, pay attention to these guidelines:

1. Carefully plan how they're to be used.
2. Make it clear what's expected of participants (e.g., saying that everyone is to participate, that it's okay and expected that they might have to work at it to carefully move into the process).
3. Create a relaxed, nonthreatening atmosphere so participants will feel at ease taking on roles.
4. Be aware that some people have difficulty getting into playing roles. If encouragement doesn't work, don't force someone to play a role.
5. Give participants as much background information as possible to help them assume their respective roles.

Learning Names and Using Them

Perhaps you've known people who could walk into a room and meet twenty strangers, then a short time later go around the room and call each person by name without a mistake. We're not all like that, but there are a number of tricks to learning names for training purposes. Because people respond much more positively when you address them by name, knowing names is vital. In fact, you may discover that some people won't say a word until you say their name. If you stop to think about this, you will realize that you too feel much better about any situation when the people around you, especially the leader or facilitator, can associate your face with the proper name. Personalization takes a lot of discomfort out of any situation, and training settings are no different. (This gets back to the reason that icebreakers can be so valuable.)

There are books and courses available to teach you techniques for remembering names if you're interested. And here are some easy-to-apply tips:

1. Get a list of the participants before the training begins and get familiar with their names. Learn as much as you can about each participant (e.g., where they're from, what they do, any positive information you've heard about them, and what expertise you might be able to count on from them).

2. Associate specific things about each person with the name (e.g., Joe who couldn't find a parking place, or Sally from accounting, which could be information gleaned from a getting-acquainted exercise).

3. Spend time at the beginning of the session (unless it's a short one) learning names (e.g., calling them out and repeating each one several times).

4. When there are multiple sessions, go over names at the beginning of each one. This repetition helps you learn them and shows learners that you care enough to learn them.

5. Repeat names several times at the start of the session.

6. Spell names out as you say them.

7. Use name tags.

8. Use name cards at the workstations, such as name tents (name cards folded into a V shape).

Providing Feedback During Training

This sounds simple, and it is. However, during the heat of a busy training session, you may forget to do this. Providing feedback can be as simple as thanking someone for a good answer to a question, accompanied by a smile. After each exercise, tell the learners how well they did. If they didn't do well, couch your feedback in terms that they got the job done but could do better, and you're sure they will next time. Use praise lavishly, and definitely when a response is excellent.

Here are some ways to provide feedback:

1. Walk around the room during group exercises, and comment on what people are doing. They need to know you're interested.

2. Use body language to show approval (e.g., smile to show approval when someone has responded to a question, and shake your head up and down, or applaud).

3. Encourage applause when a person or group has made a presentation. Try to do this always in more formal situations, such as when a learner has made a talk during a verbal communication course or a group has presented a solution to a case study.

4. Write notes and comments on written work completed during the session.

5. Summarize each segment of a session, and include it in the summary comments. Your comments will let people know how they're doing.

6. Stop people as they are leaving or walking down the hall during a break and offer feedback—even just a word or two.

7. Don't wait to give feedback. This way it's easier to remember.

8. Provide certificates or letters of completion when training is over (sending copies to their supervisors when appropriate).

Turning Instruction Over to Learners

Be careful with this technique. Never give up responsibility for facilitating the process, but use this technique to keep learners involved. One way to do this is to ask small groups to prepare a brief presentation and deliver it to the rest of the class, or to perform an exercise or demonstration. Be sure necessary reference materials are readily available so that the presenters can do a thorough job of preparing. Case studies also provide a method for learners to take over a portion of the instruction. The learners rather than the facilitator can state the lessons learned from the solution to a case or exercise. Yet another way to turn instruction over is to have a learner provide the answer when another learner asks a question.

To see how to turn instruction over to learners, consider a diversity training class. If the objective is for learners to conduct themselves properly in a meeting with people from a different culture, learners should be asked to prepare two demonstration meetings: one showing how *not* to act during such a meeting (e.g., pushing for immediate action with someone from a culture that always goes through a series of social actions first) and the other showing how to act patiently and properly. In preparation for the sessions, learners would be provided with information on key points of the culture represented in the example.

Letting Learners Perform Demonstrations

This is similar to the previous idea above. Often in technical training (e.g., computer-related or technical maintenance training), it's necessary to demonstrate the correct way to load a system or perform a specific task so that learners can see the correct procedure before doing it themselves. In this situation, there might be a system in front of the room, or perhaps a projection of the screen onto a large display. Rather than going through the steps yourself, ask a learner to come forward and do it. You are sending a message to the class that the task will be easy for them to master and you're confident in their ability. When using this method, be sure to let participants know it's okay to make mistakes. In fact, having learners perform demonstrations is an excellent way for them to see that making mistakes is okay and no harm is done.

Incorporating Writing Exercises

Writing makes people think, and most people can use practice in writing, so writing exercises are clearly valuable. When a person starts thinking about the learning objectives, involvement has a direct benefit. Writing provides variety and a change of pace too. It isn't necessary for learners to write essays or novels, but short assignments are helpful. Here are four exercises that require writing:

1. *Definitions.* When you are introducing a new subject, have learners write their definition (or understanding, perception, or whatever is appropriate) before you provide the information. For example, if you're about to introduce the concept of environmental scanning for a training course on marketing planning, have learners write their definitions of what they think (or know) it is. Review their responses before explaining the textbook definition. Often you'll find that the ones they wrote were good.

2. *Expectations.* At the beginning of a training session, have learners put down on paper (either an 8 ½- by 11-inch sheet or newsprint for posting on the wall) what they expect to gain. Refer back to these expectations from time to time, and for sure at the end. Probe to see where there might be holes in the training, as well as to determine what extra benefits the learners might have derived.

3. *Spontaneous ideas.* Have a sheet of newsprint available for participants to jot down questions that come up, new ideas, or topics they think might be appropriate for future sessions. Review these lists periodically, because some of the items might be useful to include in the current session, and at the end.

4. *Summaries.* Many segments of training end with a summary provided by the facilitator, or possibly learners, of what was just learned. Summarizing is good management practice, and training certainly gains from it. An option of summarizing is to have learners, or groups, make their executive summaries of what was just covered in writing. It doubles as a way to review material. If learners know at the beginning that they'll be doing this, they'll start giving it thought at that time, which is exactly what you want.

Many variations stem from these four, and additional activities that require writing can be developed. For example, writing short pieces is a good assignment between training sessions. What people write on a piece of paper or key into a computer is their intellectual property. It reinforces the learning process positively, so use this technique as much as possible in training.

Making Learning Contracts

When people contract to provide a service, meet a deadline, or otherwise commit themselves to keep a promise, they tend to fulfill that commitment. The same holds true in training. Learning contracts could be a matter of having learners jot down on a piece of paper what they intend to achieve during a training session and keep it for their own use, or could go so far as to specify precisely what skills or knowledge the learner expects to acquire, and at what level, recorded as a formal contract completed and signed in the presence of the trainer. Often the simple versions are all that are needed to help keep learners focused on achieving learning objectives. Have learners take out a sheet of paper (or newsprint if used as part of a flip chart session) and write out three things they expect to achieve from the training session, or perhaps what they expect to take back to their workplace that will contribute to a higher level of personal effectiveness. If practice is involved, the contract might include a statement of how they intend to keep current.

Using Instruments to Learn More About Learners

The more you know about learners, the more directed your learning can become. For example, if results of completing a learning style instrument have determined that several members of the learning group are hands-on learners, they could be selected to perform demonstrations or participate in role plays, or perhaps additional exercises could be scheduled. If an organization instrument determined that a work group undergoing training for implementing work teams was not ready to move directly into teams, the training could be altered to accommodate the fact—perhaps by including a module where the learners would interview other workers to determine their level of teamwork inclination and develop a process to start changing people to accept teams.

Simply completing an instrument before, during, or after training gets the learner involved in the process, and the more involvement, the more ownership the learner will take in the overall learning process. This is particularly true when an instrument has provided information the learner can use in some way.

Holding Individual Meetings

Sometimes you need to work one on one with a learner. Perhaps you want to give positive feedback to a person who doesn't like to be singled out in front of the group, or you're faced with dealing with problem situations where you have to go head to head with the person. Some facilitators make it a point to meet with each individual at some time during the training session. This is an excellent procedure (though time-consuming) that sends a message to the learner that you care and are concerned about his or her learning. For large groups, it's good practice at least to meet with those you notice are having problems or causing problems because, again, it shows you care about the learning that takes place.

Using Real-Time or Action Learning

The more realistic training is, the more effective it will be. This logic fits right in with adult learning theory: that adults relate learning to what they already know. Some training, of course, is automatically related directly to the workplace. For example, learning how to use a graphic presentation software package is directly related to a person who must make such presentations as a part of the job. But if the sample situations used in the class are ones that the person will actually use (e.g., diversity, management skills), this degree of realism makes the training all the more effective.

A term that is receiving a great deal of attention in training circles is *action learning* (identified in Step One)—training that uses a real-time scenario as the basis of the training. In other words, this training gives learners an actual workplace problem to solve. It's often done in teams of a diverse group of learners (e.g., middle managers from a variety of plants); they are assigned the problem, and the facilitator assesses their solution. Assessment can range anywhere from a critique to using the solution and grading it much the same as a performance review.

Following are some examples of how to apply real-time learning techniques:

- *Management development training.* Assign the group the task of developing a strategic plan for implementing a new product line. The group members, who are being groomed for higher-level positions, would then have a prescribed amount of time to develop the strategic plan. They would be provided with complete instructions, including any instructional material on how to develop such plans. Part of the assignment might be for the team to determine what resources and information they need and then find them. Upon completion of the task, the plan would be reviewed and a formal critique made by top management.

- *Problem-solving training.* Assign the group the task of developing a solution to a specific company (or department) problem, such as a conflict between the design group and the marketing group on how to package a product that is being updated. Perhaps marketing does not believe that their retail customers want the product tied to another product that needs to have its sales bolstered. The task could include a process whereby a review committee from both groups would review the proposed solution and decide whether to implement it.

- *Creativity training.* For a training course in creativity and innovation for a high-tech software company, the task for the learners could be to use a variety of creative techniques, introduced at the beginning of the course, to come up with ideas for new entertainment applications packages for consumers. Competing groups would come up with their ideas, which would be studied by the executive committee and the best ones selected for development.

- *Presentation skills training.* The training might start with several conventional classroom sessions to learn the basics of making good presentations. Individuals would be assigned the task to develop a presentation they were already scheduled to make to their departments or other work groups (e.g., a learner from the marketing group would use the requirement to give a quarterly report on new promotion campaigns and make this the basis of the presentation developed). Members of the session would critique each other's presentations.

Step Seven

Get Feedback

Feedback is what powers the system and permits individuals to continually improve their performance.

—Clay Carr, *Smart Training* (1990)

Perhaps you've heard the saying that the sale isn't complete until the customer has paid. Some version of this is a solid principle that's been around a long time because it's true. The sale has to stick. The same principle applies to training (even short training sessions), because training isn't completed until performance is improved—and it's evaluation that brings the closure we need to make that determination. Success means that learners have increased their skills, which in turn increases organization effectiveness. Using a management analogy, continuous improvement applies as much to training as to manufacturing and other business processes.

Conduct evaluation not only after training is completed, but during the process as well. Continually evaluating will greatly reduce the chance that your efforts ultimately will be ineffective. On a more positive note, good training can be turned into superb training if there are checkpoints along the way to determine how things are going and for making proper adjustments.

If you followed Steps Two, Three, and Four carefully, you will have already done all the work of preparing for training evaluation. Now, in Step Seven, you actually conduct the evaluation. (Of course, you can briefly evaluate and make improvements prior to completion; nonetheless, it's after the fact of a training course that you can determine ultimate results.)

Step Seven Summary

This step is closely related to learning objectives, which anchor the process of training. In addition, the concern is whether a person can perform better on the job, handle stress better, behave in a nonharassing manner, or perform whatever the expected outcome of the training session was. Specific elements of this step include:

- Tying training to the previous steps
- Determining what in particular is to be evaluated
- Determining whether to evaluate and to what degree
- Evaluation tools useful in training
- Time considerations (whether short- or long-term results should be evaluated)

Putting Objectives to the Test

Learning objectives are the heart of training, and directly or indirectly, they're the focus of evaluation. They were defined, in clear, measurable terms in Step Two. They were tied to learning principles in Step Three, and built into the training process during Step Four:

- *How objectives relate to Step Two.* A number of possibilities indicating the need for training were identified in Step Two. This step starts laying out a road map for training to follow. Accordingly, Step Two provides the raw input to Step Three, so it is critical in the overall training process.

- *How objectives relate to Step Three.* How to apply adult learning principles and deliver training in a variety of ways were topics addressed in Step Three. Also discussed were the concepts of core competency and mastery. Evaluation is made much easier when the appropriate methods are built into the training. The trainer can deal directly with whether skills or knowledge increased. Also, knowledge, skills, and attitude objectives may require different methods of evaluation. Evaluation helps determine if the core competencies and masteries of the organization are being achieved.

- *How objectives relate to Step Four.* One of the elements of designing training is to identify evaluation methods to use. Once this is done, the actual tools to evaluate are developed, ready to go with the training, with learning objectives providing the substance of training.

Together these three steps prepare you to evaluate and they clearly illustrate why a total systems approach to training pays off. Exhibit 7-1 shows the direct relationship between learning objectives and evaluation; it takes sample learning objectives identified in Exhibit 2-5 and shows how they can be evaluated.

Determining What to Measure

There are three distinct aspects of training to measure: training results, effectiveness of the process itself, and performance of the facilitator. All are important, but the primary one is measuring training results. Always do this, even if you merely ask a pertinent question at the end of a half-hour session. Other types of evaluation assist you in improving the process and your facilitation skills, which lead to greater assurance of achieving desired results.

Results of the Training

The first question to ask on completion of a training session is, Was the training effective? More specifically, the need may be to determine if learner skills or knowledge increased or improved as designed and expected (e.g., by evaluating the learner's presentation skills), or perhaps to discover whether the desired behaviors are being practiced after the fact (e.g., by observing a person on the job to determine if there is greater acceptance of diversity in the workplace). Training left to speculation or guesswork regarding results is virtually the same as ineffective training (which it may well have been), because no one will know if the learners gained any new skills.

Evaluation of learning objectives can be categorized into four general types: exercises, tests of various types, questioning techniques, and posttraining.

Exercises

Exercises can be used in a number of ways to evaluate training. For evaluating training results, they're essentially performance tests and work well for measuring skill-related learning objectives. The closer they are to actual workplace conditions, the better. If possible, conduct them as if they were part of the learner's regular work.

Exhibit 7-1. Sample Learning Objectives and Appropriate Tests

Learning Objective	Appropriate Test
• State Deming's fourteen steps for quality improvement *(performance)* verbatim *(standard)*, from memory *(condition)*.	Written essay
• After reading a case study *(condition)* illustrating Deming's fourteen steps, identify which of the steps were applied in the case *(performance)*, without leaving out any steps *(standard)*.	Written
• Demonstrate the correct technique for performing CPR *(performance)*, using "Annie" *(condition)* for five minutes *(standard)*.	Exercise
• Type sixty-five words per minute *(performance)* without any mistakes *(standard)*, using a standard PC keyboard *(condition)*.	Demonstration
• Develop three satisfactory learning objectives for the introductory module of a stress management training course *(performance)*, using *The First-Time Trainer (condition)*, in thirty minutes *(standard)*.	Written
• Parallel park a four-door sedan within the lines of a parking space *(performance)* during peak traffic *(condition)*, within three minutes and having to back up no more than three times *(standard)*.	Demonstration
• Demonstrate the proper response to an improper sexual advance *(performance)* during a role play (condition) in the manner acceptable to company policy *(standard)*.	Role play, demonstration, exercise
• Shut down the assembly line *(performance)* during a simulated equipment malfunction *(condition)* within five seconds after the alarm goes off *(standard)*.	Simulation, actual equipment
• Generate a budget for the planning department *(performance)* that meets the company's standard budget submission	

requirements *(standard)*, using a spread-sheet application program *(condition)*.	Written, computer
• After a viewing a video clip *(condition)*, diagnose potential sexual harassment situations *(performance)* and categorize the level of severity of each using the company policy guidelines *(standard)*.	Oral, written

The purpose of this evaluation is to see if the learner can perform a task using desired skills, applying knowledge, or exhibiting desired behaviors. For example, you could have the learner compose a business letter after completing a basic word processing training program, prepare a sample strategic plan after completing a management development program on planning, or isolate and repair a faulty circuit board using the skills just learned in a training program. A behavioral example is to determine if a person adopts healthier habits and lifestyle, as exhibited in a role play, at the end of a stress management course.

As you can see, performance tests can take many forms. What matters is finding out if learning objectives were met. Properly defined learning objectives will often state what the test should be.

Group exercises, such as those described in Step Six, can also be used to evaluate training. They offer the advantage of not only reinforcing learning but measuring it as well. They're particularly useful for measuring team training–related objectives. Use them during the training session to measure progress and at the end to measure final performance of learning objectives.

Tests

When we think of tests, we usually think back to our school days and those paper-and-pencil challenges we might well like to forget. For training, this may be the optimum way to measure training results, particularly for knowledge-related objectives. If the learning objective is to be able to identify Deming's fourteen steps for total quality management, having learners write them down, possibly with examples, will accurately evaluate the results. These can be classified as knowledge tests (as compared to skills tests). There are other forms as well:

- *Binary choice.* Right or wrong, true or false. Use sparingly, unless you use this orally during training. The answer must be clearly right; avoid trick questions.

- *Multiple choice.* For determining if learners have a solid grasp of appropriate information and can weed out unimportant information. Be sure there is just one clear answer, and be careful about terminology and jargon.
- *Matching.* Similar to multiple choice. Use it to determine if learners are acquiring specific terminology and relationships. Be careful about terminology and jargon.
- *Completion.* Similar to both matching and multiple choice.
- *Essay.* Good for behavior and manager- and executive-related training. Have predetermined key points to be made. Don't leave the essay too open-ended unless it's a creative assignment.

Evaluating tests gets more difficult as you go down the line from, say, a true-or-false test, to a case study where the answer is in essay form.

Tests can take many forms. For short sessions or for an interim evaluation, oral tests work well and simplify the process. Written tests require preparation time but are easy to maintain through word processors. Having learners take tests directly on a personal computer system also works if it is within the scope of the training to develop computer skills. Standard tests can also be used. Be careful not to ask trick or ambiguous questions, and also be aware that some cultures have difficulty with negatively phrased questions on tests.

How can you determine if a test is right for a situation? Exhibit 7-2 asks questions that will help you decide.

Questioning Techniques

Questions asked in the form of tests are excellent for measuring knowledge-related objectives. Refer to the Step Six discussion on asking questions.

Posttraining

One of the best ways to evaluate training is to follow up on learners after they have returned to work. Although it's one of the best, it is probably the least practiced because it takes time and resources to do it. A reasonable assumption is that a learner's supervisor can tell if the person's performance has improved. The supervisor was likely involved in the selection process, providing a

Exhibit 7-2. To Test or Not Test: A Dozen Questions to Help You Decide

1. Is there a faster way to obtain feedback?
2. Does the learner have to perform the task or tasks right away after returning to the job?
3. Is safety involved, for the learner and others?
4. Would failure to perform the objective(s) be costly to the organization?
5. Is the element under consideration a basic requirement before going on to a more vital element (i.e., a key building block for further objectives)?
6. Was enough knowledge provided for the learner to be properly tested?
7. Will the learner most likely do well in taking the test?
8. Are there clear-cut answers to the test?
9. If there are no clear-cut answers (e.g., a test on complex ethics issues), can you defend the answers you expect as facilitator?
10. Is there an easier way to obtain feedback?
11. Does the learning objective lend itself to testing (rather than actually performing the objective)?
12. Will the test measure it accurately?

If you answered no to either question 1 or 10 and yes to any of the other questions, testing could be of value. Another consideration is whether there is enough time to prepare, deliver, and grade the test, regardless of what type it is.

vested interest in the training outcome. A logical conclusion, then, is to ask the supervisor how well the training worked. Did the learner perform better after returning to the workplace or become more productive?

Typically these surveys are conducted at defined periods after the training and can be done more than once. For instance, a follow-up in three months might be time enough to determine what level of improvement took place. Sometimes it's appropriate to wait six months or even longer. If the training was a lengthy oral and written communications improvement course, it could take months to determine the ultimate effectiveness.

Follow-up surveys can be conducted by telephone, in formal, written forms, or by e-mail. Considering that the real test of training effectiveness is on-the-job performance, surveying supervisors is essentially more valuable than performance tests conducted during and immediately after training.

The Process Itself

Implementing the theme of continuous improvement requires that all aspects of the training process, including the actual process of delivering training, be evaluated. There are several ways to accomplish this evaluation:

- *Self-assessment by the facilitator.* A competent facilitator will be able to give a good indication of results, providing that assessment is done objectively.
- *A survey of participants.* The learners will have a sense of how well the training went and may have ideas for improving future applications. Exhibit 7-3 shows a sample form for learner feedback.
- *Outside observers.* This will cost more, but done properly can have a positive effect on future training done by the facilitator.
- *Videotape.* The video of sessions provides a relatively true picture of what transpired. There's nothing quite like listening and watching oneself perform, and this technique will show many details that the facilitator was not aware of.
- *Review of performance test results.* This is the ultimate test. If learners can meet desired objectives, then the facilitator did the job.

Using combinations of these may be more effective than applying just one.

Facilitator Performance

The purposes of this type of evaluation are to determine if you were as effective as possible in delivering training and, more important, to help you improve your facilitation efforts. Key focal points would include application of adult learning concepts, extensive learner involvement, maximum use of time, and demonstration of having achieved learning objectives.

Facilitator performance can be accomplished in two ways. The first is *self-evaluation.* A trainer, especially an experienced one, will have a sense of how well training went. Self-evaluation is an integral part of continuous improvement, since it includes trainer perfor-

Exhibit 7-3. Sample Training Evaluation Form

Training Session: _____

Facilitator: _____ Date: _____

For each item below, check the line under the number you believe best applies, using the criteria: 1 = strongly disagree, 2 = disagree, 3 = not sure, 4 = agree, 5 = strongly agree.

Item	1	2	3	4	5
1. I will be able to use these skills (knowledge) on my job.	___	___	___	___	___
2. Learning objectives were clear.	___	___	___	___	___
3. I could easily relate to examples and problems used.	___	___	___	___	___
4. Subject material was presented in an orderly manner.	___	___	___	___	___
5. The facilitator was well prepared.	___	___	___	___	___
6. The facilitator was knowledgeable in the subject matter.	___	___	___	___	___
7. The facilitator paid close attention to learner needs and questions.	___	___	___	___	___
8. The materials were useful.					
9. Audiovisuals added to the session.	___	___	___	___	___
10. The training length was just about right.	___	___	___	___	___
11. I would recommend this training to others.	___	___	___	___	___

Your comments are appreciated for future improvements, so please add anything else you feel is pertinent, including any changes you recommend: _____

_____

_____

_____

Thank you for taking time to complete this evaluation!

mance as well. Using the evaluation form shown in Exhibit 7-3 and possibly adding a few key items of interest to you is one way to do this. The other way is *learner evaluation*. If learners are considered to be competent adults who want to learn and acquire new skills, then it stands to reason that they'll have a good idea of whether the training was successful and how well it was delivered. Many learners have attended numerous training sessions and possibly have conducted training themselves. This experience gives them an excellent yardstick with which to assess trainer performance. (Again refer to the sample evaluation form shown in Exhibit 7-3.)

When and How Much to Evaluate

Since time is always of the essence—there is *never* enough of it to exhaust every aspect of each step in the training process—you are challenged to determine how much is enough. Here are some thoughts to bear in mind when designing training and paying heed to the critical evaluation element:

1. Build as much evaluation into the process as possible, which will render after-the-fact evaluation much less important (other than that done later, on the job). Several performance measurements during training will serve quite well, taking far less time than having to test participants when the training is done.

2. Prioritize evaluation according to how critical the training is to meeting organization objectives. If the company's competitiveness depends on the training (e.g., training related to shifting to a new product base and marketing it in an international arena), then evaluation is mandatory.

3. Identify evaluation methods during Step Four, so evaluation after training can be accomplished relatively quickly.

Step Eight

Improve Continuously

Training with a single-skill focus is not adequate for the work world of the 1990s. Workers need general thinking, communications, mathematical, scientific, and technical skills that can be tapped and expended to confront what is new and problematic.

—Arthur Wirth
Education and Work for the Year 2000 (1992)

Learning and growing for trainers is a constant challenge. Technology, changes in the workplace, and global competition are three prime reasons that it's essential for you to keep up with new developments. Recognizing this professional need, Step Eight addresses the vital step of professional development.

If you're a one-time trainer, you *could* ignore this step. Still, there are a few things you might want to consider for your training sessions to be the best they can be. If you'll be training regularly, the advice given in this step will help you fulfill your quest for stretching and improving your own performance. There's another consideration worth thinking about: Anticipation (such as in a learning organization) can provide vital training before a problem indicates the need for it. Everyone in the workplace, and certainly managers, are concerned with skills enhancement and competency. Thinking like a trainer and staying on top of things will serve you well in any job.

Step Eight Summary

Professionalism as a trainer encompasses many facets. Primary ones discussed in this step are:

- Review of the skills trainers need
- Ways to enhance these skills
- The portfolio concept to manage and maintain skills
- Technology and the need for trainers to keep up with what's available
- Trainers' ethics
- Summary of the eight steps to effective training

Trainer Skills Revisited

Step One identified a number of skills trainers need (actually, they are closely related to the skills all knowledge workers need). The purpose of professional development is to increase these skills, as well as take steps to acquire any newly emerging skills. As a review, here are those skills:

- *Management skills.* To ensure success within tight budgets. A trainer manages time (including time of learners who are away from their jobs for training), resources, and funds, as well as staff members.
- *Communications skills.* To motivate, among other goals.
- *Analytical and problem-solving skills.* To tackle needs assessment and more.
- *Information literacy.* To find information and implement solutions to problems.
- *Computer literacy.* To gain access to information accessible only by computer. Additionally, computers are often essential for performing on the job; communications rely on automation, and computers increasingly deliver more and more training.

Professional development should be based on these skills. Starting with an inventory of where you stand regarding them, your object is to lay out a plan to work on the ones needing the most work. These skills will form headings under your portfolio, discussed later in this step.

Strengthening Training Skills

There are numerous ways to stay up-to-date as a trainer. It could be a simple matter of finding an article on a particular aspect of training, or on a broader note, affiliating and networking with a professional association. We examine a number of ways here to strengthen skills.

Speaking and Training Opportunities

Many opportunities exist for maintaining your speaking and training skills. One available in many locations is Toastmasters. Here you'll have the chance to hone your ability to stand before a group and speak and receive valuable feedback. Many volunteer opportunities exist as well. The value is that these same skills are essential for most training situations, particularly when the instructor is central to the process, as in classroom training. These skills are also the topic of training in many organizations, since so many people need them. When you think about all the volunteer organizations and how much training they need (e.g., Scouting, senior centers, rehabilitation programs, youth sports, YMCA and YWCA, adult learning centers), you quickly realize how much opportunity there is. Also, service clubs—one example of many types of groups—may seek to put on as many as fifty programs a year, providing enormous opportunity for speaking and training.

Professional Associations

The primary national training organization, the American Society for Training and Development (ASTD), provides extensive services for trainers, from beginners to senior professionals. Most major cities have local chapters, and you can be a member of the national or local organization or both. Local chapter services include special interest groups, professional development, workshops, and meetings. Contact national ASTD at 1640 King Street, Box 1443, Alexandria, VA 22313; (703)683-8100 (voice); (703)683-1523 (fax); http://www.astd.org (Web site). Local chapter information can be obtained from the national contact. ASTD provides publications, networking opportunities, conferences, employment services, databases, and more.

Many other training-related organizations exist, but generally they are geared to specialists in various applications, such as computer-based training. Check with a local librarian or through Internet sources for assistance and information on resources. In fact, the Internet and World Wide Web offer an increasing number of potentially useful resources for trainers. In addition, you can network with other trainers through various on-line discussion groups.

Publications

Vast numbers of professional publications are available for trainers. Most major publishers of business- and workplace-related materials publish in the training field. Two magazines of interest to first-time trainers are *Training* (Lakewood Publications) and *Training and Development* (ASTD). Major libraries usually subscribe to both. For *Training and Development*, use the address already given for ASTD, including the Web page. For *Training*, the address is 50 South Ninth Street, Minneapolis, MN 55402; (612)333-0471 (voice); (612)333-6526 (fax); and TrainMag@aol.com (e-mail). Both regularly contain information on developments in the training and development field and are useful for information regarding specific training questions. A search through the annual indexes of these two magazines, both appearing in the December issues, will lead you to valuable information.

Commercial Resources

An enormous supply of materials is commercially available: workshops and seminars, certificate and degree programs, games and simulations, experiential materials, instruments, handbooks, and other materials. Professional development tools as well as off-the-shelf materials on numerous training topics are marketed that may fill your training needs. Contract trainers and consultants are widely available. These resources can be reached through the two magazines already mentioned, ASTD, electronically, and through local contacts, as well as Yellow Pages and Web sites. Training is big business, so you don't have to go far to locate most of the resources you'll need.

The Trainer's Portfolio

Professionals have long used portfolios to exhibit their skills and accomplishments. The concept is adaptable to any career and offers an effective way of presenting personal skills and qualifications. You'll still need a resumé, but it should merely reflect your current qualifications for a particular position or field. Otherwise, it's typically too broad to merit consideration from the hiring (or contracting) body. The idea is to keep adding to it. Maintaining a portfolio is an excellent way for part-time trainers to keep up with this field.

Your own portfolio (valid for both training and your profession) might include these categories (as well as others that fit your individual needs):

- Professional development
- New skills within the industry or profession (E.g., use of the workplace and trainer skills identified in Step One: information literacy, interpersonal communication, problem solving and decision making, and creativity and innovation.)
- Computer and other technology skills
- Interpersonal skills (communication, writing, motivation)
- Education—formal degree programs, certificate programs, and workshops and seminars
- Community and professional service (volunteering), which themselves might be subdivided into the categories already listed
- Other skills that are transferable to other jobs or professions (e.g., total quality management, diversity expertise, team development experience)
- Outside interests, to show you as a whole person (e.g., recreation, fitness and wellness, vocational interests)

There are plenty of opportunities to acquire skills and experiences outside the job itself—for example:

- Volunteer
- Tutor
- Religious organizations
- Industry association
- Writing
- Workshops and conferences
- Certificate programs
- Temporary firm training
- Professional mail (from associations)
- Informational interviews
- Nonprofit agencies
- Toastmasters
- Mentoring (and being mentored)
- Professional association
- Reading
- Internships (for pay and not for pay)
- Observation
- Degree programs
- Speakers' bureaus
- Adult education programs
- Coaching (and being coached)
- Networking

A Technology Update

As you've seen throughout this book, technology can be widely applied as a training tool. It creates a two-pronged challenge to trainers, including first-time ones: how best to use it to make training excellent and how to stay abreast of developments. If anything, there's too much progress and information to keep up with, but keeping up with technology is something everyone associated with the workplace must do. Two examples will illustrate the growing importance of technology to training.

Training Software Tools

Applications packages are commercially available for a broad array of training functions, from building questionnaires to administering a large training department. A representative sampling of functions includes these:

- Planning
- Tracking and administration
- Budgeting, cost estimating, and return-on-investment calculations
- Scheduling (people, facilities, and equipment)
- Maintaining training material inventories
- Testing
- Authoring and delivery of computer-based training
- Surveys and data analysis
- Evaluation
- Certificates and awards
- Self-paced learning packages

Networking Technology

Training is making extensive use of the digital, wired world of organizations. The Internet, intranets (similar to Internet, but available only to people within a specific organization), discussion groups, e-mail, and training delivery via the Internet (and intranets) are breakthroughs that can take training to a broader, more flexible plane. Learner and facilitator can discuss the learner's performance on a training class through e-mail and Web sites. Assignments can be sent through computer fax or e-mail. Training packages can be shipped (digitally) to anywhere a learner has a PC and modem. There's a virtual explosion of new training applications because of networks and being digital.

A Word About Ethics

Concern about ethics within the realm of training falls into two categories: being ethical in facilitating the learning process and delivering ethics-related training. There is no question about the need for being concerned in the workplace when it comes to ethics. Just reading the latest business news to see who tried to bilk their companies or customers out of enormous amounts of money is proof enough. From the training viewpoint, ethics is a matter of being fair in all dealings with others, including making sure every participant in a training session receives the best support and facilitation you can offer. It also means expecting participants to be ethical.

Conducting ethics training is easy to do (perhaps too easy—making it a matter of merely paying lip service). There's plenty of material—videos, cases, books, exercises—on the market and many organizations are paying attention to it, some because they want to, others because they have to. The material is uncomplicated and can be easily grasped by participants.

Here are some thoughts to keep in mind if you find yourself concerned about ethics from a training viewpoint:

1. Base everything you do, from actions to ethics training programs, on your organization's values statement.
2. Don't pass judgment on others, particularly participants.
3. Use examples that members of your training group can easily relate to.
4. Be prepared to practice what you preach.
5. Don't portray cases and people in ways that aren't true to life in your organization (unless for discussion or contrasting purposes).

Eight Steps to Effective Training: A Summary

Effective training is as easy as taking the eight steps identified in this book. Of course, it is rarely easy to do anything well, and training requires a lot of hard, but satisfying, work. The idea is that by following a series of steps, training will have a greater chance of being effective. The eight steps, summarized in Exhibit 8-1, will also serve as focal points for continuous improvement. Exhibit 8-2 notes some of the things that can be done to improve each of the steps.

Exhibit 8-1. Eight Steps to Effective Training

1. **Facilitate learning.** The key to trainer success, which includes how to implement the other seven steps. The trainer facilitates the process, depending on a well-designed program and motivated learners for the training to be effective.

2. **Focus on performance.** Establish the objective of the training and make sure you're on track—*before* you start. Objectives are derived from needs assessment, both of which must be done before attempting to do any meaningful training.

3. **Focus on learning.** Make sure the training provides the maximum possibility for participant learning, with emphasis on how adults and organizations learn. Using adult learning principles and a focus on mastery and competence will ensure the best training possible.

4. **Be prepared.** Develop the materials you'll need, bringing them all together in the most effective order, and making sure everything is ready to go. There are many things to do and many options (media, delivery methods, learners, trainers, evaluation methods). Thanks to a dedicated profession, there are plenty of tools and techniques to help get these important tasks done.

5. **Deliver effectively.** Develop the communication skills you'll need to present your training session successfully. Even if the training is fully automated, or otherwise requires little trainer intervention, communication is critical. Automated training requires that the training package be carefully communicated to the training technicians who are producing it.

6. **Get learners involved.** Develop the best in all participants, and practice different ways to deliver the training. This step is tied closely to the previous steps. Thanks to trainers who take the profession seriously, there are a number of field-tested ways to do this.

7. **Get feedback.** Determine the success of the training. Evaluation should occur all through the training process, and particularly when it's over. It's the only way you'll know if desired learning objectives are being met.

8. **Improve continuously.** Keep your trainer's portfolio up-to-date and enhance skills as a trainer.

Exhibit 8-2. Ways to Increase Professionalism in the Eight Steps

1. *Facilitate learning.* The more confidence you have as a trainer, the easier it is to think of yourself as a facilitator. At all times, keep reminding yourself that your purpose in life as a trainer is to facilitate. Try serving in a facilitator role in other things you do. All the skills identified in this step help develop facilitation skills.

2. *Focus on performance.* If you're adept at identifying learning objectives, or at least competent in recognizing them and capable of delivering training that helps learners achieve them, then you'll have focused on performance. Another way to enhance your professionalism in this regard is to think in terms of the bottom line of the training. Profit, productivity, service, or some other output must be made more effective if the training is successful.

3. *Focus on learning.* Getting fully conversant with adult learning principles and adopting the concept of the learning organization (see Step One) will help keep the focus on learning.

4. *Be prepared.* This requires diligence, patience, and much hard work. By exhibiting more of each of these three qualities, you will be better prepared.

5. *Deliver effectively.* Constant attention, including attending communication training yourself, will increase your delivery skills.

6. *Get learners involved.* This requires constant attention to the process, including always looking for new exercises and ideas.

7. *Get feedback.* Ask questions constantly and apply what you learn to improving for next time.

8. *Improve continuously.* As stated in this step.

Trainers are always looking for checklists. Good ones provide a concise, handy, and professional tool for being competent as a trainer. As a summary, a trainer's dozen items—things for a good trainer to keep in mind and apply—are listed in Exhibit 8-3. Apply all of them, and you'll be an effective trainer.

Exhibit 8-3. A Trainer's Dozen

Here is an eclectic list of things to help you become—and remain—an effective trainer.

1. Your customer is the learner. The learner replaces the sun (and everything else) as the center of your universe.

2. The trainer who can't do a passable job working somewhere within the line operations of the organization being served is suspect.

3. Technology—hard, soft, and otherwise—is nothing more than a tool. Use it as much as possible, providing you fully understand it and its effect on people. If a particular technology can make things better or more effective, use it; otherwise wait for something better to come along.

4. The trainer who stops learning is a retired trainer.

5. Things can always get better—and it's your job to make them so.

6. Practice what you preach—by coaching, managing, and growing. Otherwise turn in your pointers and markers and become a politician.

7. To be truly professional, remember the three R's: reading, 'riting, and return on investment.

8. Paper your walls with things like the Scouts' motto and the Golden Rule. Then read your walls daily.

9. Read the funny papers, go to the movies, take a hike, or go bird-watching regularly—and practice the principle of transfer of training. There's nothing more refreshing than a trainer who can relate the training situation to the bigger picture of life.

10. You *can* be replaced.

11. When all else fails, call ASTD, Dear Abby, SPCA, your shrink, or another practitioner like yourself. There's always professional help available.

12. Unlike total quality management, (where every step must be successful), seven or eight out of twelve isn't bad.

Resources for the First-Time Trainer

Experienced trainers have made a valuable contribution to their profession by being prolific writers and producers of a broad spectrum of training materials. The result? Books, articles, scripts for audios and videos, ready-made activities and training programs, experiential exercises, instruments, reports, and more. This wealth of materials comes in a variety of forms, from words on paper to exotic multimedia-based programs. The profession is awash in materials, most of which is readily available to the first-time trainer.

Because of the depth of materials, only a select few are presented here. In fact, the main intent is to show where to find materials, to point you in the right direction to find what you might need. The key to success in locating these services is to use the steps identified in Step Four regarding the critical selection process.

Discussed here are publications (books and periodicals); videos; training programs, products, and services; and on-line services.

Publications

The demand for training information is such that many publishers, large and small, offer materials for the trainer. Topics run the full range of training functions, starting with analysis and going through methods of evaluating training results. Contact the publishers to find out if they have what you need. Also, many of the organizations listed under the materials-providers section offer a wide variety of books and will be happy to provide you with a catalog. Your own needs could be in the area of technical training, supervisory training, technological aspects of training (e.g., computer-based training), or some other special area. You'll likely find one or more excellent books about your area of interest.

Books

Craig, R. L., ed. *Training and Development Handbook*, 4th ed. New York: McGraw-Hill, 1996.

Knowles, M. *The Adult Learner: A Neglected Species*, 4th ed. Houston: Gulf Publishing, 1988.

Leech, T. *How to Prepare, Stage, and Deliver Winning Presentations*, 2nd ed. New York: AMACOM, 1993.

Lorayne, H., and J. Lucas. *The Memory Book*. New York: Ballantine, 1974.

Mager, B. *Analyzing Performance Problems*, 2nd ed. (with P. Pipe); *Developing Attitude Toward Learning*, 2nd ed.; *Goal Analysis*, 2nd ed.; *Measuring Instructional Results*, 2nd ed.; and *Preparing Instructional Objectives*, 2nd ed. Belmont, Cal.: Lake Publishing, 1984.

Newstrom, J. W., and E. E. Scannell. *Games Trainers Play*. New York: McGraw-Hill, 1980. (Three other books in this series are *More Games Trainers Play* (1983), *Still More Games Trainers Play* (1991), and *Even More Games Trainers Play* (1994).

Piskwich, G. M., ed. *The ASTD Handbook of Instructional Technology*. New York: McGraw-Hill, 1993.

Tobin, D. R. *Re-educating the Corporation: Foundations for the Learning Organization*. Essex Junction, Vt.: Omneq, 1993.

Tracey, W. R., *Training Employees with Disabilities*. New York: AMACOM, 1995.

Zemke, R., and T. Dramlinger. *Figuring Things Out*. Reading, Mass.: Addison-Wesley, 1982.

Periodicals

Two periodicals, one from ASTD and the other a trade publication, have provided trainers with a wealth of vital information for several decades. *Training and Development* (formerly *Training and Development Journal*) and *Training* are valuable for any trainer who will be practicing for any length of time. For the first-and-only-time trainer, they also may provide you with just the article or piece of information you need. A major value of articles in these periodicals is that they are often presented within the context of a successful application. Either way, make the most of these two periodicals.

Contact national ASTD at 1640 King St., Box 1443, Alexandria, VA 22313; telephone 1-703-683-8100; 1-703-683-1523 (fax); http:// www.astd.org (Web site). *Training* can be contacted at 50 S. Ninth St., Minneapolis, MN 55402; 1-612-333-0471; 1-612-333-6526 (fax); and

TrainMag@aol.com (e-mail). Many libraries subscribe to both, and they are well represented in compilations of business articles that can be accessed electronically within libraries.

Videos

There are two things the first-time trainer needs to know about video and its availability. For one, it's the number one training medium, having replaced classroom and on-the-job training in recent years. This means there are plenty of videos available to use in your training. Which brings up the second thing—there are tens of thousands of them to choose from. What this means is that you either need to ask someone who uses video often or spend some time filtering through all that's available, often previewing them in order to select what you need. Fortunately, there are distributors available who can help you narrow down the process. For planning's sake, you can assume that there is a video somewhere that will fit your need, bearing in mind that it could be too long or focused on other industries or situations. Here are a few video producers whose catalogs will supply you with a broad cross section of available videos, but keep in mind that there are other companies besides these. Also, there are often local distributors of videos which can be found through telephone books or through trainer networks.

American Media, Inc.
4900 University Ave.
West Des Moines, IA 50266-6769
800-262-2557
515-224-0256 (fax)
ami@ammedia.com (e-mail)
http://www.ammedia.com (Web site)

BNA Communications
9439 Key West Ave.
Rockville, MD 20830
800-233-6067
301-948-2085 (fax)
http://www.bna.com (Web site)

CRM Films
2215 Faraday Ave.
Carlsbad, CA 92008
800-421-0833
619-931-5792 (fax)

Mentor Media
800-577-8770
800-359-1937 (fax)

Video Arts
8614 West Catalpa Ave.
Chicago, IL 60656
800-588-9372
312-693-7030 (fax)

Training Programs, Products, and Services

Again, because of the growing nature of training and development, there are plenty of suppliers to call upon for off-the-shelf materials and third-party trainers to assist you. Represented here are all of the resources discussed in the eight steps, ranging from simple exercises to audiotapes to major programs, including trainer certification. A few representative samples include:

American Management Association
1601 Broadway
New York, NY 10019-7420
212-586-8100
212-903-8168 (fax)
http://www.amanet.org (Web site)

American Society for Training and Development
P.O. Box 1443
Alexandria, VA 22313
703-683-8100
703-683-8103 (fax)

Blanchard Training and Development
125 State Place
Escondido, CA 92029
800-577-5401

Center for Creative Leadership
P.O. Box 26300
Greensboro, NC 27438-6300
910-545-2810

Toastmasters International
P.O. Box 9052
Mission Viejo, CA 92690
714-858-8255
http://www.toastmasters.org (Web site)

Training House
P.O. Box 3090
Princeton, NJ 08543
800-577-5041
609-452-2790 (fax)

In addition to these organizations and the many others in the field, local educational institutions also provide training services and programs. This is often done through extension services or continuing education programs. In addition, local ASTD chapters often have available catalogs of local providers and can put you in touch with service providers.

On-Line Services

As we become more "wired" in the workplace, demand for on-line services increases accordingly. Training is well represented in the digital world. It's available through teleconferencing and various elements of the Internet. In addition, services can be obtained through Worldwide Web sites, resources can be obtained through a variety of sources, and trainers use discussion groups (also called chat groups) to exchange information. Note the number of Web sites from the small sampling of resources in this section. In addition to the ASTD organization, many local chapters have their own Web sites. Training practitioners make their wares available through electronic advertisements. Bear in mind that these Web sites come and go or change on a daily basis. There are no librarians policing the information highway to make sure it remains tidy, complete, and cataloged. Nonetheless, there is value to be gained by trainers, provided they are experienced in using these electronic means. One site worth observing and possibly joining is sponsored by Penn State University. Another is sponsored by the University of Missouri. They represent excellent examples of how information can be obtained through digital means. Their discussion groups provide lively forums (they are officially called list servers) for trainers to gain information. These two sources can be contacted via electronic mail at trdev-l@pusvm.psu.edu (Penn State) and hrd-l@mizzou1.missouri.edu (University of Missouri).

Index

THE LITTLE, BROWN
BOOK OF
❧ ANECDOTES ❦

THE LITTLE, BROWN
BOOK OF
❧ ANECDOTES ❧

CLIFTON FADIMAN
GENERAL EDITOR

LITTLE, BROWN AND COMPANY
BOSTON   TORONTO

Clifton Fadiman, *General Editor*
Jennifer Speakes, *Research Editor and Writer*
Laurence Urdang *and* Alan Isaacs, *Consulting Editors*

Library of Congress Catalog Card No. 85–45408

Copyright acknowledgments are found at the back of the book, following the indexes.

Published simultaneously in Canada by
Little, Brown & Company (Canada) Limited

PRINTED IN THE UNITED STATES OF AMERICA

❧ CONTENTS ❧

And once when saying his prayers, which he [Sydney Smith] always did out loud, he was overheard to say: "Now Lord, I'll tell you an anecdote."
—Patrick Mahony,
Barbed Wit and Malicious Humor

❧ PUBLISHER'S NOTE ❧

THIS book is for the most part a collection of anecdotes about readily identifiable people. It is organized alphabetically by person, with a brief biography of that person followed by one or more anecdotes. Where doubt exists as to whom an anecdote should be ascribed, we have usually chosen the more familiar name. Often, when one person is the victim and another the perpetrator, we have placed the anecdote with that person whose character is most revealed. Relatives of famous people are entered under their own names when they are fairly well known in their own right or when the more famous relative has no anecdote ascribed to him or her. Otherwise, they can be found under the name of the relative.

In a few dozen cases we came across anecdotes connected with obscure or quite unfamiliar names or with places. These were in one way or another so interesting or amusing that, just for fun, we included them in no particular order. To distinguish them from the regular text, they are boxed.

Clifton Fadiman, to whom the idea for this book and its presentation belong the credit, is the General Editor. He contributed anecdotes, rewrote many, made the final selection, and edited the entire selection. Mr. Fadiman is also responsible for the translations from French and German sources.

Laurence Urdang and his associates researched anecdotes, rewrote for uniformity of style, and provided most of the biographies.

We hope *The Little, Brown Book of Anecdotes* has value as a work of reference as well as one of entertainment. It does not, however, claim to be a work of exact scholarship. All collections like this are in part the product of pilferage; we have tried to stop short of pillage.

We are especially grateful for a few exceptionally fine collections that have provided us with some anecdotes. Foremost among these is *Presidential Anecdotes*, edited by Paul F. Boller, Jr. Although we did find some stories about US presidents in other places, Mr. Boller truly has collected the best, and his extensive listing of sources attests to his thoroughgoing research. If the reader enjoys the presidential anecdotes herein, we strongly urge perusal of Boller's complete collection. *The Oxford Book of Literary Anecdotes* is a valuable assortment, and Richard Kenin and Justin Wintle's *Dictionary of Biographical Quotation* is yet another excellent one.

A complete bibliography lists all our sources. As an extra aid to the reader, the specific source for each anecdote, when known, is provided in the Source List that precedes the Bibliography. For permission to use copyrighted material, we refer the reader to the Copyright Acknowledgments, which follow the indexes.

Most of the anecdotes for the purposes of this book have been rewritten. Some are directly quoted from the source; these anecdotes are enclosed in quotation marks.

Every significant name in each anecdote will be found in the Index of Names. The Index of Subjects enables the reader interested in subject matter rather than persons to find appropriate anecdotes for a desired theme or concept. We hope that the cross-reference network will amplify both indexes.

Any venture such as this will, like *Bartlett's Familiar Quotations,* gain from response from readers. We elicit your suggestions for future editions.

And we hope that you will enjoy this book.

&✿ ACKNOWLEDGMENTS ✿&

FOR various suggestions the General Editor extends his thanks to Joe Bryan III, Annalee Fadiman, Kim Fadiman, Albert Friendly, Leo Counce Hopkins, George Lang, Open Court Publishing, Henry D. Smith II, and Don Zimmerman. He is especially grateful to Siu Zimmerman, who assisted during the making of most of this book. Her diligence was equaled only by her good judgment.

To the publisher's editorial staff and in particular to Ann Sleeper and Betsy Pitha special thanks are due.

The publisher would like to thank Colleen Mohyde and Margaret Freudenthal for the preparation of the indexes; Virginia Creeden for researching the sources and preparing the Source List and Bibliography; and Susanne McNatt and Mary George of the Reference Division of the Harvey S. Firestone Memorial Library, Princeton University.

⇒ INTRODUCTION ⇒

ANCESTRY

How far back do anecdotes go?

As with so many other good things, what we now call anecdotes may have started in classical Greece. Joseph Epstein* quotes the Italian scholar Arnaldo Momigliano, who, in his *Development of Greek Biography*, conjectures that the anecdote's founding father may have been the musical theorist Aristoxenus of Tarentum (born c. 370 BC): "Perhaps [Aristoxenus] was . . . the first to make anecdotes an essential part of biography. . . . I suspect that we owe to Aristoxenus the notion that a good biography is full of good anecdotes."

Though we borrowed the term from the French, *anecdote* ultimately derives from an almost identical Greek word meaning "things not given out," or, as we would say, unpublished. It is in this sense that Cicero uses it to describe some of his own manuscripts, a usage followed later by Renaissance scholars to denote manuscripts discovered in libraries and afterward published.

From the outset there seems also to have been attached to the word a connotation of secrecy or perhaps merely gossip. As a biographical device it was and remains anti-official, anti-panegyrical. It surprises the human being in question *en pantoufles*.

The anecdote's shady reputation probably derives from the sixth-century Byzantine historian Procopius, who called his posthumously published, scandalous account of the Emperor Justinian *Anecdota* or *Historia Arcana* ("Secret History").

It is during the Renaissance, with the rise of cities, royal courts, a true leisure class, and the cult of the individual that the anecdote, a form of condensed gossip, begins clearly to show its face. It begins to shake off its association with the merely scandalous.

In his *Dissertation on Anecdotes* Isaac D'Israeli (1766–1848) tells us that the French broadened the term to make it apply to "any interesting circumstance." In the eighteenth century Samuel Johnson defined it as "a *biographical incident;* a minute passage of *private life.*" The suggestion of amusing triviality now begins to emerge, so that two centuries later Winston Churchill could call anecdotes "the gleaming toys of history." In the transactions of biographers they function as petty cash.

The eighteenth century also marked the beginning of the association of anecdotes with the wit of old men. You can trace it in the French aphorist Rivarol (1753–1801). The frayed pejorative pun "anecdotage" may have been invented by John Wilkes (1727–1797) or perhaps by Thomas De Quincey (1785–1859). It was made fashionable

---

*"Literary Biography," *The New Criterion*, May 1983.

by Benjamin Disraeli in *Lothair* (1870): "When a man fell into his anecdotage it was a sign for him to retire from the world." But in 1835, thirty-five years earlier, an anonymous scribbler in *Blackwood's Magazine* had already made fierce play with the word: "The disgusting perversions of their anile anecdotage." It would seem that in youth we sow our wild oats, in old age our tame anecdotes.

We may conjecture that by the beginning of the eighteenth century the form had come of age in Western Europe. Continuing to develop, it becomes more and more luxuriant as we approach our own time. Hence this anthology's decided slant toward the modern.

ANATOMY OF THE ANECDOTE

An anecdote, so *Webster's Ninth New Collegiate Dictionary* informs us, is "a usually short narrative of an interesting, amusing, or biographical incident." This collection confines itself to "biographical incidents." We admit, however, that on occasion we have stretched the notion of incident so as to accommodate a reasonable number of origin stories, traditional tales, or wisecracks of the Groucho Marx–Dorothy Parker stripe.

Such witticisms gain in interest when placed in a setting, but it has not always been possible to provide one. We are, for example, ignorant of the circumstances in which the composer Mascagni stated that the Italian language has three degrees of comparison: *stupido, stupidissimo,* and *tenore*. Ditto for a learned mathematics professor, Badke by name, who once defined a point as an angle from which the two sides have been removed. These noncontextual examples failing to qualify as anecdotes, I have dishonestly smuggled them into this paragraph so that they may not be forever lost. But they really belong in *Bartlett's Familiar Quotations,* with which this book is not in competition.

Webster says: "a usually short narrative." We have in general obeyed this requirement but in a few instances violated it in order to illustrate what entertained men and women of generations long past. Our predecessors, at least to the mid-nineteenth century, valued prolixity as we do terseness. They had more time. And it was worth less money.

Furthermore, Webster's adjectives "interesting" and "amusing" may not seem to us to apply to many anecdotes that apparently gave them pleasure. A dusty collection called *The Percy Anecdotes* offers items like this: When the late Marquis of Cornwallis was leaving a nobleman's house and stepping into his carriage, a servant offered to hold an umbrella over him. "Take that thing away," said his lordship. "I am neither sugar nor salt, to suffer by a shower of rain." To us this seems flat. It is too *reasonable*. The metaphor is one you or I might have thought of without any notion that it might pass for wit. Still, our forefathers prized such conversational junk jewelry, giving it the name of anecdote.

We must keep in mind that the author of the foregoing was a marquis. That helped. The undeservedly forgotten essayist Frank Moore Colby once remarked, "Never destroy an uninteresting letter is the first rule of the British aristocracy." Second rule: Always remember to record an uninteresting action or remark. This rule has generated a revered tradition, featuring the peerage at its dullest. Horace Walpole felt the need to record for posterity that the contemporary dowager Duchess of Devonshire stayed up "every evening, till it was dark, in the skittle-ground keeping the score. . . ." Though we have salvaged a few of these antiquities — see THOMAS HERBERT PEMBROKE 1 — we must for the most part think of them as *ana* rather than anecdotes.

Our dictionary defines *ana:* "collected items of information, esp. anecdotal or bibliographical <Americ*ana*> <Johnson*iana*>." We would call it *miscellany*. The Percy miscellany is a kind of free-form substitute for a magazine. It is a potpourri of historical episodes, potted biographies, oddities of literature and history, excerpts from trial proceedings, classical legends, records of sensational events, believe-it-or-nots, travel memoirs, snippets from Plutarch, Herodotus, Macrobius; ghost and horror stories; oddities of natural history; records of the lives of eccentrics, geniuses, and other abnormals; edifying examples of virtuous speech and action; excerpts from letters; essaylets on the arts, sciences, and vocations. Indeed in many respects it is an unsystematic mini-encyclopedia of manners, persons, arts, sciences, and professions.

A representative collection such as *The Lounger's Commonplace Book; or, Alphabetical Anecdotes,* the work of Jeremiah Whitaker Newman (1759–1839), tends to conceive the anecdote as an extended short biography, often of an obscure person whose life is in some respect striking or unusual. Moralizing is a feature of the genre. The notion of point or humor hardly enters. It was not until almost the twentieth century that the anecdote became sparser, more isolated from a larger narrative context, achieving an economical effect with corresponding economy of means (see HENRY JAMES 2).

It is not always easy to distinguish between anecdote and episode. The seventh-century BC Greek poet Archilochus composed satires against his prospective father-in-law, Lycamber, so powerful that the poor man and his daughter both hanged themselves. This is beyond a doubt brief (I have told you all I know), it needs no larger context, it is far from prosy. Yet one thinks of it as an episode rather than an anecdote. If we are to admit all the striking episodes to be discovered in any eventful life (say Napoleon's), we would come up with a book quite different from the one you are now reading. Thus the story of van Gogh's ear composes a fascinating chapter in his biography, but is too complex, in a sense too *important,* to qualify as an anecdote. Many unforgettable episodes of history fall into this nonanecdotal category. In 1347 Edward III, having starved Calais into submission, required six men to deliver the keys of the town and castle dressed "in their shirts and with halters about their necks." They sacrificed themselves for their town. Though a moving story, is this an anecdote? I think not.

What makes rules interesting, however, are the exceptions. Therefore in this repository we have included a number of such anecdote-episodes whenever they seemed to us effective in brief form and diverting or striking or, as with EDITH CAVELL 1, a treasured item of our folk memory.

A career may be crowded, it may be a model of high achievement and yet in our sense produce few real anecdotes. Goethe, a titan, did not generate titanecdotes. His countrymen preserve as anecdotes his *sayings,* which range from the magnificent to the magnificently banal. Within this range you may place according to your taste this typical example: To a friend who regretted that he had never seen Italy, Goethe said, "Good, for if you had, our own sky would never seem blue enough."

However, so that certain supremely great names may be at least represented, we have on occasion smuggled in an anecdote or two that may be only moderately striking (see J. S. BACH 1). But not all greats are linked to trivia; the reader will note the absence of many famous figures.

Just as a first-rate anecdote should be more than merely a good saying, so it should be more than an odd biographical fact. It is well known, for instance, that Schiller worked better when inhaling the odor of overripe apples kept in his desk drawer. And we learn from Gordon Rattray Taylor's *The Great Evolution Mystery* that the world's leading authority on giant clams, Professor Sir Maurice Yonge, is the only man who has read *The Decline and Fall of the Roman Empire* from cover to cover while sitting on the Great Barrier Reef. Such eccentric particulars make for delightful reading but in the strict sense they are not anecdotal and few will be found in these pages.

Oddity alone, then, will not quite do. King Frederick Augustus of Saxony was in the course of his career elected king of Poland and became known as Augustus the Strong. He would astonish his dinner guests by picking up two of his state trumpeters, one in each hand. For five minutes he would keep them dangling while they played a fanfare. It is not clear just what earned Augustus his epithet — this kind of thing or his fathering of 354 bastards. The latter achievement recommends him to Guinness, but he doesn't quite fit into this book.

Similarly, we have generally ignored practical jokes, except when they are not only amusing but have some kind of narrative form and are connected with a famous personage (JOHN PARTRIDGE 1).

Finally, a book of biographical anecdotes must be just that, whether the individual created or provoked the anecdote. We have pinned each item to a single person (on occasion we were compelled to use a straight rather than a safety pin). But in the past less restrictive views obtained. Isaac D'Israeli thought "there are *anecdotes* of the art as well as the Artist; of the war as well as the General; of the nation as well as the Monarch." Such anecdotes we prefer to leave to the history books. It is true, however, that a biographical anecdote can throw light on an important *aspect* of an entire nation (see PABLO PICASSO 5).

The preceding comments underline the obvious: that the definition of anecdote shifts with the centuries. For our purposes anecdotes remain what D'Israeli called them — "minute notices of human nature and of human learning," even if today we are less interested in the latter than in the former. The witty, the humorous, those crackling with the whiplash of a tagline, tend to circulate most widely, to conform more closely to the modern sensibility. But there is plenty of room for the quieter anecdote whose value lies in the illumination of character or the inculcation of a moral lesson.

We prefer our anecdotes to be short, free-standing, with a nub or point or center. This book, nevertheless, contains many of which this cannot be said. EDWARD GIBBON 1 has no identifiable "point." But it continues to interest us as a famous statement made by a famous person about a critical event in his life. Some anecdotes are really mini-dramas appealing to our tenderest emotions (BRONSON ALCOTT 1; CHARLES DE GAULLE 5). Others — indeed, many — strip us of our dignity (ROBERT BENCHLEY 11). Some depend on mere word-play and do not rate a second reading, while others (ALBERT EINSTEIN 14) set the mind pondering. Some may not even depend on words at all (GEORGE ANTHEIL 1).

WHERE DO ANECDOTES COME FROM?

With many exceptions, anecdotes seem to be dominantly urban. Our Mountain Men, our pioneers, produce yarns, not anecdotes; desert and peasant cultures are rarely anecdotal seminaries. The atmosphere of the court, the great house, the capital, favors the anecdote as do many institutions and vocations associated with the city: the club, the dinner party, the university, the theater, the studio and gallery, the law court, parliaments and senates. The anecdote is a social product; it does not flourish in isolation. One qualifies immediately: certain personalities, irrespective of their environment or calling, may be anecdotal naturals.

Still, in these pages highly social beings are generally prominent. They tend to be associated in fair part with the arts and in consequence exhibit relatively unconventional temperaments: Tristan Bernard, Whistler, Sarah Bernhardt, George Kaufman. On the other hand, statesmen too may be loci of anecdote: Churchill (but he was also a painter); Lincoln (but he was also a great writer); Talleyrand. Money men are far less in evidence — though there is J. P. Morgan, of course, and one of our most profound and prescient anecdotes is about a banker (JAMES STILLMAN 1). Show business is replete with lively minds. It is fairly well represented in these pages. Really good sports anecdotes were hard to come by; we hope there's a fair sampling. Children, as you must know from your own childhood, are naturally brighter than adults, and in theory should provide a mine of anecdotes. However, the rules of our game require that notable names be attached to them, which limits the field.

The case of politicians is interesting. Many politicians, of course, have been vivid or witty personalities; but the general run are either by nature unamusing or are afraid to be thought amusing. That Adlai Stevenson was an interesting man with a quicksilver mind proved a political handicap. This is not true, of course, for the genuine greats, a Lincoln, a Disraeli, a Churchill. But the need to provide an image (or, as with Richard Nixon, a selection of images) tends to inhibit the kind of conduct that generates anecdotes. Still, look at Coolidge, who in some odd manner contrived to be both witty and dull.

This collection is sadly deficient in anecdotes about women. The reason is apparent: the chronicle of humankind has been written by the winners — at least up to our own day. One would wager that the index of a compilation like this, but published a century hence, will contain the names of a vast number of women. Yet even our sparse representation suggests that when women are amusing or trenchant or intellectually provocative they are often far more so than are men. The four samples from Sophie Arnould reveal a subtler spirit than the sixteen items associated with so renowned a wit as Sir Thomas Beecham.

Finally, in trying to identify the loci of anecdotes, we must keep in mind that the collector can work only with what has been recorded. Because he was a great monarch much of what Louis XIV said and did in public, whether dull or interesting, was bound to show up in memoirs of the period. It is, however, quite possible that thousands of remarkable or funny stories by or about obscure figures have been recounted in forgotten conversations. Such oral anecdote is lost forever. In the space-time continuum, one imagines, there exists a whole library of such anecdotes. But it is unwritten.

ANECDOTES AND NATIONALITY

A lady once asked Dr. Johnson why his dictionary defined "pastern" as "the knee of a horse." "Ignorance, madam, pure ignorance," he replied. This book's editors are equipped with plenty of pure ignorance. Worse still, they are not linguists. They handle adequately only three languages. Hence the anecdotes are mainly of British, American, French, and German origin.

Nevertheless, admitting our ignorance and language limitations, we consider these pages not unduly parochial. A genius for or interest in anecdote is not universal. The national traits that give birth to these airy trifles seem less marked in other countries than in those mentioned above. (On the other hand, the book's most chilling item is Russian; see KHRUSHCHEV 5.) Perhaps Scandinavians and Swiss and Poles are not so receptive to eccentricity. Or it may be that they have not chanced to evolve certain social or class institutions that tend to generate anecdotes.

One European country is almost surely underrepresented: Hungary. I have rarely met a Hungarian who was not either the subject of good anecdotes or himself a repository of them. The English-Hungarian journalist George Mikes is speaking for himself, but I think also for his countrymen: "Looking back on my life, it seems to me it has been a long string of anecdotes." Of death he says: "If I am lucky, [it] will simply be the last anecdote." We do offer a few good Hungarian stories, most of them about Molnár. But many more examples of the true paprika spirit must remain forever locked inside a formidable language. I suspect that this is true also of Czechoslovakia: any nation that can produce a Hašek and a Kundera *must* be anecdotically rich.

Even when the language is open to us our selections may be insufficiently representative. We are conditioned by an Anglo-American culture. Consequently what pleases us may not please those differently conditioned, and vice versa. For example, we include from the German many anecdotes we think entertaining or instructive. But we have also omitted many that make a special appeal to the Germanic temperament. Here is one:

> A lady suffering from headache consulted the famous Berlin physician Heim and, in some embarrassment, asked whether she could try a remedy that had been recommended to her as infallible: covering her head with sauerkraut. Heim replied: "Excellent — but don't forget to mix a bratwurst with it!"

To see why we did not find this quite as amusing as Germans do, compare HERMAN J. MANKIEWICZ 2. If you think about it, the two jokes really make the same point. But they involve rather different conceptions of wit. I might add that the German anecdote is captioned: SOMETHING LACKING. True.

As one moves eastward, the divergence of taste becomes more radical. We would have liked to find some anecdotic reflection of the magnificent cultures of India, China, and Japan. This book presents a faint reflection of that reflection. But after admittedly superficial research, one is led to conclude that anecdotically East is East, and West is

West, and never the twain shall meet. Oriental "anecdotes" tend either to be moral parables — bits and pieces of wisdom literature — or longish historical episodes. Rarely do they seem to be the bubbles that form and break on the surface of social intercourse. The East, whether Near, Middle, or Far, is not attuned to our kind of anecdote, just as it does not appear to produce our kind of light verse. (Search these pages carefully enough, however, and you may find one or two Ottomanecdotes.)

With respect to our subject, it is not true to say that Americans and British are separated by a common language. The American anecdotal *tone* differs slightly and interestingly from the British, but no vast gulf separates our mutual appreciation. However, again we must qualify. We have included a few cricket stories that will baffle many Americans — though anyone of permissive temper ought to be able to grasp the point of BRIAN JOHNSTON 2. To be fair, we have included enough baseball stories to infuriate our British cousins.

AUTHENTICITY

Leslie Stephen in his life of Milton remarks that no good story is quite true. A sobering thought.

Anecdotes are the thistledown of biography. To establish authenticity in all cases is impossible. We have done our best. Where we strongly suspect an anecdote to be apocryphal, we have so stated. We do not, however, claim to have identified every possible case and we welcome corrections from our readers.

We have tried to keep in mind the words of the venerable president of Magdalen, Oxford, Martin Joseph Routh (1755–1854). Approaching the century mark, he was once asked by a disciple what single wisdom-crammed axiom or precept he could abstract from his long life's experience. The president reflected, then, after a long pause, said, "I think, sir, since you come for the advice of an old man, sir, you will find it a very good practice *always to verify your references!*"

Well said. But difficulties abound. There is, for example, the self-effacing anecdotalist (more often simply a jokesmith) who, in the interest of wider circulation, prefers to hide his own light under another's bushel. Samuel Johnson once described the process: "Pointed axioms and acute replies fly loose about the world, and are assigned successively to those whom it may be the fashion to celebrate." Thus in the nineteenth century a *bon mot* turning on the contrast between wealth and poverty might naturally be credited to a Rothschild.

The philosopher Immanuel Kant, listening to a string of anecdotes about a famous personality of the time, remarked, "It seems to me I recall similar anecdotes about other great figures. But that is to be expected. Great men are like high church towers: around both there is apt to be a great deal of wind." In our time Churchill, Dorothy Parker, Samuel Goldwyn, have become high church towers.

Long before them came Talleyrand. He worked overtime; it was said that he never fashioned so many brilliant *mots* during his life as he did after his death. It requires great wit to utter post-mordancies. On the other hand (the authority is his brother, who may have suffered from sibling jealousy), Talleyrand is said to have abstracted many of his good things from *L'Improvisateur français,* a compilation of anecdotes in twenty-one duodecimo volumes.

We know of one interesting case in which Talleyrand created an anecdote by fiat. It has to do with the Bourbon Restoration. On the evening of the day on which the Comte d'Artois, later to become King Charles X, entered Paris, Talleyrand asked a group assembled in his drawing room what the Bourbon prince had said. "Nothing at all" was the answer. Talleyrand, not satisfied, ordered a well-known political writer to leave the room and compose an appropriately memorable remark. The writer made three tries, all inadequate. Finally he returned with the words: "Nothing is changed in France; there is only one Frenchman more." Talleyrand applauded; the Duke of Artois had been assigned his *mot;* and another famous anecdote was added to "history."

It is probable that at least five percent of the items in this book consisted originally of confected or current jokes that were then fathered on notables.

The question of authenticity arises perhaps most particularly in the case of Lincoln stories. Here the source-hunters have been busy and conscientious. Yet questions remain. We may never be able to say of certain Lincoln anecdotes, "Yes, this is authentic," but we have tried to avoid the inclusion of too many doubtful items. Those die-hards who prefer a scholarly tracking down of Lincoln stories are referred to *Abe Lincoln Laughing: Humorous Anecdotes from Original Sources by and about Abraham Lincoln,* edited by P. M. Zall (University of California Press, 1982). This is a first-rate job of scholarship.

Sometimes an anecdote may be credited to two or more different persons, though it is obvious only one can be responsible. The famous quip "And if you were my wife, I'd drink it" (WINSTON CHURCHILL 7) is (almost) surely the great man's. Yet it has also been ascribed to Senator Robert Taft, who could not have said it had the presidency come with it. The dress designer Edith Head, who knew Grace Kelly in Hollywood, was, at the time of Miss Kelly's marriage, asked for anecdotes about the princess. Said Miss Head, "Grace doesn't allow anecdotes to happen to her." Neither did Taft.

The retort "That will depend on whether I embrace your lordship's mistress or your lordship's principles" is assigned to various personages, of whom we have chosen John Wilkes as the most credible. Many such putdown retorts, in our time often attributed to Dorothy Parker, Oscar Levant, Groucho Marx, or others, were probably never actually said to anyone at all. This is shrewdly pointed out by the comedian Steve Allen in his *Funny People.*

There are legacy-anecdotes, whose birth lies in the obscure past, but are rediscovered, refurbished, and with each passing generation assigned new paternities. It was Donatus who uttered the classical curse: *Pereant qui ante nos nostra dixerunt!* (A plague on those who said our good things before we did!) Doubtless some of these good things, truly of ancient lineage, have turned up in this book dressed in modern clothes.

WHAT DO ANECDOTES DO?

Chiefly, they entertain. They form a minor genre, even a trivial one; they are not history and biography but the decoration on history and biography. Yet, when more than just good jokes, they may on occasion perform nontrivial functions.

We moderns look for the *ping* of the unexpected, the glint of heterodoxy. True enough, the Old and New Testaments contain some of the greatest *stories* ever told. Yet in one sense they are not anecdotes, and in this collection the Bible is represented only by SOLOMON 1. The ancient Hebraic temper and the anecdotal temper do not have much in common. The same appears to be more or less true with respect to early religious leaders of other faiths.

Classical figures prized their anecdotes as narrative condensations of generally acknowledged truths. That the paths of glory lead but to the grave was pointed out by Thomas Gray in 1751. But the sobering truism was more vividly expressed by Diogenes in explaining to Alexander the Great why he was examining a heap of human bones: "I am searching for the bones of your father, but I cannot distinguish them from those of his slaves." No great wit here, certainly no shock of surprise, yet a telling early statement of a universal insight.

It is by such light that we must consider the anecdotes of the ancients, some of whose bearded quips are herein collected. Besides, it is instructive to discover what amused or titillated our forefathers. You may even find some of the hoary items diverting. One man's chestnut is another man's *marron glacé*.

From its beginnings the anecdote has acted as a leveling device. It humanizes, democratizes, acts as a counterweight to encomium. Perhaps that is why it flourishes best in countries that, like Britain and the United States, enjoy a strong democratic tradition. It may bring home to our hearts social and political ideals that, expressed by politicians, elicit yawns. It may do this through phrasing of great elegance (EDWARD EVERETT 1) or of casual, bitter irony (JACKIE ROBINSON 1).

Men of high philosophic mind have valued the anecdote less for its capacity to divert, more for its power to reveal character. This value was first classically formulated by Plutarch, quoted by Boswell: "Nor is it always in the most distinguished achievements that men's virtues or vices may be best discerned; but very often an action of small note, a short saying, or a jest, shall distinguish a person's real character more than the greatest sieges, or the most important battles."

From anecdotes, thought Prosper Mérimée, one "can distinguish a true picture of the customs and characters of any given period." Nietzsche was confident that "three anecdotes may suffice to paint a picture of a man." Isaac D'Israeli, whose *Dissertation on Anecdotes* affords a perfect reflection of his time's anecdotal preferences, thought anecdotes accurate indices to character: "Opinions are fallible, but not examples." Says Ralph Waldo Emerson: "Ballads, bons mots, and anecdotes give us better insights into the depths of past centuries than grave and voluminous chronicles." His contemporary William Ellery Channing agreed: "One anecdote of a man is worth a volume of biography."

Perhaps such claims are excessive. Like statistics, an anecdote, unless measured against the whole record of a life, may be a damned lie. But a reasonable number of them, drawn from different phases of a given career, may give us an imperfect yet authentic sense of character. Try reading the sections on, let us say, Henry James, Max Beerbohm, Pablo Picasso, Johannes Brahms, Pope John XXIII. You don't get the whole man, but you do learn something valuable and generally easy to fix in the memory. The intimidating, downright character of the Iron Duke flashes out at once in WELLINGTON 16.

Beyond these functions anecdotes may perform at least three others.

The first is illustrated by such traditional stories as KING ALFRED 1. We include no more than a scattering of these quasi-legendary items, for we do not propose to compete with such massive compilations as Brewer's *Dictionary of Phrase and Fable*. But there are enough here to suggest one of the book's minor purposes. Our present educational system sees to it that Macaulay's schoolboy should not exist in our country. The editors cannot create him, either, but at least we can dig a few hundred historical and biographical postholes of traditional reference, familiar in other days to every, or at least Macaulay's, schoolboy.

An assiduous reading of anecdotes can, then, light up odd corners of the past that we should all recognize. But it can, far more valuably, shake us out of our quotidian rut, administer a slight and salutary shock of surprise or delight. At its finest, an anecdote signalizes the intervention of the unexpected. It mounts a small-scale assault on the banality of normal intercourse.

Finally, if one were asked to name the *kind* of book that within one set of covers most adequately reflects the sheer multifariousness of human personality, it might well be a book of anecdotes. *Ana* would not do, for much *ana* is mere information not revelatory of character. A biographical dictionary would not do either, for its editors do not have the space or the desire to set down the quirks and oddities of their subjects. But a reasonably ample gathering of anecdotes, drawn from many times and climes, may reconcile us to our human nature by showing us that, for all its faults and stupidities, it can boast a diversity to which no other animal species can lay claim.

Clifton Fadiman

THE LITTLE, BROWN
BOOK OF
❧ ANECDOTES ❧

A

AARON, Henry Louis ["Hank"] (1934–), *US baseball player. He broke Babe Ruth's home-run record, hitting 755 in all.*

1 During the 1957 World Series, Yankee catcher Yogi Berra noticed that Aaron grasped the bat the wrong way. "Turn it around," he said, "so you can see the trademark." But Hank kept his eye on the pitcher's mound: "Didn't come up here to read. Came up here to hit."

ABBOTT, Bud (1898–1974), and Costello, Lou (1906–59), *US comedians, the famous team of Abbott and Costello.*

1 "Bud Abbott and Lou Costello once took out a $100,000 insurance policy with Lloyds of London that stipulated payment if any of their audience should die of laughter."

ABERCROMBIE, Lascelles (1881–1938), *British poet and critic. He was professor of English literature at Leeds (1922–29) and London (1929–35) universities. His works include* Principles of English Prosody *(1922) and* Twelve Idylls *(1928).*

1 Abercrombie had expressed an opinion with which the poet Ezra Pound violently disagreed. "Dear Mr. Abercrombie," wrote Pound. "Stupidity carried beyond a certain point becomes a public menace. I hereby challenge you to a duel, to be fought at the earliest moment that is suited to your convenience. . . ." Abercrombie was rather disturbed by the challenge, knowing of Pound's skill at fencing, but then he remembered with relief that the choice of weapons lay with the party challenged. "May I suggest," he replied, "that we bombard each other with unsold copies of our own books?" Pound, having far more "weapons" than his opponent, immediately withdrew the challenge.

ABERNETHY, John (1764–1831), *British physician, especially noted as surgeon and teacher.*

1 A titled gentleman who consulted Abernethy was received by the great doctor with the rudeness for which he was notorious. The patient lost his temper and told Abernethy that he would make him "eat his words." "It will be of no use," responded Abernethy, "for they will be sure to come up again."

2 When Abernethy was canvassing for the post of surgeon to St. Bartholomew's Hospital, London, he called upon one of the governors, a wealthy grocer, in the man's shop. The grocer loftily remarked that he presumed Abernethy was wanting his vote at this important point in his life. Nettled by the man's tone and attitude, Abernethy retorted, "No, I don't; I want a pennyworth of figs. Look sharp and wrap them up. I want to be off."

3 "Mrs. J—— consulted him respecting a nervous disorder, the minutiae of which appeared to be so fantastic that Mr. A. interrupted their frivolous detail by holding out his hand for the fee. A one-pound note and a shilling were placed into it; upon which he returned the latter to his fair patient, with the angry exclamation, 'There, Ma'am! go and buy a skipping-rope; that is all you want.'"

4 Despite his brusqueness with his private patients, Abernethy was conscientious and kindly toward the poor under his care in the charity hospital. Once as he was about to leave for the hospital, a private patient tried to detain him. Abernethy observed, "Private patients, if they do not like me, can go elsewhere; but the poor devils in the hospital I am bound to take care of."

5 A patient complaining of melancholy consulted Dr. Abernethy. After an examination the doctor pronounced, "You need amusement. Go and hear the comedian Grimaldi; he will make you laugh and that will be better for you than any drugs." Said the patient, "I am Grimaldi."

6 Abernethy was renowned for his dislike of idle chatter. With this in mind, a young lady once entered his surgery and, without a word, held out an injured finger for examination. The doctor dressed the wound in silence. The woman returned a few days later. "Better?" asked Abernethy. "Better," replied the patient. Subsequent calls passed in much the same manner. On her final visit the woman held out her finger, now free of bandages. "Well?" inquired the doctor. "Well," she replied. "Upon my word, madam," exclaimed Abernethy, "you are the most rational woman I have ever met."

ॐ ॐ

ACHESON, Dean [Gooderham] (1893–1971), *US statesman and lawyer; secretary of state (1949–53). He was important in the evolution of NATO, the Truman Doctrine, and the Marshall Plan, all in pursuit of his global strategy of containing the advance of communism.*

1 On leaving his post as secretary of state, Acheson was asked about his plans for the future. He replied, "I will undoubtedly have to seek what is happily known as gainful employment, which I am glad to say does not describe holding public office."

2 In April 1963 Winston Churchill was made an honorary citizen of the United States. At the ceremony in the White House, his letter of acceptance was read by his son Randolph, as he himself was too frail to attend. It contained a passage rejecting the idea that Britain had only a "tame and minor" role to play on the international scene. Dean Acheson recognized this as an oblique allusion to his own famous and greatly resented remark that Britain had lost an

empire and failed to find a new role. "Well, it hasn't taken Winston long to get used to American ways," commented Acheson. "He hadn't been an American citizen for three minutes before he began attacking an ex-secretary of state."

3 A rather flustered elderly lady once accosted Acheson in a Washington hotel. "Pardon me," she said, "I am somewhat embarrassed. My zipper has stuck and I am due at a meeting. Could you please help me out?" As the zipper was firmly stuck halfway down her back, Acheson was obliged to undo it completely, averting his eyes as best he could, before pulling it back up to the top. The lady thanked him profusely. "I think that I should tell you," she added, "that I am vice president of the Daughters of the American Revolution."

"My dear lady," replied Acheson, "what a moment ago was a rare privilege now appears to have been a really great honor."

ॐ ॐ

ACTON, Harold (1904–), *British author, whose works include poetry, histories, memoirs, and novels.*

1 "One summer afternoon Acton, then a celebrated undergraduate poet at Oxford, was asked to perform at a Conservative Garden Fete. He decided he could do no better than recite [T. S. Eliot's] *The Waste Land* from beginning to end. His audience's good manners were severely tested, as this dirge for a godless civilization, delivered in Harold Acton's rich, resounding voice, swept irresistibly above their heads; and one or two old ladies, who were alarmed and horrified but thought that the reciter had such a 'nice, kind face,' rather than hurt the young man's feelings by getting up and leaving openly, were obliged to sink to their knees and creep away on all fours."

ॐ ॐ

ADAMS, Alexander Annan (1908–), *British air vice-marshal. A wing commander in World War II, he was head of RAF intelligence in Germany (1946–48) and became director of the Mental Health Trust in 1970.*

1 At the end of the Battle of Britain, Adams was driving to a meeting at Fighter Command Headquarters when he came upon a sign:

ROAD CLOSED—UNEXPLODED BOMB. Adams called over the policeman on duty, hoping he might be able to suggest an alternative route. "Sorry, you can't go through," said the policeman as he approached the car. "The bomb is likely to go off at any minute now." Then he caught sight of Adams's uniform. "I'm very sorry, sir," he said, "I didn't know you were a wing commander. It is quite all right for you to go through."

೩• ⊸ई

ADAMS, Ansel (1902–1984), *US landscape photographer (particularly of the mountainous Far West), a technical innovator in his field. He was also honored as a conservationist.*

1 During his early years Adams studied the piano and showed marked talent. At one party (he recalls it as *"very* liquid") he played Chopin's F Major Nocturne. "In some strange way my right hand started off in F-sharp major while my left hand behaved well in F major. I could not bring them together. I went through the entire nocturne with the hands separated by a half-step." The next day a fellow guest complimented him on his performance: "You never missed a wrong note!"

೩• ⊸ई

ADAMS, Franklin Pierce (1881–1960), *US journalist, writer of light verse, and wit. Known as FPA, he was a regular member of the* Information Please *radio program and author of such books as* In Other Words *(1912) and* The Diary of Our Own Samuel Pepys *(1935).*

1 Adams belonged to a poker club that included among its members an actor called Herbert Ransom. Whenever Ransom held a good hand, his facial expression was so transparent that Adams proposed a new rule for the club: "Anyone who looks at Ransom's face is cheating."

2 Adams accompanied Beatrice Kaufman (wife of the playwright George S. Kaufman) to a cocktail party where, feeling a little out of things, she sat down on a cane-seated chair. The seat suddenly broke, leaving Beatrice immobilized inside the frame, legs in the air. As a shocked silence gripped the party, Adams said severely, "I've told you a hundred times, Beatrice, that's not funny."

3 "Whose birthday is it today?" Adams once asked Beatrice Kaufman. "Yours?" she guessed. "No, but you're getting warm," replied Adams. "It's Shakespeare's."

4 Alexander Woollcott had been asked to sign a first-edition copy of his book *Shouts and Murmurs.* "Ah, what is so rare as a Woollcott first edition?" he sighed as he wrote. "A Woollcott second edition," replied Adams.
    {Told of others.}

5 A friend was recounting to Adams an apparently interminable tale. He finally said: "Well, to cut a long story short—"
    "Too late," interrupted Adams.

೩• ⊸ई

ADAMS, John (1735–1826), *US statesman, 2d president of the United States (1797–1801). He played a major part in winning European support for the cause of American independence, and represented his country in the peace negotiations with Britain. He served as Washington's vice president and succeeded him as president.*

1 During his presidency Adams's grand style, which contrasted unfavorably with the simpler dignity of the Washington regime, made him many enemies. A scandalous story circulated that he had sent General Charles C. Pinckney to Britain to select four pretty girls as mistresses, two for the general and two for himself. When this slander came to Adams's ears, he wrote complainingly to a friend, "I do declare, if this be true, General Pinckney has kept them all for himself and cheated me out of my two."

2 Although failing fast, Adams was determined to survive until the fiftieth anniversary of the signing of the Declaration of Independence—July 4, 1826. At dawn on that day he was awakened by his servant, who asked if he knew what day it was. He replied, "Oh, yes, it is the glorious fourth of July. God bless it. God bless you all." He then slipped into a coma. In the afternoon he recovered consciousness briefly to murmur, "Thomas Jefferson lives." These were his last words. Unknown to him, Thomas Jefferson had died that same day.
    See also THOMAS JEFFERSON 10.

೩• ⊸ई

ADAMS, John Quincy (1767–1848), *US statesman, 6th president of the United States (1825–29). Adams, son of John Adams, the second president, was a lawyer by training. As secretary of state (1817–25), he was mainly responsible for formulating the Monroe Doctrine (1823), which governed American foreign policy for nearly a century. As president, he suffered from the opposition of General Andrew Jackson, who defeated him in the election of 1828. From 1831 to his death he served in the House of Representatives.*

1 John Quincy Adams, an enthusiastic swimmer, used to bathe naked in the Potomac before starting the day's work. The newspaperwoman Anne Royall had been trying for weeks to get an interview with the president and had always been turned away. One morning she tracked him to the river bank and after he had got into the water stationed herself on his clothes. When Adams returned from his swim, he found a very determined lady awaiting him. She introduced herself and stated her errand. "Let me get out and dress," pleaded the president, "and I swear you shall have your interview." Anne Royall was adamant; she wasn't moving until she had the president's comment on the questions she wished to put to him. If he attempted to get out, she would scream loud enough to reach the ears of some fishermen on the next bend in the river. She got her interview while Adams remained decently submerged in the water.

{Anne Royall, often called the first American newspaperwoman, led an adventurous life that veered from luxury to great poverty. John Quincy Adams was among her close friends.}

2 In 1846 John Quincy Adams suffered a stroke and, although he returned to Congress the following year, his health was clearly failing. Daniel Webster described his last meeting with Adams: "Someone, a friend of his, came in and made particular inquiry of his health. Adams answered, 'I inhabit a weak, frail, decayed tenement; battered by the winds and broken in upon by the storms, and, from all I can learn, the landlord does not intend to repair.'"

ॐ ◆ॐ

ADDAMS, Jane (1860–1935), *US social reformer. A supporter of racial equality, female suffrage, and pacifism, she was president of the Women's International League for Peace and Freedom. She shared the 1931 Nobel Peace Prize with the educator Nicholas Murray Butler.*

1 In 1900 the Daughters of the American Revolution elected Jane Addams to honorary membership. However, her antiwar stance during World War I and her insistence that even subversives had a right to trial by due process of law caused them to expel her. She commented that she had thought her election was for life, but now knew it was for good behavior.

ॐ ◆ॐ

ADDISON, Joseph (1672–1719), *British writer and politician. A member of the literary circle that included Jonathan Swift and Richard Steele, he joined with the latter to produce* The Spectator *(1711–12). For* The Spectator *he wrote the famous "de Coverley" essays on the life and opinions of Sir Roger de Coverley, who typified the sensible, dignified, old-fashioned values that Addison found lacking in fashionable London society. Addison was a member of Parliament from 1708 until his death and held various offices in Whig administrations.*

1 Addison's natural diffidence made him an ineffective parliamentary debater. On one occasion he began, "Mr. Speaker, I conceive — I conceive, sir — sir, I conceive —" At this point he was interrupted by a voice saying, "The right honorable secretary of state has conceived thrice and brought forth nothing."

2 The Duke of Wharton, hoping to animate Addison into wit, plied him so generously with wine that the writer was taken ill. The duke observed with disgust that he could "get wine but not wit out of him."

3 A friend of Addison's with whom he was accustomed to have long discussions on topics of mutual interest borrowed some money from the author. Soon afterward Addison noticed a change in his behavior; before the loan the two friends had disagreed on a number of subjects, but now the borrower fell in with every line that Addison himself adopted. One day when they were talking on a point on which Addison knew his friend had previously held an opposite view to his own, he exclaimed, "Either contradict me, sir, or pay me my money!"

4   Addison's preoccupation with the principles of religion and manners extended even to his deathbed. As he lay dying, he sent for his wastrel stepson, Lord Warwick, and it was to him that his last words were spoken: "See in what peace a Christian can die."

{Doubt exists as to the authenticity of this anecdote. There is little or no evidence that Lord Warwick led the life of a wastrel, and it has been suggested that Addison's death resulted from overindulgence in brandy.}

ॐ৽ ◄ई

ADE, George (1866–1944), *US humorist and playwright. His works include* Fables in Slang *(1899),* The College Widow *(1904), and* Father and the Boys *(1907).*

1   Following a well-received after-dinner speech by George Ade, a noted lawyer rose to speak. His hands buried deep in the pockets of his trousers, he began: "Doesn't it strike the company as a little unusual that a professional humorist should be funny?" Ade waited for the laughter to die down before replying: "Doesn't it strike the company as a little unusual that a lawyer should have his hands in his own pockets?"

ॐ৽ ◄ई

ADEE, Alvey Augustus (1842–1924), *US diplomat. He served for forty-seven years in the US State Department, rising to second assistant secretary of state (1886–1924).*

1   When Adee was asked by President McKinley the best way to say "no" to six European ambassadors who were coming to see him to try to prevent war against Spain, he wrote on the back of an envelope: "The Government of the United States appreciates the humanitarian and disinterested character of the communication now made on behalf of the powers named, and for its part is confident that equal appreciation will be shown for its own earnest and unselfish endeavors to fulfill a duty to humanity

by ending a situation the indefinite prolongation of which has become insufferable."

The president read this message verbatim to the ambassadors.

ॐ৽ ◄ई

ADENAUER, Konrad (1876–1967), *German statesman and first chancellor of the Federal Republic (1949–63). He did much to advance the international prestige of West Germany and presided over its postwar economic recovery.*

1   Essentially a Rhinelander, Adenauer never liked or trusted the Prussians and his compatriots in eastern Germany. In the interwar period he used frequently to have to go by train to Berlin. It is said that every time he crossed the River Elbe on this journey he would frown and mutter to himself, "Now we enter Asia."

2   Adenauer received many marriage proposals in his mail when he was chancellor, even after he became an octogenarian. When they were brought to his notice he used to tell his secretary patiently: "Put them in the nonaggression pact file."

3   When Adenauer, still chancellor, was approaching the age of ninety, he succumbed to a heavy cold. His personal physician, unable to be of very much help, had to put up with Adenauer's impatience. "I'm not a magician," protested the harassed doctor. "I can't make you young again."

"I haven't asked you to," retorted the chancellor. "All I want is to go on getting older."

ॐ৽ ◄ई

ADLER, Hermann (1839–1911), *British rabbi, born in Hanover. He was chief rabbi of London from 1891.*

1   Adler found himself sitting beside Herbert Cardinal Vaughan at an official luncheon. "Now, Dr. Adler," said the cardinal mischievously, "when may I have the pleasure of helping you to some ham?"

"At Your Eminence's wedding," came the prompt reply.

{Told of others.}

ॐ৽ ◄ई

AESCHYLUS (525–456 BC), *Greek poet. Some of his tragedies are the earliest complete plays surviving from ancient Greece. From an output of about ninety plays, seven are extant.*

1 Aeschylus died and was buried at Gela in Sicily. Ancient biographies record the tradition that his death came about when an eagle, which had seized a tortoise and was looking to smash the reptile's shell, mistook the poet's bald head for a stone and dropped the tortoise upon him.

ॐ ◆ॐ

AGASSIZ, Jean Louis Rodolphe (1807–73), *Swiss naturalist. He made major contributions to paleontology, though his later theories on the origin of animal species conflicted with Darwin's. He became professor of zoology at Harvard in 1848, deeply influencing the teaching of natural history in the United States.*

1 An emissary from a learned society came to invite Agassiz to address its members. Agassiz refused on the grounds that lectures of this sort took up too much time that should be devoted to research and writing. The man persisted, saying that they were prepared to pay handsomely for the talk. "That's no inducement to me," Agassiz replied. "I can't afford to waste my time making money."

ॐ ◆ॐ

AGRIPPINA (AD 15–59), *mother of Emperor Nero by her first husband. Her third marriage was to her uncle, Emperor Claudius, whom she later poisoned.*

1 Agrippina was consumed by her ambition to place Nero on the imperial throne. She consulted the soothsayers, who told her, "Nero will reign, but he will kill his mother."

"Let him kill me, then," said Agrippina.

2 Agrippina proved less easy to eliminate than Nero expected. According to Suetonius, he tried poison three times (she had taken the antidote beforehand), a collapsible ceiling in her bedchamber (someone warned her), and an unseaworthy boat (she swam to safety). Finally he sent a centurion with orders to kill her. The centurion struck her first on the head, as he had been ordered, but she bared her breasts, crying out, "Strike rather these, which have nurtured so great a monster as Nero."

AIDAN, Saint (d. 651), *Irish monk who became bishop of Northumbria (635) and founded the monastery at Lindisfarne, from which he carried out missionary operations in northern England.*

1 King Oswin, ruler of the former British province of Deira and a friend of Aidan's, gave the bishop a fine horse. Soon afterward Bishop Aidan met a beggar who asked him for alms; he at once dismounted and gave the horse, with all its costly trappings, to the poor man. When this charitable deed came to the king's ears, he taxed Aidan: "Why did you give away the horse that we specially chose for your personal use when we knew that you had need of one for your journeys? We have many less valuable horses that would have been suitable for beggars." Replied Aidan, "Is this foal of a mare more valuable to you than a child of God?" The king pondered, then, suddenly casting his sword aside, knelt at Aidan's feet and begged his forgiveness. Aidan, greatly moved, begged the king to go to his dinner and be merry.

As Aidan watched the king go, he became very melancholy. When the bishop's chaplain asked why, Aidan replied, "I know that the king will not live long, for I have never seen a king so humble as he is. He will be taken from us as the country is not worthy to have such a king."

This foreboding was proved correct: King Oswin was treacherously killed by his northern neighbor, King Oswy.

ॐ ◆ॐ

ALBEMARLE, William Anne Keppel, 2d Earl of (1702–54), *British soldier and ambassador.*

1 Sent as plenipotentiary to Paris in 1748, Albemarle took with him his mistress Lolotte Gaucher, an actress described by contemporaries as cunning and rapacious. One evening, seeing her gazing pensively at a star, the earl remarked, "It's no good, my dear, I can't buy it for you."

ॐ ◆ॐ

ALBERT, Prince (1819–61), *prince consort of Great Britain; husband of Queen Victoria. The son of the Duke of Saxe-Coburg-Gotha, Albert married his cousin in 1840. She came to rely greatly upon his discreet advice and guidance.*

He did much to foster the arts and sciences and his patronage of industry culminated in the Great Exhibition of 1851. His early death was caused by typhoid.

1 Prince Albert had a chronic inability to stay awake late at night. At a concert given at Buckingham Palace and attended by various distinguished guests, Queen Victoria noticed that her husband was asleep. Half-smiling, half-vexed, she prodded him with her elbow. He woke up, nodded approval of the piece being performed, and fell asleep again, still nodding. The queen had to wake him up all over again. A guest at the concert reported, "The queen was charmed, and cousin Albert looked beautiful, and slept quietly as usual."

2 Queen Victoria and Prince Albert, visiting the British Museum, paused to admire the fossil of an ichthyosaurus. The head of the department, a Mr. König, was presented to the royal couple. Catching the German name, Prince Albert recognized a fellow countryman and asked, "From what part?"

"From the blue lias [limestone rock] at Lyme Regis in Dorsetshire, Your Royal Highness," said the fossil-keeper.

3 A picture at Balmoral portrayed all the royal children and various birds and animals. Someone asked which was Princess Helena. "There, with the kingfisher," said Albert, adding, "a very proper bird for a princess."

ॐ ॐ

ALBERT, Eugène d' (1864–1932), *German pianist and composer, born in Britain. He was noted as an interpreter of Beethoven.*

1 D'Albert was married six times. At an evening reception which he attended with his fifth wife shortly after their wedding, he presented the lady to a friend who said politely, "Congratulations, Herr d'Albert; you have rarely introduced me to so charming a wife."

ॐ ॐ

ALCIBIADES (c. 450–404 BC), *Greek general and politician who played a prominent role in Athenian affairs, including the disastrous expedition against Syracuse (415). While in exile in Phrygia, he was assassinated by order of the Persian king.*

1 Alcibiades was telling Pericles, forty years his senior, how best to govern Athens. This did not amuse Pericles. "Alcibiades," he said, "when I was your age, I talked just as you do now."

"How I should like to have known you, Pericles," replied Alcibiades, "when you were at your best."

ॐ ॐ

ALCOTT, Amos Bronson (1799–1888), *US educator and writer. His staunch adherence to his educational theories brought him and his family much disappointment and hardship, as he failed to establish a successful school. In later life he achieved some recognition and financial comfort, largely through the success of the writings of his daughter, Louisa May Alcott.*

1 The Alcott family finances were very low, but they placed great hopes on Bronson Alcott's latest lecture tour. When he arrived home one night in February, the family gathered around to welcome him, offer him food and drink, and rejoice in his homecoming. Then a little silence fell, and it was daughter May who asked the question in all their minds: "Did they pay you?" Slowly Bronson Alcott drew out his pocketbook and displayed its contents—a single dollar. "Another year I shall do better," he said. There was a stunned hush in the group around him. Then Mrs. Alcott flung her arms around his neck and said stoutly, "I call that doing very well."

ॐ ॐ

ALCOTT, Louisa May (1832–88), *US novelist, author of* Little Women (1869). *She first turned to writing to support her family impoverished by the unworldliness of her father, Bronson Alcott.*

1 When Miss Alcott became a celebrity, she often found her fame tiresome. A supporter of the fight for women's suffrage, she attended the Women's Congress in Syracuse, where she was accosted by an effusive admirer. "If you ever come to Oshkosh," said the lady, "your feet will not be allowed to touch the ground: you will be borne in the arms of the people. Will you come?"

"Never," replied Miss Alcott.

ॐ ॐ

Jono Abel was the son of the well-known US actor Walter Abel. At age seven he had never seen a play, although he had watched his father in films. The first time his mother, Marietta, took him to the theater to see his father he cried out in astonishment, "Look, Mom! Round actors!"

—Clifton Fadiman

ALEMBERT, Jean le Rond d' (1717–83), *French mathematician. He collaborated with Diderot on the* Encyclopédie *and made important contributions to gravitational theory.*

1 The illegitimate son of an aristocrat, d'Alembert was abandoned by his mother soon after his birth and was brought up by a glazier named Rousseau and his wife. When d'Alembert's extraordinary talents became known, his mother attempted to claim him. D'Alembert rejected her, saying, "My mother is the wife of the glazier."

❧

ALENÇON, Sophie-Charlotte, Duchesse d' (died 1897), *Bavarian-born duchess, who married the Duc d'Alençon in 1868.*

1 On May 4, 1897, the duchess was presiding over a charity bazaar in Paris when the hall accidentally caught fire. Flames spread to the paper decorations and flimsy walls of the booths and in seconds the place was an inferno. In the hideous panic that followed many women and children were trampled as they rushed for the exits, while workmen from a nearby site performed incredible acts of heroism, rushing into the blaze to carry out the trapped women. Some rescuers reached the duchess, who had remained calmly seated behind her booth. "Because of my title, I was the first to enter here. I shall be the last to go out," she said, rejecting their offer of help. She stayed and was burned to death, along with more than 120 others, mainly women and children.

❧

ALEXANDER I (1777–1825), *czar of Russia* (1801–25). *In 1807 Alexander was forced by Napoleon to accede to the humiliating Treaty of Tilsit. Napoleon's abortive invasion of Russia five years later, however, enabled Russia to join in the overthrow of French imperialism. Alexander played an active role in the diplomatic settlement of Europe after Waterloo.*

1 The way for Alexander's accession to the throne was cleared through the murder of his savage, megalomaniac father, Czar Paul I, by a group of aristocratic conspirators. Thus in two generations history repeated itself, for Alexander's grandmother, Catherine the Great, had connived at the murder of her husband, Peter III, in order to seize power herself less than forty years before. The youthful archduke had had prior warning of the plot against Czar Paul, but had preferred to think that the conspirators' intention was merely to depose and imprison his father. When news of the murder was brought to him, he almost collapsed with horror. This incident haunted him for the remainder of his life, but the strongest proof of his complicity was in his treatment of the conspirators; they all continued in his favor and some became his closest counselors. A French spy, the Countess de Bonneuil, reported to her master Fouché on the situation in St. Petersburg: "The young emperor goes about preceded by the murderers of his grandfather, followed by the murderers of his father, quite surrounded by his friends."

{A similar remark, though without the telling ambiguity, is attributed to Talleyrand.}

2 When Alexander was in Paris following the defeat of Napoleon, he attended anniversary celebrations at one of the hospitals. The ladies who had organized the affair passed plates around for contributions. An extremely pretty girl was delegated to take a plate to the czar. Alexander dropped in a handful of gold and whispered, "That's for your beautiful bright eyes." The young lady curtsied and immediately presented the plate again. "What? More?" said the czar. "Yes, sire," she replied, "now I want something for the poor."

❧

ALEXANDER III [Alexander the Great] (356–323 BC), *king of Macedon* (336–323).

Having secured the borders of Macedon and its position at the head of the Greek states, Alexander embarked (334) on the invasion of Asia originally projected by his father, Philip. He crushed the Persians at the battle of Issus (333), conquered Syria and Egypt (332–331), finally defeated the Persians at Gaugamela (331), and in the following years made himself master of all the former Persian lands. Between 327 and 325 he campaigned successfully in India, but his weary soldiers eventually insisted on turning homeward. Alexander died at Babylon from a fever while drawing up further plans for consolidating his empire.

1 Gossip surrounded the birth of Alexander. Doubt as to whether Philip was really his father later allowed Alexander to declare that he was a god and the son of Jupiter. Alexander's mother, Olympias, preferred to leave the matter obscure. When news was brought to her of Alexander's claim to divine paternity, she said, "Please — I don't want to get into any trouble with Juno."

2 A Thessalian brought an exceptionally beautiful horse, named Bucephalus, to the Macedonian court, offering to sell it to King Philip. However, when the royal grooms tried to test its paces it proved wild and unmanageable. The young Alexander asked his father for permission to try his skill. Philip reluctantly agreed, saying that if the prince failed to ride Bucephalus he was to pay his father a forfeit equal to its price. Alexander walked quickly to the horse's head and turned it to face into the sun, for he had noticed that the horse's own shadow was upsetting it. He calmed it, then mounted it, and Bucephalus obediently showed off his paces.

The court, which had feared for the prince's safety, broke into loud applause. Philip was overjoyed. He kissed his son, saying, "Seek another kingdom that may be worthy of your abilities, for Macedonia is too small for you."

3 Alexander, setting out on his conquest of Asia, inquired into the finances of his followers. To ensure that they should not be troubled over the welfare of their dependents during their absence, he distributed crown estates and revenues among them. When he had thus disposed of nearly all the royal resources, his friend General Perdiccas asked Alexander

what he had reserved for himself. "Hope," answered the king. "In that case," said Perdiccas, "we who share in your labors will also take part in your hopes." Thereupon he refused the estate allocated to him, and several other of the king's friends did the same.

4 At Gordium in Phrygia (Asia Minor) a chariot was fastened with cords made from the bark of a cornel tree. The knot was so cunningly tied that no ends were visible, and the tradition was that the empire of the world should fall to the man who could untie it. When Alexander conquered Gordium, he confronted the famous puzzle. Unable to untie the knot, he drew his sword and with one slash severed it.

{Hence the phrase "cut the Gordian knot" for finding a quick and drastic solution to an intricate problem.}

5 On his march through Asia Minor, Alexander fell dangerously ill. His physicians were afraid to treat him because if they did not succeed, the Macedonian army would suspect them of malpractice. Only one, Philip the Acarnanian, was willing to take the risk, as he had confidence in both the king's friendship and his own drugs.

While the medicine was being prepared, Alexander received a letter from an enemy of Philip's that accused the physician of having been bribed by the Persian king to poison his master. Alexander read the letter and slipped it under his pillow without showing it to anyone. When Philip entered the tent with the medicine, Alexander took the cup from him, at the same time handing Philip the letter. While the physician was reading it, Alexander calmly drank the contents of the cup. Horrified and indignant at the calumny, Philip threw himself down at the king's bedside, but Alexander assured him that he had complete confidence in his honor. After three days the king was well enough to appear again before his army.

6 After Alexander had conquered Egypt, the Persian king, Darius, sent a letter offering generous terms for peace and future friendship with the Macedonian king: 10,000 talents to be paid in ransom for Persian prisoners, all the countries west of the Euphrates to be ceded to Alexander, and Darius's daughter to be given to him in marriage. Alexander consulted his friends about how he should respond. His general Parmenion said, "If I were Alexander, I would accept these offers."

"So would I," retorted Alexander, "if I were Parmenion."

{A similar retort is ascribed to others.}

7   The captured Indian king Porus was brought before Alexander, who asked how he wished to be treated. "Like a king," was the reply. Alexander asked if he had anything else to request. "Nothing," said Porus, "for everything is comprehended in the word 'king.'" Alexander restored Porus's lands to him.

8   Alexander's final command before a certain battle was that the beards of his soldiers should be shaved off. "There is nothing like a beard to get hold of in a fight," he explained.

9   Alexander the Great was marching across the desert with a thirsty army. A soldier came up to him, knelt down, and offered him a helmet full of water. "Is there enough for ten thousand men?" asked Alexander. When the soldier shook his head, Alexander poured the water out on the ground.

See also CONFUCIUS 2; SIR PHILIP SIDNEY 1.

ॐ ◆§

ALEXANDER VI (c. 1431–1503), *pope (1492–1503). Born Rodrigo Borgia, Alexander obtained the papacy as the summit of a career notable for its immorality and extravagance. He used his office to advance the prospects of his illegitimate children, especially his son Cesare Borgia.*

1   Alexander VI's illegitimate daughter Lucrezia was married in 1502 to her third husband, Alfonso d'Este, son and heir of the Duke of Ferrara. Not long after the marriage the Ferrarese envoy to the papal court reassured Pope Alexander that all was well with the newlyweds; Alfonso, he reported, made love to Lucrezia nightly. Alfonso, the envoy added, also made love with equal regularity to other women during the day, but that was unimportant. "Well, he is young," said the pope, "and that is how it should be."

ॐ ◆§

ALEXANDER, Sir George (1858–1919), *British actor, and manager of the St. James's Theatre from 1891 until his death. He was noted for his encouragement of English playwrights.*

1   "On the first night of that unfortunate play [Henry James's] *Guy Domville,* produced by George Alexander, it was soon evident from the attitude of the gallery that the play was not going to be a success, but the seal of failure was set on it when Sir George uttered the line, 'I am the last of the Domvilles.' Scarcely were the words out of his mouth than a voice came from the gallery, 'Well, at any rate, that's a comfort to know.'"

ॐ ◆§

ALEXANDER, Grover Cleveland (1887–1950), *US baseball pitcher, prominent in the major leagues (1911–30).*

1   Although he became an alcoholic during his twenty-year career, Alexander remained one of the best pitchers until the end. At thirty-five he pitched superbly in the World Series of 1926 between his St. Louis Cardinals and the New York Yankees. After winning the full sixth game of the best-of-seven set and tying the series at three games each, Alexander spent that night celebrating. Since pitchers usually rested three days between starts, he went out to the bullpen next day, with the relief pitchers, and snoozed away the final game until he was, surprisingly, summoned to pitch the seventh of the nine innings. There were three men on base, one out needed to end the inning, and a one-run lead. Alexander faced the feared Tony Lazzeri and struck him out, ending the inning to the cheers of the crowd. He then stopped the Yankees in their last two innings to win the game and give his team the title.

Afterward Alexander was asked how he felt. "I feel fine," he said. "It's Lazzeri you should ask how he feels," and added, "I owe it all to clean living." And he went out and got drunk.

ॐ ◆§

ALEXANDER, Harold, 1st Earl [Alexander of Tunis] (1891–1969), *British field marshal. In command of the evacuation of Dunkirk during World War II, he was Allied supreme commander in the Mediterranean at the end of the war. Later he was governor general of Canada*

(1946–52) and Conservative minister of defense (1952–54).

1   Alexander's assistant once commented on his habit of tipping into his Out tray any letters remaining in his In tray at the end of the working day. "Excuse me, sir," he asked. "Why do you do that?"

"It saves time," explained Alexander. "You'd be surprised how little of it comes back."

※　※

ALEXANDER, Samuel *(1859–1938), Australian-born philosopher of Jewish parentage, who lived most of his life in England. He was primarily a metaphysician, and his most important work,* Space, Time, and Deity *(1920), traces the evolution of the universe from space-time toward (as yet unrealized) deity. He was professor of philosophy at Manchester for thirty-one years (1893–1924).*

1   The professor of philosophy on his beloved bicycle was a familiar sight around Manchester. On one occasion he rode over to Liverpool to dine and spend the night at the house of a wealthy shipowner. The host's valet noticed that the professor had arrived without luggage and reported the fact to his employer, who courteously said that he would not dress for dinner that evening. He also instructed the valet to put out a spare pair of pajamas in the professor's room. A short time later, however, the valet rushed into his master's dressing room with the message: "I have just seen Professor Alexander going downstairs and he's wearing a dinner jacket." The host made a rapid change.

The following morning the valet returned the spare pajamas, unused, to his master, remarking: "The professor had his own, after all." Curiosity finally overcame the shipowner. As he was seeing his guest off on his bicycle, he asked, "Do you not have any luggage?"

"I'm wearing it," replied the professor.

※　※

ALEXANDRA *(1844–1925), Danish princess, who in 1863 married the Prince of Wales (later King Edward VII of Great Britain.)*

1   On May 10, 1910, King Edward VII died. At first, as he lay on his deathbed, his long-suffering queen, who had turned a blind eye to his infidelities and his pursuit of his pleasures in every fashionable resort on the Continent, was stricken with grief. But it was not long before her sense of humor reasserted itself. She remarked to Lord Esher, "Now at least I know where he is."

※　※

ALFONSO X *(c. 1221–84), King of Castile and León (1252–84), known as Alfonso the Wise. He is particularly famous for his patronage of the arts and sciences, his revision of the Castilian legal code, and his encouragement of translations of Arabic works.*

1   The most celebrated of the works undertaken under Alfonso's sponsorship was the compilation of the "Alfonsine Tables," which were published on the day of his accession to the throne and remained the most authoritative planetary tables in existence for the following three centuries. The preparation of the tables was very laborious and was based, of course, upon the Ptolemaic scheme of the universe. Alfonso remarked that if God had consulted him during the six days of creation, he would have recommended a less complicated design.

※　※

ALFONSO XIII *(1886–1941), king of Spain (1886–1931). Having survived many assassination attempts, he was outlawed by the Republicans and forced to flee the country.*

1   One would-be assassin leaped suddenly in front of the king's horse as he was riding back from a parade and pointed a revolver at him from barely a yard away. "Polo comes in very handy on these occasions," said Alfonso afterward. "I set my horse's head straight at him and rode into him as he fired."

※　※

ALFRED [Alfred the Great] *(849–899), king of Wessex. During his reign (871–899) Alfred defeated the Danes who were threatening to overrun England and established his kingdom of Wessex in the south of the country as a bastion of Anglo-Saxon civilization.*

1   At one time during his wars with the Danes, Alfred was forced to seek refuge incognito in a hut belonging to a poor Anglo-Saxon family.

The woman of the house, who had to leave for a short time, asked the fugitive to keep an eye on some cakes she was baking. Alfred, deep in thought, did not notice that the cakes were burning. When his hostess returned, she gave the unrecognized king a hearty scolding for being an idle good-for-nothing.

2 As a young boy Alfred received little formal schooling. He did possess a highly retentive memory and particularly enjoyed listening to the court bards reciting poetry. One day his mother, holding a fine manuscript book in her hand, said to Alfred and his elder brothers, "I will give this book to whichever one of you can learn it most quickly." Although he could not read, Alfred was greatly attracted to the book and was determined to own it. Forestalling his brothers, he took it to someone who read it through to him. Then he went back to his mother and repeated the whole thing to her. This talent was the foundation of Alfred's later reputation as scholar, translator, and patron of learning.

છ્ક ન્જ

ALI, Muhammad (1942–), *US boxer; world heavyweight champion (1964–71, 1974–78, 1978–80). As Cassius Clay, he was a gold medalist in the 1960 Olympic Games before turning professional. He changed his name on becoming a Black Muslim and for three years was deprived of his heavyweight title for refusing to serve in the US Army. He is renowned for his clowning and joking both in and out of the ring.*

1 In the fight film *Rocky II*, a character apparently based on Muhammad Ali taunts the hero with the words "I'll destroy you. I am the master of disaster." After seeing a private screening of the film, Ali wistfully remarked, " 'Master of disaster': I wish I'd thought of that!"

2 Just before takeoff on an airplane flight, the stewardess reminded Ali to fasten his seat belt. "Superman don't need no seat belt," replied Ali. "Superman don't need no airplane, either," retorted the stewardess. Ali fastened his belt.

3 Irritated by Ali's perpetual boasts of "I am the greatest," a colleague asked the boxer what he was like at golf. "I'm the best," replied Ali. "I just haven't played yet."

4 At a New York party, violinist Isaac Stern was introduced to Ali. "You might say we're in the same business," remarked Stern. "We both earn a living with our hands."

"You must be pretty good," said Ali. "There isn't a mark on you."

5 (Al Silverman, Chief Executive Officer of the Book-of-the-Month Club, recalls a brief conversation with Ali.)

"This happened *years* ago when Muhammad Ali was still Cassius Clay, pink-cheeked (well, not exactly) and sassy.

"I was doing a magazine piece on sex before the big athletic event — is it good or bad for the athlete? I surveyed a lot of athletes, and I don't, of course, remember anything anyone told me — except this philosophical triplet from Clay.

"I caught him fairly early one morning at his New York hotel, and it sounded as if the phone had awakened him. After brief feints and ripostes, I asked him the fateful question — 'What do you think about a fighter having sex the night before a big fight?'

"Pause. Then in his then kind of squeaky, Gospel boy voice, he said, 'Man, are you crazy?
Only the nose knows
Where the nose goes
When the door close.'
"And he hung up on me."

છ્ક ન્જ

ALLAIS, Alphonse (1854–1905), *French humorist, writer, and dramatist.*

1 In Alphonse Allais's library was a volume of Voltaire in which he had inscribed: "To Alphonse Allais, with regrets for not having known him. Voltaire."

2 Asked to deliver a lecture on the subject of

"MARRIED: Moses Alexander, aged 93, to Mrs. Frances Tompkins, aged 105, in Bata, N.Y., on June 11, 1831.

"They were both taken out of bed dead the following morning."

—John Train,
True Remarkable Occurrences,
from *Kentucky Marriages, 1797–1865*

the theater, Allais began: "I have been asked to talk to you on the subject of the theater, but I fear that it will make you melancholy. Shakespeare is dead, Molière is dead, Racine is dead, Marivaux is dead—and I am not feeling too well myself."

ఈం ఆ

ALLEN, Ethan (1738–89), *US patriot, leader of the "Green Mountain Boys" during the Revolutionary War.*

1   Ethan Allen with a group of associates attended a Sunday service led by a stern Calvinist preacher. He took as his text "Many shall strive to enter in, but shall not be able." God's grace was sufficient, observed the preacher, to include one person in ten, but not one in twenty would endeavor to avail himself of the offered salvation. Furthermore, not one man in fifty was really the object of God's solicitude, and not one in eighty—here Allen seized his hat and left the pew, saying, "I'm off, boys. Any one of you can take my chance."

2   In the early morning of May 10, 1775, Ethan Allen led a small force in a surprise attack on the British garrison at Ticonderoga. Having overpowered the sentries, Allen demanded to be taken to the commanding officer's quarters. He shouted at him to come out immediately or he would kill the entire garrison. The commander appeared, his breeches still in his hand. Allen ordered the instant surrender of the fortress. "By what authority?" asked the British officer. "In the name of the great Jehovah, and the Continental Congress," said Ethan Allen. The garrison surrendered.
    {This account of the surrender demand is uncorroborated.}

3   When Allen's first wife, notorious for her sourness and bad temper, died, a local man offered to help transport the coffin to the church. "You could call on any of the neighbors," he said to the widower. "There's not a man in town wouldn't be glad to help out."

4   Allen lay ill. The doctor examined him and said, "General, I fear the angels are waiting for you."
    "Waiting, are they?" said the bluff frontiersman. "Waiting, are they? Well—let 'em wait."

ఈం ఆ

ALLEN, Fred (1894–1956), *US comedian and radio star. He had a long-running mock feud with Jack Benny.*

1   "If somebody caught him in an act of kindness, he ducked behind a screen of cynicism. A friend was walking with him when a truck bore down on a newsboy in front of them. Allen dashed out and snatched the boy to safety, then snarled at him, 'What's the matter, kid? Don't you want to grow up and have troubles?'"

2   Spying a haggard, long-haired cellist in the orchestra pit of a vaudeville house in Toledo, Ohio, Allen called out to him, "How much would you charge to haunt a house?"

3   The radio and TV comic Jack Parr, of *Tonight Show* fame, idolized Allen. On their first meeting he stammered, "You are my God!" Allen replied: "There are five thousand churches in New York and you have to be an atheist."

4   The script for one of Allen's radio shows was returned to him with extensive alterations scrawled across the pages in blue pencil. Allen flipped through it impatiently. "Where were you fellows when the paper was blank?" he asked.

ఈం ఆ

ALMA-TADEMA, Sir Lawrence (1836–1912), *Dutch painter who adopted British nationality in 1873. He favored subjects from Greek and Roman antiquity, using the mythological content for some startlingly erotic paintings. His later work was influenced by the Pre-Raphaelites.*

1   A friend of Alma-Tadema had just become the proud father of twins. The painter made his congratulatory visit immediately after concluding a rather excessive drinking bout. Though still a bit muzzy, he was prudent enough to exclaim, "What an enchanting baby!"

ఈం ఆ

ALTENBERG, Peter (?1862–1919), *Austrian poet.*

1   Though in fact he maintained a very solid bank balance, Altenberg had a mania for beg-

ging. The poet and critic Karl Kraus tells how Altenberg besought him again and again to give him a hundred kronen, and on every occasion Kraus refused him. Finally, his patience at an end, Kraus burst out, "Look, Peter, I'd gladly give it to you, but I *really, really,* don't have the money."

"Very well, I'll lend it to you," said Altenberg.

৯৬ ৩৬

ALVANLEY, William Arden, 2d Baron (1789–1849), *British aristocrat and society leader.*

1 After emerging unscathed from a duel fought in a discreetly secluded corner of London, Lord Alvanley handed a guinea to the hackney coachman who had conveyed him to the spot and home again. Surprised at the size of the largesse, the man protested, "But, my lord, I only took you a mile." Alvanley waved aside the objection: "The guinea's not for taking me, my man, it's for bringing me back."

2 Owing to the careless driving of their coachmen, Lord Alvanley and another nobleman were involved in a collision. The other peer jumped out of his coach, rolling up his sleeves and making ready to thrash his negligent servant, but on seeing that he was elderly and abjectly apologetic, contented himself with saying significantly, "Your age protects you." Alvanley likewise hopped out of his coach, ready to thrash his postilion, but, finding himself confronting a very large, tough-looking lad, he thought better of it. "Your youth protects you," he said, and climbed back into his coach.

৯৬ ৩৬

AMBROSE, Saint (?340–397), *Italian cleric, born at Trier (Trèves) in Germany. An ardent champion of the church against the power of the state, he even compelled the great Theodosius I to do public penance for his massacre at Thessalonika in 390.*

1 The emperor appointed Ambrose provincial governor of northern Italy, residing at Milan. In this capacity he was called out in 374 to the cathedral, where a riot was threatening between two rival factions of Christians, each intent on winning its own candidate's nomina-

tion to the bishopric. Ambrose quelled the riot but was unable to persuade the warring parties to agree on a bishop. Finally someone suggested Ambrose himself, and the nomination was enthusiastically greeted on all sides. In vain Ambrose protested that he was not even christened. He was hurriedly baptized, then ordained, and finally consecrated bishop—all within the space of a single week.

৯৬ ৩৬

ANAXAGORAS (500–428 BC), *Greek philosopher. He spent most of his life in Athens, where he was the friend and teacher of Pericles. In 450 he was accused of impiety and banished, despite Pericles' efforts to protect him.*

1 Anaxagoras took refuge at Lampsacus on the Hellespont, and the Athenians condemned him to death in absentia. When he heard the news of the sentence he observed, "Nature has long since condemned both them and me."

৯৬ ৩৬

ANAXIMENES (4th century BC), *Greek philosopher, born at Lampsacus in Asia Minor.*

1 Anaximenes accompanied Alexander the Great on his expedition against the Persians, in the course of which the Macedonian forces captured Lampsacus. Anxious to save his native city from destruction, Anaximenes sought an audience with the king. Alexander anticipated his plea: "I swear by the Styx I will not grant your request," he said. "My lord,"calmly replied Anaximenes, "I merely wanted to ask you to destroy Lampsacus." And so he saved his native city.

৯৬ ৩৬

ANDERS, William A[llison] (1933–), *US astronaut. A member of the crew of Apollo 8, he circumnavigated the moon in December 1968.*

1 Anders received his fair share of publicity after the Apollo 8 moon trip. Tired of being accosted by pressmen, photographers, and the admiring public, he "escaped" with his wife for a brief vacation in Acapulco. A few days after their arrival, however, as they relaxed on the patio of their holiday villa, a young man called and asked if he could take some photographs. Groaning, Anders replied, "Okay, come on in."

"Thanks," said the young man enthusiastically as he marched across the patio. "You've got the best view of the bay in the whole place."

❧ ❧

ANDERSEN, Hans Christian (1805–75), *Danish writer. The son of a shoemaker, Andersen failed as a singer and actor before a benefactor helped him gain the education he had missed as a child. He traveled widely in Europe and produced plays and novels. His reputation rests, however, upon his fairy tales, written over a long period (1835–72) and translated into scores of languages.*

1   As a young man Hans Christian Andersen read one of his plays to the wife of another Danish writer. She soon stopped him: "But you have copied whole paragraphs word for word from Oehlenschläger and Ingemann!" Andersen was unabashed: "Yes, I know, but aren't they splendid!"

2   Visiting with Charles Dickens's family in England, Andersen rather overstayed his welcome. One of Dickens's daughters summed up the guest as "a bony bore, and [he] stayed on and on." Dickens himself wrote on a card that he stuck up over the mirror in the guest room: "Hans Andersen slept in this room for five weeks — which seemed to the family AGES."

3   Hans Christian Andersen was discussing the march for his funeral with the musician who was to compose it: "Most of the people who will walk after me will be children, so make the beat keep time with little steps."

❧ ❧

ANDERSON, Sherwood (1876–1941), *US author. He abandoned his job and family to become a writer (1906) and eventually settled as a newspaper proprietor in Virginia, where Faulkner and Hemingway were among his protégés.* Winesburg, Ohio *(1919), his best-known book, is a chronicle of the lives of small-town Americans. He also wrote* Poor White *(1920) and* Dark Laughter *(1925).*

1   (Anderson describes a chance meeting in New Orleans with Horace Liveright, the publisher, who was a well-known womanizer.)

"He was with a beautiful woman and I had seen him with many beautiful women. 'Meet my wife,' he said and 'Oh yeah?' I answered. There was an uncomfortable moment. It *was* Mrs. Liveright. I was sunk and so was Horace."

2   Anderson's first publishers, recognizing his potential, arranged to send him a weekly check in the hope that, relieved of financial pressure, he would write more freely. After a few weeks, however, Anderson took his latest check back to the office. "It's no use," he explained. "I find it impossible to work with security staring me in the face."

❧ ❧

ANDREW, Father Agnellus (1908–   ), *British Franciscan.*

1   Father Andrew was the BBC's adviser on Roman Catholic affairs. A producer who was planning programs on the subject wrote him asking how he could ascertain the official Roman Catholic view of heaven and hell. The answering memorandum contained just one word: "Die."

❧ ❧

ANGOULÊME, Marie Thérèse Charlotte, Duchesse d' (1778–1851), *daughter of Louis XVI and Marie Antoinette and wife of the last dauphin of France. Imprisoned as a child with her parents, she was finally released in 1795, two years after their execution.*

1   Playing with a maid one day, the young Marie Thérèse took one of her hands and counted the fingers. "What?" she exclaimed. "You have five fingers, too, just like me?"

❧ ❧

ANNE, Princess (1950–   ), *daughter of Queen Elizabeth II of the United Kingdom. She shares her love of equestrian sports with her husband, Captain Mark Phillips.*

1   Watching the annual show-jumping event at Hickstead in Sussex one afternoon, Princess Anne was accosted by a fellow spectator. "Has anyone ever told you that you look like Princess Anne?" he inquired. Anne replied: "I think I'm a bit better-looking than she is."

❧ ❧

ANTHEIL, George (1900–59), *US composer. After living in Paris for eleven years, he returned to the United States in 1933. In 1936 he moved to Hollywood where he made a name as a writer of film music.*

1 Among Antheil's early avant-garde pieces, none caused a greater sensation than his *Ballet mécanique,* scored for automobile horns, airplane propeller, fire siren, ten grand pianos, and other instruments. When it was performed at Carnegie Hall in 1924, a concertgoer near the orchestra could stand no more than a few minutes of the racket. Tying his handkerchief to his cane, he raised the white flag.

る→ →ら

ANTHONY, Susan B. (1820–1906), *US reformer. For more than fifty-seven years she lectured and campaigned for women's suffrage and temperance.*

1 "You are not married," the well-known abolitionist Samuel May once said to Susan Anthony. "You have no business to be discussing marriage."

"You, Mr. May, are not a slave," she retorted. "Suppose you quit lecturing on slavery."

る→ →ら

ANTISTHENES (c. 440–c. 360 BC), *Greek philosopher. He founded the Cynic school of philosophers at Athens, advocating a simple and austere life.*

1 Antisthenes dressed with ostentatious poverty. Socrates once mocked him, saying, "I can see your vanity, Antisthenes, through the holes in your cloak."

2 Overcome by a distaste for life, Antisthenes was offered a dagger by Diogenes with the words: "Perhaps you have need of this friend?" Antisthenes replied, "I thank you, but unfortunately the will to live is also part of the world's evil, as it is part of our nature."

る→ →ら

APELLES (4th century BC), *Greek painter.*

1 While Apelles was being acclaimed at the court of Alexander the Great, Protogenes, the only man worthy to be considered his rival, was living poor and obscure on Rhodes. Apelles went to visit him, but when he arrived Protogenes was away from home. The old woman servant asked Apelles who she should tell her master had called on him in his absence. In reply Apelles took a brush and traced upon a panel, with a single continuous line, a shape of extreme delicacy. When Protogenes returned and saw the panel he remarked, "Only Apelles could have drawn that line." He then drew an even finer line inside that of Apelles, telling the old woman to show it to his visitor if he returned. In due course Apelles came back and added a third line of even greater fineness between the first two. When Protogenes saw it, he admitted that Apelles was his master and he hurried out to find him so that they could celebrate together.

{It is said that Apelles helped Protogenes by offering him such generous sums for his paintings that the Rhodians at last realized what a genius was living in their midst. The panel with the triple outline was preserved as a masterpiece until it was brought to Rome, where it was destroyed by fire.}

2 A certain cobbler had found fault with the shoes of a figure in one of Apelles' paintings. Not wishing to disregard the advice of an expert, Apelles corrected the mistake. The cobbler, flattered, went on to criticize the shape of the figure's legs. This was too much for Apelles. "Cobbler, stick to your last!" he cried, dismissing the would-be critic from his workshop and contributing a phrase that has endured for more than two millennia.

る→ →ら

AQUINAS, Saint Thomas (c. 1225–74), *Italian Dominican theologian and scholastic philosopher. He wrote voluminously, his best-known works being the* Summa contra gentiles *(1259–64) and the* Summa theologiae *(1265–73). He aimed to reconcile human reason and Christian faith, and his arguments for the existence of God have exercised theologians and philosophers for many centuries. As a Doctor of the Church, he was given the sobriquet "the Angelic Doctor" (Doctor Angelicus), and was canonized in 1323.*

1 As the pupil of the scholastic teacher Albertus Magnus in Paris, Aquinas made a poor

impression on his fellow students, who nicknamed him "the dumb ox." Albertus summoned him to a private interview at which they discussed all the subjects in the university curriculum. At the next lecture the master announced, "You call your brother Thomas a dumb ox; let me tell you that one day the whole world will listen to his bellowings."

કરે ન્ડ

ARCHELAUS (5th century BC), *king of Macedon (413–399 BC).*

1   A barber, talkative like the rest of his profession, asked King Archelaus how he would like his hair cut. "In silence," replied the king.
   {Possibly the earliest record of this well-known joke.}

કરે ન્ડ

ARCHER, William (1856–1924), *British drama critic and playwright, best known for his translations of Ibsen's plays. His own works include the melodrama* The Green Goddess *(1923).*

1   (Max Beerbohm relates an anecdote about Archer to his biographer, S. N. Behrman.)
   " 'Did you know that Archer, who always wished to demonstrate that, though a drama critic, he could write a play, had one night of triumph when he felt that he had achieved a beautiful play? He told me this himself. One night, between sleeping and waking, it seemed to him that he had evolved a perfect plot, saw the whole thing from beginning to end. He saw that it only remained to write it — like that!' Max snapped his fingers. 'Then he fell into a blissful sleep. When he wakened he went over the whole plot again in his mind. He had a disillusioning, a frightful revelation. What he had dreamt was *Hedda Gabler.*' "

કરે ન્ડ

ARCHIMEDES (287–212 BC), *Greek mathematician and scientist, who worked in Sicily under the patronage of the tyrant Hiero of Syracuse. He made numerous inventions and discoveries, including the form of water-pump known as an Archimedes screw, still in use in some third-world countries.*

1   Hiero believed that an artisan to whom he had given a quantity of gold to shape into a crown had adulterated the metal with silver. He asked Archimedes if there was any way that his suspicions could be proved or disproved. According to the traditional story, the answer occurred to Archimedes while he was taking a bath. He noticed that the deeper he went into the water, the more water overflowed, and that his body seemed to weigh less the more it was submerged. Leaping from the bath, he is said to have run naked through the streets of Syracuse crying, "*Eureka!*" (I have found it!) The concept he had grasped, now known as Archimedes' Principle, is that the apparent loss of weight of a floating body is equal to the weight of water it displaces, and that the weight per volume (density) of a body determines the displacement. Archimedes realized that by immersing first the crown, then the same weights of silver (less dense) and gold (more dense), different volumes would be displaced, and so he was able to demonstrate that the crown was indeed adulterated.

2   His vision of the possibilities opened up by his inventions of the lever and the pulley led Archimedes to make his famous utterance: "Give me a place on which to stand, and I will move the earth." Hiero challenged him to put his words into action and help the sailors to beach a large ship in the Syracusan fleet. Archimedes arranged a series of pulleys and cogs to such effect that by his own unaided strength he was able to pull the great vessel out of the water and onto the beach.

3   The lack of a suitable surface could not deter Archimedes from drawing mathematical diagrams. After leaving his bath he would anoint himself thoroughly with olive oil, as was the custom at the time, and then trace his calculations with a fingernail on his own oily skin.

4   When the Roman general Marcellus eventually captured Syracuse, he gave special orders that the life of Archimedes should be protected. A Roman soldier, sent to fetch the scientist, found him drawing mathematical symbols in the sand. Engrossed in his work, Archimedes gestured impatiently, indicating that the soldier must wait until he had solved his problem, and murmured, "Don't disturb my circles." The soldier, enraged, drew his sword and killed him.

કરે ન્ડ

ARDITI, Luigi (1822–1903), *Italian composer and conductor. He conducted opera in New York, London, and Vienna. His compositions include operas, songs, and waltzes.*

1 While staying in Birmingham, England, Arditi was advised by a friend to spend a day at Stratford-on-Avon. "It would be a pity to leave the area without visiting the birthplace of Shakespeare," said his friend. "But who is this Shakespeare?" asked the conductor. His friend looked at him in amazement. "Haven't you heard of the man who wrote *Othello* and *Romeo and Juliet* and *The Merry Wives of Windsor?*" he asked. "Ah," replied Arditi after a moment's thought, "you mean ze librettist."

ARETINO, Pietro (1492–1556), *Italian poet, playwright, and satirist. His obscene* Sonnets *(1523) lost him the patronage of Pope Leo X.*

1 Laughing at a remark by the Duke of Urbino, Aretino suffered a stroke and collapsed. A priest administered extreme unction. The rite completed, Aretino's eyes flickered open for the last time. "Now I'm oiled," he said, "keep me from the rats!" With that he relapsed into unconsciousness.
See TITIAN 1.

ARISTIDES (?530–?468 BC), *Athenian statesman. Known as "Aristides the Just," he was at first loved and respected by the Athenians. Then, influenced by his rival, Themistocles, they banished him in 483 or 482 BC. He was later recalled, led the Greek resistance to the Persians, and commanded the Athenian forces at the battle of Plataea (479).*

1 Under the Athenian system of ostracism every free adult male could specify the man he wished to see ostracized by scratching the name on a potsherd and dropping it into an urn. An illiterate Athenian, not recognizing Aristides, asked him to write on the potsherd on his behalf. Asked what name the man wanted written, he replied, "Aristides." Surprised, the statesman inquired whether Aristides had ever injured him that he should wish to see him banished. "No," replied the man, "I don't even know him, but I am sick and tired of hearing him called 'the Just.'" Aristides in silence wrote his own name on the potsherd and handed it back to the man.

ARISTIPPUS (?435–?356 BC), *Greek philosopher. He founded the Cyrenaic school of philosophy, based on the concept of hedonism, which held that pleasure is the chief good in life.*

1 Aristippus, asked by a rich Athenian to teach his son philosophy, demanded 500 drachmas. The Athenian protested, "What! I could buy a slave for that much."
"Do so," replied Aristippus. "Then you will have two slaves."

2 During his sojourn at the court of Dionysius, tyrant of Syracuse, Aristippus requested a favor for a friend. Dionysius refused. Aristippus pleaded with the tyrant, abasing himself at his feet, until the favor was granted. Criticized for this conduct as being unworthy of a philosopher, Aristippus retorted, "But that is where the tyrant's ears are."

3 Dionysius asked Aristippus why it was that philosophers paid court to princes, but not vice versa. Aristippus answered, "It is because philosophers know what they need, and princes do not."

ARLEN, Michael [Dikran Kouyoumdjian] (1895–1956), *British writer born in Bulgaria of Armenian parents. He was educated in England (at Malvern College) and naturalized a British subject in 1922. He wrote popular short stories, as well as novels, such as* The Green Hat *(1924) and* The Flying Dutchman *(1939). He also worked in Hollywood on film scripts.*

1 Down on his luck, Arlen went to New York in 1944. To drown his sorrows he paid a visit to the famous restaurant "21." In the lobby, he ran into Sam Goldwyn, who offered the somewhat impractical advice that he should buy racehorses. At the bar Arlen met Louis B. Mayer, an old acquaintance, who asked him what were his plans for the future. "I was just talking to Sam Goldwyn —" began Arlen. "How much did he offer you?" interrupted Mayer. Arlen hesitated. "Not enough," he replied evasively. "Would you take fifteen

thousand for thirty weeks?" asked Mayer. No hesitation this time. "Yes," said Arlen.

2 After his sudden rise to fame with *The Green Hat,* Arlen arrived at Chicago station, an imposing figure in a large hat and expensive astrakhan overcoat. Asked by a reporter there to sum up his artistic achievements, he replied, "Per ardua ad astrakhan."

{A twist on the proverbial *Ad astra per ardua.*}

3 Arlen had had lunch with William Saroyan, the American author of Armenian origin, and gave his wife a glowing account of the encounter. "What are you so excited about?" she asked him. "After all, the day before you lunched with the king of Greece!" Arlen replied, "For an Armenian to lunch with a king — that's natural, but for an Armenian to lunch with another Armenian — that's something to be proud of!"

ॐ ᘐ

ARMOUR, Philip Danforth (1832–1901), *US industrialist. He developed the family meat-packing business into the highly successful firm of Armour and Co. and made numerous improvements in the preparation of canned meats.*

1 Noting that the employees in a certain department of Armour and Co. had greatly increased their efficiency, Armour decided to present each of them with a new suit of clothes. Every man was asked to order the suit of his choice and send the bill to Armour. One particularly greedy young man decided on a suit of evening clothes costing eighty dollars. Armour agreed to pay the bill, commenting to his clerk as he did so, "I've packed a great many hogs in my time, but I never dressed one before."

ॐ ᘐ

ARMSTRONG, Louis ["Satchmo"] (1900–71), *US black jazz trumpeter and singer. He learned to play the cornet in a New Orleans Waifs' Home, where he was sent at the age of thirteen after firing a gun belonging to his mother. He subsequently performed in Chicago, New York, and London, and made numerous recordings. He was also famous as a band leader, film star, comedian, and composer of songs.*

1 (Satchmo recalls this incident from his earlier years.)

"One night this big, bad-ass hood crashes my dressing room in Chicago and instructs me that I will open in such-and-such a club in New York the next night. I tell him I got this Chicago engagement and don't plan no traveling. And I turn my back on him to show I'm so cool. Then I hear this sound: SNAP! CLICK! I turn around and he has pulled this vast revolver on me and cocked it. Jesus, it look like a cannon and sound like death! So I look down at that steel and say, 'Weelllll, maybe I do open in New York tomorrow.'"

2 When Armstrong's band played a command performance for the king of England, Satchmo was not too overawed by the sense of occasion. "This one's for you, Rex," he called out to George VI as the band took up their instruments.

3 Armstrong was once asked whether he objected to the impressions of him frequently given by other singers and comedians. "Not really," he replied, shrugging his shoulders. "A lotta cats copy the Mona Lisa, but people still line up to see the original."

ॐ ᘐ

ARMSTRONG, Neil (1930–), *US astronaut.*

1 On July 20, 1969, Neil Armstrong became the first human being to set foot on the moon. President Nixon authoritatively acclaimed the event as the greatest since the Creation. Armstrong himself, as he took the last step from the ladder of his lunar module onto the moon's surface, said, "That's one small step for a man, one giant leap for mankind."

2 Photographer Yousuf Karsh and his wife were having lunch with Neil Armstrong after a photographic session. Armstrong politely questioned the couple about the many different countries they had visited. "But Mr. Armstrong," protested Mrs. Karsh, "you've walked on the moon. We want to hear about *your* travels."

"But that's the only place I've ever been," replied Armstrong apologetically.

ॐ ᘐ

ARNE, Thomas Augustine (1710–78), *British composer of operas, masques, oratorios, and incidental music. His most famous composition is "Rule, Britannia!" from the masque* Alfred *(1740).*

1   Arne's father, who was both an upholsterer and an undertaker, wanted his son to become a lawyer. Thomas Arne, therefore, had to acquire his early musical training by stealth. His violin teacher, the eminent violinist Michael Festing, found Arne on one occasion practicing with his music propped up on the lid of a coffin. Not a little disturbed, Festing said he himself would be unable to play under such conditions for fear there might be a body in the coffin. "So there is," replied Arne coolly, raising the lid to provide proof.

৯৯ ৵৯

ARNIM, Harry Karl Kurt Eduard, Count von (1824–81), *German diplomat. At the end of the Franco-Prussian War he was sent to arrange the peace treaty with France and was appointed ambassador to Paris in 1872.*

1   At the close of the Franco-Prussian War Bismarck had an interview with Arnim at Versailles. Lord John Russell, the British prime minister, happened to be waiting in the anteroom. As Arnim emerged from his meeting, he said to Russell, "I don't know how Bismarck can stand it! He never stops smoking those strong Havanas of his. I had to request him to open the window." When it was Russell's turn, he walked in to find Bismarck standing at the open window, laughing. "Russell, Arnim was just in here, and he had so much scent on him that I simply couldn't stand it. I had to open the window."

৯৯ ৵৯

ARNO, Peter [Curtis Arnoux Peters] (1904–68), *US cartoonist whose work appeared regularly in* The New Yorker *in the 1930s and 1940s.*

1   Peter Arno imported a racing car from Europe for his own personal use. Among its unique features were fenders made of platinum. Once the car was safely through customs at New York, Arno had the fenders taken off and replaced by ordinary steel fenders. He then sold off the platinum at a large profit.

ARNOLD, Matthew (1822–88), *British poet and critic, who was professor of poetry at Oxford (1857–67) but spent most of his working life as a government inspector of schools. His major prose works were* Essays in Criticism *(1865, 1888) and* Culture and Anarchy *(1869). As a poet he excelled in philosophical verse, as in "Empedocles on Etna" (1852), and in narrative verse, for example,* Sohrab and Rustum *(1853).*

1   Arnold's cold reserve and critical eye did not endear him to the Americans on his American tour in 1883. There is a story that when his hostess offered him pancakes, Arnold passed the plate on to his wife with the comment: "Do try one, my dear. They're not nearly as nasty as they look."
   {An early researcher into Arnold found this incident recounted as at firsthand by several people and concluded it was apocryphal.}

2   As critic and moralist, Arnold attacked the philistinism of the British middle class of his time, upholding rather severe, even dismaying standards of intellectual rigor and moral seriousness. Shortly after his death Robert Louis Stevenson remarked, "Poor Matt. He's gone to Heaven, no doubt—but he won't like God."

৯৯ ৵৯

ARNOULD, [Madeleine] **Sophie** (1740–1802), *French actress and opera singer. She created the role of Eurydice in Gluck's* Orfeo ed Euridice *(1762) and of Iphigénie in the same composer's* Iphigénie en Aulide *(1774), and enjoyed tremendous popularity throughout her long career (1757–78).*

1   The dancer Marie Guimard was a star of the Paris Opéra; her art consisted mainly in rhythmical arm movements and graceful poses, and her fame resided principally in her celebrated liaisons with members of the aristocracy. When Mlle Guimard's arm was broken by some falling scenery, Sophie Arnould remarked, "What a pity it wasn't her leg; then it wouldn't have interfered with her dancing."

2   After a supper she had given for several distinguished personages, Sophie Arnould was visited by the lieutenant of police, demanding

their names. She replied that she could not remember one. Said the lieutenant, "But a woman like you ought to remember things like that."

"Of course, lieutenant, but with a man like you I am not a woman like me."

3 A rival actress had been presented by her lover with a magnificent diamond *rivière*. The necklace was rather too long and as worn by the actress it seemed to be about to disappear down her cleavage. Sophie Arnould commented, "*C'est qu'elle retourne vers sa source*" (It's just returning to its source).

4 Another actress consistently produced a child every year, with predictable consequences to her figure. The result was that she regularly lost both theatrical engagements and lovers. "She reminds me of those nations that are always extending their boundaries but cannot retain their conquests," remarked Sophie Arnould.

ठ॰ ॰ड़

ARRIA (died AD 42), *wife of the Roman senator Cecina Paetus.*

1 Accused of involvement in a plot against the emperor, Paetus was ordered to commit suicide. When he hesitated, Arria took the dagger from him, stabbed herself, and handed the dagger back with the words: "*Paete, non dolet*" (Paetus, it does not hurt).

ठ॰ ॰ड़

ASCHE, [John Stanger Heiss] **Oscar** (1872–1936), *Australian actor, playwright, and theatrical manager. His works included the immensely successful musical play* Chu Chin Chow *(1916).*

1 Asche was once playing a particularly bad game of golf on a Scottish course. After an uncharacteristically good stroke, he risked a casual remark to his caddie: "You'll have seen worse players than I am." When the caddie, an elderly Scot, did not reply, Asche assumed that he had not heard and repeated his remark. "I heard ye afore," said the caddie. "I was just considerin'."

ठ॰ ॰ड़

ASHE, Arthur [Robert] (1943–   ), *black US tennis player. He won the US singles title in 1968 and the men's singles title at Wimbledon in 1975.*

1 The members of the Association of Tennis Professionals represent such a wide range of nationalities that all kinds of remarks can be exchanged without malice. At a meeting of the ATP, Ashe paused in his address to search for the right word to describe a controversial new rule. "Come on, Arthur," came a voice from the floor, "don't be afraid to call a spade a spade."

ठ॰ ॰ड़

ASOKA (died c. 232 BC), *emperor of India (c. 273–c. 232 BC). The greatest of the kings of the Mauryan dynasty, Asoka ruled most of India except the extreme south. His reign is documented by the numerous stone pillars that he had engraved with his edicts and set up throughout his empire.*

1 At the outset of his reign Asoka ruled with the savagery that had characterized the previous rulers of the kingdom of Magadha in northern India. At his capital (modern Patna), there was a fearful prison called "Asoka's Hell," from which, it was decreed, none could emerge alive. One of its victims was a Buddhist saint who had been wrongfully accused. When the torturers threw him into a cauldron of boiling water, he remained unscathed. The jailer informed the king that he should come and see this miracle. Asoka came and wondered. He was about to depart when the jailer reminded him of the edict that no one was to leave the prison alive. Asoka thereupon gave orders that the jailer was to be thrown into the boiling cauldron.

His experience in the prison deeply affected Asoka's outlook. Shortly afterward, he gave orders that the prison was to be demolished and he himself became a convert to Buddhism. The pillars containing his edicts bear witness to the humanity and justice of his rule after his conversion.

ठ॰ ॰ड़

ASQUITH, Herbert Henry, 1st Earl of Oxford and Asquith (1852–1928), *British statesman and Liberal prime minister (1908–16). Asquith's administration introduced important*

*social and constitutional reforms, but suc-
cumbed to the pressures of World War I, although Asquith himself remained head of the
Liberal party until 1926.*

1 "The nineteenth century Rothschild family
kept great state in, among other places, their
home in Waddesdon, where Alfred Rothschild
lived. One day Prime Minister Asquith, who
was staying from Friday till Monday, was
waited on at teatime by the butler. The following conversation ensued: 'Tea, coffee or a
peach from off the wall, sir?' 'Tea, please.'
'China, Indian or Ceylon, sir?' 'China, please.'
'Lemon, milk or cream, sir?' 'Milk, please.'
'Jersey, Hereford or Shorthorn, sir? . . .'"

ASQUITH, **Margot** (1864–1945), *second wife
of Lord Herbert Henry Asquith (1852–1928),
British Liberal prime minister (1908–16). She
wrote an outspoken* Autobiography *(1922),
which Dorothy Parker reviewed in* The New
Yorker, *describing the affair between Margot
Asquith and Margot Asquith as one of the pret-
tiest love stories in all literature. Margot Asquith
was the mother of movie director Anthony Asquith (1902–68).*

1 When Jean Harlow, the platinum-blonde
American movie star of the 1930s, met Lady
Asquith for the first time, she addressed Lady
Asquith by her Christian name. She made the
further mistake of pronouncing the word as if
it rhymed with *rot*. Lady Asquith corrected her:
"My dear, the *t* is silent, as in *Harlow*."

2 Margot Asquith did not like the famous
British sportsman Lord Lonsdale, renowned
for his fine horses and his courage in the hunting field. Someone in Lady Asquith's hearing
once praised his prowess as a rider to hounds.
"Jump?" she interrupted. "Anyone can jump.
Look at fleas."

3 Her stepdaughter, Violet Bonham-Carter,
once asked if she planned to wear a certain hat
trimmed with ostrich feathers to Lord Kitchener's memorial service. Margot replied, "How
can you ask me? Dear Kitchener saw me in that
hat twice!"

4 Lady Asquith had a poor opinion of several

of George V's advisers. After his death the
king's doctor, Lord Dawson, was one of those
who fell victim to her sharp tongue. She once
remarked to Lord David Cecil, "Lord Dawson
was not a good doctor. King George himself
told me that he would never have died had he
had another doctor."

ASTAIRE, **Fred** [Frederick Austerlitz]
(1899–), *US stage and film dancer, whose
partnership with Ginger Rogers produced a
series of films that charmed the world. Invariably playing the role of an elegant playboy, Astaire achieved such remarkable skill that both
Balanchine and Nureyev have described him as
the world's greatest dancer.*

1 Attracted by Hollywood as a young dancer,
Astaire submitted himself for the usual screen
test. The verdict has become part of film history: "Can't act. Slightly bald. Can dance a
little."

2 (David Niven tells a story about his good
friend Astaire, who had become the owner of a
winning string of racehorses.)
    "The most balanced of men in every sense of
the word, he only once to my knowledge went
mad. At dawn one day Fred called me and announced his mental aberration.
    "'I'll never know what made me do it," he
moaned, "but I had this overpowering urge
. . . so I got up in the middle of the night and
drove all over Beverly Hills painting the mail-
boxes with my racing colors.'"

3 (Of Fred Astaire and his wife, Phyllis, who
had a little problem with her *r*'s:)
    Phyllis Astaire and David Niven came to
RKO to watch the filming of his "Cheek to
Cheek" number in the musical *Top Hat,* with
his partner, Ginger Rogers. Ginger came in for
the first take in a dress composed almost entirely of red feathers. "She looks like a wooster," giggled Phyllis.
    It turned out the dress was ready only just in
time. The dance began. "Slowly, one at a time
at first, the feathers parted company with the
parent garment. Then, as Fred whirled Ginger
faster and faster about the gleaming set, more
and more flew off. It became reminiscent of a
pillow fight at school, but they pressed bravely
on with the number, and by the end Ginger

looked ready for the spit. . . . Phyllis pulled my sleeve. 'Let's get out of here,' she said, 'Fwed will be so embawassed.'"

છે ન્ક્ષ

ASTOR, John Jacob (1763–1848), *US financier. He made his fortune with the American Fur Company and was reputed to be the richest man in the United States.*

1 Astor once observed to Julia Ward Howe, "A man who has a million dollars is as well off as if he were rich."

2 Astor sold a lot near Wall Street for $8,000. The buyer, confident that he had outsmarted Astor, could not resist a little self-congratulation after the signing of the papers. "Why, in a few years this lot will be worth twelve thousand dollars," he gloated. "True," said Astor, "but with your eight thousand I will buy eighty lots above Canal Street, and by the time your lot is worth twelve thousand, my eighty lots will be worth eighty thousand dollars."
{There are a number of versions of this story about John Jacob Astor's real estate dealing; although probably apocryphal, it was accepted as true during his lifetime.}

છે ન્ક્ષ

ASTOR, Mary Dahlgren (c. 1850–94), *wife of William Waldorf Astor, the financier who built the Waldorf section of the Waldorf-Astoria Hotel and served as US minister to Italy from 1882 to 1885.*

1 When her friends Elizabeth Marbury and Elsie de Wolfe (Lady Mendl) began to throw large and rather daring parties at Irving House (their Manhattan home), with colorful personalities as the attraction, Mrs. Astor was determined not to be left out. "I am having a bohemian party, too," she announced. Asked who would be there to provide the necessary spice, she said, "J. P. Morgan and Edith Wharton."

છે ન્ક્ષ

ASTOR, Nancy Witcher Langhorne, Viscountess (1879–1964), *US-born politician who became the first woman to take a seat in the British House of Commons (1919) and devoted herself to the welfare and rights of women.*

1 Male antagonism toward Nancy Astor as the first woman to gain a seat in the House of Commons showed itself on several occasions, Winston Churchill in particular being guilty of discourtesy. When she challenged him about his behavior, he told her that it was because he found her intrusion into the all-male preserve embarrassing — as embarrassing as if she had burst into his bathroom when he had nothing to defend himself with. "Winston," she retorted, "you are not handsome enough to have worries of that kind."

2 Particularly irksome to the antifeminists in the House of Commons was Lady Astor's opinion that it was unnecessary for her to prove herself the equal of her male colleagues since women are the superior sex. "I married beneath me — all women do," said she.

3 Since Lady Astor believed in making her presence felt in the House of Commons, she rather too frequently interrupted other speakers. Castigated for this on one occasion, she protested that she had been listening for hours before interrupting. "Yes, we've *heard* you listening," said an exasperated colleague.

4 During a formal dinner, Lady Astor remarked to her neighbor that she considered men to be more conceited than women. Noticing that her comment had been heard around the table, she continued in a loud voice: "It's a pity that the most intelligent and learned men attach least importance to the way they dress.

"A traffic problem existed in the narrow, twisted streets of Paris even in the pre-revolutionary days of King Louis XVI. It was the custom for society ladies of the time to chauffeur their own carriages, and not even the king dared risk their displeasure by forbidding them to drive. Summoning one of his shrewdest ministers, Count d'Argenson, the king asked him whether he could diplomatically unsnarl the traffic jams. 'Of course,' said d'Argenson. 'I will simply promulgate this law: Ladies under thirty years of age are forbidden to drive carriages.'"

— James C. Humes, *Speaker's Treasury*

Why, right at this table the most cultivated man is wearing the most clumsily knotted tie!" The words had no sooner left her lips than every man in the room surreptitiously reached up to adjust his tie.

5 At a dinner given by Theodore Roosevelt, Nancy Astor was given precedence over Grace Vanderbilt. By way of excuse and consolation she remarked to Mrs. Vanderbilt, "The Astors skinned skunks a hundred years before the Vanderbilts worked ferries."

6 "[During the early thirties Winston] Churchill's critics called him rash, impetuous, tactless, contentious, inconsistent, unsound, an amusing parliamentary celebrity who was forever out of step. 'We just don't know what to make of him,' a troubled Tory MP told Lady Astor. She asked brightly: 'How about a nice rug?'"

ॐ৵ ৵ঌ

ATKINSON, Christopher Thomas (1874–1964), *British academic, fellow of Exeter College, Oxford.*

1 During one course of lectures Atkinson found himself confronted with a group of girl students. He began by saying that his talk that morning would be on the sexual prowess of the natives of the Polynesian islands. The shocked ladies made a concerted rush for the door. Atkinson called after them, "It's all right, ladies, you needn't hurry. There's not another boat for a month."

ॐ৵ ৵ঌ

ATLAS, Charles (1894–1972), *US circus strongman, born Angelo Siciliano.*

1 In his early days Atlas performed with the Coney Island Circus Side Show. His demonstrations of strength included lifting two men off the floor, tearing telephone books in half with his bare hands, and lying on a bed of nails with three members of the audience standing on his chest. Of this last feat he once remarked: "Women used to faint when I did that. They couldn't stand watching a beautiful body like mine being abused."

ॐ৵ ৵ঌ

AUBER, Daniel François Esprit (1782–1871), *French composer. He wrote about fifty operas and operettas, most of which were very popular in his own time but are now hardly ever heard. In 1857 Napoleon III appointed Auber his maître de chapelle.*

1 An infant prodigy had written a score that caused a sensation on account of the "originality" displayed by one so young. Said Auber, "This lad will go far when he has less experience."

2 A friend of Auber's engaged him in conversation as they descended the grand stairway at the Opéra. "My friend, we're all getting older, aren't we?" he observed. Auber sighed. "Well, there's no help for it. Aging seems to be the only available way to live a long time."

3 Auber was having tea one day with Prince Metternich, who was a chain-smoker. The prince asked if he might drop his ash in the other's saucer as there was no ashtray. "*Certainement,*" Auber instantly replied, "*mais j'aime mon thé mieux que des cendres*" (I like my tea better without ashes), a neat pun on the more usual "*j'aime monter mieux que descendre*" (I prefer going up to coming down).

4 Auber refused to think about death and whenever reminded of the approach of his last hour would say, "I'll pay no attention to it." But in his late old age he began to accommodate himself to his own mortality. At a funeral service that he was compelled to attend, he remarked to one of his fellow mourners, "I believe this is the last time I'll take part as an amateur."

ॐ৵ ৵ঌ

AUBERNON, Euphrasie (1825–99), *French salonnière and woman of letters. She may have suggested to Proust some aspects of Mme Verdurin.*

1 Mme Aubernon presided as an absolute autocrat over her salon: she decided the topics to be discussed, dictated who should speak and for how long, prohibited any asides or tête-à-têtes, and enforced her guests' attention by ringing a little hand bell. A surprising number of the Parisian intelligentsia meekly submitted to this conversational tyranny, but there were occasional rebellions. On one occasion the witty and charming Mme Baignières arrived rather late. Before she had time to catch her breath, Mme Aubernon rang her bell and said, "We are discussing adultery, Mme Baignières. Will you give us your opinions?" Mme Baignières replied, "I'm so sorry. I've only come prepared with incest."

{According to George D. Painter in his biography of Proust the guest was Geneviève Halévy Straus.}

2   A young matron keen to set herself up as a salonnière came to Mme Aubernon for counsel. Mme Aubernon's advice: "Don't try. You have far too luscious a bosom to keep the conversation general."

3   One of Mme Aubernon's guests was relating a conversation with his young son. "Papa," the child had asked, "when you and Maman went on your honeymoon in Italy, where was I?"

"What did you tell him?" asked Mme Aubernon eagerly.

"I thought for a moment," replied the guest, "then I said, 'You went there with me and came back with your mother.'"

கூ ஃ

AUBIGNÉ, Jean Henri Merle d' (1794–1872), *Swiss Protestant divine who wrote major historical works on the Reformation, Cromwell, and the Scottish church.*

1   When Dr. d'Aubigné was staying with the Scottish divine and preacher Thomas Chalmers, he was served a kippered herring for breakfast. He asked his host the meaning of the word "kippered" and was told "kept" or "preserved." This item of information had a sequel at morning prayer, when the guest, leading the household in their devotions, prayed that Dr. Chalmers might be "kept, preserved, and kippered."

கூ ஃ

AUDEN, Wystan Hugh (1907–73), *British poet. He became a leading voice among the poets of the 1930s with such publications as* Poems *(1930),* The Dog Beneath the Skin *(with Christopher Isherwood; 1933), and* Look, Stranger *(1936). Like his friend and collaborator Isherwood, Auden was much influenced by the café society of left-wing homosexuals in Germany between the wars. In 1939 he and Isher-*wood *went to the United States. In 1946 he obtained US citizenship, but returned to England as professor of poetry at Oxford (1956–61). Auden died in Vienna.*

1   The Nazis, opposed to the anti-Nazi material in her routines, deprived the cabaret artiste Erika Mann, daughter of novelist Thomas Mann, of her passport. She appealed to the homosexual Isherwood as an available Englishman to marry her so that she could obtain an English passport. Isherwood dodged, but Auden generously agreed to marry her and she duly obtained her English passport. Soon afterward a former stage associate of Erika's, who had also lost her passport on account of her anti-Nazi stand, appealed to the Audens for help. Searching around among his acquaintances, Auden found another member of their homosexual circle who gallantly agreed to marry the second lady. "What else are buggers for?" observed Auden.

2   Auden was surprised to learn from a third party that Mike De Lisio, his sculptor friend, wrote poetry in his spare time and had had some of his verses published in *The New Yorker*. "How nice of him never to have told me," said Auden.

3   Auden, about to begin a course of lectures on Shakespeare at the New School for Social Research in New York City, noted that every seat was filled. Surveying the sea of faces extending right to the back of the large auditorium, Auden announced: "If there are any of you who do not hear me, please don't raise your hands because I am also nearsighted."

4   As a young, little-known writer, Auden was once asked what effect fame might have upon him. "I believe," he said after a moment's reflection, "that I would always wear my carpet slippers." When fame did eventually come, Auden was always to be seen in carpet slippers, even when wearing evening dress.

கூ ஃ

AUERBACH, Arnold Jacob ["Red"] (1917–   ), *US basketball executive. Having studied physical education at George Washington University, he began coaching basketball in 1941. He joined the Boston Celtics in 1950 as coach, later becoming general manager.*

1 On tour with the Boston Celtics, Auerbach met three of his players, each with an attractive young woman on his arm, in the hotel lobby at five o'clock in the morning. One of the players covered his embarrassment by introducing the young woman as his "cousin." Auerbach nodded politely. The player, desperately trying to make the unlikely tale sound more convincing, continued, "We were just on our way to church."

Auerbach, relating this story on a later occasion, remarked, "I couldn't take that. I fined him twenty-five dollars for insulting my intelligence."

სₐ ₔₛ

AUGUSTINE OF HIPPO, Saint (354–430), *North African theologian; one of the fathers and doctors of the Church. His mother, Saint Monica, was a Christian; Augustine himself was attracted to the pagan philosophers until his conversion. Returning to his native town, he lived as a monk, was ordained (391), and then consecrated bishop of Hippo (396). His* City of God *and his* Confessions *are among the greatest Christian documents.*

1 In his *Confessions* Augustine recounts the sins of his youth and how even his prayers for repentance were tainted with insincerity: "*Da mihi castitatem et continentiam, sed noli modo*" (Give me chastity and continence, but not yet).

სₐ ₔₛ

AUGUSTUS [Gaius Julius Caesar Octavianus] (63 BC–AD 14), *first Roman emperor (31 BC–AD 14). Named heir of Julius Caesar, Augustus had to fight for his position. After defeating Mark Antony at the battle of Actium (31 BC), he became sole ruler of the Roman world. In 27 BC he adopted the title of Augustus. His rule brought many benefits to Rome, and the boundaries of the empire were considerably expanded and strengthened.*

1 The evening before the crucial battle of Actium Octavian (the young Augustus) set up his camp on a hill overlooking the bay and the two fleets — his own and Antony's — near what is now the town of Preveza in northwestern Greece. In the morning as he emerged from his tent he met a peasant driving a donkey. He asked the man his name. "Eutyches" (Good Fortune) was the answer. And the donkey's name? "Nikon" (Victor).

{Cynics observe that this excellent omen must have been arranged by a thoughtful member of young Caesar's staff.}

2 An old soldier was involved in a lawsuit that seemed likely to go against him. He therefore accosted his former commander, Augustus, in a public place, asking him to appear in court on his behalf. The emperor at once selected one of his suite to appear for the man and introduced him to the litigant. But the soldier, rolling back his sleeve to reveal his scars, shouted, "When you were in danger at Actium, I didn't choose a substitute but fought for you in person." Chagrined, Augustus appeared in court on the veteran's behalf.

3 Several people trained birds to make complimentary greetings to the emperor. Augustus would often buy the birds for generous sums of money. A poor cobbler acquired a raven, intending to train it to make such a remark. The bird turned out to be such a slow learner that the exasperated cobbler often used to say to it, "Nothing to show for all the trouble and expense." One day the raven began to repeat its lesson as Augustus was passing. This time the emperor declined to buy, saying, "I get enough of such compliments at home." The bird, however, also remembering the words of his trainer's usual complaint, went on, "Nothing to show for all the trouble and expense." Amused, Augustus bought the raven.

4 Augustus had ordered a young man of bad character to be dismissed from his service. The man came to him and begged for pardon, saying, "How am I to go home? What shall I tell my father?"

"Tell your father that you didn't find me to your liking," the emperor replied.

5 A certain Roman nobleman died, leaving enormous debts that he had successfully concealed during his lifetime. When the estate was put up for auction, Augustus instructed his agent to buy the man's pillow. To those who expressed surprise at the order he explained, "That pillow must be particularly conducive to sleep, if its late owner, in spite of all his debts, could sleep on it."

6 The conduct of Augustus's daughter Julia was so blatant that a group of influential Romans threatened to denounce her as an adulteress in front of the whole court. Augustus anticipated them by banishing his daughter to a barren island. Her lovers were variously punished. One of Julia's attendants, the freedwoman Phoebe, hanged herself rather than give evidence against her mistress. "Oh, that I had been Phoebe's father, not Julia's," exclaimed Augustus when he heard of the suicide.

હે⋗ ⋖ફ

AUMALE, Henri, Duc d' (1822–97), *French aristocrat, son of King Louis Philippe.*

1 The Duc d'Aumale was one of the most aristocratic of the lovers of Léonide Leblanc, a fashionable courtesan. Léonide eventually hit on a subtle way to discourage unwanted lovers. She had a lifelike wax model of the duke set up at a table in a room of her house. When pestered by a suitor, she would half-open the door to that room, then close it quickly, and say, "Ssh! The duke is here."

2 The Duc d'Aumale's residence at Chantilly was at a distance from Paris convenient for the visits of Léonide Leblanc. One day she traveled out to Chantilly by train, sharing the compartment with a group of society ladies who began vying with each other to prove on what friendly terms they were with the duke. "We dined with His Highness last night," said one. "We shall be lunching there tomorrow," said another. "Of course, we went to the ball there last week," said a third. Léonide Leblanc held her peace until the train drew into Chantilly station. Then she stood up, said, "And I, ladies, am sleeping with His Highness tonight," and stepped lightly from the train.

3 During the Franco-Prussian War Marshal Achille Bazaine commanded the French troops in the fortress of Metz. It was his hesitations, misjudgments, and ultimate surrender that deprived France of the last forces capable of withstanding the German advance. In 1873 the marshal was arraigned before a French military court presided over by the Duc d'Aumale; he was charged with neglecting to do everything required by duty and honor before capitulating to the enemy. At one stage in the proceedings the marshal sought to exonerate himself by reminding the court of the state of affairs at the time of his surrender: "There was no government, there was no order, there was nothing."

"There was still France," said the Duc d'Aumale.

4 Aumale, a great patriot, yearned for military glory in the cause of his beloved France. Commissioned as a sublieutenant in the infantry at the age of fifteen, he announced, "My only ambition is to be the forty-third Bourbon to be killed on the field of battle."

5 The Duc d'Aumale was renowned for his youthful love affairs, but in his old age he felt his powers failing. "As a young man I used to have four supple members and one stiff one," he observed. "Now I have four stiff and one supple."

હે⋗ ⋖ફ

AUSTIN, Alfred (1835–1913), *British poet, dramatist, and prose writer. One of his least happy poetic ventures was written shortly after he was appointed poet laureate (1896)—a lengthy ode on the Jameson Raid. He is remembered for two lines on the illness of the Prince of Wales, which he probably did not write: "Across the wires the electric message came:/ 'He is no better, he is much the same.'"*

1 Someone once chided the poet laureate for grammatical errors in his verses. Austin excused himself by saying, "I dare not alter these things; they come to me from above."

હે⋗ ⋖ફ

AUSTIN, Warren Robinson (1877–1962), *US politician, diplomat, delegate to the United Nations from 1947 to 1953.*

1 In a debate on the Middle East question, Austin exhorted the warring Jews and Arabs to sit down and settle their differences "like good Christians."

2 Someone once asked Austin whether he did not become tired during the apparently interminable debates at the UN. "Yes, I do," he replied, "but it is better for aged diplomats to be bored than for young men to die."

હે⋗ ⋖ફ

AVEMPACE [Abu Bekr Ibn Bajja] (c. 1095–1138), *Spanish Muslim scholar.*

1 The Muslim governor of Saragossa was so delighted by the excellence of Avempace's verses that he swore the young scholar should walk on gold whenever he entered his presence. Avempace feared that the governor would soon regret his exuberant vow and that his own welcome at court would suffer as a result. He therefore sewed a gold piece into the sole of each of his shoes, so that the governor's oath could be kept at no expense to himself.

ॐ ◆᠍

AVERY, Oswald [Theodore] (1877–1955), *Canadian-born bacteriologist. He was one of the founders of immunochemistry and, as a pioneer in the field of molecular genetics, the discoverer of DNA as the basic genetic material of the cell, thus clearing the path for the great biological revolution wrought by Francis Crick and James Dewey Watson.*

1 Professor Avery worked for many years in a small laboratory at the hospital of the Rockefeller Institute in New York City. Many of his experimental predictions turned out to be wrong, but that never discouraged him. He capitalized on error. His colleagues remember him saying, "Whenever you fall, pick up something."

ॐ ◆᠍

AYMÉ, Marcel (1902–67), *French novelist, essayist, and playwright.*

1 A journalist was complaining to Aymé that the modern world hinders the free development of the human being. "I don't agree," said Aymé mildly. "I consider myself perfectly free."

"But surely you feel some limits to your freedom."

"Oh, yes," replied Aymé, "from time to time I find myself terribly limited by the dictionary."

ॐ ◆᠍

AZEGLIO, Massimo Taparelli, Marchese d' (1798–1866), *Italian statesman and writer. A leader of the Risorgimento, he became premier of Sardinia (1849–52). His writings include historical novels and polemic works.*

1 Azeglio's second marriage, to Luisa Blondel, was not very successful and the couple separated. In 1866, however, hearing that Azeglio was dying, Luisa rushed to his deathbed. "Ah, Luisa," sighed the marchese, "you always arrive just as I'm leaving."

B

BABBAGE, Charles (1792–1871), *British inventor and mathematician. He is best remembered for his invention of an "Analytical Engine" that was the forerunner of modern computers.*

1   Babbage objected to Tennyson's lines from *The Vision of Sin,* "Every moment dies a man,/ Every moment one is born," saying that if that were true "the population of the world would be at a standstill." In the interests of accuracy, he wrote to Tennyson, the lines should be emended to read, "Every moment dies a man,/ Every moment one and one-sixteenth is born."

2   Babbage liked to talk. At a dinner he was completely outtalked by Thomas Carlyle, who spent the whole meal haranguing the company on the merits of silence. After dinner Babbage went up to Carlyle and thanked him grimly for his interesting lecture on silence.

BACALL, Lauren (1924–   ), *US movie actress. She made her screen debut in* To Have and Have Not *(1944) with Humphrey Bogart, whom she subsequently married.*

1   Lauren Bacall attended a New Year's Eve party at which the Shah of Iran was one of the distinguished guests. He complimented her on her dancing: "You dance beautifully, Miss Bacall."

"You bet your ass, Shah," she replied.

2   When Humphrey Bogart died, Lauren Bacall placed in the urn with his ashes a small gold whistle inscribed, "If you want anything, just whistle." She had spoken this line to him in their first film together, *To Have and Have Not.*

BACH, Carl Philipp Emanuel (1714–88), *German composer; third son of Johann Sebastian Bach.*

1   As court musician to Frederick the Great in Berlin, one of C. P. E. Bach's duties was to accompany the king when the latter played the flute. Since Frederick prided himself on his ability, Bach's services as accompanist were frequently requested. At the end of one such royal performance a sycophantic courtier burst out with "What rhythm!"

"*What rhythms!*" grumbled Bach sotto voce at the piano.

BACH, Johann Sebastian (1685–1750), *German composer and instrumentalist. Orphaned at the age of nine, after a period as a chorister at Lüneburg Bach joined the Weimar court first as violinist (1703) and later as organist. From there he moved to the court of Prince Leopold of Anhalt in 1717 and in 1723 became cantor at the Thomasschule, Leipzig, and director of the city's church choirs. The originality and power of his compositions did not become widely recognized until the nineteenth century. His output was astonishing, including more than 200 cantatas, the* Saint John Passion *(1723), the* Saint Matthew Passion *(1729), the* Mass in B Minor *(1733–38), and Christmas and Easter oratorios. He also wrote extensively for the harpsichord, clavichord, violin, cello, and lute.*

1   While at school at Lüneburg, Bach more than once walked to Hamburg, fifty kilometers away, primarily to hear J. A. Reincken, organist of the Katharinen-Kirche there. One day, returning almost penniless to Lüneburg, he rested outside an inn. Someone threw two herring heads onto the rubbish heap. Picking up this unsavory offering to see if any part was edible, Bach found a coin in each head. Not only did he have his meal, he was able "to undertake another and more comfortable pilgrimage to Herr Reincken."

ৡ৵ ৵ঌ

BACON, Francis, 1st Baron Verulam and Viscount St. Albans (1561–1626), *English lawyer and experimental philosopher. He rose to the summit of the legal profession, becoming lord chancellor (1618), but was deprived of office in 1621 after being accused of corruption. The most famous of his literary works is his* Essays, *first published in 1597. His philosophical writings in English and Latin (*The Advancement of Learning, *1605;* Novum Organum, *1620) laid the foundations of the experimental approach to science, which, during the seventeenth century, gradually replaced the old Aristotelian method of induction.*

1   While lord chancellor, Bacon presided over a criminal appeal in which the plaintiff was a man called Hogg. Hogg facetiously pleaded that he should be let off on the grounds of his kinship with the judge. "For," he claimed, "Hogg must be kin to Bacon."

"Not until it has been hung," was the chancellor's reply.

2   Sir John Hayward's *History of Henry IV*, published in 1599, immediately landed its author in serious trouble with Queen Elizabeth, who believed that under the pretense of writing history he was criticizing her own policies. Summoning her legal officers, she consulted them as to whether it might not be possible to prosecute Hayward for treason. Bacon demurred: "I cannot answer for there being treason in it, but certainly it contains much felony."

"How?" asked the queen. "And wherein?"

"In many passages," Bacon replied, "which he has stolen from Tacitus."

3   Queen Elizabeth visited her lord chancellor at his house at Gorhambury in Hertfordshire. "What a little house you have gotten," she remarked, being used to the lavish establishments of the great lords who vied to entertain her. Bacon replied with consummate tact, "The house is well, but it is you, Your Majesty, who have made me too great for my house."

4   In the court of James I there was present a rather unremarkable envoy from France. After giving audience to this lanky, overgrown nobleman, the king asked Bacon his opinion of the marquis. "Your Majesty," replied Bacon, "people of such dimensions are like four- or five-story houses — the upper rooms are the most poorly furnished."

5   Bacon's experimental method was directly responsible for his death. In March 1626, as he was being driven in a coach past snowy fields near Highgate, north of London, the idea occurred to him that snow might be used as a means of preserving food. He stopped the coach at the foot of Highgate Hill and entered a poor woman's house where he bought a chicken, killed and drew it, and then packed the interior of the carcass with snow. This endeavor brought on such a chill that he was unable to return home. He went instead to the Earl of Arundel's house in Highgate, where he was installed in a somewhat damp bed. An attack of pneumonia followed, from which he died within three days.

ৡ৵ ৵ঌ

BADER, Sir Douglas Robert Stuart (1910–82), *British aviator. In 1931 he lost both his legs in a flying accident. Fitted with artificial limbs, he learned to walk, played golf and tennis, and continued to fly. He rejoined the RAF at the outbreak of World War II and made twenty-two kills before crashing in a collision over France in 1941. He was knighted in 1976.*

1   Warring countries usually communicate with bombs, bullets, and propaganda. In World War II this rule was briefly broken when an RAF plane flew over a German airfield and dropped a package by parachute. It was addressed "To the German flight commander of the Luftwaffe at St. Omer," where Bader was held prisoner in the hospital. The package contained an artificial leg, bandages, socks, and straps. The Germans, after capturing Bader, had radioed England that he was well but missing one of his tin limbs. The parachute drop followed shortly.

Once back on both tin legs, Bader made four attempts to escape before the Germans deprived him of his artificial limbs at night. After three years and eight months in a maximum-security prisoner-of-war camp, he was freed by the American Third Army.

੬ੳ ੴ

BAEYER, Johann Friedrich Wilhelm Adolf von (1835–1917), *German chemist, whose many contributions to the science include the synthesis of indigo. Professor of chemistry at Munich from 1875 to 1915, he was awarded the Nobel Prize for Chemistry in 1905.*

1 Entering his laboratory one morning, Baeyer found his assistants using mechanical stirrers operated by water turbines. Such complex machines would not normally have received the professor's approval, but he was soon fascinated by them. Anxious to communicate this new discovery to his wife, he summoned her from their neighboring apartment. Frau Baeyer watched the apparatus at work in silent admiration for a while, then exclaimed, "What a lovely idea for making mayonnaise!"

੬ੳ ੴ

BAHR, Hermann (1863–1934), *Austrian playwright, author, and theater director.*

1 Bahr once received from a young poet a historical tragedy together with a request for his opinion: "If you find any faults, please tell me the truth. Words of criticism from a source so judicious would make me feel ennobled." Bahr returned the manuscript with a brief comment: "I'd like to make you at least an archduke."

੬ੳ ੴ

BAILLY, Jean Sylvain (1736–93), *French astronomer. He also played an active part in the French Revolution, but retired from his position as mayor of Paris (1789–91) after he had ordered the National Guard to fire on a rioting mob in July 1791. In November 1793 he was condemned to death by the Revolutionary Tribunal.*

1 Bailly remarked to his nephew the day before his appointment with the guillotine, "It's time for me to enjoy another pinch of snuff. Tomorrow it will be impossible. My hands will be bound."

੬ੳ ੴ

BAKER, Josephine (1906–75), *US dancer and singer. The first black woman to appear in the Folies-Bergère, she took Paris by storm in the 1920s. She lived a large part of her life in France.*

1 In 1929 Crown Prince Adolf of Sweden visited her in her dressing room. Late that night she boarded his private railway carriage and was installed in an enormous swan-shaped bed to await his return. When the prince arrived, she complained of being cold — a condition he attempted to remedy by attaching a three-stranded diamond bracelet to her arm. He was greatly amused when she complained that the other arm was still cold. She got the matching bracelet.

2 In World War II Josephine Baker joined the French Resistance. Her marriage to a Jewish businessman, Jean Léon, brought her to the notice of Goering and the Gestapo, who decided to murder her. Goering invited her to dinner, having arranged to put cyanide in her fish course. Forewarned, Josephine excused herself as the fish was served, planning to drop down the laundry chute in the bathroom to a rendezvous with Resistance workers below. Goering produced his gun and ordered her to eat the fish before allowing her to retire to the bathroom. She managed to reach the chute, slid down, and her colleagues rushed her to a doctor, who pumped out her stomach. After a month of sickness she recovered, but lost all her hair (she always wore a wig thereafter).

੬ੳ ੴ

BAKER, Newton D. (1871–1937), *US lawyer and administrator. As secretary of war during World War I he was in charge of conscription.*

1 A deputation of American chemists called on Newton Baker and volunteered their services during World War I. He thanked them for their offer: "But the army already has a chemist."

੬ੳ ੴ

BAKST, Léon (1866–1924), *Russian artist and designer, court painter to the Romanovs. His greatest achievement was in theatrical design; his dazzlingly innovative sets for the ballets Diaghilev staged in Paris are his most famous successes.*

1 Diaghilev was sitting with Bakst watching a rehearsal when he suddenly turned to the designer and asked, "What are the three most beautiful things in this theater today?"

"Olga Spessiva [the great ballerina], the little boy with the big brown eyes [dancer Anton Dolin], and me," replied Bakst without hesitation.

ह॰ ॰ई

BALANCHINE, George (1904–83), *choreographer, born in Russia. His major achievements came about through his leadership of the New York City Ballet.*

1 (Bernard Taper, in his biography of Balanchine, tells the following story.)

"I was complaining to Balanchine one day about the scarcity of documentary materials pertaining to his life, particularly his inner life. I had been reading some biographies of literary figures — abounding in quotations from the subjects' diaries, letters, journals, and memoirs — and, as a biographer, I was feeling deprived. Balanchine had never journalized, had written perhaps fewer letters than the number of ballets he had choreographed, and had kept no scrapbooks to preserve what others had said about him. Balanchine listened to my complaint and then replied, 'You should think of your task as if you were writing the biography of a racehorse. A racehorse doesn't keep a diary.'"

ह॰ ॰ई

BALDWIN, Stanley, 1st Earl (1867–1947), *British politician, three times Conservative prime minister (1923–24, 1924–29, 1935–37). Although he adroitly handled the General Strike (1926) and the abdication of Edward VIII (1936), Baldwin was blamed for allowing World War II to happen since he condoned Mussolini's conquest of Ethiopia and without rearming Britain permitted Hitler to rearm Germany.*

1 As financial secretary to the treasury, Baldwin was appalled at the extent of the British war debt after the 1914–18 war. In 1919 he wrote an anonymous letter to *The Times* urging the wealthy to impose a voluntary tax upon themselves to help relieve the national burden. Estimating his own personal estate at £580,000, Baldwin realized 20 percent of its value and invested £150,000 in government war-loan stock. He then destroyed the stock certificates, thus making his £150,000 a gift to the treasury. The rich, however, did not stampede to follow Baldwin's example.

2 (Stanley Baldwin's daughter, Lady Lorna Howard, tells a story that illustrates the relationship between her father and the workers at the family plant.)

"An embarrassed newlywed employee came to Baldwin and told him he had broken the bridal bed. Baldwin said it could be repaired free at the family ironworks, but the man feared it would make him the laughing stock of all his mates. So the broken bed was brought to the back door of Baldwin's house at night, wheeled through the hall the following morning, and taken across the road for repair as if it were Baldwin's own."

3 During a by-election speech in 1931 Baldwin attacked the press lords in these words: "The proprietors of the national newspapers are aiming at power, and power without responsibility, the prerogative of the harlot throughout the ages." When the Duke of Devonshire, a stalwart of the Conservative party, heard a report of this speech he remarked, "That's done it. He's lost us the tarts' vote now."

ह॰ ॰ई

BALFOUR, Arthur James, 1st Earl of (1848–1930), *British statesman; prime minister (1902–05). Balfour was prominent in the Irish Home Rule conflicts and as foreign secretary (1916–19) was responsible for the Balfour Declaration (1917), which promised British support for the establishment of a Jewish state in Palestine.*

1 Balfour was once asked if the rumor that he intended to marry Margot Tennant (later Asquith) had any foundation. He replied, "No, I rather think of having a career of my own."

ह॰ ॰ई

BALMAIN, Pierre (1914–), *French couturier.*

1 "During the years of cold and shortages Gertrude [Stein] and Alice [B. Toklas] became

friends with a neighbour at Aix, a simple young man named Pierre Balmain, with a taste for antiques and a natural bent for designing women's clothes. In fact he made with his own hands heavy tweeds and warm garments for Gertrude and Alice to wear during the hard winters. Now he has opened a shop in Paris. At his first showing to the Press Gertrude and Alice arrived with their huge dog, Basket. Gertrude in a tweed skirt, an old cinnamon-coloured sack, and Panama hat, looked like Corot's self-portrait. Alice, in a long Chinese garment of bright colours with a funny flowered toque, had overtones of the Widow Twankey. Gertrude, seeing the world of fashion assembled, whispered, 'Little do they know that we are the only people here dressed by Balmain, and it's just as well for him that they don't!' "

&ᴗ ᴈᴗ

BALSAN, Consuelo (1878–1964), *US society leader. She married the 9th Duke of Marlborough in 1895; they were divorced in 1920 and a year later she married Lieutenant Colonel Jacques Balsan.*

1 (Cass Canfield, who was connected with Harper and Row, the publishers of her book, *The Glitter and the Gold,* entertained Mme Balsan, whose ideas were still colored by the grandeur of her first marriage.)

"At Fishers Island, New York, where we have a tiny two-room house on a beach, she came to tea; we chatted on the terrace adjoining our cottage, and after a pleasant hour she rose to leave. 'I've had such a nice time,' she said, 'and your place is lovely. But *where* is the house?' "

&ᴗ ᴈᴗ

BALZAC, Honoré de (1799–1850), *French novelist. After a miserable childhood in Tours, he became a lawyer's clerk in Paris. An attempt at business (a Sardinian silver mine) ended in bankruptcy, and he returned to writing, achieving his first success with* Les Chouans (1829). *His subsequent forty novels, including* La comédie humaine, *established him in Parisian society, a position he exploited to the full, being almost perpetually both in love and in debt.*

1 When he was thirty-three, Balzac received an interesting letter from the Ukraine signed

"The Stranger." Following it up, he found that the writer, Evelina Hanska, was the wife of a baron. Their affair lasted for seventeen years, and although the baron died in 1841 the couple did not marry until five months before Balzac's death. "It is easier," wrote Balzac, "to be a lover than a husband, for the same reason that it is more difficult to show a ready wit all day long than to produce an occasional *bon mot.*"

2 During his years of poverty Balzac lived in an unheated and almost unfurnished garret. On one of the bare walls the writer inscribed the words: "Rosewood paneling with commode"; on another: "Gobelin tapestry with Venetian mirror"; and in the place of honor over the empty fireplace: "Picture by Raphael."

3 A Parisian bookseller, hearing of Balzac as a young writer of outstanding promise, decided to offer him 3,000 francs for his next novel. He found Balzac's address, situated in an obscure quarter of the city. Realizing that he was not dealing with a gentleman of fashion, he dropped his price to 2,000 francs. He went to the house, saw that the writer was living on the top floor, and dropped the price another 500 francs. When he entered Balzac's garret, he found him dipping a bread roll in a glass of water. He thereupon dropped the price to 300 francs. The manuscript sold in this way was *La Dernière fée* (1823).

4 Balzac, who enjoyed his own celebrity, was discoursing one evening on fame. "I should like one of these days to be so well known, so popular, so celebrated, so famous, that it would permit me . . . to break wind in society, and society would think it a most natural thing."

5 One night a thief broke into Balzac's single-room apartment and tried to pick the lock on the writer's desk. He was startled by a sardonic laugh from the bed, where Balzac, who he had supposed was asleep, lay watching him. "Why do you laugh?" said the thief. "I am laughing to think what risks you take to try to find money in a desk by night where the legal owner can never find any by day."

6 (Edmond de Goncourt writes in his journal:)

"I have had happily confirmed the confidences of Gavarni on the economical manner in which Balzac dispensed his sperm. Lovey-dovey and amorous play, up to ejaculation, would be all right, but only up to ejaculation. Sperm to him meant emission of purest cerebral substance, and therefore a filtering, a loss through the member, of a potential act of artistic creation. I don't know what occasion, what unfortunate circumstance caused him to ignore his pet theory, but he arrived at Latouche's once, exclaiming 'This morning I lost a novel.'"

7   On his deathbed Balzac is reported to have said to the doctor attending him, "Send for Bianchon." (Doctor Bianchon was a character in *La Comédie humaine*.)

᪣᪣

BANCROFT, Sir Squire (1841–1926), *British theater manager.*

1   Sir Squire Bancroft was notoriously tight-fisted, his style of management being in complete contrast to that of another contemporary theatrical impresario, Sir Herbert Beerbohm Tree. Tree once took Bancroft to view His Majesty's Theatre, which Tree had recently had built and lavishly equipped. Gazing at the building from the opposite side of the street, Bancroft remarked, "There'll be an awful lot of windows to clean."

᪣᪣

BANKHEAD, Tallulah (1903–68), *US actress famous for her flamboyant life-style—"more of an act than an actress,"* as an anonymous wit said.

1   At the opening-night party for Lillian Hellman's *The Little Foxes,* in which she starred, Tallulah got into an argument with the writer Dashiell Hammett. Hammett, commenting on her addiction to cocaine, told her that he did not much like people who took drugs. Tallulah retorted, "You don't know what you're talking about. I tell you cocaine isn't habit-forming and I know because I've been taking it for years."

2   At a party given by Dorothy Parker, Tallulah Bankhead became rather drunk and behaved indecorously. As she was being escorted out, Dorothy Parker called out, "Has Whistler's mother left yet?"

The following day the actress, observing herself in a small mirror, said, with a glance at Mrs. Parker, "The less I behave like Whistler's mother the night before, the more I look like her the morning after."

3   Alexander Woollcott took Tallulah Bankhead to see a rather bad revival of a Maeterlinck tragedy. They decided to leave, and as they rose to go, Tallulah murmured, "There's less here than meets the eye."

4   Tallulah's volubility was notorious. The magician Fred Keating came away from an interview with her saying, "I've just spent an hour talking to Tallulah for a few minutes."

5   When Tallulah Bankhead first became successful in London, she bought herself a Bentley, which she greatly enjoyed driving. The London streets bewildered her, however, and she tended to get lost. After a while she took to hiring a taxi to lead the way while she drove behind in the Bentley.

6   When British premier Ramsay MacDonald and his spinster sister came to visit Tallulah in her dressing room, a certain Dr. Jones was also announced. The MacDonalds tactfully offered to leave. "Oh, don't go," cried Tallulah. "I'd like you to meet Dr. Jones. He's the best abortionist in London."

7   Dropping a fifty-dollar bill into the tambourine held out to her by a Salvation Army player, Tallulah waved aside the man's thanks. "Don't bother to thank me. I know what a perfectly ghastly season it's been for you Spanish dancers."

8   (The TV *Tonight Show* host Jack Paar relates a Tallulah story for which he cannot personally vouch. Miss Bankhead was in a booth in a ladies' room.)

"She could not find any toilet paper in her stall, and asked the lady in the next booth, 'Darling, is there any tissue in there?'

"'Sorry, no.'

"'Then have you any Kleenex?'

"'Afraid not.'

"Then Tallulah said, 'My dear, have you two fives for a ten?'"

9   Miss Bankhead's father, William Brockman Bankhead, was Speaker of the US House of Representatives. Checking in at a New York hotel one evening, he was pleasantly surprised by the receptionist's exclamation: "Not *the* Mr. Bankhead?" He replied, "Why, yes—Congressman Bankhead." The receptionist's face fell. "Oh," she said. "I thought, maybe, you were Tallulah's father."

10   A fellow actress once said of Miss Bankhead: "She's not so great. I can upstage her any time."

"Darling," retorted Tallulah, "I can upstage you without even being on stage." At the next performance, she set out to prove her point. In one scene, while the other actress was engrossed in a long telephone conversation, Tallulah had to put down the champagne glass from which she had been drinking and make her exit upstage. That evening, she carefully placed the half-full glass in a precarious position at the edge of the table, half on and half off. The audience gasped, their attention riveted to the glass, and the other actress was totally ignored. She later discovered that Miss Bankhead had surreptitiously stuck a piece of adhesive tape on the bottom of the glass to ensure the success of her moment of triumph.

11   Miss Bankhead had been to see a screen adaptation of Tennessee Williams's play *Orpheus Descending,* and was unimpressed. She later told the playwright: "Darling, they've absolutely ruined your perfectly dreadful play."

12   Actor Donald Sutherland had a memorable first encounter with Tallulah Bankhead. He was making up in his dressing room when he heard a noise behind him. Turning around, he was astonished to see Tallulah standing there, stark naked. "What's the matter, darling?" she asked. "Haven't you ever seen a blonde before?"

❧   ❦

BANKS, Sarah Sophia (1744–1818), *sister of Sir Joseph Banks, the British naturalist and explorer. She amassed a considerable natural history collection in her own right.*

1   A visitor once idly remarked to the eccentric Sophia, "It is a fine day, ma'am," to which she retorted, "I know nothing at all about it.

You must speak to my brother upon that subject when you are at dinner."

❧   ❦

BARBIROLLI, Sir John (1899–1970), *British conductor of French-Italian descent. He was principal conductor of the Hallé Orchestra, Manchester, from 1943, and was also associated with several other major orchestras and opera companies in Britain and the United States.*

1   One of the players in the Hallé Orchestra had an affair with a singer and after a time his wife heard of it. Intending to enlist Sir John Barbirolli's help, she went to his room in Manchester's Free Trade Hall and sobbed out her story. Sir John listened sympathetically and when she had finished tried to find words of comfort for her. He concluded, "You know, there's nothing to worry about. He's playing better than ever."

2   Barbirolli was conducting the New York Philharmonic in a rehearsal of Schubert's Fifth Symphony. "Sounds like a Moz'," murmured the first oboist, an Italian gentleman who had never learned to finish his words in the English way. "It may sound like a Moz'," replied Barbirolli, "but it's a Schube'."

❧   ❦

BARHAM, Richard Harris (1788–1845), *British clergyman and humorist. His* Ingoldsby Legends *(1840) are mainly retellings in comic verse of medieval tales.*

1   At Oxford Barham regularly failed to attend morning chapel. His tutor demanded an explanation. Barham excused himself. "The fact is, sir, it's too late for me," he said. "Too late!" said the astonished tutor. "Yes, sir," Barham continued. "I'm a man of regular habits and I can't sit up until seven o'clock in the morning. Unless I get to bed by four, or five at the latest, I'm good for nothing next day."

2   Richard Bentley, the publisher of *Bentley's Miscellany,* in which many of the *Ingoldsby Legends* first appeared, mentioned to Barham that he had had trouble in selecting the name for his magazine, and had at first intended to call it *The Wits' Miscellany.* "Well, you needn't

have gone to the other extreme," remarked Barham.

{This riposte is attributed by Charles Cowden Clarke to Douglas Jerrold, and is often given as Jerrold's.}

ॐ ॐ

BARNES, Djuna (1892–1982), *US novelist; author of* Nightwood *and other experimental works.*

1 Eccentric and reclusive, Djuna Barnes lived for many years in a tiny Greenwich Village apartment. Her neighbor E. E. Cummings would occasionally shout across to her from his window: "Are ya still alive, Djuna?"

2 Guy Davenport, learning that poet Louis Zukofsky frequently saw Djuna Barnes when he went for his morning paper, inquired whether they ever exchanged pleasantries. "No," replied Zukofsky. "What do you say to the Minister's Black Veil?"

ॐ ॐ

BARNUM, Phineas Taylor (1810–91), *US showman. He founded his famous circus— "the Greatest Show on Earth"—in 1871.*

1 In 1841 Barnum purchased Scudder's American Museum in New York, soon turning it into a prize attraction. So many people flocked to see the exhibits that it was a problem to keep them moving, and long lines built up outside the entrance. Barnum solved the problem by posting up inside the museum a sign reading "TO THE EGRESS."

2 For a time Barnum employed an elephant to do the plowing on his farm. A neighboring farmer, a friend of Barnum's, noticed the beast at work. He then got into an argument with its owner, who insisted the elephant was just another working animal about the farm. After wrangling for a time about the economics of feeding it and the amount of work it could do, the farmer said to Barnum, "I would just like to know what it can draw." Barnum smiled. "It can draw the attention of twenty million American citizens to Barnum's Museum," he said.

3 Barnum's business instincts did not desert him on his deathbed. His last reported words were: "How were the receipts today in Madison Square Garden?"

ॐ ॐ

BARR, Stringfellow (1896–1981), *US educator; co-founder of the Great Books program at St. John's College, Annapolis, Maryland.*

1 The four-year Great Books program was based on the works of great writers and thinkers from Homer to such twentieth-century giants as Freud. Someone once asked Barr, why a Great Books program? "Don't you feel sorry for all the students in all the other colleges who have no one to teach them but oafs like me?" Barr asked.

ॐ ॐ

BARRIE, Sir J[ames] M[atthew] (1860–1937), *British journalist and playwright. His stage successes include* Quality Street *(1901) and* The Admirable Crichton *(1902), but his lasting fame rests on his dramatic fantasy for children,* Peter Pan *(1904).*

1 Barrie had for a long time looked forward to meeting A. E. Housman. When this was eventually arranged and the two placed next to each other at a dinner in Cambridge, neither found much to say to the other. Barrie, returning to London with this unprofitable encounter weighing on his mind, penned the following note to Housman: "Dear Professor Houseman, I am sorry about last night, when I sat next to you and did not say a word. You must have thought I was a very rude man: I am really a very shy man. Sincerely yours, J. M. Barrie." Back from Cambridge came Housman's reply: "Dear Sir James Barrie, I am sorry about last night, when I sat next to you and did not say a word. You must have thought I was a very rude man: I am really a very shy man. Sincerely yours, A. E. Housman. P.S. And now you've made it worse for you have spelt my name wrong."

2 The pallbearers at Thomas Hardy's funeral included distinguished writers (Rudyard Kipling, G. B. Shaw, A. E. Housman) and politicians (Stanley Baldwin, Ramsay MacDonald). Shaw, the tallest and most obviously impressive, later remarked that he himself had looked well at the ceremony, but "Barrie, blast him!

looked far the most effective. He made himself look specially small."

3 *Peter Pan* premiered in London in 1904. In it Peter told the Darling children that if they believed strongly enough that they could fly, they *would* fly. Barrie soon began to hear from parents with children who had taken Peter's word literally, and hurt themselves in consequence. Barrie at once included in the play a cautionary statement that the children could fly, but only if they had first been sprinkled with "fairy dust." From then on, fairy dust being in short supply, all has gone well.

4 The success of Barrie's plays owed a great deal to the author's close attention to production details and his presence at rehearsals. Late one night after an exhausting and unsatisfactory rehearsal of *Peter Pan,* when the director had just told the cast that they could go, Barrie suddenly demanded that they all be brought back onto the stage. "Impossible," shouted the weary director. "Why?" asked Barrier. "Crocodile under fourteen — gone home," was the response.

5 One of the reactions to *Peter Pan* that Barrie most enjoyed was that of a small boy who had been given a seat in the author's box to watch the play. At the end he was asked which bit he had liked best. The child replied, "What I think I liked best was tearing up the program and dropping the bits on people's heads."

6 (Peter, one of the sons of the Davies family of whom Sir James Barrie was very fond, recalls an incident that throws a curious light on Barrie's sense of humor.)

"One evening at dusk I was summoned to J. M. B.'s room, to find him sitting in a somehow dejected attitude, at the far end of the room in the half light. As I entered he looked up, and in a flat lugubrious voice said: 'Peter, something has happened to my feet,' and glancing down I saw to my horror that his feet were bare and swollen to four or five times their natural size. For several seconds I was deceived, and have never since forgotten the terror that filled me, until I realized that the feet were artificial (bought at Henley's), made of the waxed linen masks are made of, and that I had been most successfully hoaxed."

7 Barrie, valuing the privacy of his home, tended to react violently when it was invaded. A reporter turned up on his doorstep and when Barrie came to the door said brightly, "Sir James Barrie, I presume?"

"You do," said Barrie, and slammed the door.

See also HILAIRE BELLOC 3.

8 Barrie was sitting next to George Bernard Shaw at a dinner party. The vegetarian Shaw had been provided with a special dish of salad greens and dressing. Eyeing the unpleasant-looking concoction, Barrie whispered to Shaw, "Tell me, have you eaten that or are you going to?"

{A variant of this story tells of a publisher's messenger who called on Shaw one dinnertime. Staring in amazement at the writer's plate of vegetables, he inquired politely, "Sir, have you just finished or are you just starting?"}

9 "You'll be sick tomorrow, Jack, if you eat any more chocolates," said Sylvia Llewelyn-Davies to her young son. "I shall be sick tonight," said the child calmly, as he helped

---

One morning, Yale University Professor of English John Berdan read to his English composition class a particularly inept theme and, as usual, called for comments. The students panned it unmercifully.

"Interesting," commented Berdan, "because I wrote the theme myself." As the critics began to blush, he continued, "You are quite right. This theme is incredibly bad. I spent two hours of painstaking effort last night to make sure I had not omitted a single feature of poor writing, and I believe I succeeded." The professor paused for dramatic effect.

"What astounds me," he resumed, "is how you men can dash these things off day after day in ten minutes."

— Jacob M. Braude, *Speaker's and Toastmaster's Handbook*

himself to yet another. Barrie, who overheard this exchange, was so delighted with it that he incorporated it in *Peter Pan* and paid the young Llewelyn-Davies a copyright fee of a halfpenny a performance.

10 While producing one of his own plays, Barrie was approached by an inexperienced member of the cast. Although his part was a very minor one, the young actor, anxious to give it the right interpretation, sought Barrie's advice. Sir James gave the matter some thought. "I am glad you have asked me," he finally replied. "I should like you to convey when you are acting it that the man you portray has a brother in Shropshire who drinks port."

৯৬ ৩৪

BARROW, Isaac (1630–77), *English clergyman and mathematician; Lucasian Professor of Mathematics at Cambridge (1664–69). Besides numerous works on geometry, he wrote a large number of sermons, which still enjoy a high reputation.*

1 There was no love lost between Barrow and King Charles II's favorite, the Earl of Rochester, who had called the clergyman "a musty old piece of divinity." One day at court, where Barrow was serving as the king's chaplain, he encountered the earl, who bowed low and said sarcastically, "Doctor, I am yours to my shoe-tie."
"My lord," returned Barrow, "I am yours to the ground."
"Doctor, I am yours to the center."
"My lord, I am yours to the antipodes."
"Doctor, I am yours to the lowest pit of hell."
"And there, my lord, I leave you," said Barrow, turning smartly on his heel.

৯৬ ৩৪

BARRYMORE, Ethel (1879–1959), *US actress, member of a remarkable acting family (Lionel and John were her brothers). Among her most notable stage successes are* Déclassée *(1919),* The Constant Wife *(1928), and* The Corn Is Green *(1942). She also appeared in vaudeville, film, radio, and television.*

1 Miss Barrymore was in her Hollywood dressing room one day when a studio usher knocked on the door and called: "A couple of gals in the reception room, Miss Barrymore, who say they went to school with you. What shall I do?"
"Wheel them in," came the reply.

2 Ethel Barrymore was exact in manners and expected from others the same courtesy. When she invited a young actress to dinner, her guest not only failed to appear but did not even bother to account for her absence. Several days later, the two women met unexpectedly at New York's Gallery of Modern Art. Lamely, the young woman began, "I think I was invited to your house to dinner last Thursday night."
"Oh, yes," replied Ethel. "Did you come?"
{Also told of Beatrice Lillie.}

৯৬ ৩৪

BARRYMORE, John (1882–1942), *US actor. Throughout his successful career on stage and screen he always thought of himself primarily as a great classical actor.*

1 In his youth Barrymore was extremely lazy and had already acquired an unhealthy taste for alcohol. In 1906 a heavy night of drinking enabled him to sleep through the great San Francisco earthquake. The next morning he was pressed by the army into helping clear the rubble — an event that caused his uncle to remark, "It took a calamity of nature to get him out of bed and the US army to make him go to work."

2 Although Hamlet was to become one of Barrymore's most famous roles, the actor was not at all happy with his first performance. He was sitting despondently in his dressing room after the show, when a distinguished-looking gentleman came in. Throwing himself at the actor's feet, the stranger kissed Barrymore's hand and gushed, "O Master! I enjoyed your performance so much!"
"Not half so much as I am enjoying yours," replied Barrymore.

3 During rehearsals for a play the leading lady and Barrymore had a furious row. Barrymore told her pungently what he thought of her parentage and her offstage pursuits. "Kindly remember I am a lady!" snapped the actress. "I will respect your secret, madam," retorted Barrymore.
{This anecdote is told of others, notably

Charles Frohman and Mrs. Patrick Campbell.}

4 In accord with his frequently professed contempt for the film medium, Barrymore refused to learn his lines for any of his movie roles. This necessitated having a small army of stagehands hold up boards with the star's lines written on them so that Barrymore could see and read them during filming. When directors or his fellow actors remonstrated with him about his inconvenient habit, he always produced the same answer: "My memory is full of beauty—Hamlet's soliloquies, the Queen Mab speech, King Magnus' monologue from *The Apple Cart,* most of the Sonnets. Do you expect me to clutter up all that with this horseshit?"

5 When the filming of *A Bill of Divorcement* was complete, Katharine Hepburn turned to co-star John Barrymore, saying, "Thank God I don't have to act with you anymore!"

"I didn't know you ever had, darling," he replied.

6 The assistant to a movie mogul telephoned Barrymore, explained that she was speaking for her boss, and invited Barrymore to a party the following day. Barrymore replied, "And I am speaking for John Barrymore, who has a previous engagement which he will make as soon as you have hung up."

See also EDWARD VII 1.

7 Attending a funeral, Barrymore was about to depart with the other mourners when he noticed a very old, very frail man lingering by the side of the open grave. Going over to him, Barrymore said softly, "I guess it hardly pays to go home."

{This cruel jest has been attributed to others.}

8 In 1938 Orson Welles broadcast throughout the United States a radio production of H. G. Wells's story *War of the Worlds,* which tells of a Martian invasion. The broadcast was so realistic that it almost caused a coast-to-coast panic. John Barrymore was among those convinced that the Martians had landed. He managed to contain his fear until it came to the point at which the invaders are marching down Madison Avenue. Rushing out to the kennel in which he kept his twenty St. Bernards, he flung open the gate and released the dogs, crying, "Fend for yourselves!"

9 On one occasion John Barrymore was being interviewed by a young newspaper reporter, who asked him whether he still found acting as much fun as it used to be. "Young man," said Barrymore, "I am seventy-five. Nothing is as much fun as it used to be."

10 Barrymore faced his end with a last gesture of gallantry. In the hospital and aware that he was dying, he called for a priest, who came to his bedside accompanied by an old and extremely ugly nurse. Asked if he had anything to confess, Barrymore replied, "Yes, Father, I confess to having carnal thoughts."

"About whom?" asked the nervous priest.

"About her," said Barrymore, pointing to the nurse.

ॐ॰ ◦ॐ

BARRYMORE, Maurice (1847–1905), *English-born actor. He won the English amateur boxing championship (1872), moved to the United States, and became an actor. He was the father of John, Lionel, and Ethel Barrymore.*

1 An English friend once scoffed at Maurice Barrymore's enthusiasm for his adopted country. "Why," he said, "we could go over to America and beat the daylights out of it any day."

"Again?" inquired Maurice.

2 Maurice Barrymore once took his young children to the zoo. While he was busy expounding on the llamas, young John was fascinated by the large birds in the adjacent and very dirty aviary. He kept badgering his father to come and tell them about the pelicans, cormorants, and similar exotic creatures. "Please," persisted John, "what kind of birds are they?" Maurice peered at the cage and the festoons of bird droppings. "Presumably," he said, "they are birds of passage."

3 When Maurice Barrymore was being laid to rest, the straps supporting the coffin became twisted. The coffin, already lowered into the grave, had to be raised again so an adjustment could be made. As it reappeared, Lionel impulsively nudged John and whispered, "How like Father—a curtain call!"

BARTÓK, Béla (1881–1945), *Hungarian composer and pianist. Much of his music for piano and strings draws upon themes from eastern European folk music. He also wrote ballet and opera. In 1940 he moved to the United States, where he died in poverty.*

1 (Isidore Philipp, a great teacher of piano, was visited by Bartók in Paris.)

"[Philipp] offered to introduce the young Hungarian composer to Camille Saint-Saëns, at that time a terrific celebrity. Bartók declined. Philipp then offered him Charles-Marie Widor. Bartók again declined. 'Well, if you won't meet Saint-Saëns and Widor, who is there that you would like to know?' 'Debussy,' said Bartók. 'But he is a horrid man,' said Philipp. 'He hates everybody and will certainly be rude to you. Do you want to be insulted by Debussy?' 'Yes,' said Bartók."

BARTON, Clara (1821–1912), *founder and president (1882–1904) of the US Red Cross.*

1 Miss Barton, who never bore grudges, was once reminded by a friend of a wrong done to her some years earlier. "Don't you remember?" asked her friend. "No," replied Clara firmly. "I distinctly remember forgetting that."

BARUCH; Bernard Mannes (1870–1965), *US financier and presidential adviser.*

1 Baruch was telephoned one night when giving a dinner party. His side of the conversation was clearly audible to his guests. "Consolidated Gas — good," they heard him say, then, "Yes — good — fine." A lady who was present rushed out the following morning and bought a substantial holding of Consolidated Gas. Over the next few months the stock fell disastrously. When the lady next met Baruch, she reproached him, saying she had bought Consolidated Gas on his recommendation.

Baruch was puzzled, but when she reminded him of the telephone conversation, light dawned. The call had been from a consultant whom he had briefed to investigate Consolidated Gas and who had said that Baruch's suspicions were well founded. Baruch's words had been his expression of satisfaction that his hunch had proved correct.

2 A man who had often spoken to Baruch about his love for hunting was eventually invited to the financier's South Carolina estate for a turkey shoot. For two days the hapless guest toiled around the plantation, firing at every gobbler he saw, but without hitting a single one. Baruch said nothing. On the third morning, however, the guest noticed a particularly fine turkey sitting motionless in a tree right by the path. He crept up silently to the turkey and fired point-blank. The bird dropped at his feet. With great joy he hastened to stuff his trophy into his bag and it was only then that he noticed the card tied around the bird's neck. It read: "With the compliments of Bernard Baruch."

BASIE, "Count" [William] (1904–84), *US jazz pianist. Count Basie first played in Harlem dance halls, taking piano lessons from Fats Waller. In 1935 he and his band arrived in New York and, after an initially unenthusiastic reception, had their first hit, "One O'Clock Jump," which became his signature tune. He was leader of his band for forty-nine years.*

1 On tour in London in 1957, Basie went shopping for gifts for his family. He had decided on fur gloves for his daughter, but in several shops he was advised that mittens were more practical for children. "Yeah?" said Basie. "How're they going to count in the wintertime?"

BAUGH, Sammy (1914–), *US football player. An outstanding passer, Baugh played superbly in sixteen seasons (1937–52) of professional American football for the Washington Redskins.*

1 Baugh's Washington Redskins were one of the dominant teams in the National Football League of the 1930s and 1940s. In 1940, however, they lost to the Chicago Bears, 73 to 0, in by far the most surprising and one-sided championship game the league had had. Everything the Bears tried worked. In the final minutes the Redskins drove seventy-five yards to the six-inch line, only to have a pass by Baugh intercepted by the Bears and thus ending the Redskins' threat to score at least six points before the final gun. In the dressing room afterward, dejected by the humiliating defeat, Baugh managed a little smile and said, "Maybe if we could have gotten that touchdown at the end it would've turned the tide."

❧ ❧

BAUM, L[yman] Frank (1856–1919), *US writer and journalist, author of* The Wonderful Wizard of Oz *(1900).*

1 Baum had a weak heart and was not allowed to smoke, but he often held an unlit cigar in his mouth. Once, when standing on a lakeshore, he was asked whether he ever actually lit the cigar. "I only light up when I go swimming," replied Baum. "I can't swim, so when the cigar goes out I know I'm getting out of my depth." To illustrate this bizarre explanation, he lit the cigar, walked into the lake until the water reached the level of his mouth, then returned to the dry land, the cigar extinguished. "There, now," he said triumphantly, "if it hadn't been for the cigar I would have drowned."

❧ ❧

BAYLIS, Lilian (1874–1937), *British theater manager. She founded the first Old Vic Company in London (1912) and established its reputation for Shakespearean productions. In 1931 she founded with Ninette de Valois the Sadler's Wells Company for ballet and opera.*

1 Miss Baylis was notoriously discouraging of romances between members of her companies. A young actor and actress went hand in hand to her office. For a time she affected not to notice them, then, scarcely looking up from her desk, said, "Well, what is it?"

"We're in love, Miss Baylis," stammered the actor, "and we — er — want to get married."

"Go away," said Miss Baylis. "I haven't got time to listen to gossip."

2 Chronic financial problems beset Lilian Baylis's theatrical ventures. For these, as for other matters, she was unabashed about seeking divine aid. Members of her company were frequently embarrassed by her habit of going down on her knees in her office. It was said that at one particularly stressful moment she was overheard to pray, "O Lord, send me a good tenor — cheap."

3 Elated by her recent acquisition of Sadler's Wells as an opera and ballet house, Miss Baylis stepped off the sidewalk outside London's Old Vic theater without looking and was knocked down by a passing cab. An elderly gentleman rushed to her aid. "Blimey," he exclaimed, "if it ain't Miss Lilian Baylis of the Old Vic." Raising her head with some difficulty, Miss Baylis announced proudly, "And Sadler's Wells, too!" And lapsed unconscious.

❧ ❧

BAYLOR, Elgin (1934–   ), *US basketball player.*

1 When Baylor was the leader of the Los Angeles Lakers, he agreed to take a vote among the players as to whether to buy blue or gold blazers. The vote went for gold, but Baylor ordered blue. When his rival, Bill Russell, heard about it, he asked Baylor to explain. "I told 'em I'd give 'em the vote, I didn't say I'd count it," Baylor replied.

❧ ❧

BEAN, Roy (?1825–1903), *US frontier judge and saloon keeper.*

1 Bean was the proprietor of the Jersey Lily tavern in Langtry, Texas, close to the railroad. One day when a train stopped to take on water, a passenger rushed into Bean's bar for a bottle of beer. Bean lazily told him to help himself, which the man did, rushing out again without paying. Incensed, Bean grabbed his gun and ran up to the train, telling the conductor to hold it. He found his customer in the smoking bar and, cocking his gun, demanded the money for the beer. Alarmed, the man handed over a ten-dollar bill. Bean took it and said, "Fifty cents for the beer, nine dollars and fifty for collecting. This squares your account. You can keep the bottle." Then stepping down from the train, he told the conductor, "You can go ahead now as soon as you damn well please."

❧ ❧

BEATON, Sir Cecil (1904–80), *British photographer and designer. He first won fame as a society portraitist in the 1920s.*

1 In 1926 the young Beaton, uncertain about his future plans, begged the advice of a friend, Kyrle Leng. "What on earth can I become in life?" he asked in a letter, and received the reply, "I wouldn't bother too much about *being* anything in particular, just become a friend of the Sitwells, and wait and see what happens."

2 (At an informal dinner party soon after the engagement of Princess Margaret and Anthony Armstrong-Jones was announced, Cecil Beaton was shown one of the first wedding presents, painted by one of the guests.)
   "One of the painters present had given them a large picture of a great number of hysterical-looking naked figures milling together in what appeared to be a blue haze or an earthquake or a trench scene of the 1914–18 war. Princess Margaret said, 'They're all dancing.' I took a gulp of champagne and said, 'Oh, I'm so glad it isn't a disaster.' Princess Margaret laughed so much that she had to lie flat in an armchair."

ॐ ⋘

BEATTY, David Beatty, 1st Earl (1871–1936), *British admiral; First Sea Lord (1919–27). He commanded a cruiser squadron during World War I, inflicting a number of losses upon the German navy, and in 1918 received the surrender of the German fleet.*

1 Beatty commanded one arm of the British fleet at the battle of Jutland in 1916. He was not wholly prepared with all ships in position when he encountered the German fleet, and a brisk battle soon developed. The *Lion* was hit first and then the *Indefatigable* was blown up; soon afterward the *Queen Mary*, with her crew of 1,200, was sunk. Admiral Beatty observed to his flag captain, "There seems to be something wrong with our bloody ships today, Chatfield."
   {Despite their early losses the British held their own and the outcome of the battle was inconclusive. The "something wrong" was the fact that the British naval designers had not recognized that long-

range shells would drop from above onto their targets, not blast them from the sides; they had therefore heavily armored the sides of the warships and left the decks and superstructures comparatively unprotected.}

ॐ ⋘

BEAUMARCHAIS, Pierre-Augustin Caron de (1732–99), *French dramatist. His greatest successes,* The Barber of Seville *(1775) and* The Marriage of Figaro *(1778), inspired operas by Rossini and Mozart respectively.*

1 Beaumarchais had suffered at the hands of the aristocratic Duc de Chaulnes, but had refused to fight him. Some time afterward, after another imbroglio, he received a challenge from a certain M. de la Blache. "Not a chance," replied Beaumarchais, "I've refused better men than you."

ॐ ⋘

BEAUMONT, Francis (1584–1616), *British dramatist who collaborated between about 1607 and 1612 with John Fletcher in the writing of several plays.*

1 At one stage in their collaboration Beaumont and Fletcher were arrested on suspicion of treason. As they were sitting in a tavern working out the plot of a tragedy, one had been heard to remark to the other, "I'll kill the king."

ॐ ⋘

BEAVERBROOK, William Maxwell Aitken, 1st Baron (1879–1964), *British newspaper publisher and politician, born in Canada. Having already made his fortune as a stockbroker, he came to Britain in 1910 and entered Parliament. After World War I he went into journalism and took over the* Daily Express, *dramatically increasing its worldwide circulation. A few years later he founded the* Sunday Express *and subsequently bought the* Evening Standard. *He was a member of Churchill's cabinet during World War II.*

1 In the washroom of his London club, Beaverbrook happened to meet Edward Heath, then a young MP, about whom he had printed a rather insulting editorial a few days earlier. "My dear chap," said Beaverbrook, embar-

---

Ernie Byfield, who used to run Chicago's legendary Pump Room, was once asked why real caviar was so expensive. His reply: "After all, it's a year's work for the sturgeon."

rassed by the encounter, "I've been thinking it over, and I was wrong. Here and now, I wish to apologize."

"Very well," grunted Heath. "But next time, I wish you'd insult me in the washroom and apologize in your newspaper."

{Told of others.}

৵৵ ৽৻

BECKETT, Samuel (1906–   ), *Irish novelist, playwright, and poet. In 1937 he made Paris his permanent home. His works are characterized by nihilism, expressed in savage humor, as in* Waiting for Godot *(1954). He was awarded the Nobel Prize for literature in 1969.*

1 Beckett was listening while his friend Walter Lowenfels expounded at length his views on the relationship of art and the desolate condition of society. Beckett nodded but said nothing, until his friend burst out, "You sit there saying nothing while the world is going to pieces. What do you want? What do you want to do?" Beckett crossed his long legs and drawled, "Walter, all I want to do is sit on my ass and fart and think of Dante."

2 In 1961 Beckett married his long-time companion, Suzanne. Soon afterward their relationship became soured by her jealousy of his growing fame and success as a writer. One day in 1969 the telephone rang. Suzanne answered it. She listened for a moment, spoke briefly to the caller, and hung up. Then she turned to face Beckett, looking stricken, and whispered, "*Quel catastrophe!*" (What a catastrophe!) She had just been told that the Swedish Academy had awarded him the Nobel Prize for literature.

৵৵ ৽৻

BECKFORD, William (1760–1844), *British eccentric and collector; author of the Oriental romance* Vathek *(1786). Enormously wealthy, he spent much of his fortune on his house at Fonthill, a few miles from Bath. Built by the architect James Wyatt, Fonthill was a Gothic dream with a huge central tower. Some twenty-five years after its completion the tower collapsed and the whole abbey fell into ruins.*

1 Beckford built a high wall around his estate at Fonthill to discourage visitors. One determined young man managed to slip unobserved through the main gate during a tradesman's call. Heading across the park, he came to a walled vegetable garden. A man who had been digging potatoes came over and asked the intruder to identify himself. The young man explained that he had heard a great deal about the beauties of Fonthill and finding the gate open had taken the opportunity of having a look. The gardener seemed sympathetic, showed him around the greenhouses, and then said, "Would you like to see the house and its contents?"

After a comprehensive tour of the house, the young man's guide pressed him to stay and have some dinner, then revealed his true identity; he was, of course, William Beckford. The young man readily agreed to stay, and he and Beckford had a magnificent meal and thoroughly enjoyable conversation. On the stroke of eleven Beckford withdrew to bed. A footman showed the guest to the door. "Mr. Beckford ordered me to present his compliments to you, sir," he told the young man, "and I am to say that as you found your way into Fonthill Abbey without assistance, you may find your way out again as best you can, and he hopes that you will take care to avoid the bloodhounds that are let loose in the gardens every night. I wish you good evening, sir."

With the door resolutely shut behind him, the young man ran as fast as he could to the nearest tree and climbed up out of reach of the hounds. There he spent a night of acute terror and discomfort until day dawned and he was able to make his way in safety to the main gate and escape.

2 Beckford's vast and assorted collection did not win universal admiration. After financial constraints forced its owner to disperse it, the essayist William Hazlitt remarked, "The only proof of taste he has shown in this collection is his getting rid of it."

৵৵ ৽৻

BEECHAM, Thomas (1820–1907), *British industrialist; grandfather of the conductor Sir Thomas Beecham.*

1 Beecham's fortunes were founded on his pills, which became a popular panacea and were sold with the slogan "Worth a guinea a box." It is said that this phrase was suggested to Beecham by a satisfied customer who came up to him while he was peddling the pills in the marketplace at St. Helens, Lancashire. When

Beecham became wealthy, he used to send samples of the pills to the old people of the Oxfordshire village in which he had once been a shepherd. In the bottom of each box he would put a guinea.

❧ ❧

BEECHAM, Sir Thomas (1879–1961), *British conductor and impresario. As guest conductor with the New York Philharmonic from 1928, founder of the London Philharmonic Orchestra (1932), and artistic director of the Royal Opera House, Covent Garden, Beecham was influential in promoting classical music for US and British audiences.*

1 Thomas Beecham's sister had a friend called Utica Welles. When they were out walking one day, Beecham said to her, "I don't like your Christian name. I'd like to change it."

"You can't," the girl replied, "but you can change my surname."

And so they were married.

2 As a young man Beecham was the subject of many stories relating to his dashing style. One tells how he was walking in London's Piccadilly on a balmy summer evening when he began to feel that he was too warmly dressed. He hailed a cab, tossed his redundant topcoat into it, and ordered the driver, "Follow me." He then completed his stroll unencumbered.

3 On one occasion Sir Thomas was asked if it was true that he preferred not to have women in the orchestra. "The trouble is," he said, "if they are attractive it will upset my players and if they're not it will upset me."

4 Beecham was not a great admirer of the music of the British composer Ralph Vaughan Williams. During a rehearsal of a Vaughan Williams symphony he seemed to be doing no more than listlessly beating time — indeed, he was still beating time after the orchestra had stopped. "Why aren't you playing?" Beecham mildly asked the first violinist. "It's finished, Sir Thomas," came the reply. Beecham looked down at his score, turned the page, and found it empty. "So it is, thank God!" he said.

5 Sir Thomas Beecham was traveling in a nonsmoking compartment on a train belonging to the Great Western Railway. A lady entered the compartment and lit a cigarette, saying, "I'm sure you won't object if I smoke."

"Not at all," replied Beecham, "provided that you don't object if I'm sick."

"I don't think you know who I am," the lady haughtily pointed out. "I am one of the directors' wives."

"Madam," said Beecham, "if you were the director's *only* wife, I should still be sick."

6 One day there was a face strange to Beecham among the woodwinds. "Er, Mr.—?" he began.

"Ball," came the reply.

"I beg your pardon?"

"Ball, Sir Thomas."

"Ball? Ah — *Ball.* Very singular."

7 When rehearsing Handel's *Messiah* Beecham said to the choir, "When we sing 'All we, like sheep, have gone astray,' might we please have a little more regret and a little less satisfaction?"

See also MALCOLM SARGENT 2.

8 Riding in a New York cab, Beecham irritated his companion by repeatedly whistling a passage from Mozart. Eventually the man exclaimed, "Must you do that?" Beecham replied, "You may be able to hear only my whistling; I can hear the full orchestra."

9 In the foyer of a Manchester hotel Beecham saw a distinguished-looking woman whom he believed he knew, though he could not remember her name. He paused to talk to her and as he did so vaguely recollected that she had a brother. Hoping for a clue, he asked how her brother was and whether he was still working at the same job. "Oh, he's very well," she answered, "and still king."

{A similar story is told of President Taft.}

10 The rehearsal had not been going well, with some players apparently unable to keep time. Beecham addressed one of the main offenders: "We cannot expect you to be with us the whole time, but maybe you would be kind enough to keep in touch now and again?"

11 In the first half of a concert Beecham was conducting a Mozart concerto. He and the pianist did not get on together; his conducting lacked luster and the pianist's playing was me-

diocre. During the intermission some adjustments to the stage became necessary. The person in charge asked Beecham, "Should we take the piano off or leave it on?" Beecham mentally ran over the second half of the program, for which a piano was not required. "You might as well leave it on," he said. "It will probably slink off by itself."

12 Beecham and violinist Jean Pougnet were appearing with an orchestra that seemed overawed at rehearsal. The start of the main piece was disastrous. Sir Thomas kept going, and after a while the players began to settle down. He leaned forward to Pougnet and said: "Don't look now, Mr. Pougnet, but I believe we're being followed."

13 A lady asked Sir Thomas's advice on an instrument for her son, concerned about the misery his first efforts on the violin or trombone might inflict upon the household. What instrument would Sir Thomas recommend? Beecham replied, "The bagpipes; they sound exactly the same when you have mastered them as when you first begin learning them."

14 When Beecham conducted the opening night of Richard Strauss's *Elektra* at Covent Garden in 1910, he judged the singing not up to standard. He urged the orchestra to play louder and louder: "The singers think they are going to be heard, and I'm going to make jolly well certain that they aren't."

15 Beecham spent much of World War II in Australia and the Americas. Asked by an Australian journalist why he had left England when his country was at war, Beecham replied: "The government declared a state of emergency, so I obediently emerged."

16 Beecham was once asked why he always chose such generously built ladies for the leading soprano roles in his productions, rejecting the more shapely and attractive candidates. "Unfortunately," replied the conductor with a wistful sigh, "those sopranos who sing like birds eat like horses — and vice versa."

&ﬂ ﻭﺵ

BEECHER, Henry Ward (1813–87), *US Congregational minister and author. Like his sister Harriet Beecher Stowe, he was a fervent campaigner for the abolition of slavery.*

1 In the middle of one of Henry Ward Beecher's most eloquent political speeches, a member of the crowd gave a perfect imitation of a cock crow. The audience roared with laughter, but the speaker gave no sign of annoyance, simply pulling out his watch and studying it until the noise had died down. Then he said, "That's odd. My watch says it's ten o'clock. But there can't be any mistake. It must be morning, for the instincts of the lower animals are absolutely infallible."

2 Arriving at Plymouth church one Sunday, Beecher found in his mail a letter containing just one word: "Fool." During the service that morning, he related the incident to his congregation, adding the remark: "I have known many an instance of a man writing a letter and forgetting to sign his name, but this is the only instance I have ever known of a man signing his name and forgetting to write the letter."

3 During the Civil War, Beecher traveled to England with the aim of arousing British support for the Northern cause. Addressing a turbulent crowd of rebel sympathizers in Manchester, he was asked: "Why didn't you whip the Confederates in sixty days, as you said you would?"

"Because," retorted Beecher, "we found we had Americans to fight instead of Englishmen."

4 Beecher possessed a beautiful globe depicting the various constellations and stars of the heavens. Robert Ingersoll, visiting Beecher one day, admired the globe and asked who had made it. "Who made it?" said Beecher, seizing the opportunity to attack his guest's well-known agnosticism. "Why, nobody made it; it just happened."

&ﬂ ﻭﺵ

BEERBOHM, Sir Max (1872–1956), *British writer, caricaturist, and wit. He wrote several books of essays and parodies and the fanciful romance* Zuleika Dobson *(1911).*

1 When Max was a schoolboy at Charterhouse, his mother came to visit him on a day of school festivities. His housemaster's wife was

wearing a fine new pearl necklace. "Do you see that?" said Max, pointing out the necklace to his mother. "Every pearl represents a boy's empty stomach."

2 (Sir James Barrie, although a Scot, was frequently to be seen as a pallbearer at the funerals of major figures of the English literary establishment. Max recounts an incident at the funeral in 1909 of George Meredith.)
"As I left . . . a young woman rushed up to me, crying, 'Mr. Barrie, Mr. Barrie — you are Mr. Barrie, aren't you? — will you write something for me in my autograph book. Here it is!' . . . I know it was in poor taste; I said nothing, but when I took the volume my pen ran away with me, and I wrote, 'Ay, Lassie! It's a sad day the noo. J. M. Barrie.'"

3 Max had no time for the new psychological theories that pervaded literature in his latter years. Reflecting on his own happy family life, he wondered aloud to a friend what the psychologists would make of him. "I adored my father and mother and I adored my brothers and sisters. What kind of complex would they find me a victim of? Oedipus and what else?" He paused for a moment and then went on, "They were a tense and peculiar family, the Oedipuses, weren't they?"

4 Max's eccentricities may in part have been inherited from his father, Julius Beerbohm. On one occasion, at a party he was not enjoying, one of Julius's daughters-in-law came across him groping his way around the room. She asked if he was looking for something. "The door," exclaimed Mr. Beerbohm.

5 Elisabeth Jungmann, reading about Newton, observed to Max that she would have liked to have met the great scientist. Max, to whom scientific matters were a closed book, said that he would not have understood him. "He would have liked you," persevered Elisabeth. Max was amused: "I would have taught him the law of levity," he said.

6 Beerbohm was entertaining his biographer, S. N. Behrman, at tea. Elisabeth Jungmann, then mistress of the house, brought in a bowl of strawberries that she proudly declared to be from their own garden. "I always say," remarked Max mischievously, "that things from

gardens just haven't got that special something which you find in things bought in a shop, have they?"

❧ ☙

BEETHOVEN, Ludwig van (1770–1827), *German composer. Beethoven's musical talent manifested itself by the time he was five years old. His father had him given a thorough musical training in the hope of exhibiting the boy as an infant prodigy. In 1792 Beethoven moved to Vienna, where he studied with Haydn. After 1798 he was troubled by increasing deafness. Despite this handicap he produced a huge volume of music in many forms: two masses, two ballets, an opera (Fidelio), nine symphonies, five piano concertos, a violin concerto, thirty-two piano sonatas, ten sonatas for violin and piano, and seventeen string quartets. His last years were plagued by financial problems and ill health.*

1 On one occasion when Beethoven was walking with Goethe, Goethe expressed his annoyance at the incessant greetings from passersby. Beethoven replied, "Do not let that trouble Your Excellency; perhaps the greetings are intended for me."

2 When Beethoven composed, he considered himself at one with the Creator and took endless pains to perfect his compositions. On one occasion a violinist complained to him that a passage was so awkwardly written as to be virtually unplayable. Beethoven replied, "When I composed that, I was conscious of being inspired by God Almighty. Do you think I can consider your puny little fiddle when He speaks to me?"

3 Beethoven's Third Symphony, *Eroica*, composed in 1803, was originally entitled "Bonaparte." This was intended as a tribute to the hero of revolutionary France, then First Consul and almost exactly the same age as Beethoven. But Beethoven's admiration soon gave way to disillusionment when Napoleon proclaimed himself emperor in May 1804. Beethoven was in Vienna when he heard of this; in a rage he went to the table where the score lay and tore the title page in two.
{On publication the symphony was given its present title, *Eroica* (Heroic), and it was described as having been composed

"to celebrate the memory of a great man."}

4 Performing a new piano concerto at the Theater An der Wien, Beethoven forgot that he was the soloist and began to conduct. At the first *sforzando,* he threw out his arms with such force that he knocked down the lights on the piano. He began the concerto again, this time with two choir boys holding the lights. On reaching the same *sforzando,* Beethoven repeated his dramatic gesture. He hit one of the boys, who was so frightened that he dropped his light. The other boy anticipated what would happen and dodged the blow. Enraged by the audience's laughter, Beethoven struck the piano with such force that at the first chord six strings broke.

5 His Ninth Symphony (the *Choral*) completed, Beethoven was urged to conduct his latest work at a Vienna concert. After a particular passage, unaware of the thunderous ovation, the composer stood still turning the leaves of his score. Finally one of the singers pulled at his sleeve and pointed to the audience. Beethoven turned, and bowed.

৯৯ ৼ৯

BEGIN, Menachem (1913–), *Israeli statesman; prime minister (1977–83). A hardline Zionist, when he became prime minister he nonetheless engaged in peace negotiations with President Anwar Sadat of Egypt and with him was awarded the 1979 Nobel Peace Prize.*

1 In September 1940 Begin was playing chess with his wife when Russian soldiers burst into his home to arrest him. As they dragged him away, he shouted to Mrs. Begin that he conceded the game.

৯৯ ৼ৯

BEHAN, Brendan (1923–64), *Irish playwright. The Quare Fellow (1954) was based on his experiences under detention for IRA offenses. He also wrote The Hostage (1956) and an autobiography, Borstal Boy (1958).*

1 (During one of his alcoholic periods, Behan arrived at his publisher's office en route for Euston station, wearing his pajamas under his suit. The publicity director, a friend of the family, was to accompany Behan to the station to meet his parents. She had the task of making him a little more presentable.)

"On our way to the station we stopped at an outfitter's in a side street off the Euston Road, and although the clothes in the window had little in common with Brendan, we went in. As I busied myself informing the immaculately dressed assistant that we wanted an overcoat, shirt, and a tie, I did not notice that Brendan was preparing himself enthusiastically for the fitting until, too late, he stood in front of us with not a stitch between himself and his Maker, his suit and his pajamas bunched in a pile by his tiny bare feet. With a dignity that is essentially the mark of a perfect English gentleman, the assistant did not raise an eyebrow as he helped Brendan into his new shirt and back into his trousers as though the sight of a naked customer in his shop was an everyday occurrence."

2 Behan was originally a housepainter by trade, and while in Paris was asked to paint a sign on the window of a café to attract English tourists. He painted, "Come in, you Anglo-Saxon swine / And drink of my Algerian wine. / 'Twill turn your eyeballs black and blue, / And damn well good enough for you." After receiving payment for the job, Behan fled before the café proprietor had time to have the rhyme translated.

3 Behan was asked what he thought of drama critics. "Critics are like eunuchs in a harem," he replied. "They're there every night, they see it done every night, they see how it should be done every night, but they can't do it themselves."

4 Just before he died, Behan looked up at the nursing nun who was taking his pulse. "Bless you, Sister," he said with a weak smile. "May all your sons be bishops!"

৯৯ ৼ৯

BELINSKY, Robert ["Bo"] (1936–), *US baseball player, who became famous when he pitched a no-hit game for the California Angels in 1962.*

1 When Bo was dating the movie actress Mamie van Doren, she came to visit him during preseason training in Palm Springs, and they made the rounds of the night spots. All the players were due in their rooms by midnight. As the witching hour approached, Bo was dancing with Mamie. "I'm sorry, I gotta go, or I'll miss bed check," he explained. "I know, honey," replied Mamie, "I'm dancing as fast as I can."

৯৬ ৪৫

BELL, Alexander Graham (1847–1922), *Scottish inventor, who worked most of his life in North America. Most noted for his invention of the telephone (patented 1876), he also researched the fields of sound recording, aerodynamics, and electro-optical communication.*

1 On March 10, 1876, Bell made the first telephone communication over a line set up between two rooms in a building in Boston. The epoch-making words recorded by Mr. Watson, Bell's assistant, were simply: "Mr. Watson, come here; I want you."

2 As professor of vocal physiology at Boston University, Bell had many deaf pupils, including Mabel Hubbard, who later became his wife. They lived happily together for forty-five years. As Bell lay dying after a long illness, Mabel whispered to him, "Don't leave me." Unable to speak, Bell traced with his fingers the sign "No." With this last silent message, the inventor of the telephone took his final leave of his wife.

৯৬ ৪৫

BELL, Joseph (1837–1911), *Scottish surgeon, the model for Sir Arthur Conan Doyle's Sherlock Holmes. He was consulting surgeon to the Royal Infirmary of Edinburgh.*

1 Bell used a standard experiment to test the powers of perception of each new class of medical students. He held up a tumbler of liquid, explaining that it contained a potent drug with a very bitter taste. "We might easily analyze this chemically," he said, "but I want you to test it by smell and taste and, as I don't ask anything of my students which I wouldn't be willing to do myself, I will taste it before passing it around." The students watched uncomfortably as Dr. Bell dipped a finger into the liquid, put his finger to his lips, and sucked it. Grimacing, he then passed the tumbler around the class and each student in turn dipped a finger into the unknown substance, sucked it, and

shuddered at the bitter taste. The experiment over, Dr. Bell announced: "Gentlemen, I am deeply grieved to find that not one of you has developed this power of perception, which I so often speak about. For, if you had watched me closely, you would have found that, while I placed my forefinger in the bitter medicine, it was the middle finger which found its way into my mouth!"

{In a variant of this story, the liquid in the tumbler is revealed to be urine.}

2 Dr. Bell once attempted to demonstrate the deductive method of diagnosis to a group of students gathered around the bed of one of his patients. "Aren't you a bandsman?" he asked the sick man. His patient nodded. "You see, gentlemen, I am right," said Dr. Bell triumphantly. "It is quite simple. This man has a paralysis of the cheek muscles, the result of too much blowing at wind instruments. We need only inquire to confirm. What instrument do you play, my man?"

"The big drum, doctor."

{This anecdote is also told of others.}

৯৬ ৪৫

BELLOC, [Joseph] **Hilaire** [Pierre] (1870–1953), *English writer of French and British descent. His numerous works include novels, biographies, travelogues, books of light verse, and literary criticism.*

1 Belloc's passionate convictions prompted him in 1906 to seek election as an MP, although he knew that, as a Roman Catholic, he would have a struggle to overcome the voters' religious prejudices. On the occasion of his first campaign speech at Salford he appeared on the rostrum with a rosary in his hand and made the following declaration: "I am a Catholic. As far as possible I go to Mass every day. As far as possible I kneel down and tell these beads every day. If you reject me on account of my religion, I shall thank God that he has spared me the indignity of being your representative." He was elected.

2 At a dinner in Trinity College, Cambridge, Bertrand Russell observed that he had been in a chapel in which the Ten Commandments were written up on two boards and placed where the congregation could read them. Hilaire Belloc, who strongly disapproved of Russell's permissive views on marriage, said, "And I always think when I see boards like that, that there should be a third board over them: 'Candidates should not attempt more than six of these.' "

3 Belloc was a master of insult. The novelist and critic Wilfrid Sheed recalls that an unidentified man came up to Belloc, saying, "You don't know me."

"Yes, I do," replied Belloc, turned on his heel, and walked off.

See also JAMES BARRIE 7.

4 (A. N. Wilson, in his biography of Belloc, states that he heard the following story from several sources but has never been able to substantiate it. It illustrates the strain under which Belloc often worked, turning out book after book, not always up to his highest standard, merely in order to make a difficult livelihood.)

During the 1930s in a railway carriage Belloc noticed a man in front of him reading a volume of his *History of England*. He leaned forward, asked him how much he had paid for it, was informed of the price, took a corresponding sum out of his pocket, gave it to the man, snatched the book from his hand, and tossed it out the window.

৯৯ ৺৪

BELLOWS, George Wesley (1882–1925), *US painter and lithographer, known for his pictures of high-speed action, as in his prizefight series. He was associated with the so-called Ashcan School.*

1 Joseph Pennell once accused Bellows of nonauthenticity for having painted the execution of nurse Edith Cavell by the Germans in 1915 without having been an eyewitness of the event. Bellows retorted that although he had not been present at the execution, "neither had Leonardo da Vinci been present at the Last Supper."

৯৯ ৺৪

BELMONT, August (1813–90), *US financier, born in Prussia of Jewish descent. He came to New York (1837) as agent for the Rothschilds, amassed a huge fortune, and became an American citizen (1844).*

1 An apocryphal story illustrates Belmont's ambiguous position in fashionable New York society, to which his wealth gave him an entrée but in which he was an outsider by reason of his origins. When the invitation committee denied Belmont an invitation to their City Ball, he wrote them: "I have been investigating the accounts of you gentlemen on the Street. Either I get an invitation to the Assembly this year, or else the day after the Assembly each of you will be a ruined man." He got his invitation to the ball. No one else showed up.

৯৯ ৺৪

BEMBO, Pietro (1470–1547), *Italian scholar. He wrote an official history of Venice (published posthumously, 1551) and a treatise on Italian prose, besides poems, essays, and dialogues. In 1539 he was created cardinal.*

1 In Rome Cardinal Bembo gave a splendid dinner. Among the distinguished guests was the Count Montebello, famous for his perfect breeding. During the banquet the count rose from his seat and looked around. He observed the priceless carpets, the mirrors, the bronzes —and shook his head. He let his gaze wander over the wall tapestries, the gold and crystal table service, and shrugged his shoulders. Then his eyes roved over the servants, dressed in silk and satin, ranged against the walls. Finally he walked up to one of the lackeys and spat straight into his mouth. The cardinal, shocked, looked in astonishment at his guest. Montebello explained, "My lord, it was the only place I could find in the whole room where I could spit."

{Apparently this story actually goes back to Aristippus and Diogenes.}

৯৯ ৺৪

BENCHLEY, Robert Charles (1889–1945), *American humorist. He was editor of* Vanity Fair, *drama critic for* Life *and* The New Yorker, *and a member of the famed Algonquin Round Table. He published fifteen volumes of his collected humorous essays and acted in several films.*

1 As an undergraduate at Harvard, Benchley was much given to practical jokes. One day he and a friend were walking in Boston's elegant Louisburg Square. "Come on," said Benchley, "let's get the davenport." Knocking on the door of the nearest house, he told the maid that they had come to fetch the davenport. The maid hesitated, then asked, "Which one?" Robert indicated one that stood just inside the front door. The maid let them in and the two men carried the davenport across the square to another house. When the maid there came to the door, Robert said, "We've brought the davenport. Where shall we put it?" The confused maid showed them the sitting room, and duly depositing the davenport, the two young men left.

2   When Benchley visited Venice for the first time, he sent a cable to Harold Ross, the editor of *The New Yorker,* reading, "Streets full of water. Please advise."

3   At a Hollywood party the guests were playing a game in which each one had to compose his or her own epitaph. An actress, whose marriages and love affairs were notorious, sat next to Benchley. She complained that she could not think what to write about herself. The humorist suggested: "At last she sleeps alone."

4   (Benchley had himself admitted to the hospital to escape an engagement.)
    "The doctor who examined him was the kind that interprets a hangnail as the early symptom of something obscure and hideous. 'Lucky for you this case fell into my hands,' he told Benchley. 'I don't want to alarm you, but all we can do is prescribe in a general way and watch the effects of the treatment, although we don't know precisely what they'll be. Now, these pills —.'
    "Next day the patient was moaning feebly. 'Those pills!' he managed to gasp. 'Doctor, they must have been — you don't suppose —' The frightened doctor whipped back the sheets. Benchley had glued pillow feathers from his shoulder blades to his knees."

5   Passing Ulysses S. Grant's tomb in New York, Benchley was seen to be scribbling something on the back of an envelope, which he slipped under the door of the monument. The note read: "Please leave 2 quarts Grade A and 1 pint whipping cream. U. S. G."

6   Leaving the Algonquin after a particularly alcoholic session, Benchley found himself face to face with a uniformed man whom he took to be the doorman. "Would you get me a taxi, my good man?" he requested. The other drew himself up proudly. "See here, I happen to be a rear admiral in the United States navy," he snapped. "Perfectly all right," said Benchley, "just get me a battleship then."

7   Caught in a rain shower one afternoon, Benchley arrived home soaking wet. "George," he called to his servant, "get me out of this wet suit and into a dry martini."
    {Robert Benchley, in fact, disclaimed credit for this now classic line, stating that it had definitely been said by his friend Charles Butterworth.}

8   Benchley was attending the Broadway premiere of a play during which a telephone rang on an otherwise deserted stage. "I think that's for me," remarked Benchley, and he rose and left the theater.

9   Benchley and Dorothy Parker were visiting a speakeasy when a man showed them what he said was an indestructible watch. They tested this by hitting it against the table top, then throwing it on the floor and stamping on it. The owner picked it up, put it to his ear, and said in incredulous dismay, "It's stopped."
    "Maybe you wound it too tight," said Benchley and Mrs. Parker in chorus.

10   Attending the premiere of *The Squall* in 1926, Benchley was exasperated by the play's use of pidgin English. He whispered to his wife that if he heard one more word of it he was going to leave. At that moment a gypsy girl on stage prostrated herself at the feet of another character and announced, "Me Nubi. Nubi good girl. Me stay." Benchley rose to his feet and said, "Me Bobby. Bobby bad boy. Me go." And he went.

11   A scene in one of Benchley's movie shorts required that he be strung up in a mess of telephone wires above a street. While waiting for the final camera, he said to his wife, Gertrude, "Remember how good at Latin I was in school?"
    "Yes."
    "Well, look where it got me."

12   The office Benchley shared with Dorothy Parker in the Metropolitan Opera House building was so tiny that Benchley observed of it, "One cubic foot less of space and it would have constituted adultery."

13 Someone asked whether Benchley knew the playwright Robert Sherwood, distinguished for his great height — he was six feet seven inches tall. Benchley hopped onto a chair and raised his hand to a level just below the ceiling. "Sure," he said, "I've known Bob Sherwood since he was *this* high."

14 Benchley was horrified when his request for a bank loan was promptly and unconditionally granted. He immediately closed his account. "I don't trust a bank that would lend money to such a poor risk," he said.
See also GROUCHO MARX 4.

15 (In his later years Robert Benchley increasingly succumbed to alcoholism and despair, despising his career in Hollywood as a writer of shorts and a character-part player. Nathaniel Benchley describes a scene at a Hollywood party attended by Robert Sherwood.)
   "At one point, late in the evening, Benchley was heard to say, 'Those eyes — I can't stand those eyes looming at me!' Everybody stopped and turned, and saw Benchley was backing away from Sherwood. They waited, already smiling and set to laugh at the joke that was about to come, but Benchley was serious. He pointed at Sherwood and said, 'He's looking at me and thinking of how he knew me when I was going to be a great writer . . . And he's thinking, now *look* at what I am!' "

ぎ ⊷

BEN-GURION, David (1886–1973), *Israeli socialist statesman, born in Poland. He founded the Israeli Workers' Party in 1930 and became chairman of the Zionist Executive in 1935. When the new Jewish state of Israel was established in 1948, Ben-Gurion became its first prime minister (1948–53) and was prime minister again, from 1955 to 1963.*

1 Members of the Israeli Cabinet did not hesitate to register their disapproval when Ben-Gurion addressed Parliament wearing neither jacket nor tie. Parrying their protests, the prime minister claimed to have Winston Churchill's permission for his unconventional state of dress. "On my last visit to London," he explained, "I wanted to take off my jacket and tie. Churchill stopped me. 'Mr. Prime Minis-

ter,' he said, 'you can only do that in Jerusalem.' "

ぎ ⊷

BENNETT, [Enoch] **Arnold** (1867–1931), *English writer and theater critic. His novels are set in the pottery towns of the English Midlands. Perhaps his finest work is* The Old Wives' Tale.

1 In his review of Arnold Bennett's *The Old Wives' Tale,* the critic Frank Harris complained that the famous public execution scene was obviously written by someone who had never witnessed such an event. He accused Bennett of having a warped imagination and proceeded to write his own version of the scene. This was so appalling and so explicit that Bennett wrote to Harris saying that if Harris's description had been published before *The Old Wives' Tale* had been written, he would have gladly utilized it in the book. He wound up by admitting that he had never actually seen an execution. "Neither have I," wrote back Harris.

2 Bennett usually took great pleasure in getting detail perfect in his fiction. He used to boast that Darius Clayhanger's death in the Clayhanger series could not be bettered: "I took infinite pains over it. All the time my father was dying I was at the bedside making copious notes."

3 Bennett had a serious speech impediment. Once while being presented at court, he saw the Duke of York, later George VI, moving in his direction. The duke also had a speech impediment.
   "Great Scott," Bennett confided to a neighbor, "if he s-s-speaks to me I'll p-p-probably spend my last days in the Tower of London."

4 Irascible and nervous, Bennett was intensely wary of approaches by strangers. One day in London a luckless passerby asked Bennett to tell him the quickest way to Putney Bridge. "There are e-e-eight million people in London," erupted Bennett. "Why the devil can't you ask somebody else?"

5 At a literary luncheon one day, Bennett was autographing copies of his latest book. One young man had arrived clutching three copies of the first edition, but was too embarrassed to ask the author to sign all three at once. Having received his first autograph, he returned to the end of the line, hoping that Bennett would not recognize him when his turn came again. The author signed the second book without comment, and the young man patiently repeated the procedure. Presented with the third copy, however, Bennett paused for a moment. Then he penned on the flyleaf: "To——, who is fast becoming an old friend."

છ્ક ન્ડ

BENNETT, James Gordon (1841–1918), *US newspaper owner and eccentric. In 1887 he launched the Paris edition of the* New York Herald. *He financed a number of expeditions and established international trophies in yachting and automobile racing.*

1 During World War I, whenever news was lacking, Bennett filled in the empty space with "Deleted by French censor."

2 Since Bennett and William Randolph Hearst were never on the best of terms, it did not come as welcome news to the former that Hearst was trying to buy Bennett's paper, the ailing *Herald*. When Hearst tried to find out what it would cost, Bennett cabled him: "Price of Herald three cents daily. Five cents Sunday. Bennett."

3 Bennett's primary goal was to spend all his money. On one occasion he gave a tip of $14,000 to the guard on the Train Bleu between Paris and Monte Carlo. The guard stepped off the train, resigned from his job, and opened a restaurant.

4 Night after night Bennett would return to the same restaurant in Monte Carlo because of the perfect way it prepared a mutton chop. One evening someone else was occupying his favorite table. He ordered the owner to sell him the restaurant and purchased it for $40,000. Bennett then asked the diners at his table to leave, even though they were only halfway through their meal. When Bennett had finished his meal of mutton chops, he left a very large tip: he gave the restaurant back to the owner.

5 One time when he was interviewing a young man for a job on the Paris *Herald,* Bennett suddenly began to squirm in his chair. Then he pulled a bundle of thousand-franc notes from his back pocket, where they'd obviously made him uncomfortable, and threw them into the fire. The surprised young man immediately sprang from his chair and saved them from the flames. "Give them to me," the billionaire shouted. "That's where I want them to be." And he flung them back into the fire.

છ્ક ન્ડ

BENNY, Jack (1894–1974), *US comedian, highly successful in vaudeville, radio, and television. He was also successful in films.*

1 Although generous in real life, Benny was best known for his persona as miser. On one occasion, just before leaving a hotel, the comedian had to visit the rest room. A few minutes later in the cab Benny realized that he did not have his wallet. Surmising that he had dropped it in the toilet cubicle, he asked the driver to go back. Once in the rest room, lacking a dime to get back in the cubicle, Benny peered through the two-foot gap below the door and saw his wallet lying inside. He was flat on his stomach, reaching under the door for the wallet, when another man entered the rest room. The newcomer recognized the tightwad of all tightwads apparently attempting to sneak into a pay toilet. Nothing Benny could say could convince him otherwise.

2 Benny had refused to accept any payment for a certain charity performance. "But just in case I *was* accepting money," he asked, "how much was I refusing?"

3 Benny was never able to make fellow-comedian George Burns laugh. "I thought I had him once in Milwaukee," he told an interviewer. "George telephoned me from downstairs to say that he was coming up. I got undressed and stood naked on a table posing like a statue holding a rose in my hand. I figured when he came in the door, he'd *have* to laugh."
"What happened?"
"He sent the maid in first," replied Benny.

4 Benny was very proud of the fact that a school in his home town of Waukegan, Illinois, was named after him. He made a point of visiting it and speaking to the children whenever he was in the neighborhood. Some ten years after the school opened, Benny found himself addressing a class of twelve-year-olds. His speech

over, he asked if there were any questions. One little boy immediately put up his hand. "Mr. Benny," he asked, "why did they name you after our school?"

5   Benny's wife, Mary, was very fond of expensive jewelry. In 1963, she was held up in her New York hotel suite and robbed of her most treasured piece, a magnificent diamond ring. Benny, in Pittsburgh at the time, learned of the robbery from a reporter. He called Mary several times, only to be told on each occasion that she was out. When he finally got through, his first question was: "Where on earth have you been?"

"At the jeweler's," she replied, "looking for another ring."

"What! At a time like this you're out shopping for a diamond?"

"Sure. It's like when you fall off a horse. If you don't get right back on, you never ride again."

6   On the morning after Benny's death, his widow, Mary, received a single long-stemmed rose, sent without a card from the local florist's. The following day, a second rose was delivered. Mystified, Mary called the florist. She was told that Jack had once said, on leaving the florist's shop, "If anything should happen to me, I want you to send Mary a single rose every day." (He had actually made provision in his will for the florist to supply "one perfect red rose daily for the rest of Mary's life.")

ह‍ও ওई

BENTON, Thomas Hart (1782–1858), *US statesman. He was Democratic senator from Missouri for thirty years (1821–51) and ardently promoted the opening up of the West. Benton accurately foresaw the dangers into which the slavery question was leading the Union.*

1   When Benton's house in Washington was destroyed by fire, he was summoned from Congress to view the ruin. He gazed at it for a while, then said, "It makes dying easier. There's so much less to leave."

2   Benton had never been on good terms with Senator Henry S. Foote of Mississippi. Foote once threatened to write "a little book in which Mr. Benton would figure very largely."

Benton was unperturbed. "Tell Foote," he replied, "that I will write a very large book in which he shall not figure at all."

ह‍ও ওई

BERGEN, Edgar [John] (1903–78), *US ventriloquist and comedian. He made his name on the radio and in films with his dummy Charlie McCarthy.*

1   Invited to the White House, Bergen was stopped by the Secret Service men at the gate because he had no identification. Having searched in vain through all his pockets for some suitable document, he finally opened up his case and took out Charlie McCarthy. The dummy looked at Bergen, then turned to the Secret Service men and said, "Yeah, fellows, he's Edgar Bergen." The ventriloquist was ushered into the White House without further ado.

ह‍ও ওई

BERIA, Lavrenti Pavlovich (1899–1953), *Russian bureaucrat. He was appointed head of the secret police (1938) and became a member of the Presidium (1946). After the power struggle following Stalin's death (1953) he lost favor and was executed.*

1   Stalin's death is reputed to have been caused by a seizure suffered during a fit of rage brought on by an argument with Kliment Voroshilov during a Presidium meeting. Livid with fury, Stalin leaped from his seat, only to crash to the floor unconscious. While other members of the Presidium stared at the apparently dead figure, Beria jumped up and danced around the body shouting, "We're free at last! Free at last!" Stalin's daughter forced her way into the room and fell on her knees by her father. At this point Stalin stirred and opened one eye. Beria at once dropped down beside him, seized his hand, and covered it with kisses.

{Details of this extraordinary scene were supplied to the newspaper *France-Soir*, allegedly by a member of the Presidium present at the meeting.}

ह‍ও ওई

BERLE, Milton (1908–   ), *US performer, lyricist, and author, who began his acting career as a child. He appeared in vaudeville, on Broadway, in motion pictures and television, and in nightclubs.*

1 At dinner one night Berle asked his wife for a glass of water. "Milton," replied Mrs. Berle, "just for tonight why don't you get it yourself?" Berle started for the kitchen door, stopped, and said, "Where do we keep the water?"

છ્ર જ્જ

BERNADOTTE, Jean Baptiste Jules (c. 1763–1844), *French general who became King Charles XIV John of Sweden (1818–44). Rising from humble origins in the French provinces, Bernadotte became connected with Napoleon by marriage and by his military successes. In 1810, with Napoleon's support, he was elected crown prince of Sweden to succeed Charles XIII. In this role and later as king he increased Sweden's territories and internal prosperity.*

1 During the days of the Terror, Bernadotte fought in the French revolutionary army. Later, when king of Sweden, he fell ill and to the consternation of the attending physician, steadfastly refused to be bled. As his condition grew worse, the doctor begged the king to allow him to bleed him. At last the king capitulated. "You must swear," he said, "that you will never reveal to anyone what you have seen." The doctor swore, picked up his lancet, and rolled back the patient's sleeve. On the king's upper arm was a tattoo: the red Phrygian cap and under it the words: "Death to all kings."

છ્ર જ્જ

BERNARD, Tristan (1866–1947), *French dramatist and novelist. His best plays are satires on bourgeois manners and morals, including* Monsieur Codomat *(1907),* Le Prince charmant *(1914), and* La Volonté de l'homme *(1917).*

1 Taking tea one day with a stingy hostess, Bernard was offered a plate of babas au rhum, each cake cut in two. Helping himself, Bernard said politely, "Thank you, madame, I will have a ba."

2 A young playwright sent Bernard a play of his to read and some time later asked Bernard for suggestions for a title. Bernard, who had not read the manuscript, thought for a few seconds, then asked: "Are there any trumpets in your play?"

"No," said the young dramatist, rather puzzled.

"Or any drums?"

"No."

"Well, then, why not call it *Without Drums or Trumpets*?"

{A similar anecdote is told of J. M. Barrie.}

3 One afternoon, during a rather unsettled phase in his first marriage, Bernard was found by a friend gazing despondently into a shop window in the pouring rain. Having ascertained that Bernard had no specific reason for being there, his friend offered to take him for a meal, or at least a drink. The dejected writer declined both invitations. "Surely you're not going to stand out here in the rain!" exclaimed his friend. "Why don't you go home?"

"I don't dare," replied Bernard. "My wife's lover is there." His friend was about to voice some expression of sympathy when Bernard continued, ". . . and he's a goddam bore!"

4 A friend saw Tristan Bernard on the promenade at Deauville wearing a jaunty new yachting cap. When he remarked on it, Bernard replied that he had just bought it with his winnings from the previous night's play at the casino. The friend congratulated him. "Ah," said Bernard, "but what I lost would have bought me the yacht."

5 Bernard once amused a friend with a particularly witty remark. "Only you could have said that!" exclaimed the friend admiringly. Bernard admitted that he had in fact just read the observation in that morning's paper. "But you used it as your own," protested the friend. "Yes, to make it authentic," Bernard replied.

6 Applications to join the French Academy are a serious business, and the elaborate formalities required were antipathetic to Tristan Bernard's temperament. Eventually, succumbing to the urgings of a friend, he scribbled off an application and sent it to the secretary. The latter was still in a state of shock at the casualness of Bernard's approach when a second note arrived, withdrawing the application; Bernard had decided that the academy with its formal

rules, elaborate eighteenth-century costume, and intense seriousness was not for him. The friend rebuked Bernard for his change of heart. "Me an academician?" said Bernard, shaking his head. "No. The costume is too expensive. I'll wait until someone dies who's my size."

7   Bernard was always casual, not to say untidy, about his dress. One day a dandy was boasting that his turnout was so immaculate that his tailor allowed him a discount because he was such an excellent advertisement for the firm. "My tailor also allows me a discount," said Bernard. "It's on condition that I never tell anyone where I buy my suits."
See also EARL OF SANDWICH 2.

8   Tristan Bernard strongly disliked female journalists. One was seated next to him at a press luncheon and said, "Forget that I am a woman; treat me as you would a male colleague." Bernard steadily ignored her existence throughout the meal. At the end, he tapped her on the shoulder and said, *"Allons pisser."*

9   Bernard's frankness often went to extremes. One evening, he had been invited to a dinner party at a house renowned for its excellent cuisine. An hour after the appointed time, Bernard still had not arrived, and his hostess, anxious that the meal should not be ruined, telephoned him to ask what had happened. "I'm so sorry," said Bernard, "but I'm not coming."
"Not coming?"
"No," replied Bernard. "I'm not hungry."

10   The generosity of Bernard, who could never resist the entreaties of a beggar, was one of the causes of his own financial difficulties. One poor wretch, taking advantage of this weakness, would always be found at Bernard's gate at certain fixed times. On one occasion, the old man's eyes widened with delight as he watched his benefactor take a sizable bill from his wallet instead of the usual coins. "We're leaving tomorrow for Normandy," explained Bernard, dropping the bill into the beggar's hat. "Here's two months' donation in advance. You have a right to your vacation, too."

11   Bernard was about to start off in a fiacre one day when the horse either took fright or

---

"A notorious tiepin was once flaunted by Barney Barnato, the cockney 'card' who sold the Kimberley tip to Cecil Rhodes for a bucket of the sparklers. After he had retired to Park Lane, this man with a heart of pure diamond became a famous giver of gifts and a well-known wag. Once, when he was bidden out on the town by some friends, the invitation arrived too late for him to go home and dress, so on his way to dinner Mr. Barnato popped into an outfitter on the Charing Cross Road and bought a pair of paste studs and a paste tiepin of splendiferous vulgarity. Over dinner, as the champagne flowed and the Whitstable oysters slipped smoothly down the throats of one and all, the Diamond King's fellow roisterers were unable to take their eyes off the beacon of light glittering on his shirt front.

" 'By Jove, that's a cracker — good old Kimberley!' one of them finally exclaimed.

"Barnato waved his Romeo y Julieta expansively. 'Anyone who wants it — all he has to do is pay for the wine tonight,' he said.

"They almost knocked the wine steward over in their rush to pick up the tab; and only when copious Krug for six had been duly paid for did Barnato reveal that the tiepin, together with the studs, had cost him ninepence."

— David Frost and Michael Deakin,
*David Frost's Book of
Millionaires, Multimillionaires,
and Really Rich People*

---

had some sort of insane seizure. It reared, kicked, pawed the air with its front hoofs, then fell onto its knees and eventually flopped over, supine, on the ground. Climbing down from the fiacre, Bernard quietly asked the coachman, "Is that all the tricks he knows?"

12   Bernard hated the effort of writing. His apparently spontaneous output was, in fact, a grim, plodding labor, which he would post-

pone whenever he could. If anyone suggested coming to see him, he would say, "Please do. And preferably in the morning. That's when I work."

13 Bernard once won a newspaper competition by providing the best answer to the question: "If a fire broke out in the Louvre and you could save only one painting, which one would it be?" His reply was, "The one nearest the exit."

14 Bernard suffered severe financial embarrassment in later life and at one stage was obliged to withdraw all the money that he had in his account at the Banque de France. With the check for the total amount in his pocket Bernard paused to return the salute of the armed guard stationed outside the bank. "Thank you, my friend," he said. "You may go home now."

15 Bernard and his wife were interned by the Gestapo during World War II. "The time of fear is over," Bernard told his wife when they were arrested. "Now comes the time of hope."
{Bernard survived his ordeal in a concentration camp; other members of his family were less fortunate.}

৯৯ ৩ৎ

BERNERS, Gerald Tyrwhitt-Wilson, 14th Baron (1883–1950), *British musician and artist. He made important contributions to ballet music, notably* A Wedding Bouquet *(1937), for which he also designed the costumes.*

1 "One of his acquaintances was in the impertinent habit of saying to him, 'I have been sticking up for you.' He repeated this once too often, and Lord Berners replied, 'Yes, and I have been sticking up for you. Someone said you aren't fit to live with pigs, and I said that you are.'"

2 "A pompous woman of his acquaintance, complaining that the head waiter of a restaurant had not shown her and her husband immediately to a table, said, 'We had to tell him who we were.' Gerald, interested, inquired, 'And who were you?'"

3 Lord Berners was lunching with guests one day when his butler came in with a large placard. "The gentleman outside says would you be good enough to sign this, my lord," he said. Lord Berners read the message on the placard, "An appeal to God that we may have Peace in our Time," and shook his head. "It wouldn't be any use," he replied. "He won't know who I am — probably has never heard of me."

4 (Ballet dancer Robert Helpmann had been invited to take tea with the eccentric Lord Berners.)
"Helpmann was shown into the drawing room of the peer's mansion near Oxford and found him with an elegant silver tea service and a horse. Lord Berners greeted Helpmann, asked whether he took cream and sugar, and fed buttered scones to the horse. No explanation was offered, and after the animal had been told it had eaten enough, it was led out through the french windows. Much later, Helpmann asked about the horse's presence.
"'I'm very nervous,' Lord Berners explained. 'When people see the horse, they become as nervous as I am, so that after a while I get over it. Then we can have a normal conversation.'"

৯৯ ৩ৎ

BERNHARDT, Sarah (1844–1923), *French actress, famous for her interpretation of great tragic roles, her beautiful voice, and her striking personality.*

1 Bernhardt's debut in the title role of Racine's *Iphigénie* was unimpressive. The scrawny figure of the seventeen-year-old girl was not flattered by the classical Greek dress that she wore, and at the beginning she was plainly suffering from stagefright. At one point in the drama Iphigénie stretches out her arms imploringly to Achilles. As she did this a voice from the balcony called out, "Careful, monsieur, or you'll impale yourself on her toothpicks!"

2 When Bernhardt was twenty-two, she persuaded Félix Duquesnel, the owner of the Odéon, to give her a contract. His partner, Charles-Marie de Chilly, demurred, as he had no wish to gamble on the continuing success of a young actress who already had a reputation for a difficult temperament. "If I were alone in this, I wouldn't give you a contract," he told Sarah. "If you were alone in this, monsieur, I wouldn't sign," was the retort.

3 Sarah Bernhardt was playing Cleopatra in Shakespeare's *Antony and Cleopatra* (one of her most celebrated emotional roles) to a packed theater in Victorian London. She stabbed the messenger who brought her the news of Antony's marriage to Octavia, stormed hysterically, smashed some of the props, and finally, as the curtain fell, flung herself to the floor in a fury of despair. As the rapturous applause died away, a lady's voice was heard to remark, "How different, how very different, from the home life of our own dear queen!"

4 A friend, watching Bernhardt making up for the part of Cleopatra, was intrigued to see her painting the palms of her hands a terra-cotta red. "No one in the audience will possibly see that," objected the friend. "Maybe not," replied the actress, "but if I catch sight of my hands, then they will be the hands of Cleopatra."

5 The actress Madge Kendal, though an admirer, once complained that Bernhardt always acted in roles requiring such displays of passion that Mrs. Kendal felt she could not take her daughter to see her. Bernhardt replied, "But, madame, you should remember that were it not for passion, you would have no daughter to bring."

6 In the United States a clergyman spoke of Bernhardt as "an imp of darkness, a female demon sent from the modern Babylon to corrupt the New World." Sarah responded with a note: "My dear confrère, why attack me so violently? Actors ought not to be hard on one another. Sarah Bernhardt."

7 Clergymen across the United States, in fact, denounced Sarah Bernhardt from their pulpits as the "whore of Babylon," thereby ensuring massive attendance at her performances. The Episcopalian bishop of Chicago having delivered a particularly effective piece of publicity, Bernhardt arranged for her agent to send him a note and a bank draft. "Your Excellency," the note read, "I am accustomed, when I bring an attraction to your town, to spend $400 on advertising. As you have done half the advertising for me, I herewith enclose $200 for your parish."

8 After a magnificent performance in Victorien Sardou's *Fédora,* Sarah Bernhardt received a thunderous ovation. The applause gradually turned to laughter, however, as members of the audience noticed two one-armed men in the front row of the gallery. Eager to show their appreciation of the actress's performance, the two were enthusiastically clapping their remaining hands together.

9 During a rehearsal of one of his plays, Oscar Wilde quarreled with Miss Bernhardt over how her part should be interpreted. An impasse having been reached, Wilde asked, "Do you mind if I smoke, madame?"
  "I don't care if you burn," snapped Sarah.

10 It was such common knowledge that Sarah Bernhardt, celebrated for her almost skeletal thinness, was given to wild exaggeration that Dumas *fils* was driven to comment, "You know, she's such a liar, she may even be fat!"

11 In 1915, as the result of an accident while Sarah Bernhardt was playing the title role in Victorien Sardou's drama *La Tosca,* one of her legs had to be amputated. While she was convalescing, the manager of the Pan-American Exposition at San Francisco asked permission to exhibit her leg, offering a fee of $100,000. Sarah cabled two words in reply: "Which leg?"

12 An admirer of a certain young English performer was discussing her acting with Sarah Bernhardt, who was not at all convinced of the young woman's talent. "But surely," said the man, "you will at least admit that she has some wonderful moments."
  "Maybe, but also some terrible half-hours," countered Sarah.

13 Sarah Bernhardt went to see Nijinsky dance Michel Fokine's ballet *Petrushka.* Her comment: "I'm afraid, I'm afraid, for I am watching the world's greatest actor."

14 Sarah Bernhardt was so idolized by her colleagues in the Paris theater that the callboy would notify her of the first-act curtain with the words: "Madame, it will be eight o'clock when it suits you."

15 Shortly after World War I, Lucien Guitry was asked to play opposite Bernhardt in a charity performance. The great actress was by now

in her seventies, her former beauty had vanished, and she walked on a wooden leg. The magical quality of her voice, however, and her ability to deliver even the most ordinary lines with emotion still shone through. At the first rehearsal of the scene, Bernhardt read to the end of her first long speech and waited for Guitry's reply. Hearing no response, she looked up from her script to find him overcome, tears running down his cheeks.

16   In her later years, Sarah Bernhardt lived high up in a Paris apartment block. An old admirer arrived at her door one day, gasping for breath after the long climb. When he had recovered his strength a little, he inquired, "Madame, why do you live so high up?"

"My dear friend," replied the actress, "it is the only way I can still make the hearts of men beat faster."

৵ ৶

BERNOULLI, Jacques (1654–1705), *Swiss mathematician of Flemish descent and one of a notable family of mathematicians. He is known for his work on the calculus of variations and the theory of complex numbers.*

1   "[Bernoulli] had a mystical strain which . . . cropped out once in an interesting way toward the end of his life. There is a certain spiral (the logarithmic or equiangular) which is reproduced in a similar spiral after each of many geometrical transformations. [Bernoulli] was fascinated by this recurrence of the spiral, several of whose properties he discovered, and directed that a spiral be engraved on his tombstone with the inscription *Eadem mutata resurgo* (Though changed I shall arise the same)."

৵ ৶

BERNSTEIN, Henri (1876–1953), *French dramatist. After his early success with melodramas, Bernstein was mainly concerned to attack anti-Semitism and nazism in a number of serious plays.*

1   Shortly before his death Bernstein visited Hollywood. He was unimpressed. "Genius and geniuses every way I turn!" he lamented. "If only there were some talent!"

৵ ৶

BERNSTEIN, Leonard (1918–   ), *US conductor, composer, and pianist. His compositions include the symphony* Jeremiah *(1942) and the musical* West Side Story *(1958).*

1   Bernstein's father was criticized for not having given his talented son more encouragement when he was a child. "How was I to know he would grow up to be Leonard Bernstein?" he protested.

2   Arriving at an airport one day, Bernstein was asked by a photographer if he would mind posing for a picture astride a motorcycle. Bernstein objected. "I don't ride a motorcycle," he said. "It would be phony." The photographer tried to persuade him. He showed him the con-

"The perils of irony were never better illustrated than in the following example: Lord Justice Bowen, when acting as a Puisne Judge, had before him a burglar who, having entered a house by the top story, was captured below stairs in act of sampling the silver. The defence was more ingenuous than ingenious. The accused was alleged to be a person of eccentric habits, much addicted to perambulating on the roofs of adjacent houses, and occasionally dropping in 'permiscuous' through an open skylight. This naturally stirred the judge to caustic comment. Summing up, he is reported to have said:

"'If, gentlemen, you think it likely that the prisoner was merely indulging in an amiable fancy for midnight exercise on his neighbour's roof; if you think it was kindly consideration for that neighbour which led him to take off his boots and leave them behind him before descending into the house; and if you believe that it was the innocent curiosity of the connoisseur which brought him to the silver pantry and caused him to borrow the teapot, then, gentlemen, you will acquit the prisoner!'

"To Lord Bowen's dismay, the jury *did* instantly acquit the prisoner."

— Daniel George,
A Book of Anecdotes

trols, explaining briefly how to operate them. "I'm sure you could ride it if you tried," he said encouragingly. Bernstein climbed onto the machine and, to the horror of his colleagues, shot off at top speed across the airfield. After a few other maneuvers he returned, grinning broadly. "Now you can take your picture," he announced. "I'm a motorcycle rider."

ॐ ॐ

BERNSTEIN, Robert (1923–), *US publisher, currently president of Random House, New York City.*

1 As a quite young man, Robert Bernstein had a job at New York's radio station WNEW. Albert Leventhal, head of sales of the publishing house of Simon and Schuster, liked the looks of the tall, red-headed, engaging Bernstein and enticed him into publishing. Bernstein turned out to be a phenomenon of energy. Once Leventhal, happening to enter the office at the early hour of 7:30 A.M., found his protégé already busy at work. Bernstein looked up at his boss and said: "I'm ambitious. What's your excuse for being here at this unearthly hour?"

ॐ ॐ

BERRA, Lawrence ["Yogi"] (1925–), *US baseball player. A great catcher and hitter, Berra was three times nominated Most Valuable Player in the American League, but is perhaps most famous for his verbal confusions.*

1 On one occasion when the New York Yankees were not drawing well, Berra said, "If the people don't want to come out to the park, nobody's gonna stop them."
{Variants of this remark are attributed to other entertainers.}

2 Taken to a famous restaurant of which he had never heard, Yogi looked around the packed place and observed, "No wonder nobody comes here—it's too crowded."

3 Yogi Berra read only the sports pages, so he was clearly at a loss when introduced to novelist Ernest Hemingway in a restaurant. Someone asked Berra if he had ever heard of the famous author. "I don't think so," Berra admitted. "What paper does he write for?"

4 On "Yogi Berra Day" in St. Louis, his home town, Berra opened his acceptance speech by saying, "I want to thank all the people who made this night necessary."

5 Berra once received a twenty-five-dollar check for a radio interview with sportscaster Jack Buck. Berra glanced at the check, which was made out to "Bearer," and promptly complained: "How the hell long have you known me, Jack? How could you spell my name like that?"

6 Having ordered a pizza, Berra was asked whether he would like it cut into four or eight pieces. "Better make it four," said Yogi. "I don't think I can eat eight."

ॐ ॐ

BETTY, William Henry West (1791–1874), *English actor, nicknamed "the Child Roscius." As a child prodigy, Betty was such a success that the military had to be called out to restore order among the crowd that flocked to his Covent Garden debut in London (1804).*

1 After Betty's triumph, the English stage was beset by a multitude of juvenile imitators. Dorothea Jordan, the actress who was mistress of the Duke of Clarence (later William IV), surveying the throng of would-be Bettys, exclaimed, "Oh, for the days of King Herod!"
{The opening night of J. M. Barrie's *Peter Pan* in 1904 wrung a similar comment from novelist Anthony Hope Hawkins: "Oh, for an hour of Herod." See Matthew 2:16.}

ॐ ॐ

BEUNO, Saint (died c. 640), *abbot of Clynnog (North Wales).*

1 When the chapel in which the saint's bones were believed to be interred was being renovated, it was necessary to open the tomb itself. This offered an opportunity to discover more about the relics. An anthropologist was called in to inspect the skeleton. He pointed out that its pelvis contained the bones of a fetus. The man in charge of the renovation was unsurprised. "Saint Beuno was a very remarkable man," he observed.

ॐ ॐ

BEVAN, Aneurin ["Nye"] (1897–1960), *British Labour statesman. The son of a miner, he* *was born in Wales and himself became a miner at thirteen. Renowned as an orator, he represented Ebbw Vale in Parliament from 1929 until his death. As minister of health (1945–51) he introduced the National Health Service (1948).*

1   Bevan once asked Harold Wilson: "Were you really born in Yorkshire?"

"Not just born, Nye," replied Wilson proudly, "forged."

"I always thought there was something counterfeit about you," remarked Bevan.

2   While minister of health, Bevan often brought work home with him. Almost every night he would retire to a small bedroom at the top of the house, clutching a briefcase bulging with cabinet documents. One night, after several hours' work, he asked his wife to bring up a second batch of papers. "No," she replied firmly. "One you may have. But taking two to bed is positively immoral."

გა ❧

BEVIN, Ernest (1881–1951), *British trade-union leader and statesman. He founded the powerful Transport and General Workers' Union and served as its general secretary from 1921 to 1940. In Churchill's wartime government he was minister of labor and in the first postwar government the prime minister, Clement Attlee, made him foreign secretary.*

1   Bevin never cultivated an upper-class accent and had few aspirates in his speech. At an early meeting of Attlee's cabinet, it was decided that a subcommittee of two should be formed to investigate a certain problem. When Attlee suggested this, Bevin spoke up, proposing that it should consist of "You and I." Half the cabinet thought that the subcommittee would consist of Attlee and Bevin, while the other half thought the proposal was for 'Ugh (Hugh Dalton) and Nye (Aneurin Bevan).

2   Nor did it faze Bevin a bit to mix his metaphors. Once, in rejecting a Foreign Office recommendation, he said: "I ain't 'avin' it. If you open up that Pandora's box you'll find a lot of Trojan 'orses inside."

3   There was little love lost between Bevin and Aneurin Bevan. When another member of

the cabinet described Bevan as his own worst enemy, Bevin was heard to mutter, "Not while I'm around."

{This anecdote is told of others.}

4   Shortly after taking up his post as foreign secretary, Bevin returned to his office one Friday afternoon and found a heap of documents on his desk. The attached note read: "The Secretary of State may care to peruse these at his leisure before Monday." Bevin added a note of his own and left the office without having looked at the documents. His note read: "A kindly thought, but erroneous."

გა ❧

BEWICK, Thomas (1753–1828), *British wood engraver. He revived wood engraving as an art form and used it to excellent effect to illustrate his volumes of natural history.*

1   When Bewick died, he left his last wood engraving unfinished. Its title was *The Old Horse Waiting for Death.*

გა ❧

BIALIK, Chaim Nachman (1873–1934), *Jewish poet, born in the Ukraine. His work, in particular* The Talmud Student *(1894), was fundamental to the establishment of a modern Hebrew literature. From 1924 he lived in Palestine.*

1   (A few days before Bialik's death, the newspapers were full of speculation that he would be awarded the Nobel Prize for literature.)

"When the prize was awarded to another writer, Bialik was asked for his reaction. 'I'm very glad I didn't win the prize,' he said. 'Now everybody's my friend and feels sorry for me. My, my how angry they are on my behalf! "Now isn't that a scandal," they say. "Imagine such a thing—Bialik, the great poet Bialik, doesn't get the Nobel Prize! And—tsk! tsk!—just look who they gave it to! To X, that so-and-so! Why, he can't even hold a candle to Bialik!"

"'On the other hand, what if I had been awarded the Nobel Prize? Then, I'm sure, some of the very same people who are now so indignant on my account would have said, "Nu, nu, what's so wonderful about getting the Nobel Prize? Why, even that poet Bialik got one!"'"

See also CATO THE CENSOR 3; BENJA-
MIN DISRAELI 9; ABBÉ GABRIEL BON-
NET DE MABLY 1.

ào ·oś

BING, Sir Rudolf (1902–   ), *Austrian-born
opera administrator. He was manager of
the Glyndebourne Festival Opera (1935–39,
1946–49), artistic manager of the Edinburgh
Festival (1947–49), and general manager of the
Metropolitan Opera, New York (1950–72).*

1 At one of the early Glyndebourne seasons,
Bing engaged the Italian singer Salvatore Baccaloni. Artistically the engagement was a success, but Baccaloni could be very temperamen-
tal. The problems were exacerbated by the fact
that he could speak only Italian while Bing
spoke none at all. Baccaloni would storm into
Bing's office and deliver a flood of Italian, to
which Bing would listen uncomprehendingly.
When he seemed to have finished what he had
to say, Bing would solemnly hand him a five-
pound note. This always seemed to appease
Baccaloni.

2 (In *5000 Nights at the Opera,* Sir Rudolf
Bing tells the following story about the Munich
crisis in 1939:)
  "Edwards had volunteered Glyndebourne as
an evacuation center for London children in
the event of war. . . . The day after Nina and
I returned to Glyndebourne, the buses arrived
from London; and some three hundred children and seventy-two adults from south
London — the children ranging in age from
upper-nursery-school down to ten days —
were dumped on the Glyndebourne lawn.
There were not enough rooms for so many,
of course — and nowhere near enough bathrooms. I raced to Woolworth's in Lewes, and
asked the shop assistant, 'Do you keep
chamber pots?' She said the store did have
chamber pots available, and I said, 'Give me six
dozens, please.' It made quite a sensation."

3 When Bing arrived in the United States in
November 1949 to take up his appointment at
the Metropolitan Opera, he was interviewed
on board ship before it docked. The reporter
began, "I am supposed to ask tactless questions." Bing replied, "And I am supposed to
give evasive answers."

4 The Secret Service men were worried about
security at a Washington performance of *La
Bohème* that President Eisenhower was to attend. They interrogated Bing: "We hear the girl
dies. How is she killed?" He replied, "She dies
of consumption. It isn't contagious at a distance."

5 (Birgit Nilsson had a magnificent success in
Tristan and Isolde in New York. A few days
later Tristan, sung by Ramon Vinay, fell ill, and
each of the two possible substitutes was similarly sick. It was too late by then to change the
program.)
  "I consulted with Miss Nilsson and then
spoke with my three tenors again. None of
them felt up to an entire *Tristan;* could each of
them take an act? They agreed. When the house
lights went down, before the music began, I
came onto the stage, and was greeted by a great
moan from all corners of the house — the
general manager appears only to make the
most important announcements, and everyone
thought he knew that this announcement had
to be: Miss Nilsson has canceled.
  "So I began by saying, 'Ladies and gentlemen, Miss Nilsson is very well,' which brought
a sign of relief from almost four thousand people. Then I went on: 'However, we are less
fortunate with our Tristan. The Metropolitan
has three distinguished Tristans available, but
all three are sick. In order not to disappoint
you, these gallant gentlemen, against their doctors' orders, have agreed to do one act each.'
There was laughter in the house. I added, 'Fortunately, the work has only three acts.'"

6 Bing disliked the negotiations with the
trade unions at the Metropolitan Opera because of the hysteria and sense of confrontation they generated. At one session with representatives of the stagehands, he leaned across
the table toward the trade union's lawyer and
said, "I'm awfully sorry, I didn't get that.
Would you mind screaming it again?"

7 Bing was mugged one day while walking his
dog in Central Park, losing his money and his
watch. Although the watch was worth only
about twenty-five dollars, its loss particularly
grieved Bing since it was a British Army watch,
a souvenir of his time as a fire warden in Britain
during World War II. This incident found its
way into the newspapers. Next day at the opera

house he was severely rebuked by soprano Zinka Milanov. "The general manager of the Metropolitan Opera does not carry a watch worth only twenty-five dollars," she said sternly.

8 In Sir Rudolf Bing's *5000 Nights at the Opera* there is a photograph of the author sitting all alone in the old Metropolitan Opera House, a solitary figure in a sea of empty seats. On seeing this picture his brother commented, "No wonder you have a deficit."

9 When Bing engaged Maria Callas to sing the Queen of the Night in *The Magic Flute,* the star expressed mild surprise at the fee he offered her: "It doesn't make sense for you to pay me such a big fee for such a small part."

"I have a solution," said Bing, "reduce your fee."

10 When Bing canceled Maria Callas's contract with the Metropolitan Opera, in 1958, he engaged Leonie Rysanek to sing Lady Macbeth in Verdi's opera. He was fearful, however, that the audience, resenting the absence of Callas, would give Rysanek a hostile reception. He therefore hired a claqueur to shout *"Brava, Callas,"* as Rysanek made her first entrance. As he had guessed, the Met audience rallied to the stand-in, and the performance was a great success.

11 A flu epidemic hit the cast of the New York Met, so Bing pinned up a list of precautions to prevent further spread of the infection. The last item on the list read: "Confine your kissing to the irresistible."

ঌ ❧

BION (2d century BC), *Greek philosopher, born in what is now southern Russia. When a boy, he was sold as a slave to a teacher of rhetoric who realized his talents and freed him. He studied at Athens and lived some time at the royal court of Macedon, where he became famous for his pithy sayings.*

1 Bion undertook a sea voyage on a vessel manned by a particularly dissolute and wicked crew. A storm blew up and the sailors began to pray loudly to the gods for deliverance. Bion advised them to keep quiet: "Rather let them *not* know where you are."

BISMARCK, Otto Eduard Leopold, Prince von (1815–98), *German statesman; first chancellor of the German Empire (1871–90). Bismarck was the architect of Prussian supremacy among the German states, successfully undermining Austria's dominance. Following Austria's defeat in the Austro-Prussian War (1866), Prussia's William I became president of the North German Confederation. After the Franco-Prussian War (1870–71), William became emperor, with Bismarck as his chancellor. Known as the Iron Chancellor, Bismarck set his face against liberalism; he also encountered opposition from the Roman Catholic Church. In 1890 he resigned when he and the new emperor, William II, clashed over the abolition of antisocialist legislation.*

1 Bismarck's career in the Prussian civil service was unsuccessful and brief. He fell in love, overstayed his leave, got into debt, and eventually tendered his resignation. He was then twenty-four years old. Five years later he tried to make a fresh start in the civil service, but resigned in less than a month, saying, "I have never been able to put up with superiors."

2 The Seven Weeks' War between Prussia and Austria in 1866 was almost entirely engineered by Bismarck, who wished to establish Prussia's position as leader of the German states instead of Austria. Sanctioning the advance of the divisions under General Manteuffel's command across the River Elbe into Austrian territory, Bismarck telegraphed the general: "Treat them as fellow countrymen, homicidally if necessary."

3 During the Franco-Prussian War of 1870 a German prince complained to Bismarck that the Iron Cross was being too freely awarded to the undeserving. Bismarck replied that unfortunately this was unavoidable; a certain number of persons would have to be decorated for reasons of protocol or out of mere politeness. He added, "After all, Your Highness, you and I have it too."

4 At a ball in St. Petersburg Bismarck entertained his attractive partner with the usual pleasant flatteries. But she would have none of it, exclaiming, "One can't believe a word you diplomats say."

"What do you mean?" said Bismarck.

"Well, when a diplomat says 'Yes,' he means 'perhaps.' When he says 'perhaps,' he means 'no.' And if he should say 'no'—well, he's no diplomat."

To which Bismarck replied, "Madam, you are quite right, it's part of our profession, I fear. But with you ladies the exact opposite is the case."

"How so?"

"When she says 'no,' she means 'perhaps.' When she says 'perhaps,' she means 'yes.' And if she says 'yes'—well, she's no lady."

{This story is probably apocryphal.}

5   An American visitor to Berlin in the days when Bismarck was chancellor was eager to hear him speak. She obtained two tickets for the Reichstag visitors' gallery, employing an interpreter to accompany her. Soon after they arrived, Bismarck rose to intervene in a debate. He spoke with force and at some length, and the interpreter sat listening with intense concentration, ignoring the nudges of the American, who was anxious for him to begin translating. At last she could keep quiet no longer and burst out, "What is he saying?"

"Patience, madam," replied the interpreter. "I am waiting for the verb."

{Probably an old joke.}

6   Bismarck, a stickler for formality, was once seated at dinner next to a young, ebullient American lady. At first she addressed him correctly as "Your Highness." With the next course he became "Mr. Chancellor" and with the third course "My dear Mr. Bismarck." As the plates were changed once more, he smiled and said amiably, "My first name is Otto."

7   He had been conversing for rather a long time with the English ambassador when the latter posed the question: "How do you handle insistent visitors who take up so much of your valuable time?" Bismarck answered, "Oh, I have an infallible method. My servant appears and informs me that my wife has something urgent to tell me." At that moment there was a knock at the door and the servant entered with a message from his wife.

8   In 1878 Disraeli and Bismarck were among those representing their countries at the Berlin Conference. As part of the Berlin settlement Britain managed to win Cyprus from Turkey. Bismarck seemed very pleased on Disraeli's behalf and told him, "You have done a wise thing. That is progress. It will be popular. A nation likes progress." Describing this encounter later to Queen Victoria, Disraeli observed of Bismarck, "His idea of progress was evidently seizing something."

9   A friend greeting Bismarck on his eightieth birthday wished him many more happy years. Bismarck thanked him, adding, "But, you know, the first eighty years of a man's life are always the happiest."

❧   ❦

BLACK, Hugo (1886–1971), *US jurist, politician, and Supreme Court justice.*

1   Justice Black was attending the funeral of a dignitary whom he had heartily disliked and whose funeral he would not have attended had it not been expected of him. Another judge, arriving late, tiptoed into his place next to Black and whispered, "How far has the service got?" Black whispered back, "They've just opened for the defense."

❧   ❦

BLACKWELL, Alexander (died 1747), *British adventurer. He failed as a printer in London and spent two years in jail, from which he was rescued by the efforts of his wife, Elizabeth, who produced a popular herbal, the sales of which paid off his debts. He later became involved in a mysterious plot in Sweden and was tortured and executed.*

1   Sentenced to be decapitated, Blackwell came to the block and laid his head on the wrong side. The executioner pointed out his mistake. Blackwell moved around to the correct side, observing that he was sorry for the mistake, but this was the first time that he had been beheaded.

❧   ❦

BLAKE, Eubie [James Hubert Blake] (1883–1983), *black American jazz pianist and composer. The son of former slaves, he studied the piano with a classical musician, but his first musical engagement involved playing in a* *brothel. His "Charleston Rag" was written in 1899; perhaps his best-known song is "I'm Just Wild about Harry," which Harry S. Truman later used as his election theme song.*

1 Asked why he played so many of his compositions in complicated sharp or flat keys, Eubie replied, "Down South where I come from, you don't go round hittin' too many white keys."

2 On Sunday, February 13, 1983, the London *Observer* carried in its feature "Sayings of the Week" a quotation from centenarian Eubie, who had smoked since he was six and refused to drink water. "If I'd known I was going to live this long, I'd have taken better care of myself," he was reported as saying.

ঌ ✑

BLAKE, William (1757–1827), *English artist, poet, and mystic. He engraved his own illustrations to his poetical works, which included* Songs of Innocence *(1789),* Songs of Experience *(1794), and* Jerusalem *(1808–18). Among other books he illustrated were Gray's* Poems, *Dante's* Divina commedia, *and the Book of Job. His mystical philosophy is set out in* The Marriage of Heaven and Hell *(1790). The abstruse symbolism of his work won him few admirers during his lifetime.*

1 Blake and his wife, Catherine, were once sitting naked in their garden, reciting to each other passages from *Paradise Lost*. Blake was not at all embarrassed when a visitor called on them. "Come in!" he cried. "It's only Adam and Eve, you know."

2 When Blake was fourteen years old, his father planned to apprentice him to the engraver William Ryland. He took the boy to visit Ryland's studio and the arrangement seemed acceptable to both parties, when young Blake suddenly took a violent dislike to his future master. The only justification he could make to his father was: "I do not like the man's face. He looks as if he will live to be hanged." Ryland was then a famous and respected figure, so the boy's objection seemed totally irrational, but his father was obliged to forgo his original intention and apprentice William to the comparatively unknown engraver James Basire. Many years later Ryland became bankrupt

after the failure of his business and in his desperation committed a forgery. His crime was discovered and he was hanged.

3 From childhood Blake had seen visions. One of the earliest stories recounted of him was that he told his parents he had seen a tree full of angels. This angered his father, who thought the boy was willfully telling lies. In later years Blake habitually talked about the supernatural subjects of his pictures as being actually present in his studio when he was drawing them. A visitor once surprised him hard at work on a picture of an invisible sitter. He looked and drew, drew and looked, apparently intent on capturing a likeness. "Do not disturb me, I have one sitting to me," he said. "But there's no one here," exclaimed the visitor. "But I see him, sir," replied Blake haughtily. "There he is — his name is Lot — you may read of him in the Scriptures. He is sitting for his portrait."

ঌ ✑

BLAND-SUTTON, Sir John (1855–1936), *British surgeon.*

1 (For five years Bland-Sutton carried out examinations of animals that had died at London Zoo, and from these dissections gained considerable knowledge of comparative anatomy and the health of various species. He also took an interest in the living animals.)

"The lemurs are pretty animals and very liable to suffer from cataract. I was very much attached to a ring-tailed lemur with a cataract in each eye, and asked . . . the Superintendent to allow me to remove them. He asked me if I had removed a cataract from a man's eye successfully. I replied, 'No.' He said indignantly, 'How can you expect me to let you operate on a lemur, if you have not operated on a man successfully! This lemur is worth £50.'"

ঌ ✑

BLECH, Leo (1871–1958), *German composer and conductor.*

1 At a rehearsal of the orchestra of the Berlin State Opera Company, one of the players could not follow Blech's beat. "You're new here?" asked Blech. "Yes, I started only yesterday," replied the player. "Well, your difficulty is understandable," said Blech. "Let's work at it till we get it right." He spent two hours working with the performer, then said, "Now it sounds right and tomorrow at the premiere you'll be perfect." The player replied, "But I won't be here tomorrow. I'm only here to help out with the rehearsals."

❧ ☙

BLESSINGTON, Marguerite, Countess of (1789–1849), *British author and society leader. At Gore House, where she lived with Count d'Orsay, husband of her stepdaughter, Lady Blessington was the center of a cosmopolitan set who did not mind that she kept the bailiffs at bay by writing for money (then considered rather shocking in a lady). In 1849, overwhelmed by debts, she fled to Paris, where she died.*

1   In the late 1830s, between his first and second abortive attempts to regain the French throne, the future Emperor Napoleon III frequented Lady Blessington's salon. But when she arrived in Paris, pursued by scandal and debts, Napoleon, then returned from exile and president of the Republic, felt it would be an embarrassment to recognize her. After waiting in vain for an invitation from her former protégé, Lady Blessington managed to accost him at a reception. "*Ah, Miladi Blessington!*" said Napoleon distantly. "*Restez-vous longtemps à France?*" (Are you staying in France for some time?) Lady Blessington curtsied. "*Et vous?*" (And you?) she inquired sweetly.

❧ ☙

BLUME, Judy (1938–   ), *US writer of realistic stories for and about young teenagers.*

1   Judy Blume was once accosted by a woman who had been so upset by two pages about wet dreams in Ms. Blume's novel *Then Again Maybe I Won't* that she had torn them out of her son's copy. "What if they had been about a girl's menstruation?" inquired the author. "Would you still have torn the pages out?"
"Oh, no, that's normal," said the mother.

❧ ☙

BLUMENTHAL, Oskar (1852–1917), *German playwright, journalist, and critic.*

1   Blumenthal and his friend, critic Ludwig Sternaux, were discussing a play that had opened the previous night. "I'm amazed the audience didn't hiss it," observed Sternaux. "Well, you can't yawn and hiss at the same time," said Blumenthal.

❧ ☙

BOAS, Franz (1858–1942), *US anthropologist. Boas specialized in American Indian culture and primitive cultures in general. In effect he founded the American school of cultural relativism and helped destroy, at least for the reflective, the myth of racial superiority. His writings include* The Mind of Primitive Man *(1911) and* Anthropology and Modern Life *(1928).*

1   When the United States entered World War I in 1917, Boas was professor of anthropology at Columbia University, New York City. At that time the university's president was Nicholas Murray Butler, a paragon of orthodoxy and general respectability. He sent a questionnaire to the entire faculty, asking what they proposed to do to help the war effort. Boas drew a line through the question and filled in his answer: "Mind my own business."

❧ ☙

BOGARDE, Dirk (1921–   ), *British film actor of Dutch descent. From mainly lightweight romantic or adventure films in the 1940s and 1950s Bogarde graduated to major roles in such superior pictures as* The Servant *(1963) and* Death in Venice *(1970).*

1   Dirk Bogarde was of two minds as to whether he should accept the part of the barrister in the film *Victim,* since the story concerned a secret homosexual relationship, a very daring theme for the time. Most of the actors who had been approached for the part had turned it down flat. Bogarde decided to ask his father's advice: "Pa . . . would you mind if I made a rather difficult film . . . I mean difficult in the moral sense — serious stuff?"
"I don't think I quite follow you. Political, do you mean?"
"Homosexual."
His father mopped his brow and took a refreshing sip of beer. "Oh, my dear boy, we get so much of that sort of thing on television. Mother and I find it dreadfully boring, all those doctors and psychiatrists bumbling on. Now if you want to do something really serious, why

on earth don't you do *The Mayor of Caster-bridge?*"

2 After his rise to fame, pictures of Bogarde appeared all over London, including the Underground stations. One day he received an irate phone call from his father. "I've just come through Charing Cross Underground," he said. "I suppose you realize that you have brought the family name down as low as you possibly could?" Distressed, Bogarde made no further reference to the incident for some time. "My dear boy," cried his father when the subject was finally broached. "It was just a joke. Charing Cross is the *deepest* station in London — didn't you know?"

છ્ક ≈§

BOGART, Humphrey (1899–1957), *US film star. After years of playing gangsters in second-rate Hollywood films he emerged as everyman's (or more particularly everywoman's) image of a tough guy with a big heart. His greatest hits were* Casablanca *(1942), with Ingrid Bergman;* To Have and Have Not *(1944), with his future wife, Lauren Bacall, and* The African Queen *(1952), with Katharine Hepburn.*

1 Taking Verita Peterson, his hairdresser and mistress, to Romanoff's restaurant for the first time, Bogart introduced her to Mike Romanoff as Petée Gonzales, a Mexican actress who spoke very little English. Somewhat surprised, Verita played along with the joke, talking in mock Spanish to Bogart and in very broken English to Romanoff. As they left, she complained to Bogart that she would now have to take on this persona every time she went to Romanoff's. Bogart said he had a solution. When they returned to Romanoff's a few days later, "Good evening, Señorita Gonzales!" cried the proprietor. A look of horror passed across Bogart's face. "What the hell's the matter with you, Mike?" he growled. "You getting senile or something? This is my executive secretary, Verita Peterson. Christ! Can't you tell one broad from another? This is really *embarrassing!*"

છ્ક ≈§

BOHR, Niels Henrik David (1885–1962), *Danish physicist. With British physicists J. J. Thomson and Ernest Rutherford, he suggested a version of atomic structure that is the forerun-ner of the current model, and was awarded the Nobel Prize in 1922. In the 1930s Jewish and other refugees from Nazi-controlled countries came to work at Bohr's Institute of Theoretical Physics in Copenhagen. During World War II Bohr himself had to flee to the United States, where he worked at Los Alamos on the atomic bomb. In 1955 he chaired the first Atoms for Peace conference.*

1 A visitor to Niels Bohr's country cottage, noticing a horseshoe hanging on the wall, teased the eminent scientist about this ancient superstition. "Can it be that you, of all people, believe it will bring you luck?"

"Of course not," replied Bohr, "but I understand it brings you luck whether you believe or not."

છ્ક ≈§

BOILEAU [-Despréaux], **Nicolas** (1636–1711), *French satirist and critic. His influential* L'Art poétique *(1674) formulated the basic principles of classic French literary criticism. In 1677 Louis XIV appointed Boileau and Jean Racine joint official historians of his reign.*

1 Boileau once introduced an impoverished poet to a prospective patron with the words: "I present to you a person who will give you immortality; but you must give him something to live on in the meantime."

2 When Jean Racine's third play, *Alexandre,* was produced, it attracted the favorable notice of Boileau, who took the aspiring playwright under his wing. Racine once boasted to Boileau that he wrote his verses with astonishing ease. Replied Boileau, "I want to teach you to write them laboriously."

3 Part of the duties of Boileau and Racine as the Sun King's official historiographers was to visit battlefields with the monarch. Nicknamed the "Messieurs du Sublime," they were figures of fun on these occasions, getting in the soldiers' way, pestering preoccupied generals for information, and falling off their horses. They were also widely suspected of being too frightened to take proper notice of what was going on. Louis once inquired of Boileau, "Were you far from the cannon?"

"About a hundred paces, Sire."

"Were you not afraid?"

"Sire, I trembled greatly for Your Majesty, and even more for myself."

4 Louis XIV showed Boileau some poems he had written, and asked his opinion of them. The great poet was also an accomplished courtier: "Sire, nothing is impossible for Your Majesty. Your Majesty has set out to write bad verses and has succeeded."

৯ৎ ৎৡ

BOLEYN, Anne (1507–36), *second queen consort of Henry VIII. It was in order to marry Anne that Henry divorced his first wife, Catherine of Aragon, and thus initiated the quarrel with the pope that led to the English Reformation. Henry and Anne married in 1533 and the same year Anne gave birth to the future Elizabeth I. After that she suffered a series of miscarriages and a stillbirth.*

1 Henry, desperate for a male heir, decided that Anne was no better as a "broodmare" than Catherine of Aragon had been. He therefore had Anne accused of infidelity with five men, one of them her own brother. She and all her supposed lovers were convicted of treason and condemned to death. For Anne's execution the services of the executioner of Calais were engaged. He used a sword for the beheading, according to French practice, instead of the ax used by English executioners. Anne refused to be blindfolded and the executioner found her so disarming that he persuaded someone to attract her attention so that he could steal up silently behind her to carry out the death penalty.

2 Anne did not repine at her fate and cheerfully acknowledged the boon that Henry granted her in allowing her to be decapitated by a sword instead of an ax. "The king has been very good to me," she said. "He promoted me from a simple maid to be a marchioness. Then he raised me to be a queen. Now he will raise me to be a martyr."

৯ৎ ৎৡ

BOLINGBROKE, Henry St. John, Viscount (1678–1751), *British orator and statesman who held important offices under Queen Anne. A Jacobite sympathizer, he went into exile in France on the accession of George I, returning to*

England only in 1725. In France he came under the influence of such thinkers as Voltaire.

1 Bolingbroke's marital infidelities were a source of considerable scandal. Voltaire reports that when Bolingbroke took office, a courtesan remarked to her friends, "Seven thousand guineas a year, my girls, and all for us!"

৯ৎ ৎৡ

BOLT, Tommy (1919–), *US golfer, known for his graceful swing and terrible temper.*

1 Anecdotes of Tommy Bolt's quirky temperament still light up darkened clubhouses. Once, after lipping out six straight putts, he shook his fist at the heavens and shouted, "Why don't You come on down and fight like a man!"

2 Another time, trying to enliven a clinic, he asked his fourteen-year-old son to "show the nice folks what I taught you." The son obediently hurled a nine-iron into the blue sky.

৯ৎ ৎৡ

BONNER, John (1920–), *US professor of biology, Princeton University, and world authority on what are called "colonial organisms."*

1 Bonner's specialty is the slime-mold *Distyostelium,* discovered in 1935 by Kenneth Raper. It may contain as many as 40,000 amoebae which under certain circumstances form themselves into a sausage-shaped slug, crawl about, and exhibit other remarkable talents. Bonner was once explaining his work to two Russian university rectors. They betrayed no sign of interest until he wrote on the blackboard the words "social amoebae." At this they at once perked up, delighted with the idea that even one-celled animals could form collectives. Apparently a slime-mold too may be used to justify Karl Marx.

৯ৎ ৎৡ

BOONE, Daniel (1734–1820), *US pioneer. He led settlers into Kentucky in 1775 and later moved on into Missouri.*

1 The American artist Chester Harding, painting Daniel Boone's portrait, asked the old frontiersman, then in his eighties, if he had ever been lost. Boone replied, "No, I can't say I was ever lost, but I was bewildered once for three days."

❦ ❦

BOOTH, John Wilkes (1838–65), *US actor. A supporter of the South in the Civil War, he assassinated President Lincoln and was cornered and shot while on the run twelve days later.*

1 After firing the fatal shot at Lincoln, Booth jumped from the president's box onto the stage at Ford's Theatre and shouted, "*Sic semper tyrannis!* The South is avenged!" (*Sic semper tyrannis* [Thus always to tyrants] is the motto of the Commonwealth of Virginia.)

❦ ❦

BOOTH, Junius Brutus (1796–1852), *US actor, born in Britain, father of John Wilkes Booth. He was regarded as one of the greatest tragedians of his day, particularly in Shakespearean roles.*

1 A young actor playing a minor role with Booth in *Richard III* inadvertently made his entry from the wrong side of the stage. After the scene he apologized abjectly to the great actor, expecting to be given a royal dressing-down. "Young man, it makes no difference to me," said Booth kindly. "Only come on; I'll find you."

2 (Booth's profile was marred by a broken nose.)
"You're such a wonderful actor, Mr. Booth," gushed a female admirer one day, "but to be perfectly frank with you, I can't get over your nose."
"There's no wonder, madam," replied Booth. "The bridge is gone."

3 Booth was famous for his eccentricities, many of them doubtless a consequence of his wholehearted addiction to the bottle. Once, it is said, when playing Othello, he prolonged his death scene for quite some time. Finally terminating it, he got up and asked the audience, "How did you like *that?*"

4 In later life Booth's addiction to rum made him a problem to theater managers, though his vast experience often enabled him to perform when a lesser man would have been incapaci-

tated. One story tells how the aged actor, putting the last touches to his makeup, staggered from his dressing room at curtain time, inquiring, "Where's the stage, and what's the play?"

❦ ❦

BORGE, Victor (1909–), *US comedian and pianist, born in Denmark.*

1 Explaining why the keys of his piano were so yellow, Borge insisted that it was not that the piano was old, but because "the elephant smoked too much."

2 When Victor Borge was just starting his career as a comedian in America, he was pleased to be given a booking at the Everglades Club, Palm Beach, for which he was to be paid a dollar a head for each member of the audience. About three hundred guests saw his show, which was a tremendous success. When the management came to pay Borge the agreed fee, the comedian pointed out that the club's forty waiters had also greatly enjoyed the performance. He got $340.

3 Borge always made a point of observing his audience closely. If any members of it responded poorly, he would try different lines of approach. One evening he found himself confronted by a table of six, all totally unsmiling. After fifteen minutes during which he failed, despite his best efforts, to elicit any response, Borge appealed to them in desperation to tell him why they were not enjoying the show. One man replied in English so heavily accented as to be almost unintelligible, "We come to hear you play piano. Please play piano." They were Latin Americans and had not understood a word of what Borge had been saying. He played the piano, and the faces of the six lit up with smiles.

4 Borge had just completed the purchase of a chicken farm. "Do you know anything about breeding chickens?" asked a friend, astonished to learn of this new acquisition. "No," replied Borge, "but the chickens do."

❦ ❦

BORGES, Jorge Luis (1899–), *Argentinian poet, short-story writer, and scholar. Educated in Europe, he returned to Argentina in 1921 and published a book of poems (1923). His other works include the short-story collections* Fictions *(1944, 1966) and* The Aleph *(1949, 1970). By 1955 he was almost completely blind.*

1 During the Perón era, Borges's refusal to hang a portrait of the dictator in his office led to his expulsion from the presidency of the Society of Writers. One night an ardent Peronista called on his mother and threatened to kill her and her son. "Well," she replied, "if you want to kill my son, it's very easy. He leaves home for his office every morning at eight; all you have to do is wait for him. As for myself, señor, I have turned eighty, and I advise you to hurry up if you want to kill me, because I might very well die on you beforehand."

{The gallant old lady died of natural causes at the age of ninety-nine.}

જી જી

BORGHESE, Princess Marie Pauline (1780–1825), *French–Italian noblewoman. She was a sister of Napoleon and in 1803 married Prince Camillo Borghese (1775–1832) as her second husband.*

1 A lady expressed surprise that the princess should have posed naked while Antonio Canova modeled his famous statue of her as Venus Victrix. "But," said Princess Pauline demurely, "there was a fire in the room."

જી જી

BORODIN, Alexander (1833–87), *Russian composer. Although a professor of chemistry and medicine who composed only in his spare time, Borodin won acceptance as a member of the Five, the group of Russian composers who revitalized Russian music. His most famous composition is probably the opera* Prince Igor, *completed after his death by Rimsky-Korsakov and Glazunov.*

1 Borodin was once called as an expert witness in the case of two young composers, each accusing the other of musical plagiarism. Both compositions were played. Asked who was the injured party, Borodin replied, "My friend Mussorgsky."

જી જી

BORROMEO, Saint Charles (1538–84), *Italian churchman; archbishop of Milan (1560–84). One of the foremost figures in the Counter-Reformation, he was canonized in 1610.*

1 Cardinal Borromeo was once rebuked for the great pleasure he took in exercising his skill at chess. "What would you do if you were busy playing and the world came to an end?"

"Continue playing," replied Borromeo.

જી જી

BOSQUET, Pierre François Joseph (1810–61), *French soldier, who distinguished himself as a divisional commander during the Crimean War (1853–56).*

1 The British cavalry attack on the Russian guns at Balaclava, the charge of the Light Brigade, was carried out with parade-ground steadiness of pace and discipline, despite the murderous fire from all sides. Watching the doomed advance of his allies, General Bosquet was moved to the memorable utterance, "*C'est magnifique, mais ce n'est pas la guerre*" (It's magnificent, but it's not war).

જી જી

BOSSUET, Jacques Bénigne (1627–1704), *French Roman Catholic bishop and preacher. He played a prominent role in French ecclesiastical affairs after 1681, when he was appointed bishop of Meaux, but is best remembered for his sermons and funeral orations.*

1 Bossuet was a precocious child, already preaching with skill and grace at the age of eight. Vincent Voiture was present at one of the boy's sermons, which on this occasion went on until midnight. The poet was heard to remark on leaving, "I have never heard a sermon so early — or so late."

2 Shortly after Louis XIV had collated Bossuet to the bishopric of Meaux, the king asked some of the citizens whether they were pleased with their new bishop. They replied, rather uncertainly, that they liked him pretty well. "'Pretty well!' Why, what's wrong with him?" asked the monarch. "To tell Your Majesty the truth, we should have preferred a bishop who had completed his education. Whenever we call to see him we are told that he is at his studies."

જી જી

BOSWELL, James (1740–95), *Scottish lawyer who published his famous biography of Dr. Johnson in 1791. This book and Boswell's lively* *account of their joint* Tour to the Hebrides *(1785) give an incomparable picture of "the Great Cham of Literature" and of the literary life of the eighteenth century.*

1 After their first meeting in the back of Tom Davies's bookshop, Boswell assiduously cultivated the acquaintance of Johnson. Johnson enjoyed his company and conversation, and decided to grant him friendship. "Give me your hand," he said. "I have taken a liking to you." Some of Johnson's other friends were less impressed by the new arrival in their circle. "Who is this Scotch cur at Johnson's heels?" asked someone. "He is not a cur," replied Oliver Goldsmith, "he is a burr. Tom Davies flung him at Johnson in sport, and he has the faculty of sticking."

2 During their Scottish tour, Boswell took Johnson to his home in Edinburgh, and Johnson there met Boswell's wife. Mrs. Boswell did not much care for Johnson, although she received him civilly enough. She was scornful of her husband's devotion to this ungainly, lumbering, ill-complexioned man whose manners displeased her. "I have seen many a bear led by a man, but I never before saw a man led by a bear."

{For more Boswell, *see* SAMUEL JOHNSON's anecdotes.}

ॐ ॐ

BOTTICELLI, Sandro [Alessandro di Mariano Filipepi] (c. 1445–1510), *Italian painter, born in Florence. He worked mainly for the Medici before moving to Rome to work on the Frescoes of the Sistine Chapel (1481–82). His* Primavera, Birth of Venus, *and* Mars and Venus *epitomize the mystical neoplatonic symbolism of the Florentine Renaissance. His later works are more religious and emotional in appeal.*

1 A weaver set up his eight-loom workshop next to Botticelli's house. The noise drove the painter nearly mad, but his protests remained unheeded. Botticelli hoisted a vast rock onto the roof of his own house, balancing it in such a way that it overhung the neighbor's roof and threatened to come crashing down upon it at the slightest disturbance. The weaver, eyeing this novel sword of Damocles, came to terms.

See also BUFFALMACCO 1.

The great fashion photographer, Norman Parkinson, tells the following story about Bettina Ballard when she was Fashion Editor of *Vogue:*

"One afternoon we were working in the Versailles gardens and I complained to Bettina Ballard that a particular Dior ball gown would look much better if the bodice was pulled down tighter into its enormous skirt. 'You're right,' she said, taking hold of the model's arm. 'Come with me.'

"Nearby there was a small copse with bushes which Bettina immediately thought might offer the necessary 'cover'. She half-dragged the somewhat unwilling model into the shade and, facing the girl, bent down, throwing the many petticoats upwards as she dived forward to grab hold of the bodice. The two of them locked in this extraordinary position presented a bizarre shape. Bettina, bent like a croquet hoop, was under the model's many petticoats, and as she fumbled for the base of the bodice, only her posterior was visible. A passing pedestrian, having stopped for a few seconds to take in the scene, became as fascinated by this extraordinary sight as we were. His curiosity got the better of him, and walking forward, he tapped Bettina on the back: '*Pardon, puis-je intervenir, madame? Je suis médecin.*' (Pardon, may I be of help, madame? I am a doctor.)"

— Norman Parkinson,
Fifty Years of Style and Fashion

BOTTOMLEY, Horatio William (1860–1933), *British journalist and financier. His name constantly cropped up in the courts in connection with bankruptcy writs and fraud charges. His talents as a writer and orator and his position as an MP did not save him finally from being sentenced in 1922 to seven years' penal servitude.*

1 Horatio Bottomley called to see Lord Cholmondley. "I wish to speak to Lord Cholmond-ley," he said to the butler. "Lord *Chum*-ley, sir," said the butler, correcting his pronunciation. "Oh, all right," said Bottomley. "Tell him that Mr. Bumley would like to see him."

2 An acquaintance found Bottomley in prison stitching mail bags. "Ah, Bottomley," he said, "sewing?"

"No," Bottomley replied, "reaping."

ಶ್ಲ ೇ

BOUHOURS, Dominique (1628–1702), *French Jesuit grammarian, who promoted a high standard of correctness and purity in French.*

1 On his deathbed Bouhours announced, "I am about to — or I am going to — die; either expression is used."

See also FRANÇOIS DE MALHERBE 1.

ಶ್ಲ ೇ

BOULANGER, Georges Ernest Jean Marie (1837–91), *French general. A blatant political opportunist, Boulanger seized upon the discontent of the populace in the 1880s, after the Franco–Russian War, to create a considerable following for himself. It seemed for a time that he might overthrow the parliamentary constitution of the republic.*

1 When Boulanger's mistress, Marguerite de Bonnemain, died of tuberculosis in 1891, the heartbroken general had her tombstone inscribed with the simple message: "Marguerite. See you soon." He returned to the grave two and a half months later to fulfill his promise. Drawing his pistol, he held it to his head and pulled the trigger. (Another version of the story says he stabbed himself.)

Boulanger's tombstone, erected beside that of his beloved Marguerite, was inscribed as requested: "Georges. Could I really live two and a half months without you?"

ಶ್ಲ ೇ

BOULANGER, Nadia [Juliette] (1887–1979), *French composer, conductor, and teacher of composition. Her long list of pupils included Aaron Copland and Lennox Berkeley.*

1 (US composer Roy Harris once described how Nadia Boulanger selected her pupils.)

"Nadia Boulanger told me this way she has of deciding who to accept for students. Those who have no talent, and those who have no

money; these are not acceptable. There are those who have talent but no money. These she accepts. Those who have little talent but much money she also accepts. But those who have much talent and much money she says she never gets."

ಶ್ಲ ೇ

BOULT, Sir Adrian (1889–1983), *British conductor. Known especially for his interpretation of the compositions of his British contemporaries, Boult was conductor of the BBC Symphony Orchestra (1930–49) and the London Philharmonic (1949–57).*

1 At the BBC Boult frequently found himself in conflict with the administrators over their parsimony and their ignorance of music. On one occasion, when Boult was planning to perform a piece scored for two piccolo players, he was told that the budget allowed for only one. He protested, but the administrators were adamant. He took his complaint to the head of the department, Charles Carpendale. Carpendale was torn between his wish to oblige Boult and his dislike of overruling his subordinates. Having pondered for a minute, he proposed a compromise: "How about using one piccolo, and placing it closer to the microphone?"

ಶ್ಲ ೇ

BOWEN, Elizabeth Dorothea Cole (1899–1973), *British writer, born in Ireland. She wrote short stories and novels, notably* The Death of the Heart *(1938) and* The Heat of the Day *(1949).*

1 (Howard Moss describes a dinner party given by Elizabeth Bowen one hot summer evening.)

"She had been detained and had to shop at the last minute. When I arrived, the drinks were impeccable, everything went swimmingly. After drinks, you went into another room for a stand-up dinner. And that was rather unbelievable. Elizabeth was notoriously near-sighted and she must have gone into some delicatessen and ordered a buffet. There was a salad that looked as if it had been briefly shampooed. The lettuce leaves had suspicious ruffles. I was standing next to her, and she tasted the salad first. She turned to me and said, 'You know, this just doesn't have that *je ne sais quoi.*'"

ಶ್ಲ ೇ

BOWEN, Louise de Koven (1859–1953), *US grande dame of the Midwest, active social worker, and suffragist.*

1 Mrs. Bowen, originally from Chicago, spent her summers from 1882 to the 1940s in fashionable Bar Harbor. Though very rich and well-connected, she met with some difficulty in establishing friendly relations with the tonier eastern seaboard families.

Once, driving her pony-cart down a country road, she was dumped out of it when the pony shied and upset the cart. Two Philadelphia ladies came along in their carriages, noticed the dazed figure lying on the road, stopped, got out, and examined Mrs. Bowen briefly. Said one to the other, "Who *is* she?" Her companion shook her head.

They took no further action. Finally a native islander happened to come along and sent for help.

> ট— —ঙ

BOWLES, William Lisle (1762–1850), *British clergyman whose graceful poetry was admired by Coleridge. He wrote a hostile study of Pope that embroiled him in controversy with Byron.*

1 When Bowles gave a Bible to Bessie Moore, wife of the poet Tom Moore, she asked him to inscribe it. She was startled to see that the absentminded divine had written: "from the Author."

2 Bowles's usual daily ride took him along a road through a turnpike gate at which he had to pay twopence to the tollkeeper to allow his horse through. One day he passed that way on foot and tendered the twopence as usual. The gatekeeper, puzzled, asked: "What's this for, sir?"

"For my horse, of course!"

"But, sir, you have no horse!"

"Oh, am I walking?" exclaimed Bowles.

> ট— —ঙ

BOWRA, C. Maurice (1898–1971), *British classical scholar, warden of Wadham College, Oxford (1938–71), professor of poetry (1946–51), and the author of several important books on the history of poetry. He was knighted in 1951.*

1 Parsons' Pleasure, the stretch of river at Oxford set aside for men's bathing, is out of bounds for women. One day Bowra and a group of other dons were bathing there *au naturel* when a boatload of women, disregarding the "Men Only" signs, rowed into their midst. The dons on the bank hurriedly grabbed towels and fashioned impromptu loincloths — with the exception of Bowra, who threw his towel over his face. When the intruders had gone, Bowra explained, "I believe, gentlemen, that I am recognized by my face."

{This story is sometimes told of other well-known Oxford characters.}

> ট— —ঙ

BRADFORD, John (?1510–55), *English Protestant martyr.*

1 Bradford was in the habit of saying, when he saw criminals going to their execution, "But for the grace of God, there goes John Bradford."

{This saying, in various forms, has been uttered by a number of people, and the version "There but for the grace of God go I" has attained semiproverbial status. *See also* SIR WINSTON CHURCHILL 25.}

> ট— —ঙ

BRADLEY, Henry (1845–1923), *British philologist. His review of the first part of the* Oxford English Dictionary *attracted the attention of Sir James Murray, who appointed him an editor in 1889. After Murray's death he became chief editor.*

1 Bradley was very helpful to other scholars, supplying them with advice and material to such an extent that he once remarked that some of his best work was in other men's books. When another scholar attacked the competence of a certain philologist, Bradley put up some defense for the victim. "Well," said the detractor, "I suppose the man can't be an absolute fool as he did supply that brilliant reading in —" naming a particular work. Bradley shifted uneasily in his chair: "To tell you the truth, I sent him that."

> ট— —ঙ

BRADY, William A. (1863–1950), *US theatrical producer, husband of actress Grace George.*

1 "To keep up morale in my staff," Brady once recalled, "and to fool rival producers and

theatrical reporters, I always instructed managers of my road companies to add three hundred dollars to their nightly reports of box-office receipts. The system worked fine until one of them wired, 'Only theatre in town burned to the ground this afternoon. No performance. Receipts $300.'"

ઓ ન્ও

BRAHMS, Johannes (1833–97), *German composer. As a young man Brahms came to the attention of violinist Joachim, Liszt, and the Schumanns, who helped him find a footing in the musical world. In 1863 Brahms settled in Vienna. A prolific composer of orchestral and chamber music, he is noted for lyrical melody and harmonic inventiveness. He also wrote many songs and choral works, including* A German Requiem *(1868) and the* Alto Rhapsody *(1869).*

1 Brahms came from a humble background, and the financial welfare of his parents was an anxiety to him. As he made his way in music, he contributed to the upkeep of their home out of his increasing but still slender resources. Knowing that his father was rash in money matters, he provided against an unforeseen economic crisis in his own way, before leaving home. "If things go badly with you the best consolation is always in music," he advised his father. "Read carefully in my old *Saul* and you'll find what you want." His father found this advice rather puzzling. Nonetheless when difficulties arose he took down the score of *Saul* and opened it; there between the pages was a substantial supply of banknotes.

2 During the period in which Brahms was still considered advanced, the Boston Symphony Orchestra ventured to play one of his compositions. Some wag changed the exit sign to read: EXIT IN CASE OF BRAHMS.

3 As a celebrated composer, Brahms conducted his two piano concertos in Berlin and attended a dinner given for him. His host proposed a toast to "the most famous composer." Brahms, seeing what was coming, interposed hastily, "Quite right: here's to Mozart!" and clinked glasses all round.

4 Although Brahms could be agreeable and interesting, he could also be difficult, sarcastic,

and rude. Even his friends were not immune to unprovoked verbal attacks. On one occasion he upset a gathering of friends with a series of offensive remarks, then rose to his feet and left the room, stopping briefly at the door to say, "If there is anyone here whom I have not insulted, I beg his pardon."

5 A great wine connoisseur invited Brahms to dinner and in his honor brought out some of his choicest bottles. "This is the Brahms of my cellar," he announced to the company as wine from a venerable bottle was poured into the composer's glass. Brahms scrutinized the wine closely, inhaled its bouquet, took a sip, and then put down his glass without comment. "How do you like it?" anxiously asked the host. "Better bring out your Beethoven," murmured Brahms.

6 A singer asked Brahms to give her some of his least-known songs for a forthcoming recital. "Have some of my posthumous ones," suggested the composer. "No one will know them."

7 A young musician complained bitterly to Brahms about delays in the publication of his first opus. Brahms counseled him to be patient. "You can afford not to be immortal for a few more weeks," he said.

8 Brahms and Johann Strauss the Younger, each of whom had great admiration for the other's work, once met in Vienna. Strauss handed Brahms his autograph book and asked if he would do him the honor of signing it. Opening the book at a blank page, Brahms transcribed the first few bars of *The Blue Danube* and wrote underneath, "Unfortunately not by Johannes Brahms."

9 Brahms, who enjoyed his food, was distressed when he became ill and his doctor prescribed a strict diet. "But this evening I am dining with Strauss and we shall have chicken paprika," he protested. "Out of the question," said the doctor. "Very well, then," said Brahms. "Please consider that I did not come to consult you until tomorrow."
See also OTTO ERICH HARTLEBEN 1.

10 Finding himself cornered by a group of rather talkative ladies, Brahms made several

vain attempts to escape. Finally, in desperation he took out a large cigar and lit it. Engulfed in smoke, the ladies reproached the composer for this lack of courtesy. "A gentleman doesn't smoke in the presence of ladies," they reminded him. Continuing to puff at his cigar, Brahms replied: "Ladies, where there are angels there must also be clouds."

11 In his old age Brahms announced to his friends that he was going to stop composing music and enjoy the time left to him. Several months went by without Brahms's writing a note. But there came the day when a new Brahms composition made its debut. "I thought you weren't going to write any more," a friend reminded him. "I wasn't," said the composer, "but after a few days away from it, I was so happy at the thought of no more writing that the music came to me without effort."

ভিও উৎ

BRAITHWAITE, Dame [Florence] **Lilian** (1873–1948), *British actress. She made her name in Noël Coward's play* The Vortex; *her greatest success was in* Arsenic and Old Lace.

1 It was the opening night of *The Vortex* in Washington, D.C. At one of the most dramatic moments of the play, Miss Braithwaite had to snatch a box of drugs from Coward's hands and hurl them out of an open window. One of the stagehands, unfamiliar with the script, helpfully threw the box back into Miss Braithwaite's hands. The bewildered actress had no option but to throw the box again, this time with such force that it broke the edge off the window as it sailed through.

2 Drama critic James Agate, finding himself alone with Miss Braithwaite, made the controversial remark: "My dear lady, may I tell you something I have wanted to tell you for years: that you are the second most beautiful woman in the United Kingdom." Expecting the actress to ask the obvious question, Agate had prepared a suitable reply. Miss Braithwaite, however, did not take the bait. "Thank you," she said. "I shall always cherish that, as coming from the second-best dramatic critic."

ভিও উৎ

BRAKHAGE, Stan (1933–   ), *US underground filmmaker. His films include* Flesh of Morning *(1956) and* Dog Star Man *(1964).*

1 Brakhage had been hired by the Scott Paper Company, maker of Scotties, to film a commercial, the main aim of which was to persuade the buying public that not every paper handkerchief on the market was a Kleenex. Giving last-minute instructions to the star of the commercial, Brakhage said, "Now, sweetheart, when I hold up my hand, blow your nose on the Kleenex."

ভিও উৎ

BRANCUSI, Constantin (1876–1957), *Rumanian sculptor. His wooden sculptures show the influence of African art. His works in stone and bronze are more abstract and have a massive simplicity of form.*

1 Brancusi moved to Paris in 1904. In 1906 Auguste Rodin invited him to work in his studio. Brancusi refused, remarking: "Nothing grows well in the shade of a big tree."

ভিও উৎ

BRANDEIS, Louis Dembitz (1856–1941), *US jurist. He served as an associate justice of the US Supreme Court from 1916 until his retirement in 1939.*

1 Brandeis was once criticized for taking a short vacation just before the start of an important trial. "I need the rest," explained Brandeis. "I find that I can do a year's work in eleven months, but I can't do it in twelve."

"Victor Biaka-Boda, who represented the Ivory Coast in the French Senate, set off on a tour of the hinterlands in January 1950 to let the people know where he stood on the issues, and to understand their concerns — one of which was apparently the food supply. His constituents ate him.

"[His colleagues, according to an account in *Time* magazine in July 1951, remembered Biaka-Boda, a former witch doctor, as a 'small, thin, worried-looking man.']"

—John Train, *True Remarkable Occurrences*

BRANDT, Willy (1913–   ), *German states-man. During World War II he led the resistance movement against the Nazis. As socialist chancellor for West Germany (1969–74), he was awarded the Nobel Peace Prize in 1971.*

1   On a visit to Israel as mayor of West Berlin, Brandt was invited to view the great new Mann auditorium in Tel Aviv. Having expressed his appreciation of Israel's naming the concert hall for Thomas Mann, the German writer, Brandt was politely corrected by his host. The hall was actually named for a certain Frederic Mann of Philadelphia. "What did he ever write?" exclaimed Brandt. "A check," came the reply.

৯৯ ৽৾

BRAQUE, Georges (1882–1963), *French painter. With Picasso he originated Cubism, although he later took an independent line in his use of large flat planes of color.*

1   The painter Roland Penrose, calling on Picasso, found that Braque and his wife were also visiting. "You know Penrose?" Picasso said to Braque as greetings were being exchanged. "Oh, yes," said Braque, "but I haven't seen him for about twenty years and at first sight I didn't recognize him; he's changed so little."

৯৯ ৽৾

BRESHKOVSKAYA, Catherine (1844–1934), *known as Babushka or "Grandmother of the Russian Revolution." She left her wealthy home to support the revolutionaries; she was later imprisoned, banished to Siberia, and released. She finally fled to Switzerland in 1917 to escape the Bolsheviks. Thereafter she lived in exile, always hoping to return to Russia.*

1   In 1919 Breshkovskaya toured the United States, giving lectures. A wealthy admirer gave her a trunkful of beautiful clothes. "What in the world will I do with all these dresses?" she cried in dismay. Then her face brightened. "I know! I will use them for my disguises when I return to Russia."

৯৯ ৽৾

BRIAND, Aristide (1862–1932), *French statesman; socialist prime minister (1909–11, 1913, 1915–17, 1921–22, 1925–26, 1929). After World War I he did much to promote international cooperation.*

1   In September 1926 Briand arranged to meet the German statesman Gustav Stresemann, with whom he shared that year's Nobel Peace Prize. They met at a small village in the Jura where they could discuss postwar problems in privacy. After lunch the two statesmen wrangled amicably about the bill. "No, I'll pay for the lunch," said Briand. "You take care of the reparations."

2   Briand tended to be somewhat lazy. He once rebuked a Latin American diplomat who brought him a massive armful of documents to study, "You don't suppose I've lost my incapacity for work, do you?"

৯৯ ৽৾

BRIDGER, Jim (1804–81), *US frontiersman and fur-trapper.*

1   A man dressing a serious wound that Bridger had received in the course of one of his numerous skirmishes with hostile Indians or wild animals expressed the fear that the wound would suppurate. Bridger told him not to worry: "In the mountains meat never spoils."

2   Bridger sold a yoke of cattle worth $125 to obtain a copy of the complete works of Shakespeare and then engaged a wagon boy at $40 a month to read the plays to him. In the middle of *Richard III,* Bridger gave up the business in disgust. "I won't listen anymore to the talk of a man who was mean enough to kill his mother."

৯৯ ৽৾

BRIDGES, Robert (1844–1930), *British poet. In 1913 he was appointed poet laureate. His crowning achievement was the philosophical poem* The Testament of Beauty *(1929).*

1   By the beginning of the twentieth century Bridges's reputation had undergone almost total eclipse because of the shift in readers' tastes toward more robust and accessible verse. When an anthology was published in 1906 under the title *Bridges to Kipling,* one baffled reader was heard to ask, "But what do we need bridges to Kipling for?"

2   When *The Testament of Beauty* was published, its difficult and experimental meter attracted hostile criticism. Dean William Inge of St. Paul's Cathedral, known as "the Gloomy

Dean" on account of his attitude toward all things modern, remarked, "I hate loose meter even more than loose living."

੩~ ~੩

BRIGHT, John (1811–89), *British politician and orator who was at the forefront of nine-teenth-century moves for parliamentary reform. His efforts were crowned by the 1867 Reform Act, considerably extending the franchise.*

1 Bright was among the crowd of onlookers at the scene of a street accident in which the victim was seriously injured. He removed his hat, put ten pounds in it, and then went around the crowd saying, "I'm ten pounds sorry. How sorry are you?"

੩~ ~੩

BRILLAT-SAVARIN, Anthelme (1755–1826), *French writer and gastronome. His Phy-siologie du goût (1825) is a classic exposition on food and the art of dining.*

1 A lady inquired whether he preferred Bur-gundy or claret. Brillat-Savarin replied, "That, madame, is a question that I take so much plea-sure in investigating that I postpone from week to week the pronouncement of a verdict."

੩~ ~੩

BRODIE, Sir Benjamin Collins (1783–1862), *English surgeon.*

1 Brodie, deeply immersed in the preparation of a paper, was dragged away from his work to attend a fashionable evening party. After drinking with the gentlemen there for a while, he went to the men's room. Intending then to make his escape, he tucked his hat under his arm, emerged, and walked past a number of arriving guests. The men all sniggered and the women tittered and turned their heads away. In the hall he was accosted by his host: "Good Lord, Brodie, is that a usual part of your at-tire?" Brodie looked, too. Instead of his hat, he had absentmindedly picked up the toilet-seat cover.

੩~ ~੩

BRODIE, Steve (fl. 1880s), *US saloonkeeper.*

1 In 1886 Steve Brodie jumped off the Brooklyn Bridge into the East River, a fall of

some 135 feet, to win a two-hundred-dollar wager. This is the origin of the phrase "to do (or pull) a Brodie," meaning to attempt a risky stunt. The police arrested him for this suicidal leap, though at the time many people doubted whether Brodie had actually jumped; some people believed that he had just thrown a dummy off the bridge.

Some time later the father of the heavy-weight boxer Jim Corbett met Brodie. "So you're the fellow who jumped over Brooklyn Bridge," he said. "I jumped *off* it," corrected Brodie. Old Mr. Corbett was disgusted: "I thought you jumped over it. Any damn fool could jump off it."

੩~ ~੩

BRODIE, William (died 1788), *Scottish head of the Incorporation of Edinburgh Wrights and Masons.*

1 A respected figure in Edinburgh, Brodie was also a highly successful burglar. No suspi-cion fell upon him until an accomplice turned king's evidence. Brodie fled to Amsterdam but was apprehended, brought back to Edinburgh for trial, and condemned to death. He is cred-ited with an invention that was first tested at his own execution—the drop. Before that time, the person to be hanged was simply pushed off a height; Brodie thought up the sys-tem of trapdoor and lever that became stan-dard wherever hanging was the means of legal execution. On the gallows the hapless inventor inspected the arrangements, pronounced them satisfactory, and was efficiently launched into eternity.

੩~ ~੩

BRONTË, Charlotte (1816–55), *British nov-elist and poet. The daughter of an Irish clergy-man, Charlotte spent most of her life, between soul-destroying stints as a governess, at her fa-ther's rectory at Haworth (Yorkshire). Her mother and two sisters died when she was a child. With Emily, Anne, and Branwell, the sur-viving Brontë children, Charlotte presided over a peculiarly close-knit family group. In 1846 Charlotte, Emily, and Anne brought out a vol-ume of verses under the pseudonyms of Currer, Ellis, and Acton Bell. The following year Char-lotte's great novel Jane Eyre was published, achieving instant success. Charlotte later wrote Shirley (1849) and Villette (1853). In 1854 she* *married her father's curate but died within the year as a result of childbirth.*

1   During one of Charlotte Brontë's spells as a governess, a child whom she had scolded burst into penitent tears and ran to her crying, "I love you, I love you, Miss Brontë."

"Love the *governess,* my dear?" icily queried the mother, who was in the room.

2   In her first desperate rebellion against her role as a teacher Charlotte wrote in 1836 to the poet laureate Robert Southey, asking whether he thought she could earn her living as a writer. Southey wrote back: "Literature cannot be the business of a woman's life, and it ought not to be. The more she is engaged in her proper duties, the less leisure will she have for it, even as an accomplishment and recreation. To those duties you have not yet been called, and when you are you will be less eager for celebrity."

{Southey congratulated himself on having administered "a dose of cooling admonition to that poor girl." To do him justice, when Charlotte wrote again, he did reply in friendlier terms and asked her to visit him.}

ঌ৽ ৶ঌ

BROOKFIELD, Charles Hallam Elton (1857–1913), *English actor, known for his performances with the Haymarket Company (1879–85); he also wrote and produced some forty plays.*

1   Chatting to Brookfield one day, a theatrical colleague sensed that the actor was looking at him rather oddly. "What's up?" he asked. "Is my tie wrong?"

"No," replied Brookfield, "but you have a little dried soap in your right ear."

"How filthy!" exclaimed his colleague.

"Oh, no," said Brookfield, "not filthy at all; a little ostentatious perhaps."

ঌ৽ ৶ঌ

BROOKS, Mel (1927–   ), *US movie director of such offbeat comedies as* Blazing Saddles *(1974) and* Young Frankenstein *(1975).*

1   Finding an abandoned box of German rifles and ammunition while on patrol in France in 1945, Brooks and his men organized a sharp-shooting contest, using the white insulation caps on the telephone wires as their targets.

Brooks was doing quite well when an urgent call came through on the jeep radio from their headquarters: German guerrillas had destroyed communications with the Ninth Army by bringing down the telephone lines. Guiltily, the patrol hurried back to camp. Had they seen anything? No, but Brooks was willing to take out another patrol to see if he couldn't stop the sabotage. This offer was accepted and Brooks spent some time searching the countryside. The "guerrillas" had mysteriously disappeared.

2   Asked what he thought of critics, Brooks replied, "They're very noisy at night. You can't sleep in the country because of them." His interviewer politely corrected him: "I said *critics,* not crickets."

"Oh, critics! What good are they? They can't make music with their hind legs."

3   (Carl Reiner, film and television actor, tells the following story.)

"In 1959, I appeared in a movie called *Happy Anniversary,* and Mel came to the wrap party for the cast and crew at a restaurant in the Village. Moss Hart was dining with his wife on the other side of the room. Mel recognized him. All of a sudden, he got up and walked across to Hart's table and said, very loudly, 'Hello. You don't know who I am. My name is Mel Brooks. Do you know who you are? Your name is Moss Hart. Do you know what you've written? You wrote *Once in a Lifetime* with George Kaufman, and *You Can't Take It with You* and *The Man Who Came to Dinner.* You wrote *Lady in the Dark* and you directed *My Fair Lady.*' And he ran right through the list of Hart's credits. 'You should be more arrogant!' he shouted. 'You have earned the right to be supercilious! *Why are you letting me talk to you?*'"

ঌ৽ ৶ঌ

BROOKS, Phillips (1835–93), *US Episcopal bishop. His writings include* The Light of the World *(1890) and the hymn* "O Little Town of Bethlehem."

1   Recovering from a serious illness, Brooks refused to receive any visitors, even his closest friends. When the agnostic Robert Ingersoll called, however, the bishop did not turn him away. Ingersoll, conscious of the privilege, was curious to know the reason behind it. Said the bishop, "I feel confident of seeing my friends in the next world, but this may be my last chance of seeing you."

৯ৈ ৩৬

BROUGHAM, Henry Peter, Baron Brougham and Vaux (1778–1868), *British lawyer and statesman; lord chancellor (1830–34). Advocate in Parliament of many reforms and good causes, including the abolition of slavery, and founder of the Society for the Diffusion of Useful Knowledge, he acted in a spirit of such self-aggrandizement that, according to Donald H. Reiman, he "appears to rank as a leading claimant for the title of the person who has done the most good in the world from mean and selfish motives." In 1838 he invented the compact one-horse carriage named after him.*

1 When Lord Brougham arrived at the theater for a performance of Handel's *Messiah*, Sydney Smith remarked, "Here comes counsel for the other side."

2 When Sydney Smith was living in London he saw Lord Brougham's one-horse carriage pass him in the street and noticed the splendid B surrounded by a coronet on the panel of the coach. "There goes a carriage with a B outside and a wasp within," he commented to a friend.

3 It distressed Lord Brougham to learn that his eldest son was having an affair with a young French actress. To bring the erring youth to his senses, his father wrote to him tersely: "If you do not quit her, I will stop your allowance." His son wrote back: "If you do not double it, I will marry her."

4 Brougham's greatest speech was made for the second reading of the Reform Bill in 1830. At the climax of his peroration, he fell on his knees, lifting up his voice in prayer. Since he had kept himself going throughout the speech by generous drafts of mulled port, and since he remained kneeling for some time, his colleagues not unnaturally assumed that the port had gone to his head. To his vast displeasure, they picked him up bodily and set him back on his woolsack.

৯ৈ ৩৬

BROUN, [Matthew] Heywood Campbell (1888–1939), *US journalist. He worked on a number of newspapers, including the* New York Morning Telegraph *(1908–09; 1910–12),* Tribune *(1912–21), and* World *(1921–28).*

1 Reviewing a play in 1917, Broun described the performance of actor Geoffrey Steyne as "the worst to be seen in the contemporary theater." Steyne immediately sued. While the case was pending Broun had occasion to review the actor's performance in another play. This time he wrote: "Mr. Steyne's performance was not up to his usual standard."

2 A large, shambling, awkward man, Broun was noted for the disarray of his dress. During World War I, serving as a correspondent, he resisted wearing an officer's cap with his uniform, preferring a fedora. His son recalls: "The dishevelment of that uniform, bought at the Galeries Lafayette department store, led one exasperated major at an inspection of correspondents to ask fretfully, "Mr. Broun, have you fallen down?"

৯ৈ ৩৬

BROWN, John Mason (1900–69), *US critic and lecturer.*

1 One of Brown's first important appearances as a lecturer was at the Metropolitan Museum of Art. He was pleased, but also rather nervous, and his nerves were not helped when he noticed by the light of the slide projector that someone in the room was mimicking his every gesture. At length he broke off, announcing with dignity that if anyone was not enjoying the lecture he was free to leave. Nobody did, and the mimicking continued. It was only after another ten minutes that Brown realized that the mimic was his own shadow.

2 At a party given by a collector of modern art, Brown paused to study a large sculpture by Jean Arp that was supposed to depict the female form. Peering through a large hole in the middle of the sculpture, he exclaimed, "Ah, a womb with a view!"

৯ৈ ৩৬

BROWNE, Lewis (1897–1949), *US rabbi and author, born in England. Having been a rabbi for six years, in 1926 he decided to become a writer. His works include* This Believing World *(1926) and* Blessed Spinoza *(1932).*

1 At a literary dinner Browne was questioned by another rabbi about his early career. "You were a rabbi, eh," he remarked. "Were you unfrocked?"

"No," replied Browne. "Just unsuited."

છે. જે

BROWNING, Elizabeth Barrett (1806–61), *British poet. After a childhood accident, Elizabeth Barrett led a life of semi-invalidism, watched over by her tyrannical father. In 1845 she began a correspondence with Robert Browning, and they fell in love. Their wedding (1846) was held in secret because of Mr. Barrett, and they left immediately for Italy, where they lived for the rest of her life. Her Sonnets from the Portuguese (1850) were inspired by her love for her husband.*

1 During the early months of 1846, encouraged by Browning and in preparation for their elopement, Elizabeth Barrett began to rid herself of the habits acquired as an invalid, practicing standing without assistance and then walking where she had previously been carried. In January she reported to Browning a notable advance: "I put on a cloak and walked downstairs into the drawing-room — walked, mind!" Her brother, who was in the room, was so startled by the unexpected sight that he exclaimed, "So glad to see you!" as if she were a stranger.

છે. જે

BROWNING, Robert (1812–89), *British poet. Browning's early work included poetic tragedies and several long poems that won limited critical acclaim. Some of the poems written during his marriage to Elizabeth Barrett, particularly his love lyrics, are the most beautiful and accessible pieces that he produced. After her death (1861) he returned to England. Browning specialized in dramatic verse monologues, enabling him to give full vent to his preoccupation with human emotions and motives.*

1 Browning's *Sordello* was published in 1840. On the face of it the story is simple enough, the tale of an unknown heir to a dukedom in thirteenth-century Italy. But it is considerably complicated by Browning's interest in the development of the human soul and the motives that sway it toward a practical or disinterested course of action. Tennyson is reported to have

said that there were only two lines in it that he could understand, and both of them were lies: "Who will may hear Sordello's story told" and "Who would has heard Sordello's story told." Baffled readers resorted to the poet for an explanation. Members of the London Poetry Society asked Browning for an interpretation of a particularly obscure passage. Browning read it through twice, frowned, and then shrugged his shoulders. "When I wrote that, God and I knew what it meant, but now God alone knows."

See also DOUGLAS JERROLD 1.

2 Cornered by a bore at a party, Browning had to listen to a volley of questions concerning his work. Eventually the poet managed to escape. "But my dear fellow, this is too bad. I am monopolizing you," he exclaimed, and fled.

3 (During the months of suspense before his marriage to Elizabeth Barrett, Browning was one day seized with a whimsical notion of attempting divination while he was at work in his library.)

" 'What will be the event of my love for Her?' he questioned the book that fell under his hand, opening it at a random passage. The volume, of all inauspicious ones, turned out to be Cerutti's Italian grammar. He hoped he might come upon a word like *conjunction* or at least a possessive pronoun. To his amazement his eyes lighted upon the sentence in an exercise for translation: 'If we love in the other world as we do in this, I shall love thee to eternity.' "

છે. જે

BRUCE, James (1730–94), *British explorer who discovered the source of the Blue Nile at Lake Tana in northwestern Ethiopia (1770).*

1 Someone once asked Bruce what musical instruments were used in Abyssinia. Bruce, unprepared for the question, hesitated before saying, "I think I only saw one lyre there." George Selwyn whispered to his neighbor, "Yes, and there is one less since he left the country."

છે. જે

BRUMMELL, George Bryan (1778–1840), *British society figure known as Beau Brummell, arbiter of fashion during the Regency period and a friend of the prince regent (later George IV). In*

1816 he fled to France to escape his creditors, dying there in poverty.

1   A friend, seeing Beau Brummell limping, inquired the reason. He recounted the story of the injury, concluding, "And the worst of it is that it is my favorite leg."

2   Beau Brummell found the fashionable romantic raptures about scenery rather boring. An acquaintance, knowing he had recently visited the English Lake District, asked which of the lakes he had most admired. Beau Brummell summoned his valet. "Which of the lakes did I most admire?" he asked. "Windermere, sir," replied the valet. "Ah, yes, Windermere," said Beau Brummell to the inquirer.

3   Beau Brummell's quarrel with his former friend the prince regent shook fashionable society. Various versions of the row were current. Brummell himself said that the prince delivered the first cut; he was riding with a friend in the park in London when they met the regent, who spoke to the friend but ignored Brummell. When the regent moved on but was not yet quite out of earshot, Brummell asked loudly, "Who's your fat friend?"

4   After his quarrel with the prince regent, Beau Brummell found that many London hostesses who had previously been eager for his presence now excluded him from their guest lists. Among these was a certain Mrs. Thompson. Beau Brummell managed to discover that she had invited the regent to a party. Near the time that he might be expected to arrive, Beau Brummell sauntered into her house. In terror lest the regent encounter his enemy, the hostess bustled up to eject the unwanted guest, telling him to leave at once as he had not been invited. "Not invited, ma'am? But surely there must be some mistake. I have a card." Brummell began to feel in all his pockets, very leisurely, while Mrs. Thompson was on tenterhooks in case the regent arrived. At length Beau Brummell found a card and handed it to her. "But this is from Mrs. Johnson," she exclaimed. Beau Brummell appeared deeply surprised and contrite. "From Mrs. Johnson? How very unfortunate, Mrs. John — er, Thompson, I mean. Johnson and Thompson, Thompson and Johnson, so very much the same kind of thing." He bowed low and made a dignified exit.

5   Someone commiserated with Beau Brummell for having a cold. He explained that he had caught it at an inn on the Brighton road: "My infidel valet put me in a room with a damp stranger."

6   Beau Brummell at one period had a whim to eat no vegetables. A lady asked him if he had ever in his life eaten any. "Yes, madam," replied the dandy, "I once ate a pea."

7   At Ascot a fashionable man-about-town complimented Brummell on his exquisite turnout. Brummell replied, "I cannot be elegant, since you have noticed me."

8   (An acquaintance asked Beau Brummell where he had dined the previous night.)
    "Why with a person of the name of R —. I believe he wishes me to notice him, hence the dinner; but to give him his due, he desired that I would make up the party myself, so I asked Alvanley, Mills, Pierrepoint, and a few others, and I assure you the affair turned out quite unique; there was every delicacy in and out of season; the Sillery was perfect, and not a wish remained ungratified; but, my dear fellow, conceive my astonishment when I tell you that Mr. R — had the assurance to sit down and dine with us."

ॐ ∽

BRUNO, Giordano (1548–1600), *Italian philosopher, theologian, and astronomer. His belief that a philosophical view could and should be published irrespective of its theological implications eventually cost him his life at the hands of the Inquisition. Heretical views discussed by Bruno included the Copernican theory and the idea that religion was an acceptable means of manipulating the ignorant masses, while philosophy was limited to the governing elect.*

1   Denounced to the Venetian Inquisition in 1592, Bruno put up a plausible defense. However, the much more relentless Roman Inquisition demanded that he be handed over to them. Over the next seven years Bruno's trial progressed to its inevitable conclusion. On February 8, 1600, eight cardinals excommunicated him (yet again) and with customary hollow recommendation to mercy turned him over to the secular law. "Perhaps your fear in passing

judgment is greater than mine in receiving it," commented the unrepentant ex-monk. On February 17 Bruno was led barefoot to the stake and burned alive — gagged to restrain him from uttering further heresies in his final agony.

৯৯ ৶৶

BRYAN, William Jennings (1860–1925), *US politician. Bryan, a perennial presidential candidate, was for many years the acknowledged leader of the Democratic party. Woodrow Wilson appointed him secretary of state in 1913, and he worked hard to preserve peace. In 1915 he resigned over Wilson's second* Lusitania *note to Germany. Toward the end of his life he assisted the prosecution in the case of John T. Scopes, the Dayton, Tennessee, teacher who was tried for teaching the theory of evolution to his class.*

1   Admiral Togo, whose brilliant tactics had destroyed the Russian fleet at the battle of the Sea of Japan, visited the United States shortly after the Russo–Japanese War. At a state dinner arranged in his honor Bryan was asked to propose the toast. A strict Prohibitionist, he absolutely refused to drink champagne, and it was feared that an embarrassing breakdown of protocol was about to occur. When Bryan rose to propose the toast he held up his glass, saying, "Admiral Togo has won a great victory on the water, and I will therefore toast him in water. When Admiral Togo wins a victory on champagne, I will toast him in champagne."

2   On a campaign Bryan was asked to speak to a crowd of people assembled in a field. As he climbed up onto the manure spreader that served as an impromptu dais, he remarked, "This is the first time I have ever spoken from a Republican platform."
   {Ascribed to others.}

3   In a burst of patriotism, J. P. Morgan announced, "America is good enough for me!"
   "Whenever he doesn't like it, he can give it back to us," was William Jennings Bryan's comment.

৯৯ ৶৶

BUCHANAN, James (1791–1868), *US politician, 15th president of the United States (1857–61). He was US minister to Russia (1832–33) and Great Britain (1853–56) before becoming president as a compromise Democratic candidate. His attempts to hold the country together over the slavery question failed and with the secession of South Carolina in December 1860 his administration virtually fell apart.*

1   In 1845 President Polk appointed Buchanan secretary of state. Ex-President Andrew Jackson made a strong protest. "But you yourself appointed him minister to Russia in your first term," said Polk defensively. "Yes, I did," said Jackson. "It was as far as I could send him out of my sight, and where he could do the least harm. I would have sent him to the North Pole if we had kept a minister there."

2   On leaving the White House in March 1861, Buchanan said to the incoming president, Abraham Lincoln, "If you are as happy, my dear sir, on entering this house as I am in leaving it and returning home, you are the happiest man in this country."

৯৯ ৶৶

BUCHWALD, Art (1925–   ), *US columnist and author.*

1   Buchwald, talking about taxes to the National Association of Beverage Importers at a New York convention, told of just how far a businessman can go these days to justify writing off a lunch tab. Buchwald said the man at the next table asked him, "Would you like to buy this restaurant?" Buchwald declined. Then the stranger said, "Well, can I have your name so that I can say we discussed business?"

৯৯ ৶৶

BUCKINGHAM, George Villiers, 2d Duke of (1628–87), *British nobleman and statesman, member of the Cabal, for which his name supplied the middle letter. (The Cabal was a group of five ministers chosen by King Charles II to advise him. The other members were Clifford, Arlington, Ashley-Cooper, and Lauderdale.) Buckingham's loyalty during Charles II's exile made him an influential figure.*

1   On a royal ceremonial occasion Charles II was being addressed by the full battery of his titles. When the master of ceremonies got to the epithet "Father of his people," Buckingham added, in an undertone, "or quite a lot of them." Even Charles could not overlook this

lèse-majesté, and Buckingham was told to withdraw from the court for a while.

೩ ಆನ

BUCKLAND, William (1784–1856), *British geologist and paleontologist.*

1 Professor Buckland had great gastronomic curiosity. John Ruskin, once his student, tells us (in *Praeterita*) that he "always regretted a day of unlucky engagement on which I missed a delicate toast of mice."

The professor, who disdained virtually nothing organic, once decided that a mole was the nastiest thing he had ever tasted. Later on he awarded the palm to blue-bottles. He was once shown the heart of a king of France, preserved in a snuff box. Said the professor, "I have eaten some strange things, but never the heart of a king." And swallowed it.

{There are other stories told about the disappearance of the preserved heart, generally assumed to be that of Louis XIV.}

2 Buckland once gave a dinner party at which a delicious but unusual soup was served. He challenged his guests to name the chief ingredient, but none guessed correctly. They were subsequently horrified to learn that they were eating the remains of an alligator Buckland had dissected earlier in the day. Two or three were obliged to make a hasty exit from the room. "See what imagination is," said Buckland. "If I told them it was turtle, or terrapin, or bird's-nest soup, they would have pronounced it excellent, and their digestion would have been none the worse." One of the remaining guests ventured to ask if the soup had really been made from the dissected alligator. "As good a calf's head as ever wore a coronet," answered Buckland with a smile.

೩ ಆನ

BUCKLEY William F[rank] (1925–), *US editor, author, and lecturer. The son of a multimillionaire, he founded the journal* National Review *in 1955. His conservative and Roman Catholic opinions are well known to many readers of newspapers and magazines. He is also a familiar radio and television figure.*

1 In 1965, Buckley stood as Conservative candidate for the office of mayor of New York City. The likelihood of victory being almost nonexistent, the campaign was not taken very seriously, even by Buckley himself. A reporter asked him what his first action would be if elected. "I'd demand a recount," replied Buckley.

2 Buckley once sent fellow-author Norman Mailer a copy of his latest book. Mailer, disappointed to find that Buckley had not written any message on the flyleaf, promptly turned to the index to see if he had been mentioned. Alongside Mailer's name in the index was the handwritten greeting "Hi!"

೩ ಆನ

BUDDHA, Gautama (563–483 BC), *Indian prince whose teachings formed the basis of Buddhism. Gautama married his cousin, Princess Yasodhora, at the age of sixteen. At twenty-nine he left home, renouncing his life of luxury to seek solutions to the problems of human existence. After six years of asceticism he came to the conclusion that self-mortification was unlikely to answer his questions. He therefore sought enlightenment within himself, and this he achieved, according to tradition, while seated beneath a banyan tree. The rest of his life was spent in teaching the principles of his enlightenment.*

1 After his enlightenment the Buddha decreed, as an act of personal humility, that no one was to make an image of him or to paint him. However, one nameless artist, seeing him sitting deep in contemplation on the banks of the Ganges at Benares, was so moved by his saintly demeanor that he could not resist attempting to portray the Buddha in some way. He reasoned that if he used as his model, not the Buddha himself, but his reflection in the rippling waters of the Ganges, he would be able to secure for posterity a portrait of the great man without defying the injunction. For this reason many representations of the youthful Buddha have folds in their garments known as the water-ripple effect.

2 A man interrupted Buddha's preaching with a flood of abuse. Buddha waited until he had finished and then asked him, "If a man offered a gift to another but the gift was declined, to whom would the gift belong?"

"To the one who offered it," said the man.

"Then," said Buddha, "I decline to accept your abuse and request you to keep it for yourself."

❧ ☙

BUDÉ, Guillaume (1467–1540), *French humanist scholar. As royal librarian he established the nucleus of the Bibliothèque Nationale and encouraged the study of classical Greek in France.*

1 Budé's servant came running to him one day to tell him that the house was on fire. "Tell your mistress," Budé replied, waving him away. "You know I leave all household matters in her hands."

❧ ☙

BUDGE, J. Donald (1915–), *US tennis player. In 1938 he crowned his achievements by winning the Grand Slam (the four major singles championships — US, British, Australian, and French) before turning professional.*

1 In 1937 Budge met Baron Gottfried von Cramm of Germany in the deciding match of the Davis Cup final at Wimbledon. Just as the game was due to begin, watched by Queen Mary, von Cramm was called to the telephone. "You can't keep Queen Mary waiting," said an official severely. "I can't keep der Fuehrer waiting," responded von Cramm. The caller was Adolf Hitler, ordering the baron to win for the honor of Germany.

{The match was one of the finest in the history of lawn tennis. The German led, two sets to love, before Budge evened the score and eventually won in the fourteenth game of the final set after having had five match points. As he made the

winning shot, he fell. Von Cramm ran to help him up and embraced and congratulated him. Walter Pate, the US team captain, commented on the match, "No other man could have beaten either man," and Budge paid tribute to his sporting opponent by saying that no man had ever faced such pressure in a tennis court as von Cramm faced that day.}

❧ ☙

BUFFALMACCO, Buonamico (?1262–?1340), *Italian painter.*

1 Buffalmacco once lived next door to a rich woolworker, whose wife worked throughout the night at her spinning wheel. The noise of the wheel frequently kept the painter awake. In desperation he devised a plan to remedy the nuisance. Having noticed a small hole in the communicating wall, directly above the neighbors' cooking pot, Buffalmacco hollowed out a cane, pushed it through the wall, and was thus able to add a large amount of salt to the woolworker's dinner every evening. After two or three inedible meals, the woolworker began to beat his wife for her carelessness, and her screams brought a number of their neighbors, including Buffalmacco, to their door. "This calls for a little reason," said the painter when he had heard his neighbor's case. "You complain that the pot is too much salted, but I marvel that this good woman can do anything well, considering that the whole night she sits up over that wheel of hers and has not an hour's sleep. Let her give up this all-night work and sleep her fill, so she will have her wits about her by day and will not fall into such blunders." The woolworker accepted Buffalmacco's advice, and from that time on the painter enjoyed an undisturbed night's rest.
See also BOTTICELLI 1.

❧ ☙

BULL, John (?1563–1628), *English composer. He was organist at the Chapel Royal (1591–92).*

1 "The queen's will being to know the music, her Grace was at that time at the virginals: whereupon, he, being in attendance, Master Bull did come by stealth to hear without, and by mischance did sprawl into the queen's majesty's presence, to the queen's great disturbance. She demanding incontient the

---

The old Duc de Broglie, reminiscing in company about memorable letters he had received, recalled, "The one that gave me the greatest satisfaction was one I got from a very lovely lady. It consisted of only one word."

"And that was?" said one of the guests.

"Friday."

— W. Scholz, *Das Buch des Lachens*

wherefore of such presumption, Master Bull with great skill said that wheresoever majesty and music so well combined, no man might abase himself too deeply; whereupon the queen's majesty was mollified."

2 Hearing of a famous musician at St. Omer's, Dr. Bull, pretending to be a novice, visited him. The man showed Bull a song with forty parts, boasting that it was so complete and full that no one could add to it or improve it. Bull requested pen, ink, and ruled paper and then asked to be locked up in the cathedral music school for two or three hours. The musician locked Bull in as he desired. Before his return Bull had added another forty parts to the original song. The musician tried the music, examined it, then exclaimed that the hand that had added the extra forty parts must be either that of the devil or of Dr. Bull. Bull thereupon disclosed his identity and the St. Omer man fell at his feet in homage.

ॐ ৺

BULLER, Sir Redvers Henry (1839–1908), *British general. A gallant soldier who won the Victoria Cross for his bravery in the Zulu War (1879), Buller had less success as commander during the Boer War (1899–1902) and was replaced in October 1900.*

1 On one of the numerous occasions when Buller was forced to retreat by the Boers, he put the best face possible on the setback by saying that he had retreated without losing a man, a flag, or a cannon. "Or," added Whistler, when the story was told to him, "a minute."

ॐ ৺

BÜLOW, Hans Guido, Baron von (1830–94), *German conductor and pianist. Until his wife, Cosima, eloped with Richard Wagner in 1866, von Bülow was a foremost interpreter of Wagner's work. He subsequently became a great champion of Brahms.*

1 The kaiser wearied of von Bülow's eccentricities and let fall a heavy hint: "If anyone doesn't care for the way things are in Germany, let him shake the dust from his shoes." At the end of von Bülow's last concert in Berlin, he laid down his baton, took out a handkerchief, and elaborately dusted his shoes. And left next day for Egypt.

2 Invited to play for Napoleon III, von Bülow was annoyed to find that the emperor soon ceased to attend to the music and began talking animatedly to one of his guests. Von Bülow stopped playing. "When his majesty speaks," he said, "all must be silent."
{There are a number of versions of this story, some of them featuring other musicians.}

3 A young composer asked von Bülow to listen to his latest composition, a piece that turned out to be notable mainly for the extent of its borrowings from other composers. "How do you like it?" asked the man when he had played it through. "I have always liked it," replied von Bülow.

4 Musicians could assure themselves of the approval of a certain music critic only by taking moderately priced lessons from him. "That's not too bad," observed von Bülow. "His fees are so low one might almost call him incorruptible."

ॐ ৺

BUNSEN, Robert Wilhelm (1811–99), *German chemist; the Bunsen burner is named for him. With Gustav Kirchhoff he developed the science of spectroscopy and discovered the elements rubidium and cesium. He became professor of chemistry at Heidelberg in 1852.*

1 At the end of one of Bunsen's courses, a student of completely unfamiliar appearance presented his certificate to the professor for endorsement. "But, Herr Dingskirch," said Bunsen, glancing at the name on the card, "I've never seen you at any of my lectures."
"Quite so," replied the student. "You see, I always sit behind the pillar."
"What a lot of you sit there," remarked Bunsen, endorsing the certificate with a sigh of resignation.
{This anecdote is also told of Max Herrmann, among others.}

ॐ ৺

BUÑUEL, Luis (1900–83), *Spanish film director. His early surrealist films include* L'Age d'or *(1930). He worked largely in Mexico in the 1950s; his later films include* The Exterminating Angel *(1962) and* The Discreet Charm of the Bourgeoisie *(1972).*

1 Buñuel was brought up as a Catholic by the Jesuits. When asked, in later life, if he had been deeply affected by his Jesuit education, he replied, "I am an atheist, thanks be to God."

ৡৈ ৵ঌ

BURKE, Edmund (1729–97), *British statesman, political philosopher, and writer. He campaigned against maladministration in India and the American colonies and against George III's concept of the king's role in government. Opposed to democracy because he thought it brought irresponsible mob leaders to power, he believed that good government could be best secured under an aristocracy. In his* Reflections on the Revolution in France *(1790) he condemned the French Revolution.*

1 The barrister Arthur Murphy opposed Burke in the discussion during the early 1770s on the question of whether perpetual copyright could exist in literary property. Murphy argued the case of those who contested the booksellers' endeavor to establish such a principle. Discussing the question with Murphy, Burke observed, "But you must remember the booksellers deal in commodities they are not supposed to understand."

"True," said Murphy, "some of 'em do deal in morality."

2 David Hartley, son of the famous philosopher of the same name, was an exceptionally dull speaker. As member of Parliament for Hull, he regularly emptied the House of Commons when he rose to speak. On one occasion in 1783 his audience had dwindled from about three hundred to eighty, most of these half asleep. He seemed about to wind up his oration when he demanded that the clerk of the House read the text of the 1715 Riot Act to illustrate some point he had made. At this Burke leaped to his feet, shouting, "The Riot Act? The Riot Act? To what purpose? Don't you see that the mob is already quietly dispersed?"

3 Someone observed to Burke that the democratic faction in Parliament never seemed to hold together for any length of time. Burke replied, "Birds of prey are not gregarious."

4 Burke's celebrated nine-day speech made in 1794 at the trial of Warren Hastings, the former colonial administrator in India, on charges of corruption, was widely acclaimed as a masterpiece of eloquence. The greatest tribute, however, came from Hastings himself. "For half an hour," he confessed, "I looked up at the orator in a reverie of wonder, and during that space I actually felt myself the most culpable man on earth."

5 Edward Thurlow was moved to the patriotic exclamation: "When I forget my king, may my God forget me!"

"And the best thing God can do for him," muttered Burke.

ৡৈ ৵ঌ

BURNETT, Carol (1934–), *US comedienne.*

1 Climbing out of a cab one day, Miss Burnett inadvertently caught her coat in the door. As the driver continued on his way, unaware of the accident, the comedienne was obliged to run alongside the moving vehicle to avoid being pulled off her feet. A quick-thinking passerby, noticing her plight, hailed the cab and alerted the driver. Having released Miss Burnett's coat, the driver asked her anxiously, "Are you all right?"

"Yes," she replied, still gasping for breath, "but how much more do I owe you?"

ৡৈ ৵ঌ

BURNS, George (1896–), *US actor and radio comedian.*

1 Burns worked in radio for many years with his wife, Gracie Allen. After her death he visited her grave regularly. An interviewer jokingly asked him if he told her what had been going on. "Sure, why not?" was the reply. "I don't know whether she hears me, but I've nothing to lose and it gives me a chance to break in new material."

2 George Burns was lunching one day at a restaurant with his friend Jack Benny. Benny could not make up his mind about whether he should put butter on his bread. "I hate bread without butter," he sighed. On the other hand, his wife, Mary, had put him on a diet specifying no butter. What should he do? Perhaps he should ring up Mary? At this point George Burns cut across his deliberations with,

"Please, Jack, just make this one decision your-self!" So Benny had the butter.

At the end of the meal when the bill was brought, Burns told the waiter to give it to Benny. "Why should I pay?" asked Benny. "If you don't, I'll tell Mary about the butter," said Burns.

3 On reaching the age of eight-five, George Burns observed that this was a very comfort-able stage of life: "I was always taught to re-spect my elders and I've now reached the age when I don't have anybody to respect."

4 Ed Sullivan happened to mention in his newspaper column one day that George Burns wore a toupee. Burns later reproached Sullivan for publicizing this embarrassing piece of in-formation. "But, George," said Sullivan, "I didn't think you'd mind."

"If I didn't mind," retorted Burns, "why would I wear a toupee?"

ও৶ ৶ও

BURR, Aaron (1756–1836), *US politician and lawyer. His checkered political life was effec-tively ended when he killed his bête noire, Alex-ander Hamilton, in a duel (1804). Thomas Jef-ferson distrusted Burr and soon afterward had him arrested on a charge of treason. Although acquitted, he was compelled to spend four years abroad, then returned to a quiet legal practice for the rest of his life.*

1 Burr was inordinately proud of his reputa-tion as a lady-killer. A friend asked him, shortly before his death, why he had allowed a woman to saddle him with the paternity of a child when he knew he was not its father. Burr re-plied, "Sir, when a lady does me the honor to name me the father of her child, I trust I shall always be too gallant to show myself ungrateful for the favor."

ও৶ ৶ও

BURTON, Richard (1925–84), *British stage and screen actor, born in Wales. He was mar-ried twice to actress Elizabeth Taylor, with whom he starred in such films as* Cleopatra *(1962),* Who's Afraid of Virginia Woolf? *(1966), and* The Taming of the Shrew *(1967).*

1 During the filming of *The Assassination of Trotsky*, Burton was playing a scene with

French actor Alain Delon. Delon, as the ner-vous killer, was swinging an ice ax around; at one point the ax came dangerously close to Burton's head. "You'd better be careful how you handle that ax," cried Burton. "There are plenty of French actors around, but if you kill me, there goes one-sixth of all the Welsh actors in the world."

ও৶ ৶ও

BURTON, Sir Richard (1821–90), *British scholar and explorer. He traveled extensively, in India, the Near East, and South America; vis-ited Mecca disguised as a Moslem; and trans-lated into English* The Arabian Nights *(1885) and the* Kama Sutra *(1883). After his death his wife — afraid that he would be remembered for his scandalous works — burned all his journals and diaries.*

1 In Boulogne after his return from Sind, Burton was attracted by a young woman called Louisa, cousin of his future wife, Isabel Arun-dell. Unsavory rumors about Burton's adven-tures in Sind had spread through the fashion-able English colony in Boulogne, and Louisa's mother summoned the young man to her pres-ence, "because," she said, "I think it my duty to ask what your intentions are with regard to my daughter." Burton, who regarded his relation-ship with the lively young Louisa as little more than a pleasant flirtation, was amused and somewhat taken aback by the formality of the interview. "Your duty, madam?"

"Yes, sir."

"Alas," sighed Burton. "Strictly dishonor-able."

2 Isabel Arundell always wanted to marry Richard Burton, and her joy was boundless when at last he proposed to her. Their engage-

---

Anthony Burgess was taking a bath in a Leningrad hotel when the floor con-cierge yelled that she had a cable for him. "Put it under the door," he cried. "I can't!" she shouted. "It's on a tray."

— Anthony Burgess, Preface,
   in *Modern Irish Short Stories,*
   ed. Ben Forkner

ment somewhat prolonged by Burton's continued traveling, Isabel spent the time actively preparing for the marriage she so ardently desired. She learned to milk cows, groom horses, ride astride. She sought out a celebrated fencer and demanded he take her on as a pupil. "What for?" he asked. "So that I can defend Richard when he is attacked," said she.

ಶಿ ⋖ई

BUSBY, Richard (1606–95), *headmaster of Westminster School, London, from 1640. He had a great reputation as both teacher and disciplinarian.*

1 As Dr. Busby was showing King Charles II around his school, it was noticed that, contrary to etiquette, the headmaster kept his hat on in the royal presence. Busby excused himself in these words: "It would not do for my boys to suppose that there existed in the world any greater man than Dr. Busby."

2 Dr. Busby was very short. One day in a crowded London coffeehouse he was addressed by an Irish baronet of huge stature: "May I pass to my seat, O giant?"

"Certainly, O pygmy!" said the doctor, making way.

The bulky baronet started a clumsy apology: "My expression alluded to the size of your intellect."

"And my expression to the size of yours," retorted Busby.

ಶಿ ⋖ई

BUSCH, Fritz (1890–1951), *German-born Swiss conductor of orchestras in several European cities and of the Glyndebourne Festival Opera from 1934 until his death.*

1 One of the favorite stories at the Glyndebourne Festival Opera concerned Busch's very first orchestral rehearsal. He raised his baton and then quickly dropped his arms to his sides before anyone had played a note. Addressing the orchestra, he said in his thickly accented English, "Already is too loud."

ಶಿ ⋖ई

BUTLER, Benjamin Franklin (1818–93), *US general. He became governor of Massachusetts in 1882.*

1 As commander of the Union forces occupying New Orleans in 1862, Butler made himself thoroughly unpopular. After some women had abused Northern soldiers he issued the notorious proclamation that if any woman insulted or showed contempt for "any officer or soldier of the United States, she shall be regarded and shall be held liable to be treated as a woman of the town plying her avocation." This provoked a furious outcry; Butler was dubbed "Beast" Butler, and the enraged ladies all turned their backs on him whenever they met him. He remarked, "These women know which end of them looks best."

2 A Confederate soldier, brought before Butler to take the oath of allegiance at the end of the Civil War, impudently remarked, "We gave you hell at Chickamauga, General!" The furious Butler warned him that if he did not take the oath immediately he would be shot. With some reluctance, the rebel duly took the oath. Then he looked Butler in the eye and said, "General, I suppose I am a good Yankee and citizen of the United States now?" The general replied benignly, "I hope so." "Well, General, the rebels did give *us* hell at Chickamauga, didn't they?"

ಶಿ ⋖ई

BUTLER, Henry Montagu (1833–1918), *British academic. He was headmaster of Harrow (1859–85), then Master of Trinity College, Cambridge (1886–1918). In both posts he was outstandingly successful, inspiring the respect and affection of generations of young men.*

1 Dr. Butler used to invite freshmen at Trinity to have breakfast with him. Finding a nervous group awaiting him one wintry day in the breakfast room, he glanced toward the window and remarked, "Well, we have a little sun this morning." At this the shyest of the young men responded with "I hope Mrs. Butler is all right."

ಶಿ ⋖ई

BUTLER, Richard Austen (1902–82), *British statesman. He became an MP in 1929 and had a distinguished parliamentary career. "Rab" failed, however, to win the leadership of the Conservative party, and with it the chance of becoming prime minister. As minister of education he was responsible for the 1944 Education*

Act, guaranteeing universal secondary education in Britain.

1 In 1957 Butler was defeated by Harold Macmillan in his bid to become leader of the Conservatives, and had to be content with the post of home secretary in Macmillan's administration. Labour statesman Harold Wilson observed of this situation, "Every time Mr. Macmillan comes back from abroad, Rab Butler goes to the airport and grips him warmly by the throat."

৯৯ ৶৶

BUTLER, Samuel (1835–1902), *British novelist. Greatly interested in the scientific controversies of the day, Butler wrote a number of works on these topics, but is best known for his utopian satires* Erewhon *(1872) and* Erewhon Revisited *(1901). He also translated Homer and wrote an autobiographical novel,* The Way of All Flesh *(1903).*

1 (Butler and his companion Henry Festing Jones visited the Palazzo Reale in Palermo. They were cheated by the custode at the entrance to the Capella Palatina, who gave Butler a bad lira in his change and refused to exchange it despite their remonstrances.)

"When we came out we had recovered a little, and the custode . . . returned our umbrellas to us with an obsequiousness capable of but one interpretation. 'I shall not give him anything,' said Butler severely to me. 'Oh yes, I will though,' he added, and his eyes twinkled as he fumbled in his pocket. Then, with a very fair approach to Sicilian politeness, he handed the bad lira back to the old gentleman. The custode's face changed and changed again like a field of corn on a breezy morning. In spite of his archiepiscopal appearance he would have been contented with a few soldi; seeing a whole lira he beamed with delight; then, detecting its badness, his countenance fell and he began to object; almost immediately he identified it as his own coin and was on the point of bursting with rage, but suddenly realizing that he could have nothing to say, he laughed heartily, shook hands with both of us, and apologized for not being able to leave his post as he would so much have liked to drink a glass of wine with us.

"'There, now we have made another friend for life,' said Butler as he drove away."

2 As a result of his studies in Homer, Butler became convinced that the *Odyssey* was written by a woman. In 1897 he published *The Authoress of the Odyssey*. Shortly after this work appeared, Anne Thackeray Ritchie, Thackeray's intelligent and witty daughter, asked him what he was working on now, and was told a book of Shakespeare's sonnets. "Oh, Mr. Butler," she said playfully, "do you know my theory about the sonnets? They were written by Anne Hathaway." Butler never understood that she was mocking him and told the story everywhere against her: "Poor lady, that was a silly thing to say!"

3 (An admirer asked Samuel Butler to write her "a rule of life." Butler thought that her own common sense ought to be a better guide than any precepts he might deliver, and wrote back in a lighthearted tone.)

"'Get as many nice people about you as you can, more particularly Jones and myself. Snub snobs. Stick to the Ten Commandments — they never forbid swearing — and really I do not know what else there is!' She said she did not find my letter as comforting as she hoped it would be."

{For an even more entertaining "rule of life" *see* SATCHEL PAIGE 1.}

4 "The first time that Dr. Creighton asked me to come down to Peterborough before he became Bishop of London, I was a little doubtful whether or not to go. As usual I consulted Alfred [his servant and confidant], who said: 'Let me have a look at his letter, sir.'

"I gave him the letter, and he said: 'I see, sir, there is a crumb of tobacco in it; I think you may go.' I went and enjoyed myself very much."

5 (Samuel Butler's notebooks reveal him as not the most comforting of deathbed companions.)

"'Promise me solemnly,' I said to her as she lay on what I believed to be her death bed, 'if you find in the world beyond the grave that you can communicate with me — that there is some way in which you can make me aware of your continued existence — promise me solemnly that you will never, never avail yourself of it.' She recovered and never, never forgave me."

৯৯ ৶৶

BYNG, John (1704–57), *British admiral, court-martialed and shot for failing to relieve the island of Minorca, then under French attack (1756). He was the subject of Voltaire's witticism that in England "il est bon de tuer de temps en temps un amiral pour encourager les autres" (it is thought desirable to kill an admiral from time to time to encourage the others).*

1 When Byng came to stand before the firing squad, some officers suggested that his face be concealed with a handkerchief lest the sight of him breed reluctance in his executioners. Byng replied, "If it will frighten *them*, let it be done; *they* will not frighten me."

ঌ৽ ৵৾

BYRD, William (1674–1744), *US tobacco planter, diarist, and colonial official. In 1709 he became a member of the council of state and in 1743 its president.*

1 The entry for July 30, 1710, in *The Secret Diary of William Byrd of Westover 1709–1712*, reads:

"In the afternoon my wife and I had a little quarrel which I reconciled with a flourish. Then she read a sermon in Dr. Tillotson to me. It is to be observed that the flourish was performed on the billiard table."

ঌ৽ ৵৾

BYRON, George Gordon, Lord (1788–1824), *British Romantic poet. His first collection of verse,* Hours of Idleness *(1807), was followed by his attack on the literary establishment,* English Bards and Scotch Reviewers *(1809).* Childe Harold's Pilgrimage *(1812) was the fruit of two years' travel in Europe. In his verse romances Byron developed the persona of the Byronic hero: courageous, noble, doomed — and irresistibly attractive to women. Byron's personal life was correspondingly dramatic. After a series of liaisons, including one with his half-sister, Augusta Leigh, he made a disastrous marriage (1815) with Anne Isabella Milbanke, which broke up the following year. Byron left England for Italy, where he began his great verse satire* Don Juan. *In 1823 he volunteered his services to assist the Greeks in their struggle for independence against the Turks, and died from fever at the northern Greek town of Missolonghi the following year.*

1 While he and Robert Peel were schoolmates at Harrow, one day Byron saw Peel being beaten unmercifully by a senior boy. Having no hope of fighting because of his clubfoot, Byron nevertheless approached the bully and bravely asked how many stripes he was intending to inflict upon his poor friend. "What's that to you?" thundered the bully. "Because, if you please," replied Byron, trembling with rage and fear, "I would take half."

2 (Byron was to meet Thomas Moore at the house of Samuel Rogers, although he did not know his host. Rogers describes the evening.)

"When we sat down to dinner I asked Byron if he would take soup? 'No, he never took soup.'—'Would he take some fish?' 'No, he never took fish.' Presently I asked if he would eat some mutton? 'No, he never ate mutton.' — I then asked if he would take a glass of wine? 'No, he never tasted wine.' It was now necessary to inquire what he *did* eat and drink; and the answer was, 'Nothing but hard biscuits and soda water.' Unfortunately neither hard biscuits nor soda water were at hand; and he dined upon potatoes bruised down on his plate and drenched with vinegar.— My guests stayed till very late discussing the merits of Walter Scott and Joanna Baillie.— Some days after, meeting [Byron's friend John Cam] Hobhouse, I said to him, 'How long will Lord Byron persevere in his present diet?' He replied, 'Just as long as you continue to notice it.' I did not then know what I now know to be a fact — that Byron, after leaving my house, had gone to a club in St. James's Street, and eaten a hearty meat supper."

3 After the well-publicized breakup of his marriage, Byron was cut by London society. At one social gathering, he was standing near a doorway through which a group of aristocratic ladies were passing, all of whom ostentatiously ignored him. The procession ended with a pert brunette who nodded to him and whispered, "You see, you should have married me, and then this wouldn't have happened to you."

4 Byron gave his publisher, John Murray, a handsomely bound Bible with a flattering inscription. Murray was rather proud of this gift and used to leave it on a table where his guests might see it. One day a visitor who was admiring the book remarked that at John 18:40, in the sentence "Now Barabbas was a robber," Byron had deleted the word "robber" and substituted "publisher." After this discovery Byron's present no longer appeared on Murray's table.

5 After visiting one of his ladies at a palazzo in Venice, Byron upon departing threw himself fully clothed into the Grand Canal and swam home. The next night he did the same thing, but in order to avoid being wounded by the oars of the gondolieri, this time he swam with his right hand and held a torch aloft in his left hand to give himself light.

C

CABELL, James Branch (1879–1958), *US novelist. His reputation rests on* Jurgen *(1919), a book made famous by attempts to suppress it on account of its supposed immorality.*

1 None of Cabell's other works quite lived up to the success of *Jurgen*. In later years he was amused to receive a letter from a fan: "Dear Mr. Cabell, I have chosen you as my favorite author. Please write to me immediately and tell me why."

CADBURY, George (1839–1922), *British Quaker, cocoa manufacturer, and social reformer. He initiated substantial improvements in the housing and working conditions of his employees.*

1 When King George V and Queen Mary visited the Cadbury works, George Cadbury led the way with the queen while his wife walked behind with the king. Cadbury had removed his hat as a mark of respect for royalty. It was, however, very cold, and Queen Mary was concerned lest the old man should get a chill. "Mr. Cadbury, please put on your hat," she said. George Cadbury demurred. "Please, Mr. Cadbury — or I'll ask the king to command you to do so!" Her host still hesitated. Then from behind them came the ringing tones of Elizabeth Cadbury: "George, put your hat on." He did.

CAEN, Herbert Eugene (1916–   ), *US journalist.*

1 (Herb Caen followed hard on the heels of the troops at the D-Day landings in Normandy. The writer Barnaby Conrad records the contents of a postcard that Caen sent describing an incident just after the landing.)

"When we landed at Carentan it was so great — I was elated and excited and scared and I had to go to the bathroom desperately. I saw an old guy there who was too old-world-French to be true, with the smock and the white mustache and the beret, and I rushed up to him and said, '*Monsieur, pardon, où est le lavabo?* [Excuse me, sir, but where is the bathroom?]' And he answered, tears of happiness streaming down his cheeks and gesturing around him expansively, '*Mais, toute la belle France, mon ami, toute la belle France!*'" (All of beautiful France, my friend, all of beautiful France!)

CAESAR, Gaius Julius (100–44 BC), *Roman general and statesman. Weathering the political storms that destroyed the late Roman republic, Caesar became the leader of the popular party in Rome. His conquest of Gaul (58–50) brought him command of a loyal and powerful army. When his erstwhile political colleague Pompey, backed by the Roman senate, demanded that he resign his command, he invaded Italy, thus sparking civil war. Defeats of the Pompeian forces at Pharsalus (48), Thapsus (46), and Munda (45) left Caesar as sole ruler of the Roman world. He returned to Rome, where he initiated an ambitious program of reform and reconstruction. He was assassinated by a republican group on the Ides (the fifteenth) of March in 44 BC.*

1 At one stage in Caesar's early career political feelings were running so high against him that he thought it expedient to leave Rome for a while and go to Rhodes to take a course in rhetoric. En route the ship was attacked by pirates. Caesar was captured and held for a ransom of 12,000 gold pieces. His staff were sent away to arrange the ransom, and Caesar spent nearly forty days with his captors. During this time he would often jokingly say to the pirates that he would capture and crucify them, a threat they found greatly amusing. When the ransom was paid and Caesar was set at liberty, the first thing he did was to gather a fleet and go after the pirates. He caught them and crucified them to a man.

2 In 61 BC Caesar's second wife, Pompeia, was involved in a scandal concerning the religious rites known as the Feast of the Great Goddess. Only women were admitted to the rites, but on this occasion it was rumored that the notorious profligate Publius Clodius had attended them in female dress and had there committed adultery with Pompeia. Caesar divorced Pompeia. At the subsequent inquiry into the desecration various members of Caesar's family gave evidence. Caesar himself declined to offer any testimony against Pompeia. The court therefore asked him why he had divorced her. "Caesar's wife must be above suspicion," was the reply.

3 Caesar's confrontation with the senatorial party came to a head in 49 BC, when he was ordered to relinquish control of the armies he had commanded as governor in Gaul. Realizing that his opponents would not rest until they had destroyed him, Caesar decided to invade Italy. However, when he reached the Rubicon River, which formed the boundary between Gaul and Italy itself, he could scarcely bring himself to issue the fatal order to cross. As he hesitated, a figure of superhuman size was seen on the bank. It snatched a trumpet from a soldier, blew a mighty blast on it, and then ran into the river and crossed over. Caesar accepted this as a sign from the gods and led his troops over with the words: "*Iacta alea est*" (The die is cast).

4 When Caesar sailed from Italy at the end of 49 BC to attack Pompey in northwestern Greece, he was hampered by lack of transport for his troops and by the midwinter storms that made crossing the Adriatic a hazardous enterprise. When the transports he had sent back to Brindisi to fetch reinforcements failed to return (some had been lost to enemy action and the remainder were afraid to sail), Caesar resolved to return to Brindisi himself and reorganize them. Disguised as a slave, Caesar set out in a small boat against the wind. The sea became so stormy that the pilot gave orders to turn back, but Caesar stood up and encouraged him to persevere. "Go on and fear nothing," he cried. "You carry Caesar and his fortune."

{Despite this famous exhortation, the weather eventually forced the boat to turn back to the Greek shore, where, according to Plutarch, his soldiers met him and scolded him for exposing himself to so much danger and for trusting them so little.}

5 Gossip was rife in Rome about Caesar's sexual appetites and the streets resounded with ribald songs about him; as one opponent remarked, "He was every woman's husband and every man's wife." One of Caesar's mistresses was Servilia, the mother of Marcus Junius Brutus, and it was also rumored that she had prostituted her daughter, Tertia, to him. Caesar gave Servilia many costly gifts and during the civil war had certain profitable estates sold to her at a price far below their market value. "No wonder they were cheap," observed Cicero, "since a third [*tertia*] had been discounted."

6 In 47 BC Caesar decisively defeated the king of Pontus, Pharnaces II, at Zela in Asia Minor. He announced his victory in Rome with the immortal "*Veni, vidi, vici*" (I came, I saw, I conquered).

7 In the Alps Caesar came upon a poor and miserable village. One of his company idly wondered whether there was competition for civic honors in such a place, whether the village's men struggled and schemed to be head of their wretched community. With great earnestness, Caesar said, "For my part, I would rather be the chief man in this village than the second man in Rome."

8 While he was dining with friends on the evening of March 14, the question arose: "What is the best kind of death?"

"A sudden one," exclaimed Caesar before the others could answer. The next day he was assassinated.

9 Early in March of 44 BC the augur Spurinna warned Caesar that a great danger would befall him on the Ides of that month. On the Ides Caesar set off as usual for the Senate house; he encountered Spurinna and said to him with a smile, "The Ides of March have come."

"True, they have come," answered Spurinna, "but not yet gone."

{Or as Shakespeare has the line, "Ay, Caesar; but not gone."}

10 Among the conspirators who attacked Caesar on the fatal Ides of March in the Roman Senate house was Marcus Junius Brutus, whom Caesar had trusted and favored as a son. In the accounts of the assassination by Roman historians, Caesar is said at first to have resisted the onslaught of the assassins. But when he saw Brutus among them with his dagger drawn to deliver a blow, he ceased to struggle, and pulling the top part of his robe over his face, said, "You too, Brutus?"

{These words, which if spoken at all would have been said in Greek, are well known in their Latin form: "*Et tu, Brute?*" The Greek form is "*Kai su, teknon?*" (You too, my son?)}

ह० ००१

CAGLIOSTRO, Alessandro (1743–95), *Italian alchemist and adventurer. Among his other adventures, he was implicated (in 1785, while on a visit to Paris) in the notorious scandal involving Marie Antoinette, the Comtesse de La Motte, and a diamond necklace. He was acquitted.*

1 Among the stories attaching to this famous charlatan was a rumor that he was three hundred years old. One of his servants, asked to confirm this, replied, "I can't. I've only been in his service a hundred years myself."

ह० ००१

CAGNEY, James (1899–   ) *US film actor. Among his many famous roles are those he played in* The Public Enemy *(1931),* Yankee Doodle Dandy *(1942), and* Ragtime *(1982).*

1 (His wife is proud of Cagney's incredible memory. She recently recalled one instance of it.)

"One day not long ago, we were getting into the car in New York, and he saw a man across the street. 'You see that fellow over there?' Jimmy said to me. 'He sat next to me in school. His name is Nathan Skidelsky.' 'Prove it,' I told him. 'Go say hello.' So he did. And you know what? It *was* Nathan Skidelsky. The only problem was, he didn't remember who Jimmy Cagney was."

ह० ००१

CAINE, Hall (1853–1931), *British novelist and dramatist who often used the Isle of Man as a setting. His best-known works were* The Manxman *(1894),* The Prodigal Son *(1904) and* The Woman of Knockaloe *(1923).*

1 Fame, it seems, can vanish as quickly as it comes. Few people now know the name of Hall Caine, for instance, who was internationally admired in the first half of this century. His books were translated into every known language and his appearance (not unlike Shakespeare's) was familiar to everyone. When Maksim Gorki visited London and was introduced at a party to such literary greats as Hardy, Conrad, Shaw, Wells, and Bennett, he inspected the guests for the famous face and, not finding it, demanded, "Where is Hall Caine?"

ह० ००१

CALHERN, Louis (1895–1956), *US actor.*

1 Calhern was starring in an obviously doomed play that was having its first — and as it turned out, its last — night in Boston. Halfway through the first act the actors realized that the audience consisted of three people. Advancing to the proscenium, Calhern courteously invited them to join the cast so they wouldn't feel so lonely.

ह० ००१

CALIGULA [Gaius Caesar] (AD 12–41), *Roman emperor. His nickname means "Little Boots," a reference to the small military boots he wore as a boy. His reign (37–41) was marked by capricious cruelty, and he seems to have been more than half mad.*

1 Caligula was much addicted to gladiatorial games and other gory sports. On one occasion when the assembled Romans cheered on a team that the emperor did not support, he leaped to his feet in a rage, shouting, "I wish all you Romans had only one neck!"

2 At full moon, in accordance with his claim to be on an equal footing with the gods, Caligula used to invite the moon goddess to his bed. "Did you not see her?" he demanded of Aulus Vitellius (himself later to become emperor). "No," said Vitellius tactfully, "only you gods can see one another."

3 At a banquet Caligula was suddenly seized with a fit of helpless laughter. The consuls reclining next to him asked if they might share in the imperial merriment. Caligula, wiping the tears from his eyes, managed to gasp, "You'll never guess! It suddenly occurred to me that I had only to give a single nod, and both your throats would be cut on the spot."

ॐ ॐ

CALLAS, Maria (1923–77), *operatic soprano born in the United States of Greek parentage and trained in Greece. Her brilliant coloratura singing and powerful dramatic presence brought her acclaim in opera houses around the world. Her personal life was dogged by unhappiness.*

1 When Maria Callas was singing at the Metropolitan Opera in New York, she was interviewed by a reporter who said, "You were born in the United States, you were brought up in Greece, you are now practically an Italian. What language do you think in?" Miss Callas replied, "I count in English."

2 Signing a contract to perform at the 1958 Festival of Two Worlds at Spoleto, Italy, Callas explained to Gian Carlo Menotti that he was actually saving money by employing her. He would not need to spend vast amounts on elaborate decor, which might distract the audience's attention from her voice. An expensive tenor would also be unnecessary, as the crowds would flock to hear the great Callas regardless of the quality of the other performers. "I've signed up Luchino Visconti as director," said Menotti. "Wonderful!" cried Callas. Then, after a moment's thought, she added, "But he lacks just one thing. He lacks humility."

ॐ ॐ

CALVERLEY, Charles Stuart (1831–84), *British writer of light verse, known for his parodies and translations.*

1 On an undergraduate frolic, Calverley and some accomplices stole the inn sign hanging outside a public house in Cambridge and bore it off to their college. The irate landlord collected a group of brawny friends and set off after the students. The college porter barred the college gates against the townsmen. They hammered on the gates and the master of the college came to see what was the matter. The porter told him, and the master sent for Calverley. "Mr. Calverley, what is the meaning of this disturbance?"

"Master, an evil and adulterous generation seeketh a sign, but a sign shall not be given unto them," replied Calverley. (See Matthew 12:39.)

2 Showing a party of tourists around the colleges of Oxford University, Calverley is said to have announced: "That is Balliol College. That is the Master's house . . ." Here he paused to throw a stone at the study window. "And that," he continued, "is the Master."

{This story has been ascribed to other famous undergraduates.}

ॐ ॐ

CAMBRIDGE, George William Frederick Charles, 2d Duke of (1819–1904), *British field marshal. After distinguished service in the Crimean War, the duke, who was first cousin to Queen Victoria, took on the reorganization of the War Office and was in charge of military administration until his reluctant retirement at the age of seventy-six.*

1 Making the rounds of a hospital with Florence Nightingale during the Crimean War, the duke recognized a sergeant of the guard who had had a third of his body shot away. The duke addressed him by name, and asked jovially, "Aren't you dead yet?" Later the wounded man said to Miss Nightingale with tears in his eyes, "So feelin' of 'is Royal 'ighness, wasn't it, ma'am? Bless 'is 'eart, 'e wondered why I ain't dead yet!"

ॐ ॐ

CAMBRONNE, Pierre-Jacques, Baron de (1770–1842), *French general.*

1   Cambronne commanded the French imperial guard at Waterloo. The circumstances of his capture by Colonel Hugh Halkett, a Hanoverian officer serving in the British army, are confused. The traditional account is that when Halkett called upon Cambronne to surrender, the Frenchman replied, "*La garde meurt, mais ne se rend pas.*" (The guard dies but does not surrender.)

"Damned humbug," Halkett later remarked of this famous utterance, leaving it unclear whether he was referring to its authenticity or its sentiment.

{Cambronne himself denied the saying twenty years later at a banquet in Nantes. The possibility remains that the words were uttered earlier as an encouragement to the guard; it has also been plausibly suggested that what Cambronne actually said when Halkett grabbed him by the aiguillette was "*Merde!*" Hence *le mot de Cambronne* as a euphemism for "shit" (*merde*).}

ॐ ঙ্গ

CAMBYSES II (died 522 BC), *king of Persia (529–522 BC), son of Cyrus the Great. His conquests added Egypt and part of the Nile Valley to the Persian empire, but subsequent expeditions against Ammon and Ethiopia were unsuccessful.*

1   Cambyses was a drunken despot, yet one of his actions shows that he was not without a sense of poetic fitness. When a judge was found guilty of corruption, Cambyses ordered him to be flayed alive. After the sentence had been carried out, the skin was used to cover the seat from which judgments were handed down. Cambyses then appointed the dead judge's son to his father's position.

ॐ ঙ্গ

CAMERON, Julia Margaret (1815–79), *British photographer. A pioneer in the field, she took up photography quite late in life. She was noted for her eccentricity.*

1   Mrs. Cameron used to present her friends with inappropriate and rather eccentric gifts that had caught her eye — a pair of yew trees for the poet Alfred Tennyson to plant, old cat-

alogues for his children to read, rolls of wallpaper, legs of mutton from her sister's estate, a violet poncho for Mrs. Tennyson's father. Her gifts were not always graciously received. Thomas Carlyle once unwrapped a Christmas parcel and found a prayer book. "Either the Devil or Julia Cameron must have sent me this!" he exclaimed.

ॐ ঙ্গ

CAMERON OF LOCHIEL, Sir Ewan (1629–1719), *Scottish highland chieftain, reputed to have killed the last wolf in Scotland. He fought with Graham of Claverhouse in the battle of Killiecrankie (1689), when William III's troops were massacred by the Jacobite highlanders.*

1   Sir Ewan was out camping in the highlands with his young grandson, Donald Cameron (1695–1748), later known as "the Gentle Lochiel." There had been a heavy fall of snow and the Cameron of Lochiel noticed that his grandson had rolled up a snowball to make a pillow. Sir Ewan kicked the snowball away. "I'll have no effeminacy here, boy," he snarled.

ॐ ঙ্গ

CAMPBELL, Donald (1921–67), *British engineer who followed his father, Sir Malcolm Campbell (1885–1948), in building record-breaking racing cars and speedboats, invariably called* Bluebird. *He was killed trying to break his own water-speed record at Coniston Water, crashing at the speed of 328 mph.*

1   The night before his fatal run, Campbell, playing Russian patience, turned up the combination of ace of spades and queen of spades — considered to be the unluckiest card combination. "One of my family is going to get the chop," said Campbell, who was extremely superstitious.

ॐ ঙ্গ

CAMPBELL, Mrs. Patrick [Beatrice Stella Campbell, *née* Tanner] (1865–1940), *English actress, famous for her wit as well as her dramatic tantrums. She created the role of Eliza Doolittle in George Bernard Shaw's* Pygmalion.

1   Mrs. Patrick Campbell was rehearsing William Butler Yeats's *Deirdre* at the Abbey

Theatre, Dublin. After a particularly wild display of her famous temperament, she walked downstage and peered out at the author, who was pacing up and down the stalls. "I'd give anything to know what you're thinking," she shouted. "I'm thinking," replied Yeats, "of the master of a wayside Indian railway station who sent a message to his company's headquarters saying: 'Tigress on the line: wire instructions.' "

2   When Mrs. Campbell went to Hollywood in the early 1930s to be considered for film roles, she was handed the customary mimeographed publicity form. As requested, she gave details of her name, the color of her hair and eyes, her height, her hobbies, and so forth. When she came to the sheet headed "Experience," she wrote, "Edward VII."

3   At dinner Mrs. Patrick Campbell was sitting next to a biologist who could talk of nothing but the marvelous social organization of ant colonies. "Do you know," he said enthusiastically, "they have their army and their own police force?"
"What, no navy?" said Mrs. Campbell.

4   Mrs. Campbell once attempted to smuggle her pet Pekingese through customs by tucking him inside the upper part of her cape. "Everything was going splendidly," she later remarked, "until my bosom barked."

5   During the course of an American tour, Mrs. Pat once lost her usual control of the situation. A rather shy, unobtrusive little man was taking her in to dinner. She turned her magnetic eyes on him and, in her most effective histrionic tones, said, *"Tell* me which would you sooner do — love passionately or be loved passionately?" The little man took a deep breath, considered, then ventured, "I'd rather be a canary."

6   Sara and Gerald Murphy, talented in their own right, were wealthy, well-connected friends of the novelist F. Scott Fitzgerald. Sara was also a favorite of Mrs. Pat Campbell, so much so that Mrs. Pat, whenever out shopping for clothes for her theater appearances, would insist on Sara's accompanying her. "Sara, darling," she would say, "does the dress walk? Or does it make me look just like a cigar?"

Chertkov, a disciple of Tolstoy, was a wealthy aristocrat. Tolstoy once reprimanded him for traveling first class, suggesting that, to demonstrate his humility, he should go second. On his next journey the obedient Chertkov hired an entire second-class coach for himself.

— from Michael Scammel, *Alexander Solzhenitsyn: A Biography*

7   Mrs. Campbell was once asked by a rather pompous gentleman why it was that women were so devoid of any sense of humor. "God did it on purpose," replied the actress, "so that we may love you men instead of laughing at you."

8   Her genius did not always include tact. In her latter years, during an American tour, she was introduced to a distinguished gentleman who happened to be virtually bald. They had met many times before, but each time she had failed to recognize him. So it was in this latest encounter. The gentleman finally muttered something expressing irritation. Mrs. Pat's lovely voice filled with tears as she murmured brokenly, "I'm so sorry — I think it's because you do your hair differently!"

9   Even when she was in her seventies, an imposing ruin, Mrs. Pat's wit did not desert her. In 1937, in New York, the English drama critic James Agate accompanied her on a drive across the George Washington Bridge. He remembers her comment on Moses. She decided that there were only ten commandments because Moses must have said to himself, "Must stop or I shall be getting silly."

❧ ❧

CAMPBELL, Thomas (1777–1844), *British poet, known especially for his war songs and narrative poems. An educational reformer as well, he played an active part in the foundation of London University.*

1   At the height of the Napoleonic wars Campbell attended a literary dinner at which he proposed a toast to "Napoleon Bonaparte." An angry clamor broke out among the patriotic guests. Campbell raised his voice and contin-

ued: "Gentlemen, you must not mistake me. I admit that the French emperor is a tyrant. I admit that he is a monster. I admit that he is the sworn foe of our nation, and, if you will, of the whole human race. But, gentlemen, we must be just to our enemy. We must not forget that he once shot a bookseller."

The audience, nearly every one of them an author, broke into applause.

{The executed bookseller was Johann Palm of Nuremberg.}

2 Campbell once explained to a friend why he did not like to be associated with his famous work, *The Pleasures of Hope*. "When I was young," he said, "I was always greeted among my friends as Mr. Campbell, author of *The Pleasures of Hope*. When I married, I was married as the author of *The Pleasures of Hope*; and when I became a father, my son was the son of the author of *The Pleasures of Hope*." His friend could not help but recall these words as he stood beside the poet's grave at his funeral. The inscription on the coffin read: "Thomas Campbell LLD, author of *The Pleasures of Hope*, died, June 15, 1844, aged 67."

3 Attending Paisley races with John Wilson, Campbell bet his companion fifty pounds that a certain horse, Yellow Cap, would win the first race. When the race was over, Campbell, thinking his horse had lost, turned to Wilson and said, "I owe you fifty pounds; but really, when I reflect that you are a professor of moral philosophy, and that betting is a sort of gambling only fit for blacklegs, I cannot bring my conscience to pay the bet."

"I very much approve of your principles," replied Wilson, "and I mean to act upon them. In point of fact, Yellow Cap has won the race, and, but for conscience, I ought to pay you the fifty pounds. But you will excuse me."

ह्ल्र ॐ

CANE, Facino (1360–1412), *Italian condottiere*.

1 Facino Cane's marauding bands of soldiers were greatly feared. One day a rich man, dressed in a fine doublet, came to complain that one of Cane's soldiers had held him up and robbed him of his coat. "Were you wearing that doublet on the day of the robbery?" inquired Facino Cane. The complainant said that

he was. "Get out," said the condottiere. "It wasn't one of my soldiers who robbed you. None of *them* would have left you that doublet."

ह्ल्र ॐ

CANNING, George (1770–1827), *British statesman, foreign secretary twice (1807–09, 1822–27) and Tory prime minister (1827)*.

1 Sydney Smith said that Canning in office was like a fly in amber: "Nobody cares about the fly. The only question is — how the devil did it get there?"

2 Canning was a master of the putdown. He once attended a church service, following which the clergyman asked his opinion of the sermon. Canning replied, "You were brief."

"Yes," said the clergyman, "you know I avoid being tedious."

"But you *were* tedious," said Canning.

ह्ल्र ॐ

CANNON, Cornelia James (1876–1969), *US novelist, wife of Walter B. Cannon, eminent neurologist and professor of medicine*.

1 (The Cannons' daughter Marian Cannon Schlesinger, ex-wife of historian Arthur Schlesinger, Jr., tells this story about her mother.)

"A year or two later [she was about ninety], when sitting in the car waiting for my sister, who was buying apples in an orchard farm near Franklin [New Hampshire] my mother suddenly called out to her, 'I'm dying, Linda. We must go home. This is such an undignified place to die!' When my sister exclaimed, 'Mother, how do you know you're dying?' she said, 'How *can* I know, I've never died before.'"

When Vera Czermak learned that her husband had betrayed her, she decided she would end it all by jumping out of her third-story window. Some time later she awoke in the hospital to discover that she was still alive, having landed upon her husband. Mr. Czermak, however, was dead.

— John Train, *True Remarkable Occurrences*

CANTOR, Eddie (1892–1964), *US comedian. He began his career as a vaudeville entertainer and went on to perform in films such as* Whoopee *(1930),* The Kid from Spain *(1932), and* Show Business *(1944).*

1 As he left the theater after a vaudeville show in Wichita, Kansas, Cantor stopped to sign autographs for a group of children gathered around the stage door. One of the children, a small boy, was standing apart from the rest. "Don't you want my autograph too?" called Eddie.

"Hell, no," replied the boy scornfully. "I was waiting for you to get through with your act so I can see *Donald Duck.*"

2 Hearing of the birth of producer Irving Thalberg's son, Cantor sent the following telegram: "Congratulations on your latest production. Sure it will look better after it has been cut."

છે. ✑

CANUTE [Cnut] (?994–1035), *Danish king of England (1014–35).*

1 The story of how Canute rebuked the flattery of his retainers is told in a twelfth-century chronicle. Tiring of their extravagant praises of his greatness, power, and invincibility, Canute ordered his chair to be set down on the seashore, where he commanded the waves not to come in and wet him. The incoming tide soon proved the futility of human commands, and the chronicler adds that from this time on Canute never wore his crown again, but hung it upon a statue of the crucified Christ.

છે. ✑

CAPA, Robert (1913–54), *US photo-journalist, born Andrei Friedmann in Hungary. He made some of the best-known photographic records of twentieth-century slaughter, from the Spanish Civil War, through World War II, and later in Palestine. He was killed by a land mine while covering the French Indochina conflict for* Life.

1 Capa was in the Basque town of Bilbao in 1937 during the German bombing. He was out photographing when a German plane swooped low overhead. With two other men he jumped for shelter into a ditch. Thinking that he needed somehow to introduce himself, Capa turned to his companions. "I am a photographer," he said. "I am a Basque Catholic," said the second man. The last man snarled, "Those are two professions that are of no use at this moment."

છે. ✑

CAPONE, Al (1899–1947), *US gangster of Italian birth. He dominated the Chicago underworld in the 1920s.*

1 The US Bureau of Internal Revenue astounded Capone by demanding millions of dollars in back taxes. "They can't collect legal taxes from illegal money," he objected.

{They could; in 1931 Capone was imprisoned for tax evasion.}

છે. ✑

CAPUS, Alfred (1858–1922), *French playwright and novelist.*

1 Capus attended a rehearsal of a play in which an incredibly bad performance was given by the ingenue in the main female role. "How could such an important part be given to such an inexperienced ninny?" Capus demanded of the director. The director explained that the show's producer was "interested" in the girl. "Ah, *bon*," said Capus, "but that's not brought out enough in the first act."

છે. ✑

CARDANO, Girolamo (1501–76), *Italian mathematician and astrologer. His addiction to gambling led him to formulate a mathematical theory of chance.*

1 Cardano was renowned throughout Europe as an astrologer, even visiting England to

---

Caesarius of Heisterbach (c. 1170–c. 1240), Cistercian monk and medieval chronicler, tells of a Cistercian lay brother who was heard to pray to Christ: "Lord, if Thou free me not from this temptation, I will complain of Thee to Thy mother."

— Will Durant, *The Story of Civilization*, IV

cast the horoscope of the young king, Edward VI. A steadfast believer in the accuracy of his so-called science, Cardano constructed a horoscope predicting the hour of his own death. When the day dawned, it found him in good health and safe from harm. Rather than have his prediction falsified, Cardano killed himself.

ॐ ॐ

CARDOZO, Benjamin (1870–1938), *US Supreme Court Justice.*

1 A group of Supreme Court justices once took an outing by boat as a break from the pressures of the law. Justice Cardozo, well known for his courtroom dispassionateness, began to feel seasick. A colleague, noticing his discomfort, hurried over to him and asked whether there was anything he could do. "Yes," replied the judge, "overrule the motion."

ॐ ॐ

CARLETON, Henry Guy (1856–1910), *US playwright and wit.*

1 Carleton suffered from a stutter, but he did not let that worry him unduly. Greeting his friend Nat Goodwin, the comedian, he said, "G-G-Goodwin, c-c-can you sp-p-pare m-m-me f-f-fifteen m-m-minutes?"

"Certainly, what is it?"

"I w-w-want f-f-five m-m-minutes' c-c-conversation w-w-with you."

ॐ ॐ

CARLOS I (1863–1908), *king of Portugal (1889–1908). After suspending the Portuguese constitution (1907) in order to bring about some urgent reforms, King Carlos and his eldest son were assassinated.*

1 At the end of a visit to England King Carlos was asked by his host, King Edward VII, which aspects of the country had impressed him most. "The roast beef," replied the Portuguese monarch. "Is that all?" pursued his host, mildly disappointed. King Carlos pondered, then said, "Well, the boiled beef is quite good too."

ॐ ॐ

CARLYLE, Thomas (1795–1881), *British historian, born in Scotland. In 1826 he married Jane Welsh, renowned for her wit and talents as*

a letter-writer. In 1834 the Carlyles moved to London, where Carlyle completed his most famous work, The French Revolution (1837). His writings on contemporary politics were flavored by his view that justice and progress could not be obtained by popular movements, but only by the rule of a strong man, the hero. Other major works include Oliver Cromwell's Letters and Speeches (1845) and the History of Frederick the Great (1858–65). With Mrs. Carlyle's death in 1866 Carlyle ended his career as a major writer.

1 (When Carlyle had completed the first part of *The French Revolution,* he lent the whole manuscript to John Stuart Mill, who had aided him with advice and loans of books. Carlyle's *Journal* for March 7, 1835, takes up the story:)

"Last night at tea, Mill's rap was heard at the door: he entered pale, unable to speak; gasped out to my wife to go down and speak with Mrs. Taylor [whom Mill later married]; and came forward (led by my hand, and astonished looks) the very picture of desperation. After various inarticulate utterances to merely the same effect, he informs me that my First Volume (left out by him in too careless a manner, after or while reading it) was except four or five bits of leaves irrevocably ANNIHILATED! I remember and can still remember less of it than of anything I ever wrote with such toil. It is gone, the whole world and myself backed by it could not bring that back: nay the old spirit too is fled. I find it took five months of steadfast, occasionally excessive, and always sickly and painful toil. — Mill very injudiciously stayed with us till late; and I had to make an effort and speak, as if indifferent, about other common matters: he left us however in a relapsed state. . . ."

{By the latter part of September the same year, Carlyle had rewritten the destroyed manuscript, though the second version was considerably different from the first.}

2 Carlyle told the Irish poet William Allingham that he was intending to write a life of Michelangelo. When Allingham expressed interest and enthusiasm, Carlyle went on discouragingly, "Mind ye, I'll no' say much about his art."

3 Carlyle found that the American Civil War

confirmed his somber views on the human condition. "There they are cutting each other's throats, because one half of them prefer hiring their servants for life, and the other by the hour."

4 Commenting on the marriage of Thomas and Jane Welsh Carlyle, a mutual acquaintance suggested to Tennyson that it was a pity because with anybody else each might have been quite happy. Tennyson disagreed: "By any other arrangement *four* people would have been unhappy instead of two."

5 Carlyle was among those who used to provide financial aid to Leigh Hunt, who was notoriously careless about money. (He suggested the character of Harold Skimpole to Charles Dickens when the latter was writing *Bleak House*.) A friend calling on Carlyle, who was not rich himself at that time, noticed two gold sovereigns lying on the mantel and inquired what they were for. Carlyle tried to fob him off with an evasive answer, but his visitor persisted. "Well," said Carlyle reluctantly, "the fact is, Leigh Hunt likes better to find them there than that I should give them to him."

&ℰ⇔

CARNEGIE, Andrew (1835–1919), *Scottish-born US businessman and philanthropist. He considered that the rich had a responsibility toward society, a view put forward in his book* The Gospel of Wealth (1900). *He provided capital for numerous social and educational projects, including many libraries.*

1 Andrew Carnegie was a generous supporter of the New York Philharmonic Society, meeting its annual deficits in its early years. One year the society's secretary came as usual to Carnegie's mansion, this time requesting a subvention of $60,000. Carnegie was just about to sign the check when he paused and said, "No, I've changed my mind. Surely there are other people who like music enough to help with their own money." He then told the secretary to go out and raise half the necessary amount, promising to match it with the other half when this had been done.

The following day the secretary was back at the Carnegie mansion, announcing that he had raised the requisite money. Carnegie commended the man's enterprise and wrote out

and signed his check for $30,000. As he handed it over he said, "Would you mind telling me who gave you the other half?"

"Not at all. Mrs. Carnegie."

2 Carnegie did not marry until he was fifty-one, although in earlier years he had sought the company of various eligible girls. When one of these married a rival, he said complacently, "If anybody else in the world can win her, I don't want her."

3 A fervent socialist, visiting Carnegie, spoke at some length about the evils of capitalism and the need for the fair distribution of wealth. Carnegie called his secretary and asked for two figures: the total value of his assets and possessions, and the latest estimate of the world population. After a simple calculation he instructed his secretary: "Give this gentlemen sixteen cents. That's his share of my wealth."

4 Questioning Frank Doubleday about the publishing business, Carnegie asked bluntly, "How much did you make last month?" Doubleday tried to dodge the question, explaining that publishing profits could not be calculated on a month-to-month basis. Carnegie was unimpressed. "Frank," he said, "I'd get out of it."

&ℰ⇔

CAROL II (1893–1953), *king of Rumania (1930–40). After divorcing Mme Zizi Lambrino, with whom he had contracted a morganatic marriage in 1917, he married Princess Helen of Greece. In 1925 he renounced his right of succession to the throne in favor of their son Michael, and went to live in Paris with Mme Magda Lupescu. In 1930 he flew back to Rumania and replaced his son as king. Driven from the throne by the Germans, he spent the rest of his life in exile with Mme Lupescu.*

1 While in exile King Carol told his friend, the British diplomat Sir Robert Bruce Lockhart, that during his reign he had selected fourteen of the brightest Rumanians for special training in the government service. He sent seven to England and seven to the United States, to study their political and economic systems. "The seven who went to England were very smart — they all achieved great success in the government in Bucharest," said Carol.

"What about the seven you sent to the States?" asked Lockhart.

"They were even smarter," said the king. "They stayed there."

§ ≈ ≈§

CAROLINE, Duchesse de Berri (1798–1870), *Italian wife of Charles Ferdinand, Duc de Berri (1778–1820), son of Charles X of France. Her husband was assassinated, but Caroline bore him a posthumous son on whom the hopes of French royalists were centered after Charles X was exiled (1830).*

1 The Duc de Berri was a notorious libertine, a fact to which his wife was quite resigned. In 1820 she was visited by about a score of women from Nantes, all of them claiming to be with child by the duke. The duchess asked one of her household how long the duke had been at Nantes. "A week, madame."

"Ah, then in that case, it's quite possible," sighed the duchess.

§ ≈ ≈§

CAROLINE of Ansbach (1683–1737), *wife of George II, king of Great Britain and Ireland (1727–60), whom she married in 1705.*

1 Queen Caroline went to see an exhibition of portraits of English royalty by the painter Jonathan Richardson. She observed the picture of the plain-looking Cromwell hung between Charles I and Charles II. To the artist she said, "Surely that personage is not a king."

"No, madam," replied Richardson. "He is no king, but it is good for kings to have him among them as a memento."

2 Though George II was notoriously unfaithful to Queen Caroline and kept a series of mistresses, when she lay on her deathbed he was sincerely grieved and sat weeping. The dying queen begged him to marry again, but George replied through his tears, "No, I shall have mistresses."

"Ah, that need not hinder you," said Queen Caroline.

§ ≈ ≈§

CAROLINE of Brunswick (1768–1821), *wife of King George IV of Britain. George detested her and from 1796 they lived apart. Her incautious conduct provoked the so-called Delicate Investigation, and in 1814 she left England to travel abroad. On George's accession (1820) she returned to claim her rightful place as queen, provoking the king to bring an action for divorce on the grounds of adultery. Although the bill dissolving the royal marriage had to be abandoned because popular feeling favored Caroline, she was excluded from the coronation ceremony. She died shortly afterward.*

1 When the then Prince of Wales first set eyes on his future wife at St. James's Palace in April 1795, he was appalled at her graceless appearance. As etiquette demanded, he kissed her and then, stepping back, called out to his aide, "I am unwell; bring me a glass of brandy."

2 At her trial in 1820 before the House of Lords, various salacious details of Caroline's behavior on her foreign travels were produced in evidence against her. One line of inquiry concerned her conduct with the dey (governor) of Algiers. The chief justice, Lord Norbury, remarked, "She was happy as the dey was long."

3 When Caroline returned to England in 1820, popular enthusiasm for her was intense. George IV and his ministers, determined to prevent her establishing her position as queen, were threatened by mobs on the London streets. The Duke of Wellington was accosted by a group of men armed with pickaxes, who demanded that he express his loyalty to Caroline. The duke replied, "Well, gentlemen, since you will have it so, 'God save the Queen' — and may all your wives be like her!"

4 George IV's groom of the bedchamber announced to him the portentous news of Napoleon's death: "Sir, your bitterest enemy is dead."

"Is she, by God!" exclaimed Caroline's husband.

§ ≈ ≈§

CAROTO, Giovanni Francesco (c. 1480–1555), *Italian painter of the Veronese school. His works were influenced by Mantegna, Leonardo da Vinci, and Raphael, but his handling of landscape was definitely original. He painted numerous frescoes and paintings for churches and secular buildings in Verona.*

1   A priest objected to Caroto's figures on the grounds that he made them too lascivious. "If painted figures move you so," retorted the artist, "how are you to be trusted with living flesh and blood?"

2   Caroto had executed a painting for the Chapel of the Cross at San Bernadino. The picture, portraying Christ kneeling before his mother, was criticized by the guardian of the monastery, who thought that Christ should have been kneeling on both knees to show true reverence to her. By way of reply Caroto asked the guardian to kneel down and stand up again. This he did, grudgingly, lowering his right knee to the ground first as he knelt and raising his left leg first as he rose. When he was standing again, Caroto said to him, "Did you observe, Father Guardian, that you neither knelt down nor stood up with both knees together? This Christ of mine is correct, because one might say he is either coming to his knees before his mother or, having knelt a while, is in the process of rising."

≈

CARROLL, James (1943–   ), *US novelist. His books include* Fault Lines *(1980),* Family Trade *(1982), and* Prince of Peace *(1984).*

1   (Carroll once told the following story:)
"On the occasion of the publication of my novel *Mortal Friends* in 1978, I was honored with a special tour of the Little, Brown warehouse in a suburb of Boston. My host and tourguide, a Little, Brown executive, showed me the assembly line along which workers wrapped, boxed, and mailed off books to wholesalers and bookstores. At one point he introduced me to one of the workers who said, 'Mr. Carroll, we all just love your book.'
"I took that as the greatest compliment an author could receive. To think that these workers had actually troubled to read my book.
"But then she went on. 'We just love it. It's the perfect size for packing.'"

≈

CARROLL, Lewis [Charles Lutwidge Dodgson] (1832–98), *British author, don, and mathematician. At Oxford (1855–81) he made friends with the young daughter of Dr. Henry George Liddell, dean of Christ Church. The stories he made up to entertain her formed the basis of the children's classics* Alice in Wonderland *(1865) and* Through the Looking-Glass *(1872).*

1   Queen Victoria was so delighted with *Alice in Wonderland* that she had a letter sent to the author stating that Her Majesty would be graciously pleased to accept any other works by the same pen. She was somewhat disconcerted to receive in due course a copy of Dodgson's *Syllabus of Plane Algebraical Geometry*.
{Carroll, however, denied emphatically that this episode had ever taken place.}

2   (The amusement Lewis Carroll derived from logical problems is illustrated in an anecdote related by his younger cousin, Alice Raikes.)
"The room they had entered had a tall mirror standing in one corner. Dodgson gave his cousin an orange and asked her which hand she held it in. When she replied, 'The right,' he asked her to stand before the glass and tell him in which hand the little girl in the mirror was holding it. 'The left hand,' came the puzzled reply. 'Exactly,' said Dodgson, 'and how do you explain that?' Alice Raikes did her best: 'If I was on the *other* side of the glass,' she said, 'wouldn't the orange still be in my right hand?' Years later she remembered his laugh. 'Well done, little Alice,' he said. 'The best answer I've had yet.'"

≈

CARSON, Johnny (1925–   ), *US television entertainer, star of the* Tonight *Show.*

1   When Carson signed for the *Tonight* Show, he was so beset by reporters that he compiled a list of ten answers to which the journalists could furnish the questions to suit. They were: "1. Yes, I did. 2. Not a bit of truth in that rumor. 3. Only twice in my life, both times on Saturday. 4. I can do either, but I prefer the first. 5. No. Kumquats. 6. I can't answer that question. 7. Toads and tarantulas. 8. Turkestan, Denmark, Chile, and the Komandorskie Islands. 9. As often as possible, but I'm not very good at it yet. I need much more practice. 10. It happened to some old friends of mine, and it's a story I'll never forget."

2   On a visit to Harvard to receive an award, Carson was asked by a reporter what he would like his epitaph to be. "I'll be right back," he replied.

{Kenneth Tynan observes that this line is "the traditional cliché with which talk-show hosts segue into the commercial break." Although Carson had used this joke before, he delivered it as if it were newly coined for the occasion.}

CARTER, Jimmy (1924–   ), *US statesman; 39th president of the United States (1977–81). After being governor of Georgia (1970–74), Carter ran for president on a manifesto promising ambitious social reforms. His plans were frustrated by the serious rise in inflation and his own vacillations, which alienated Congress. In foreign policy he succeeded in bringing about the Camp David Accords (1979) between Israel and Egypt and committed the United States to surrendering control of the Panama Canal by the year 2000.*

1   Carter's devout Southern Baptist background frequently led reporters to question him on his stance on moral issues. "How would you feel if you were told that your daughter was having an affair?" a reporter asked him. "Shocked and overwhelmed," replied Carter, adding, "but then, she's only seven years old."

2   Before moving into the White House Mrs. Carter was anxious to discover whether the chef there could cook the kind of meals the Carters enjoyed at home in the South. "Yes, ma'am," was the reply. "We've been fixing that kind of food for the servants for a long time."

3   Carter was asked, in the spring of 1979, whether his young daughter, Amy, ever boasted about her father's presidential status. Mindful of the heavy criticism that his administration was attracting, Carter replied, "No, she probably apologizes."

4   With candor rare among celebrities, the president's daughter, Amy Carter, when asked by a reporter if she had any message for the children of America, answered: "No."

CARTLAND, Barbara (1902–   ), *British novelist, specializing in popular romances.*

1   Barbara Cartland came into remote contact with royal circles when her daughter Raine's stepdaughter became the Princess of Wales in 1981. When Miss Cartland was interviewed for the BBC radio program *Today,* the woman interviewer asked her whether she thought that class barriers had broken down in Britain. "Of course they have," replied Miss Cartland, "or I wouldn't be sitting here talking to someone like you."

CARUSO, Enrico (1873–1921), *Italian tenor, renowned for his roles in the operas of Verdi and Puccini.*

1   Caruso was caught in the great 1906 San Francisco earthquake and fire. He swore he would never again go back to such a city, "where disorders like that are permitted."

2   A group of reporters once asked him what he thought of Babe Ruth. Caruso, who was unfailingly polite and amiable, replied that he didn't know because unfortunately he had never heard her sing.

3   During the twenties one of the most beloved men of New York's literary and newspaper crowd was a warm-hearted minor actor and singer named Ed MacNamara. At one time the unambitious MacNamara was seized by the feeling that he should develop his vocal talents. The ambition subsided but not before he had managed an informal coaching session with Caruso. He would recount the great tenor's simple recipe for successful singing: "Mac, you know whatta you do when you shit? Singing, it's the *same* thing, only up!"

4   Caruso once reported an extraordinary conversation with a lady who was anxious to learn to sing, believing it possible that within a month she would be a recognized artist. "I'm leaving the country next month," she said, "and need twenty-five lessons before my departure."
"Impossible, madam."
"Why? Couldn't I take two lessons each day?"

"True enough," said Caruso. "I hadn't thought of that. But in that case why not take all twenty-five lessons in one day?"

"Splendid," exclaimed the future diva. "We do it tomorrow."

&> <&

CARVER, George Washington (1864–1943), *US agricultural researcher, the son of black slaves. Reared by his master, he went on to gain a degree in agriculture (1896). He worked for the Bureau of Plant Industry in the US Department of Agriculture from 1935, specializing in the industrial uses of the peanut.*

1 Carver lost his entire life savings, some seventy thousand dollars, in the crash of the Alabama bank in which the money was deposited. Carver, however, was apparently unperturbed. "I guess somebody found a use for it," he remarked. "I was not using it myself."

&> <&

CASALS, Pablo (1876–1973), *Spanish cellist, conductor, and composer.*

1 Casals found his greatest fulfillment in conducting, which he always wanted to do even when, at the height of his career as a cellist, he had little time for anything outside his cello performances. On his first American tour in 1901 a falling rock injured the fingers of his left hand. His first reaction was: "Thank God I won't have to play the cello anymore."

2 At his Viennese debut Casals suffered from nerves. When he came to pick up his bow to play the first note, he found that his hand was too tense. To loosen it he tried a little twirl, but the bow flew from his fingers and landed in the middle of the orchestra. As it was carefully passed back to him along the rows of musicians, he remembered his mother's maxim about calmness and steadiness in the pursuit of one's purpose. By the time the bow was returned to him his hand was steady. The concert was one of his greatest triumphs.

3 While playing a piece that she knew well and had played many times, a pupil suffered a lapse of memory. Casals said, "Fine — everything should be new every time you play it."

4 (The famous photographer Yousuf Karsh remembers photographing Casals with his back to the camera. Karsh recalls:)

"I was so moved on listening to him play Bach that I could not for some moments attend to photography. I have never posed anyone else facing away from the camera, but it seemed just right.

"Years later when the photograph was on exhibition at the Museum of Fine Arts in Boston, I was told that every day an elderly gentleman would come and stand for many minutes in front of it. Full of curiosity, a curator finally inquired gingerly, 'Sir, why do you come here and stand in front of this picture?'

"He was met with a withering glance and the admonition, 'Hush, young man. Can't you see I am listening to the music!' "

&> <&

CASSATT, Mary (1845–1926), *expatriate US artist and promoter of the Impressionists; much influenced by Degas and Monet, with whom she worked.*

1 Mary Cassatt was always generous in her praise of her fellow Impressionists, but never of her own work. At an exhibition one day she was talking with some people who did not know her. "But you are forgetting a foreign painter that Degas ranks very high," said one of the strangers in the course of the conversation. "Who is that?" Mary Cassatt inquired with in-

---

Frank Case was manager of the Algonquin Hotel in New York City. He would never charge the Algonquin Round Table celebrities for their lunches, but this did not stop them from saying what they thought of the food he served. On one occasion they declared it inedible and arranged to have their food sent over from the Colony the following week. The week after that the group, doubtless feeling that they had made their point, assembled at the Algonquin as usual and were greeted by small cards that Case had put on their table, saying, "Basket parties welcome." No one was embarrassed.

—Caskie Stinnett, *Travels with Marc*

terest. "Mary Cassatt," came the reply. "Oh, nonsense!" exclaimed the artist with conviction. "She's jealous," murmured the stranger as he turned away.

ॐ ॐ

CASTIGLIONE, Nicchia, Countess di
(1837–99), *aristocratic beauty at the court of Empress Eugénie, wife of Napoleon III.*

1 The countess's public appearances in a state of virtual undress caused considerable scandal. At a diplomatic ball she appeared dressed as the Queen of Hearts, her breasts covered only by a strip of gauze onto which two hearts had been sewn to conceal the nipples, and another heart sewn onto her transparent skirt concealing her vaginal mound, but leaving her pubic hair clearly visible. Empress Eugénie looked at her and said, "Countess, your heart seems a little low."

ॐ ॐ

CASTLEROSSE, Valentine Browne, Lord
(1891–1943), *Irish nobleman, who in 1941 succeeded his father as the 6th Earl of Kenmare.*

1 "Gross in appetite and appearance, with nimble wit concealed beneath buffoon's exterior, Lord Castlerosse was Beaverbrook's court jester. 'What is your handicap?' Nancy Cunard asked him on the golf-course. 'Drink and debauchery,' he answered sadly but correctly."

ॐ ॐ

CASTRACANI, Castruccio (1281–1328),
Italian condottiere, later nobleman.

1 The Quatigiani family of Lucca had been Castracani's friends and supporters. They quarreled, and after Castracani defeated them, he treated them with the utmost severity. One of his advisers warned him that people were censuring him for dealing so harshly with his old friends. "I am not dealing with old friends," was the reply, "but with new enemies."

ॐ ॐ

CASTRO, Fidel (1927–), *Cuban revolutionist and political leader. He led the guerrilla campaign that toppled the Batista regime on January 1, 1959, and as premier has established a government and economy based on Marxist-Leninist principles, closely allied with the Soviet Union.*

1 A meeting in 1959 between then Vice President Richard Nixon and Fidel Castro turned out, as might have been expected, to be a disaster. Just before the meeting, as the Cuban delegation waited, a functionary entered, announced as "Mister So-and-So, in charge of Cuban Affairs." To which Castro replied, "And I thought I was in charge of Cuban affairs."

2 On a flight to New York in 1960, Fidel turned to Ramiro Valdes and asked if there would be an escort plane accompanying them. Valdes stuttered out a no. "We're in danger. If I were running the CIA, I'd shoot down the plane at sea and report the whole thing as an accident." Silence. Fidel went on, "At least we should have had an escort. What a mistake." Everybody started to look around. Suddenly there was a huge roar: a squadron of planes was heading toward them. Yankee fighters. Everybody panicked. The fighters came closer, but US territory was just ahead. Fidel was calm, probably having said all those things just to see the reaction. There were too many planes for an attack. They were an honorary escort. The plane entered US territory literally under the CIA's wing.

ॐ ॐ

CATHERINE of Aragon (1485–1536), *first queen of Henry VIII of England, whom she married in 1509. She bore him a daughter, Mary (later Mary I), but no living male heir, so Henry tried to divorce her. The divorce proceedings started the defiance of papal authority that led to the separation of the Church of England from Rome.*

1 Catherine was imprisoned, deprived of her titles and the company of her daughter, and died in suspicious circumstances. One of her last acts before her death was to dictate an affectionate letter to Henry VIII, beseeching him to be kind to their daughter, Mary. The last words were: "*Oculi mei te solum desiderant. Vale*" (Mine eyes desire thee only. Farewell).

ॐ ॐ

CATHERINE II [Catherine the Great]
(1729–96), *empress of Russia (1762–96). The daughter of a German prince, Catherine mar-*

ried (1745) the future Czar Peter III, who humiliated and neglected her. He was deposed and killed in the year of his accession (1762), and Catherine assumed power. With a series of advisers who were also her lovers, Catherine expanded Russian territory by wars against the Turks and in Poland. Influenced by the ideas circulating in Western Europe, she entertained writers and philosophers at her court.

1   As part of her plans for reform in Russia, Catherine dreamed of founding great cities that would be centers of industry and progress in her backward country. During a state visit from the Austrian emperor Joseph II, the two rulers proceeded to lay the foundation stones of one of these proposed metropolises. Catherine laid the first stone, the emperor laid the second. Joseph commented, "I have finished in a single day a most important business with the empress of Russia; she has laid the first stone of a city and I have laid the last."

{Sure enough, this city, like most of the others, was never built, and even the proposed site is now unknown.}

る～ ∽ら

CATO [the Censor] (234–149 BC), *Roman statesman. Later Romans looked upon him as embodying the integrity, discipline, and incorruptible independence that were the chief virtues of the Roman Republic.*

1   Cato was the chief instigator of the third Punic War, convinced that Rome could never be secure while the great city of Carthage on the North African coast remained its rival. Whenever called upon to speak in the Senate, whatever the subject under debate, he always concluded his speech with the words: "*Carthago delenda est*" (Carthage must be destroyed).

2   The eighty-year-old Cato surprised his friends by setting himself the task of studying Greek. Asked how he could contemplate such a lengthy course of study at his advanced age, he replied that it was the youngest age he had left.

3   As Cato had deserved well of the Republic, someone once asked him why no statue had been erected to him. Cato replied, "Better that question than the question: 'Why have they erected a statue?'"

See also CHAIM NACHMAN BIALIK 1; BENJAMIN DISRAELI 9; ABBÉ GABRIEL BONNET DE MABLY 1.

る～ ∽ら

CAVELL, Edith Louisa (1865–1915), *British nurse.*

1   As a Red Cross nurse in Belgium during World War I, Edith Cavell helped Allied soldiers to escape from behind the enemy lines. The Germans captured her, and in a court-martial sentenced her to death. As she was led before the firing squad, she is reputed to have said, "I realize that patriotism is not enough; I must have no hatred or bitterness towards anyone."

る～ ∽ら

CECIL, William (1863–1936), *bishop of Exeter.*

1   Traveling by rail to a confirmation ceremony, the absentminded bishop mislaid his ticket and was unable to produce it for the ticket collector. "It's all right, my Lord," said the collector, "we know who you are."

"That's all very well," replied the bishop, "but without the ticket how am I to know where I'm going?"

{This story is also told of Ambassador Dwight Morrow.}

る～ ∽ら

CERVANTES SAAVEDRA, Miguel de (1547–1616), *Spanish writer. Author of* Don Quixote *and many lesser works.*

1   When King Philip III of Spain noticed a man reading beside the road and laughing so much that the tears were rolling down his cheeks, he commented: "That man is either crazy or he is reading *Don Quixote.*"

る～ ∽ら

CETEWAYO (1826–84), *king of the Zulus. During his reign, confrontation with the British settlers in Natal led to war. The great Zulu victory at Isandhlwana was followed by their crushing defeat at Ulundi (1879) and Cetewayo's capture. In 1883, after his visit to Queen Victoria in England, part of his kingdom was restored to him, but strife with rivals drove him out again and he died a refugee.*

1   Cetewayo, like the Zulu kings before him, would not allow the young men in his regiments to marry until they had "washed their spears," that is, killed enemy warriors in battle. When one of his regiments had passed this test, he ordered the men to find wives. One of the women chosen did not want to marry the man allotted to her. To avoid marriage she put on the *isidwaba*, the long full skirt worn by married women. Her deception discovered, she was taken to a high waterfall and thrown over. The *isidwaba* billowed out as she fell, breaking her fall and saving her from being drowned or smashed on the rocks. When night came she crept away and found refuge with some European settlers. The waterfall, in the Mangeni Gorge in Zululand, is still called the Isidwaba Falls.

2∞ ∞3

CÉZANNE, Paul (1839–1906), *French painter. Around 1872 he worked for a short time in the Impressionist style, but quickly rejected it in favor of a more solid, geometrical approach. His Provencal landscapes, late portraits, and the Bathers series are considered some of the finest works of Postimpressionism.*

1   Cézanne worked very slowly. His friend, the famous art dealer Ambroise Vollard, underwent no fewer than 115 sittings for a single portrait. Cézanne commented, "I am not entirely displeased with the shirt front."

2∞ ∞3

CHALIAPIN, Feodor Ivanovich (1873–1938), *Russian bass of peasant origins. He left Russia after the Revolution and settled in Paris. His greatest role was as the hero in Mussorgsky's* Boris Godunov.

1   Once when Chaliapin was on tour, he spent a night with a young woman of the town. In parting he offered her two tickets for the opera in which he was singing that evening. The girl said she was poor and hungry, and opera tickets did not buy bread. "If it was bread you wanted," retorted Chaliapin, "why didn't you spend last night with a baker?"

2   During a seemingly interminable delay in a rehearsal, the singers began to show signs of impatience. A stagehand offered to fetch a chair so that Chaliapin could sit down until the difficulty was worked out. Chaliapin said, "It is not my body that is tired, it is my soul. But my soul has no ass. So forget the chair."

3   Chaliapin was afflicted with lifelong stagefright, which he eased with vodka. On one occasion, he was dozing comfortably after a particularly strong dose of vodka while Eddie ("Papa") Senz, the makeup man at the Metropolitan Opera in New York, made him up. Suddenly, he opened his eyes and inspected his reflection in the mirror. "Vot is dis face you giff me?" he exclaimed.

"Mefistofele," replied Senz.

"Not Boris?" asked the great bass, apparently expecting to appear in the name part of Mussorgsky's *Boris Godunov*. "Holy mother! Send for de *Faust* score! I must see de score."

2∞ ∞3

CHALONER, John Armstrong (1862–19??), *US financier.*

1   In 1897 Chaloner was certified as insane and incarcerated in a New York lunatic asylum. There was a tremendous family and public scandal over the episode; speculation was revived when he escaped, fled across the state border, and was pronounced sane by two other doctors. Sometime later Chaloner's brother, known as Sheriff Bob, announced that he was intending to marry the tempestuous singer Lina Cavalieri. Chaloner sent his brother a telegram: "Who's loony now?"

2∞ ∞3

CHAMBERLAIN, [Arthur] Neville (1869–1940), *British statesman; prime minister (1937–40). Chamberlain refused to embroil Britain in the Spanish Civil War and led the Conservative strategy of appeasement of Mussolini and Hitler. Forced to abandon appeasement after Hitler's invasion of Czechoslovakia, Chamberlain was pilloried in Parliament for his direction of the war effort and resigned.*

1   When Chamberlain returned on September 30, 1938, from his visit to Munich to see Hitler, he waved the agreement that he had made with the Nazi leader and said, "I believe it is peace for our time."

{Less than a year later Britain and Germany were at war after Hitler had demonstrated his total disregard for the promises of nonaggression made at Munich, and the phrase "peace for (or in) our time" became an obscene irony.}

❧ ⹊

CHAMBERLAIN, Joseph (1836–1914), *British politician. He was a leading Liberal until he quarreled with Gladstone over Irish Home Rule and joined the Conservatives (1886). Appointed colonial secretary (1895), he handled the Boer War and its aftermath with considerable skill.*

1   Chamberlain was once guest of honor at an important civic dinner. The main part of the meal over, the mayor whispered to Chamberlain as the coffee was being served, "Shall we let the people enjoy themselves a little longer, or had we better have our speech now?"

{A similar anecdote is told of others.}

❧ ⹊

CHAMBERLAIN, Sir [Joseph] Austen (1863–1937), *British statesman. As foreign secretary (1924–29), he negotiated the Locarno Pact (1925).*

1   Offered the post of chancellor of the exchequer in 1919, Austen complained that the prime minister, David Lloyd George, had not sent for him with the customary formality, but had simply thrown the office at him — like a bone to a dog. "Stop a minute, Austen," said Lloyd George to him, "there is a good deal of meat on that bone."

2   Chamberlain and his wife were dining one evening with the well-known London hostess Mrs. Ronnie Greville. The excellent food and wine were marred only by the fact that the butler had obviously been drinking.
Rather than make a scene in front of her guests, Mrs. Greville surreptitiously scribbled a note and handed it to him. The message read: "You are drunk — leave the room at once." The butler dutifully laid the slip of paper on a silver salver, tottered around to the other side of the table, and presented it to Austen Chamberlain.

❧ ⹊

CHAMBERLAIN, Wilt (1936–   ), *US basketball star. Seven feet, one inch tall, Chamberlain dominated the sport during his professional career (1959–73), setting many of the National Basketball Association's records for scoring and rebounding.*

1   Despite his personal successes, Chamberlain was criticized for not taking his team to titles. Then in 1967, when his Philadelphia team finally won a championship, someone asked Chamberlain if he thought that everybody would get behind him now. "No way," he said.
"Why not?"
"Nobody roots for Goliath," was the answer.

❧ ⹊

CHANEL, Coco [Gabrielle Chanel] (1883–1971), *French dress designer. Her Paris fashion house led a trend toward simplicity and comfort in the design of women's dresses and suits.*

1   When Coco's nephew, a country child, visited his aunt in Paris, he found it difficult to adapt to the unfamiliar society life. Taken to lunch at the Rothschilds', he refused to eat with the other children in the nursery because the boys were wearing what appeared to him to be girls' shoes. Sitting instead at the table with the adults, he looked in horror at the fingerbowls. "I've behaved very well up to now," he said, "but I'm not going to drink that!"

2   Coco's friend the Duke of Westminster detested any form of extravagance, and continued to have his shoes resoled long after the uppers were worn out. Exasperated by this obsession, Coco secretly ordered twelve new pairs of shoes for him and hid them in his wardrobe. Some time later she saw the duke, wearing one of his new pairs of shoes, and unaware that he was being watched, jump purposefully into a large puddle to take the offending shine off them.

3   When Cocteau's *Antigone* was produced in Paris in 1924 the playwright specified that Mlle Chanel was to make the gowns worn by the princesses in the play. "She is our leading couturière," he said, "and I cannot imagine Oedipus's daughters patronizing a 'little dressmaker.'"

4   When the mini-skirt came into fashion in the mid-1960s, Chanel was asked whether she approved of girls' exposing their knees and

thighs in this way. "Thighs — of course," she replied. "But knees — never!"

&> <&

CHANNING, Carol (1921–), *US actress and singer.*

1 As part of a nightclub act, Carol Channing sometimes encouraged the members of the audience to ask her personal questions. "Do you remember the most embarrassing moment you ever had?" asked one man. "Yes, I do," replied Miss Channing. "Next question?"

&> <&

CHAPLIN, Charlie (1889–1977), *British-born film actor, who went with Fred Karno's troupe to the United States in 1910. He became legendary as a downtrodden little man in baggy trousers and a bowler hat in such silent comedies as* The Gold Rush *(1924) and* City Lights *(1931). He spoke for the first time in* The Great Dictator *(1940), a film ridiculing Hitler. Knighted in 1976, he is considered to be the screen's greatest comic.*

1 In 1931 Chaplin invited Albert Einstein, who was visiting Hollywood, to a private screening of his new film *City Lights*. As the two men drove into town together, passersby waved and cheered. Chaplin turned to his guest and explained: "The people are applauding you because none of them understands you and applauding me because everybody understands me."

2 Charlie Chaplin entered a Charlie Chaplin look-alike competition in Monte Carlo. He came in third.

3 (The playwright Charles MacArthur had been brought to Hollywood to do a screenplay, but was finding it difficult to write visual jokes.)

" 'What's the problem?' asked Chaplin.

" 'How, for example, could I make a fat lady, walking down Fifth Avenue, slip on a banana peel and still get a laugh? It's been done a million times,' said MacArthur. 'What's the best way to *get* the laugh? Do I show first the banana peel, then the fat lady approaching: then she slips? Or do I show the fat lady first, then the banana peel, and *then* she slips?'

" 'Neither,' said Chaplin without a moment's hesitation. 'You show the fat lady approaching; then you show the banana peel; then you show the fat lady and the banana peel together; then she steps *over* the banana peel and disappears down a manhole.' "

4 Chaplin was entertaining guests at a Hollywood dinner party with his impressions of familiar figures. He concluded his performance with an excellent rendering of an operatic aria. "Why, I never knew you could sing so beautifully!" exclaimed one of his guests. "I can't sing at all," replied Chaplin. "I was only imitating Caruso."

&> <&

CHAPMAN, John (1774–1845), *US frontiersman and folk character. Having wandered through the Ohio River countryside planting apple seeds and pruning the young trees, he became known as "Johnny Appleseed."*

1 Johnny Appleseed once entered a house in Washington Territory, Ohio, barefoot, and introduced himself to the occupants. The man of the house asked why he was wearing no shoes. Johnny Appleseed, who had recently trodden on a snake, held out one of his feet and said, "Sir, this foot had been guilty of offense in treading unmercifully upon one of God's creatures, and as a corresponding punishment I am now exposing it to the inclemency of the weather."

2 Johnny Appleseed carried his reverence for other forms of life to what other people would consider extremes. It is said that once when he had been bitten by a rattlesnake, someone asked him what had become of it. "The poor thing!" replied Johnny Appleseed, his eyes filling with tears. "Hardly had it touched me than I, overcome by godless passion, cut off its head with my sickle. The poor, poor innocent thing!"

&> <&

CHAPMAN, John Jay (1862–1933), *US dramatist, critic, and political reformer. Memories and Milestones (1915) is perhaps his best collection of essays.*

1 After a high-spirited dinner at Harvard's Porcellian Club in 1887, Chapman horse-whipped a classmate who he thought had made insulting remarks about his fiancée. Sobering up, Chapman was so ashamed of his behavior that he went to the open fireplace and held his left hand in the flames. It was so badly burned that it had to be amputated.

૯౨ ౨૭

CHARLEMAGNE (?742–814), *king of the Franks (768–814) and Holy Roman Emperor (800–814). He campaigned against the Saxons (772–81) and the Lombards (773), and by 800 had conquered most of western Christendom. His court at Aachen became a center of culture and learning, and he was responsible for many judicial and ecclesiastical reforms.*

1   The great French white wine Corton-Charlemagne owes its existence, according to local legend, not to the emperor but to his wife. The red wines of Corton stained his white beard so messily that she persuaded him to plant vines that would produce white wines. Charlemagne ordered white grapes to be planted. Thus Corton-Charlemagne.

૯౨ ౨૭

CHARLES, Prince of Wales (1948–), *eldest son of Queen Elizabeth II and heir apparent to the throne of the United Kingdom. In 1981 he married Lady Diana Spencer.*

1   Actress Susan Hampshire, wearing an extremely low-cut dress, was presented to Prince Charles at a show-business function. Without a trace of embarrassment, the prince greeted Miss Hampshire with the words: "Father told me that if I ever met a lady in a dress like yours, I must look her straight in the eyes."

2   Charles briefly attended a school in Australia. One Sunday, the rector of the local parish church was surprised to see the prince at his morning service. There was only a scanty congregation that day, for which the rector apologized as his royal visitor left the church. "Being bank holiday weekend," he explained, "most of the parishioners are away."

"Not another bank holiday!" said the prince. "What's this one in aid of?"

"Well," replied the rector, a little embarrassed, "over here we call it the queen's birthday."

૯౨ ౨૭

CHARLES II (1630–85), *king of England, Scotland, and Ireland (1660–85). After his father's execution (1649) Charles attempted to regain the throne by force. Having failed to do so, he lived in exile until the monarchy was restored in 1660. Charles's Roman Catholic sympathies (acknowledged openly on his deathbed) brought conflict with Parliament and caused disquiet that culminated in the Popish Plot (1678). His pro-French foreign policy embroiled England in some ignominious wars with Holland. The king himself is summed up in the Earl of Rochester's phrase, "A merry monarch, scandalous and poor."*

1   Charles's attempt to recover the throne by force ended in his defeat at Worcester in 1651. Despite the reward offered for his capture and the extreme penalties threatened to any who concealed or aided him, Charles eventually made his escape to the continent. An early part of his journey was accomplished with the aid of some brothers, one of whom lent him the horse from his mill. Charles, accustomed to more sprightly steeds, complained after a while of the heavy, lumbering pace of his mount. The miller at once defended his horse with the words: "No wonder, sire, that the horse goes so heavily, as it bears the weight of three kingdoms on its back."

2   (John Aubrey tells a charming story:)
"Arise Evans had a fungous nose, and said, it was revealed to him, that the king's hand would cure him, and at the first coming of King Charles II into St. James's Park, he kissed the king's hand, and rubbed his nose with it; which disturbed the king, but cured him."

3   Charles II enjoyed talking and in particular telling anecdotes of his own life. His courtiers, who had all heard the stories many times, found them very tedious, and used to withdraw from the king's presence if they could, leaving him with a much diminished audience. The Earl of Rochester said of this trait that he wondered that a man could so well remember every detail of a story yet not remember that he had told it to the same people only the day before.

4   In contemporary satires Charles sometimes features under the name of "Old Rowley," a stallion with a reputation for breeding fine foals. One of the king's young ladies was sitting

in her apartment singing the satirical ballad "Old Rowley the King," when Charles II knocked at her door. She asked who was there. "Old Rowley himself, madam," the king replied with his customary good humor.

5   There are several versions of Charles's encounter with the Quaker William Penn, whose creed enjoined him to refuse to remove his hat as a mark of respect to his social superiors. Seeing Penn's hat remaining on his head, the king with a flourish removed his own. "Friend Charles, why dost thou uncover thyself?" asked the Quaker. "Friend Penn," replied the king, "in this place it is the custom for only one man at a time to keep his hat on."

6   On his morning walk one day in London, Charles dismissed most of his attendants and strolled into Hyde Park with just two lords attending him. As he crossed the road, his brother, James, Duke of York, drove up in his carriage, attended by an armed guard. The duke stopped his coach, expressed surprise at seeing the king almost alone, and hinted that it was unwise to expose himself to danger in this way. "No danger," said King Charles, "for no man in England would take away my life to make *you* king."

7   The king asked Edward Stillingfleet, bishop of Worcester and a popular preacher, why when Stillingfleet preached at court he always read his sermons. He had heard that when he preached elsewhere he always delivered his sermons extempore. Stillingfleet explained that awe of the king made him afraid of forgetting what he had to say, so he preferred to read when he had royalty in the audience. Emboldened by the king's favorable reaction to this diplomatic reply, the bishop then asked if he might put a question of his own. Why, he asked Charles, did he always read his speeches to the House of Commons, when it could not be that he was in awe of his audience? Charles replied good-naturedly, "I have asked them so often, and for so much money, that I am ashamed to look them in the face."

8   The Earl of Rochester once wrote on the door of the king's bedchamber: "Here lies our sovereign lord the king,/ Whose promise none relies on;/ He never said a foolish thing,/ Nor ever did a wise one." Charles skillfully replied

to the insult with the observation: "This is very true, for my words are my own, and my actions are those of my ministers."

9   Seventeenth-century monarchs died as they had lived, very much in the public eye. To the attendants and notables gathered around his deathbed Charles II said, "I have been a most unconscionable time a-dying; but I beg you to excuse it."
   {Another candidate for the title of the Merry Monarch's last words is the injunction about his mistress, Nell Gwyn, spoken to his brother and successor, James: "Let not poor Nelly starve."}

ॐ ✦

CHARLES V (1500–58), *Holy Roman Emperor (1519–56) and king of Spain (1516–56). Having inherited vast and far-flung estates in Europe, Charles spent much of his reign in warfare and diplomacy; in the east his empire was threatened by the Ottoman Turks and in Italy the French determinedly challenged him for hegemony. Charles tried to prevent the spread of the Reformation, but was eventually compelled to take up arms against the Protestants (1546). The Peace of Augsburg (1555) established the coexistence of Lutheranism and Roman Catholicism in Germany; Charles then abdicated and retired to a Spanish monastery.*

1   In 1521, when Charles renewed his struggle with the French king, Francis I, over the empire's Italian lands, the emperor remarked, "My cousin Francis and I are in perfect accord — he wants Milan, and so do I."

2   When Hernando Cortéz, the celebrated explorer of the New World, returned to Spain and made a report of his findings to the king, one of his chief recommendations was that a passage to India be effected by digging a canal across the Isthmus of Panama. Charles considered this suggestion with his advisers and finally rejected it: "What God hath joined together let no man put asunder."

ॐ ✦

CHARLES X (1757–1836), *king of France (1824–30). As Comte d'Artois, Charles was the leader of the reactionary party, which was forced into exile by the French Revolution. During the reign of his brother Louis XVIII, he* *embarrassed him by his ultraroyalist policies. Succeeding Louis as king, Charles adopted a course of extreme reaction, which led to his deposition.*

1   When Louis XVIII became king, the Comte d'Artois continued to treat his brother with easy familiarity, bordering on disrespect. Eventually this became so marked that M. de Maurepas was entrusted with the delicate task of dropping a hint to Charles that now that Louis was king, he should observe a more formal approach. Maurepas put his case to the count, concluding by saying that if he continued in his informal ways, the king might be offended. "Offended, eh?" said Charles. "Well, and what if he is? What can he do to me?"

"He can pardon you, sir," replied Maurepas suavely.

2   Charles X, oblivious of his brother's flight on March 20, 1815, justified his absolutist policies to Talleyrand by saying that for the Bourbons "there is no middle course between the throne and the scaffold."

"Your Majesty is forgetting the postchaise," Talleyrand reminded him.

≈

CHARLES FRANCIS JOSEPH [Charles I of Austria] (1887–1922), *Austrian emperor. He succeeded his great-uncle, Francis Joseph, in the middle of World War I (1916), struggled unsuccessfully to hold together his crumbling empire, and in 1921 was formally deposed.*

1   Informed of the death of Francis Joseph, Charles, now elevated to the throne, was deeply moved. He seized his adjutant's hand and in his emotion stammered, "What should I do? I think the best thing is to order a new stamp to be made with my face on it."

≈

CHARLOTTE of Mecklenburg-Strelitz (1744–1818), *wife of George III, king of Great Britain and Ireland (1760–1820), whom she married in 1761.*

1   Queen Charlotte was never a beauty, being short, pale, and very thin at the time of her marriage. As she grew older, her appearance improved, inspiring her chamberlain to re-

mark, "I really do think that the bloom of her ugliness is going off."

≈

CHARONDAS (6th century BC), *Greek legislator, who gave laws to Catana and other Greek cities in Italy and Sicily.*

1   One of Charondas' laws forbade citizens to carry weapons into the public assembly. Forgetting this, he wore his sword into the public meeting one day. A fellow citizen reproached him for violating his own law. "By Zeus, I will confirm it," said Charondas instantly, and, drawing his sword, killed himself.

≈

CHASE, Ilka (1903–78), *US actress, novelist, and playwright.*

1   A short while after her just-divorced husband, Louis Calhern, married Julia Hoyt, Miss Chase was going through some boxes and found a packet of visiting cards on which was engraved the name "Mrs. Louis Calhern." Thinking it a pity to let them go to waste, she wrapped them up and mailed them to her successor with a note: "Dear Julia, I hope these reach you in time."

≈

CHASE, Salmon Portland (1808–73), *US statesman and jurist; Chief Justice of the Supreme Court (1864–73). As secretary of the treasury under Lincoln (1861–64), he was largely responsible for the establishment of a national banking system.*

1   Shortly after the Civil War Chief Justice Chase was introduced to a striking beauty from Alabama. "I must warn you that I'm an unreconstructed rebel," she archly informed him. "In your case, madam," responded Chase gallantly, "reconstruction — even in the slightest degree — would be nothing short of sacrilege."

≈

CHATEAUBRIAND, François René, Vicomte de (1768–1848), *French author and statesman. A visit to America in 1791 furnished him with material for one of his most famous works,* Atala *(1801), an epic on North American Indian themes. He lived in exile in England* *from 1793 to 1800, then returned to France, where under the restored monarchy he was rewarded with diplomatic and other posts. His Mémoires d'outre-tombe (1849–50) give a brilliant, if biased, picture of his life and times.*

1 Chateaubriand's exalted opinion of himself drew some acerbic comments from his contemporaries, among them Napoleon, who gave him a post in the French legation in Rome in 1803. Chateaubriand soon became disaffected. Napoleon observed, "The difficulty lies not so much in buying Monsieur Chateaubriand, but in paying him the price he thinks he's worth."

2 In his later years Chateaubriand suffered from deafness, an affliction that evoked a biting comment from his old enemy Talleyrand: "He thinks he's deaf now that he no longer hears himself talked about."

৪৯ ৵৪

CHATTERTON, Thomas (1752–70), *British poet. He wrote and published the "Rowley Poems," which purported to be the work of a fifteenth-century Bristol poet, Thomas Rowley. Rowley, like the poems, was the product of Chatterton's imagination, but the poems, appealing to the fashionable antiquarianism of the day, had a considerable vogue. His patrons, however, proved less forthcoming with money than they were with praise and after two months in London, Chatterton, poverty-stricken and in despair, swallowed arsenic.*

1 Walking with a friend in a London churchyard one day, engrossed in the melancholy pastime of reading the inscriptions on the gravestones, Chatterton stumbled and fell into a newly dug grave. His friend immediately came to his rescue, and in an attempt to make light of the matter, said he was glad to have been present at the resurrection of a genius. Chatterton took a more gloomy view of the accident: "I have been at war with the grave for some time, and I find it not so easy to vanquish it as I imagined. We can find an asylum to hide from every creditor but that." Three days later he killed himself.

৪৯ ৵৪

CHEKHOV, Anton Pavlovich (1860–1904), *Russian short-story writer and dramatist. His*

plays — The Seagull (1896), Uncle Vanya (1897), The Three Sisters (1901), and The Cherry Orchard (1904) — were produced by the Moscow Art Theater company. Chekhov died of tuberculosis.

1 Once a plump, healthy, handsome, well-dressed lady addressed him à la Chekhov. "Life is so boring, Anton Pavlovich. Everything is so gray: the people, the sea, even the flowers seem to be gray. . . . And I have no desires . . . my soul is in pain . . . it is like a disease."

"It is a disease," said Anton Pavlovich with conviction. "In Latin it is called *morbus fraudulentus*."

2 In Chekhov's story "The Malefactor," a peasant removes the nuts from railroad ties to use as weights for his fishing lines, unaware that this comparatively trivial theft could endanger the lives of hundreds of railroad travelers. A lawyer asked Chekhov how he would have punished the peasant had he been judge at his trial. "I would have acquitted him," said Chekhov. "I would say to him: 'You have not yet ripened into a deliberate criminal. Go — and ripen!'"

৪৯ ৵৪

CHERUBINI, Maria Luigi (1760–1842), *Italian composer known mainly for his choral works. He became head of the Paris Conservatoire in 1822.*

1 An acquaintance of Cherubini's handed him a score, saying that it was by Étienne Méhul. Cherubini studied it. "This isn't by Méhul, it's too bad!" he said. "Then will you believe me if I tell you that it is mine?" asked the other man. "No," Cherubini replied, "it's too good."

2 Cherubini once granted an audition to a man possessed of a very powerful voice. Asked for a demonstration of his talents, he sang so forcefully that the windowpanes rattled. "Do you think anything can be made of me?" he asked Cherubini at the conclusion. "Certainly," was the reply. "An auctioneer."

3 During Cherubini's directorship of the Paris Conservatoire, a student who had written an opera that was being considered for production begged him to be present at the tryout. Cherubini consented. He listened to the first act, then the second, but uttered not a word of comment. The young composer, nervously haunting the box in which Cherubini sat, could no longer conceal his impatience. "Master, haven't you anything to say to me?" Cherubini grasped the young man's hands, replying kindly, "My poor chap, what can I say to you? I've been listening to you for two hours and you haven't said anything to me either."

4   "What is worse than a flute?" mused Cherubini, and immediately supplied his own answer: "Two flutes."

≈≫ ≪≋

CHESTERFIELD, Philip Dormer Stanhope, 4th Earl of (1694–1773), *English politician and writer. Lord Chesterfield held several important diplomatic posts, but at home his political career was frustrated by the enmity of George II. From the mid-1750s Chesterfield gradually withdrew from politics and society, devoting himself to writing. His witty and elegant* Letters to his Son *(1774) instruct his illegitimate son Philip in all aspects of a gentleman's conduct and accomplishments.*

1   The popularity of the preacher George Whitefield was such that the Privy Council debated whether steps should be taken to prevent his vast evangelical rallies. Chesterfield listened, then struck in with a practical suggestion: "Make him a bishop, and you will silence him at once."

2   Addressing the House of Lords on some knotty issue, Lord Chesterfield observed, "We, my lords, may thank heaven that we have something better than our brains to depend upon."

3   Lord Chesterfield's sister, Lady Gertrude Hotham, was an active Methodist. When her brother fell ill, she tried to coax him into going to a Methodist seminary in Wales to recuperate, partly because she genuinely believed that the environment would improve his health, but also because she hoped to convert him to Methodism. She extolled the virtues of the place, in particular its views and its mountains. Lord Chesterfield, guessing her intentions,

broke in, "I do not love mountains. When your ladyship's faith has removed them, I will go thither with all my heart."

4   Increasing deafness, political disappointment, and the unsatisfactoriness and eventual death of his son and namesake Philip clouded Lord Chesterfield's last years. His friend and contemporary Lord Tyrawley also suffered setbacks, being ignominiously dismissed from his post in Portugal in 1763 on the grounds that he was too old. Near the end of his life Chesterfield was asked by a mutual acquaintance how Lord Tyrawley was. He replied, "Tyrawley and I have been dead these two years, but we do not choose to have it known."

5   In the last few months of his life Lord Chesterfield was so infirm that when he rode in his carriage the horses were usually led at a slow walking pace. An acquaintance, meeting him on such an expedition, congratulated him on being able to take the air. His lordship thanked the man, adding, "I do not come out so much for the air, as for the benefit of rehearsing my funeral."

6   Lord Chesterfield's last visitor was his godson and protégé, Solomon Dayrolles. With the passion for politeness that had governed his life, the dying man roused himself to instruct a servant, "Give Dayrolles a chair." These were, we are told, his final words.

≈≫ ≪≋

CHESTERTON, G[ilbert] **K**[eith] (1874–1936), *British essayist, novelist, critic, and poet. He wrote a series of detective stories centered in the character of Father Brown, a Roman Catholic priest. In 1922 he himself became a Roman Catholic and thereafter wrote chiefly on religious themes.*

1   Chesterton's prosperous middle-class parents, wedded to respectability, attached great importance to "proper" speech and the right accent. At the age of three GKC must have known this. He once screamed for his hat: "If you don't give it to me, I'll say 'AT'!"
    {Considerably later, remembering the world into which he was born, he wrote that it was one in which "nobody was any more likely to drop an *h* than to pick up a title."}

2   Chesterton was an imposing figure, very tall and burly. "Oh, Mr. Chesterton," gushed an admirer, "how wonderful it must be to be so famous that everyone knows who you are."

"If they don't, they soon ask," he replied.

3   Despite his large bulk, Chesterton had a mild falsetto voice, which he sometimes used to surprising effect. Before giving his first lecture on a tour of the United States, he was introduced in embarrassingly florid terms by a pompous and long-winded chairman. Sensing the audience's restlessness, Chesterton got to his feet and murmured, "After the whirlwind, the still, small voice." ·

4   Bernard Shaw, tall and thin, stood in vivid contrast to the corpulent Chesterton. They differed about other matters too. Once Shaw is reported to have said to Chesterton, "If I were as fat as you, I'd hang myself." Chesterton replied amiably, "And if I had it in mind to hang myself, I'd use you as the rope."

5   Once when G. K. Chesterton's economic views were abused in print by George Bernard Shaw, his friends waited in vain for him to reply. Historian Hilaire Belloc reproached him.

"My dear Belloc," Chesterton said, "I have answered him. To a man of Shaw's wit, silence is the one unbearable repartee."

6   Chesterton's vast bulk afforded him certain consolations. He once remarked that it gave him opportunity for gallantry. "Just the other day in the Underground I enjoyed the pleasure of offering my seat to three ladies."

7   During World War I, a young lady handing out white feathers in Fleet Street accosted Chesterton with the question: "Why are you not out at the front?"

"My dear madam," replied the portly novelist, "if you will step round this way a little, you will see that I *am*."

8   G. K. Chesterton was not embarrassed by his girth. In Pittsburgh he told a delighted audience: "I want to reassure you I am not this size, really—dear me, no. I'm being amplified by the mike."

9   Chesterton's mind was so preoccupied that he frequently forgot to keep appointments and was obliged to write apologetic notes explaining his absence. He once astonished his publisher by arriving punctually at the agreed hour. He then handed the man a letter containing an elaborate explanation of why he was unable to keep the appointment.

10   The absentminded Chesterton was devoted to his mother. When he became engaged to be married, he was so eager to share the happy event with her that he went straight home and wrote her a long letter. Mrs. Chesterton was delighted with her son's news, although she was not at all surprised to receive his letter. She was in the room with him when he wrote it.

11   "Chesterton relied on his wife in all practical matters. Once on a lecture tour he sent her the following telegram: 'Am in Birmingham. Where ought I to be?' She wired back: 'Home.'"

12   Alexander Woollcott met Chesterton for lunch at a London restaurant. Chesterton expounded on various philosophical topics, including the relationship between power and authority. "If a rhinoceros were to enter this restaurant now, there is no denying he would have great power here. But I should be the first to rise and assure him that he had no authority whatever."

13   Chesterton was once asked what books he would most like to have with him if he were stranded on a desert island. "Thomas's *Guide to Practical Shipbuilding*," he replied.

14   On his American travels, Chesterton was taken one night to view the brilliant lights of Broadway blazing the names of brand products and shows through the blackness. After staring at the spectacle for a few minutes Chesterton remarked, "How beautiful it would be for someone who could not read."

৵   ৽

CHEVALIER, Maurice (1888–1972), *French singer and actor, whose lilting French accent and famous straw hat became his trademarks. Having made his name in Paris revues before World War I, he went to Hollywood in the thirties and appeared in such films as* The Love Parade *(1930) and* Folies Bergère *(1935).*

1 Chevalier was once asked to explain the French practice of kissing friends of either sex on both cheeks. "It is simply that we like to renew acquaintances, we Frenchmen," replied Chevalier. "We may kiss a man we haven't seen for five years — or a girl we haven't seen for five minutes."

2 Chevalier was once asked why he had chosen to remain a bachelor. "You're not going to believe this," he replied, "but it's for a very good reason. When I get up in the morning, I like to have the choice of getting out of bed from either side."

3 Chatting to comedian Phil Silvers backstage, the seventy-three-year-old Chevalier heaved a deep sigh as a group of pretty showgirls trooped past them. "Ah, if only I were twenty years older," he said. "Don't you mean twenty years younger?" asked Silvers. "No," replied Chevalier. "If I were twenty years *older,* then these girls would not bother me the way they do."

8❧ ❧8

CHIGI, Agostino (1465?–1520), *wealthy Italian banker, who lived at the Villa Farnese in Rome.*

1 When Agostino Chigi held dinner parties *al fresco* at the Villa Farnese, overlooking the Tiber, he would impress his guests by instructing them to jettison their dishes and cutlery into the river at the end of each course. The gesture was less extravagant than it seemed,

---

"The *Andrea Doria,* sunk in collision, its beauty now rusting on the Nantucket shoals, was a major disaster. Yet whenever that disaster comes to mind, I also think of poor Captain Piero Calamai, the master of the doomed ship. He was brought ashore, dazed and in shock, and the newspapermen clamored at him — 'What happened? What happened?'

" 'Somebody sinka my ship,' said the captain."

— Robert Sylvester,
Notes of a Guilty Bystander

---

however, for the banker had had the servants rig up nets just below the surface of the water before each party, so that none of his valuable tableware was lost forever in the mud of the Tiber.

8❧ ❧8

CHOATE, Joseph Hodges (1832–1917), *US lawyer and diplomat. He was ambassador to Great Britain (1899–1905). Many stories are told of his wit in court and his skill as an after-dinner speaker.*

1 Choate was asked at a private dinner who he would like to be if he were not himself. He thought rapidly through a list of world celebrities, and then, catching his wife's eye, said, "If I could not be myself, I would like to be Mrs. Choate's second husband."

2 Once during a Supreme Court hearing it was pointed out to Choate that he was arguing directly contrary to what was stated in his brief. Choate was not at all abashed. "Oh well, I have learned a great deal about the case since the brief was prepared."

3 Fellow-lawyer Chauncey M. Depew was a rival wit with whom Choate had many skirmishes. At one dinner Depew introduced Choate with the words, "If you open Mr. Choate's mouth and drop in a dinner, up will come a speech." When Choate rose to speak he began, "Mr. Depew says that if you open my mouth and drop in a dinner, up will come a speech. But I warn you that if you open your mouths and drop in one of Mr. Depew's speeches, up will come your dinners."

4 Chauncey Depew was billed to speak before Choate at a dinner. Choate, expecting the usual witticisms at his expense, made preparations beforehand by obtaining a prospectus for a concern called "The Depew Natural Gas Company Ltd." When Depew had finished, Choate rose, prospectus in hand, glanced at Depew, looked around the company, and asked mildly, "Why 'limited'?"

5 Visiting at a certain ducal residence, Choate happened to be standing near the front door when an English nobleman came into the hall and, mistaking him for the butler, said to him, "Call me a cab."

"You are a cab," Choate obligingly replied. The nobleman complained to his host and was gently told that Choate was the American ambassador. At this the nobleman returned to Choate to apologize. Choate said, "Pray don't apologize. If I had known who *you* were, I would have called you a hansom cab."

{Choate always denied this story about his period as ambassador in London, but it is commonly associated with his name.}

6   In London Choate was amused by the cockney accent, in particular the dropping of *h*'s. Noticing a box marked "Drop Letter Box" on a street one day he observed, "That box must be full of *h*'s."

7   In a case at the New York courts Choate was opposed by an attorney from Westchester County, a residential area lying north of New York City. The attorney, having a poor case, fell back upon an attempt to belittle Choate, ending with a warning to the jury not to be taken in by Choate's "Chesterfieldian urbanity." Choate waited until his summing up, then urged the jury not to be unduly influenced by "my opponent's Westchesterfieldian suburbanity."

෩ ⚬ঌ

CHOPIN, Frédéric (1810–49), *Polish composer and pianist. He lived mainly in France, but his music was inspired by Polish folk themes. Composing primarily for the piano, he is best known for his romantic polonaises, mazurkas, waltzes, ballades, and nocturnes. From 1838 to 1847 he had a celebrated affair with the novelist George Sand, and died of pulmonary disease shortly after they parted.*

1   Chopin was lionized by Parisian hostesses who imposed upon him by inviting him to dinner and then asking him to play something by way of free entertainment. One lady was particularly unsubtle in her approach, so much so that Chopin murmured in response to the inevitable request, "But, madame, I have eaten so little!"

2   Chopin was extremely fastidious; one point on which he was particularly sensitive was the physical appearance of his manuscripts. Knowing this, a friend to whom Chopin lent the manuscript score of his Concerto in E Minor donned white gloves to turn the pages and returned the manuscript to the composer without a spot or mark upon it. On opening it Chopin grimaced with displeasure. "My dear fellow, you were smoking when you read it!" he exclaimed.

෩ ⚬ঌ

CHRISTIAN X (1870–1947), *king of Denmark (1912–47). During the German occupation of Denmark the king's courage and dignity won him international respect. He was imprisoned by the Germans from 1943 to 1945 for rejecting their anti-Semitic legislation.*

1   During the occupation, but before his imprisonment, the king noticed a Nazi flag flying over a Danish public building. He immediately called the German commandant, demanding that the flag be taken down at once. The commandant refused to comply with the king's request. "Then a soldier will go and take it down," said the king. "He will be shot," returned the commandant. "I think not," replied the king, "for I shall be the soldier."

The flag was taken down.

෩ ⚬ঌ

CHRISTIE, Dame Agatha (1891–1976), *British writer of detective fiction. Her novels are admired for the ingenuity of their plots. The Belgian detective Hercule Poirot, first introduced in* The Mysterious Affair at Styles *(1920), is the most famous of the several fictional detectives she created. Her play* The Mousetrap *had the longest London run of any play (from 1952), and several Christie books have been filmed, including* Murder on the Orient Express.

1   Agatha Christie's second husband, Max Mallowan, was a distinguished archaeologist who made his name excavating in Mesopotamia. On her return with her husband from the Middle East Miss Christie was asked how she felt about being married to a man whose interest lay in antiquities. "An archaeologist is the best husband any woman can have," she said. "The older she gets, the more interested he is in her."

2   In 1977, a young Arab girl was flown to England in a semiconscious state and admitted

to a London hospital. The doctors were baffled by her condition, which continued to deteriorate over the next five days. On the sixth day, the child began to lose her hair. The nurse watching over her was suddenly struck by the similarity of her symptoms to those of a series of murder victims in Agatha Christie's *The Pale Horse,* which she was reading at the time. The fictional characters had been killed by thallium poisoning; subsequent tests on the Arab girl revealed that she had high levels of thallium in her urine. Three weeks later, the child was fit enough to return home, and the case was written up in the *British Journal of Hospital Medicine,* with a note of thanks to the observant nurse and the late Dame Agatha Christie.

CHRISTIE, John (1882–1962), *British music lover who founded the Glyndebourne Festival Opera at his country estate (1934) for his wife, the opera singer Audrey Mildmay (1900–53).*

1 Christie was a Mozart devotee and the Glyndebourne Opera specialized in Mozart's works. He was much less favorably inclined to modern music, though contemporary operas were occasionally staged. During an interval in the performance of Hans Werner Henze's *Elegy for Young Lovers,* a patron wandered through the gardens and happened on Christie, then an old man, looking out across the fields of the estate. "Do you see those cows off in the distance?" Christie asked. "Well, when we do Mozart, they are always right here."

CHRISTINA (1626–89), *queen of Sweden (1644–54). Despite her encouragement of science, literature, and industry her reign was marred by her personal extravagance, indifference to the wishes of her people, and jealousy of some of her wisest counselors. Wearying of the government, she abdicated, forswore Protestantism, and thereafter led a wandering and dissipated life, finally settling in Rome, where she lived on papal charity and died forgotten.*

1 Having abdicated, Christina journeyed south through Europe and in Innsbruck was received into the Roman Catholic Church, no doubt to the huge satisfaction of the local priests, who made a grand ceremony out of her abjuration. After the solemn ritual in the cathe-

dral, the next item on Christina's agenda in Innsbruck was a visit to the theater. "It is only fair," she remarked, "that you should treat me to a comedy, after I have treated you to a farce."

CHURCHILL, Randolph Frederick Edward Spencer (1911–68), *British journalist, son of Sir Winston Churchill. Failing to follow his father in politics, Randolph Churchill was for many years a forceful and abrasive commentator on the political scene. His last years were dedicated to writing the official biography of Sir Winston.*

1 Randolph Churchill never won a contested election, though he was member of Parliament for Preston during the wartime coalition in the 1940s. People naturally speculated that this failure to emulate his father was an embittering factor in his life. Someone unkindly remarked, "I'm so fond of Randolph. He's quite unspoiled by his many failures."
{This remark is attributed to Noël Coward, among others.}

2 Lord Beaverbrook's valet habitually referred to his master as "the Lord." Randolph telephoned Beaverbrook one day only to be told by the valet that "The Lord is out walking in the park."
"On the waters, I suppose," remarked Randolph.

3 Randolph Churchill's friends were not spared his notorious rudeness and this occasionally led to angry words and broken friendships. By way of apology after disrupting some social event, Randolph said, "You know, I ought not to be allowed out in private."
{Several people recall his saying this to them.}

4 Habitually extravagant, Randolph resolved at one point to curb his lavish life-style. "And how do you intend to do that?" inquired his wife. Randolph thought for a while. "I have it," he said. "We'll stop taking the *Sunday Dispatch.*"

CHURCHILL, Lord Randolph Henry Spencer (1849–95), *British politician; secretary for India (1885–86). Entering Parliament in*

1874, he led a Conservative group known as the Fourth Party, which urged that more power be given to the rank and file. His political advance ended in 1886, when he resigned his post as chancellor of the exchequer after his cuts in the defense budget were opposed by Lord Salisbury, the prime minister. In 1874 he married an American, Jennie Jerome; their eldest son was Winston Churchill.

1   Lord Randolph Churchill was buttonholed on the stairs of his club by the resident bore, who embarked on a long-winded tale. In desperation Lord Randolph summoned a footman. "Listen until his lordship finishes," he instructed the man and made his escape.

2   As a guest at a country house party Lord Randolph was called away from his book to take part in the fashionable Victorian pastime of thought-reading. His hostess blindfolded him and stood him in the middle of the drawing room. "Don't resist your thoughts," she instructed him. "Just do exactly as you feel." Stepping forward, he wrapped her in a warm embrace. After that he was allowed to read unmolested.

§⁂ ⁂§

CHURCHILL, Sir Winston (1874–1965), *British statesman. A direct descendant of the first Duke of Marlborough, Churchill served in the Boer War before being elected to Parliament in 1900. After holding various offices he became First Lord of the Admiralty (1911–15). From 1929 until the outbreak of World War II he was out of office. When World War II began, Churchill was again appointed First Lord of the Admiralty. In 1940 he replaced Neville Chamberlain as prime minister, becoming head of the coalition government. His remarkable powers of oratory and outstanding qualities as a leader made him the personification of British resistance to tyranny and a symbol of the free world's opposition to Nazi Germany's brutality.*

1   In the early 1900s, Churchill gave a lecture on his escape from prison during the Boer War. He had been provided with a large map of the relevant part of South Africa, which he used from time to time during the talk. Describing his movements immediately after the escape, he suddenly broke off, looked closely at the map, and carefully placed the tip of his pointer on a tiny dot. "That's me!" he announced.

2   As a young subaltern Churchill sported a mustache. At a smart dinner he fell into argument with a grand dowager who, thinking to quell him, snapped, "Young man, I care for neither your politics nor your mustache."

"Madam," responded Churchill, "you are unlikely to come into contact with either."

3   Soon after Edward Marsh became Churchill's private secretary in 1905, he accompanied Churchill on an election campaign in his Manchester constituency. Their canvassing took them into the slums. Churchill looked at the rows and rows of squalid little houses with horror. "Fancy living in one of these streets," he observed to Marsh, "never seeing anything beautiful, never eating anything savory — never saying anything clever!"

4   Edward Marsh was waiting at a railroad station with Mrs. Churchill for Churchill to join them to catch a train. It was getting late and Mrs. Churchill began to worry that her husband would miss the train. Marsh soothed her by observing, "Winston is such a sportsman that he always gives the train a chance to get away."

5   (Violet Asquith describes a conversation with Churchill at the dinner-table.)

"For a long time he remained sunk in abstraction. Then he appeared to become suddenly aware of my existence. He turned on me a lowering gaze and asked me how old I was. I replied that I was nineteen.

"'And I,' he said almost despairingly, 'am thirty-two already.'

"On reflection he added thoughtfully, 'Younger than anyone else who counts, though.' Then, savagely, 'Curse ruthless time! Curse our mortality. How cruelly short is the allotted span for all we must cram into it!' He burst into a diatribe about the brevity of life and ended: 'We are all worms. But I do believe that I am a glowworm.'"

6   A group of political friends who had achieved high office comparatively early in life were discussing their careers. Someone asked whether they had ever expected to be where they were then. They all said, "No," with the exception of Churchill, who was then home secretary at the age of thirty-five. "Yes," he said. "Napoleon won Austerlitz at my age."

7   Shortly before World War I Nancy Astor, the American-born wife of Waldorf, Viscount Astor, visited Blenheim Palace, the ancestral home of the Churchill family. In conversation with Churchill, she expounded on the subject of women's rights, an issue that was to take her into the House of Commons as the first woman member of Parliament. Churchill opposed her on this and other causes that she held dear. In some exasperation Lady Astor said, "Winston, if I were married to you, I'd put poison in your coffee." Churchill responded, "And if you were my wife, I'd drink it."

{This anecdote has been ascribed to others, but is eminently Churchillian.}

8   Despite holding important posts in the Liberal administration just before World War I, Churchill found that his salary from the government did not cover the expenses of his growing family. He was obliged to supplement his income by lecturing and journalism. "I live from mouth to hand," he remarked.

9   At one stage of World War I Churchill went across to France as a volunteer to observe the fighting at first hand. In his sandbagged shelter at the front line, he was brought a message from a visiting general, a former acquaintance, who wanted to see him. He was to walk to a crossroads about three miles away, where a car would pick him up and take him to the general. After waiting at the crossroads for nearly an hour, Churchill was joined by one of the general's officers. The car had been sent to the wrong crossroads and now it was too late for the meeting to take place.

Churchill began the long trudge back to the trenches in the dark and the rain, in a very bad humor, cursing the thoughtless general. When he got back to his shelter, however, he found that it no longer existed. Five minutes after he had left a shell had come through the roof, killing the man left inside. As Churchill records, "Suddenly I felt my irritation against General X pass completely from my mind. All sense of grievance departed in a flash. As I walked to my new abode, I reflected how thoughtful it had been of him to wish to see me again, and to show courtesy to a subordinate when he had so much responsibility on his shoulders."

10   In the House of Commons one afternoon, Churchill was attacking a certain aspect of government policy. Referring to Stanley Baldwin, then prime minister, Churchill declared: "History will say that the right honorable gentleman was wrong in this matter." After a brief pause, he added, "I know it will, because I shall write the history."

11   In 1938 Churchill published a collection of his speeches under the title *Arms and the Covenant*. There was to be an American edition of the work, but the publishers felt that the title would not mean much to US readers, who were not very interested in the League of Nations. Churchill was asked to suggest an alternative. In due course he sent a cable suggesting "The Years of the Locust." Somehow the phrase got garbled in transmission and arrived in the publishers' offices as "The Years of the Lotus." The editors puzzled over what was intended and eventually, following through the association of lotuses and slumber, came up with the title *While England Slept*. The book duly appeared under this title and was a great success.

12   When Winston Churchill became First Lord of the Admiralty at the outbreak of World War II, he visited a naval base to see the Asdic antisubmarine defense system in operation. He was taken on board a warship, which sailed to an area in which there were known to be submerged wrecks. In due course the Asdic located one. Churchill asked what happened next. The naval officer in charge explained that they would then depth-bomb the target. Churchill asked to see this part of the operation as well, so a depth-charge was dropped overboard. A few seconds later there was a tremendous underwater explosion and quantities of water and wreckage erupted. Amid the wreckage was an apparently intact door bearing upon it the letters W. C. Churchill afterward observed, "The navy always knew how to pay proper compliments, bless them."

13   Churchill made his first address to the US Congress on Boxing Day 1941. He remarked on this occasion, "If my father had been American and my mother British, instead of the other way round, I might have got here on my own."

14   In the summer of 1941 Sergeant James Allen Ward was awarded the Victoria Cross for climbing out onto the wing of his Wellington

bomber, 13,000 feet above the Zuider Zee, to extinguish a fire in the starboard engine. Secured only by a rope around his waist, he managed not only to smother the fire but also to return along the wing to the aircraft's cabin. Churchill, an admirer as well as a performer of swashbuckling exploits, summoned the shy New Zealander to 10 Downing Street. Ward, struck dumb with awe in Churchill's presence, was unable to answer the prime minister's questions. Churchill surveyed the unhappy hero with some compassion. "You must feel very humble and awkward in my presence," he said.

"Yes, sir," managed Ward.

"Then you can imagine how humble and awkward I feel in yours," said Churchill.

15   Combining the jobs of prime minister and minister of defense in 1942, Churchill faced a motion of censure in the House of Commons just as the war in North Africa was at its most critical stage. He delivered a ninety-minute oration that confounded his critics and opponents. In the course of it an MP interjected a query about the so-called Churchill tank. Churchill said, "This tank, the A22, was ordered off the drawing board and large numbers went into production very quickly. As might be expected, it had many defects and teething troubles, and when these became apparent, the tank was appropriately rechristened the 'Churchill.' These defects have now been largely overcome. I have no doubt that this tank will prove, in the end, a powerful, massive, and serviceable weapon of war."

This joke against himself brought delighted laughter from all sides of the House, and in the ensuing vote the censure motion was thrown out by a majority of 475 to 25.

16   Comment was made during the war that although Churchill was a magnificent war leader, he had failed to provide the country with the strong spiritual guidance some people felt it needed. Churchill's reaction: "Since I became prime minister, I have appointed no fewer than six new bishops. What more do they want?"

17   During World War II Lord Mancroft's duties in the War Office included visiting the prime minister's residence, 10 Downing Street, while Churchill was out and putting the latest information on Churchill's war maps. One day

Mancroft was busy doing this with the maps spread out on the floor of the Cabinet Room, his hat upturned beside him, and colored chalks in his hand, when Churchill unexpectedly appeared. Seeing the engrossed figure on the floor, Churchill reached into his pocket and without saying a word tossed a penny in Mancroft's hat.

18   "Before the Battle of El Alamein, he summoned General Montgomery and suggested that he study logistics. Montgomery doubted that he should become involved in such technical matters. 'After all, you know,' he said, 'they say that familiarity breeds contempt.' Churchill replied: 'I would like to remind you that without a degree of familiarity we could not breed anything.'"

19   Churchill was accosted at a wartime reception by a rather overbearing American lady. "What are you going to do about those wretched Indians?" she demanded. "Madam," replied Churchill, "to which Indians do you refer? Do you refer to the second greatest nation on earth, which under benign and munificent British rule has multiplied and prospered exceedingly? Or to the unfortunate North American Indians, which under your present administration are almost extinct?"

20   Once when Churchill was visiting the White House, President Roosevelt wheeled himself along to the British premier's bedroom and opened the door unexpectedly. Churchill was standing in the middle of the room stark naked and unembarrassed. "You see, Mr. President," he said, "we British have nothing to hide."

21   During a tour of the battlefields between Maastricht and Aachen at the beginning of March 1945, Churchill's party happened to pass a section of the Siegfried Line. Churchill halted the procession so that he might take a closer look at a German pillbox. Once out of the car, however, he turned to his companions with a mischievous grin and said, "Let's all go and piss on the West Wall." As he proceeded to put his suggestion into action, photographers rushed to record the scene. Churchill sent them away. "This is one of the operations connected with this great war," he said, "which must not be reproduced graphically."

22 F. D. Roosevelt had expressed hopes that the Yalta conference would not last more than five or six days. Remarked Churchill: "I do not see any way of realizing our hopes about world organization in five or six days. Even the Almighty took seven."

23 Contrary to almost everyone's expectations, the Conservatives lost the general election held in 1945 in the aftermath of World War II. By way of consolation, Churchill was offered an honor by the Crown. "How can I take the Order of the Bath from His Majesty," he asked, "when the electorate has given me the order of the boot?"

24 President Charles de Gaulle, a six-foot-four-inch humorless Frenchman with "a head like a banana and hips like a woman" (as Hugh Dalton remarked), did not hit it off with the much more compact and sparkling Churchill. Each had his own ego problem; each saw himself as the embodiment of his nation. On one occasion, during dinner at Chequers, Churchill was informed by his butler that de Gaulle wished to speak to him on the phone. Churchill, in the middle of drinking his soup, refused to take the call. De Gaulle, vehemently persisting through the intermediary of the butler, eventually persuaded the British leader to abandon his soup. When Churchill returned to the table ten minutes later, he was still crimson with rage. "Bloody de Gaulle! He had the impertinence to tell me that the French regard him as the reincarnation of Joan of Arc." Pause. "I found it necessary to remind him that we had to burn the first one."

25 Churchill was no admirer of Sir Stafford Cripps, minister for aircraft production in Churchill's government during World War II. After the war Cripps rejoined the Labour party. Churchill was standing with a friend in the House of Commons when Cripps went by; Churchill pulled a face and remarked, "There, but for the grace of God, goes God."

{This remark is attributed to others about others.}

26 Queen Salote Tupou was on Tonga's throne when Elizabeth II was crowned. As a commoner, Prime Minister Churchill sat below royal witnesses from abroad. The ceremonies dragged on past noon, Churchill was hungry. It was what he called his "tummy time." Finally their majesties filed out, the black queen followed by an even blacker small boy carrying her train. His companion nudged the Prime Minister, pointed to the boy, and asked, "Who's that?" Churchill growled: "That's her lunch."

27 Churchill's actress daughter Sarah was married for a time to the music-hall entertainer Vic Oliver. Churchill did not particularly like him. Out walking one day, Oliver asked his father-in-law whom he had admired in the war. "Mussolini," growled Churchill surprisingly, adding, "He had the courage to have his son-in-law shot."

{Count Galeazzo Ciano, husband of Edda Mussolini, had been convicted on a charge of high treason and executed in 1944.}

28 During a visit to America, Churchill was invited to a buffet luncheon at which cold fried chicken was served. Returning for a second helping, he asked politely, "May I have some breast?"

"Mr. Churchill," replied his hostess, "in this country we ask for white meat or dark meat." Churchill apologized profusely.

The following morning, the lady received a magnificent orchid from her guest of honor. The accompanying card read: "I would be most obliged if you would pin this on your white meat."

29 George Bernard Shaw sent Churchill a note inviting him to the first-night performance of *Saint Joan*. He enclosed two tickets, "One for yourself and one for a friend — if you have one." Expressing his regret at being unable to attend, Churchill replied, asking if it would be possible to have tickets for the second night — "if there is one."

30 A critic (or editor) once had the temerity to correct a Churchillian sentence on the grounds that he should not have ended the sentence with a preposition. Churchill scribbled a note of his own: "This is the sort of English up with which I will not put."

31 A proud mother remarked that her baby looked exactly like Churchill. "Madam, all babies look like me," said Churchill.

32 He had few illusions about his oratorical effectiveness. When one of his friends asked, "Aren't you impressed to see ten thousand people gather to hear you speak?" he replied, "No — because ten times as many would come to see me hanged."

33 At a dinner for Commonwealth dignitaries, a chief of protocol approached Churchill, who was presiding, and whispered in his ear that one of the distinguished guests had been seen to slip a silver salt shaker into his pocket. Churchill promptly pocketed the matching pepper shaker. At the end of the meal he slid up to the offending guest, murmuring, "Oh, dear, we were seen. Perhaps we had both better put them back."

34 Churchill tended to talk of historical figures, such as Sir Walter Raleigh and Henry VIII, as though they were his contemporaries. Just after Harold Macmillan had been chosen over Rab Butler as the new Conservative leader, a private secretary entered Churchill's office and overheard Churchill muttering, "Intelligent, yes. Good-looking, yes. Well-meaning, yes. But not the stuff of which prime ministers are made."

"But would Rab have been any better?" asked the secretary.

Churchill looked at him blankly. "I was thinking of Melbourne," he said.

35 During an after-dinner conversation Churchill's son Randolph was trying to make a point when his father interrupted him to express his own opinion. Randolph listened for a moment, then attempted to bring the conversation back to his own line of reasoning. "Don't interrupt me when I am interrupting!" snapped his father.

36 Churchill, irritated by the noise of staplers, insisted on fastening his papers together with tape threaded through punched holes. He referred to his paper punch as his "klop"; most of his subordinates were familiar with this onomatopoeic term. On one occasion, however, a new secretary was somewhat surprised to hear Churchill call, "Bring me my klop." Some time later, she staggered into Churchill's office clutching all fourteen volumes of Onno Klopp's *Der Fall des Hauses Stuart.*

37 Entering the men's room in the House of Commons one day, Churchill found Clement Attlee already standing at the urinal. Churchill took up his stance at the opposite end of the urinal. "Feeling standoffish today, are we, Winston?" asked Attlee. "That's right," replied Churchill. "Every time you see something big, you want to nationalize it."

38 At a dinner party one evening, there was a heated exchange between Churchill and a female MP. At the end of the exchange the lady scornfully remarked, "Mr. Churchill, you are drunk."

"And you, madam," replied Churchill, "are ugly. But I shall be sober tomorrow."

{This anecdote is also told of others.}

39 Of the Greek prime minister Plasteras, Churchill once remarked, "Well, I hope he doesn't have feet of clay, too."

40 Returning home exhausted one evening, Churchill felt he could not face his last appointment of the day — a visit from a rather tiresome colleague who always outstayed his welcome. "When Sir —— arrives," he told his valet, "tell him I'm out." Then, after a moment's thought, he added, "And to convince him, smoke one of my cigars when you open the door."

41 While in New York, Churchill visited publisher Henry Luce, who had one of the former prime minister's landscapes hanging in his private office. "It's a good picture," remarked Luce, "but I think it needs something in the foreground — a sheep, perhaps." The following morning, Luce was horrified to receive a call from Churchill's secretary, requesting him to send the painting back. Luce complied, distressed to think that his criticism had caused such offense. A few days later, however, the canvas was returned — with a single sheep grazing placidly in the foreground.

42 "The poodle ate in the dining room with the rest of the family. A cloth was laid for him on the Persian carpet beside the head of the household, and no one else ate until the butler had served Rufus's meal. One evening at Chequers the film was *Oliver Twist.* Rufus, as usual, had the best seat in the house, on his master's lap. At the point when Bill Sikes was about to drown his dog to put the police off his track, Churchill covered Rufus's eyes with his hand. He said, 'Don't look now, dear. I'll tell you about it afterwards.' "

43 One of Churchill's bodyguards also enjoyed painting in his spare time. He showed a few of his canvases to the former prime minister, who was quite impressed. "They're much better than mine," he remarked. "But yours will have to be judged on merit."

44 Asked why he chose to paint landscapes rather than portraits, Churchill replied: "Because no tree has ever complained about its likeness."

45 The photographer who had been photographing Churchill on his eightieth birthday said courteously that he hoped he would photograph him on his hundredth. "I don't see why not, young man," said Churchill. "You look reasonably fit to me."

46 (Sir Robert Menzies tells us that after a dinner at Buckingham Palace in the mid-1950s Churchill started a conversation with the Muslim prime minister of Pakistan.)
"Will you have a whisky and soda, Mr. Prime Minister?"
"No, thank you!"
"What's that?"
"No, thank you!"
"What, why?"
"I'm a teetotaler, Mr. Prime Minister."
"What's that?"
"I'm a teetotaler."
"A teetotaler. Christ! I mean God! I mean Allah!"

47 The older Churchill grew, the stronger the bond he felt with others of his own generation. Told that a man over seventy-five years of age had been arrested in Hyde Park for making improper advances toward a young girl in subzero weather, he chuckled, "Over seventy-five and below zero! Makes you *proud* to be an Englishman!"

48 Even toward the end of his life Churchill retained his powers of repartee. As he was sitting in the smoking room of the House of Commons with his fly buttons undone, someone pointed out to him that his dress needed

adjusting. "Dead birds don't fall out of nests," said the elder statesman.

49 In his eighties, Churchill paid a visit to the House of Commons. His appearance distracted attention from the debate then in progress. An MP said irritably, "After all, they say he's potty."
"They say he can't hear either," said the aged former prime minister.

ॐ ✺

CHWOLSON, Daniel Abramovich (1819–1911), *Russian archaeologist, of Jewish descent. After his conversion to Christianity, he became professor of Oriental languages at the University (1855) and professor of Hebrew and biblical archaeology at the Academy (1858) in St. Petersburg.*

1 Asked whether his decision to join the Orthodox Church had been made through conviction or for expediency, Chwolson replied: "I accepted baptism entirely out of conviction — the conviction that it is better to be a professor in the Academy in St. Petersburg than a teacher in a *cheder* in Vilna."

ॐ ✺

CIBBER, Colley (1671–1757), *British actor and dramatist, who became poet laureate (1730) and was immortalized in Alexander Pope's* Dunciad *(1743 edition) as the* supremo *of dullness.*

1 Colley Cibber worked his way up in the theater from the humblest of beginnings. His very first role was a brief appearance to hand a message to a character played by the great Thomas Betterton. Paralyzed with stage fright, he made a mess of it and upset the other actors. Afterward, Betterton angrily asked the prompter for the name of the youth who had caused the disturbance. "Master Colley," replied the prompter.
"Master Colley. Then fine him!"
"But, sir, he has no salary."
"No?" said Betterton. "Then put him down for ten shillings a week and fine him five shillings."

ॐ ✺

CICERO, Marcus Tullius (106–43 BC), *Roman orator and statesman. He played an im-*

portant role in the events leading up to the collapse of the Roman Republic, using his powers as an orator and his political influence to counter the popular party and Julius Caesar. While consul in 63 BC he defeated the notorious Catalinian conspiracy. After the murder of Caesar, Cicero devoted himself to maintaining the ideal of liberty against the ambitious Mark Antony, whom he attacked in a series of speeches known as the Philippics. He was assassinated on Antony's orders.

1   While Cicero was dining with a friend, the host produced a bottle of mediocre wine with the words, "Try this Falernian; it's forty years old." Cicero tasted it and commented, "Young for its age."

2   Caesar greatly increased the number of Roman senators, a practice that caused much resentment among those who were already entitled to senatorial rank. One day at the games a newly created senator walked along the rows, looking for a seat. As he passed Cicero, the latter said to him, "I should have been happy for you to sit beside me were I not already short of room," intending both to snub the interloper and to make plain his contempt for the enlarged senate. Mindful of Cicero's reputation for political fickleness, the man replied, "I am surprised that you of all people should be short of room, since you make a habit of sitting on two seats at once."

3   Caninius Revilus was consul for only one day. Cicero, who deplored the disintegration of the ancient and dignified offices of the Roman Republic, made several observations on this event, including, "We have a consul of such vigilance that during his entire term he never slept a wink." And, on being reproached for not practicing the usual courtesy of calling on the consul during his consulship, Cicero explained, "I was on my way, but night overtook me."

4   Metellus Nepos, whose mother had a reputation for licentiousness, once teased Cicero on his low birth. "Who, after all, *was* your father?"

"It would be much harder for me to tell you who yours was," replied Cicero.

ॐ ◌

CIMON (died 449 BC), *Athenian admiral and statesman who won important victories over the Persians and did much to consolidate Athens's supremacy over the other Greek cities and islands.*

1   A barbarian prince who had formerly supported the Persian cause abandoned his ally and came to Athens, seeking to place himself under Cimon's protection. To ensure his welcome he brought two vessels, one filled with gold pieces and the other with silver, and placed them before Cimon's door. Cimon looked at them and smiled. "Would you prefer to have me as your mercenary or as your friend?" he asked.

"As my friend," replied the man.

"Go," said Cimon, "and take these things away with you. For if I am your friend, your money will be mine whenever I have need of it."

ॐ ◌

CINQUE, Joseph (?1813–80), *African slave who led a mutiny aboard the Spanish ship* Amistad *in 1839. The slaves seized the vessel, killed the captain and cook, and ordered the crew to go to Africa. Instead, they entered American waters, were taken into custody, and were eventually freed by a Supreme Court decision.*

1   In his later years Cinque became an interpreter at a Christian mission in Sierra Leone. He was asked whether, if he were faced with the situation aboard the *Amistad* again, he would not now pray for the captain and cook instead of killing them. "I would pray for them," he replied, "and kill them too."

ॐ ◌

CLAIRE, Ina (1895–1985), *US actress. She made her reputation as a stage comedienne before moving to Hollywood as one of the stars of the first generation of "talkies."*

1   Between 1929 and 1931 Ina Claire was married to John Gilbert, the romantic hero of the silent screen. A reporter asked her how it felt being married to a celebrity. "Why don't you ask my husband?" replied Mrs. Gilbert.

ॐ ◌

CLARK, A[lbert] C[urtis] (1859–1937), *British classical scholar; professor of Latin at*

Oxford (1913–34). His chief work was his edition of Cicero's speeches.

1 Once while visiting a college farm, Clark and his party witnessed a bull servicing a cow. Clark turned to Alan Blakeway (a younger Oxford classicist), who was with him, and said, "Blakeway, *omne animal post coitum triste.* There was, Blakeway, a firm of solicitors in London called Mann, Rogers, and Greaves."

੬ঌ ঌ੬

CLARK, George Rogers (1752–1818), *US soldier. He organized the defense of the Ohio area against English forces and their Indian allies during the Revolution. Clark received no pay during this period, and the Virginia legislature never reimbursed him for his expenses, so that his later life was harassed by debt. In 1786 he was relieved of his military command through the misrepresentations of a subordinate, and spent the rest of his life in embittered retirement.*

1 Impoverished and crippled, Clark applied to the Virginia legislature for a military pension. He was sent a ceremonial sword in token of his many heroic exploits. "When Virginia needed a sword, I gave her one. Now she sends me a toy," the old hero said. "I want bread." So saying, he broke the sword in two with his crutch.

੬ঌ ঌ੬

CLARK, Mark Wayne (1896–1984), *US general. After graduating from West Point in 1917 he served briefly in World War I. He was given command of the US ground forces in Europe in World War II, and subsequently served in North Africa, Italy, Austria, and the Far East.*

1 Clark was once asked what was the best advice he had ever been given. "To marry the girl I did," he replied.
  "And who gave you that advice?" was the next question.
  "She did," said the general.

੬ঌ ঌ੬

CLAY, Cassius Marcellus, Sr. (1810–1903), *US abolitionist and political campaigner. He was US minister to Russia (1861–62, 1863–69).*

1 A cousin of the great Henry Clay, he remained loyal to the Union during the Civil War

and fought numerous duels with fellow Kentuckians who disagreed with him. Though he was an expert duelist (he never lost an encounter), his first confrontation was a failure. As both he and his opponent missed their allowed three shots, the encounter was called off. It was well known that Clay could normally hit a suspended string at ten paces three times out of five. Asked to explain his inaccurate fire, he replied, "That damned string never had no pistol in his hand."

੬ঌ ঌ੬

CLAY, Henry (1777–1852), *US statesman and orator. A popular and fluent speaker, he had a brilliant, virtually unbroken career in Congress from 1806 until his death. He promoted the cause of national unity and prestige, advocating the 1812 war with Britain, and, as secretary of state (1825–29), establishing the policy of Pan-Americanism. Despite his efforts to gain the presidency between 1824 and 1848, he never achieved this, his highest ambition. He was nicknamed "the Great Compromiser" on account of his compromises to preserve the Union over the issue of slavery.*

1 Henry Clay's forceful and brilliant style of oratory won him the acclaim of the House but also the jealousy of certain older and more ponderous speakers whose long-windedness showed up badly in comparison. One such speaker approached Clay and tried to deflate him by pointing out that Clay's speeches, aimed at immediate impact, were for the present generation while most senior orators were speaking for posterity. "And it seems, sir, that you are resolved to speak until the arrival of your audience," retorted Clay.

2 John Randolph of Roanoke and Henry Clay were deadly rivals. On one occasion the two politicians found themselves walking toward each other on a footpath so narrow that they could not pass. "I never give way to scoundrels," said Randolph, standing stock-still. "I *always* do," said Clay, stepping off the curb.

3 Jefferson's vision of the westward expansion of America fired the imagination of the young Henry Clay. On his way home from Washington to Kentucky he stepped from the stagecoach, bent down, and put his ear to the

ground. "What are you listening for?" inquired the driver. "I'm listening for the tread of un-numbered thousands of feet that will pass this way westward," said Clay.

4   "You don't remember my name," said a lady to Henry Clay. "Madam, I do not," said Clay, bowing, "for when we last met, I was certain that your beauty and accomplishments would soon cause you to change it."

5   In about 1850 Clay observed in a speech, "I would rather be right than be president," a sentiment not borne out in his own unsuccessful struggle to achieve the supreme political office. John C. Calhoun, who had been vice president in 1824, commented, "I guess it's all right to be half right, and vice president."

See also THOMAS B. REED 2 and NORMAN THOMAS 4.

6   Speaking at a meeting one day, Clay found himself struggling against a number of slave-owners who were trying to drown out his voice by hissing. "Gentlemen," he cried, "that is the sound you hear when the waters of truth drop upon the fires of hell."

7   Clay was sitting outside the old National Hotel in Washington with Daniel Webster, then US senator from Massachusetts. Watching a man walk by with a pack of mules, Webster remarked, "Clay, there goes a number of your Kentucky constituents."

"They must be going up to Massachusetts to teach school," commented Clay.

৪৵ ৩৯

CLEMENCEAU, Georges (1841–1929), *French statesman, prime minister (1906–09, 1917–20), known as "the Tiger." As a member of the Chamber of Deputies (1876–93) he became renowned for his vehement polemics, which he also exercised in journalism. He strengthened ties with Britain during his first premiership and during the early years of World War I attacked the defeatism of the French government. He played a major role in the treaties after the war ended.*

1   Clemenceau told the following story of himself, and it perhaps illuminates his diplomatic methods. On a tour in the East he took a liking to a statuette offered for sale by a dealer. The man said he could have it for only seventy-five rupees, "because it's you." Clemenceau offered forty-five rupees. The bargaining went on, with Clemenceau firmly sticking to his forty-five-rupee offer. Eventually the dealer flung up his hands indignantly. "Impossible! I'd rather give it to you!" he exclaimed. "Done!" said Clemenceau, pocketing the statuette. "You are exceptionally kind and I thank you, but such a gift could only come from a friend. I hope you will not be insulted if I offer you a gift in return." The bemused dealer said that he would not. "Here," said Clemenceau, "are forty-five rupees for you to use in charitable works." The dealer accepted the rupees and they parted on excellent terms.

2   Clemenceau once awarded the Legion of Honor to a business magnate whose only claim was his large contribution to the Tiger's political funds. Pinning on the decoration, Clemenceau said, "Sir, you wanted the Legion of Honor. Here it is. Now all you have to do is deserve it."

3   At a Paris railroad station on the way to one of his numerous duels, Clemenceau surprised his second by asking for a one-way ticket. "Isn't that a little pessimistic?" asked the second. "Not at all," replied Clemenceau. "I always use my opponent's return ticket for the trip back."

4   Clemenceau fought a duel with his long-time political rival Paul Deschanel. Every time Clemenceau lunged, Deschanel retreated a little farther. Eventually Clemenceau shrugged, tucked his sword under his arm, and said, "Monsieur is leaving us."

5   When Clemenceau was appointed home secretary, he arrived punctually at the department to inspect his new offices and staff. As he and his aide walked around the building, flinging open door after door, they found every office empty. At last they entered a room to discover a staff member slumped over his desk, fast asleep. As the aide darted forward to rouse him, Clemenceau put out a restraining hand. "Don't wake him," he said. "He might leave."

6   A supporter rushed into Clemenceau's office in great excitement, crying out, "Your son has just joined the Communist party."

Clemenceau looked up calmly. "Monsieur, my son is twenty-two years old. If he had not become a Communist at twenty-two I would have disowned him. If he is still a Communist at thirty I will do it then."

7 Although Clemenceau was in his seventies during World War I, he liked nothing better than to tour the battlefields. His dauntless insistence on being taken right up to the front line was a major worry to those responsible for his safety. Churchill accompanied him on a tour of inspection in 1918 in the course of which they left their car to go and talk to some British cavalry officers. Shells were coming over intermittently and the French staff officers became anxious about Clemenceau. As they headed back to the car, a shell burst among a group of riderless horses standing nearby and scattered it. One of the wounded animals, covered with blood, came at a lurching trot toward Clemenceau's escort. The elderly statesman leaped into its path, seized its bridle, and brought it to a halt. The general escorting him remonstrated, and Clemenceau reluctantly continued to his car. As he got in he murmured unrepentantly to Churchill, "*Quel moment délicieux!*"

8 President Woodrow Wilson's Fourteen Points (1918) outlined the proposals for a peace settlement after World War I. Clemenceau, unimpressed, remarked, "Even God Almighty only has ten."

9 Clemenceau's contrariness was invaluable in shaking France out of its torpor during World War I, but it was altogether less of an asset during the subsequent peace. This trait emerged even in trivial matters. Going into a grand garden party at Versailles, the bowler-hatted Clemenceau met the British foreign secretary, Lord Balfour, wearing a top hat. "They told me top hats would be worn," said the British diplomat. "They told me too," said Clemenceau.

10 After Wilson's departure from the Versailles conference following World War I, Clemenceau, on his way to a meeting with Colonel House, Wilson's adviser, was fired on by a young anarchist, Emile Cottin. As Clemenceau's car sped away, Cottin fired seven (some

say eight) more shots. One hit Clemenceau near his heart. Cottin was apprehended and the death penalty demanded. Clemenceau intervened: "We have just won the most terrible war in history, yet here is a Frenchman who misses his target six times out of seven. . . . Of course the fellow must be punished for the careless use of a dangerous weapon and for poor marksmanship." He recommended eight years in prison "with intensive training in a shooting gallery."

11 Clemenceau loathed flying and always avoided it whenever possible. Before one flight he was heard to admonish the pilot, "Fly very cautiously, very slow, and very low."

ड़ॐ ॐड़

CLEVELAND, Frances Folsom (1864–1947), *wife of Grover Cleveland, 22d and 24th president of the United States.*

1 At a White House dinner given during one of the Cleveland terms of office a young European attaché was served a salad that included a worm. He was on the point of raising a protest when he caught Mrs. Cleveland's eye, fixed on him in a challenging stare. The attaché then proceeded to devour the salad, worm and all. Mrs. Cleveland smiled approvingly. "You will go far, young man," she told him. Fifteen years later that same attaché returned as a full ambassador.

ड़ॐ ॐड़

CLEVELAND, [Stephen] Grover (1837–1908), *US politician; 22d and 24th president of the United States (1885–89, 1893–97). His determination to stamp out corruption made him many powerful enemies even among his fellow Democrats. His second term of office was dogged by labor unrest and financial problems that brought him considerable unpopularity.*

1 Cleveland, though constantly at loggerheads with the Senate, got on better with the House of Representatives. A popular story circulating during his presidency concerned the night he was roused by his wife crying, "Wake up! I think there are burglars in the house."

"No, no, my dear," said the president sleepily, "in the Senate maybe, but not in the House."

2   A reporter was pestering President Cleveland to make a statement on a major issue of foreign policy. "That, sir, is a matter of too great importance to discuss in a five-minute interview — now rapidly drawing to its close," said Cleveland firmly.

ۮ ۮ

CLIVE, Robert, Baron Clive of Plassey (1725–74), *British administrator in India. He joined the East India Company in 1743 and achieved fame first as a military commander. He captured Calcutta from the nawab of Bengal and then defeated him at Plassey (1757), leaving the East India Company the dominant force in Bengal. As governor of Bengal (1764–67), Clive made important reforms, but was subsequently impeached by the British Parliament. Although vindicated, he soon afterward committed suicide.*

1   In polite eighteenth-century society diners were called upon for "sentiments," that is, epigrammatical observations or wishes expressed in the manner of toasts at the end of the meal. Clive's used to be: "Alas and alackaday!" (a lass and a lac — 100,000 rupees — a day).

2   The opportunities for corruption on the part of British officials in India were astounding. When Clive was being cross-examined on this score during the parliamentary proceedings against him in 1773, he burst out, "By God, Mr. Chairman, at this moment I stand astonished at my own moderation."

ۮ ۮ

CLURMAN, Harold (1901–80), *US theatrical director and drama critic.*

1   With Lee Strasberg and Cheryl Crawford, Clurman was one of the directors of the Group Theatre, an influential theatrical force in the thirties. Out of it came the playwright Clifford Odets as well as a host of actors who later achieved fame on stage and screen.

One of these, Stella Adler, married Clurman. Her affection was not alloyed by sentimentality. Robert Lewis, one of the youngest members of the Group, once asked her why Clurman continually studied his face, turning it from side to side, in the mirror. Stella Adler replied, "He's trying to imagine how he's going to look on that horse when he's a statue in Central Park."

2   Robert Lewis, visiting Clurman in Hollywood, shared a bedroom with him. He noted with some alarm that throughout the night in his sleep Curman would emit a variety of dramatic sounds, including those of clicking teeth, affection, and rage. Stella Adler reported that she once awakened him and suggested, "Harold, don't sleep like a great man. Just sleep."

ۮ ۮ

COBB, Irvin S[hrewsbury] (1876–1944), *US humorist and writer. His Judge Priest stories, depicting life in a southern community, were particularly successful.*

1   As a young reporter in New York, Cobb suffered from the ill humor of his boss at the *World*, Charles E. Chapin. Arriving for work one day, Cobb found that Chapin was home ill. "Nothing trivial, I trust," commented Cobb.

{Possibly the first appearance of this familiar riposte.}

2   As a correspondent during World War I, Cobb was sent to Belgium to cover the German invasion. Traveling to the Belgian army headquarters by taxi, he and his three colleagues were captured by the Germans and questioned. The interrogation lasted throughout the night and well into the next day, and Cobb's nervousness grew increasingly apparent. Finally he called out to the interrogating officer: "Sir, whether or not you intend to shoot us, will you at least grant us one request?" The German, a little surprised, asked, "What is that?" Replied Cobb: "Will you please tell the driver of our taxicab to stop the meter?"

ۮ ۮ

COCKCROFT, Sir John (1897–1967), *British nuclear scientist. He worked under Lord Rutherford in the famous Cavendish Laboratory at Cambridge, where with E. T. S. Walton he demonstrated that accelerated protons could split an atomic nucleus. They were awarded the Nobel Prize for physics for this work in 1951.*

1   (Cockcroft used to tell this story of a visit to the United States in 1933 to illustrate what he called the Old Stone Age of nuclear physics, before it became big business.)

"A letter from Oliphant asked me whilst in Berkeley to purchase or steal a gallon or so of heavy water, since it was needed desperately for dozens of experiments. He added kindly that Rutherford would willingly spend some money on it. So I collected about a gallon of 2 percent D_2O and paid G. N. Lewis $10 for it. After passing through the Customs with difficulty, since they did not understand why I should be importing a liquid which looked very like water, I presented the heavy water and the bill personally to Rutherford, only to find that he considered the price to be too high and I should have asked his authority for purchasing it."

ཉ৯ ৎৡ

COCTEAU, Jean (1889–1963), *French writer, artist, and occasional film director. He worked with Sergei Diaghilev's Ballets Russes, writing sketches such as* Parade *(1917), and during World War I also became acquainted with many leading artists. He wrote poetry, plays, and a number of novels, notably* Les Enfants terribles *(1929), which he later turned into a film (1950).*

1 Someone asked Cocteau what he would take if his house were on fire and he could remove only one thing. "I would take the fire," replied Cocteau.

2 Dissatisfied with one of his productions, Cocteau confided his disappointment to a group of his film students: "It's my worst work." One of his loyal disciples said, "Among us it's generally understood that you aren't its author."

3 Cocteau was once asked if he believed in luck. "Of course," he replied. "How else do you explain the success of those you don't like?"

4 William Fifield recounted the following anecdote in *In Search of Genius:* "When I asked Cocteau what he thought of [Raymond] Radiguet, who had written a French classic *The Devil in the Flesh,* before he died at twenty, would have done next had he lived, he surprised me by saying, 'Oh, seen to his publicity.' I had been innocent enough to think he might say, 'Try to write even better.' "

5 Cocteau's publisher, Bernard Grasset, had put forward the view that publishers are more important than authors. "In that case," retorted Cocteau, "perhaps you ought to imitate the film producers. Announce a BOOK BY GRASSET in big characters, and then, in tiny letters, 'Words by Cocteau.' "

6 When the subject of heaven and hell was broached in conversation one day, Cocteau politely declined to offer any opinion. "Excuse me for not answering," he said. "I have friends in both places."

ཉ৯ ৎৡ

COHAN, George M. (1878–1942), *US playwright, actor, songwriter, and theatrical producer. Among his memorable achievements is his starring appearance in Eugene O'Neill's* Ah, Wilderness!

1 Cohan auditioned an actor for a role and finally dismissed him. As the door closed, Cohan said to one of his staff, "I hate that rat. Remind me never to hire him again unless we need him."

2 When the Actors' Equity Association was officially organized in 1913, one of its foremost opponents was George M. Cohan. He ran a signed advertisement in the New York newspapers reading: "Before I ever do business with the Actors' Equity, I will lose every dollar I have even if I have to run an elevator to make a living." The next day a sign appeared hanging out of the office window of the Equity headquarters: "WANTED — ELEVATOR OPERATOR. GEORGE M. COHAN PREFERRED."

3 At the height of his success as a theatrical producer, Cohan was dining with his father at an expensive hotel. Listening to the violinist playing skillfully in the background during their meal, Cohan was reminded of the unsuccessful violin lessons of his own childhood. "Say, Dad," he remarked, "perhaps if I had given more attention to my violin lessons I might be playing here."

"Yes, you might," replied his father. "But you wouldn't be eating here."

4 Jim Moore, founder of a famous New York restaurant, had many friends in the theatrical world. As he grew older several of them died and were sorely missed by Moore. One Friday afternoon he made a pilgrimage to the graves of these departed friends, remonstrating with them for their thoughtlessness in dying. When he got to George M. Cohan's grave he took out a parcel of fish and thumped it against the headstone. "In case you don't know," he shouted, "today's Friday, and I just want you to see what you're missing."

ॐ ☙

COHEN, Morris Raphael (1880–1947), *US philosopher and educator, born in Russia. He was professor of philosophy at the College of the City of New York (1912–38) and at the University of Chicago (1938–47).*

1 At the end of an introductory course in philosophy, one of Cohen's students complained, "Professor Cohen, you have knocked a hole in everything I've ever believed in, and you have given me nothing to take its place!"

"Young lady," replied the professor sternly, "you will recall that among the labors of Hercules he was required to clean out the Augean stables. He was not, let me point out, required to fill them."

ॐ ☙

COHN, Harry (1891–1958), *US movie producer, head of Columbia studios.*

1 Though Harry Cohn was greatly disliked in Hollywood, there was a large turnout for his funeral. An observer remarked: "It only proves what they always say — give the public something they want to see and they'll show up to see it."

{This remark exists in numerous variants, attributed to several people, including Joan Fontaine and Red Skelton. It is also, of course, applicable to funerals of other unpopular characters; see LOUIS B. MAYER 5, for example.}

2 Cohn's brother Jack once suggested to Harry that they produce a biblical epic. "What do you know about the Bible?" cried Harry. "I'll lay you fifty dollars you don't even know the Lord's Prayer." After a moment's thought, Jack began, "Now I lay me down to sleep . . ." Harry pulled fifty dollars out of his pocket. "Well, I'll be damned," he said, hand-ing the money to his brother. "I didn't think you knew it."

3 Cohn announced to his staff one day that he was planning a trip to New York. "Take me with you, Mr. Cohn?" asked screenwriter Norman Krasna. "You? What the hell do I need *you* for?" stormed Cohn. "You'll need me, Mr. Cohn, because on trains you have to write out your order for your meals," replied Krasna. "So what?" demanded Cohn. "So what?" replied the screenwriter. "*You* can't write. You'll starve to death!"

4 Frank Capra remembers a day when Cohn ordered him to his office at once. Capra arrived to find that Cohn, evidently having forgotten that he had called Capra, was quarreling furiously with his brother Jack over some creative differences. The tinkling bell of an ice-cream wagon was heard from the street. Cohn stopped in his tracks, took orders, ran to the window, yelled down, "One chocolate! Two strawberry!" and then went back to throttling his brother while they waited for the ice creams.

"That," Frank Capra said, "was Harry Cohn."

ॐ ☙

COKE, Sir Edward (1552–1634), *English lawyer. He became attorney general (1594) and was chief justice (1613–16) until James I dismissed him for upholding common law against royal prerogative. He vehemently supported the liberties of Parliament against encroachments by both James I and Charles I. His reputation, however, has suffered because of his browbeating of Sir Walter Raleigh at his trial in 1603.*

1 In 1598 Coke (pronounced "cook") married as his second wife Lady Elizabeth Hatton, the widow of Sir William Hatton and granddaughter of Lord Burghley. There was much speculation at the time as to why a lady with such grand connections should ally herself with a man of Coke's plebeian origins. An anecdote preserved by John Aubrey suggests a reason. In bed with his new wife, Coke put his hand on her belly and felt a child stir. "What? Flesh in the pot?" he exclaimed. "Yes," said the lady, "or else I would not have married a cook."

{The marriage did not prosper after this inauspicious start.}

COLE, Dr. Harry (?1500–1580), *English clergyman. Under Henry VIII and Edward VI Cole acquiesced in the Reformation, but with the accession of the Roman Catholic Queen Mary reverted to Catholicism. He preached the notorious sermon at Oxford justifying the execution of Archbishop Cranmer (1556) and was appointed dean of St. Paul's, London, the same year. After Elizabeth's accession he lost his preferments, was imprisoned, and eventually died obscurely.*

1   In 1558 Cole was given a commission to suppress the Protestants of Ireland. En route to Dublin, he stopped for the night at Chester, where he lodged with the mayor, to whom he showed his commission, boasting, "Here is what shall lash the heretics of Ireland." The mayor's wife, overhearing these words, feared for her brother, a Protestant living in Dublin. Seizing an opportunity when Cole's back was turned, she opened the box, removed the commission, substituted a pack of playing cards, and resealed the box. The following day Cole went on his way unsuspecting.

As soon as he landed in Ireland he went to a meeting of the Privy Council, where he announced his errand to the lord deputy. When the lord deputy opened the box, all he found was the pack of cards, with the knave lying uppermost. "Let us have another commission," said he, "and in the meantime we will shuffle the cards." So Cole was obliged to return to England, but before he could reach Ireland again with a fresh commission Queen Mary died and Elizabeth ascended the throne. It is said that Elizabeth gave the resourceful wife of the Chester mayor an annual pension for her part in preserving the Irish Protestants from persecution.

જે⊷ ⊷ઙ

COLERIDGE, Samuel Taylor (1772–1834), *British poet, critic, and philosopher. As a young man Coleridge dreamed about forming with his friend Robert Southey an ideal communistic society ("Pantisocracy") in America. With Wordsworth he wrote* Lyrical Ballads *(1798), which announced their determination to break with the artificial poetic conventions of the time; Coleridge's contribution to the volume was "The Ancient Mariner." Much of his literary criticism appears in* Biographia Literaria *(1817). In addition he translated, wrote plays,*
edited periodicals, and did much to introduce German philosophy to an English audience. Contemporaries record the brilliance of his conversation, but poverty, the failure of his marriage, and his addiction to opium blighted his career.

1   In 1796 Coleridge launched a periodical called *The Watchman,* a collection of prose and verse with the motto: "That all might know the truth, and that the truth might make us free." The enterprise was a total failure; it was discontinued after the ninth issue and a large number of unsold copies lay around Coleridge's house. One morning the poet saw his servant-girl laying a fire and it seemed to him that she was being unnecessarily prodigal with the amount of paper she was using. "Don't worry, sir," she reassured him, "it's only *Watchmen.*"

2   (Coleridge tells the story of the genesis of "Kubla Khan.")

"In the summer of 1797, the author, then in ill health, had retired to a lonely farm-house between Porlock and Linton, on the Exmoor confines of Somerset and Devonshire. In consequence of a slight indisposition, an anodyne had been prescribed, from the effects of which he fell asleep in his chair at the moment of reading the following sentence, or words of the same substance, in Purchas' *Pilgrimage:* 'Here the Khan Kubla commanded a palace to be built, and a stately garden thereunto. And thus ten miles of fertile ground were inclosed with a wall.' The author continued for about three hours in a profound sleep, at least of the external senses, during which time he has the most vivid confidence that he could not have composed less than from two to three hundred lines; if that indeed can be called composition in which all the images rose up before him as *things,* with a parallel production of the correspondent expressions, without any sensation or consciousness of effort. On awaking he appeared to himself to have a distinct recollection of the whole, and taking his pen, ink, and paper, instantly and eagerly wrote down the lines that are here preserved. At this moment he was unfortunately called out by a person on business from Porlock, and detained by him above an hour, and on his return to his room, found, to his no small surprise and mortification, that though he still retained some vague and dim recollection of the general purport of the vision, yet, with the exception of some eight or ten scattered lines and images, all the rest had passed away like the images on the surface of a stream into which a stone has been cast, but, alas! without the restoration of the latter."

{Scholars have recently questioned the accuracy of Coleridge's recollection.}

3 (Charles Lamb recalls an encounter with Coleridge in London.)

"Brimful of some new idea, and in spite of my assuring him that time was precious, he drew me within the door of an unoccupied garden by the road-side, and there, sheltered from observation by a hedge of evergreens, he took me by the button of my coat, and closing his eyes commenced an eloquent discourse, waving his right hand gently, as the musical words flowed in an unbroken stream from his lips. I listened entranced; but the striking of a church clock recalled me to a sense of duty. I saw it was of no use to attempt to break away, so taking advantage of his absorption in his subject, I, with my penknife, quietly severed the button from my coat, and decamped. Five hours afterwards, in passing the same garden on my way home, I heard Coleridge's voice, and on looking in, there he was, with closed eyes — the button in his fingers — and his right hand gracefully waving, just as when I left him. He had never missed me!"

4 Coleridge was once involved in discussion with a man who firmly believed that children should not be given formal religious instruction of any kind. They would then be free to choose their own religious faith, he reasoned, when they reached the age of discretion. Coleridge did not disagree, but later invited the man into his somewhat neglected garden.

"Do you call this a garden?" exclaimed the visitor. "There are nothing but weeds here!"

"Well, you see," explained Coleridge, "I did not wish to infringe upon the liberty of the garden in any way. I was just giving the garden a chance to express itself and to choose its own production."

5 Shortly after Coleridge's tragedy *Remorse* appeared, he was sitting in a public room of a hotel when he heard his name being read out by a gentleman who was studying a newspaper report of a coroner's inquest. Coleridge asked if he might see the paper, and the stranger handed it over to him. "Extraordinary that Coleridge should have hanged himself just after the success of his play, but he always was a strange mad fellow," he remarked. "Indeed, it is the most extraordinary thing," said Coleridge, "that he should have hanged himself, be the subject of an inquest, and yet should be here at this moment speaking to you." Greatly disconcerted, the other man began to apologize, but Coleridge had taken no offense and was scanning the coroner's report. It seemed that the body of a man had been cut down from a tree in Hyde Park, and no papers had been found in his pockets to identify him, but inside his shirt was a label reading "S. T. COLERIDGE." Coleridge could readily explain that; in his travels he very frequently mislaid or otherwise lost shirts.

6 Coleridge was out riding with a friend near his home in the Lake District, wearing his customary shabby clothes. Seeing some people approaching, Coleridge suggested that he pass himself off as his friend's servant. "No," said his companion. "I am proud of you as a friend, but would be ashamed of you as a servant."

COLETTE [Sidonie Gabrielle Claudine Colette] (1873–1954), grande dame *of French letters.*

1 In a memoir written in her forties, Colette said that she owed all her success as a writer to

Samuel Butler told this story about the poet Herbert Clarke's little boy aged ten: "His mother had put him to bed and, as he was supposed to have a cold, he was to say his prayers in bed. He said them, yawned and said, 'The real question is whether there is a God or no,' on which he instantly fell into a sweet and profound sleep which forbade all further discussion."

— *Samuel Butler's Notebooks: Selections,* ed. Geoffrey Keynes and Brian Hill the appeal that her mother made to her constantly in her childhood, as she did her farm chores, to "Look, look!" Colette died in Paris in 1954, during the worst thunderstorm to visit Paris in sixty-seven years. She was eighty-one then, but her passion for observation was undiminished. Her last conscious act was to gesture toward the flashing lightning and exclaim, "Look, look!"

છ્ય   ઉડ

COLLINS, Joan (1933–   ), *British-born stage and film actress. She has also appeared on television, notably in the US soap opera* Dynasty. *Many of her numerous affairs are candidly revealed in her autobiography,* Past Imperfect *(1978).*

1   Miss Collins had been friendly with the director George Englund. When his wife, Cloris Leachman, revealed symptoms of pregnancy, Miss Collins understandably lost her temper. "That's *my* baby she's having!" she screamed at Englund.

છ્ય   ઉડ

COLLINS, Michael (1890–1922), *Irish nationalist leader. Imprisoned by the British for his role in the Easter Rising of 1916, he subsequently played a major part in the negotiations that led to the establishment of the Irish Free State (1921).*

1   One of the leading figures on the British side during the 1921 negotiations over the Irish treaty was F. E. Smith, who supported a compromise on the basis of a division that allowed Ulster to remain under British control. This encountered opposition in Britain, and after signing the treaty Smith observed as he laid down his pen, "I may have signed my political death warrant tonight."

"I may have signed my actual death warrant," said Collins.

Eight months later Collins was gunned down by republican extremists opposed to the compromise with Britain.

છ્ય   ઉડ

COLUMBUS, Christopher (1451–1506), *Italian-born navigator who was a discoverer of America (1492). He convinced Spanish monarchs Ferdinand and Isabella of the viability of* his plan to sail westward to reach India and after the initial voyage made several further exploratory expeditions (1493–96, 1498–1500, 1502–04), landing on Guadeloupe, Puerto Rico, Jamaica, Trinidad, and mainland South America.

1   On Columbus's first voyage west, in 1492, his crew was understandably uneasy about the trip through unknown waters, to an unknown destination, and for an unknown period of time. To reassure the sailors and disguise the true length of the journey, Columbus kept two logs: one the real distances traveled as he reckoned them, and the other giving shorter ones so that the crew would think they were closer to home than they actually were. The irony is that it turned out the falsified figures were more accurate than the ones Columbus kept in the "true" log.

2   At a banquet given by the grand cardinal of Spain, Columbus was seated at the most honored place at table and served with great deference and ceremony. A courtier, jealous of the foreigner's success, asked him rudely whether he thought that if he had not discovered the New World somebody else would have done so. Columbus did not reply at once, but, taking an egg in his hand, invited the guests to make it stand on one end. All tried and failed, whereupon Columbus cracked the egg against the table in such a way as to flatten one end. Then he set it standing on the crushed part. The moral was plain to the company: once he had shown the way, anyone could follow it.

{Giorgio Vasari tells a similar story of Filippo Brunelleschi.}

3   At his anchorage off Jamaica in 1504 Columbus faced a dangerous situation with supplies of food running low and the Jamaican Indians refusing to sell him any more. Consulting his almanac, he noticed that a lunar eclipse was due a few days later. On the day predicted he summoned the leaders of the Jamaicans, telling them that that night he would blot out the moon unless they resumed food trading. The Jamaicans laughed at him, but that night, when the lunar eclipse began, they came hurrying back in a state of great terror. Columbus said he would restore the moon if they would bring him food, an offer that they gladly accepted. The moon was duly restored and the Jamaicans hurried to bring the food supplies they had withheld.

{Similar anecdotes crop up in connection with other explorers.}

COMTE, Auguste (1798–1857), *French philosopher, whose pioneer study of social structures and their evolution is considered the foundation of modern sociology.*

1 Knowing that he was about to die, Comte murmured, "What an irreparable loss!"

CONDORCET, Marie Jean Antoine de Caritat, Marquis de (1743–94), *French writer, mathematician, and philosopher. He worked on the* Encyclopédie, *published an important essay on the doctrine of probability (1785), and wrote a popular life of Voltaire (1787). A Girondist (moderate republican), Condorcet played an active role in the Revolution until the triumph of extremism forced him into hiding. He died in prison, probably by his own hand.*

1 After the Jacobins came to power, Condorcet was sheltered by a widow who bravely insisted that the outlaw remain with her despite the knowledge that she would certainly be killed if he were discovered. Concerned for her safety, Condorcet slipped away and went into hiding for three days in a stone quarry until hunger forced him out to a tavern in the village of Clamart. Here he ordered an omelet. The cook asked how many eggs he wanted. With an aristocrat's ignorance of the usual number of eggs for such a dish, Condorcet ordered a dozen. Suspicions aroused, the taverner demanded his trade. "Carpenter," lied Condorcet. The man snatched the fugitive's hands and studied them. "You're no carpenter," he declared, and Condorcet was dragged off to prison. The next day he was found dead on the floor of his cell.

CONFUCIUS (c. 551–479 BC), *Chinese philosopher and administrator. He spent his life partly in quest of a ruler who would allow him to put into practice his vision of a just and humane society. In his wanderings Confucius was ac-companied by a number of disciples to whom he taught the ethical and philosophical foundations of Confucianism.*

1 Ejected from yet another state, Confucius and his disciples were passing through a remote and deserted region when they came upon an old woman weeping beside a grave. The master asked her why. A tiger had killed her husband, she explained, and her husband's father; now it had recently slain her only son. "Why then do you live in this savage place?" asked Confucius. "Because there is no oppressive government here," was the reply. "My children," said Confucius to his followers, "remember that oppressive government is worse than a tiger."

2 Confucius and his disciples, traveling through dry country, were all suffering from thirst. One disciple, however, managed to discover a hidden rain puddle, filled his rice bowl, and offered it to the Master. Confucius was about to raise it to his lips when he observed the faces of his disciples. At once he emptied the bowl on the ground, saying, "It would be too much for one, too little for all of us. Let us continue our walk."

See also ALEXANDER THE GREAT 9; SIR PHILIP SIDNEY 1.

CONGREVE, William (1670–1729), *British dramatist. Congreve's tragedy* The Mourning Bride *(1697) was immensely successful, but he is now best remembered for his sophisticated comedies, including* Love for Love *(1695) and* The Way of the World *(1700).*

1 After 1700 Congreve wrote little, preferring to lead the life of a gentleman supported by various pensions and sinecures obtained for him by his friends. Voltaire had the highest admiration for Congreve's comedies and on his visit to England sought out the elderly ex-dramatist. Much to Voltaire's disgust, Congreve spoke slightingly of the profession of author, although he owed to it his lasting fame and worldly fortunes, telling Voltaire that he wished to be thought of merely as an ordinary gentleman. Voltaire told Congreve sharply that if he had been so unfortunate as to have been only "a mere gentleman," he would never have come to visit him.

CONNELLY, Marc (1890–1980), *US dramatist, author of* Green Pastures.

1 Connelly was almost totally bald. One afternoon at the Round Table in the Algonquin dining room a man ran his hand over the dramatist's bare head and observed, "That feels just like my wife's behind." Connelly stroked his head thoughtfully. "So it does," he replied. {This anecdote is also told of Nicholas Longworth, husband of Alice Roosevelt Longworth.}

2 Neysa McMein, whose memory for names was a bit shaky, was rattling off a list of stage stars to appear in a benefit she was helping to organize: "We've got Beatrice Lillie, Ethel Barrymore, Helen Hayes, Bobby Clark, N. B. Fields, the Lunts —"
"Wait a minute," interrupted a listener. "Did you say 'N. B. Fields'?"
"Certainly," interposed Connelly. "Would you expect a lady like Neysa to say 'W. C.'?"

3 Connelly was traveling in Portugal with a group of US pressmen, although his own credentials for joining the party were nonexistent. At a formal dinner all the members were invited by their Portuguese hosts to say a few words about the publications they represented. Some of the touring Americans wondered how Connelly would get out of what was potentially an embarrassing situation. When his turn came, Connelly got to his feet with perfect dignity, announced his name, and said, "I am editor of *Popular Wading,* the magazine of shallow water sports." He then went on to deliver a fifteen-minute oration on the imaginary publication, praising its editorial policy and excoriating the rival magazine *True Wading,* which catered only to "those sports reaching the ankle." When he sat down, the touring press group gave him an enthusiastic ovation. The Portuguese maintained a bemused silence.

4 While Connelly was in Portugal he was invited to a lecture about the recently completed bridge over the Tagus at Lisbon. The lecture was highly technical, lengthy, and boring. The speaker concluded by saying that no color had yet been chosen for the bridge, and suggestions would be welcome. Connelly rose majestically to his feet. "I think puce would be nice," he said.

❧ ❧

CONNOLLY, Cyril (1903–74), *British writer and critic.*

1 (Connolly was easily moved to tears, sometimes for the most trivial reasons. Stephen Spender recalls such an occasion.)
"At a restaurant dinner given on some fairly grim PEN Club Conference occasion, he [Connolly] was sitting opposite me and I noticed the tears start in his eyes and then trickle down each cheek. Suddenly he got up from the table, came over to me, and insisted on changing places. Intense boredom with the conversation of the lady journalist on his left had driven him to this extreme course of action."

❧ ❧

CONSTABLE, John (1776–1837), *British artist. The son of a miller, Constable captured the beauty of the English rural scene, in particular the area around his birthplace in Essex.*

1 Before the opening of the Royal Academy's annual exhibition, Constable and the other artists were there doing the final touching-up to their work. Constable paused to look at a landscape by Clarkson Stanfield and particularly singled out the sky for praise. A little while later he met his friend Ramsay Reinagle and told him to look at Stanfield's work. "Take particular note of the sky; it looks just like putty," he

---

"Primo Carnera was the hulking giant who captured the boxing world's imagination during the 1930's. Not much on defensive skills, he seemed willing to absorb a hundred punches if he could get off one good one himself. It was during his fight with Max Baer, with Baer giving Primo a thorough boxing lesson, that Grantland Rice remarked, 'The big fellow sure can take it.' 'Yes,' said another writer, Heywood Broun, 'but he doesn't seem to know what to do with it.'"

—R. L. Crouser, *It's Unlucky to Be Behind at the End of the Game* added. Reinagle went to look. "But I like the sky!" he exclaimed, half to himself, after studying the picture. Stanfield overheard him and demanded to know what he meant. "Well, Constable told me the sky was like putty," Reinagle said. Incensed, Stanfield sought out Constable and accused him of being a humbug. "You singled out the sky for particular praise, and then you tell Reinagle it looks like putty!"

"So what?" said Constable. "I happen to like putty."

2   It is said that Constable and William Blake met on only one occasion. Constable showed the older artist some of his drawings, and Blake exclaimed enthusiastically, "Why, this is not drawing, but inspiration!"

"I never knew it before," replied the prosaic Constable. "I meant it for drawing."

చ్చు ఆర్

CONSTANTINE [Constantine the Great] (c. 285–337), *Roman emperor in the West (312–24), and sole emperor at Byzantium (312–37). He was the first emperor to be converted to Christianity. In 313 he issued the edict of Milan guaranteeing toleration of Christians within his realms. He founded the city called after him — Constantinople (now Istanbul) — in 324, moving his government there from Rome in 330.*

1   In the first decade of the fourth century AD six men claimed the leadership of Rome. Chief among them were Maxentius, proclaimed emperor by the Roman Praetorian Guard, and Constantine. In 312 Constantine advanced across the Alps toward the forces of Maxentius and challenged him at the Mulvian bridge over the Tiber. On the afternoon before the battle Constantine saw a flaming cross outlined against the sun; on it were the Greek words *"En toutoi nika"* (In this sign you shall conquer). The next morning Constantine heard a voice in a dream commanding him to have his soldiers mark upon their shields the chi rho — the monogram for Christ. Constantine obeyed, fought Maxentius, and won.

{The authority for these visions is Constantine himself, as told to his panegyrist Eusebius of Caesarea. The words "In this sign you shall conquer" are also well known in their Latin form: *In hoc signo vinces.*}

CONSTANTINE, Learie Nicholas, Baron (1901–71), *West Indian cricketer. He was a brilliant all-rounder, known especially for his fast bowling. After retiring from cricket he led an active public life, becoming high commissioner in London for Trinidad and Tobago (1962–64).*

1   When Learie Constantine was bowling, he had a trick that greatly endeared him to the English crowds who first saw him in 1928. Sometimes when the ball had been played to a fieldsman and Constantine was walking back to his mark, the fieldsman would throw the ball at Constantine's back. Just as it seemed certain to hit him in the small of the back, he would whip his hand behind him and catch it, without having given the slightest hint that he had seen it coming.

చ్చు ఆర్

CONTI, Prince Louis-Armand II de (1695–1727), *a member of one of the most influential French families, who was often called a monster of vice.*

1   The prince was as ugly as his wife was witty. One day, about to depart on a journey, he said to her in jest, "Madame, I would advise you above all things not to make me a cuckold during my absence." Her reply: "Monsieur, you may leave without any anxiety, for it is only when I look at you that I have any wish to deceive you."

చ్చు ఆర్

COOK, Thomas (1808–92), *British tour operator. In 1841 Cook launched the package-tour industry when he arranged for his temperance society an excursion from Leicester to Loughborough by special train.*

1   Cook himself was a zealous supporter of temperance, but his non-teetotal clients on continental tours took a different view. At an Italian railroad station his flock surged toward the buffet in search of cheap local wine. He tried to halt them with the cry: "Gentlemen, don't invest your money in diarrhea!"

చ్చు ఆర్

COOLIDGE, [John] Calvin (1872–1933), *30th president of the United States (1923–29). A Republican, he led a conservative administration that promoted American business interests* *but failed to check the financial speculation that ended in the 1929 Wall Street crash. He was nicknamed "Silent Cal" for his extreme taciturnity, of which many stories, some no doubt apocryphal, are told. Alice Roosevelt Longworth once commented: "He looks as if he'd been weaned on a pickle." Coolidge was not without a sense of humor on this point, remarking, "I think the American people want a solemn ass as a president. And I think I'll go along with them."*

1   On returning from church one day, Coolidge was asked on what topic the minister had preached. After a moment's thought he replied, "Sin."
    "And what did he say about sin?"
    "He was against it."
    {Coolidge's interlocutor has been variously identified as his father and his wife. Coolidge himself denied the truth of the anecdote.}

2   A lady sitting next to Coolidge at dinner tried to coax him into talking to her. "I have made a bet, Mr. Coolidge, that I could get more than two words out of you."
    "You lose," said Coolidge.

3   While Coolidge was governor of Massachusetts, two of the state senators had an argument, which ended in one telling the other that he could "go to hell." The insulted politician went to see Coolidge to ask him to do something about it. Coolidge said calmly, "I have looked up the law, senator, and you don't have to go."

4   When Coolidge became vice president, he was succeeded as governor of Massachusetts by Channing H. Cox, who came to Washington to call on his predecessor. Cox was impressed by the fact that Coolidge was able to see a long list of callers every day and yet finish his work at five P.M., while Cox found that he was often detained at his desk up to nine o'clock. "How come the difference?" he asked Coolidge. "You talk back," said Coolidge.

5   During the first days of his presidency, Coolidge and his family had not yet left their third-floor suite at the Willard Hotel in Washington. In the early morning hours the president awoke to see a cat burglar going through his clothes, removing a wallet and a watch chain. Coolidge spoke: "I wish you wouldn't take that. . . . I don't mean the watch and chain, only the charm. Read what is engraved on the back of it." The burglar read: "Presented to Calvin Coolidge, Speaker of the House, by the Massachusetts General Court." Coolidge then identified himself as the president, persuaded the burglar to relinquish the watch charm, led him into a quiet conversation, found out that the young man and his college roommate were unable to pay their hotel bill and buy train tickets back to their campus, counted out thirty-two dollars from the wallet (which the dazed young man had also relinquished), declared it to be a loan, and advised the student to leave (in order to avoid the Secret Service) as unconventionally as he had entered.

The episode was confided to only two friends, one of them Frank MacCarthy, freelance writer, who wrote out the story fifteen years after Coolidge's death. But Mrs. Coolidge preferred that it not be publicized. Richard C. Garvey, a colleague of MacCarthy's, reconstructed the story and released it in 1982, long after all reasons for secrecy had vanished. According to MacCarthy's notes Coolidge stated that the young cat burglar repaid the loan in full.

6   During his presidency Coolidge was taken around the horticultural conservatories of Pierre S. Du Pont's estate at Longwood, Pennsylvania. The party passed through greenhouses containing magnificent orchids, extraordinary and grotesque cacti, and exquisite tropical ferns, none of which brought a word of comment from the president. At last they came to the conservatory devoted to tropical trees. The president gazed about him for a few seconds and observed with interest, "Bananas."

7   Visiting the Amherst home of the poet Emily Dickinson, Coolidge was given a special guided tour of the house and allowed to see and handle many relics normally kept under lock and key. In the small room upstairs where Emily Dickinson had done most of her writing he was shown the greatest treasures of all: the holograph manuscripts of some of her most famous poems. He studied the handwritten sheets with some interest and then made the

only observation of his entire visit: "Wrote with a pen, eh? I dictate."

8   A lady admirer burst into Coolidge's office to congratulate him on a speech he had made the previous day. She reported that the hall had been so crowded she had been unable to get a seat, so "I stood up all through your speech."
    "So did I, madam," said the president.
    See also MARK TWAIN 7.

9   President and Mrs. Coolidge, visiting a government farm, were taken around on separate tours. At the chicken pens Mrs. Coolidge paused to inquire of the overseer whether the rooster copulated more than once a day. "Dozens of times," said the man. "Tell that to the president," requested Mrs. Coolidge. The president came past the pens and was told about the rooster. "Same hen every time?" he asked. "Oh, no, a different one each time." Coolidge nodded. "Tell that to Mrs. Coolidge," he said.
    {This incident gave the president lasting fame he could never have foreseen. From it arose the technical term "the Coolidge effect" to describe the rearousal of a male animal by a new female.}

10   The ambassador of a great nation called at the White House one day for an important and private conversation with the president. Mrs. Coolidge came in as the ambassador was preparing to leave. 'Why don't you offer the ambassador a drink?' she suggested. 'He's already had one,' said the president testily. The next day, correspondents asked if he had anything to say about the conference. 'No,' said Coolidge. 'I have nothing to say about anything else either.' As they were leaving, he called after them, 'And don't quote me!' "

11   An overnight guest at the White House was mystified when he saw the president at breakfast pouring some milk from his cup into a saucer. Fearful of committing some breach of etiquette, the guest imitated him. Coolidge said nothing but smiled slightly. Bending down, he placed the saucer on the floor for the cat, which had been waiting quietly under the table.
    {A similar story is told of a young officer in the British army invited by Queen Elizabeth II to dine at Buckingham Palace. Seeing Her Majesty take a couple of dry

biscuits from a plate placed in front of her, he followed suit, only to realize that he had helped himself to dog biscuits intended for the royal corgis. Other variants of the story exist.}

12   Senator Selden P. Spencer of Missouri, walking around the White House grounds with Coolidge, pointed to the Executive Mansion. "I wonder who lives there," he said facetiously. "Nobody," replied Coolidge glumly. "They just come and go."

13   When Will Rogers was to be presented to President Coolidge, a friend bet him that he would not be able to make Coolidge laugh inside two minutes. "I'll make him laugh in twenty seconds," retorted Rogers. The introduction was performed: "Mr. President, this is Mr. Will Rogers; Mr. Rogers, President Coolidge." Rogers held out his hand, then a look of embarrassment and confusion stole over his face. "Er, excuse me, I didn't quite get the name." Coolidge grinned.

14   A smooth-talking salesman had persuaded Mrs. Coolidge to buy an expensive medical handbook. Regretting the purchase, she decided not to mention it to her husband. Coolidge noticed the book on the parlor table, but made no comment. Opening it some days later, however, Mrs. Coolidge saw that her husband had written inside: "This work suggests no cure for a sucker."

15   One of Coolidge's associates objected when the name of a certain industrialist was put forward for inclusion in the cabinet. "But, Mr. President, he's a son of a bitch!"
    "Well, don't you think they ought to be represented, too?" said Coolidge.

16   Coolidge became an enthusiastic angler, but his skill did not match his keenness. Asked how many trout there were in one of his favorite fishing places, Coolidge replied that there were estimated to be about 45,000. Then he added, "I haven't caught them all yet, but I've intimidated them."

17   A visitor to the White House asked President Coolidge for a cigar, explaining that he wanted it for a friend who collected bands from cigars of well-known smokers. Coolidge

pondered for a moment. Then, opening his cigar box, he selected a cigar, removed the band, returned the cigar to the box, and gave the band to the visitor.

18 Coolidge was asked to consider easing the terms of a large debt owed by a foreign power to the United States. "Why?" he asked. "They hired the money, didn't they?"

19 Coolidge was once invited to break ground for the cornerstone of a public building. Having performed this ceremonial duty, he was expected to make a speech. Pointing to the broken earth, he observed solemnly, "That's a mighty fine fishworm," and then departed.

20 A biography of George Washington containing libelous observations having recently been published, a group of reporters visited Coolidge to get his reaction. The president merely moved to the window, pulled back one of the curtains, revealing the Washington Monument, and murmured, "I see it's still there."

21 "President Coolidge had a group of guests on the presidential yacht cruising the Potomac. As he stood alone at the rail, looking out at the expanse of water, someone exclaimed, 'Look at that slight and slender figure! Look at that head, bowed over the rail! What thoughts are in the mind of this man, burdened by the problems of the nation?'

"Finally, Coolidge turned around, and joined the others, saying, 'See that sea gull over there? Been watching it for twenty minutes. Hasn't moved. I think he's dead!'"

22 A talkative young lady had failed to get any response from Coolidge throughout the course of a dinner party. "You go to so many dinners," she finally remarked. "They must bore you a great deal." Without lifting his eyes from the table, Coolidge replied, "Well, a man has to eat somewhere."

23 Asked at a press conference whether he would be attending a certain trade fair the following day, Coolidge replied, "I think the press already knows that I am expecting to attend."

"It isn't likely you will say anything tomorrow at the fair?"

"No," replied the president. "I am just going as an exhibit."

24 At the end of his elected term of office, President Coolidge issued his famous "I do not choose to run" statement. Anxious reporters pressed persistently for a more detailed statement. One managed to bar his way: "Exactly why don't you want to be president again, Mr. Coolidge?"

"Because," answered the president, brushing him aside, "there's no chance for advancement."

25 Soon after he had left the White House, Coolidge had to fill out a form confirming his membership in the National Press Club. After writing his name and address, he moved on to the space marked "Occupation," in which he wrote "Retired." Next came "Remarks." Coolidge paused for a moment and then wrote, "Glad of it."

26 A newspaper reporter visited Coolidge in his retirement and noted the number of sightseers driving past the house. "It must make you proud to know that even as an ex-president you are not forgotten. Just look at the number of those cars."

"Not as many as yesterday," replied Coolidge, "there were sixty-three then."

27 Someone came up to Dorothy Parker and blurted out the news that Coolidge was dead. "How can they tell?" she inquired.

{This remark is also attributed to Wilson Mizner in the form: "How do they know?"}

ॐ ৺

COOPER, Lady Diana (1892–), *British social leader. Born Lady Diana Manners, she was renowned for her beauty and wit. In 1919 she married Alfred Duff Cooper, the politician and diplomat who became Viscount Norwich.*

1 As part of a publicity stunt for a play due to open in New York with Diana Cooper as leading lady, the rumor was put about that another actress had been engaged for the role. Alarmed, Lady Diana cabled the impresario Morris Gest to know if she was still wanted. He replied, "Come to America and I'll treat you like a queen."

"Which queen?" Lady Diana cabled back. "Mary Queen of Scots?"

2   Staying with their friends the Guinnesses on their new yacht, Duff and Diana joined in the discussion about naming it. Should it be called *Diana*? *Gloria*, after their host's wife? *Gloria Mundi*? *Sick Transit* would be better, Diana suggested.

3   After the return of the Conservatives to power in 1951, Duff Cooper was made a viscount. His wife, the daughter of a duke, was not overly impressed at the prospect of being a mere viscountess. She suggested various fanciful titles for Duff — Lord Ladydiana, Unicorn, Lackland, Sansterre, Erewhon, St. Firmin, and so on. Without consulting her, Duff settled for "Viscount Norwich." This did not meet with Diana's approval at all. She said she would even have preferred "Porridge" (which rhymes with the correct pronunciation of "Norwich"). Duff retorted, "A little Norwich is a dangerous thing."

{She continued to dislike the name, and after Duff Cooper's ennoblement announced that she wished still to be known as Lady Diana Cooper and not Viscountess Norwich.}

೩> ⊷§

COOPER, Gary (1901–61), *US actor and film star. His most famous roles were those of brave and sensitive heroes in such films as* The Virginian *(1929) and* High Noon *(1952).*

1   When Gary Cooper first came to Hollywood from Montana, he was taken under the wing of a glamorous member of the international set, the Countess di Frasso. She wanted her handsome but gauche young lover to acquire the proper poise and sophistication. To this end she took him with her to Europe. Gene Fowler remarked one day that he had not seen the countess and her young man recently, and was told where they had gone. "Oh, well," he said, "everyone knows the best way to go to Europe is on the Countess di Frasso."

2   While he was writing the script for *Along Came Jones*, Nunnally Johnson lent Cooper, who was to produce and act in the film, a copy of the novel on which it was based. A couple of weeks later, Johnson asked Cooper: "How did you like the book?"

"Oh, fine, I'm about halfway through," came the reply. "I'm reading it word by word."

೩> ⊷§

COOPER, Dame Gladys (1888–1971), *British actress. She first appeared on stage in 1905 and made her name in* The Second Mrs. Tanqueray *(1922).*

1   In 1928, Miss Cooper appeared in the play *Excelsior,* with her sister Doris in a minor role. Doris was not well known as an actress, but she gave a creditable performance as the maid and hence was rather distressed to hear a hissing sound from the audience whenever she made an entrance. In the intermission one evening she asked a friend in the audience what she was doing wrong. "It's all right," said her friend, "they're not actually hissing you: it's just a lot of people whispering to each other, 'That's Doris Cooper, Gladys Cooper's sister!'"

2   As Dame Gladys, weakened by illness, brushed her hair on the last evening of her life, she peered into the mirror and remarked to her nurse, "If this is what virus pneumonia does to one, I really don't think I shall bother to have it again." She then tottered back to her bed and died peacefully in her sleep.

೩> ⊷§

COOPER, Sir William (died 1664), *British merchant; alderman of London.*

1   Sir William Cooper was a guest at a banquet held by the London Clothworkers' Company. Having partaken liberally of his hosts' brandy, he made his way home, where he dropped dead on arrival. Lady Cooper accused the Clothworkers of killing her husband with their noxious brandy, and when she died left a sum of money to the company with which to buy gin as a wholesome alternative.

The choice of brandy or gin is still offered at the Clothworkers' feasts with the words, "Do you dine with Alderman or Lady Cooper?"

೩> ⊷§

COOTE, Robert (1909–), *British character actor. His films include* A Yank at Oxford *(1938),* The Prisoner of Zenda *(1952), and* Theatre of Blood *(1973).*

1   The British arrived in Hollywood as an invading army of expert settlers who formed

themselves rapidly into polo clubs and cricket teams and gave tea parties for each other on Sunday afternoons. During one of these weekly gatherings, Robert Coote called across to Gladys Cooper in tones of disapproval: "Darling, there seems to be an American on your lawn."

> ২০ ৫৩

COPE, Edward Drinker (1840–97), *US paleontologist who built up a massive collection of fossils from the western United States.*

1 A Quaker, Cope refused to take a gun with him on his fossil-hunting forays, despite the fact that these led him into territories populated with hostile Indians. On one occasion, finding himself surrounded by a distinctly unfriendly band, Cope distracted his captors from their murderous intentions by removing and putting back his false teeth. Enthralled by this performance, they made him do it over and over again and eventually released him unharmed.

> ২০ ৫৩

COPELAND, Charles Townsend (1860–1952), *US educator. A greatly beloved professor of English at Harvard from 1925, he was known for his translations from the classics.*

1 For many years Copeland used a couple of cramped and inconvenient rooms on the top floor of Harvard's Hollis Hall. He resisted all attempts to move him to more spacious accommodations, maintaining that the top floor suited him perfectly. "It's the only place in Cambridge where God alone is above me. He's busy — but he's quiet."

2 Copeland for many years called his favorite beverage shop each Friday night and greeted the clerk with the same phrase: "Hello. Charles Townsend Copeland. Send down a fifth of the usual." On the Friday after his retirement, he made his regular call. "Hello, Charles Townsend Copeland. Do you know what emeritus means?"

"No," said the clerk.

"It means on the shelf," said Copeland. "Send down two fifths of the usual."

> ২০ ৫৩

COPLAND, Aaron (1900–   ), *US composer. His works include three symphonies, the ballet* Billy the Kid *(1938), the suite* Quiet City *(1941), concertos for piano and clarinet, and an assortment of chamber and piano music.*

1 Browsing in a bookshop one day, Copland noticed a woman buying a copy of his book, *What to Listen for in Music,* together with a paperback edition of a Shakespeare play. As the customer left the shop, Copland stopped her and asked, "Would you like me to autograph your book?" Looking blankly into the composer's beaming face, the woman asked, "Which one?"

> ২০ ৫৩

COPPÉE, François Edouard Joachim (1842–1908), *French writer. His poetry includes the collections* Intimités *(1868) and* Les Humbles *(1872). In 1884, he became a member of the French Academy.*

1 The wife of a not too distinguished writer once asked Coppée to support her husband's candidacy for a place in the French Academy. "I beg you, vote for my husband," she pleaded. "He'll die if he's not elected." Coppée agreed, but his vote failed to ensure the writer's success.

A few months later, another seat became vacant and the lady returned to Coppée to ask him to vote for her husband again. "Ah, no," replied the academician. "I kept my promise

---

Sebastien Roch Chamfort was a French aphorist and playwright, an ardent supporter of the Revolution and an enemy of high society. One of his favorite stories was that of the marquis at the court of Louis XIV who, on returning to his wife, found her in the arms of a bishop. The nobleman walked calmly to the window and began blessing the people in the street below. When the startled wife asked what he was doing, the marquis replied: "Monseigneur is performing my function, so I am performing his."

— Sigmund Freud, *Wit and Its Relation to the Unconscious*

but he did not keep his. I consider myself free of any obligation."

ह‍ॐ ॐॳ

CORBET, Richard (1582–1635), *English cleric, bishop successively of Oxford (1628–32) and Norwich (1632–35). He was a friend of Ben Jonson's and a minor poet of some distinction.*

1 (Corbet's conviviality was well known, as John Aubrey recalls.)

"After he had become a bishop he would sometimes take the key of the wine cellar and he and his chaplain (Dr. Lushington) would go and lock themselves in and be merry. Then first he laid down his episcopal hat — 'There lies the doctor.' His gown followed — 'There lies the bishop.' Then it was 'Here's to thee, Corbet,' and 'Here's to thee, Lushington.' "

ह‍ॐ ॐॳ

CORDAY, Charlotte (1768–93), *French noblewoman. A Girondist, she assassinated the Jacobin leader Marat in his bath and was guillotined.*

1 Corday and Samson, the executioner, sat side by side in the tumbril on the way to the guillotine. To make conversation he said politely, "Perhaps you find the trip too long?"

"Bah, we're sure to get there," was the reply.

ह‍ॐ ॐॳ

CORNELIA (2d century BC), *Roman aristocrat, daughter of Scipio Africanus, wife of Tiberius Sempronius Gracchus.*

1 Most of Cornelia's children died young, but two, Tiberius and Gaius, grew up to become the famous reformers of Rome's agrarian laws. When the two Gracchi were still boys, Cornelia once received at her house a wealthy Roman lady, who proudly showed off her jewelry to her hostess. She then challenged Cornelia to show off her own jewels. Cornelia gestured toward her sons, who had just entered the room. "These are my jewels," she said.

{After her death a statue was erected in her memory, bearing the simple inscription: "Cornelia, the mother of the Gracchi."}

ह‍ॐ ॐॳ

COROT, Jean-Baptiste Camille (1796–1875), *French landscape painter of the Barbizon school. Coming to art comparatively late in life, he did not achieve real acclaim until he was in his fifties. He was friendly with and influenced many younger artists, including the Impressionists.*

1 The caricaturist Honoré Daumier was very poor in his old age. On his sixty-fifth birthday, nearly blind, he was threatened with eviction from his little cottage at Valmondois because he could not pay the rent. Then he received a letter from Corot: "I have a little house at Valmondois which I could not, for the life of me, think what to do with. Suddenly I thought to give it to you, and liking the idea, I have had your ownership legally confirmed. I had no idea of doing you a good turn. The whole scheme was carried out to annoy the landlord. Ever yours, Corot." In his reply, Daumier wrote, "You are the only man from whom I could accept such a gift and not feel humiliated."

2 Even when very short of money, Corot found so much pleasure in having his pictures around him he could not rejoice unreservedly when he at last made a sale. "Alas, my collection has been so long complete, and now it is broken!" he exclaimed.

3 To a lady admirer who persisted in searching for hidden meanings in Corot's pictures, he replied: "*Non, madame, la peinture est plus bête que cela*" (No, madame, painting is too stupid for that).

ह‍ॐ ॐॳ

CORRIGAN, Douglas (*dates unknown*), *US aviator.*

1 In 1937 Corrigan applied to the Bureau of Air Commerce for permission to make a solo flight across the Atlantic in his 1929 Curtis-Robin monoplane (nicknamed *Lizzy*). After inspecting the aircraft the bureau refused permission on the grounds that it could not condone suicide: *Lizzy* lacked any safety devices, radio, or beam finders, and the extra fuel tanks that Corrigan had put on completely obscured the pilot's forward view, so he had to look out of the side windows to see where he was going. Undaunted, Corrigan flew from Los Angeles to New York in twenty-seven hours in mid-July

1938. The following morning he told the airfield manager at New York that he was returning home. *Lizzy* was so weighed down with fuel that she traveled 3,200 feet along the runway before achieving takeoff. Just twenty-three hours and thirteen minutes later, Corrigan landed at Baldonnel Airport, Dublin. "I've just flown from New York," Corrigan announced to the airport officials. "Not in that thing!" said someone, and told Corrigan where he was. "I flew the wrong way!" exclaimed the man who shortly (and forever after) would be known as Wrong-way Corrigan.

ঌ   ঌ

CORTOT, Alfred (1877–1962), *Swiss-born French pianist and conductor. Founder of the Ecole Normale de Musique (1919), he is remembered particularly for his interpretation of Chopin.*

1   Cortot was notorious for lapses of memory during performances. Sir Thomas Beecham recalled how he had once conducted a performance of a Beethoven piano concerto with Cortot. "We started with Beethoven, and I kept up with Cortot through the Grieg, Schumann, Bach, and Tchaikovsky, but then he hit on one I didn't know, so I stopped dead."

ঌ   ঌ

COURTELINE, Georges [Georges Moineaux] (?1858–1929), *French playwright and humorous writer.*

1   A pretentious young writer, hoping to gain publicity, wrote to Courteline demanding satisfaction for some minor insult. The handwriting of the letter was barely legible and the spelling atrocious. Courteline picked up his pen and replied: "My dear young sir. As I am the offended party, the choice of weapons is mine. We shall fight with orthography. You are already dead."

ঌ   ঌ

COURTNEIDGE, Dame Cicely (1893–1980), *British actress born in Australia. The wife of Jack Hulbert, she performed with her husband in many musical comedies and films.*

1   (Christopher Milne—son of A. A. Milne and hero of his children's books—loved going to the theater with his parents to see musical comedies.)

"Once it was Jack Hulbert and Cicely Courtneidge, and I enjoyed myself so much

---

Gay Talese tells this story about Frank Costello, US racketeer:

"Even in jail Costello baffled the law. He continued to smoke English Ovals, although nobody knew how he smuggled them in. He ate steak—ebony on the outside, claret on the inside, just as he'd ordered at '21'—and yet it was impossible to uncover the source of the steaks. The unbelievable power that Costello was able to wield despite his imprisonment was demonstrated some years later when he performed a behind-bars miracle for his attorney, Edward Bennett Williams.

"Williams, during a visit to Costello's jail, seemed concerned about something, and Costello, detecting it, asked, 'What's bothering you, Mr. Williams?'

"Williams explained that he and his wife were taking her parents out that night to celebrate their thirty-fifth wedding anniversary and that he had promised them tickets to *My Fair Lady;* but the particular agent who had promised Williams the tickets—a person who'd always been reliable in the past—had suddenly failed on this occasion.

"'Mr. Williams,' Costello said, 'you shoulda told me; maybe I coulda helped.'

"Williams admitted it had never occurred to him that a man in jail could help get four tickets at the last minute to a hit Broadway show.

"Costello shrugged.

"It was then 5 P.M.

"When Williams returned to his hotel room, he heard a soft rap on the door. Upon opening it, a broad-shouldered man under a slouch hat grunted something, handed over an envelope containing four tickets to that evening's performance of *My Fair Lady,* then quickly disappeared down the hall."

—Gay Talese, *Fame and Obscurity*

that in the interval a box of chocolates was brought round for me. 'For *me*?' 'Yes, sir. It is from Miss Courtneidge. She said it was for the little boy who is laughing so loudly.' "

ॐ ক্ষ

COWARD, Sir Noël (1899–1973), *British playwright and actor. He is famous for his witty and sophisticated comedies of high-society life, including* Hay Fever (1925), Private Lives (1930), *and* Blithe Spirit (1941).

1   Actors are reluctant to perform with children or animals because they inevitably upstage the rest of the cast. On its second night Coward attended a play written around a fourteen-year-old "prodigy" who was on stage for most of the action. He remarked, "Two things should have been cut. The second act and that youngster's throat."

2   During rehearsal a young actor kept interrupting Coward with questions about the motivation behind the character he was playing. Finally Coward snapped, "Your motivation is your pay packet on Friday. Now get on with it."

3   With the choreographer Wendy Toye Coward was watching the first dress rehearsal of the revue *Sigh No More*. The young and inexperienced actor in the role of the Fourth Harlequin, never having worn tights before, did not know that he ought to be wearing something under them. Coward turned to the choreographer and said in a piercing whisper, "For God's sake, go and tell that young man to take his Rockingham tea service out of his tights."

4   The author Edna Ferber was fond of wearing tailored suits. Noël Coward, meeting her on an occasion when she was wearing a suit very similar to the one he himself was wearing, greeted her with the words: "You look almost like a man."
   "So do you," said Miss Ferber.
   {This story is also told of Miss Ferber and writer Michael Arlen.}

5   After seeing a certain actress in the role of Queen Victoria, Coward murmured as he left the theater, "I never realized before that Albert married beneath him."

6   Lady Diana Cooper, the society beauty who played a starring role in Max Reinhardt's famous production of *The Miracle,* observed to Coward that she had seen him in *The Vortex* (his domestic drama of the 1920s) and did not think that he had been very funny. Coward replied, "I saw you as the Madonna in *The Miracle,* and I thought you were a scream."

7   (The press unanimously damned Coward's *Home Chat* and *Sirocco,* but when he starred in S. N. Behrman's *The Second Man,* the critics praised his performance in extravagant terms. Raymond Massey describes an incident in Coward's dressing room after the second night.)
   "Hannen Swaffer, a critic and theatre writer on the *Daily Express,* entered unannounced. He had been insufferable in his abuse of Noël (and of me too). 'Nowley,' he sneered in his assumed cockney accent, 'I've always said you could act better than you write.' 'And I've always said the same about you,' was Noël's instant reply."

8   Rehearsing *Hay Fever,* Edith Evans kept on spoiling the rhythm of Coward's line, "On a clear day you can see Marlow." Every time she spoke this sentence she gave it as "On a very clear day you can see Marlow." At last Coward, the perfectionist, could bear it no longer, and remonstrated from his seat in the stalls: "Edith dear, the line is 'On a clear day you can see Marlow.' On a *very* clear day you can see Marlowe *and* Beaumont and Fletcher."

9   A rather dim-witted impresario, no friend of Coward's, blew his brains out. Remarked Coward, "He must have been a marvelously good shot."

10   Coward was walking along the seafront at Brighton with Laurence Olivier and Olivier's young son. Observing two dogs copulating, the boy innocently asked what they were doing. "It's like this, dear boy," explained Coward. "The one in front is blind and the kind one behind is pushing him."

11   During a rather stormy rehearsal of *Blithe Spirit,* actress Claudette Colbert screamed at Coward, "If you're not very careful, I may throw something at you!"
   "You might start with my cues," replied Coward.

12 Coward was strolling around an art exhibition at the Victoria and Albert Museum in London when a friend rushed up to him with an invitation to dinner. Noël politely declined, explaining that he was about to leave for Jamaica. "When will you be back?" asked his friend. "In the spring," replied Coward. "With the swallows. You'll recognize me easily among them."

13 Actor Clifton Webb was devoted to his mother, who had campaigned on his behalf with producers and directors throughout his career. A tireless exhibitionist, she was still dancing the cancan at Hollywood parties in her ninetieth year. When she finally died, Webb's health rapidly declined. "Poor dear," remarked Coward. "The late sixties is rather late to be orphaned."

14 The American writer Barnaby Conrad was badly gored in a bullfight in Spain in 1958. The columnist Leonard Lyons recorded a subsequent conversation between Eva Gabor and Noël Coward at a New York restaurant. "Noël dahling," said Eva, "have you heard the news about poor Bahnaby? He vass terribly gored in Spain."
"He was *what?*" asked Coward in alarm.
"He vass gored!"
"Thank heavens. I thought you said he was bored."

15 Coward once spent a rather uncomfortable night at a bug-ridden hotel in the Seychelles. "May I put up a sign reading 'Noël Coward Slept Here'?" asked the manager as his distinguished guest checked out. "Certainly," replied Coward, "if you'll add one word — fitfully."

16 A London journalist once approached Coward and asked: "Mr. Coward, would you like to say something to the *Star?*"
"Of course," Coward replied. "Twinkle."

❧ ❧

COWELL, Henry (1897–1965), *US composer, writer, and pianist.*

1 Cowell wrote a piece for flute and piano entitled *A Bit.* His publisher complained that the composition was too short and asked him to write a companion piece. Cowell complied and called the resulting work *Two Bits.* He also specified that the end product should sell for 50 cents. Accordingly, the title page read: "*Two Bits for Flute and Piano.* Price 50 cents."

❧ ❧

COWL, Jane (1884–1950), *US actress.*

1 When John Barrymore was starring in *Hamlet* on Broadway, Jane Cowl attended one of the matinee performances. Her arrival caused a considerable stir in the theater and her audible comments throughout the play further distracted the audience. Barrymore himself gave no sign of noticing her presence until he took his curtain call. After thanking the audience, he bowed deeply in the direction of Miss Cowl's box and said, "Finally, I would like to take this opportunity to thank Miss Cowl for the privilege of co-starring with her this afternoon."

❧ ❧

CRANMER, Thomas (1489–1556), *archbishop of Canterbury (1532–1556), who won the office as reward for his supporting Henry VIII in the latter's divorce from Catherine of Aragon. He promoted the translation and dissemination of the English Bible and virtually created the liturgy of the Church of England. Mary I loathed him for his role in her mother's divorce and had him tried as a heretic, excommunicated, and burned at the stake.*

1 In peril of his life Cranmer signed a recantation, but when brought to St. Mary's Church, Oxford, to make a public declaration of his former errors, he said that his conscience would not let him save his life by recanting. He bitterly regretted having signed the recantation, promising that when he was brought to the stake the hand that had done the signing would be the first to burn. This promise he kept, holding his right hand steadfastly in the flames.

❧ ❧

CRAWFORD, Joan (1904–77), *US film actress. Her films include* Our Dancing Daughters *(1928),* Grand Hotel *(1932),* Mildred Pierce *(1945), for which she won an Academy Award, and* Whatever Happened to Baby Jane? *(1962).*

1 Leaving New York's "21" one day, Miss Crawford decided to take advantage of the sunny weather and walk home. "But, madam," protested her chauffeur, "you'll be mobbed."

"I should certainly hope so," she replied.

৵৶ ৶৶

CROCKETT, Davy (1786–1836), *US frontierman, member of Congress, and folk hero. He was killed at the Alamo.*

1 When he first returned from Washington, Crockett remarked on the curiosity of the people in his home town about how people in the capital lived. Crockett told them, "They have breakfast when the sun is one or two hours high, or when you fellows have done practically half a day's work. About one or two o'clock in the day they have what they call lunch, and 'way in the night, they have their dinner."

"Then when do these people have their supper?" asked a constituent. "They don't get that until the next day," Crockett replied.

2 At a menagerie exhibition in Washington, Crockett amused his friends by pointing out a similarity between the features of one of the monkeys on display and those of a certain member of Congress. Turning around, Crockett found the member in question standing right behind him. "I suppose I ought to apologize," he said, "but I don't know whether to apologize to you or to the monkey."

৵৶ ৶৶

CROCKFORD, William (1775–1844), *British gambler whose successes enabled him to abandon his original profession of fishmonger and found the famous gambling club that still bears his name.*

1 Crockford's horse Ratan was favorite for the 1844 Derby. A few days before the race the horse was poisoned. Crockford's rage and disappointment brought on a fit of apoplexy that proved fatal. This put his gambling friends in a quandary as Crockford also had a heavily backed filly entered for the Oaks, which is run at the same Epsom meeting as the Derby itself. If the owner's death became known, the filly would be disqualified. They therefore propped Crockford's body up at a window in his house at Epsom, overlooking the racecourse, where it would be clearly visible to the crowd, who would thus discount any rumor of Crockford's

demise. The filly won the race and the punters duly collected their winnings before their ruse was discovered.

৵৶ ৶৶

CROESUS (6th century BC), *king of Lydia in Asia Minor (560–546 BC). He lost his throne in an ill-advised campaign against the Persians. From his great wealth comes the phrase "rich as Croesus."*

1 Deliberating whether to attack the Persians, Croesus asked the oracle at Delphi if the undertaking would prosper. The oracle replied that if he went to war, he would destroy a great empire. Encouraged, Croesus invaded the Persian realms. He was decisively beaten and the Persians then invaded Lydia, captured its capital, and threw Croesus himself into chains. Croesus again sent an embassy to Delphi, this time with the question, "Why did you deceive me?" The priestess of the oracle replied that she had not deceived him — Croesus had indeed destroyed a great empire.

৵৶ ৶৶

CROLL, James (1821–90), *Scottish geologist and meteorologist. Largely self-taught, he wrote a number of books, including* Climate and Time *(1875).*

1 As he lay dying he was offered a glass of whiskey, although he had been a strict teetotaler all his life. "I'll take a wee drop o' *that*," he said. "I don't think there's much fear o' me learning to drink now."

৵৶ ৶৶

CROMWELL, Oliver (1599–1658), *lord protector of England (1653–58). A talented soldier, he was largely responsible for the parliamentary army's successes over Charles I. Although at first he sought a reconciliation with the king, he eventually signed Charles's death warrant. The constitutional uncertainty that followed finally compelled Cromwell to assume the office of lord protector. His rule was based on his own prestige and personality, having no settled constitutional basis, and his death heralded the collapse of the Commonwealth and the restoration of the monarchy.*

1 Cromwell sat for Peter Lely, the portraitist. The painter already had a reputation for his

portraits of the handsome noblemen and beautiful ladies of Charles I's court. Cromwell said, "Mr. Lely, I desire you would use all your skill to paint my picture truly like me, and not flatter me at all; but remark all these roughnesses, pimples, warts, and everything as you see me, otherwise I will never pay a farthing for it."

2   In April 1653 the Long Parliament had sat for more than twelve years, presiding over Britain's decline into civil war and constitutional chaos. It looked ready to entrench itself and its incompetence forever. Cromwell, with the army behind him, intervened and dissolved the Parliament by force, with a band of musketeers. The musketeers led away the Speaker and ejected the MPs. In front of the Speaker's chair lay the mace, emblem of parliamentary authority. "What shall we do with this bauble? Take it away," Cromwell commanded, and it was removed.
{This is often quoted in the form: "Take away this bauble."}

3   Cromwell addressed his troops as they were about to cross a river to attack the enemy. He concluded with the famous exhortation: "Put your trust in God, but mind you keep your powder dry."

4   There is an old but probably unreliable tradition that toward two A.M. on the night after the execution of Charles I, when the body was lying in the banqueting hall at Whitehall, a dark figure, closely muffled, entered the room and gazed upon the face of the dead king. The Earl of Southampton and the other man keeping vigil by the body could not see his face, but they heard him sigh the words: "Cruel necessity!" before he glided out of the room. The earl swore that the mysterious visitor had the figure and gait of Cromwell.
{This does not accord with other sources, which state that Charles's body was hustled away to the embalmers immediately after he was beheaded.}

5   One of the changes that came with the rise to power of Oliver Cromwell was the nation's coinage. New coins were struck on the obverse of which was engraved "God with Us" and on the reverse, "The Republic of England." One old nobleman, a Royalist and anti-Puritan to the core, saw the coins and commented: "Quite proper that God and the Republic should be on different sides."

ह∾ ≼§

CROSBY, Bing [Harry Lillis] (1904–77), *US singer and actor who starred in many films. His fame as a crooner was achieved primarily in the 1930s and 1940s.*

1   Crosby was asked once by the interviewer on a television show why he had such a calm and unruffled air. He reached into his pocket and pulled out an enormous wad of dollar bills. "That helps!" he said.

ह∾ ≼§

CUKOR, George Dewey (1899–1983), *US motion-picture director. His films include* The Philadelphia Story *(1940) and* My Fair Lady, *for which he won an Academy Award in 1964.*

1   In 1953 Jack Lemmon came to Hollywood to make his first film, *It Should Happen to You,* co-starring with Judy Holliday. The director was George Cukor. During the first rehearsals Cukor, after each of Lemmon's tries, would cry, "Less, less, less!" Lemmon, frustrated and bewildered, finally broke out with "Don't you want me to act at *all?*"
"Dear boy," said Cukor, "you're beginning to understand."

ह∾ ≼§

CULBERTSON, Ely (1891–1955), *US bridge player, born in Rumania. He used his wealth and skill as a player to make contract bridge a popular and social game. He also wrote many books on the subject.*

1   Playing bridge with some sharpers in London, Culbertson suspected that they were cheating by signaling to each other. But even watching them closely, he could see no telltale gestures. Then he realized that they were playing to a regular rhythm; information was being passed by the number of seconds allowed to elapse before a bid or a play was made, the length of the silence indicating weakness or strength in a particular suit. Once sure of this, he timed the next silent count, then continued out loud, "Eight, nine . . . that knocks me

out, gentlemen; you play too high for me." And he left the table.

CUMMINGS, E[dward] E[stlin] (1894–1962), *US poet and painter. His poetry is characterized by unorthodox devices, such as the absence of capitals and punctuation.*

1 Departing with Marion, his wife, from a fashionable New Year's Eve party, Cummings realized that he did not have enough money for the subway fare. They stepped into the elevator, which was already occupied by a portly gentleman. "Excuse me," said Cummings politely, placing his hat with a flourish at the man's feet, "would you care to step on my hat?" The man, somewhat taken aback but nevertheless impressed by Cummings's aristocratic demeanor, nodded assent. "I'm afraid it will cost you five dollars," added Cummings. The portly fellow stepped on the hat and paid his fee, enabling Cummings and his wife to travel home by taxi.

CUNARD, Emerald, Lady (1872–1948), *British society hostess, born Maud Burke in the United States.*

1 Lady Cunard was a guest at one of the first balls to be given in London after World War II had ended. Encouraged by limitless champagne, patricians of English high society danced away the night in elegant surroundings. A fellow guest, the diarist Henry ("Chips") Channon, gestured toward the glittering assembly and said, *"This* is what we fought the war for."

"Oh, do you mean they are all Poles?" inquired Lady Cunard.

{The memoirs of many London fashionables contain this exchange, though they differ as to the exact occasion on which it was spoken; this is Nancy Mitford's version.}

2 (Edward Marsh tells the following story:)
"Later in life I had a beautiful object-lesson in behaviour to the unpunctual. The scene was a luncheon-party at the Broughams': the appointed time, 1:30. Till 1:45 we waited for Lady Cunard; and at two o'clock she arrived, full of apologies—she had been buying a chandelier. Old Lord Brougham, a handsome patriarch with magnificent silver hair, looked straight in front of himself and said in a pensive tone: 'I once knew a man who bought a chandelier *after* luncheon.'"

CUNNINGHAME GRAHAM, Robert Bontine (1852–1936), *Scottish writer. A descendant of the earls of Glencairn, he succeeded to the family estates in 1883. He was a member of Parliament (1886–92), after which he spent a number of years traveling in South America, Spain, and Morocco. His writings include* Mogreb-el-Acksa *(1898),* Success *(1902), and* The Conquest of the River Plate *(1924).*

1 A dinner partner, impressed by tales of Cunninghame Graham's aristocratic ancestry, asked him: "Is it true that there is royal blood in your family?"

"Madam," replied Cunninghame Graham, "if I had my rights I should be king of England —and what a two weeks *that* would be!"

CURIE, Marie (1867–1934), *Polish chemist. She emigrated to France in 1891 and after studying at the Sorbonne married (1895) a French physicist, Pierre Curie. In 1903 she shared the Nobel Prize for physics with the discoverer of radioactivity, Henri Becquerel. Marie Curie also isolated the highly radioactive element polonium, for which she won the 1911 Nobel Prize for chemistry. She died from the effects of the radiation to which she had been exposed.*

1 An American newspaperman tracked the Curies down to the remote cottage in Brittany where they were vacationing. He found a rather dowdy woman sitting outside the door. "Are you the housekeeper?" he began.

"Yes."

"Is your mistress inside?"

"No."

"Will she be back soon?"

"I don't think so."

The reporter sat down. "Can you tell me something confidential about your mistress?" he went on.

"Madame Curie has only one message that she likes to be given to reporters," said Marie Curie. "That is: be less curious about people and more curious about ideas."

CURLEY, James Michael (1874–1958), *Boston politician, also known as "The Purple Shamrock" and "The Master." He provided the model for the hero-villain in Edwin O'Connor's novel* The Last Hurrah.

1 In 1946 "the Purple Shamrock" managed to get reelected as mayor of Boston, only to find himself facing fraud charges and appearing in the dock. Convicted, the new mayor was obliged to fulfill his duties from a prison cell. This was clearly inconvenient, so he sent a demand to the court for his release on the grounds that he was suffering from twelve potentially fatal illnesses. Summoned before the court (wearing a shirt three times too large for him), the former governor of Massachusetts was asked to name one of his twelve illnesses. "An imminent cerebral hemorrhage," the mayor declared. He was not released.

∂৯ ৩চ

CURRAN, John Philpot (1750–1817), *Irish lawyer and judge. He was a renowned orator and wit, his speeches on behalf of the accused in state trials in the aftermath of the abortive Irish revolt of 1798 being particularly famous. He fought hard for Catholic emancipation.*

1 Curran detested all those who had voted for the union of Ireland with the rest of Britain. One day as he was in the part of Dublin near the disused Parliament Building, he was accosted by one of the pro-union peers who happened to remark on the building's present uselessness and how he disliked the sight of it. "No wonder, my lord," said Curran. "I never heard of a murderer who was not afraid of a ghost."

2 One of the high court judges had a dog he occasionally brought into the courtroom. During a trial in which Curran was expounding a particularly involved argument, the judge, perhaps intending to indicate disregard of Curran's case, bent down and began ostentatiously to pet the dog. Curran stopped. The judge looked up inquiringly. "I beg pardon, my lord," said Curran. "I thought your lordships were in consultation."

3 A gentleman was boasting of his marriage into a distinguished family, stressing their wealth, status, and importance. "Sir John has given me his eldest daughter," he announced with great self-satisfaction. "Indeed," said Curran, bored by this display of vanity, "and no doubt if he'd had an even older one he'd have given her to you instead."

4 During Curran's last illness, his doctor, paying an early morning call, observed that he was coughing with difficulty. "That is surprising," retorted Curran, "for I have been practicing all night."

৯চ ৩চ

CURTIZ, Michael (1888–1962), *Hungarian-born US film director. After working in Europe he moved to Hollywood, where his many movies included* Elizabeth and Essex *(1939) and* Casablanca *(1942). His English always remained somewhat eccentric.*

1 During the filming of *The Charge of the Light Brigade,* Curtiz directed the release of a hundred riderless chargers by ordering, "Bring on the empty horses." David Niven and Errol Flynn, the stars of the film, doubled up with laughter. Curtiz saw them and yelled, "You and your stinking language! You think I know fuck nothing. Well, let me tell you, I know fuck all!"

2 Curtiz, always keen on realism, had extras throw authentic spears at Errol Flynn during a characteristic scene of derring-do. The star, dodging the hail of lethal weapons, felt the stress of real peril and started across the set after Curtiz. "Lunch!" yelled Curtiz, beating a hasty retreat.

৯চ ৩চ

CUSHMAN, Charlotte (1816–76), *US actress, noted for her interpretation of the great tragic roles.*

1 Charlotte Cushman's final appearance on the New York stage was an emotional occasion with presentations, speeches, a torchlit parade, and finally a huge display of fireworks organized by the theater's business representative, Joseph H. Tooker, who was also one of the Tammany Hall stalwarts. The finale of the firework display was a huge portrait bust. "Who's that?" asked Miss Cushman. "Shakespeare," replied Mr. Tooker, and Miss Cushman's delight knew no bounds. Actually it was a gigantic head of Boss Tweed, left over from a Tammany Hall festivity.

CUVIER, Georges Léopold, Baron (1769–1832), *French zoologist. His work at the Museum of Natural History in Paris laid the foundations of the sciences of comparative anatomy and paleontology. Le Règne animal (1817) was a major step forward in the classification of animal species, including those known only from fossils.*

1 Cuvier's outstanding achievement resulted from his ability to reconstruct whole skeletons from fragmentary remains through his understanding of the way in which any particular feature entailed the presence or absence of other characteristics. This logical approach brought no little discomfiture to a group of students bent upon a practical joke. They broke into Cuvier's rooms in the middle of the night, and one, dressed in a devil's outfit with horns, tail, and hoofed feet, approached his bed, intoning, "Cuvier, I have come to eat you!" Cuvier woke up, gave him a single glance, and announced, "All animals with horns and hooves are herbivorous. You won't eat me." Then he promptly went back to sleep.

2 During his final days as leeches were being applied to him, Cuvier murmured, "Nurse, it was I who discovered that leeches have red blood."

৪৯ ৪৯

CYRUS II [Cyrus the Great] (died 529 BC), *king of Persia and founder of the Achaemenian Empire. After staging a revolt against his overlord, he went on to conquer the empires of the Medes, Lydia, Ionia, and Babylonia. As conqueror he was humane; as ruler, tolerant.*

1 On one occasion Cyrus reprimanded his son, Cambyses, for his arrogant behavior and rudeness. Like many fathers before and since, Cyrus told his son that he would never have spoken to his own father in the way that Cambyses spoke to him. "But you were the son of a nobody," replied Cambyses, "whereas I am the son of Cyrus the Great."

৪৯ ৪৯

CYRUS of Panopolis (5th century AD), *Praetorian prefect of the emperor Theodosius II at Constantinople.*

1 In 441 palace intrigues caused Cyrus to lose his office. Despite the well-founded suspicion that he favored the old pagan religion over Christianity, he was consecrated bishop and packed off to a remote see in Phrygia in Asia Minor. He demonstrated his contempt for his exiled state by delivering to his new congregation what must surely be one of the tersest sermons on record: "Let the birth of our Savior Jesus Christ be commemorated in silence, because the Word of God was conceived in the Holy Virgin through hearing alone. Amen."

D

DAHN, Felix (1834–1912), *German jurist and historian.*

1 After a lecture in Hamburg, Dahn was invited to be the guest of honor at a dinner. He declined, giving as his reason that he had once spent six weeks in Hamburg doing nothing but sleeping and drinking; he did not want to repeat this time-wasting experience. His host, troubled, asked him when this had happened. "During the first six weeks of my life," was the answer.

DALE, Valentine (died 1589), *British diplomat.*

1 When his employment in Flanders was first proposed, Dale was told by Queen Elizabeth that he would receive twenty shillings a day expenses. "Then, madam, I shall spend nineteen shillings a day," he said. "What will you do with the odd shilling?" inquired the queen. "I will reserve that for my wife and children," replied Dale. Elizabeth took the hint and increased the allowance.

DALI, Salvador (1904–), *Spanish surrealist painter. Dream landscapes containing hallucinatory objects constitute his most characteristic work.*

1 (Luis Buñuel tells this story:)
"As a young man [Dali] was totally asexual. . . . Of course he's seduced many. . . . But these seductions usually entailed stripping [American heiresses] in his apartment, frying up a couple of eggs, putting them on the women's shoulders and without a word showing them to the door."

2 (Dali was staying in the same New York hotel as the Igor Stravinskys. One day as they were walking down a corridor Dali suddenly appeared before them carrying a small silver bell. Stravinsky recounted the episode to a friend.)
"'It was the little silver bell carried before the priest when he goes through the street to bring the viaticum to a dying person,' said Stravinsky.
"He paused and greeted Dali, who replied, 'Bonjour, Igor, bonjour, Madame,' and then stood waiting. . . . It was in the period when Dali wore waxed spikes of mustache which reached to the corners of his eyes. 'But I said nothing, and Vera said nothing, we smiled très doucement, and started to go by.'
"At that Dali rang his little silver bell.
"'What is your little silver bell doing there?' asked Stravinsky.
"'I carry it and I ring it,' replied Dali, and Stravinsky imitated him, 'so people will see my mustaches.'"

3 Dali went into a New York bookstore one day and asked for a copy of his *Secret Life of Salvador Dali.* The young clerk, instantly recognizing his distinguished customer, fetched the book and began to wrap it up.
"Have you read it?" asked the artist.
"No, I'm afraid not," replied the young man, handing over the package.
"Take it," said Dali magnanimously, pushing the book back across the counter. "It is my gift to you. Would you like me to autograph it for you?" The clerk eagerly tore open the package and handed the artist a pen.
Only after Dali had left the store did the young man, gazing at the treasured autograph, realize that the artist had omitted one important detail. He had neglected to pay for the book.
{The General Editor of this volume, once *invited* to lunch by Dali, left the restaurant paying the check.}

4 Dali had bought a castle in Spain for his wife, Gala. In one of the rooms there was a rather obtrusive radiator, and Gala asked her husband if he would paint a screen for it. Dali obliged with what he later called "Le more realistic of my paintings"—a picture of the radiator itself.

5 A female admirer asked Dali, "Is it hard to paint a picture?"

"No," replied the artist. "It's either easy or impossible."

6 Dali once took his pet ocelot with him to a New York restaurant and tethered it to a leg of the table while he ordered coffee. A middle-aged lady walked past and looked at the animal in horror. "What's that?" she cried. "It's only a cat," said Dali scathingly. "I've painted it over with an op-art design." The woman, embarrassed by her initial reaction, took a closer look and sighed with relief. "I can see now that's what it is," she said. "At first I thought it was a real ocelot."

DALTON, John (1766–1844), *British chemist known for his research on gases. He is the originator of modern atomic theory.*

1 Dalton shunned the honors that the scientific world attempted to bestow upon him and refused to be presented to the king on the grounds that as a Quaker he could not wear the elaborate court dress etiquette then demanded. In 1832, however, he was presented with a doctor's degree at Oxford, and since the scarlet doctoral robes were considered sufficiently formal dress it was arranged that Dalton should also be presented to King William IV on the same occasion. A hitch arose when it was pointed out that Quakers could not wear scarlet any more than they could wear court dress. Dalton's color-blindness saved the day. The scarlet robes appeared to him as gray and he consented to wear them and meet the king.

DANA, Richard Henry (1815–82), *US author and lawyer. He wrote the maritime classic* Two Years Before the Mast *(1840) and used his legal talents to improve the conditions of sailors. Later he helped slaves seized under the Fugitive Slave Act and brought out an important edition of Wheaton's* International Law *(1865).*

1 In 1876 Dana was nominated for the post of minister to England. His campaigns on behalf of sailors and slaves and his attitude with respect to the legal aspects of the Civil War had made him objectionable to many senators. Senator Simon Cameron helped to quash the nomination with the remark, "One of those damn literary fellers."

D'ANNUNZIO, Gabriele (1863–1938), *Italian poet, dramatist, novelist, and fascist politician. He was a World War I flying ace. Short, bald (at twenty-three), and handsome, he was regarded as irresistible by the many women with whom he had affairs, the details of which often featured in his novels.*

1 Isadora Duncan told the story of D'Annunzio's adoption of a goldfish belonging to a hotel where he stayed. The poet would feed the goldfish, which he christened Adolphus, talk to it, and watch it swimming around its bowl. After his return to Italy, he telegraphed the hotel at frequent intervals asking: "How is my beloved Adolphus?" Eventually the goldfish sickened and died and the maître d'hôtel threw the corpse out. Almost immediately there arrived a telegram from D'Annunzio: "Feel Adolphus is not well." The maître d'hôtel cabled back: "Adolphus dead. Died last night." D'Annunzio telegraphed: "Bury him in the garden; arrange his grave." The maître d'hôtel took a sardine, wrapped it in silver paper, and buried it in the garden under a little cross inscribed: "Here lies Adolphus." When D'Annunzio returned he asked to see the grave, laid flowers upon it, and stood over it, weeping.

2 At the end of one of his love affairs D'Annunzio sought refuge in a decaying castle in the Italian hills. The flutter that this arrival caused among the local peasantry and neighbors died down, winter set in, and the prospect seemed bleak and tedious. Suddenly the neighborhood was electrified by news of a lady in a flowing white cloak seen riding a white horse into the castle courtyard at midnight. She appeared again on subsequent nights, and speculation was rife about the poet's new mistress and her secret visits to him. The explanation? It was

D'Annunzio himself in disguise seeking to re-create the atmosphere of romantic mystery in which he loved to live.

஻ ௸

DANTE ALIGHIERI (1265–1321), *Italian poet. Exiled from his native Florence by his political enemies (1307), Dante spent many years wandering before finally settling in Ravenna (c. 1318). During this time he wrote* La divina commedia [The Divine Comedy], *his vision of hell, purgatory, and paradise, which is generally held to be the greatest medieval work of literature. His fictional guide in the Paradise section of* La divina commedia *is Beatrice, the Florentine aristocrat for love of whom he wrote* La vita nuova *(c. 1292). His creative writings and his two critical treatises on Italian as a literary language were the forerunners of the Italian literary renaissance.*

1   Dante had an uneasy relationship with his patron and protector, Can Grande della Scala, at whose court he lived for some time. Another member of Can Grande's court was a conceited ignoramus who nonetheless delighted his master with his jests and fooleries and was lavishly rewarded with gifts of money. One day this man said to Dante, "How is it that I, who am so ignorant and foolish, should be so rich and favored, while you, who are so learned and wise, should be a beggar?" Dante replied, "The reason is that you have found a lord who resembles you, and when I find one who resembles me, I shall no doubt be as rich as you are."

2   Deeply immersed in meditation during a church service, Dante failed to kneel when the holy sacrament was elevated. His enemies at once hurried to the bishop and demanded that Dante be punished for his sacrilege. When Dante was brought before the bishop, he excused himself by saying, "If those who accuse me had had their eyes and minds on God, as I had, they too would have failed to notice events around them, and they most certainly would not have noticed what I was doing."

{As this anecdote suggests, genius and sanctimoniousness may be quite compatible. For an offbeat view of the dour Florentine, *see* LOPE DE VEGA 1.}

஻ ௸

DANTON, Georges Jacques (1759–94), *French revolutionary leader. After the storming of the Bastille (1789) Danton became the accepted leader of the Parisian mob and pursued a policy of dedicated republicanism. In the end his enemies, led by Robespierre, and the fickleness of his friends brought about his downfall.*

1   At his trial before the revolutionary tribunal on the charge of having betrayed the people, Danton treated the accusations with haughty contempt. Condemned to death, he maintained on the guillotine his unflinching calm. "Show my head to the people," he instructed the executioner. "It is worth it."

஻ ௸

DARIUS I (550–486 BC), *king of Persia (521–486). He crushed the Babylonian empire (c. 516), invaded Scythia (now the southern part of the Soviet Union), and put down a revolt of the Greek city-states of Ionia (Asia Minor). His first invasion of Greece itself was foiled at the battle of Marathon (490). Preparations for another expedition were deflected by a revolt in Egypt, and he died before he could put his plans into action.*

1   In about 512 BC, as Darius led his armies north of the Black Sea, the Scythians sent the Persian king a message comprising a mouse, a frog, a bird, and five arrows. Darius summoned his captains. "Our victory is assured," he announced. "These arrows signify that the Scythians will lay down their arms; the mouse means the land of Scythia will be surrendered to us; the frog means that their rivers and lakes will also be ours; and the Scythian army will fly like a bird from our forces." But a cunning adviser to the king put a different interpretation on the message. "The Scythians mean by these things that unless you turn into birds and fly away, or into frogs and hide in the waters, or into mice and burrow for safety in the ground, you will all be slain by the Scythian archers."

Darius took counsel and decided that the second was the more likely interpretation. By beating a prudent retreat, he managed to extricate his army from the Scythian territory.

{This is the version of the story given in Herodotus; other writers give slightly different accounts.}

2   The tomb of Nitocris, queen of Babylon, bore the following inscription: "If any king of Babylon after me should be short of money, he

may open this tomb and take as much as he wants, but only if he really is in need of it." Darius, although he had no genuine need for the money, thought it a shame that such riches should go to waste. He had the tomb opened, only to find no money there at all. Beside the body of the queen, however, was a second message: "If you had not been greedy of gold and fond of base gain, you would not have thought of ransacking the graves of the departed."

႙ ⚬§

DARROW, Clarence Seward (1857–1938), US *lawyer renowned for his conduct of labor litigation and murder cases.*

1 Reporters would on occasion tease the energetic and hard-working Darrow about his disheveled appearance. Darrow retorted, "I go to a better tailor than any of you and pay more for my clothes. The only difference is that you probably don't sleep in yours."

2 A female client whose legal problems Darrow had solved burbled, "How can I ever show my appreciation, Mr. Darrow?"
"Ever since the Phoenicians invented money," replied Darrow, "there has been only one answer to that question."

3 In 1925 Darrow defended John T. Scopes of Tennessee, tried for teaching the theory of evolution. The prosecution attempted to discredit Darrow by labeling him an agnostic. He replied, "I do not consider it an insult but rather a compliment to be called an agnostic. I do not pretend to know where many ignorant men are sure."

4 After a speaking engagement at a Women's Club meeting, Darrow was cornered by a couple of ladies who wanted to discuss birth control. One asked him what he thought of birth control for the masses. "My dear lady," replied Darrow, "whenever I hear people advocating birth control, I always remember that I was the fifth child."

5 Darrow was being interviewed for a magazine article on the reasons given by prominent men for their success. "Most of the men I've spoken to so far attribute their success to hard work," said the interviewer.

"I guess that applies to me, too," said Darrow. "I was brought up on a farm. One very hot day I was distributing and packing down the hay which a stacker was constantly dumping on top of me. By noon I was completely exhausted. That afternoon I left the farm, never to return, and I haven't done a day of hard work since."

႙ ⚬§

DARWIN, Charles Robert (1809–82), *British naturalist. Moving from the study of medicine and theology, Darwin became interested in current theories explaining the diversity of animal species, living and extinct. His observations during the famous* Beagle *voyage (1831–36) led him to conclude that living things evolve by a process of natural selection. In 1859 Darwin's* On the Origin of Species *appeared. Years of bitter controversy with the church ensued, for Darwinism was seen as a threat to orthodox Christian belief in biblical creationism. The controversy was intensified in 1871 when* The Descent of Man *applied Darwin's theories to human beings.*

1 Darwin spent the eight years from 1846 to 1854 in a detailed study of barnacles. At one time there were no fewer than 10,000 barnacles in the house. His children accepted their presence as a part of normal life. One of Darwin's sons, on a visit to a friend's house, once inquired of the other boy where his father "did his barnacles."

2 Emma Darwin, though a loving wife, did not share Darwin's enthusiasm for his work, nor did she pretend to find his experiments interesting. One day she accompanied him to a scientific lecture, during the course of which he turned to her and said, "I am afraid this must be very wearisome to you."
"Not more than all the rest," she replied politely.

3 Charles Darwin was standing near the hippopotamus cage at the zoo one day when he overheard a little boy and girl talking. The hippopotamus had closed its eyes for a minute. "That bird's dead," said the little girl. "Come along."

႙ ⚬§

DARWIN, Erasmus (1731–1802), *British poet and physician, grandfather of Charles Darwin.*

He versified the principles of botany in The Botanic Garden *(1789, 1791) and the laws of organic existence in* Zoonomia *(1794–96).*

1 Darwin was once offended by a young man's asking him whether he did not find his stammer very inconvenient. "No, sir," he replied. "It gives me time for reflection, and saves me from asking impertinent questions."

ॐ ◌

DAUDET, Alphonse (1840–97), *French writer. His works include* Tartarin de Tarascon *(1872), the humorous* Lettres de mon moulin *(1866), and plays such as* L'Arlésienne *(1872).*

1 Alphonse Daudet's *L'Arlésienne,* for which Bizet composed the incidental music, was far from a success when it opened at the Odéon theater. This was in 1872, at a time when the politician and polemical journalist Victor-Henri Rochefort was beginning to regain some of the popularity he had enjoyed a few years before. At a social gathering Rochefort boasted, "I have only to raise my little finger and one hundred thousand Parisians will leave their homes and follow me wherever I wish." Daudet, also present as a guest, was heard to murmur, "Oh, if you could only lead them to the Odéon."

ॐ ◌

DAVENANT, Sir William (1606–68), *British dramatist, whose plays were successful at the courts of Charles I and Charles II. He also wrote the earliest English opera,* The Siege of Rhodes *(1656). He composed his romantic epic* Gondibert *(1651) while imprisoned for the royalist cause, at which time his life is said to have been saved by Milton's intervention.*

1 As the result of an illness Davenant lost his nose — a misfortune that evoked much merriment and ribaldry among his literary friends. A simple old countrywomen once blessed Davenant's eyesight. Rather surprised, the poet inquired why. She explained that if his eyesight should fail he would be in serious difficulty, as he lacked the means to support a pair of spectacles.

2 Apologizing because he could not finish a poem on which he was working, Davenant said, "I shall ask leave to desist, when I am interrupted by so great an experiment as dying."

ॐ ◌

DAVID, Sir Edgeworth (1858–1934), *Australian geologist and explorer. He accompanied Ernest Shackleton on his expedition to the South Pole (1907–09).*

1 During the South Polar expedition, Sir Edgeworth's assistant, Douglas Mawson, was working in his tent one day when he heard a muffled cry from outside. "Are you very busy?" called the voice, which Mawson recognized as that of Sir Edgeworth.

"Yes I am," he replied. "What's the matter?"

"Are you really *very* busy?"

"Yes," snapped Mawson, losing his patience. "What is it you want?"

After a moment's silence, David replied apologetically, "Well, I'm down a crevasse, and I don't think I can hang on much longer."

ॐ ◌

DAVIES, Lady Eleanor (died 1652), *English religious fanatic; wife of the poet Sir John Davies. She published several books of prophecy and in 1633 was imprisoned and fined £3,000.*

1 As a result of her prophecies, considered potentially dangerous in the troubled religious climate of Charles I's reign, Lady Eleanor found herself before the Court of High Commission. She had discovered that the letters of her name, with an *I* substituted for the final *s*, could be rearranged to form the words: "Reveal, O Daniel!" On the strength of this anagram, she attempted to persuade the court that she was possessed by the spirit of the prophet Daniel. The bishops, convinced that she was quite mad, tried to reason with her, but she had a ready reply for all their arguments. At last, one of the deans of the Arches, who had been scribbling furiously for some time, announced that he had irrefutable "proof" of Lady Eleanor's insanity, and read out the anagram: "Dame Eleanor Davies — never so mad a ladie!" The prophetess's pretensions were dismissed in a wave of ridicule.

ॐ ◌

DAVIES, Marion (1897–1961), *US film actress. A talented comedienne, she was the mis-*

tress of William Randolph Hearst, who used his great influence to advance her career and obtain (often quite unsuitable) parts for her. The result was a long string of unmemorable films made between 1917 and 1936.

1   Marion Davies was among the first of the silent screen stars to realize the impact that talking pictures would have on their careers. She asked the MGM publicity manager to accompany her to see *The Jazz Singer,* the first film of the sound era, and sat quiet and totally absorbed throughout the performance. At the end she turned and said in a small voice, "M-m-mister Voight, I-I-I have a p-p-problem."

{She need not have worried; her stammer scarcely affected her at all when she was speaking lines she knew.}

꙳   ꙴ

DAVIS, Bette (1908–   ), *US movie actress. She made her name in dramatic films (Of Human Bondage; Dark Victory) in the 1920s and 1930s. In later years she specialized in characterizing intense, sinister, or neurotic elderly women, as in* Whatever Happened to Baby Jane? *(1962).*

1   Bette Davis's attorney told her a rumor was spreading throughout New York that she had died. Miss Davis was unworried: "With the newspaper strike on I wouldn't consider it."

꙳   ꙴ

DAVY, Sir Humphry (1778–1829), *British chemist. The discoverer of the use of nitrous oxide as an anesthetic, he was invited to join the Royal Institution in London (1801), where he became professor of chemistry. He invented the miner's safety lamp, known as the Davy lamp (1815), discovered potassium and several other chemical elements, and advanced the understanding of electricity.*

1   Davy's fame was international. A letter reached him safely from Italy although it bore only the direction:

"SIROMFREDEVI/LONDRA."
Compare MARK TWAIN 15.

2   One clear night Davy was passing through the London streets when he saw a man showing the moon through a telescope. He stopped to look and offered the showman the penny fee. The man, recognizing his customer as the great Sir Humphry Davy, refused the money, saying, "I could not think of taking money from a brother philosopher."

3   On his return from a visit to Paris Davy was asked how he had liked the picture galleries there. "The finest collection of frames I ever saw," was his reply.

꙳   ꙴ

DAYAN, Moshe (1915–81), *Israeli statesman. Minister of defense (1967, 1969–74) and foreign minister (1977–79), he was easily recognized by the eyepatch that covered the eye he lost fighting in the British army during World War II.*

1   Stopped for speeding by a military policeman, Dayan argued: "I have only one eye. What do you want me to watch — the speedometer or the road?"

꙳   ꙴ

DEAN, Jay Hanna ["Dizzy"] (1911–74), *US baseball player. He and his brother Paul pitched for the St. Louis Cardinals.*

1   Asked how the Cardinals expected to fare against Detroit in the World Series of 1934, Dizzy Dean replied, "Me and Paul'll win two games apiece."

{They won the first, second, sixth, and seventh games, thus clinching the Series for the Cardinals, 4–3.}

2   After Dizzy Dean had pitched a one-hitter in the first game of a double-header, Paul Dean pitched a no-hitter in the nightcap. Dizzy commented, "Shucks, if I'd known Paul was gonna pitch a no-hitter, I'd a pitched one too."

3   Accused of corrupting English language students with his unruly diction and grammar, Dean retorted, "A lot of people who don't say ain't ain't eatin'."

4   An English interviewer, frustrated by Dizzy Dean's idiosyncratic relationship with language, exclaimed, "Mr. Dean, don't you know the king's English?" Dizzy reflected for a moment. Then, "Sure I do, and so's the queen."

DEBS, Eugene Victor (1855–1926), *US socialist, trade unionist, and frequent presidential nominee of the Socialist party.*

1 In 1918 the pacifist Debs made a speech condemning World War I and criticizing the persecution of persons charged with sedition in violation of the 1917 Espionage Act. This brought him a ten-year prison sentence. He ran his 1920 presidential campaign as Convict 2273 in the federal penitentiary in Atlanta, receiving nearly a million votes. On Christmas Day 1921 Debs was released on the orders of President Harding. Surprised but unrepentant, he remarked, "It is the government that should ask me for a pardon."

ॐ ॐ

DEGAS, [Hilaire Germain] **Edgar** (1834–1917), *French painter and sculptor. His most characteristic pictures are scenes from the ballet, and his intimate studies of women at their toilet are also highly regarded.*

1 By nature Degas was conservative. His friend the etcher Jean-Louis Forain believed in progress. Forain had recently installed that newfangled invention, the telephone. Arranging to have a friend phone him during the meal, he invited Degas to dinner. The phone rang; Forain rushed to answer it, then returned, beaming with pride. Degas merely said, "So that's the telephone. It rings and you run."

2 Degas attended an auction at which one of his pictures was sold for an enormous sum. Asked what it felt like to witness such a transaction, Degas replied, "I feel as a horse must feel when the beautiful cup is given to the jockey."

3 When Degas knew he was dying, he called his friend Forain to him, instructing him that there was to be no funeral oration. Then he added, "But if there has to be one, Forain, you get up and say, 'He greatly loved drawing. So do I.' Then go home."

ॐ ॐ

DE GAULLE, Charles André Joseph Marie (1890–1970), *French statesman and general; president (1958–69). A professional soldier, de Gaulle advocated mechanization in warfare, gaining respect as a military theorist with such* books as Vers l'armée de métier *(1934). He was promoted to general in 1940, but his opposition to an armistice with Germany led him to exile in London, where he gathered the Free French forces to fight on the Allied side. De Gaulle received a hero's welcome after liberation, becoming briefly president in the postwar provisional government (1945–46). After an unsuccessful attempt to form his own political party, he resigned from politics in 1953, but was summoned from retirement in 1958 to save France from the engulfing chaos caused by the Algerian war. As president, de Gaulle pursued a course of independent nationalism. Distrustful of international organizations, he took France out of NATO (1966). Student unrest and labor troubles made his position untenable and he resigned in 1969, leaving to France a powerful legacy of national pride and right-wing politics.*

1 Clementine Churchill was sitting next to General de Gaulle at luncheon, and during one of the many silences found herself thinking how difficult Mme de Gaulle's life must be. Her reverie was interrupted by the general's observation to her, "*Vous savez*, madame, it must be very difficult, being the wife of Mr. Churchill."

{Clementine Churchill told this to Cecil Beaton while he was photographing her at No. 10 Downing Street in 1940.}

2 De Gaulle's touchiness about the honor of France and his own position during World War II made him a difficult ally, and personal antagonism frequently flared between him and Churchill. After one such incident Churchill remarked, "Of all the crosses I have to bear, the cross of Lorraine is the heaviest."

{There are a number of variants of this remark. And *see* WINSTON CHURCHILL 24 for another remark about de Gaulle.}

3 During an official tour of Iran, de Gaulle spent a day in the ancient city of Persepolis. The members of de Gaulle's party were obliged to stand in the baking sun while the curator gave an exhaustive account of the history of the city from the earliest settlements to the present day. By the time he had reached the conquest of Persepolis by Alexander the Great, his illustrious visitor had had enough. "Thus Alexander conquered the city and destroyed it," announced the curator in dramatic tones.

"Fine," interrupted de Gaulle. "Let's go and see what's left." With that, the entire group departed.

See also HENRI IV 5.

4 De Gaulle was once likened by a speaker to Robespierre. The general's reaction was, "I always thought I was Jeanne d'Arc and Bonaparte. How little one knows oneself!"

5 The de Gaulles' daughter Anne, born in 1928, was retarded from birth and needed constant care and attention, for she could not feed or clothe herself and was unable to speak properly. Mme de Gaulle devoted herself to caring for the child and so did her husband. The pains that the aloof soldier took to entertain the little girl astonished those who knew him only in his dealings with adults; he would spend hours playing simple games with her and at night would hold her hand until she fell asleep. In 1948 Anne contracted a lung ailment and died. After her body had been placed in the family vault at Colombey-les-Deux-Eglises, de Gaulle turned to his wife and said, "Now at last our child is just like all children."

6 When Jacques Soustelle was governor-general of Algeria (1955–56), he complained to de Gaulle that all his friends were attacking him for supporting the general's Algerian policies. De Gaulle's reply was brief: "*Changez vos amis*" (Change your friends).

7 In 1960, philosopher Jean-Paul Sartre publicly urged French troops in Algeria to desert. Asked why he had taken no action against Sartre for this seditious behavior, de Gaulle replied, "One does not arrest Voltaire."

8 A French diplomat, about to take up a new ambassadorship, visited President de Gaulle before leaving the country. "I am filled with joy at my appointment," he said enthusiastically. The president frowned. "You are a career diplomat," he said. "Joy is an inappropriate emotion in your profession."

9 At the height of one of the many crises that beset de Gaulle's political career, he exclaimed in frustration, "How can one govern a country that has three hundred and fifty kinds of cheese?"

10 Mrs. Sargent Shriver, the wife of the US ambassador to France, was seated beside de Gaulle at a state banquet. Charmed by his conversation, she found herself saying, as the meal drew to a close, "Mr. President, my only regret is that you're not twenty years younger and that I'm not twenty years younger." Without thinking, she repeated the remark to Mme de Gaulle later that evening. "Ah, yes, Mrs. Shriver," said the president's wife. "But just remember, I would then be twenty years younger, too."

11 Lunching with English friends at the time of her husband's retirement, Madame de Gaulle was asked what she was looking forward to in the years ahead. "A penis," she replied without hesitation. The embarrassed silence that followed was finally broken by the former president. "My dear," he murmured, "I think the English don't pronounce the word quite like that. It's ''appiness.'"

12 An assassination attempt on de Gaulle was made in August 1962 when he and Mme de Gaulle were being driven through the outskirts of Paris. Bullets punctured the car tires, it swerved violently, and the bodyguard in the front seat yelled at the de Gaulles to get down. Neither moved. When the car came to a stop they got out, brushing the glass from a shattered rear window out of their clothing. "They really are bad shots," observed the general calmly.

Mme de Gaulle, asked later if she had been frightened, retorted, "Frightened of what? We'd have died together, and no old age."

৯৯ ৩৯

DÉJAZET, Pauline Virginie (1798–1875), *French actress. In the 1820s her success in male parts was such that these roles were nicknamed "Déjazets." She managed and acted successfully at the Théâtre Déjazet until 1868.*

1 At a dinner party in Berlin Virginie Déjazet was chagrined to find that her most amusing sallies made no impression upon the stolid Germans around the table. "My German friends," she cried at last, "what you have been listening to is known as wit. Why don't you club together in order to understand it?"

৯৯ ৩৯

DE LA MARE, Walter (1873–1956), *British poet, novelist, and anthologist. He retired on a government pension at the age of thirty-six to devote himself to writing.*

1 De la Mare suffered a severe illness and for some time his life lay in the balance. During his convalescence, his daughter came to see him and asked if there was anything she could get him — fruit or flowers. "No, no," said the poet weakly, "too late for fruit, too soon for flowers."

੩੦ ੬ੲ

DE MOIVRE, Abraham (1667–1754), *British mathematician of French Huguenot descent. His major work was* The Doctrine of Chances *(1716); he also made significant contributions to trigonometry.*

1 (In his old age, twenty hours' sleep a day became habitual with De Moivre.)
"Shortly before [his death] he declared that it was necessary for him to sleep some ten minutes or a quarter of an hour longer each day than the preceding one. The day after he had reached a total of over twenty-three hours he slept up to the limit of twenty-four hours and then died in his sleep."

੩੦ ੬ੲ

DEMOSTHENES (c. 384–322 BC), *Greek orator. His most famous speeches were the Philippics, denunciations of Philip of Macedon, who was determined to subjugate the free cities of Greece.*

1 Demosthenes is generally considered the greatest orator of classical antiquity, but in his day he had a strong rival in the Athenian general Phocion. "One of these days the Athenians will kill you when they are in a rage," observed Demosthenes. "And you too," retorted Phocion, "when they are in their right minds."

2 Demosthenes' first success as a speaker came when he made a claim against his guardian, who had defrauded him. The fortunate outcome prompted him to embark on the career of an orator. When he first took part in the public debates, his speech was so tortuous and feebly delivered that the audience could not understand him and laughed him out of the assembly. The actor Satyrus caught up with him as he was going disconsolately homeward and then and there gave him a lesson in how to deliver a speech. Demosthenes thereupon made himself an underground study where he stayed for weeks at a time, practicing his oratory. To protect himself against the temptation of going out into society, he shaved one side of his head so that he would be too embarrassed to show himself in public. He cured his stammer by speaking with pebbles in his mouth and his shortness of breath by declaiming poetry while running uphill. Thus he eventually acquired the skill to hold an Athenian audience spellbound.

੩੦ ੬ੲ

DEMPSEY, Jack [William Harrison] (1895–1983), *US boxer, world heavyweight champion from 1919 to 1926.*

1 On September 23, 1926, Dempsey lost his title to Gene Tunney. To his wife he explained, "Honey, I just forgot to duck."
{This remark was quoted by President Ronald Reagan after he was wounded in an assassination attempt in 1981.}

2 When Dempsey was training for his first fight with Gene Tunney, he sent a spy to watch Tunney work out and pick up tips on his opponent's style. The spy returned in great good humor to make his report. "It's a set-up," he said. "I seen the lug readin' a book."

3 J. Paul Getty was one of the wealthy men who frequently came to watch Dempsey train. Himself a keen amateur boxer, he asked to be allowed to spar for a round with the champion. Getty put up quite a creditable performance until he made the mistake of saying, 'Hit me a little harder, Jack." Dempsey knocked him out.

4 Dempsey was staying overnight in a California hotel. Just after midnight, he received a call from the reception clerk. "There's a man down here who says he can lick you," said the clerk, "and he won't go away." Tired of being challenged by drunks wherever he went, Dempsey replied wearily, "Tell you what you do — tell him he can have my title, but I want it back in the morning."

੩੦ ੬ੲ

DENHAM, Sir John (1615–69), *English poet. A minor name in English verse, his chief claim to fame is his topographical poem, "Cooper's Hill."*

1 The Puritan poet George Wither was imprisoned in the Marshalsea and sentenced to death for his rather innocuous anti-Royalist satires. Sir John Denham, though on the king's side, nevertheless successfully interceded with Charles I for his fellow poet's life on the ground that "If Your Majesty kills Wither, I will then be the worst poet in England."

DENIS, Marie-Louise (c. 1710–90), *French femme du monde. She was Voltaire's niece, for a time his mistress, and kept house for him in his old age.*

1 In the course of an English lesson Mme Denis grew impatient over the difficulty of pronouncing the words of this uncouth language. She said to her teacher, "You write *bread,* but say *bred.* Wouldn't it be simpler just to say *du pain?*"

2 Mme Denis was once complimented on the skill with which she had played the role of Zaïre at one of her uncle's private theatricals at Ferney. She replied, "Alas, to handle the role properly one must be young and pretty."
"Ah, madame, you are a complete proof of the contrary."

DENNIS, John (1657–1734), *British playwright and critic. His own plays failed to achieve much success, but he gained a reputation as a critic. He antagonized some of the leading literary figures of the day, including Alexander Pope, from whom he acquired immortality of a kind in* The Dunciad, *a long poem satirizing contemporary literary and social characters. He did, however, make one lasting contribution to the English language.*

1 In one of Dennis's plays, *Appius and Virginia* (1709), a clap of thunder is called for. This Dennis provided by a machine he had invented. However, in a later performance of *Macbeth* at the same theater he heard an identical clap of thunder, which he correctly assumed emanated from his own machine. "Damn them," he is reported to have cried. "See how the rascals use me! They will not let my play run, and yet they steal my thunder!"

2 On one occasion Dennis visited a tavern with the composer Henry Purcell. Purcell rang the bell to summon the drawer (waiter) to provide them with two glasses of ale. The summons was not answered. Purcell with some annoyance tapped the table. "Why does the table remind you of this tavern?" he asked his companion. Dennis looked blank. "Because it has no drawer," said Purcell.
{Dennis once made a comment that is perhaps the most widely known remark on puns: "Any man who would make such an execrable pun would not scruple to pick my pocket!" The remark is often attributed, erroneously, to Dr. Johnson.}

DEPALMA, Ralph (1883–1956), *US racing driver, born in Italy. He was the US champion in 1912 and 1914 and in 1915 won the Indianapolis 500.*

1 DePalma was leading the Indianapolis 500 by five miles in 1912 when his car began losing oil and stopped with less than one mile to go. DePalma and his riding mechanic of the day, Rupert Jeffkins, got out and pushed the car toward the finish line, but before they reached it Joe Dawson had circled the 2½-mile track twice in his car and passed them to win. After receiving a standing ovation, DePalma said, "I'd rather receive the winner's trophy. I can drive these things, but I can't carry them."

DEPEW, Chauncey Mitchell (1834–1928), *US lawyer, politician, and wit. He held various posts in connection with the Vanderbilt railroad empire and was senator from New York State for two terms (1899–1911).*

1 Chauncey Depew and Mark Twain were both billed to speak at a banquet. Twain spoke first for about twenty minutes and was loudly applauded. When Depew was called upon, he rose and said: "Before this dinner Mark Twain and I agreed to trade speeches. He has just delivered mine and I am grateful for the reception that you have given it. Unfortunately I have lost his speech and I cannot remember a word of what he had to say." And he sat down.

2 When Chauncey Depew was quite old, he was sitting at dinner next to a young woman wearing a very low-cut, off-the-shoulder dress. The old lawyer peered at her décolletage, leaned toward her, and asked, "My dear, what is keeping that dress on you?"

"Only your age, Mr. Depew."

৫৯ ৯৫

DESCARTES, René (1596–1650), *French philosopher and mathematician. His Medita-tions (1641) undermined the Aristotelian con-cept of reality European thought had adhered to for two millenia. His approach was summed up in his famous line: "Cogito, ergo sum" (I think, therefore I am). In his youth, Descartes mainly lived quietly in Holland, though he corre-sponded with scholars all over Europe. Queen Christina of Sweden lured him to Stockholm in 1649 as her philosophy tutor. The Swedish cli-mate and the rigors of court hours killed him.*

1 To Queen Christina Descartes tried to ex-plain his mechanistic philosophy: the view that all animals are mechanisms. The queen coun-tered this by remarking that she had never seen a watch give birth to baby watches.

> {As a gloss on this anecdote, the General Editor offers his clerihew:
> Said Descartes, "I extoll
> Myself because I have a soul
> And beasts do not." Of course
> He had to put Descartes before the horse.}

2 Descartes's coordinate system was one of his main contributions to the development of mathematics. It is said that the idea came to him during a period of idleness in his military service as he lay on his bed watching a fly ho-vering in the air. He realized that the fly's posi-tion at every moment could be described by locating its distance from three intersecting lines (axes). This insight was the basis of Carte-sian coordinates.

3 Descartes once constructed a robot in the form of a girl, which he later had occasion to transport by sea. The ship's captain, out of cu-riosity, looked into the chest in which the robot was packed and was horrified by the

lifelike form, which moved like an animated being. Thinking that this could only be the devil in disguise, he threw the chest and its contents into the sea.

৫৯ ৯৫

DE SEVERSKY, Alexander Procofieff (1894–1974), *US aviator and aeronautical engi-neer, born in Russia. The president of Seversky Aircraft Corporation (1931–39), he invented a number of aeronautical devices, including a bomb sight.*

1 De Seversky was visiting a fellow aviator in the hospital. The young man had just had his leg amputated; de Seversky, who had been walking on an artificial limb for some time, tried to cheer him up. "The loss of a leg is not so great a calamity," he said. "Look at me. I dance, I fly, I drive a car, I go everywhere. And another thing: if you get hit on a wooden leg, it doesn't hurt a bit! Try it!" The patient raised his walking-stick and brought it down on de Se-versky's leg with considerable force. "You see," said de Seversky cheerfully. "If you hit an ordinary man like that, he'd be in bed for five days!" With these words he took his leave of the young man and limped out into the corri-dor, where he collapsed in excruciating pain. The aviator had struck him on his good leg.

৫৯ ৯৫

DETOURBEY, Jeanne (d. 1908), *Comtesse de Loynes, salonnière of the Second Empire, and mistress of the writer Jules Lemaître, twenty years her junior.*

1 "Once while discussing the wave of anti-clericalism which was sweeping the country, an ardently Romanist guest declared that when it came to his loyalties, he was a Catholic before he was a Frenchman. "Catholic before being French?" the comtesse exclaimed. "Oh, happy the man who has been baptized before being born!""

৫৯ ৯৫

DE VALERA, Eamon (1882–1975), *Irish statesman. He was thrice prime minister of Ire-land (1932–48, 1951–54, 1957–59) and subse-quently president (1959–73).*

1 As a young man De Valera visited France. On his return he announced, "All I can say is that sex in Ireland is as yet in its infancy."

2 In the middle of a fiery political speech at Ennis, De Valera was arrested. After a year's imprisonment, he was released. At once he hastened back to Ennis, summoned a meeting, and began to speak: "As I was saying when I was interrupted —"

{This anecdote is also told of others, including the Spanish philosopher Unamuno.}

3 After the Easter rebellion of 1916 De Valera was sentenced to penal servitude. En route to his prison he took out his pipe and was about to light it when he stopped suddenly and said, "I will not let them deprive me of this pleasure in jail!" He immediately threw away the pipe and from that day never smoked again.

4 De Valera held meetings with Lloyd George at which the Irishman was seen to be doing most of the talking. Someone later asked Lloyd George how he was getting along with De Valera. "We have talked for two days," replied Lloyd George gloomily, "and he has got up to Brian Boru."

ও্য়ও ওপ্ত

DE VALOIS, Dame Ninette (1898–   ), *British ballet dancer and choreographer. With Lilian Baylis, Ninette de Valois founded the Sadler's Wells Ballet, which became the Royal Ballet in 1956. Dame Ninette continued to direct it until her retirement in 1963.*

1 Ninette de Valois always disliked publicity and the cult of the star performer; she herself resolutely shunned the limelight. After one of the Royal Ballet's triumphant tours, the audience at Covent Garden clamored for the company's director after their first performance back in their home theater. Ninette de Valois came reluctantly to the front of the stage and made one of the briefest curtain speeches on record: "Ladies and gentleman, it takes more than one to make a ballet." And then she withdrew.

ও্য়ও ওপ্ত

DEVONSHIRE, Spencer Compton Cavendish, 8th Duke of (1833–1908), *British statesman. He rose to political prominence in Victorian Britain, became war secretary (1866) in Lord Russell's government, secretary of state for India (1880–82) under Gladstone, and three times refused the premiership during the 1880s.*

1 The Duke of Devonshire was renowned for his passion for sleep — a passion he often indulged in the House of Lords. One afternoon he fell asleep in the chamber. When he awoke he was heard by Lord Portland, who was sitting nearby, to complain: "Good heavens, what a bore, I shan't be in bed for another seven hours." Earlier on in his career he impressed Disraeli when he yawned in the middle of his maiden speech in the House of Commons. "He'll do," said Disraeli. "To anyone who can betray such languor in such circumstances the highest posts should be open."

2 In 1894 the Liberal chancellor of the exchequer, Sir William Harcourt, introduced death duties that gravely threatened the privileged position of the upper classes, as they saw it. The budget incorporating this tax was of course vigorously opposed by the enormously wealthy Duke of Devonshire.

One evening at dinner the duke was seated next to Lady Harcourt. She remarked, "Your Grace, I feel you would like to hang my husband."

"No, madam," he replied, "merely suspend him for a period."

ও্য়ও ওপ্ত

DEWEY, John (1859–1952), *US philosopher and educator; professor of philosophy at Columbia University (1904–30). He expounded his pragmatist views in a number of influential books, such as* Reconstruction in Philosophy *(1920).*

1 Dewey's theories of education also influenced his own home life. His study was directly below the bathroom. One day as he was sitting at his desk he felt a trickle of water running down his back. Dashing upstairs, he found his young son, Fred, with a fleet of toy boats in the overflowing bathtub and the child struggling to shut off the water. As he saw his father, Fred said sternly, "Don't argue, John. Get the mop."

2 Dewey and some philosophical colleagues walked half a mile down Broadway one sunny afternoon to attend an open-air movie. It was not until they arrived that they realized, in the words of Thomas Reed Powell, "that movies require darkness, which in this part of the world is not rampant in the daytime."

3 In retirement Dewey sold eggs and vegetables to his neighbors on Long Island. On one occasion he received an urgent call from a wealthy neighbor for a dozen eggs. As there were no children available to take them around, Dewey delivered them himself. He went from force of habit to the front door, but was told sharply to make deliveries at the back. Sometime later he was giving a talk to a local women's club and as he rose to speak was amused to hear his rich customer saying in a stage whisper to her neighbor, "Why, he looks exactly like our egg man!"

છ્ર જ

DEWEY, Mrs. Thomas E. [Frances E. Hutt] (1903–70), *wife of US politician Tom Dewey, governor of New York (1942–1954), who twice ran unsuccessfully for US president.*

1 In the 1948 presidential contest between Truman and Dewey, the latter looked like a winner. On election night, Dewey asked his wife, "How will it be to sleep with the president of the United States?" She replied, "A high honor, and quite frankly, darling, I'm looking forward to it."

Next morning, at breakfast, after Dewey's defeat, Mrs. Dewey said, "Tell me, Tom, am I going to Washington or is Harry coming here?"

છ્ર જ

DE WOLFE, Elsie (1865–1950), *US designer and fashion leader. In 1926 she married British diplomat Sir Charles Mendl.*

1 In 1933 Elsie traveled to Greece with some friends. Like most visitors, Elsie found her first sight of the Acropolis a stirring experience. "It's beige! My color!" she cried.

છ્ર જ

DIAGHILEV, Sergei [Pavlovich] (1872–1929), *Russian impresario. After organizing art exhibitions in Russia, he moved to Paris and in 1908 staged Mussorgsky's* Boris Godunov *at the Paris Opéra. The next year his season of Russian ballet was so successful that a permanent company, the Ballets Russes, was formed in 1911. Diaghilev remained director of this until his death; among the talents he nurtured were Nijinsky, Pavlova, Fokine, and Balanchine.*

1 Diaghilev was a notorious woman-hater. The suspicion that any of his young men was favoring female companionship over his own elicited considerable petulance. When he brought his ballet company to London, one of the constant attenders at the rehearsals was the critic and writer Sacheverell Sitwell, then stationed at Aldershot, the army training center in Hampshire. Military hours meant that Sitwell sometimes had to leave early, making the excuse to Diaghilev that he must "get back to Aldershot." Eventually the Russian's jealous suspicions boiled over. "*Qu'est-ce que c'est que cette Aldershot?*" he snapped waspishly. "*C'est une femme?*"

2 In the twenties in Paris, when Diaghilev was triumphing with his Ballets Russes, his problem was to continue to surprise a sophisticated public. Jean Cocteau, who had undertaken to provide a scenario for a new ballet, asked the great impresario for some direction. Diaghilev replied only, "*Etonne-moi!*" (Astonish me!)

This phrase epitomized the era.

3 Henri Matisse once visited a rehearsal of *Parade,* by Erik Satie and Jean Cocteau, with sets by Picasso, which Diaghilev was choreographing. At a break in proceedings, Matisse asked the great choreographer what was meant "when that little ballerina skips and then falls down and kicks her legs in the air?" Diaghilev adopted a tone of amazement that Matisse had not understood. "Why," he cried, "it's quite simple. That's the *Titanic* disaster."

છ્ર જ

DIANA, Princess of Wales [*née* Lady Diana Spencer] (1961–   ), *wife of Prince Charles. Before her marriage in 1981 she worked as a kindergarten assistant in London.*

1 In 1983, the Prince and Princess of Wales visited Australia and New Zealand on a royal tour. Walking freely among the crowds in South Australia, the princess made for a group of young children, the nearest of whom she patted affectionately on his tousled head. "Why aren't you at school today?" she inquired.

"I was sent home," the lad replied, "because I've got head lice."

> As Count Jean Dauger lay dying, he spoke these last words to his son: "You'd better not wait . . . better be off to bed . . ." Then: "On the other hand, maybe you're right. You'd better stay. Nobody can watch a father die twice."

DICKENS, Charles (1812–70), *English novelist. He achieved recognition and financial security with the success of* The Pickwick Papers *(1836–37), in which his genius for comic characterization was fully displayed. His greatest works, which include* Oliver Twist *(1837–38),* Barnaby Rudge *(1841),* Martin Chuzzlewit *(1843–44),* David Copperfield *(1849–50),* Bleak House *(1852–53),* Little Dorrit *(1857–58), and* Great Expectations *(1860–61), combine intense vitality and wide-ranging comedy with penetrating criticism of social abuses and human folly. His public readings from his works were enormously popular.*

1   Dickens's childhood was overshadowed by his father's inability to keep out of debt and subsequent imprisonment. Hardship and frequent changes of address were visited upon John Dickens's family, and the future novelist at the age of ten was forced to work at a factory pasting labels on pots of shoe blacking. When old John Dickens was later asked where his famous son had been educated, he replied, "Well, he may be said to have — ah — educated himself."

2   Like most of Dickens's works, *The Old Curiosity Shop* (1841) was first published in serial form. The novel won a vast readership in both Britain and the United States, and interest in the fate of the heroine, Little Nell, was intense. In New York, six thousand people crowded the wharf at which the ship carrying the magazine with the final installment was due to dock. As it approached, the crowd's impatience grew to such a pitch that they cried out to the sailors, "Does Little Nell die?"

3   The monthly installments of *The Pickwick Papers* were also eagerly awaited by all. A clergyman spent some time administering spiritual comfort to a sick parishioner. When he got up to leave, he felt satisfied that he had done some good. As the door closed behind him, he heard the invalid say, "Well, thank God, *Pickwick* will be out in ten days anyway."

4   While Dickens was acting as editor of the weekly periodical *Household Words,* a young poet called Laman Blanchard sent him a contribution entitled "Orient Pearls at Random Strung." Dickens's rejection slip read, "Dear Blanchard, too much string — Yours, C. D."

5   An elderly charwoman who could not read used to go every month to a subscription tea at a snuff shop, at which the proprietor would read aloud that month's installment of *Dombey and Son.* She was much surprised to learn that the author of the book was one man. "I thought that three or four men must have put together *Dombey.*"

6   When Charles Dickens moved into Tavistock House, he made sure that every detail of it was to his taste. One of the features he installed was a hidden door to his study, made to look like part of an unbroken wall of books, complete with dummy shelves and fictitious titles. Dickens clearly derived much amusement from the invention of titles for these volumes. They ranged from the purely facetious — *Five Minutes in China,* three volumes, and *Heaviside's Conversations with Nobody* — to straight puns such as *A Carpenter's Bench of Bishops* and *The Gunpowder Magazine.* These stood alongside more satirical titles such as *The Quarrelly Review* and *Hansard's Guide to Refreshing Sleep* in "as many volumes as possible." Further additions in later years included *Strutt's Walk, Noah's Arkitecture, Shelley's Oysters, Cat's Lives* (nine volumes), *History of a Short Chancery Suit* (twenty-one volumes), and *The Wisdom of Our Ancestors,* which consisted of volumes on ignorance, superstition, the block, the stake, the rack, dirt, and disease. The companion *The Virtues of Our Ancestors* was so narrow the title had to be printed sideways.

7   (G. K. Chesterton tells the following:)
    "It is related of him . . . that in his last visit to America, when he was already reeling as it were under the blow that was to be mortal, he remarked quite casually to his companions that a row of painted cottages looked exactly like the painted shops in a pantomime. No sooner

had the suggestion passed his lips than he leaped at the nearest doorway and in exact imitation of the clown in the harlequinade, beat conscientiously with his fist, not on the door (for that would have burst the canvas scenery of course), but on the side of the door-post. Having done this he lay down ceremoniously across the doorstep for the owner to fall over him if he should come rushing out. He then got up gravely and went on his way."

ठॐ ◌ई

DIDEROT, Denis (1713–84), *French philosopher. With Voltaire, Diderot was the guiding spirit of the French Enlightenment. After 1750 he held the enormously influential post of editor of the* Encyclopédie, *through which the tenets of the Enlightenment and the triumph of rationalism and science were propagated.*

1 In 1773 Diderot spent some months at the court of St. Petersburg at the invitation of the Russian empress, Catherine the Great. He passed much of his time spreading his gospel of atheism and materialism among the courtiers, until it was suggested to the empress that it would be desirable to muzzle her guest. Reluctant to take direct action, Catherine requested the aid of another savant, the Swiss mathematician Leonhard Euler, a devout Christian. As Diderot was almost entirely ignorant of mathematics, a plot was hatched to exploit this weakness. He was informed that a learned mathematician had developed an algebraical demonstration of the existence of God, and was prepared to deliver it before the entire court if Diderot would like to hear it. Diderot could not very well refuse. Euler approached Diderot, bowed, and said very solemnly, "Sir, $(a + b^n)/n = x$, hence God exists. Reply!" Diderot was totally disconcerted, and delighted laughter broke out on all sides at his discomfiture. He asked permission to return to France, and the empress graciously consented.

ठॐ ◌ई

DIETRICH, Marlene [Maria Magdalene von Losch] (1904–), *German actress and singer. The film* The Blue Angel *(1930) established her image as a sultry beauty; her subsequent films, of varying quality, included* Destry Rides Again *(1939),* A Foreign Affair *(1948),* Witness for the Prosecution *(1957), and* Judgment at Nuremberg *(1961).*

1 Asked whether she objected to being imitated by other performers, Dietrich replied, "Only if they do it badly."

2 In August 1944, just days after the liberation of Paris, Marlene Dietrich, still wearing her American GI uniform, strode into the House of Hermès on the rue du Faubourg Saint-Honoré and ordered a blue leather dress to be especially made by the couturier department. A few weeks later, when she returned to pick it up, she was presented with the bill from the firm's owner, Emile-Maurice Hermès. Dietrich took one look at the bill and paled. "Madame," suggested M. Hermès politely, "you'll be able to wear it more than once."

ठॐ ◌ई

DIETZ, Howard (1896–1983), *US writer and publicist. He is best known for his musical-comedy lyrics, especially those written with Jerome Kern and Arthur Schwartz.*

1 During the course of an argument, critic Alexander Woollcott asked Dietz, "Are you trying to cross me?" Surveying Woolcott's ample girth, Dietz replied, "Not without an alpenstock."

ठॐ ◌ई

DIGBY, Sir Everard (1578–1606), *English gentleman, conspirator in the Gunpowder Plot (1605) to blow up James I and the Houses of Parliament.*

1 (Sir Everard Digby was a most gallant gentleman and one of the handsomest men of his time.)
"'Twas his ill fate to suffer in the Powder-plott. When his heart was pluct out by the Executioner (who *secundum formam*, cryed, Here is the heart of a Traytor!) it is credibly reported, he replied, Thou liest!"

ठॐ ◌ई

DiMAGGIO, Joseph (1914–), *US baseball player, one of the greatest heroes of the game. He was an enormously popular star of the New York Yankees, dominant baseball team of the 1930s and 1940s.*

1 In January 1946 Joe DiMaggio married movie actress Marilyn Monroe. She knew nothing about baseball, but was attracted to

the tall, elegant, reserved DiMaggio. With his blessing, she interrupted their honeymoon to make a tour of American troop installations abroad. Returning in triumph, she told him, "Oh, Joe, it was so exciting. The boys were thrilled. You never heard such cheers." Quietly DiMaggio observed, "Yes, I have."

છે ુ

DIOGENES (?412–323 BC), *Greek philosopher, principal exponent of the Cynic school of philosophy. He held that happiness consisted in the satisfaction of one's basic needs and decried the pursuit of wealth and success. His unconventional life and acid temper caused many legends to grow up around him.*

1 When Alexander the Great visited Corinth, Diogenes was living in a large earthenware tub in one of the city suburbs. Alexander went to see the philosopher and found him sunning himself. The king politely asked if there was any way in which he could serve him. "Stand out of my sun," replied the surly Cynic. Alexander's courtiers began ridiculing Diogenes as a monster, but the king said, "If I were not Alexander, I should wish to be Diogenes."

2 On being asked of what country he was a citizen, Diogenes replied, "I am a citizen of the world."

3 Someone was speaking enthusiastically of Callisthenes, Alexander the Great's historian. "What a fortunate man, a part of Alexander's household, privileged to be present at his feasts!"

"Say rather, how unfortunate a man," said Diogenes, "who can neither dine nor sup except at Alexander's pleasure."

4 By assiduous flattery the hedonistic philosopher Aristippus had won himself a comfortable sinecure at the court of Dionysius, tyrant of Syracuse. One day, observing Diogenes preparing some lentils for a meager meal, Aristippus offered some worldly wisdom to his fellow sage: "If you would only learn to compliment Dionysius, you wouldn't have to live on lentils."

"And if you would only learn to live on lentils, you wouldn't have to flatter Dionysius," retorted Diogenes.

5 One day a woman, accompanied by her small son, came to Diogenes, complaining that the boy was rude and ill-behaved and asking what she should do to improve his conduct. Diogenes' answer was to strike the mother in the face.

6 Alexander the Great was puzzled to find Diogenes examining a heap of human bones. "What are you looking for?" he inquired.

"I am searching for the bones of your father," replied the philosopher, "but I cannot distinguish them from those of his slaves."

7 Diogenes was once noticed begging from a statue. Asked the reason for this pointless conduct, he replied, "I am exercising the art of being rejected."

8 Diogenes observed a child drinking from his cupped hands. At once he drew his goblet from his satchel and threw it away, saying, "In the practice of moderation a child has become my master."

છે ુ

DIONYSIUS II (c. 395–343 BC), *tyrant of Syracuse (367–356, 346–343), known also as Dionysius the Younger to distinguish him from his father of the same name. His misrule resulted in his expulsion from Sicily and a ten-year exile in Locri (southern Italy).*

1 Dining one day with Dionysius, Philip II of Macedon spoke scornfully of the tyrant's father, who had spent his leisure time writing poetry and plays. "How could the king find leisure to write such trifles?" he asked. "In those hours that you and I spend in drunkenness and debauchery," replied Dionysius.

છે ુ

DIRICHLET, Peter Gustav Lejeune (1805–59), *German mathematician.*

1 Dirichlet was opposed to writing letters; many of his friends had in the course of their entire lives received no communications from him. However, when his first child was born he broke his silence; he wired his father-in-law: "$2 + 1 = 3$."

છે ુ

DISNEY, Walt[er Elias] (1901–66), *US film producer. He is remembered for his animated cartoons featuring such characters as Mickey Mouse and Donald Duck, and for his full-length cartoon films, among them* Snow White and the Seven Dwarfs *(1937),* Fantasia *(1941), and* Bambi *(1942). He also organized the first Disneyland at Anaheim, California.*

1 "How does it feel to be a celebrity?" Disney was once asked. "It feels fine," he replied, "when it helps to get a good seat for a football game. But it never helped me to make a good film or a good shot in a polo game, or command the obedience of my daughter. It doesn't even seem to keep fleas off our dogs — and if being a celebrity won't give one an advantage over a couple of fleas, then I guess there can't be much in being a celebrity after all."

DISRAELI, Benjamin, 1st Earl of Beaconsfield (1804–81), *British Conservative statesman and prime minister (1868, 1874–80). Of Italian-Jewish descent, Disraeli became a Christian at the age of thirteen, a member of Parliament at thirty-three, and prime minister at sixty-four. A flamboyant personality and a staunch supporter of the monarchy, the Empire, and the Church, he won the respect of the nation and the queen. Before attaining political power he wrote a number of novels, the best known of which are* Coningsby *(1844) and* Sybil *(1845).*

1 In 1835 Daniel O'Connell, the Irish Roman Catholic leader, attacked Disraeli in the House of Commons. In the course of his unrestrained invective he referred to Disraeli's Jewish ancestry. Disraeli replied, "Yes, I am a Jew, and when the ancestors of the right honorable gentleman were brutal savages in an unknown island, mine were priests in the temple of Solomon."
{A pointed riposte others have used for similar racial slurs.}

2 Disraeli made his maiden speech to the House of Commons in December 1837, delivering a high-flown and ambitious response to an old adversary, Daniel O'Connell. He was greeted with roars of derision from O'Connell's supporters and eventually forced to sit down. Before he did so, he looked across at his persecutors and said loudly, "Though I sit down now, the time will come when you will hear me."

3 The widowed Mary Anne Wyndham Lewis was twelve years Disraeli's senior. When they married in 1839, she brought him a considerable fortune and a handsome house in London. The marriage was a very happy one. In later years Disraeli used to joke with his wife, saying he had only married her for her money. "But if you had to do it again, you'd do it for love," she would always reply.

4 On the first morning of a house party Mrs. Disraeli said to her hostess at breakfast, "I find that your house is full of indecent pictures." Alarm and dismay spread across the faces of the assembled guests. Mrs. Disraeli went on, "There is a most horrible picture in our bedroom. Disraeli says it is *Venus and Adonis*. I have been awake half the night trying to prevent his looking at it."
{Frank Muir, who quotes the passage from William Fraser's *Disraeli and his Day* from which the above is taken, comments, "The account does not specify the method Mrs. Disraeli adopted to divert her husband's attention from the vile painting."}

5 Gladstone once accosted Disraeli on the topic of the latter's renowned wit, observing that Disraeli had the reputation of being able to make a joke on any subject. Disraeli responded that that was quite possible. "Then I challenge you," said Gladstone. "Make a joke about Queen Victoria."
"Sir," replied Disraeli, "Her Majesty is not a subject."
{Told of others.}

6 Gladstone and Disraeli frequently clashed in parliamentary debates. "Mr. Disraeli cannot possibly be sure of his facts," roared Gladstone in one debate. "I wish," responded Disraeli, "that I could be as sure of anything as my opponent is of everything."

7 Disraeli was onced asked to define the difference between a calamity and a misfortune. Taking the name of his great rival, Gladstone, as his example, Disraeli said, "If, for instance, Mr. Gladstone were to fall into the river, that

would be a misfortune. But if anyone were to pull him out, that would be a calamity."
Compare EUGÈNE NAPOLEON 3.

8   Disraeli had a standard acknowledgment for people who sent him unsolicited manuscripts for his opinion: "Thank you for the manuscript; I shall lose no time in reading it."

9   Disraeli, plagued by an applicant for a baronetcy, found various reasons why it was impossible to confer the desired honor. "You know I cannot give you a baronetcy," said Disraeli, "but you can tell your friends that I offered you one and you refused it. That's much better."
    See also CHAIM NACHMAN BIALIK 1; CATO 3; ABBÉ GABRIEL BONNOT DE MABLY 1.

10   Disraeli had a standard method of covering up if he forgot the name of the person to whom he was talking. "When I meet a man whose name I can't remember, I give myself two minutes; then, if it is a hopeless case, I always say, 'And how is the old complaint?'"
    {A similar instance of portmanteau solicitude was suggested in the Diary column of the London *Times* in 1981, for use by the intelligentsia on the cocktail circuit: "How's the book?"}

11   Like many prominent Victorians, Disraeli was an anti-Darwinian, seeing the question in terms of a contest between those who thought of man as occupying the middle ground between material and spiritual beings and those who maintained the evolutionary line. Alluding to the debate in a speech made in November 1864, Disraeli said, "Is man an ape or an angel? Now I am on the side of the angels."

12   When asked about his motives for writing novels, Disraeli explained that every so often he was overcome by the urge to read a novel, and in order to have one at hand he would write it himself.

13   Disraeli had been criticized for his harsh verbal attacks on John Bright, who was, after all, a self-made man. "I know he is," retorted Disraeli, "and he adores his maker."
    {This familiar retort seems to have been made by others.}

14   Disraeli was the guest of honor at a public dinner. As the kitchen was some way from the banqueting hall, most of the food was stone-cold by the time it reached the table. Sipping his champagne after the meal, Disraeli murmured, "Thank God! I have at last got something warm."

15   A young lady was taken to dinner one evening by Gladstone and the following evening by Disraeli. Asked what impressions these two celebrated men had made upon her, she replied, "When I left the dining room after sitting next to Mr. Gladstone I thought he was the cleverest man in England. But after sitting next to Mr. Disraeli I thought I was the cleverest woman in England."
    {This story was recounted by Princess Marie Louise, Queen Victoria's granddaughter.}

16   Queen Victoria once paid Disraeli the honor of visiting him at his country house near Beaconsfield. On his deathbed he declined another royal visit. "No, it is better not. She will only ask me to take a message to Albert."

৯০ ৶৫

DIVINE, Father (1877–1965), *US black revivalist preacher, born George Baker. He founded the Peace Mission movement.*

1   Father Divine taught that heaven was on earth and established "heavens" for his followers in which spiritual life was centered on the worship of himself. The segregation by sexes, even of married couples, in these "heavens" caused considerable scandal. One of his confidential lady "secretaries" revealed Father Divine's favorite seduction technique. "Mary wasn't a virgin," he would murmur.

2   The goings-on at Father Divine's house of worship in Saybrook drove his neighbors to bring a court case against him as causing a public nuisance. On November 16, 1931, Justice Lewis J. Smith fined the preacher $500 and sentenced him to a six-month jail term. Four days later, on November 20, the judge, without warning, pain, or premonition, dropped dead. This extraordinary coincidence unleashed a storm of publicity. Father Divine kept his head and told the reporters clamoring for his comments on the affair, "I hated to do it."

DIX, Dorothea Lynde (1802–87), *US philanthropist, noted for her work on behalf of the insane and for her organization of the nursing corps during the Civil War.*

1 The diarist and philanthropist George Templeton Strong described Miss Dix as a "philanthropic lunatic." Her impulsive ways led her into conflict with the Sanitary Commission, "because we do not leave everything else and rush off the instant she tells us of something that needs attention." Miss Dix once burst into a meeting of the commission in great excitement to report that a cow was dying of sunstroke in the Smithsonian grounds. She was very peeved when the commission did not immediately adjourn to investigate.

DODGE, Mary Mapes (1831–1905), *US writer. She wrote* Hans Brinker; or, The Silver Skates *(1865) and founded the famous children's magazine* St. Nicholas, *which she edited for many of its sixty-four years.*

1 Among the eminent writers published in *St. Nicholas* were Mark Twain, Longfellow, Whittier, Emerson, and Thoreau. When Rudyard Kipling asked Mrs. Dodge whether she would like him to contribute to her magazine, she answered, "Do you think you are up to it?"

DOHERTY, John (1783–1850), *Irish lawyer and politician. In 1830 he was appointed Lord Chief Justice of Ireland.*

1 Attending a ball at Dublin Castle, Doherty and another gentleman were scandalized by the décolletage of a certain young lady. "Did you ever see anything like it since you were born, Doherty?" exclaimed the friend. "I can't say since I was *born*," Doherty answered, "but certainly since I was weaned."

DONATELLO (c. 1386–1466), *Italian Renaissance sculptor. A pioneer of the new humanist style, Donatello worked in marble, bronze, and wood. Among his greatest works are the statues on the exterior of Or San Michele in Florence (1415), the bronze* David *(early 1430s) in the Bargello in Florence, and the* Gattamelata *equestrian statue in Padua.*

1 The Signori of Venice commissioned Donatello to make the equestrian statue of the condottiere Erasmo da Narni ("Gattamelata") and plagued the artist with their demands that he hurry up and finish it. Exasperated by their importunities, Donatello smashed with a hammer the nearly completed head of the statue. The Signori threatened him with similar treatment, to which Donatello retorted, "Quite agreeable, as long as you feel you will be able to reshape my head as I will do Gattamelata's."

DONNE, John (1572–1631), *British poet, who entered the Church (1615) and became dean of St. Paul's, London (1621–31). As a young man Donne was the foremost "metaphysical" poet, noted for his beautiful and witty love lyrics. His sermons are also distinguished.*

1 Donne secured the post of secretary to Sir Thomas Egerton, Keeper of the Great Seal, in 1598. He outraged his employer's family by a clandestine marriage to Anne More, the niece of Sir Thomas's wife, and lost his job. The young couple took refuge in a house at Pyrford in Surrey. There Donne scratched on a pane of glass the words: "John Donne/An Donne/Undone."

2 Donne was persuaded, after he took holy orders and repudiated his former ambitious and worldly life, to have his portrait painted. He posed for the painter in a winding sheet with his body and hands arranged like those of a corpse. When the picture was completed, he had it placed beside his bed as a constant reminder of mortality.

DONOVAN, William Joseph ["Wild Bill"] (1883–1959), *US lawyer and general, decorated for his services in both world wars. In World War II, as director of the Office of Strategic Services (OSS), he was raised to the rank of major general.*

1 On D-day, during the Allied invasion of Europe, Donovan asked David Bruce, chief of the OSS in Europe, if he had arranged to be buried in Arlington cemetery. Taken aback, Bruce said that he had not — and why did he ask. "Well," said Donovan, "I have; that's where I want to be buried. David, you've got to

get a plot near mine. Then we can start an Underground together."

৯৯ ৵৽

DOOLEY, Thomas Anthony (1927–61), *US physician. His lectures and books, such as* De-liver Us From Evil *(1956), brought home to the Western world the tragic turmoil in Southeast Asia and the problems confronting "jungle doc-tors" like him who were concerned to bring medical aid to poor and primitive societies. He died young of cancer.*

1 A newspaperwoman was expressing doubts about whether the food served in the Laotian capital of Vientiane was "safe." "Have no qualms, my dear," said Dooley, "I've been eat-ing here for five years and all I've got is cancer."

৯৯ ৵৽

DOUGLASS, Frederick (c. 1817–95), *US ora-tor and journalist. The son of a white man and a black slave, he spent his early years in slavery but escaped in 1838 and became a leading figure in the antislavery movement. After the Civil War he enjoyed a distinguished career in public service, including a period as minister general in Haiti (1889–91).*

1 Douglass was traveling by boat from New York to Boston on a stormy night. As his Negro blood disqualified him from occupying a cabin or any of the public rooms, he was obliged to curl up in a corner of the deck to sleep. An officer came across him there and took pity on him. Knowing that he could find Douglass a stateroom if he could pass him off as an American Indian, the officer approached him with the words, "You're an Indian, aren't you?" Douglass at once grasped the signifi-cance of the question. Looking the officer straight in the eyes, he replied, "No, sir, I'm a nigger," and curled up in his corner again.

৯৯ ৵৽

DOYLE, Sir Arthur Conan (1859–1930), *Brit-ish writer, creator of the detective Sherlock Holmes and his colleague Dr. Watson. Conan Doyle is remembered for his many stories fea-turing the famous sleuth, such as* The Sign of the Four *(1889) and* The Hound of the Basker-villes *(1902), but he felt that his historical ro-mances, such as* Micah Clarke *(1888) and* The White Company *(1890), had greater literary merit. He was knighted in 1902.*

1 Joking with Doyle during a rehearsal for one of his plays, a young three-pound-a-week actor called Charlie suggested that he and Sir Arthur should pool their incomes and take half each for the rest of their lives. Though amused by the proposal, Doyle declined for obvious reasons. "I don't think so, Mr. Chaplin," he replied.

2 In later life, Doyle became a fervent spiritu-alist and gave many public lectures on the sub-ject. At one of these meetings, gesticulating enthusiastically as he spoke, he accidentally spilled a glass of water over some of the re-porters in the front row. "So sorry," said Doyle. "I seem to have baptized you, even if I don't succeed in converting you!"

3 When Doyle did not arrive for a scheduled lecture on spiritualism, Cambridge students mounted a placard bearing the announcement: "Sir Arthur Conan Doyle has failed to mate-rialize."

4 As part of his belief in the spiritual world, Doyle thought communication with the dead was possible. A friend once asked him to visit a fellow author who was seriously ill. "I'll call in tomorrow," promised Doyle.
"Tomorrow could be too late — he may not last the night," said his friend.
"In that case," replied Doyle breezily, "I'll speak to him next week."

৯৯ ৵৽

DRAKE, Sir Francis (?1540–1596), *English ad-miral, who made a series of successful expedi-tions to plunder Spanish settlements in the New World and to prey on their shipping. In 1577 he set out for South America on the first leg of the voyage that was to take him around the world. Queen Elizabeth knighted him (1581) and he played an active part in the war against Spain. In 1587 Drake sailed into Cadiz harbor, where the Spanish Armada was preparing to invade England, and destroyed thirty-three ships. He was second in command of the fleet that de-feated the Armada in 1588. Drake died in the West Indies on a disastrous expedition against the Spaniards.*

1 Drake's most famous exploit, the "singeing of the king of Spain's beard," by which he destroyed thirty ships in Cadiz harbor where they were fitting out for the invasion of England, was carried out in the face of Queen Elizabeth's reluctance to provoke the Spaniards. She hoped, despite the evidence of Spain's warlike preparations, to reach a negotiated settlement. It was only with the utmost unwillingness that she gave the order allowing Drake, who had been hanging around in Plymouth harbor for some time, to set off on his hostile errand. No sooner had she given the order than she had second thoughts, and another dispatch rider was sent racing off toward Plymouth to countermand it. Drake however had guessed that such a second order might be forthcoming and as soon as he received the first he put to sea. A speedy boat was sent after him, but curiously enough it failed to locate his fleet. The queen was very angry, but there was nothing she could do to stop him.

2 With the English fleet in harbor, Drake and the other commanders were playing bowls on Plymouth Hoe when news was brought on July 19, 1588, that the Spanish Armada was sailing up the English Channel. Lord Howard of Effingham, lord admiral, wanted to put to sea at once, but Drake insisted on finishing his bowls. "There is plenty of time to win this game and beat the Spaniards after." Only when the game was over did the English captains go to their ships.

{According to David Howarth in *The Voyage of the Armada: The Spanish Story*, Drake's remark "does not appear in a written history until 1736. One can only say it was just the sort of thing he would have said . . . [and] it is much easier to believe he said it than that somebody years afterward made it up."}

ริ⊶ ⊷ริ

DREISER, Theodore (1871–1945), *US novelist. His best-known works*, Sister Carrie *(1900) and* An American Tragedy *(1925), reflect his uncompromising dedication to realism.*

1 During World War I Dreiser became friendly with H. L. Mencken, made him his literary executor, and confided to him that he had chosen his own last words. They were to be "Shakespeare, I come!"

During the early years of the twentieth century aspiring poets, musicians, and artists frequented the Dill Pickle Club on Chicago's Near North Side — a nightspot that served coffee, cider, and toasted cheese sandwiches to the hungry artists and also put on their experimental, avant-garde plays. Next door to it was the Bush Conservatory dormitory, at which equally aspiring young women studied to become musicians; indeed, some of them earned pin money by playing the piano at the Dill Pickle. One cold winter night in 1917 the dormitory caught fire. Roused by one of their roommates, the girls seized the pictures of their boyfriends, rushed downstairs, and went en masse into the Dill Pickle Club, where they danced the night away in their nightgowns with the surprised and delighted yet-to-be-famous Chicago literati.

DREW, John (1853–1927), *US actor. He was a renowned comedy star, much admired for his elegant bearing and meticulous dress.*

1 To play in *Rosemary* Drew shaved off his mustache, which greatly altered his appearance. Soon afterward he met Max Beerbohm but failed to recall who the latter was. Beerbohm, however, recognized Drew and said, "Mr. Drew, I'm afraid you don't recognize me without your mustache."

ริ⊶ ⊷ริ

DREYSCHOCK, Alexander (1818–69), *Czech pianist.*

1 "At Dreyschock's first court appearance [in Vienna] he played before the emperor [Francis Joseph] in a very hot room, with closed windows. Dreyschock began to perspire. The emperor listened intently and watched him even more closely. When the pianist got up and faced the emperor, he was afraid to wipe his face. The emperor approached. 'My dear Dreyschock, I have heard Moscheles play.' Dreyschock bowed. 'I have heard Thalberg.' Dreyschock bowed lower. 'I have heard

Liszt,' Dreyschock bowed very low indeed. 'I have heard all the great players. But I never, never, never saw anybody perspire as you do.' "
{In a version of this story told by George Robey the pianist is one Liebling and the punch line is attributed to W. S. Gilbert.}

ða æð

DRYDEN, John (1631–1700), *English poet and critic. His panegyrics on Charles II earned him in 1668 the title of poet laureate. His plays* Marriage à la Mode *(1673) and* All for Love *(1677) have remained part of the repertory of the theater. His verse satires — notably* Absalom and Achitophel *(1681) — were very influential in their time.*

1 Dryden often played hooky from classes at Westminster School in London and rarely spent much time preparing his lessons. Once when the class had been told to compose a poem on the gospel story of the conversion of water into wine, Dryden hastily scribbled: "The modest water, awed by power divine,/ Beheld its God, and blushed itself to wine." By comparison with the turgid effusions of his classmates, this couplet brought Dryden an accolade from the master, who saw in it a portent of future poetic greatness.

2 Dryden described himself as a man of grave demeanor without much of a sense of humor. However:
    On one occasion his wife, Lady Elizabeth Howard, bustled into his study, feeling herself to be somewhat neglected. "Lord, Mr. Dryden," she exclaimed, "how can you always be poring over those musty books? I wish I were a book, and then I should have more of your company." Dryden replied, "Pray, my dear, if you do become a book let it be an almanac, for then I shall change you every year."

3 Dryden was enjoying a convivial meeting with a group of fashionable wits, including the earls of Buckingham and Dorset. Someone proposed a poetic competition, each man present to write an impromptu composition, and Dryden to judge which was the best. The Earl of Dorset was the first to hand in his piece of paper. Dryden waited until all the contributions had been completed before he began to read them. His face showed his pleasure as he studied the succession of witty or beautiful

verses, but the broadest smile spread over his countenance as he opened the Earl of Dorset's paper. "I will have to award the prize to my Lord Dorset," he said and then read out the earl's contribution: "I promise to pay John Dryden, or order, on demand the sum of £500. Dorset."

ða æð

DU BARRY, Marie Jeanne Bécu, Comtesse (?1743–93), *French aristocrat, mistress of Louis XV from 1768. Banished from court after Louis's death (1774), she was guillotined during the French Revolution.*

1 Louis XV always maintained that women could never attain to the highest excellence as cooks. Mme du Barry took the opposite view and invited the king to a supper that had been prepared by the best cuisinière in France. At the end of the meal Louis said, "Who is your cook? I must have him in the royal household." Mme du Barry replied, "It is not a cuisinier, but a cuisinière. I demand a recompense worthy both of Your Majesty and of her. I cannot accept anything less than a cordon bleu." The king agreed, and it was in this way that the cordon bleu — the blue ribbon of the grand cross of the Order of the Holy Spirit, the highest chivalric order under the Bourbon kings — became the accolade of an outstanding cook.

ða æð

DUCLOS, Charles Pinot (1704–72), *French writer and historian. His* Histoire de Louis XI *(1745), although initially badly received, won him in 1750 the title of historiographer of France. In 1755 he was created perpetual secretary of the French Academy.*

1 Jean-Pierre Bougainville, eminent man of letters and elder brother of the famous explorer, suffered from ill health. While electioneering for admission to the French Academy, he never failed to stress this fact. As he had not long to live, he would plead, he would soon give place to another. Duclos was unmoved by this argument: "Apparently, sir, you imagine that among the Academy's other prerogatives is that of giving extreme unction."

ða æð

DU DEFFAND, Marie Anne, Marquise (1697–1780), *French noblewoman and salon-*

nière. Her friends included Voltaire, Montesquieu, Fontenelle, D'Alembert, and Horace Walpole.

1   Cardinal de Polignac told Mme du Deffand, at great length and in inordinate detail, the story of how Saint Denis was decapitated at Montmartre and then walked a whole league to the village named after him, carrying his head in his hands. Seeing his narrative was evoking no response, the cardinal explained, "Do you deny that he carried his head in his hands for a whole league?"

"It's only the first step that counts," said Mme du Deffand.

2   Asked whether she believed in ghosts, Mme du Deffand replied, "No — but I'm afraid of them."

{This anecdote is told of others. For a variation see NIELS BOHR 1.}

3   Mme du Deffand once tried to have a conversation with Jacques de Vaucanson, celebrated for his invention of automatons. No matter how she tried, she could extract from the great inventor only monosyllables. Later she was asked about her impression of Vaucanson. "I think he made himself," she said.

᠀ ᠀

DUDLEY, John William Ward, 1st Earl of (1781–1833), *British politician.*

1   Lord Dudley was notoriously absentminded. One of his eccentricities was his habit of rehearsing audibly, using two voices, one gruff and one shrill, what he was going to say to others. On one occasion, when he had been asked to present a country gentleman at court, everything went smoothly until their carriage became stuck in a fearful traffic jam as they were leaving the palace. Dudley's protégé was startled to hear his companion say, "Now this tiresome country squire will be expecting me to ask him to dine. Shall I? Or shall I not? On the whole I think not; I think he might be a bore." The country squire was momentarily confounded, then he too soliloquized, "Now this tiresome old peer will of course be asking me to dine with him today. Shall I or not? No; I am pretty sure it would be a bore." It was the earl's turn to be startled, but he quickly recollected

himself, laughed, and with genuine pleasure asked the squire to dine with him.

᠀ ᠀

DUKE, Vernon [Vladimir Dukelsky] (1903–69), *US composer, born in Russia. He is remembered for his popular songs, notably "April in Paris."*

1   Inspired by Duke's famous song, a friend of the composer's decided to spend a few weeks in Paris one April. The weather was appalling. On his return, the traveler complained at some length about his disappointing trip. "Whatever made you go to Paris in April?" asked Duke. "The weather is always terrible then." His friend looked at him in astonishment. "I went because of your song," he replied. "Ah, well," explained the composer apologetically, "we really meant May, but the rhythm required two syllables."

᠀ ᠀

DULLES, John Foster (1888–1959), *US politician; secretary of state (1953–59) under President Eisenhower. From 1945 to 1949 he represented the United States at the United Nations, which he helped to establish.*

1   Asked whether he had ever been wrong, Dulles considered the question for some time before replying. "Yes," he finally admitted, "once — many, many years ago. I thought I had made a wrong decision. Of course, it turned out that I had been right all along. But I was wrong to have *thought* that I was wrong."

᠀ ᠀

DUMAS, Alexandre [*père*] (1802–70), *French novelist and playwright, often called Dumas père to distinguish him from his illegitimate son and namesake, Dumas fils. He wrote historical melodramas and romances. Among the latter* The Count of Monte Cristo *(1844–45),* The Three Musketeers *(1844), and* The Black Tulip *(1850) were outstandingly successful.*

1   At the production of one of Alexandre Dumas's plays, another playwright, coincidentally named Adolphe Dumas, came up to the successful dramatist and complimented him on his work. The great seventeenth-century

French playwright, Pierre Corneille, had had a much younger brother called Thomas, a rather less successful dramatist. Adolphe Dumas's compliment revolved around the pleasure it gave him to think of his name being linked with that of Alexandre Dumas just as the two Corneilles had been. Alexandre Dumas bowed, but said nothing. At the end of the evening he went across to his namesake and said, "Goodnight, Thomas."

2   Dumas's prodigious output was greatly assisted by his corps of ghost writers. Meeting his son and namesake, Dumas inquired, "Have you read my new novel yet?" Alexandre *fils* replied, "No. Have you?"

3   A reporter was questioning Dumas about his ancestry. "Is it true that you are a quadroon?" he asked. Dumas replied that it was.
"So your father was a mulatto?"
"Yes."
"And your grandfather was a negro?"
"Yes."
Incautiously the reporter persisted: "And your great-grandfather was — ?"
"A baboon, sir," roared Dumas, his patience exhausted. "A baboon! Which means that my family begins where yours ends."
{Variations of this story have been attributed to many people of honorable attainments but what some might think socially dubious origins. *See,* for example, IPHICRATES 1.}

4   A well-known theater manager visited Dumas and, without removing his hat, rather unceremoniously asked if it was true that the famous playwright had sold his latest play to another, smaller theater company. Dumas confirmed this. The manager then made an enormous rival bid, but was unable to change Dumas's mind. "Your competitor," said Dumas, "got the play much more cheaply by a very simple procedure."
"And that was — ?"
"While enjoying the honor of conversing with me, he took off his hat."

5   A committee asked Dumas to contribute toward the funeral of a man who had died in poor circumstances. Dumas asked whether the deceased had been a member of the artistic circle of Paris. "Not exactly," was the reply, "but he sort of moved in and out among us. He was the district bailiff."
"How much will it cost to bury him?" inquired Dumas.
"Twenty-five francs."
"Here are fifty francs," said Dumas. "Go bury two bailiffs."
See also EARL OF NORBURY 2.

6   Dumas's quarrel with a rising young politician became so intense that a duel was inevitable. As both were superb shots, they decided to draw lots, the loser agreeing to shoot himself. Dumas lost. Pistol in hand, he withdrew in silent dignity to another room, closing the door behind him. The rest of the company waited in gloomy suspense for the sound of the shot that would end Dumas's career. It rang out at last. They ran to the door, opened it, and there was Dumas, smoking revolver in hand. "Gentlemen, a most regrettable thing has happened. I missed."
{The authenticity of this anecdote is not guaranteed.}

7   When the acrobat Charles Blondin, fresh from his triumphant North American tour, visited Paris, Dumas called on him and characteristically ventured some skeptical remarks about Blondin's achievements on the high wire. "Monsieur Dumas," burst out the irritated Blondin, "if you wish I would be glad to have you accompany me over Niagara Falls."
"Delighted," replied Dumas, "but only on condition that I carry you."

8   During the premiere of one of his plays at the Théâtre Français, Dumas mentioned to a friend that on the previous night at the same theater he had witnessed Fournet's *Gladiator.*
"How was it?"
"Tedious," answered Dumas. "People simply fell asleep."
At this moment the friend noticed a member of the audience sunk in deep slumber and remarked with a smirk, "Well, apparently your own play doesn't seem especially gripping either."
"My dear friend, you are mistaken. He's left over from last night."

9   "How do you grow old so gracefully?" ex-

claimed an admirer of the elderly Dumas. "Madame, I give all my time to it," was the reply.

❧ ❧

DUMAS, Alexandre [*fils*] (1824–95), *French novelist and playwright, often known as Dumas* fils *to distinguish him from his father. His best-known work,* La Dame aux camélias *(1848), was the basis of Verdi's opera* La Traviata, *and explores the themes of love and sexual morality, which dominate Dumas's work.*

1 At a Paris salon Dumas overheard a woman describe him as a "boor with whom one could never spend more than an hour." Some months later Dumas found himself staying in the same seaside hotel as the woman. Her husband was away in Paris for most of the week; she was thoroughly bored and ready for a little intrigue. Dumas exerted all his charm to seduce her, and in the end gained his objective of an assignation. At the end of exactly one hour he got up and marched to the door. "Madame, the time is up. Good day." He bowed and left the room.

2 Before the first night of a Dumas play a pretty young actress rushed up to Dumas all aflutter with stage fright. "Oh, Monsieur Dumas," she gasped, "just feel how my heart is beating." Dumas, of course, was only too happy to oblige. "How does it feel?" pursued the soubrette after a pause. "Round," said Dumas.

3 One night Dumas *fils* set out to go to the theater, but, deterred by pouring rain, returned home. His wife, Ida, had already gone to bed, so Dumas settled down to read by the fire in their bedroom. Suddenly the closet door burst open, Dumas's friend Roger de Beauvoir, clad only in a shirt, emerged, shaking with cold. "I don't see why I should die of pneumonia while you sit there warming yourself by the fire," he exclaimed. A heated altercation ensued, at the end of which Dumas started to hustle de Beauvoir outside. Seeing the pelting rain, however, he paused to reflect; after all, de Beauvoir was an old friend. "You can explain tomorrow," he said, "in the meanwhile I am going to bed and you can sleep in the armchair."

At first all was peaceful, but as the fire died down de Beauvoir's teeth began to chatter again. Dumas awoke. "Come to bed," he called

magnanimously to de Beauvoir, who hopped in at once beside Ida. The three of them slept cosily till morning, when Dumas woke up the guilty pair. "As old friends, Roger, we shouldn't quarrel, even about a wife," he said. "Let us be reconciled as the ancient Romans were — on the public thoroughfare." So the two of them shook hands across the still sleeping Ida.

4 Dumas listened in silence as his friends discussed the physical attributes of two courtesans. One of the ladies had a magnificent figure, the other a beautiful face. The young men finally turned to Dumas. "Which would you prefer?" they asked. "I would prefer to go out with the second," replied the writer, "and come home with the first."

❧ ❧

DUNCAN, Isadora (1878–1927), *US dancer, famous worldwide for her interpretive dancing and flamboyant life-style.*

1 At her home in Nice in September 1927, Isadora Duncan stepped into her brand-new, low-slung Bugatti racing car, driven over from the dealer's by a mechanic. She wrapped her beloved long red scarf around her neck, flung back the end of it, waved gaily to her friends, crying, "*Adieu, mes amis! Je vais à la gloire!*" The driver started up and the car moved off with a roar. The long red scarf became entangled in the spokes of the oversized rear wheel, twisted, and snapped Isadora's neck, killing her instantly.

❧ ❧

DUNSANY, Edward John Moreton Drax Plunkett, 18th Baron (1878–1957), *Irish poet, short-story writer, and playwright. His works include the plays* The Glittering Gate *(1909) and* The Laughter of the Gods *(1919).*

1 Dunsany Castle, the home of Lord Dunsany in County Meath, Ireland, was sacked by the Black and Tans (a British armed force sent to Ireland to combat the republican movement, Sinn Fein). As the soldiers departed, leaving a trail of destruction in their wake, Lord Dunsany's butler politely inquired, "Who shall I say called?"

> Mme du Martel, one of Mme du Deffand's circle in eighteenth-century France, shared her gentle, smiling philosophy. Very ill and facing death, she said to a friend at her bedside, "My consolation is that I am confident that somewhere at this very moment people are making love."

DU PONT, Thomas Coleman (1863–1930), *US entrepreneur and politician; senator from Delaware (1921–22, 1925). He built the Delaware highway named after him and donated it to the state.*

1 On arrival at a Chicago hotel, Du Pont found that a lady who had previously occupied his room had left behind a frilly nightgown. He summoned the manager, handed him the garment, and instructed, "Fill it, and bring it back."

ಕ್�   ಆ

DURANTE, Jimmy ["Schnozzola"] (1893–1980), *US comedian, known for his large nose.*

1 (When Eddie Cantor and Jimmy Durante as young beginners were singing and playing together in cafés, Cantor would encourage Durante to quit piano playing and try something more ambitious on the vaudeville stage.)

" 'I know you want to be a piano player, but piano playing is going to get you nothing. You'll be a piano player till you're a hundred years old. You gotta look further than that. People like you a whole lot. So why don't you get up on the floor and say something to the people? Make remarks while you're playing the piano?' To this Jimmy answered, 'Gee, Eddie, I couldn't do that. I'd be afraid people would laugh at me.' "

2 (Clifton Fadiman recalls an occasion when Jimmy Durante was one of the two guest experts on his radio program *Information Please.*)

"Hoping for some typically Durantean entanglement with the English language, I asked the experts, 'Can you touch your scapula with your patella?' Jimmy's comment was unexpected: 'I hope your program ain't getting off-color.' "

3 Jimmy Durante's father, Bartolomeo Durante, arrived in America in his twenties. One of the first jobs he had was as a day laborer for a contractor's agent. He joined a construction crew on the Third Avenue El in New York and later became the nightwatchman, a duty he took very seriously. "Pop told me," Jimmy recalled later, "that in all the nights he stood guard on the El nobody ever stole a girder off'n him."

4 The climax of one of Durante's television shows was a sketch with Helen Traubel, the great opera diva. They sang a duet, a song called "The Song's Gotta Come from the Heart." The unlikely combination proved a tremendous success, and the song was later recorded as a Victor Red Seal record. On this occasion the grateful Mme Traubel said, "It's a pleasure to record with a great *artiste* whose voice sounds the same with bad needles."

5 Jimmy stepped into a crowded Waldorf Astoria elevator on his way to a dinner party on the Starlight roof. In the elevator he was of course recognized at once. One man said, "Mr. Durante, I saw you on television and I just want to shake your hand." A lady gushed, "Mr. Durante, I've never laughed so hard in my life." The compliments multiplied; Jimmy blushed, held up his hands, and said, "Folks, folks — save them adjectives — we got thoity floors to go!"

ಕ್ಷ   ಆ

DUROCHER, Leo (1906–   ), *US baseball manager, formerly a feisty player known for his aggressive style and tough tactics.*

1 Asked if he didn't feel sorry to have beaten such a "nice bunch of guys" as the New York Giants when he was manager of the Brooklyn Dodgers in the 1940s, Durocher coined the classic: "Nice guys finish last."

ಕ್ಷ   ಆ

DUSE, Eleonora (1859–1924), *Italian actress. She won international fame for her tragic and romantic roles, especially in the plays of contemporary French dramatists, Ibsen, and her lover, Gabriele D'Annunzio.*

1 On her California tour Eleonora had as her personal press representative a charming journalist named Sam Davis. He was the editor of

the *Carson Appeal* and also wrote for the *San Francisco Examiner*. Duse grew very fond of him and when it came time for her to return to New York, just before the "All aboard!", she kissed him first on one cheek, then on the other, and finally on the mouth. "The right cheek is for the *Carson Appeal,* the left for the *Examiner,* and the mouth, my dear friend, for yourself." Davis thanked her, then added, "I also represent the Associated Press, which serves three hundred and eighty newspapers west of Kansas."

2 Eleonora Duse offered to look after the year-old baby of some friends while they went out. The parents wondered about the famous actress's competence with babies, but she assured them that she was full of dodges for entertaining infants. When the parents returned, they found their child sitting up gazing transfixed at the baby-sitter, who was lying on the sofa, snoring sonorously. Duse opened one eye. "Ssh," she said. "If I stop snoring for an instant she yells." She had, she reported, run through her whole gamut of singing, dancing, face-pulling, and other tricks and the baby had wailed throughout. The moment she had begun pretending to snore the baby had sat quite silent, mesmerized.

ಶಿ ⊷ई

DUVAL, Claude (1643–70), *British highwayman, born in Normandy.*

1 Duval's exploits were the subject of many ballads and pamphlets around the time of his trial and execution. The most famous of these concerns his reputation for gallantry toward ladies and his appreciation of the finer arts of life, which he had no doubt learned when he was page to the Duke of Richmond. It was said that one day on Hounslow Heath Duval and his gang stopped a coach in which sat a knight and his young wife. The lady, to show her unconcern, took a flageolet from her pocket and proceeded to play upon it. Thereupon, Duval also took out a flageolet and the highwayman and his victim played very prettily together. "Sir," said Duval, "your lady plays excellently and I doubt not she dances quite as well. Will you please to get out and let me have the honor of a dance with her upon the Heath?" The knight did not think it prudent to oppose the highwayman's wishes, so the lady got out and

she and the highwayman danced upon the Heath. When the dance was over, Duval turned to the husband. "You have forgotten to pay for the music," he said. "No, I have not," replied the knight, and handed Duval a bag containing £100. Now Duval knew well that the couple had another £300 concealed in their coach, but he accepted the £100 with a good grace, bade the lady a courteous farewell, and rode off.

ಶಿ ⊷ई

DUVEEN, Joseph, Baron Duveen of Millbank (1869–1939), *British art dealer.*

1 Duveen's advice and help were sought by millionaires anxious to build up their own art collections. Told that Edsel Ford was beginning to acquire a collection, Duveen is said to have remarked, "He's not ready for me yet. Let him go on buying. Some day he'll be big enough for me."

2 Shortly after Duveen had sold a Dürer painting for several hundred thousand dollars to an important New York client, he attended a gathering at the client's home. One of the fellow guests was a young French art scholar to whom the client's daughter showed off the Dürer. He studied it closely for several minutes and then whispered, "You know, I don't think this Dürer is right." The girl promptly reported his verdict to her father, and the collector, somewhat shaken, turned to Duveen. Duveen laughed and said, "How very amusing. Do you realize, young man, that at least twenty other art experts here and in Europe have been taken in too, and have said that painting isn't genuine? And now you've made the same mistake." His breezy confidence made everyone else in the room feel uncomfortably ignorant, and soon had even the young Frenchman apologizing for his "error."

3 A rival firm of art dealers had sent an Old Master religious painting to one of their clients, a rather straitlaced duke. The duke, not sure whether to buy, asked Duveen for an opinion. Duveen examined the painting and pronounced it very nice. "But," he added, "I assume you are aware that cherubs are homosexual." The duke did not buy the painting.

4 Duveen was a brilliant showman when it came to displaying his pictures to his clients.

One afternoon as they were walking around Andrew Mellon's extensive collection, a shaft of light from a stormy sky happened to fall onto an Old Master, illuminating its rich and dramatic colors. "Ah," said Mellon a bit wistfully, "the pictures always look better when you're here."

5   In 1920 Duveen and some of the other major art dealers decided on a determined attempt to divert some of Henry Ford's millions into the art market. They clubbed together to produce exquisite full-color reproductions of the "hundred greatest paintings in the world" and had these plates bound into three magnificent volumes, which they took along to the Ford residence. Ford was delighted, admired the pictures extravagantly, and thanked the delegation of dealers for showing him their splendid books. The dealers thought the time ripe to broach the real business. By a curious coincidence, they explained, every one of the pictures represented in the books was for sale and they would be happy to assist Mr. Ford in any way they could to acquire these art treasures for his own. A look of puzzlement spread over Ford's face. He explained courteously that he was not really in the market for buying such big expensive books. Duveen hastened to reassure him: the books were a gift. Ford protested that he could not possibly accept such a valuable present from strangers. At this impasse Duveen was obliged to come clean and explain that the books had been specially made up to interest him in buying the originals of the pictures. At last Ford understood. "But, gentlemen," he protested, "why would I want to buy originals when the pictures here in these books are so beautiful?"

෯ ෯

DYSON, Sir Cyril (1895–?), *British jeweler. He joined the family business of jewelers, watchmakers, and opticians in 1919 and was managing director from 1948 to 1972. He was also president of the National Association of Goldsmiths of Great Britain and Northern Ireland (1957–70).*

1   Presenting the graduation prizes at a girls' school, Dyson found it difficult to think of something different to say to each girl. As an attractive seventeen-year-old approached him across the platform, he could come up with nothing more original than: "And what are you going to do when you leave school?" With a coy flutter of her eyelids, the girl replied, "Well, I *had* thought of going straight home."

E

EDDINGTON, Sir Arthur Stanley (1882–1944), *British astrophysicist and popularizer of science. He was responsible for discovering that the sun's temperature must be millions of degrees Celsius or it would collapse. His* Expanding Universe *(1933) propounds the theory that the galaxies are flying apart.*

1 Eddington was once asked how many people could really understand his theory of the expanding universe. He paused, then said, "Perhaps seven."

❦

EDDY, Mary Baker (1821–1910), *US religious leader. In 1879 she founded the Church of Christ, Scientist, in Boston.*

1 Bronson Alcott, the philosopher and father of Louisa May Alcott, came one day to visit the Massachusetts Metaphysical College, which Mrs. Eddy had established to train practitioners of Christian Science. He encountered by chance a young man named George Barry and fell into conversation with him. Much impressed by Barry's mental ability, he asked him his age. "Five years old," was the response. Then, noting Alcott's puzzlement, Barry continued: "It's five years since I first met Mrs. Eddy."

❦

EDEN, [Robert] Anthony, 1st Earl of Avon (1897–1977), *British statesman; prime minister (1955–57). The Suez crisis of 1956 led to his downfall. He was created Earl of Avon in 1961.*

1 Shortly before Eden became prime minister, the journalist Alistair Cooke asked the aging Bertrand Russell his opinion of Eden. "Not a gentleman; dresses too well," was the verdict.

EDEN, Sir William (1849–1915), *British baronet, father of Anthony Eden (later Lord Avon).*

1 As the father of a future prime minister, Sir William Eden could be surprisingly undignified at times. Although he usually restricted himself to dry comments, such as "the progress of civilization is the decay of taste," he could be stirred to more violent action. On one occasion, when the weather had looked promising but then turned to rain, Sir William shook his fist at the clouds beyond the window and yelled, "Just *like* you, God!" He then tore the barometer, which still indicated "Fair," off the wall and threw it through that same window with the cry, "There, you damned fool, see for yourself!"

❦

EDISON, Charles (1890–1969), *US politician. The son of Thomas Alva Edison, he was governor of New Jersey from 1941 to 1944.*

1 Campaigning for the governorship in 1940, Edison was anxious to dissociate himself from his father's renown. "I would not have anyone believe I am trading on the name Edison," he would explain as he introduced himself. "I would rather have you know me merely as the result of one of my father's earlier experiments."

❦

EDISON, Thomas Alva (1847–1931), *US inventor responsible for about thirteen hundred inventions, the most famous of which is the electric light bulb (1879). He also invented the gramophone and motion pictures, and his carbon transmitter enabled Bell's telephone to be brought into practical use.*

1 Edison was asked to sign a guest book that had the usual columns for name and address, as

well as one for "Interested in." In this last column Edison entered the word: "Everything."

2   Edison was concerned about the way in which acquaintances visiting his office helped themselves to his Havana cigars. As he could not be bothered to lock them up, his secretary suggested that a friend of his in the cigar trade should roll some cigars made from cabbage leaves in brown paper and that these should be substituted for the Havanas. Edison agreed, then forgot about it, and only remembered some time later when the Havanas started vanishing again. He called his secretary and inquired why the bogus cigars had not arrived. The secretary said that they had and that he had handed them over to Edison's manager. The manager explained that, not knowing what they were, he had packed them in Edison's bag when he had gone away on a visit. "And do you know," Edison concluded, "I smoked every one of those damned cigars myself!"

3   Someone remarked on the huge number of failures Edison had encountered in his search for a new storage battery — fifty thousand experiments before he achieved results. "Results?" said the inventor. "Why, I have gotten a lot of results. I know fifty thousand things that won't work."

4   Edison had a summer residence of which he was very proud. He enjoyed showing visitors around his property, pointing out the various labor-saving devices. At one point it was necessary to pass through a turnstile in order to take the main path back to the house. Considerable effort was needed to move the turnstile. A guest asked Edison why it was that, with all the other clever gadgets around, he had such a heavy turnstile. Edison replied, "Well, you see, everyone who pushes the turnstile around pumps eight gallons of water into the tank on my roof."

5   After a series of electrical storms at Orange, New Jersey, the vestrymen of a certain church there discussed the desirability of placing lightning rods on the structure. They then sought Edison's advice, who asked them what sort of building it was. "A church," was the reply. "By all means put lightning rods on," said Edison. "You know Providence is absentminded at times."

6   The great journalist Henry Morton Stanley went to hear Edison's phonograph tested. After the demonstration he asked Edison whose voice, out of all the people in history, Edison would most like to have heard. "Napoleon's," replied Edison instantly. "The voice that I should most like to hear," said Stanley in a reproving tone, "is that of our Savior." Edison, slightly embarrassed by Stanley's display of piety, said deprecatingly, "Well, you know I like a hustler."

7   Henry Ford had Edison's electrical laboratory moved from Menlo Park to Dearborn. The reassembled building was opened on October 29, 1929. After the ceremony Henry Ford asked Edison what he thought of it. "It's ninety-nine and a half percent perfect," replied Edison. "Why, what's wrong?" asked Ford, who prided himself on the accuracy of the reconstruction. "Well, we never used to keep the place so clean," said Edison.

8   Edison found formal dinners extremely tedious. On one occasion, the company was so dull that the inventor made up his mind to escape to his laboratory at the earliest opportunity. Unfortunately, his host accosted him as he hovered near the door. "It certainly is a delight to see you, Mr. Edison," he said. "What are you working on now?"
"My exit," replied Edison.

9   The Western Union Company had offered Edison a hundred thousand dollars for one of his inventions. Such a sum was beyond the inventor's comprehension. "The money is safer with you," he replied. "Give me six thousand dollars a year for seventeen years."

৩৯ ৎৡ

EDMAN, Irwin (1896–1954), *US philosopher and educator. On the Columbia University faculty from 1920, he became a professor in 1935.*

1   By a private arrangement Professor Edman had access to the swimming pool of his friend, the book publisher Bob Haas. On one occasion Edman bathed alone and, still in his wet bathing suit, wandered into Haas's living room. There he spotted a volume of Thucydides and sat down to read a few pages. Later on, after Edman had left, Mrs. Haas returned to find a pool of water in the middle of her living room.

"It's that dog again!" she cried angrily. The French maid quickly put her right: "No, madame, not the dog. The professor!"

2 Professor Edman's absentmindedness, in fact, was his trademark and the source of much humor at Columbia University. One day he stopped a student on Riverside Drive and asked, "Pardon me, but am I walking north or south?" The student answered, "North, Professor." "Ah," replied Edman, "then I've had my lunch."

3 Another time, at a dinner party, the host was insisting to publisher Bennett Cerf that Irwin Edman couldn't possibly be as absentminded as Cerf's stories made him out to be.

"Of course they're true," Cerf countered.

At that moment ice cream was being offered to the guests, and Professor Edman, who happened to be present, took a generous helping from the server and plopped it directly into his finger bowl.

"See what I mean?"

୬~ ∽૬

EDWARD I (1239–1307), *king of England (1272–1307). He encouraged parliamentary institutions at the expense of feudalism, subdued Wales, and campaigned against the Scots.*

1 After the death in 1282 of Prince Llewelyn ab Gruffydd, leader of the Welsh resistance to English encroachments, Edward I promised the Welsh a new Prince of Wales "who would not speak a word of English." In fulfillment of this promise he presented the assembled Welsh chieftains with his infant son (later Edward II) a few days after his birth in Caernarvon Castle. According to some reports he held the royal baby aloft in his arms and proclaimed in Welsh, "*Eich dyn*" (literally, "This is your man").

{The Prince of Wales's emblem is the motto *Ich dien* (I serve), surmounted by three white ostrich feathers, but the foregoing story for the origin of the Prince of Wales is probably not true. According to other reports, the motto and emblem first became associated with the heir to the British throne when Edward the Black Prince, Edward II's grandson, took them from the heraldic insignia of the king of Bohemia, whom the Black Prince slew at the battle of Crécy in 1346.}

EDWARD III (1312–77), *king of England (1327–77). He assumed power by imprisoning his mother (Isabella of France, wife of Edward II) and executing her lover, Mortimer, after they had murdered his father. His claim to the French throne started the Hundred Years' War, which saw great English victories at Crécy (1346) and Poitiers (1356) during Edward's reign. He also campaigned in Scotland, planning to effect a union between Scotland and England.*

1 Edward's military adventures made him eager to attract Europe's best soldiers into his service. He therefore decided to found an order of knighthood based on King Arthur's legendary Round Table. On St. George's Day, 1344, he arranged a grand jousting tournament and banquet at Windsor Castle. By some accounts, it was at this banquet that the order of the Knights of the Garter was founded. The Countess of Salisbury, accidentally or otherwise, dropped her garter while dancing with the king. He instantly retrieved it. Observing the knowing nudges and looks of the bystanders, Edward fastened the garter around his own leg, saying (in Old French), "*Honi soit qui mal y pense*" (Shame on him who thinks ill of it).

{A different account of the origin of the Order of the Garter relates to the battle of Crécy, at which the king is reported to have displayed his garter as a signal for the battle to commence. The subsequent success of the English army led Edward to commemorate the event by founding the Order of the Garter.}

2 Edward the Black Prince, Edward's eldest son, sixteen years old at the battle of Crécy, was in the forefront of the fighting. A messenger hurried up to the English king, reporting that the Black Prince was in some danger. Edward refused to send reinforcements or to recall his son. "Let the boy win his spurs," was all he said.

୬~ ∽૬

EDWARD VII (1841–1910), *king of the United Kingdom (1901–10). In his youth his mother, Queen Victoria, excluded him from active participation in public affairs because of his indiscreet life. Nevertheless, he and his wife, Queen Alexandra, became popular monarchs.*

He played an active role in diplomacy, strengthening Britain's ties with France against his hated German nephew, Kaiser William.

1 While Edward VII was Prince of Wales, one of his closest associates was Lord Charles Beresford. Once when the prince invited him to dinner, Beresford cabled back: "VERY SORRY CANT COME LIE FOLLOWS BY POST."
{Told of others.}

2 In turn-of-the-century Paris one of the most dedicated social climbers was Mrs. Kate Moore, an American millionairess. After energetically pursuing him for some time she captured her prize trophy: the Prince of Wales accepted an invitation to dine at her Biarritz palace. The future Edward VII, far from being irritated by her assiduousness, was amused at her good-natured vulgarity. "Madam, you should have lived in the days of Louis the Fourteenth," he remarked. "In those days there were kings everywhere."

3 Edward's self-permissive conduct, as Prince of Wales and king, was partly a reaction to his mother's impossibly virtuous standards of conduct. When Lady Beaconsfield once suggested that her son must be a great comfort to her, Queen Victoria replied, "Comfort! Why, I caught him smoking a fortnight after his dear father died!"

4 During the 1897 Diamond Jubilee Edward often had to represent his mother at public events. One of the hymns frequently sung and played on these occasions was "Eternal Father, Strong to Save." He once muttered, "It's all very well about the Eternal Father. But what about my eternal mother?"

5 As Queen Victoria lay dying, a member of the royal household discussed the imminent event with Edward, the Prince of Wales. "I wonder if she will be happy in heaven?" he mused.
"I don't know," said the prince. "She will have to walk *behind* the angels—and she won't like that!"

6 Even the great, confronted by the unfamiliar in foreign parts, can become confused. Edward VII, recalling a visit he paid to Colonel James Biddle and his family, certainly did. "In Philadelphia, when I was the Prince of Wales, I met a large and interesting family named Scrapple. They served me a rather delicious native food, too—something, I believe, called biddle."
{Philadelphia scrapple is a seasoned mixture of ground meat and cornmeal set in a mold and served sliced and fried.}

7 As king, Edward would alternate social charm with an irritable demandingness that often made things hard for his friends and courtiers. One of his hostesses, Lady Brougham, noticing his black mood, sought to cheer him up. "Did you notice, sir, the soap in Your Majesty's bathroom?"
"No!"
"I thought you might, sir. . . . It has such an *amorous* lather!"
It is reported that the king's cheerfulness was restored.

8 A fashionable hostess who had spent a fortune on redecorating her house entertained the king for the first time. Was everything to his liking, she asked. He thought for a moment, and then said it might be a good idea to put a hook in the bathroom door.

9 When the opera *The Wreckers* was first staged in 1909, influential friends of the composer, Dame Ethel Smyth, persuaded Edward VII to grace the opening night. Later, conductor Sir Thomas Beecham asked the king's private secretary, who had accompanied him to the opera, what the king had thought of it. "I don't know," said the private secretary. "Didn't he say anything?" persisted Beecham. "Well, yes," admitted the private secretary. "He did say something. He suddenly woke up three-quarters of the way through and said, 'Fritz, that's the fourth time that infernal noise has roused me.'"

10 A pompous young minister once used the royal pronoun "We," referring only to himself, in the presence of Edward VII. The king picked him up at once: "Only two people are permitted to refer to themselves as 'We'—a king, and a man with a tapeworm inside him."
{Possibly an old joke.}

11 Edward was not remarkable for his wit, but there is something endearing in his mild rebuke to a footman who accidentally emptied a jug of cream over him: "My good man, I'm not a strawberry."

છ્ક્ર   જ્વ

EDWARD VIII (1894–1972), *king of the United Kingdom (1936). He abdicated because of the furor over his liaison with the American divorcée Wallis Warfield Simpson, whom he married in France in 1937. Given the title of Duke of Windsor, he was governor of the Bahamas during World War II. Later he lived in France.*

1   On a visit to the United States in the twenties, while Prince of Wales, Edward was nearly caught in a raid on a nightclub run by the celebrated hostess Texas Guinan. The police, however, never realized his identity, thanks to the quick thinking of Texas, who hurried him out to the kitchen, put a chef's hat on his head and a skillet in his hand, and told him to keep cooking eggs until the raid was over.

2   Addressing a group of friends on the subject of remaining on friendly terms with one's wife, the Duke of Windsor remarked, "Of course, I do have a slight advantage over the rest of you. It helps in a pinch to be able to remind your bride that you gave up a throne for her."

3   The Homestead is a luxurious resort hotel in Hot Springs, Virginia, the haunt of many distinguished visitors, among whom have been counted the Duke and Duchess of Windsor. In 1943 they spent an entire happy month there. As they prepared to leave, the bill was presented. The duke looked at it blankly and muttered, "Now what do I do with *this?*"
   The bill has not yet been paid.

છ્ક્ર   જ્વ

EINSTEIN, Albert (1879–1955), *German-born physicist of Jewish descent, who lived in the United States after Hitler's accession to power in 1933. In 1905 Einstein published four papers that held revolutionary implications for physics. Among them was his special theory of relativity. In 1915 he published his general theory of relativity. He won the Nobel Prize for physics in 1921.*

1   (Otto Neugebauer, the historian of ancient mathematics, told a story about the boy Ein-

stein that he characterizes as a "legend," but that seems fairly authentic.)
   As he was a late talker, his parents were worried. At last, at the supper table one night, he broke his silence to say, "The soup is too hot." Greatly relieved, his parents asked why he had never said a word before. Albert replied, "Because up to now everything was in order."

2   An expedition to observe the 1919 solar eclipse verified Einstein's prediction, based on his general theory of relativity, concerning the curvature of space. A pupil asked him, "What would you have said if there had been no confirmation of this kind?"
   "I would have been obliged to pity our dear God," replied Einstein. "The theory is correct."

3   When Einstein and his friend and colleague Philipp Frank were to visit the Berlin Astrophysical Observatory, they agreed to rendezvous on a certain bridge at Potsdam. Frank, who did not know the town well, was worried that he might be late, but Einstein told him not to worry, that he would wait on the bridge. Frank said he was concerned that that might waste Einstein's time. Einstein dismissed the objection. "The kind of work I do can be done anywhere. Why should I be less capable of reflecting about my problems on the Potsdam bridge than at home?"

4   "On a visit to Palestine in 1921 Einstein went to look at a kibbutz. . . . He asked a great many questions of the 22-year-old girl who was head of the young community. One of his questions was, 'What is the relationship here of men to women?' Thinking that he was one of the many visitors who were of the opinion that women were common property in the kibbutz she stammered with embarrassment,

---

"The late Eddie Erdelatz was the Naval Academy football coach in the 1950s. When his team played West Point to a 7–7 tie Eddie was asked his reaction. 'A tie game,' he said, 'is like kissing your sister.'"

— James C. Humes, *Speaker's Treasury*

'But, Herr Professor, each man here has one woman.' Einstein's eyes twinkled. He took the girl's hand and said, 'Don't be alarmed at my question. We physicists understand by the word "relationship" something rather simple, namely, how many men are there and how many women.'"

5   In 1927 the physicist Werner Heisenberg enunciated his principle of uncertainty, or indeterminacy. This states (roughly) that the position and velocity of an object cannot both be measured exactly at the same time.

Einstein never accepted the principle, for it would play havoc with the strict determinism in which he believed. As he often said and wrote, "God does not play dice with the universe." He and Niels Bohr carried on a controversy for many years. In 1930 at the Solvay conference in Brussels they had a celebrated discussion of the matter. Einstein had invented an imaginary device involving clocks and scales, which, he affirmed, appeared to violate the uncertainty principle. But, following a sleepless night, Bohr found that Einstein in the course of his argument had forgotten to take into account the consequences of one of his own discoveries — in a gravitational field clocks run slower.

The uncertainty principle still stood firm.

6   (When L. L. Whyte was a young theoretical physicist studying in Berlin in the late 1920s, an acquaintance arranged for him to meet Einstein. Whyte, diffident about intruding upon the great man, was delighted to receive a friendly letter from Einstein, inviting him to call. The letter concluded, "Don't be put off by Frau Einstein. She's there to protect me." Whyte recounts what happened during his visit to Einstein's home.)

"After we had been talking for about twenty minutes the maid came in with a huge bowl of soup. I wondered what was happening and I thought that this was probably a signal for me to leave. But when the girl left the room Einstein said to me in a conspiratorial whisper, 'That's a trick. If I am bored talking to somebody, when the maid comes in I don't push the bowl of soup away and the girl takes whomever I am with away and I am free.' Einstein pushed the bowl away, and so I was quite happy and much flattered and more at my ease for the rest of the talk."

7   Speaking at the Sorbonne during the 1930s, Einstein said, "If my relativity theory is verified, Germany will proclaim me a German and France will call me a citizen of the world. But if my theory is proved false, France will emphasize that I am a German and Germany will say that I am a Jew."

8   After Einstein had gone into exile, a hundred Nazi professors published a book condemning his theory of relativity. Einstein was unconcerned. "If I were wrong," he said, "one professor would have been enough."

9   The classical scholar Gilbert Murray one day encountered Einstein sitting in the quadrangle of Christ Church, Oxford. The exiled scientist was deep in thought, with a serene and cheerful expression on his face. Murray asked him what he was thinking about. "I am thinking that, after all, this is a very small star," Einstein answered.

10   On August 6, 1945, the world's first nuclear weapon was dropped on Hiroshima, Japan. Two hundred and eighty-two thousand human beings died and tens of thousands more were left burned, maimed, and homeless. Einstein, whose letter to Roosevelt had initiated the American effort that resulted in the atom bomb and whose special theory of relativity formed its theoretical basis, heard the news on the radio. For a long time he could find only the two Yiddish words traditionally used by Jews in such circumstances: "Oi vey."

11   Einstein's wife was once asked if she understood her husband's theory of relativity. "No," she replied loyally, "but I know my husband and I know he can be trusted."

12   It is alleged that when Einstein and his wife visited the Mount Wilson Observatory in California, Mrs. Einstein pointed to a particularly complex piece of equipment and asked its purpose. Their guide said that it was used to determine the shape of the universe. "Oh," she said, not at all impressed, "my husband uses the back of an old envelope to work that out."

13   Einstein and an assistant, having finished a paper, searched the office for a paper clip. They finally found one, too badly bent for use. They looked for an implement to straighten it, and

after opening many more drawers came upon a whole box of clips. Einstein at once shaped one into a tool to straighten the bent clip. His assistant, puzzled, asked why he was doing this when there was a whole boxful of usable clips. "Once I am set on a goal it becomes difficult to deflect me," said Einstein.

{Einstein said to an assistant at Princeton that this was the most characteristic anecdote that could be told of him.}

14 A certain distinguished astronomer once declared at a scientific meeting: "To an astronomer, man is nothing more than an insignificant dot in an infinite universe."

"I have often felt that," said Einstein. "But then I realize that the insignificant dot who is man is also the astronomer."

15 "The laws of physics should be simple," said Einstein, lecturing at Princeton. "But what if they are not simple?" came a voice from the audience. Replied Einstein: "Then I would not be interested in them."

16 During his stay in Princeton, New Jersey, Einstein used to play his violin in a string quartet. He enjoyed these sessions, but the other musicians were less enthusiastic about his skills. Complained one of the other players after a private performance, "He can't count."

17 Einstein's scientific theories and investigations were an impenetrable mystery to his second wife, Elsa. "Couldn't you tell me a little about your work?" she complained one day. "People talk a lot about it, and I appear so stupid when I say I know nothing." Einstein thought for a minute or two, frowning deeply as he searched for a way to begin his explanation. Suddenly, his face cleared. "If people ask," he said, "tell them you know all about it, but can't tell them, as it is a great secret!"

18 The journal *Scientific American* once ran a competition for the best exposition of relativity in three thousand words. A prize of several thousand dollars was at stake. "I'm the only one in my entire circle of friends who is not entering," remarked Einstein ruefully. "I don't believe I could do it."

19 In the course of conversation at an American dinner party Einstein's neighbor, a young girl, asked the white-haired professor: "What are you actually by profession?" Einstein replied: "I devote myself to the study of physics." The girl looked at him in astonishment. "You mean to say you study physics at your age?" she exclaimed. "I finished mine a year ago."

20 A young friend of Einstein's proudly presented his eighteen-month-old son to the great scientist. The child looked up into the old man's smiling face and promptly began to howl. Einstein patted him on the head and said fondly, "You're the first person for years who has told me what you really think of me."

ॐ॰ ॰ॐ

EISENHOWER, Dwight David (1890–1969), *US general and statesman; 34th president of the United States (1953–61). During World War II he commanded US troops in Britain and Allied troops in North Africa and Italy (1942–43) before becoming supreme Allied commander in charge of the Normandy landings (1943–44). In 1951 he assumed supreme command of NATO. As president, he tried to stabilize the Middle East against Communist influence by offering economic and military aid —the Eisenhower Doctrine (1957).*

1 After the successful landings in France, Eisenhower was inspecting a British section of the Allied lines when German planes came over and strafed them. The party dived for cover. As soon as it was safe to emerge a senior British officer hurried across to see if Eisenhower was all right. Finding him unharmed, he expressed his relief in fervent terms. Ike thanked him for his solicitude. "Oh," said the officer, "my concern was just that nothing should happen to you in *my* sector."

2 General Eisenhower was called upon to address a graduating class at an illustrious university. "Your business is to put me out of business," he told them.

3 During his first term Eisenhower appointed Arthur Burns as his first chairman of the Council of Economic Advisors. (Dr. Burns later served as chairman of the Federal Reserve and ambassador to Germany under President Reagan.) At their first meeting Burns suggested that he send Ike a memo outlining a plan for organizing the flow of economic advice to the president. Said Ike, "Keep it short. I can't read." Replied Burns, "We'll get along fine. I can't write." (It worked out well: the two settled on a one-hour weekly conference of the council and the president.)

4 Some months after the end of his term as president, Eisenhower was asked if leaving the White House had affected his golf game. "Yes," he replied, "a lot more people beat me now."

ફ્રેબ્ડ ન્જ્જ્

ELEANOR of Aquitaine (c. 1122–1204), *French queen consort. She was first the wife of Louis VII of France, then divorced him in 1152 and married Henry II of England in 1154. In later years she fomented rebellion against Henry among his sons and he imprisoned her. When her eldest son, Richard Coeur de Lion, came to the throne, he released his mother, who became regent of England while he was crusading.*

1 Eleanor's petition for divorce from Louis VII was based on the pretext that they were too closely related for their marriage to be legal in the eyes of the church. The divorce was granted. Two years later, when Eleanor married Henry II, she remarked with satisfaction, "I am queen of England by the wrath of God."

ફ્રેબ્ડ ન્જ્જ્

ELIOT, Charles William (1834–1926), *US educator. President of Harvard for forty years (1869–1909), he instituted major reforms, including raising the standards for entry and introducing science courses into the curriculum. On the other hand, under his influence all required courses were abolished.*

1 At a dinner in Eliot's honor the professors at Harvard vied with each other in proposing toasts to their president. One speaker congratulated him on achieving miracles at the university: "Since you became president, Harvard has become a storehouse of knowledge." Eliot responded: "What you say is true, but I can claim little credit for it. It is simply that the freshmen bring so much and the seniors take so little away."

2 During his many years as president of Harvard, Charles W. Eliot expressed frequent misgivings about sports. At one point Eliot announced at the end of a successful baseball season that he was thinking of dropping the sport. Pressed for an explanation, he said, "Well, this year I'm told the team did well because one pitcher had a fine curve ball. I understand that a curve ball is thrown with a deliberate attempt to deceive. Surely that is not an ability we should want to foster at Harvard."

ફ્રેબ્ડ ન્જ્જ્

ELIOT, John (1604–90), *British missionary. Emigrating to America in 1631, he devoted the rest of his life to proselytizing the American Indians.*

1 While translating the Bible into a language of the American Indians, Eliot found himself unable to translate the word "lattice" in the sentence: "The mother of Sisera looked out at a window, and cried through the lattice." He described the object in question to a number of Indian friends, one of whom offered what he thought to be an appropriate translation. Years later Eliot discovered, to his great amusement, that his rendering of the passage in the Indian Bible read: "The mother of Sisera looked out at a window, and cried through the eel-pot."

ફ્રેબ્ડ ન્જ્જ્

ELIOT, T[homas] S[tearns] (1888–1965), *American-born poet. He worked briefly as a bank clerk in London before his volume of poetry,* Prufrock and Other Observations *(1917), appeared.* The Waste Land *(1922) is a commentary on the spiritual sterility of contemporary life. From 1922 he edited* The Criterion, *a critical review that influenced the development of modern poetry. His* Four Quartets *(1935–41) was his major poetic achievement. In later years he turned to writing verse dramas, among them* Murder in the Cathedral *(1935) and* The Cocktail Party *(1949). He won the 1948 Nobel Prize for literature.*

1 I. A. Richards, the eminent literary critic and scholar, knew T. S. Eliot when he was a junior member of the staff of Lloyd's Bank in Queen Henrietta Street, London, at the end of World War I. By chance he met one of Eliot's superiors on holiday in Switzerland and the two men discovered that the poet was a mutual acquaintance. The senior banker was a pleasant man who seemed unable to frame a question that he obviously wanted to put to Richards. Eventually it came out: did Richards think that Eliot was a *good* poet? Richards replied that in his opinion, which would not be shared by everyone, Eliot was a good poet. The other man was pleased to hear it. Some of his colleagues considered that banking and poetry did not go together, but in his view if a man had a hobby and did it well it helped him in his work. He ended by telling Richards that he could tell Eliot that if he continued to do as well as he was doing at the bank, "I don't see why — in time, of course, in time — he mightn't even become a branch manager." Richards found great delight in relating this conversation to Eliot.

2   Critics and admirers of Eliot's work both found *Four Quartets* obscure. During his lecture tours students took the opportunity to question Eliot on the meaning of the poems. Louis Untermeyer repeated to Eliot a story he had heard of how a student at a midwestern university had volunteered a lengthy analysis of a passage from "East Coker." Eliot was said to have listened patiently. At the end the young man had said, "Isn't that what it means?" and Eliot responded, "It may very well mean that." Eliot smiled as Untermeyer finished his story, then remarked, "I may very well have said that."

3   On his way to Stockholm for the Nobel prize-giving ceremony, Eliot was interviewed by a reporter who asked him for which of his works the prize had been awarded. Eliot replied that he believed it was for the entire corpus. "And when did you publish that?" asked the reporter. Eliot observed afterward that *The Entire Corpus* might make rather a good title for a mystery story.

4   At a meeting of the Oxford Poetry Club Eliot was the guest of honor and agreed to answer questions about his work. An undergraduate asked him what he meant by the line from *Ash-Wednesday:* "Lady, three white leopards sat under a juniper-tree." Eliot answered, "I mean, 'Lady, three white leopards sat under a juniper-tree.'"

5   An American arriving in England in 1961 for postgraduate study went to visit Eliot. As he was leaving, he noticed that the poet was apparently searching for the right remark with which to bid him farewell. "Forty years ago I went from Harvard to Oxford," Eliot began. "Now, what advice can I give you?" There was a prolonged pause while the younger man waited breathlessly for the poet's words of wisdom. Finally Eliot said, "Have you any long underwear?"

6   W. H. Auden, finding Eliot engrossed in a game of patience, expressed surprise at his apparent enjoyment of this trivial occupation. "Well," said Eliot thoughtfully, "I suppose it's the nearest thing to being dead."

7   Asked why he did not go the movies more often, Eliot replied, "Because they interfere with my daydreams."

8   Publisher Robert Giroux once asked Eliot whether he agreed with the widely held belief that most editors are failed writers. Eliot pondered for a moment, then said, "Yes, I suppose some editors are failed writers — but so are most writers."

ॐ ✍

ELISABETH (1876–1965), *wife of King Albert I of Belgium (reigned 1909–34), whom she married in 1900. She won the affection of the Belgians by her devotion to duty as a nurse during World War I. Even after King Albert's death in a climbing accident, she exercised considerable influence over the affairs of the Belgian monarchy.*

1   In 1956 Elisabeth visited Soviet-dominated Warsaw. A chief of protocol was assigned to accompany her to mass. She asked him, "Are you a Catholic?"
"Believing," replied the functionary, "but not practicing."
"Of course," said Elisabeth, "then in that case you must be a Communist."
"Practicing, Your Majesty, but not believing."

ॐ ✍

ELIZABETH I (1533–1603), *queen of England and Ireland (1558–1603). The daughter of Henry VIII and Anne Boleyn, she brought about a religious compromise that restored harmony to England after the troubled reign of her Roman Catholic half-sister, Mary. Her champi-*

onship of the Protestant cause in the Netherlands and her aggressive promotion of trade and exploration in the New World resulted in conflict with Spain. From this England emerged with considerable glory after the naval victory over the Spanish Armada (1588). Elizabeth's court took its character from the veneration centered on the queen, a cult she herself assiduously encouraged. Her most favored courtiers, men like Sir Walter Raleigh and the earls of Leicester and Essex, were all successful soldiers or naval commanders.

1   Shortly after Elizabeth came to the throne, a knight who had behaved insolently toward her when she was living in disgrace and obscurity during the reign of her half-sister Mary threw himself at her feet to beseech her pardon. Elizabeth gestured to him to rise, dismissing him with the words, "Do you not know that we are descended of the lion, whose nature is not to prey upon the mouse or any other such small vermin?"

2   On one occasion, as he was bowing low to Queen Elizabeth, Edward de Vere, the Earl of Oxford, audibly broke wind. Deeply embarrassed, the earl withdrew from court and traveled abroad for several years. Upon his return he went to court to pay his respects, and was greeted by the queen. Her first words were: "My lord, I had forgot the fart."

3   The diplomat Valentine Dale, on a mission to Flanders, found himself running short of money. The queen's notorious parsimony was such that he feared he would be unlikely to receive a draft before he became seriously embarrassed for cash. Nonetheless, he wrote to the queen about the affairs of state and his financial position; by the same packet he also sent an affectionate letter to his wife, giving an intimate account of his state of health and mentioning his monetary difficulty. However, the letter intended for the queen was addressed to his wife and vice versa, so that Elizabeth was startled and amused to find herself reading a familiar letter interspersed with such endearments as "sweetheart" and "dear love." The mix-up appealed to her sense of humor, and Dale's financial problem to her sense of diplomatic honor. She promptly sent off a further supply of money, never suspecting that the "mistake" of course had been deliberately contrived by the artful diplomat.

❦ ❦

ELIZABETH II (1926–   ), *queen of the United Kingdom (1952–   ). She has greatly enhanced the prestige of the British monarchy. Her popularity was amply demonstrated at the silver jubilee of her reign (1977).*

1   Toward the end of World War II, the young Princess Elizabeth, anxious to make some contribution to the war effort, joined the Auxiliary Territorial Service. She took a course in heavy mechanics, learning how to service engines and drive military vehicles. On the last day of the course, George VI came upon his daughter, clad in her greasy overalls, working underneath a car. Try as she would, she could not make the engine start. "What, not got it going yet?" asked the king with a smile. He had surreptitiously removed the distributor.

2   The regulations of some of the older London clubs are sacrosanct. One has the rule that no visitors are allowed in the lounge. The queen, arriving at the club for a private dinner party, quickly looked into the room to admire the pictures. "Not in there, Bet," said Prince Philip, and the queen retreated. An elderly member of the club, dozing by the fire, caught

> "The nineteenth century produced great preachers in Wales, some of whom are remembered to this day. John Elias was one such. It is said that the power of his oratory was so great that people would come from miles around to hear him preach. But then, 'preach' is hardly the right word. It was not a sermon, it was a performance with a sense of theatre and enough dread to give it spice. The story is told of his preaching in a small village in mid-Wales on the way the finger of God touched every man. At the height of his peroration he flung out his arm, having carefully arranged the candles beforehand so that the huge shadow of his finger fell upon the wall. Seeing this monstrous arm, the congregation fled."
>
> — Ivor Richard, *We, the British*

sight of her as she left. "Who was that woman? What's she doing here?" he rumbled. "That was the queen, my lord," said a waiter. "Well, dammit, she shouldn't be here," snapped the old man. "Members only, you know."

3 During a visit to the Bahamas the queen's host was seen to take a silver pencil from his pocket and use it to swizzle the bubbles out of a drink. "That's all right in our company," said Queen Elizabeth, "but what happens in high society?"

4 In old age, the former society beauty and ambassadress, Lady Diana Cooper, suffered from failing eyesight. Attending a reception in honor of Sir Robert Mayer's one hundredth birthday at the Festival Hall in London, she fell into conversation with a friendly lady who apparently knew her well and whom, she felt vaguely, she ought to know too. It was only when she peered closely at the magnificent diamonds that she realized she was talking to the queen. Overcome with embarrassment, she managed to curtsy and blurted out, "Ma'am, oh, ma'am, I'm sorry, ma'am. I didn't recognize you without your crown!"

"It was so much Sir Robert's evening," said the queen sweetly, "that I decided to leave it behind."

5 The queen and Prince Philip paid a visit to the White House during Gerald Ford's presidency. Dressing for dinner that evening, the Fords' son Jack mislaid the studs for his dress shirt and rushed to his father's room to see if he could borrow some. He stepped into the elevator, his shirt unfastened and his hair in disarray, only to find it already occupied by his parents and their royal guests. Mrs. Ford, visibly embarrassed, introduced her son. Taking in at a glance the young man's unkempt appearance, the queen remarked sympathetically: "I have one just like that!"

6 "During an interview with the Queen, a British ambassador returning from the Middle East was struggling to explain the character of the head of government with whom he had to deal. He approached it from this angle, and that angle, and roundabout, using increasingly long words with a psychological tinge, until his sovereign extricated him from his misery. 'Are

you trying to tell me,' Her Majesty enquired, 'that the man is just bonkers?'"

ELIZABETH the Queen Mother (1900–   ), *wife of George VI of the United Kingdom, whom she married in 1923. On the unexpected accession of her husband to the throne, she worked hard to help him restore the prestige of the monarchy, badly tarnished by Edward VIII's abdication. After George VI's death (1952) she continued to play an active role, supporting her daughter Elizabeth II and remaining one of the best-loved figures in the British royal family.*

1 As Duchess of York, Elizabeth paid a visit to Marshal Lyautey's Colonial Exhibition at Vincennes. During tea at the lakeside, she said to the marshal, "Monsieur le Maréchal, you are so powerful. You created the beautiful country of Morocco and you have made this fine exhibition. Would you do something for me?" The marshal, a little taken aback, asked what he could do. "The sun is in my eyes," replied the duchess. "Could you make it disappear?" At that moment a cloud passed in front of the sun. The other guests within earshot looked at Lyautey in amazement. Elizabeth smiled graciously. "I saw the cloud coming," she whispered to her neighbor.

2 The queen and her then small daughter Margaret Rose were out walking one day. An effusive lady, recognizing them, approached and exclaimed, "So this is the lovely little lady we've heard so much about!" Margaret at once spoke up firmly: "I'm *not* a little lady. I'm a pr—" The queen interrupted with equal firmness: "She's not *quite* a little lady yet. But she's learning."

{This anecdote is possibly apocryphal.}

3 During the Blitz of London in 1940 the king and queen set an example of steadfastness and devotion to duty. Queen Elizabeth was particularly affected by the sufferings and gallantry of the poor people of London's East End, many of whom lost their homes and all they possessed. One day Buckingham Palace received a direct hit from a bomb. The queen, surveying the damage, remarked that she was not entirely sorry: "Now we can look the East End in the face."

4 When asked whether the little princesses (Elizabeth and Margaret Rose) would leave England after the Blitz, the queen replied: "The children will not leave unless I do. I shall not leave unless their father does, and the king will not leave the country in any circumstances whatever."

{For a similar statement that runs in the opposite direction, *see* THEMISTOCLES 2.}

5 During World War II, the Hungarian-born film director Vincent Korda helped to stage a private pantomime in which the princesses Elizabeth and Margaret took part, together with other children connected with the royal household. Afterward he was invited to have tea with King George and Queen Elizabeth. Feeling uneasy in his exalted surroundings, Korda squirmed on his chair and in his heavily accented English did his best to make conversation. Queen Elizabeth noticed his distress and asked if he was uncomfortable. "My feet hurt," he replied, making the first excuse that came into his head. "Mine do too," said the queen, and she at once slipped off her shoes so that her guest might feel at liberty to do the same — which he did.

6 On a royal tour of South Africa in 1947, King George VI and Queen Elizabeth did much of their traveling by train. A warm welcome was not always assured at some of the stops where the Nationalist sentiments of Afrikaners ran high.

One of the first stops was at Swellendam, well known for Nationalist leanings. At the station, where the queen greeted the crowd, an old Afrikaner farmer said bluntly that, much as he was delighted to meet the Royal Family, he did not like the overseeing from Westminster. The queen, daughter of a Scottish earl, sweetly replied, "I understand perfectly. We feel the same in Scotland."

7 King George and Queen Elizabeth went to see a Noël Coward–Gertrude Lawrence production at a London theater. As they entered the royal box, the whole audience rose to its feet to honor them. Gertrude Lawrence, standing in the wings, said, "What an entrance!"

"What a part!" said Coward.

8 During a state visit to Australia, the Queen Mother found herself surrounded by a group of inquisitive Australians at a garden party. Still nodding and smiling graciously as the circle pressed closer, she remarked in an undertone: "Please don't touch the exhibits."

9 Cecil Beaton was showing the Queen Mother a selection of photographs of herself from a sitting she had recently given him. After she had chosen one, Beaton suggested that he could have the picture discreetly retouched to conceal a few wrinkles. The Queen Mother rejected the proposal. "I would not want it to be thought that I had lived for all these years without having anything to show for it," she explained.

ಶ್ಞ   ೩ಶ್

ELLENBOROUGH, Edward Law, 1st Baron (1750–1818), *British lawyer, lord chief justice (1802–18).*

1 Ellenborough had a redoubtable reputation for sarcasm and severity. A young lawyer, making his first appearance in court, was petrified and, rising to speak, could only stammer, "My lord, my unfortunate client — my lord, my unfortunate client — my lord —"

"Go on, sir, go on," said Ellenborough. "As far as you have proceeded hitherto, the court is entirely with you."

{Sydney Smith, who liked to tell this story, commented, "How wicked! How cruel! It deserves a thousand years' punishment at least."}

2 Asked to identify himself, a witness in a case began pompously, "I employ myself as a surgeon."

"But does anyone else employ you as a surgeon?" interrupted Ellenborough.

ಶ್ಞ   ೩ಶ್

ELLIOT, Hugh (1752–1830), *British diplomat.*

1 In 1777 Elliot was sent as envoy to the court of Frederick the Great at Berlin. His opposite number in London was a notoriously disreputable individual whom Frederick had sent thither to annoy and indicate his contempt for the British government. Frederick mockingly asked Elliot what he thought of the Prussian envoy. "Worthy to represent Your Majesty," replied Elliot suavely.

ELLISTON, Robert William (1774–1831), *British actor.*

1   Elliston was excessively chivalrous toward ladies, believing he was expected to make a declaration of love even to chance acquaintances. In a stagecoach he was embarked upon such a declaration to a fellow passenger when he observed that the lady was reacting very unfavorably. He wound up his speech by saying that he hoped he had not exceeded the limits of decorum. "Perhaps not, sir," the lady retorted, "but your limits of decorum are so extremely liberal that you may possibly lose your way in the excursion."

2   Elliston sat down to play at cards with Charles Lamb. His hands were excessively grimy. Lamb looked at them with distaste for some time and then observed, "If dirt were trumps, what a hand you'd have!"

᠂ᠣ ᠅ᠪ

ELMAN, Mischa (1891–1967), *US violinist. Born in Russia, he became one of the best-known soloists of the 1920s and 1930s.*

1   As a child of seven, Elman was asked to give a violin recital for friends of the family. He embarked on Beethoven's *Kreutzer* sonata, which he played with ease and great virtuosity. During one of the many long rests in the piece, one of his listeners, a kindly old lady, tapped him on the shoulder and whispered confidentially, "Play something you know, dear."
{Told of others.}

2   Concert managers in the United States tend to spare no expense when communicating with their artistes, the practice being that all such communications are charged to the musicians themselves. Elman, like many of his fellow musicians, resented having to pay for unnecessary telegrams and long-distance phone calls. By way of retaliation, he once sent his manager the following collect telegram: "Am sitting in the dining room of my hotel having French onion soup, wholewheat toast, filet mignon medium rare, mixed salad with Thousand Island dressing, French apple pie à la mode, coffee without cream and sugar. Weather marvelous. Have splendid room with magnificent view. Now how do you like telegrams collect? Yours cordially, Mischa Elman."

> "Henry Erskine, Lord Advocate of Scotland toward the close of the eighteenth century, had a tutor who was very absent-minded. So much so that Erskine, who thought a great deal of the old man, was one day flabbergasted to hear him say: 'I was very sorry, my dear boy, you have had the fever in your family; was it you or your brother who died of it?' 'It was I,' Erskine replied. 'Ah, dear me, I thought so—very sorry for it—very sorry for it.' And the old man walked away."
>
> —Herbert V. Prochnow,
> *The Public Speaker's Treasure Chest*

3   Just before Elman was to give a recital a man burst into his dressing room and greeted him: "We're related, Mr. Elman! Your wife's aunt is married to the uncle of my ex-wife's first husband's present wife." Mr. Elman responded to this announcement with a deeply furrowed brow, then smiled with relief. "It's not so close that I have to give you a free ticket to the concert this evening," he said.

᠂ᠣ ᠅ᠪ

EMERSON, Ralph Waldo (1803–82), *US writer, Transcendentalist philosopher, and exponent of individualism, known as "the Sage of Concord." He wrote his main Transcendentalist work,* Nature (1836), *after a European tour on which he met Wordsworth, Coleridge, and Carlyle. He was influenced by the German romantic philosophers, especially Schelling. Emerson was also distinguished as poet, essayist, and lecturer.*

1   As a child, Ralph Waldo once watched a sawyer cutting up some wood. The task was beyond young Emerson's strength, but finally he saw a way to be useful. "May I," he asked, "do the grunting for you?"

2   When he moved to his house in Concord, Emerson was particularly delighted with the orchard. He spent an hour each morning tending the trees; he did his writing in the orchard when possible, and received his friends there.

He sent some of his pears to the local cattle show, and was pleased when he received a visit from the committee of the horticultural society who asked whether they might examine his pear trees. Emerson received them with modest pride, and then discovered that they had not come to congratulate him — they had come to look at the soil that had produced such poor specimens of such a fine species.

3   Among the sages whom Emerson sought out on his visit to Europe was the notoriously reticent and difficult Thomas Carlyle. He called on Carlyle one evening and was given a pipe, while his host took one himself. They sat together smoking in perfect silence until bedtime, and on parting shook hands most cordially, congratulating each other on the fruitful time they had enjoyed together.

4   Emerson was asked to speak on the occasion of the two hundredth anniversary of the founding of Concord, which was also the sixtieth anniversary of the famous battle. He considered this a great honor and, determined to do his very best, decided to produce a fresh literary version of the encounter. He began by questioning the surviving veterans, and in the course of his researches came across a barefooted farmer who was driving his oxen in Concord. Emerson asked him whether all the people thereabouts went without shoes and stockings, and the farmer replied, "Wal, some on 'em doos, and the rest on 'em minds their own business."

5   The sculptor David Chester French made a bust of Emerson, which met with his subject's approval. "Yes," said Emerson, after scrutinizing the work for a few minutes, "that is the face that I shave every morning."

6   While at Harvard, Oliver Wendell Holmes, Jr., wrote a fifteen-page critical essay on Plato and showed it to Emerson for his comments. Emerson returned it with the observation: "When you shoot at a king, you must kill him." Holmes destroyed his essay.

7   John Greenleaf Whittier once asked Emerson what he prayed for. "When I first open my eyes upon the morning meadows and look out upon the beautiful world," replied Emerson, "I thank God I am alive and that I live so near Boston."
See also FRANCES WILLARD 1.

8   A lady once asked a scrubwoman who regularly attended Emerson's lectures at Concord if she understood Mr. Emerson. "Not a word," was the reply, "but I like to go and see him stand up there and look as though he thought everyone was as good as he."

9   Warned by a member of a religious cult that the world was going to end in ten days' time, Emerson calmly replied, "Well, no doubt we will get on very well without it."

10   In Emerson's later years his memory began increasingly to fail. He used to refer to it as his "naughty memory" when it let him down. He would forget the names of things, and have to refer to them in a circumlocutory way, saying, for instance, "the implement that cultivates the soil" for plow. Worse, he could not remember people's names. At Longfellow's funeral, he remarked to a friend, "That gentleman has a sweet, beautiful soul, but I have entirely forgotten his name." Perhaps most touching was his term for umbrella — "the thing that strangers take away."

෬   ෫

EMPEDOCLES (5th century BC), *Greek philosopher and scientist of Acragas (Agrigentum) in Sicily. Empedocles was a polymath to whom several discoveries in physics and biology were credited. As a philosopher he propounded the theory that all natural phenomena can be attributed to the opposing forces of Love and Discord operating upon four basic elements: earth, air, fire, and water.*

1   Various accounts of Empedocles' death are given in ancient sources. His enemies said that his desire to be thought a god led him to throw himself into the crater of Mount Etna so that he might vanish from the world completely and thus lead men to believe he had achieved apotheosis. Unfortunately the volcano defeated his design by throwing out one of the philosopher's sandals.
{Matthew Arnold's long philosophical poem "Empedocles on Etna" makes use of this tradition.}

෬   ෫

ENESCO, Georges (1881–1955), *Rumanian violinist, composer, and conductor. After 1895 he lived mainly in France, gaining an international reputation for his interpretations of Bach.*

1 Enesco, wishing to help a young friend making his debut at Carnegie Hall, offered to accompany him on the piano. The idea diverted the pianist Walter Gieseking, who said he would turn the pages. A review next morning read: "The man who should have been playing the piano was turning the pages, and the man who should have been turning the pages was playing the violin."

ঌ৯ ৽ঌ

ENGELS, Friedrich (1820–95), *German socialist leader and political philosopher. He collaborated with Karl Marx on the* Communist Manifesto *(1848), and spent much of the later part of his life translating and editing Marx's works. From the mid-1840s he lived in England. He published* The Condition of the Working Classes in England *in its German form in 1845; the English translation appeared in 1887.*

1 Friedrich Engels was the son of a prosperous manufacturer of textiles. The father, to familiarize the six-year-old Friedrich with his eventual inheritance, once showed him through the factory. The little boy was profoundly shocked by the miserable working conditions under which children hardly older than himself had to labor. Before his stern father he disguised his feeling, but on his return home in great agitation he asked his beloved mother, "Must I too go to work soon in the factory?"

"No, my dear, thank God you won't have to. You can be glad that the factory belongs to us."

"And how about the children? Are they glad?"

"No, Friedrich, not like you. But it's better for you not to trouble your little head about it. No one can change things, even you."

The boy slept little that night. In the morning his mother awakened him. He looked at her. "Mother, suppose I *want* to change things — then what . . . ?"

ঌ৯ ৽ঌ

EPICTETUS (c. AD 55–c. 135), *Greek philosopher, an eminent exponent of Stoicism. His principal doctrines are contained in his* Encheiridion.

1 In his youth Epictetus, a slave, was cruelly treated by his master. One day the latter twisted his leg violently. Epictetus remonstrated, "If you continue to do that, you will break my leg." His master took no notice, went on twisting, and broke the leg. "Didn't I tell you that you would break my leg?" observed Epictetus mildly.

ঌ৯ ৽ঌ

EPSTEIN, Sir Jacob (1880–1959), *British sculptor, born in New York of Russo-Polish descent. A number of his early works, such as the eighteen nude figures for the British Medical Association building (1907–08), aroused great controversy. His bronze portrait busts of celebrities, however, were highly acclaimed, as were his later* Christ in Majesty *(1957) for Llandaff Cathedral and his* Saint Michael and the Devil *(1958) for Coventry Cathedral.*

1 On a visit to Epstein's studio, George Bernard Shaw noticed a huge block of stone standing in one corner and asked what it was for. "I don't know yet," said the sculptor. "I'm still making plans." Shaw was astounded. "You mean you plan your work? Why, I change my mind several times a day!" he exclaimed. "That's all very well with a four-ounce manuscript," replied Epstein, "but not with a four-ton block."

ঌ৯ ৽ঌ

ERASMUS, Desiderius (1466–1536), *Dutch humanist scholar and writer. His translation of the Greek New Testament (all previous ones had been from the Latin Vulgate version) was a landmark in biblical scholarship, and his* Encomium Moriae (The Praise of Folly, *1509), a satire on the state of Europe in his time, became a best-seller.*

1 Reproached for not observing the Lenten fast, Erasmus replied, "I have a Catholic soul, but a Lutheran stomach."

ঌ৯ ৽ঌ

ERIC the Red (late 10th century AD), *Norwegian navigator. Brought up in exile in Iceland, he led an expedition westward around 982 and* *discovered Greenland, where he established a Viking colony a few years later.*

1   The terrain of Greenland is covered mainly with glaciers and barren rock, with only a few patches of tundra and habitable land. Eric named it Greenland on the principle that colonists would be keen to go there if the country bore an attractive name.

෪ ෧

ERSKINE, John (1879–1951), *US educator and writer, professor of English at Columbia University (1909–37). His works include* The Moral Obligation to Be Intelligent *(1915) and* The Private Life of Helen of Troy *(1925).*

1   Erskine was to lecture at the University of Tennessee at Chattanooga, and the president of the university went to the station to meet him. He had some difficulty in recognizing his guest, however, and told Erskine about it at dinner that evening: "I asked one gentleman if he were John Erskine and he said, with emphasis, 'I should say not.' I asked another, and he said, 'I wish I were.' Which shows that at least one man had read your books."

"It does indeed," replied Erskine, "but which one?"

2   Erskine was once asked if he found it disconcerting to see members of the audience looking at their watches during a long lecture. "No," replied Erskine, "not until they start shaking them."

෪ ෧

ERSKINE, Thomas, 1st Baron (1750–1823), *British lawyer and politician who became lord chancellor (1806–07). He made important contributions to commercial law.*

1   Lord Erskine had a standard practice for dealing with letters soliciting his subscription to various causes. "Sir, I feel much honored by your application to me, and I beg to subscribe" —here the reader had to turn over the notepaper—"myself your very obedient servant."

2   Erskine, who was fond of puns, was told that such word-play was the lowest form of wit. "That's very true," he replied, "and therefore it is the foundation of all wit."

ESHKOL, Levi (1895–1969), *Israeli politician. A Zionist pioneer in Palestine in 1914, Eshkol later became minister of finance (1952–63) and succeeded David Ben-Gurion as prime minister of Israel (1963–69).*

1   The economic interdependence of the nations of the world is illustrated by a story the Israelis like to tell about Eshkol. Shortly after becoming prime minister, he received some bad news. One of his aides informed him that a serious drought was imminent. Eshkol, upset, asked, "Where?"

"In the Negev."

Eshkol's face cleared. "For a moment I thought you meant in *Kansas.*"

෪ ෧

ESPOSITO, Phil (1942–   ), *Canadian-born ice-hockey player. He was a high-scoring star of the National Hockey League in the United States and Canada for eighteen years until his retirement (1980).*

1   Esposito was one of the North American ice-hockey players who went to Moscow to play the Soviet team in the early 1970s. Assigned a hotel room, they suspected that it might be bugged. Esposito recalls, "We searched the room for microphones. In the center of the room, we found a funny-looking, round piece of metal imbedded in the floor, under the rug. We figured we had found the bug. We dug it out of the floor. And we heard a crash beneath us. We had released the anchor to the chandelier in the ceiling below."

෪ ෧

ESTE, Borso d' (1413–71), *Duke of Modena and Reggio and Duke of Ferrara, under whom Ferrara reached the height of its splendor and prosperity.*

1   Duke Borso sent a letter in Latin to the mayor of an outlying village asking him to catch a sparrowhawk (*accipetrem*) and send it to Ferrara trussed up in a sack to prevent its escape. When the letter was delivered, it caused great consternation; the villagers read it as a demand for the surrender of their archpriest (*arciprete*). Although they knew of no reason for the duke's apparent displeasure with the popular priest, they thought they had better

obey his command. The luckless cleric, protesting his innocence, was duly popped into a sack and taken to Ferrara. At the ducal palace, the official to whom the package was delivered was totally perplexed. "Have you a letter?" he asked. The letter, of course, made all things clear. Duke Borso, to save the villagers' face, solemnly sent back a message saying that he had changed his mind and they could set their victim free. After that he took care to write to his rustic subjects in the vernacular.

ह ह

EUCLID (fl. 300 BC), *Greek mathematician who lived and worked in Alexandria, Egypt. His principal work, the* Elements, *remained the standard textbook on geometry until the end of the nineteenth century.*

1 Euclid was employed as tutor of mathematics in the royal household. King Ptolemy I complained about the difficulty of the theorems that Euclid expected him to grasp, wondering whether there was not an easier way to approach the subject. Euclid gently rebuked him: "Sire, there is no royal road to geometry."

ह ह

EUGÉNIE (1826–1920), *empress of France (1853–70), wife of Napoleon III. The Spanish-born empress presided over the glittering society of the Second Empire and several times acted as regent in the emperor's absence. When the empire collapsed as a result of the Franco-Prussian War, she took refuge in England, where Queen Victoria became a faithful friend. Her years in exile were saddened by the deaths of her husband and of her son, the Prince Imperial.*

1 The empress and her lady-in-waiting, Mme de Pourtalès, were playing patience in a remote corner of the palace garden at Saint-Cloud when a masked man appeared brandishing a gun. He demanded their jewels, which they duly handed over. He then told them to undress. They had begun to do so when Mme de Pourtalès suddenly recognized the intruder. "It's Poché!" she exclaimed, naming a young courtier who was known for his pranks. As they scolded him, the sound of running feet was heard—the imperial security guards alerted by the women's raised voices. Realizing that even Poché might find it difficult to ex-

plain his mask and gun, Eugénie said, "Quick, hide under my crinoline!" So, until the guards had withdrawn, there he remained.

2 The day after an attempt by Felice Orsini and two accomplices to assassinate the imperial couple, Napoleon was implacably resolved to seek the death penalty for the conspirators, a step Eugénie implored him not to take. The argument grew heated. Eugénie, seeking an ally, burst from their private apartments, wearing nothing but a transparent peignoir, and ran into the adjacent library where her private secretary, a plain, rather stolid man, was working. She begged him to help her make her case to the emperor. He was deeply embarrassed by the virtually naked empress and scarcely knew where to look. "Your Majesty seems to forget that there is a man under the secretary," he mumbled in painful confusion. Eugénie, her nerves on edge, glanced at the solid secretaire in the corner. "What? A man hidden in here under the furniture?" she shrieked.

ह ह

EULER, Leonhard (1707–83), *Swiss mathematician. He worked mainly in Russia (1727–41, 1766–83) and in Frederick the Great's Berlin Academy (1741–66). Although blind in his last years, he labored strenuously until his death, making major contributions in geometry, calculus, and number theory. The number* e, *the base of natural logarithms, is sometimes called Euler's number.*

1 When Euler first came to Berlin from Russia, Frederick the Great's mother, the dowager queen Sophia Dorothea, took a liking to him and tried to draw him out on a number of topics. Euler, no courtier, replied in monosyllables. "Why," asked the dowager queen, "do you not wish to speak to me?" Euler replied, "Madame, I come from a country where, if you speak, you are hanged."

2 (Says E. T. Bell:) "After having amused himself one afternoon calculating the laws of ascent of balloons—on his slate, as usual—[Euler] dined with Lexell [a mathematical colleague] and his family. 'Herschel's Planet' (Uranus) was a recent discovery. Euler outlined the calculation of its orbit. A little later he asked that his grandson be brought in. While playing with the child and drinking tea he suffered a stroke. The pipe dropped from his hand, and with the words, 'I die,' Euler ceased to live and calculate."

੩੦   ੨੧

EURIPIDES (c. 480–406 BC), *Greek tragic playwright. He wrote some ninety plays, of which fewer than twenty survive, among them* Medea *and* The Trojan Woman. *He was renowned for his portrayal of people, especially women, in the grip of powerful emotion, and for his skill as a stylist.*

1   Euripides once confessed that it had taken him three days to write three verses. His astonished interlocutor, a poet of inferior abilities, exclaimed, "I could have written a hundred in that time!"

"I believe it," replied Euripides, "but they would have lived only three days."

੩੦   ੨੧

EVANS, Sir Arthur [John] (1851–1941), *British archaeologist. While Evans was keeper at Oxford's Ashmolean Museum (1884–1908), his interest in sealstones in Crete led him to excavate the site of Knossos, bringing to light the hitherto unknown civilization that he christened Minoan. His* Palace of Minos *(1921–36) established the outlines of Minoan chronology and culture that have been largely confirmed by subsequent excavations.*

1   "[Evans] kept his powers into extreme old age and on his ninetieth birthday on 8 July 1941 welcomed a party of friends who went to pay honour to him. He seemed remarkably spry and talked about a new Roman road which he had discovered. Very soon afterwards a man in the Intelligence Corps, with Greece as his special province, who liked to be a bit of a 'know-all,' told him that the Germans had destroyed Knossos. Evans was stricken to the heart, believing that his life's work had been ruined. He died three days later, and the tragic irony was that, so far from destroying Knossos, the Germans had taken pains to see that nothing was damaged."

੩੦   ੨੧

EVANS, Dame Edith (1888–1976), *British actress, celebrated for her Shakespearean performances. In the course of her long career she played most of the great classic roles of the British stage.*

1   When Dame Edith was introduced to Dr. Billy Graham, the evangelist told her, "We in the ministry could learn a good deal from you about how to put our message across."

"You in the ministry have an advantage over us," replied Edith Evans. "You have long-term contracts."

2   When Edith Evans was playing the role of Miss Betsey Trotwood in a film adaptation of Dickens's *David Copperfield,* she had to carry a cat in a basket on her arm during one scene. The cat was sedated but in the middle of a long speech the effects of the drug began to wear off and it began making efforts to climb out of its prison. Scarcely pausing in her speech, Edith Evans shoved it back into the basket. "Don't be such an ambitious pussy. You're not in *Dick Whittington,*" she hissed in an aside.

3   Told that writer Nancy Mitford was staying at a friend's villa to finish a book, Dame Edith remarked: "Oh, really? What exactly is she reading?"

4   Out walking with a friend one day, Dame Edith paused at the window of a London art gallery. After studying a rather drab modern watercolor, the actress gave her critical assessment of the picture. "I couldn't have that in my house," she said. "It would be like living with a gas leak."

5   (In 1966 Bryan Forbes directed Edith Evans, then seventy-eight, in the role of Mrs. Ross in the film *The Whisperers.*)

"We only had one meeting prior to shooting when we discussed the script. Edith asked if I would insert one additional line of dialogue for her. Although she greatly admired Eric Portman [her co-star] as an actor she was not . . . enamoured of his private personality. 'Do you think,' she said, 'you could add a line to indicate that she married slightly beneath her?' I promised to consider it. A few days later I met with Eric to discuss his reactions to the script. He admired Edith as an actress without qualification, but confessed, with more bluntness than Edith, that there were aspects of her off-stage personality that grated on him. 'Do you think, dear boy,' he said, 'you could somehow insert an extra line which would indicate she married a much younger man?' I kept both confidences to myself, duly made the amendments and neither of them ever referred to it again."

৵৽ ৽৵

EVARTS, William Maxwell (1818–1901), *US lawyer and statesman, secretary of state (1877–81).*

1 Evarts was a popular after-dinner speaker. At an important Thanksgiving function he rose and said, "You have been giving your attention to a turkey stuffed with sage; you are now about to consider a sage stuffed with turkey." {Told of others.}

2 A lady asked Evarts, a bon vivant, whether drinking so many different wines did not make him feel ill the next day. "Not at all, madam," he replied, "it's the indifferent wines that produce that result."

৵৽ ৽৵

EVERETT, Edward (1794–1865), *US statesman and orator. A scholar by inclination, Everett nonetheless followed a mainly political career after his election to the House of Representatives in 1825. He was governor of Massachusetts (1835–39), US minister in London (1841–45), president of Harvard (1846–49), and followed Daniel Webster as secretary of state for a few months (1852–53).*

1 While Everett was president of Harvard, a storm arose over the proposed admission of a Negro to the college. Everett replied, "If this boy passes the examination he will be admitted; and if the white students choose to withdraw, all the income of the college will be devoted to his education."

❧ F ❧

FAGIUOLI, Giovanni Battista (1660–1742), *Italian poet, renowned for his burlesques. His works include* Rime piacevoli *(1729).*

1 As court poet to Archduke Cosimo III of Tuscany, Fagiuoli was also a kind of court clown. One day he presented his master with a list of names. "What do these names stand for?" asked the archduke.

"They're a list of all the fools of my acquaintance."

"But," exploded the archduke, "my name heads the list!"

"Your Highness, that's because yesterday you commissioned that botanist in England to collect and bring you a collection of rare plants. But — you paid him in advance!"

"I see nothing foolish in that. Suppose he delivers them in accord with my instructions?"

"In that case I'll erase your name and substitute his."

❧ ❧

FAIRBANKS, Douglas (1883–1939), *US film actor. He played the handsome, athletic hero in many productions by the United Artists Corporation, which he cofounded in 1919. His romance with the star Mary Pickford ("America's sweetheart") caught the imagination of fans all over the world.*

1 While on their honeymoon in 1920, Douglas Fairbanks and Mary Pickford stayed in the Hôtel de Crillon in Paris. In the suite next door was General Pershing. Naturally a large crowd gathered. The general figured this was due to the presence of the famous film pair. The famous film pair figured it was due to the presence of Pershing. None of the three therefore appeared on the balcony. The crowd waited, nothing happened, everybody went home.

2 As he was driving back to his mansion, Pickfair, Fairbanks saw an Englishman of aristocratic mien and familiar face trudging along the road in the heat. He stopped to offer him a ride, which the stranger accepted. Still unable to remember the man's name, Fairbanks invited him in for a drink, and in the course of conversation attempted to elicit some clues as to his visitor's identity. The Englishman seemed to know many of Fairbanks's friends and was evidently well acquainted with the estate, for he made approving comments on some recent changes. Eventually Fairbanks managed a whispered aside to his secretary, who had just entered the room. "Who's this Englishman? I know he's Lord Somebody, but I just can't remember his name."

"That," replied the secretary, "is the English butler you fired last month for getting drunk."

❧ ❧

FAISAL Ibn Abdul Aziz (1905–75), *king of Saudi Arabia (1964–75). During his reign, Saudi Arabia gained considerable importance as one of the world's major oil producers. Faisal was assassinated by his nephew.*

1 In 1945, Faisal visited San Francisco for the drafting of the UN charter. As he passed through the foyer of the St. Francis Hotel, dressed in his customary flowing robes, he overheard a young teenager ask her friend, "I wonder what he wears under that robe?"

Turning majestically toward the girl, the prince replied: "BVDs, young lady."

❧ ❧

FALLA, Manuel de (1876–1946), *Spanish composer.* The Three-Cornered Hat *is his most celebrated work.*

1 As Falla was very bad at replying to his correspondents, a large pile of letters awaiting an answer was always upon his desk. Receiving news of the death of the painter Ignacio Zuloaga, Falla was deeply distressed. "What a pity!" he lamented. "He died before I answered his letter, which he sent me five years ago!"

જે છ

FALLIÈRES, [Clement] **Armand** (1841–1931), *French statesman; eighth president of the Third Republic (1906–13).*

1 Fallières, visiting sculptor Auguste Rodin's studio, looked around him at the assemblage of unfinished work — hands, feet, heads, torsos. Then he remarked, "Well, I can see that the movers haven't been particularly careful."

જે છ

FANGIO, Juan Manuel (1911–   ), *Argentinian motor-racing driver. He won twenty-four Grand Prix races and was world champion five times (1951, 1954–57).*

1 In the lead after the opening lap of the 1950 Monaco Grand Prix, Fangio was approaching a particularly dangerous bend for the second time when he suddenly became aware that something was wrong. The faces of the spectators, which he usually saw as a whitish blur as he drove down the straight, were all turned away from him. "If they are not looking at me," Fangio must have instantly thought, "they must be looking at something more interesting around the corner." He braked hard. As he carefully rounded the bend, he saw that his split-second assessment of the situation had been accurate. The road was blocked by a pileup of most of the other cars in the race.

જે છ

FARADAY, Michael (1791–1867), *British chemist and physicist. Apprenticed as a bookbinder, he persuaded Sir Humphry Davy to make him his assistant, and eventually (1833) succeeded Davy as professor of chemistry at the Royal Institution in London. He did important work on the liquefaction of gases, discovered benzene (1825), and made the first electric generator (1831).*

1 Faraday's interest in knowledge for its own sake sometimes baffled people with a more practical turn of mind. William Gladstone, watching Faraday at an experiment from which he could discern no practical result, asked, "Of what use is such a discovery?" Faraday retorted, "Why, you will soon be able to tax it."

જે છ

FAROUK I (1920–65), *king of Egypt (1936–52). After the military coup of 1952 he was forced to abdicate; he spent the remainder of his life as an enormously fat playboy in Monaco.*

1 After being driven from his throne in 1952, Farouk remarked bitterly, "One day there will be only five kings left: hearts, spades, diamonds, clubs, and England."

જે છ

FARQUHAR, Sir Walter (1738–1819), *British physician.*

1 One of Sir Walter's patients, an elderly lady with an ill-defined complaint, took it into her head that it would do her the world of good to take the waters at Bath for a few weeks. Sir Walter encouraged her in this scheme, and to allay her worries at the prospect of being separated from her usual physician, he promised to recommend her to a very clever doctor in Bath, a friend of his, and to write a letter for her to take with her, detailing her case. The old lady set out happily for Bath, but on the way fell to thinking that although Sir Walter had been her physician for years, he had never told her precisely what was wrong with her. Her curiosity about the contents of the letter grew. At the first overnight stop she announced to her traveling companion that she was going to open it. Her companion protested about the breach of trust, but to no avail. The letter was opened. It read: "Dear Davis, Keep the old lady three weeks and send her back again."

જે છ

FARRAGUT, David Glasgow (1801–70), *US Union admiral during the Civil War.*

1 In August 1864 Admiral Farragut led the attack on Mobile Bay, to give the Union forces control over a large slice of Confederate territory. The bay was well defended by mines, forcing any approaching ships to sail close to Fort Morgan, the Confederate fortress that dominated the channel. The Confederate iron-

clad, the *Tennessee*, also covered the approaches. Farragut's first ship, the *Tecumseh*, eager to attack the *Tennessee*, incautiously crossed the minefield and was blown up. Then the *Brooklyn* faltered, and in an instant the lines of ships were in disarray, with the tide sweeping them closer to the guns of Fort Morgan. "Damn the torpedoes, go ahead!" shouted Farragut, swinging his own ship, the *Hereford*, clear of the *Brooklyn* and heading straight across the minefield. They heard the mine cases clatter against the hull of the *Hartford*, but none exploded, and the rest of the attacking force sailed into Mobile Bay after Farragut. In a very short time the *Tennessee* and the shore forts had surrendered.

{Farragut's exclamation has become immortalized as "Damn the torpedoes, full speed ahead!"}

ε∾ ⵄⵇ

FAULKNER, William (1897–1962), *US novelist. He based many of his stories in Yoknapatawpha County, a fictionalized version of his native northern Mississippi. His major novels include* The Sound and the Fury *(1929) and* Absalom, Absalom! *(1936). He was awarded the Nobel Prize for literature in 1949.*

1   One of the many jobs Faulkner took before he established himself as a writer was as postmaster at the University of Mississippi post office. When he found that his official duties interfered with his writing, he wrote the following letter to the postmaster general: "As long as I live under the capitalistic system I expect to have my life influenced by the demands of moneyed people. But I will be damned if I propose to be at the beck and call of every itinerant scoundrel who has two cents to invest in a postage stamp. This, sir, is my resignation."

2   "I [Leland Hayward, literary and dramatic agent] got a call one day from Metro. They were completely confused over there and they wanted to know where in hell was my client, [William] Faulkner! They were pretty sore — nobody was supposed to walk out of Metro without letting the front office know where he'd gone. I didn't know where Bill was. He hadn't told me he was going anywhere. I got the office to start making calls all over the damned place, and finally we thought of trying him at

his home in Mississippi, and sure enough, there he was. 'What the hell are you doing down there?' I yelled on the phone, and he said, 'Well, ah asked my producer if ah could work at home, and he said fine, so heah ah am.'"

3   Frank Case, the manager of the Algonquin Hotel in New York, met Faulkner one morning in the hotel lobby looking decidedly sorry for himself. Case asked him what was the matter. "I feel like the devil. My stomach's upset," Faulkner grumbled. "Too bad," sympathized Case. "Something you wrote, no doubt."

4   One spring evening Faulkner invited a woman to come with him to see a bride in her wedding dress. Driving over back roads, Faulkner finally turned off into a meadow, where he doused the headlights and drove cautiously forward in the darkness. At length he stopped the car and announced that the bride was in front of them. He switched on the lights, and there in their beam stood an apple tree in full blossom.

5   Faulkner was on a shooting expedition with director Howard Hawks and actor Clark Gable. In the course of conversation, Gable asked Faulkner to name the five best authors of the day. Replied Faulkner: "Ernest Hemingway, Willa Cather, Thomas Mann, John Dos Passos, and myself."

"Oh," said Gable maliciously, "do you write for a living?"

"Yes," retorted Faulkner, "and what do *you* do?"

ε∾ ⵄⵇ

FAURÉ, Gabriel Urbain (1845–1924), *French composer, known especially for his songs, though he produced distinguished work in every branch of chamber music. His* Requiem Mass *(1887–90) is greatly loved.*

1   Fauré was once asked what the ideal tempo for a song should be. He replied, "If the singer is bad — very fast."

ε∾ ⵄⵇ

FAVRAS, Thomas de Mahay, Marquis de (1744–90), *French aristocrat. Commissioned to negotiate a loan that would enable Louis XVI to escape at the outbreak of the French Revolution, Favras was betrayed, tried for high treason, and hanged.*

1 Favras's trial lasted nearly two months; the evidence against him was inconclusive and the witnesses disagreed, but in the end he was found guilty. Before being led to the scaffold he was handed his death sentence, written down by the clerk of the court. He read it through, then said, "I see, monsieur, that you have made three spelling mistakes."

ॐ ৺

FAWKES, Guy (1570–1606), *English Roman Catholic conspirator.*

1 Guy Fawkes was disenchanted with the lot of the Roman Catholics in England under James I. Serving with the Spanish army in the Netherlands, he was invited by one Robert Catesby to join a conspiracy to blow up the king and Parliament. Fawkes agreed. Having rented a cellar under the Houses of Parliament, the conspirators managed to secrete thirty-six barrels of gunpowder there behind a stack of wood and coal. The day that King James was due to open Parliament (November 5, 1605) was the date set for the explosion. However, one of the conspirators wrote an anonymous note to a friend who was a member of Parliament, warning him not to attend the opening. The MP alerted the authorities, the cellar was searched, and the conspirators arrested. Catesby was killed resisting arrest and Fawkes was captured and tortured. He betrayed the names of the other conspirators and all were tried and executed. This is the origin of the celebrations in Britain on November 5 with fireworks and bonfires, during which an effigy, called a guy, is burned.

ॐ ৺

FERDINAND I (1793–1875), *emperor of Austria (1835–48). Ferdinand suffered bouts of insanity and even when sane was so feeble of mind that affairs of state during his reign were managed by a council. This brought Austria to a state of revolution, and he was forced to abdicate in favor of his nephew Francis Joseph.*

1 Ferdinand's one recorded notable saying was: "I am the emperor, and I want dumplings."
{A. J. P. Taylor maintained that this was the most lucid utterance of his reign.}

ॐ ৺

Robert Fitzerald (1911–1985), the poet and translator of the *Odyssey,* the *Iliad,* and the *Aeneid,* worried sometimes that these classic tales were lost on young people. But he was heartened, not long before his death, by an incident his wife related. Two young women were wheeling their bicycles ahead of her through a college campus. Just before they turned off the path one young woman said to the other, "You know what I said to him? I said, 'You know that scene where Hector got dragged by his ankles through the blood and the dust? Well,' I said, 'I hope that happens to you.'"

—from *The New Yorker,* February 5, 1985

FERDINAND I (1861–1948), *king of Bulgaria (1908–18). He was elected prince of Bulgaria in 1887, an election for a long time challenged by Russia. In 1908 he assumed the title of king. His expansionist policies caused the other Balkan states to combine against him, and the humiliation of the treaty of Bucharest (1913) brought Bulgaria into World War I on the German side. After the defeat of the Bulgarian armies, Ferdinand abdicated and spent the rest of his life in exile in Germany.*

1 Led by Russia, the European powers withheld recognition of Ferdinand's status in Bulgaria. When Ferdinand entered a room at Chantilly on a visit to his elderly uncle, the Duc d'Aumale, who did not like him, the old man seemed not to recognize him. An aide whispered in the duke's ear. "Ah, Ferdinand," said Aumale, "I am behaving like the rest of Europe; I did not recognize you."

ॐ ৺

FERDINAND IV (?1286–1312), *king of Castile (1295–1312). His short reign was marked by anarchy and rebellion.*

1 Ferdinand had rejected an appeal by two prisoners, Peter and John de Carvajal, condemned to death on circumstantial evidence. The two men, still proclaiming their innocence, summoned Ferdinand to appear before

God within thirty days. On the thirtieth day the king, still fit and well, appeared to have defied the "summons." The following morning, he was found dead in his bed.

{This story may be myth. Ferdinand's nickname, however, was "the summoned."}

ॐ ॐ

FERGUSSON, George, Lord Hermand (died 1827), *Scottish judge.*

1 Lord Hermand was convivial to the point of believing that drinking could improve one's behavior. He was a member of a panel of judges trying a young man who had accidentally killed a drinking companion. A verdict of culpable homicide was brought in and the majority of the panel thought a lenient sentence would be appropriate; a short term of imprisonment was imposed. Lord Hermand dissented: "We are told that there was no malice, and that the prisoner must have been in liquor. In liquor! Why, he was drunk! And yet he murdered the very man who had been drinking with him! They had been carousing the whole night; and yet he stabbed him! After drinking a whole bottle of rum with him! Good God, my laards, if he will do this when he's drunk, what will he not do when he's sober?"

ॐ ॐ

FERMAT, Pierre de (1601–65), *French mathematician renowned for his contribution to the theory of numbers.*

1 As Fermat engaged in mathematics for his own amusement, many of his most important contributions were recorded in margins of books or in notes to his friends. In about 1637 he scribbled in his copy of Diophantus's *Arithmetic*, "The equation $x^n + y^n = z^n$, where x, y, and z are positive integers, has no solution if n is greater than 2," and added, "I have discovered a most remarkable proof, but this margin is too narrow to contain it." The problem has gone down in mathematical lore as "Fermat's Last Theorem," and generations of mathematical adepts have taxed their ingenuity to reconstitute the proof.

{The theorem has been proved for many values of n, but not for all values; Fermat himself proved the theorem for $n = 4$, and computers have proved it for all values of n up to 2,000, but this does not constitute a general proof. The despairing and the skeptical have doubted whether Fermat was correct in believing that he had a proof.}

ॐ ॐ

FERMI, Enrico (1901–54), *Italian-born physicist. After winning the 1938 Nobel Prize for physics for his work on uranium fission he emigrated to the United States, where he lived for the rest of his life. Using a converted squash court at the University of Chicago as his laboratory, he was the first person to achieve a controlled nuclear chain reaction (1942). He later played a key role in the development of the atom bomb.*

1 As early as March 1939 Enrico Fermi tried to see Admiral Hooper in the office of the Chief of Naval Operations to explain to him the military significance of uranium fission. He got no further than two young lieutenant commanders, who listened courteously as Fermi explained his case in his fractured English. They then politely but firmly showed him the door. As he left, one turned to the other and said, "That wop's crazy!"

2 In 1942 in his laboratory at the University of Chicago stadium, Fermi built the first atomic pile, using specially produced graphite blocks into which several tons of uranium were inserted. The first controlled nuclear chain reaction began on December 2 at 2:20 P.M. and lasted twenty-eight minutes. Afterward Arthur Compton, the American physicist who collaborated with Fermi, put through a call to James Bryant Conant at Harvard's Office of Scientific Research and Development. "The Italian navigator has reached the New World," he announced. "And how did he find the natives?" asked Conant. "Very friendly," came the reply. Thus was the atomic age announced.

ॐ ॐ

FERNANDEL [Fernand Joseph Désiré Contandin] (1903–71), *French comedian. The role for which he was best known internationally is that of Don Camillo in the series of films about an Italian priest engaged in a battle of wits with the Communist mayor of his village.*

1 Fernandel visited a new barbershop. The barber was palpably anxious that his handiwork should be well received by his famous client. Finished, he produced a mirror and held it with a flourish to the back of Fernandel's head. Fernandel studied the effect, then smiled his celebrated toothy smile and said, "Just a little longer at the back, please."

❧ ☙

FEYDEAU, Georges (1862–1921), *French playwright. Between 1881 and 1916 he wrote a number of brilliant farces. Many have been translated into English and are still performed. In its day* The Girl from Maxim's *enjoyed a great success.*

1 There was some question hanging over Feydeau's parentage, as his mother had a reputation as a flirt and Emperor Napoleon III had been seen to pay her marked attention. Mme Feydeau was indignant at the suggestion: "How could anybody imagine that a child as intelligent as Georges could be the son of such an idiotic monarch?"

2 At a restaurant Feydeau was served a lobster with only one claw. When he protested, the waiter explained that sometimes the lobsters fought in their tank, and such mutilations resulted. "Take this one away," ordered Feydeau, "and bring me the victor."

3 A tiresome acquaintance, whose wife was notorious for her infidelities, was boring Feydeau with a recital of the virtues of his small son. "He's so devoted to his mother and so loving," said the proud father. "He's always under her skirts."

"Where he must meet a lot of others," murmured Feydeau.

4 In Feydeau's early days as a playwright, his comedies were not always well received. At one such disastrous opening night he stationed himself in the aisle and joined in the hissing and booing. "Have you taken leave of your senses!" exclaimed a friend who had run down the aisle after him. Feydeau shook his head. "This way I can't hear them," he explained, "so it doesn't hurt so much."

❧ ☙

FIELD, Eugene (1850–95), *US versifier and journalist. Much of his writing was for children.*

1 Field once reviewed in the *Denver Tribune* a production of *King Lear* starring actor Creston Clarke in the title role. Of Clarke's inadequate performance, Field wrote, "All through the five acts of that Shakespearean tragedy he played the king as though under a momentary apprehension that someone else was about to play the ace."

2 When Field was living in a dreary boardinghouse in Kansas City, he was invited to dine at a mansion the hostess of which prided herself on the excellence of her fare. At the dessert course a bowl of fine strawberries was passed around. Field looked at them wistfully, but passed them on. "Don't you like strawberries, Mr. Field?" asked his attentive hostess. "I love them," replied Field. "Well, then, why not have some?" she said. Field shook his head sadly: "I'm afraid that if I did, it would spoil my appetite for prunes."

❧ ☙

FIELD, John (1782–1837), *British pianist and composer, considered one of the finest pianists of the nineteenth century. His* Nocturnes *are believed to have been the model for much of Chopin's work. He spent much of his life teaching music in St. Petersburg.*

1 Field's friends, attending him during his last hours, felt the need of a clergyman to administer the last rites. But they were not sure of Field's religious affiliation. "Are you a Papist or a Calvinist?" they asked him. "I am . . . a pianist," replied the dying artist.

❧ ☙

FIELD, Marshall, III (1893–1956), *US founder of the* Chicago Sun (*afterward the* Chicago Sun-Times).

1 "When Marshall Field III was a small child, he displayed some of the cautious shrewdness which made his grandfather the greatest merchant prince in America.

"Being left alone in a hotel lobby for half an hour, young Marshall approached an old lady and asked if she could crack nuts.

"'No, dear,' replied the old lady. 'I lost all my teeth years ago.'

"'Then,' said master Field, extending both hands full of pecans, 'please hold these while I go and get some more pecans.'"

> "I had a very elderly and esteemed relative who once told me that while walking along the Strand he met a lion that had escaped from Exeter Change menagerie. I said, 'What did you do?', and he looked at me with contempt as if the question were imbecile. 'Do?' he said. 'Why, I took a cab.'"
>
> — Ford Madox Ford, *Ancient Lights*

FIELDING, Henry (1707–54), *British novelist, playwright, and lawyer. His first success as a novelist was a parody of Samuel Richardson's* Pamela; *his masterpiece,* Tom Jones, *appeared in 1749. Fielding's clear-eyed, humorous depiction of characters from all ranks of society drew in part on his experiences as a justice of the peace at Westminster.*

1 Andrew Millar, the publisher, bought Fielding's novel *Amelia* in 1751 for the then enormous sum of £800, relying upon the previous success of *Tom Jones* and the great reputation Fielding currently enjoyed. He ordered a large number of copies printed, but then became nervous and showed the manuscript to a friend whose judgment he trusted. The friend said that *Amelia* was by no means up to the standard of *Tom Jones.* Millar decided to dispose as quickly as possible of the whole edition. When next he was auctioning some of his stock to other members of the trade, he began by saying, "Gentlemen, I have several works to put up for which I shall be glad if you will bid. But as to *Amelia*, every copy is bespoke." The ploy worked, as rival booksellers rushed to get their names put down for the next edition. In this way Millar disposed of the whole stock of *Amelia.*

2 When he was once in the company of the Earl of Denbigh, whose family name was Feilding, the conversation turned to Fielding's membership in the same family. The earl inquired why the names were spelled differently. Fielding replied that he could give no reason, "except maybe that my branch of the family was the first to know how to spell."

FIELDS, W. C. [William Claude Dukenfield] (1879–1946), *US film actor and comedian. He made many successful movies, including* My Little Chickadee *(1940).*

1 A reporter interviewing Fields asked him, off the record, for his views on sex. "On or off the record," replied Fields, "there may be some things better than sex, and there may be some things worse. But there's nothing exactly like it."

2 During Prohibition, Fields and a friend heard that an acquaintance on Long Island had just received two cases of contraband Irish whiskey. They drove over to his place and helped him put part of the liquor beyond reach of the law. About dawn they left for home, taking along several bottles from which they refreshed themselves from time to time. After several hours they remarked upon the surprising length of Long Island — but kept going. When they asked filling-station attendants how far it was to the Queensboro Bridge, they got only blank stares or laughter in response. Eventually they found themselves in a hotel room. Fields fell asleep. His friend noticed a palm tree outside the window, went out to buy a paper, and learned that they were in Ocala, Florida. "We're in Ocala, Florida!" he said, shaking Fields awake. "I always said those Long Island roads were poorly marked," observed Fields.

3 Fields always kept a thermos of martinis at hand when he was filming, maintaining that it contained nothing but pineapple juice. One day someone tampered with the flask and Field's anguished cry rang out across the set: "Somebody put pineapple juice in my pineapple juice!"

4 "Can I fix you a Bromo-Seltzer, sir?" asked a waiter of Fields, who was groaning in the grip of a fearful hangover. "No," moaned Fields, "I can't stand the noise."

5 After a performance one evening Fields quarreled with his assistant, Shorty. "You're fired!" he growled. "Then I'll get a job at RKO," retorted Shorty. "They're all Jews at RKO," said Fields. "They're not Jews, they're Roman Catholics," replied Shorty.
"The worst kind of Jew," countered Fields.

6 A lifelong agnostic, Fields was discovered reading a Bible on his deathbed. "I'm looking for a loophole," he explained.

৵৹ ৹৵

FILLMORE, Millard (1800–74), *US politician; 13th president of the United States (1850–53). Becoming president only because of Zachary Taylor's death in office, Fillmore has no claims to fame, except that during his presidency the first bathtub was installed in the White House.*

1 Fillmore's presidency is regrettably encapsulated in a story (possibly of malicious invention) that circulated in Washington soon after he was sworn in. He decided that he needed a new carriage, and a White House attendant, Edward Moran, was detailed to find a suitable one. He discovered a handsome equipage that was being sold off quite cheaply since its owner was leaving the town. Fillmore inspected it, approved it, but was troubled. "How would it do, Edward, for the president of the United States to ride around in a secondhand carriage?" Moran replied reassuringly, "But sure, Your Excellency is only a secondhand president!"

৵৹ ৹৵

FIRBANK, Ronald (1886–1926), *British novelist. His witty and decadent novels, including* Caprice *(1917),* Valmouth *(1919), and* Prancing Nigger *(1924), together with his flamboyant homosexuality, helped to make him a cult figure in some circles.*

1 Firbank very much wanted to have his portrait painted by Augustus John, but was overcome by dismay at the idea of having to introduce himself to John and explain what he wanted. He summoned a cab to take him to the great artist's studio, but on the way again lost his nerve. Augustus John recorded his mild astonishment when the cab driver was sent up to introduce his fare and explain his business, while Firbank himself sat blushing in the vehicle.

2 Firbank had offended writer Eddie Marsh by speaking irreverently of the poet Rupert Brooke. Meeting Firbank in a theater foyer some weeks later, Marsh resolutely turned his back and thrust his right hand into his pocket.

Firbank ignored the snub. He crept up behind Marsh, gently pulled Marsh's right hand out of his pocket, shook it, and politely slipped it back again.

৵৹ ৹৵

FISKE, Minnie Maddern (1865–1932), *US actress. She did much to popularize Ibsen's plays in the United States.*

1 The actress Margaret Anglin once left a message attached to the mirror in Minnie Fiske's dressing room. It read: "Margaret Anglin says Mrs. Fiske is the best actress in America." Mrs. Fiske read it, added two commas, and returned it to Miss Anglin. The revised note read: "Margaret Anglin, says Mrs. Fiske, is the best actress in America."

৵৹ ৹৵

FITZGERALD, Ella (1918–), *US black jazz singer, especially famous for her "scat" singing. She has performed with a number of jazz groups, notably those of Duke Ellington and Oscar Peterson.*

1 Ella once performed at Columbia, South Carolina, before an audience of children. The show seemed to go well, the children all joining in such songs as "Old MacDonald Had a Farm." A television interviewer went around the audience afterward. "What did you think of Ella Fitzgerald?" one little boy was asked. "Well, I liked her singing all right," he replied, "but she didn't break no glass."

৵৹ ৹৵

FITZGERALD, F[rancis] **Scott** [Key] (1896–1940), *US writer, whose successful first novel,* This Side of Paradise *(1920) enabled him to marry Zelda Sayre and live in style in France. The Great Gatsby (1925) was equally successful. Zelda, however, became increasingly unstable and by 1930 was confined to a psychiatric hospital. Fitzgerald became a Hollywood scriptwriter and eventually succumbed to alcoholism.*

1 Producer Joseph L. Mankiewicz, stubbornly convinced that the film *Three Comrades* would make more money if the leading female character did not die, asked Fitzgerald to change the script. "*Camille* would have made twice as much if Garbo had lived," he argued. "How about *Romeo and Juliet*—you wouldn't have wanted Juliet to live, would you?" asked Fitzgerald. Mankiewicz, whose cultural experience did not extend beyond the film world, cast his mind back to the unsuccessful 1936 film version of the play. "That's just it," he retorted triumphantly. "*Romeo and Juliet* didn't make a cent."

2 When Thomas Wolfe dedicated his first, very lengthy, novel to his editor, Maxwell Perkins, a proof copy was sent to F. Scott Fitzgerald for his views. "Dear Max," ran Fitzgerald's reply, "I liked the dedication, but after that I thought it fell off a bit."

ॐ ॐ

FITZGERALD, Zelda (1900–47), *US writer, wife of F. Scott Fitzgerald.*

1 Both Scott and Zelda suffered from self-destructive urges. Once, when they were guests of Gerald and Sara Murphy on the Riviera, Sara reproached them for their habit, after returning late from a party, of diving into the sea from thirty-five-foot rocks. Zelda, wide-eyed and innocent, replied, "But, Sara, didn't you know? We don't believe in conservation."

ॐ ॐ

FITZSIMMONS, Robert (1862–1917), *British heavyweight boxer.*

1 Due to meet James J. Jeffries, a considerably bigger man, in San Francisco in July 1902, Fitzsimmons was asked if he was worried about the disparity in size. "The bigger they are, the harder they fall," he is supposed to have said.

ॐ ॐ

FLAHERTY, Robert (1884–1951), *US film director.*

1 As a young man Robert Flaherty spent many months making arduous journeys in the far north in a search for iron ore and cod. He found neither, but in the course of his travels he shot over 70,000 feet of film. To salvage something from the wasted enterprise, Canadian financier Sir William Mackenzie encouraged him to edit the film and make a documentary. Flaherty toiled for weeks in a garret room and at last had an edited motion picture. Lighting a celebratory cigarette, he dropped the match on the floor. There was a tiny spurt of flame and in an instant the room was an inferno; every scrap of the highly inflammable celluloid was destroyed and Flaherty himself was badly burned, surviving only because he managed to jump out through a window onto the fire escape. His reaction to this disaster was a determination to return to the far north and make a film of Eskimo life "that people will never forget."

He did just that, and the result was the classic documentary *Nanook of the North* (1922).

ॐ ॐ

FLANNER, Janet (1892–1978), *US writer, for many years the Paris correspondent for* The New Yorker *magazine, under the pseudonym Genet.*

1 Jill Krementz, noted New York photographer, specializes in literary portraits. One of her subjects was Janet Flanner. Ms. Krementz asked if she had ever been married. Ms. Flanner replied, "I'm sure I have, but the precise details of the union quite escape me."

ॐ ॐ

FLAUBERT, Gustave (1821–80), *French writer. His most famous novel,* Madame Bovary *(1857), describes Emma Bovary's attempts to escape her drab existence through adultery and finally suicide.*

1 Flaubert was once asked outright who the real-life Emma Bovary was. With a wistful smile the author replied, "*I* am Madame Bovary."

ॐ ॐ

FLEETWOOD, Sir William (?1535–1594), *British lawyer, Recorder of London (1571).*

1 Fleetwood was famous for his rigorous prosecution of highwaymen. Determined to get their own back, a gang of them, halter at the ready, waylaid him near the gallows at Tyburn, bound his servants, tied his hands behind his back, and led him on his horse under the gallows. They then fixed the rope around his neck and left him to the mercy of his horse. Obedient to his master's desperate "Whoa, whoa," the horse stood quite still for a quarter of an hour or more until someone passed by and released Fleetwood from his predicament.

FLEMING, Sir Alexander (1881–1955), *British microbiologist. In 1928 he observed that a mold, which he identified as* Penicillium notatum, *destroyed bacteria around it in a contaminated culture. The antibacterial agent, which Fleming called "penicillin," was eventually isolated and identified by two other scientists, Sir Howard Florey and Ernst Chain, with whom Fleming shared the Nobel Prize in 1945.*

1 Fleming's discovery of penicillin was made by accident when a speck of dust happened to land on an uncovered culture plate. Touring a modern research laboratory some years later, he observed with interest the sterile, dust-free, air-conditioned environment in which the scientists worked. "What a pity you did not have a place like this to work in," said his guide. "Who can tell what you might have discovered in such surroundings!"

"Not penicillin," remarked Fleming with a smile.

ஃ ❧

FLEMING, Ian (1908–1964), *English suspense-story writer, famous for his creation of Secret Service agent James Bond.*

1 The English literary critic Peter Quennell was a guest at the Flemings' country house. Queried on the point by Mrs. Fleming, Quennell stated that he was an early riser. Mrs. Fleming then gently requested, in case he should care to walk about outside in the early morning, that he not disturb the dew on the spiderwebs on the lawn. Ian, it seemed, liked to look at them first thing in the morning when he awoke.

ஃ ❧

FLETCHER, Henry Prather (1873–1959), *US diplomat; ambassador to Italy (1924–29).*

1 Charles Gates Dawes, while ambassador to Great Britain, grumbled, "American diplomacy is easy on the brain but hell on the feet."

"It depends on which you use," commented Fletcher.

ஃ ❧

FOCH, Ferdinand (1851–1929), *French marshal. As commander of the French forces at the start of World War I, he was mainly responsible for the Allied victory at Ypres (1915). In 1918 as commander in chief of the Allied armies he led the decisive movement that forced the Germans back to the Rhine and final defeat.*

1 Marshal Foch's driver was often bothered by newspapermen anxious to get inside information on his master and his thinking about the war. "When does the marshal think the war will end?" they would ask, and the driver would promise to tell them if Foch divulged anything to him. One day he said, "This morning the marshal spoke." The reporters clustered around eargerly. "He said, 'Pierre, what do you think? When is this war going to end?'"

2 A young officer had been disciplined by his colonel for showing fear in battle. When Foch learned of the incident, however, he chose to reprimand the colonel rather than the officer. "None but a coward," he said, "dares to boast that he has never known fear."

3 (Sir Basil Thomson tells the following:)
"When the German delegation came to Marshal Foch at the end of the war to ask for armistice terms, the Frenchman picked up a paper from his desk and read a set of conditions.

"'But—there must be some mistake,' the leader of the German officers stammered in dismay. 'These are terms which no civilized nation could impose on another!'

"'I am very glad to hear you say so,' replied Foch gravely. 'No, gentlemen, these are not our terms. These are the terms imposed on Lille by the German commander when that city surrendered.'"

4 On a visit to the United States, Marshal Foch was escorted on a sight-seeing tour by a colonel who spoke French fluently. The distinguished visitor was taken to see the Grand Canyon. He gazed thoughtfully down into its depths. The colonel waited for his pronouncement. At length Foch stepped back from the brink and spoke: "What a marvelous place to drop one's mother-in-law!"

5 An American once complained to Marshal Foch about the insincere politeness of the French. "There is nothing in it but wind," he said.

"There is nothing but wind in a tire," replied Foch, "but it makes riding in a car very smooth and pleasant."

FONDA, Henry (1905–82), *US movie actor and director. His films include* The Grapes of Wrath *(1940);* War and Peace *(1956);* Twelve Angry Men *(1957), which he also directed; and* On Golden Pond *(1981), for which he received an Academy Award.*

1 Henry Fonda was asked to say in one phrase the one most important thing that any young actor has to know. Fonda answered, "How to become an old actor."

2 Fonda's father disapproved of his son's decision to take up acting as a career. He grudgingly agreed, however, to attend Henry's debut with the rest of the family. At home after the performance, which had been a great success, Fonda's mother and sisters congratulated him enthusiastically on his triumph. His father remained buried in silence behind a newspaper, until one of Fonda's sisters dared to make a tiny criticism of her brother's performance. "Shut up!" snapped the elder Fonda, tossing the paper aside. "He was perfect."

ॐ ॐ

FONTANNE, Lynn (1887–1983), *US actress, who with her husband, Alfred Lunt, made a highly successful team, performing mostly comedies.*

1 The fees paid by the film studios to actors sometimes amazed those accustomed to the comparatively slender Broadway salaries. When the Lunts made *The Guardsman* for MGM, they were asked by a reporter if it was true that they were getting $60,000 for their part in the film. Lynn Fontanne dumbfounded the MGM executives sitting in on the interview by replying, "Alfred and I would have worked for less, but nobody asked us."

ॐ ॐ

FONTENELLE, Bernard de (1657–1757), *French writer and philosopher. His scientific writings did much to spread the theories of Newton and Descartes.*

1 Fontenelle was conversing one day with Louis XIV when the king remarked that he had little faith in the existence of honorable men. "Plenty of honorable men exist, sire," said Fontenelle, "but they do not seek the company of kings."

2 A collection at the French Academy was found to be slightly short of the expected total, and one of the more miserly members was accused of having failed to make his contribution. He protested his innocence. "I didn't see it, but I believe it," said another academician generously. Remarked Fontenelle, "I, on the other hand, saw it, but I don't believe it."

3 In his great old age Fontenelle feebly but gallantly tried to pick up a fan a young lady had dropped. As she moved to help him, he exclaimed, "Ah, if I were only eighty again!"
See also OLIVER WENDELL HOLMES, JR. 6.

4 At a reception in his ninety-eighth year, Fontenelle spent the first part of the evening saying gallant things to an attractive young lady. When the guests were summoned to dinner, however, he passed ahead of her to secure his place at table. "So that's what your gallantries are worth!" said the lady. "You walk straight past me without even looking at me."
"Madame, if I had looked at you I could not have passed you," replied the old man.

5 "Death has forgotten us," said an aged friend to the equally aged Fontenelle. "Sh-sh!" said Fontenelle, bringing his finger to his lips.

6 Fontenelle died just a few weeks short of his hundredth birthday. When asked how he was feeling, he replied, "I feel nothing, apart from a certain difficulty of being."

ॐ ॐ

FONTEYN, Dame Margot [*née* Margaret Hookham] (1919–), *British ballerina. Joining the Sadler's Wells Ballet (now the Royal Ballet) in 1934, she has since performed with leading European and US companies, frequently dancing with Rudolf Nureyev. Her repertoire includes most of the classical roles.*

1 Asked whether she was in favor of the women's liberation movement, Miss Fonteyn replied, "Not if it means I have to carry the male dancers instead of them carrying me!"

2 (In Paris after the war, Margot Fonteyn went out one night with some friends.)
"At the Bal Nègre I was entranced as I watched the black dancers. One of them in-

vited me on to the floor. I thought it rude to refuse, and nervously stepped out, trying to follow his rhythm and movement. He steered me once around the hall then returned me to my table saying, 'You're an attractive girl, it's too bad you can't dance!' "

ॐ ◄६

FOOTE, Samuel (1720–77), *British actor and playwright. Having failed to establish himself as a tragic actor, Foote found himself much in demand as a comedian, particularly in his own farces. He was dubbed by his contemporaries "the English Aristophanes."*

1   In 1755 Charles Macklin, the famous actor, boasted in Foote's presence that he could repeat any speech after hearing it only once. Foote challenged Macklin to repeat the following: "So she went into the garden to cut a cabbage leaf to make an apple pie; and at the same time a great she-bear, coming up the street, pops its head into the shop — What! no soap? So he died and she very imprudently married the barber; and there were present the Picninnies, and the Joblillies, and the Garyalies, and the grand Panjandrum himself, with the little round button at top. . . . "

Macklin had to own himself defeated by this nonsense, but the speech has been responsible for two phrases still current in colloquial English: "no soap" (meaning unsuccessful, a failure) and "the grand Panjandrum" (meaning an important, or particularly a self-important, person).

2   The Duke of Cumberland once applauded Foote's wit with the words: "Mr. Foote, I swallow all the good things you say."

"Indeed, sir," said Foote, "then Your Royal Highness has an excellent digestion, for you never bring any of it up again."

3   Foote once asked a man why he was continually singing one particular tune. "Because it haunts me," the man replied. "No wonder," retorted Foote, "since you are forever murdering it."

4   The author of a rather foolish book entitled *Thoughts* asked Foote if he had read it. "No, I wait for the second volume," Foote replied. Somewhat baffled, the author asked

why. "Because I have heard that second thoughts are best," said Foote.

5   A group of people were discussing the long and happy marriage of a lady who had led a wild life before her wedding. They ascribed the successful outcome of the match to the fact that she had confessed all her previous affairs to her husband before they married. They were loud in her praise: "What candor! What courage!"

"Yes, and what a memory!" added Foote.

6   Foote went into White's Club in London with a friend, who wished to write a note. While his friend was busy at the desk, Foote stood around uneasily; since he was not a member of White's, which had a very different political complexion from his own, many of the men in the room were strangers to him. The compassionate Lord Carmarthen thought of a pretext for approaching him with a few friendly words. "Mr. Foote, your handkerchief is hanging out of your pocket," he began. "Thank you, my lord, thank you," said Foote, misunderstanding the casual remark as a warning against pickpockets and quickly pushing the handkerchief back into the pocket. "You know the company here better than I do."

7   A member of the royal court complained to Foote that he had been thrown out of a second-floor window for cheating at cards, and asked for his advice. "Do not play so high," replied Foote.

8   Samuel Foote was equaled in tightfistedness by his friend and fellow-actor David Garrick. On one occasion when they were out together Foote, reluctantly pulling out his purse to pay for the entertainment, dropped a guinea. Both men fell to their knees and started groping about on the floor. "Where on earth is it?" exclaimed Foote in exasperation after they had hunted vainly for some time. "Gone to the devil, I suppose," muttered Garrick. "Well, you always were one for making a guinea go further than anyone else," Foote remarked.

ॐ ◄६

FORD, Gerald R. (1913–   ), *US politician; 38th president of the United States (1974–77). He was appointed vice president to replace the* *disgraced Spiro Agnew in 1973 and ten months later took over as president when Nixon resigned. He devoted himself to the task of restoring Americans' faith in the presidency after the Watergate scandal but failed to be elected at the end of his term of office.*

1   President Ford was playing golf with ice-hockey star Gordie Howe. At the twelfth hole, Howe conceded a two-foot putt to his distinguished opponent. Ford insisted on taking the shot—and missed. "We won't count that one," said Howe generously. Pointing toward the reporters and Secret Service men at the edge of the green, Ford replied, "Maybe *you* won't, but *they* will."

৯৯ ৩৩

FORD, Henry (1863–1947), *US automobile manufacturer. The Ford Motor Company, founded in 1903, pioneered the mass production of automobiles with the assembly line set up to make the celebrated Model T in 1912.*

1   In the early stages of World War I, Henry Ford launched his chartered Peace Ship, which sailed to Europe with a passenger list of eminent pacifists. The intention was to appeal to heads of state to "get the boys out of the trenches by Christmas." Three weeks later Henry Ford was back in the United States. "I didn't get much peace," he said, "but I learned that Russia is going to be a great market for tractors."

2   A man of action, Ford is also remembered for his terse epigram, "History is bunk." He is supposed to have said this in 1919 on the witness stand during the course of his libel suit against the *Chicago Tribune*. What he actually said, in an interview with Charles N. Wheeler published in the *Chicago Tribune* (May 25, 1916), was: "History is more or less bunk. It's tradition. We don't want tradition. We want to live in the present and the only history that is worth a tinker's damn is the history we make today."

3   Henry Ford once called in an efficiency expert to examine the running of his company. The expert made a favorable report, but had reservations about one employee. "It's that man down the corridor," he said. "Every time I

go by his office he's just sitting there with his feet on his desk. He's wasting your money."

"That man," replied Ford, "once had an idea that saved us millions of dollars. At the time, I believe his feet were planted right where they are now."

4   A visitor to the factory of the Ford Motor Company happened to meet Henry Ford himself. Pointing to a finished car, Ford proudly declared, "There are exactly four thousand, seven hundred and nineteen parts in that model." Impressed that the president should have such details at his fingertips, the visitor subsequently asked a company engineer if the statement were true. The engineer shrugged his shoulders. "I'm sure I don't know," he replied. "I can't think of a more useless piece of information."

5   While on vacation in Dublin, Ireland, Ford was asked if he would contribute to a collection for a new orphanage. Judging the cause worthy, Ford promptly wrote out a check for two thousand pounds. His generosity made headline news in the local paper the following day. The amount of the check, however, was wrongly quoted as twenty thousand pounds. The director of the orphanage called on Ford at his hotel to apologize. "I'll phone the editor straight away and tell him to correct the mistake," he said.

"There's no need for that," replied Ford, taking out his checkbook and pen. "I'll give you a check for the remaining eighteen thousand pounds, but only on one condition. When the new building opens, I want this inscription on it: I WAS A STRANGER, AND YOU TOOK ME IN."

6   Ford was once asked why he made a habit of visiting his executives when problems arose rather than calling them to his own office. "I go to them to save time," explained Ford. "I've found that I can leave the other fellow's office a lot quicker than I can get him to leave mine."

৯৯ ৩৩

FORD, John (1895–1973), *US movie director. He specialized in westerns, but also made several films with more serious themes, such as the much-acclaimed The Grapes of Wrath (1940).*

1 While Ford was directing a film for Sam Goldwyn, the shooting schedule fell one day behind. Goldwyn visited the set, pointed out this fact, and inquired what the director was going to do about it. "Sam, about how many script pages do you think I should shoot a day?" asked Ford. "About five," was the rather uncertain response. Ford picked up the script and ripped out five pages. "Okay," he said, "now we're on schedule."

෪~ ᦞ

FORDYCE, George (1736–1802), *British physician.*

1 Dr. Fordyce sometimes drank a great deal at dinner. It was after one of these heavy sessions that he received an urgent summons to a lady patient taken ill with an unspecified complaint. Dr. Fordyce hurried to her house, aware that he was far from sober. He had considerable difficulty locating her pulse, and was then unable to count its beats. Muttering under his breath, "Drunk, by God!" he wrote out a prescription and hurriedly left the room. The following morning a letter came for the doctor from his patient. He opened it in expectation of a severe rebuke. Instead, the gist of the letter was as follows: she well knew the unfortunate condition in which he had found her the previous day and she begged him to keep the business confidential in consideration of the enclosed—a bank note for a hundred pounds. {This anecdote is told of others.}

෪~ ᦞ

FORGY, Howell Maurice (1908–83), *US naval chaplain.*

1 Forgy was a chaplain aboard the cruiser *New Orleans* when the Japanese attacked Pearl Harbor on December 7, 1941. As the Japanese planes roared overhead, it was discovered that the man with the keys to the ammunition locker had gone ashore. A group of crewmen managed to break into the locker, only to face a second obstacle—the power ammunition hoist was out of action. So the men, Forgy among them, formed a human chain, passing the shells from hand to hand up to the gun deck. Noticing that some of the men were weakening under the weight of the shells, Forgy slapped his neighbor on the back and cried, "Praise the Lord and pass the ammunition!"

{This catchphrase became the title of a popular song and was later adapted, when London was under attack from Hitler's flying bombs, as "Praise the Lord and keep the engine running"—said by Londoners as they waited for the engine to cut out, followed by ominous silence before the sound of the explosion.}

෪~ ᦞ

FORREST, Nathan Bedford (1821–77), *US general. He was an outstandingly successful cavalry commander in the Confederate army.*

1 Forrest was reminiscing with General John Hunt Morgan about their respective exploits in Tennessee and Kentucky in the summer of 1862. Morgan was keen to know how Forrest had achieved his remarkable success at Murfreesboro, where he had captured the garrison and stores in defiance of the federal forces that filled the surrounding countryside. Forrest's terse reply was "I just took the short cut and got there first with the most men."

{This is usually recorded as "I got there fustest with the mostest."}

෪~ ᦞ

FORSTER, John (1812–76), *British historian, biographer of his great friend, Charles Dickens.*

1 One evening, when Dickens was dining at Forster's house, Mary, the maid, served boiled beef without any carrots. Forster instantly recalled her and demanded an explanation. "Weren't none," the girl replied simply. With a dignified wave of the hand, Forster commanded: "Mary, let there be carrots."

෪~ ᦞ

FOSDICK, Harry Emerson (1878–1969), *US Protestant minister and teacher. He was a prominent force on the liberal side of the liberal-fundamentalist debate of the 1920s, wrote a large number of theological works, and was the moving spirit behind the interdenominational church at Columbia University.*

1 One winter night Fosdick was awakened by a tipsy young student banging on his door.

After Dr. Fosdick had admitted him, the young man asked him to explain to him the difference between modernism and fundamentalism. "Go home and sober up," advised Fosdick, "and come back when you have slept it off and I will gladly give you the answer." The young man began to sob: "The trouble is, doctor, when I'm sober, I won't give a damn!"

⋯ ⋯

FOSTER, Stephen Collins (1826–64), *US composer. His songs, such as "Swanee River" (1851), drew upon black slave melodies for their inspiration.*

1 Though an accomplished flutist, Stephen Foster composed his melodies without needing to work them out on any instrument. At the height of his popularity he was invited to a party at which he suspected it was not his company that was sought but his flute-playing ability. He stayed home and sent his flute to the party.
See also PABLO DE SARASATE Y NAVASCUÉS 1.

⋯ ⋯

FOUCHÉ, Joseph, Duc d'Otrante (1763–1820), *French politician and police functionary. Until the French Revolution, Fouché was a priest and teacher. In 1792 he was elected to the National Convention and two years later played an active role in overthrowing Robespierre. Napoleon made him minister of police, and he ran an exceptionally successful intelligence service. His political career ended with the restitution of the monarchy in 1816.*

1 Napoleon found Fouché an able minister, but resented his freedom of speech and independent attitude. Seeking to disconcert him, the emperor once reminded Fouché that he had been one of those who had voted in favor of executing Louis XVI. "True," said Fouché, unabashed. "That was the very first service that I had occasion to perform for Your Majesty."

2 On Napoleon's escape from Elba, Fouché, who had been making overtures to the victorious allies, turned coat with his customary promptitude. During the Hundred Days he was employed in compiling a list of those whom Napoleon intended to punish once he had reestablished his ascendancy. After the battle of Waterloo, this list was something of an embarrassment to its compiler, particularly when it fell into the hands of Talleyrand, whose name of course was on it. Running his eyes over the list, Talleyrand remarked, "One must at least do him the justice of acknowledging that he has omitted none of his friends."

⋯ ⋯

FOWLER, Gene (1890–1960), *US journalist, biographer, and novelist.*

1 At a high-school dance Gene Fowler sat next to a ravishing young girl who began to make a play for him. Young Fowler sat silent under her flattery. At last she offered him a penny for his thoughts. "I was just wondering," came the reply, "whether a horse's legs ever go to sleep on him."

2 Fowler was a master of creative expense-account writing. In 1921, while on Hearst's *New York American,* he traveled to northern Canada to interview three US navy balloonists who had turned up, after being missing for a month, at a remote spot called Moose Factory. While most of their fellow journalists waited at Toronto, Fowler and five colleagues loaded a private railroad car with choice food and drink and set out for Moose Factory.
    The cost of the expedition worked out at $7,200 — $1,200 for each of them. Fowler got back to the *American* offices and began drawing up his expense account. He listed all manner of items that might be thought necessary for an expedition to the far north — mittens, parkas, snowshoes — but was still short of the necessary total. He added on the purchase of a secondhand dogsled and a team of huskies to draw it. The *American's* auditor returned the account; it still did not balance. Fowler added a mention of the death of the lead dog and compensation of $80 paid to its owner, plus a commemorative headstone for the same dog — $20. Again the account was returned, this time just a trifle short. Fowler added the final item: "Flowers for the bereft bitch — $1.50."

3 In the mid-1930s there was an influx of homosexuals to Fire Island, where Gene Fowler had made his home. His biographer, H. Allen Smith, asked him how he felt about it.

Fowler frowned. "I'm worried. I lie in bed at night and worry about them."

"You think they are ruining the island?"

"No, it's not that. The thing that bothers me is: suppose it turns out they're right!"

≈≈ ≈≈

FOX, Charles James (1749–1806), *British statesman. His independent attitude prevented him from holding high office for any length of time or from achieving his political aims. He constantly opposed William Pitt and supported the French Revolution until it became plain that Napoleon was planning to invade Britain. Many tales circulated about his wit, his immoral life, and his passion for gambling.*

1 Fox's father severely reprimanded him for his immense debts, concluding his rebuke by saying that he wondered that he could sleep or take any pleasure in life with these hanging over him. "Your lordship need not be surprised," his son coolly replied. "You should rather be astonished that my creditors can sleep."

2 In November 1779 William Adam, a politician who had lately become one of Lord North's supporters, challenged Fox to a duel over a speech he had made attacking the government. When the pistols had been loaded and handed to the combatants, Fox took his position facing Adam squarely. He was told to stand sideways, to lessen the chance of his opponent's shot hitting him. Fox, who had done his best to find an honorable way to avert the duel, merely said, "I am as thick one way as the other."

The signal to fire was given. Adam fired; Fox did not. The seconds called to Fox that he must fire. "I'll be damned if I do; I have no quarrel," he said. The combatants then advanced to shake hands. Fox said, "Adam, your shot would have killed me if you had not been using *government* powder."

{Actually, Fox had been hit and slightly wounded in the groin. In later years Adam became a devoted adherent of Fox.}

3 On September 15, 1784, Fox went with his brother to Moorfields in London to watch the Italian Lunardi make an ascent in a balloon. As they were standing in the dense crowd, Fox felt a hand at his pocket. He quickly turned and grabbed the would-be pickpocket's wrist. "You have chosen an occupation that will bring you to utter ruin, my friend," he observed. The thief begged for mercy, saying that he had been driven by desperation to turn to crime, his wife was starving, his children were ill, and he was penniless. Moved by this tragic tale, Fox gave the man a guinea and warned him to mend his ways.

At the conclusion of the show Fox felt for his watch and found it gone. His brother said that he had seen his "friend" take it. "You saw him take it, and yet you made no move to stop him?" said Fox, astounded. "Well," replied his brother, "you and he appeared to be on such good terms with each other that I did not choose to interfere."

4 When Fox went to see the play *The Gamester,* the newspapers sensed the opportunity for an edifying paragraph on how the notorious gambler had been moved to tears at this theatrical depiction of a gambler's career. In fact, Fox just watched attentively and in silence until the point at which the hero announces that he will borrow money upon the reversion of his uncle's estate. Fox turned to his friend Richard Brinsley Sheridan and whispered, "Rather odd, eh, that he had not thought of that before?"

5 While canvassing, Fox asked a respectable tradesman for his vote. "I admire your abilities," the man replied, "but damn your principles." Fox replied, "And I applaud your sincerity, but damn your manners."

6 While canvassing in London's Haymarket, Fox entered a saddler's shop to persuade the man to vote for him. The saddler thought very little of Fox and even less of his Whiggish policies. Producing a halter with a running noose, the saddler indicated that Fox could not have his vote but he might like to take the halter and put himself out of his misery. Fox courteously declined the offer. "I return thanks for your present, but I should be sorry to deprive you of a family piece," he said.

≈≈ ≈≈

FOX, George (1624–91), *English religious leader; founder of the Quakers. Dissatisfied with the formalism in current religious practice, Fox taught that human conduct could, if people were receptive, be brought under the immediate* *guidance of the Holy Spirit. His Journal (1674) is a powerful and fascinating account of his life, his religious experiences, and the persecution he suffered for his beliefs.*

1 Among the people influenced by Fox's teachings was William Penn. The son of a distinguished admiral, Penn used to wear a sword as a reminder of his own and his family's martial tradition. As he came further under the spell of the Quaker doctrine of nonviolence, he began to doubt whether it was appropriate for him to wear such an ornament. He sought Fox's counsel. "Wear thy sword as long as thou canst," was the Quaker leader's advice. A few weeks later when Fox met Penn, he asked him with a smile, "Where is thy sword?" Replied Penn, "I wore it as long as I could."

ॐ ∽

FRAGUIER, Claude François (1666–1728), *French scholar. Having entered the Jesuit order in 1683, he found relaxation from his theological studies in reading the Latin poets. Increasingly drawn toward literature, he subsequently left the Jesuits and devoted the rest of his life to translating and writing critical studies of the classics.*

1 Over a twenty-year period the Abbé Fraguier persisted in prosecuting a case at law that he could not, as his friends continued to tell him, possibly win. Finally it was decided against him. His friends all reminded him that had he never engaged in the case he could have spared himself much sorrow and heartbreak. The abbé replied, "Every night before falling asleep I've managed to win this case. Do you call that nothing?"

ॐ ∽

FRANCE, Anatole (1844–1924), *French novelist, born Jacques Anatole Thibault. His novels, admired for their elegance and erudition, are deeply marked by pessimism. After the Dreyfus case (1897), France underwent a change in his views of society that led him to espouse socialism and even to be drawn toward communism. He won the 1921 Nobel Prize for literature.*

1 Visiting Lourdes, Anatole France surveyed the ex-votos and crutches and remarked, "Don't see any wooden legs."

2 Anatole France was in a modest way a collector of antiquities. A friend with similar interests once brought a newly purchased Roman cameo along for him to inspect. "Whose head do you think it is?" he asked. France studied the miniature intently. "Well, whose do you want it to be?" he inquired affably.

3 His books having brought in little revenue, France was still a poor man when he was awarded the cross of the Legion of Honor. His friends sympathized with his plight; one of them suggested that it would have been more generous to have given the writer a cash prize instead of the cross, which served no useful purpose. "Oh, I wouldn't say that," said France. "When I wear the sash, it will cover the stain on my jacket. That's useful."

ॐ ∽

FRANCIS I (1494–1547), *king of France (1515–47). Much of his reign was dominated by his conflict with the Holy Roman Emperor Charles V over the control of Italy. Despite such setbacks as his imprisonment at Pavia (1525), he is remembered as a model Renaissance ruler, mainly on account of his patronage of writers and artists who sang his praises.*

1 Francis, a great lover of strenuous exercise, was a proficient tennis player. Once when he was playing tennis with a monk as a partner, the monk hit a fine stroke that decided the set in Francis's favor. The king applauded his partner: "That is the stroke of a monk!"

"Sire," said the man of God, "whenever it shall please you, it shall be the stroke of an abbot." Francis took the hint and the monk received his preferment.

ॐ ∽

FRANCIS II (1768–1835), *Holy Roman Emperor (1792–1806) and, as Francis I, emperor of Austria (1804–35). After successive defeats by Napoleon, Francis allied himself with France. His daughter, Marie–Louise, became Napoleon's second wife in 1810. After 1814 Francis, in conjunction with his minister Metternich, sought to make Austria a point of stability in the turmoil of post-Napoleonic Europe.*

1 Even the Austrian army's fearful defeat by Napoleon at Austerlitz in 1805 failed to impress the Austrians with the seriousness of war.

Francis II, arriving back at Vienna at the head of his vanquished troops, announced quite cheerfully to his courtiers, "Well, here we are! Well beaten!"

2   A certain distinguished person was recommended to the emperor as a fine patriot, intensely loyal to the empire. "But is he a patriot for *me*?" inquired the great autocrat.

&

FRANCIS FERDINAND (1863–1914), *archduke of Austria. The nephew of Emperor Francis Joseph, Francis Ferdinand unexpectedly became heir to the Austro-Hungarian monarchy after the deaths of Crown Prince Rudolf (1889) and his own father (1896). He was assassinated at Sarajevo in 1914.*

1   On the fatal day at Sarajevo, the conspirators had placed a number of assassins in the crowd. The first one to act was a young man who threw a bomb at the archduke and his wife. The bomb bounced off the vehicle in which they were traveling and failed to explode. The would-be assassin ran off into the crowd and the day's ceremonial duties continued. In the course of the mayoral reception Francis Ferdinand was told the bomb-thrower had been captured. He commented wryly, "Wait and see: instead of locking that fellow up, they'll be proper Austrians and award him the medal of merit."

&

FRANCIS JOSEPH (1830–1916), *emperor of Austria (1848–1916). During his reign the rise of nationalism led to the decline of Austria's hegemony in central Europe and it fell increasingly under the influence of Prussia and the nascent German empire. The assassination of his nephew and heir Francis Ferdinand in 1914 evoked his ultimatum to Serbia that led to World War I.*

1   The emperor, having heard the conversational abilities of the famous comedian Girardi much praised, asked the actor to tea, in expectation of a flood of brilliant talk. But Girardi said almost nothing, speaking only when spoken to, and then replying in tones of the greatest respect. The disappointed emperor finally remarked, "But my dear Girardi, I've been told

so much about your extraordinary conversational gifts." Girardi wiped his forehead and replied, "Majesty, sometime you just try chatting with an emperor."

2   The emperor was basically a simple man. On one occasion he and two companions were out hunting near Bad Ischl in Austria, dressed in hunting clothes. A passing peasant stopped his cart to offer them a lift. As they were some way from their lodge, they accepted and soon fell into conversation with their benefactor. The peasant asked one of his passengers who he was. "The king of Saxony," was the supercilious reply. The peasant nodded and asked the next man the same question. "The king of Bavaria," said the second passenger. "And you?" said the peasant, indicating Francis Joseph. "I suppose you are the emperor of Austria?"

&

FRANCIS of Assisi, Saint (c. 1182–1226), *Italian friar; founder of the Franciscan order. After a wild and dissipated youth, he was converted in 1205 and began to devote himself to prayer and works of charity. In acknowledgment of his love for the countryside and wild creatures, he was designated patron saint of ecology in 1980.*

1   Saint Francis, who traveled quite extensively on missionary work, in 1219 visited Egypt, where he hoped to convert the sultan, al-Malik al-Kamil. The sultan laid a trap for the saint, spreading a carpet decorated with crosses in front of his divan. "If he treads on the crosses, I will accuse him of insulting his God, and if he refuses to tread on the carpet, I will accuse him of insulting me." Saint Francis walked straight onto the carpet, to the jeers of the sultan. "Our Lord was crucified between two thieves," said the saint, undisturbed. "We Christians have the True Cross. The crosses of the thieves we have left to you, and I am not ashamed to tread on those."

&

FRANCO, Francisco (1892–1975), *Spanish general and statesman. Commander in chief of the Falangists in the Spanish Civil War, he established a dictatorship (1939) after the defeat of the Republican government. He maintained Spain's neutrality during World War II and remained head of state until his death.*

1 Franco had remarkable powers of endurance and persisted in surviving long after the time that even many of his supporters considered appropriate. On his deathbed his aide announced that a General García wanted to be admitted to say goodbye to him. Franco asked, "Why, is García going on a trip?"

৯৯ ৫৩

FRANKLIN, Benjamin (1706–90), *US statesman, diplomat, and scientist. Franklin's first trade was printing; he published the* Pennsylvania Gazette *from 1729 and in 1733 started the immensely popular* Poor Richard's Almanac. *He represented the American colonists in London (1757–62, 1764–75) and on his return home actively promoted the revolutionary cause, being one of the five who drafted the* Declaration of Independence *(1776). Sent to win France's support for the Revolution, he brought about the vital alliance in 1778. He returned to take part in the Constitutional Convention (1787) and retired from public life the following year. Franklin found time to make important contributions to physical theory, identified lightning as an electrical charge, drew the first printed chart of the Gulf Stream, and invented bifocal spectacles and the lightning rod, among many other things.*

1 In Paris in the early 1770s after the death of his wife, Franklin thought seriously of marrying Madame Helvétius, the attractive widow of the famous philosopher. Meeting him after a few days during which the pressure of his other commitments had prevented him from seeing her, she chided him for not paying her a visit. "Madam, I am waiting until the nights are longer," was the reply.

2 When a committee sat to examine the wording of Jefferson's draft of the Declaration of Independence, the proud author was somewhat discomfited by their editorial revisions. Franklin noticed his colleague's distress and told him a little story. When he was a young man, Franklin said, he had a friend who had completed his apprenticeship as a hatter and was about to open up in business for himself. He was anxious to have a fine signboard and composed one with the inscription "John Thompson, hatter, makes and sells hats for ready money" over the depiction of a hat. He then showed it to his friends and asked them

what they thought. The first one remarked that "hatter" was superfluous, as "makes and sells hats" showed the nature of the business. The second pointed out that "makes" could be left off the sign, as customers were unlikely to be interested in who had made the hats. The third friend said that as it was not the custom locally to sell on credit, the words "for ready money" were superfluous, and they too were struck out, leaving just: "John Thompson sells hats." "No one would expect you to give them away," said the fourth friend, "so what is the point of 'sells?'" Finally someone said that it seemed unnecessary to have the word "hats" on the board since there was the painted picture of a hat. So the board eventually read "John Thompson" with a picture of a hat underneath the name. Jefferson was much mollified by this story, and it was generally agreed that the committee's editorial work had improved the wording of the Declaration of Independence.

3 At the signing of the first draft of the Declaration of Independence John Hancock, one of the signatories, observed, "We must be unanimous, we must all hang together." Franklin replied, "We must indeed all hang together — or, most assuredly, we shall all hang separately."
   {Doubt has been cast on the authenticity of this story.}

4 After the Declaration of Independence each state assembly busied itself with drafting new constitutions and laws to take the place of the old. The Pennsylvania Assembly passed two or three months in such business, but at the end of the time the delegates were no closer to agreeing on a new form of government than they had been when they started. The citizens of Pennsylvania, on the other hand, had gone quietly about their daily lives, and affairs in the state had run pretty smoothly without the benefit of a new constitution. Franklin pointed out to his fellow delegates the dangers of this situation: "Gentlemen, you see we have been living under anarchy, yet the business of living has gone on as usual. Be careful; if our debates go on too much longer, people may come to see that they can get along very well without us."

5 A French well-wisher remarked enthusiastically to Franklin in 1776 that the revolution-

ary states of America offered a great spectacle. "Yes," Franklin agreed, "but the spectators don't pay."

6 Shortly after Washington's victory at Yorktown, Benjamin Franklin, as America's minister in Europe, attended a dinner in Paris at which the French foreign minister and the British ambassador were also present. The Frenchman proposed a toast to his king: "Louis XVI, who like the moon fills the earth with a soft benevolent glow." The British ambassador followed with: "George III, who like the noonday sun spreads his light and illumines the world." Franklin rose and said, "I give you George Washington, general of the armies of the United States, who, like Joshua of old, commanded both the sun and the moon to stand still, and both obeyed."

{Several authorities have commented on the inherent unlikeliness of this sequence of toasts. After all, the United States and France were allies at the time of Franklin's residence in Paris, and neither George III nor Louis XVI seems a particularly obvious candidate for comparison with their respective celestial bodies. Could it be an adaptation of a possible earlier toast from the period of the Seven Years' War, with Louis XV of France [sun], Maria Theresa of Austria [moon], and Frederick the Great of Prussia [Joshua]?}

7 When Franklin was dining out in Paris, one of the other diners posed the question: "What condition of man most deserves pity?" Each guest proposed an example of such a pitiable condition. When Franklin's turn came, he offered: "A lonesome man on a rainy day who does not know how to read."

8 Franklin was walking with friends along the banks of a small stream. The wind that day was strong enough to form waves on the surface of the water. Announcing that he had the power to calm the waves, Franklin walked a little way upstream and solemnly waved his walking stick three times over the water. His companions watched in amazement as the surface of the stream became as smooth as glass. Franklin later enlightened them: he had shaken a few drops of oil from the hollow joint of his bamboo cane.

9 When Franklin was in France, he frequently used to play chess with the elderly Duchess of Bourbon. On one occasion Franklin put her king in check and then took it. "We do not take kings so," remonstrated the duchess. "We do in America," replied Franklin.

10 Franklin was taken to a meeting of the French Academy at which Voltaire was also present. The members of the Academy all wished to see the two famous men introduced to each other, and there was a buzz of expectation as the introduction was made. The two bowed and spoke, as politeness demanded, but the onlookers, who felt they were witnessing a historic moment, thought there ought to be something more. The great men, slightly embarrassed and puzzled, took each other by the hand. Still the onlookers felt cheated and the noise increased. "*Il faut s'embrasser, à la française,*" someone explained. So Franklin and Voltaire threw their arms around each other and kissed each other on the cheeks, to the tumultuous applause of the Academy members. One witness exclaimed, "*Qu'il était charmant de voir embrasser Solon et Sophocle!*" (How delightful to see Solon and Sophocles embracing!) and these words spread throughout Europe as epitomizing this momentous encounter.

{The allusion to Solon, the great lawgiver of ancient Athens, was a tribute to Franklin's part in shaping the 1776 Pennsylvania constitution.}

11 At a meeting of a Parisian literary society Franklin found himself a bit at sea as flowery compliments in French were exchanged. He decided that it would be safest to clap only when he saw a lady of his acquaintance applauding. After the gathering was over, Franklin's little grandson said, "But, Grandpapa, you always applauded, and louder than anyone else, when they praised you."

12 According to the *American Jest Book* (1789): "[On the day the Constitutional Convention agreed to the new constitution to present to the public] Dr. Franklin asked a gentleman who sat next to him, whether he had taken notice of the picture of the sun in the recess at the back of the president's chair? He replied that he had, but not with a particular attention. The doctor then observed that

painters had been puzzled to paint a single sun in such manner that the spectator could determine whether it was a rising or a setting sun; he added, that he had viewed the picture before mentioned as often as he had been in the hall, and never had been able to come to a determination, but *now* he was sure it was a *rising* sun."

13 At the conclusion of the Constitutional Convention, a lady asked Franklin, "Well, doctor, do we have a republic or a monarchy?"

"A republic — if we can keep it," Franklin replied.

14 An English peer invited Franklin, during his stay in London, to admire a house the peer had recently had built for himself. Behind the handsome colonnaded facade, the house was oddly and inconveniently laid out on account of the narrow and irregular plot on which it had been constructed. "All you need to do to enjoy your house, my lord," Franklin observed, "is to rent a spacious apartment directly across the street."

15 Seeing Franklin lying in an awkward position during his last hours, his daughter tried to raise him into a more comfortable attitude, hoping, as she said, to enable him to lie easier. "A dying man can do nothing easy," said Franklin.

౩৯ ◄৭

FRANKS, Sir Oliver Shewell (1905–   ), *British diplomat. He entered the civil service in 1939 and was British ambassador to the United States (1948–52).*

1 In December 1948, a Washington radio station telephoned various ambassadors in the capital, asking what they would like for Christmas. The unedited replies were recorded and broadcast in a special program the following week. "Peace throughout the world," proclaimed the French ambassador. "Freedom for all people enslaved by imperialism," demanded the Russian ambassador. "Well, it's very kind of you to ask," came the polite voice of Sir Oliver. "I'd quite like a box of crystallized fruit."

౩৯ ◄৭

FREDERICK II [Frederick the Great] (1712–86), *king of Prussia (1740–86). He pursued a program of enlightened despotism that brought* *Prussia for the first time to the forefront of the European powers and confirmed its military supremacy. His palace of Sans Souci, near Potsdam, was a center for musicians and intellectuals, including Voltaire.*

1 On a campaign in Silesia, Frederick gave orders that all fires and lights were to be extinguished in his camp by a certain hour. To make certain that his order was obeyed he himself went the rounds. Passing by the tent of a certain Captain Zietern, he saw the glimmer of a candle, and upon entering found the officer sealing a letter to his wife. Frederick demanded to know what he thought he was doing; did he not know the orders? The captain threw himself at the king's feet, unable to deny or excuse his disobedience. Frederick told him to sit down and add a postscript to the letter, which he dictated: "Tomorrow I shall perish on the scaffold." Zietern wrote what he was told and was duly executed the following day.

2 Frederick arranged a tour of inspection of the prison in Berlin. The prisoners fell on their knees before him, all vigorously protesting their innocence. One man alone remained silent and aloof. Frederick called to him, "You there. Why are you here?"

"Armed robbery, Your Majesty."

"And are you guilty?"

"Yes, indeed, Your Majesty. I entirely deserve my punishment."

Frederick summoned the warder. "Guard, release this guilty wretch at once. I will not have him kept in this prison where he will corrupt all the fine innocent people who occupy it."

3 One of Frederick's worst setbacks during the Seven Years' War was in 1757 at the battle of Kolin, when he was forced to abandon the siege of Prague. As his cavalry streamed past him in full retreat, Frederick tried to rally them with shouts of "Rogues! Cowards! Would you live forever?"

{The phrase has been used in later periods by other commanders.}

4 Rossbach (1757) was one of Frederick's greatest victories, when, with very little damage to itself, the Prussian army inflicted heavy losses on the opposing French and German forces. Many French officers were captured.

Frederick, who had justifiable hopes of weaning the French away from the alliance against him, invited them to share his table. He apologized for the scanty provisions, saying, "But, gentlemen, I did not expect you so soon, and in such large numbers."

5 After the disastrous defeat suffered by Frederick's forces at Kunersdorf, many men deserted from the Prussian army. One was caught and taken before the king, who asked him why he had deserted. "Because things were going badly for Your Majesty." Frederick reflected for a moment, then said mildly, "I suggest that you wait a week. Then, if things are still going badly, we'll desert together."

6 His cook Noël one day served some marvelous pastry to which the king paid due honor. After complimenting Noël, he added, "But don't serve this too often. Gluttony is a sin, and we may both in consequence have to burn in hell." The cook replied, "That shouldn't frighten us — everyone knows that neither of us is afraid of fire."

7 The worthy General von Winterfeldt had long been in disfavor with the king. Happening to encounter the monarch in Potsdam, he saluted him with the greatest respect, but Frederick simply turned his back on him. "I am happy to see that Your Majesty is no longer angry with me," murmured Winterfeldt. "How so?" demanded Frederick. "Because Your Majesty has never in his life turned his back on an enemy," replied the general.
{It is said that this reply led to a reconciliation.}

8 A soldier in one of the Prussian regiments had a watch chain of which he was very proud. Because he could not afford a watch he used to wear a bullet attached to the chain's free end. One day Frederick noticed this curious ornament and, deciding to have some fun with the man, took out his own diamond-studded watch. "My watch tells me that it is five o'clock," he said. "What time does yours tell?" Replied the soldier: "My watch does not tell me the hour, but tells me every minute that it is my duty to die for Your Majesty." Frederick was so pleased with this response that he handed his own watch over to the man, saying,

"Take this so you may be able to tell the hour also."

9 In 1770 Frederick's court was visited by General Gideon von Laudon. Before his retirement in 1763 Laudon had been one of Austria's most successful military commanders and had inflicted heavy defeats on Frederick himself at Kunersdorf and Landshut during his country's Seven Years' War with Prussia. At a formal dinner the general was placed across the table from Frederick. When the king, never slow to acknowledge military skill even in an adversary, saw where Laudon had been seated, he called out for all his court to hear, "Pray, sir, take place here at my right. I do not feel at ease to have you opposite me, even at table."

10 When the time came to sign the treaty for the first partition of Poland in 1772, Maria Theresa, Archduchess of Austria, wept. "I sign because so many great and wise men want me to," she said. "But a long time after my death, the world will witness the results of an act that has gone against all precedent of what is accepted as sacred and just." Frederick the Great was unmoved by her tears. "She is always weeping," he observed, "but always annexing."

11 The great physician Georg von Zimmermann was summoned to attend Frederick the Great on his deathbed. The king remarked ironically, "You have, I presume, sir, helped many a man into the next world."
"Not as many as Your Majesty," replied the doctor, "nor did so much glory accrue to me."

&⋯⋯&

FREDERICK AUGUSTUS I (1750–1827), *elector (1763–1806) and king (1806–27) of Saxony. Forced to fight against Napoleon, he became the latter's ally after the battle of Jena (1806), and remained loyal to the French emperor, with the result that he lost much of his territories following Napoleon's final defeat. A conscientious administrator and a cultured man, the king was known as "the Just."*

1 The king had a barber who, like himself, had no prejudice against wine. Once the barber happened to nick the monarch badly. The latter broke out, "That comes from all that damned alcohol!"

"Unfortunately true, Your Majesty," said the barber humbly. "Alcohol does tend to dry the skin."

੩੦ ੦੬

FREDERICK WILLIAM I (1688–1740), *king of Prussia (1713–40). His strict and vigorous rule turned Prussia into a powerful state. He reinforced its position in Europe by modernizing and enlarging its army.*

1 Frederick William was deeply disappointed by his son, the future Frederick the Great, who in his youth seemed more interested in French culture, music, and literature than in the military virtues. The father's disaffection turned to actual hatred, and his treatment became so harsh that the young prince decided to run away, with the aid of two accomplices, Lieutenants Katte and Keith. Their plan was discovered; Keith escaped, but the prince and Katte were captured and court-martialed. Katte was sentenced to life imprisonment, Frederick to solitary confinement. Frederick William, deciding that Katte's sentence was too lenient, had him beheaded in the presence of Prince Frederick.

This drastic measure had the desired effect; Frederick asked the king's pardon and began to apply himself to acquiring the Prussian military philosophy.

2 The pastor attending Frederick William on his deathbed warned him that if he wished to go to heaven he must forgive all his enemies. The king's thoughts immediately turned to his hated brother-in-law, George II of England. "In that case," he told his wife reluctantly, "write to your brother and tell him I forgive him, but be sure not to do it until after my death."

3 The priest sent to console the dying Frederick William read to him out of the Book of Job: "Naked came I out of my mother's womb and naked shall I return thither." The king replied, "No, not quite naked. I shall have my uniform on." And died.

੩੦ ੦੬

FREDERICK WILLIAM IV (1795–1861), *king of Prussia (1840–61). His liberal views did much to further the popular demands for German nationhood. However, the king's concessions after the revolutionary outbreaks in 1848 were negated by Austrian hostility.*

1 The citizens of the town of Gumbinnen petitioned the king for leave to change the name of their local river, the Pissa. Frederick William endorsed the petition: "Granted. Recommend Urinoco."

2 The king attended the performance of a lengthy, tedious, and now justifiably forgotten play. As he left the royal loge, he noticed the loge attendant slumped in his chair, fast asleep. "An eavesdropper," whispered the king to his aide.

੩੦ ੦੬

FREUD, Sigmund (1856–1939), *Austrian psychiatrist of Jewish descent, founder of modern psychoanalysis. With the Viennese physician Josef Breuer he wrote* Studies in Hysteria *(1895) and* The Interpretation of Dreams *(1899); these works outline the theory he subsequently developed that neuroses originate in childhood experiences and desires, often of a sexual nature, which have been deliberately or unconsciously repressed. Much of Freud's work was controversial, particularly his theories about children's sexuality, but his concept of the unconscious mind underlies most modern inquiries into human behavior and motives.*

1 On a visit to the United States Freud admitted to Carl Jung that he found American women disturbing and that they gave him erotic dreams. "I continue to dream of prostitutes," he complained. "Why don't you do something about it then?" asked Jung. Freud was shocked. "But I'm a married man," exclaimed the crusader against repression.

2 Cigar-smoking is often thought of as a symbolic activity, the cigar itself frequently interpreted as a phallic symbol or emblem of masculinity. Freud himself was an inveterate cigar-smoker. A curious student once asked him if his cigar-smoking carried any particular symbolic weight for him. He puffed reflectively, then replied, "Sometimes a cigar is just a cigar."

3 In a raid on Vienna in 1938, the Germans ransacked Freud's office and emptied his safe. On his return, Freud simply shrugged his shoulders and remarked, "I would never have taken so much for a single visit."

❧ ❦

FRICK, Henry Clay (1849–1919), *US industrialist. He was chairman of the Carnegie Steel Company (1889–1900) and played an important role in the formation of the US Steel Corporation (1901).*

1 Frick had an estate at Pride's Crossing, Massachusetts, where he liked to spend the summer months. Each year, he would load up a custom-built railroad car with his priceless collection of art treasures and transport them from New York to Pride's Crossing. Journalist Oswald Garrison Villard once asked him if he was not afraid that the paintings might be stolen or damaged in transit. "Oh, no," replied Frick with confidence. "They're insured."

❧ ❦

FRISCO, Joe (1891–1958), *US comedian, born Louis Wilson Josephs in Rock Island, Illinois. From 1918 until his death he was known to all as Joe Frisco, and considered by many the fastest natural wit in the history of comedy. Robert Sylvester tells two anecdotes.*

1 "It was always argued among the hip set as to whether Frisco's stutter was natural or a planned affectation to make his timing more effective. . . . Almost at the end of the line, he was living in a scrubby hotel in Hollywood where the clientele was mostly former vaudevillians on the downbeat. Joe sneaked an old pal into his room and bedded him down on the floor.

"'Mr. Frisco,' the hotel manager said firmly on the phone one day, 'if you have an extra guest in your room it will be one dollar a day extra.'

"'All right,' agreed Joe, 'b-b-but send up another B-B-Bible.'"

2 "Behind the bar the lodge had mounted a deer head on the wall to aid the place's outdoorsy atmosphere. Frisco would look at this deer head in wonderment.

"'He m-m-must have been c-c-coming pretty fast,' he would decide, 'to g-g-go right through that wall.'"

❧ ❦

"Some years ago — I'm sure they order these things better now — I had occasion to visit the kindergarten class of a highly progressive school, attended by my small son Jonathan. The tots were engaged in what I believe is termed rhythmic play. They were following the lead of their teacher, an energetic young woman, who danced and marched about the room clapping her hands in time to the music of a phonograph record. The docile pupils straggled along behind her in somewhat ragged formation.

"After the rhythmic play was over, I drew my five-year-old son Jonathan aside — his countenance had seemed particularly knowing and stoical — and said: 'I guess you have lots of fun doing that, don't you?' He turned his face up to me and replied, with philosophic resignation: 'No, we don't, but' — he pointed to the teacher — 'she does.'"

— Clifton Fadiman

FRITH, William Powell (1819–1909), *British artist. He had a special talent for depicting crowds, as in* Derby Day *(1858), but also painted some notable portraits.*

1 The superstition that if thirteen people sit down to a meal together the first one to rise from the table will die within the year is supported by an anecdote told of Frith's wife, Isabelle. The Friths were dining with eleven others and at the end of the meal Mrs. Frith got up saying, "I will be the first because I can best be spared." Her friend, the widowed Mrs. Brooks, immediately leaped up too. "Well, I'll be the second, for if you died, I shouldn't want to live."

Within a month Mrs. Frith was dead, and Mrs. Brooks died five months later.

❧ ❦

FROHMAN, Charles (1860–1915), *US theatrical manager. Between 1890 and 1915 most of the major stars of the burgeoning US theater worked for him.*

1　When the unarmed British passenger ship *Lusitania* was sunk by a German submarine in the Atlantic, Charles Frohman was among the nearly twelve hundred people who perished. Trying to encourage a group of passengers as the ship was sinking, he shouted, "Why fear death? Death is only a beautiful adventure," thus paraphrasing a line from Barrie's *Peter Pan* ("To die will be an awfully big adventure").

ε❧　❦ϡ

FROST, Robert Lee (1874–1963), *US poet. Much of his work reflects the New England countryside, where he spent a large part of his life.*

1　After a dinner party Robert Frost and the other guests went out onto the veranda to watch the sunset. "Oh, Mr. Frost, isn't it a lovely sunset?" exclaimed a young woman. "I never discuss business after dinner," Frost replied.

2　A journalist once called at Frost's house for an interview. "Do you have one of those machines—those tape recorders?" asked the poet suspiciously as he opened the door. "No, sir," replied the journalist. Frost's manner changed instantly. "Well, come on in!" he cried. "Those people who take down every word never get anything right."

3　Frost had just recited one of his poems, and was asked to explain it. "What do you want me to do?" he replied. "Say it over again in worser English?"

ε❧　❦ϡ

FRY, Roger (1866–1934), *British painter and art critic. His writings exerted a major influence upon British artists and he was largely responsible for promoting the exhibitions (1910, 1912) that introduced the French Postimpressionists to the British public.*

1　"[Roger Fry] was taking Lady Violet Bonham-Carter round the Post-Impressionist Exhibition, in which Cézanne, Van Gogh, Gauguin, etc., first blazed upon London, and finally led her up to [Matisse's] *La Ronde,* which was hanging in the place of honour on the end wall of the Grafton Gallery. 'What do you think of *that?*' Lady Violet, whose soul was already a little fatigued by its adventures among

so many novel masterpieces, gazed upon it in stupefaction, and at last brought out apologetically, 'I don't think I quite like the shape of their legs.' 'Ah!' said Roger in a tone of triumph, 'but don't you like the shape of the spaces *between* their legs?' "

2　Roger Fry once asked a little girl how she set about drawing. She replied, "First I have a think, and then I put a line around it."

ε❧　❦ϡ

FUGGER, Johann (late 11th century), *German bishop.*

1　In the year 1110 Bishop Fugger set out from his German diocese for Rome to attend the coronation of Emperor Henry V. He sent his majordomo ahead to sample the fare provided by the taverns along the proposed route and to write "*Est*" (it is) over the doors of all those that served good wine. When the man reached the little hill town of Montefiascone in Lazio, just north of Rome, he was so enthusiastic about the local wine that he wrote, "*Est! Est! Est!*" over the inn door. His master agreed with the recommendation; during the remainder of his life he drank the Montefiascone vintage and was buried in the town. Under the terms of the bishop's will, a barrel of wine was to be poured over his grave once a year, but this wasteful stipulation was later altered and the barrel of Est! Est! Est!, as the wine is still called, was diverted to the local seminary where it could be enjoyed by trainee priests.

ε❧　❦ϡ

FULLER, Margaret, Marchioness d'Ossoli (1810–50), *US writer and philosopher. She played a leading role in the New England transcendentalist movement and was an early advocate of women's rights. Traveling in Europe, she met and married the Marquis d'Ossoli, a follower of Giuseppe Mazzini. En route to America the Ossolis were shipwrecked and drowned.*

1　Margaret Fuller cried out enthusiastically, "I accept the universe." Hearing of this, Thomas Carlyle, the Scottish historian, snarled, "By God, she'd better!"

2　Meeting her by chance in the street one day, Mrs. Horace Greeley noticed that Miss

Fuller was wearing kid gloves. "Skin of a beast!" she said, shuddering with distaste.

"Why, what do you wear?" asked Margaret.

"Silk," replied Mrs. Greeley.

Miss Fuller wrinkled her nose with equal distaste. "Entrails of a worm!" she said.

୫∾ ∾ई

FULLER, Melville Weston (1833–1910), *US lawyer; Chief Justice of the US Supreme Court (1888–1910).*

1 Chief Justice Fuller was chairing a church conference at which one of the speakers launched into a tirade against the pernicious influence of higher education, thanking God that his own mind had never been polluted by contact with a university. "Are we to understand that the speaker is thanking God for ignorance?" broke in Fuller. "Well, yes, I suppose you could put it like that," was the reply. "In that case," said Fuller, "the speaker has a very great deal to thank God for."

୫∾ ∾ई

FULLER, Richard Buckminster (1895–1983), *US writer, architect, and engineer. His many projects and inventions include the Dymaxion house and car, designed to make the best use of energy sources, and the geodesic dome, which spans a large area and can be made of cheap and lightweight materials.*

1 A student at the Massachusetts Institute of Technology once asked Fuller whether he took aesthetic factors into account when tackling a technical problem. "No," replied Fuller. "When I am working on a problem, I never think about beauty. I think only of how to solve the problem. But when I have finished, if the solution is not beautiful, I know it is wrong."

୫∾ ∾ई

FULTON, Robert (1765–1815), *US inventor. His* Clermont *was one of the earliest steamships, and his work was primarily responsible for demonstrating that steam could be a practicable source of power at sea.*

1 Fulton constructed a submarine for the French to use against the British. In 1801 it was tested in Brest harbor. After the trial the inventor was withered by a French admiral who snorted, "Thank God, sir, France still fights her battles above the waves, not beneath them."

୫∾ ∾ई

FURTWÄNGLER, Wilhelm (1886–1954), *German conductor and composer. He conducted the Berlin Philharmonic Orchestra (1922–54) and became renowned for his interpretations of Beethoven and Wagner.*

1 Gregor Piatigorsky was present at a rehearsal in which Furtwängler pulled the orchestra up over a certain phrase. "Gentlemen, this phrase must be — it must be — it must — you know what I mean — please try it again." Afterward, Furtwängler remarked to Piatigorsky complacently, "You see how important it is for a conductor to convey his wishes clearly?"

୫∾ ∾ई

FUSELI, Henry [Johann Heinrich Füssli] (1741–1825), *British painter and illustrator, born in Switzerland. His paintings include illustrations of the works of Shakespeare and Milton.*

1 Following the death of Reynolds, the Royal Academy in London met in 1794 to elect a new president. There was one vote for the American John Singleton Copley, one for the royal coach-painter Catton, and one for the Swiss painter Mary Moser. But most of the votes went to the previously nominated Benjamin West, the renowned historical painter. The vote for Mary Moser came from Fuseli — not because he had any particular esteem for her, but out of sheer animosity toward West. Asked why he had cast his vote for one whose sex obviously (in those days) made her unelectable, he replied, "Because I thought one old woman might be as good as another."

2 At the Royal Academy Fuseli showed the great portrait-painter George Romney a sketch he had made, which he called "The First Kiss." It was notable for the distorted, almost acrobatic pose of the two figures. Romney examined the sketch attentively, then said "Looks to me more like 'The Kiss of the Laocoön Family.'"

⇜ G ⇝

GABIN, Jean (1904–76), *French film actor. He is particularly remembered for his performances in Jean Renoir's* La Grande Illusion *(1937) and Marcel Carné's* Le Jour se lève *(1939). He also played the part of Inspector Maigret in several films of Georges Simenon's famous novels.*

1 Arriving in New York during World War II, Gabin was asked by a reporter about the French attitude toward the British. "We are both pro-British and anti-British," Gabin replied. "Those who are pro-British say every night in their prayers, 'Dear God, let the gallant British win quickly,' and those who are anti-British pray, 'Dear God, let the filthy British win very soon.'"

⇜ ⇝

GABOR, Zsa Zsa (1919–   ), *Hungarian-born US movie and television star, noted for her accent, her sexiness, and her numerous marriages. Her mother and her two sisters are also remarkable for their beauty.*

1 Zsa Zsa was asked if she was not embarrassed to have had so many marriages — seven at the last count. She replied, "Why should I be, dah-link? Other women have many more affairs. They are the ones who should be embarrassed. At least I marry my affairs."

2 Asked how many husbands she had had, Miss Gabor looked puzzled. "You mean apart from my own?" she inquired.

3 A women's magazine once printed the replies of a number of famous women to the question: "What is the first thing you notice about a woman?"

"Her way of speaking," was Agatha Christie's answer.

"Her hands," said Maria Callas.

"Her husband," replied Zsa Zsa.

4 Asked which of the Gabors is the oldest, Zsa Zsa replied: "Well, she'd never admit it — but it's Mama."

5 Miss Gabor once appeared on a television program in which guest celebrities attempted to solve viewers' conjugal problems. The first question came from a young lady: "I'm breaking my engagement to a very wealthy man who has already given me a sable coat, diamonds, a stove, and a Rolls-Royce. What should I do?"

"Give back the stove," advised Zsa Zsa.

⇜ ⇝

GAINSBOROUGH, Thomas (1727–88), *British portraitist and landscape painter. His fashionable sitters included members of the royal family. He was much influenced by the early seventeenth-century portraitist Anthony Van Dyck.*

1 Gainsborough, who found actors difficult subjects, experienced some problems with his portrait of Sarah Siddons. At one sitting he finally burst out in exasperation, "Damn your nose, madam; there's no end to it!"

2 Having discovered a malignant tumor on his neck, Gainsborough began with courage and composure to prepare himself for death. He had not been on good terms with Sir Joshua Reynolds, his rival for royal favor, but he sent for him and the two artists were reconciled. Turning to Sir Joshua with a contented smile, Gainsborough said, "We are all going to heaven and Van Dyck is of the company."

"Jack Good, after a period of top secret work for the British Navy and a Fellowship at Oxford, zoomed off to the USA and is now a Distinguished Professor of Statistics at the Virginia Polytechnic Institute. His impeccable scientific credentials — he has a list of about a *thousand* published scientific papers, reports and notes in his curriculum vitae — do not prevent his enjoying an idiosyncratic approach to life. His keen interest in palindromes (phrases like ABLE WAS I ERE I SAW ELBA) led him on one occasion to write to Her Majesty the Queen suggesting that she appoint him a peer of the realm. His reason for making his request was that when people saw him approaching they would certainly remark, 'Good Lord, here comes Lord Good.'"

— Christopher Evans,
The Micro Millennium

GAISFORD, Thomas (1779–1855), *English classical scholar. He was Regius Professor of Greek at Oxford and dean of Christ Church (1831–55).*

1   Gaisford once ended a sermon with the following advice: "Nor can I do better, in conclusion, than impress upon you the study of Greek literature, which not only elevates above the vulgar herd, but leads not infrequently to positions of considerable emolument."

ॐ ◄ई

GALBRAITH, John Kenneth (1908–), *Canadian-born US economist and diplomat. His economic theories, which follow the tradition established by John Maynard Keynes, are set out in* The Affluent Society *(1958) and* Economics and the Public Purpose *(1973). He became professor of economics at Harvard in 1949 and was also US ambassador to India (1961–63) and adviser to President John F. Kennedy.*

1   William F. Buckley, Jr., tried to make an appointment with Galbraith during a particular week in June. "That week I'll be teaching at the University of Moscow," Galbraith said. "Oh?

What do you have left to teach them?" inquired the right-wing Buckley.

2   On the morning that *The New York Times* published a profile of Galbraith, he was having breakfast with President Kennedy. When Kennedy asked him what he thought of the article, Galbraith said it was all right but he could not understand why they had to call him arrogant. "I don't see why not," said the president, "everybody else does."

3   During a European tour, Galbraith was presented with a tiny gold-plated music box attached to a key ring. Some time later, while in Sweden, he visited the men's room in a hotel. As he stood at the urinal beside a blond, sad-looking Swede, Galbraith played with his car keys, which were now attached to the new key ring, and accidentally set off the music box. As the first notes of *Tales from the Vienna Woods* struck up, Galbraith's neighbor glanced down at the apparent source of the music and fled from the room. Galbraith hurried after the Swede in order to explain but was brought up short by his wife, who, having just witnessed the flight of the other man from the washroom, eyed him with the deepest suspicion. It was some time before all was untangled.

ॐ ◄ई

GALEN (c. AD 129–199), *Greek physician who practiced at Rome. His voluminous writings on medicine were standard medical textbooks up to the Renaissance.*

1   Galen was called to attend the wife of a Roman aristocrat. Her doctor had been treating her for an organic complaint, but she had not improved. Galen, while taking her pulse, mentioned the name of an actor with whom her name was linked in the gossip of the town. Her pulse immediately bounded. Then Galen leaned down and whispered something in her ear that made her laugh. That laugh began her cure and is one of the earliest instances of a psychiatric treatment for psychosomatic illness.

ॐ ◄ई

GALIANI, Ferdinando (1728–87), *Italian writer, economist, wit, and friend of the Encyclopédistes.*

1 Even after Sophie Arnould, the famous eighteenth-century opera singer, was no longer in full control of her voice, she continued to charm audiences with the appeal of her stage presence and the allure of her figure. After one concert, the Abbé Galiani, noted as a connoisseur of music, was asked his opinion of her performance. He replied: "It's the most beautiful asthma I have heard in my whole lifetime."

෨෪ ෫ඁ

GALILEO [Galileo Galilei] (1564–1642), *Italian astronomer and physicist. By dropping different weights from the top of the Leaning Tower of Pisa he is said to have shown that the rate of fall of a body is independent of its mass. He also made a number of important astronomical discoveries, which convinced him of the truth of Copernicus's theory that the earth moved around the sun. The view brought him into conflict with the Church and in 1616 the Inquisition pronounced his theory a heresy.*

1 In 1632, after years of silence on the Copernican issue, Galileo published his *Dialogo dei due massimi sistemi del mondo* (Dialogue on Two Chief World Systems). The Inquisition summoned the aged author to Rome, where he was examined and threatened with torture. Galileo recanted and was sentenced to house arrest for the remainder of his life. As he rose from his knees after making a solemn renunciation of the Copernican doctrine, he was heard to mutter, "*Eppur si muove*" (But still it moves).

{This classic story is considered by many to be legendary. The *Columbia Encyclopedia,* however, states that the words were found on a portrait of Galileo c. 1640. The circumstances may lend some credibility to the anecdote.}

෨෪ ෫ඁ

GALLI-CURCI, Amelita (1889–1963), *Italian operatic soprano. She made her debut in Rome at the age of seventeen; in 1920 she joined the New York Metropolitan Opera Company.*

1 Relaxing in her dressing room after a concert one evening, Galli-Curci heard a knock at the door. Quite accustomed to receiving visits from aspiring young singers seeking free advice and encouragement, she sighed wearily and opened the door. There stood a rather timid young girl clutching a small bunch of roses. Galli-Curci invited her in, taking the flowers from her admirer's trembling hand. "Do you sing?" she asked. "Oh, no!" exclaimed the girl, a little taken aback by the question. "Well then, do you play?" asked the soprano, gesturing toward the piano. "No," replied her visitor, adding somewhat apologetically, "I just listen." Galli-Curci smiled and impulsively embraced the girl. "I had quite forgotten," she said, "that there were people left who *only* listen."

෨෪ ෫ඁ

GALLUP, George Horace (1901–84), *US statistician, founder of the American Institute of Public Opinion (1935). Polls conducted by the institute and its British counterpart are called Gallup polls after their founder.*

1 The Gallup poll conducted before the presidential election of 1948 wrongly predicted a win for Thomas E. Dewey. Shortly after the announcement of Harry Truman's victory, Gallup was stopped by a policeman for driving down a one-way street in the wrong direction. On reading the name on Gallup's driving license, the policeman grinned broadly and exclaimed, "Wrong again!"

෨෪ ෫ඁ

GALOIS, Évariste (1811–32), *French mathematician. He founded the branch of modern mathematics known as group theory. Dogged by tragic ill luck, he died of peritonitis after a duel, leaving his revolutionary mathematical discoveries to be published posthumously.*

1 At the hospital to which Galois, fatally wounded, was taken, his younger brother sat weeping at his bedside. Galois tried to comfort him. "Don't cry," he told him, "I need all my courage to die at twenty."

෨෪ ෫ඁ

GALVANI, Luigi (1737–98), *Italian anatomist and physiologist, for whom the galvanometer is named.*

1 (Wilder Penfield tells this story:)
"One evening in the late eighteenth century an Italian woman stood in her kitchen watching the frogs' legs which she was preparing for

the evening meal. 'Look at those muscles moving. . . . They always seem to come alive when I hang them on the copper wire.'

"Her husband [Luigi Galvani] looked. . . . The cut end of the frog's nerve was in contact with the copper wire, and electric current produced by the contact was passing along the nerve to the muscle. As a result, the muscle was twitching and contracting. . . .

"He had discovered the key to electricity, and to nerve conduction, and to muscle action. Here was the basis of all animal movement, reflex and voluntary, in frog and man."

ह ़

GANDHI, Indira (1917–84), *Indian stateswoman; prime minister (1966–77, 1980–84). Daughter of Jawaharlal Nehru, the first prime minister of independent India, Indira Gandhi won sweeping victories in the elections of 1971 and 1972, but was subsequently accused of electoral malpractices. She suspended the constitution, ruling under a state of emergency (1975) until her position became untenable. Her political eclipse was short-lived, since her successor failed to cope with India's many problems. She was returned to power in 1980, her popularity undiminished among her peasant supporters, but in 1984 was assassinated by a member of her own bodyguard.*

1 Throughout Indira Gandhi's childhood and youth, members of her family were in and out of prison on account of their opposition to the British raj, with Nehru himself serving no fewer than nine prison sentences between 1921 and 1945. A caller at their house on one occasion asked why the house was so deserted. "What else could it be when Papa, Mama, and Grandpa are all in prison?" said young Indira.

2 Shortly after Mrs. Gandhi declared a state of emergency, a customer in a major Delhi bookstore asked the assistant for a copy of the constitution of India. "I am sorry, sir," replied the bookseller, "but we don't stock periodicals."

ह ़

GANDHI, Mohandas Karamchand [Mahatma] (1869–1948), *Indian statesman and spiritual leader. He led India's struggle for independence with campaigns of civil disobedience ("passive resistance") against the British raj.*

His own political power was based on his immense spiritual and moral authority. Among many issues, he campaigned for improvement of the lot of the Untouchables (the downtrodden outcasts of Hindu society), increase of small-scale handicraft industries in the chronically poor rural areas, and reconciliation between the warring Muslim and Hindu factions of India. In the last he failed and was forced to agree to the partition that brought into existence the state of Pakistan. Shortly afterward he was assassinated by a Hindu fanatic.

1 Even after becoming an internationally recognized statesman, Gandhi persisted in following an extremely spartan life-style. He wore the simple clothes of the poor, traveled on foot whenever possible, preferred staying in the slum areas of cities, and always used the cheapest class of railway travel. In view of the danger to which such behavior exposed Gandhi, Lord Louis Mountbatten, the British viceroy, expressed surprise to an eminent member of Gandhi's party on one occasion at a railroad station. He was told that all the Untouchables in the carriage had been carefully selected and checked by the security services: "You have no idea what it costs to keep that old man in poverty!"

2 Gandhi gave a lecture to a select gathering of maharajahs, exhorting them to give up their money and possessions and embrace a life of poverty and simplicity. One by one his distinguished audience slid out until there was nobody left except (as Gandhi afterward said) "God, the chairman, and myself." After another few minutes the chairman himself melted away. "Poor fellow," observed Gandhi, "he must have been very uncomfortable in that strange company."

3 In 1931 Gandhi went to call on Mussolini, complete with the goat that he took around with him at the time. Mussolini's children laughed at the incongruous figure, but *Il Duce* reproved them: "That man and his goat are shaking the British empire."

4 The American sculptor Jo Davidson, who made sculpture portraits of many of the greatest political and artistic figures of his day, took some photographs of his work to show Gandhi. "I see you make heroes out of mud," Gandhi observed. "And sometimes vice versa," said Davidson.

5   As Gandhi stepped aboard a train one day, one of his shoes slipped off and landed on the track. He was unable to retrieve it as the train was moving. To the amazement of his companions, Gandhi calmly took off his other shoe and threw it back along the track to land close to the first. Asked by a fellow passenger why he did so, Gandhi smiled. "The poor man who finds the shoe lying on the track," he replied, "will now have a pair he can use."
    {This may well have happened. It is, however, a familiar story, usually told about a glove.}

6   Mahatma Gandhi was once asked what he thought about Western civilization. "I think," he replied, "that it would be a very good idea."
    {A variation on this witticism has been attributed to George Bernard Shaw.}

ॐ

GARBO, Greta [Greta Louisa Gustafsson] (1905–   ), *Swedish film actress, widely acclaimed for her beauty. Her films include* Flesh and the Devil *(1927),* Grand Hotel *(1932), and* Anna Karenina *(1935). She retired from the film world in 1941.*

1   After such films as *The Torrent* and *Flesh and the Devil,* Garbo decided to exploit her box-office power and asked Louis B. Mayer for a raise — from three hundred and fifty to five thousand dollars a week. Mayer offered her twenty-five hundred. "I tank I go home," said Garbo. She went back to her hotel and stayed there for a full seven months until Mayer finally gave way.

2   David Niven speaks of a conversation with Greta Garbo one day in a rainstorm: "I often wondered if something of [vertigo] had overtaken Garbo at the pinnacle of her career, so seeing her before me, carefree and happy, munching away contentedly with the rain cascading off the table, I decided it might be a propitious moment to try and find out.
    "'Why *did* you give up the movies?' I asked.
    "She considered her answer so carefully that I wondered if she had decided to ignore my personal question. At last, almost to herself, she said, 'I had made enough faces.'"

GARDNER, Erle Stanley (1889–1970), *US lawyer and writer of detective stories. His best-known character is lawyer-detective Perry Mason, who features in some eighty novels, including* The Case of the Velvet Claws *(1933) and* The Case of the Duplicate Daughter *(1960).*

1   In the early days of his career, Gardner churned out stories for pulp magazines at the rate of 200,000 words a month. As he was paid by the word, the length of the story was more important to him than its quality, and he tended to draw the maximum potential from every incident. His villains, for example, were always killed by the last bullet in the gun. Gardner's editor once asked him why his heroes were always so careless with their first five shots. "At three cents a word," replied Gardner, "every time I say *bang* in the story I get three cents. If you think I'm going to finish the gun battle while my hero has got fifteen cents' worth of unexploded ammunition in his gun, you're nuts."

ॐ

GARDNER, Isabella Stewart ["Mrs. Jack"] (1840–1924), *US social leader and art collector.*

1   New York–born Mrs. Jack Gardner, who once out of boredom walked a lion cub down Tremont Street, Boston, on a leash, never felt secure in Boston society. Once when she was visited by a grande dame who told her, "I am here to accept your donation to Boston's Charitable Eye and Ear Association," she replied: "Really? I didn't know there was a charitable eye or ear in Boston."

2   "Isabella Stewart of New York never thought much about ancestry until she married into the Gardner family of Boston. In Boston, she endured a good deal of fairly dull conversation on the subject, so, eventually, she had her Stewart descent traced directly back — all the way to King Fergus I of Scotland, a contemporary of Alexander the Great! . . . After having the Stewart lineage engrossed and illuminated in colors on a long scroll, Isabella Stewart Gardner was in a position to make one of her famous, much-quoted remarks. She had listened to a monologue by a Boston dowager concerning that lady's American Revolutionary ancestry. 'Ah yes,' said Isabella. 'They were

much less careful about immigration in those days, I believe.' "

3 It is stoutly averred by Boston traditionalists—and equally stoutly denied by Boston's noted Episcopal Church of the Advent—that every Ash Wednesday Mrs. Jack, in her chauffeur-driven limousine, would arrive at the church with a bucket and mop, and would wash the steps of the church as a penance for her sins of the preceding year. The event was always duly reported in the newspapers.

4 Mrs. Jack, received by Chicago's "queen of the White City," Berthe Honore (Mrs. Potter) Palmer, in her battlemented castle, summed up her feelings about Midwest splendor and contemporary social art when shown the pantry. Mrs. Palmer's eighteen-year-old son exhibited gold and silver plates and endless towers of porcelain dishes. "Mother has fifty of everything," said he. "What does she do," asked Mrs. Gardner, "when she has a really *big* party?"

ॐ ॐ

GARFIELD, James Abram (1831–81), *20th president of the United States (1881). Garfield was elected after a vicious electoral campaign, but shortly afterward was shot and died a few months later.*

1 When President Lincoln was assassinated in 1865, Garfield was staying in New York. There was an excited crowd in the street and Garfield was implored to address them. When he had won their attention, he said simply, "My fellow citizens, the President is dead, but the Government lives and God Omnipotent reigns."

{Woodrow Wilson called this "one of the noblest sentences ever uttered." The anecdote, however, may be apocryphal.}

ॐ ॐ

GARLAND, Judy [Frances Gumm] (1922–69), *US entertainer and film actress. The daughter of vaudeville performers, she first appeared on stage at the age of three and made her first film in 1936. Her star quality became evident with her performance as Dorothy in the film* The Wizard of Oz *(1939); subsequent successes included* Meet Me in St. Louis *(1944) and* A Star is Born *(1954). The later years of her life were marred by emotional breakdowns, suicide attempts, and drug dependence.*

1 The *Tonight Show* TV luminary Jack Paar recalls discussing with Judy Garland another actress, notorious for her bed-hopping. "Isn't she a nymphomaniac?" asked Paar. Replied Judy, "Only if you can calm her down."

2 Comedian Alan King once took Judy Garland to Chinatown in New York for dinner. King ordered as a first course stir-fried chicken, lobster, and Chinese vegetables. The magnificent dish arrived. On top was a big, black, round thing. Judy asked what it was. "That's a very rare and exotic Chinese mushroom," King told her. "It's such a delicacy they only use one to a portion, just as a French chef uses a slice of truffle." As he spoke, the exotic mushroom began to move, off the plate, across the table, and up the wall. Judy began to scream, tears rolling down her cheeks. The alarmed King was sure she was hysterical and slapped her. She stopped, then slapped him back. "What the hell's the matter with you, you idiot? I'm not hysterical. I'm laughing."

ॐ ॐ

GARNER, John Nance (1868–1967), *US politician; vice president (1933–41).*

1 "When . . . Mr. Garner visited Tokyo en route to the Philippines, he told friends in his jovial way that when he was received by the Emperor he was going to take an American dollar watch from his pocket, and say, 'Your Majesty, here is one thing you folks can't imitate and undersell!' Horrified, the Americans in Japan told Mr. Garner that he must under no circumstances do this, since, if he did, the Emperor's aides in the room would consider that the Emperor had been insulted and would have to commit suicide. In any case Garner gave up the idea—after finding several Japanese watches that *were* imitation Ingersolls selling for thirty cents."

ॐ ॐ

GARRICK, David (1717–79), *British actor and theater manager. He was particularly famous for his Shakespearean roles.*

1 The actor and wit Samuel Foote kept a small bust of Garrick on his bureau. "You may wonder," he said, "that I allow him so near my gold, but see—he has no hands."

2 A nobleman tried to persuade Garrick to put himself forward as a candidate for election to Parliament. Garrick declined, saying, "I had rather play the part of a great man on stage than the part of a fool in Parliament."

৯৯ ৯৫

GARRISON, William Lloyd (1805–79), *US abolitionist. He founded the antislavery paper* The Liberator *in 1831, and was president (1843–65) of the American Anti-Slavery Society.*

1 At antislavery meetings Garrison was well used to handling insults and dodging missiles from the crowd. The British Anti-Slavery Society gave a banquet in his honor and presented him with a gold watch. "Well, gentlemen," said Garrison, "if this had been a rotten egg I should have known what to do with it, but as it is a gold watch, I am at a loss for words."

৯৯ ৯৫

GARROD, Heathcote William (1878–1960), *British classical scholar and literary critic, who taught for most of his life at Merton College, Oxford.*

1 During World War I, Garrod, already a distinguished scholar, worked at the Ministry of Munitions in London. The practice of handing white feathers to able-bodied men who were not in uniform was in full swing. Garrod was handed one by a woman in a London street with the withering comment, "I am surprised that you are not fighting to defend civilization." Garrod replied, "Madam, I am the civilization they are fighting to defend."
{This anecdote is also told of others.}

৯৯ ৯৫

GARTH, Sir Samuel (1672–1719), *British physician and poet. His works include the satirical poem* The Dispensary *(1699).*

1 At a convivial meeting of the Kit-Kat Club Garth announced early on in the proceedings that he would have to leave shortly to attend to his practice. However, under the influence of absorbing conversation and excellent wine, he stayed on until Sir Richard Steele thought to remind him of the waiting patients. At that, Garth pulled from his pocket a list containing fifteen names. Said he, "It is no great matter whether I see them tonight or not, for nine of them have such bad constitutions that all the physicians in the world can't save them, and the other six have such good constitutions that all the physicians in the world can't kill them."

৯৯ ৯৫

GATES, John Warne (1855–1911), *US industrialist, speculator, and gambler. Nicknamed "Bet-you-a-million" Gates, he made and lost a fortune on the New York stock exchange before entering the Texas oil industry.*

1 He once bet the wealthy John Drake, whose family founded Drake University, $11,000. The wager turned on whose bread, dunked in coffee, would attract the most flies. Gates won. He had not bothered to let young Drake know that he had put six spoonfuls of sugar in his own cup.

৯৯ ৯৫

GATTI-CASAZZA, Giulio (1869–1940), *Italian-born operatic manager. He was director of La Scala at Milan (1898–1908) and general manager of the Metropolitan Opera House, New York (1908–35).*

1 While general manager of the Met, Gatti-Casazza had occasion to audition a rather mediocre tenor. Trying to break the news gently, Gatti-Casazza suggested to the singer that he was not quite ready for the Met. "Not ready!" thundered the tenor. "Why, I'll have you know that when I was with La Scala they thought so much of my voice that they insured it for fifty thousand pounds."
"Oh?" replied Gatti-Casazza. "And what did La Scala do with the money?"

৯৯ ৯৫

GAUSS, Karl Friedrich (1777–1855), *German mathematician. He made major contributions in most fields of mathematics and physics, and is regarded as one of the greatest mathematicians of all time.*

1 At school, Gauss showed little of his precocious talent until the age of nine, when he was admitted to the arithmetic class. The master had set what appeared to be a complicated problem involving the addition of a series of numbers in arithmetical progression. Although he had never been taught the simple formula for solving such problems, Gauss handed in his slate within seconds. For the next hour the boy sat idly while his classmates labored. At the end of the lesson there was a pile of slates on top of Gauss's, all with incorrect answers. The master was stunned to find at the bottom the slate from the youngest member of the class bearing the single correct number. He was so impressed that he bought the best available arithmetic textbook for Gauss and thereafter did what he could to advance his progress.

2 Someone hurrying to tell Gauss that his wife was dying found the great mathematician deep in an abstruse problem. The messenger blurted out the sad news. "Tell her to wait a minute until I've finished," replied Gauss absently.

See also FÉDÉRIC MOREL 1.

ぶ ✑

GEHRIG, [Henry] Lou[is] (1903–41), *US baseball player. He played in 2,130 consecutive games (June 1, 1925, to May 2, 1939) for his team, the New York Yankees, the longest such sequence in American sports history, and is accounted the game's all-time great star.*

1 At an exhibition game against a Texas university, the college team, surprisingly enough, was succeeding in holding the Yankees to a close score. Lou Gehrig came to bat with two runners on base and it was three and two for Gehrig. At that moment the pitcher threw one straight toward home plate. Gehrig sent the ball sailing clear out of sight. The college catcher stormed up to the pitcher, raging at him for not watching his signals. The pitcher was unrepentant. "Yeah, I know," he said, "but I got to thinking: I'll never pitch a Big League game and maybe I'll never get to see a game at the Yankee Stadium, and I sure did want to see Gehrig bust just one!"

2 Gehrig had been playing poorly when he asked his manager not to use him on a certain day in early May 1939. He said that he did not know why he was not playing well, but it would not be fair to his team or himself to go on. It was then discovered that he was suffering from a fatal illness; he was to die within twenty-five months. Before that he was given a "day" in his honor before a full house in New York's Yankee Stadium. Hearing the cheers, Gehrig said,

"Today I consider myself the luckiest man on the face of the earth."

ぶ ✑

GELON (died 478 BC), *tyrant of Syracuse (485–478).*

1 Gelon suffered from bad breath, but was unaware of it for a long time until one of his foreign mistresses mentioned the fact to him. Gelon went to Bilia, his wife, and scolded her for never telling him, when she was the person with the best opportunities for doing so. She replied that as she had never been at close quarters with any other man, she had assumed that all men had disagreeable breath.

ぶ ✑

GEOFFRIN, Marie-Thérèse (1699–1777), *French* salonnière, *whose salon attracted leading artists and writers, including the influential Encyclopédistes.*

1 Mme Geoffrin one day was overheard quarreling vigorously with one of her intimates, a man of letters who responded with equal warmth and vivacity. Baron d'Holbach, who had been listening for a while in silence, approached them, smiling, and inquired, "By any chance are you two secretly married?"

ぶ ✑

GEORGE I (1660–1727), *king of Great Britain and Ireland (1714–27). George's claim to the throne of England was through his mother, the granddaughter of James I of England. Even after he ascended the throne, however, his main interest lay in his German principality of Hanover. He found the English uncongenial, refused to learn their language, and left policy almost wholly in the hands of powerful ministers.*

1 The collapse in 1720 of the South Sea Company, of which George I was governor, was a financial disaster that affected many people in Britain. The king was overheard to say, "We had very good luck, for we sold out last week."

ぶ ✑

GEORGE II (1683–1760), *king of Great Britain and Ireland. Of Hanoverian origin, he had little political ability but was an ardent soldier*

and the last British monarch to appear on the battlefield. He was a patron of music, notably of George Frideric Handel.

1   George II was invited to attend the first performance of Handel's *Messiah* in London in 1743. The audience was extremely moved by the music, as was the king. When the words "And he shall reign for ever and ever" were sung in the "Hallelujah Chorus," he leaped to his feet, believing, because of his poor command of English, that this was a personal tribute to him from his protégé. The audience, seeing the king on his feet but perhaps not understanding his motive, also rose to their feet. It is still the custom for the audience to stand during this part of the performance, although not everyone knows why.

2   The keeper of a village inn at which King George stopped for a brief meal served him an egg, for which he charged a guinea. His Majesty smiled and commented, "Eggs must be very scarce around here."

"Oh, no, sire," said the innkeeper, "it is kings that are scarce."

{Told of others.}

৵ ৵

GEORGE III (1738–1820), *king of Great Britain and Ireland (1760–1820). Principal events of his long reign were the loss of the American colonies and Britain's great victories in the wars against Napoleon. From the 1780s George suffered bouts of insanity, and after 1811 his son, later George IV, acted as regent.*

1   Greatly impressed by astronomer William Herschel's forty-foot telescope, George invited the archbishop of Canterbury to view the magnificent new instrument. "Come, my lord bishop," he urged. "I will show *you* the way to Heaven."

2   In the stables at Windsor George III met a boy and asked him what he did and what he was paid. "I help in the stable," replied the lad, "but they give me only my food and clothes."

"Be content," said the king, "I have no more."

3   When Lord Eldon received the Great Seal of the office of lord chancellor from George IV

in 1801, the king was very affable. At the conclusion of the interview, he said, "Give my remembrance to Lady Eldon." Lord Eldon thanked the king for his kindness and condescension. "Yes," said the king, "I know how much I owe to Lady Eldon. You would have made yourself a country curate; she has made you my lord chancellor."

4   The acclaimed musician Johann Peter Salomon gave violin lessons to George III, but found the king neither an apt nor a diligent pupil. Torn between exasperation and the wish to encourage the royal fiddler, Salomon delivered the following pronouncement: "Your Majesty, fiddlers may be divided into three classes: the first, those who cannot play at all; the second, those who play badly; the third, those who play well. You, sire, have already attained the second class."

5   During a fit of madness George insisted on ending every sentence with the word "peacock." This was a grave embarrassment to his ministers whenever he spoke in public until one of them thought of telling him that "peacock" was a particularly royal word and should therefore only be whispered when the king addressed his subjects. The suggestion helped.

৵ ৵

GEORGE IV (1762–1830), *king of Great Britain and Ireland (1820–30). In 1795, in return for having his debts paid off by his father, he reluctantly married his cousin, Princess Caroline of Brunswick. As regent (1811–20) for his insane father, George III, he presided with taste and elegance over the glittering society of London, but his dissipation, extravagance, callousness, and weak-mindedness made him unable to govern effectively.*

1   In the closing months of his life George IV kept almost entirely to his overheated apartments, where he consumed vast draughts of cherry brandy. He was troubled by delusions of riding a winning horse in a race and of commanding a battalion at the battle of Waterloo. His physician and confidant, the levelheaded Sir William Knighton, observed, "His Majesty has only to leave off cherry brandy, and, rest assured, he will gain no more victories."

2   Frequent repetition of his supposed feats at the battle of Waterloo reinforced the king's belief that he had actually been there. After one such recital he turned to the Duke of Wellington and said, "Was it not so, duke?"

"I have often heard Your Majesty say so," replied Wellington.

છે ૭

GEORGE V (1865–1936), *king of the United Kingdom (1910–36). During World War I he and his wife, Queen Mary, set an example of quiet determination. His policy of conciliation helped to unify the British people during the other financial and constitutional crises of his reign.*

1 When George V was in his early forties and still Prince of Wales, he and his father, Edward VII, dined at the Elysée Palace as guests of President Armand Fallières of France. The lady seated next to Edward VII turned to him and, indicating the prince, inquired sweetly, "And what do you have in mind for that fine big boy of yours?"

2 George V was an enthusiastic stamp collector. A private secretary once remarked to him, "I see in *The Times* today that some damn fool has given fourteen hundred pounds for a single stamp at a private sale."

"I am that damn fool," said the king.

3 During a dinner-table conversation with the US ambassador to Britain during World War I, George V asked, "How long a term is it that your American president serves?"

"Four years."

"My God!" said the king. "If I could get through in four years, I'd never run again."

4 When Charles Lindbergh, first aviator to fly across the Atlantic Ocean alone, was presented to the king, George asked the usual questions including one that must have put the young aviator immediately at ease. "Now tell me," said the king, "there is one thing I long to know. How did you *manage?*"

5 The young Prince of Wales never got along with his father, a no-nonsense type, abrupt and cold with his children. Lord Derby once mildly suggested that the king might be a little more relaxed with Prince Edward. George replied, "My father was frightened of his mother; I was frightened of my father; and I am damned well

going to see to it that my children are frightened of me."

6 In 1935 the British foreign secretary, Sir Samuel Hoare, came to an agreement with his French counterpart, Pierre Laval, settling Mussolini's territorial claims in Abyssinia. By the Hoare-Laval Pact, signed in Paris, Abyssinia was virtually handed over to the Italians. George V is said to have commented in disgust, "No more coals to Newcastle, no more Hoares to Paris."

7 In 1917 George V proclaimed that he was changing the surname of the royal family from the Germanic Saxe-Coburg-Gotha to the solidly British Windsor. When his cousin and enemy, Kaiser Wilhelm of Germany, heard the news, he observed that he would look forward to the next performance of *The Merry Wives of Saxe-Coburg-Gotha.*

8 The great between-the-wars Cunard liner R.M.S. *Queen Mary* was originally to have been christened *Queen Victoria*. George V was told by a Cunard executive that the company wanted to name it after "the greatest of all English queens." The delighted king exclaimed, "Oh, my wife *will* be pleased."

9 Pedestrian crossings marked by black-and-white poles surmounted by an orange globe (called "Belisha beacons" for the minister of transport, Leslie Hore-Belisha) were introduced toward the end of George's reign. Driving through London with Queen Mary one day, the king, eager to test one of the new crossings, ordered the chauffeur to stop the car and let him out. He returned a few minutes later, chuckling with delight. "One of my devoted subjects," he declared, "has just called me a doddering old idiot."

10 His doctor assured the dying George V that he would soon be convalescent and able to go to his favorite seaside resort of Bognor Regis on the south coast of England. "Bugger Bognor," said the monarch and expired.

{This, one of the most *juste* of deathbed *mots,* is generally considered apocryphal. Other candidates for the distinction of being George V's last words are: "How is the empire?" and "Gentlemen, I am sorry for keeping you waiting like this. I am unable to concentrate."}

"Two gangsters, James Gallo and Joe Conigliaro, set about to murder a stool pigeon, Vinny Ensulo, alias Vinnie Ba Ba, alias Vincent Ennisie.

"On November 1, 1973, they jumped him on Columbia Street, Brooklyn, and took him for a ride. Gallo pointed a gun at his head from the right, and Conigliaro covered him from the left. The car swerved violently. The two gangsters shot each other.

"*The New York Daily News* described the sequel: 'Conigliaro, hit in the spine, was paralyzed. Every year after that Vinny Ensulo sent wheelchair batteries to Conigliaro. A small card with the batteries always said, "Keep rolling, from your best pal, Vinny Ba Ba." ' "

— John Train,
True Remarkable Occurrences

GEORGE VI (1895–1952), *king of Great Britain and Northern Ireland. He unexpectedly succeeded to the throne after the abdication of his brother, Edward VIII, in 1936. A diffident and retiring man with a painful stammer, he and Queen Elizabeth inspired great love and loyalty in the British people, especially during World War II.*

1   King George VI was not a great connoisseur of music, but in the course of duty he and other members of the Royal Family attended the inaugural concert for the 1951 Festival of Britain. To the great delight of the audience Sir Malcolm Sargent conducted "Rule Britannia" in its authentic eighteenth-century setting. The king, meeting Sargent a few days later, mentioned how much he had enjoyed it. He went on, "Whenever I come to one of your concerts you must play it again, just like that." Sargent replied that he would love to, but that it might not be suitable.

"Not suitable, Sir Malcolm? What do you mean?" asked the king.

"I mean, sir," said the conductor, "that I might for instance be playing the *Saint Matthew Passion*."

The king's face cleared. "Oh, that's all right," he said. "I shouldn't be there then."

2   Although George VI was distinguished in several fields, he could not claim to be well versed in modern art. Looking at the paintings of the modernist John Piper, who specialized in storm scenes, all the monarch could think of to say was, "Pity you had such bloody awful weather."

3   In 1939 King George VI and Queen Elizabeth, on a tour of the United States, were entertained at cocktails, mixed by their host, President Franklin D. Roosevelt. The president's mother looked on with disapproval. "My mother," Roosevelt explained, "thinks you should have a cup of tea. She doesn't approve of cocktails." The king accepted the drink gratefully. "Neither does my mother," he said.

֍   ֍

GEORGE-BROWN, Baron (1914–   ), *British statesman, born George Alfred Brown. He was deputy leader of the Labour party (1960–70) and foreign secretary (1966–68). He was created a life peer in 1970, but in 1976 left the Labour party.*

1   Lord George-Brown, at one stage of his career, was known to be a heavy drinker. At a certain diplomatic function when the orchestra struck up, he felt that as the senior British minister present he should start the dancing. Spying a gorgeously robed figure, he said, "Beautiful lady in scarlet, will you do me the honor of waltzing with me?"

"Certainly not," was the sharp response. "In the first place you are drunk; in the second this is not actually a waltz but the Venezuelan national anthem; and, thirdly, I am not a beautiful lady in scarlet, I am, in fact, the papal nuncio."

{This story is told of other diplomatic and ministerial dignitaries and is probably apocryphal.}

֍   ֍

GERARD, James Watson (1867–1951), *US lawyer and diplomat. He was US ambassador to Germany during the four years preceding the outbreak of hostilities between the United States and Germany in 1917.*

1   In 1916 Arthur Zimmerman became German foreign minister. Gerard once described him as "just and friendly toward America." But

relations between the two countries deteriorated. Zimmerman, whose intelligence service was unreliable, once remarked to the ambassador that if the United States entered the war, "there are half a million trained Germans in America who will join the Irish and start a revolution." Gerard replied, "In that case there are half a million lamp-posts to hang them on."

જાજ જાજ

GERSHWIN, George (1898–1937), *US composer and songwriter. Among his numerous successes were* Rhapsody in Blue *(1924),* An American in Paris *(1928), and* Porgy and Bess *(1935). He wrote music for films and stage shows and such well-known songs as "I Got Rhythm" and "Lady Be Good."*

1 The pianist and wit Oscar Levant, Gershwin's close friend, once asked the composer confidentially, "Tell me, George, if you had to do it all over, would you fall in love with yourself again?"

2 When Gershwin started psychoanalysis, Oscar Levant, who used to scoff at it, asked him, "Does it help your constipation, George?" Gershwin replied, "No, but now I understand why I have it."

3 A girl whom Gershwin had admired married someone else. Gershwin's only comment was, "If I wasn't so busy, I'd be upset."

4 Oscar Levant complained to Gershwin that when they traveled together on trains he always had to take the upper berth while Gershwin had the lower. "That's the difference between talent and genius," said Gershwin.

5 At one time Gershwin thought of taking some lessons from Ravel in Paris, but nothing came of it. Later a story went the rounds explaining what happened. Gershwin had asked the French composer for lessons, and was answered with the question: "How much do you earn a year from your compositions?"

"Between one hundred and two hundred thousand dollars," replied Gershwin.

"Then it is I who must ask you to teach me to compose."

6 At the end of a magnificent piano recital by a Spanish virtuoso, Gershwin's companion turned to him and said enthusiastically, "Isn't he great, George?"

"Yes, he's a genius," agreed the composer. "A Spanish Gershwin."

7 After Gershwin's death an admirer with musical aspirations wrote an elegy for him and took it to Oscar Levant. Levant reluctantly agreed to hear the piece. After the man had finished playing it, he turned to Levant, looking for his approval. "I think," said Levant, "it would have been better if you had died and Gershwin had written the elegy."

{Variants of this story, featuring others, are numerous. *See,* for example, FRANZ LISZT 1.}

જાજ જાજ

GERSHWIN, Ira (1896–1983), *US lyric-writer. He collaborated with his brother, George Gershwin, on a number of the latter's songs and musical comedies.*

1 Gershwin was a keen poker player, but very unlucky. After a particularly disastrous evening, he announced to his friends: "I take an oath. I'll never pick up a card again." After a moment's pause, he added, "Unless, of course, I have guests who want to play. . . . Or unless I am a guest in another man's house." He paused again. "Or whatever circumstances arise."

જાજ જાજ

GESVRES, Bernard François Potier, Marquis de (1655–1739), *French aristocrat and courtier.*

1 (The diarist Saint-Simon records a blunder made by the marquis.)

"In the king's apartments one day, he was holding forth in praise and criticism of the fine pictures there. Pointing to several Crucifixions by great masters, he maintained that they had all been painted by the same artist. People began to mock him, pointing out the various painters and how they might be recognized by their personal styles. 'Nonsense,' exclaimed the marquis, 'The painter of all of them was called "INRI," cannot you read his signature?' You may imagine the silence that followed this gross blunder, and what became of the ignoramus."

{The letters INRI frequently appear, of course, on Christ's cross in medieval and later depictions of the Crucifixion, and stand for *Iesus Nazarenus Rex Iudaeorum — Jesus of Nazareth, King of the Jews.*}

๛ ๏

GETTY, J[ean] Paul (1892–1976), *US oil executive, millionaire, and art collector.*

1 Getty once received a request from a magazine for a short article explaining his success. A check for two hundred pounds was enclosed. The multimillionaire obligingly wrote: "Some people find oil. Others don't."

2 A newspaper reporter once asked Getty if it were true that the value of his holdings, at that time, amounted to a billion dollars. Getty was silent for a minute or two. "I suppose so," he replied thoughtfully. "But remember, a billion dollars doesn't go as far as it used to."

๛ ๏

GHIBERTI, Lorenzo (c. 1378–1455), *Italian Renaissance sculptor and goldsmith.*

1 Awarded the commission for the baptistry doors of the Duomo in Florence in 1402, Ghiberti spent most of the rest of his life working on them. When he saw them, Michelangelo exclaimed, "These designs are worthy to adorn the gates of paradise."

๛ ๏

GIAMPETRO, Joseph (1866–1913), *German actor, born in Vienna.*

1 Elegant and accomplished, Giampetro was an indefatigable Don Juan. A friend, encountering him in a coffeehouse looking somewhat worried and holding a letter in his hands, asked sympathetically if he had received bad news. "No," was the reply, "but the sender of this letter says that he will strangle me if I keep on paying attentions to his wife."
   "Well," advised the friend, "I'd lay off the lady, if I were you."
   "But *which* lady?" cried Giampetro. "The damn letter is anonymous."

๛ ๏

GIBBON, Edward (1737–94), *British historian. He is remembered for his epic and ironic treatment of Christianity in* The History of the Decline and Fall of the Roman Empire, *of which the first volume appeared in 1776. Initially the work caused considerable controversy, but its vast scale, the painstaking accuracy of its detail, and the rich, stately style of the exposition have ensured its survival.*

1 When Gibbon was staying in Lausanne in 1757, he met and fell in love with an accomplished and beautiful French girl, Suzanne Curchod. He was invited to her home, and had some hopes that she would agree to marry him. However, when he raised the subject with his father, Gibbon senior emphatically refused to agree to allow his son to marry a foreigner. Destitute without his father's consent to the match, Gibbon gave up his love, later writing, "After a painful struggle I yielded to my fate: I sighed as a lover, I obeyed as a son."
   {Mlle Curchod eventually married Jacques Necker, the French statesman and economist, and became the mother of Mme de Staël.}

2 Gibbon's ventures in the direction of matrimony were ill-fated. In middle age he wooed Lady Elizabeth Foster, who at the time was governess in the Duke of Devonshire's family. On an occasion when Gibbon was engaging the lady in close conversation, one of his rivals, a French doctor, could not contain his irritation: "*Quand mi lady Elizabeth Foster sera malade de vos fadaises, je la guérirai*" (When my lady Elizabeth Foster becomes sick of your nonsense, I shall cure her). Gibbon's riposte was: "*Quand mi lady Elizabeth Foster sera morte de vos recettes, je l'immortaliserai*" (When my lady Elizabeth Foster dies from your prescriptions, I shall immortalize her).
   {Alas, neither the doctor nor Gibbon won the lady; after a long period as the mistress of the Duke of Devonshire, she became his second duchess.}

3 William, Duke of Gloucester, brother of King George III, permitted Gibbon to present him with the first volume of *The Decline and Fall*. When the second volume appeared in 1781, Gibbon not unnaturally sought an audience with the prince to present him with a copy. He was received affably: "Another damned, thick, square book!" said the prince. "Always scribble, scribble, scribble! Eh! Mr. Gibbon?"

> "*Clientelismo* [patronage] offers the only safety, and the one sin Naples inevitably punishes is ambition. Some years ago, a *millemestieri* nicknamed Giovanni the Immortal made a good economic thing out of stepping in front of moving automobiles. He survived twenty-six accidents and was regarded as something of a local hero in his *vicolo* because he not only supported his family by sticking the insurance companies but also provided an income for the neighborhood cronies who inevitably testified in court on his behalf. The day inevitably came when he misjudged a car's speed and was fatally run over on the Via del Duomo. At his funeral, a reporter for a local television program asked one of the mourners, an old man who had been a frequent witness at Giovanni's court appearances, how he felt about his benefactor's demise. The old man shrugged and said, 'This time he exaggerated.'"
>
> — William Murray,
> *Italy: The Fatal Gift*

GIBBS, Josiah Willard (1839–1903), *US mathematical physicist; professor at Yale (1871–1903). He is considered the founder of chemical thermodynamics, which is based mainly upon the Gibbs free-energy function.*

1   At a Yale faculty meeting the language departments had been making out a strong case for being given more money. "Mathematics is also a language," remarked Gibbs.

છે ન્ડ

GIDE, André (1869–1951), *French novelist and leader of French liberal thought.* Les Faux-Monnayeurs (The Counterfeiters, *1926) is probably his best-known work.*

1   Paul Claudel, the Catholic mystic poet, once tried to convert the free-thinking Gide. He was unsuccessful. On February 19, 1951, Gide died. A few days later, on a bulletin board in a hall of the Sorbonne, a telegram appeared bearing Gide's signature. It read: "Hell doesn't exist. Better notify Claudel."

GIELGUD, Sir John (1904–   ), *British actor, noted for his Shakespearean roles as well as for his parts in many modern plays and films.*

1   Gielgud's first production was the Oxford University Dramatic Society's *Romeo and Juliet* in 1932. The youthful cast was a glittering one and the production launched several people on their theatrical careers, notably Peggy Ashcroft in the role of Juliet. For the role of the Nurse, Gielgud had the inspired idea of asking Edith Evans, already a considerable star, and she agreed to play the part. There were various hitches at the first performance and by the time of the final curtain Gielgud was in a state of acute nervous tension. All the flowery compliments that he had intended to pay Edith Evans and Peggy Ashcroft flew out of his head as he stepped to the front of the stage. What he actually ended up doing was thanking "two leading ladies, the like of whom I hope I shall never meet again."

2   When Gielgud told the actors in a play that all the men must wear jockstraps under their leotards, a voice asked: "Please, Sir John, does that apply to those of us who only have small parts?"

3   After the evening performance, a man came to Gielgud's dressing room to offer his congratulations. "How pleased I am to meet you," said Sir John, recognizing the man's face. "I used to know your son, we were at school together."
     "I don't have a son," replied the man coldly. "*I* was at school with you."

4   Comedienne Carol Channing once invited Gielgud to a sports event at which she was to award the prizes. Sir John, suffering from a virus infection at the time, scribbled the following note in reply: "Sorry, love, cannot attend. Gielgud doesn't fielgud."

5   Discussing the character of Othello, Gielgud once remarked, "I don't really know what jealousy is." A moment of reflection. Then: "Oh, yes, I do! I remember! When Larry [Olivier] had a success as Hamlet, I wept."

6   (Sir John tells the following story:)
     "When Clement Attlee was prime minister, I was asked to meet him at Stratford-upon-Avon at a supper at the Falcon Hotel after he had

attended a performance (one I was not in myself). I sat next to his daughter and the conversation turned on where we lived.

"'I have a very convenient home in Westminster,' I remarked. 'So easy to walk to the theatre. And where do you live?'

"Miss Attlee looked distinctly surprised and replied curtly, 'Number ten, Downing Street.'"

ह्ब ॐ

GILBERT, Sir Humphrey (?1539–83), *English soldier and navigator, half-brother of Sir Walter Raleigh. He distinguished himself as a soldier in Ireland and the Netherlands and in 1578 led an unsuccessful expedition to the New World. In 1583 he achieved his objective, landing in Newfoundland and claiming it for England.*

1 Despite the advice of his lieutenants, Gilbert refused to abandon his little ten-ton frigate, the *Squirrel,* which was overloaded and unseaworthy. Having paid a visit to his men on board the other remaining ship in his fleet, the *Golden Hind,* he insisted on returning to the *Squirrel.* On the afternoon of September 9, 1583, the frigate was almost overwhelmed by the waves, but finally was recovered. Gilbert, sitting near the stern with a book in his hand, shouted out to the *Golden Hind* as it came within earshot, "We are as near to heaven by sea as by land." That night the watch on the *Golden Hind* saw the lights of the *Squirrel* suddenly vanish, and he cried out, "The general is cast away." This was indeed true, and of the five ships that set out on the expedition, only the *Golden Hind* returned to England to tell the tale, together with Gilbert's noble last words.

ह्ब ॐ

GILBERT, John (1895–1936), *US film actor. A great screen lover of the silent film days, Gilbert found his career ruined by the advent of sound, which revealed his light, rather high voice to be totally unlike the husky romantic tones imagined by his millions of admirers.*

1 Gilbert was once called upon at short notice to play the role of the heroine's father in a Chicago production. He learned his lines in record time, but was still struggling to remember the name of the character he was playing, Numitorius, when the play opened. A colleague having helpfully suggested the Book of Numbers as a mnemonic, Gilbert rushed on stage with renewed confidence that evening and delivered his opening line: "Hold, 'tis I, her father — Deuteronomy."

ह्ब ॐ

GILBERT, Sir W[illiam] S[chwenck] (1836–1911), *British writer famous mainly for his humorous verse collected in* Bab Ballads *(1869, 1873) and for his collaboration with Sir Arthur Sullivan in the Savoy operas.*

1 Soon after the death of a well-known composer, someone who did not keep up with the news asked Gilbert what the maestro in question was doing. "He is doing nothing," was the answer.

"Surely he is composing," persisted the questioner.

"On the contrary," said Gilbert, "He is decomposing."

{This riposte may be a composite of several similar ones.}

2 At the Garrick Club in London, Gilbert was once baiting a group of Shakespeare admirers. "Take this passage, for example," he said. "I would as lief be thrust into a quickset hedge, As cry 'Plosh' to a callow throstle." One of the group at once sprang to Shakespeare's defense: "That's perfectly clear. It just means that the speaker would prefer to be scratched all over in a thorny bush rather than disturb the bird's song. Er — what play is that from?" Gilbert smiled triumphantly. "No play," he said. "I made it up — and jolly good Shakespeare it is, too!"

3 The Gilbert and Sullivan partnership was frequently stormy, with Gilbert particularly irritated by Sullivan's oft-repeated intention of pulling out so that he could write "better music." Gilbert observed, "He is like a man who sits on a stove and then complains that his backside is burning."

4 *Ruddigore* met a hostile reception, certain critics even complaining about the "vulgarity" of the title. Someone frivolously asked Gilbert how "Bloodygore" was going. Gilbert, sensitive on this point, brusquely corrected him.

"*Ruddigore*—Bloodygore—pretty much the same thing," persisted the other man. "Indeed?" said Gilbert. "Then if I say I admire your ruddy countenance—which I do—it means I like your bloody cheek—which I don't."

5 An actor whom Gilbert was attempting to browbeat turned on his tormentor and said, "See here, sir, I will not be bullied. I know my lines."

"Possibly," retorted Gilbert, "but you don't know mine."

6 The actress Henrietta Hodson had a long-running feud with Gilbert, whose dictatorial methods in the theater she strongly resented. At a rehearsal for a Gilbert comedy she missed the chair and sat down heavily on the stage. Gilbert applauded from the stalls. "I always thought you would make an impression on the stage someday," he said.

7 When Gilbert lived in his mansion, Grims Dyke, in Stanmore just outside London, his neighbors on the adjoining estate were the Blackwells, a family of solid tradespeople who had built up a thriving business in jams and pickles, which sold under the trade name "Cross and Blackwell." They were totally unaware that their attempts to pass themselves off as landed gentry caused a considerable amount of local amusement. On several occasions Gilbert's dogs wandered onto the Blackwells' land, an intrusion not permitted to pass unnoticed. Gilbert received a stiff note of complaint. His reply was brief: "Dear Sir, I will take care that in future my dogs do not trespass on your preserves. Kindly pardon the expression."

8 At rehearsals one day, Gilbert was anxious to speak to a particular actress and asked a stagehand where she might be found. "She's round behind," replied the stagehand.

"Yes, I know that," said Gilbert, "but where is she?"

9 Gilbert watched one of his actors give an appalling performance. Bursting into the man's dressing room after the show, he cried, "My dear chap! Good isn't the word!"

❧

GILES, Frank Thomas Robertson (1919–   ), *British journalist.*

1 Frank Giles married Lady Katharine Sackville, who, as the daughter of an earl, retained her title after her marriage. Once on a journey abroad they received an invitation from the British embassy addressed to Mr. and Mrs. Giles. Concerned at the breach of protocol, Giles rang the embassy and started to explain: "She isn't exactly *Mrs.* Giles—"

"That's all right," said the voice at the other end cheerily. "Bring her along anyway. We're not at all stuffy here."

❧

GILOT, Françoise (1921–   ), *French artist, mistress of Pablo Picasso for nearly ten years and mother of two of his children, Paloma and Claude. She is married to Jonas Salk, discoverer of the Salk vaccine for poliomyelitis.*

1 One day while Françoise was painting in her studio, her son Claude knocked on the door.

"Yes?" Françoise answered, but continued working.

"Mama, I love you."

She kept painting but answered, "I love you too, my darling."

Then: "Mama, I like your painting."

"Thank you, darling. You're an angel."

A minute later: "Mama, what you do is very nice. It's got fantasy in it but it's not fantastic." Françoise stopped painting but didn't say anything. Claude continued: "It's better than Papa's."

She went to the door and let him in.

❧

GIOLITTI, Giovanni (1842–1928), *Italian statesman; prime minister in a number of short-lived administrations between 1892 and 1921.*

1 Someone mindful of Giolitti's tumultuous political career once asked him if it was difficult to govern Italy. "Not at all," replied the old statesman, "but it's useless."

{This witticism was also attributed to Giolitti's rival, Mussolini.}

❧

GIORGIONE [Giorgione da Castelfranco] (c. 1477–1510), *Italian painter of the Venetian school, which he greatly influenced. He worked with Titian on the frescoes for the German exchange in Venice. His paintings, even those on* *conventional religious subjects, have a characteristically poetic and romantic atmosphere.*

1 On one occasion a group of sculptors were maintaining the superiority of their art to that of the painter. Giorgione was not impressed, claiming that a painting could show at once all that was necessary, without obliging the viewer to walk around the object. He offered to show in a single view the front, back, and both sides of a figure in one painting. The sculptors were skeptical, but Giorgione fulfilled his promise by painting a nude with her back turned to the viewer, a pool of water at her feet to reflect the front, a burnished corselet reflecting one side, and a mirror the other.

{For another artist's handling of a comparable problem, *see* JEAN-BAPTISTE ISABEY 1.}

GIOTTO [Giotto di Bondone] (c. 1266–1337), *Italian painter and architect. His surviving frescoes include a cycle in the upper church of St. Francis at Assisi and scenes of the Holy Family in the Arena Chapel, Padua. In 1334 he became city architect in Florence, designing the campanile for the cathedral. He is sometimes regarded as the first of the Renaissance painters.*

1 Pope Boniface VIII, thinking to employ Giotto, sent a messenger to the painter to ask for a sample of his work. With one continuous stroke of his hand, Giotto drew a perfect circle. When this was shown to the pope, he realized that Giotto was preeminent among painters of the time.

{Professional artists do not find this anecdote persuasive evidence of Giotto's genius.}

2 While studying with Giovanni Cimabue, Giotto painted a fly on the nose of a figure in one of his master's paintings. So realistic was the insect that when Cimabue returned to work on the picture, he tried repeatedly to brush the fly away. It was some time before he realized that he had fallen victim to one of Giotto's practical jokes.

{Similar stories are told of other painters. *See also* ZEUXIS 1.}

3 When he first encountered Giotto's children, Dante was struck by their ugliness. "My friend," he exclaimed, "you make such hand-some figures for others — why do you make such plain ones for yourself?" The unruffled Giotto replied, "I paint for others by day."

GIPP, George (1895–1920), *US football player, whose brilliant play gave Notre Dame, "The Fighting Irish," unbeaten seasons in 1919 and 1920.*

1 In December 1920 a throat infection turned to pneumonia and Gipp died at the height of his career. On his deathbed he told Notre Dame's coach, Knute Rockne, "Someday, when things look real tough for Notre Dame, ask the boys to go out there and win one for the Gipper." In 1928 Notre Dame had had a catastrophic season. They were in New York to play Army, burdened with the memory of a 18–0 defeat in the previous year's Army game. In the locker room Rockne gathered the team around him and repeated to them Gipp's deathbed request. "I've never used Gipp's request until now," he concluded. "This is that game. It's up to you." The Notre Dame team went out and played like men inspired. The final score was Army 6, Notre Dame 12. The following day the *New York Daily News* headline read: "Gipp's Ghost beats Army." The game was known thereafter as "the Gipp Game" and "Win one for the Gipper" entered the American language.

GIRAUDOUX, Jean (1882–1944), *French novelist, playwright, and diplomat. He established his reputation in the 1920s with his poetic novels. His elegant, witty plays —* Amphitryon 38 *(1929),* Ondine *(1939), and* La Folle de Chaillot *(1945) among them — are still regularly performed.*

1 During his tenure as France's minister of information shortly before World War I, Giraudoux attended a meeting to discuss the problem of unemployment. After a long debate one speaker summed it up: "If things go on this way another year, we'll all be begging."

"From whom?" asked Giraudoux.

GLADSTONE, William Ewart (1809–98), *British statesman; four times Liberal prime minister (1868–74, 1880–85, 1886, 1892–94). Renowned for his abilities as an orator, Glad-*

stone, *with his rival Disraeli, dominated British politics between 1850 and 1900. He was responsible for disestablishment of the Irish Church (1869); the Education Act (1870), which established universal elementary education; and various acts to regulate electoral procedure and parliamentary reform.*

1 (C. M. Bowra remembers this story:)

"A visitor was telling Gladstone about a crank school which existed in 1812 in Devonshire; its rule was that if anyone did anything wrong, he was not punished but all the boys in the school wrote home about it. So one day dear old Canon Denniston of Durham, who had six boys at the school, received six letters, each of which said, 'Yesterday Jones minor cheated,' and on each letter he had to pay one and threepence. At this point Gladstone commented, 'But in eighteen hundred and twelve the postage from Devonshire to Durham was a great deal more than one and threepence.' His children, feeling that this was a little unkind to the story-teller, said, 'But, father, this is a funny story,' and he said, 'I am perfectly aware of the humorous aspects of the story but what particularly interests me are the financial aspects.'"

2 Mrs. Gladstone was presiding over a gathering in her drawing room when some of her visitors launched into a spirited controversy over the interpretation of a biblical passage. Presently one of the party, feeling that the discussion was becoming too heated, tried to put a stop to it by remarking piously, "Well, there is One above who knows all things." Mrs. Gladstone's face brightened. "Yes," she said, "and Mr. Gladstone will be coming down in a few minutes."

3 Gladstone, visiting an antique dealer's shop, admired an early seventeenth-century oil painting depicting an aristocrat dressed in old Spanish costume with a ruff, plumed hat, and lace cuffs. He wanted it badly but thought the price too high.

Sometime later, at the house of a rich London merchant, he came upon the portrait he had so admired. His host, noticing Gladstone's absorption, approached him. "You like it? It's a portrait of one of my ancestors, a minister at the Court of Queen Elizabeth." Said Gladstone: "Three pounds less and he would have been *my* ancestor."

Walter Winchell reported in his column of December 17, 1947:

"Leopold Godowsky (son of the late pianist-composer) asked his sister to drive his three-year-old twins to their Westport home. 'By the way,' said Leopold, 'please drive carefully as I have two violins worth fifty thousand dollars in the luggage compartment.'

"'Which,' inquired his sister, 'should I watch first, the twins or the fiddles?'

"'The twins, of course, of course!' said Godowsky. 'The violins are insured.'"

— From Nicholas Slonimsky, *A Thing or Two about Music*

GLEASON, Jackie (1916–), *US comedian. He appeared in films such as* The Hustler *(1961) and also enjoyed a long and successful career in* The Honeymooners, *a television comedy series.*

1 While performing at a nightclub in a seaside town, early in his career, Gleason stayed at a local boardinghouse. Finding himself unable to pay the rent, he devised a way of escaping from his lodgings without raising suspicion. He packed up his belongings, lowered the suitcase out of his bedroom window into the arms of a waiting friend, then strolled nonchalantly out of the house in his swimming trunks, heading for the beach. Some three years later, anxious to pay off his debt, he returned to the boardinghouse. The landlady, recognizing him at once, stepped back in horror as if she had seen a ghost. "Oh, my Lord!" she exclaimed. "I thought you were drowned!"

GLUCK, Christoph Willibald (1714–87), *German composer. He is chiefly renowned for his operas, notably* Orfeo ed Eurydice *(1762) and* Alceste *(1767), which in their dramatic power heralded a distinct break with the older, more artificial operatic tradition.*

1 Walking along the rue St. Honoré one day, Gluck accidentally broke a shopkeeper's glass pane. The value being put at thirty sous, Gluck offered him a coin worth about double that.

The shopkeeper was about to run next door to get change when Gluck stopped him. "Why bother? I'll make it even." And he broke another pane.

{A similar story is told of others.}

❧

GLYN, Elinor (1864–1943), *British writer of feverish romances, who popularized the term "it" for sex appeal. Her novels include* Three Weeks *(1907),* It *(1927), and* Did She? *(1934).*

1 Mrs. Glyn's first manuscript was rejected by a number of publishing houses. Trying a bolder approach, she sent it to another publisher with the following note attached: "Would you please publish the enclosed manuscript or return it without delay, as I have other irons in the fire." The manuscript was returned a few days later, together with a rejection slip on which the editor had scribbled: "Put this with your other irons."

❧

GODARD, Jean-Luc (1930–   ) *French movie director, known for his experimental techniques.*

1 Filmmaker Georges Franju, laying down the law at a symposium, said, "Movies should have a beginning, a middle, and an end."

"Certainly," agreed Godard, "but not necessarily in that order."

❧

GODIVA, Lady (c. 1040–80), *English noblewoman. With her husband, Leofric, Earl of Mercia, she founded a monastery in their home town of Coventry.*

1 A story first mentioned in 1236 by the chronicler Roger of Wendover relates how Lady Godiva, in the year 1057, exasperated her husband by persistently pleading with him to reduce the taxes on the people of Coventry. To silence her, Leofric declared he would do so only if she rode naked through the town's market place. The seventeen-year-old Godiva called his bluff and set out for the town next day on horseback completely naked. However, by concealing most of her body with her long and copious tresses of hair, she preserved both her own modesty and her husband's pride, en-abling Leofric to reduce the taxes without loss of face.

{A later, probably seventeenth-century, embellishment of this almost certainly apocryphal tale suggests that Lady Godiva made a pact with the townspeople that they would remain indoors, behind shuttered windows, if they wanted their taxes reduced. Everyone complied except a tailor called Tom. This prurient citizen peeped through his curtains, drawing upon himself instant calamity by an unspecified agent; he was struck blind (or, in some versions, dead) on the spot. Poor voyeuristic Tom, blind or dead as the case may be, left the epithet "a peeping Tom" as a permanent legacy to the English language.}

❧

GODOWSKY, Leopold (1870–1938), *Russian-born piano virtuoso and composer, who came to the United States and settled in St. Louis.*

1 When the child prodigy Jascha Heifetz made his American debut at Carnegie Hall in 1917, the audience included Mischa Elman, the violinist, and Leopold Godowsky. As the sixteen-year-old Heifetz played, Elman grew restless, fidgeting and wiping his brow. "It's awfully hot in here," he whispered to Godowsky, who shared his box. "Not for pianists," replied Godowsky.

{This, the *ne plus ultra* of anecdotes about professional rivalry, has been ascribed to many performers.}

❧

GOERING, Hermann Wilhelm (1893–1946), *German politician, founder of the Nazi secret police force, the Gestapo. He joined the Nazi party in 1922 and held a number of important posts in Hitler's government before becoming economic dictator (1937) and marshal of the Reich (1940). Condemned to death for war crimes at the Nuremberg trials, he committed suicide before his execution by taking poison.*

1 Making his way along a crowded railroad platform in Rome, Goering happened to collide with an Italian aristocrat. The nobleman demanded an apology. "I am Hermann Goering," snapped the marshal.

"As an excuse that is not enough," replied the Italian coldly, "but as an explanation it is ample."

2 Goering's many titles included that of Master of the German Forests. He was particularly concerned with the Bialowieza National Park, which had lost much of its wildlife during World War I. Goering had the forest restocked with game and put a restriction on the number of hunting permits issued. So it was that one of the most powerful members of the Nazi party had on the wall of his office the notice: "He who tortures animals wounds the feelings of the German people."

ชจ ชจ

GOETHE, Johann Wolfgang von (1749–1832), *German poet, novelist, playwright, and scholar. With his friend Friedrich Schiller, Goethe was the leading spirit in the* Sturm und Drang *period of German literature. His autobiographical novel,* The Sorrows of Young Werther *(1774), was acclaimed all over Europe. In 1775 he settled at the court of Weimar and turned this small German town into a major cultural center. He wrote a number of plays and translated works in other European languages into German, but his greatest fame rests on his poetic drama* Faust *(1808, 1832) and his* Wilhelm Meister *novels (1795–96, 1829), which explore in their different ways the pilgrimage of the human soul. He also made contributions to botany and comparative anatomy.*

1 At the battle of Valmy in September 1792 the army of revolutionary France confronted the combined forces of Austria and Prussia and eventually compelled them to retreat. Goethe, present at the battle, made the immortal remark, "From today and from this place there begins a new epoch in the history of the world."

2 Goethe admired Napoleon, whom he saw in the light of a defender of civilization against the barbaric Slavs. When they finally met at Erfurt, Napoleon's comment on Goethe was simply: *"Voilà un homme!"* (There is a man!)

3 As Goethe's mother lay on her deathbed, a servant girl brought her an invitation to a party. The old lady directed her thus: "Say that Frau Goethe is unable to come; she is busy dying at the moment."

4 In 1830 Goethe's dissipated son August, who had caused his father much disappointment and care, died in Rome. When the news was brought to Goethe, he said, "I was not unaware that I had begotten a mortal."

5 During Goethe's last years a disciple, Johann Peter Eckermann, recorded his conversations and also took down his last words: "Open the second shutter so that more light may come in."

{This is usually quoted simply as "More light!"}

6 When a new edition of Goethe's autobiography was produced by the greatest of the German annotators, a curious footnote crept in. After Goethe's confession, "With her, for the first time in my life, I really fell in love!" the scholarly editor added an asterisk and the information: "Here Goethe was in error."

ชจ ชจ

GOGARTY, Oliver [Joseph] St. John (1878–1957), *Irish poet. The character of Buck Mulligan in James Joyce's* Ulysses *is based on him.*

1 Entering a tavern one day, Gogarty caught sight of a friend wearing a patch over one eye. He greeted him: "Drink to me with thine only eye."

2 (In January 1923 during the Irish civil war Gogarty, who had played a prominent role in the founding of the Free State, was seized by Republican extremists. William Butler Yeats continues:)

"[He was] imprisoned in a deserted house on the edge of the Liffey with every prospect of death. Pleading a natural necessity, he got into the garden, plunged under a shower of revolver bullets and as he swam the ice-cold December stream promised it, should it land him in safety, two swans. I was present when he fulfilled that vow."

{The title of Gogarty's volume of poems, *An Offering of Swans,* recalls this event.}

ชจ ชจ

GOLDBERG, Arthur J[oseph] (1908–), *US politician and lawyer. He was US ambassador to the United Nations (1965–68) and chairman of the US United Nations Association (1968–70).*

1 Goldberg was waiting in line for sandwiches in a New York delicatessen when he was recognized by an elderly lady in front of him. "If it will help straighten out the problems of the world any quicker, Ambassador Goldberg," she said obligingly, "you can go ahead of me."

2 As secretary of labor, Goldberg was congratulated by President Kennedy for averting a labor strike. "How do you do it, Arthur?" he asked. Goldberg smiled. "The trick is to be there when it's settled," he replied.

ह~ ~ई

GOLDEN, John (1874–1955), *US playwright and theatrical producer. He also composed songs.*

1 Golden had invited Rose Franken, author of the *Claudia* novels, to lunch. As they chatted in his office before leaving for the restaurant, Golden handed his guest a bar of chocolate. Mrs. Franken, pleasantly surprised, thanked him and put the chocolate in her purse. "I don't want to spoil my appetite," she explained. "I'll save it for later." Golden frowned. "You're supposed to spoil your appetite," he snapped. "Give it back."

ह~ ~ई

GOLDSMITH, Oliver (1728–74), *English poet, playwright, and novelist, born in Ireland. He was an intimate of the Samuel Johnson circle, and is best known for his comedy* She Stoops to Conquer *(1773) and his novel* The Vicar of Wakefield *(1766).*

1 Goldsmith was talking about the writing of fables, and how necessary it was to make the animals talk in character so that little fishes spoke like little fishes. Samuel Johnson was overcome by laughter. "Why, Dr. Johnson," said Goldsmith smartly, "this is not so easy as you seem to think, for if you were to make little fishes talk they would talk like WHALES."

ह~ ~ई

GOLDWYN, Samuel (1882–1974), *US film producer. Goldwyn Pictures, the company he cofounded in 1916, merged with others to become Metro-Goldwyn-Mayer (MGM) in 1924. Among his many successes were* Wuthering Heights *(1939) and* Guys and Dolls *(1955). The Polish-born Goldwyn never completely mastered idiomatic English. Many famous "Goldwynisms" are apocryphal or categorically disowned by their reputed author. Some well-known examples are: "In two words, impossible!"; "Any man who goes to a psychiatrist ought to have his head examined"; "Include me out"; and "A verbal contract isn't worth the paper it's written on."*

1 In place of his original surname, which was Polish and unpronounceable, Goldwyn adopted the name Goldfish on arrival in the United States. Goldwyn, the company name, was an amalgam of Goldfish and the name of an early partner, Edgar Selwyn. A lawsuit was brought challenging his right to use the invented name. In the course of the hearing, the judge, who eventually ruled in Goldwyn's favor, observed, "A self-made man may prefer a self-made name."

2 Goldwyn had a technique for handling people from whom he needed a favor. On one occasion he wanted an actor who was under contract to Darryl Zanuck. He telephoned Zanuck, made a great fuss, and demanded that Zanuck's secretary call him out of a meeting. There was a long wait. Eventually Zanuck came on the line. Goldwyn said, "Yes, Darryl? What can I do for you today?"

3 In Goldwyn's office the rows with his top director, William Wyler, were so noisy that Merritt Hulbert, head of Goldwyn's story department, asked to have his office moved to another floor. "Quiet story conferences make quiet pictures," retorted Goldwyn firmly. Eventually, however, he and Wyler arranged a truce. "Look, Willie," he said, "from now on when we meet, we each put a hundred-dollar bill on my desk, and the first one to shout loses his money."

"Okay," said Wyler.

As a result Hulbert stayed on in his office while, next door, appalling insults were traded in whispers.

4 Edward G. Robinson told Goldwyn that his studio was going to make Shakespeare's *Merchant of Venice* and that they wanted him to play Shylock. Did Goldwyn think he ought to accept the part? Goldwyn's response: "Screw 'em—tell 'em you'll only play the Merchant."

5   Goldwyn is said to have been eager to buy the film rights to Radclyffe Hall's *The Well of Loneliness,* a controversial novel dealing with lesbianism. "You can't film that," a studio adviser said. "It's about lesbians."

"All right," said Goldwyn, "where they got lesbians, we'll use Austrians."

{The authenticity of this anecdote is not guaranteed.}

6   A ghostwriter was employed to write a series of articles purporting to be by Samuel Goldwyn. Halfway through the assignment the ghostwriter fell ill and a substitute had to be found. Goldwyn, reading a piece by the stand-in writer, expressed dismay: "That's not at all up to my usual standard."

7   Goldwyn, coaxed to change his mind about a particular script, stood firm: "I am willing to admit that I may not always be right," he conceded, "but I am never wrong."

8   As Goldwyn and another studio chief both wanted a certain big star at the same time, there was a wrangle about the contract. In the end someone suggested that the dispute be settled by arbitration. Goldwyn agreed reluctantly: "Okay, as long as it's understood that I get him."

9   Goldwyn boasted that the greatest living writers were on his team of authors and he would spare no expense to get them, even if his ideas about their output were rather vague. One of the literary celebrities he lured to Hollywood was the Belgian writer Maurice Maeterlinck, winner of the 1911 Nobel Prize for literature and author of the enormously successful *La Vie des abeilles (The Life of the Bee).* When Maeterlinck arrived, fearful of his ignorance of motion-picture technique, Goldwyn reassured him: "I know you don't understand picture technique. That doesn't matter. All I want you to do is just go away and write your greatest book over in the form of a scenario."

A few weeks later Maeterlinck returned with a manuscript. Goldwyn was delighted and retired beaming into his office, taking the manuscript with him to read. A couple of minutes later he rushed out again screaming. "My God," he yelled, "the hero is a bee!"

10   Goldwyn's secretary came to him to ask if she could destroy the files that were more than ten years old. "Yes," said Goldwyn, "but keep copies."

11   Goldwyn, showing off his picture collection to a guest, announced proudly, "And this is my Toujours-Lautrec."

12   David Selznick was once greatly alarmed when Goldwyn telephoned him at midnight and said in ominous tones, "David, you and I are in terrible trouble." His mind racing over possible disasters, Selznick asked what was the matter. "You've got Gable, and I want him," replied Goldwyn.

13   When *The Best Years of Our Lives,* probably Goldwyn's greatest film, was due for release, the producer called a mammoth press conference. "I don't care if it doesn't make a nickel," he told the assembled reporters. "I just want every man, woman, and child in America to see it!"

14   Goldwyn found on his office desk one morning a copy of *The Making of Yesterday: The Diaries of Raoul de Roussy de Sales, 1938–1942,* which someone had submitted as possible movie material. Goldwyn looked at the book in amazement. "How do you like that?" he said. "Four years old and the kid keeps a diary!"

15   Goldwyn had invited writer Louis Bromfield to Hollywood. After two months, however, Bromfield had still been given nothing to do. Exasperated, he finally complained to Goldwyn. "Be patient," said Sam, "take your time."

"But why did you hire me?" asked Bromfield.

"For your name, Mr. Bronstein, for your name."

{The story is considered apocryphal, but this book's General Editor is inclined to believe in it, for he once himself worked for Mr. Goldwyn. At their first meeting Goldwyn opened the conversation with: "I'm glad to meet you, Mr. Freedman. I've been reading you in the *Times* for years." The General Editor's name is not Freedman and he had at that period not written for the *Times.*}

16   His inability to get names straight was part of the Goldwyn legend. One of his stars, Joel

McCrea, was always Joe MacRail. Once, in a meeting, Mr. McCrea gently corrected him: "It's Joel McCrea, Mr. Goldwyn." At which Goldwyn burst out, "Look! He's telling me how to pronounce his name, and I've got him under contract!"

17 Director William Wyler had been trying in vain to explain a particular scene to Goldwyn. Exasperated, he finally turned to Goldwyn's fifteen-year-old son and asked, "Do *you* understand it, Sammy?"

"Sure," replied the boy. "It's perfectly clear to me."

"Since when are we making pictures for kids?" growled Goldwyn.

18 During the making of a film, Goldwyn had a habit of phoning his associates whenever an idea came to him, regardless of the hour. N. Richard Nash, who was writing the screenplay for *Porgy and Bess,* was the unfortunate recipient of such a call, at three o'clock in the morning. "Do you know what time it is?" he snapped. Goldwyn paused for a moment, then turned to his wife. "Frances," he said, "Mr. Nash wants to know what time it is."

19 Goldwyn was not given to flights of (uncalculated) sentiment. He and some colleagues, visiting him at his home, were once engaged in a bitter dispute over a script. One of them walked over to the window looking out on Goldwyn's luxurious lawn. He stood there for a moment, then called out to the other, "Come look. Here we are fighting, and this marvelous, peaceful event is taking place in nature right under our noses. We should be ashamed of ourselves." The others, Goldwyn last, trooped over. Parading across the lawn were a mother quail and her five little chicks. They stood there for a short time; then the silence was broken by the unappeasable Goldwyn: "They don't belong here."

20 Goldwyn and Louis B. Mayer did not love each other. In the locker room at the Hillcrest Country Club in Los Angeles, Mayer backed Goldwyn into a corner and then pushed him into a laundry hamper. Later, chided by a friend about the noisy altercation, Goldwyn said, apparently honestly astonished, "*What?* We're like friends, we're like brothers. We love each other. We'd do anything for each other.

We'd even cut each other's throats for each other!"

21 A certain actor, negotiating a contract with Goldwyn, declared, "I'm asking fifteen hundred a week."

"You're not asking fifteen hundred a week," snapped Goldwyn, "you're asking twelve, and I'm giving you a thousand."

22 Frances Goldwyn was once asked by actress Shirley MacLaine what it was like to be married to the same man for more than thirty-five years. "It gets worse every day," Mrs. Goldwyn told her. "Thirty-five years ago I told Sam to come home and I'd fix him lunch. He's been coming home for lunch every day for thirty-five years."

కావ్ ఆర్

GOMEZ, Vernon ["Lefty"] (1910–), *US baseball pitcher for the New York Yankees in the 1930s.*

1 Gomez was once asked, after a poor year, to take a cut in salary — from twenty thousand dollars to seven and a half thousand. "Tell you what," said Gomez, recovering from the shock, "you keep the salary and pay me the cut."

కావ్ ఆర్

GOODMAN, Benny [Benjamin David] (1909–), *US jazz clarinetist. In 1934 he led his first band and subsequently became an important figure in the development of swing. He is also noted as a classical musician.*

1 In the early part of his career, Goodman shared a flat with fellow-musician Jimmy Dorsey. Both played clarinet and saxophone, so there was fierce competition when any job came up. Rather than share the work fairly, they operated on the basic rule that whoever answered the telephone first got the job. Goodman recalls an occasion when there was a tie: "Jimmy got the mouthpiece of the phone and accepted the date. But I had the receiver and knew where the job was."

కావ్ ఆర్

GOODMAN, Dodie (*dates unavailable*), *US entertainer, who appeared often on Jack Paar's TV talk show.*

1 (Jack Paar relates an anecdote:)

"One night in the dressing room she said to me: 'You have a speck on your eyelash.'

"I couldn't see anything, but batted at my eyelashes to brush it away.

"'You still didn't get it,' she said, brushing at my left eye. I still couldn't see anything.

"'Oh, mercy,' she finally said, touching her forehead. 'It's on *my* eyelash.'"

❧ ❦

GORDON, Lord George (1751–93), *British political agitator responsible for fomenting the anti–Roman Catholic Gordon Riots in London in 1780. He was tried for treason, but acquitted.*

1 After his release from the Tower of London, Gordon was accosted by a beggar. "God bless you, my lord," he said. "You and I have been in all the prisons in London."

"What do you mean?" said Gordon. "I was never in any prison but the Tower."

"That is true, my lord, and I have been in all the rest."

❧ ❦

GORDON, John Brown (1832–1904), US *Confederate general.*

1 During the fighting around Spotsylvania in 1864, Gordon rode off with a young officer called Jones to ascertain the enemy's position. Jones, who was sitting in a slouched position on his horse, was greatly concerned when a bullet passed through Gordon's coat from side to side. Gordon assured him that the bullet had only grazed his back, and went on to use the incident as an object lesson in deportment. "Suppose my back had been in a bow like yours," he said, "the bullet would have gone straight through my spine. Sit up, or you'll be killed." Jones straightened himself with a jerk, and Gordon never had cause to criticize his posture again.

❧ ❦

GORDON, Richard (1921–), *British author. He qualified as a doctor but left medical practice in 1952 to begin his highly successful series of "Doctor" books. These include* Doctor in the House *(1952),* Doctor at Sea *(1953),* Doctor at Large *(1955), and* Doctor in Love *(1957).*

1 (Gordon relates an embarrassing experience at the *viva voce* examination at his gynecology finals. He describes his examiner as "a red-faced fellow in tweeds and a striped tie.")

"'Well, my boy,' started the jovial professor amiably, pushing a bottle towards me. 'What do you think of that?'

"'Fibroids, sir,' I replied proudly.

"He frowned. I was puzzled. My answer, impregnably correct, had not gone over too well. . . .

"'How would you treat a case of endometriosis?'

"'Progestogens, sir. But if I may say, sir, the results are often disappointing.'

"My examiner glared. . . .

"'Have I said something wrong, sir?' I asked.

"'Not professionally,' my tweedy examiner snapped. 'But I don't think you have much future as a gynaecologist.'

"My shamed eyes looked down in confusion. They encountered a pair of brogues, stout stockings, the hem of a tweed skirt. It frightened me off gynaecology for the rest of my career, and off medical woman for life."

❧ ❦

GORE-BOOTH, Paul Henry, Baron (1909–), *British diplomat. He held a number of posts in the Foreign Office before becoming permanent undersecretary of state for the department (1965–69). He was head of the Diplomatic Service in 1968–69.*

1 During his days in the Foreign Office, Gore-Booth once received an urgent telegram from the Middle East. The message ran: "Ruler has died suddenly. Please advise." Gore-Booth replied immediately. "Hesitate to dogmatize," he said, "but suggest burial."

❧ ❦

GORKI, Maksim [Aleksei Maksimovich Peshkov] (1868–1936), *Russian novelist and short-story writer. He wrote an autobiographical trilogy covering his hard early life and novels such as* Mother *(1906) and* The Lower Depths *(1906). After intervals in exile (1906–13, 1921–28) he returned to Russia, becoming president of the Soviet Writers' Union and a supporter of Stalinism.*

1 On a visit to the United States Gorki was taken by his hosts to spend a day at Coney

Island. The huge amusement park was thronged with tourists in holiday mood, and Gorki and his hosts joined in, spending the whole day sampling the sights. As they were leaving the park, they asked Gorki what he had thought of it all. After a moment's pause he said simply, "What a sad people you must be!"

৵ ⋖৵

GOSSE, Sir Edmund (1849–1928), *British critic and translator. He wrote lives of Congreve (1888), Donne (1899), Jeremy Taylor (1904), Sir Thomas Browne (1905), Ibsen (1908), and Swinburne (1917), and translated Ibsen's plays. In his day he was a ubiquitous figure on the British literary scene, numbering Swinburne, Robert Louis Stevenson, and Henry James among his friends.*

1 The scholar W. P. Ker was walking with a friend across Exmoor when a fog came down. They saw a figure of vast size ahead of them. When they caught up with it, it turned out to be Gosse, whose shadow had been magnified by the atmospheric conditions — the phenomenon known as a Brocken specter. Ker greeted Gosse, saying, "I couldn't think what you could be, whether the Specter of the Brocken or an Oxford don returning to nature."

Afterward, when they were alone, Ker remarked to his friend, "Did you notice how pleased Gosse was to be taken for an Oxford don — even in a fog?"

2 Gosse was asked his opinion after he had been taken to see a private performance of a new play by Swinburne. "We were as nearly bored as enthusiasm would permit," he replied.

3 After Swinburne's death Gosse worked on an edition of the poet's works in collaboration with the bibliographer and forger T. J. Wise. One afternoon when Gosse was entertaining at his house, a maid took a message from Wise on the telephone that she, not knowing of Swinburne's death, misunderstood. She announced loudly to Gosse, "Mr. Swinburne to speak to you on the telephone, sir." There was a startled hush in the room. Gosse said, "Mr. Swinburne to speak to me on the telephone? I shall certainly not speak to Mr. Swinburne. I don't know *where* he may be speaking from."

4 The Anglo-Saxon scholar Walter William Skeat, knowing Gosse's propensity for ferocious literary controversy, tried to embroil him in argument. Gosse on this occasion decided that silence was the wiser course; he maintained a lofty indifference to Skeat's carefully planted goads and made no response, either public or private, to his attacks. In the end Skeat acknowledged that he was beaten. He sent Gosse a postcard reading: "What? Not one kind word? W. W. S."

৵ ⋖৵

GOULD, Jay (1836–92), *US financier and railroad magnate.*

1 Gould built up a vast railroad empire, the Gould system, in the southwestern states. Just before an impending strike he is said to have observed, "I can hire one half of the working class to kill the other half."

2 The rector of Gould's church sought the magnate's advice concerning the investment of his life's savings, amounting to about $30,000. Gould suggested, in the strictest confidence, that he should buy Missouri Pacific. The preacher followed this advice and the stock began to rise steadily, only to fall disastrously some months later. The preacher complained to Gould that he had lost all his savings. He was somewhat taken aback when Gould promptly presented him with a cheque for $40,000 to cover his losses. Guiltily he confessed that he had also told several members of his congregation about Gould's tip. "Oh, I know that," said Gould. "They were the ones I was after."

৵ ⋖৵

GRABLE, Betty (1916–73), *US actress, singer, and dancer, who, largely because of her splendid legs, was known as "the Pin-Up Girl."*

1 Betty Grable's five-year-old niece, who was staying with her, asked her aunt if she could join her in the bathtub. "Sure," was the reply. "Climb right on in." The little girl did as she was invited. Betty noticed the child staring at her very intently. She asked what was the matter. "I'm just wondering," said the child, "why it is that I'm so plain and you're so fancy."

৵ ⋖৵

GRACE, W[illiam] G[ilbert] (1848–1915), *British cricketer, known as the Doctor. His career spanned forty-two seasons and he is consid-*

ered to be the greatest all-rounder who ever lived.

1 Grace was a doctor — hence his nickname — and he originated a number of stories about the clash of his cricketing commitments with his medical career. On one occasion a patient was said to have come to his office and asked his assistant whether the doctor was in. "Of course he's in," was the reply, "he's been batting since Tuesday lunchtime."

2 The fast bowler C. J. Kortright of Essex was bowling to Grace and made several vain appeals for leg-before-wicket. Eventually he knocked Grace's middle stump out of the ground with a yorker. As Grace began to walk away, Kortright called after him, "You're surely not going, Doctor? There's a stump still standing."

3 There is a famous portrait of Grace painted for the long room of Lord's Cricket Ground, London, depicting the great batsman in his characteristic relaxed stance, bat held high. "Would you stand as easily as that if the game was in a tight spot?" asked the artist who was painting the picture. "Certainly," said Grace, "because after all I'd only be facing the next ball."

4 Grace was accosted by an anxious young woman on his way to the cricket ground one day. "I think my twins have got measles," she said. "Can you come?"

"Not just now," replied the doctor. "But contact me at the ground if their temperatures reach 210 for two."

ઠ્ટ ક્ટ

GRAINGER, Percy Aldridge (1882–1961), *Australian composer and pianist. After studying in Germany he moved to London (1900–15) and thence to the United States, where he took out citizenship. He made an important contribution to the study of British folk music, on which many of his own compositions were based.*

1 A friend who went to hear Grainger play for a women's club matinee audience on suburban Long Island accused him of giving them a shortened rendering of Grieg's "Ballade." "That's right," said Grainger serenely, "I dropped six pages out of the middle so I could catch the 4:58."

GRANGE, Red [Harold] (1903–   ), *US football player, nicknamed "The Galloping Ghost" for his fleetness on the field.*

1 "All Grange can do is run," said a detractor in the early 1920s when Grange was at the height of his success. "All Galli-Curci can do is sing," retorted Illinois coach Bob Zuppke.

2 Asked to explain his astonishing ability to elude tacklers, Grange modestly replied: "I can't explain it or take credit for it. You can teach a man how to block or tackle, run or pass, but you can't teach a man how to run so tacklers can't tackle him. No one ever taught me and I can't teach anyone. If you can't explain it, how can you take credit for it?"

ઠ્ટ ક્ટ

GRANT, Cary [Archibald Leach] (1904–   ), *US actor, born in Britain. His many films include* She Done Him Wrong *(1933),* The Philadelphia Story *(1941), and* North by Northwest *(1959).*

1 After watching Cary on a television broadcast, his mother, then in her nineties, reprimanded him for letting his hair get so gray. "It doesn't bother me," he replied carelessly.

"Maybe not," said his mother sternly, "but it bothers *me*. It makes me seem so old."

ઠ્ટ ક્ટ

GRANT, Ulysses Simpson (1822–85), *18th president of the United States (1869–77). Grant came to prominence as an outstandingly able general in the American Civil War, during which he rose to become commander in chief of the Union forces. Throughout his life he was a heavy drinker.*

1 Out driving in a buggy with Julia Dent, whom he was courting, Grant found that their route took them across a flooded creek spanned by a flimsy bridge. Grant assured the apprehensive Julia that it was safe. "Don't be frightened, I'll look after you," he said. "Well," said the girl, "I shall cling to you whatever happens," and she held tightly onto his arm with both hands as they drove across. Safely on the other side Grant drove on in thoughtful silence for some minutes, then cleared his throat, and spoke: "Julia, you said back there that you would cling to me whatever happened. Would you like to cling to me for the rest of our lives?" They were married in August 1848.

2 At Cairo, Illinois, in 1861 Grant had cause to reprimand a young recruit for deserting his post while on guard duty. Rather than punish the lad, he gave him a lesson in handling a gun and warned him, "Orders must be strictly and promptly obeyed always." Some days later the same recruit was put on guard of a steamboat laden with ammunition. His orders were to prevent anyone with a lighted pipe or cigar from approaching the boat. In due course General Grant appeared and made to board the vessel, one of his beloved cigars between his teeth. "Halt!" cried the recruit, and raised his gun. The general, surprised and annoyed at this apparent impertinence, demanded an explanation. "I have been taught to obey orders strictly and promptly," replied the soldier, "and my orders are to allow no one to approach this boat with a lighted cigar. You will please throw yours away." Grant was forced to smile on hearing his own words quoted back at him, and obediently tossed his cigar into the river.

3 In February 1862 the Confederate commander of Fort Donelson, Tennessee, sent a message to Grant, commander of the besieging Northern forces, suggesting an armistice. Grant replied, "No terms except an unconditional and immediate surrender can be accepted. I propose to move immediately upon your works." This message became famous and won Grant the nickname of "Unconditional Surrender Grant."

4 Shortly before the attack on Fort Donelson in 1862, a deserter from the fort turned up in Grant's camp. At this point Grant had not decided whether to attack the fort immediately or give his tired men a day's rest. However, on learning that the deserter, along with the other troops in the fort, had been given six days' rations, Grant made up his mind. He addressed his men: "Gentlemen, troops do not have six days' rations served out to them in a fort if they mean to stay there. These men mean to retreat, not to fight. We will attack at once."

5 Grant had major successes in 1862 with his capture of the Confederate stronghold of Fort Donelson and at the battle of Shiloh, where he averted a disaster for the Union side, turning likely defeat into a narrow victory. Nevertheless, his heavy drinking caused many of President Lincoln's advisers to urge the general's dismissal. This step Lincoln could scarcely afford to take, in view of the incompetence of the other Union generals. "I can't spare this man; he fights."

The complaints continued, but so did Grant's successes. Lincoln is said to have exclaimed, "If I knew what brand of whiskey he drinks, I would send a barrel or so to my other generals!"

{The second remark, quoted in several forms, is probably apocryphal.}

6 Grant's repeated efforts to have a particular officer relieved of his command had met with failure. In exasperation he eventually sent the War Department a dispatch that read: "I beg that you will relieve General ——, at least until all danger is over."

7 Undistinguished and often shabby in appearance, Ulysses S. Grant did not recommend himself to strangers by his looks. He once entered an inn at Galena, Illinois, on a stormy winter's night. A number of lawyers, in town for a court session, were clustered around the fire. One looked up as Grant appeared and said, "Here's a stranger, gentlemen, and by the looks of him he's traveled through hell itself to get here."

"That's right," said Grant cheerfully.

"And how did you find things down there?"

"Just like here," replied Grant, "lawyers all closest to the fire."

8 On his way to a reception held in his honor, Grant caught in a rain shower, offered the shelter of his umbrella to a stranger walking in the same direction as himself. The stranger was also bound for the reception, but confided that he was going only to satisfy a personal curiosity, having never seen Grant. "Between us, I have always thought that Grant was a very much overrated man," he explained. "That's my view also," Grant said.

9 For a great general, Grant took surprisingly little interest in military affairs, an attitude that he seemed to reveal especially when meeting other military notables. Introduced to the second Duke of Wellington, he said with bland innocence, "They tell me that your father was also a military man."

10 Someone remarked in Grant's hearing that Charles Sumner did not believe in the Bible. "Why should he?" inquired Grant. "He didn't write it."

11 Grant, having no appreciation of music, found it hard when he was obliged, as president, to attend concerts. After one such occasion someone asked him if he had enjoyed the evening. "How could I?" was the response. "I know only two tunes; one of them is 'Yankee Doodle' and the other one isn't."

See also ABRAHAM LINCOLN 17.

12 A friend of Grant's once took the president to a golf course in the hope of encouraging him to take up the game. After watching a beginner hack the grass around the tee for several minutes without touching the ball, Grant remarked: "That does look like very good exercise. But what is the little white ball for?"

13 After the close of Grant's presidency, in the spring of 1877, the Grants embarked on a world tour, in the course of which they were entertained at dinner by Queen Victoria at Windsor Castle. The queen retired early, pleading "fatiguing duties." Mrs. Grant is said to have assured the queen that she quite understood: "I too have been the wife of a great ruler."

14 When Grant lay dying of cancer of the throat, he was attended by a popular Methodist minister who sprinkled water over the unconscious patient and then announced to the press that he had been converted and baptized. A little while later the doctor who was also in attendance succeeded in temporarily reviving him. When the minister was informed of this rally, he cried, "It is Providence. It is Providence."

"Not at all," said the doctor, "it was the brandy."

ॐ ◈

GRASSINI, Giuseppina (1773–1850), *Italian contralto.*

1 Following his second victorious Italian campaign, Napoleon brought back with him to Paris an Italian opera company. The Parisians, starved for pleasure and entertainment after the terrible years of the Revolution, enthusiastically stormed the opera house.

Napoleon, proud of his grasp of mass psychology, bestowed upon Girolamo Crescendi, the company's great bel canto star, the Cross of the Legion of Honor. While this pleased the opera lovers, the same was not true of the army. One staunch old warrior complained to the beautiful singer Giuseppina Grassini (with whom Napoleon was wont to console himself for Josephine's infidelities): "It's unheard of! To think that this decoration, intended for the bravest of the brave who have suffered wounds on the battlefield, should be given to a castrato!"

Replied Grassini: "And how about the wound Crescendi endured for art's sake? Doesn't that count?"

ॐ ◈

GRAVES, Robert Ranke (1895–), *British poet and novelist. His works include* Goodbye to All That *(1929), a memoir of his World War I experiences;* I, Claudius *and* Claudius the God *(1934), set in ancient Rome; and* Sergeant Lamb of the Ninth *(1940).*

1 Graves's mother tried not to appear shocked when four-year-old Robert, after saying his evening prayers, casually asked her if she would leave him any money when she died. "If you left me as much as five pounds, I could buy a bicycle," he said. "Surely you'd rather have me, Robby," protested Mrs. Graves. "But I could ride to your grave on it," reasoned the child.

ॐ ◈

GRAY, Thomas (1716–71), *English lyric poet. His fame rests on a single poem,* "Elegy Written in a Country Churchyard" *(1751).*

1 Gray once attended a sale of books with a friend. One lot particularly appealed to him: an elegant bookcase containing a collection of finely bound volumes of French classics. The hundred guineas demanded, however, was far beyond Gray's means, and his disappointment on learning the price was obvious. The Duchess of Northumberland, who had witnessed the incident and was acquainted with Gray's companion, asked the identity of the disconsolate bibliophile. Later the same day, Gray was over-

whelmed with delight to find that the coveted bookcase had been delivered to his lodgings. The gift was accompanied by a note from the duchess, in which she apologized for making so small an acknowledgment of the intense pleasure she had derived from reading Gray's "Elegy Written in a Country Churchyard."

ক্ক

GRAZIANO, Rocky [Thomas Rocco Barbella] (1922–), *US boxer; world middleweight champion (1947–48).*

1   Like many fighters Graziano came from a poor background and had little education, and like many fighters he was proud of it. In a restaurant, Graziano was approached by a youthful amateur boxer who reminded him of himself when he was young. "Spell 'school,'" Graziano suddenly demanded. The lad struggled and came up with "s-k-u-l." Graziano said, "Fifteen years, and he can't even spell 'school.'" He pointed to a fellow fighter nearby. "See him. He can't even read or write." The boy said, "I bet I read and write worse than him even." Graziano, annoyed, said, "I read and write worse than either of you."

2   (R. L. Crouser tells this anecdote:)
    "Rocky Graziano was making the perilous leap from the sweet science of boxing to the precarious world of show biz. So someone asked him if he planned to polish up his syntax with some training at a place like the famous Actors Studio. 'Why should I go to a place like that?' said the Rock. 'All they do is learn guys like Brando and Newman to talk like me.'"

ক্ক

GREELEY, Horace (1811–72), *US journalist and politician, founder of the* New York Tribune *(1841), which he edited until 1872. He mobilized public opinion against slavery, provoked great hostility by his insistence on universal amnesty as a basis for reconstruction after the Civil War, and in 1872 ran unsuccessfully against Grant for the presidency.*

1   Traveling on a train in New York, Greeley observed a fellow passenger reading the *Sun.* Always interested to discover what made people buy the rival newspaper, Greeley opened a conversation, at first on general topics and then leading up to the question, "Why don't you read the *Tribune?* It's a much more informative paper than the *Sun.*"
    "I take the *Tribune* too," replied the other man. "I use it to wipe my arse with."
    "Keep it up," said Greeley, "and eventually you'll have more brains in your arse than you have in your head."

2   Greeley served in Congress for three months. In the course of conversation one day, another congressman boasted that he was a self-made man. "That, sir," replied Greeley, "relieves the Almighty of a great responsibility."

3   Under the will of Stephen Girard endowing Girard College in Philadelphia, no clergymen were to be admitted to the campus. Greeley, who affected a rather clerical style of dress, one day approached the portals and was challenged by the guard. "You can't come in here," he said. "The hell I can't," retorted Greeley angrily. "I beg your pardon, sir," said the guard. "Go right in."

4   Greeley had one linguistic quirk: he insisted that the word "news" was plural. Accordingly, he once sent a cable to a member of the *Tribune* staff that read: "ARE THERE ANY NEWS?" Back came the reply: "NOT A NEW."

5   Greeley, renowned for his illegible handwriting, once wrote a note to a member of his staff on the *New York Tribune,* dismissing him for gross neglect of duty. Meeting Greeley several years later, the journalist told his former chief how useful his note of dismissal had proved. "I took it with me," he said. "Nobody could read it, so I declared it a letter of recommendation, gave it my own interpretation, and obtained several first-class situations by it. I am really very much obliged to you."

6   Greeley's notorious handwriting was, in fact, unreadable by all but one of the *Tribune*'s compositors. One day, while this expert was at lunch, two of his colleagues caught a couple of pigeons, inked their claws, and allowed them to scamper back and forth across a sheet of paper. This page was then substituted for Greeley's copy.
    That afternoon, the compositor struggled

through most of the inky scrawl, but there was one "paragraph" that he was totally unable to decipher. In desperation, he consulted Greeley. Casting his eye over the inky claw-marks, Greeley snapped impatiently: "What's the matter with you? Do you expect me to print it myself? Here, I'll rewrite the whole page."

7   A collector for a certain charitable organization once asked Greeley for a donation. "Your money will save millions of your fellow men from going to hell," was the encouraging promise. "Then I'll not give a damned cent," retorted Greeley. "Not half enough of them go there now."

ঌ৯ ৵ঌ

GREEN, Hetty [Henrietta Howland] (1834–1916), *US multimillionairess. Her reclusive lifestyle and shrewd investment technique earned her the nickname "the Witch of Wall Street."*

1   Like J. P. Morgan, Jr., and many other exceedingly wealthy people, Hetty Green was wary of giving financial tips. Asked to suggest a good investment, she replied, "The other world."

2   Mrs. Green's most faithful friend was a mongrel dog, which had the unfortunate habit of biting her visitors. Most of the dog's victims, anxious not to offend the millionairess, tolerated the animal, but one friend had had enough. "Hetty," she said reproachfully, "that dog just bit me again. You've got to get rid of him."
   Hetty refused. "He loves me," she explained, "and he doesn't know how rich I am."

ঌ৯ ৵ঌ

GREEN, Joseph Henry (1791–1863), *British surgeon. Distinguished as a surgeon, Green was also the friend and literary executor of Samuel Taylor Coleridge.*

1   On his deathbed Green behaved very coolly. "Congestion," he observed, and then took his own pulse. "Stopped," he said, and died.

ঌ৯ ৵ঌ

GREENE, Graham (1904–   ), *English writer. His major novels include* Brighton Rock *(1938),* The Power and the Glory *(1940) and* The Heart of the Matter *(1948). He also wrote*

"entertainments," such as Stamboul Train *(1932) and* The Third Man *(1950); plays, such as* The Living Room *(1933); and short stories.*

1   An English magazine had run a competition for the best parody of Graham Greene's work. A week after the prizewinning entry was published, a letter appeared from Greene himself. He was delighted that Mr. John Smith had won the contest, although he felt that two of the other competitors, Mr. Joe Doakes and Mr. William Jones, also deserved prizes. Greene had sent in all three entries himself — they were not parodies, but passages from some of his earlier novels, which he had not considered fit for publication.

2   Graham Greene has never been awarded the Nobel Prize, despite widespread opinion that he ought to have it. Asked if he was disappointed, Greene replied that he was awaiting a much better prize than the Nobel. "What prize?" he was asked. "Death."

ঌ৯ ৵ঌ

GREENWOOD, Frederick (1830–1909), *British journalist; editor of the* Pall Mall Gazette *(1864–89).*

1   In the early 1900s Lord Riddell acquired the sensational London newspaper *The News of the World*. Meeting Greenwood at his club one day, Riddell mentioned that he owned a newspaper, told Greenwood its name, and offered to send him a copy. The next time they met Riddell asked Greenwood what he had thought of *The News of the World*. "I looked at it and then I put it in the wastepaper basket," said Greenwood, "and then I thought, 'If I leave it there the cook may read it,' so I burned it."

ঌ৯ ৵ঌ

GREGORY I, Saint (?540–604), *pope (590–604). He instituted major reforms in the Italian church, greatly increasing papal authority. He introduced Gregorian plainchant into the liturgy and his writings continued to be influential throughout the Middle Ages.*

1   In 586 Gregory was appointed abbott of the monastery of St. Andrew's in Rome. The traditional story is that he happened to see some beautiful Angle children put up for sale as

slaves in Rome's market. Struck by their appearance, he asked what nation they came from, and was told that they were Angles. "*Non Angli, sed angeli* [not Angles, but angels]," said Gregory, and he decided then and there to convert this pagan nation to Christianity.

2   Inspired by his sight of the Angle children, Gregory received permission to lead a mission to England. The party had not gone far when Gregory was halted by a sign: a locust dropped onto the Bible that he was reading. "*Locusta!*" he exclaimed, "That means *loco sta* [remain in your place]." He returned to Rome and was soon elected pope.

> {Gregory's abortive mission is historical, but the locust is probably an embroidery pandering to the monkish predilection for bad Latin puns.}

ॐ ॐ

GRENFELL, Joyce Irene (1910–79), *British actress, comedienne, and writer. She appeared in a number of comedy films and performed on stage in solo shows all over the world. In the 1970s she was a regular panelist on BBC television's* Face the Music.

1   During World War II, Miss Grenfell toured hospitals in southern Europe, North Africa, and India with her accompanist Viola Tunnard. Invited to a hospital dance at Poona, the two ladies were delighted to find the men queuing up to dance with them. Not so flattering, however, was an announcement made during the course of the evening. "We are lucky enough to have with us tonight," declared the announcer, "two well-known artistes who have been flown out from home to entertain men in bed."

ॐ ॐ

GREVILLE, Mrs. Ronald [Maggie] (1867–1942), *one of the great London hostesses of the twenties, heiress to the tremendous fortune of her father, John McEwen, a Scottish beer baron. She would say, "I would rather be a beeress than a peeress."*

1   Mrs. Greville did not care for ladies whose jewels were more spectacular than hers. On one occasion after dinner, a very rich and famous American lady suddenly discovered that the principal diamond had dropped from her necklace. Everyone got on their hands and knees and then Maggie's voice was heard, speaking to a footman. "Perhaps this," she was saying, "might be of some assistance." She was handing him a large magnifying glass.

ॐ ॐ

GREY, Edward, 1st Viscount Grey of Fallodon (1862–1933), *British statesman, foreign secretary (1905–16). To reverse Britain's isolation at the beginning of the twentieth century, he negotiated the Triple Entente between France, Russia, and Britain, and supported France against Germany in the years leading up to World War I.*

1   (On August 3, 1914, Grey made his appeal to the British Parliament to support France and Belgium against Germany; a few hours later Germany declared war on France, making the violation of Belgium's territory certain.)

"In Whitehall that evening, Sir Edward Grey, standing with a friend at the window as the street lamps below were being lit, made the remark that has since epitomized the hour: 'The lamps are going out all over Europe; we shall not see them lit again in our lifetime.'"

ॐ ॐ

2   Grey was deeply attached to his country estate at Fallodon in Northumberland. Once when Lloyd George was inveighing against Grey's policies during World War I, Churchill came to the foreign secretary's defense. If the Germans held a gun to Grey's head, stated Churchill, and threatened to shoot him if he did not sign a treaty, Grey would absolutely refuse to be intimidated and would simply tell them that a British minister would not bow to such pressure. "Ah, but the Germans wouldn't threaten to shoot him if he didn't sign," said Lloyd George. "They'd threaten to scrag all the squirrels at Fallodon. That would break him."

ॐ ॐ

GRIMM, Charlie (1899–), *US baseball figure, one-time manager for the Chicago Cubs.*

1   Win or lose (and when he was manager it was mostly lose), Charlie Grimm always kept his sense of humor. One time, when the Cubs were digging deep in the barrel for new talent, one of Grimm's scouts excitedly phoned him from somewhere in the sticks.

"Charlie," he shouted, "I've landed the greatest young pitcher in the land. He struck out every man who came to bat — twenty-seven in a row. Nobody even got a foul until two were out in the ninth. The pitcher is right here with me. What shall I do?"

Back came Grimm's voice. "Sign up the guy who got the foul. We're looking for hitters."

❧ ❧

GROTE, Harriet (1792–1878), *British writer. She published a number of biographies and did much to promote the work of her husband, historian George Grote (1794–1871).*

1   Mrs. Grote was noted for her eccentricity, which extended to her dress. Sydney Smith, after a few seconds' contemplation of her turban, remarked, "Now I know the meaning of the word 'grotesque.'"

❧ ❧

GUGGENHEIM, Peggy (1898–1979), *US art collector and patron of modern artists. After leaving New York for Venice in 1946, she maintained her collection in the Palazzo Venier dei Leoni.*

1   Among the pieces Peggy Guggenheim displayed in her garden in Venice was a horse and rider that had been cast for her by Marino Marini (1901–1980). To express the rider's ecstasy the artist had cast him with an erect penis. The fact that the penis was detachable saved the collector much embarrassment on holy days, when a group of nuns habitually passed the garden.

❧ ❧

GUIMOND, Esther (fl. 19th c.), *French courtesan.*

1   Traveling in Italy, Esther Guimond was detained at a customhouse by an officious bureaucrat because her passport did not list her occupation. "I am a courtesan," she told him clearly. "Now please repeat that to the Englishman over there, who appears to be rich."

❧ ❧

GUINES, Adrien-Louis de Bonnières, Duke of (1735–1806), *French diplomat; ambassador in London (1770–76).*

1   Guines was enormously fat, but nonetheless a great dandy. His wardrobe contained two pairs of breeches for each outfit — one for days when he would have to sit down and the other, much tighter, for days when he would only have to stand. In the morning his valet's first question would be: "Will monsieur be sitting down today?"

{A contemporary describes how, on days when he was to remain standing, Guines would get into his breeches by climbing onto two chairs and then descending into the garment held up by a couple of servants.}

❧ ❧

GUINNESS, Sir Alec (1914–   ), *British actor. Having made his name as a stage actor in the 1930s, he embarked on a successful film career after World War II. His films include* Kind Hearts and Coronets *(1949), in which he played eight different roles;* The Bridge on the River Kwai *(1957), for which he won an Academy Award; and* Tunes of Glory *(1960). He also played the leading role of Smiley in the award-winning television adaptations of John Le Carré's* Tinker, Tailor, Soldier, Spy *and* Smiley's People.

1   After Guinness received an honorary degree at Boston College, along with the Pulitzer Prize poet Phyllis McGinley, the youngest of Mrs. McGinley's three daughters slipped up to Guinness. "Oh, Sir Alec," she gushed, "how does it feel to know the whole world adores you?"

"If you want to know the answer to that," Guinness said kindly, "you must ask your mother."

❧ ❧

GUITRY, Lucien (1860–1925), *French actor; father of the dramatist and actor Sacha Guitry. Lucien Guitry's style of acting was notable for its expressiveness and restraint.*

1   A silly and talkative woman had been boring Lucien Guitry with her vacuous chatter. "You know, I simply talk the way I think," she burbled. "Yes, but more often," he replied.

2   A fellow actor sent Guitry the manuscript of a play he had written, with a note saying, "I'll bet you a louis that you don't read this script."

Guitry promptly returned it, unopened; attached to it was an envelope containing a louis and a note: "You win."

3 Many great actors have been famous for their powers of observation. Lucien Guitry was no exception. Given the role of Rostand's Chanticleer, he studied farmyard cocks in Normandy. "Have you ever observed that a rooster runs with his hands in his pockets?"

�უ ჟ

GUITRY, Sacha (1885–1957), *French actor and playwright, born in Russia, the son of actor Lucien Guitry. His stage debut was made with his father's company. His plays are mainly light comedies; he also wrote and directed a number of films.*

1 Guitry was married five times. When his fifth wife exhibited signs of jealousy of her four predecessors, Guitry consoled her with the words: "The others were only my wives. But you, my dear, will be my widow."
{Variants of this anecdote are ascribed to others.}

2 An avid collector, Guitry, toward the end of his life, held an exhibition of all his treasures. One of his visitors remarked: "A splendid exhibition, Monsieur Guitry, but you have left out one thing—your collection of wives."
"Dear sir," replied Guitry, "although women are the collector's items most easily assembled, they are also the hardest to keep, for the number of collectors is incalculable."

3 A young reporter apologized to Guitry for calling on him during what was to be his final illness. "I know, sir, that your moments are precious," he said. "No, my friend," replied Guitry. "It isn't that they're precious—it's that they're numbered."

�უ ჟ

GULBENKIAN, Nubar Sarkis (1896–1972), *British industrialist and philanthropist, commercial attaché to the Iranian embassy (1926–51, 1956–65). His father, multimillionaire Calouste Sarkis Gulbenkian, financed the Gulbenkian Foundation for the advancement of the arts, science, and education.*

1 One of the wealthiest men in the world, Gulbenkian denied himself none of the pleasures that money could buy. He came home one day with a magnificent new car, the latest and most expensive model. "It has disk brakes, whatever they are," he announced excitedly. "It has automatic transmission, whatever that is. It has power steering, whatever that is. And it can turn on a sixpence, whatever *that* is."

2 Filling out a market research form, Gulbenkian came across a section labeled "Position in life." After a moment's thought he wrote: "Enviable."

3 In his *Lords, Ladies and Gentlemen,* Clifton Daniel recalls meeting Nubar Gulbenkian. Daniel said, "I'm sorry I hadn't met you when I was recently in Lisbon. I saw your father, and would have been fascinated to meet him. If I had known you, I could have said, 'I know your son in London,' and introduced myself."
To which Nubar replied, "That wouldn't have done you any good. My father has instructed all the members of his family that we are not to introduce anybody to him. He says he has met everybody he wants to know."

�უ ჟ

GUNTHER, John (1901–1970), *US journalist, author of* Inside Europe (1936) *and other successful similar volumes.*

1 Many of the most diverting puns ever ad-libbed were shot into the air week after week by the four experts on the radio show *Information Please.* Once they were required to identify a certain Middle Eastern potentate. John Gunther confidently supplied the correct answer. "Are you Shah?" ventured emcee Clifton Fadiman. "Sultanly," Gunther replied.

2 Assessing his busy career as a chronicler of world affairs, John Gunther recalls that soon after publication of his seventh "Inside" book, Clifton Fadiman asked him, "What are you going to do when you run out of continents?"
Quipped Gunther, "Try incontinence."

3 "John and Frances Gunther's son, Johnny, died in his eighteenth year, and was buried on July 2nd [1947]. He was a handsome, tall, fair-haired boy. He went to Deerfield Academy where he majored in mathematics and chemistry. For fourteen months he had suffered from a brain tumor for which he had had two operations. But even after the second, and about two weeks before he died, he passed his examinations for Columbia. He was one of the finest, bravest boys we've ever known. After his first operation, the doctors asked John and Frances about the advisability of telling Johnny what was the matter with him. He was so intelligently interested that the doctors thought it wiser to explain, and the older Gunthers agreed. The surgeon went to Johnny alone and told him the full gravity of a brain tumor. The boy listened carefully, then looked the doctor in the eye and asked, 'How shall we break it to my parents?' "

{Gunther himself tells the story of Johnny's illness and death in the moving *Death, Be Not Proud* (1949).}

ॐ ✦

GWENN, Edmund (1875–1959), *Welsh-born actor, best remembered as a Hollywood character actor of the 1940s. In 1947 he won an Academy Award for his role as Santa Claus in* Miracle on 34th Street.

1 On his deathbed Gwenn was visited by the American actor Jack Lemmon, who asked him frankly how hard it was to be facing death. "Oh, it's hard," Gwenn said in the whispery voice that was left to him, "very hard indeed. But not as hard as doing comedy."

ॐ ✦

GWYN, Nell [Eleanor] (1650–87), *English actress and mistress of Charles II.*

1 In 1675 Nell Gwyn paid a visit to Oxford with Charles II. The crowd, believing that the king was accompanied by Louise de Kérouaille, his unpopular Roman Catholic mistress, angrily shook the coach in which Nell was riding. With an instant appraisal of the situation, she leaned out of the window, calling, "Pray, good people, be civil; I am the Protestant whore."

2 One day in the king's presence Nell Gwyn shouted at her son by Charles, "Come here, you little bastard." The king rebuked her for her language. "But, sire, I have no better name to call him by," Nell protested. King Charles took the hint and soon afterward created the boy Baron of Headington and Earl of Burford.

H

HADRIAN (76–138), *Roman emperor (117–138). He was adopted as Trajan's heir under the influence of Plotina, Trajan's wife, and his reign was considered to be a golden era of peace and prosperity for the empire. Hadrian spent much time traveling through his realm and initiated many legal and administrative reforms.*

1 A woman came to Hadrian with a petition, but the harassed emperor brushed her aside, saying that he had no time to listen to her. "Cease then to be emperor," she retorted. Hadrian accepted the rebuke and heard her petition.

HAESELER, Count Gottlieb von (1836–1919), *German general.*

1 Count Haeseler was sitting in a railway waiting room, enjoying a cigar. The room's other occupant, a young lieutenant, was not quite so comfortable. "You shouldn't be smoking that cabbage-leaf of yours in good company," he said, offering Haeseler one of his own cigars. The count accepted it, slipped it into his pocket, and continued to smoke his own. "Sir, why are you not smoking my cigar?" demanded the lieutenant angrily. "I think I'll wait, as you suggest, until I'm in good company," Haeseler replied.

HAGEN, Walter (1892–1969), *US golfer. The first great golfing professional in the United States, he won the US Open twice and the British Open four times, as well as the US Professional Golfers' Association five times.*

1 Hagen won and spent more than a million dollars during his career. After winning one of his major titles, he was asked the secret of his success. Said Hagen, "You're only here for a short visit, so don't hurry, don't worry, and be sure to smell the flowers along the way."

HALBE, Max (1865–1945), *German naturalistic playwright.*

1 As a young man Halbe had difficulty making ends meet and was continually behind with his rent. Eventually his usually amiable landlady lost patience: "Herr Halbe, if you don't pay up now, I'm afraid I shall have to sue you."

"My dear lady, please don't," cried Halbe. "Let me make another suggestion — raise my rent."

HALDANE, J[ohn] B[urdon] S[anderson] (1892–1964), *British biochemist. Professor of genetics (1933–57) and biometry (1937–57) at London University, he was an ardent Marxist, but left the Communist party after the Lysenko affair. His many writings include* Science and Ethics *(1928) and* Heredity and Politics *(1938). In 1957 he emigrated to India as a protest against British policies.*

1 Haldane was engaged in discussion with an eminent theologian. "What inference," asked the latter, "might one draw about the nature of God from a study of his works?" Haldane replied: "An inordinate fondness for beetles."

2 A discussion between Haldane and a friend began to take a predictable turn. The friend said with a sigh, "It's no use going on. I know what you will say next, and I know what you will do next." The distinguished scientist promptly sat down on the floor, turned two back somersaults, and returned to his seat. "There," he said with a smile. "That's to prove that you're not always right."

> "In one of his autobiographical works, the English author Augustus John Cuthbert Hare described the experience of a certain lady who awoke in the middle of the night with the sense that someone else was in her room. The sound of footsteps going to and fro across the room and the impression of hands moving over the bed terrified the poor lady so much that she fainted. Only when morning came was it discovered that the butler had walked in his sleep and set the table for fourteen places upon her bed."
>
> — Daniel George, *A Book of Anecdotes*

HALDANE, Richard Burdon, Viscount Haldane (1856–1928), *British statesman; lord chancellor (1912–15); uncle of J. B. S. Haldane. As secretary for war (1905–12), he was responsible for creating a military organization similar to that in Germany. Haldane was also a philosopher.*

1 At a dinner in London, Lord Haldane was teased by some of his peers on account of his considerable bulk. He countered by maintaining that fatness did not necessarily mean unfitness. To prove it he offered to set off then and there to walk the sixty miles to Brighton in his evening clothes, resting no more than two minutes in every hour, and to send his dining companions a telegram when he got there. And that is precisely what he did.

ॐ ॐ

HALE, Nathan (1756–76), *US Revolutionary patriot.*

1 In September 1776 Hale volunteered for a spying mission behind the British lines in New York. He was disguised as a Dutch schoolteacher, but was betrayed, arrested, and hanged on the following day. On the scaffold he is reported to have said, "I only regret that I have but one life to lose for my country."

{This inspiring utterance, known to every American schoolchild, may be apocryphal.}

ॐ ॐ

HALEY, Alex (1921–), *black American writer, famous for* Roots, *an investigation of his ancestral background.*

1 Alex Haley's uncle, a rather self-satisfied person, always wore his Phi Beta Kappa key on a chain around his neck. Another of Haley's relatives, a woman of a realistic turn of mind, eyed the key, then said, "Real pretty. But what does it unlock?"

ॐ ॐ

HALIFAX, Charles Montague, 1st Earl of (1661–1715), *British statesman; First Lord of the Treasury (1697–99, 1714–15). Halifax was one of the leaders of the Whig party.*

1 In the Glorious Revolution of 1688 Lord Halifax was one of the first to take up arms on behalf of the prince of Orange. Once the prince was established on the English throne as William III, office-seekers swarmed to court claiming rewards for assisting the revolution. Referring to the sacred geese whose cackling alerted the Roman garrison in time to repulse a night attack by Celts in 390 BC, Halifax remarked, "Rome was saved by geese, but I do not remember that these geese were made consuls."

ॐ ॐ

HALIFAX, Edward Frederick Lindley Wood, Earl of (1881–1959), *English Conservative statesman. As viceroy of India (1926–31), he cooperated with Mahatma Gandhi. In Neville Chamberlain's government he held the post of foreign secretary (1938–40). He subsequently became ambassador to the United States.*

1 On a train journey to Bath, Halifax shared a compartment with two rather prim-looking middle-aged ladies. All three were strangers to one another, and the journey passed in silence until the train went through a tunnel. In the total darkness of the compartment, Halifax placed a number of noisy kisses on the back of his hand. As the train emerged from the tunnel, the former ambassador turned to his companions and asked, "To which of you charming ladies am I indebted for the delightful incident in the tunnel?"

ॐ ॐ

HALL, Sir Benjamin (1802–67), *British politician, chief commissioner of Public Works in the 1850s.*

1   The tall and portly "Big Ben" Hall was involved with the building of the Houses of Parliament after a fire in 1834. In September 1856 Parliament was much concerned with the pressing question of a name for the new fourteen-ton bell being installed in the clock tower. "How about Big Ben?" someone offered. To a man, Parliament rang with delighted applause, and Sir Benjamin's nickname was immortalized.

HALSEY, William Frederick, Jr. (1882–1959), *US naval commander in the Pacific during World War II.*

1   In October 1944 the Japanese put out claims to the effect that most of the American Third Fleet had been sunk or was retiring. Admiral Halsey countered with the message: "Our ships have been salvaged and are retiring at high speed toward the Japanese fleet."

HAMILTON, Alexander (1755–1804), *US statesman. The first secretary of the Treasury (1789–95), he established the first national bank (1791) and set up the national debt. Leader of the Federalist party, he was instrumental in obtaining the ratification of the Constitution. He was killed in a duel with Aaron Burr.*

1   Talleyrand had met Hamilton while visiting the United States, and was much impressed by him. He observed to George Ticknor, in a conversation recorded in the latter's journal, that although he had met many distinguished men in his time, none had been Hamilton's equal. Ticknor felt that as a fellow American he ought to demur; surely, he said, the statesmen and generals of Europe had been involved with wider issues and larger numbers of people than Hamilton had ever encountered. "*Mais, monsieur, Hamilton avait deviné l'Europe* [But, sir, Hamilton had foretold Europe]," replied Talleyrand.

HAMMERSTEIN II, Oscar (1895–1960), *US lyricist; collaborated with several musical-*comedy composers, most notably Richard Rodgers. He was the librettist for many famous successes, including* Oklahoma! *(1943),* Carmen Jones *(1943),* South Pacific *(1949), and* The Sound of Music *(1959).*

1   For years Hammerstein had failed to receive his proper due from the critics. With *Oklahoma!* and *Carmen Jones* he made the breakthrough; praise was lavished on him for his part in the shows' successes, and offers of work suddenly flooded in. That year Hammerstein took space in the traditional annual issue of *Variety* in which show-business people sent season's greetings to one another and also announced the work that they had done in the past twelve months. The advertisement ran: "Holiday Greetings from Oscar Hammerstein II, author of *Sunny River* (6 weeks at the St. James), *Very Warm for May* (7 weeks at the Alvia), *Three Sisters* (7 weeks at the Drury Lane), *Ball at the Savoy* (5 weeks at the Drury Lane), *Free for All* (3 weeks at the Manhattan). I've Done It Before and I Can Do It Again!" The advertisement caused a sensation.

Hammerstein himself offered two explanations, not necessarily contradictory. The first was that on Broadway a person is either very, very good or terrible and "I'm the same guy I used to be, except now I've got hits instead of flops. The ad was just a gentle reminder that times change and keep changing." The second, less subtle motive was to "thumb my nose and say: 'Well, you hyenas, so you thought I was all washed up?'"

2   Hammerstein's wife, Dorothy, was always ready to speak out for her husband when she felt that he was being pushed out of the limelight by one of his collaborators. Whenever somebody referred to Jerome Kern's "Ol' Man River," Dorothy would immediately retort, "Oscar Hammerstein wrote 'Ol' Man River.' Jerome Kern wrote 'Ta-ta dumdum, ta ta-ta dumdum.'"

HAMMETT, Dashiell (1894–1961), *US novelist. His own career as a private detective supplied material for his fiction. Two of his most successful works,* The Maltese Falcon *(1930) and* The Thin Man *(1932), were filmed. In 1951* *he fell afoul of the anticommunist zeal of the McCarthyites and served some time in jail.*

1 During the eight years that Hammett worked as a detective for the Pinkerton agency, he found out how resourceful a sleuth must be. A man he had been assigned to tail wandered out into the country and managed to lose himself completely. Hammett had to direct him back to the city.

2 The chief of police of a southern city once sent Hammett a detailed description of a wanted criminal, which included even the mole on the man's neck. The description omitted, however, the fact that the wanted man had only one arm.

3 During World War II Hammett served on Adak in the Aleutian Islands, where he edited a newspaper for the forces in the area. One serviceman recalls that in the paper Hammett would favor the progress of our Russian allies, but rarely mention the American forces. When the general of the Alaskan Command demanded to know the reason, Hammett replied, "Well, sir, this paper has a policy not to publish any ads."

4 Hammett lived for many years with playwright Lillian Hellman. During a quarrel when they had both been drinking heavily, she was raging at him and pacing about the room when she noticed that he was grinding a burning cigarette into his cheek. "What are you doing?" she demanded. "Keeping myself from doing it to you," was his reply.

હ્ય ∙ે

HAMSUN, Knut (1859–1952), *Norwegian author. He is best known for his novel* Growth of the Soil *(1917). In 1920 he won the Nobel Prize for literature.*

1 During the winter of 1894–95 Hamsun visited Paris for the first time. On his return home someone asked him, "At the beginning, didn't you have trouble with your French?"

"No," replied Hamsun, "but the French did."

હ્ય ∙ે

Greek orator and satirist Lucian described an ill-fated debut: "Harmonides, a young flute-player and scholar of Timotheus, at his first public performance began his solo with so violent a blast that he breathed his last breath into his flute, and died upon the spot."

—from Charles Burney,
A General History of Music

HANCOCK, John (1737–93), *US statesman, first governor of Massachusetts (1780–85, 1787–93).*

1 As president of the Continental Congress, Hancock was the first signatory of the Declaration of Independence. Having written his name in a fine, bold hand, the paradigm for signatures thereafter, he commented, "There, I guess King George will be able to read that."

હ્ય ∙ે

HANDEL, George Frideric (1685–1759), *German composer, who lived in England after 1712. He received numerous royal commissions and became the first director of the Royal Academy of Music (1720). His Italian operas were highly acclaimed. After 1739 he turned to writing oratorios with equal success; his most famous work in this genre is* Messiah *(1742). His large and varied output also included much chamber music.*

1 Handel once sent word to a local tavern ordering dinner for two. When he arrived, he asked for the dinner to be brought. The landlord came up, begged his pardon, and said he had understood that his honor had been expecting company. "I am the company," said Handel, and duly ate his way through the dinner for two.

2 (Charles Burney tells a story about the preparation at Chester Cathedral for the first performance of *Messiah* in Dublin.)
"During this time, [Handel] applied to know whether there were any choirmen in the cathedral who could sing *at sight;* as he wished to prove some books that had been hastily tran-

scribed, by trying the choruses which he intended to perform in Ireland. . . . Among them [was] a printer of the name of Janson, who had a good bass voice. . . . A time was fixed for this private rehearsal . . . but alas! on trial of the chorus in the Messiah, 'And with his stripes we are healed,' poor Janson, after repeated attempts failed so egregiously, that Handel, . . . after swearing in four or five languages, cried out in broken English, 'You shcauntrell, tit you not dell me dat you could sing at soit?' 'Yes, sir,' says the printer, 'and so I can, but not at *first sight.*' "

3   The famous soprano Francesca Cuzzoni, who came to England in 1722, treated Handel to a display of prima-donna temperament by refusing to sing the song that he had written for her London debut. Handel picked her up bodily and threatened to drop her out of the nearby window unless she did as she was told.
She sang the song.

4   While rehearsing his opera *Flavio*, Handel, accompanying the singers upon a harpsichord, fell afoul of the tenor, who objected to the composer's playing. "If you don't follow me better than that," he grumbled, "I'll jump on your harpsichord and smash it up."
"Go right ahead," retorted Handel, "only please let me know when and I will advertise it, for more people will come to see you jump than to hear you sing."

৪৽ ৵঳

HANNIBAL (247–?183 BC), *commander of the initially successful Carthaginian army against Rome during the Second Punic War (218-201 BC). The scorched-earth policy of Quintus Fabius Cunctator eventually forced Hannibal to withdraw to Africa, where he was defeated at Zama (202). Later exiled, he spent the last years of his life advising the Syrian king, Antiochus III, on how to conduct his war against Rome.*

1   After the final defeat of King Antiochus III's forces by the Romans at Magnesia in 189 BC, the victors insisted that the aged Hannibal be surrendered to them. Hannibal fled to Crete and then to Bithynia in Asia Minor, where a detachment of Roman soldiers caught up with him and surrounded his hiding place. Hannibal

took out the phial of poison that he always carried with him and drank it. "Let us relieve the Romans of the fear which has so long afflicted them," he said, "since it seems to tax their patience too hard to wait for an old man's death."

৪৽ ৵঳

HARDIE, [James] **Keir** (1865–1915), *British politician, one of the founders of the Labour party. A former coal miner and active trade-unionist, he entered Parliament in 1892 and became the first parliamentary leader of the Labour party in 1906.*

1   On Hardie's first day at the House of Commons, the policeman at the gate took one look at the former miner, dressed in his ordinary working clothes and cloth cap, and asked suspiciously, "Are you working here?"
"Yes," replied Hardie.
"On the roof?"
"No," said the new MP. "On the floor."

৪৽ ৵঳

HARDY, Thomas (1840–1928), *British novelist and poet. His great tragic novels —* The Return of the Native *(1878),* The Mayor of Casterbridge *(1886),* Tess of the d'Urbervilles *(1891), and* Jude the Obscure *(1896) — reflect Hardy's sense of the underlying forces that rule events.* Jude the Obscure *caused such an outcry that Hardy abandoned novels in disgust, thereafter concentrating on poetry and his epic drama* The Dynasts *(1903–08).*

1   During the furor that followed the publication of *Jude the Obscure,* the novel was burned by a bishop. Hardy took this phlegmatically, ascribing the action to the ecclesiastic's chagrin, "presumably, at not being able to burn me."

৪৽ ৵঳

HARRIMAN, W[illiam] **Averell** (1891–   ), *US diplomat. He was ambassador to the Soviet Union (1943–46) and to Britain (1946), was instrumental in negotiating the 1963 nuclear test ban treaty, and conducted negotiations in Paris during the Vietnam peace talks (1968–69).*

1   Averell Harriman, a phenomenally hard worker, expected his staff to be the same. One

afternoon he left his office at the unprecedented time of 5:30. "I'm not coming back tonight," he called to his staff, "so you can declare a half-holiday."

2   During his ambassadorial stint in Moscow, Harriman was shadowed everywhere by the Soviet secret police. One weekend he was invited to visit a British diplomat at his country retreat. The house was accessible only by means of a four-wheel-drive vehicle, a fact of which Harriman considerately warned his shadows. Nonetheless, the police followed Harriman's jeep in their customary heated sedan, which soon became hopelessly bogged down. A resolute operative set off doggedly on foot, and the jeep slowed down to allow him to keep up. Harriman, concerned that the policeman would freeze to death before they reached their destination, offered him a ride, promising that he would tell no one about the incident. The man accepted, and ambassador and policeman rode together for the rest of the journey.

ﺥ﮼   ﯼ

HARRIS, Frank [James Thomas] (1856–1931), *British writer and critic. As editor of the* Saturday Review *(1894–99), Harris was at the heart of fin de siècle literary London.*

1   Frank Harris was an unashamed plagiarist in his conversation, on one occasion relating as his own an anecdote everyone in his audience recognized as the property of Anatole France. There was a slightly embarrassed silence, broken by Oscar Wilde's saying, "You know, Frank, Anatole France would have spoiled that story."

2   In later years someone asked Max Beerbohm, an acquaintance of Harris's during the 1890s, whether Harris had ever been known to speak the truth. "Sometimes," replied Max, "when his invention flagged."

ﺥ﮼   ﯼ

HARRIS, George (1844–1922), *US Congregational clergyman and educator. He was president of Amherst College (1899–1912).*

1   Addressing Amherst students at the beginning of a new academic year, Harris broke off after the first few sentences of his prepared homily. "I intended to give you some advice,"

he said, "but now I remember how much is left over from last year unused."

ﺥ﮼   ﯼ

HARRIS, Jed (1900–1979), *US theatrical producer. At the age of twenty-eight he had produced four straight hits on Broadway in eighteen months, a feat not yet matched by any other producer. He worked with playwrights Moss Hart, George Kaufman, and Arthur Miller, among others, and produced such classics as* The Front Page *and* Our Town.

1   Arthur Miller and the completely out-of-funds Jed Harris were driving to Boston to check out a possible actor for Miller's *The Crucible*. Shortly after Miller pulled away from a toll booth, Harris shouted, "Stop the car!"
    "What's the matter?" replied Miller.
    "The toll. I've got the money right here."
    "I've already paid the toll," Miller said, driving on.
    "But you forgot the tip!" Harris cried, waving a dollar bill. "We have to go back and give him a tip!"

2   "Jed Harris . . . became convinced he was losing his hearing. He went to a specialist who gave him a thorough checkup. The doctor pulled out a gold timepiece and asked, 'Can you hear this ticking?' 'Of course,' said Harris. The specialist walked to the door and held up the watch again. 'Now can you hear it?' Harris concentrated and said, 'Yes, I can hear it clearly.' The doctor walked out the door into the next room and said, 'Can you hear it now?' 'Yes.' 'Mr. Harris,' the doctor said, 'there is nothing wrong with your hearing. You just don't listen.'"

ﺥ﮼   ﯼ

HARRISON, Benjamin (?1726–91), *US statesman, known as "the Signer" to distinguish him from other members of his family with the same first name who also served as congressmen.*

1   The English government offered a large reward for the names of those who had signed the Declaration of Independence, which it declared an act of high treason, punishable by death. Benjamin Harrison, who had played an active role in drafting the declaration, was amused at the threat. He was a large, heavy

man, while his fellow signatory, Elbridge Gerry, was a small, frail one. "When the hanging comes," he said to Gerry, "it will be all over with me in a minute, but you will be kicking the air for an hour after I'm gone."

᠈᠊

HARRISON, Benjamin (1833–1901) *US politician; 23d president of the United States (1889–93). Grandson of President William Henry Harrison, he had a deserved reputation for incorruptibility, but was hampered by the venality and opportunism of some of his Republican supporters.*

1 Harrison took the 1888 election results very calmly. His chief interest seemed to be in his own state of Indiana. When the results from Indiana were safely announced, around 11:00 P.M., he went to bed. The following morning a friend, having called to congratulate him at midnight, asked why he had retired so early. The president-elect explained, "I knew that my staying up would not alter the result if I were defeated, while if I was elected I had a hard day in front of me. So a night's rest seemed the best in either event."

᠈᠊

HARRISON, George (1943–), *British rock musician, member of the Beatles (1962–70).*

1 At the start of the Beatles' first major recording session George Martin, the executive of the record company, explained minutely what effect he was trying to achieve. He wound up with, "Let me know if there's anything you don't like."

"Well, for a start," said George Harrison, "I don't like your tie."

᠈᠊

HART, Moss (1904–61), *US playwright and theatrical producer.*

1 Hart, though later a happily married man, for many years prized his independent bachelor life. Oscar Levant was a guest at a dinner party when Hart entered, the beautiful actress Edith Atwater on his arm. "Ah," said Levant, "here comes Moss Hart and the future Miss Atwater."

᠈᠊

HARTE, [Francis] **Bret** (1836–1902), *US writer. His most acclaimed work consisted of short stories depicting the lives of the miners, prostitutes, gamblers, and others attracted by the California gold rush.*

1 Bret Harte once attended a lecture in Richmond, Virginia, suffering from a miserable headache. Afterward, to clear his head, he took a walk with a Richmond friend, who expatiated on the city's wholesome air and location, adding proudly that its mortality statistics reflected only one death per day. Harte, still in agony with his headache, exclaimed, "Heavens, let's hope today's candidate is already dead."

2 Bret Harte was often credited with the popular poem, "Little Breeches," although the real author was John Hay. One admirer approached Harte and said effusively, "My dear Mr. Harte, I am so delighted to meet you. I want to tell you how much I loved reading 'Little Breeches.'"

"Thank you, madam," responded Harte, "but I have to tell you that you have put the little breeches on the wrong man."

᠈᠊

HARTLEBEN, Otto Erich (1864–1905), *German poet.*

1 The poet, feeling quite ill, consulted a doctor who after a thorough examination prescribed complete abstention from both smoking and drinking. Hartleben picked up his hat and coat and started for the door. The doctor called after him, "My advice, Herr Hartleben, will cost you three marks."

"But I'm not taking it," retorted Hartleben, and vanished.

{For a comparable riposte to medical advice, *see* JOHANNES BRAHMS 9.}

᠈᠊

HARTNELL, Norman (1901–), *English couturier, dressmaker to the Queen Mother and Queen Elizabeth II. He also designed the "utility" dresses of World War II and the WRAC uniform.*

1 (Hartnell told this story to Robert Morley.)

"I was lunching one day at a country house when a lull in the conversation left this well-practiced designer to compliment my hostess on a silver trophy in the center of the table.

" 'I won it for one of my jumpers,' my hostess explained.

" 'How clever,' I replied. 'Could you knit one for me?' "

୫ଓ ଓ୫

HATTO (?850–913), *archbishop of Mainz (891–913), who played a prominent role in German politics as regent (899–911) for King Louis the Child.*

1 The story of the mice is the best known of many apocryphal tales about Hatto's cruelty and treachery. At a time of famine, Bishop Hatto was besieged by poor people who wanted him to release some of the grain stored in the archiepiscopal granaries. Hatto assembled his petitioners in a large barn to which he set fire, burning them all to death. He then retired to a fortified tower in the middle of the Rhine, thinking himself safe from retribution. But a great army of mice swam across the river, gnawed their way into the tower, and ate Bishop Hatto alive.

୫ଓ ଓ୫

HAVEMEYER, Louisine Waldron Elder (1855–1929), *US art collector, suffragist, and philanthropist.*

1 "Mrs. Havemeyer, whose collection of paintings is today the pride of New York's Metropolitan Museum, was once confronted by a wealthy, bejewelled dowager who asked, rather scornfully, why she spent so much money on dabs of paint on paper and canvas. Mrs. Havemeyer examined the dowager's pearl necklace for a long and studious moment before answering: 'I prefer to have something made by a man than to have something made by an oyster.' "

୫ଓ ଓ୫

HAWTHORNE, Nathaniel (1804–64), *US novelist, best known for* The Scarlet Letter *(1850) and* The House of the Seven Gables *(1851). He was appointed consul in Liverpool (1853) and later traveled in Italy, the setting for his romance* The Marble Faun *(1860).*

1 As Hawthorne's son, Julian, was also a writer, father and son were frequently mistaken for each other. "Oh, Mr. Hawthorne, I've just read *The Scarlet Letter,* and I think it's a real masterpiece," gushed a lady to whom Julian Hawthorne had just been introduced. "Oh, that," said Julian, shrugging modestly, "that was written when I was only four years old."

୫ଓ ଓ୫

HAWTREY, Sir Charles Henry (1858–1923), *English actor, producer, and theater manager. He made his name in* The Private Secretary *(1884), which he had adapted from a German farce, and remained famous for his comedy roles. He was manager of the Globe Theatre, London (1884–87), and the Comedy Theatre (1887–93; 1896–98).*

1 Hawtrey directed the first production of Ben Travers's farce *The Dippers* in 1922. At the first rehearsal, Travers was disturbed to see Hawtrey cutting some of his favorite scenes from the script. As the director's pencil slashed through the best line of the play, Travers cried, "Oh, Mr. Hawtrey, must that line go? I always thought it was rather a good line."

"A good line?" repeated Hawtrey. "A good line? It's a very good line indeed, dear boy. You mustn't on any account lose it. Put it in another play."

୫ଓ ଓ୫

HAY, Lord Charles (died 1760), *British soldier.*

1 At the battle of Fontenoy in 1745, Lord Charles Hay was leading the 1st Footguard Regiment over a low hill when he suddenly and unexpectedly came face to face with the French Guards, who were as little prepared for action as were their English counterparts. Hay immediately stepped forward from the ranks. His French opposite number, M. d'Auteroches, did the same. "Gentlemen of the French Guards, fire," said Hay, bowing low. "Monsieur," said the Frenchman, "we never fire first; do you fire."

{A variant of this story has d'Auteroches making the initial approach to the English.}

୫ଓ ଓ୫

HAYAKAWA, S. I. (1906–), *US scholar and politician. Having achieved recognition for his development of the field of general semantics, Hayakawa was president of San Francisco State College from 1968 to 1973, and senator from California from 1977 to 1983.*

1   Hayakawa once openly lamented the fact that even in Japan, his ancestral home, one hundred fast-food eating places had been established by a US chain. "That seems," he said, "a terrible price to pay for Pearl Harbor."

2   In Washington on one occasion, Hayakawa failed to recognize Russell B. Long, the chairman of the Senate Finance Committee. Admonished by a friend, he shrugged. "All you middle-aged white men look alike," he said.

֍

HAYDN, Franz Joseph (1732–1809), *Austrian composer. From 1761 he was kapellmeister to the Esterházy family. Visiting England in 1791 and 1794, he wrote a number of symphonies first played in London. He composed a great deal of piano music, string quartets, concertos, 104 symphonies, and some major choral works, including the oratorio* The Creation *(1798).*

1   Haydn was composing a passage to give the effect of a storm at sea. He tried various arrangements of discords and harmonies on the piano, but the librettist kept shaking his head. In exasperation, Haydn eventually threw his hands to the far ends of the keyboard and brought them rapidly together, exclaiming, "The deuce take the tempest; I can make nothing of it!"

"That is the very thing!" cried his delighted collaborator.

{Painters have similar problems of expression. *See,* for example, NICOLAS POUSSIN 1.}

2   The musicians for the Esterházy family spent much of the year at Schloss Esterházy in a remote corner of northwestern Hungary, separated from their wives and families. During one particularly long spell of service, Haydn composed his "Farewell" Symphony (no. 5), in the last movement of which the instruments drop out of the score one by one. At the first performance each player, on completing his part, blew out his candle and tiptoed away from the orchestra. Prince Esterházy took the hint, and granted his musicians leave of absence.

{In much the same way the members of the famous von Trapp family began their escape from Nazi Germany by leaving the stage one at a time after being forced to compete in a talent festival.}

3   Haydn enjoyed traveling because it took him away from his difficult wife. One day a caller remarked on the large pile of unopened letters on Haydn's desk. "They're from my wife," the composer explained. "We write to each other monthly, but I do not open her letters and I am certain she doesn't open mine."

4   Sir Joshua Reynolds painted a famous portrait of soprano Elizabeth Billington in the character of Saint Cecilia, patron saint of music. Haydn, seeing the picture in the artist's studio, observed to Sir Joshua, "I like the portrait much, but you have painted Billington listening to the angels; you should rather have made the angels listening to her."

֍

HAYES, Helen (1900–), *US actress, acclaimed for her work on stage, screen, radio, and television. She is perhaps best known for her performance in the title role of Laurence Housman's* Victoria Regina.

1   Helen Hayes's daughter was just under five when her father, Charles MacArthur, took her to a rehearsal of Maxwell Anderson's *Mary of Scotland,* in which Miss Hayes had the title role. The little girl watched attentively as her mother played a tempestuous scene in which Mary confronted Elizabeth I. Turning to her father, she said, "Mama's angry."

2   When Helen Hayes first went to Hollywood, she already had a reputation as a stage star. At first Hollywood did not quite know what to make of her, so different was she from any conventional image of a film star. Louis B. Mayer decided that he must discover whether she had sex appeal. There was, he said, only one way to find out: he would make her a present of a white satin gown exactly like the one Norma Shearer had worn in *A Free Soul.* Miss Hayes firmly turned down the offer: "That wasn't a dress; that was an invitation," and when he persisted, she told him, "I'm going to save you a

lot of money. I can tell you right now that there won't be anything under that dress." Mayer was forced to relinquish his idea.

3 As she retired to the kitchen to put the finishing touches to the dinner preparations, Helen Hayes warned her family: "This is the first turkey I've ever cooked. If it isn't right, I don't want anybody to say a word. We'll just get up from the table, without comment, and go down to the hotel for dinner." She returned some ten minutes later to find the family seated expectantly at the dinner table — wearing their hats and coats.

HAYES, Rutherford B. (1822–93), *US politician; 19th president of the United States (1877–81). Hayes made it into the White House by just a single electoral vote. He found more satisfaction in his distinguished military record during the Civil War than in his presidency.*

1 Hayes and his wife were fervent advocates of temperance. During Hayes's presidency liquor and tobacco were banned from the White House. William M. Evarts, secretary of state, observed of one official dinner, "It was a brilliant affair; water flowed like champagne."

HAYWARD, Leland (1902–71), *US impresario, agent, and producer of such films as* Mister Roberts *(1955). As an agent, he had among his clients actresses Ginger Rogers and Judy Garland and writer Ernest Hemingway.*

1 Hayward acted as agent for so many different actors, writers, and other clients that some confusion was inevitable. Ginger Rogers was once sent a script that she found totally unacceptable. Hayward went straight to the producer's office to complain. "How can you insult Ginger with such trash, such drivel, such rot?" he said indignantly. "Get out of here before I throw you out," roared the producer. "*You* sold us that story!"

HAYWORTH, Rita (1918–), *US movie star, known for her seductive roles in such movies as* Gilda *(1946).*

1 At their wedding singer Dick Haymes was asked whether Rita Hayworth had ever cooked

anything for him. "Who'd marry Rita for her cooking?" he replied.

2 Comedian Jack Lemmon once found Miss Hayworth working her way through a heap of correspondence, tearing up most of the letters unopened. "Stop!" he cried, horrified. "There may be checks in there."

"There are," replied Rita, shrugging her shoulders. "But there are also bills. I find it evens up."

HAZLITT, William (1778–1830), *British critic and essayist. He worked as a journalist on several papers, including the* Edinburgh Review, *and wrote notable literary criticism on the Elizabethan dramatists and his own contemporaries. Some of his best essays appeared in* Table Talk *(1812–22) and* The Spirit of the Age *(1825).*

1 Hazlitt's literary friends were confirmed book borrowers. He observed plaintively that he visited them from time to time, "just to look over my library."

2 Editor William Gifford once criticized Hazlitt's work with the terse observation: "What we read from your pen, we remember no more." Hazlitt completed the couplet with the caustic line: "What we read from your pen, we remember before."

HEARST, William Randolph (1863–1951), *US newspaper proprietor whose nationwide empire based its commercial success on sensationalism.*

1 Hearst sent the artist Frederic Remington, who made a specialty of depicting soldiers and warfare, to cover events in Cuba after the US battleship *Maine* had been blown up in Havana harbor in February 1898. The expected conflict between the United States and Spain did not immediately materialize and Remington cabled Hearst, asking whether he should return. Hearst cabled back: "Please remain. You furnish the pictures and I'll furnish the war."

(Sure enough, on April 20 the US ultimatum for the withdrawal of Spanish troops brought about open conflict. The Hearst newspapers' demands for war against

Spain had undoubtedly created a climate of opinion in which a declaration of war was popular. The episode was used by scriptwriter Herman Mankiewicz in writing Orson Welles's screen masterpiece *Citizen Kane*.}

2 In the 1890s Hearst's *New York Journal* was locked in a titanic circulation battle with Joseph Pulitzer's *World,* with Hearst pouring his resources into the struggle. Someone observed to his mother that he was losing a million dollars a year. Mrs. Hearst was unmoved. "Is he?" she said. "Then he will only last about thirty years."

3 Hearst offered columnist Arthur Brisbane a six-month vacation on full pay as a reward for his dedicated and successful work. When Brisbane refused, Hearst asked him why. The journalist advanced two reasons: "The first is that if I quit writing for six months it might damage the circulation of your newspapers." He paused for a moment; then: "The second reason is that it might not."

4 Considering the high moral tone expected of people in public life at that time, Hearst's thirty-year relationship with actress Marion Davies evoked surprisingly little scandal, even in newspapers owned by rivals. Hearst himself refused to discuss it. "I'm not saying it's right, I'm saying it *is*," he declared flatly.

5 In an idle moment Hearst bought St. Donat's Castle in Glamorgan but never used it as a family home. Indeed, he never mentioned the purchase to his wife. When she was told it was Norman, she is said to have asked, "Norman who?"

෨ ෯

HEATH, Edward (1916–   ), *British statesman; Conservative prime minister (1970–74).*

1 A new choral work was being performed for the first time at the Three Choirs Festival in Gloucester Cathedral. At the end of the concert, an enterprising music critic caught sight of Edward Heath in the audience and asked him for his opinion. The former prime minister, not at all impressed by the new piece, replied: "I was interested in being present for its first, and I trust only, performance."

> The actual origin of one of the most famous slogans in American history took place in 1898 in a Broadway bar. An unknown man lifted his drink and intoned to the other patrons, "Gentlemen, remember the *Maine!*" From that moment W. R. Hearst and the Yellow Press had their battle cry.
>
> — David Wallechinsky and Irving Wallace, *The People's Almanac*

HECHT, Ben (1894–1964), *US playwright, novelist, and scriptwriter.*

1 Although Ben Hecht was paid $2,500 a week to promote Florida real estate during the Florida property boom of the early 1920s, he himself never believed the boom would last. Soon people began remarking how plump Hecht was becoming; this was because he hid all his earnings in bankrolls about his person and never deposited any of the money in a bank. When the crash came, he was one of the few people to escape with the money he had made during the boom years, some thirty thousand dollars.

෨ ෯

HEGEL, Georg Wilhelm (1770–1831), *German idealist philosopher. His writings are notorious for their obscurity, in particular* The Phenomenology of Mind *(1807), which has had an important influence upon Marxism.*

1 On his deathbed Hegel complained, "Only one man ever understood me." He fell silent for a while and then added, "And he didn't understand me."

෨ ෯

HEGGEN, Thomas (1919–49), *US writer.*

1 When Heggen's *Mister Roberts* appeared, the publishers arranged for him to make some public appearances to advertise the book. His first speaking engagement was at a luncheon in a New York hotel. Throughout the meal he sat among the ladies at the head table, paralyzed with apprehension and unable to swallow anything. Called upon to speak, he stood up and, overcome with nerves, failed to utter a single word. A neighbor, seeing his agony, tried to get him started by saying kindly, "Perhaps you can tell us how you wrote your book." Heggen gulped and the words suddenly came: "Well, shit, it was just that I was on this boat . . ."

જ⊷   ⊷ઙ

HEIDEGGER, John James (?1659–1749), *Swiss impresario known as the "Swiss Count." He became manager of the opera house in London's Haymarket in 1713. His masked fancy-dress balls became so notorious that the authorities banned them. They were carried on, nonetheless, under the new title of "ridottos."*

1   Heidegger was famous for his ugliness, recorded for posterity in a number of William Hogarth's prints. He once bet Lord Chesterfield that he would not be able to produce anyone uglier. The earl eventually came up with an old woman who was said to be marginally more hideous. Heidegger quickly borrowed his rival's bonnet, settled it on his head, and was awarded the victory.

જ⊷   ⊷ઙ

HEIFETZ, Jascha (1901–   ), *world-famous Russian-born violinist who obtained US citizenship in 1925. He commissioned major works for the violin.*

1   Jascha Heifetz once attended a vaudeville show at which a man performed various acrobatic feats while playing a violin: standing on his head, holding the instrument behind his back, turning somersaults. Heifetz watched for some time, frowned, and then said to his companion, "Why doesn't he play it straight?"

2   Heifetz told his new secretary that there was no need to compliment him after every performance. "If I play well," he said, "I know it myself. If I don't, I shall only be disappointed if you flatter me." The young man, anxious to please his new employer, complied with these instructions. Halfway through his next tour, after a particularly successful concert, an enraged Heifetz accosted his secretary. "What's the matter?" he roared. "You don't like music?"

3   When he played in trios with pianist Arthur Rubinstein and cellist Gregor Piatigorsky, Heifetz complained that Rubinstein always got first billing. "If the Almighty himself played the violin," he once said, "the credits would still read 'Rubinstein, God, and Piatigorsky,' in that order."

4   In New York for a Carnegie Hall recital, Heifetz was still practicing in his hotel room at midnight on the eve of the concert. An irate fellow guest phoned to complain about the noise. "But I am Jascha Heifetz," said the violinist. "I don't care if you're Lawrence Welk," retorted the female voice at the other end of the line. "I want to get some sleep."

5   Shortly after his appointment as professor of music at the University of California, Los Angeles, Heifetz was asked what had prompted this change of direction in his career. "Violin-playing is a perishable art," said Heifetz solemnly. "It must be passed on as a personal skill; otherwise it is lost." Then, with a smile, he continued: "I remember my old violin professor in Russia. He said that someday I would be good enough to teach."

જ⊷   ⊷ઙ

HEINE, Heinrich (1797–1856), *German poet. After 1831 he lived in Paris, where he was involved in radical political journalism, wrote essays on French and German culture, and composed satirical verse.*

1   A composer friend, visiting Heine, found the poet at his desk gloomily surveying a blank page. Asked what the trouble was, Heine replied, "Well, I just met X in the street, I stopped for a moment to exchange ideas, and now I feel like a complete idiot."

2   In 1841 Heine married Eugénie Mirat, a saleswoman in a Parisian bootshop. She was uneducated, foolish, and vain. Heine's affection for her did not preclude an awareness of her shortcomings. At his death he left her his whole estate on condition that she marry again, "because then there will be at least one man who will regret my death."

3   In 1845 Heine first showed the symptoms of the crippling spinal disease that condemned

him to a "mattress grave" for many years before his end. He viewed the approach of death calmly, refusing to be drawn into a display of religious zeal. "God will pardon me," he said. "It's his profession." It was with less equanimity, however, that he viewed the possibility of leaving things unsaid. His last words were, "Write . . . write . . . pencil . . . paper."

4   Heine died in poverty, deserted by his friends. The sole person to attend his deathbed in his squalid Parisian garret was the composer Berlioz. "I always thought you were an original, Berlioz," observed the dying man.

 controls

HELLMAN, Lillian (1905–84), *US dramatist, whose successful plays include* The Little Foxes *(1939),* Watch on the Rhine *(1941), and* The Searching Wind *(1944).*

1   *Harper's Magazine* once sent out a questionnaire to a selected number of prominent men. One question was: "During what activity, situation, moment, or series of moments do you feel most masculine?" Having processed the replies, the editor felt it might be interesting to send the questionnaire to a similar group of celebrated women. Lillian Hellman was among the chosen number. She replied: "It makes me feel masculine to tell you that I do not answer questions like this without being paid for answering them."

controls

HELLMESBERGER, Joseph (1828–93), *Austrian composer and violinist. He was a member of a prominent Viennese musical family, and became director of the conservatory in Vienna.*

1   Joseph Hellmesberger was notorious for suspecting every other composer of plagiarism. When Leo Delibes visited Vienna, the whole musical world was anxious to meet him. One of the local composers who knew Hellmesberger asked the latter to introduce him to the famous Frenchman. Hellmesberger performed the introduction: "Monsieur Delibes, meet Monsieur le Dieb" (i.e., the thief).

controls

"Most of the rich have liked partying, and since the less rich like being the admiring guests of their financial betters, there is a never-ending stream of party fodder. Though perhaps not always with the happiest of results — as the slightly down-market guests of the Emperor Heliogabalus discovered when one of them remarked how pleasant it would be to be smothered in the scent of roses that adorned the imperial table, and the rest agreed. Taking them at their word, the next time the same guests came to dinner the emperor had several tons of petals dumped over the dinner table. The guests' reaction on this occasion passed unrecorded. They had suffocated."

— David Frost and Michael Deakin,
David Frost's Book of Millionaires, Multimillionaires, and Really Rich People

HELPRIN, Mark (1947–   ), *US novelist and short-story writer. His novels include* Refiner's Fire *and* A Winter's Tale. *Some of his best shorter fiction is collected in* Ellis Island and Other Stories.

1   At the age of two young Mark observed his father spearing a lobster before throwing it into the cooking pot. He burst out: "Wun for your wife, wobster, wun for your wife!"

controls

HEMINGWAY, Ernest (1899–1961), *US writer. His longer fictional works include* The Sun Also Rises *(1926),* For Whom the Bell Tolls *(1940), and* The Old Man and the Sea *(1952). A keen sportsman and hunter, he extolled courage and stoicism in his books, which were written in a simple, terse style. Subject always to severe depressions, he committed suicide in 1961.*

1   The threat of starvation can bring unusual foods to the table, as Hemingway discovered during the course of a particularly hard Paris winter. In order to feed his family, which he was unable to do by selling stories, he resorted to catching pigeons in the Luxembourg

Gardens when the gendarme on duty went into a café for a glass of wine. Having lured the pigeons with a handful of corn, Hemingway dispatched the luckless creatures with an expert twist of the neck. He then concealed the bodies under the blanket in his son Bumby's baby carriage in order to take them home to be cooked and eaten.

2   Hemingway left his wife, Hadley, and their small son in 1926 and moved to 2 *bis* rue Feron, Paris, where Pauline Pfeiffer, whom he would later marry, awaited him. He was asked why he had left Hadley. In his best Hemingway prose the novelist answered, "Because I am a bastard."

3   Hemingway's contract with his publishers, Scribner's, contained a clause prohibiting the publishers from changing a single word in his manuscripts. Maxwell Perkins, then an editor with Scribner's, was reading *Death in the Afternoon* when he came across the word "fuck." He decided to apply to the highest authority to get a ruling on whether to delete it. He read the passage to the elderly Charles Scribner, head of the firm, who was just about to leave the office and did not feel capable of reaching an immediate decision. "We will have to discuss this fully when I come back from lunch," said the distinguished publisher, and on his notepad headed "What To Do Today" jotted down the one word: "Fuck."

4   F. Scott Fitzgerald remarked to Hemingway that the rich "are not as we are."

"No," replied Hemingway, unimpressed. "They have more money."

{A footnote in *Bartlett's Familiar Quotations* glosses this famous exchange: "In 1936 Maxwell Perkins . . . lunched with Hemingway and the critic Mary Colum. When Hemingway announced, 'I am getting to know the rich,' Mary Colum replied, 'The only difference between the rich and other people is that the rich have more money.'— Matthew J. Bruccoli, *Scott and Ernest* [1978]."}

5   In 1918, toward the end of World War I, Hemingway was wounded at Fossalta di Piave on the Austro-Italian front. Some thirty years later, passing the same spot on his way to Venice, he got out of his car and buried a 1,000-lira note in the ground. With this gesture, he reasoned, he had now contributed both blood and money to Italian soil.

{The hero of Hemingway's novel *Across the River and into the Trees* (1950) performs an almost identical action, the main difference being that his monetary contribution is a 10,000-lira note.}

6   Hemingway won the Nobel Prize for literature in 1954. Five years earlier it had been awarded to another American novelist, William Faulkner. The two writers did not have a very high opinion of each other. Faulkner said of Hemingway that he had no courage, that "he had never been known to use a word that might send the reader to the dictionary." When Hemingway heard this, he said, "Poor Faulkner. Does he really think big emotions come from big words? He thinks I don't know the ten-dollar words. I know them all right. But there are older and simpler and better words, and those are the ones I use."

7   Hemingway's son Patrick asked his father to edit a story he had written. Hemingway went through the manuscript carefully, then returned it to his son. "But, Papa," cried Patrick in dismay, "you've only changed one word."

"If it's the right word," said Hemingway, "that's a lot."

8   (Yousuf Karsh tells of preparing to photograph Hemingway.)

"I had gone the evening before to La Floridita, Hemingway's favorite bar [in Havana] to do my 'homework' and sample his favorite concoction, the daiquiri. But one can be overprepared! When, at nine the next morning, Hemingway called from the kitchen, 'What will you have to drink?' my reply was, I thought, letter-perfect: 'Daiquiri, sir.' 'Good God, Karsh,' Hemingway remonstrated, 'at *this* hour of the day?'"

9   In a Sun Valley restaurant a stranger asked Hemingway for his autograph. "Thanks, Mr. Hemingway," the pleased visitor said cheerily when he got the signature. He passed the table again and said, "Hello, Mr. Hemingway." Intoxicated by being so near the great man, the stranger permitted himself another walk past, this time calling out, "Hi, Ernest!" Further

giddied by Hemingway's acknowledging nod, the man made one final pass, this time calling, "Hello, Papa!" Hemingway lowered his beard and raised his arms. "Hellooo!" he roared. "And goodbyyyyye!"

☙ ❧

HENRI IV (1553–1610), *king of France. Heir to the small kingdom of Navarre, he was brought up as a Protestant and became the main hope of the Protestant party during the French wars of religion. Henri III of France recognized him as his heir, but he had to fight for more than ten years to establish his control over his kingdom.*

1   One of the turning points in Henri's struggle to assert his claim to the throne of France was at Arques in September 1589, when his force of 7,000 men defeated the 23,000–strong army of the Duke of Mayenne. Henri announced his victory to an absent comrade-at-arms with the famous message: *"Pends-toi, brave Crillon; nous avons combattu à Arques, et tu n'y étais pas"* (Hang yourself, brave Crillon; we fought at Arques and you were not there).

2   Paris was one of the centers that held out most stubbornly against the Protestant forces. Henri, who had made a feigned abjuration of his faith to escape the massacre of the Protestants in 1572, decided once again that a lasting peace between the warring religious groups was more important than his personal religious inclinations. In July 1593 he solemnly converted to Roman Catholicism. All opposition collapsed and Paris opened its gates to him. As he rode into his capital city, he is said to have remarked, "Paris is well worth a mass."

3   Greatly taken by the beauty of one of the young ladies of his court, the king asked her to tell him how to reach her bedchamber. "Through the church, sire," was the reply.

4   As the king passed through a small town, a deputation of burgesses was drawn up at the gates to receive him. Just as the leading dignitary began his speech of welcome, a donkey nearby started to bray. The king turned toward the noisy creature and said with great gravity, "Gentlemen, one at a time, please."

5   On his way to dinner, Henri was accosted by a suppliant who began his address with

"Sire, Agesilaus, king of Lacedaemon—" Alert to the danger signs of a bore, Henri interrupted, "I have heard of him—but he had dined, and I have not."

See also CHARLES DE GAULLE 3.

6   Henri IV, who disliked long-windedness, happened to meet an ecclesiastic on the road one day. "Where do you come from? Where are you going? What is your purpose?" demanded the king. "From Bourges—to Paris—a benefice," replied the priest. Delighted at this terse response, the king exclaimed, "You shall have it!"

☙ ❧

HENRY II (1133–89), *king of England (1154–89). He succeeded to the throne after his mother, Matilda, daughter of Henry I, persuaded her nephew Stephen to adopt him as his heir. He inherited a confused and fragmented administration, but managed to extend royal control and set up a strong, centralized government at the expense of the feudal aristocracy. By his marriage (1152) to Eleanor of Aquitaine, he acquired large tracts of land in France. Eleanor's influence fomented the family strife that dogged Henry's later years.*

1   One of Henry's advisers and friends in the early part of his reign was Thomas à Becket. He appointed Becket chancellor in 1154 and archbishop of Canterbury in 1162, hoping to bring the powers of church and state into harmony under his control. Becket, however, resigned the chancellorship and went into exile in France. After nearly seven years abroad, he and Henry were reconciled. Becket returned, only to defy the king again over his attempts to exert control over the church. Henry was spending Christmas near Bayeux, in France, when a deputation of bishops came to him to tell him of Becket's continuing intransigence. "Will no one rid me of this turbulent priest!" Henry raged. Four knights, members of his household, took him literally. They crossed the Channel, rode posthaste to Canterbury, and murdered Becket at the altar of Cantebury cathedral.

{Authorities differ as to the actual words spoken by Henry, but the above version, with its variants, has been approved by popular tradition. The *Dictionary of National Biography* gives a longer version:

"What a parcel of fools and dastards have I nourished in my house that not one of them will avenge me of this one upstart clerk!"}

❧ ❦

HENRY IV (1367–1413), *king of England (1399–1413). Grandson of Edward III, Henry seized the throne from his cousin Richard II after the latter had banished him and appropriated his inheritance. Henry's reign was marked by civil war as he saw his authority challenged by the Welsh and the feudal aristocracy.*

1 Henry's cherished wish was to lead a crusade to the Holy Land and recapture Jerusalem from the infidel, as an expiation for his deposition of Richard. Since the threats to his throne from internal feuding made it seem impossible that he would realize this ambition, he was encouraged when a soothsayer told him he would die only in Jerusalem. Early in 1413 he suffered a stroke while praying in Westminster Abbey, and was carried into the abbot's house. The name of the room in which he died was the Jerusalem Chamber.

❧ ❦

HENRY VIII (1491–1547), *king of England (1509–47). His military and diplomatic successes against France and Scotland set England on the road to becoming a major European power. His divorce from the first of his six wives, Catherine of Aragon, who had failed to bear him a male heir, precipitated the repudiation of papal authority that led to Henry's becoming head of the church in England, and thence to the establishment of the Anglican Church, no longer in communion with Rome.*

1 Henry VIII designated a particular nobleman as his ambassador to King Francis I of France, at a time when relations between the two countries were at a very low ebb. The peer, listening to Henry's aggressive message, begged to be excused because, he said, the hot-tempered French king might well have him executed if he delivered it. Henry reassured him by saying that if Francis killed him, there were a dozen Frenchmen in England whose heads Henry could strike off. "But of all these heads, there may not be one to fit my shoulders," persisted the reluctant ambassador.

2 Henry's powerful minister, Thomas Cromwell, wishing to strengthen England's links with Protestant Europe, arranged that Henry should marry the Flemish Anne of Cleves as his fourth wife. Hans Holbein painted a delightful portrait of the princess, which was sent to Henry and encouraged him to look forward to his new bride with joyful anticipation. When she finally arrived, the princess turned out to be much homelier than her portrait. "You have sent me a Flanders mare," exclaimed the disappointed bridegroom in disgust.

{This episode was the end of Cromwell; Henry soon afterward had him executed on a trumped-up charge of treason.}

❧ ❦

HENRY, Camille (1933–), *US professional ice-hockey player.*

1 "During a tense, rough and brawling hockey game, courageous Camille Henry, one of the tiniest players in the National Hockey League, lost his temper and tangled with big tough defenseman Fernie Flaman, one of the most feared sluggers in the league. As they grappled, shoulder to shoulder, pint-sized Henry suddenly shouted a warning at his huge opponent, who outweighed him by more than seventy pounds: 'Watch out, Fernie, or I'll bleed all over you!'"

❧ ❦

HENRY, O. (1862–1910), *US writer, born William Sidney Porter. He published many volumes of short stories.*

1 Characteristic of O. Henry are the words he is reputed to have uttered just before his death: "Don't turn down the light. I'm afraid to go home in the dark."

{He was quoting the words of a popular song of the day.}

2 Henry wrote to his publisher, Frank Munsey, requesting an advance of fifty dollars. Munsey replied that as Henry was already several stories in arrears, there would be "no advance unless I know what you want it for." He received by return mail a sealed envelope containing a single long blonde hair. Henry got the advance.

❧ ❦

Thomas Jefferson Hogg, biographer of Percy Bysshe Shelley, once told the story of a Cambridge mathematician who, having never read Milton's *Paradise Lost,* was finally prevailed upon to do so. "I have read your famous poem," the mathematician is reported to have said. "I have read it attentively: but what does it prove? There is more instruction in half a page of Euclid! A man might read Milton's poem a hundred, aye, a thousand times, and he would never learn that the angles at the base of an isosceles triangle are equal!"

HENSON, Josiah (1789–1883), *US orator. An ex-slave, Henson was a leader in the early abolitionist movement. He was reputed to be the original of Uncle Tom in Harriet Beecher Stowe's* Uncle Tom's Cabin.

1 Henson was introduced to the archbishop of Canterbury, who was so impressed by his bearing and speech that he inquired the name of the university at which he had studied. "The university of adversity," replied Henson.

ဆ ⋖ဇ

HEPBURN, Katharine (1909–), *US actress. She co-starred with Spencer Tracy in a number of films, such as* Pat and Mike *(1952) and* Guess Who's Coming to Dinner *(1967). Her other films include* The Philadelphia Story *(1940),* The African Queen *(1951), and* The Lion in Winter *(1968). She has won four Academy Awards.*

1 During the earlier part of her great career, Katharine Hepburn made a series of pictures she herself considered "boring." In the trade she was put down as "Box Office Poison." Reviews were not flattering. Just about this time, however, the writer Cleveland Amory noticed in a Hartford, Connecticut, paper a glowing pro-Hepburn notice. Amory, in conversation with Kate's father, a Hartford urologist, commented on this pleasant shift in journalistic appreciation of Miss Hepburn. Dr. Hepburn fixed his gaze on Mr. Amory. "Do you know what I do?"

"No."

"I specialize in what is known as the 'Old Man's Operation.' I have operated on half of the newspaper publishers of this city and I confidently expect to operate on the other half."

2 A reporter noticed that Miss Hepburn, during the filming of *The Lion in Winter,* was wearing sneakers under her twelfth-century robes. Asked why she had made such an odd choice of footwear, Miss Hepburn replied, "I play Eleanor of Aquitaine, queen of England —and also a practical woman who believed in comfort."

ဆ ⋖ဇ

HERBERT, A[lan] P[atrick] (1890–1971), *British humorist and legal reformer. His* Holy Deadlock *(1934) wittily drew attention to the injustices and hypocrisy of British divorce law. The rights of authors and prevention of pollution in rivers and canals were other issues on which A.P.H. (as he was always known) vigorously campaigned. He also wrote plays and review sketches, and contributed for more than sixty years to the humorous weekly* Punch.

1 In 1935 A.P.H. was elected one of the two members of Parliament for Oxford University. By tradition a new MP makes his or her maiden speech in the House of Commons on some noncontroversial topic, but Herbert seized the chance to make an impassioned appeal for reform of the divorce laws. Some members were shocked, believing that Herbert's unconventional tactics had jeopardized the bill's chances. (They were wrong: Herbert and his allies got the bill through Parliament within twenty months.) Among the people who came up to congratulate Herbert was Winston Churchill. Complimenting him on his aplomb, Churchill growled, "Call that a maiden speech? It was a brazen hussy of a speech. Never did such a painted lady of a speech parade itself before a modest Parliament."

ဆ ⋖ဇ

HERFORD, Oliver (1863–1935), *US humorist, illustrator, and writer of light verse, born in Britain.*

1 Herford was short of money in the early days of his career. The manager of his hotel, aware of his guest's precarious financial situation, did not insist on immediate payment, but simply added any money owing at the end of a week to the bill for the following week. One day, as the two men passed in the hotel foyer, the manager asked Herford if he had received his latest bill. Herford simply replied, "Yes."

"Is that all you have to say?"

"At the moment, yes," said the humorist. "But if the bill gets any larger, I'll have to ask you for a larger room."

2 Herford was a guest of honor at a banquet along with a famous general. Suddenly the hostess without prior warning announced, "Mr. Oliver Herford will now improvise a poem in honor of this occasion." Herford, a shy and modest man, protested. "Oh no," he said, shrinking back in his chair, "have the general fire a cannon."

{This anecdote is also told of Carl Sandburg.}

3 Herford was traveling on a trolley one day with his young nephew on his lap. The car was so crowded that when an attractive blonde entered, she was obliged to stand. Herford gave her an admiring look and said to his nephew, "My boy, why don't you get up and give the lady your seat?"

4 A serious-minded young lady once solemnly asked Herford whether he really had no ambition beyond making people laugh. "Oh, yes, I have," said Herford with equal gravity, "and one day I hope I may fulfill it."

"Oh, what is your ambition, Mr. Herford? Do tell me."

"I would like to throw an egg into an electric fan."

5 A notorious bore at Herford's club bustled up to him, complaining of having been insulted. "I've just overheard someone in the lobby saying that he'd offer me fifty dollars to resign my membership," he said plaintively. "What do you think I should do about it, Oliver?"

"Hold out for a hundred," advised Herford.

6 Herford was asked his opinion of Arnold Bennett's work. "Well," he confessed, "something I once wrote about him in a critical way so prejudiced me against him that I never read a word he wrote."

❧ ❦

HERSCHEL, Sir William (1738–1822), *British astronomer, born in Germany. Herschel went to England (1757) as a musician and became a leading figure in the musical world at the fashionable resort of Bath. His real interest, however, lay in astronomy, a field in which he was entirely self-educated. Finding contemporary telescopes inadequate, he constructed his own, with the aid of his sister, Caroline. In 1781 he made his greatest discovery, the planet Uranus, and the following year was appointed astronomer to George III.*

1 As news of Herschel's discoveries became known in the 1780s, what most caught the popular imagination was that the astronomer's powerful new telescopes revealed stars to be circular objects instead of the rayed or spiky shapes that they appeared to the naked eye. At a dinner Herschel was placed next to the great physicist Henry Cavendish. Conversation between these two scientific giants did not flourish, no doubt mainly on account of Cavendish's notorious awkwardness in public. At length Cavendish leaned forward. "Is it true, Dr. Herschel, that you see the stars round?" he asked, very slowly. "Round as a button," replied Herschel. Cavendish lapsed into a silence that lasted until the end of the meal. Then he leaned forward again. "Round as a button?" he asked. "Round as a button," affirmed Herschel. And that was the end of their conversation.

❧ ❦

HESS, Dame Myra (1890–1965), *English pianist. During World War II she gave regular lunchtime recitals at the National Gallery in London; they continued throughout the bombing.*

1 Dame Myra approached Sir Thomas Beecham before a concert one evening. "Are you going to conduct by heart again tonight, Sir Thomas?" she asked. "Of course," replied the conductor. "In that case," announced Dame Myra, "*I* am going to use my music."

❧ ❦

HEVESY, Georg de (1885–1966), *Hungarian chemist. With the physicist Dirk Coster he discovered the element hafnium (1923). For his work on radioactive tracers he was awarded the 1943 Nobel Prize for chemistry.*

1 Suspecting the quality of food served at his lodgings, Hevesy decided to conduct a simple experiment at dinner one evening. While his landlady's back was turned he slipped a microscopic amount of a certain radioactive substance into a piece of rather fatty meat that he had left at the side of his plate. The following day, meat hash was served for dinner. Hevesy passed a Geiger counter over his plate: its ominous clicks confirmed his worst suspicions. Within a few days he had changed his lodgings.

HEYERDAHL, Thor (1914–   ), *Norwegian anthropologist. In 1947, he suggested that the original inhabitants of Polynesia could have been migrants from Peru. To demonstrate the feasibility of this theory he built a raft of balsa wood, which he named* Kon-Tiki, *and sailed it from Peru to the Pacific Tuamotu Islands. This voyage and his later ones in 1969 and 1977–78 led to successful books and documentary films.*

1 On a visit to London, Heyerdahl had a busy schedule of appointments. Shortly after recording a program for the Independent Television Network, he was due at the BBC studios for an interview. Having been assured by the BBC that a taxi would be sent to pick him up from the ITN studios, Heyerdahl waited expectantly in the lobby. As the minutes ticked by, however, he began to grow anxious. He approached a little man in a flat cap, who looked as if he might be a taxi driver and was obviously searching for someone. "I'm Thor Heyerdahl," said the anthropologist. "Are you looking for me?"

"No, mate," replied the taxi driver. "I've been sent to pick up four Airedales for the BBC."

HIDEYOSHI (1536–98), *Japanese warlord. The son of a peasant, Hideyoshi rose to exercise civil and military control over the whole of Japan by 1590. His last years were taken up with a bloody but fruitless invasion of Korea.*

1 Hideyoshi commissioned a colossal statue of Buddha for a shrine in Kyoto. It took 50,000 men five years to build, and Hideyoshi himself sometimes worked incognito alongside the laborers. The work had scarcely been completed when the earthquake of 1596 brought the roof of the shrine crashing down and wrecked the statue. In a rage Hideyoshi loosed an arrow at the fallen colossus. "I put you here at great expense," he shouted, "and you can't even look after your own temple!"

HILBERT, David (1862–1943), *German mathematician whose work as teacher and theorist (especially in geometry) during his tenure at Göttingen made him probably the most influential mathematician of the first half of the century.*

1 The Hungarian-American mathematician George Pólya likes to tell stories about Hilbert's absentmindedness. At a party at the great mathematician's house his wife noticed that her husband had neglected to put on a clean shirt. She ordered him to do so. He went upstairs; ten minutes passed; Hilbert did not return. Mrs. Hilbert went up to the bedroom to find Hilbert lying peacefully in bed. As Pólya puts it, "You see, it was the natural sequence of things. He took off his coat, then his tie, then his shirt, and so on, and went to sleep."

2 George Pólya tells another story about the Göttingen of more than half a century ago. Each new member of the faculty, dressed in black coat and top hat, was supposed to make a brief, formal call on the senior professors. One such knocked on Hilbert's door; Mrs. Hilbert decided for her husband that he was at home. The new colleague entered, sat down, put his top hat on the floor, started a conversation. Hilbert, whose mind may well have been on some profound mathematical problem, listened to the flow of talk with growing impatience. Finally he took the top hat from the floor, put it on his head, took his wife's arm, said, "My dear, I think we have delayed our good colleague long enough," and walked out of his own house.

HILL, John (?1716–75), *British botanist, miscellaneous writer, and charlatan. After receiving the order of Vasa from the king of Sweden for a botanical treatise (1774), Hill called himself Sir John and set himself up as a "doctor."*

1 Failing to secure a nomination to the Royal Society, Hill switched his considerable satirical powers from the theater, hitherto his favorite target, to the sciences. From Portsmouth he sent a bogus communication to the society describing the case of a sailor who had broken a leg in a fall from the rigging and who had had it treated with bandages and tarwater to such good effect that within three days he was able to use the leg as well as ever. This revelation occasioned some solemn discussion, in the midst of which another letter arrived from the joker: he had forgotten to mention in his first communication that the leg in question was wooden.

ঙ৯ ৵ও

HILL, Rowland (1744–1833), *British preacher. His evangelical sermons earned him much hostility from the Anglican establishment.*

1 During a heavy rainstorm a number of people took shelter in the chapel where Hill was preaching. "People who make religion their cloak are rightly censured," he remarked, "but I consider that those who make it their umbrella are not much better."

2 Hill received an anonymous letter attacking him for driving to chapel in his carriage and reminding him that this was not the example set by Christ. Hill agreed, adding, "If the writer of this letter would come to my house saddled and bridled next Sunday, I will gladly follow our Lord's example."

ঙ৯ ৵ও

HILLARY, Sir Edmund (1919–), *New Zealand explorer and mountaineer. In 1953 he and his Sherpa guide, Tenzing Norgay, became the first men to climb Mount Everest.*

1 The dramatic photograph of Tenzing Norgay on the summit of Everest went around the world. Later people wondered why there was no companion picture of Hillary. The explorer wrote that he had not asked the Sherpa to reciprocate because "as far as I knew, he had never taken a photograph before, and the summit of Everest was hardly the place to show him how."

ঙ৯ ৵ও

HINDEMITH, Paul (1895–1963), *German composer and musical theorist. His outstanding work is the opera* Mathis der Maler *(1938).*

1 "The composer Paul Hindemith was once conducting a rehearsal of one of his more dissonant orchestral compositions. At one point, he rapped his baton and said, 'No, no, gentlemen; even though it sounds wrong, it's still not right!'"

ঙ৯ ৵ও

HITCHCOCK, Sir Alfred (1889–1980), *British film director who worked mainly in the United States after 1940. He was a master of sophisticated cinematic effects used to produce an atmosphere of tension. Among the best known of his brilliant thrillers were* Psycho *(1960) and* The Birds *(1963).*

1 Hitchcock, who enjoyed food, was put out to find totally inadequate quantities served up at a private dinner he attended. Toward the end of the evening the host said, "I do hope you will dine with us again soon."

"By all means," assented Hitchcock. "Let's start now."

{*See also* GIOACCHINO ROSSINI 6 and JACQUELINE SUSANN 3 for other hungry guests.}

2 Working with Hitchcock early in her career, actress Ingrid Bergman was uncomfortable about the way he had asked her to play a certain scene. "I don't think I can do that naturally," she told him, and went on to explain her difficulties and suggest possible alternatives. Hitchcock listened solemnly, nodding from time to time; Miss Bergman felt she had won her case. "All right," he finally said, "if you can't do it naturally, then *fake* it."

{Much later, Miss Bergman admitted that this was the best piece of acting advice she ever received.}

3 At a French airport one day, the customs official looked suspiciously at Hitchcock's passport, in which his occupation was listed simply as "Producer." "What do you produce?" he asked. "Gooseflesh," Hitchcock replied.

4 Hitchcock had a habit of falling asleep at parties. On one occasion, he had been asleep for nearly four hours when his wife woke him and suggested that they go home. "But it's only one o'clock," protested Hitchcock. "They'll think we aren't enjoying ourselves!"

5 Hitchcock watched with fascination as his wife prepared a cheese soufflé. After she had put the dish into the oven, his eyes remained glued to the oven door. "What *is* going on behind that door?" he asked every few minutes, lowering his voice to a whisper in case a sudden noise should prevent the soufflé from rising. By the time the dish was ready, and Mrs. Hitchcock opened the oven door to reveal a perfect soufflé, Hitchcock was in a state of nervous exhaustion. "No more soufflés until we have an oven with a glass door," he said. "I can't *stand* the suspense."

6 Hitchcock never sat among the audience to watch his films. "Don't you miss hearing them scream?" he was once asked. "No," replied Hitchcock. "I can hear them when I'm making the picture."

7 (Though at the time he was still a church-going Catholic, Hitchcock's attitude toward religion may be illustrated by this anecdote.)

Driving through a Swiss city one day, Hitchcock suddenly pointed out of the car window and said, "That is the most frightening sight I have ever seen." His companion was surprised to see nothing more alarming than a priest in conversation with a little boy, his hand on the child's shoulder. "Run, little boy," cried Hitchcock, leaning out of the car. "Run for your life!"

8 When the shooting of *The Thirty-nine Steps* began, Hitchcock amused himself by handcuffing the star, Madeleine Carroll, to her co-star Robert Donat and pretended to lose the key until the end of the day. He was particularly interested in seeing how the unfortunate couple would cope with the inevitable demands of nature.

ะৈ ৎই

HOAR, George Frisbie (1826–1904), *distinguished US congressman (1869–77) and senator (1877–1904), who helped organize the Republican party in Massachusetts.*

1 Hoar was once greeted effusively by a man he barely knew but who certainly seemed at first to recognize him. "How are you,

Senator?" the man inquired, and then: "And how is Mrs. W.?"

ะৈ ৎই

HOBBS, Jack [Sir John Berry] (1882–1963), *British cricketer. During his long career (1905–34) he scored more than 61,000 runs. He was the first cricketer to receive a knighthood (1953).*

1 As a young player Hobbs did not achieve his first century until he was eighteen. During one evening game he was within striking distance of the longed-for total when he was given out, leg-before-wicket. He had then scored 90. The decision was a bad one, but Hobbs went back to the pavilion without argument. However, a journalist friend covering the match was so incensed that he reported the score was "Hobbs 90 not out."

ะৈ ৎই

HOBSON, Laura Z. (1900–), *US writer. Her novels include the famous* Gentleman's Agreement *(1947), which turns on the issue of anti-Semitism.*

1 Laura Zametkin married Thayer Hobson and thenceforward used the name Hobson both socially and professionally. During the pre-World War II period, when Hitler's Nazis were beginning their murderous attacks on Jews, she was a guest at a fashionable New York dinner party. Some deplored "those awful Germans." Others took their excesses lightly. One remarked, "The chosen people ask for it, wherever they are." Another came up with the conventional cliché: "Some of my best friends are Jews." At which point Mrs. Hobson spoke up quietly: "Some of mine are, too. Including my father and mother."

There was a moment's silence. Then the conversation resumed.

ะৈ ৎই

HOBSON, Thomas (?1544–1631), *English carrier. A famous Cambridge figure, Hobson was the subject of two mock epitaphs by Milton.*

1 When customers came to Hobson to hire a horse, he would take them into the stable to make their choice, telling them that they must take the horse standing nearest to the stable door. Thus Hobson ensured that each customer had an equal chance of hiring a good or bad horse and that each horse had an equal chance of receiving good or bad treatment.

{From this practice arose the expression "Hobson's choice," meaning a situation in which one has the choice of taking what is offered or nothing.}

૭♥ ౿ఠ

HOCKING, William Ernest (1873–1966), *US philosopher, professor of philosophy at Harvard from 1914 until his retirement in 1943. His wife, Agnes, founded the Shady Hill School in Cambridge.*

1 (Marian Cannon Schlesinger tells this story about the distinguished philosopher.)

"Ernest Hocking took up painting, and Agnes Hocking, ever the worshipper at his shrine, used to startle the philosophy graduate students when Professor Hocking addressed one of their monthly meetings. She would creep silently across the platform in front of the lectern where he stood speaking, doubled over in order not to interfere with his flow of words, with one of his paintings clasped to her bosom. Having reached the other side, she would snatch up another painting in exchange, and noiselessly repeat the exhibition. No reference was made to this unusual phenomenon by Professor Hocking, who imperturbably carried on the discussion of the evening as though it were the most natural happening in the world. One has heard of 'action painting,' but this seems to have been an example of 'action showing.'"

૭♥ ౿ఠ

HOFFMANN, Ernst Theodor Wilhelm (1776–1822), *German novelist, composer, and theatrical manager. His opera* Undine *(1816) was a considerable success, and he also wrote music for other theatrical performances. He is best remembered for his novels and stories, many of them tales of the gruesome and supernatural. Offenbach's* Tales of Hoffmann *is based on three of them.*

1 Hoffmann was once the guest of a Berlin *nouveau riche,* who after dinner showed him around his lavishly decorated house. Speaking of his domestics, the millionaire mentioned casually that he needed three servants for his personal attendance. Hoffmann replied that he had four just to take care of his bath: one to lay

out the towels, one to test the temperature of the water, and the third to make sure the faucets were in good order.

"And the fourth?"

"Oh, he's the most important of all — he takes my bath for me."

૭♥ ౿ఠ

HOFMANN, Josef Casimir (1876–1957), *Polish-born pianist who also composed under the name of Michael Dvorsky. He became a US citizen in 1926.*

1 Hofmann was just five feet five inches tall, his hands so small that he had to have a keyboard specially made for him. A musician called Felix Salmond went backstage after a Hofmann concert. Salmond was a very tall man, more than a foot taller than Hofmann. As he bent over to congratulate the pianist, he said solemnly, "You are a giant."

2 During a train ride Hofmann sat gazing straight ahead, motionless, his eyes apparently unfocused. "What are you doing?" inquired his traveling companion. "Practicing," said the pianist.

3 At a concert one evening, members of the orchestra were concerned to see a look of bewilderment pass over Hofmann's face as he settled himself at the piano. Leaning toward a lady in the front row of the audience, the pianist whispered, "May I please see your program, madam? I forget what comes first."

૭♥ ౿ఠ

HOGARTH, William (1697–1764), *British painter and engraver. His works satirizing contemporary society were highly popular; among the best known are* The Harlot's Progress, The Rake's Progress, Marriage à la Mode, *and* Gin Lane, *showing the effeteness and debauchery of the upper classes and the brutality of the lower.*

1 Hogarth was commissioned to paint the portrait of an exceptionally ugly nobleman. As was his custom, he depicted the sitter with the utmost frankness and realism. When the nobleman saw the portrait, he refused to pay for it. An acrimonious discussion ensued. Eventually Hogarth, needing the money, sent a letter to his client, saying that a certain showman who specialized in exhibiting wild beasts and freaks or monstrosities was interested in the portrait. Unless Hogarth received payment within three days, he proposed to embellish the picture with a tail and other appendages and to sell it to the showman for exhibition. The nobleman paid up, took delivery of the portrait, and burned it.

ॐ ॐ

HOKUSAI (1760–1849), *Japanese painter and illustrator. His early studies of women and the theater were superseded by an interest in landscapes, which influenced the Impressionist and Postimpressionist artists of Europe.*

1   Looking back toward the end of his long life on his artistic output, Hokusai dismissed as nothing all the work he had done before the age of fifty; it was only after he had reached seventy that he felt he was turning out work of note. At age eighty-nine, on his deathbed, he lamented, "If heaven had granted me five more years, I could have become a real painter."

{Hokusai left a memorable description of himself: "the old man mad with painting."}

ॐ ॐ

HOLLAND, George (1791–1870), *US actor. Born in England, he came to the United States in 1827, where he was a popular comedian until his death.*

1   When George Holland died, his family first intended to arrange the funeral at a fashionable Fifth Avenue church. However, the rector objected to conducting a service for an actor. He told the family friend delegated to call on him, "There's a little church around the corner where you may get it done." This was the Church of the Transfiguration on Twenty-ninth Street, and here the bereaved family had a cordial reception from the rector, the Reverend George H. Houghton, who agreed to conduct the funeral service. The story got out and aroused much indignation; the name "Little Church around the Corner" stuck.

ॐ ॐ

HOLLES, Denzil Holles, 1st Baron (1599–1680), *British statesman. He was one of the early leaders of parliamentary opposition to Charles I, but later tried to make peace between*

the king and Cromwell. When this attempt failed he fled to join the royalist party abroad. At the Restoration he was made a peer.

1   The first great constitutional crisis of Charles I's reign occurred in 1629 when the king, finding that Parliament would not do as he wished but instead had produced a document censuring his policies, tried to dissolve the sitting. Uproar ensued in the House, as the Speaker made as if to obey the king's command and leave the chamber. Denzil Holles shouted, "God's wounds! You shall sit here till we please to rise," and, going to the Speaker's chair, he and another man held the Speaker down in it while the paper condemning illegal taxes and Roman Catholicism was read.

ॐ ॐ

HOLLIDAY, Judy [Judith Tuvim] (1922–65), *US comedienne. She appeared in a number of films of the fifties, notably* Born Yesterday *(1950),* It Should Happen to You *(1953), and* The Solid Gold Cadillac *(1956).*

1   At a movie interview, Judy Holliday found herself being chased around the room by a lecherous studio head. Unperturbed, she put her hand inside her dress and pulled out her falsies. "Here," she said, handing them to her dumbfounded pursuer, "I think this is what you want."

ॐ ॐ

HOLMES, Fanny Dixwell (1841–1929), *wife of Oliver Wendell Holmes, Jr.*

1   When her husband was appointed Supreme Court justice, Fanny Holmes was rather apprehensive about the social life she would encounter in Washington. Their first White House function was a big formal dinner to welcome the new justice. Fanny was greeted by President Theodore Roosevelt, who chatted with her, asking her whether she had seen much of Washington yet, whether she had been to Congress, whether she had met many people. Fanny replied politely that a number of congressmen's wives had called on her. But there was a certain note in her voice that caused the president to ask, "You found the ladies pleasant?" Fanny replied, "Washington is full of famous men and the women they married

when they were young." The president laughed heartily and, with Fanny on his arm, led everyone in to dinner. Fanny was never again nervous attending functions in Washington.

2   Justice Holmes was very fussy about his books. One day in their Washington home, discovering that a volume that he wanted was either lost or misplaced, he made an uproar, worrying his secretary, the butler, and the servants about it before he went off to the Supreme Court. Fanny did not say a single word, but when her husband returned, he found the book in its place on the shelf. An American flag stuck out above it, and underneath Fanny had hung a neatly printed sign: "I am a very old man. I have had many troubles, most of which never happened."

3   Mr. Larcum, who ran the livery stable at Beverly Farms where the Holmeses spent their summers, used to drive Mrs. Holmes about on various errands. One afternoon when he was driving her to meet Justice Holmes, the horse bolted and could not be stopped until they reached their destination. Mrs. Holmes did not panic, nor even appear to be scared; she just leaned out, waving her parasol, and called, "Larcum! If you kill me, tell him I loved him."

೭ℯ   ⋅ઙ

HOLMES, John (1812–99), *US lawyer; brother of Oliver Wendell Holmes, Sr.*

1   A kind, unassuming man, John Holmes learned early on to live with his brother's fame and reputation. At a party attended by numerous celebrities, a boy went around collecting autographs. When offered the piece of paper to sign, John Holmes wrote simply, "John Holmes, *frère de mon frère*" (my brother's brother).

2   Mrs. Dixwell, Justice Holmes's mother-in-law, was always trying, without success, to marry off John Holmes. John lived in a little alley in an unpretentious house that had a gentle air of dilapidation: it was filled with cats, books, and birds in cages. His mother's old housekeeper looked after him, and he was perfectly content as he was, but Mrs. Dixwell told him severely, "You should move to better quarters, John." He replied gravely, "Oh, I can't move to better quarters until I have a better half."

3   John Holmes was most often described as "homely." Contented to be outshone by his elder brother, he claimed that he had been paid only one compliment in his life. When he was six, the maid brushing his hair turned to his mother and said, "I don't think John's so *awful* cross-eyed, ma'am."

4   When John Holmes lay dying, he had been comatose and motionless for such a long time that the people around his bed began to wonder whether he might not already have died. The nurse, finding no pulse, announced that she would just feel his feet to see if they were warm. "If they are, he's alive," she said. "Nobody ever died with warm feet."
    "John Rogers did," said Holmes distinctly. He never spoke again.
    { John Rogers, the first Protestant martyr of Mary Tudor's reign, was burned at the stake in 1555.}

೭ℯ   ⋅ઙ

HOLMES, Oliver Wendell, Sr. (1809–94), *US writer and physician. He achieved sufficient distinction in medicine to be appointed professor of anatomy and physiology at Harvard, a post he held for many years (1847–82). After the great success of his essays entitled* The Autocrat of the Breakfast Table, *which first appeared in* The Atlantic Monthly *(1857–58), he devoted his principal energies to authorship and to being a literary celebrity. In the* Breakfast Table *series* The Autocrat *was succeeded by* The Professor *(1860) and* The Poet *(1872). Oliver Wendell Holmes also wrote novels, poems, and memoirs of other eminent New Englanders.*

1   Holmes arrived at the house of a poor patient one morning to find the priest about to depart. "Your patient is very ill," said the priest solemnly. "He is going to die." Holmes nodded. "Yes, and he's going to hell," he said. The priest was horrified. "I have just given him extreme unction," he exclaimed. "You must not say such things!" Holmes shrugged his shoulders. "Well, you expressed a medical opinion," he retorted, "and I have just as much right to a theological opinion."

2   Dr. Holmes, who suffered all his life from asthma, was asked how hay fever could be cured. In the authentic voice of one afflicted by such ailments, he answered, "Gravel is an

effective remedy; it should be taken eight feet deep."

3 A hostess who had arranged a particularly lavish afternoon tea in honor of Dr. Holmes asked him, "What do you think of afternoon tea?" The reply may have taken her aback. "It's giggle — gabble — gobble — 'n' git!"

4 To pay tribute to the discoverer of anesthesia, the Massachusetts Historical Society commissioned a monument. There was some dispute, however, as to whose bust should adorn it, for both William Morton and Charles Jackson claimed the discovery. Holmes came up with a simple solution: busts of both men should be used, with the inscription "To Ether."

5 Oliver Wendell Holmes proved that money has a universal appeal that can affect the great as well as the lowly. On receiving an invitation to deliver a lecture, he sent back the following reply: "I have at hand your kind invitation. However, I am far from being in good physical health. I am satisfied that if I were offered a $50 bill after my lecture, I would not have strength enough to refuse it."

6 Holmes's love of flattery continued unabated into his old age, and he used his hardness of hearing to indulge it. "I am a trifle deaf, you know," he would say to someone who had just praised his latest work. "Do you mind repeating that a little louder?"

7 In old age, Holmes was often bothered by the attentions of devoted admirers who would follow him home from church and even attempt to follow him into his house. On one occasion he tried to elude some pursuers by taking back alleys, but found them still on his trail as he neared home. He summoned enough energy to run up the steps and open the front door. Then he turned to confront the group who rushed after him. "Don't come in," he said. "It's catching and I've got it."

8 A few days before his death, Dr. Holmes said to his son, "Well, Wendell, what is it, King's Chapel?"

"Oh, yes, father."

"All right, then, I am satisfied. That is all I am going to say about it."

Content with these final arrangements, Oliver Wendell Holmes died a few days later, and his funeral took place at King's Chapel in Boston, where a tablet was set up to his memory.

કે૦ ૦ડૃ

HOLMES, Oliver Wendell, Jr. (1841–1935), *US jurist. He combined the roles of practicing and academic lawyer for many years after 1870, and also wrote and edited influential legal texts, notably* The Common Law *(1881). As a judge in the Massachusetts Supreme Judicial Court, and afterward (from 1902) in the US Supreme Court, he enjoyed a reputation for humane interpretation of the Constitution.*

1 Oliver Wendell Holmes, Jr., fought in the Civil War and was wounded three times. While he was recovering at home from his second injury, visitors came to the family home to pay their respects to the wounded hero. Expecting reflections on glory and patriotism, they were offended by what he said: "War? War is an organized bore."

2 When he recovered from his third Civil War wound Oliver Wendell Holmes, Jr., decided to return to law school as the army did not need him for a while. He knocked on the door of his father's study so that he could inform him of this decision. He found his father at work, and said without preamble, "I am going to the law school." Dr. Holmes looked up from his desk. "What's the use of that, Wendell?" he said. "A lawyer can't be a great man."

{Dr. Holmes made the remark without thinking, but if he had tried he could not have produced anything more provocative to say to his son. At the age of ninety Justice Holmes quoted those words, and remarked that his father had kicked him upstairs into the law and he supposed he should be grateful.}

3 When Emile Zola's novel *Germinal* reached the United States, it caused a considerable stir, being concerned with the sordid, poverty-stricken life of French miners. Mrs. Bell, a leading lady of Boston society, remarked one evening to Holmes, "I hear you have been reading *Germinal*. Boston is still shocked by

Zola. What do you think of him, Judge Holmes?"

"Improving, but dull," Holmes replied.

4 (After his father's death Wendell had to settle into the house that his father had so dominated by his presence.)

"Gradually [Wendell assumed] the privileges of the manor. Things he had not dared to touch he began now to use as his own. Grandfather Jackson's high desk stood in a corner of the library. Wendell had always been proud of Judge Jackson, pleased when in court he had to refer to his opinions. Now he stood at the desk to write his opinions. 'Doesn't it tire you?' Fanny asked, watching him write, one knee propped against the desk. 'Yes,' Wendell replied. 'But it's salutary. Nothing conduces to brevity like a caving in of the knees.' "

5 Charles Hopkinson's impressive portrait of Justice Holmes, which hangs in the library of the Law School at Harvard, is a full-length picture of the judge in judicial robes, with distinguished white hair and mustache. When Justice Holmes saw the finished picture, he said, "That isn't me, but it's a damn good thing for people to think it is."

6 In his eighty-seventh year Justice Holmes was out walking with another elderly friend when a pretty girl passed them. The judge turned to watch her and then sighed, "Oh, to be seventy again!"

See also BERNARD DE FONTENELLE 3.

7 Throughout his judicial career Holmes had a reputation for independence of judgment that earned him the title of "the Great Dissenter." It is said that when he was in his eighty-eighth year, a newspaperman in search of copy about the old judge asked passersby in Capitol Square whether they had heard of Justice Holmes. "Holmes?" replied an overalled mechanic, looking up from the sports page of his newspaper. "Oh, sure! He's the young judge on the Supreme Court that's always disagreeing with the old guys."

8 At the age of ninety-one, Justice Holmes resigned from the Supreme Court and spent the following summer at his country house in Massachusetts. Old friends from Boston came to see him, bringing their grandchildren, whose company Holmes greatly enjoyed. Sitting on the porch with Betsy Warder, aged sixteen, and discussing life with her, he said, "I won't refrain from talking about anything because you're too young, if you won't because I'm too old."

9 Soon after Justice Holmes's retirement his legal secretary, Dean Acheson, came to read to him. Holmes chose Plato's *Symposium*. Acheson was unenthusiastic about the choice and asked why they should take that as their text. "To improve our minds, sonny," replied the judge.

≈• •≈

HOME, Alec Douglas-, Baron Home of the Hirsel (1903–), *British statesman; prime minister (1963–64). Lord Home was foreign secretary (1960–63) before renouncing his peerage to accept the premiership. After his electoral defeat in 1964 he resigned the leadership of the Conservative party (1965). In 1974 he received life peerage.*

1 Watching a recorded television program featuring Sir Alec, Lady Douglas-Home was horrified by her husband's haggard appearance. She ran up to the bedroom, where Sir Alec was changing for an evening engagement, and asked, "Are you all right? You look terrible downstairs."

≈• •≈

HOME, William Douglas- (1912–), *British playwright, brother of Sir Alec Douglas-Home. His plays include* The Chiltern Hundreds *(1947),* The Secretary Bird *(1968), and* Lloyd George Knew My Father *(1972).*

1 (Home and his wife, Rachel, were invited to join friends for dinner. Home tells this story:)

"Having been to Oxford for a matinee, I duly arrived, dined, chatted and then rose to go around eleven.

" 'Thank you, Rachel, for a lovely dinner,' said my host to my wife.

" 'What do you mean?' I inquired. 'I brought it over from home,' Rachel explained, 'as their cook was off.'

" 'In that case,' I said, 'I am at liberty to say that the fish was the most disgusting thing I've ever eaten.'

" 'That was the only dish I provided,' said my host."

HOMER, Winslow (1836–1910), *US painter. He worked in New York as an illustrator and was an artist-correspondent during the Civil War before settling in Maine. There he produced some of his most famous pictures of the sea and fishermen.*

1   The artist Leon Kroll was having trouble with a seascape. "My boy," said Winslow Homer, "if you want to make a great sea, use only two waves."

ॐ ๛

HOOK, Theodore Edward (1788–1841), *British journalist and wit. As a young man Hook was a renowned practical joker and man-about-town in Regency London. During his tenure as treasurer of Mauritius (1813), he was held responsible for the embezzlement of a deputy, brought back to England, and imprisoned. In later life he supported himself by novel-writing and journalism.*

1   Hook's most famous practical joke was the Berners Street hoax. A certain Mrs. Tottenham, who lived on this fashionable London thoroughfare, had offended Hook. He took his revenge by sending out hundreds of letters inviting people of all ranks of society on various pretexts to visit her house on the same day. Hook and his friends then watched from a vantage point opposite as the carriages of the Duke of Gloucester, the lord mayor of London, and other notables struggled through the bedlam of chimney sweeps, draymen, and tradesmen of all sorts, besieging Mrs. Tottenham's house and bringing the usual business of Berners Street to a chaotic standstill.

2   Hook was rowing up the Thames on an excursion with the comic actor Charles Mathews when their attention was caught by a notice in a waterside garden forbidding unauthorized landings. Incensed, the two men moored, disembarked, and, using their fishing lines as impromptu surveyor's tape, paced to and fro across the lawn, measuring and working out distances. Out came the owner of the property, an alderman of London, to demand what they were doing. Hook introduced himself as an official of a canal company that he said was planning to cut a new canal. This — as far as he could judge it — would go straight through the alderman's garden, right underneath the windows of his house. The poor alderman, dumbfounded, was unable to decide whether to wheedle or bluster. In an attempt to propitiate these unwelcome emissaries, he invited them to dinner, served them excellent food and wine, and tried to dissuade them from ruining his property. It was only over the last bottle of wine that Hook owned up to the hoax.

3   Hook was the guest of an alderman who entertained him with much ostentation and plied him lavishly with food and drink. When Hook was already surfeited, his overattentive host pressed yet another delicacy upon him. "I thank you," said Hook, "but if it's all the same to you, I'll take the rest in money."

4   Spying an exceedingly pompous-looking gentleman making his self-important way along a London street, Hook went up to him and said with an exquisite bow, "I beg your pardon, sir, are you anyone in particular?" He then bowed again and passed on, before his startled victim could collect his wits.

5   Toward the end of a successful dinner party, Hook observed that one of his fellow guests, a bookseller, had had rather too much to drink. Leaning toward his host, Hook remarked in a whisper: "You appear to have emptied your wine cellar into your bookseller."

ॐ ๛

HOOKER, Joseph (1814–79), *US federal commander.*

1   At the height of the battle of Williamsburg in 1862, reports on the fighting were circulated to the newspapers every few hours. At one point a dispatch arrived relating to an earlier report on General Hooker, whose troops were heavily engaged. The dispatch was labeled "Fighting — Joe Hooker," indicating that it was the continuation of the previous report. However, the typesetter mistook this for a heading, and the dispatch duly appeared in print under the title "Fighting Joe Hooker." Hooker was subsequently nicknamed "Fighting Joe," and the sobriquet remained with him for the rest of his life.

ॐ ๛

HOOVER, Herbert (1874–1964), *US states-man; 31st president of the United States (1929–33). Following a career as a mining engineer, Hoover supervised relief measures in Europe after World War I. Shortly after he became president, the collapse of the stock exchange led to the Great Depression of the 1930s. This made Hoover's election promises about prosperity ring very hollow.*

1   Hoover lamented to former President Calvin Coolidge that his attempts to promote economic recovery seemed to be making little impact and that his critics were becoming increasingly angry. "You can't expect to see calves running in the field the day after you put the bull to the cows," said Coolidge soothingly. "No, but I would at least expect to see contented cows," replied the unhappy president.

2   During the Boxer Rebellion Hoover had been in China. In later years his campaign managers wanted to boost his political image by describing in dramatic terms an incident during which Hoover had rescued a Chinese child trapped by gunfire. Hoover read the draft of the story, then threw it into the wastebasket. "You can't make a Teddy Roosevelt out of me," he said.

3   Hoover's caution in speaking was sometimes attributed to his Quaker upbringing. On a train journey a traveling companion remarked to Hoover that sheep in a field they were passing had been sheared. Hoover looked and then said, "Well, on this side, anyway."
{This anecdote is also told of Calvin Coolidge and Cordell Hull, among others.}

4   An autograph collector sent a request to President Hoover asking for three signatures; he explained that he wanted one for himself and two to trade for one of Babe Ruth's since "it takes two of yours to get one of Babe Ruth's." Hoover, amused, obliged with three signatures.
{For Babe Ruth's view of the relative values of himself and President Hoover, *see* BABE RUTH 1. The anecdote is also told of others.}

5   After suffering some particularly torrid criticism, Hoover pointed from the South Portico of the White House toward the Washington Monument and said, "This, apparently, is the only stable thing in my administration."

❧ ☙

HOPE, Bob [Leslie Townes] (1903–), *US comedian. He also appeared in many films, including* Road to Singapore *(1940), the first of a series of "Road to . . ." films with Bing Crosby and Dorothy Lamour;* The Paleface *(1948); and* The Facts of Life *(1960).*

1   On a show one evening, Hope cracked the classic joke about theatrical accommodation: "The hotel room where I'm staying is so small that the rats are round-shouldered." The hotel proprietor was not amused, however, and threatened to sue for damages. Hope agreed to take back the remark. At the beginning of his next show he announced: "I'm sorry I said that the rats in that hotel were round-shouldered. They're not."

❧ ☙

HORNE, Lena (1917–), *US black singer and entertainer.*

1   (Al Duckett, a freelance journalist during World War II, recounts the following story about Lena Horne.)
"She had been sent to a camp in the south to entertain the troops. She was scheduled to do a performance for the white troops and a separate performance for the black troops and the German prisoners of war. When I was in the service in Fort Dix, the German prisoners would be in the mess line with black troops and you'd have a separate line for white troops. Lena entertained the blacks and the German prisoners and then she left."

❧ ☙

HOROWITZ, Vladimir (1904–), *Russian-born pianist who settled in the United States after 1940.*

1   As a young pianist Horowitz was shocked by the advice he was given by Artur Schnabel: "When a piece gets difficult, make faces."

2   Horowitz was to perform at Chicago after a long absence from the public stage. Franz Mohr, the chief concert technician of Steinway

and Sons, was given the task of ensuring that the piano was in perfect condition. This he did to the best of his ability, but he was not able to relax until Horowitz had given a brilliant rendering of his first number. As was his custom, the pianist then left the stage — but on this occasion did not return. Mohr was summoned backstage. "Where have you been?" exclaimed Horowitz. "I cannot play again. The piano stool is far too high!" Mohr nervously enquired as to the magnitude of the problem. Horowitz held up his hand, his thumb and forefinger about a quarter of an inch apart.

3   Horowitz occasionally had trouble with the English language. At an audience with Mrs. Hoover, wife of the then president of the United States, Herbert Hoover, he bowed and said courteously, "I am delightful."

ॐ◆ ◆ও

HORTHY DE NAGYBÁNYA, Miklós (1868–1957), *Hungarian statesman and admiral. After the collapse of Austro-Hungary in World War I, Admiral Horthy led the resistance to the Communist regime of Béla Kun, and was appointed regent of Hungary in 1920. He maintained a precarious independence from Nazi Germany until the Germans deposed him in 1944 for attempting to surrender to the advancing Russians.*

1   Admiral Horthy always retained his loyalty to the concept of the Hapsburg empire and the Austro-Hungarian axis that had seemed so immutable in his youth. His reactionary yearnings were the target of many malicious tales. Once on a hunting party Horthy shot a big bird, which someone told him was an eagle. "What? An eagle? I always thought an eagle had two heads!" he is reputed to have said.
{The two-headed eagle was the symbol of the Hapsburg monarchy.}

ॐ◆ ◆ও

HORTON, Edward Everett (1887–1970) *American film and stage actor.*

1   Recalling numerous straw-hat tours with *Springtime for Henry,* actor Edward Everett Horton said one particular evening at Cambridge's Brattle Theater stood out in his memory. The show, a benefit performance, wasn't getting the usual laughs. Horton used every

trick experience had taught him, but apparently without success. After the show, a woman approached him. "Mr. Horton," she began, "you were so funny we could hardly keep from laughing."

ॐ◆ ◆ও

HOUDINI, Harry [Ehrich Weiss] (1874–1926), *US escape artist and magician, whose name became an international byword for daring and ingenious feats of escapology.*

1   Houdini had a reputation for not paying his fair share of the bill when he dined out with friends. On one occasion, however, a conjuror called Meyenberg managed to get the better of him. After lunching in a restaurant with Houdini and a number of other vaudeville artists, Meyenberg turned to the escapologist and asked, "Would you like to see a new trick? Lay your hands flat on the table, with your palms down." Houdini did as he was told. The conjuror then filled two glasses with water and carefully balanced one on each of Houdini's hands. "Let's see you get out of *that* without paying the bill!" he cried as he and the other performers beat a hasty retreat.

2   Broadway producers Charles Dillingham and Florenz Ziegfeld were among the pallbearers at Houdini's funeral. As they carried the coffin out of the church, Dillingham leaned across to Ziegfeld and whispered, "Ziggie, I bet you a hundred bucks he ain't in here."

ॐ◆ ◆ও

HOUSMAN, A[lfred] **E**[dward] (1859–1936), *English poet and classical scholar. Professor of Latin at University College, London (1892–1911) and at Cambridge (1911–36), Housman is best remembered for his books of lyrics,* A Shropshire Lad *(1896) and* Last Poems *(1922). He had an awesome reputation for aloofness and verbal ferocity (he kept notebooks primed with devastating phrases to be used against those whose behavior or scholarship had displeased him).*

1   In an after-dinner speech at Trinity College, Cambridge, Housman described his dual career:
"This great college, of this ancient university, has seen some strange sights. It has seen Wordsworth drunk and Porson sober. And

here am I, a better poet than Porson, and a better scholar than Wordsworth, [somewhere] betwixt and between."

2 Housman's rooms in Trinity were in the part of the college known as Whewell's Court, up several flights of stairs. The year before his death was a sad time for Housman, who was suffering from increasing ill health and the loss of several of his closest friends and relatives. That summer he wrote to his brother Laurence: "I still go up my 44 stairs two at a time, but that is in hopes of dropping at the top."

3 As Housman lay dying in a Cambridge nursing home, his doctor, Dr. Woods, remembering his patient's pleasure in risqué anecdotes, repeated to him a witticism ascribed to an English actor who had been asked what actors did to pass the time when they were not working: "We spend half our time lying on the sands looking at the stars and the other half lying on the stars looking at the sands." Housman gasped out, "Indeed — very good. I shall — have to repeat — that — on the Golden Floor."

᠅

HOWARD, Catherine (1520–42), *the fifth queen consort of Henry VIII. After his political marriage with Anne of Cleves, the twenty-year-old Catherine brought new life to the ailing and aging monarch (then nearing fifty).*

1 After two happy years with Catherine, Henry discovered that she had previously had an affair with a certain Francis Dereham. Henry tried to laugh this off, but flew into a rage when he found out that she was still in love with a favorite courtier, Thomas Culpeper, who had been her fiancé. Catherine and her two lovers were ordered to be beheaded. Defiant as she stood before the block, Catherine announced, "I die a queen. But I would rather die the wife of Thomas Culpeper."
{This report of Catherine's last words is apocryphal; eyewitnesses of her execution remark on her humble confession of her faults.}

᠅

HOWARD, Leslie (1890–1943), *British actor, noted for his romantic roles in such films as* The

Scarlet Pimpernel *(1935) and* Gone with the Wind *(1939).*

1 The small repertory company in which Howard obtained his early acting experience put on a different show every night and sometimes two different shows in a day. One afternoon Howard forgot his lines. He froze on the stage, but no help came from the prompt corner. "What's my line?" he hissed desperately to the prompter. "What's the play?" came back the equally desperate whisper.
{A similar anecdote is told of John Barrymore.}

᠅

HOWARTH, Humphrey (fl. 1800), *British surgeon.*

1 Challenged to a duel, Howarth appeared at the appointed venue stark naked. His challenger, understandably nonplussed, asked what he thought he was doing. Howarth solemnly explained that if any bit of cloth is carried into the body by a gunshot, festering inevitably follows. His opponent averred it would be ridiculous to fight a naked man and the duel was called off.

᠅

HOWE, Elias (1819–67), *US inventor of the sewing machine.*

1 A major problem in the development of Howe's sewing machine was the location of the eye of the needle. The inventor was rapidly running out of money and ideas when one night he had a peculiar dream. He was being led to his execution for failing to design a sewing machine for the king of a strange country. He was surrounded by guards, all of whom carried spears that were pierced near the head. Realizing instantly that this was the solution to his problem, Howe woke up and rushed straight to his workshop. By nine o'clock that morning, the design of the first sewing machine was well on the way to completion.

᠅

HOWE, Julia Ward (1819–1910), *US writer and social reformer. She is remembered chiefly for "The Battle Hymn of the Republic," first published in 1862. She also wrote and lectured on many of the major issues of the day: abolition, women's suffrage, and prison reform.*

1 Senator Charles Sumner was one of Mrs. Howe's New England circle. On one occasion she invited him to meet the actor Edwin Booth, who was just beginning to become known. Sumner wrote back declining the invitation, remarking loftily, "The truth is, I have got beyond taking an interest in individuals." Mrs. Howe commented in her diary on this arrogant remark: "God Almighty has not got so far."

2 At the age of ninety Mrs. Howe was still playing an active part in public life. On her birthday that year an admirer sent her a card reading, "Greetings to Boston's greatest trinity: Howe, Higginson, and Hale." The other two also were of very advanced age. Mrs. Howe smilingly remarked, "Well, they can't say we drop our *H*s in Boston."

ᢀᠵ ᢀᠵ

HOWELLS, William Dean (1837–1920), *US novelist and critic. He was editor of* The Atlantic Monthly *(1871–81), a position that brought him into contact with the main literary talents of his day. An influential critic, he encouraged realism in fiction and his interest in social interactions motivated some of his own best novels, notably* The Rise of Silas Lapham *(1885) and* A Hazard of New Fortunes *(1890).*

1 An author was boring Howells with his efforts to extract a compliment from him. "I don't seem to *write* as well as I used to," said the man fretfully. "Oh, yes, you do," said Howells reassuringly. "You write as well as ever you did. But your *taste* is improving."

2 Mrs. Howells engaged a young girl to do housework for her. For several weeks the newcomer observed the novelist constantly about the house. One day she came to Mrs. Howells, and after some preamble and embarrassment said, "You pay me four dollars a week, madam, and—"

"I'm afraid I really can't afford to pay you more," broke in Mrs. Howells apologetically.

"Well, what I was wanting to say, madam," the girl went on, "was that I would be willing to take three until Mr. Howells lands a job."

HRUSKA, Roman Lee (1904–), *US politician. Elected to the House of Representatives in 1952, he later was US senator from Nebraska from 1955 to 1977.*

1 On January 19, 1970, President Richard Nixon submitted to the Senate the nomination of G. Harrold Carswell to the Supreme Court. That Mr. Carswell was hardly qualified was apparent to most, though not to Mr. Nixon. He was rejected, of course, but has attained a certain immortality through his defense by Senator Hruska: ". . . even if he was mediocre, there are a lot of mediocre judges and people and lawyers. They are entitled to a little representation, aren't they, and a little chance? We can't have all Brandeises and Cardozos and Frankfurters and stuff like that there."

ᢀᠵ ᢀᠵ

HUGHES, William Morris (1864–1952), *Australian statesman. He was prime minister from 1915 to 1923, initially as head of the Labour party and then (1916–23) as head of the Nationalist party, which he helped to form.*

1 While prime minister of Australia, Hughes was once the victim of a vicious verbal attack in Parliament by a member of his own party. When the traitor had finished speaking, Hughes rose to his feet and cupped his hand to his ear, as if listening for something. Knowing the prime minister to be rather deaf, one of his colleagues asked what he was waiting for. "I'm waiting for the cock to crow," replied Hughes.

ᢀᠵ ᢀᠵ

HUGO, Victor (1802–85), *French poet, novelist, and dramatist. The drama* Hernani *(1831) confirmed Hugo's position as the leader of the Romantic movement in French literature. Subsequent involvement in politics—he was an ardent republican—forced him to spend many years in exile in the Channel Islands (1850–71). During this time he wrote some of his best verse, published in* Les Contemplations *(1856), and his greatest novels:* Les Misérables *(1862) and* Les Travailleurs de la mer *(1866). In his last years in France he was idolized as a national figure, somewhat to the detriment of his work.*

1 When Victor Hugo wanted to know what his publishers thought of the manuscript of *Les*

Misérables, he sent them a note reading simply: "?" They replied: "!"

2   Victor Hugo enjoyed a reputation as a tireless lover. When he was eighty, one of his grandsons surprised him in the arms of a young laundress. Not at all abashed, Hugo exclaimed, "Look, little George, this is what they call genius!"

3   (Richard Monckton Milnes, the British writer and politician, went to call on Victor Hugo in Paris.)
"I was shown into a large room . . . with women and men seated in chairs against the walls, and Hugo at one end throned. No one spoke. At last Hugo raised his voice solemnly, and uttered the words: '*Quant à moi, je crois en Dieu!*' (As for me, I believe in God!). Silence followed. Then a woman responded as if in deep meditation: '*Chose sublime! un Dieu qui croit en Dieu!*' (How sublime! A God who believes in God!)"

4   Hans Christian Andersen on his travels around Europe met Victor Hugo and asked the great French writer for his autograph. Hugo, suspicious of the strange young Dane, worried that he might later write an acknowledgment of debt above the signature or make some other improper use of the autograph. To prevent this he squeezed the name "Victor Hugo" into one corner at the top of a sheet of paper.

5   Goethe was not among Hugo's favorite writers. "Goethe never wrote anything worth reading except *The Robbers*," he once declared. One of his listeners immediately pointed out that *The Robbers* was written by Schiller, not Goethe. Undaunted, Hugo continued, "And even that is Schiller's."

৪৽ ৽৪

HULL, Cordell (1871–1955), *US statesman; secretary of state (1933–44). He won the 1945 Nobel Peace Prize for his work in helping to found the United Nations.*

1   A biographer of Cordell Hull submitted his manuscript to his subject for approval. It was returned with just one correction; in a passage describing an incident during the Spanish–American War in which Cordell Hull had won all his company's money at poker, the word "company" was struck out and in Cordell Hull's own handwriting the word "regiment" had been written in.

৪৽ ৽৪

HUMBOLDT, Friedrich Heinrich Alexander, Baron von (1769–1859), *German naturalist, traveler, and statesman. He explored Central and South America and central Asia in the course of his studies; the Humboldt Current in the South Pacific and the Humboldt Glacier in Greenland were named for him. In Kosmos (1845–62) he put forward his views on the physical universe.*

1   In the course of conversation with a doctor friend in Paris, Humboldt once expressed a desire to dine with a lunatic. His friend, who specialized in mental disorders, was only too pleased to satisfy the naturalist's curiosity. On the appointed day, Humboldt found himself eating with two strangers. One conducted himself in a polite but aloof manner throughout the meal, saying nothing; the other, unkempt and eccentrically dressed, chattered continuously. Toward the end of the meal Humboldt whispered to his host, his eyes on this second stranger, "I like your lunatic, he amuses me." The doctor, following his friend's gaze, replied, "But it's the other one who's the lunatic. The man you're looking at is Monsieur Honoré de Balzac."

৪৽ ৽৪

HUME, David (1711–76), *Scottish philosopher and historian. His* Treatise of Human Nature *(1739–40) tackles major problems in human perception and existence. Some aspects of his philosophy still pose challenges to twentieth-century philosophers, in particular his explanation of cause and effect as "constant conjunction." While librarian of the Advocates' Library in Edinburgh, he wrote his best-selling* History of Great Britain *(1754–62).*

1   Hume, who enjoyed an annual income of £1,000 from his pensions and literary productions, was on all sides urged to continue his *History* and bring it up to date. "Gentlemen, you do me too much honor," said Hume, "but I have four reasons for not writing: I am too old, too fat, too lazy, and too rich."

2 Hume regularly attended church services conducted by a sternly orthodox minister. A friend once suggested to the skeptical philosopher that he was being inconsistent in going to listen to such a preacher. Hume answered, "I don't believe all he says, but *he* does, and once a week I like to hear a man who believes what he says."

3 Hume was visited by the poet Thomas Blacklock, who complained at great length about his misfortunes: blind and penniless, he no longer had the means to support his large family and did not know where to turn for help. Hume, in financial difficulties himself at that time, had just managed to secure, through the influence of a friend, a university appointment worth about forty pounds a year. Nevertheless, he was so moved by the poet's tale of woe that he offered him the only means of assistance within his power to give. Taking from his desk the grant for the university post, he handed it to his unfortunate friend and promised to have the name changed from Hume to Blacklock. This generous sacrifice almost certainly saved Blacklock and his family from destitution.

4 While Hume was living in Paris, some of the *philosophes* grew jealous of him and made fun of his stoutness. Once when he entered a room d'Alembert quoted from the beginning of St. John's Gospel: "*Et verbum caro factum est* [And the word was made flesh]."

"*Et verbum carum factum est* [And the word was made lovable]," riposted a lady admirer of Hume's.

5 At a supper party at Hume's shortly before his death, a guest complained of the spitefulness of the world. Hume contradicted him: "No, no, here am I who have written on all sorts of subjects calculated to excite hostility, moral, political, and religious, and yet I have no enemies, except, indeed, all the Whigs, all the Tories, and all the Christians."

❧ ❧

HUMES, John (1921–), *US statesman, ambassador to Austria.*

1 "Ambassador John Humes at the U.S. Embassy in Austria found himself in a difficult situation. He was the recipient of several boxes of Havana cigars. Since his country had no formal relations with Cuba, this gift could be embarrassing to an American diplomat. But he was resolute. He knew what had to be done. He gave his deputy chief of mission these instructions: 'Burn them . . . one by one . . . slowly.'"

❧ ❧

HUMPHREY, Hubert Horatio (1911–78), *US politician. He was US senator from Minnesota (1949–64) and vice president in the Lyndon B. Johnson administration (1964–68). Nominated as the Democratic presidential candidate in 1968, he was defeated by Richard Nixon.*

1 During the 1964 American presidential campaign Hubert Humphrey was the vice-presidential candidate on the Democratic ticket. It was a period of racial unrest and urban rioting, with much talk of "backlash" and "frontlash." The Republican candidate assailed Humphrey with a sarcastic reference to Humphrey's middle name, Horatio. Replied Humphrey: "In the name of charity I must warn him. The hidden middle-name vote — all those youngsters blessed by loving parents with a middle name they choose to convert into an initial — may rise against him. He should beware of the midlash."

2 During his term as vice president, Humphrey was invited to address a meeting of teachers in Washington. In the early part of his speech he spoke at some length about his own teaching experience. Feeling the need to account for this digression, Humphrey explained: "I mention my teaching background because, considering the precarious future of public office, I thought you might like to look me over."

❧ ❧

HUNDLEY, Rodney (1934–), *US basketball player, nicknamed "Hot Rod." He played six seasons of professional basketball in the late 1950s and early 1960s.*

1 Rod Hundley and Bob Leonard were notorious for their off-court activities when they were teammates on the Minneapolis Lakers.

Having missed a team plane flight after a night out, they were summoned to the offices of team owner Bob Short. Hundley was called in first. After observing that they had been warned for their misbehavior many times, Short told Hundley that he was being fined $1,000. (Hundley noted that he was making $10,000 a season at that time; so a player earning the $500,000 usual today would have to be fined $50,000 to match that fine. Relative to earnings, Hundley's fine was the largest ever.)

When Hundley left Short's office to call Leonard in, he found him worrying over how much money he could afford to pay without his wife's finding out. "How much?" he asked anxiously.

"A big one, baby, a big bill," replied Hundley.

"A hundred dollars?" asked Leonard.

"A hundred, hell. A thousand," Hundley told him. Tears came to Leonard's eyes. "It's a record," said Hundley consolingly.

Leonard brightened. "Let's go out and celebrate," he said.

2 Hundley roomed for a while with Elgin Baylor, one of the greatest scorers in the history of the National Basketball Association. One night in New York in 1971, Baylor set a league record by scoring seventy-one points in one game. That night Hundley scored two points. As they got into a taxi for the ride back to their hotel, he put an arm around Elgin and noted triumphantly, "What a night we had, buddy! Seventy-three points between us!"

3 Hundley picked up a lady at a bar and as they talked he realized that she was a prostitute. "How much do you get?" he asked.

"Twenty-five bucks," she replied.

"Too rich for my blood," said Hundley.

"How much do *you* get?" asked the woman, laughing.

"Twenty-five cents," he said.

"You're on," the woman replied.

After they had spent the night in a hotel bedroom, he awoke to find her gone. On the dresser she had left a shiny new quarter. ("I saved it as a souvenir for years," said Hundley.)

HUNTER, John (1728–93), *British physician. He was responsible for developing surgery*

as a branch of medicine, and was surgeon extraordinary to George III.

1 A sufferer from angina, Hunter found that his attacks were often brought on by anger. He declared, "My life is at the mercy of any scoundrel who chooses to put me in a passion." This proved prophetic: at a meeting of the board of St. George's Hospital, London, of which he was a member, he became involved in a heated argument with other board members, walked out of the meeting, and dropped dead in the next room.

HUSTON, John (1906–), *US motion picture director. Among his classic films are* The Maltese Falcon *(1941),* The Treasure of the Sierra Madre *(1948), and* The African Queen *(1951), all with Humphrey Bogart, and* The Misfits *(1960).*

1 (David Niven recalls the moment of Huston's call-up for military service during World War II.)

"The word came by phone when he was in the middle of directing Bogie in a scene in which the Japanese enemy had surrounded hero Bogart in a small building. His escape had been carefully rehearsed—who he shot, who he knifed and through which window he would jump, etc.

"Huston never said a word about the receipt of his 'call-up,' he just tripled the number of Japanese around the building, boarded it up with the hero inside and left for Europe. A hastily summoned take-over director found a note on the door: 'I'm in the Army—Bogie will know how to get out.'"

HUTCHINS, Robert Maynard (1899–1977), *US educator. In 1929 he became president of the University of Chicago, where he was responsible for many reforms. He was the author of* Education for Freedom *(1943), and founded the Center for the Study of Democratic Institutions at Santa Barbara, California (1959).*

1 When Hutchins was dean of Yale Law School, he had a brief conversation with William Howard Taft, then Chief Justice of the Supreme Court. "Well, Professor Hutchins," said Taft, "I suppose you teach your students that the judges are all fools."

"No, Mr. Chief Justice," replied Hutchins, "we let them find that out for themselves."

2   As president of the University of Chicago, Hutchins kept a little sign in his desk drawer, waiting for appropriate moments to display it to possible donors. It read: "WE WASH MONEY."

3   The eminent Greek scholar Professor Paul Shorey, meeting Hutchins on the campus at Chicago, remarked, "I understand that you and Mr. Adler are reading and discussing great books with the freshmen at the rate of one a week."

"That's right," replied Hutchins.

"I don't see how you can do that," said Shorey. "When I was a senior at Harvard it took us a whole year to study the *Divine Comedy.*"

"The difference, Professor Shorey," said Hutchins, "is that our students are bright."

4   After his retirement from the University of Chicago, Hutchins was asked by an acquaintance if communism was still being taught at the university. "Yes," replied Hutchins, "and cancer at the medical school."

5   When Hutchins was head of the Ford Foundation in the 1950s, one of his friends, the journalist Milton Mayer, asked for a grant of $250 for coal for the freezing students of Professor Carl Friedrich von Weizsäcker, nuclear physicist and philosopher of science at Göttingen University. Hutchins replied, "There is no way for the Ford Foundation to give anyone $250. Tell Carl Friedrich to apply for $250,000." He later quietly gave von Weizsäcker his own check for $250.

৯৯ ৶৪

HUXLEY, Aldous Leonard (1894–1963), *British writer, grandson of Thomas Henry Huxley. He spent much of his life outside England, living in California from 1937 to his death. He wrote successful satirical novels —* Antic Hay (1923) *and* Point Counter Point (1928) *among them — short stories, and essays, and a nightmare Utopia,* Brave New World (1932). *In* The Doors of Perception (1954) *and* Heaven and Hell (1956) *he recorded his experiments with psychedelic drugs.*

1   As a child Aldous Huxley was precocious and thoughtful. A member of the family once asked him (he was about four) what he was thinking about. "Skin," replied Aldous.

2   Aldous Huxley's brother, Julian, the eminent zoologist, talking on one occasion about genes, used the phrase "the aristocracy of genes."

"You mean blue genes?" queried Aldous.

3   Huxley's cousin commiserated with him on his near-blindness. "But it is not without compensations," replied Huxley. "Being able to read Braille, I can read in bed with the book beneath the blankets. So my hands are kept warm on even the coldest nights."

4   (Aldous Huxley seems to have developed an individual approach to visiting the sick, which, from the description Osbert Sitwell gave of Huxley's visits to him in the hospital, can hardly have failed to distract the sufferer from his ailments.)

"Versed in every modern theory of science, politics, painting, literature, and psychology, he was qualified by his disposition to deal in ideas and play with them. Nor would gossip or any matter of the day be beneath his notice: though even these lesser things would be treated as by a philosopher, with detachment and an utter want of prejudice. But he preferred to discourse on more erudite and impersonal scandals, such as the incestuous mating of melons, the elaborate love-making of lepidoptera, or the curious amorous habits of cuttle-fish. He would speak with obvious enjoyment, in a voice of great charm, unhurried, clear, without being loud, and utterly indifferent to any sensation he was making. Thus the most surprising statements would hover languidly in air heavy with hospital disinfectants. 'From his usual conduct,' I remember his announcing on one occasion, 'one must presume that every octopus has read Ovid on Love.'"

5   Aldous Huxley's fame rested largely upon his novels, such as *Brave New World,* in which he examined humanity's choice between a fully human life and the mechanized servitude of the anthill. In his sixties he admitted, "It is a bit

embarrassing to have been concerned with the human problem all one's life and find at the end that one has no more to offer by way of advice than 'Try to be a little kinder.' "

๛

HUXLEY, Sir Julian (1887–1975), *British zoologist, brother of Aldous Huxley. He was for many years associated with schemes to improve and enlarge the London Zoo. In 1946 he was appointed the first director of UNESCO.*

1 Julian Huxley was a difficult small boy, but his tantrums did not harm him in the opinion of his famous grandfather. "I like the way he looks you straight in the face and disobeys you."

2 Huxley was presiding over a UNESCO session in Mexico City. The debate grew long and tedious and all the delegates were slumped at their desks under their headphones. Huxley beckoned to a messenger and handed him a brief note addressed to a member of the French delegation: "Please come here. I have something important to ask you." The Frenchman left his place, walked around the chamber, and approached Huxley. "When I was driving here this morning, do you know what I saw?" said Huxley to him. "Of all things, a hoopoe. Did you see it too?"

๛

HUXLEY, Thomas Henry (1825–95), *British biologist, philosopher, and paleontologist. Known as "Darwin's bulldog," he staunchly defended his friend Charles Darwin in the controversy surrounding the theory of evolution. Delighting in polemic, in later years he attacked religious dogma, coining and putting into circulation the term "agnostic" to describe his own position.*

1 The controversy between the supporters of Darwin and the Church came into the open at a famous meeting in Oxford in June 1860. No one took down what was said, so accounts are based on recollections of the participants as pieced together afterward. Samuel Wilberforce, bishop of Oxford and professor of mathematics, was on the platform to support the religious viewpoint; Huxley was the spokesman for the Darwinian side. As Wilberforce was expected to smash the scientific forces, the room was packed to capacity. His speech was a savage invective against Darwin and Huxley; at the end he asked Huxley, "If anyone were to be willing to trace his descent through an ape as his *grandfather,* would he be willing to trace his descent similarly on the side of his *grandmother?*" The audience greeted this with rapturous applause.

Although Huxley had come to the meeting with the idea of averting a head-on clash between religion and science, Wilberforce's arrogance and the inadequacy of his answer to the Darwinian position stung Huxley into fighting back. "A man has no reason to be ashamed of having an ape for his grandfather," he said. "If there were an ancestor whom I should feel shame in recalling, it would rather be a man who, not content with an equivocal success in his own sphere of activity, plunges into scientific questions with which he has no real acquaintance."

At this slur on the clergy bedlam broke out in the lecture room and ladies fainted from shock. From that moment the relationship of science to religion would never again be the same.

2 Huxley was late setting off to give a lecture. He jumped into a cab, crying, "Top speed!" The cabman whipped up his horse and they set off as fast as the horse could go. A thought then dawned on Huxley; sticking his head out of the window, he called to the cabman, "Hey, do you know where I want to go?"

"No, your honor," shouted back the cabman, "but I'm driving as fast as I can!"

๛

HUYSMANS, Joris Karl (1848–1907), *French novelist. His novels, such as En Ménage (1881) and À Rebours (1884), created much controversy. He also wrote percipiently of art and architecture.*

1 Léon Bloy was at one time friendly with Huysmans, but, an irascible man, he later wrote a savage article about him. Nevertheless, Bloy's friends, arranging a subscription list for one of his books, did not hesitate to apply to Huysmans first. Huysmans at once generously put his name down for fifty francs. The entire sum collected, together with the list of subscribers' names, was taken to Bloy, who looked at it and exploded with fury. "What's wrong with you, Bloy?" his friends asked. "Huysmans was not only the first to sign, but also the most generous."

"The bastard! He set a maximum," raged Bloy.

“❧

HYDE, Lady Catherine (1700–77), *British noblewoman who became Duchess of Queensberry by her marriage (1720) to Charles Douglas, the third duke. A celebrated beauty, she was the friend and ally of Gay, Congreve, Pope, Thomson, and other literary figures.*

1 She kept her beauty into her seventies, and her friend Horace Walpole drank her health, wishing that she might live long enough even to grow ugly. "I hope then that you will keep your taste for antiquities," the duchess replied.

“❧

HYDE, William (*dates unknown*), *English painter, who customarily depicted placid, somber landscapes in line and wash drawings.*

1 William Hyde often told the tale of an odd literary coincidence that happened to him when he came to live in Westminster. On the evening of his very first day in London, returning to his new lodgings, he found the slumped form of a stranger on his step. Noting that the man was evidently ill, and assuming him to be a fellow lodger, Hyde summoned the maid to help him. "Why," exclaimed the woman with some concern on seeing the sick man, "it's Dr. Jekyll. He lives here, poor gentleman."

“❧

HYDE-WHITE, Wilfrid (1903–), *English actor who enjoyed a long and happy stage and screen career in both England and the United States. He appeared in numerous films, notably as Colonel Pickering in* My Fair Lady *(1964).*

1 Hyde-White was a well-known horse-fancier. During his long career as a racehorse owner he made an unfortunate appearance in the Bankruptcy Court. In the course of his examination the somewhat exasperated official receiver remarked, "Mr. Hyde-White, if you cannot tell us how you spent such a large sum in so short a time, perhaps you could tell us what will win the Gold Cup at Ascot this afternoon, since I understand you would already like to be on your way?"

"Of course, dear fellow," Hyde-White replied and went on to name the horse that later turned out to be the winner. "But only have a small bet," he added. "We don't want to have to change places, do we?"

“❧

HYLAN, John F. (1868–1936), *US lawyer and politician, mayor of New York (1918–25).*

1 "Honest John" Hylan was, if not the worst, surely one of the least bright mayors New York City has ever had. In 1922, during his administration, he solemnly swore to the citizenry that the much-publicized crime wave did not exist. He went on to assert, "The police are fully able to meet and compete with the criminals."

“❧

HYRTL, Joseph (1810–94), *Austrian anatomist, who spent most of his life as professor of medicine at Vienna.*

1 Hyrtl was examining a candidate for the medical degree who seemed more than ordinarily nervous. "What can you tell me about the function of the spleen?" was the first question. The candidate wiped his forehead. "Herr Professor, I did know exactly what it was, I knew it just a minute ago, but now I've forgotten," he stammered.

"Miserable creature," cried Hyrtl. "You're the only man in the whole world who knows anything about the function of the spleen — and now you've forgotten it!"

{An anecdote also told of other similar mysteries and other people.}

IBN SAUD (?1880–1953), *first king of Saudi Arabia (1932–53). In 1891 Ibn Saud's father was exiled from Riyadh in Arabia. It was Ibn Saud who played a crucial role in the reconquest of the city (1900). From his base at Riyadh he consolidated his power and drove back the Turks from Arabian territory, a process accelerated by Saudi participation in World War I. In 1932 the lands under Ibn Saud's sway became the kingdom of Saudi Arabia.*

1 A woman came to Ibn Saud, asking a death sentence for the man who had killed her husband. The man had been in a palm tree gathering dates when he had slipped and fallen upon her husband, fatally injuring him. Ibn Saud inquired: Was the fall intentional? Were the two men enemies? The widow knew neither the man nor why he fell, but, according to the law, she demanded the blood price due her. "In what form will you have the compensation?" Ibn Saud asked. The widow demanded the head of the guilty party. Ibn Saud tried to dissuade her, pointing out that she needed money and that exaction of a life for a life would profit neither her nor her children. But the widow, set on vengeance, would not listen.

Ibn Saud said, "It is your right to exact compensation, and it is also your right to ask for this man's life. But it is my right to decree how he shall die. You shall take this man with you immediately and he shall be tied to the foot of a palm tree and then you yourself shall climb to the top of the tree and cast yourself down upon him from that height. In that way you will take his life as he took your husband's." There was a pause. "Or perhaps," Ibn Saud added, "you would prefer after all to take the blood money?" The widow took the money.

2 Ibn Saud, advanced in years, visited the town of Hofuf to bathe in its hot springs. During the cure one of the men of Hofuf presented the king with a handsome gray horse. Ibn Saud, delighted with the gift, called for the ledger in which he personally recorded the details of the presents that he bestowed upon visitors and well-wishers. Against the name of the donor of the horse he wrote "300 riyals," a sum greatly in excess of the real worth of the beast. As he was writing, the nib of his pen sputtered and a shower of little ink blobs scattered across the page, turning "300 riyals" into "300,000 riyals" (the Arabic sign for zero is a dot, like a period, rather than an open 0). The vizier respectfully drew his lord's attention to the spattered page. "I see my pen has clearly stated 300,000," said Ibn Saud, "so that is what you must pay. My hand wrote it, and I cannot have anyone say that my hand is more generous than my heart."

ꕥ ꕥ

IBRAHIM PASHA (1789–1848), *Egyptian general. He subdued the Wahhabi movement in Arabia (1816–19), campaigned in Greece against the revolutionaries there (1824–28), and conquered the Turks in Syria (1831–33).*

1 The sultan at Constantinople commanded his viceroy in Egypt, Muhammad Ali, to punish the Wahhabis, who had defied his authority. Although he had some success, Muhammad Ali found that he could make no impression upon the heartland of Wahhabi power, the area called Nejd, where the strength of these desert fighters was greatest.

One day Muhammad Ali was sitting in his apartments with his generals, each one contending that if *he* were given command of the armies in Arabia, he would conquer Nejd with no difficulty. Muhammad Ali placed an apple in the center of a large carpet and said, "The task of conquering Nejd is a difficult one. It is like seizing this apple without setting foot on the carpet. The man who is able to perform such a thing is the man capable of capturing Nejd." The generals were puzzled, but Muhammad Ali's son, Ibrahim Pasha, asked permission to attempt it. This was granted. The young man went to one side of the carpet and began to roll it up. When the carpet was half rolled up, he reached out and grasped the apple with ease. His father appointed him commander of the Egyptian forces in Arabia, and after a bloody two-year campaign Ibrahim Pasha captured Nejd and completely crushed Wahhabi power.

෨ ෴

IBSEN, Henrik (1828–1906), *Norwegian playwright. He achieved international fame with such dramas as* Brand *(1866),* Peer Gynt *(1867),* A Doll's House *(1879), and* An Enemy of the People *(1882). The social issues in the last two (women's emancipation and corruption of public officers) caused considerable controversy; later plays, such as* Hedda Gabler *(1890), concentrate on psychological studies of individuals.*

1   Two middle-class ladies were discussing a revival of *A Doll's House,* which they had recently seen. "I just loved it," said the first. "Ibsen is so timeless, isn't he?"

"I'm not so sure," said the second lady doubtfully. "It's a good deal easier to borrow money these days."

2   In Rome one day, Ibsen noticed a number of people gathered around a large red poster. Intrigued, he reached for his spectacles, only to find that he had left them in his hotel room. "Signore," he said, turning to the man beside him, "could you please tell me what those signs say? I've forgotten my glasses."

"Sorry, signore," replied the Italian in a confidential whisper, "I don't know how to read either."

3   After suffering a stroke in 1900, Ibsen was forced to abandon his writing and spent the remaining six years of his life as a helpless invalid. One day he heard his nurse suggest that he was feeling a little better. "On the contrary!" he snapped, and promptly died.

෨ ෴

IKKU, Jippensha (died 1831), *Japanese writer.*

1   Shortly before his death Ikku entrusted a number of small packages to his disciples, asking that they be placed unopened upon his funeral pyre. When the prayers had been said, the disciples reverently placed the packets around the body of their deceased master, and the pyre was then set alight. At that point the funeral proceedings broke up in disorder: Ikku's packages contained firecrackers.

෨ ෴

INCHBALD, Elizabeth (1753–1821), *English playwright and novelist best known for her prose romance* A Simple Story *(1791).*

1   Mrs. Inchbald was discussing her latest play with a theatrical manager when the man suddenly tried to make violent love to her. Finding her remonstrances unheeded, she seized him by the little plait that gentlemen then wore at the

---

"Prince Michael Golitsyn of Russia had taken an Italian Catholic wife, to the intense displeasure of Czarina Anna Ivanovna. Although the prince's bride soon died, the czarina remained bent on punishing him. She had a vendetta against the prince and his family, who opposed her rule; she also had a vicious sense of humor. She ordered an ice palace built in St. Petersburg in the winter of 1739, completely outfitted with ice furnishings —dishes, toilets, tables, even a four-poster ice bed. When all was finished, she selected the ugliest woman she could find to be the prince's second bride and forced the couple to parade about town on an elephant before the wedding. Accompanying them was a procession of freaks.

"The procession made its way to the ice palace, where 'the Bridal Pair of Fools' were stripped and sent to their icy nuptial chamber. Then all exits were sealed. The couple survived the frigid night, and nine months later, the prince's wife gave birth to twins."

— Irving Wallace,
David Wallechinsky,
and Amy Wallace, "Significa"

back of their coiffures, and with the other hand rang the bell until help arrived. Speaking of this incident afterward, she said, in her habitual stammer, "How f-f-ortunate for me he did not w-w-ear a w-w-ig."

§~ ~§

INGE, William Ralph (1860–1954), *British clergyman; dean of St. Paul's (1911–35), whose pessimism earned him the sobriquet of "the gloomy dean." He was a contributor to the* Evening Standard *for many years.*

1 One of the gloomy dean's articles provoked the wrath of a lady who wrote to him: "I am praying nightly for your death. It may interest you to know that in two other cases I have had great success." Inge was delighted with this missive.

§~ ~§

INGERSOLL, Robert Green (1833–99), *US lawyer and orator.*

1 Ingersoll was famous as a free-thinker and for his attacks on the Bible. His extensive library reflected his views and interests. A reporter once asked him if he would mind telling him how much his library had cost him. Ingersoll looked over the rows of shelves for a moment and then said, "These books cost me the governorship of Illinois, and maybe the presidency of the United States as well."

§~ ~§

INGYO (mid-5th century AD), *Japanese emperor.*

1 The administration was much bothered during Ingyo's reign by families who laid claim to nobility to which they were not entitled. In the end Ingyo announced that it had been revealed to him that he could separate those with true claims from the pretenders by having all claimants immerse their arms in boiling water; only those with genuine claims would suffer no ill effects. This had the result of drastically reducing the number who turned up on the day appointed for the trial, as only those with legitimate claims saw fit to appear.

IPHICRATES (died 353 BC), *Athenian general. During the Corinthian war (394–387 BC) he used peltasts (lightly armed troops) to great effect against the Spartans. He is credited with having equipped the peltasts with light shields and long javelins to increase their mobility.*

1 Harmodius and Aristogiton were greatly revered in Athens for their attack on the tyrant Hippias in 514 BC. As a result, their descendants were granted certain privileges. A descendant of Harmodius scoffed at Iphicrates for being the son of a shoemaker. The general replied, "The difference between us is that my family begins with me, whereas yours ends with you."
{This rejoinder has been borrowed by others; *see* ALEXANDER DUMAS *père* 3.}

§~ ~§

IRVING, Sir Henry (1838–1905), *British actor, manager of the Lyceum Theatre in London (1878–1902). Famed for his Shakespearean interpretations, he was the first actor to receive a knighthood (1895).*

1 In London's Garrick Club, the haunt of actors, a new member, anxious to establish himself on a familiar footing with the great Irving, approached him, greeted him casually, and launched into an anecdote about having been stopped in the street by a total stranger who had said, "God bless me, is that you?" Irving said: "And — er — was it?"

§~ ~§

ISABEY, Jean-Baptiste (1767–1855), *French painter best known for his miniature portraits.*

1 Isabey visited Vienna in 1815 to make a pictorial record of the participants in the Congress. The great French diplomat Talleyrand indicated that he expected to have the place of honor at the center of the picture. A similar stipulation was made by the Duke of Wellington. Isabey solved the difficulty with masterly diplomacy. He showed the Duke of Wellington entering the hall, with every eye turned toward him, and Talleyrand sitting in an armchair at the center of the picture.
Compare GIORGIONE 1.

ಶ J ಶ

JACKSON, Andrew (1767–1845), *US states-man, 7th president of the United States (1829–37). Jackson first won fame as a military hero when he defended New Orleans against the British during the War of 1812. "Old Hickory," as he was called, based his political life on popular support and states' rights. His distribution to local banks of federal deposits in the Bank of the United States caused serious financial crises.*

1 In 1791 Jackson married his dearly loved Rachel Donelson Robards in the belief that her first husband had deserted and divorced her. A legitimate divorce was eventually obtained and the Jacksons remarried, but the affair caused much scandal. Jackson was touchy about his wife's reputation, and when a certain Charles Dickinson made an insulting allusion to Rachel, Jackson immediately challenged him to a duel. The knowledge that Dickinson was a crack pistol shot did not deflect him from his defense of his wife's name.

Dickinson took aim quickly and fired, but the impact of his bullet was blunted by the loose coat Jackson was wearing and it merely broke one of his ribs. Jackson then took very slow and deliberate aim and shot Dickinson dead. He later said, "I intended to kill him. I would have stood up long enough to kill him if he had put a bullet in my brain."

2 While Jackson was presiding judge at a small town in Tennessee in 1798, a notorious badman called Russell Bean created a disturbance outside the courthouse. The sheriff was unable to arrest him single-handed. Nor could he assemble a posse, as no one wanted to tackle the heavily armed Bean, who was swearing to shoot the first person to come within ten feet of him. Finally, Jackson took his pistols and sought out Bean himself. Making his way through the crowd, he walked coolly up to the

troublemaker, pistols in hand, and commanded, "Surrender this instant, or I'll blow you through!" To everyone's amazement, Bean eyed Jackson for a moment, then meekly allowed himself to be led away. Asked later why he had allowed himself to be cowed by Jackson, Bean answered, "When he came up I looked him in the eye, and I saw shoot, and there wasn't any shoot in nary other eye in the crowd; and so I says to myself, says I, hoss, it's about time to sing small, and so I did."

3 When the British admiral Sir Alexander Cochrane was about to attack New Orleans, he boasted that he would eat his Christmas dinner in the town. The remark was reported to Jackson, who said, "It may be so, but I shall have the honor of presiding at that dinner."

4 As his artillery pounded the British lines at the battle of New Orleans, Jackson stood beside the gunners to watch the effect of their fire. Not entirely satisfied, he gave the order, "Elevate them guns a little lower."

5 Scandal broke out during Jackson's first administration because of his friendship with Peggy Eaton, the attractive wife of Jackson's secretary of war. This lady had a rather dubious background, and John Eaton's marriage to her did not restore her reputation; all the Washington ladies boycotted receptions at which she was present and clergymen denounced her in public. Jackson called two of the latter into a cabinet meeting to discuss the question. The ministers admitted that there was no evidence of improper behavior on the part of John Eaton. "Nor Mrs. Eaton, either!" said the angry president. "I would prefer not to venture an opinion on that point," replied the clergyman. "She's as chaste as a virgin!" snapped Jackson. When this last remark was repeated to

Daniel Webster, he paraphrased the line from Shakespeare's *Antony and Cleopatra:* "Age cannot wither her, nor custom stale her infinite virginity."

6 Thomas Hart Benton became an enthusiastic Jackson supporter, but in 1813 they had had a fight that left one of Benton's bullets lodged in Jackson's left arm. There it remained for many years, until in 1832 a surgeon removed it. It was suggested that the bullet be returned to Benton as it was his property. Benton thanked Jackson, who by now was his friend, but declined the offer, saying that twenty years' possession of the bullet had made it Jackson's property. It was pointed out that it was only nineteen years since the duel. Benton replied, "In consideration of the extra care he has taken of it — kept it about his person and so on — I'll waive the odd year."

7 The attractive niece of the British minister said to President Jackson, "Mr. President, you and General Washington enjoy a unique fame: no one else has ever defeated my countrymen."

"That, my dear, is because we are both descended from your countrywomen," said the president.

ॐ ॐ

JACKSON, Joe (1887–1951), *US baseball player.*

1 Some reporters and a group of small boys were waiting in the courthouse corridor when Jackson emerged after giving testimony in the "Black Sox Scandal" case, in which Jackson and other White Sox players were accused of accepting bribes to throw the World Series. One of the boys came forward and asked, "It ain't true, is it, Joe?" to which the player replied, "Yes, I'm afraid it is."

{The boy's question was later rephrased as the famous "Say it ain't so, Joe."}

ॐ ॐ

JACKSON, Thomas Jonathan ["Stonewall"] (1824–63), *American Confederate general.*

1 At the first battle of Bull Run in 1861 the fierceness of the Union onslaught caused some confusion in the Confederate ranks. General Barnard Bee, commanding a battalion adjacent

to Jackson's, rode up to him. "General, they are beating us back," he cried.

"Give them the bayonet," shouted Jackson. Heartened by this, Bee galloped back to his own men and encouraged them: "There is Jackson standing like a stone wall! Rally behind the Virginians!" The Confederates rallied and beat off the enemy, and the nickname "Stonewall" was permanently attached to Jackson.

{General Bee himself was later killed in battle.}

2 Jackson blamed the failure of an attempt to destroy the canal leading to Washington on the fact that the raid had taken place on a Sunday. In order not to break the Sabbath a second time, he planned the next attempt for early Monday morning, and ordered that the necessary gunpowder be obtained on Saturday. Unfortunately the quartermaster was unable to find a suitable supply of powder that day and was obliged to procure it on Sunday. Jackson learned of this and sent for more powder first thing on Monday morning. He commanded the colonel in charge of the expedition, "I desire that you will see that the powder which is used for this expedition is not the powder that was procured on Sunday."

3 General Ewell was so impressed by the conspicuous gallantry of a certain Federal cavalry officer in rallying his troops on the field of battle that he ordered his soldiers not to shoot at the man. Jackson later reprimanded Ewell for this quixotic action, remarking shrewdly, "Shoot the brave officers and the cowards will run away and take their men with them!"

4 Jackson had strictly forbidden his men to ride into the fields alongside the roads so as not to damage the crops. Returning to his camp near Richmond one day, Jackson became impatient with the slow progress he was making along a road cluttered with wagon trains and led his men through a nearby field of oats. The farmer, witnessing this blatant violation of well-publicized orders, rushed over and blocked Jackson's path. Purple with rage, he threatened to report the miscreant to Stonewall Jackson himself and have all his men arrested. With some embarrassment the general admitted that *he* was Stonewall Jackson. The farmer's manner changed instantly. With tears in his eyes and waving his bandanna around his

head, he cried, "Hurrah for Stonewall Jackson! By God, general, please do me the honor to ride all over my damned old oats!"

5   An enemy sergeant had been captured and was taken to Jackson's tent for further questioning. While waiting for the general to arrive, the prisoner began to stroke the rump of Jackson's horse and run his finger through the tail in an absentminded manner. One of Jackson's staff noticed that he was actually pulling a few hairs out of the tail every time he did this and ordered him to stop. At this point Jackson arrived, and, seeing the prisoner's hand full of horsehair, asked for an explanation. The man replied, respect and admiration in his voice, that every hair from the general's horse would be worth a dollar in New York. Jackson was so moved by this tribute to his renown that he sent the prisoner away without further interrogation, still clutching his handful of horsehair.

6   General J. E. B. Stuart arrived at Jackson's camp late one night. Everyone was asleep, and Stuart lay down beside Jackson's bed to get some rest. It was a cold night. In his sleep Stuart gradually began to pull Jackson's blankets over himself and unconsciously slipped in between the sheets. When he awoke in the early morning, he was astonished to find himself in Jackson's bed, still fully clothed, and got out as quickly as possible. Emerging from the tent some time later, he was greeted by Jackson with the words: "General Stuart, I'm always glad to see you here. You might select better hours sometimes, but I'm always glad to have you. But, general, you must not get into my bed with your boots and spurs on and ride me around like a cavalry horse all night!"

7   After a brilliantly successful maneuver Jackson outflanked a greatly superior number of Union troops at Chancellorsville, Virginia. On May 2, 1863, as dusk was falling, the Federals began to flee and Jackson rode out to organize the pursuit. Some of his own men, not recognizing their general in the twilight, shot and wounded him so badly that he lost his left arm. Pneumonia set in and Jackson died. His last words were: "Let us cross over the river and sit under the shade of the trees."

❧ ⚬

JACOBI, Karl Gustav Jacob (1804–51), *German mathematician. Professor of mathematics at Königsberg (1827–42), he was acclaimed as one of the greatest algorists of all time.*

1   Jacobi's brother, M. H. Jacobi, had a prodigious contemporary reputation as the founder of the fashionable "science" of galvanoplasty. The professor of mathematics was constantly being mistaken for M. H. Jacobi or even congratulated on having such a famous sibling. Conscious of the lasting value of his own work, K.G.J. found this tiresome. When a lady complimented him on having such a distinguished brother, he retorted, "Pardon me, madame, but *I* am my brother."

❧ ⚬

JAMES I (1566–1625), *king of England and Ireland (1603–25) and, as James VI, king of Scotland (1567–1625). The son of the luckless Mary, Queen of Scots, James succeeded to the throne as an infant at his mother's deposition, but for many years was under the control of various warring factions in Scotland. Elizabeth I of England made him her heir and he united the hitherto separate thrones.*

1   Shortly after ascending the throne of England, James was attending the hearing of a court case. The counsel for the plaintiff spoke so eloquently that when he had finished, James said, "'Tis a clear case," and made as if to leave the court. His advisers insisted that he stay and hear the other side, which the king with a bad grace agreed to do. The counsel for the defendant also spoke very eloquently. When he had finished, James jumped to his feet, crying out, "They are all rogues alike," and left the courtroom.

2   A preacher as renowned for his fearless attacks on personalities and abuses as James was for his irresolution was invited to preach before the king. He entered the pulpit and gave as his text: "James One, Six. 'But let him ask in faith, nothing wavering. For he that wavereth is like a wave of the sea, driven with the wind and tossed.'"
   "God's faith!" exclaimed the monarch. "He's at me already."

3   A young girl was presented to James I as a prodigy. Impressed by her proficiency in Latin,

Greek, and Hebrew, the king was not without reservation. "These are rare attainments for a damsel," he remarked, "but pray tell me, can she spin?"

ৡৈ এৡ

JAMES, Henry (1843–1916), *US novelist and critic. After a visit to Paris in 1875, which profoundly influenced him, James lived mainly in England. His novels and shorter works of fiction are characterized by their intricate style and elaborate psychological explorations. The encounter between the values of Americans and European culture is a theme developed in such novels as* Portrait of a Lady *(1881),* The Wings of the Dove *(1902),* The Ambassadors *(1903), and* The Golden Bowl *(1904). The prefaces to his novels are subtle and influential analyses of the craft of the novelist.*

1 (According to David Cecil:)
"Henry James was all that Max [Beerbohm] liked a great man to be: majestic, benignant and slightly comical. . . . Henry James, on his side, took to Max. He liked courteous, elegant, intelligent young men. He treated Max on flatteringly equal terms. Once, at a wedding reception, a woman friend saw the two standing together. 'How terribly distinguished you look,' she said. 'We *are* distinguished,' Henry James replied. 'But you need not look so terribly so,' said the friend. 'We are shameless, shameless!' said Henry James."

2 Though invitations to the literary parties of Sir Edmund Gosse were eagerly sought by aspiring writers, the parties themselves were often somewhat uncomfortable occasions. At one party, crushed against the wall in the overcrowded room, Henry James was among those forced to watch a rather dreary puppet show. After a time he groaned, "An interesting example of economy. Economy of means and . . . economy of effect."

3 When James suffered his first stroke, he thought he was dying. He told a friend that the thought had come into his mind: "So it has come at last — the Distinguished Thing." He lived for a further three months.

4 After James's stroke the literary establishment rallied around and recommended him for the Order of Merit. When the honor was an-nounced, Sir Edmund Gosse went to his bedside to deliver the news. James paid him no attention, apparently not even taking in the honor that was being paid him, but after Gosse had left, the invalid called out, "Nurse, take away the candle and spare my blushes."

ৡৈ এৡ

JAMES, Jesse (1847–82), *US train- and bank-robber. The feats of the James-Younger gang, under Jesse's leadership, are part of the legendry of the West.*

1 On one occasion Jesse James and his gang sought food and rest at a lonely farmhouse. The woman there gave them what food she could and apologized for the poor hospitality. A widow and deeply in debt, she was even then waiting for the debt collector to visit her to demand $1,400, which she could not possibly afford to pay. Jesse James had the spoils of one of his bank raids with him. He gave the astonished woman enough money to pay off her debt, telling her to be sure to get a receipt from the debt collector. Then he and his gang withdrew to watch the road leading to the farmhouse. Along came the debt collector, looking very grim. A short while later he emerged from the farm, looking altogether more pleased with himself. Jesse James and his men stopped him, recovered their $1,400, and rode off.

2 The St. Louis–Texas express train was robbed by Jesse James's gang on January 31, 1874. As they boarded the train, one of the gang members handed the conductor an envelope. It contained the following press release, which appeared in the newspapers the next day: "THE MOST DARING TRAIN ROBBERY ON RECORD! The southbound train of the Iron Mountain Railroad was stopped here this evening by five heavily armed men and robbed of — — dollars. The robbers arrived at the station a few minutes before the arrival of the train, arrested the agent, put him under guard and then threw the train on the switch. The robbers were all large men, all being slightly under six feet. After robbing the train they started in a southerly direction. They were all mounted on handsome horses. P.S. There is a hell of an excitement in this part of the country."
{There were actually ten men in the gang and they headed westerly, not southerly, after the robbery.}

> In England in the years following World War I, the universal obsession was dancing—as Thomas Beecham once described it, "a funereal assemblage of creatures, tightly packed together in an exiguous space, bumping and banging into one another, hardly moving the while and all looking as if they were practicing some painful penitential exercise." Beecham in turn related a French diplomat's comment on the phenomenon, *"Les visages sont si tristes, mais les derrières sont si gais."*
>
> —Thomas Beecham, *A Mingled Chime*

JAMES, William (1842–1910), *US philosopher and psychologist, the brother of Henry James. He taught successively comparative anatomy, philosophy, and psychology at Harvard. His most influential books were* The Varieties of Religious Experience *(1902) and* Pragmatism *(1907).*

1   Josiah Royce, who succeeded James in the Harvard chair of philosophy, was among a group of philosophers who were close personal friends of James, even though they might disagree on philosophical matters. On one occasion Royce was standing in for James at a lecture, using the latter's copies of texts for reference. He picked up one of his own works, opened it at a page marked by James, was about to read from it, then paused. After a long look at the passage, he glanced up at the class, smiled, and said, "Gentlemen, the marginal note says 'Damn fool!'"

2   At Radcliffe, Gertrude Stein was a favorite pupil of William James. Confronted with an exam paper the day after a session of opera-going and parties, she wrote on her paper, "Dear Professor James, I am so sorry but I do not feel a bit like writing an examination paper on philosophy today." James wrote back, "Dear Miss Stein, I understand perfectly. I often feel like that myself."

3   James was walking along a Cambridge, Massachusetts, street accompanied by a pair of his students, a boy and a girl. A large, imposing figure, white-bearded, swinging his cane, talking to himself, oblivious to the others, approached them. Remarked the girl: "Whoever he is, he's the epitome of the absentminded professor." "What you really mean," said James, "is that he is present-minded somewhere else."

4   Professor James was once asked by a young writer what his views were about the use of dictation in writing. "Never dictate any of your creative work," the professor answered. "Now let me tell you, I have a brother [Henry James] who used to be a pretty good novelist. But of late he has taken to dictating his stuff, and it has ruined his style. I can't read him anymore!"

❧ ❦

JARRY, Alfred (1873–1907), *French surrealist writer. His* Ubu Roi *(1896) caused a scandale with its satire of bourgeois conventions. Jarry is regarded as the forerunner of the Theater of the Absurd.*

1   Jarry demonstrated his eccentricity one day in a Paris restaurant. Wishing to communicate with a woman fellow diner who was engaged in staring contemplatively at her reflection in a mirror on the wall, Jarry drew out a pistol and shot at the mirror. In the stunned silence that followed Jarry repocketed the pistol and smiled engagingly. "Now that the mirror is gone," he said to the lady, "can we talk to each other?"

2   Another time Jarry fired his pistol into a hedge. From behind it appeared a furious woman shouting, "My child is playing here. You might have killed him!"
"Madame, I would have given you another!" responded Jarry gallantly.

3   Jarry was a small man, only five feet tall. In his room on the mantel he displayed an enormous stone phallus. A lady visitor inquired if this were a cast. Jarry at once rapped out, "No, madame, it is a re-duc-tion."

❧ ❦

JEFFERSON, Joseph (1829–1905), *US actor. So successfully did he create the role of Rip van Winkle in a dramatized version of Washington Irving's story that after 1859 he was always identified with the part.*

1 (Jefferson once told this story to a friend:)
"'I was coming down the elevator of the Stock Exchange building, and at one of the intermediate floors a man whose face I knew as well as I know yours got in. He greeted me very warmly at once, said it was a number of years since we had met, and was very gracious and friendly, but I couldn't place him for the life of me. I asked him as a sort of feeler how he happened to be in New York, and he answered, with a touch of surprise, that he had lived there for several years. Finally, I told him in an apologetic way that I couldn't recall his name. He looked at me for a moment and then he said very quietly that his name was U. S. Grant.'
'What did you do, Joe?' his friend asked.
'Do?' he replied, with a characteristic smile. 'Why, I got out at the next floor for fear I'd ask him if he had ever been in the war.'"

ॐ ॐ

JEFFERSON, Thomas (1743–1826), *US statesman, chief author of the Declaration of Independence (1776), and 3d president of the United States (1801–09). A lawyer by training, Jefferson began his political career in the Virginian House of Burgesses (1769), and went on to serve as governor of Virginia (1779–81), minister to France (1785–89), secretary of state (1789–93), and vice president (1797–1801) under John Adams. As president, Jefferson insisted on what he called "Republican simplicity" in institutions and manners. His greatest achievement was probably the Louisiana Purchase (1803), by which the United States gained extensive territories ceded to France by Spain. In his retirement, he founded the University of Virginia. Jefferson was a man of wide interests and many talents, a scholar, musician, and architect. See JOHN F. KENNEDY 15 for a notable tribute.*

1 While Jefferson and his mother were away from home, the house caught fire and was destroyed with all its contents. One of their slaves came to report the bad news. "Not one of my books saved?" cried Jefferson in distress. The slave shook his head: "No, master — but we saved the fiddle."

2 The young widow Martha Skelton, whom Jefferson married in 1772, had many suitors. Two gentlemen among their number decided to visit her together. Arriving at her house, they heard as they stood in the hall the sound of music — a violin accompanied by a harpsichord, and a lady and a gentleman singing. At once the gentlemen realized who it was: Jefferson was the only violinist in the vicinity. Acknowledging to each other that they were wasting their time, they stole out of the house and returned home.

3 When Jefferson arrived to represent his country in France in 1785, he went to pay his respects to the French minister for foreign affairs. "You replace Monsieur Franklin?" asked the minister.
"I succeed him," was Jefferson's reply. "No one can replace him."

4 During his term as vice president, Jefferson once asked for a room in Baltimore's principal hotel. Not recognizing the vice president, who had no servants with him and was dressed in soiled working clothes, the proprietor, a Mr. Boyden, turned him away. Soon after Jefferson's departure, Boyden was informed that he had just sent away the vice president. Horrified, Boyden promptly dispatched a number of his servants to find Jefferson and offer him as many rooms as he required. Jefferson had already taken a room at another hotel and sent the man who found him back with the message: "Tell Boyden that I value his good intentions highly, but if he has no room for a dirty farmer, he shall have none for the vice president."

5 One morning Thomas Jefferson woke up in a modest Washington rooming house, dressed, and then left the house in order to attend his inauguration as the third president. When he got back, duly sworn in, he found no space left for him at the dinner table. Quietly accepting the democratic principle of first come, first served, the president of the United States went up to his room without dinner.

6 In bygone days affairs of state were tackled with a good deal less frenetic haste than they are today, as this remark by Thomas Jefferson, speaking of the US minister to Spain, illustrates: "I haven't heard from him in two years. If I don't hear from him next year, I will write him a letter."

7 Baron Alexander von Humboldt, the German scientist and explorer, was surprised to

find in Jefferson's office a newspaper containing the most scurrilous abuse of the president. "Why is this libelous journal not suppressed?" asked the baron. "Or why do you not fine the editor, or imprison him?" Jefferson smiled. "Put that paper in your pocket, baron," he said, "and if you hear the reality of our liberty, the freedom of the press, questioned, show them this paper and tell them where you found it."

8   Jefferson and his grandson were out riding one day when a slave took off his hat and bowed to them. Jefferson courteously raised his hat and bowed in acknowledgment. His grandson, engrossed in conversation, ignored the man. Jefferson said severely, "Do you permit a slave to be more of a gentleman than you?"

9   The code of discipline at the University of Virginia was at first very lax, as Jefferson trusted that the students would take their studies seriously. This trust proved misplaced and the misbehavior of the students culminated in a riot in which the professors who tried to restore order were attacked with bricks and canes.
     The following day a meeting was held between the university's board of visitors, of which Jefferson was of course a member, and the defiant students. Jefferson began by saying, "This is one of the most painful events of my life," was overcome by emotion, and burst into tears. No amount of oratory or scolding could have had such an extraordinary effect. Another member of the board took over the meeting and asked the rioters to come forward and give their names. Nearly every one of them did so. As one of the students said afterward, "It was not Mr. Jefferson's words, but his tears."

10   By a strange coincidence Jefferson and his old rival John Adams both died on the fiftieth anniversary of the Declaration of Independence — July 4, 1826. On the evening of July 3 Jefferson was in bed, his life ebbing rapidly. "This is the Fourth?" he whispered to a young friend watching by his bedside. The man could not bring himself to say that it was not yet, so kept silent. Jefferson repeated the question, and this time the friend nodded. A look of deep satisfaction came over Jefferson's face, he

sighed deeply, lay back, sank into a deep sleep, and died shortly after noon on the Fourth.
     {As the news of this extraordinary coincidence spread, a sense of reverent awe seemed to pervade the country. "Newspaper columns were edged in black and memorial services were held in city, town, and hamlet from Maine to Florida and westward. . . . Established statesmen, ministers of the Gospel, and ambitious local politicians vied with each other for the honor of commemorating the occasion by the spoken word. In Boston, by common consent, it was Daniel Webster who was invited to deliver the eulogy." See also JOHN ADAMS 2.}

ॐ ও

JEFFREYS, George, 1st Baron Jeffreys of Wem (?1645–89), *English judge, notorious for his brutality. He presided at the "Bloody Assizes" (1685): the trial of those involved in Monmouth's rebellion. The rebels were executed after the downfall of James II.*

1   Pointing with his cane at a man about to be tried, Jeffreys remarked, "There is a rogue at the end of my cane." The accused looked Jeffreys straight in the eye. "At which end, my lord?" he asked.

ॐ ও

JÉRÔME (1784–1860), *king of Westphalia (1807–13), brother of Napoleon Bonaparte. He failed to support Napoleon's attack on Russia and lost power on his brother's fall. Jérôme lived mainly abroad until 1847 and the Bonapartist restoration in France, after which his nephew, Napoleon III, appointed him to several high offices.*

1   When Napoleon III heard that his uncle was on his deathbed, he sent for Cardinal Moriot, told him that he wished Jérôme to die with the full benefit of the last rites of the Roman Catholic Church, and dispatched him to attend on the dying man. Arriving at Jérôme's house, the cardinal asked his majordomo, "*Le roi a-t-il sa connaissance?*" (Is the king in possession of his senses?) But the majordomo, interpreting *connaissance* in its more colloquial sense as "mistress," replied, "Yes, your eminence, Mme de Plancy has spent the whole night at his bedside."

JERROLD, Douglas (1803–57), *English writer and humorist, author of many successful plays. His fame rests primarily on* Mrs. Caudle's Curtain Lectures *(1846), which appeared originally as sketches in* Punch *magazine.*

1 Jerrold had been seriously ill and was recuperating at a seaside resort, with reading prohibited. One day a parcel arrived containing Robert Browning's abstruse philosophical poem *Sordello,* and Jerrold indulged in the illicit pleasure. After reading a few lines he was seized with a mounting panic. He could not understand the poem at all. He sat down on his sofa, murmuring, "Oh, God, I *am* an idiot!" Had the illness softened his brain? When Mrs. Jerrold came in, he thrust the book into her hands, demanding to know what she made of it. She read it carefully under the anxious scrutiny of her husband. "I don't understand what the man means," she declared at last. "It is gibberish." A delighted smile broke out on Jerrold's face. "Thank God, I am *not* an idiot!" he cried.

2 A man was speaking to Jerrold of a mutual acquaintance who had absented himself from his family for a long time. "Why," he exclaimed indignantly, "he has been away from his family and has never sent them a farthing. Call that kindness?"
"Yes, I do," replied Jerrold. "Unremitting kindness."

3 "What's going on, Jerrold?" asked a talkative bore, stopping Jerrold one day in the street. "*I* am," said Jerrold firmly, and did.

4 A certain member of Jerrold's acquaintance was notorious for his demands upon his friends' purses. Finding himself once again short of money, he sent an intermediary to Jerrold to ask him to subscribe. Jerrold viewed the go-between with disfavor as he made his case. "How much does he want this time?" he asked. "Just a four and two noughts will put him straight," said the man uneasily. "Put me down for one of the noughts," Jerrold replied.

৯৯ ৶

JESSEL, George (1898–1981), *US entertainer. He performed in vaudeville from childhood, and appeared in such films as* The Other Man's Wife *(1919),* Love, Live and Laugh *(1929), and*

The Busy Body *(1957). He also produced a number of musicals.*

1 Out of work and depressed, Jessel sat with a group of friends at his club. An announcement came over the public address system that there was a telephone call for him, but Jessel made no move to respond. "Why don't you answer the phone, George?" said one of his friends. "It might be a job for you."
"The way things have been going for me lately," replied Jessel gloomily, "it not only wouldn't be a job — I'd also tear my coat going into the phone booth."

2 Jessel arrived at the Stork Club one day with the beautiful and talented Lena Horne. Sherman Billingsley, the owner of the Stork Club, and his headwaiters were not fervent believers in racial equality, but Jessel was a regular customer. The headwaiter stalled, paging through his reservation book, pretending that all the tables were filled. Finally, the headwaiter said to Jessel, "Mr. Jessel, who made the reservation?" And Jessel answered, "Abraham Lincoln." Billingsley signaled the headwaiter from across the room, and Mr. Jessel and Miss Horne were seated.

৯৯ ৶

JOAD, Cyril Edwin Mitchinson (1891–1953), *British philosopher, teacher, and radio personality. His writings include* Matter, Life and Value *(1929) and* Guide to Philosophy *(1936). He was well known to millions of radio listeners for his invariable "It depends what you mean by . . ." in the BBC program* Brains Trust.

1 An express train to London once made an unscheduled stop at Reading station and Joad, who had just missed his own train, hopped aboard. "I'm afraid you'll have to get off, sir," called a porter. "This train doesn't stop here."
"In that case, don't worry," replied Joad. "I'm not on it."

৯৯ ৶

JOHN XXIII [Angelo Roncalli] (1881–1963), *pope (1958–63). A popular and innovative leader of the Church, he instigated a number of reforms and worked tirelessly for Church unity and reconciliation between world powers.*

1 As papal nuncio to France, the future pope was once invited to a banquet. His dinner partner wore an extremely low-cut dress, which the prelate affected not to notice during the course of the meal. When dessert was served, however, he selected a rosy apple and offered it to the lady. She politely refused. "Please do take it, madam," he urged. "It was only after Eve ate the apple that she became aware of how little she had on."

2 While serving as papal nuncio in Paris, Pope John, then Monsignor Roncalli, was created a cardinal. At a reception given in his honor the new cardinal was asked if he had any family connections with the Marquis of Roncalli. Roncalli, a farmer's son, smiled. "Up to now we did not belong to the same family," he replied, "but I think that starting from this moment we will become more and more related."

3 Photographer Yousuf Karsh had been commissioned to take an official portrait of the pope. He was accompanied to the Vatican by Bishop Fulton Sheen. Pope John watched uneasily as Karsh set up his equipment. Turning to Sheen, he remarked with a sigh, "God knew seventy-seven years ago that someday I would be pope. Why couldn't he have made me a little more photogenic!"

4 Pope John reported that frequently when he was drowsing off some important thought would come into his mind and he would make a mental note, "I must speak to the pope about that." "Then," he went on, "I would be wide awake and remember that I am pope."

5 Pope John had some confidential advice for an ambitious young priest who was trying rather too hard to impress the Vatican dignitaries. "My dear son," he said, "stop worrying so much. You may rest assured that on the day of judgment Jesus is not going to ask you, 'And how did you get along with the Holy Office?'"

6 Pope John once received a courtesy visit from the Anglican bishop of Gibraltar, whose see covers the whole Mediterranean region. Stepping forward to greet his guest, the pope cried heartily, "Ah, good day, Bishop. I believe I'm in your diocese?"

7 Pope John had expressed a wish to take a short walk around his garden each day. Vatican officials hastily made arrangements to erect a

barrier around the path so that the daily constitutional would not be observed by neighbors or passersby. The pope learned with some surprise of this proposal. "What's the matter?" he asked. "Don't I look respectable?"

❧ ≼

JOHN III SOBIESKI (1624–96), *king of Poland (1674–96). His brilliant military talents saved central Europe from the invading armies of Turks.*

1 In 1683 John Sobieski drove the Turks back from the walls of Vienna. He announced his victory to the pope with a paraphrase of Caesar: "I came; I saw; God conquered."

❧ ≼

JOHN, Augustus [Edwin] (1878–1961), *painter. Having studied art at the Slade School in London, John taught at Liverpool University until 1904. He then took to roaming around Wales and Ireland with gypsies, absorbing their life-style and language. He was official war artist during World War I, and was elected to the Royal Academy in 1928. His most important works are bold portraits of artistic intellectuals of the time, such as James Joyce, G. B. Shaw, and Dylan Thomas.*

1 Augustus John had a reputation for exaggeration. One of his favorite stories featured a meeting he claimed to have had with Abdul Hamid II, sultan of Turkey, before the latter was deposed in 1909. The sultan was known to be a ruthless man and several of his wives had disappeared in mysterious circumstances. John was asked to paint the beheading of John the Baptist. All went well until the two men began to argue over the appearance of a severed neck after decapitation. Before the artist had time to protest the sultan had sent for one of his wives and had her beheaded on the spot. "See how right I was?" said the sultan calmly.

❧ ≼

JOHNSON, Andrew (1808–75), *US statesman; 17th president of the United States (1865–69). A tailor by trade and proud of his humble origins, Johnson considered himself a spokesman for ordinary Americans during the Reconstruction period after the Civil War. Radical Republican opposition to Johnson's mild Reconstruction program was triumphant over the* *president's vetoes. In 1868 Johnson was impeached for his challenge to the Tenure of Office Act, which he held to contravene the Constitution. Though acquitted, he lost power the following year and was not even reelected to Congress until 1875.*

1 Johnson fiercely denounced secession and as senator from Tennessee courageously did his best to keep his state in the Union. This made him exceedingly unpopular in the southern states and for a period his life was in danger from mobs. In one incident at Lynchburg, Virginia, the mob actually succeeded in dragging him out of the train in which he was traveling to his home town of Greenville, Tennessee, assaulted him, and was about to hang him, when an old man in the crowd shouted, "His neighbors at Greenville have made arrangements to hang their senator on his arrival. Virginians have no right to deprive them of that privilege." Swayed by this argument, the mob released its victim and he resumed his journey.

ॐ ॐ

JOHNSON, Lyndon Baines (1908–73), *US statesman; 36th president of the United States (1963–69). Succeeding to the presidency after the assassination of John F. Kennedy, Johnson initiated his Great Society program to stimulate economic growth and promote civil rights legislation. His administration, however, lost popularity as Americans increasingly rejected involvement in the Vietnam War. Johnson liked to remind people that he was the first Texan to get to the White House.*

1 Appointed director of the National Youth Administration for Texas at the age of twenty-six, LBJ sometimes seemed to his staff to deliver cutting remarks for their own sake. Passing a colleague whose desk was piled high with papers, he commented in a voice intended to be heard by others in the room, "I hope your mind's not as messy as that desk." By tremendous exertion the man managed to deal with the papers and clear the desk before Johnson made his next round of the office. Viewing the vacant surface, the boss remarked, "I hope your mind's not as empty as that desk."

2 (David Halberstam tells this story:)
"Early in 1961, Russell Baker, then covering Capitol Hill for *The New York Times,* was coming out of the Senate when he ran into Vice-President Johnson. Johnson grabbed him, cried, '*You,* I've been looking for *you,*' pulled him into his office, and began a long harangue about how important he was to the Kennedy administration and what an insider he really was. While talking, he scribbled something on a piece of paper and rang the buzzer. His secretary came in, took the paper, and left the room; she returned a few minutes later and handed the paper back to him. Still talking, LBJ glanced at the paper, crumpled it up, threw it away, and finally finished his monologue. Later Baker learned that Johnson had written on the paper: 'Who is this I'm talking to?' "

3 The Senate worked hard and late when Johnson was majority leader. One weary senator complained to a colleague, "What's all the hurry? Rome wasn't built in a day."
"No, but Lyndon Johnson wasn't foreman on that job," said the other.

4 At one stage Johnson looked for a way to get rid of the head of the FBI, J. Edgar Hoover, but the difficulties appeared insuperable. Philosophically accepting Hoover's continuance in office, he observed, "It's probably better to have him inside the tent pissing out, than outside pissing in."

5 Johnson tried to persuade his secretary of defense, Robert McNamara, to let a certain Pentagon speechwriter move over to the White House. McNamara was anxious not to lose the young man, but he could not give the president a straight refusal. Instead, he implied that the speechwriter's work was not up to the high standards of the White House. Some weeks later, Johnson repeated his request, taking McNamara by surprise. "But I can't spare him," he protested. "Why, you told me yourself he wasn't any good at all," replied Johnson triumphantly. "I just want to take him off your hands." McNamara admitted defeat, and the speechwriter was transferred.

6 Johnson's daughter was once asked by an inquisitive journalist to describe her relationship with her famous father. After no more than a moment's hesitation, she replied: "Blood."

7 Bill Moyers, Johnson's press secretary, was saying grace at lunch one day. "Speak up, Bill,"

shouted Johnson. "I can't hear a damn thing."

"I wasn't addressing you, Mr. President," replied Moyers quietly.

೮ッ ⋖§

JOHNSON, Nunnally (1897–1977), *US screenwriter and film producer. His films include* The Desert Fox *(1951) and* The Three Faces of Eve *(1957), both of which he wrote and produced; he also wrote the screenplay for* The Dirty Dozen *(1967).*

1   When first asked how he would adjust to writing for the wide screen, Nunnally replied: "Very simple. I'll just put the paper in sideways."

2   Johnson had arranged to have lunch with a lady friend, unaware that she was intending to use the occasion to air certain grievances concerning their relationship. He had ordered shad roe, his favorite dish, and was tucking in with a hearty appetite when the emotional scene was launched. Unable to abandon the roe, which was delicious, he attempted between mouthfuls to make the right noises of contrition and regret. The young lady was fully aware, however, that she was not receiving her lover's undivided attention. "Look at you," she cried, "our very lives are at the crossroads, and you sit there smacking your lips like a pig!" Johnson was genuinely distressed. "I'm so sorry," he replied. "If I'd known it was going to be like this, I'd have ordered something I didn't like."

೮ッ ⋖§

JOHNSON, Samuel (1709–84), *English journalist, critic, poet, and lexicographer. Born in Lichfield, the son of a bookseller, Johnson went to Oxford briefly but left without a degree. He had to support his family, left impoverished by his father's death (1731), and in 1735 married a wealthy widow considerably older than himself. Two years later he settled in London, supporting himself mainly by contributing to* The Gentleman's Magazine. *His first notable poem,* London, *was published in 1738. His biography of Richard Savage (1744) won much acclaim, and in 1747 he issued the "Plan" of his famous* Dictionary, *on which he worked until 1755. In 1749 his long poem* The Vanity of Human Wishes *appeared, together with his tragedy* Irene. *He started the periodical* The Rambler *and ran it almost single-handedly for two years*

(1750–52), subsequently contributing papers to other journals. He also wrote the tale Rasselas *(1759), edited Shakespeare's plays (1765), and composed a series of* Lives of the Poets *(1779–81). His* Journey to the Western Islands of Scotland *(1775) recounts a tour made with his biographer, Boswell, whose great* Life of Samuel Johnson *appeared in 1791. His position for many years as doyen of London literary society won him the title of the "Great Cham of Literature."*

1   When Johnson was a very young child in petticoats and had just learned to read, his mother gave him the Book of Common Prayer, pointed to the collect for the day, and told him to learn it by heart. Leaving him with that task, she went upstairs, but by the time she reached the second story, she heard him following her. "What's the matter?" she asked. "I can say it," he replied, and repeated the collect from memory although he had not had time to read it more than twice.

2   Johnson was explaining to his former tutor from Oxford how he would complete his dictionary in three years. The other objected, "But the French Academy, which consists of forty members, took forty years to compile their dictionary."

"Sir, thus it is. This is the proportion. Let me see; forty times forty is sixteen hundred. As is three to sixteen hundred, so is the proportion of an Englishman to a Frenchman."

{ Johnson was optimistic in his estimate: his dictionary took eleven years to produce.}

3   Andrew Millar, the bookseller who published Johnson's *Dictionary,* had great difficulty in extracting the copy for this work from the author. At last a messenger was dispatched to Millar with the final page. Upon the messenger's return Johnson asked, "Well, what did he say?"

"Sir," replied the messenger, "he said, 'Thank God I have done with him.' "

"I am glad," said Johnson, "that he thanks God for anything."

4   Two ladies were complimenting Dr. Johnson on his *Dictionary,* then recently published. In particular they praised his omission of all naughty words. "What! My dears! Then you have been looking for them?" exclaimed Johnson. The ladies, deeply embarrassed, changed the subject.

5 Dr. Johnson was taken to task by a lady who asked why he had defined "pastern" as "the knee of a horse" in his dictionary. She expected an elaborate defense. He replied, "Ignorance, madam, pure ignorance."

6 Johnson once offered a lift in his coach to a poor woman who was trudging along in the rain with her baby, but only on condition that she refrain from indulging in baby talk, to which he had a strong aversion. At first the woman sat quietly in her corner and the baby slept, but after a while the motion of the coach awakened the infant. "The little dearie, is he going to open his eyesy-pysies then," said the woman, forgetting her benefactor's prohibition. "Stop the coach," Johnson ordered, and promptly turned her and the child out onto the road.

7 Johnson started work on a new edition of Shakespeare, and, to pay for the project, took subscriptions. A bookseller's apprentice, calling with yet another subscription for him, was startled to see him pocket the money without making any note of the subscriber's name or address. Diffidently he suggested that Johnson should take a note of this for the printed list of subscribers that should appear in the completed work. "I shall print no list of subscribers," said Johnson emphatically and abruptly, and then, supposing that some explanation was required, he added, "Sir, I have two very cogent reasons for not printing any list of subscribers — one, that I have lost all the names, the other, that I have spent all the money."

8 Johnson had no great feeling for music and tended to be somewhat dismissive of it. When someone tried to impress upon him the virtuosity of a celebrated violinist's performance, he replied, "Difficult, do you call it, sir? I wish it were impossible."

9 A lady who had just performed to perfection on the harpsichord in Johnson's presence asked the philosopher if he was fond of music. "No, madam," he replied frankly, "but of all the noises I think music is the least disagreeable."

10 Johnson maintained the superiority of England and the English at all times. Visiting North Wales with friends and viewing the local scenery, he inquired, "Has this *brook* e'er a name?" He was assured that it was the *River* Ustrad. "Let us jump over it directly," he said to his companions, "and show them how an Englishman should treat a Welsh river."

11 After several attempts to meet Johnson, Boswell was finally introduced to him and, knowing how much Johnson disliked Scotland, begged the friend who was performing the introductions, "Don't tell where I come from."
   "From Scotland," his friend announced immediately, and Boswell, anguished, cried, "Mr. Johnson, I do indeed come from Scotland, but I cannot help it."
   "That, sir, I find," retorted Johnson, "is what a very many of your countrymen cannot help."

12 A Scot talking to Johnson unfortunately chose his native land as a topic of conversation. He claimed that Scotland had a great many noble wild prospects. "I believe, sir, you have a great many," said Johnson. "Norway, too, has noble wild prospects; and Lapland is remarkable for prodigious noble wild prospects. But, sir, let me tell you, the noblest prospect which a Scotchman ever sees, is the high-road that leads him to England."

13 On his tour of Scotland with Boswell, Johnson visited the island of Mull, which amply justified his prejudices about the bleakness of Scottish landscapes. While they were there, Johnson mislaid his stout oak staff. Boswell was hopeful that they might recover it, but Johnson immediately gave it up for lost. "It is not to be expected that any man in Mull who had got it will part with it. Consider, sir, the value of such a piece of timber here."

14 Boswell and Johnson on an excursion to Bristol were not at all pleased with the inn in which they stayed. Writing his journal, Boswell wondered out loud how he should describe it. "Describe it, sir?" said Johnson. "Why, it was so bad, that Boswell wished to be in Scotland!"

15 At a party held in his honor during his tour of the Hebrides, Johnson found himself with a

pretty little married girl of sixteen sitting on his knee. She had taken a bet to do this and to kiss him because some other girls had said that he was too ugly for any woman to kiss. So the girl put her arms round his neck and kissed his cheek. "Do it again," he said, "and let us see who will tire first."

16   It was mentioned to Johnson that a certain female political writer, whose doctrines he disliked, had become very fond of her appearance and her clothes, and would spend many hours on them. "She is better employed at her toilet, than using her pen," said Johnson. "It is better that she should be reddening her own cheeks, than blackening other people's characters."

17   Johnson and Boswell were discussing Bishop Berkeley's theory of the nonexistence of matter, which held that all things in the universe exist solely in the mind as ideas. Boswell remarked that he found it impossible to refute this theory, although it was clearly untrue. Johnson promptly aimed a hefty kick at a large stone and, as his foot struck it, announced, "I refute it *thus.*"

18   One Sunday morning Boswell went to a Quaker meeting, where he heard a woman preach. He hastened to tell Johnson about this singular experience. "Sir," said Johnson, "a woman's preaching is like a dog's walking on his hind legs. It is not done well, but you are surprised to find it done at all."

19   One of Johnson's great friends was the actor David Garrick, who frequently took him to the greenroom and to rehearsals at his theater. Here he made the acquaintance of many actors and actresses, greatly relishing their company. But he finally relinquished this pleasure on moral grounds, telling Garrick, "I'll come no more behind your scenes, David; for the silk stockings and white bosoms of your actresses excite my amorous propensities."

{There is some debate whether Johnson actually used the final phrase or whether it is Boswellese for a much more earthy expression.}

20   The volume of poems allegedly written by the Highland bard Ossian and translated by James Macpherson attracted a large number of admirers. Johnson, however, was quick to see through its spurious antiquity, and denied that the poems (which were entirely the work of the "translator") had any literary merit. In this he was in a minority and found himself arguing with one of Ossian's admirers, who asked, "Do you think, sir, that any man of a modern age could have written such poems?"

"Yes, sir," replied Johnson, "many men, many women, and many children."

21   Dr. Johnson was once asked his opinion of Laurence Sterne's *Sermons of Mr. Yorick.* He replied that he knew nothing about them, but was later heard censuring the work. On being reminded of his earlier assertion, he explained, "I did read them, but it was in a stagecoach. I should not have even deigned to have looked at them had I been at large."

22   On being told that a gentleman who had been very unhappy in marriage married again immediately after his wife died, Johnson observed that it was the triumph of hope over experience.

23   Dr. Johnson's attention was once directed to the discrepancy between the epitaph that had been carved upon the tombstone of a certain gentleman and the way in which the deceased had actually conducted his life. With typical wryness, the doctor observed that "in lapidary inscriptions a man is not upon oath."

24   Johnson's wife in later years insisted that her failing health made it impossible for her to sleep with him, and Johnson's friends accordingly commiserated with him on this "conjugal infelicity." Garrick related a conversation with Johnson in which, when asked what was the greatest pleasure in life, "he answered fucking and the second was drinking. And therefore he wondered why there were not more drunkards, for all could drink tho' all could not fuck."

JOHNSON, Sir William (1715–74), *British soldier who became an administrator of American Indian affairs. Having acquired considerable influence over the Mohawks and Iroquois, from 1740 to 1770 he was the key figure in the colonists' dealings with the Indian tribes.*

1 Sir William Johnson had ordered some suits of rich clothing from England. When they were unpacked, the Mohawk chief Hendrick admired them greatly. Shortly afterward he told Sir William that he had had a dream in which Sir William had given him one of the suits. Sir William took the hint and presented Hendrick with one of the handsomest outfits. Not long after that when Sir William and Hendrick were again together, Sir William said that he too had had a dream. Hendrick asked him what it was. Sir William explained that he had dreamed that Hendrick had presented him with a certain tract of land on the Mohawk River, comprising about five thousand acres of the most fertile terrain. Immediately Hendrick presented the land to Sir William, remarking as he did so that he would dream no more with him. "You dream too hard for me, Sir William," he observed.

કે ⋅ર્ડ

JOHNSTON, Brian [Alexander] (1912–   ), *British broadcaster and commentator, specializing in cricket commentaries on radio and television.*

1 During an England–New Zealand cricket match at Lords in 1969, batsman Glenn Turner was hit in the groin by a very fast-moving cricket ball and collapsed in pain. As the television cameras focused on the writhing figure, Johnson described the accident in fairly circumspect terms, taking care not to be too explicit. It was with some relief that he saw Turner pick up his bat and return to the wicket to take the last ball of the over. "Turner looks a bit shaky and unsteady," announced Johnston, "but I think he's going to bat on — one ball left."

2 British television viewers joined the England–West Indies match at the Oval in 1976 in the middle of an over. Michael Holding was bowling to Peter Willey. Johnston hastily set the scene with one of those memorable phrases that can only occur during live commentary: "The bowler's Holding, the batsman's Willey."

કે ⋅ર્ડ

JOLLEY, Smead (1902–   ), *US baseball player of the 1930s, known for his good hitting and bad fielding.*

1 Smead Jolley could hit, but the problem was finding a position for him where he could get by in the field. He was being tried as an outfielder in Boston's Fenway Park, where there was an incline leading to the wall. The coaches worked with him at running back and taking the little hill in stride, when he had to go to the wall to catch a fly ball. In the game Jolley ran back for one, but went too far. Realizing this, he came forward again, down the incline, and fell flat on his face. The ball hit him on the head and bounced away. Afterward Jolley came to the bench, rubbing his head and muttering, "Ten days you guys spend teaching me how to go up the hill and there isn't one of you with the brains to teach me how to come down."

કે ⋅ર્ડ

JOLSON, Al [Asa Yoelson] (1886–1950), *US singer and songwriter, born in Russia. He became famous for his blackface minstrel-show routines and the song "Mammy." Subsequently he made a number of films, including the first full-length sound film,* The Jazz Singer *(1927).*

1 At one point during the making of *The Jazz Singer,* Al Jolson called out to the technicians and extras on the set, "Wait a minute! Wait a minute! You ain't heard nothin' yet." The unscripted words went into the sound track, from which they were due to be cut. By a last-minute decision they were left in, and became part of movie history.

કે ⋅ર્ડ

JONES, Henry Arthur (1851–1924), *English playwright. His first success,* The Silver King *(1882), was followed by* Saints and Sinners *(1884) and several other notable plays.*

1 As he lay dying Jones was asked whether he would prefer his niece or his nurse to spend the night at his bedside. "The prettier," he replied. "Now fight for it."

કે ⋅ર્ડ

JONES, James (1921–77), *US author. His first book,* From Here to Eternity *(1951), was by far his most successful. Subsequent works include* Some Came Running *(1957) and* The Thin Red Line *(1962).*

1 Shortly after the publication of *From Here to Eternity,* Jones was known to carry around

with him a pocketful of envelopes, each containing 67 cents, which he handed to friends who had bought a copy of his book. "That's my royalty on each copy," he explained. "I don't want to make money on my friends."

૪૦ ૯ફ

JONES, John Paul (1747–92), *US sailor. Of Scots origin, Jones took a commission in the colonial navy in 1775 and harassed British shipping with considerable daring and resourcefulness.*

1   On September 23, 1779, off Flamborough Head in northeast England, Jones, sailing the rather ramshackle *Le Bonhomme Richard,* encountered a convoy of British merchantmen under the escort of the royal naval ship *Serapis.* The commander of the *Serapis,* Richard Pearson, recognized the *Richard* and attacked. His ship battered by forty-four hostile guns, Jones closed on his enemy and lashed the *Richard's* bowsprit to the mizzenmast of the *Serapis.* The sides of the *Richard* had been so pounded by the *Serapis's* guns that Pearson sent a signal inviting Jones to surrender. Back came the immortal reply, "I have not yet begun to fight."
   {Jones did not claim to have said these words. His own version was: "I answered him (Pearson's aide) in the most determined negative. . . ." In any event, Jones's courage was justified. Locked together, the two ships mauled each other until an explosion aboard the *Serapis* so disheartened Pearson's men that it was they who surrendered. Although the *Richard* sank shortly afterward, Jones had enough men left to seize the British ship and sail it away as a prize.}

2   When Pearson eventually returned to England, the loss of the *Serapis* was forgotten in the general praise for the heroic fight he had put up. Despite his ill luck, he received a knighthood. When Jones heard that his opponent had been made a knight, he remarked, "Should I have the good fortune to fall in with him again, I'll make a lord of him."

૪૦ ૯ફ

JONSON, Ben (1572–1637), *British dramatist. In his early years Jonson was closely connected with the theatrical company of his rival, Shakespeare, but after 1605 spent most of his* time *writing masques for court entertainments, with Inigo Jones. He also wrote tragedies, which have been largely forgotten. He is best remembered for satiric comedies such as* Volpone *(1606),* Epicoene *(1609),* The Alchemist *(1610), and* Bartholomew Fair *(1614). In 1616 he was given a pension by James I and thereby is often referred to as the first poet laureate.*

1   When Ben Jonson asked his benefactor, Charles I of England, for a square foot in hallowed Westminster Abbey after he died, that is exactly what he got. He was buried in an upright position in order that he take up no more space than he had bargained for.

2   A certain Sir John Young, who happened to be in Westminster Abbey when Jonson's grave was being covered over, paid the mason eighteen pence to inscribe upon the gravestone the words: "O rare Ben Jonson."
   {It was later thought that the first two words of the inscription should have been joined together as the Latin word *orare* (pray). The epitaph would then translate as "Pray for Ben Jonson."}

૪૦ ૯ફ

JOSEPH II (1741–90), *Holy Roman emperor (1765–90). He was co-ruler with his mother, Maria Theresa, until 1780, and tried to conduct himself as an enlightened despot. His reforms evoked considerable opposition from the Church and other vested interests.*

1   During his travels in France in 1781, the emperor reached the town of Bethel ahead of his entourage. The talkative hostess of the inn asked if he belonged to the emperor's suite. "No, I precede it." Shortly afterward she passed the door of his room while he was shaving and again inquired whether he was in the employ of the emperor. "Yes," replied Joseph, "I shave him sometimes."

2   Joseph II proposed to open the royal gardens in Vienna to the public. A certain nobleman, hearing of the scheme, exclaimed in dismay, "If the common people are permitted to have free access, where can I walk with my equals?" The emperor commented, "If I wish to walk with my equals, I have to go to the Capuchin crypt."

JOWETT, Benjamin (1817–93), *English classical scholar. He was Master of Balliol College, Oxford (1870–93), Regius Professor of Greek from 1855, and published important translations of Plato, Thucydides, and Aristotle.*

1 The scholar and educator Frederick Denison Maurice took pains to dissociate himself from any of the factions then raging in ecclesiastical circles — to the irritation of those more partisanly inclined. When Jowett was asked the subject of a sermon that Maurice had recently given at Oxford, he replied, "All that I could make out was that today was yesterday, and this world the same as the next."

{Another critic observed that listening to Maurice was like eating pea soup with a fork.}

2 Jowett was once approached by a rather conceited young student. "Master," he said, "I have searched everywhere in all philosophies, ancient and modern, and nowhere do I find the evidence of a God." Jowett, who had little time for such pretentious attitudes, issued the following ultimatum: "If you don't find a God by five o'clock this afternoon you must leave the college."

༈ ⚜

JOYCE, James (1882–1941), *Irish novelist. Leaving Ireland in 1902, he spent the remainder of his life on the Continent. His works, which have profoundly influenced modern literature, include* A Portrait of the Artist as a Young Man *(1916),* Finnegans Wake *(1939), and his masterpiece,* Ulysses, *published in Paris in 1922.*

1 In his impoverished youth, Joyce once applied for a job in a bank. "Do you smoke?" asked the bank manager.

"No," replied his would-be employee.

"Do you drink?"

"No."

"Do you go with girls?"

"No."

The manager was unimpressed by this display of virtue. "Away with you!" he cried. "You'd probably rob the bank."

2 (The story of the first meeting in Dublin between the youthful James Joyce and William Butler Yeats, then at the height of his poetic powers, exists in a number of versions. George Russell wrote from memory a version of this encounter that is published in Richard Ellmann's biography of Joyce.)

"Yeats asked Joyce to read him some of his poems. 'I do so since you ask me,' said Joyce, 'but I attach no more importance to your opinion than to anybody one meets in the street.' Yeats made him some compliments on the verses, which were charming. But Joyce waved aside the praise. 'It is likely both you and I will soon be forgotten.' He then questioned Yeats about some of his later poetry. Yeats began an elaborate and subtle explanation, the essence of which was that in youth he thought everything should be perfectly beautiful but now he thought one might do many things by way of experiment. 'Ah,' said the boy, 'that shows how rapidly you are deteriorating.' He parted from Yeats with a last shaft. 'We have met too late. You are too old for me to have any effect on you.'"

{The most widely known version of this meeting puts Joyce's brashness in an even worse light, having him say to Yeats, "You are too old for me to help you." However, both Joyce and Yeats denied that this was said, although Joyce did admit that he said something to that effect but that he really had a profound admiration for Yeats at the time in question and his words were certainly not spoken in the tone of contempt implicit in the generally reported version.}

3 At the age of twenty-two, "asked what he was thinking about when C. P. Curran photographed him, Joyce replied, 'I was wondering would he lend me five shillings.'"

4 A woman was singing one evening at a private gathering, when a moth headed straight for her open mouth. She stopped abruptly, and there was an awkward silence, broken by Joyce's saying, "The desire of the moth for the star."

5 When Joyce was sitting for the painter Patrick Tuohy, the artist "began to philosophize about the important to an artist of capturing his subject's soul. Joyce replied, 'Never mind my soul. Just be sure you have my tie right.'"

6 Asked about the demands his writing made upon the reader, Joyce replied, "The demand I make of my reader is that he should devote his whole life to reading my works."

7 "Joyce had no patience with monuments. Valery Larbaud said to him as they drove in a taxi in Paris past the Arc de Triomphe with its eternal fire, 'How long do you think that will burn?' Joyce answered, 'Until the Unknown Soldier gets up in disgust and blows it out.'"

8 "When a young man came up to him in Zurich and said, 'May I kiss the hand that wrote *Ulysses*?' Joyce replied, somewhat like King Lear, 'No, it did lots of other things too.'"

9 "One night drinking with Ottocaro Weiss, who had returned from the army in January 1919, he sampled a white Swiss wine called Fendant de Sion. This seemed to be the object of his quest, and after drinking it with satisfaction, he lifted the half-emptied glass, held it against the window like a test tube, and asked Weiss, 'What does this remind you of?' Weiss looked at Joyce and at the pale golden liquid and replied, '*Orina.*' '*Si*,' said Joyce laughing, '*ma di un'arciduchessa*' ('yes, but an archduchess's'). From now on the wine was known as the Archduchess, and is so celebrated in *Finnegans Wake*."

10 "Once or twice Joyce dictated a bit of *Finnegans Wake* to Samuel Beckett, though dictation did not work very well for him; in the middle of one such session there was a knock at the door which Beckett didn't hear. Joyce said, 'Come in,' and Beckett wrote it down. Afterwards he read back what he had written and Joyce said, 'What's that "Come in"?' 'Yes, you said that,' said Beckett. Joyce thought for a moment, then said 'Let it stand.'"

ঙ‍ ‍ড়

JOYCE, John (1849–1931), *father of Irish writer James Joyce. The character of John Joyce appears in Joyce's* Portrait of the Artist as a Young Man.

1 (John Joyce, who worked as a tax collector in Dublin, had a dry native wit.) "On one occasion someone complained that his name had been spelled with two *ll*'s instead of one. 'Which *l* would you like to have removed?' asked John Joyce gravely."

2 The Rumanian sculptor Brancusi and James Joyce were friends during the twenties. Harry and Caresse Crosby, wealthy American expatriates, proposed to illustrate their Black Sun edition of Joyce's *Tales Told of Shem and Shaun* with a portrait of the author by Brancusi. Brancusi's portrait was a sketch of an abstract spiral intended to suggest the labyrinthine nature of Joyce's thought processes. When the portrait was shown to John Joyce in Dublin, he remarked, "The boy seems to have changed a good deal."

3 John Joyce was renowned as a heavy drinker and was frequently in debt. After his death, when his son was asked what his father had been, James Joyce replied, "He was a bankrupt."

ঙ‍ ‍ড়

JOYNSON-HICKS, William (1865–1932), *British statesman. His distinguished parliamentary career culminated in five eventful years as home secretary (1924–29).*

1 Born William Hicks, he added the name Joynson on his marriage (1895) to heiress Grace Joynson, and during an election campaign he acquired the nickname "Jix," by which he was generally known. Jix was a long-standing antagonist of Lloyd George. When the latter was speaking in a budget debate Jix once interrupted him with the question: "Would the right honorable gentleman define what he means by the term 'unearned increment'?" Lloyd George pondered for a moment, then replied, "Certainly; unearned increment is the hyphen in the honorable gentleman's name."

ঙ‍ ‍ড়

JUANG-ZU (4th century BC), *Chinese philosopher, a major interpreter of Taoism.*

1 Juang-zu's disciples wished to give their master an elaborate burial, but when the dying sage's views were asked he vetoed the idea of interment. "Above ground I shall be food for kites; below I shall be food for mole-crickets and ants. Why rob one to feed the other?"

ঙ‍ ‍ড়

JULIA (39 BC–AD 14), *daughter of Augustus Caesar, the first Roman emperor. Married three times, she engaged in such licentious behavior and extravagance that her puritanical father* *banished her in 2 BC to an island off the Italian coast.*

1 By Marcus Vipsanius Agrippa, her second husband, Julia had three sons and two daughters. Her infidelities were common gossip among Roman high society. Someone once observed that it was remarkable in the circumstances how like Agrippa all her children looked. "That," said Julia, "is because passengers are never allowed on board until the hold is full."

2 One day Julia came into her father's presence wearing a rather immodest dress. Though shocked, the emperor did not rebuke her. The following day, to his great pleasure, she appeared in a dress entirely suitable to her age and status. "This dress," he said to her, "is much more becoming to the daughter of Augustus." Julia excused herself: "Today I dressed to meet my father's eyes; yesterday it was for my husband's."

3 At a gladiatorial display, the groups of people attending the two first ladies of Rome — Julia and her stepmother, Livia — appeared in striking contrast. Livia was surrounded by mature men who held important positions in public life, while Julia's suite comprised mainly wild and pleasure-loving youngsters. Augustus sent Julia a note, remarking on this difference. Julia countered: "These friends of mine will be old men too, when I am old."

4 A friend once tried to persuade Julia that she should abandon her extravagant life-style and live more in accordance with her father's simple tastes. Julia refused: "He sometimes forgets that he is Caesar, but I always remember that I am Caesar's daughter."

❧

JULIAN (c. 332–363), *Roman emperor at Constantinople (361–63), known as Julian the Apostate for his attempts to bring back the ancient pagan religion in place of Christianity.*

1 A former provincial governor was accused of embezzlement, which he strongly denied. He was put on trial and his evidence could not be faulted under examination. Eventually the judge, irritated by the absence of proof and the accused's protestations of innocence, turned to Julian and demanded, "Can anyone ever be proved guilty if it is enough just to deny the charge?" Julian replied, "Can anyone be proved innocent if it is enough just to accuse him?"

{This anecdote shows Julian's acceptance of the idea that an accused person is innocent until proved guilty, one of the fundamental principles of Western legal systems.}

❧

JULIUS II (1443–1513), *pope (1503–13), born Giuliano della Rovere. Julius became a cardinal (1471) under the nepotistic patronage of his uncle Pope Sixtus IV. During his papacy he repelled an attempt by Louis XII of France to dethrone him and considerably extended the area of the papal lands in Italy. He was a famous patron of artists, including Michelangelo and Raphael, and began the building of St. Peter's, Rome.*

1 Michelangelo was commissioned to make a statue of Julius II in bronze. He suggested a design showing the pope's right hand raised and a book held in his left hand. The pope did not approve. "Put a sword there," he said, "for I know nothing of letters."

❧

JULIUS III (1487–1555), *pope (1550–55), born Giammaria Ciocchi del Monte.*

1 When the shoemaker appointed to make the special papal slippers for the new pope brought them for Julius III to try on, it was found that they were too tight. "I am afraid they don't fit you, Holy Father," apologized the shoemaker. "On the contrary," replied the pope, "no shoes ever fitted me better than these in my life."

❧

JULLIEN, Louis Antoine (1812–60), *French composer and conductor. As a virtuoso conductor Jullien was immensely successful, particularly with his London promenade concerts. Though he did well financially for a time, in the end he went mad and died in poverty.*

1 Jullien was born at Sisteron in the Basses Alpes. His father, a violinist, had been invited to play a concerto with the local Philharmonic Society orchestra and thought it only proper that he should ask one of the musicians to be the child's godfather. A problem arose, however, when all thirty-six members of the orchestra claimed the privilege. In the end the society's secretary held the infant at the font and he was duly baptized with all thirty-six names.

{Although his full name was decidedly cumbersome, it nevertheless was useful when he wanted to select pseudonyms under which to publish some of his musical compositions.}

2   In his last year Jullien toyed with the scheme of setting the Lord's Prayer to music. He said it was the idea of the wording on the title page that really attracted him: "THE LORD'S PRAYER. Words by Jesus Christ. Music by Jullien."

JUSSERAND, Jean Adrien Antoine Jules (1855–1932), *French diplomat and scholar; ambassador to Washington (1902–25). He was an enthusiastic student of English literature and wrote on a number of medieval English topics.*

1   Theodore Roosevelt's enthusiasm for exercise was a challenge to which the Washington diplomatic corps never became fully accustomed. When Jusserand, garbed in afternoon suit, top hat, and kid gloves, turned up one day for a stroll with the president, he was not a little disconcerted to find Roosevelt in a rough tweed suit and stout boots. The stroll soon became something of a marathon as Roosevelt bounded off cross-country, with his unhappy companions toiling fretfully in his wake. At a stream too wide to jump and too deep to ford, they were sure that there would be a respite. But Roosevelt merely said, "We'd better strip, so as not to wet our things in the creek." With the honor of his country at stake, the urbane Jusserand removed his clothing, except for the kid gloves. As Roosevelt cast a disapproving eye at him, Jusserand forestalled comment by saying, "With your permission, Mr. President, I will keep these on, otherwise it would be embarrassing if we should meet ladies." Thus they crossed the stream.

2   Jusserand eventually found Roosevelt's phenomenal energy too much for him. After two sets of tennis at the White House, Roosevelt invited Jusserand to go jogging. Then they had a workout with the medicine ball. "What would you like to do now?" the president asked his guest when his enthusiasm for that exercise seemed to be flagging. "If it's all the same to you," gasped the exhausted Frenchman, "lie down and die."

3   When Jusserand was once talking with Mrs. Theodore Roosevelt, she said, "Why don't you learn from the United States and Canada? We have a three-thousand-mile unfortified peaceful frontier. You people arm yourselves to the teeth." The ambassador replied: "Ah, madame. Perhaps we could exchange neighbors!"

K

KAC, Mark (1914–), *Polish-born mathematician who has spent most of his working life in the United States. Many of his achievements lie in the domain shared by mathematics and physics.*

1 (Kac spent several years as a professor of mathematics at Cornell University. He records one of his experiences as an examiner of Ph.D. candidates.)

"The candidate shall remain anonymous. He was not terribly good—in mathematics at least. After he had failed to answer a couple of questions, I asked him a really simple one which was to describe the behavior of the function l/z in the complex plane. 'The function is analytic, sir, in the whole plane except at $z = 0$ where it has a singularity,' he answered and it was perfectly correct. 'What is the singularity called?' I continued. The student stopped in his tracks. 'Look at me,' I said, 'What am I?' His face lit up. 'A simple Pole, sir,' which is, in fact, the correct answer."

KAHN, Otto H. (1867–1934), *US financier.*

1 The great magnate was incensed one day to notice on the front of a run-down store the sign: "ABRAM CAHN. COUSIN OF OTTO H. KAHN." As soon as he arrived home, he directed his lawyer to get the offending sign removed, under threat of legal proceedings. A few days later Kahn drove past the store again to make sure that the sign had been taken down. It had. In its place was a new one: "ABRAM CAHN. FORMERLY COUSIN OF OTTO H. KAHN."

KALLIO, Kyösti (1873–1940), *Finnish statesman; prime minister (1924–25, 1929–30, 1936–37) and president (1937–40).*

1 In the Winter War of 1939–40 the Finnish army with nine divisions held off forty-five Soviet divisions for 105 days after the unprovoked Soviet onslaught. The Finns, inevitably, were crushed, and terms were imposed upon them in a treaty signed in Moscow in March 1940. As President Kallio picked up the pen to sign, he exclaimed, "Let the hand wither that signs this monstrous treaty!" Within a few months his arm had become paralyzed.

KAMES, Henry Home, Lord (1696–1782), *Scottish lawyer and psychologist. His best-known works are* Introduction to the Art of Thinking *(1761) and* Elements of Criticism *(1762).*

1 Meeting his old rival Lord Monboddo in an Edinburgh street shortly after the publication of *Elements of Criticism,* Lord Kames inquired whether Lord Monboddo had read it. "I have not, my lord," was the response. "You write a great deal faster than I am able to read."

KANT, Immanuel (1724–1804), *German transcendentalist philosopher. The fullest expression of his complex and subtle approach to metaphysics is to be found in his* Critique of Pure Reason *(1781).*

1 Kant, a confirmed bachelor, had a very regular mode of life. He used to walk every day along an avenue lined with linden trees, known as the Philosopher's Walk. When he appeared each afternoon at his door dressed for this excursion, his Königsberg neighbors knew it was exactly three-thirty.

2 In 1802 Kant discharged Lampe, the faithful servant who had been with him for years. But he could not dismiss him from his mind,

and this began to trouble him greatly. He therefore made an entry in his memorandum book: "Remember, from now on the name of Lampe must be completely forgotten."

See also CLARA BARTON 1.

ৡ৯ ঌ৵

KARL ALEXANDER (1818–1901), *grand duke of Saxe-Weimar (1853–1901). A patron of the arts, he made Weimar a center of culture.*

1 About Karl Alexander cluster many anecdotes, most of them based on his absentmindedness and the difficulty he found in paying attention to matters that didn't interest him. In the course of his duties he frequently had to receive and welcome the reserve officers of his Eisenach battalion. One such occasion is well remembered:
  "Your name?"
  "Schulze, Your Highness."
  "And what do you do?"
  "I am chief forester, Your Highness."
  "Where do you come from?"
  "Strassburg, Your Highness."
  A look of joyful recognition appeared on the archduke's face. He gave the young officer a hearty handshake and exclaimed, "Ah, then you must be Chief Forester Schulze from Strassburg!"

ৡ৯ ঌ৵

KARSAVINA, Tamara (1885–1978), *one of the great ballerinas in Diaghilev's Ballets Russes; she often danced with Nijinsky.*

1 Karsavina possessed the typical prima ballerina's temperament. Asked if she had been helped by the American dancer Lydia Sokolova, as the latter claimed, in interpreting a particularly successful role of hers, Karsavina snapped back: "Lyydia has vairy good myemory; but she tyends to relyye upon it too muarch."

ৡ৯ ঌ৵

KASNER, Edward (1878–1955), *US mathematician. A renowned topologist, he held a professorship at Columbia University for many years.*

1 At an informal evening attended by half a dozen logicians and mathematicians, one of the latter ventured the opinion that to become a good mathematician you should *not* have good teachers, as they prevented you from learning by yourself. He then added, courteously, "I was lucky. I had only one great teacher — Dr. Kasner here. Kasner looked up, his eyes twinkled. He said mildly, "I had none."

2 The eccentric Kasner liked to take his summer vacations in Brussels, where he had become especially attached to a particular chair in a certain outdoor café. He also maintained that he liked Brussels because it was a convenient base from which to organize a mountain-climbing expedition to the highest point in Belgium. "How high is that?" he was asked. "Twelve feet above sea level," he replied.

ৡ৯ ঌ৵

KAUFMAN, George S[imon] (1889–1961), *US dramatist, wit, director, and journalist. He was one of the brightest ornaments of the famous Algonquin Round Table group of wits. He collaborated with Moss Hart on many successful Broadway comedies and with George Gershwin on* Of Thee I Sing *(1932).*

1 Kaufman looked in at the theater while William Gaxton was starring in *Of Thee I Sing* to make sure that all was running smoothly. He was appalled at the liberties that Gaxton was taking with the script. In the intermission Kaufman hurried out and sent Gaxton a wire: "Am sitting in the last row. Wish you were here."

2 A gold-mine promoter was praising the productivity of the mine with an eye to persuading Kaufman to take shares in it. "Why, it's so rich you can pick up the chunks of gold from the ground."
  "Do you mean I'd have to bend over?" asked Kaufman.

3 At his bridge club Kaufman lapsed into freezing disapproval of a fellow member's play. When the hand was over, the offender burst out with, "All right, George, how would you have played it?"
  "Under an assumed name," was the response.

4 Walking on Fifth Avenue one day, Mrs. Kaufman saw so many acquaintances from her home town of Rochester that she observed,

"All Rochester seems to be in New York this week."

"What an excellent time to visit Rochester," suggested George Kaufman.

5 A self-made millionaire was boasting to a circle of people, "I was born into the world without a single penny."

"Really," mused Kaufman. "When I was born, I owed twelve dollars."

6 During the warm-up period of the radio quiz program *Information Please,* guest star George Kaufman failed to answer a single question. Just before the show went on the air, the host, Clifton Fadiman, asked kiddingly, "May I ask what you have been doing for the past fifteen minutes, Mr. K?"

"You may," answered Mr. K. "I've been listening to *Information Please.*"

7 The head of the great Bloomingdale's department store in New York once backed a Kaufman production, which opened out of town. Early the following morning Bloomingdale was in touch with Kaufman for news of how the play had fared. "Close the play and keep the store open nights," advised Kaufman.

8 (Marc Connelly tells this story:)

"George C. Tyler [a producer] commissioned George Kaufman to adapt Jacques Deval's French farce *Someone in the House.* George did a good job, but a weak cast plus a city-wide epidemic of influenza shortened its life. Tyler reluctantly turned down George's suggestion for an advertising slogan for the faltering play: 'Avoid crowds, see *Someone in the House* at the Knickerbocker Theater.' "

9 Kaufman went on business to the office of theatrical producer Jed Harris, notorious for doing outrageous things to attract attention to himself. When Kaufman was ushered in, he found Harris seated at his desk completely nude. "Jed, your fly is open," said Kaufman.

10 A guest at an Algonquin lunch bored everyone by his monologue on the antiquity and eminence of his family, which, he said, he could trace back to the Crusades. Kaufman broke in: "I had a famous ancestor, too. Sir Roderick Kaufman. He also went off to the Crusades." He paused for a moment, then added, "As a spy, of course."

11 Though Dorothy Parker was half-Jewish, Kaufman could not always count on her support against Alexander Woollcott, who liked to pretend to be anti-Semitic. At the Round Table one day Woollcott loudly addressed Kaufman as "you Christ-killer." Kaufman stood up and announced, "I will not stay here and listen to any more slurs on my race. I am now leaving this table and the Algonquin." He turned on his heel, then paused and glared at Dorothy Parker, who was sitting silent. "And I hope Mrs. Parker will follow me — halfway."

12 Kaufman, though deploring the liberties taken by the Marx brothers with the text of *Animal Crackers,* which he and Morrie Ryskind had written specially for them, could do little to control their ad-libbing. At one performance, he and Ryskind were talking quietly together at the back of the theater, when Kaufman suddenly broke into what Ryskind was saying: "Excuse me, Morrie, but I think I just heard one of the original lines."

13 Dropping in on a matinee performance in New York, Kaufman was incensed to discover that the Marx Brothers were up to their usual tricks and went backstage to protest. "Well, they laughed at Edison, didn't they?" said Groucho defensively. "Not at the Wednesday matinee, they didn't," replied Kaufman.

14 During a game of bridge Kaufman's partner asked to be excused to make a visit to the men's room. "Gladly," said Kaufman. "For the first time today I'll know what you have in your hand."

15 Hollywood mogul Adolph Zukor offered a mere $30,000 for the movie rights to one of Kaufman's plays. Kaufman replied with a telegram offering Zukor $40,000 for Paramount.

16 Actress Ruth Gordon was telling Kaufman about her latest play. "In the first scene I'm on the left side of the stage," she explained, "and the audience has to imagine I'm eating dinner in a crowded restaurant. Then in scene two I run over to the right side of the stage and the audience imagines I'm in my own drawing room."

Kaufman was unimpressed. "And the second night," he said, "*you* have to imagine there's an audience out front."

17 Leaving the White House after a dinner party, Kaufman remarked to Eleanor Roosevelt: "You have a good location, good food, and I'm sure the place should be a great success when it's noised around a bit."

18 Kaufman had offered to go shopping with his second wife, actress Leueen McGrath, who was redecorating their apartment. In one of New York's big stores, however, he began to regret his decision. While his wife agonized over color schemes and fabrics, Kaufman grew increasingly bored and impatient. "Can I do anything for you, Mr. Kaufman?" inquired the manager sympathetically. The playwright thought for a moment, then asked: "Do you have any good second-act curtains?"

19 The Canadian stage and screen actor Raymond Massey clearly reveled in his tremendous success in the role of Abraham Lincoln. "Massey won't be satisfied until he's assassinated," commented Kaufman.
{This *mot* is ascribed to others.}

20 Kaufman became embarrassingly famous when the diary of the film actress Mary Astor was disclosed, revealing the playwright as Public Lover No. 1. Subpoenaed to appear at Miss Astor's divorce trial, he fled Hollywood and remained secluded for some time. When the case was settled, he returned to Hollywood, and thereafter is said to have asked every woman who attracted him, "Do you keep a diary?"

21 Eddie Fisher, in his youth, appeared on a US television program in which entertainers sought the advice of a panel on various problems. Fisher's complaint was that chorus girls refused to go out with him because he was too young. Kaufman, one of the panelists, replied: "Mr. Fisher, on Mount Wilson there is a telescope that can magnify the most distant stars up to twenty-four times the magnification of any previous telescope. This remarkable instrument was unsurpassed in the world of astronomy until the development and construction of the Mount Palomar telescope — an even more remarkable instrument of magnification. Owing to advances and improvements in optical technology, it is capable of magnifying the stars to four times the magnification and resolution of the Mount Wilson tele-scope." Here Kaufman paused, surveying the puzzled faces around him. "Mr. Fisher," he continued, "if you could somehow put the Mount Wilson telescope *inside* the Mount Palomar telescope, you *still* wouldn't be able to detect my interest in your problem."

22 Bedridden in his last years, Kaufman was annoyed one night by a radio request program that played just a few bars of each piece of music before fading it out. Too weak to get out of bed and turn off the radio, Kaufman in desperation phoned the number the program announcer had given to his listeners. When he identified himself as George S. Kaufman, the announcer was delighted to have such a celebrity on his show. "What is your request, sir? I'll honor it right away."
"My request is for five minutes' silence," said Kaufman to the announcer — and to a rather large audience.

23 Asked to suggest his own epitaph, Kaufman came up with "Over my dead body!"

ॐ ॐ

KAUNITZ-RIETBURG, Wenzel Anton, Prince von (1711–94), *Austrian statesman and diplomat. He dominated eastern European diplomacy, protecting Austria's interests successfully against Prussia for more than forty years (1750–92).*

1 Empress Maria-Theresa relied greatly upon Prince von Kaunitz, but she disapproved of his personal morals. Once she rebuked him for riding openly through the Viennese streets with his mistress seated beside him. To this von Kaunitz replied, "I have come here, madame, to speak about your affairs, not mine."

ॐ ॐ

KEATS, John (1795–1821), *British Romantic poet. He studied to be a surgeon, but abandoned the career for poetry. His first two volumes,* Poems *(1817) and* Endymion *(1818), were rejected by the public and critics, but Keats persisted.* Lamia and Other Poems *(1820), including his great odes and the narrative poems "La Belle Dame Sans Merci" and "The Eve of St. Agnes," secured his reputation. By then Keats was seriously ill with tuberculosis, a condition exacerbated by his tormented love for Fanny Brawne. In search of health he went to Rome, where he died.*

1   In the spring of 1819 Keats was staying with his friend Charles Armitage Brown and found great pleasure in listening to the song of a nightingale that had built its nest near Brown's house. One morning he took his chair out into the garden for two or three hours. When he returned, Brown noticed that he had some scraps of paper in his hand that he was quietly tucking behind some books. Knowing Keats's habits of composition, Brown got his friend to show him the almost illegible scraps and together they arranged the stanzas. The poem was "Ode to a Nightingale," and at once Brown instigated a search for other scraps of paper tucked into books or carelessly abandoned, and in that way rescued a number of poems. After that Keats agreed that Brown should make fair copies of everything he wrote.

2   (Keats's medical training left him in no doubt about the nature of the disease that was to kill him. Charles Armitage Brown was with Keats at the moment that he realized that he had tuberculosis.)
    "On entering the cold sheets, before his head was on the pillow, he slightly coughed, and I heard him say, 'That is blood from my mouth.' I went towards him; he was examining a single drop of blood upon the sheet. 'Bring me the candle, Brown, and let me see this blood.' After regarding it steadfastly, he looked up in my face, with a calmness of countenance that I can never forget, and said, 'I know the color of that blood; it is arterial blood; I cannot be deceived in that color; that drop of blood is my death-warrant — I must die.'"

3   Keats's room in Rome was near the Spanish Steps, and he could hear from his sickbed the sound of the water playing in the fountain there. Lines from the play *Philaster* by the seventeenth-century playwrights Beaumont and Fletcher came into his mind: "All your better deeds/Shall be in water writ." He told his friend Joseph Severn, who was nursing him, that he wished for no inscription upon his grave, nor even his name, but simply the words: "Here lies one whose name was writ in water."

ॐ ॐ

KEKULÉ VON STRADONITZ, [Friedrich] **August** (1829–96), *German chemist. The first chemist to establish the concept of valence, he also introduced the idea of single, double, and* triple bonds, enabling him to work out the structural formulas of many organic molecules.

1   The structural formula for benzene eluded Kekulé for a long time. He claimed that the initial insight came to him in 1858 while he was dozing on a London bus traveling to Clapham Road. He saw atoms dancing before his eyes and then things like snakes, which contorted and took their tails in their mouths, thus creating rings. The ancient alchemical symbol of the snake biting its tail suggested that the two ends of the benzene chain were joined, and the Kekulé formula for benzene was thus established.

ॐ ॐ

KELLAND, Clarence Budington (1881–1964), *US popular writer. His novels include* Dynasty *(1929),* Catspaw *(1934), and* Star Rising *(1938).*

1   Acting as toastmaster at a large dinner party, Kelland rose to speak at the end of the meal. "Gentlemen," he began, "the obvious duty of a toastmaster is to be so infernally dull that the succeeding speakers will appear brilliant by contrast." An appreciative chuckle rose from the speakers' table. "However," continued Kelland, clutching the slip of paper on which the speakers' names were listed, "I've looked over the list and I don't believe I can do it."

2   Introducing educator Nicholas Murray Butler, who had been invited to speak at a literary luncheon, Kelland announced: "For years organizations, societies, clubs, distinguished groups of all kinds have been beseeching Dr. Butler to address them — with remarkable success."

ॐ ॐ

KELLER, Helen Adams (1880–1968), *US social worker and writer. In her infancy she lost her sight, hearing, and most of her ability to utter sounds. Nevertheless she learned to speak, read, and write, graduated from Radcliffe College (1904), and wrote a number of books and articles.*

1   With her teacher, Anne Mansfield Sullivan, Helen Keller lectured all over the country, answering questions from the audience that were communicated to her by Miss Sullivan. A stock

question was: "Do you close your eyes when you go to sleep?" Helen Keller's stock response was: "I never stayed awake to see."

જ્જ ૯જ

KELLY, George (1887–1974), *US playwright and author of the 1920s; uncle of actress Grace Kelly.*

1 On his deathbed Kelly was visited by his sister Mary's daughter, who had come to see her uncle for the last time. As she leaned forward to kiss him the old man whispered softly, "My dear, before you kiss me goodbye, fix your hair. It's a mess."

જ્જ ૯જ

KELLY, Michael (?1764–1826), *Irish singer, actor, and composer. For many years he was musical director and manager of the Drury Lane Theatre in London.*

1 In 1802 Kelly embarked on a new venture as wine merchant. He proposed to put up a shop sign reading, "Michael Kelly, Composer of Music, Importer of Wine." His friend and colleague Richard Brinsley Sheridan suggested that this should be amended to read "Michael Kelly, Importer of Music, Composer of Wine," for "none of his music is original and all his wine is, since he makes it himself."

જ્જ ૯જ

KELVIN, William Thomson, 1st Baron (1824–1907), *British physicist. Professor of natural philosophy at Glasgow for fifty years (1849–99), he was renowned for his work in thermodynamics and as a pioneer of undersea telegraphy. He was knighted in 1866 and raised to the peerage in 1892. The Kelvin temperature scale is named after him; he also made numerous contributions to navigation.*

1 When Kelvin was professor at Glasgow, he sometimes left the actual teaching to his assistant, Dr. Day. One morning, as Day drew toward the end of a course of lectures, he found the following inscription written on the blackboard: "Work while it is yet Day, for the Knight cometh when no man can work."

2 Kelvin worked out an improved method for measuring the depth of the sea, using piano wire and a narrow-bore glass tube, stoppered at the upper end. While experimenting with this invention, he was interrupted one day by his colleague James Prescott Joule. Looking with astonishment at the lengths of piano wire, Joule asked him what he was doing. "Sounding," said Thomson. "What note?" asked Joule. "The deep C," returned Thomson.

3 Lost in a scientific reverie at lunch one day, Kelvin suddenly became aware that his wife was discussing plans for an afternoon excursion. Looking up, he asked abstractedly, "At what time does the dissipation of energy begin?"

4 (Kelvin was a great admirer of the nineteenth-century French mathematician Joseph Liouville.)

"'Do you know what a mathematician is?' Kelvin once asked a class. He stepped to the board and wrote

$$\int_{-\infty}^{+\infty} e^{-x^2} dx = \sqrt{\pi}.$$

"Putting his finger on what he had written, he turned to the class. 'A mathematician is one to whom *that* is as obvious as that twice two makes four is to you. Liouville was a mathematician.'"

5 At Glasgow University one day, a certain Dr. Campbell was delivering a chemistry lecture in the room above Lord Kelvin's. At the end of the lecture, Campbell's students showed their appreciation in the customary way — by stamping vigorously on the floor. "Ah," remarked Kelvin, as flakes of plaster fell from the ceiling above him, "I see Dr. Campbell's conclusions don't agree with my premises."

જ્જ ૯જ

KEMBLE, Charles (1775–1854), *English actor, father of Fanny Kemble. He acted at Drury Lane and Covent Garden, London, and excelled in comic roles. In 1822 he became manager of Covent Garden.*

1 Kemble had received and ignored insistent demands for income-tax payment. Eventually, however, he was forced to give in. As he presented the money to the tax collector he remarked: "Sir, I now pay you this exorbitant charge, but I must ask you to explain to Her Majesty that she must not in future look upon me as a source of income."

> Richard Kowalski was one of the greatest black marketeers in the history of modern Poland. He was a totally illiterate poor Jew whose wife, mother, and three children had been slaughtered by the Germans. He blamed his fate on poverty. In the 1960s he sold to the state 26 million zlotys' worth of water, a remarkable coup in view of the fact that the contract called for wine. When his increasing wealth could no longer be ignored, the militia called him in for interrogation. The interrogator said, "Mr. Kowalski, do us a favor. Stop making money. Don't you understand our economic system?" Kowalski reflected sadly, then said, "I never learned to read and I never learned to write. What else is there left for me to do but make money?"
>
> — from Stewart Steven, *The Poles*

KEMBLE, Fanny [Frances Anne] (1809–93), *British actress. She played many of the principal women's roles in Shakespearean and later English drama. Having married an American, she lived between 1832 and 1877 in the United States.*

1   Wishing to explore the countryside of Massachusetts, where she was spending a summer vacation, Miss Kemble hired a local farmer to drive her around. As they set off on their first excursion, the farmer embarked on a detailed description of the area. Fanny brusquely interrupted him: "I hired you to drive me, not talk to me." The farmer said no more until the end of the holiday, when he presented his bill. Miss Kemble studied it for a moment or two. Pointing to one entry, she asked: "What is this item?"

"Sass, five dollars," drawled the farmer. "I don't often take it, but when I do I charge."

2   The Swedish novelist Fredrika Bremer had suffered a heavy cold, and the versatile Miss Kemble, then at the height of her many-faceted fame, came to call on her. "I hope you are feeling sufficiently recovered to see people," said the actress as she entered. "Oh, yes, certainly," said Miss Bremer, "though I am not sure that I ought to see as many people as you are."

❧

KEMBLE, John Philip (1757–1823), *British tragic actor and theatrical manager, brother of Sarah Siddons and uncle of Fanny Kemble.*

1   Playing one of his celebrated roles in a country theater, Kemble was constantly interrupted by the crying of a young child. Finally Kemble came to the front of the stage and announced, "Ladies and gentlemen, unless the play is stopped, the child cannot possibly go on."

2   Kemble was once in conversation with a gentleman who had just returned from a visit to Sydney, Australia, and who spoke of the flourishing condition of the theater there. "Yes," remarked Kemble, "the performers ought to be all good, for they have been selected and sent to that situation by very excellent judges."

❧

KEMBLE, Stephen (1758–1822), *British actor and theatrical manager; brother of John Philip Kemble.*

1   As an actor Stephen Kemble was eclipsed by other members of his illustrious clan. His main claim to fame was his huge bulk, which enabled him to play Falstaff without any padding. One night, Kemble awoke early at the country inn at which he was staying to find a diminutive figure standing at his bedside. Raising his massive body to a sitting position, Kemble asked for an explanation. "I am a dwarf come to exhibit at the fair tomorrow, and I have mistaken the bedchamber," replied the intruder. "I suppose you are a giant come for the same purpose."

❧

KENNEDY, John Fitzgerald (1917–63), *35th president of the United States (1961–63). The first Roman Catholic to become president, Kennedy made a great impact on the nation before he was assassinated in 1963.*

1   During World War II Kennedy held a commission in the US navy and served in the Pacific. In August 1943 in Blackett Strait in the

Solomon Islands, a Japanese destroyer rammed his ship. Kennedy, with some others, reached a nearby island but found it was held by the Japanese. He and another officer then swam to another island, where they persuaded the inhabitants to send a message to other US forces, who rescued them. Kennedy's comment on his reputation as a hero: "It was involuntary. They sank my boat."

2   When John F. Kennedy was first persuaded to enter politics, his father orchestrated the campaigns that took him into Congress. Joseph Kennedy remarked, "We're going to sell Jack like soap flakes," and did so.

3   After he had lost the vice-presidential nomination to Estes Kefauver in 1956, Kennedy flew to Europe to rest. He was basking in the sun at his father's rented Riviera home when Michael Canfield, former husband of Jackie Kennedy's sister, Lee, came by. Canfield asked Jack why he wanted to be president. His eyes still closed, Jack replied, "I guess it's the only thing I can do."

4   During the contest for the 1960 Democratic presidential nomination, Kennedy visited a mine in West Virginia. "Is it true you're the son of one of our wealthiest men?" asked one of the miners there. Kennedy admitted that this was true.

"Is it true that you've never wanted for anything and had everything you wanted?"

"I guess so."

"Is it true you've never done a day's work with your hands all your life?"

Kennedy nodded.

"Well, let me tell you this," said the miner. "You haven't missed a thing."

5   As Democratic candidate for the presidency in 1960, Kennedy was surprised to receive the endorsement of *The New York Times,* which usually supported the Republicans. Once elected, the new president remarked: "In part, at least, I am one person who can truthfully say, 'I got my job through *The New York Times.*'"

6   Kennedy enjoyed telling this story against himself. He said that during an election campaign his father sent him the following telegram: "Don't buy a single vote more than

necessary. I'll be damned if I'm going to pay for a landslide."

7   Sir Rudolf Bing, manager of the Metropolitan Opera House in New York, invited the whole company to a party to watch the ticker-tape parade for President Kennedy soon after his inauguration. As the cavalcade went by, Bing was standing next to one of the Italian ladies who sang in the chorus. He overheard her say to her little daughter, "Now watch. This is President Kennedy and he's the first Catholic president of the United States."

"All the others were Jews?" asked the child in surprise.

8   When Kennedy made his brother Robert attorney general in 1961, a great cry of "nepotism" went up across the land. Kennedy retorted, "I can't see that it's wrong to give him a little legal experience before he goes out to practice law."

9   Shortly after Kennedy blocked the hike in steel prices in 1961, he was visited by a businessman who expressed wariness about the national economy. "Things look great," said JFK. "Why, if I wasn't president, I'd be buying stock myself."

"If you weren't president," said the businessman, "so would I."

10   Senator Barry Goldwater, a talented amateur photographer, once took a picture of President Kennedy and sent it to him, requesting an autograph. Back it came with this inscription: "For Barry Goldwater, whom I urge to follow the career for which he has shown so much talent — photography. From his friend, John Kennedy."

11   Kennedy resigned from the Metropolitan, an exclusive Washington club, as a gesture of disapproval of its refusal to admit blacks. At around the same time he refused Moise Tshombe, the rebel Congolese leader, an entry visa to the United States. Arthur Krock of *The New York Times* remained a member of the Metropolitan and took up Tshombe's cause with the president. "Arthur," said Kennedy, "I'll give Tshombe a visa if you'll take him to lunch at the Metropolitan Club."

12   After the fiasco of the Bay of Pigs invasion of Cuba, the American people rallied around

their president. Kennedy's popularity rating was never higher, with eighty-two percent expressing their approval of him. Kennedy was dumbfounded. "My God! It's as bad as Eisenhower. The worse I do, the more popular I get."

13 When President Kennedy and his wife visited Paris in 1962, Jacqueline charmed everyone, including President de Gaulle. At departure time, Kennedy held a press conference. He began: "I do not think it is altogether inappropriate to introduce myself to this audience. I am the man who accompanied Jacqueline Kennedy to Paris, and I have enjoyed it."

14 In October 1962 the world was brought to the brink of nuclear war when the United States confronted the Soviet Union over the Russian decision to install ballistic missiles in Cuba. President Kennedy made plain his determination to have the missiles removed. After days of acute tension, the Soviet premier, Nikita Khrushchev, ordered their withdrawal. At the height of the crisis Kennedy observed, "I guess this is the week I earn my salary."

15 When Kennedy entertained a group of Nobel Prize–winners at the White House in December 1962, he welcomed them as the most distinguished gathering of intellects to have dined at the Executive Mansion—"with the possible exception of when Mr. Jefferson dined here alone."

16 Joseph Kennedy once remarked of his granddaughter Caroline, Jack's daughter: "Caroline's very bright, smarter than you were, Jack, at that age."
"Yes, she is," agreed Jack. "But look who *she* has for a father!"

17 William Haddad was an associate of Kennedy's. After JFK was assassinated, his young son, John, asked Mr. Haddad, "Are you a daddy?" Haddad admitted that he was. Said little John, "Then will you throw me up in the air?"

ड़ॐ ॐई

KENNEDY, Joseph Patrick (1888–1969), *US businessman and diplomat; ambassador to Britain (1937–40); father of President John F.*

Kennedy, and Senators Robert and Edward Kennedy.

1 Kennedy objected to being referred to as an Irishman in the Boston newspapers. Although he could not claim to be a "Proper Bostonian," he felt he was at least eligible for American status. "I was born here," he complained. "My children were born here. What the hell do I have to do to be an American?"

2 In 1926 Joseph Kennedy became involved in the film industry, rising to the chairmanship of Pathé, Inc. Many Hollywood people disliked him and his methods. Marcus Loew is said to have inquired, "What's Kennedy doing in the movie business? He's not a furrier."

3 In 1926 Kennedy and his family moved from Boston to New York, which offered wider financial horizons. Shortly before he left, a friend asked him, "What is it you really want?" Kennedy reflected a moment. Then he replied, "Everything."

4 Joseph Kennedy, on reading the latest bills that had been charged to him, often would lecture his family about extravagance as they sat at the dinner table. On one occasion his son Bobby's wife, Ethel, was subjected to one of these tirades and fled from the room, very distressed. Only after much soothing from her indignant husband did she return to the table. Father and son confronted each other in an ominous silence. Then Jack shrugged his shoulders and, breaking the tension, told Bobby: "We've found the solution. Dad's just got to go out and make more money."

ड़ॐ ॐई

KEPLER, Johannes (1571–1630), *German astronomer. He was one of the first to support Copernicus's heliocentric theory and published (1609, 1619) the three laws of planetary motion named after him. He inherited the astronomical records of his master Tycho Brahe and from 1610 used a telescope for his own observations.*

1 Kepler also believed in the Pythagorean music of the spheres, that each celestial body in its course gave out a characteristic note or notes. The notes sounded by Earth, he said, were *mi, fa, mi,* indicating *mi*sery (*miseria*), *fa*mine (*fames*), and *mi*sery.

"It was one thing to knock down old-time boxer Stanley Ketchel. It was quite another thing to keep him down. On those rare occasions when he did suffer the indignity of being decked, he usually came off the canvas in a rage. An incredulous friend, hearing of Ketchel's death, offered a suggestion. 'Stand over him and start counting,' he said. 'He'll get up at nine.'"

—R. L. Crouser, *It's Unlucky to Be Behind at the End of the Game*

KEPPEL, Augustus Keppel, 1st Viscount (1725–86), *British statesman and admiral; First Lord of the Admiralty (1782–83). He circumnavigated the globe with Baron George Anson (1740) and was appointed commander in chief of the grand fleet (1778).*

1 When Keppel was still in his mid-twenties, he was sent as an emissary to the dey of Algiers to insist that he restrain his corsairs, who were then a major menace on the high seas. The dey scornfully queried the wisdom of the king of England who had sent a beardless boy to negotiate with him. "Had my master supposed that wisdom was measured by the length of the beard, he would have sent your deyship a he-goat," retorted Keppel.

{This remark so enraged the dey that he threatened Keppel with instant death; Keppel pointed toward the naval squadron riding in the bay and observed that there were enough Englishmen there to make a glorious funeral pyre for him. The dey thought better of it.}

KER, William Paton (1855–1923), *British scholar; professor of English at University College, London (1889–1922). Ker's most important work was in the field of medieval poetry, and his wide knowledge of European literatures is seen in such works as* Epic and Romance (1897).

1 Visiting a natural history museum, Ker and a young woman acquaintance paused in front of a display of seafowl. "What's that bird?" the girl inquired.

"That's a guillemot."

"That's not my idea of a guillemot."

"It's God's idea of a guillemot," said Ker.

2 An energetic walker and lover of mountain scenery, Ker revisited the Italian Alps in 1923. Walking up the slopes of the Pizzo Bianco at Macugnaga, he paused to remark to his companions, "I thought this was the most beautiful spot in the world, and now I know it." So saying, he dropped dead of a heart attack.

KERN, Jerome [David] (1885–1945), *US composer, best known for his musical comedy* Show Boat *(1925). Among his most famous songs are* "Smoke Gets in Your Eyes," "The Last Time I Saw Paris," *and* "Ol' Man River."

1 An actress had been irritating Kern all afternoon with her theatrical gestures and affected articulation, particularly the exaggerated rolling of her *r*'s. "Tell me, Mr. Kern," she cried at one point, "you want me to cr-r-ross the stage, but I'm behind a table. How shall I get acr-r-ross?"

"Why, my dear," replied Kern, "just r-r-roll over on your *r*'s."

KEROUAC, Jack (1922–69), *US writer and leading chronicler of the Beat Generation of the 1950s.*

1 (In *The Origins of the Beat Generation* Kerouac recalled how he borrowed the term that labeled an entire decade from a broken-down drug addict named Herbert Huncke and how he then went on to use it himself.)

"John Clellon Holmes . . . and I were sitting around trying to think up the meaning of the Lost Generation and the subsequent existentialism and I said, 'You know, this is really a beat generation': and he lept up and said, 'That's it, that's right.'"

KEYNES, John Maynard, 1st Baron (1883–1946), *British economist. His* General Theory of Employment, Interest, and Money *(1936) profoundly influenced postwar economic thinking.*

1 In his late twenties Keynes was traveling in Africa with a Cambridge friend, Walter John

Sprott. At one point they had their shoes polished by the native boys. The economist handed the boys a miserly tip. Sprott suggested a more generous handout, but Keynes firmly declined: "I will not be a party to debasing the currency."

2 During the panic and uncertainty of the first days of the Great Depression, a reporter asked Keynes whether anything like it had ever happened before. "Yes, it was called the Dark Ages, and it lasted four hundred years," was the response.

❧ ☙

KHRUSHCHEV, Nikita Sergeyevich (1894–1971), *Soviet statesman. He pursued a policy of destalinization and as premier of the Soviet Union (1958–64) generally promoted peaceful coexistence with the West, while attacking Western involvement in Third World countries.*

1 Khrushchev furiously denounced the United Nations for acting to prevent Russian intervention in the postindependence crisis in the Congo. Shortly afterward he sent Dag Hammarskjöld, then UN secretary general, a protocol invitation to a Soviet reception. Hammarskjöld attended the reception and was greeted with great cordiality by the Russian leader. Someone asked Khrushchev why he behaved so warmly toward a man whom he had recently been attacking so bitterly in public. Khrushchev replied, "Do you know the tradition of the mountain people of the Caucasus in our country? When an enemy is inside your home, sharing your bread and salt, you should always treat him with the greatest hospitality. But as soon as he steps outside the door, it is all right to slit his throat."

2 Khrushchev had no qualms about exacerbating international tensions by often deliberate tactlessness. At a reception during the Suez Canal crisis in 1956, Khrushchev called out loudly to a French dignitary, "I must tell you a good joke I have just heard. Eden [the British prime minister] is sick. What is he suffering from? Inflammation of the Canal."

3 On a trip to Russia, Stewart Udall, US secretary of the interior, visited the Black Sea in Khrushchev's company. Khrushchev asked Udall if he would like to have his photograph taken with him. Udall said he would, so the photographer lined them up. Just as he was about to take the picture, the Russian premier stopped him. "If it will help you out," he said to Udall, "you can go ahead and shake your finger in my face."

4 During a fiery exchange in a summit meeting between Khrushchev and President Kennedy, Kennedy said to the Russian premier, "Do you ever admit a mistake?"

"Certainly I do," Khrushchev replied. "In a speech before the Twentieth Party Congress, I admitted all of Stalin's mistakes."

5 Censuring Stalin at a public meeting, Khrushchev was interrupted by a voice from the audience. "You were one of Stalin's colleagues," shouted the heckler. "Why didn't you stop him?"

"Who said that?" roared Khrushchev. There was an agonizing silence in the room. Nobody dared to move a muscle. Then, in a quiet voice, Khrushchev said, "Now you know why."

6 (Khrushchev and his family were visiting the Twentieth Century–Fox lot in Hollywood while in the United States. David Niven goes on:)

"The publicity department, scenting a big break for their forthcoming picture *Can-Can*, herded the visitors across to a sound stage where Shirley MacLaine and a large troupe of carefully rehearsed dancers were 'just by chance' about to shoot a take of the famous dance of the same name.

"The Khrushchev party were seated in a specially built box and looked down with undisguised horror as Shirley and Company, complete with garter belts and black fishnet stockings, kicked their legs, swirled their petticoats, waggled their knees, and ended up with their skirts over their heads and their bottoms pointing directly at the guest of honor and his family.

"As the publicity department gathered around for Khrushchev's eagerly awaited quote, he gave it to them in one word: 'DISGUSTING.' "

❧ ☙

KIERAN, John (1892–1979), *US sports writer and columnist; regular member of the radio program* Information Please.

1   Anybody who ever heard Kieran confound the experts on *Information Please* knows he was a Latin wizard. To the headmaster of a certain prep school, however, he was only a sports writer, invited to address the Latin class as a favor to the football coach. When the headmaster introduced him to the class, he threw in a Latin phrase, for the boys' amusement, that meant in English, "Let's make the best of this ordeal."

Kieran stood up, bowed stiffly to the headmaster, and said, "Gentlemen, the only thing that outraged me more than the boorishness of the man who introduced me was his inexcusable use of the present participle instead of the past pluperfect in the quotation." Kieran then delivered his entire speech ın Latin and stalked out of the classroom.

KINER, Ralph (1922–   ), *US baseball player for the Pittsburgh Pirates.*

1   "Former Pirate slugger Ralph Kiner was telling his broadcasting buddy Lindsey Nelson, about his wife, the former tennis star Nancy Chaffee. 'When I married Nancy, I vowed I'd beat her at tennis someday. After six months, she beat me 6–2. After a year, she beat me 6–4. After we were married a year and a half, I pushed her to 7–5. Then it happened — she had a bad day and I had a good one, and I beat her 17–15.' 'Good for you, Ralph,' exclaimed Lindsey. 'Was she sick?' 'Of course not!' Kiner snapped indignantly. 'Well, she was eight months pregnant.'"

ॐ❧

KINGLAKE, Alexander William (1809–91), *British writer. In addition to his well-known travel book* Eothen *(1844), he wrote an authoritative multivolume account of the Crimean War.*

1   A skeptic by nature, Kinglake suggested that all churches should bear the inscription: "IMPORTANT IF TRUE."

ॐ❧

KINGSALE, Michael William de Courcy, 32nd Baron [or 28th by some reckonings] (1822–1895), *Victorian representative of a long line of Irish peers, the premier barons of Ireland. The Lords Kingsale claim as an ancient privilege the right to appear before the monarch with their heads covered. The right, apparently granted by Henry VIII, was bestowed not because of royal favor but because the king was afraid of catching the ringworm that afflicted the baron of that time.*

1   Determined to exercise his rights, the 32nd Baron Kingsale appeared before Queen Victoria without removing his hat, explaining to the austere queen that he was asserting the ancient privilege. "Don't be so silly," snapped the queen. "It may be your right to keep your hat on before the monarch, but I am a lady, too. Take it off at once." The privilege has not been tested since.

ॐ❧

KIPLING, [Joseph] Rudyard (1865–1936), *British poet and short-story writer, born in India. Much of his work draws upon his experiences as a journalist in India in the 1880s, during which time he published a number of short stories. His most successful novel,* Kim *(1901), has an Indian setting, as do his two* Jungle Books *(1894, 1895), written for children. He was awarded the 1907 Nobel Prize for literature.*

1   A newspaper to which Kipling subscribed published by mistake an announcement of his death. Kipling wrote at once to the editor: "I've just read that I am dead. Don't forget to delete me from your list of subscribers."

2   At the height of Kipling's success, a journal published a report that his earnings worked out at a dollar a word. An autograph hunter who had vainly tried to extract a signature from the great man wrote again to him: "I see you get $1 a word for your writing. I enclose a check for $1. Please send me a sample." Kipling wrote back a single word on an unsigned postcard: "Thanks."

{This story exists in a number of versions. According to one, the resourceful autograph collector sold the anecdote for two dollars and sent Kipling half the profit on the transaction, minus postage — 45 cents.}

ॐ❧

KIRCHHOFF, Gustav Robert (1824–87), *German physicist. His work in electricity and in* experimental and mathematical physics is important, but he is best remembered for his invention, jointly with Robert Bunsen, of spectroscopy.

1   One of the important results of Kirchhoff's work on spectrum analysis was that for the first time it became possible to ascertain the chemical elements present in celestial bodies. Kirchhoff's banker, however, was skeptical about his customer's work. "What good is gold in the sun if I can't bring it down to earth?" he asked. When Kirchhoff's work became internationally recognized, he was awarded a medal and a prize paid in gold sovereigns. "Here is the gold from the sun," he observed as he handed the money to his banker.

ﻬ ﻬ

KISSINGER, Henry (1923–   ), *US diplomat, born in Germany. He was assistant to President Nixon for national security affairs (1968–75) and secretary of state (1973–77). In 1972 he shared the Nobel Peace Prize.*

1   In Moscow for arms control negotiations in 1972, Kissinger, then secretary of state, joked with some of his hosts about bugging. During one session Kissinger held a document up in the air toward the chandelier and said, "Can I have two copies of this delivered to my suite?" Soviet Foreign Minister Andrei Gromyko, who had a sense of humor, said no, he couldn't. The hidden cameras had been installed in the Kremlin, said he, during the time of Ivan the Terrible, and their lenses were not good enough to pick up the fine print.

2   The day after Kissinger was nominated as secretary of state, he held a news conference. Newsman Richard Valeriani wound up the conference by asking, "Do you prefer being called 'Mr. Secretary' or 'Dr. Secretary'?"
   "I don't stand on protocol," Kissinger deadpanned. "If you will just call me 'Excellency,' it will be okay."

ﻬ ﻬ

KITCHENER, Horatio Herbert, 1st Earl of Khartoum and Broome (1850–1916), *British general. His reconquest of the Sudan (1898) made him a national hero, although his actions after the second Boer War left a legacy of bitterness in South Africa. Appointed war secretary*

in 1914, he became indelibly associated with the recruiting poster captioned: "YOUR COUNTRY NEEDS YOU."

1   On June 5, 1916, the British ship *Hampshire* was sailing to Arkhangelsk when she struck a mine shortly after leaving Scapa Flow and sank. Lord Kitchener, along with most of the crew, drowned. When the news broke the following morning, newspaper magnate Lord Northcliffe announced it to his sister with the words: "Providence is on the side of the British Empire after all."

ﻬ ﻬ

KITTREDGE, George Lyman (1860–1941), *US scholar; professor of English at Harvard (from 1894). He is best known for his work on medieval English poetry.*

1   Someone once asked Kittredge why, although he was such a great scholar, he had never gotten a Ph.D. "My dear sir, who could examine me?" replied Kittredge.
   {Told of others. Kittredge always maintained that the question was never asked and if it had been he would never have dreamed of answering in such a manner.}

ﻬ ﻬ

KLEIN, Charles (1867–1915), *US playwright, born in Britain. His greatest success was* The Music Master *(1904). Klein was drowned in the sinking of the* Lusitania.

1   Klein wrote a play called *The Ne'er Do Well,* which flopped. As the final curtain fell, a young lady sitting behind him tapped him on the shoulder. "Are you Mr. Klein?" The disconsolate playwright admitted that he was. "Before the curtain rose," the girl went on, "I took the liberty of cutting off a lock of your hair. Now I would like to give it back."

ﻬ ﻬ

KLEMPERER, Otto (1885–1973), *German-born conductor, famous for his interpretations of Beethoven's symphonies. Having conducted in a number of German opera houses, he was expelled by the Nazis at the beginning of World War II and took refuge in the United States. He returned to Europe in 1947 as conductor of the Budapest Opera, and subsequently conducted the Philharmonia Orchestra (1959–73). In 1970 he became an Israeli citizen.*

1 Expecting nothing but the best from his musicians, Klemperer was very sparing with his praise. On one occasion, however, after a particularly excellent performance, he congratulated the orchestra with an enthusiastic "Good!" The players burst into spontaneous applause, and Klemperer's smile faded into the more familiar frown. "Not *that* good," he growled.

2 Klemperer went into a music shop one day accompanied by a recording company executive called George de Mendelssohn-Bartholdy. "Do you have Klemperer conducting Beethoven's Fifth?" he asked the young man behind the counter.

"No," said the clerk. "We have it conducted by Ormandy and Toscanini. Why do you want it by Klemperer?"

Replied the indignant conductor: "Because I *am* Klemperer!"

The clerk looked at him skeptically, then nodded toward George. "And that, I suppose, is Beethoven," he said.

"No," replied Klemperer with a triumphant smile. "That's Mendelssohn."

3 In the middle of a performance of a modern work that he hated, Klemperer heard a member of the audience leave the hall. "Thank God somebody understands it!" exclaimed the conductor.

❧

KLÖPFER, Eugene (1886–1950), *German actor.*

1 Klöpfer once dried up on the stage and paused for the prompter, a certain Frau Wesemeier, to help him out. She had apparently lost her place in the prompt book and the embarrassing silence dragged on. To cover the lapse, Klöpfer addressed the fellow actor with whom he was playing the scene: "I wanted to ask you, how is Frau Wesemeier? Is she ill?" The other actor shrugged noncommittally. With increasing desperation Klöpfer went on, "I haven't heard from her for quite some time."

❧

KNELLER, Sir Godfrey (1646–1723), *German-born British portrait painter, known for his paintings of royalty and high-society figures. His series of forty-eight portraits of members of the Kit-Cat Club is the origin of the name "kit-cat," applied to a type of portrait depicting the sitter's head and shoulders.*

1 Alexander Pope had wagered that there was no flattery so gross that Kneller would not believe it. One day as Kneller was painting, Pope observed, "Sir Godfrey, I believe if God Almighty had had your assistance the world would have been formed more perfect."

" 'Fore God, sir," said Kneller, "I believe so."

2 A visitor to Kneller's house remarked on a full-length portrait of Lady Kneller, the bottom of which had been very considerably damaged by scratches. The marks, Kneller explained, had been made by his wife's little lapdog, which used to paw at the painted skirt, asking to be taken up into its mistress's arms. The visitor observed that that reminded him of the story of Zeuxis, who painted grapes on a boy's head so realistically that birds came to peck at them. Kneller disparaged this legend: "If the boy had been painted as well as the grapes, the birds would have been afraid to meddle with them."

3 Kneller was greatly attached to his country house at Whitton. When he lay dying, a friend exhorted him to think of death merely as the passage to a better place. "Ah, my good friend, I wish God would let me stay at Whitton," the painter sighed.

❧

KNOPF, Alfred A. (1892–1984), *US book publisher, famous for many creative innovations in design and promotion, and for the high literary quality of his offerings.*

1 Traveling by train one day, Knopf entered the smoking car and seated himself next to a gentleman of pleasant appearance and manners. He took out one of his special cigars, lit it, and then on an impulse offered one to his neighbor. The man accepted, lit up, and after a few puffs remarked, "A magnificent cigar."

"It should be," replied Knopf. "These cigars are specially put up for me by Upmann."

"Indeed?" said the stranger. "May I ask your name?"

"Alfred Knopf. May I ask yours?"

"Upmann."

❧

KNOX, Philander Chase (1853–1921), *US lawyer and political leader. He was attorney general (1901–04) and secretary of state (1909–13).*

1   In 1903 Theodore Roosevelt acquired the Panama Canal Zone. Though proud of his achievement, he knew that not all citizens approved of it. Philander Knox, his attorney general, was a corporation lawyer, and it was to him that Roosevelt went for a defense of his action. Knox is said to have replied, "Oh, Mr. President, do not let so great an achievement suffer from any taint of legality."

৵৽ ৵ৡ

KNOX, Ronald (1888–1957), *British Roman Catholic priest and author. A convert to Catholicism at the age of twenty-nine, he became Roman Catholic chaplain at Oxford University in 1926. He is best known for his modern translation of the Vulgate, his books relating the history of his conversion (such as* A Spiritual Aeneid, *1918), and his detective stories.*

1   As a boy of four, Knox suffered quite seriously from insomnia. Asked by a friend of the family how he managed to occupy himself during his sleepless nights, he answered, "I lie awake and think about the past."
Compare ALDOUS HUXLEY 1.

2   (Knox taught for seven years at St. Edmund's College, a Roman Catholic boys' school in Hertfordshire. He did not receive a very promising impression of the place on his first visit in February 1918.)
"He was taken for a walk by one of the priests on the staff, and as they went down the avenue of bare chestnuts, his companion felt moved to remark: 'Come on ye buds, bust. There's a fine line for a *Punch* poem.'
"Ronald appeared to be a little depressed by this sally. They walked for an hour through dismal lanes and footpaths, talking of general matters. Ronald seemed preoccupied. At length they returned in chill twilight up the avenue. Ronald then said: 'Come on ye buds, bust./ You really must/ And show this unfortunate newcomer/ How beautiful this place can be in summer.'"

3   (While Knox was teaching Latin at St. Edmund's, there was an official inspection of the school by representatives of an examining board.)
"One of the inspectors proved to be his old friend Mr. Thomas Higham of Trinity. The meeting was a complete surprise to both of them. Ronald was taking his form in *Aeneid*. He gave no sign of recognition, but quietly said: 'Pay no attention to this gentleman. He's stone deaf.' Mr. Higham played up, sat blankly cupping his hand on his ear while a boy construed, then rose, said, 'I have not been able to hear anything you have said, but I perceive by the intelligent look on your faces that you have fully mastered the text,' and left them."

4   Knox was engaged in a theological discussion with scientist John Scott Haldane. "In a universe containing millions of planets," reasoned Haldane, "is it not inevitable that life should appear on at least one of them?"
"Sir," replied Knox, "if Scotland Yard found a body in your cabin trunk, would you tell them: 'There are millions of trunks in the world — surely one of them must contain a body?' I think they would still want to know who put it there."

5   Traveling by train from Oxford to London one morning, Knox opened his copy of *The Times* and turned straight to the crossword puzzle, reputed to be the most difficult in the world. One of his fellow passengers, noticing that the priest had been staring at the puzzle for several minutes without filling in any of the answers, offered to lend him a pencil. "No, thanks," replied Knox, looking up with a smile. "Just finished."

6   (Watched over by devoted friends, Knox died of cancer of the liver.)
"For three days he lay in a coma, but once Lady Eldon saw a stir of consciousness and asked whether he would like her to read to him from his own [translation of the] New Testament. He answered very faintly, but distinctly: 'No,' and then after a long pause in which he seemed to have lapsed again into unconsciousness, there came from the deathbed, just audibly, in the idiom of his youth: 'Awfully jolly of you to suggest it, though.'
"They were his last words."

৵৽ ৵ৡ

KNOX-JOHNSTON, Robin (1939–), *British yachtsman.*

1 In 1968–69, taking part in the (London) *Sunday Times* race, Knox-Johnston made the first nonstop solo circumnavigation of the world in his old-fashioned ketch *Suhaili*, starting from Falmouth, England. It took him 313 days to sail the 30,000-odd miles, finishing at 3:30 P.M. on April 22, 1969. As he neared Falmouth, he was accompanied by other boats, a Royal Naval Reserve ship, planes, and so on. When he berthed, he was of course boarded by the customs officers, who, as per regulation, questioned him: "Where from?" Knox-Johnston replied, "Falmouth."

᪥

KOESTLER, Arthur (1905–83), *British writer, born in Vienna. In 1940 he settled in Britain, where his novel* Darkness at Noon *(1940) was first published. In addition to several novels he wrote a number of books on political and broadly philosophical topics, including* The Yogi and the Commissar *(1945),* The Act of Creation *(1964),* The Ghost in the Machine *(1967), and* The Roots of Coincidence *(1972). Koestler suffered in later life from Parkinson's disease, and in 1983 he and his wife committed suicide together.*

1 (Koestler tells the following story:)
"It is reported that John Stuart Mill wrote Latin verse at the age of three. I can offer no equally impressive feat. Still, my first words in French, also pronounced at the age of three, are reliably recorded. They were addressed to the governess and consisted of the laconic statement: '*Mademoiselle, pantalons mouillés.*'"

2 Koestler once quelled a gushing fan by saying, "Liking a writer and then meeting the writer is like liking goose liver and then meeting the goose."

3 In Palestine early in August 1945, Koestler managed to get a seat on a plane bound for England. On the way to the airfield he bought a copy of the *Jerusalem Post* carrying the news of the dropping of the atomic bomb on Hiroshima. "That's the end of the world war," he said to the friend seeing him off, "and it's also the beginning of the end of the world."

KOO, Wellington [Ku Wei-chün] (1887–), *Chinese statesman and ambassador.*

1 When Wellington Koo was representing his country at the 1921 Washington Conference, he found some Americans were ill at ease when talking to a sophisticated foreigner. At a banquet he was placed next to a young woman who, after some minutes of embarrassed silence, attempted to begin a conversation with "Likee soupee?" Koo, feeling that there was not much to be said on this level, just nodded and continued with his soup. At the end of the meal he was called upon to address the guests, which he did for ten minutes in perfect English. As he sat down, he turned to the young woman and said: "Likee speechee?"
{This famous story has been attributed to many notable Chinese.}

᪥

KOPPAY, Joszi Arpád, Baron von Drétoma (1859–?), *Hungarian portrait painter.*

1 On an Atlantic crossing Koppay met the sixteen-year-old Iphigene Ochs, daughter of Adolph Ochs, the owner of *The New York Times.* He offered to paint her portrait free of charge, saying he could never be fulfilled as an artist until he had captured such beauty on canvas. Adolph Ochs, flattered, consented. When the portrait was finished Ochs received a bill for $1,000. Koppay met his objection: "Your daughter has such a beautiful face, it was a joy to paint it. But the body was dull and bored me. It is for this that I charge you one thousand dollars."

᪥

KORDA, Sir Alexander (1893–1956), *British film producer and director, born in Hungary. Forced to leave his native land during Nicholas Horthy's "White Terror" after World War I, Korda went to the United States before settling in Britain (1930). His forte was opulent productions with big stars and strong story lines;* The Private Lives of Henry VIII *(1932),* The Scarlet Pimpernel *(1934), and* Anna Karenina *(1948) were among his great successes.*

1 Having offered a part to the English actress Ann Todd, Korda changed his mind and made the film with another actress. Understandably hurt and angry, Miss Todd raged at Korda for his perfidy. "I wouldn't have done it to anyone else," said Korda. Miss Todd was taken aback by this unexpected response. "What do you mean?" she asked. "You and I are such good friends," Korda continued placatingly, "I knew you would forgive me."

2 In 1942 Korda was given a knighthood for his services to the British film industry. Proud of the honor, he resisted the temptation to take it overseriously, though it made a considerable impression upon his Hollywood colleagues. One evening he won nearly $10,000 from Sam Goldwyn at poker. The next day a check arrived, written in red ink with the note: "Signed in my blood. Sam." Soon afterward Korda lost a similar amount of money to Goldwyn. Korda sent a check in blue ink with the inscription: "This check is signed in my blood, too."

3 When Korda was filming Kipling's *Jungle Book,* a rubber and wire python was operated from a barge moored in midstream. On the barge stood the technicians, the camera crew, and Korda's brother Zoli. Korda, on the bank, remarked that the barge appeared rather unstable with so many people on it. A few minutes later it capsized. Everyone swam to the shore, with the exception of Zoli Korda, who remained in the deep water near the python, splashing and shouting. Korda watched his brother's foolery with an indulgent smile. Suddenly someone asked, "Can he swim?" Alexander Korda pondered: "No, we never learned to swim as children. I don't believe he can. Someone help him." A long pole was fetched and Zoli Korda was fished out. As soon as he could speak, he demanded, "Why didn't you bloody help?" Korda replied coolly, "You should have shouted in Hungarian. Always cry for help in your native language — they're the only people who understand."

4 Gossip said that Alexander Korda had an infallible seduction technique. After inviting a woman to stay for a drink at his apartment, he would look wistful, sigh, and say what a sadness it was for him to be impotent. Some of the most desirable women in the world had tried and failed with him, Korda would continue. Most of his guests accepted the irresistible challenge. After a while a "miracle" would happen.

5 On a visit to Marc Chagall's studio, Korda admired a painting that he said he would like to buy. The artist, declaring that negotiations about money embarrassed and upset him, promptly left the room, leaving Mme Chagall to discuss the price. Leaning forward to speak to her, Korda suddenly noticed a reflection in a mirror. It was Chagall, standing, as he thought, unseen in the hall, and signaling to his wife. First he sketched a dollar sign in the air, then held up five fingers, then ten, and finally crossed his index fingers to indicate that she should multiply. Before Mme Chagall could say anything, Korda offered $50,000. "Why, that's the sum I was going to ask you for," exclaimed Mme Chagall in some surprise. "How did you guess?"

"Ah, madame, sometimes a painting simply speaks for itself."

୬ଡ଼ ୬ଟ

KOUSSEVITZKY, Sergei (1874–1951), *Russian composer and conductor. After leaving Russia in 1920 he worked in Paris and the United States, where he conducted the Boston Symphony Orchestra (1924–49). He commissioned many pieces of music from contemporary composers.*

1 Boston held him in the highest regard. Not only because of his long stay there but also because of his imposing presence and musical inspiration, he was a genuine idol. At one reception, a Boston matron came up to him and with awe said: "Mr. Koussevitzky, you are a god to me." To which Koussevitzky replied: "Ah, madame, what a responsibility!"

2 Koussevitzky was known for his interesting turns of phrase. Once, during rehearsals of Ravel's *Bolero,* Koussevitzky, losing patience with a struggling tympanist, blurted out, "If you make me more nervous I send you bill from my doctor."

3 Another time, a clarinetist, goaded to the limit, glared at Koussevitzky in the midst of Shostakovitch's First Symphony. Koussevitzky finally said, "Kill me; it will make me more pleasure than listen to you!"

୬ଡ଼ ୬ଟ

KREISLER, Fritz (1875–1962), *US violinist of Austrian birth. His interpretations of Beethoven and Brahms were particularly applauded. In 1910 he gave the first performance of Sir Edward Elgar's violin concerto, which was dedicated to him. He wrote a number of concert pieces for the violin.*

1 Setting out from Hamburg one day to give a concert in London, Kreisler found that he had an hour to kill before the boat sailed. He wandered into a music shop, where the proprietor asked if he could look at the violin Kreisler was carrying. Having looked, he vanished and then reappeared with two policemen, one of whom said to the violinist, "You are under arrest."
"What for?" asked Kreisler.
"You have Fritz Kreisler's violin."
"I am Fritz Kreisler."
"You can't pull that one on us. Come along to the station."
As Kreisler's boat was sailing soon, there was no time for prolonged inquiries and explanations. Kreisler asked if the music shop had any of his records. The proprietor found one, "The Old Refrain," and put it on the Victrola. When it had finished playing, Kreisler asked for his violin and, mustering all the skill at his command, played the piece through again. "Now are you satisfied?" he asked. They were.

2 A society hostess asked Kreisler how much he would charge to play at a private musical evening. The fee was $5,000. To this the lady reluctantly agreed, adding, "Please remember that I do not expect you to mingle with my guests." Kreisler smiled: "In that case, madam, my fee will be only two thousand dollars."

{A similar anecdote is told of other famous musicians.}

3 Jascha Heifetz and Mischa Elman were dining together when the waiter brought over a note with the superscription: "To the greatest violinist in the world." Heifetz glanced at it and handed it to Elman: "For you, Mischa." Elman passed it back. "No, no, for *you*, Jascha," he said. The note went back and forth a few more times before they agreed to open it together. The first words were: "Dear Fritz."

4 Kreisler's devoted wife refused to sit next to him at his seventy-fifth birthday party. "I want him to have a good time with other women fussing over him," she explained. "That's my birthday gift."

❧ ❧

KURLAND, Bob (1924–), *US basketball player. He was a leader on the US Olympic teams of 1948 and 1952, both of which won gold medals.*

1 Kurland was the first seven-foot-tall player to star in American basketball. Playing at Oklahoma A&M, he blocked so many shots that the National Collegiate Athletic Association introduced a rule that a shot could not be legally blocked on its downward path toward the basket. At one point they built a platform over the basket and stationed an official there to watch Kurland. Kurland observed, "The rule was designed to stop me, but it really started the big man in basketball because it encouraged bringing in taller players who shot down at the basket instead of smaller ones who shot up."

❧ L ❧

LABOUCHERE, Henry (1831–1912), *British politician and journalist. He founded the influential journal* Truth *(1876) and was an MP for many years, representing Northampton between 1880 and 1905.*

1 As a student at Cambridge, Labouchere was stopped by one of the university proctors as he was strolling through the town arm in arm with a local tart. Challenged to account for his companion, Labouchere promptly introduced her as his sister. "Nonsense, she's one of the most notorious whores in the town," said the proctor. Labouchere looked grieved. "I know, sir," he said disconsolately, "but it is unkind of you to throw my family misfortunes in my face."

2 When Labouchere was an attaché at the British legation in St. Petersburg, a pompous nobleman paid a call, stating that he wished to see the ambassador immediately. "Pray take a chair," Labouchere told him, "the ambassador will be here soon." The visitor took exception to this offhand treatment. "Young man, do you know who I am?" he demanded, and recited a list of his titles and appointments. "Pray take two chairs," said Labouchere.

{A similar story is told of Abraham Lincoln and others.}

3 "[Labouchere] was one of the stiffest opponents of votes for women. In Northampton he kept them at a distance as long as he could, but at last a deputation of two ladies found him in at his hotel and were shown to his sitting-room. Labouchere received them with grave courtesy. Each in turn stated the reasons why in their view they should have the vote. Silence followed for a minute or so. Labouchere, who had listened with the closest attention, and appeared to be carefully considering their appeal, then leaned forward and murmured, 'Pretty dears!'"

4 In public Labouchere treated Gladstone respectfully, but in private attacked his political methods and style. He once said that he did not object that Gladstone always seemed to have the ace of trumps up his sleeve; what he did object to was Gladstone's pretense that God had put it there.

5 Labouchere, away from home when his father died, came back in time to see his body. The butler showed him into the room where it lay in the open coffin. Labouchere gazed at his parent's face for a few moments, then remarked to the butler, "The right man in the right place."

6 On the day before Labouchere's death A. L. Thorold (nephew as well as biographer) was sitting by his bedside. A burning spirit lamp was accidentally overturned. Labouchere opened his eyes, murmured, "Flames? — not yet, I think," laughed, and went to sleep.

❧

LAEMMLE, Carl (1908–79), *US film producer.*

1 A new writer came from Australia. Laemmle asked him how long he had been in America and was told two weeks. "It's amazing how well you talk English after only two weeks," said Carl.

❧

LAFAYETTE, Marie Joseph Gilbert du Motier, Marquis de (1757–1834), *French general and politician. In 1777 he joined the American Revolution and became a great friend of George Washington. Known as the "hero of both* *worlds," he returned to France, where as a committed liberal he helped to found the revolutionary National Assembly. In 1792, he was forced to defect to Austria, where he was kept prisoner until Napoleon insisted on his return in 1799. Always a man of great influence, he commanded the national guard that helped to install Louis-Philippe on the French throne in 1830.*

1   The harvest of 1783 was a poor one, but the bailiffs of Lafayette's estates at Chavaniac had managed to fill the barns with wheat. "The bad harvest has raised the price of wheat," said the bailiff. "This is the time to sell." Lafayette thought about the hungry peasants in the surrounding villages. "No," he replied, "this is the time to give."

2   In the heady days of the French Revolution the followers of Lafayette once went to unusual lengths to indicate their admiration. Stopping his carriage in the street, they unhitched the horses and pulled the vehicle to its destination. Some weeks later it was suggested to Lafayette that he must have been much pleased by the gesture. The great man considered for a moment. "Yes, it was delightful, delightful," he agreed slowly, "but one thing disturbs me a little — I never saw anything more of my horses."

ॐ ✎

LA FONTAINE, Jean de (1621–95), *French poet, renowned for his* Fables *(1668–94), which retold traditional stories from Aesop, Phaedrus, and other writers, and his* Contes *(1664).*

1   La Fontaine, engaged to make a speech before the French Academy, had first to attend a society gathering that soon began to bore him. He excused his departure by explaining the circumstances of his engagement. "But," objected his hostess, "the Academy isn't scheduled to meet for a whole hour. Taking the quickest way, you'll need only twenty minutes to get there." La Fontaine made a courteous bow, replying, "But you see, I prefer the longest way."

ॐ ✎

LA GUARDIA, Fiorello (1882–1947), *US politician and mayor of New York (1933–45), nicknamed the "Little Flower." A popular figure, he introduced labor safeguard schemes and* improved housing in the city. He was director of the US Office of Civilian Defense (1941–42) and director-general of UNRRA.*

1   (Bennett Cerf records an occasion on which La Guardia was presiding at the police court.)

"One bitter cold day they brought a trembling old man before him, charged with stealing a loaf of bread. His family, he said, was starving. 'I've got to punish you,' declared La Guardia. 'The law makes no exception. I can do nothing but sentence you to a fine of ten dollars.'

"But the Little Flower was reaching into his pocket as he added, 'Well, here's the ten dollars to pay your fine. And now I remit the fine.' He tossed a ten-dollar bill into his famous sombrero. 'Futhermore,' he declared, 'I'm going to fine everybody in this courtroom fifty cents for living in a town where a man has to steal bread in order to eat. Mr. Bailiff, collect the fines and give them to this defendant!' The hat was passed and an incredulous old man, with a light of heaven in his eyes, left the courtroom with a stake of forty-seven dollars and fifty cents."

2   (Journalist John Gunther, interviewing La Guardia, asked him about the large collection of files in his office.)

"I'll tell you a little story. Files are the curse of modern civilization. I had a young secretary once. Just out of school. I told her, 'If you can keep these files straight, I'll marry you.' She did, and so I married her."

3   An important German diplomat was to pay a visit to New York. It was the mid-1930s, and anti-Nazi feeling ran high in the city. La Guardia, as mayor, was duty-bound to protect his visitor, but he found it hard to swallow his own hatred of the Nazis. As a compromise, he surrounded the diplomat with a bodyguard of specially selected policemen. They were all Jewish.

4   La Guardia felt that the New York police were being rather too hard on young offenders, and tried to point out to them the difference between a mischievous prank and true juvenile delinquency. "When I was a boy," he said, "I used to wander around the streets with my friends until we found a horse tied up to a post. We'd unhitch him, ride him around town, then tie him up again."

"Are you trying to tell us," asked one of the policemen, "that the mayor of New York was once a horse thief?"

"No," replied La Guardia. "I'm telling you that he was once a boy."

ৡ৶ ৶ৡ

LAIRD, Melvin (1922–   ), *US secretary of defense for four years during the Nixon presidency.*

1   When Richard Nixon visited the Vatican in 1970, it was decided that the presidential party should leave from St. Peter's Square in a US military helicopter. In order not to embarrass the Curia with further reminders of warfare, it was suggested to the secretary of defense that he should not accompany the rest of the party to the papal audience. However, Laird was not so easily spurned. When the group gathered inside the Vatican, there he was, smoking his inevitable cigar and ready with the excuse that he was only looking for the president's helicopter. He was persuaded at least to pocket the cigar as the pope began to speak. Unfortunately, the cigar was still alight and in a few moments Laird's jacket was issuing ominous clouds of smoke. Alarmed, Laird began slapping at his pocket. Many of the guests present, interpreting the sound as applause, joined in enthusiastically. Ingrained Vatican decorum, thus challenged, was maintained only with difficulty.

ৡ৶ ৶ৡ

LAÏS (5th century BC), *famous Corinthian beauty.*

1   When she moved to Athens, Laïs posed for several well-known Athenian sculptors. The elderly Myron, who had created the classic *Discus Thrower,* was high on her list. When she removed her clothes and prepared to pose, the old man was instantly rejuvenated and offered her the entire contents of his studio if she would stay the night with him. Glancing at the old man's tangled gray hair and beard and tattered garments, she put her clothes back on and walked out.

The following day, the eager Myron had his hair cut, his beard shaved, and his new robe perfumed. Then, donning a gold chain, he found Laïs and declared his love for her. "My

friend," she said, "you are asking me to do for you what I refused your father yesterday."

ৡ৶ ৶ৡ

LAMAR, Lucius Quintus Cincinnatus (1825–93), *US statesman and judge. After the Civil War he did much to promote reconciliation between North and South. He served as secretary of the interior (1885–88) in Grover Cleveland's first administration.*

1   When Lamar was appointed secretary of the interior on a salary of $8,000, he looked for a residence to rent. It happened that the widow of Admiral J. H. Dahlgren had a property to let in the neighborhood that Lamar liked. She informed him that the house was indeed for rent —at $7,500 per annum. Secretary Lamar sat quite motionless, eyes downcast, saying nothing, until Mrs. Dahlgren finally asked if he had been taken ill. "No, madam," he replied, "I was simply wondering what I could do with the remainder of my salary."

ৡ৶ ৶ৡ

LAMB, Lady Caroline (1785–1828), *British novelist. In 1805 she married William Lamb, later Lord Melbourne. After her notorious affair with Lord Byron ("mad, bad, and dangerous to know"), her behavior became so outrageous that Lamb decided on a legal separation. Although they were reconciled on this occasion, she became increasingly eccentric and after Byron's death lived apart from her husband. Her novel* Glenarvon *(1816) caricatures Byron.*

1   (The *Boston Globe* told this story:)
"Lady Caroline, renowned for her flamboyant style, once celebrated the birthday of her husband, the English prime minister Lord Melbourne, by having herself served to him as a birthday banquet dish. On that occasion, she emerged naked from a large tureen."

2   Lady Caroline was staying with her cousin Lord Hartington at Lismore Castle in Ireland. One evening, after a dispute with Hartington, Lady Caroline suddenly went to the door, opened it wide, and said, "Pray walk in, sir. I have no doubt that you are the rightful possessor, and my cousin only an interloper, usurping your usual habitation." Nothing happened for some minutes, then in hopped a frog. Caroline

walked behind it with two lighted candles, "to treat the master of the castle with proper respect."

❦ ❧

LAMB, Charles (1775–1834), *English essayist, poet, and literary critic. From 1796 he had charge of his sister, Mary, who had killed their mother in a fit of madness. His attempts as a dramatist were failures, but he wrote, with Mary, the popular book for children called* Tales from Shakespeare *(1807). His essays for the* London Magazine *were published in volume form as* Essays of Elia *(1823; second series, 1833).*

1   When Charles Lamb was little more than a toddler, his sister, Mary, took him for a walk in the graveyard. The precocious little boy read the laudatory epitaphs on the tombstones, commemorating the deceased as "virtuous," "charitable," "beloved," and so on. As they came away, he asked, "Mary, where are all the naughty people buried?"

2   A superior in the office where Lamb worked reproached him for bad time-keeping. "You arrive late, Mr. Lamb," the senior clerk began. Lamb is reputed to have replied, "But see how early I leave!"

3   Lamb had been advised for medical reasons to take a course of sea-bathing at Hastings. Shivering with cold and trepidation, he stood at the door of his bathing machine and issued instructions to the men who were to "dip" him. Unfortunately, his stammer got the better of him: "Hear me, men! Take notice of this. I am to be d-d-d-dipped . . ." Tired of waiting, the two men assumed their instructions to be complete and plunged the protesting writer into the sea. Emerging from the icy water, Lamb was only able to stutter, "I tell you I am to be d-d-d-dipped . . ." before being plunged for a second time. After his third ducking, Lamb was finally allowed to complete his sentence: "I tell you that I am — no, that I *was* — to be d-d-d-dipped only *once*."

4   A lady asked Lamb, "Mr. Lamb, how do you like babies?" He replied, "B-b-boiled, ma'am."

5   Lamb's farce *Mr. H* — was a complete failure on its first night. Sitting in the pit at Drury Lane Theatre, he joined in the hissing, because, as he later explained, he was "so damnably afraid of being taken for the author."

6   "Don't introduce me to him," said Lamb urgently when a friend offered to present a man whom Lamb had for a long time disliked by hearsay. "I want to go on hating him, and I can't do that to a man I know."

7   Someone told Lamb about the hardheartedness of the Duke of Cumberland. It seems he had prevented his duchess from rushing to embrace her son, whom she had not seen for some time, and had insisted on greeting him formally. "Wasn't that terribly cold?" said the friend. "I don't know," said Lamb, stammering as usual. "After all, he is the Duke of Cu-cumberland."

8   Lamb was a generally acquiescent audience for the garrulous Coleridge. One day when Coleridge had been particularly voluble, he suddenly interjected the question, "Charles, have you ever heard me preach?"
    "I've never heard you do anything else," replied Lamb resignedly.

9   In the course of a lecture, Lamb was interrupted by a hiss from the audience. "There are only three things that hiss," said Lamb calmly, "a goose, a snake, and a fool. Stand forth, and let us identify you."

❦ ❧

LANDERS, Ann [Esther Pauline Lederer, *née* Friedman] (1918–   ), *US columnist. Author of a problems column for the Chicago* Sun-Times *Syndicate since 1955, she has claimed a readership of 70 million in over a thousand papers. She has also made political speeches on behalf of the Democratic party and served as a volunteer with the US Red Cross.*

1   At an embassy reception, Miss Landers was approached by a rather pompous senator. "So you're Ann Landers," he drawled. "Say something funny." Without hesitation, Miss Landers replied, "Well, you're a politician. Tell me a lie."

2   Miss Landers was fond of making political bets. In the 1968 presidential election she bet on Richard Nixon but, as a Democrat, was not altogether pleased when he won. On receiving a check for a hundred dollars from one of the losers, she replied: "This morning I received your check for $100 — your payment on the election bet. Enclosed is my check for $50. It was a half-assed election."

3   Miss Landers spent some time visiting wounded US soldiers in Vietnam. A young corporal in one of the hospitals asked her to lean a little closer to him so that he could smell her perfume. "How long has it been since you've smelled perfume, fella?" she asked. "Ten and a half months," he replied. Miss Landers rose with a smile. "That's all for you, brother," she said. "You could be dangerous."

ஒ ஐ

LANDIS, Kenesaw Mountain (1866–1944), *US jurist, district judge for the Northern District of Illinois (1905–22). He was also the first commissioner of baseball (1920–44).*

1   An old offender was severely reprimanded by Landis and sentenced to five years in prison.
"But I'm a sick man, I'll be dead long before that," he protested. "I can't do five years!"
Landis fixed the felon with an icy glare. "You can try, can't you?" he thundered.

ஒ ஐ

LANDOR, Walter Savage (1775–1864), *British poet, essayist, and critic. His fiery temper involved him in numerous quarrels, marital and literary. Imaginary Conversations (1824–29) is his most impressive work. He also wrote a tragedy,* Count Julian *(1812), and lyric and narrative verse.*

1   Landor's cook displeased his master one day by serving an indifferent meal. Landor in a passion threw him through an open window. The cook landed awkwardly in the flower bed below and broke a limb. Landor cried out, "Good God, I forgot the violets!"

ஒ ஐ

LANDOWSKA, Wanda (1879–1959), *Polish harpsichordist. She was largely responsible for reviving interest in the harpsichord repertoire, and played and taught in Europe and the United States.*

1   Landowska was famous for her interpretation of Bach. Meeting a woman who also was a Bach specialist, she was soon deeply engrossed in discussion. The other lady's views on Bach ornamentation differed from Landowska's. "Well, my dear," said Landowska, "you continue to play Bach your way, and I'll continue to play him his way."

ஒ ஐ

LANDRU, Henri Désiré (1869–1922), *French multiple murderer, guillotined for at least eleven murders.*

1   Landru's trial was a popular sensation, with fashionable ladies, complete with picnic baskets and pet dogs, contending for seats in the courtroom. Landru's comment: "If any lady would care to have my place, I would willingly surrender it."

ஒ ஐ

LANG, [William] Cosmo Gordon, Baron Lang of Lambeth (1864–1945), *British clergyman, archbishop of Canterbury (1928–42).*

1   When William Orpen painted Lang's portrait, the archbishop had strong reservations. He asked the bishop of Durham what he thought of it, saying it seemed to portray him as "proud, arrogant, and worldly."
"To which of the three does Your Grace take exception?" inquired the bishop.

ஒ ஐ

LANGRISHE, Sir Hercules (1731–1811), *Irish politician.*

1   Someone expressed amazement to Sir Hercules that he had managed to consume three bottles of port at a sitting, asking if he had had any assistance. "None," he replied, "save that of a bottle of Madeira."

ஒ ஐ

LANGTRY, Lillie [Emilie Charlotte le Breton] (1853–1929), *British actress known as the Jersey Lily, her beauty contributing largely to her success on the stage. She moved in the highest social circles.*

1   Lillie Langtry was the mistress of the Prince of Wales (later King Edward VII). During a quarrel, the prince complained, "I've spent

enough on you to buy a battleship." Lillie retorted, "And you've spent enough in me to float one."

ॐ ◌

LAPLACE, Pierre-Simon, Marquis de (1749–1827), *French mathematician and astronomer. His major contribution to science was a detailed study of gravitation in the universe; his conclusions were published in his five-volume* Traité de mécanique céleste (Celestial Mechanics, 1798–1827). *Neutral in his views, he escaped execution during the Revolution. He served for a brief period as minister of the interior under Napoleon and was created a marquis by Louis XVIII.*

1   Laplace presented a copy of an early volume of his *Mécanique céleste* to Napoleon, who studied it very carefully. Sending for Laplace, he said, "You have written a large book about the universe without once mentioning the author of the universe."
  "Sire," Laplace replied, "I have no need of that hypothesis" (*Je n'ai pas besoin de cet hypothèse*).

2   Joseph-Louis Lagrange worked with Laplace on the *Mécanique céleste* and indeed made an original contribution to the thinking behind it. Laplace failed to acknowledge this contribution, an omission that the generous Lagrange appears not to have resented. When Lagrange heard of Laplace's reply to Napoleon, he is said to have shaken his head at his colleague's skepticism, commenting, "But it is a beautiful hypothesis just the same. It explains so many things."

ॐ ◌

LARDNER, Ring [Ringgold Wilmer] (1885–1933), *US writer. He is known for the biting, sardonic humor of his short stories, which through their conversational speech reveal the foibles and follies of "average" Americans.*

1   Lardner was drinking at a club frequented by actors when an individual came in whose flamboyance of dress and hairstyle were remarkable even in those theatrical surroundings. Lardner scrutinized the man for some minutes and then said to him, "How do you look when I'm sober?"

2   On an excursion Ring Lardner and Arthur Jacks stocked their hotel room with supplies of liquor, including a good Canadian whiskey and some inferior Midwestern corn. They made a heavy night of it. When Jacks awoke the following morning, he felt rather ill and in need of a drink. He poured himself some of the Canadian whiskey, which promptly made him sick. He tried again, with the same result. On Jacks's third or fourth unsuccessful attempt to keep the liquor down, Lardner opened one eye and said, "Arthur, if you're just practicing, would you mind using the corn?"

3   When the sportswriter Grantland Rice was invited to play golf with President Warren Harding, Ring Lardner arranged to join the party. "This is an unexpected pleasure, Mr. Lardner," said the president as they went around the course. "I only knew Granny was coming. How did you happen to make it, too?"
  "I want to be ambassador to Greece."
  "Greece?" said Harding. "Why Greece?"
  "Because my wife doesn't like Great Neck."

ॐ ◌

LARWOOD, Harold (1904–), *English cricketer. Larwood was an outstanding fast bowler, who played many times for England in the 1920s and early 1930s. He is remembered for his "body-line" bowling and the controversy it raised in the 1932–33 test matches against Australia.*

1   Larwood generously agreed to take part in a charity match. It soon became clear that the umpire regarded Larwood and his bowling with some disfavor when a dead-straight ball was intercepted by the batsman's pad. "How's that?" called Larwood, confident that he had dismissed the batsman on the leg-before-wicket rule. "Not out," said the umpire. Larwood bowled again, faster this time, and the batsman made a slash at the ball with his bat, snicked it, and sent it straight into the wicket-keeper's hands. "How's that?" again called Larwood. "Not out," said the umpire. Larwood took his full run and sent down one of his deadly fast deliveries. The batsman's wicket was blasted from the ground, bails and stumps flying through the air. Larwood turned to the umpire, "I darned near bowled him that time."

ॐ ◌

During the 1984 Olympic Games, held in Los Angeles, the gymnasts from China fielded a magnificent team. However, one of their stars, Yun Lou, scored a low 9.20 on the pommel horse exercise. Yun explained it: "Suit too big. Grabbed pants instead of pommel."

LATIMER, Hugh (?1485–1555), *English cleric, bishop of Worcester (1535–39), supporter of Henry VIII by declaring that Henry's marriage to Catherine of Aragon was illegal. He was a major figure in ecclesiastical reform during Edward VI's reign, but was executed under Queen Mary.*

1 After a show trial at Oxford, Latimer and the bishop of London, Nicholas Ridley, were condemned to be burned at the stake for heresy. As the fire was lighted, Latimer turned to his co-martyr and said, "Be of good comfort, Master Ridley, and play the man; we shall this day light such a candle, by God's grace, in England as I trust shall never be put out."

෯෨ ෧෯

LAUGHTON, Charles (1899–1962), *British character actor. His many successful films include* The Sign of the Cross *(1932),* Mutiny on the Bounty *(1935),* The Hunchback of Notre Dame *(1939), and* Hobson's Choice *(1954).*

1 Laughton, married to actress Elsa Lanchester, was once asked the hypothetical question: "Would you ever consider marrying again?" Having answered emphatically in the negative, the actor was asked his reasons. "During courtship," replied Laughton, "a man reveals only his better qualities. After marriage, however, his real self gradually begins to emerge, and there is very little his wife can do about it." After a moment's pause he concluded: "I don't believe I would ever put a woman through that again."

2 When the writer Ben Irwin lured his parents from rural New England to the West Coast, he took them to meet Charles Laughton. Laughton greeted all three warmly and showed them around his huge house and magnificent collection of art, discoursing at considerable length. Irwin watched his parents closely for some sign of enthusiasm, but found none. Only when they got back in their car and were driving away did his mother speak. "Did you notice?" asked Mrs. Irwin of her husband. "Notice what?" Mr. Irwin replied. "All that furniture," she went on, "and no doilies."

3 Having invited Laughton and a number of other film stars to dinner one evening, pianist Arthur Rubinstein entertained his guests before the meal by showing home movies of his children's amateur stage performances. The "audience" was visibly relieved when the last reel came to an end and dinner was served. "I've always regretted that I never had children," remarked Laughton to his host as they passed into the dining room, "and never more so than now. Because, Mr. Rubinstein, if I had children, I would make them play the piano for you."

෯෨ ෧෯

LAUZUN, Armand Louis de Gontaut, Duc de (1747–93), *French aristocrat and soldier. He went with Rochambeau to America during the Revolutionary War and brought back to France the news of the British surrender at Yorktown (1781). For a while he commanded an army for the French Revolutionary Committee, but military failures led to his fall and execution.*

1 When the executioner came to fetch the duke from his cell, he found him eating oysters and drinking wine. "Allow me to finish, citizen," said the condemned man. "And take a glass of this wine. In your profession you must need courage."

෯෨ ෧෯

LAVOISIER, Antoine Laurent (1743–94), *French chemist, discoverer of the two gases he named oxygen and nitrogen. During the French Revolution he was arrested for his membership in the Ferme Générale (the main tax-gathering agency) and guillotined.*

1 "But I'm a scientist," protested Lavoisier to the officer who had been sent to arrest him on the charge of tax-farming. "The Republic has no need of scientists," replied the man.

෯෨ ෧෯

LAW, [Andrew] Bonar (1858–1923), *British statesman; prime minister (1922–23).*

1 Bonar Law's elder daughter, Isabel, informed her father that she was going to marry Sir Frederick Sykes, who had made his mark as a capable administrator and politician during World War I. Bonar Law's only reaction to the news of this quite appropriate engagement was "Oh, Isabel, how could you — when you knew I was so worried about Ireland!"

8~ ~8

LAWRENCE, D[avid] H[erbert] (1885–1930), *British novelist and poet, son of a Nottinghamshire miner. His early novel* Sons and Lovers *(1913) is based on his own youthful experiences. He spent much of his life abroad, since his explicit treatment of sex and marriage caused a scandal in Britain.* Lady Chatterley's Lover *(1928), for instance, was not published in Britain in unexpurgated form until after the famous trial in 1961.*

1 Lawrence's first novel, *The White Peacock*, was published in 1911. He was able to give it to his mother on her deathbed. His father, after struggling through half a page, asked Lawrence how much he had got for the book. "Fifty pounds, father," he replied. The old miner was incredulous: "Fifty pounds! An' tha's niver done a day's hard work in thy life!"

8~ ~8

LAWRENCE, James (1781–1813), *US naval hero.*

1 During the War of 1812 the US frigate *Chesapeake* engaged the British frigate *Shannon* off Boston and was badly beaten. In the fighting James Lawrence, the *Chesapeake's* captain, was mortally wounded. His dying words are now part of American legend: "Don't give up the ship."

{There is some doubt whether this famous naval saying was actually Lawrence's or whether it was coined by Benjamin Russell, the editor of the *Columbian Centinel.*}

8~ ~8

LAWRENCE, T[homas] E[dward] (1888–1935), *British soldier and writer, known as "Lawrence of Arabia." While excavating (1911–14) the site of ancient Carchemish, he learned Arabic. In 1916 he joined the Arab revolt against the Turks, and led the Arabs'* *triumphal entry into Damascus in 1918, but failed to secure Arab independence. His* Seven Pillars of Wisdom *(privately published, 1926), is a classic of warfare that made Lawrence an almost legendary figure. Enlisting in the ranks of the RAF and later the Royal Tank Corps, Lawrence was killed in a motorcycle accident.*

1 (It was Lawrence's greatest source of pride that he was a Fellow of All Souls College, Oxford; it is, with his birth and death dates, the only fact about his career recorded on his tombstone in the quiet country churchyard in Dorset. Robert Graves (who tells the first two anecdotes here), recalls how, shortly after World War I, Lawrence acquired the two heavy leather chairs that were part of the furnishing in his rooms in All Souls.)

"An American oil-financier had come in suddenly one day when I was there and said, 'I am here from the States, Colonel Lawrence, to ask a single question. You are the only man who will answer it honestly. Do Middle-Eastern conditions justify my putting any money in South Arabian oil?' The always self-assured Lawrence, without rising, quietly answered, 'No.' 'That's all I wanted to know; it was worth coming for. Thank you, and good day!' In his brief glance about the room he missed something and, on his way home through London, chose the chairs and had them sent to Lawrence with his card."

2 "[Lawrence and I] planned to collaborate in a burlesque on contemporary writers in the style of a Government Blue-book. I said, 'First we must get a Blue-book and study it.' [Lawrence] agreed to buy one next time he went to London. When he asked at the Stationery Office for a Blue-book, the clerk asked, 'Which Blue-book? We have hundreds.' 'Whichever you like.' Mistaking his indifference for guilty embarrassment, the clerk handed him the report of a Royal Commission on Venereal Disease."

3 (Edward Marsh relates this story:)

"On one of his spells in the ranks [Lawrence] was assigned as batman to an officer of the class who used to be known in the War as 'temporary gentlemen.' Lawrence hated him at sight, and on the first evening, when he was unpacking his kit, looked round and said: 'I beg your pardon, sir, but I can only find one of your razors.' 'I've only got one razor.' 'Indeed, sir? I thought most gentlemen had a razor for every day in the week.' After a moment he looked round again. 'Sir, I can't find your left-handed nail-scissors.' The poor man rushed out of the tent and applied for a less exacting batman."

4   At a cocktail party in Egypt on a day of intense heat, Lawrence was approached by a lady of uncertain age who had the reputation of perseveringly courting the acquaintance of celebrities. Seizing upon the heat wave as a conversational gambit, she remarked, "Ninety-two today, Colonel Lawrence. Just think of it! Ninety-two."

"Many happy returns, madam," responded Lawrence.

෧ ๑

LAWRENCE, William (1850–1941), *US Episcopal bishop of Massachusetts from 1893 to 1927.*

1   (A pleasant, possibly apocryphal, story is told of Bishop Lawrence.)

Driving somewhere along Massachusetts' North Shore one day in the early 1900s, Lawrence happened upon a driver swearing profusely as he struggled to pry a flat tire from the rim. "Have you tried prayer, my good man?" gently inquired the bishop — upon which the poor fellow, in the desperation of his plight, fell to his knees, clasped his hands, and lifted his eyes heavenward. He then picked up the iron, inserted it, and off popped the tire. "Well, I'll be Goddamned!" exclaimed the bishop.

෧ ๑

LAWSON, Wilfrid [Wilfrid Worsnop] (1900–66), *British character actor. He first appeared on stage in 1916 and excelled in eccentric roles on stage and screen. His films include* Pygmalion *(1938),* The Great Mr. Handel *(1942), and* The Wrong Box *(1966).*

1   Lunching in a pub before a matinee performance, Lawson met fellow-actor Richard Burton and invited him to the show that afternoon. As Lawson was not due to appear at the beginning of the play, he sat with Burton to watch the opening scenes. Some twenty minutes into the performance, however, Burton

was a little concerned to find Lawson still sitting beside him, having made no move to leave and prepare for his entrance. A few moments later, Lawson tapped Burton on the arm. "You'll like this bit," he whispered excitedly. "This is where I come on."

෧ ๑

LAZAR, Irving Paul ["Swifty"] (1907–   ), *one of the most remarkable US literary and dramatic agents operating on the New York–Hollywood circuit.*

1   Former President Nixon, planning his memoirs, received the dynamic, short-statured Lazar at his Pacific Coast compound to listen to the agent's proposals. Lazar envisioned a two-million-dollar advance. After three hours of talk, they shook hands on the deal. Lazar was no admirer of Nixon but he was impressed by his spirit, his appearance, and particularly by his toughness and stamina. As he rose to take leave, Lazar said, "You know, there is one way you could make even more money than you can on this book." "What's that?" asked Nixon. "Leave your body to the Harvard Medical School."

෧ ๑

LEAHY, William Daniel (1875–1959), *US admiral; personal chief of staff to President Franklin D. Roosevelt during World War II and, after Roosevelt's death in 1945, to President Truman.*

1   When Truman came to office in 1945, Leahy was present at meetings at which the new president was briefed upon the development of an atomic weapon. Leahy's comment: "That is the biggest fool thing we have ever done. . . . The bomb will never go off."

෧ ๑

LEAR, Edward (1812–88), *British artist and poet. Much of his life was spent traveling in Europe and the Middle East. Although excelling as a landscape painter, he is best remembered for his delightful nonsense verse for children.*

1   In 1846 Lear was asked to give Queen Victoria a course of drawing lessons. These progressed very well and Lear soon felt quite at ease in the royal apartments. He liked to stand in front of the fire, warming his coattails, but

every time he took up his position on the hearthrug, facing the queen, one of the lords-in-waiting would invite him to look at something on the far side of the room, thus obliging him to move. No one explained, and the episode was repeated several times before it dawned upon Lear that etiquette forbade a subject to adopt such a relaxed and comfortable posture in his sovereign's presence.

2   Queen Victoria took a liking to Lear. Following one of the drawing lessons, she showed him some miniatures and other treasures kept in display cases in her apartments. Lear in his enthusiasm exclaimed, "Oh, where did you get all these beautiful things?" The queen replied, "I inherited them, Mr. Lear."

3   Traveling in southern Italy in 1847, Lear was overtaken by the beginnings of the Italian revolution at Reggio. He returned to his hotel to find the waiter deliriously drunk, and his pleas for the keys to his room fell on oblivious ears. "*Non ci sono più chiavi; non ci sono più passaporti, non ci sono più Ré — più legge — più giudici — più niente! Non x'e altro che l'amore, la libertà — l'amicizia e la constituzione . . .*" (There are no more keys, there are no more passports, no more kings, no more laws, no more judges, no more nothing! Nothing but love, liberty, friendship, and the constitution.)

4   When a man is in full flight upon some learned topic that tests the intellect and demands the greatest concentration, he does not especially welcome another's irrelevant witticisms. Just such a man was Lear's old friend Lord Westbury, the ex–lord chancellor. One evening, in the midst of a discussion on Tennyson, Lear could not help slipping in a small pun or two. "Lear," said the old man sternly, "I abominate the forcible introduction of ridiculous images calculated to distract the mind from what it is contemplating."

❧   ❧

LEDERER, Charles (1910–76), *US playwright and director.*

1   During the rehearsals for *Jumbo*, Lederer watched comedian Jimmy Durante trying to spirit the elephant past the sheriff, who was trying to serve a writ of attachment. "You could have the sheriff say, 'Where are you going with that elephant?'" suggested Lederer, "and then you could have Jimmy say, '*What* elephant?'" The suggestion was taken up and provided the biggest laugh in the show. Ben Hecht and Charles MacArthur, the writers, acknowledged their friend's contribution with a note in the program: "Joke by Charles Lederer."

❧   ❧

LEDRU-ROLLIN, Alexandre Auguste (1807–74), *French politician. Elected to the Chamber of Deputies in 1841, he quickly became associated with radical groups. A leader during the Revolution of 1848 and minister of the interior in the subsequent provisional government, he made a bid for the presidency in December 1848, which failed. He was later largely responsible for the adoption of universal suffrage in France.*

1   During the Revolution of February 1848 Ledru-Rollin was caught up in a mob at the barricades. Amid the confusion he was heard to shout, "Let me pass, I have to follow them, I am their leader!"

{The phrase has been used by many politicians, including John F. Kennedy.}

❧   ❧

LEE, Gypsy Rose [Rose Louise Hovick] (1919–1970), *US entertainer, professional celebrity, and author.*

1   In his book about his mother, Gypsy's son, Erik Lee Preminger, recalls that one of her favorite (and always financially productive) hobbies was sewing. In the spring of 1955 her friend Mr. John, the famous milliner, showed her his spring collection in advance. Gypsy bought one of the hats, took it apart, made a dozen copies, and distributed them to her friends as Easter gifts. Mr. John noticed one of these friends, complete with hat, walking past his shop and at once phoned Gypsy. She cut him off with, "Oh, John darling, I'm so glad you called. I made a few copies of your marvelous hat, and I need some labels. The hats look so naked without them." The labels arrived shortly. They read: "A Mr. John design stolen by Gypsy Rose Lee." Gypsy put one inside each hat.

> Thérèse Lachmann, one of the *grandes horizontales* of the era of Napoleon III, played with francs like a child playing with sand. Once an impecunious admirer pursued her for months, passionately. At length she instructed him to bring her ten thousand francs in small notes. "We'll waste them together," she promised him. He somehow acquired the necessary investment and arrived at Thérèse's boudoir to find her gracefully arranged on a couch beside which a marble table had been placed. On this altar she piled the crumpled notes and set a match to them. "I promise that your flame shall be allowed to burn as long as the notes," she told him. In very short order, money and passion were consumed, and she looked ironically at her lover. To her astonishment his face wore the same expression. "They were counterfeit," he said.

LEE, Nathaniel (?1653–92), *British playwright, author of a number of successful verse dramas, including* Sophonisba *(1676) and* The Rival Queens *(1677). After 1684 he suffered prolonged bouts of insanity, and was confined in the London asylum Bedlam.*

1 A friend visited Lee in Bedlam and, finding him calm and reasonable, hoped he had recovered. Lee offered to show him around the asylum. As they proceeded, Lee's conversation was so rational that the friend's hopes soared. At length they came out on the lofty roof of the building. Lee suddenly gripped his visitor's arm. "Let us immortalize ourselves; let us leap down this moment!" he burst out excitedly. "Any man could leap *down*," said Lee's friend coolly, "so we should not immortalize ourselves that way. But let us go down and try if we can leap *up*." Delighted with the idea, Lee at once ran down the stairs to see if he could put into practice his friend's novel idea for achieving immortality.

୫ ୶

LEE, Robert E[dward] (1807–70), *US Confederate general. His outstanding abilities as a strategist and leader made him the most success-ful Confederate commander during the Civil War (1861–65), although after losing 25,000 men at Gettysburg (July 1863) he was increasingly forced on the defensive.*

1 Confederate troops held a low ridge called Marye's Heights at Fredericksburg (1862). The Union divisions sent to assault it had exposed ground to cross before they could reach the Confederate positions. Wave after wave of federal troops charged with bayonets and were cut down by the Confederate fire before any could reach the stone wall marking the enemy front line. More than 12,000 were killed. Watching the dying federal soldiers, Lee remarked to General James Longstreet, whose men were holding Marye's Heights, "It is well that war is so terrible; else we would grow too fond of it."

2 One day in 1864 Lee visited General Henry Heth at Petersburg to inspect his defenses. As they rode down the line, Lee was displeased to see a large stretch without fortification. Heth was surprised, for he had given orders for the defenses to be completed. He assured the general that the work would be undertaken immediately, but when Lee returned a few days later nothing had been done. He was obviously very annoyed, and Heth waited anxiously for the storm to break. However, much to Heth's relief, Lee began talking instead about the rather boisterous horse being ridden by Heth's wife. To quiet the horse down, Lee recommended plenty of exercise. He concluded, "For the sake of your wife, as well as your own, I beg you to try the experiment; and I know of no better place for you to ride the horse than just up and down in front of the gap I ordered you to have closed, until a good breastwork has been completed."

3 Shortly before the battle of Spotsylvania in 1864, it was reported that General Grant had lost many men and was preparing to retreat. General John Gordon was therefore surprised when Lee ordered him to move his troops to Spotsylvania Courthouse. Lee, however, having great faith in Grant's military genius, had reasoned thus: "General Grant ought to move to Spotsylvania. That is his best maneuver and he will do what is best. I am so sure of it that I have had a short road cut to that point, and you will move by that route." The prediction was fulfilled: Grant's troops arrived at Spotsylvania at almost exactly the same moment as the Confederate forces under Gordon.

4 Toward the end of the Civil War, when meat was an almost unobtainable luxury for Lee, he lived chiefly on boiled cabbage. One day, when he had several important guests dining with him, the table was set with the usual heap of cabbage and a very small piece of meat. The guests politely refused the meat, and Lee looked forward to having it all to himself the following day. However, on the next day there was nothing but the usual cabbage. Lee inquired as to the whereabouts of the meat. He learned to his dismay that his servant had only borrowed the meat to impress the guests, and had duly returned it, untouched, to its rightful owner.

5 One Sunday morning in 1865, a black man entered a fashionable Episcopalian church in Richmond, Virginia. When Communion was served, he walked down the aisle and knelt at the altar. A rustle of resentment swept the congregation—how dare he! Episcopalians use the common cup. Then a distinguished layman stood up, stepped forward to the altar, and knelt beside the black man. It was Robert E. Lee. Said he to the congregation, "All men are brothers in Christ. Have we not all one Father?" Humbly, the congregation followed his lead.

6 After the Civil War Lee was encouraged to write his memoirs. He refused: "I should be trading on the blood of my men."

ॐ॰ ॰ॐ

LE GALLIENNE, Richard Thomas (1866–1947), *British poet and essayist. He was associated with many of the prominent literary figures of the 1890s. He describes the decadents and their literature in* The Romantic '90s *(1926).*

1 Despite his flowing hair and unconventional clothes, Richard Le Gallienne was a lay preacher. One of his sermons was published as "If I were God, by Richard Le Gallienne." A reviewer remarked, "If I were Richard Le Gallienne, by God I'd get my hair cut."

ॐ॰ ॰ॐ

When black boxers first began to dominate the heavyweight scene, many followers of the sport felt that the honor of the white race was at stake. Managers trained "white hopes" to challenge the black titleholders. One such challenger, advertised by his manager as a future world champion, fought Sam Langford, nicknamed "The Boston Tar Baby," and was hopelessly outclassed. Langford maneuvered the challenger around the ring to the point where his manager was seated and then with a cry of "Here comes your champion!" knocked him over the ropes into his manager's lap.

—*New Yorker,* July 29, 1950

LEGROS, Alphonse (1837–1911), *French painter and etcher. He settled in London in 1863 and was subsequently appointed Slade Professor of Fine Arts at University College, London (1876–93).*

1 During his time as Slade Professor, Legros became a naturalized British citizen. Asked by another French artist what he expected to gain by this "defection," Legros replied, "To begin with, I win the battle of Waterloo!"

ॐ॰ ॰ॐ

LEHMANN, Lilli (1848–1929), *German coloratura soprano, who specialized in Wagnerian roles. She studied under Wagner and appeared in the first complete performance of the Ring cycle at Bayreuth in 1876.*

1 At a reception given by Wagner's widow, Cosima, during the 1894 Bayreuth festival, soprano Lillian Nordica, who was singing Elsa in *Lohengrin* at the festival, approached Lilli Lehmann and asked if she might call on her. Glaring frostily at her potential rival, Lehmann replied: "I am not taking any pupils this season."

ॐ॰ ॰ॐ

LEIGHTON, Frederic, Baron Leighton of Stretton (1830–96), *British painter and sculptor. His elaborately finished paintings on classical subjects, often with a subdued erotic appeal,* *were enormously popular. Elected president of the Royal Academy (1878), he was ennobled shortly before his death.*

1   Leighton, who prided himself on the thoroughness of his draftsmanship, met Whistler one day in Piccadilly, and took it upon himself to remark upon the other artist's technique. "My dear Whistler, you leave your pictures in such a crude, sketchy state. Why don't you ever finish them?"

"My dear Leighton," was the response, "why do you ever begin yours?"

{The authenticity of this exchange is doubtful.}

ぎ✦ ✦ß

LENCLOS, Ninon de (1620–1705), *French courtesan whose salon attracted many prominent literary and political figures, including the playwright Molière and the philosopher Saint-Évremond. Her disregard for religion prompted Anne of Austria, mother of Louis XIV, to have her confined in a monastery. Her friends soon arranged her release, but not before she had seduced (or been seduced by) 439 monks; she apparently kept detailed records.*

1   Ninon de Lenclos's sexual expertise was so renowned that daughters of the aristocracy were sent to her to learn the art of love. One such student asked, "How large should a woman's breast be to attract a lover?"

"Large enough to fill the hand of an honest man," replied her instructress.

2   Ninon de Lenclos had no time for the fashionable group of writers known as the *précieuses,* and poked fun at their literary and social affectations. When a man complained to her that his daughter had lost her memory, she answered, "Be thankful, monsieur, for that will prevent her from quoting."

3   A nobleman forced to flee Paris entrusted half his savings of twenty thousand crowns to a clergyman and the other half to Ninon, asking them both to look after the money for him until he returned. When the nobleman eventually came back to Paris, he found that the clergyman had given away his ten thousand crowns to the poor to enhance his own charitable reputation. If this was how the saint behaved, then what could he expect from the sinner? Ninon,

however, had kept her share intact and was delighted to be able to hand back his ten thousand crowns.

4   In her sixties Ninon de Lenclos still received a few young men, the sons of close friends, to educate them in the skills of being a gentleman. One, a certain Monsieur de Gersay, fell in love with her. Knowing him to be her own son, Ninon ridiculed him, pleading that at her age no sexual relationship could even be contemplated. The youth persisted until his mother had no alternative but to say, "This dreadful love cannot continue. Do you realize who you are and who I am?" The boy, stunned, murmured the word "Mother," ran outside into the garden, drew his sword, and fell upon it.

5   In her will Ninon de Lenclos left only ten écus to provide for her funeral. She wished it to be as simple as possible. However, she did ask her attorney, M. Arouet, if she might leave a thousand francs to his son, a clever lad who was studying with the Jesuits, so that he could buy books. The attorney's son grew up to be Voltaire.

ぎ✦ ✦ß

LENYA, Lotte (1900–81), *Austrian-born actress and singer. She is famous for her interpretations of songs composed by her first husband, Kurt Weill. Outstanding successes in her long career included roles in the Brecht-Weill Three-penny Opera (1928) and the American revue Brecht on Brecht (1962).*

1   Although she had a magnetic stage personality, Lotte Lenya was no beauty. She would often tell the story of how Kurt Weill proposed to her. They were boating one afternoon on a lake, Weill wearing his thick glasses, since he was very nearsighted. Accidentally, she knocked them into the water. Later that afternoon he asked her to marry him. Sometime afterward she asked him, "Would you have married me with your glasses on?" He peered at her closely and said, "I *think* so."

ぎ✦ ✦ß

LEO X (1475–1521), *pope (1513–21). Born Giovanni de' Medici, second son of Lorenzo the Magnificent, Leo in 1489 was made a cardinal through family interest. As pope he was a noted* *patron of the arts, but allowed the papacy to suffer some major political and financial setbacks.*

1 As Leo was a smiling sybarite infected with the popular neopagan culture of his day, his pontificate was a gorgeous carnival that left the Church bankrupt. To his flair for bacchanalian diversions, he added a reckless patronage of the arts, worked Raphael to death, and adorned his court with all the entertainers, scholars, and poets money could buy. When he was enthroned, he remarked: "Since God has given us the papacy, let us enjoy it."

ε≫ ≪з

LEONIDAS (died 480 BC), *king of Sparta (487–480). He led the last stand of the Greek troops at Thermopylae, where he and his three hundred Spartan followers were killed by the Persians. Over their tomb is the most famous of Greek epitaphs: "Go, stranger, and tell the Lacedaemonians that here we lie, obedient to their commands."*

1 The Persians sent an envoy to Leonidas urging the futility of resistance to the advance of their huge army. "Our archers are so numerous," said the envoy, "that the flight of their arrows darkens the sun."

"So much the better," replied Leonidas, "for we shall then fight in the shade."

ε≫ ≪з

LEOPOLD II (1835–1909), *king of the Belgians (1865–1909). Leopold sponsored Henry Stanley's exploration of the Congo and ruled the vast area as a personal estate until 1908, when it became a Belgian colony.*

1 A zealous republican once observed to King Leopold that although he had no liking for monarchies he did acknowledge Leopold's superior qualities. "I admit you would make an excellent president of a republic," he went on. "Really?" said the king. "I must remember to pass that compliment along to my doctor. 'Thiriar,' I'll say, 'you are an excellent doctor and I think you would make an admirable vet.'"

2 Once while King Leopold was in consultation with his ministers, a breeze blew a pile of documents from his desk onto the floor. "You

pick them up," said the king, pointing to his nephew, the heir apparent, Prince Albert. "Leave him alone," he went on, addressing the ministers, who were clearly embarrassed to see their future monarch groveling on the floor. "A constitutional king must learn to stoop."

ε≫ ≪з

LESCHETIZKY, Theodor (1830–1915), *Polish pianist. He was an influential teacher, numbering Paderewski among his pupils.*

1 Leschetizky considered that there were three essentials for pianistic greatness. He used to ask prospective pupils three questions: "Were you a child prodigy? Are you of Slavic descent? Are you a Jew?" If the answer to all three was "Yes," Leschetizky was delighted and would undertake the young player's tuition.

ε≫ ≪з

LESSING, Gotthold Ephraim (1729–81), *German dramatist, historian, and theologian. His* Laokoön *(1766) reacted against the formality of French classical aesthetics and influenced the Romantic movement. In later life he wrote some important theological works.*

1 Many stories are told of Lessing's absentmindedness. One evening, returning home after dark without his key, he knocked on the front door of his house. A servant looked out of a window and, not recognizing his master in the gloom, called out, "The professor is not at home."

"Oh, very well," said Lessing, turning away. "No matter. Tell him I'll call another time."

ε≫ ≪з

LEVANT, Oscar (1906–72), *US pianist, writer, and wit, author of* A Smattering of Ignorance *(1940), and premier interpreter of the music of George Gershwin.*

1 During World War II Oscar Levant appeared before the draft-board examiner. "Do you think you can kill?" the official asked. "I don't know about strangers," replied Oscar, "but friends, yes."

2 Levant was playing a virtuoso passage at a college concert when a telephone began ringing offstage. The pianist carried on, but the ringing continued and soon the audience became restless. Levant, without pausing in his playing, glanced at the audience and said, "If that's for me, tell them I'm busy."

3   Every conductor interprets the first four bars of Beethoven's Fifth Symphony in a different way. Oscar Levant and Bernard Herrmann, the movie composer, were discussing the differences. "How would *you* play them, Oscar?" asked Herrmann. "Oh, I'd omit them," replied Oscar.

4   The model for the face on the Liberty Head dime was Mrs. Wallace Stevens, wife of the famous poet. Introduced once to Stevens, Oscar Levant's first words were: "Why shouldn't you be a great poet? I'd be inspired too if my wife had little wings where her ears should be."

5   Oscar Levant once escorted Beatrice Kaufman, the wife of George S. Kaufman, to a performance of Bach's Mass in B Minor. Mrs. Kaufman, no music lover, enjoined him, "In heaven's name, let's hurry, or we'll miss the intermission."

6   As a houseguest in the Kaufman household, Levant rather overstayed his welcome. At the end of one of his prolonged visits, Mrs. Kaufman hinted, "The servants always expect a little something, and I know you haven't any money, so I tipped them each three dollars and told them it was from you." Levant was outraged. "You should have given them five!" he exclaimed. "Now they'll think I'm stingy."

7   (Oscar Levant describes his reprisals against a woman who arrived late for one of his recitals and distracted the audience as she walked down the center aisle.)
"I stopped my performance of a Poulenc piece and began choreographing her walk by playing in time with her steps. She hesitated and slowed down—I slowed down. She stopped—I stopped. She hurried—I hurried. By the time she reached her seat, the audience was in hysterics and the matron in a state of wild confusion."

8   Jack Paar, host of the *Tonight Show,* recalls Levant's story of the time he and June, his wife, were guests of President and Mrs. Truman at

the White House. As they were bidding their hosts goodnight, Oscar turned to June and said resignedly, "Now we have to have them over to dinner."

ଓଓ   ଙଓ

LÉVIS, Duc Gaston Pierre Marc de (?1764–1830), *French aristocrat and author of works such as* Maximes et réflexions *(1808) and* Voyages de Kang-hi *(1812).*

1   The de Lévis family considered itself to be the oldest in Christendom. Their château was reputed to contain two paintings to prove it: one of Noah going into the Ark with a box full of the Lévis papers under his arm; the other of the Virgin Mary addressing the founder of the house as *mon cousin* and begging him to put his hat back on.

ଓଓ   ଙଓ

LEWIS, C[live] S[taples] (1898–1963), *British writer and scholar. After teaching at Oxford for thirty years (1925–54), he became professor of medieval and Renaissance English at Cambridge (1954–63). Besides literary criticism, he wrote a number of popular works on religious themes, the most successful being* The Screwtape Letters *(1942). He also published science fiction and children's books about the imaginary land of Narnia, which combined themes and motifs from his other writings.*

1   An important part of the selection procedure for Oxford fellowships—and one much dreaded by shy candidates—was dinner at the high table with the assembled dons, who would put aspirants through their social paces. When C. S. Lewis was a candidate for a fellowship in English at Magdalen College, Oxford, he was placed next to the elderly and formidable Sir Herbert Warren, president of the college. Throughout the first two courses the president did not speak a word. Then, as the meat course was served, Warren spoke: "Do you like poetry, Mr. Lewis?" Lewis replied, "Yes, President, I do." As there seemed to be no further reaction from his eminent neighbor, he added, "I also like prose." That was the whole extent of their conversation. Lewis was awarded his fellowship.

2   The medievalist Nevill Coghill once encountered C. S. Lewis walking in the grounds

of Magdalen College. Lewis was wearing a happy smile. Coghill greeted him with, "You're looking very pleased with yourself. What is it?"

"I believe," Lewis replied modestly but triumphantly, "I have proved that the Renaissance never happened in England." Coghill was about to interrupt in astonishment, but Lewis checked him and went on: "Alternatively, that if it did it had no importance."

3 Lewis had been on a walking tour. As he boarded the train for his return journey, his unkempt appearance startled an old lady in the first-class compartment. "Have you a first-class ticket?" she asked. "Yes, madam," replied Lewis, "but I'm afraid I'll be needing it for myself."

ह‍ॐ ॐई

LEWIS, Joe E. (1902–71), *US nightclub entertainer.*

1 In his early barnstorming days, Lewis stopped once at a boardinghouse whose proprietress could make a pound of food go farther than could any other landlady in history. One Sunday she produced a platter full of cold cuts that were actually transparent. "Did you cut these?" asked Lewis politely, indicating the slices. "I did," said the landlady. "Okay," said Lewis. "Then I'll deal."

ह‍ॐ ॐई

LEWIS, Matthew Gregory (1775–1818), *British novelist and poet, known as "Monk" Lewis for his horror-romance,* The Monk *(1796).*

1 The immensely successful *Monk* brought its author the adulation of high society, an attention he greatly enjoyed. Byron records seeing Lewis with red eyes and air "sentimental" and asking him what was the matter. "I am so deeply affected by kindness," said the author, "and just now the Duchess of York said something so kind to me — " Here he broke off as his tears began to flow again. "Never mind, Lewis," said a colonel who was standing nearby, "never mind, don't cry. She couldn't mean it."

ह‍ॐ ॐई

LEWIS, Sinclair (1885–1951), *US novelist. His novels of social satire include* Main Street *(1920) and* Babbitt *(1922). He was awarded the* 1930 Nobel Prize for literature, the first American author to receive the award.

1 Sinclair Lewis met journalist Dorothy Thompson a few days after her divorce had come through and immediately proposed marriage to her. She hesitated, saying that she knew him only as a public figure, not as a private person. He replied that he would continue to ask her in public and private to marry him until she consented. Shortly afterward, called upon at a dinner party to make a speech, he stood up, said, "Dorothy, will you marry me?" and sat down again.

2 In 1927, when he began his courtship of Dorothy Thompson, Sinclair Lewis followed her across Europe, all the way to Moscow. At Moscow airport, says John Jakes in *Great Women Reporters,* the press was waiting to greet him. "What brought you to Russia?" Lewis was asked.

"Dorothy," he said.

"We mean, what's your business here?" the press persisted.

"Dorothy," said Lewis.

"You misunderstand. What do you plan to see in Russia?"

"Dorothy," said Lewis.

{Lewis's eventual marriage to Dorothy Thompson ended in divorce.}

3 Lewis, staying at a hotel that boasted a swimming pool, heard that the pool was at the moment occupied by a contingent of policemen using the hotel as a convention headquarters. Lewis promptly descended to the pool, somehow secured admittance, took off his clothes, jumped in, introduced himself as Patrolman So-and-so, and spent a happy hour exchanging professional anecdotes with two hundred nude cops. By dinnertime they were all buddies. Everybody clambered out. The policemen got into their uniforms. Lewis got into his sack suit. He grinned at his colleagues and made a quick beeline for his room.

4 Booked to give a lecture at Columbia University on the writer's craft, Sinclair Lewis began by asking, "How many of you here are really serious about being writers?" A forest of hands shot up. "Well, why the hell aren't you all home writing?" said Lewis, and sat down.

5 After Lewis's death in Rome from alcoholism, his body was cremated and the urn containing his ashes sent to the US embassy for safekeeping until their final disposal. A caller was surprised to find one of the consular officials on her knees, busy with a broom and pan, an overturned funerary urn beside her. "Whatever are you doing?" he said. "Sweeping up Sinclair Lewis," was the response.

સ્જ ·ৡ

LIBERACE, Wladziu Valentino ["Liberace"] (1919–), *US pianist, renowned for his sequined suits and flamboyant life-style as much as for his piano-playing.*

1 Liberace's concert in Madison Square Garden, New York, in June 1954 was vastly successful with his fans, but the critics loathed him. Some time later Liberace observed to the latter, "What you said hurt me very much. I cried all the way to the bank."

સ્જ ·ৡ

LI BO (701–762), *Chinese poet. He led a wandering life, briefly enjoying spells of court employment. He is considered one of China's greatest poets.*

1 A lover of beauty and wine, Li Bo met his death appropriately. According to popular tradition, he was out in a boat one evening. Trying to embrace the reflection of the moon, which shone full on the water, he fell in and drowned.

સ્જ ·ৡ

LICHTENBERG, Georg Christoph (1742–99), *German physicist and satirist. As a scientist, he investigated electricity. As a satirist, he attacked Greek pronunciation, Johann Lavater's science of physiognomy, and the* Sturm und Drang *writers. His reputation rests largely on his aphorisms.*

1 One day a person not noted for his tact made a slighting remark to Lichtenberg about his notably large ears. Lichtenberg replied: "Well, just think of it — with my ears and your brains we'd make a perfectly splendid ass, wouldn't we?"
Compare GEORGE BERNARD SHAW 9.

સ્જ ·ৡ

LIEBERMANN, Max (1847–1935), *German painter and etcher of Jewish descent. He specialized in depicting the lives of the poor and obscure — peasants, factory workers, orphans, and the occupants of almshouses. From 1884 he lived in Berlin, where he became president of the Berlin Academy.*

1 Despite the growing anti-Semitism in Germany in the early 1930s, President Paul von Hindenburg sent emissaries to Liebermann, asking him to make a portrait of Hindenburg, but specifying that it must be done within a very short space of time. Liebermann promptly showed Hindenburg's agents the door. As he flung it open, he pointed to the snow that lay deep outside and said, "If I were to piss on that snow, I could do a very good likeness of Hindenburg."

સ્જ ·ৡ

LIEBLING, Abbott Joseph (1904–63), *US journalist, noted for his work on* The New Yorker.

1 (Brendan Gill describes how he and Liebling were trying to cross the street when they got caught up in one of the numerous "ethnic" parades that periodically snarl up the New York streets.)
"We waited in vain on the curb as the band of Our Lady of Sorrows blocked every foot of space in front of us. 'One of the great things about the Jews,' I said to Liebling, 'is that they're the only large group in New York that doesn't insist on a parade. Why should that be?' Liebling thought and thought. 'Their feet hurt,' he said at last."

સ્જ ·ৡ

LIEVEN, Dariya Khristoforovna, Princess de (1784–1857), *Russian aristocrat. At the age of sixteen she married the Russian diplomat Khristofor de Lieven, ambassador to Berlin (1809) and London (1812–34). After his death in 1839, she lived in Paris, where her salon was frequented by the leading diplomats of Europe.*

1 The widowed Princess de Lieven was asked whether she would now marry François Guizot, the utterly middle-class politician and historian with whom she had been living for several years, and with whom she continued to live until her death. "Oh! my dear," she replied, "can you see me being announced as Mrs. Guizot?"

Jean Cocteau, in his old age, related the following in conversation with William Fifield:

"I will recount one thing. Then you must let me rest. You perhaps know the work of the painter Domergue? The long girls? Calendar art, I am afraid. He had a domestic in those days — a 'housemaid' — who would make the beds, fill the coal scuttles. We all gathered in those days at the Café Rotonde. And a little man with a bulging forehead and a black goatee would come there sometimes for a glass and to hear us talk. This was the 'housemaid' of Domergue, out of funds. We asked him once (he said nothing and merely listened) what he meant to do with himself. He said he meant to overthrow the government of Russia. We all laughed, because of course we did too. That is the kind of time it was. It was Lenin."

— William Fifield,
In Search of Genius

LILIENCRON, Detlev von (1844–1909), *German lyric poet and novelist.*

1 Dining one evening with a group of local noblemen, Liliencron listened while one of them boasted at length about his aristocratic ancestors who had fought in the Crusades, sailed with Columbus, and so forth. "You remind me of a potato," Liliencron said at last.
"How so?"
"The best part is underground."

2 Liliencron was often in dire financial straits. One of his creditors stopped him in the street and demanded payment. "Sorry, but I have no money," said Liliencron. "Please be patient."
"But that's what you said four weeks ago."
"Well," said Liliencron triumphantly, "haven't I kept my word?"

LILLIE, Beatrice (1898–), *Canadian-born actress and outstandingly successful comedienne in revues. She married the British peer Sir*

Robert Peel in 1920. Her autobiography, Every Other Inch a Lady, *was published in 1973.*

1 Beatrice Lillie, carrying her Pekinese puppy, took a cab to a smart London hotel. As she got out, she noticed a small puddle on the seat. The driver noticed it at the same time and began to complain. Slipping a large tip into his hand, Miss Lillie said firmly, "*I* did it," and whisked into the hotel.

2 Beatrice Lillie was dining at Buckingham Palace, wearing an exquisite model gown, when a waiter spilled a ladleful of soup down her dress. There was a horrified silence as he desperately mopped at the stain. Miss Lillie broke the hush by saying in ringing tones, "Never darken my Dior again."

3 Miss Lillie, in a Chicago beauty salon with several members of her company, overheard a conversation between the receptionist and a client who was annoyed at being kept waiting. "Oh, if I'd known all these theatrical people would be here today, I'd never have come," said the woman in a loud and affected voice. Miss Lillie found out that she was Mrs. Armour, wife of the Chicago meat-packing tycoon. As Miss Lillie was leaving, she saw Mrs. Armour still in the reception area. Without looking at her, she said to the receptionist in her clear English tones, "You may tell the butcher's wife that Lady Peel has finished."

4 A pigeon blundered in through the open window of a room where Miss Lillie was sitting. She looked up brightly and said, "Any messages?"

5 Miss Lillie was already an established star when she befriended the child actor Brandon de Wilde in New York. She took him out on several excursions, including a visit to the Coney Island Tunnel of Love. A radio interviewer asked the child what Miss Lillie did in the Tunnel of Love. The little boy patiently explained, "Well, you see, it's very dark in there, so naturally she doesn't do anything."

6 Beatrice Lillie was very much an international actress. Once, while in Philadelphia with the play *Inside U.S.A.*, she was asked by a newspaperman for a particular picture, which he wanted for his story. "It's right up in my

London apartment," she told him. "Why don't you go there and pick it up?"

7 At a reception given for Josephine Baker on one of her trips to New York, many theatrical personalities were invited. Among them was Beatrice Lillie, who patiently waited her turn to greet the fabulous Josephine. Unfortunately, Miss Baker chose this occasion to put on her well-known regal air. Holding out her hand for Beatrice to kiss, she purred, "Ah, Lady Peel, eet *is* a great plaisir." Bea Lillie glanced at the proffered hand: "Ah likes you too, honey," she said.

8 (Clifton Daniel tells the following story.)

"One bright day on Piccadilly I saw an unmistakable figure approaching — Bea on the arm of a man. She had been abroad entertaining the 'troooops,' as she called them, and I hadn't seen her for a long time.

"As she came down the street I maneuvered myself so that she could not avoid running into me. When she did she threw open her arms and embraced me.

"'Darling,' she cried, 'how *are* you?' Still holding me, she leaned back and examined my face. 'And *who* are you?'"

9 In Hollywood one day, Miss Lillie was absentmindedly driving on the left-hand side of the road when she suddenly noticed another car bearing down on her. She swerved to the left and crashed, wrecking the car but escaping with a few cuts and bruises. She staggered to the nearest house, which happened to be that of film star John Gilbert. "Why, Bea! What's up?" cried Gilbert as he opened the door. "Heard there was a party," gasped Miss Lillie. "Came."

৪ ৵

LINCOLN, Abraham (1809–65), *US statesman; 16th president of the United States (1861–65). Born in a log cabin, Lincoln was a self-educated man. He became a lawyer and in 1847 entered Congress as a representative from Illinois. An opponent of slavery, he was elected president on an antislavery ticket, an election that precipitated the secession of the Southern states and the Civil War. In 1863 Lincoln issued the Emancipation Proclamation, freeing Southern slaves, and two years later masterminded the Thirteenth Amendment, prohibiting slavery anywhere in the United States. He proposed a generous settlement to the defeated Southerners, hoping to heal the wounds caused by the war, but only a few days after its end he was assassinated while attending the theater in Washington. The most famous of Lincoln's speeches is the Gettysburg Address (1863). A vast fund of anecdotes and humorous stories by him or told of him have accumulated under his name. Many are doubtless apocryphal.*

1 As a young man Lincoln was captain of a militia company during the Black Hawk War of 1832. He was not well versed in military procedures. One day, as he was leading a squad of some twenty men across a field, the appropriate word of command for getting them into position for marching through a gate went right out of his mind. In desperation, he shouted, "This company is dismissed for two minutes, and will fall in again on the other side of the gate."

2 When Lincoln was a lawyer, an out-of-town case required him to hire a horse from the local livery stables. Returning the animal, he asked the liveryman whether he kept the horse for funerals. "Certainly not," said its owner indignantly. "I am glad to hear it," said Lincoln, "because if you did, the corpse would not get there in time for the resurrection."

3 Lincoln's friend and fellow-lawyer Ward Lamon was on circuit in Illinois. While waiting outside the courtroom, Lamon was challenged to a wrestling match and in the struggle tore the seat of his trousers. Immediately afterward he was summoned into court for a case. His short coat did not conceal the damaged condition of his trousers. One of the other lawyers facetiously started a subscription paper to buy him a new pair, and it was passed around the various members of the bar. When the paper reached Lincoln, he wrote his name and under the column for the amount the words: "I can contribute nothing to the end in view."

4 In his legal practice Lincoln was never greedy for fees and discouraged unnecessary litigation. A man came to him in a passion, asking him to bring a suit for $2.50 against an impoverished debtor. Lincoln tried to dissuade him, but the man was determined upon revenge. When he saw that the creditor was not to be put off, Lincoln asked for and got $10 as his legal fee. He gave half of this to the defendant, who thereupon willingly confessed to the debt and paid up the $2.50, thus settling the matter to the entire satisfaction of the irate plaintiff.

5   (A clerk of the court relates the only occasion on which he was fined for contempt of court.)
"Davis fined me five dollars. Mr. Lincoln had just come in, and leaning over my desk had told me a story so irresistibly funny that I broke out into a loud laugh. The judge called me to order, saying, 'This must be stopped. Mr. Lincoln, you are constantly disturbing this court with your stories.' Then to me: 'You may fine yourself $5.00.' I apologized, but told the judge the story was worth the money. In a few minutes the judge called me over to him. 'What was that story Lincoln told you?' he asked. I told him, and he laughed aloud in spite of himself. 'Remit your fine,' he ordered."

6   A New York firm wrote to Lincoln, then practicing law, requesting information about the financial circumstances of one of his neighbors. The reply was as follows: "I am well acquainted with Mr.——, and know his circumstances. First of all, he has a wife and baby; together, they ought to be worth $50,000 to any man. Secondly, he has an office in which there is a table worth $1.50, and three chairs, worth $1.00. Last of all, there is in one corner a large rat-hole which will bear looking into. Respectfully yours, A. Lincoln."

7   During his time as a lawyer in Springfield, Lincoln was walking into town one day when he was overtaken by a man driving in the same direction. Lincoln hailed him and asked, "Will you have the goodness to take my overcoat to town for me?"
"With pleasure," responded the stranger, "but how will you get it again?"
"Oh, very easily; I intend to remain in it."
{This may be a standard joke, attributed —like many others—to Lincoln.}

8   On hearing the anguished cries of children in the street, one of Lincoln's neighbors in Springfield rushed out of his house in alarm. There he found Lincoln with two of his sons, both of whom were sobbing uncontrollably.

"Whatever is the matter with the boys, Mr. Lincoln?" he asked. "Just what's the matter with the whole world," replied Lincoln resignedly. "I've got three walnuts, and each wants two."

9   When Lincoln ran for Congress as a Whig in 1846, his Democratic opponent was an evangelical Methodist, Peter Cartwright. During the campaign Lincoln attended a religious meeting at which Cartwright, after a stirring address, invited all those who wished to go to heaven to stand up. A few people rose self-consciously to their feet. "Now all those who do not wish to go to hell will stand!" The rest of the audience, with the exception of Lincoln, stood up. Cartwright saw an opportunity to embarrass his rival. "May I inquire of you, Mr. Lincoln, where you are going?" Lincoln stood up and said calmly, "I came here as a respectful listener. I did not know I was to be singled out by Brother Cartwright. I believe in treating religious matters with due solemnity. I admit that the questions propounded by Brother Cartwright are of great importance. I did not feel called upon to answer as the rest did. Brother Cartwright asks me directly where I am going. I desire to reply with equal directness: I am going to Congress."
{One of many Lincoln anecdotes of doubtful authenticity.}

10   In 1858 the Illinois legislature elected Stephen A. Douglas senator instead of Lincoln. A sympathetic friend asked Lincoln how he felt. "Like the boy who stubbed his toe; I am too big to cry and too badly hurt to laugh."
{Adlai Stevenson, when defeated by Dwight Eisenhower in 1952, ruefully recalled this story.}

11   Stephen Douglas was attempting to discomfit Lincoln by making allusions to his lowly start in life. He told a gathering that the first time he had met Lincoln it had been across the counter of a general store in which Lincoln was serving. "And an excellent bartender he was too," Douglas concluded. When the laughter had died away, Lincoln got up and said, "What Mr. Douglas says is quite true: I did keep a general store and sold cotton and candles and cigars and sometimes whiskey, and I particularly remember Mr. Douglas, as he was a very good customer. Many a time I have been on

one side of the counter and sold whiskey to Mr. Douglas on the other side. But now there's a difference between us: I've left my side of the counter, but he sticks to his as tenaciously as ever."

12   Lincoln was called in as arbiter in many disputes, serious and frivolous. Two men who had been arguing for hours about the correct proportion of the length of a man's legs to the size of his body called on Lincoln to settle the question. Lincoln listened gravely to the points on both sides, and then gave his summing up in full legal fashion. It seemed to him, he said, that this was a question of the utmost significance and one that had caused much bloodshed in the past and would doubtless do so again in the future, so it was not without much mental anguish and exertion that he reached his opinion. Nonetheless, he concluded, "It is my opinion, all side issues being swept aside, that a man's lower limbs, in order to preserve harmony of proportion, should be at least long enough to reach from his body to the ground."

13   Holding the copy of his speech, his hat, and a cane, Lincoln arrived at the rostrum to be sworn in as president. He laid the cane down, but there was nowhere to put the hat. Senator Stephen A. Douglas quickly came forward and relieved him of it. As he sat down, he observed to one of Mrs. Lincoln's cousins, "If I can't be president, I can at least hold his hat."

14   As Lincoln was walking down a corridor in the War Department building, an army officer in a hurry barged straight into him. When the man saw who it was, he offered "ten thousand pardons."
    "One is quite enough," said Lincoln, adding, "I wish the whole army would charge like that!"

15   At the conclusion of his tour of America, an aristocratic young Englishman secured an audience with President Lincoln. The talk turning to social conditions, the visitor expressed amazement that many gentlemen in America customarily blacked their own boots. "True," replied Lincoln, "but would gentlemen in England not do that?"
    "Certainly not."
    "Then, whose boots do they black?" asked Lincoln.

{This is a rather more plausible version of a popular story that depicts Lincoln being interrupted by a foreign diplomat in the act of cleaning his own boots; the punch line is the same.}

16   A delegation called on Lincoln to ask that the commissionership of the Sandwich Islands be given to a particular man. After setting out his qualifications they concluded by saying that their candidate was in poor health and the climate in the Sandwich Islands would be beneficial to him. "I am sorry to say, gentlemen," said Lincoln, "that there are eight other applicants for the post, and they are all sicker than your man."

17   The singer Lillie de Hegermann-Lindencrone records in a letter a conversation she had with Lincoln. Lincoln remarked that if he heard her sing often he might have to become a musician himself. "But," he added, "so far I only know two tunes."
    " 'Hail, Columbia'?" she asked. "You know that, I am sure."
    "Oh, yes," he replied, "I know that, for I have to stand up and take off my hat."
    "And the other one?"
    "The other one? Oh, that is the one when I don't stand up."
    See also ULYSSES S. GRANT 11.

18   President Lincoln turned down an applicant for a job and gave as his reason: "I don't like his face." One of the members of his cabinet indicated that he did not think this was a sufficient and satisfactory explanation. Lincoln disagreed: "Every man over forty is responsible for his face."

19   Lincoln particularly enjoyed a story that circulated in Washington during the Civil War concerning him and the president of the Confederate States, Jefferson Davis. Two Quaker ladies were discussing the relative merits and prospects of the opposing leaders. "I think Jefferson will succeed because he is a praying man," said one. "But so is Abraham a praying man," said the other. "Yes," rejoined the first lady, "but the Lord will think that Abraham is joking."

20   A woman once approached Lincoln, demanding a colonel's commission for her son.

"My grandfather fought at Lexington, my father fought at New Orleans, my husband was killed at Monterey. I ask the commission not as a favor, but as a right."

"I guess, madam," answered Lincoln, "your family has done enough for the country. It's time to give somebody else a chance."

21 When the Confederate forces were attacking Fort Stevens, Lincoln made a tour of inspection of the Union defenses. He was shown around by the general's aide, Oliver Wendell Holmes, Jr. As Holmes pointed out the enemy lines, Lincoln, wearing his customary tall hat, stood up to get a better view. At once there was a crackle of musketry fire from the opposing trenches. "Get down, you fool!" shouted Holmes, grabbing the president and hauling him under cover. An instant later he realized what he had said, and wondered what kind of disciplinary action would be taken against him. As Lincoln was leaving, he bade the young officer farewell with the words, "Goodbye, Captain Holmes. I'm glad to see you know how to talk to a civilian."

22 In a discussion on the manpower and resources in the Civil War someone asked Lincoln how many men the Confederates had in the field. "Twelve hundred thousand," was the prompt and astonishing reply. Seeing the amazement and disbelief on the faces of those around him, Lincoln went on, "No doubt of it — twelve hundred thousand. You see, all our generals, every time they get whipped, they tell me that the enemy outnumbered them at least three to one, and I must believe them. We have four hundred thousand men in the field, and three times four equals twelve. Twelve hundred thousand men, no doubt about it."

23 In the later months of 1862 Lincoln was angered by General George B. McClellan's inactivity, despite his superiority in numbers over the Confederate forces. In the end he wrote McClellan a single-sentence letter: "If you don't want to use the army, I should like to borrow it for a while. Yours respectfully, A. Lincoln."

24 When General Joseph Hooker, nicknamed "Fighting Joe," was appointed commander in chief of the Union army, he was anxious to dispel the impression of incompetence and inaction left by his predecessors in the post, though, as it turned out, he was temperamentally unsuited to supreme command. On one occasion he reported his energetic activities to Lincoln in a dispatch datelined "Headquarters in the saddle." Lincoln received it and sighed: "The trouble with Hooker is that he has got his headquarters where his hindquarters ought to be."

25 In September 1862 Lincoln called a special session of his closest advisers. When they arrived, he was reading a book. At first he paid little attention to their entrance, then started to read aloud to them a piece by the humorist Artemus Ward entitled "A High-Handed Outrage at Utica," which Lincoln found very funny. At the end he laughed heartily but no one joined in; the cabinet members sat in stony disapproval of the president's frivolity. Lincoln rebuked them: "Why don't you laugh? With the fearful strain that is upon me night and day, if I did not laugh I should die, and you need this medicine as much as I do." Then turning to business, he told them that he had privately prepared "a little paper of much significance." It was the draft of the Emancipation Proclamation.

26 The Emancipation Proclamation was laid before Lincoln for his signature at noon on January 1, 1863. Lincoln twice picked up the pen and twice laid it down. To the secretary of state he said, "I have been shaking hands since nine o'clock this morning, and my right arm is almost paralyzed. If my name ever goes into history, it will be for this act, and my whole soul is in it. If my hand trembles when I sign the Proclamation, all who examine the document hereafter will say, 'He hesitated.'" He then picked up the pen again and slowly and firmly wrote his signature.

27 Lincoln was much plagued by people seeking offices or favors. He was unwell one day and not feeling inclined to listen to such requests. One petitioner, however, managed to get into his office. Just as the man was settling down for a lengthy interview, Lincoln's physician entered. Holding out his hands to him, Lincoln asked what the blotches on them were. The doctor instantly diagnosed varioloid, a mild form of smallpox. "It's contagious, I believe?" asked Lincoln. "Very contagious," was the answer. The visitor got to his feet at this point. "Well, I can't stop now, Mr. Lincoln, I just called to see how you were," he said. "Oh, don't be in a hurry," said Lincoln affably. "Thank you, sir, I'll call again," said the visitor, heading speedily for the door. As it closed behind him, Lincoln observed, "A good thing about this is that I now have something that I can give to everybody."

28   Lincoln's secretary of war, Edwin Stanton, had some trouble with a major general who accused him, in abusive terms, of favoritism. Stanton complained to Lincoln, who suggested that he write the officer a sharp letter. Stanton did so, and showed the strongly worded missive to the president, who applauded its powerful language: "What are you going to do with it?" he asked. Surprised at the question, Stanton said, "Send it." Lincoln shook his head. "You don't want to send that letter," he said. "Put it in the stove. That's what I do when I have written a letter while I am angry. It's a good letter and you had a good time writing it and feel better. Now, burn it, and write another."

29   A Prussian nobleman, who had been involved in revolutionary activities in his own country, came to the United States seeking a commission in the Union army. In an audience with the president, he expatiated on the high and ancient nobility of his family. Lincoln eventually broke in, saying, "That need not trouble you. It will not stand in your way if you behave yourself as a soldier."

30   Lincoln's mail one day contained a letter from a lady requesting not only his autograph but also a "sentiment" with his signature. Irritated by this demand at a time of national crisis, the president responded: "Dear Madam: When you ask from a stranger that which is of interest only to yourself, always enclose a stamp. There's your sentiment, and here's my autograph. A. Lincoln."

31   (The following story exists in many versions but is usually attributed to Lincoln.)
   On the night of December 23, 1863, Lincoln dreamed that he was in a party of undistinguished, unattractive people; when they found out who he was, they commented on his appearance. One of them said, "He's a very common-looking man." Lincoln retorted, "The Lord prefers common-looking people; that's the reason that he makes so many of them."

32   A guest at a reception told Lincoln that in his home state people said that the welfare of the nation depended on God and Abraham Lincoln. "You are half right," said Lincoln.

33   During the Civil War Lincoln had occasion at an official reception to refer to the Southerners rather as erring human beings than as foes to be exterminated. An elderly lady, a fiery patriot, rebuked him for speaking kindly of his enemies when he ought to be thinking of destroying them. "Why, madam," said Lincoln, "do I not destroy my enemies when I make them my friends?"

34   A delegation of businessmen from Wilmington, Delaware, came to see Lincoln to give him their views on winning the war. Their spokesman announced pompously that they represented the "weighty men" of Delaware. "So you're the weighty men of Delaware," said Lincoln when he had heard them out. "All from New Castle County?"
   "Yes, all from the same city."
   "Did it ever occur to you gentlemen," asked the president, "that there was danger of your little state tipping up in your absence?"

35   When a gentleman called on the president, asking for a pass to allow him to visit Richmond (the Confederate capital), the president replied, "I would be very happy to oblige you if my passes were respected; but the fact is, sir, I have, within the last two years, given passes to two hundred and fifty thousand men to go to Richmond, and not one has got there yet."

36   During Lincoln's visit to Richmond after it had been evacuated by the Confederate troops, an old black man approached him and, removing his hat, bowed and said, "May de good Lord bless you, President Linkum." The president took off his own hat and bowed silently in return.

37   Just a week before he was assassinated Lincoln had a dream that he discussed with several people. It seemed that he was walking through the silent White House toward the

sound of sobbing. When he entered the East Room he was confronted by the sight of a catafalque covered in black. He asked the guard on duty there who was dead. "The president," said the soldier.

38 On April 13, 1865, the Civil War being over, orders were given to end the draft of soldiers. The following day Lincoln made his fatal visit to the theater to see *Our American Cousin.* At one point in the play the heroine, reclining on a garden seat, calls for a shawl to protect her from the draft. The actor Edward Sothern, to whom the request was addressed, replied on this occasion with the impromptu line: "You are mistaken, Miss Mary, the draft has already been stopped by order of the president!" Lincoln joined in the audience's appreciation of this remark with what was to be his last laugh.

਩ ਤ

LINCOLN, Robert Todd (1843–1926), *US politician and businessman, son of Abraham Lincoln. He was minister to Great Britain (1889–93).*

1 Robert Todd Lincoln was home from Harvard on a visit at the time that his father was assassinated. After the shooting he sat by his father's bedside until he died. He had no political ambitions, preferring the life of a lawyer. But President James Garfield called him away from his practice to occupy the post of secretary of war in 1881. He reluctantly accepted. Later that same year Robert Lincoln arrived at the Washington railroad station just in time to see Garfield shot. Twenty years later, as president of the Pullman Company, Robert Lincoln was invited to bring his family to meet President William McKinley. As they arrived they heard the news: the president had just been shot. Robert Lincoln observed, "There is a certain fatality about presidential functions when I am present."

਩ ਤ

LIND, Jenny (1820–87), *Swedish operatic soprano. Known as "the Swedish nightingale," she toured throughout Europe and in the United States (1850–52), before finally settling in England.*

1 A group of American tourists knocked on Jenny Lind's door. The star asked them what

they wanted. The spokesman said that they merely wanted to have a look at her. "This is my face," she said, and then turned around: "This is my back. Now you can go home and say you have seen me." With that she shut the door.

਩ ਤ

LINDEMANN, Frederick Alexander, Viscount Cherwell (1886–1957), *German-born British physicist, known as "the Prof." He became personal assistant to Winston Churchill, who appointed him paymaster-general in his wartime government. Some of his advice was good, some bad. As his colleague, Sir George Paget Thomson, said of him, "He was better as critic than as creator."*

1 In 1931 Churchill was hit by a taxi on Fifth Avenue in New York and taken to a hospital. From there he sent a cable to Lindemann asking him to calculate the shock, to a stationary body weighing two hundred pounds, of a car weighing 2,400 pounds traveling between thirty and thirty-five miles an hour. He also asked the professor to bear in mind that the brakes did not operate before he was hit by the car and that he had been "carried forward on the cowcatcher" until he dropped off, adding that the information "must be impressive." Lindemann soon sent the following reply, "Collision equivalent falling thirty feet on pavement. Equal six thousand foot pounds energy. Equivalent stopping ten-pound brick dropped six hundred feet or two charges buckshot pointblank range. Rate inversely proportional thickness cushion surrounding skeleton and give of frame. If assume average one inch your body transferred during impact at rate eight thousand horsepower. Congratulations on preparing suitable cushion and skill in bump."

਩ ਤ

LISTER, Joseph, 1st Baron Lister (1827–1912), *British surgeon. Influenced by the work of Pasteur, he used carbolic acid as an antiseptic in surgery and greatly reduced the incidence of infection.*

1 Lister was once summoned to attend a rich lord who had a fishbone stuck in his throat. Dextrously the great surgeon removed the bone. Overcome with gratitude, the patient asked Lister what was owed him. Lister replied, with a smile, "My lord, suppose we settle for half of what you would be willing to give me if the bone were still lodged in your throat."

৯৯ ৩৯

LISZT, Franz (1811–86), *Hungarian pianist and composer. He was acclaimed as the greatest virtuoso pianist of his time. His compositions included symphonic poems (a form he invented), symphonies, and much piano music. Cosima, his daughter by the Comtesse d'Agoult (1805–76), became the wife of Hans von Bülow and, later, of Richard Wagner.*

1   (According to Samuel Butler:)
    "It is said, with what truth I know not, that Liszt got Verdi to give him a letter of introduction to Rossini and went to call on him. Rossini was exceedingly polite, asked him to play, and when he had done inquired what the piece was. Liszt said, 'It is a march I have written on the death of Meyerbeer; how do you like it, maestro?' Rossini said he liked it very much, but presently added, 'Do you not think it would have been better if it had been you who had died, and Meyerbeer who had written the music?'"
    {This is probably a standard musical chestnut, adaptable to any three characters in similar circumstances. *See also* GEORGE GERSHWIN 7.}

2   It has been said of Liszt that Wagner was indebted to him for much besides money—including sympathy and a wife. The two men were friends, if somewhat tempestuously on Wagner's part, and Wagner came to rely on Liszt as mentor and guide. Musically they influenced each other considerably. Wagner, by far the more popular composer, once wrote to Liszt to say that he had unconsciously used a theme of his. Liszt replied, "Now at least it will be heard."

৯৯ ৩৯

LIVERMORE, Mary Ashton Rice (1821–1905), *US reformer, active in the agitation for women's suffrage and in temperance reform.*

1   (May Saxton tells this story:)
    "One of Mary Livermore's favorite stories was about the time she and five other girls had

gone to see President Josiah Quincy of Harvard about studying at the university. They demonstrated their learning for him and he said, 'Very smart girls. . . unusually capable, but can you cook?' They assured him they were expert domestics. 'Highly important,' he said. He continually diverted them from asking their questions until finally Mary burst out that they wanted to go to college with their brothers: 'You say we are sufficiently prepared, is there anything to prevent our admission?' He told them that the place for girls was at home. 'Yes, but, Mr. Quincy, if we are prepared, we would not ask to recite but may we not attend the recitations and sit silent in the classes?'
    " 'No, my dear, you may not.'
    " 'Then I wish —'
    " 'What do you wish?'
    " 'I wish I were God, for the instant, that I might kill every woman from Eve down and let you have the masculine world all to yourselves and see how you would like that!' "

৯৯ ৩৯

LLOYD, Chris[tine] Evert (1954–), *US tennis player, who won the Wimbledon singles championship in 1974, 1976, and 1981, and the doubles championship in 1976. She was US singles champion in 1975–78, 1980, and 1982.*

1   Chris Evert developed at an early age the powers of concentration that enable her to close her mind to any potential distraction, physical or mental, during a match. At a junior tournament one day someone had left a chair near the back line; every time she went back for a shot, Chris ran into it. "Why didn't you move the chair back against the fence?" she was asked after the match. "What chair?" she replied.

৯৯ ৩৯

LLOYD GEORGE, David, 1st Earl (1863–1945), *British statesman; prime minister (1916–22). Entering Parliament in 1890, Lloyd George quickly established his reputation as orator, Welsh nationalist, and champion of the underdog. While chancellor of the exchequer (1908–15) he introduced the so-called People's Budget (1909), which proposed higher death duties and a supertax. At the beginning of World War I he was minister for munitions, and became prime minister at the end of 1916. He led the coalition government through the* *war and its immediate aftermath, but was forced to resign after growing dissatisfaction over his handling of the Irish question and Turkish nationalism.*

1 In the early days of his political career Lloyd George appeared as a speaker at a rally in favor of Home Rule. His speech advocated extension of the principle to other parts of the British Empire: "Home Rule in Ireland, Home Rule in India, Home Rule in South Africa—" At this point he was interrupted by a heckler shouting, "'Ome Rule for 'Ell." Lloyd George's glance swept round the audience until he had picked out the speaker. "Yes," he thundered back, pointing his finger at the interrupter, "Home Rule for Hell. I like every man to speak for his own country."

{Other politicians seem to have been confronted with the same situation and to have been inspired to similar repartee.}

2 When popular patriotism was at its zenith at the outbreak of World War I, and the slogan "The war that will end war" was on every tongue, Lloyd George expressed a gloomy skepticism. "This war, like the next war, is a war to end war," he remarked.

{While often attributed to Lloyd George, this remark may have originated elsewhere.}

3 During his ministry Lloyd George had to contend with World War I, the economic crisis, and the Sinn Fein movement for Irish liberation, among other difficulties. Asked how he retained his good spirits, he replied, "Well, I find that a change of nuisances is as good as a vacation."

4 The chairman of a meeting introduced Lloyd George with the jocular remark: "I had expected to find Mr. Lloyd George a big man in every sense, but you see for yourselves he is quite small in stature."

"In North Wales," replied Lloyd George, "we measure a man from his chin up. You evidently measure from his chin down."

5 Lloyd George was once approached by explorer Ernest Shackleton, seeking a sponsor for his next expedition. Proud to be considered a friend of the rich and famous, Lloyd George introduced the explorer to a millionaire of his acquaintance. Some time later, Lloyd George inquired of Shackleton how the meeting had gone. "Very well indeed," replied the explorer, "your friend was most charming and considerate. He offered me ten thousand pounds for my expenses, provided I would take you along with me to the Pole. And he promised me one million pounds if I were to leave you there by mistake."

6 During Lloyd George's term as prime minister, a colleague once said to him, "If you treated me half as badly as you treat Curzon [the foreign secretary], I'd resign tomorrow morning."

"Oh, he does resign," replied Lloyd George. "But there are two messengers at the Foreign Office. One has a limp; he comes with the resignation. The other was a champion runner; he always catches him up."

LOBENGULA (c. 1836–94), *king of the Matabele (1870–94). Lobengula granted land and mineral rights in his kingdom (now part of Zimbabwe) to the British South Africa Company. Nevertheless war broke out between the Matabele and the Europeans and Lobengula's kingdom was annexed (1893).*

1 Lobengula was anxious until the last minute to avoid open conflict with the encroaching Europeans. Unfortunately, a party of *indunas* (chiefs) whom he sent as emissaries to the British were attacked and killed through a misunderstanding. Lobengula, enraged at what he saw as treachery, declared war. He did this in the traditional way, by driving an *assegai* (short stabbing spear) into the ground in sight of the assembled army. The shaft of the *assegai* snapped. Despite this bad omen the Matabele warriors marched out to war—and defeat.

LOCKE, John (1632–1704), *British philosopher. His* Essay Concerning Human Understanding *(1690) is an inquiry into the origins, nature, and status of ideas; its conclusions stimulated a fruitful philosophical controversy about the learning process that still echoes today.*

1 Locke had been introduced by his patron Lord Shaftesbury to two other noblemen.

Rather than take the opportunity to converse with the philosopher, the three men sat down to play cards. Locke said nothing, but began to scribble in his notebook. Some time later, intrigued by the philosopher's behavior, one of the players asked what he was doing. "My lord," replied Locke, "I am endeavoring, as far as possible, to profit by my present situation; for having waited with impatience for the honor of being in company with the greatest geniuses of the age, I thought I could do nothing better than to write down your conversation, and indeed I have set down the substance of what you have said for this hour or two." This remark had the desired effect, and the noblemen, suitably embarrassed, abandoned their game.

ॐ ॐ

LOMBARDI, Vince (1913–70), *US football coach. His Green Bay Packers won five National Football League championships.*

1 Lombardi was a stern disciplinarian but also an inspirational leader who hated to lose. After one noteworthy victory, he was asked how important it was to him to win. He said, "Winning isn't everything, but wanting to win is."

{Apparently the original line, "Winning isn't everything, it's the only thing," was said by Red Sanders while coaching the University of California at Los Angeles football team. It is not known if Lombardi had heard of Sanders's statement, but it is known that Lombardi said it in the 1960s and the widely used line is attributed to him.}

2 One of the Green Bay Packers remarked on Lombardi's fairness, the fact that he treated every man the same. "He treats us all like dogs."

ॐ ॐ

LONG, Huey Pierce (1893–1935), *US lawyer and politician. Governor of Louisiana from 1928 to 1931, he subsequently served as a US senator until his assassination in 1935.*

1 Before beginning his electoral campaign in southern Louisiana, Long was reminded by a colleague that a large number of the voters

there were Catholics. In accordance with this advice, he opened his first speech with the words: "When I was a boy, I would get up at six o'clock in the morning on Sunday, and I would hitch our old horse up to the buggy and I would take my Catholic grandparents to mass. I would bring them home, and at ten o'clock I would hitch the old horse up again, and I would take my Baptist grandparents to church."

"Why, Huey," remarked his colleague later, "you've been holding out on us. I didn't know you had any Catholic grandparents."

"Don't be a damn fool," replied Long. "We didn't even have a horse."

2 Although an ardent supporter of the New Deal, Long was wary of wholehearted support for Roosevelt. The only difference between Hoover and Roosevelt, he once said, was that Hoover was a hoot owl while Roosevelt was a scrootch owl. "A hoot owl bangs into the roost and knocks the hen clean off, and catches her while she's falling. But a scrootch owl slips into the roost and talks softly to her. And the hen just falls in love with him, and the first thing you know, *there ain't no hen.*"

ॐ ॐ

LONGWORTH, Alice Roosevelt (1884–1980), *US society hostess, daughter of Theodore Roosevelt.*

1 Alice's antics scandalized the staid society of Washington during her father's tenure at the White House. When a visitor objected to the girl's wandering in and out of the president's office while he was discussing important business with her father, Roosevelt said, "I can be president of the United States or I can control Alice. I cannot possibly do both."

2 Alice's barbed comments on political figures quickly became current Washington gossip. When Thomas E. Dewey was seeking the Republican presidential nomination, she exclaimed, "How can the Republican party nominate a man who looks like the bridegroom on a wedding cake?"

{Mrs. Longworth herself always disclaimed this and several other of the well-known remarks attributed to her, saying that she merely enjoyed repeating them and giving them currency. It is more probable that the wedding cake *mot* originated with Clare Boothe Luce.}

3 Alice suffered from breast cancer in her old age, and her second breast was removed when she was eighty-six. After this operation she said, "I am the only topless octogenarian here."

੭ॐ ৽ই

LONSDALE, Frederick (1881–1954), *British dramatist known for his witty comedies of high society.*

1 At the Garrick Club (a famous London club of which several leading actors were members) on New Year's Eve Freddy Lonsdale was asked by Seymour Hicks to make up a quarrel he had previously had with one of his fellow members. "You must," Seymour said. "It is very unkind to be unfriendly at such a time. Go over now and wish him a happy New Year." Freddy crossed the room and spoke to his enemy. "I wish you a happy New Year," he said, "but only one."

2 (Frances Donaldson tells the following:)
"The only deadly sin in the eyes of the membership of the Garrick Club was to be a bore. Anyone who told long stories, showed too much eagerness for familiarity with famous people, mistook simple rudeness for rudeness coupled with wit, boasted of his own success, failed gracefully to conceal malicious envy of other people's, or quailed before the onslaughts of his fellow members was ripe for massacre. . . . Freddy was welcomed into the Garrick because of his natural understanding of the rules. On one occasion, he was accosted by a stranger who said to him, 'Aren't you Freddy Lonsdale?' Freddy surveyed him swiftly, and replied, 'No, not tonight.'"

੭ॐ ৽ই

LOSCH, Tilly (?1907–75), *Austrian dancer and actress.*

1 (The designer Cecil Beaton was helping Tilly Losch with her costume for an Oriental ball in Paris in 1935).
"Tilly has a smouldering, Slavic face. In costume as an *ouled nail,* her appearance becomes barbarically *fatale.* Unfortunately she is completely helpless — either lazy and spoilt or else

clever at getting things done for her. After creating her costume the whole morning I said, 'Now you are complete. All you have to do for the Ball is glue a sequin between your brows.' Tilly whispered, 'But how can I do that? Won't you come to the hotel and bring some glue?' "

੭ॐ ৽ই

LOUIS XI (1423–83), *king of France (1461–83). Louis did much to unite France and revive its prosperity after the ravages of the Hundred Years' War.*

1 A devout believer in astrology, Louis was deeply impressed when an astrologer correctly foretold that a lady of the court would die in eight days' time. Deciding that the too-accurate prophet should be disposed of, he summoned the man to his apartments, having first told his servants to throw the visitor out of the window when he gave the signal. "You claim to understand astrology and to know the fate of others," Louis said to the man, "so tell me at once what your fate will be and how long you have to live."
"I shall die just three days before Your Majesty," answered the astrologer. Louis decided not to risk defenestration.

੭ॐ ৽ই

LOUIS XIV (1638–1715), *king of France (1643–1715), known as* Le Roi Soleil *(the Sun King) because of the brilliance of his court and the prestige that France achieved during his reign. In a succession of wars he made his country the greatest power in Europe. France's commerce and industry prospered, and the court at Versailles attracted writers and artists from all over France. Louis's revocation (1685) of the Edict of Nantes (guaranteeing toleration to France's Protestants) had serious long-term effects, his autocratic rule seriously weakened the country's constitutional stability, and the alliance of the other European powers against him in the last two decades of his life challenged France's supremacy. Still, his reign is regarded as the Golden Age of French culture.*

1 When Louis's father, Louis XIII, knew himself to be dying, he took much consolation and pleasure in the precocious energy and intelligence of the four-year-old dauphin. "What is your name?" the king asked playfully. "Louis the Fourteenth," replied the child promptly. "Not quite yet, my son," said the king with a smile.

2 The etiquette that attended every portion of the king's day was minutely prescribed. The *grand lever* ceremony, at which the king dressed and made ready, was attended by over a hundred courtiers. Despite living surrounded by grandeur and formality, Louis was capable of showing genuine concern for the feelings of others. A valet who had made a mistake in the details of the royal *lever* was immediately abused and scolded by the assembled courtiers. "Let us not forget," Louis interposed, "that he is far more upset about it than I am."

3 Louis's great general, Maréchal Villars, made enemies among the king's favorites. A pretext was found to send him off to a dangerous posting in Germany. The marshal took his leave of Louis with these words: "I leave Your Majesty surrounded by my enemies, and I go to be surrounded by yours."

4 Louis XIV was one day expatiating to his courtiers on the absolute power great kings have over their subjects. The Comte de Guiche objected that such power must have its limits, to which Louis replied, "If I commanded you to throw yourself into the sea, you would be the first to obey me." The count, instead of replying, turned his back and walked toward the door. Astonished, Louis asked him where he was going. "To learn to swim, sire," replied de Guiche.

5 The insatiable ambition of one of his courtiers was well known to the king. "Do you know Spanish?" Louis asked.

"No, sire."

"What a pity."

The courtier at once concluded that Louis had an ambassadorship in mind for him. He devoted himself strenuously to learning the language, and then presented himself before the monarch, stating that he was now master of it.

"Do you know it so well that you can actually converse with Spaniards?"

"Yes, sire."

"I congratulate you. Now you can read *Don Quixote* in the original."

6 When hunting, Louis XIV never wore gloves, even in the coldest weather. Two peasants watched him ride by; one voiced his surprise that the king took no precautions against the cold. The other replied, "Why should he? He always has his hands in our pockets."

7 Louis was very fond of billiards. On one occasion a dispute arose over a shot, and Louis asked the Comte de Gramont, who was sitting nearby, to adjudicate. "Sire, you are in the wrong," said Gramont immediately, without budging from his seat. "Why, sir, you didn't even see the shot!" exclaimed the king. "No, sire," replied Gramont, "but if there had been the slightest doubt about the shot, the gentlemen who did see it would have all cried out that you were in the right."

8 The English ambassador Lord Stair was described to Louis as being one of the best-bred men in Europe. Louis decided to put this to the test. The next time Lord Stair was in attendance as Louis was about to set out in his coach, the king gestured for the ambassador to go ahead of him into the conveyance. Lord Stair bowed and climbed in, as bidden. "It is true what they say of Lord Stair," observed Louis afterward. "Another man would have troubled me with ceremonious objections."

9 News of the French army's crushing defeat at Blenheim was brought to Louis. "How could God do this to me," he exclaimed, "after all I have done for him?"

10 As Louis lay dying in great pain, with his left leg gangrenous, he noticed that the two attendants at the foot of his bed were weeping. "Why are you weeping?" he said. "Did you imagine that I was immortal?"

కావ్ ఆన్

LOUIS XV (1710–74), *king of France (1715–74). His long reign was marked by indecisiveness and court intrigues. Abroad, France lost prestige and territory during the Seven Years' War (1756–63). Louis left a legacy of disaffection and financial instability that led to the French Revolution.*

1 Mme d'Esparbés, one of Louis's many mistresses, did not confine her favors to the royal couch. "You have slept with all my subjects," protested Louis one day. Mme d'Esparbés denied this.

"You have slept with the Duc de Choiseul?"

"Yes, sire, but he is so powerful!"

"The Maréchal de Richelieu?"

"But he is so witty!"

"Mainville?"

"But he has such beautiful legs!"

"Very well, but how about the Duc d'Aumont, who has none of these attractions?"

"Ah, sire, he is so devoted to Your Majesty!"

2 Louis XV once asked the elderly Marquis de Souvre where he was going to be buried. "At your feet, sire," was the unfortunate reply.

3 The Comte de Charolais, the king's cousin, was a notorious eccentric. One of his oddities was to order his coachman to run over any monks they might encounter on the road. He went too far, however, when, for the pleasure of seeing him fall, he shot a man who was putting tiles on a roof. Louis pardoned him but said, "Let it be understood: I will similarly pardon anyone who shoots you."

4 Aware of the deplorable social and economic state of France, Louis was given to remarking, "*Les choses, comme elles sont, dureront autant que moi*" (Things as they are will see out my time).

{Madame de Pompadour's expression of the same sentiment is perhaps better known: "*Après nous le déluge.*"}

5 Louis was playing cards with members of his entourage when a certain M. de Chauvelin was stricken by a fit of apoplexy, of which he died. "M. de Chauvelin is ill," exclaimed a courtier, seeing him fall. Louis turned and surveyed the fallen body coldly. "Ill?" he said. "He is dead. Take him away. Spades are trumps, gentlemen."

6 Marie Antoinette was on her way from Austria to marry Louis XV's grandson, the future Louis XVI. The elderly roué greatly looked forward to seeing the fifteen-year-old dauphine-to-be. A courtier who had been in the party sent from France to meet Marie Antoinette at the French border galloped back ahead of the bridal party to report to his master. "What do you think of her?" was Louis's first question. "Has she any bosom?"

કરે છે

LOUIS XVI (1754–93), *king of France (1774–93). Louis, a weak character and an idle ruler, allowed the reactionary forces of the aristocracy, led by his wife, Queen Marie Antoinette, to plunge the kingdom into economic crisis and political turmoil. After the Revolution broke out, he was at first retained as constitutional monarch, but later deposed, tried for treason against the nation, and guillotined.*

1 The Maréchal de Richelieu suggested that Louis take a certain lady as his mistress. "No," said the king, "she would be too expensive to dismiss."

2 On July 14, 1789, a Paris mob stormed and captured the Bastille, the old royal prison in Paris. That day Louis XVI, who had been out hunting, returned to Versailles and entered a note in his diary: "July 14: Nothing." Then the Duc de La Rochefoucauld-Liancourt hurried in from Paris to tell the king of the successful attack. "Why, this is a revolt!" said the monarch. "No, Sire," replied the duke. "It is a revolution."

3 When the arrangements were being made in December 1792 for the trial of Louis XVI before the Revolutionary Convention, the distinguished lawyer Chrétien de Malesherbes came out of retirement to offer his services to his king. Louis accepted sadly and reluctantly. "Your sacrifice is the greater," he said, "for you are jeopardizing your own life while you cannot possibly save mine."

{Louis's prediction was correct; sixteen months later Malesherbes and most of his family were guillotined.}

કરે છે

LOUIS XVIII (1755–1824), *king of France (1814–24). Louis became nominal king of France in 1795 on the death of Louis XVII in prison during the Revolution. In the Bonaparte years he was unable to assert his claim to the throne. Restored in 1814, Louis was temporarily ousted during the Hundred Days, but returned for good after Waterloo.*

1 At his restoration "fat Louis" was fully and sympathetically aware of his subjects' need to let bygones be bygones. The elderly M. de Barentin was stumblingly explaining to Louis how it was that he had not — strictly speaking — in actual fact — sworn an oath of allegiance to Napoleon Bonaparte. "I quite understand," Louis broke in. "At our age one only does things by halves. You didn't swear an oath to Bonaparte, you swore an oathlet."

ॐ ⚕

LOUIS, Joe (1914–81), *US boxer. He was world heavyweight champion from 1937 until he retired in 1949, during which time he successfully defended his title twenty-five times.*

1 Joe Louis defended his heavyweight title against Billy Conn, "the Pittsburgh Kid," in June 1941. Although Conn was much smaller and lighter than Louis, his speed and agility made him a serious challenger. As his opponent darted around him and managed to get in some telling punches, Louis grew increasingly confused and his own punches appeared to have no effect. By the end of the twelfth round Conn was a long way ahead on points and the huge crowd of fans were confident they would see a new champion. At the start of the thirteenth round Conn delivered a heavy punch to Louis and went in for the kill, only to meet a tremendous uppercut from Louis that stretched him out cold on the canvas.

Some years later the two boxers were talking about this famous battle, and Conn asked jokingly why Louis had not let him win that one fight. "You could have sort of loaned me the crown for six months," he said. Louis replied seriously, "Billy, you *had* that title for twelve rounds."

2 Joe Louis defended the rights of his race before there really was a civil rights movement. Touring the army bases of the South during World War II, giving boxing exhibitions, he and black fighter Sugar Ray Robinson were once confronted by a military policeman while waiting at an Alabama bus station.

"You soldiers belong in the rear of the station," said the M.P.

When the two men didn't respond, they were arrested and severely reprimanded by an officer at the provost marshal's office.

"I'm sorry, sir," Joe Louis replied. "But I'm in this war like anybody else. I expect to be treated like anybody else."

3 During his period of army service, Louis, driving with a fellow GI, was involved in a minor collision with a large truck. The truck driver got out, yelling and swearing at Louis, who just sat in the driver's seat, smiling. "Why didn't you get out and knock him flat?" asked his buddy after the truck driver had moved on. "Why should I?" replied Joe. "When somebody insulted Caruso, did he sing an aria for him?"

4 Knocked down by a surprise left from Tony Galento, Louis was back on his feet before the referee could start the count. Joe's trainer later reproached him: "I keep teaching you to take a count when you're knocked down. Now why didn't you stay down for nine like I've always taught you?"

"What," growled Louis, "and let him get all that rest?"

5 In 1946 Joe Louis once again prepared to defend his title against Billy Conn. He was warned to watch out for Conn's great speed and his tactic of darting in to the attack and then moving quickly out of his opponent's range. In a famous display of (justified) confidence, Louis replied, "He can run, but he can't hide."

ॐ ⚕

LOUIS PHILIPPE (1773–1850), *king of France (1830–48), known as the "Citizen King." After Louis XVIII's successor was ousted by the July Revolution, Louis Philippe assumed power. His initially liberal stance turned to oppression in the face of constant threats to his regime. In 1848 he was forced into exile in England.*

1 Fleeing from Paris in 1848, Louis Philippe climbed into the carriage that would take him into exile; an unknown man closed the door. "Thank you," said the king absently. "Not at all," replied the man. "I've waited eighteen years for this day."

ॐ ⚕

LOWE, Joseph (?1846–99), *US gunman, known as "Rowdy Joe."*

1 "Rowdy Joe" was celebrated for his antisocial behavior, which included shooting men who dared to pay attention to any of the light ladies he favored. In the course of one altercation, a lawman stopped the fight and suggested that the two men apologize to each other. Lowe agreed. He said to his antagonist, "Come here. I want to kiss and make up." Then he bit off the end of the man's nose.

ह्ल ४३

LOWELL, Abbott Lawrence (1856–1943), *US educator and lawyer. After practicing law (1880–97), he became a lecturer at Harvard, where he was subsequently professor of science and government (1900–09) and president (1909–33).*

1 During William Howard Taft's administration President Lowell was summoned from Harvard to the White House on business. In his absence his secretary received a visitor who asked where Lowell was. "The president is in Washington seeing Mr. Taft," was the reply.

ह्ल ४३

LOWELL, Amy (1874–1925), *US poet and critic. She wrote a major biography of Keats and was an acknowledged leader of the Imagist movement in poetry.*

1 When Amy Lowell's ancient car broke down, the garage mechanic refused to repair it until she identified herself and could guarantee payment of the bill. Miss Lowell informed the man that she was the sister of the president of Harvard and suggested that he call her brother. The mechanic duly telephoned Harvard. Abbott Lawrence Lowell asked, "What's she doing now?"
    "Sitting on a wall smoking a big cigar."
    "That's my sister, all right."

2 The Cabots, one of Boston's leading families, were held in low esteem by Miss Lowell. She would go to the extent of refusing invitations to parties and dinners if she knew that one or more Cabots had also been invited. One day, as she set off for her annual trip to Europe aboard the *Devonian,* she happened to glance at the passenger list and promptly disembarked. "There are sixteen Cabots aboard the *Devonian* this trip," she told a newspaper

reporter, "and God isn't going to miss such an opportunity."

3 "When Miss Lowell traveled . . . her wardrobe was always carefully sorted and packed for speed and efficiency . . . gowns in one suitcase, toilet articles in another, underwear in a third. The trunk containing the underwear once slipped into the harbor at Piraeus when the landing net broke, and Miss Lowell stood on the Greek pier wringing her hands and moaning, 'My drawers, oh, my drawers!' She had the harbor dredged and recovered them."

4 The American writer Kay Boyle vouches for this story. At the time of the declaration of war in 1914 Miss Lowell was in London. Late for an appointment, hindered by the crowds in the street, indignant at the police for not helping her, as she returned to her hotel she burst out, "Don't they know I'm Amy Lowell? And it was this month that my book of poems was coming out here! What attention will it get with this going on? What has happened to England? Why doesn't she simply stop the war?"

ह्ल ४३

LOWELL, Robert (1917–77), *US poet. His early poetry was complex and abstract.* Life Studies *(1959) marked a transition to the more relaxed and "confessional" style for which he became famous. During the 1960s he was deeply involved in left-wing politics.*

1 Due to present the Duff Cooper Memorial Prize before an illustrious gathering that included Duff Cooper's widow, Lady Diana, Lowell suffered a serious nervous breakdown and was taken to a mental home. A substitute was arranged, but at the last moment Lowell discharged himself and set off for the ceremony. Lady Diana's son was informed of this and told that Lowell must on no account touch alcohol. He rushed to pass the news to his mother, and found her talking to Lowell, then on his third glass of champagne. "Darling," she said brightly, "I've just been telling this gentleman how the principal speaker has lost his marbles and been carted off to a loony-bin!"

2 As a punishment for refusing to serve in the army, Lowell was imprisoned for five months by the US courts. While waiting to be transferred to Connecticut to serve the sentence, Lowell spent a few days in New York's West Street Jail. During his stay there he was put in a cell next to Louie Lepke, a convicted member of Murder Incorporated. "I'm in for killing," Lepke told the poet. "What are you in for?" Lowell answered: "Oh, I'm in for refusing to kill."

છે. ત્ર

LUBITSCH, Ernst (1892–1947), *German film director, originally a comic actor. His films include* Trouble In Paradise *(1932),* Ninotchka *(1939), and* To Be or Not to Be *(1942).*

1 (Lubitsch's command of the English language was far from perfect, as playwright Edward Knoblock recalls.)

"Another time, when Lubitsch and I had a difference about the interpretation of a scene, he lost his temper and started rushing off the set, but turned to face me and by way of an annihilating farewell exclaimed, 'How do you do.'"

છે. ત્ર

LUCE, Clare Boothe (1903–), *US journalist, playwright, and politician, wife of Henry R. Luce. After her conversion to Roman Catholicism, her writing was dominated by religious themes.*

1 Lady Jeanne Campbell, the granddaughter of Lord Beaverbrook, worked as a researcher on *Life* and it was well known that Henry Luce was having an affair with her. It is said that he even went so far as to ask Clare for a divorce so that he could marry Jeanne. Clare replied that, curiously enough, Lord Beaverbrook had been showing considerable interest in *her,* and if she married him that would make her the grandmother of Luce's intended bride. Luce decided against the marriage.

2 A certain congressman, intending to flatter Mrs. Luce, said of her in the House of Representatives one day: "She has the best mind of any woman in the House." Mrs. Luce was enraged by the patronizing tone of the compliment. "The mind knows no sex," she retorted. "If the lady believes that," remarked a second congressman, "she doesn't know the mind of man."

3 Asked by a reporter to comment on a certain senator's move from the Republican to the Democratic party, Mrs. Luce replied: "Whenever a Republican leaves one side of the aisle and goes to the other, it raises the intelligence quotient of both parties."

છે. ત્ર

LUCE, Henry R. (1898–1967), *US publisher, founder of the Time-Life publishing concern.*

1 Stanley Karnow, once based in Hong Kong for *Time* magazine, told Sterling Seagrave of a trip made to Taiwan with his boss Henry Luce. (Chiang Kai-shek had fled after losing China to the Communists. He had been, of course, a hero to Luce.) On their way to the Palace Hotel in Taipei, Luce noticed that their luggage seemed to be missing and muttered peevishly, "I think they've lost our bags." Karnow commented, "It won't be the first thing they've lost."

"Within a year," Karnow told Seagrave, "I was no longer working for *Time.*"

છે. ત્ર

LUCULLUS, Lucius Licinius (c. 114–57 BC), *Roman general and statesman, celebrated for his conquest of Mithridates, king of Pontus in Asia Minor. On returning to Rome (67 BC), he devoted the great wealth he acquired in Pontus to a life of luxury. He was also a famous patron of literature.*

1 Lucullus's dinners became proverbial for their sumptuousness. On one of the rare occasions when Lucullus was dining alone, he noticed to his displeasure that the preparations for the meal were not up to their usual standard. He summoned the servant responsible, who explained that as no one had been invited, he had assumed that his master would want a less lavish meal. Lucullus frowned: "Do you not know that this evening Lucullus sups with Lucullus?"

છે. ત્ર

LUISETTI, Hank (1916–), *US basketball player. He was the star of the Stanford University team and is known for having developed the one-handed shot.*

1 Until Luisetti came along, basketball players mainly shot the ball with both hands.

Luisetti said he did not know why he started to shoot with one hand, but that it just seemed natural to him. His high-school coach allowed him to continue because the shot worked. When Luisetti asked his college coach, John Bunn, if he could continue with the shot, he was asked to demonstrate it. Luisetti did so, putting the ball in the basket several times. "Stay with it," Bunn said. Later he commented, "That's what makes a great coach, not changing a great player."

2 Luisetti's first appearance in New York's Madison Square Garden drew a capacity crowd, but Stanford was given little chance of defeating Clair Bee's championship Long Island University team, undefeated in three seasons. "No one is going to beat us one-handed," warned Bee. But Luisetti scored fifteen points and his all-around play led Stanford to a stunning 45–31 upset. "I hate to think how badly they'd have beaten us if he'd used both hands," said Bee.

ॐ ॐ

LULLY, Jean-Baptiste (1632–87), *French composer. He became court composer to Louis XIV in 1653 and director of the Paris Opera in 1672. His ballet music for court entertainments revolutionized concepts of dance. He was also responsible for numerous innovations in operatic music.*

1 The baton used by a seventeenth-century conductor was a much longer and heavier affair than the little wand used today. On January 8, 1687, in the course of conducting a *Te Deum*, Lully struck his foot with his baton, injuring it so seriously that gangrene set in and he died ten weeks later.

ॐ ॐ

LUNT, Alfred (1893–1977), *US actor who with his wife Lynn Fontanne (1887–1983) constituted a famous husband-and-wife acting team.*

1 The Lunts made one motion picture, *The Guardsman*. On the day of the premier Lunt was ill and Fontanne went alone. She returned distraught. "Alfred, it was a total disaster," she babbled. "I cannot imagine what they were thinking of. You were all right, just occasion-

ally it looked as if you had thin lips, but in the close-ups of me all you could see were my nostrils, or else my eyelashes cast such a shadow that it looked as if I had great bags under my eyes, and my hair was a mess, a total mess, and there is something wrong with the sound that makes my voice sound like either a squeak or a groan . . ."

She paused for breath. Lunt said thoughtfully, "Thin lips, eh?"

2 In one of the plays in which they co-starred Lynn Fontanne had to hit Alfred Lunt across the face. A devoted wife, she tried for some time without bringing herself to do it. Everyone became exasperated as the scene stuck at that point. Finally Lunt burst out, "For God's sake, you're the lousiest actress I've ever played opposite." Miss Fontanne, her hang-up overcome, struck him sharply. Thereafter at every performance Lunt used to whisper, "Don't be lousy, dear."

3 One night in 1944, a V-2 rocket landed outside the London theater where Lunt and Fontanne were performing. Miss Fontanne stood helpless on stage as the building shook and plaster fell around her. Lunt entered on cue, holding up a piece of fallen scenery, and delivered his scripted line: "Are you all right, darling?"

ॐ ॐ

LUTHER, Martin (1483–1546), *German Protestant theologian. Convinced of the corruption of the Roman Catholic Church, in particular the practice of selling indulgences, Luther embarked on a campaign for reform that effectively began with the ninety-five theses nailed to the church door at Wittenberg (1517) and ended in the establishment of a Protestant Church in schism with Rome.*

1 Luther's colleague, Philipp Melanchthon, vexed his more ebullient friend by his quiet and virtuous ways. "For goodness' sake, why don't you go and sin a little?" cried Luther in exasperation. "Doesn't God deserve to have something to forgive you for!"

2 Cornered by a persistent young theologian with the question of where God had been before the world was created, Luther snapped,

"He was building hell for such presumptuous, fluttering, and inquisitive spirits as you are."

3 Arraigned for his heresies before the Diet of Worms in 1521, Luther refused to recant. "*Hier stehe ich, ich kann nicht anders* [Here I stand, I can do no other]," he declared.

{This famous statement does not appear in the transcripts of the proceedings of the diet, but does appear in the earliest printed version of Luther's speech. If not authentic, the words are nonetheless entirely in the spirit of Luther's defiance, and are inscribed on the Luther *Denkmal* at Worms.}

ॐ ≼

LUTYENS, Sir Edwin Landseer (1869–1944), *British architect. His greatest commission was planning the official center of New Delhi (1912–30). He was also responsible for the Cenotaph in London (1919–20), as well as some notable town and country houses.*

1 Struggling through the fish course in a famous London restaurant, Lutyens observed, "You know, this piece of cod passeth all understanding."

2 Lutyens was given to childish but often funny practical jokes. Once, staying with the Sitwells, he drew some strands of horsehair from a broken sofa, wrapped them in a piece of paper on which he had written a few words, and quietly deposited it in a desk drawer. Many years later Osbert Sitwell discovered the little package. Upon it was written: "A lock from Marie Antoinette's hair, cut from her head ten minutes after execution."

ॐ ≼

"It was once suggested to Dodgers pitcher Billy Loes that since he was the sole support of his parents, he should have some life insurance.

"'They wouldn't need it,' said Billy. 'If anything happened to me, it would kill 'em.'"

— R. L. Crouser,
*It's Unlucky to Be
Behind at the End of the Game*

LYAUTEY, Louis Hubert Gonzalve (1854–1934), *French general. During World War I he saved Morocco from the Germans. He was created marshal of France in 1921.*

1 After the war was over, Lyautey asked his gardener to plant a tree in a particular part of his estate. The gardener objected that the tree the marshal had chosen was particularly slow-growing and would not reach maturity for at least a century. The marshal replied, "In that case, there is no time to lose. Plant it this afternoon."

{This was one of John F. Kennedy's favorite anecdotes.}

ॐ ≼

LYCURGUS (7th century BC), *Spartan statesman.*

1 Lycurgus is credited with having created the Spartan constitution, with its strict military discipline and repressive state control of the peasantry. When someone asked why it was that he had not made the constitution of Sparta a democratic one, Lycurgus retorted, "Try the experiment in your own family."

ॐ ≼

LYNDHURST, John Singleton Copley, Lord (1772–1863), *British lawyer; lord chancellor (1827–28, 1834–35, 1841–46). Born in the United States, the son of the artist John Singleton Copley, Lord Lyndhurst rose to eminence in the law through his outstanding talents as an orator. He pursued his parliamentary career until almost his ninetieth year.*

1 A society lady asked Lord Lyndhurst whether he believed in platonic friendship between men and women. "After, not before," replied his lordship.

ॐ ≼

LYTTON, Edward George Earle Lytton Bulwer-Lytton, 1st Baron (1803–73), *British novelist and politician. A prolific writer, he is best known for his popular historical novels, such as* The Last Days of Pompeii *(1834),* Rienzi *(1835), and* Harold *(1848).*

1 When Wilkie Collins's detective novel *The Woman in White* appeared in 1860, it created a considerable stir. A feature much remarked upon was the villain, Count Fosco. One lady reader, however, was not so impressed and wrote to tell Collins, "You really do not know a villain. Your Count Fosco is a very poor one." She then offered to supply Collins with a villain next time he wanted one. "Don't think that I am drawing upon my imagination. The man is alive and constantly under my gaze. In fact, he is my husband." The writer was Bulwer-Lytton's wife.

{The Bulwer-Lytton marriage had not been a happy one, and in 1836 there had been a legal separation. Lady Lytton was in fact offering Collins a secondhand villain; she had herself already depicted her husband in that role in her own novel *Cheveley, or the Man of Honour* (1839).}

❦ M ❧

MABLY, Gabriel Bonnet, Abbé de (1709–85), *French political writer and philosopher.*

1 It was proposed to Mably that he campaign for election to the French Academy. He replied, "If I were a member, people would ask: 'Why is he there?' I prefer them to ask: 'Why is he not there?'"

See also CHAIM NACHMAN BIALIK 1; CATO 3; BENJAMIN DISRAELI 10.

❦ ❧

MACARTHUR, Charles (1895–1956), *US playwright; husband of Helen Hayes. With Ben Hecht he wrote* The Front Page *(1928) and* Twentieth Century *(1933); he and Hecht also adapted* Wuthering Heights *for the cinema.*

1 At the theater with Charles Lederer, MacArthur was feeling the effects of the liquor he had consumed earlier in the evening. A rather prim lady, seated beside Lederer, was harassed by MacArthur's obscene remarks and called for the manager. As an army of ushers descended on their seats, MacArthur urged Lederer to take advantage of the situation. "Quick!" he cried. "Put your hand up her skirt; we're going to be thrown out anyway."

❦ ❧

MACARTHUR, Douglas (1880–1964), *US general. He was Allied commander in the Pacific (1942–45), head of the forces occupying Japan (1945–51), and commanded the UN forces in the Korean War.*

1 (Alexander Woollcott tells this story about MacArthur in World War I.)

"As the sun came up . . . he might have been seen by his fellow officers (and he certainly was seen by the Germans) standing erect, adventurous, and oblivious on a painfully exposed parapet. One hand held his field glasses to his eyes, the other was clenched in excitement as the infantry just ahead charged through a wood. His adjutant — call him Smith, for the purpose of this story — stood at his elbow. Machine-gun bullets were hissing and hitting all around. A captain jumped up out of the trench and touched the general on the arm. 'If I might suggest, sir,' he said, 'your position is dangerous. The machine guns are reaching here.'

"'Eh, eh, what's that? Oh, yes, quite right, quite right. Thank you. Smith'—this with a glare at his adjutant —'get down in that trench at once.'"

2 When it became clear early in 1942 that Bataan, the last American foothold in the Philippines, would fall to the Japanese, President Roosevelt, in order to save MacArthur for tasks elsewhere, commanded him to leave the Philippines. As he left on March 11, MacArthur promised, "I shall return."

{He did — in October 1944.}

3 (Eisenhower, who had been on MacArthur's staff before World War II, called on his former commander in Tokyo. At the time, the names of both generals were being mentioned in connection with the presidency.)

"Eisenhower could not get a word in for three-quarters of an hour, while MacArthur reminisced about old times. Then Eisenhower interrupted to say, with emphasis and much elaboration, that he did not think that any military man should be president of the United States. His sincerity was manifest. But MacArthur cocked a wary eye at him and said, 'That's the way to play it, Ike.'"

4 When MacArthur did decide to run as the dark horse in the 1944 election, the first Mrs.

MacArthur was asked to assess his chances. "It depends which end you look at," replied the ex-wife cautiously.

৯৯ ৎৎ

MACAULAY, Thomas Babington, 1st Baron (1800–59), *Scottish statesman and writer. He served on the Supreme Council for India (1834–38), was secretary of war (1839–41), and paymaster of the forces (1846–47). He wrote a* History of England *(1848, 1855, 1861);* Essays *(1843), which appeared first in the* Edinburgh Review; The Lays of Ancient Rome *(1842); and contributions on literary and political figures for the* Encyclopaedia Britannica.

1 Macaulay was an infant prodigy with a quite extraordinary memory and a passion for books and reading. When he was only about four, his father took him to see the collection at Strawberry Hill assembled by the connoisseur Horace Walpole. Having spent some time looking at the collection, they were served coffee as guests of the then owner of the house, Lady Waldegrave. A clumsy servant spilled some of the hot liquid on the child's legs, much to the distress of the hostess. When the coffee had been mopped up, Lady Waldegrave asked him how he was feeling. "Thank you, madam, the agony is abated," said the four-year-old.

2 There is a story, of unknown origin, that bears on Macaulay's fabulous memory. It seems that one day an acquaintance of his, calling on him, found the noble lord pacing up and down in his study, reciting, line after line, hundreds of alexandrines from some obscure French medieval epic romance. After listening patiently for some time, the visitor at last interrupted: "Why in God's name, Macaulay, did you ever bother to memorize all that tedious nonsense?" Macaulay at once turned to him, saying, "Sir, do you not see that I am doing my best to *forget* it?"

3 Macaulay was known as a prodigious talker. After his return from India, Sydney Smith professed to notice an improvement. "His enemies might have said before that he talked rather too much; but now he has occasional flashes of silence that make his conversation perfectly delightful."

4 As Macaulay was notoriously clumsy about shaving himself, his rooms were always scattered with fragments of strops and broken razors. On one occasion when he had injured a hand, he had to send for a barber to shave him. "What should I give you?" he asked, uncertain what fee would be expected. "Whatever you usually give the person who shaves you, sir," replied the barber equably. "In that case I should give you a great gash on each cheek," Macaulay observed.

5 At a political meeting in Macaulay's Edinburgh constituency, he was standing on a balcony beside his opponent when he suffered the unpleasant experience of being hit by a dead cat thrown by a member of the audience. The man at once apologized, explaining that he had intended the cat for Macaulay's opponent. "In that case," said Macaulay, "I wish you had intended it for me and hit him."

6 (In June 1850 huge queues formed to see the first living hippopotamus to be displayed at London Zoo. By this time Macaulay's *History of England* had made him something of a celebrity too. Macaulay wrote to his friend Thomas Flower Ellis to tell him of what he described as "the proudest event of my life.")

"Two damsels were just about to pass that doorway [to the hippopotamus's quarters] when I was pointed out to them. 'Mr. Macaulay!' cried the lovely pair. 'Is that Mr. Macaulay? Never mind the hippopotamus.' And having paid a shilling to see Behemoth, they left him in the very moment at which he was about to display himself — but spare my modesty. I can wish for nothing more on earth."

৯৯ ৎৎ

McAULIFFE, Anthony Clement (1898–), *US general.*

1 McAuliffe commanded the 101st Airborne Division at Bastogne, an important road junction, during the Battle of the Bulge in World War II. Completely surrounded and outnumbered four to one, McAuliffe and his troops were asked to surrender. McAuliffe is alleged to have rejected the German surrender demand with an emphatic "Nuts!"

{Those acquainted with the general doubted that he would have used such a mild expletive.}

৯৯ ৎৎ

Henry Wise Miller, a US stockbroker and husband of the poet-novelist Alice Duer Miller, occasionally sat in on the famous poker games played by the New York wits of the thirties and forties at the Algonquin Hotel. Harold Ross, editor of *The New Yorker,* noticing Miller's black hair and hawk nose, suggested that he was an Arab. The Massachusetts-born, Harvard-bred Miller gravely replied that his grandmother was an Arab. During the colloquy the pot had been steadily growing. Miller discarded his hand, then remarked, "I fold. I am a folding Bedouin."

— Arthur Krock, *Memoirs*

McCARTHY, Joseph R[aymond] (1908–57), *US politician, senator from Wisconsin. He was notorious as the instigator of a persecution of people suspected — often totally without cause — of Communist sympathies during the Cold War period. In 1954 the senator was censured by a congressional inquiry and McCarthyism was finally discredited.*

1 Senator McCarthy stalked out of a congressional committee room in a rage, to be met by a bevy of reporters who asked him to comment upon a shocking allegation that had just been made. "Why, it's the most unheard-of thing I've ever heard of," McCarthy exploded.

McCORMACK, John (1884–1945), *US operatic tenor, born in Ireland. Having made his operatic debut in London in 1907, he moved to the United States in 1909 and was naturalized ten years later. He sang with a number of opera companies and was also famous as a concert singer, particularly for his renderings of Irish songs.*

1 McCormack was noted for his performance as the naval officer Pinkerton in *Madame Butterfly.* Having watched a production of the opera by a different company, he sought out the tenor playing Pinkerton and told him, "You sang very well, but you must have been a rotten naval officer." The tenor looked puzzled. "You began with a little bit of braid on

your sleeve," continued McCormack, "then, years later, when you return to Japan and your little Butterfly, you're still wearing the same bit of braid. Don't you ever get promoted? When I sang Pinkerton I took good care to promote myself to commander in the third act."

McCORMICK, Edith Rockefeller (1872–1932), *daughter of John D. Rockefeller, who married the businessman Harold McCormick and was the chief promoter of civic opera in Chicago.*

1 Edith McCormick always maintained a large staff in her huge and magnificent house. One rule applied to all of them, from the first butler to the personal maid's assistant: they were not permitted to speak to her. Only once was that rule broken. One evening in 1901, when Edith McCormick's young son was suffering from scarlet fever, a dinner party was in progress at the family's country retreat in Lake Forest. During the meal the news arrived that the unfortunate boy had died. Following a discussion in the servants' quarters, the tragic news was whispered to Mrs. McCormick at the table. Mrs. McCormick merely nodded her head, and the dinner party continued without pause.

McCOY, Kid [Norman Selby] (1873–1940), *US welterweight boxer, world champion (1896).*

1 The expression "the real McCoy" originated in a barroom brawl, when a drunk insisted that the boxer was not who he said he was. McCoy flattened his opponent, who struggled back onto his feet and said, "It's the real McCoy."

2 (P. G. Wodehouse, having watched Kid McCoy training at a gymnasium at White Plains, impulsively asked if he could step into the ring with him. The world champion agreed and he and Wodehouse began to make themselves ready for the bout, when McCoy suddenly laughed.)

"He had been reminded, he said, of an entertaining incident in his professional career, when he was fighting a contender who had the misfortune to be stone deaf. It was not immediately that he became aware of the other's affliction, but when he did he acted promptly and shrewdly. As the third round entered its concluding stages he stepped back a pace and pointed to his adversary's corner, to indicate to him that the bell had rung, which of course was not the case but far from it.

"'Oh, thank you so much,' said the adversary, 'Very civil of you.'

"He dropped his hands and turned away, whereupon Kid McCoy immediately knocked him out."

శ్రీ ఆశ్రీ

McCULLERS, Carson (1917–67), *US novelist and playwright. Her novels, such as* The Heart is a Lonely Hunter *(1940), are set in the American South.*

1   Carson McCullers's mother was on a bus en route to visit her daughter in New York when she fell into conversation with a lady of aristocratic mien who said she was fond of reading. The proud mother immediately began a lengthy monologue on her daughter's extraordinary literary talents. After some time the other woman mentioned that her father had also been a writer. Carson's mother asked her name. "Countess Tolstoy," was the answer.

శ్రీ ఆశ్రీ

MACDONALD, Sir John Alexander (1815–91), *Canadian statesman, born in Scotland. He was the first prime minister of the newly created dominion of Canada (1867–73), and held the office again from 1878 until his death.*

1   Lord Dufferin, governor general of Canada in the 1870s, once addressed an audience at McGill University, Montreal, entirely in Greek. Political leader Sir Hector Langevin, who had accompanied MacDonald to the meeting, was surprised to read in a newspaper report the following day that Dufferin had spoken "the purest ancient Greek without mispronouncing a word or making the slightest solecism."

"How would the reporter know that?" asked Langevin.

"I told him," replied MacDonald.

"But you don't know any Greek."

"That's true," said Sir John, "but I *do* know a little about politics."

శ్రీ ఆశ్రీ

> "Discussing Sophocles's *Oedipus the King,* Ellen Smith, the wife of Hermon Dunlap Smith, a university trustee, expressed some puzzlement over the horror which the Greeks apparently felt about incest. Milton Mayer [the journalist and educator], sitting at my side, responded by saying, in an audible stage whisper, 'There's nothing wrong with incest just as long as you keep it in the family.'"
>
> — Mortimer Adler,
> *Philosopher at Large*

McKINLEY, William B. (1843–1901), *US politician; 25th president of the United States (1897–1901). He was a congressman and later (1891–96) governor of Ohio. His administration was marked by the war with Spain over Cuba and moves to expand American power abroad, notably in the Far East.*

1   On a visit to Niagara Falls in 1901, McKinley was careful to walk only halfway along the bridge connecting the United States with Canada. He simply didn't want to be the first president to leave the boundaries of the United States during his term of office.

2   On September 6, 1901, while greeting people at an official reception at Buffalo, McKinley was shot at point-blank range by an anarchist named Leon Czolgosz. McKinley slumped in a chair, his first thoughts for the safety of his assailant, who was being tackled by people nearby, and his second thoughts for his wife, Ida, a semi-invalid who suffered from seizures. "My wife," he gasped, "be careful how you tell her." He was taken to a hospital where he lingered for a few days. His wife was at his bedside as his end approached. "I want to go too, I want to go too," she sobbed. "We are all going," said McKinley faintly. He did not speak again.

శ్రీ ఆశ్రీ

MACMAHON, Marie Edmé Patrice Maurice, Comte de (1808–93), *French general and statesman; president (1873–79). He was responsible for the French victory at Magenta (1859) and was created marshal of France. He* *helped crush the Commune of Paris (1871) and became president.*

1 Visiting a field hospital one day, the marshal addressed a few words to a soldier who lay ill with a tropical fever. "Yes, that's a nasty disease you've got there. You either die of it, or go crazy. I've been through it myself."

ॐ ॐ

MACMILLAN, [Maurice] **Harold, 1st Earl of Stockton** (1894–), *British statesman. Having become a Conservative MP in 1924, he later served as minister of defense (1954–55), chancellor of the exchequer (1955–57), and prime minister (1957–63).*

1 At the United Nations in September 1960, Macmillan was interrupted in the middle of his speech by Nikita Khrushchev, the Soviet premier, who had taken off his shoe and was banging on the table with it. Unperturbed, Macmillan simply remarked, "I'd like that translated, if I may."

2 Among Macmillan's many critics was his own son, Maurice, who once wrote a letter to *The Times* attacking the government in general and his father in particular. By way of reply, Macmillan announced in the House of Commons, "The member for Halifax [Maurice Macmillan] has intelligence and independence. How he got them is not for me to say."

3 Told that his Labour rival Harold Wilson had been obliged as a child to go to school without boots, Macmillan remarked: "That was probably because his boots were too small for him."

ॐ ॐ

MACREADY, William Charles (1793–1873), *British actor. Noted for his tragic roles, he was called by Hazlitt the best tragic actor of his time except for his rival Kean.*

1 Macready's handwriting was notoriously difficult to decipher. When he wrote a complimentary letter of admission to a theater during one of his American tours, the recipient remarked that it looked every bit as illegible as a doctor's prescription. He and a friend thereupon decided to take it along to the apothecary to see what he made of it. The young assistant took the piece of paper and with scarcely a glance at it began pulling down phials and jars to make a compound. After mixing a number of ingredients with great confidence, he seemed to come to an item that bothered him; he paused and puzzled over it and at last summoned his boss from the back of the shop. The older man studied the paper and then with a contemptuous snort at his assistant's ignorance, pulled down another bottle and completed the mixture. Handing the result to his customers, he remarked with a smile, "A cough mixture, and a very good one. Fifty cents, if you please."

See also HORACE GREELEY 6.

2 Macready once directed a production of *Hamlet* in Norwich, playing the title role himself. His innovative ideas made him a number of enemies among the cast, notably the actor playing Claudius. On the opening night, having received his deathblow from Hamlet, Claudius staggered to center stage to die. Macready was incensed: he had made it quite clear at rehearsals that Claudius was to die upstage, leaving the center free for his own death scene. "Die further up the stage," hissed the irate director. "Get up and die elsewhere." The "dead" Claudius sat up and said, in tones heard by the entire audience, "Look here, Mr. Macready, you've had your way at rehearsals, but I'm king now, and I shall die just where I please."

ॐ ॐ

MADISON, James (1751–1836), *US statesman; 4th president of the United States (1809–17). Deeply versed in theories of government, Madison helped frame the US Constitution (1787). His presidency was flawed by the unnecessary and humiliating War of 1812 with Britain.*

1 At the Constitutional Convention Madison was one of the most active speakers, and many wise provisions owe their origin to his foresight and learning. Apt to get carried away when addressing the Convention, he asked a friend to sit by him and tweak his coattails if he seemed to be getting overexcited. After a particularly impassioned speech he sat down, almost exhausted, and reproached his friend for not pulling at his coat. "I would as soon have laid a finger on the lightning," said his friend.

> During a murder trial the defense barrister, Sir John Maynard, challenged the judge on a point of law. "Sir," said the judge, "you have grown so old you have forgotten the law." Sir John replied, "I have forgotten more law than you ever knew, but allow me to say, I have not forgotten much."
>
> — James C. Humes,
> *Speakers' Treasury*

MAETERLINCK, Maurice (1862–1949), *Belgian poet and dramatist. He first made his reputation as a poet and later became a leading figure in the Symbolist movement. His play* Pelléas et Mélisande *(1892) formed the basis for Debussy's opera of the same name. From 1890 he lived chiefly in France. In 1911 he won the Nobel Prize for literature.*

1   Modern amenities were sometimes sparse in old French country houses at the end of the nineteenth century, but Maeterlinck was nonetheless pleased to accept an invitation for a prolonged stay in a remote château to enable him to relax and write in peace. Arriving while his hostess was out, he asked the maid to direct him to the bathroom. She led him down a corridor at the end of which was a huge, apparently solid, oak throne. From behind the contraption she pulled a large cloak and a face mask. "Here you are, monsieur," she said. "You wear these so no one knows who is sitting here." Maeterlinck thanked her and was well away from the château by the time his hostess returned.

2   Maeterlinck's well-publicized romance with the French actress Georgette Leblanc came to a mysterious end after twenty years. The sixty-year-old writer then married a young girl of nineteen. He refused to speak to the press on the subject, but an enterprising young American reporter managed to secure an interview with him at his Mediterranean villa. She sent him a note bearing the following message: "I am an American writer in great difficulties. If I can do an interview on you for my paper I can pay my passage home, and all will be well. If not, my only alternative will be to commit suicide." Even Maeterlinck could not reject such an appeal. The woman duly arrived for her interview, opened up her notebook, and began: "May I ask why you left Georgette Leblanc?" Maeterlinck glared at the reporter and snapped, "Go and commit suicide, madame."

MAGRUDER, John B. (1810–71), *US Confederate commander.*

1   While Magruder was in command at Yorktown in 1861, he forbade soldiers to bring liquor into the camp. One day he noticed a certain Private Sharpe drinking from his canteen with a relish suggesting the canteen contained something more potent than water. Magruder, known to be fond of alcoholic refreshment, ordered Sharpe to let him have a drink of his "water." Magruder took a draught, returned the canteen, and promptly promoted the terrified private to the rank of corporal. Some time later Magruder called for another drink, and this time returned the canteen with the words: "You are no longer Corporal Sharpe, sir; you are Sergeant Sharpe!" Sharpe realized he would merit his instant promotions as long as the liquor in his canteen lasted. Unfortunately, he had only attained the rank of lieutenant when the canteen was found to be empty. When Magruder next called for a drink, the disappointed Sharpe, having searched the camp in vain for further supplies, could only reply, "General, it is played out, and I am sorry for it; for if it had held out I'll be damned if I would not have been a brigadier general before night!"

MAHAFFY, Sir John Pentland (1839–1919), *Irish scholar known for his work on ancient Greek literature and history. He was provost of Trinity College, Dublin (1914–19).*

1   Dr. Mahaffy was out shooting when another member of the party carelessly put some shot through the crown of his hat. He inspected the damage calmly. "Two inches lower, and you would have shot away ninety per cent of the Greek in Ireland."

2   A lady seeking to embroil Dr. Mahaffy in a feminist argument opened her attack with "You are a man. I am a woman. What is the essential difference between us?"
  "Madam," said Dr. Mahaffy urbanely, "I can't conceive."

"When John Mariucci was coaching the U.S. Olympic hockey team, there was a time or two when he became a bit impatient with his young and inexperienced squad. During one locker room tirade he screamed, 'Every day you guys look worse and worse. And today you played like tomorrow.'"

— Richard L. Crouser,
It's Unlucky to Be
Behind at the End of the Game

MAHLER, Gustav (1860–1911), *Austrian composer. He wrote nine symphonies, of which the eighth, the* Symphony of a Thousand *(1906–07), is perhaps the most famous. He also wrote song cycles, such as* Kindertotenlieder *(1901–04).*

1 Mahler found the inspiration for much of his music in the beautiful scenery of the Austrian countryside. "Don't bother looking at the view," he once told a visitor to his country house. "I have already composed it."

ॐ ॐ

MAINTENON, Françoise d'Aubigné, Madame de (1635–1719), *French noblewoman, second wife of Louis XIV. Married (1652) to the crippled poet Paul Scarron, she was widowed in her mid-twenties and put in charge of Louis XIV's illegitimate children by Mme de Montespan. Louis came to rely on her discretion and later to love her, but she refused to be his mistress. He secretly married her, probably in 1684, and they were devotedly happy together until Louis's death.*

1 Louis built a château at Marly as a country retreat. The central building, called the Sun, was flanked by twelve other buildings, each named for a sign of the zodiac and arranged six on either side of a pool of water. In this exquisite artificial pond swam Louis's favorite carp, which boasted glamorous names like Golden Sun, Beautiful Mirror, the Dauphine, Topaz, and Dawn. To the eyes of a lady walking by the pond with Mme de Maintenon, the fish looked melancholy in the crystal-clear water, and she mentioned the fact to her companion. "The

carp are like me," said Mme de Maintenon. "They regret their native mud."

{Hence the French phrase "*nostalgie de la boue*."}

2 Mme de Maintenon, an excellent conversationalist, could keep a company of witty and malicious courtiers charmed by her talk. Even the servants recognized her powers in this direction. At a private dinner when some culinary hitch had occurred, one of them whispered to her. "Madame, be pleased to tell another story. There is no roast today."

ॐ ॐ

MALHERBE, François de (1555–1628), *French poet and critic. His critical writings were influential in setting the standard for classical French poetry.*

1 Even on his deathbed Malherbe retained his passionate concern with purity of diction and style. As he lay dying, his confessor tried to encourage him with a fulsome description of the joys of paradise. Malherbe begged him to stop: "Your ungrammatical style is giving me a distaste for them."

{Other dying precisionists seem to have uttered similar severities. *See* DOMINIQUE BOUHOURS 1.}

ॐ ॐ

MALIBRAN, Maria Felicia (1808–36), *French opera singer, daughter of the Spanish tenor Manuel García (1775–1832). She made her debut in Rome (1825) in Rossini's* Barber of Seville.

1 While she was on stage at the Paris Opéra with her rival Henriette Sontag one evening, a floral wreath landed at Malibran's feet. As she bent to pick it up, a voice rang out from the audience: "Leave that alone — it isn't for you."

"I wouldn't deprive Mademoiselle Sontag of the wreath," retorted Malibran. "I'd rather place one on her."

ॐ ॐ

MALLARMÉ, Stéphane (1842–98), *French Symbolist poet.*

1 The picture dealer Ambroise Vollard was walking in the woods near Paris with a friend when they came upon a small gray-haired

gentleman spearing pieces of paper and other litter with a nailed stick and putting them into a basket. "That's Mallarmé," said the friend, and going up to the poet asked him what on earth he was doing. "I have invited some Parisians to come to tea tomorrow," Mallarmé explained, "so I am cleaning up the banquet hall."

ह~ ~ई

MALLORY, George Leigh (1886–1924), *British mountaineer. He vanished on an attempt to scale Mount Everest and speculation still continues as to whether he was killed before or after reaching the summit.*

1   Mallory, a veteran of several Everest expeditions when he went on a lecture tour of the United States in 1923, was frequently asked why he wanted to climb Mount Everest. He always gave the same answer: "Because it is there."
    {This is also attributed in the form "Because it was there" to the eventual conqueror of Everest, Sir Edmund Hillary.}

ह~ ~ई

MANKIEWICZ, Herman J. (1897–1953), *US journalist and film scriptwriter.*

1   After Mankiewicz had been out of a job for some time, his agent succeeded in getting him a post at the Columbia studio, with a warning to steer clear of Harry Cohn, head of the studio. For some weeks Mankiewicz obeyed, but the sound of laughter and talk from the executive dining room penetrated his office and finally proved too much for him. When the Columbia executives assembled one day, they found Mankiewicz seated at the end of the table. "I won't say a word," he promised. Cohn came in and immediately launched into an attack on a film he had seen the night before in his private projection room. Someone suggested he might feel otherwise if he had seen it with a public audience. Audience reaction made no difference to him, Cohn replied. "When I'm alone in a projection room I have a foolproof device for judging whether a picture is good or bad. If my fanny squirms, it's bad. If my fanny doesn't squirm, it's good. It's as simple as that." The sudden silence was broken by Mankiewicz's voice from the foot of the table: "Imagine — the whole world wired to Harry Cohn's ass!"

That was the end of Mankiewicz's job at Columbia.

2   Arthur Hornblow, Jr., film producer and epicure, gave a rather stuffy dinner party for a number of Hollywood celebrities. Mankiewicz had too much to drink and threw up at the table. An appalled hush fell on the guests. Then Mankiewicz said, "It's all right, Arthur. The white wine came up with the fish."

3   Mankiewicz's wife, Sara, had a difficult time with her husband's drinking problem and the frequent interruptions to his career caused by his falling out with studio bosses. A friend whom he had not seen for a while asked Mankiewicz, "How's Sara?"
    Mankiewicz looked puzzled: "Sara? Who?"
    "Sara. Your wife, Sara."
    "Ah, you mean Poor Sara."

ह~ ~ई

MANN, Thomas (1875–1955), *German novelist, winner of the 1929 Nobel Prize for literature. His major novels include* The Magic Mountain *(1924),* Doctor Faustus *(1947), and* The Confessions of Felix Krull *(1954). He also wrote the novella* Death in Venice *(1912). His opposition to Nazism forced him to emigrate to the United States in the 1930s.*

1   Mann was introduced to an American writer of some note who abased himself before the famous novelist, saying that he scarcely considered himself to be a writer in comparison with Mann. Mann answered him civilly, but afterward he remarked, "He has no right to make himself so small. He's not that big."

ह~ ~ई

MANNING, Hugh Gardner (1920–   ), *British actor. He has acted with a number of English companies, often in Shakespearean roles, and has also appeared in films and on television.*

1   Performing at a Birmingham repertory theater one evening, Manning found himself stranded on stage with a piano and a vase of daffodils, a fellow actor having failed to enter on cue. He strolled across to the piano and idly fingered one of the daffodils, looking anxiously toward the wings. The actor still did not appear. Manning picked up the flower, sniffed

it, and finally, in desperation, ate it. The audience roared with laughter. The improvisation was such a success, in fact, that Manning found himself expected to eat a daffodil at every subsequent performance.

෧ଈ ൴ଈ

MANSART, François (1598–1666), *French architect. He built or remodeled numerous châteaux and town houses, including the north wing of the royal château at Blois (1635–38). The type of double-angled roof in which the lower part is steeper than the upper is called a mansard roof.*

1   Louis XIV was walking with Mansart in the sun. The architect was bareheaded, as court etiquette demanded. Louis told him to put on his hat. To his courtiers, who expressed astonishment at the king's condescension, he said, "I can make twenty dukes in a quarter of an hour, but it takes centuries to make a Mansart."
{Other kings have made similar remarks to or about other creative artists.}

෧ଈ ൴ଈ

MANSFIELD, William Murray, 1st Earl of (1705–93), *British judge who became solicitor general in 1742 and attorney general twelve years later. He was lord chief justice from 1756 to 1788.*

1   On one occasion an old woman, accused of being a witch, was brought before him. She was also charged with walking through the air. The judge listened attentively to all the evidence and then dismissed the accused woman. "My opinion," he said, "is that this good woman should be suffered to return home, and whether she shall do this, walking on the ground or riding through the air, must be left entirely to her own pleasure, for there is nothing contrary to the laws of England in either."

෧ଈ ൴ଈ

MAO ZEDONG (1893–1976), *Chinese statesman, founder of the People's Republic of China and chairman of the Chinese Communist party. Mao extended his influence to every aspect of Chinese life and his writings formed the theoretical basis for the new society he aimed to build.*

1   It is reported that Mao was fond of a little set speech he would make to visitors: "Our fathers were indeed wise. They invented printing, but not newspapers. They invented gunpowder, but used it only for fireworks. Finally, they invented the compass, but took care not to use it to discover America."

෧ଈ ൴ଈ

MARCEAU, Marcel (1923–), *French mime, who achieved international fame both as a soloist and with the troupe he formed in the 1940s.*

1   "Marceau said to William Fifield, 'Genius is silence.' When Fifield smiled slightly, he went on: 'No—I don't mean mime, I mean the mime is silent because if he spoke, the expression would be so much easier, and so he is *silent*,' he said with a whispering sibilancy, 'to oblige himself to say more.'"

෧ଈ ൴ଈ

MARGARET [Rose] (1930–), *princess of Great Britain, Countess of Snowdon and sister of Queen Elizabeth II.*

1   While attending a small dinner given in her honor during a visit to San Francisco in 1966, Princess Margaret was introduced to Barnaby Conrad. "You have a very English name," the princess observed. "Are you English?"
"No, ma'am," Conrad replied, "but my sixth great-grandmother was. Then she married a lieutenant colonel and soon after became an American. His name was George Washington."
"Oh," she said, as only the English can say that word.

෧ଈ ൴ଈ

MARIA FËDOROVNA (1847–1928), *empress of Russia as the wife of Czar Alexander III (1845–94). The daughter of King Christian IX of Denmark, she returned to her native land in 1919.*

1   The czarina was known throughout Russia for her philanthropy. She once saved a prisoner from transportation to Siberia by transposing a single comma in a warrant signed by Alexander. The czar had written: "Pardon impossible, to be sent to Siberia." After Maria's

intervention, the note read: "Pardon, impossible to be sent to Siberia." The prisoner was subsequently released.

{For a similar adjustment of punctuation, *see* MINNIE FISKE 1.}

કે⊷ ⊷ક

MARIA THERESA (1717–80), *empress of Austria (1740–80). Her accession sparked the War of the Austrian Succession (1740–48) when her predatory neighbor Frederick the Great seized Silesia. Maria Theresa sought a pact with France, but suffered defeat in the Seven Years' War (1756–63). Her domestic policies were forerunners of the enlightened despotism of her son Joseph, who succeeded her.*

1   Maria Theresa spent the last few days of her life propped up in a chair as she was unable to breathe if she lay down. Her son Joseph was constantly by her side. After one particularly agonizing spasm she struggled from the chair and dropped awkwardly onto a sofa. "Your Majesty cannot be comfortable like that," said Joseph, trying to support her. "No, but comfortable enough to die," said Maria Theresa, and within a few minutes she died without further struggle.

કે⊷ ⊷ક

MARIE ANTOINETTE (1755–93), *wife of King Louis XVI of France, whom she married in 1770. As an Austrian, Marie Antoinette was disliked and suspected by the French people.*

1   Told that her people had no bread to eat, Marie Antoinette is reported to have said, "*Qu'ils mangent de la brioche*" (Let them eat cake).

{This famous saying is considerably older than Marie Antoinette, so if she did indeed say it, she was quoting. Rousseau's *Confessions* (1740), for instance, refers to a similar remark as a current saying.}

2   Marie Antoinette loved to escape from the stifling confines of court etiquette. One of her pleasures was to go for donkey rides in the Bois de Boulogne, much to the disgust of the older and more staid ladies of the court. One day the queen's donkey took it into its head to roll on the turf, and threw its royal rider, who, quite unharmed, sat on the grass laughing uncontrol-

lably. As soon as she was able to speak, Marie Antoinette asked that the grand mistress of ceremonies be brought to her. This lady presented herself with considerable hauteur. The queen, still sitting on the ground, said to her, "Madame, I have sent for you to ask you to instruct me regarding the etiquette to be followed when the Queen of France and her donkey have both fallen. Which of them is to get up first?"

3   Marie Antoinette was painted several times by Marie-Louise Vigée-Lebrun. During one sitting the artist, who was far advanced in pregnancy, dropped some of her colors. The queen at once said, "You are too far along," and stooped to pick up the fallen colors herself.

4   At her trial before the revolutionary tribunal, Marie Antoinette defended herself with skill and courage, but the verdict and sentence were a foregone conclusion. She behaved with great composure when brought to the guillotine. As she was standing on the platform, she accidentally stepped on the executioner's foot. "Monsieur," she said, "I ask your pardon. I did not do it on purpose."

કે⊷ ⊷ક

MARIE de Médicis (1573–1642), *Italian-born wife of King Henri IV of France, whom she married in 1600. After his death (1610), she was regent for their son Louis until 1614. In later years she and Louis were in a state of open or concealed hostility. Cardinal Richelieu, one of her protégés, later went over to the king's side.*

1   The queen mother was visited on her deathbed by Fabio Chigi, then papal nuncio in France. To him she vowed to forgive all her enemies, including Cardinal Richelieu. "Madame," asked Chigi, "as a mark of reconciliation, will you send him the bracelet you wear on your arm?"

"No," she replied firmly, "that would be too much."

કે⊷ ⊷ક

MARLBOROUGH, John Churchill, 1st Duke of (1650–1722), *British general and statesman. During the War of the Spanish Succession he won four great battles against the French: Blenheim (1704), Ramillies (1706), Oudenaarde (1708), and Malplaquet (1709). To his* *wife, Sarah, the friend and confidante of Queen Anne, he owed his political influence, which he lost when she fell from favor. Blenheim Palace near Oxford was built as a gift to Marlborough from the nation in gratitude for his victories.*

1 Marlborough's notorious love of money remained with him through his life. In his last years he was once playing picquet with a certain Dean Jones, with stakes of sixpence a game. When they stopped, Marlborough was one game ahead and he asked the dean for his sixpence. The dean said he had no silver at that moment, but would pay the duke next time he saw him. Marlborough replied that he needed the sixpence to pay for a sedan chair to take him home, and made such a fuss that the dean eventually went to the trouble of sending a servant out to get change for a guinea. Marlborough took his sixpence and departed. The dean watched him leave the house and walk on down the street, conserving his winnings by going home on foot.

> ❧

MARLBOROUGH, John Spencer-Churchill, 10th Duke of (1897–1972), *British aristocrat. He made a notable contribution to the restoration of the family home, Blenheim Palace, opening it to the public in 1950.*

1 The duke lived in some style at Blenheim. Once he had occasion to stay overnight in the much more modest home of one of his three daughters. Before breakfast the daughter was surprised to hear her father bellowing down the stairs that his toothbrush was "not working." Upon investigation it turned out the toothbrush was not foaming as it should and the duke was angrily demanding a new one. The daughter had to explain that toothbrushes foamed only if toothpaste or powder was applied to them—a task habitually performed for the duke by his valet at Blenheim.

> ❧

MARQUAND, J[ohn] **P**[hillips] (1893–1960), *US novelist. He specialized in satires of upper-crust New England society, of which probably* The Late George Apley *(1937) is the best known.*

1 Marquand was looked down on by his aristocratic Sedgwick in-laws, who refused to take his writing seriously. One vacation when Marquand and his wife went to stay at her parental home, his brother-in-law, A. C. Sedgwick, was also staying there, also engaged in writing a book. The two writers occupied rooms on opposite sides of the main hall, spending most of the day at their desks. One afternoon Marquand's mother-in-law came into his room with her son's dog on a leash, and asked Marquand to take the animal out for its daily exercise, since A. C. could not do it himself. "He's writing, you know," she said in explanation.

2 After his first heart attack, Marquand did his best to face his threatened mortality with high spirit. Shortly after his return from the hospital, when one of his neighbors was visiting, John suddenly jumped out of bed. In his pajamas, he seized an antique sword from the wall, unsheathed it, and struck a John Barrymore pose. "Death," he boomed, "thus do I defy you!"

3 (The novelist Louis Auchinloss recalls another incident at a party soon after Marquand was released from the hospital.)
"John was back in his old form, swinging his glass in his hand as he entertained his audience, holding forth on what he called 'the lack of taste and reticence' in younger American writers. A few minutes later, he was talking about his weeks in the Newburyport hospital and how, as part of his therapy, an abdominal massage had been prescribed. His nurse, John confided, had whispered to him during the procedure, 'How lucky I am to be able to manipulate the lower abdominal muscles of a man like you!' One of the guests at the gathering was the New York *grande dame* Mrs. August Belmont. When Marquand had finished this anecdote, Mrs. Belmont inquired, 'And where, Mr. Marquand, was the taste and reticence in that remark?'"

> ❧

MARQUIS, Don[ald Robert Perry] (1878–1937), *US journalist and poet. He created the comic characters archy and mehitabel.*

1 After a month on the wagon, Don Marquis came up to the bar at the Players' Club and ordered a double martini. "I've conquered my goddam willpower," he announced to the assembled company.

2   Don Marquis once rashly bet with an expert golfer; the stakes were five dollars a hole and in addition Don Marquis gave his opponent two strokes. As they were about to start, the other turned to Marquis and asked, "Where do I get my two strokes?"

"It doesn't matter to me where you take the second," was the answer, "so long as the first is a stroke of apoplexy."

ই ঙ্গ

MARSHALL, Herbert (1890–1966), *British actor, known for his suave English style in British and American stage and film productions. He settled in the United States in the 1930s, appearing in many Hollywood films.*

1   Marshall served in the British merchant marine in World War I and lost a leg. He talked about one stint of sea duty, in which all the men had to wear life jackets most of the time, especially on deck. He said, "They got terribly soiled and foul-smelling, and after a while you detested them. Coming to port, finally, at the conclusion of my tour of duty, I threw mine overboard. And watched it sink."

ই ঙ্গ

MARSHALL, John (1755–1835), *US lawyer; Chief Justice of the Supreme Court (1801–35). His judgments on constitutional law were of fundamental importance in molding the traditions of the US legal system. He presided over a number of important trials, most notably that of Aaron Burr (1807).*

1   On hearing it said that they were drinking too much, the justices of the Supreme Court decided that they would henceforth drink nothing on their weekly consultation day unless it was raining. The following consultation day Marshall duly asked Joseph Story to go to the window and see if there was any sign of rain. Story reported: "Mr. Chief Justice, I have very carefully examined this case, and I have to give it as my opinion that there is not the slightest sign of rain." Marshall, not content with this assessment of the situation, replied, "Justice Story, I think that is the shallowest and most illogical opinion I have ever heard you deliver; you forget that our jurisdiction is as broad as the Republic, and by the laws of nature it must be raining some place in our jurisdiction. Waiter, bring on the rum."

"The first roller skates were perfected more than two centuries ago by Joseph Merlin — who, unfortunately, failed to perfect the art of skating as well. His first public demonstration ended in diasaster.

"A renowned maker of violins and harpsichords, the Belgian-born Merlin moved to London in 1760, where he dreamed up the idea of replacing the blades on ice skates with metal wheels. To dramatize his invention, Merlin dressed as a minstrel and made a spectacular entrance on skates at an elegant masquerade ball. He dazzled the other guests as he wheeled gracefully about the ballroom floor while playing a violin. Then, as his admirers watched in horror, Merlin lost control and sailed headlong into a crystal mirror, demolishing it and his handcrafted violin.

"Whatever chances of immediate success the new invention might have had were shattered with the mirror. Fearful that Merlin's creation was unsafe, Europeans virtually ignored roller skating, and it wasn't until the 1860s — when a skating craze swept the U.S. and Europe — that the sport finally enjoyed real popularity."

— *Parade*, June 26, 1983

MARSHALL, Thomas Riley (1854–1925), *US politician; vice president (1913–21).*

1   During a tedious debate a senator embarked upon a boring enumeration of "what this country needs."

"What this country needs is a good five-cent cigar," chipped in Marshall.

{This famous remark has been echoed by many others. Franklin P. Adams noted, "What this country needs is a good five-cent nickel," and Will Rogers remarked, "Our country has plenty of good five-cent cigars, but the trouble is that they charge fifteen cents for them."}

2   Thomas Marshall was never under any illusion about the role and scope of the vice presidency. He once said, "The vice president of the United States is like a man in a cataleptic state: he cannot speak; he cannot move; he suffers no pain; and yet he is perfectly conscious of everything that is going on about him."

᠈᠊᠊᠊

MARTEN, Neil (1916–   ), *British Conservative member of Parliament (1959–   ).*

1   Marten was giving a group of his constituents a guided tour of the Houses of Parliament. During the course of the visit they happened to meet Lord Hailsham, then lord chancellor, wearing all the regalia of his office. Hailsham recognized Marten among the group of visitors and cried "Neil!" Not daring to question or disobey the command, the entire group of constituents promptly fell to their knees.

᠈᠊᠊᠊

MARTIN, Kingsley (1897–1969), *British journalist, editor and later director of* The New Statesman.

1   During the early sixties, when Kingsley Martin was editor of *The New Statesman,* he had occasion to stop at the desk of a young subeditor whom he had recently hired. He complimented him on his work. Pleased by the praise, the young editor hesitated a moment, then said, "Thank you, Mr. Martin . . . but may I say that I've recently married and we do find it hard to get by on twenty guineas a week." Martin (a Socialist, one should add) looked at him in astonishment, then said, "Good God! You mean you haven't got a private income?"

᠈᠊᠊᠊

MARTINELLI, Giovanni (1885–1969), *opera singer, born in Italy. He moved to the United States in 1913 and joined the Metropolitan Opera Company in New York.*

1   Martinelli was once questioned by a newspaper reporter about his smoking habits. "Tobacco, cigarettes, bah!" exclaimed the singer in disgust. "I would not think of it." The reporter, a little puzzled, reminded Martinelli of an advertisement in which he had asserted that a particular brand of cigarettes did not irritate his throat. "Yes, yes, of course I gave that

endorsement," said Martinelli impatiently. "How could they irritate my throat? I have never smoked."

2   At the opera one evening, Martinelli listened to a fellow Italian bellow his way through the title role of Verdi's *Otello.* "He sings it like a truck driver," remarked Martinelli scornfully. His companion, surprised by this apparently harsh criticism, asked the great tenor what he thought of a certain American's rendering of the role. "Ah, now, *he* sings it like the truck," replied Martinelli.

᠈᠊᠊᠊

MARX, Chico [Leonard] (1891–1961), *US movie comedian, one of the famous Marx Brothers.*

1   Marx's wife had caught him kissing a chorus girl. During the ensuing row, Chico declared: "I wasn't kissing her. I was whispering in her mouth."

2   A new neighbor, not recognizing Chico, asked him what he did for a living. "I'm a smuggler," announced Chico, then, reassuringly, "Nothing big. Just Mexicans."

3   Chico wrote Heywood Broun a check to pay off some gambling debts, warning him not to cash it before twelve o'clock the following day. Broun later complained to Chico that the check had bounced. Chico asked: "What time did you try to cash it?"
    "Twelve-o-five."
    "Too late."

᠈᠊᠊᠊

MARX, Groucho [Julius] (1895–1977), *US comedian, one of the famous Marx Brothers.*

1   Groucho was working in the garden of his California house, dressed in tattered and ancient clothes. A wealthy matron in a Cadillac caught sight of him, stopped, and wondered whether she might persuade the supposed gardener to come and work for her. "Gardener," she called, "how much does the lady of the house pay you?"
    Groucho looked up. "Oh, I don't get paid in dollars," he replied. "The lady of the house just lets me sleep with her."

2 Groucho was descending in the elevator of the Hotel Danieli in Venice. On the third floor the elevator stopped and a group of priests entered. One of them, recognizing Groucho, told him that his mother was a great fan of his. "I didn't know you guys were allowed to have mothers," said Groucho.

3 When Groucho wanted to join a certain beach club in Santa Monica, California, he was told by a friend that as the club was known to be anti-Semitic he might as well not bother to apply. "But my wife isn't Jewish," replied Groucho, "so will they let my son go into the water up to his knees?"

See GEORGE S. KAUFMAN 11.

{This story and the one following, however, are both probably apocryphal.}

4 Groucho sent a telegram to the exclusive Friar's Club in Hollywood, to which he belonged: "Please accept my resignation. I don't want to belong to any club that will accept me as a member."

{Robert Benchley had similar suspicions about his bank. *See* BENCHLEY 14.}

5 The maître d'hôtel stopped Groucho as he was about to enter the dining room of a smart Los Angeles hotel. "I am sorry, sir, but you have no necktie."

"That's all right," said Groucho, "don't be sorry. I remember the time when I had no pants."

"I am sorry, sir," repeated the man, "you cannot enter the dining room without a necktie."

Groucho caught sight of a bald man in the center of the dining room and yelled, "Look! Look at him! You won't let me in without a necktie, but you let him in without his hair!"

6 Groucho attended one of George Gershwin's parties, given, it seemed, for the sole purpose of letting the host play and show off his music. Someone asked him, "Do you think that Gershwin's melodies will be played a hundred years from now?"

"Sure," was Groucho's answer, "if George is here to play them."

7 A tipsy man lumbered up to Groucho Marx, slapped him on the back, and said, "You old son-of-a-gun, you probably don't remember me." Marx glared at him and said, "I never forget a face, but in your case I'll be glad to make an exception."

8 The Marx Brothers, though a closely knit group, also understood their relative values as performers. When they were working on Broadway, Zeppo, the straight man and consequently replaceable, decided to quit the show. Sam Harris, the producer, gave him permission to leave. When Groucho, Harpo, and Chico heard about it, they went to Harris. Groucho said, "Sam, if Zeppo leaves you'll have to give us more money."

9 Groucho Marx intensely disliked producer Harry Cohn, who worked for Columbia Pictures. Once, with his brother Chico, he viewed Cohn's latest film. When the words "Columbia Pictures Presents" came up, Groucho turned to Chico and remarked, "Drags, doesn't it?"

{This story invites comparison with F. SCOTT FITZGERALD 2.}

10 Warner Brothers threatened to sue Groucho Marx when they heard that the next Marx Brothers film was to be called *A Night in Casablanca,* arguing that the title was too close to their own *Casablanca.* Groucho's reply: "I'll sue you for using the word *Brothers.*"

11 During his stint as comedian in a show called "You Bet Your Life," Groucho interviewed many participants. On one occasion he interviewed a Mrs. Story, who had given birth to twenty-two children. "I love my husband," Mrs. Story said enthusiastically. "I like my cigar, too," said Groucho, "but I take it out once in a while."

{This remark, like many others, had to be cut before the broadcast. On average one and a half hours of live show were cut to about twenty-six minutes of broadcast.}

12 Invited to a bachelor dinner at a fashionable restaurant before a high-society wedding, Groucho and Harpo noted that the automatic elevator opened directly into the dining rooms on the various floors. As the elevator went up, they gleefully arranged a surprise for the assembled bachelors and emerged — carrying their clothes in valises and wearing nothing but top hats.

To their consternation, they were greeted not by raucous roars of male hilarity but by high-pitched feminine shrieks. The bride was entertaining *her* friends on the floor above the bachelor dinner, and Groucho and Harpo had pressed the wrong button. No ready escape appeared; they took refuge behind a large potted plant until they could drape themselves in tablecloths secured by a kindly waiter, murmur abject apologies to the horrified ladies, and slink ignominiously from the room.

13 Marx despised the empty clichés of business correspondence. A letter from his bank manager ended with the standard phrase, "If I can be of any service to you, do not hesitate to call on me." Marx immediately put pen to paper. "Dear Sir," he wrote, "The best thing you can do to be of service to me is to steal some money from the account of one of your richer clients and credit it to mine."

14 For many years, every time they met, Samuel Goldwyn's first words to Groucho Marx would be "How's Harpo?" Marx grew rather tired of this. Finally, on meeting Goldwyn again and facing the inevitable inquiry, he said, "Listen, Sam, every time we meet — every time for *years* — you always ask, 'How's Harpo?' You never ask me anything else, and to tell you the truth, I'm getting goddam sick and tired of it. Why don't you ever ask me how *I* am?"

"How are you?" asked Goldwyn obligingly.

"I'm fine," replied Groucho.

"And how's Harpo?"

> ॐ ॐ

MARX, Harpo [Arthur] (1893–1964), *US movie comedian, the member of the famous Marx Brothers team who often pretended to be dumb. He was a skilled harpist.*

1 Among the guests at a dinner party were Harpo Marx and his wife, Susan. The English writer Jonathan Miller quizzed one of the other guests afterward, hoping to hear firsthand of some of Harpo's witticisms. "What did Harpo say?" he asked.

"He didn't say anything."

"How about his wife?"

"She didn't say anything, either."

"Oh," said Miller in pretended disgust, "stealing Harpo's bit, eh?"

2 Meeting George S. Kaufman in New York, Oscar Levant asked if he had recently heard from his friend Harpo Marx. "How can you hear from Harpo?" asked Kaufman. "He can't write and he can't talk, so how can you hear from Harpo?"

3 Harpo Marx on a visit to New York was plagued by representatives of charities wanting him to appear at benefits. One persistent lady telephoned him no fewer than twelve times in forty-eight hours. Harpo eventually agreed to appear for her charity. To ensure that he would not escape her at the last minute, she called to escort him personally to the benefit. As they were leaving the hotel suite, the telephone began ringing. "Don't you want to go back and answer it?" the lady asked. "Why bother?" responded Harpo with a weary sigh. "It's undoubtedly you again."

> ॐ ॐ

MARY I (1516–58), *queen of England (1553–58). Brought up in the shadow of Henry VIII's divorce from her mother, Catherine of Aragon, Mary suffered humiliation and uncertainty in her youth. Succeeding her half-brother, Edward VI, she devoted herself to restoring Roman Catholicism in England. Her marriage (1554) to Philip II of Spain made her unpopular, and her persecution of Protestants won her the nickname of "Bloody Mary."*

1 Calais, England's last possession in France, was lost to the French in 1558. This disaster further undermined Mary's health, which had been weakened by a phantom pregnancy. A lady-in-waiting suggested to her during her last illness that her distress was caused by the absence of her husband, Philip, from her side. "Not only that," said the unhappy queen, "but when I am dead and opened you shall find 'Calais' lying in my heart."

> {This famous anecdote was used by Robert Browning in "De Gustibus":
> Italy, my Italy!
> Queen Mary's saying serves for me —
>   (When fortune's malice
>   Lost her — Calais) —
> Open my heart and you will see
> Graved inside of it, 'Italy.'}

In his *Encyclopedia of Eccentrics* De Morgan tells the story of the slow-witted royal duke of the previous century who was once out riding with noble members of his retinue. "The rain comes into my mouth," complained the royal rider with a grimace. An equerry politely suggested that His Highness would be wise to shut his mouth in that case. The duke did so. A few minutes later he commented thoughtfully, "It doesn't come in now."

— Augustus De Morgan,
The Encyclopedia of Eccentrics

MARY (1867–1953), *queen consort of George V of Great Britain. Born Princess Mary of Teck, she was the great-granddaughter of George III.*

1 As Prince and Princess of Wales, George and Mary once visited Portsmouth, where they were entertained by the commander in chief of the British fleet, Admiral Sir John Fisher. Sir John offered to take the prince down in a submarine, and the invitation was eagerly accepted. Mary was not altogether happy about this idea, but with true regal self-control managed to suppress her feelings. As the vessel disappeared below the surface, she simply murmured, "I shall be very disappointed if George doesn't come up again."

2 When she was informed of the death of her son, King George VI, all that escaped Queen Mary's lips was the smallest "Oh!" She looked so upset, however, that the members of her household asked her daughter, the Princess Royal, to come to her as quickly as possible. The princess, then in her mid-fifties, hurried to Queen Mary, full of concern for the old lady. To her surprise she was greeted with disapproval. "When you come before the queen," said her mother, "please do your hair properly." The princess retreated to her room.

MARY, Queen of Scots (1542–87). *The daughter of James V of Scotland, she became queen soon after her birth, with her mother as regent. Mary was brought up at the French court and married the dauphin (later Francis II). On* Francis's death (1561) Mary returned to Scotland. Her second husband, the unpopular Lord Darnley, was murdered in 1567 by the Earl of Bothwell, who became Mary's third husband. The Scottish nobles rose in rebellion, and forced Mary to abdicate in favor of her one-year-old son, James VI (later James I of England). Mary fled to England, where she was held prisoner by Elizabeth I, to whose throne she had long laid claim. Eventually Elizabeth put her on trial for complicity in the Babington plot (1586). She was found guilty and executed.

1 Surviving portraits of Mary show her with exquisite auburn hair. After she had been beheaded, the executioner stooped to pick up her head to exhibit it, as the custom was, to the crowd. As he stood up and cried, "Long live the queen!" he found he was holding only a kerchief to which was fastened an auburn wig. At his feet lay the head of the queen of Scots, almost completely bald.

MASARYK, Jan (1886–1948), *son of the founding president of Czechoslovakia. He became foreign minister in London when the Czech government was in exile during World War II. He remained foreign minister after the war but died as a result of a "fall" from a window, not long after the Communist takeover in 1948.*

1 Early in his career Jan Masaryk served as Czech ambassador to the United States. At a party he was prevailed upon by the hostess to play the violin. He graciously accepted the invitation and played a Czech nursery song, to rapturous applause from all present. He left the party with a Czech friend, who wanted to know why on earth he had been asked to play the violin. Masaryk explained: "Oh, it's all very simple—don't you see? They have mixed me up with my father; they mixed him up with Paderewski. And they mixed the piano up with the violin."

MASCAGNI, Pietro (1863–1945), *Italian composer best known for his one-act opera* Cavalleria Rusticana *(1889).*

1 Mascagni was much irritated by an organ-grinder who stood outside his apartment playing tunes from *Cavalleria Rusticana* at about half the correct speed. Eventually he could stand it no longer, went out into the street, and said to the organ-grinder, "I am Mascagni. Let me show you how to play this music correctly." He gave the handle of the hurdy-gurdy a few vigorous turns.

The following day Mascagni again heard the organ-grinder in the street outside. When he looked out, he noticed a sign over the instrument: "PUPIL OF MASCAGNI."

{Andy Warhol claims, in a famous statement, that everyone will be famous for fifteen minutes. Perhaps this anecdote and OTTO KAHN 1 indicate how.}

2 When in 1901 the time came to dedicate his opera *Le Maschere,* Mascagni solved the problem neatly. He dedicated it to himself "with highest esteem and unchanging affection."

॰৵ ৵৹

MASSENET, Jules (1842–1912), *French composer, best remembered for his operas, including* Manon Lescaut *(1884) and* Werther *(1892).*

1 Massenet was conducting a rehearsal of *Manon Lescaut* with a particularly lackluster chorus. Finally he rapped on the rostrum and exhorted them, saying, "Brother and sister artists! Sing it like an encore! Sing it as though the audience had applauded!" The appeal was immediately successful.

॰৵ ৵৹

MASTROIANNI, Marcello (1923–   ), *Italian actor. His films include* Divorce Italian Style *(1961) and* Yesterday, Today and Tomorrow *(1963).*

1 Film producer Joseph Levine once presented Mastroianni with a magnificent gold wristwatch. It could have been an embarrassing moment, for the actor was already wearing a gold watch. On seeing what was inside the package, however, Mastroianni took off his own watch and nonchalantly dropped it into the nearest wastebasket.

॰৵ ৵৹

MATHILDE, Princess (1820–1904), *French noblewoman; daughter of King Jérôme of Westphalia.*

1 Separated from her husband within five years of their marriage, Princess Mathilde had a long affair with Count Niewekerke. The liaison was public knowledge, but because of Princess Mathilde's position in the imperial family, no one was supposed to know about it. She was entertaining a group of ladies one afternoon when her dog, a miniature greyhound, came running up to her to be caressed. "Go away, you naughty dog," said the princess, pushing it from her. "Don't you know you're in disgrace?" Then turning to her guests she explained: "Last night he kept jumping on the bed all night and I couldn't get any sleep at all." A short while later Count Niewekerke joined the party. The little dog ran to fawn on him as well, but he pushed it away. "You're a very bad dog and I'm not going to pet you. You kept jumping on the bed all night and I didn't sleep a wink."

2 At the end of a pleasant social evening at Saint Gratien, her summer residence, the princess rose and said to her *chevalier d'honneur,* General Bougenel, "Now let's go to bed." Admiral Duperré was also present. "I wish I were in the general's place," he murmured. "I'm afraid you'd be cheated, *mon cher,*" said the princess, playfully slapping the admiral's wrist with her fan. "In this house we don't provide night service."

॰৵ ৵৹

MATISSE, Henri (1869–1954), *French painter. He studied with Gustave Moreau in the 1890s and in the early 1900s pioneered fauvism, a style characterized by its use of strong colors. Matisse was also a sculptor and designer of stained glass.*

1 Matisse's painting *Le Bateau* hung upside down in the Museum of Modern Art, New York, for forty-seven days before anyone noticed (October 18–December 4, 1961). In that period 116,000 people had visited the gallery.

॰৵ ৵৹

MATTHEWS, A[lfred] E[dward] (1869–1960), *British actor. He made his first stage appearance in 1886 and performed on stage and screen until his death. His films include* Quiet Wedding *(1940) and* The Chiltern Hundreds *(1949). In his ninetieth year he made the* *headlines by sitting on the sidewalk outside his lovely Georgian house in Bushey near London for several days and nights to prevent the council from installing a streetlight, the design of which did not please him.*

1 Toward the end of his career Matthews was acting in a West End play. One scene involved a crucial telephone call, which Matthews was to answer. The telephone rang on cue; he crossed the stage, picked up the receiver, and promptly dried up. In desperation, he turned to the only other actor on the stage and said, "It's for you."

2 Matthews's last memorable stage appearance was in *The Manor of Northstead* in 1953. During rehearsals, it was obvious that the eighty-four-year-old actor was having some difficulty learning his part, and his director was rather concerned. "I know you think I'm not going to know my lines," said Matthews when approached on the subject, "but I promise you that even if we had to open next Monday, I would be all right."

"But, Matty," replied his director anxiously, "we *do* open next Monday."

ॐ ॐ

MATURE, Victor (1915–   ), *US film actor specializing in heavy romantic roles.*

1 Victor Mature applied for membership in the exclusive Los Angeles Country Club, only to be told "We don't accept actors." "I'm no actor," Mature is supposed to have protested, "and I've sixty-four pictures to prove it."

2 Groucho Marx was among the audience invited to a private screening of Victor Mature's new film *Samson and Delilah,* in which he co-starred with Hedy Lamarr. "What did you think?" asked the producer buoyantly at the end. "I have one major criticism," said Groucho. "You can't expect the public to get excited about a film where the leading man's bust is bigger than the leading lady's."

3 During a break in the filming of a historical picture, Mature slipped out with one of his fellow actors for a quick drink. As time was short, they did not bother changing out of their Roman gladiator costumes and strode into the local bar in full armor, complete with helmets and swords. The barman, speechless, stood rooted to the spot. "What's the matter?" asked Mature. "Don't you serve members of the armed forces?"

ॐ ॐ

MAUGHAM, W[illiam] Somerset (1874–1965), *British novelist and playwright. His successes included* Liza of Lambeth *(1897),* Of Human Bondage *(1916),* The Moon and Sixpence *(1919), and* Cakes and Ale *(1930). His comedies were also immensely popular. Scandal arising from his homosexuality and the breakup of his disastrous marriage caused him to leave England in 1928 to live permanently in the south of France.*

1 Somerset Maugham's *Liza of Lambeth,* his first novel, was published in 1897. Drawing on his experiences as a medical student when he spent some weeks as an obstetric clerk in the London slums, it achieved sufficient success to encourage Maugham to abandon his medical career for writing. Ten years passed before that success was repeated, and in the meantime his numerous novels and plays made no further mark. Edmund Gosse, then the doyen of the literary and social circles to which Maugham aspired, had been particularly enthusiastic about *Liza of Lambeth,* but for many years after that he rubbed salt into the wounds in Maugham's self-esteem by saying every time they met, "My dear Maugham, I liked your *Liza of Lambeth* so much. How wise of you never to have written anything else!"

2 Somerset Maugham believed that early nights would keep him young, a habit his friend, the society hostess Emerald Cunard, found irritating. As he was preparing as usual to leave soon after dinner one night, Lady Cunard pressed him to stay. Maugham demurred: "I can't stay, Emerald. I have to keep my youth."

"Then why didn't you bring him with you?" Lady Cunard asked. "I should be delighted to meet him."

3 Asked why he always chose to sail in French ships, Maugham replied, "Because there's none of that nonsense about women and children first."

4 Unable to take his Spanish royalties out of the country, Maugham decided to use the money to pay for a luxury holiday there. He chose one of the best hotels and dined extravagantly every evening, until he felt satisfied that he had spent most of the accumulated sum. He informed the manager that he would be leaving the following day, and asked for his bill. The manager beamed at his distinguished guest. "It has been an honor having you here," he replied. "You have brought much good publicity to us. Therefore, there is no bill."

5 During the course of his eightieth-birthday celebrations, Maugham spoke at a dinner in his honor at the Garrick Club in London. "There are many virtues in growing old," he began, then paused and looked down at the table. The pause grew uncomfortably long. Maugham fumbled with his notes, looked around the room, shifted uneasily from one foot to the other. The guests exchanged embarrassed glances. The writer cleared his throat and continued: ". . . I'm just trying to think what they are."

ॐ ♔

MAUREPAS, Jean-Frédéric Phélippeaux, Comte de (1701–81), *French statesman. Minister of the marine under Louis XV, he incurred the enmity of the king's mistress, Mme de Pompadour, and was dismissed. Louis XVI recalled him to high office.*

1 When Louis XVI ascended the throne, he cast about for experienced advisers. Two names were suggested to him: Comte de Machault as prime minister and Comte de Maurepas as master of ceremonies to arrange the court mourning for Louis XV. Both were summoned. Maurepas arrived first and, like the experienced courtier he was, quickly insinuated himself into the young king's favor. When the king was called to a council meeting, Maurepas was still with him, and as Louis did not dismiss him, he followed him into the council chamber and sat down at the table. Seeing that Louis was nonplussed as to how to deal with him, Maurepas asked boldly, "Is Your Majesty wishing to appoint me prime minister?"

"No," said Louis, "I did not intend that."

"Ah," said Maurepas, "I understand; Your Majesty wishes me to teach him how to govern without one."

{After this Maurepas became de facto prime minister, Machault returned home empty-handed, and the consequences for Louis's government were disastrous.}

ॐ ♔

MAURY, Jean Siffrein (1746–1817), *French cardinal. He was a renowned wit and the author of* Principes de l'éloquence *(1777), a classic of French criticism. An ardent royalist, he defended the* ancien régime *and the rights of the clergy. He emigrated from France in 1792, living in exile for a number of years. In 1794 he was created cardinal and in 1810 archbishop of Paris, but he later fell out with the pope and was deposed.*

1 In 1781 Maury was the Lenten preacher at Louis XVI's court. The king observed of his preaching, "If the abbé had only said a few words about religion, he would have covered every possible subject."

2 During the period 1789–92 Maury's wit stood him in good stead in the Constituent Assembly; it was said that a single *bon mot* might preserve his life for a month. On one occasion he was followed as speaker by Mirabeau, who announced, "I shall enclose the abbé in a vicious circle."

"Ah, Mirabeau," interjected the abbé, "are you proposing to embrace me?"

ॐ ♔

MAXWELL, Robert W. ["Tiny"] (?–1922), *US football player and official, who set a standard for fairness. He was often the brunt of good-natured jokes about his enormous size and his problem with stuttering.*

1 After he transferred to Swarthmore College in 1904, Maxwell got permission from his coach to go into Philadelphia one night, provided he return by 1:00 A.M. When he eventually arrived back at school, his coach woke up and demanded to know what time it was.

"A little before wuh-wuh-one," said Maxwell.

At that point the clock struck five.

"Either you're a liar," remarked the coach, "or that clock stutters as badly as you do."

2   Maxwell was officiating at a Notre Dame–Harvard game. A lineman for the Catholic school bit the finger of one of the Harvard players. Maxwell advised the victim, "Next year, schedule the game on a Friday because they d-d-don't eat meat then."

3   Refereeing another game, Maxwell followed a Pittsburgh runner for the length of the field in a breakaway play against Penn State. The latter's captain insisted that the running back had stepped out of bounds at his own 10-yard line, and offered to show Maxwell the incriminating cleat mark.

"Young man," replied Maxwell, "if you want me to go back and look at that cleat mark, you'll have to hire a taxi."

కా ఆక

MAY, Phil[ip William] (1864–1903), *English illustrator and caricaturist. He specialized in the depiction of East London types for newspapers such as the* Daily Graphic *and later for* Punch.

1   An editor once complained that May's drawings seemed unfinished. Replied May, "When I can leave out half the lines I now use, I shall want six times the money."

కా ఆక

MAYER, Louis B. (1885–1957), *US film producer. In 1924 he joined forces with Samuel Goldwyn to found Metro-Goldwyn-Mayer (MGM), the company responsible for some of the greatest Hollywood spectaculars.*

1   When Mayer visited Franklin Roosevelt in the White House, he laid his watch down on the president's desk at the start of their meeting and said, "I'm told, Mr. President, that when anyone spends eighteen minutes with you, you have them in your pocket." Their interview lasted seventeen minutes.

2   Driving away from the funeral of Irving Thalberg, his protégé, longtime colleague, and finally rival, Mayer was very quiet. MGM executive Edgar J. Mannix, who was in the limousine with him, wondered what thoughts were going through his chief's head. Suddenly a smile broke across Mayer's face and he said, "Isn't God good to me?"

3   Trying to persuade Mayer to give money to charity, a colleague reasoned: "You can't take it with you when you go."

"If I can't take it with me," retorted Mayer, "I won't go."

4   Mayer admired "class" and wanted badly to possess it. Told that golf was a classy American sport, he at once took it up. But he never seemed to get the hang of it, never quite understood that it was scored in strokes. Instead he saw it as a kind of race. He employed two caddies. One caddy was posted down the fairway to locate the ball at once. Meanwhile caddy number two would run ahead, Mayer pelting behind him, to station himself for the next shot. The game over, Mayer would consult his watch. "We made it in one hour and seven minutes! Three minutes better than yesterday."

5   Mayer's funeral was attended by huge crowds, a fact that could not in his case be attributed to universal popularity. Goldwyn explained: "The reason so many people showed up at his funeral was because they wanted to make sure he was dead."

See also HARRY COHN 1.

కా ఆక

MAYO, Charles Horace (1865–1939), *US surgeon, cofounder (with his brother William James) of the Mayo Foundation for Medical Education and Research. He also set up, in collaboration with his brother, the Mayo Clinic at St. Mary's Hospital, Rochester, Minnesota. The hospital had been originally erected by their father, the surgeon William Worrall Mayo.*

1   In Dr. Mayo's mail one morning was a letter from a spiritualist. "Ever since your late great father passed over," it read, "he has been my doctor. What do you say to that?" Mayo picked up his pen and drafted a reply: "Fine! Please estimate what my father's services have amounted to and send the money to me."

కా ఆక

MAZARIN, Jules, Cardinal (1602–61), *French statesman. He succeeded his mentor, Cardinal Richelieu, in 1642 as chief adviser of Louis XIV's mother, Anne of Austria, regent of France during Louis's minority. Mazarin* *strengthened the power of the monarchy against the aristocracy during the Fronde (1648–53). He also built up French power abroad by his skillful foreign policy.*

1 A court gossip once told Cardinal Mazarin of a dreadful row between two ladies of the court. The ladies had bombarded each other with insults, each trying to blacken the other's reputation with accusations and slander. "Have they called each other ugly?" asked the cardinal. His informant thought for a moment. "No, Monseigneur," he replied. "Well, then," said Mazarin, "it should not be too difficult to reconcile them."

2 As Mazarin lay dying, the night skies of France were lit by a comet, which the superstitious saw as heralding the great statesman's death. When Mazarin was told of the fears aroused by the phenomenon, he remarked drily, "The comet does me too much honor."

୫ ୶

MEDICI, Lorenzo de' (1449–92), *Florentine ruler, known as "Lorenzo the Magnificent." Immoral and tyrannical, he was also a great patron of the arts, who contributed greatly to Florence's prosperity.*

1 Lorenzo was on one occasion watching a young apprentice carving the face of an old satyr. He remarked that he was surprised such an old face had a full set of teeth. When he next saw the young man at work again, he noted that one of the satyr's teeth had been knocked out and the gums carefully aged and wrinkled. Impressed, Lorenzo invited the young man to live in the Palazzo Medici with his family. The youth was Michelangelo.

୫ ୶

MEHMED II (1432–81), *Ottoman sultan (1451–81) known as the Conqueror. He captured Constantinople from the last Byzantine emperor in 1453 and extended Ottoman control in southeastern Europe.*

1 The son of Sultan Murad II and an obscure slave girl, Mehmed had an unhappy childhood and turbulent adolescence while his status as heir to the throne was being established. These early events probably instilled in him his inordinate deviousness and secretiveness. Once when asked what he intended to do, he replied, "If a hair of my beard knew, I would pluck it out."

୫ ୶

MEHTA, Zubin (1936–), *Indian-born conductor. Director of the Los Angeles Philharmonic Orchestra from 1961 to 1976, he became director of the New York Philharmonic Orchestra in 1978 and since 1968 has also been music adviser to the Israel Philharmonic Orchestra.*

1 Asked which orchestra gave him the most pleasure to conduct, Mehta tactfully refused to single out any particular favorite. "What would a devout Muslim answer as to which of his wives he preferred?" he reasoned. "One can have preferences about details only — a dimple here, an oboe there."

୫ ୶

MEIR, Golda (1898–1978), *Israeli stateswoman, born in Russia, educated in the United States. She was a founding member of the Israeli Workers' Party and its secretary general (1966–68). She became prime minister of Israel in 1969, but resigned in 1974 after the first Arab-Israeli war.*

1 During the negotiations with the Arabs, Mrs. Meir insisted on meeting her opponents face to face. A journalist suggested that this was not necessary. "Even divorces are arranged without personal confrontation," he argued. "I'm not interested in a divorce," retorted Mrs. Meir. "I'm interested in a marriage."

2 (Richard M. Nixon tells the following story.)
"When my daughter, Julie Eisenhower, interviewed Mrs. Meir for her book, *Special People*, she asked how it had felt to be appointed the first woman foreign minister in 1956. [Mrs. Meir's] reply was characteristic. 'I don't know,' she said with a smile. 'I was never a man minister.'"

3 Not long after Nixon had nominated Henry Kissinger as US secretary of state he had a meeting with Golda Meir. Nixon observed that they both now had Jewish foreign ministers. "Yes," said Mrs. Meir, and then with Kissinger's German accent in mind, added, "But mine speaks English."

The liberal views of Robert Montgomery, professor of economics at the University of Texas, made him unpopular with the Texas legislature. An investigation was set in motion. When he was asked if he favored private property, Montgomery replied, "I do—so strongly that I want everyone in Texas to have some."

— John Kenneth Galbraith,
A Life in Our Times

MELBA, Dame Nellie [Helen Porter Armstrong, *née* Mitchell] (1861–1931), *Australian opera singer. She derived her stage name from her native city of Melbourne. During her long career (1887–1926) she enjoyed worldwide fame for her interpretation of the grand opera soprano roles.*

1   According to the traditional account, the invention of Melba toast was an accident. While Dame Nellie Melba was staying at the Savoy Hotel in London, whoever prepared the star's toast left it too long in the oven and it was brought to her in a thin, dried-up, fragile state. When the maître d'hôtel hastened to apologize, Dame Nellie cut him short, saying the toast was delicious.

2   Opera, in the days before World War I, was often a much more emotional experience than it became in later years. Nellie Melba played Desdemona so heartrendingly during tours of America that many women in the audience burst into tears when she was strangled by Otello. If the applause was particularly persistent, Nellie would rise from her deathbed and signal for a piano to be brought on to the stage. She would then accompany herself for an encore by singing *Home, Sweet Home,* with the audience joining in. When the ovation following the encore died down, she would collapse again upon the bed and the unfortunate Otello was allowed to finish the act.

ঌ৯

MELBOURNE, William Lamb, 2d Viscount (1779–1848), *British statesman; prime minister (1834, 1835–41). He served as secretary for*

Ireland (1827–28). As home secretary (1830–34) he dealt sternly with labor unrest and threats to the Constitution. He was an important influence upon Queen Victoria in the early years of her reign. His wife, Caroline, had a well-publicized affair (1812–13) with Lord Byron.

1   In Dublin as secretary for Ireland, Lamb very quickly assessed the way in which the government there worked and was regarded by the Irish. The young son of one of his subordinates came in to be shown the office one day. "Is there anything here you would like?" asked Lamb, gesturing toward the top of his desk. The child selected a stick of official red sealing wax. "Quite right, my boy," said the secretary for Ireland, pressing some pens into his hand as well, "begin life early. All the things here belong to the public, and it's your business to get as much out of the public as you can."

2   Lord Melbourne had a strong distaste for religious zeal. Having been forced to sit through an evangelical sermon on the consequences of sin, he grumbled, "Things have come to a pretty pass when religion is allowed to invade private life."

3   Melbourne also had little patience with the ecclesiastical squabbles of the day and frequently ran into difficulties over the appointment of bishops, particularly as he favored the more liberal theologians in the church hierarchy. Consequently, he was distressed when the death of a bishop entailed a vacancy in the House of Lords which it was the prime minister's duty to fill. "Damn it! Another bishop dead! I think they die just to vex me."

4   When the death in 1832 of the poet George Crabbe was announced, Lord Melbourne observed, "I am always glad when one of these fellows dies, for then I know I have the whole of him on my shelf."

ঌ৯

MELLON, Andrew William (1855–1937), *US financier, secretary of the Treasury, art collector, and philanthropist.*

1   (The writer Lucius Beebe recalls a breakfast at the Mellon establishment.)
"The old man was very fond of thin little hot cakes and sausages, and their service was ritual.

One morning in the midst of their presentation, one at a time by the day footman, another lackey brought in the telephone on a cord and announced that the Minister of Finance of France wished to speak with Mr. Mellon on the transocean. 'Not with the hot cakes,' said the old gentleman testily. . . . 'These foreigners have no sense of propriety.' "

ई॰ ॰ई

MELVILLE, Herman (1819–91), *US novelist. His experiences as a member of the crew of a whaler in the 1840s are the basis of his tales of adventure in the South Seas — Typee (1846), Omoo (1847), Mardi (1849), White-Jacket (1850), and his masterpiece, Moby-Dick (1851).*

1   On a visit one evening to Nathaniel Hawthorne and his wife, Melville told them a story of a fight he had witnessed on an island in the South Seas, in which one of the Polynesian warriors had wreaked havoc among his foes with a heavy club. Striding about the room, Melville demonstrated the feats of valor and the desperate drama of the battle. After he had gone, Mrs. Hawthorne thought she remembered that he had left empty-handed, and wondered, "Where is that club with which Mr. Melville was laying about him so?" Mr. Hawthorne maintained that he must have taken it with him, and indeed a search of the room revealed nothing. The next time they saw him they asked him what had happened to the club. It turned out that there was no club; it had simply been a figment of their imagination, conjured up by the vividness of Melville's narrative.

ई॰ ॰ई

MENCKEN, H[enry] L[ouis] (1880–1956), *US critic and journalist. As editor of* The Smart Set *(1914–23) and the* American Mercury *(1924–33), he was influential in promoting the work of many young American writers. His iconoclastic wit and contagious disrespect for a variety of sacred cows gave the mortal blow to the Genteel Tradition.*

1   As editor of *The Smart Set,* Mencken gave help and publicity to Joseph Conrad at a time when he was virtually unknown in the United States. After Conrad had become an estab-

lished writer, Mencken wrote to him to ask for a story, adding that he would be grateful to have it as cheaply as possible in view of the magazine's tight budget. Months passed and then Conrad's agent wrote to say that Conrad had a story ready — fee $600. Mencken cabled back: "For $600 you can have *The Smart Set.*"

2   Mencken was scandalized by the gambling losses incurred by members of the Algonquin Round Table set. After Robert Sherwood had had a particularly costly evening, Mencken commented glumly, "None but the brave *chemin de fer.*"

3   (In 1948 Mencken suffered a stroke that crippled his mental faculties for the remainder of his life. Alistair Cooke recalls a visit to him in 1955.)
   "He asked how the food was these days at Luchow's, and that brought on memories of various literati of the *Smart Set* days, and of his particular affection for Edgar Lee Masters. He talked of him in the past tense, and I asked how long Masters had been dead. He was puzzled for a moment, and I suggested something like 1948. Said Mencken with no guile at all, 'That's right, I believe he died the year I did.' "

4   Mencken coined his own epitaph: "If after I depart this vale, you ever remember me and have thought to please my ghost, forgive some sinner and wink your eye at some homely girl."
   {It was engraved on a plaque in the lobby of the *Baltimore Sun* building.}

ई॰ ॰ई

MENELIK II (1844–1913), *emperor of Ethiopia (1889–1913). During his reign he carried out a number of important reforms; in 1896 he released Ethiopia from Italian domination.*

1   In the late nineteenth century, news of the success of the electric chair as a means of dispatching criminals reached Ethiopia; Menelik II eagerly ordered one. When it arrived, however, he was disappointed to find that it did not work: no one had warned him that Ethiopia's lack of electricity would be a problem. The criminals of the nation sighed with relief and the emperor, anxious that his new acquisition should not go to waste, had the chair converted into a throne.

2 The emperor had one eccentricity. If he felt unwell, he was convinced that he had only to eat a few pages of the Bible in order to feel better. This odd behavior did him little harm, as long as his testamentary intake was modest. However, in December 1913 he was recovering from a stroke, when he suddenly felt extremely ill. On his instructions the complete Book of Kings was torn from the Bible and fed to him, page by page. He died before he had consumed the entire book.

{An example of the truth — far more comprehensive than he thought — of Bacon's maxim: "Some books are to be tasted, others to be swallowed, and some few to be chewed and digested." Here is the only case in history of the occurrence of all three.}

୧୬ ୫୨

MENOTTI, Gian-Carlo (1911–), *US composer, born in Italy. His operas, such as* The Medium *(1946) and* The Consul *(1950), were influenced by the Italian operatic tradition.* Amahl and the Night Visitors *(1951) is a Christmas opera written for television.*

1 (Menotti describes the drawing-up of his will.)

"I have always felt that a man often betrays his friendships in his will. So there is a clause in mine in which I name all of the people I have loved or who have been nice to me. And to each of them I leave a little thing — either an object or a little money. I tried to remember them all. When I made my will, my lawyer looked at me in dismay. 'Mr. Menotti,' he said, 'this is not a will. This is a jumble sale!'"

୧୬ ୫୨

MENSHIKOV, Alexander Sergeievich, Prince (1787–1869), *Russian general, commander in chief of the Russian forces during the Crimean War.*

1 During a sortie near Sevastopol a young British army officer was captured by the Russians, who searched him and found a number of letters in his possession. The man was particularly reluctant to part with one from his sweetheart, but the Russians insisted on having it and it was sent to Prince Menshikov along with the others. When the prince read it, he was amused to find that the girl had written flippantly that she hoped her young man would have the good fortune to capture Prince Menshikov and that if he did so he was to be sure to send her one of his buttons. Much to the man's surprise the letter was returned to him, along with a note from Menshikov and a button. The note said that although events had not happened quite as the lady had envisaged, nonetheless here was one of Prince Menshikov's buttons and it was to be sent to her.

୧୬ ୫୨

MENZIES, Sir Robert Gordon (1894–1978), *Australian statesman; prime minister (1939–41 and 1949–66). As liberal prime minister in his second term, he advanced the influence of the United States in Australian affairs.*

1 While addressing a political rally in his constituency, Menzies was interrupted by a woman heckler shouting, "I wouldn't vote for you if you were the Archangel Gabriel!" Menzies riposted, "If I were the Archangel Gabriel, madam, you would scarcely be in my constituency."

See also JOHN WILKES 1.

୧୬ ୫୨

MERMAN, Ethel (1909–84), *US entertainer, famous for her dynamic performances in such musicals as* Annie Get Your Gun *and* Gypsy.

1 During Mary Martin's Broadway run in *Leave It to Me!* Ethel Merman was asked her opinion of her rival. "Well," replied Ethel rather tartly, "if you like talent . . ."

୧୬ ୫୨

MERRILL, Robert [Robert Miller] (1917–), *US operatic baritone. After success as a popular singer he made his debut at the Metropolitan Opera in New York in 1945.*

1 (In his autobiography Merrill records this incident:)

"We had a new director, 'daring' but not yet 'sensational,' for a production of *Pagliacci* at the old Met. Leonard Warren was Tonio and I was cast as Silvio, the lover of young Nedda.

"Our Nedda, however, was a woman of a certain weight, about forty pounds more than mine. For our passionate duet, the director thoughtfully placed her in a chair and instructed me, 'Get on your knees and put your head in her lap.'

"I demurred *sotto voce,* 'But she doesn't have a lap.'

" 'Well, snuggle as close as you can.'

"The only place my face could go was into her crotch. This evoked unsuppressed giggles from others in the cast. 'It looks bad,' I told the director.

"But he was determined to be creative. 'These are Italian peasants, they're passionate people.'

"I went back to my prenatal position and we started the duet. On a lovely phrase, my voice wobbled.

" 'What's the trouble?' the director yelled.

" 'I think I'm getting an echo.' "

2 Merrill once gave a concert at a university, where he was allocated one of the science laboratories for his dressing room. He was relaxing there during the intermission when a young lady arrived at the door. "I never sign autographs during the intermission," said Merrill firmly. "I don't want your autograph, Mr. Merrill," replied the girl. "I want to feed my snake."

ह‍ം

MESSIER, Charles (1730–1817), *French astronomer, the first to compile a systematic catalogue of nebulae and star clusters. He discovered a number of comets; Louis XV called him the "comet ferret."*

1 Nursing his dying wife, Messier was obliged to abandon his search for a certain comet. In the meantime, the comet was discovered by a rival astronomer, Montaigue of Limoges. A friend, hearing of the death of Mme Messier, expressed his sympathy for Messier's loss. The astronomer nodded in acknowledgment, his eyes filling with tears. "To think that when I had discovered twelve," he said, "this Montaigue should have got my thirteenth."

ह‍ം

METAXAS, Ioannis (1871–1941), *Greek general. With the reestablishment of the monarchy (1935) he became prime minister and subsequently dictator (1936–41).*

1 During a visit of inspection to an air base Metaxas was invited to test a new flying boat. He took the aircraft up for a short flight and was coming in to land when the commander of the base intervened: "Excuse me, General; it would be better to come down on the water; this is a flying boat." Metaxas, who had been about to put the aircraft down on a runway, swerved quickly upward, made another circuit, and touched the flying boat down safely on the surface of the water. Metaxas switched off the engine and turned to his host. "Thank you, Commander, for preventing me from making a stupid blunder"—and so saying, briskly opened the aircraft's door and jumped out into the water.

{This sounds like an invention by one of Metaxas's numerous political enemies, but is nonetheless *molto ben trovato.*}

ह‍ം

METTERNICH, Klemens, Prince von (1773–1859), *Austrian statesman. As foreign minister (1809–48), he made Austria a leading European power, dominating the Congress of Vienna (1814–15) and subsequent diplomatic efforts to create a stable balance of power.*

1 Metternich, who had a contempt for the average Englishman's inability to speak French fluently, observed to Lord John Dudley that he was the only Englishman he knew who could speak French well: "The common people of Vienna speak French better than the educated men of London." Lord Dudley replied, "That may be so, but Your Highness will recall that Bonaparte has not been twice in London to teach them."

ह‍ം

METTERNICH, Princess Pauline [*née Countess Sándor*] (1859–1921), *autocratic wife of Prince Richard Metternich (1829–95), with whom she played an important role in the court of Napoleon III.*

1 The princess was traveling on a train one day toward Compiègne. The other occupant of her compartment asked politely if smoking would bother her. The princess replied: "I have no idea, monsieur. No one has ever dared to smoke in my presence."

ह‍ം

MEURISSE, Paul (1912–79), *French actor.*

1   Meurisse, renowned for his taciturnity, once caught sight of a sign in a florist's window: "SAY IT WITH FLOWERS." He went in and asked for a rose. "Just one," he told the young clerk. "To be delivered to this address with my card." The girl picked out a delicate red rose and asked, "Is there any message?" Meurisse took the flower and plucked out all the petals except two. "There you are," he said, handing back the mutilated bloom. "And even then, I wonder if I haven't said too much."

಼

MEYERBEER, Giacomo (1791–1864), *German pianist and operatic composer. Having failed with his early German operas, he went to Italy, where he achieved spectacular success. Later, in Paris, he produced his grand romantic works* Robert le Diable *(1831) and* Les Huguenots *(1836). He spent some years as royal kapellmeister in Berlin, where he was the friend and patron of Weber and Wagner. His greatest work,* L'Africaine *(1865), was in preparation when he died.*

1   Meyerbeer took care to be on good terms with the Parisian critics, a policy he was able to implement with the help of his great wealth. Heinrich Heine was among those convinced by the lavishness of Meyerbeer's generosity that his forthcoming works were very good indeed. Unfortunately for the impoverished critic, Meyerbeer suddenly cut off the flow of funds just at a moment when Heine's resources were especially depleted. Heine avenged himself by remarking, "Meyerbeer will be immortal while he lives and maybe for a little while after, because he always pays in advance."

2   The rival composers Meyerbeer and Rossini, though polite, cordially disliked each other. One day Rossini was complaining to Meyerbeer that he felt in the lowest possible spirits, bored, melancholy, and so forth. Meyerbeer consoled him: "You listen to too much of your own music."

3   In 1839 a young German composer left his native land for Paris, where he hoped to obtain recognition for his work. One of his compatriots referred him to Meyerbeer, who received the young German amiably enough and gave him a sealed letter of recommendation to Léon Pillet, at that time director of the Opéra. What the letter actually contained were the words: "Take this imbecile off my hands."

The imbecile was Richard Wagner.

಼

MICHELANGELO BUONARROTI (1475–1564), *Italian sculptor, architect, painter, and poet. After an apprenticeship at Florence under Medici patronage, Michelangelo moved to Rome (1496–1501), where he produced his first important sculptures, including the* Pietà *in St. Peter's. Back in Florence, he continued to produce major paintings, including* The Holy Family, *now in the Uffizi gallery. He was again (1505) summoned to Rome by Pope Julius II, who commissioned Michelangelo to make his tomb, a project that proved both lengthy and troublesome. Michelangelo painted the ceiling of the Sistine Chapel in the Vatican (1508–12), then returned again (1516) to Florence, where he worked on architectural projects for the Medicis. He later painted the* Last Judgment *fresco in the Sistine Chapel (1534–41) and in 1547 was appointed architect in charge of St. Peter's, for which he designed the celebrated dome.*

1   One day Michelangelo happened to overhear a group of people admiring his *Pietà*. One man attributed the sculpture to Il Gobbo, much to the chagrin of Michelangelo, who took particular pride in the *Pietà*. Returning to the sculpture after dark that evening, he carved his name on it, so that no similar mistake could occur in the future.

{This is believed to be the only time that Michelangelo identified one of his works in this way.}

2   The figures Michelangelo completed for the Medici tombs ordered by Pope Clement VII represent the members of the family in highly idealized form. Someone remarked on this absence of realism. "Who will care," replied the sculptor, "in a thousand years' time, whether these are their features or not?"

3   The pope's master of ceremonies pestered Michelangelo to allow him a glimpse of the *Last Judgment* fresco before the artist was ready to unveil it. Michelangelo took his

revenge by including the official among the damned in hell, being tormented by devils. When the master of ceremonies complained to Pope Paul III, the latter replied: "God has given me authority in heaven and on earth, but my writ does not extend to hell. You will just have to put up with it."

4 Michelangelo was once assisted in his work by a marble-hewer, who, by following Michelangelo's detailed instructions—"Cut this away . . . level that . . . polish here"—was amazed to find that he had created a splendid marble figure. "What do you think of it?" asked Michelangelo. "I think it's fine," replied the man, "and I am much obliged to you. By your means I have discovered a talent that I did not know I possessed."

5 A certain painter had produced a picture that was a pastiche of details stolen from other artists. Asked by a friend his opinion of the picture, Michelangelo praised the workmanship but added wryly, "I don't know what will become of this scene on the Day of Judgement, when all the bodies shall recover their members, for there will be nothing left of it."

6 A priest once remarked to Michelangelo that it was a pity that he had not married and had many children to whom he could have bequeathed his works. Michelangelo answered, "I have too much of a wife in this art of mine, which has afflicted me throughout my life, and my children shall be the works I leave. What would have become of Lorenzo Ghiberti's reputation if he had not made the gates of San Giovanni? His children and grandchildren sold or squandered all he left, but the gates are still standing."

7 Michelangelo began the Rondanini *Pietà* when he was nearly ninety. The effort of cutting the marble exhausted him and revealed how far his power and genius had withered with age. He himself was tragically aware of his decline. One night Vasari, visiting the old sculptor, found his eyes irresistibly drawn to the unfinished *Pietà* standing in a corner. Michelangelo said, "I am so old that death often plucks at my mantle to bear me away, and one day my body will fall—like this." As he spoke he dropped the lantern he had been holding, cutting off the scene from Vasari's eyes.

MICHELET, Jules (1798–1874), *French historian. His great classic,* Histoire de France *(1833–67), is strongly nationalist in tone.*

1 The July Revolution of 1830, which ousted the autocratic Charles X and ushered in the constitutional monarchy of Louis Philippe, broke out on July 27, when Michelet was delivering a lecture at the École Normale. As the sound of cannon fire became audible, the students grew restless. "Gentlemen," Michelet said, "they are making history. We shall write it."

৵ ৶

MIES VAN DER ROHE, Ludwig (1886–1969), *German architect. He was a pioneering influence upon modern German architecture in the 1920s and 1930s, using glass and steel in strikingly original ways. After 1937 he moved to the United States, where he continued to design major buildings, such as the Seagram, New York (1958).*

1 Mies van der Rohe did not believe that an architect should indulge in self-expression. Once a student asked him for his opinion on this subject. He handed her a pencil and paper and told her to write her name. When she had done so, he said, "That's for self-expression. Now we get to work."

৵ ৶

MIKES, George (1912–), *Hungarian-born British humorist and writer.*

1 In preparation for writing a humorous book on the subject, Mikes decided to undergo psychoanalysis himself. The analyst began by asking whether Mikes had had a happy childhood. "I am still having a happy childhood," Mikes responded.

৵ ৶

MILL, John Stuart (1806–73), *British political philosopher and social reformer. He wrote an influential* System of Logic *(1843), but is perhaps better remembered for* On Liberty *(1859) and* Utilitarianism *(1863).*

1 As John Stuart Mill, in Parliament, was expounding his famous principle of "the greatest good for the greatest number," Disraeli, from the Tory benches, breathed, "Ah—the nursery governess!"

MILLAY, Edna St. Vincent (1892–1950), *US poet and dramatist. Her collections of verse include* The Harp Weaver and Other Poems *(1923), for which she received a Pulitzer Prize.*

1   The poet's middle name is that of a New York hospital. How did this come about?

On a February day in 1892 a young man named Charles Buzzell boarded the ship *El Monte,* then in New Orleans loading cotton for New York, to watch the loading. Suffering from a slight fever, he fell asleep on a bale of hay, cotton stacked all about him. He awoke in the hold, all hatches battened down. Calls for help were unheard. Nine days later the hold was opened and Charles was found at the foot of the hatchway. The captain rushed him to St. Vincent's Hospital, where he was given up for dead. But the doctors plus a strong constitution pulled him through. It was said then that he had survived "longer than anyone ever had without food or water."

At about that time a little girl was born to Mrs. Henry Tolman Millay, Charles's sister. She gave the little girl a middle name in memory of the hospital in which her brother had recovered. These facts are recorded in a letter to *The New York Times Book Review* from Edna's sister Norma, who concludes, "Had it been Doctor's Hospital or Lenox Hill, she doubtless would have reconsidered—they wouldn't scan."

❦

MILLER, Arthur (1915–   ), *US dramatist. His plays include* Death of a Salesman *(1947),* All My Sons *(1947),* The Crucible *(1953), and* After the Fall *(1964). His short novel* The Misfits *(1957, 1961) provided the script for the last film made by his wife, Marilyn Monroe.*

1   "Arthur Miller, sitting alone in a bar, was approached by a well-tailored, slightly tiddly fellow who addressed him thus:

" 'Aren't you Arthur Miller?'

" 'Why, yes, I am.'

" 'Don't you remember me?'

" 'Well . . . your face seems familiar.'

" 'Why, Art, I'm your old buddy Sam! We went to high school together! We went out on double dates!'

" 'I'm afraid I—'

" 'I guess you can see I've done all right. Department stores. What do *you* do, Art?'

" 'Well, I . . . write.'

" 'Whaddya write?'

" 'Plays, mostly.'

" 'Ever get any produced?'

" 'Yes, some.'

" 'Would I know any?'

" 'Well . . . perhaps you've heard of *Death of a Salesman?*'

"Sam's jaw dropped; his face went white. For a moment he was speechless. Then he cried out, 'Why, you're ARTHUR MILLER!' "

❦

MILLIKAN, Robert Andrews (1868–1953), *US physicist. He was awarded the 1923 Nobel Prize for his work, which included the first measurement of the charge on the electron.*

1   Millikan's wife was passing through the hall of their home when she overheard the maid answering the telephone. "Yes, this is where Dr. Millikan lives," she heard the girl say, "but he's not the kind of doctor that does anybody any good."

❦

MILNE, A[lan] A[lexander] (1882–1956), *British journalist and playwright, best known for his books for children,* When We Were Very Young *(1924),* Winnie-the-Pooh *(1926),* Now We Are Six *(1927), and* The House at Pooh Corner *(1928).*

1   (Christopher Milne explains how his father tactfully corrected his table manners.)

"Once, when I was quite little, he came up to the nursery while I was having my lunch. And while he was talking I paused between mouthfuls, resting my hands on the table, knife and fork pointing upwards. 'You oughtn't really to sit like that,' he said, gently. 'Why not?' I asked, surprised. 'Well . . . ,' he hunted around for a reason he could give. Because it's considered bad manners? Because you mustn't? Because . . . 'Well,' he said, looking in the direction that my fork was pointing, 'suppose somebody suddenly fell through the ceiling. They might land on your fork and that would be very painful.' 'I see,' I said, though I didn't really."

❦

MILNES, Richard Monckton, 1st Baron Houghton (1809–85), *British writer and politician.*

1 As he lay on his deathbed the bon vivant Monckton Milnes observed, "My exit is the result of too many entrées."

ஒ௸ ௸ஒ

MILO (late 6th century BC), *Greek wrestler, born at Crotona in southern Italy. He was six times champion wrestler at the ancient Olympic games, and many stories were told about his strength.*

1 Milo's strong-man antics were his eventual downfall. He came upon a tree trunk in which woodmen, who had been trying to split it, had left a wedge. Milo attempted to split the tree part with his bare hands, the wedge sprang out, and the trunk closed upon his hands. Trapped, he was found by a pack of wolves who tore him limb from limb.

ஒ௸ ௸ஒ

MILTON, John (1608–74), *English poet. In the 1630s he wrote "L'Allegro" and "Il Penseroso" (1632), the masque* Comus *(1634, published 1637), and the elegy* Lycidas *(1637). In the next twenty years he was chiefly involved in writing prose polemical pamphlets and in pursuing his duties as Latin secretary to the council of state formed after Charles I's execution. He also lost his sight. At the Restoration he was fined, lost his fortune and his position in the state, and thereafter devoted himself again to poetry, working on* Paradise Lost *(1667),* Paradise Regained *(1671), and* Samson Agonistes *(1671).*

1 In April 1667 Milton signed an agreement with Samuel Simmons, a London bookseller (i.e., publisher), by which he sold the copyright of *Paradise Lost* for five pounds, plus five pounds for the sale of each of three subsequent editions, an edition comprising 1,500 copies. Milton received a second five pounds in April 1669, making a grand total of ten pounds to the author of England's greatest epic. After his death, Milton's widow, his third wife, Elizabeth, sold all remaining rights for eight pounds to Simmons, who became perpetual owner of the copyright.

2 In the course of a visit to Milton, James II, then Duke of York, suggested that the poet's blindness was a divine punishment for his having written a defense of the execution of Charles I. Milton retorted, "If Your Highness thinks that misfortunes are indexes of the wrath of heaven, what must you think of your father's tragical end? I have only lost my eyes — he lost his head."

ஒ௸ ௸ஒ

MIRABEAU, Honoré Gabriel Riqueti, Comte de (1749–91), *French revolutionary statesman. He championed the cause of the Third Estate, but resisted the tide of republicanism. His early death from natural causes almost certainly saved him from the guillotine. In his youth he was a notorious libertine.*

1 Mirabeau received numerous challenges, to which he always returned the same answer: "Sir, your favor is received and your name is on my list, but I must warn you that the list is long, and I grant no preferences."

2 Mirabeau, who was badly pockmarked, addressed one of the first sessions of the constitutional convention, describing in his best oratorical style the proper qualifications of the to-be-elected president. Talleyrand remarked, "He has forgotten only one thing: he must also be pockmarked."

3 Although not noted for his own sincerity, Mirabeau was quick to recognize the quality in others. On hearing Robespierre speak for the first time, he leaned toward his neighbor and observed, "That man will go far; he believes all he says."

4 A group of students, observing the proceedings of the French Assembly, listened to the pompous and long-winded debates with expressions of disgust. Mirabeau mocked them gently for their naiveté. "Laws are like sausages," he said. "You should never watch them being made."

ஒ௸ ௸ஒ

MISES, Ludwig von (1881–1973), *Austrian economist. He was professor at the University of Vienna (1913–38) and at New York University (1945–69). His writings include* The Anti-Capitalistic Mentality *(1956) and* Planned Chaos *(1947).*

1 At the age of eighty-eight Mises was asked how he felt upon getting up in the morning. "Amazed," he replied.

MITCHELL, Sharon (1951–), *US actress, heroine of the X-rated movie* Captain Lust.

1 Sharon Mitchell experienced difficulty getting a check cashed at a New York bank because she did not have her driver's license or other means of identification with her. She did, however, have a magazine containing a nude picture of herself. Handing the magazine to the teller, she lifted her sweater up to her chin and struck the same pose. The check was cashed.

૪૦ ૯૬

MITCHUM, Robert (1917–), *US film actor. His films include* The Sundowners *(1960),* Ryan's Daughter *(1970), and* Farewell My Lovely *(1975).*

1 Mitchum, happily married for thirty years, was asked what he thought had made his marriage last, when those of so many of his show-business colleagues had failed. "Mutual forbearance," he replied. "We have each continued to believe that the other will do better tomorrow."

૪૦ ૯૬

MITFORD, Nancy (1904–73), *British author. Her three sisters were also famous: writer Jessica; Unity, a Hitlerophile who committed suicide; and Diana, who married Sir Oswald Mosley. Nancy Mitford's* The Pursuit of Love *and* Love in a Cold Climate *became successful TV serials, and her* Noblesse Oblige *started a controversy, both amusing and irate, over upper- and lower-class linguistic usage.*

1 The British police were having one of their periodic drives to stamp out prostitution in London. "But," protested Nancy Mitford, "where will the young men learn?"

2 Art Buchwald lent Nancy Mitford a copy of *The Day Lincoln Was Shot* and some time later asked her how she had liked it. "Oh," she said, "I found it fascinating, but, you see, I have always had an irrational dislike for Abraham Lincoln. I couldn't wait to finish the book; I knew that he was going to be assassinated but was kept in suspense for fear that something would happen to change the end."
{When Buchwald published this story in his column, it elicited a deluge of angry letters from Lincoln fans all over the United States.}

MITFORD, Thomas (1909–1945), *brother of Nancy Mitford. Of the seven children, Tom was the only male.*

1 (A biographer of the Mitford family tells this story.)
"As at other times, there was at Eton in Tom's day a certain amount of what was then known as 'the love that dares not speak its name', though it dares now, all right. Tom rather fancied a boy called Milton. Once in the car, when the family was passing a signpost to Milton-under-Wychwood, he is supposed to have murmured: 'Lucky Wychwood!' "

૪૦ ૯૬

MIZNER, Addison (?–1933), *US architect and entrepreneur, brother of Wilson Mizner.*

1 Despite an almost complete lack of formal qualifications, Addison Mizner sprang to wealth and fame as the chief architect employed by those who bought land in Florida during the great property boom. The rich and celebrated scrambled for the cachet of a Mizner-designed residence, despite certain structural drawbacks (engrossed in aesthetic considerations, Mizner once forgot to install a stairway between the first and second stories). When client William Gray Warden asked for a copy of the blueprints of his Palm Beach house in order to show his friends, Mizner remonstrated, "Why, the house isn't built yet! Construction first, blueprints afterward."
{Thus the King of Hearts in *Alice's Adventures in Wonderland*: "Sentence first, verdict afterwards."}

૪૦ ૯૬

MIZNER, Wilson (1876–1933), *US writer and wit who tried his hand at a score of respectable and disreputable means of earning a living.*

1 In the hospital for an appendectomy, Mizner was not reassured when a nurse came to write his name, illness, and other information on his chest for purposes of identification. He kept quiet about his misgivings and when her back was turned added a postscript to her notes: "Store in a cool place until opened."

2 Mizner's opponent at a game of draw poker took out his wallet and tossed it onto the table, saying, "I call you." Mizner calmly took off his right shoe and put it on the table and announced, "If we're playing for leather, I raise."

3 Mizner was at a party in which a discussion arose as to whether Grant or Lee was the greater general. To put an end to the debate Mizner said, "I don't know, gentlemen, but they paid off on Grant."

4 In 1907 Mizner managed the Hotel Rand on West Forty-ninth Street in New York. He put up two signs for guests: "No opium-smoking in the elevators" and "Carry out your own dead."

5 When Mizner was running the Hotel Rand, it was patronized mainly by prostitutes. Mizner warned his friends never to walk in front of the hotel if they could avoid it. "The girls throwing down keys to their customers will knock your brains out."

6 The friend and associate of boxers, Mizner was himself a talented pugilist. One night in a San Francisco bar to which he had been accompanied by a group that included the middleweight known as "Mysterious" Billy Smith, Mizner started a fight with some longshoremen. At the end only one longshoreman was left standing; although Mizner was raining punches upon him, he remained obstinately upright, causing Mizner to worry that his punch had lost its power. Suddenly Mysterious Billy Smith noticed what was happening. "Leave him alone, Wilson!" he shouted. "I knocked him out five minutes ago." On investigation it turned out that a punch from Smith had indeed knocked the longshoreman out cold, but had also wedged him vertically between two pieces of furniture.

7 The American heavyweight boxer Tom Sharkey owned a saloon with swinging doors at the entrance. Mizner said of him, "He was so dumb that he crawled under them for two years before he found out that they swung both ways."

8 Mizner, who enjoyed imparting information, found the middleweight boxer Stanley Ketchel (known as the "Michigan Assassin") an ideal subject. One day he explained to Ketchel the theory of evolution. It seemed to make a deep impression upon his protégé. Ketchel remained sunk in thought for the rest of the day and in the evening turned down an invitation to join Mizner and friends for a night on the

town. When Mizner returned home at five A.M., Ketchel sprang up from his chair next to a bowl of goldfish and strode toward Mizner in a towering rage. "That evolution is all bunk!" he shouted. "I've been watching those fish nine hours and they haven't changed one bit!"

9 For a while Mizner managed Stanley Ketchel. One day he received a phone call informing him that a jealous husband had shot Ketchel dead. Mizner advised, "Tell them to start counting to ten over him, and he'll get up."

10 When in June 1906 Harry Thaw shot the well-known architect Stanford White in a quarrel over Evelyn Nesbit, the scandal gripped the entire country. Some years later Wilson Mizner, observing with distaste a Palm Beach hotel designed by Joseph Urban, remarked, "Harry Thaw shot the wrong architect."
{This remark has been ascribed to others about other architects.}

11 Passenger liners with their cargo of the wealthy, gullible, and bored offered Mizner extensive scope for his talent for separating people from their money. A favorite form of amusement was the daily lottery in which passengers guessed the number of miles covered by the ship in each 24-hour period. On one voyage Mizner thought he detected signs of fallibility in one of the officers with access to the ship's log, and he laid his plans accordingly. With an accomplice he stood outside the officer's cabin and mentioned, very loudly, the number that he had drawn in the lottery. He concluded by saying: "You know what I'd do if I won? I'd stick a thousand bucks under the right officer's pillow." Sure enough, when the winning lottery number was announced that day, it turned out to be Mizner's. The following day Mizner and his accomplice repeated the routine and again Mizner's number was drawn. The third day too, their "luck" held, but on the fourth day as they stationed themselves outside the cabin door a voice growled out, "Clear off, you bastards. I'm four hundred miles off course already."

12 For a while Mizner was married to Myra Moore Yerkes, a woman of great wealth who owned a two-million-dollar art collection. One day Mizner, short of cash, took a version of *The Last Supper* from the living-room wall and sold it. His wife saw the empty frame and demanded to know what had happened to the masterpiece. "Some masterpiece," grumbled Mizner. "I got only fifty dollars a plate."

13 During the 1920s property boom in Florida the Mizner brothers ran an "antiquing" factory at which pieces of furniture, timber, statuary, and other items were treated to give the impression of venerable age. Showing friends around the factory, Wilson Mizner handed them air rifles and offered to let them take part in inflicting the ravages of time upon a too-new dining-room suite. "Don't shoot straight at it," he instructed. "Remember a worm always charges at a piece of furniture from an angle."

14 Addison Mizner developed many of his ideas in cooperation with Wilson. In 1933, after he had retired to Palm Beach and was succumbing to the disease that killed him, he received a telegram from his brother, then in Hollywood: "Stop dying. Am trying to write a comedy."

15 At a Hollywood premiere the important limousines kept drawing up in front of the marquee. Then came a dilapidated Ford and out of it, faultlessly dressed, stepped Wilson Mizner. He threw his keys at the parking attendant, who in turn looked with contempt at Mizner's rattletrap. "What shall I do with it?" he asked. "Keep it," said Mizner and strode into the theater.

16 On his deathbed Mizner awoke briefly from a coma to find a priest bending over him offering words of comfort. Mizner waved the man away. "Why should I talk to you? I've just been talking to your boss."

MODIGLIANI, Amedeo (1884–1920), *Italian painter and sculptor. His best work dates from his Paris period (1906–20). It was influenced by Cézanne and Brancusi as well as by African masks. He died of tuberculosis aggravated by drink and drugs.*

1 Modigliani's admiration of Utrillo was reciprocated. On the occasion of their first meeting, they began by paying each other extravagant compliments. "You are the world's greatest painter," said one.

"No, *you* are the world's greatest painter," said the other.

"I forbid you to contradict me."

"I forbid you to forbid me."

The argument became heated. "If you say that again, I'll hit you."

"You are the greatest—" and they fell to blows.

Later, they made up over several bottles of wine at a nearby bistro. As they went out into the street, one said, "You are the world's greatest painter."

"No, you are."

And so the fight broke out again, until both combatants were down in the gutter, where they went to sleep. In the early dawn they woke up to discover that they had been robbed.

MOLIÈRE [Jean-Baptiste Poquelin] (1622–73), *French actor and dramatist. His satirical comedies include* Les Précieuses ridicules *(1659),* Tartuffe *(1664),* Le Misanthrope *(1666), and* Le Malade imaginaire *(1673). His attacks on hypocrisy brought him into conflict with the religious authorities from whom the patronage of Louis XIV could not entirely shield him.*

1 On February 17, 1673, the desperately ill Molière insisted on going on stage so as not to let the rest of the company down. When the play was over he had to be carried home, where he died shortly afterward.

Religious prejudices against the theater were so powerful that it was customary for a dying actor solemnly to abjure his profession so as to obtain burial in consecrated ground. Molière's sudden death prevented this formality and appeals to the archbishop of Paris were fruitless. Molière's widow sought the aid of the king. Louis sent to the ecclesiastical authorities to ask how deep consecrated ground may run. Back came the answer: "Fourteen feet."

"Very good," said Louis. "Let Molière's grave be dug in the churchyard sixteen feet deep and then it cannot be said that he is buried in consecrated ground, nor need it scandalize the clergy."

{This tradition may be intended to account for the fact that Molière's grave has never been located. There is the suspicion that the archbishop of Paris, who would permit the funeral to take place only after nightfall and with just two priests in attendance, may after all have had the actor's body buried outside the churchyard.}

જીજી

MOLNÁR, Ferenc (1878–1952), *Hungarian dramatist and novelist. He gained international success with such plays as* Liliom *(1909) and* The Red Mill *(1923), and also wrote novels and short stories.*

1 Molnár was a late riser, never emerging until 1:00 P.M. On one occasion in Budapest, called as a witness in a lawsuit, he had to present himself at court by 9:00 A.M. The combined efforts of his servants got him out of bed and dressed, and they propelled him out of the house at 8:30 into the rush-hour crowd. Molnár looked in amazement at the hurrying workers and exclaimed, "Good heavens, are all these people witnesses in this fool case?"

2 A man called Schweiger, a notorious Budapest wastrel, pestered Molnár for a loan. Molnár gave him a paltry twenty pengos. Affronted, Schweiger exclaimed, "What? From a Molnár, twenty pengos?"
"No. To a Schweiger, twenty pengos."

3 Molnár's life in Budapest was punctuated by a series of lively literary feuds. A member of Molnár's circle who was thought to have fallen out with the irascible writer rejected the suggestion, saying, "No, Molnár isn't my enemy at the moment, Felecki is. But he has an option on me for October."
{The journalist Felecki was exceptionally thin. Molnár remarked that when Felecki was born, the midwife had thrown away the baby and kept the umbilical cord, a remark Felecki strongly resented. Hence the feud.}

4 During the Béla Kun revolution the streets of Budapest became unsafe, the haunt of thugs who attacked passersby with impunity. People went about in groups or stayed off the streets at night. Molnár remained home during much of this period, but he encouraged friends to visit him. One evening they brought a giant of a man along with them. Molnár eyed him in a worried way all evening. When he came to bid the giant farewell, he shook his hand and said in a concerned voice, "Aren't you afraid to go home by yourself? Aren't you horribly worried that you'll attack somebody?"

5 Molnár's devotion to the Café Central in Budapest was legendary. There he held court for a number of years in the period after World War I. When *Liliom* became a hit in New York, Molnár's American agent came to Budapest to try to lure the dramatist to the United States. Molnár refused on the grounds that he dreaded the journey. The agent assured him that he would travel in complete comfort, first through Europe on the Orient Express and then across the Atlantic by luxury liner. "But what about the journey from this café to the railroad station?" protested Molnár.

6 Molnár had been away from Budapest and his beautiful mistress for some weeks. On his return, his friends greeted him with tales of the lady's infidelity, listing the sexual encounters she had had during his absence. "That's all right," said Molnár, shrugging his shoulders. "She goes to bed with others because she loves them. But for money: only with me!"

7 While Molnár was living in a hotel in Vienna during the 1920s, a large contingent of his relatives came to see him in the hope of sharing some of the fruits of the playwright's fabulous success. They were prepared for a hostile reception, but to their surprise Molnár greeted them kindly, even insisting that they all sit for a group portrait to mark the occasion. The print ready, Molnár presented it to the hotel doorman. "And whenever you see any of the persons in the picture trying to get into the hotel, don't let them in."

8 Molnár was invited to the house of a well-known Viennese politician for an evening party at which Richard Tauber was to sing. During the course of the evening Molnár yielded gradually to the *gemütlich* atmosphere; standing by the piano, cigar in one hand, he let his other arm steal around the comely form of his hostess. Suddenly the host stepped across, his expression hostile, and said, "Herr Molnár, may I see you in private?" With a sinking heart, Molnár followed the husband into an adjoining room. "Herr Molnár," he said, "I must ask you not to smoke while Herr Tauber is singing; it is bad for his throat."

9 An old friend of the Molnárs listened in amazement as the couple argued violently over some trivial matter. Both were too busy shouting to hear what the other was saying. "Is this the way you always argue?" asked the friend, when the storm began to show signs of abating. "Of course," replied Molnár, "it saves time. Now that we've both unburdened ourselves we can enjoy some delicious silences."

10 Another friend of Molnár's once arrived just as the playwright was going to bed. He watched, fascinated, as Molnár took off his slippers and carefully placed them toe to toe beside the bed. "What's the idea of that?" asked the visitor. "Well, you see," explained Molnár, "if you put them side by side, both staring straight ahead, they look like a married couple who have just had words. It depresses me. But see how friendly they look nose to nose. They cheer me up and I sleep better."

11 Expatriate Hungarians, all of them coffeehouse habitués, gathered around Molnár in New York and soon established a semblance of the former café society of Budapest — gossiping, playing games, writing, and arguing for up to twelve hours a day. Once the talk turned to the topic of learning English. Molnár asked his friends which words or sentences had been the first they had learned. One man replied, "I love you." Others cited the conventional greetings — "Hello," "Goodbye," "Good morning," and so on. "The first sentence I learned," said Molnár, "was 'Separate checks, please!'"

12 Molnár and a friend had been given complimentary tickets for a particularly uninspiring play. After the opening scene, Molnár decided to leave. "You can't walk out," hissed his friend. "We're guests of the management." Molnár reluctantly returned to his seat and sat through a few more lines of dialogue. Then he stood up again. "Now where are you going?" asked his friend impatiently. "To the box office," replied Molnár, "to buy two tickets so we can leave."

≈

MOMMSEN, Theodor (1817–1903), *German historian. His monumental* History of Rome *(1845–85) was a milestone in the realistic and critical study of classical antiquity.*

1 Napoleon III, in the course of writing his *History of Julius Caesar,* consulted many scholars, among them Mommsen. After its publication a friend of Mommsen's asked him his opinion of the work, as he intended to give a copy to his young son. "How old is he?" asked Mommsen.

"Fourteen."

"Good, give it to him now. One more year and he'll be too old for it."

≈

MONROE, Marilyn (1926–62), *US film actress. She became an international sex symbol with the success of such films as* Gentlemen Prefer Blondes *(1953). Her last film was* The Misfits *(1961), written by her third husband, Arthur Miller. Soon afterward she died from an overdose of barbiturates.*

1 Marilyn Monroe rushed up to Nunnally Johnson on the set of *How to Marry a Millionaire* and gasped, "Where's the men's room?" He told her, and away she hurried in that direction. He could never figure out why she needed to know.

2 Marilyn Monroe was difficult to direct, often unsure of her lines, frequently late — yet what finally emerged on screen was usually triumphant. Director Billy Wilder once recalled an episode that occurred during the shooting of *Some Like It Hot.*

It was simple enough. The script required Miss Monroe to knock on a door, enter the room, and ask for a slug of bourbon from a bottle in a bureau drawer. But, try as she would, the line of dialogue eluded her, and it never quite came out as fitting the action. Wilder recalled: "On the fifty-third take I told her we had put the line on pieces of paper and they were in every drawer she would open. . . . She went to the wrong piece of furniture."

≈

MONTAGU, Lady Mary Wortley (1689–1762), *English letter-writer and traveler. She introduced into England the Turkish practice of inoculation against smallpox. She was the friend of many prominent literary and political figures.*

1 In Constantinople Lady Mary lost no opportunity to tell the Turkish ladies of the superior status of women in England. Her propaganda suffered a serious setback, however, when her friends invited her to go with them to a public bath. The Turkish lady who helped her undress was amazed at the sight of Lady Mary's stays, and called all her friends to come and have a look. "See how cruelly the poor English ladies are used by their husbands!" she cried. "How can you boast of your greater liberty when your husbands lock you up in a box like this?"

2 The breadth of Lady Mary's experience is perhaps best summed up in her alleged dying words: "It has all been most interesting."

இச் ஆஇ

MONTAGUE, Charles Edward (1867–1928), *British journalist and writer.*

1 At the outbreak of World War I, Montague dyed his gray hair black in order to conceal his age and join the army. H. W. Nevinson remarked that Montague was "the only man on record whose hair turned black in a single night from fearlessness."

இச் ஆஇ

MONTECUCCOLI, Raimund, Count (1609–1680), *Austrian general. He fought against the Turks in the Thirty Years' War and was given command of the imperial army in the war against France (1672–75). For his services in the latter he was created Duke of Melfi.*

1 The Roman Catholic (and ordinarily pious) general had dutifully ordered an omelet for his dinner one Friday. Being exceptionally hungry, however, he decided that there would be no harm in having a little ham sliced up in it. Just as the dish was set in front of him, an exceptionally loud clap of thunder announced the start of a storm. Without a word, the general strode to the window, opened it, and threw out the omelet. Looking up toward the source of the thunder, he exclaimed petulantly, "*Voilà bien du bruit, pour une omelette au jambon!*" (What a lot of fuss over a mere ham omelet!)

இச் ஆஇ

MONTEFIORE, Sir Moses (1784–1885), *Jewish philanthropist. He was born in Italy, lived mainly in Britain, and traveled extensively in the course of his tireless efforts to improve conditions for the Jews.*

1 At a dinner party Montefiore found himself seated next to an anti-Semitic nobleman who opened the conversation by saying, "I have just returned from Japan, and it's a most unusual country. Did you know that it has neither pigs nor Jews?"

"In that case," Montefiore replied, "you and I should go there, so it will have a sample of each."

இச் ஆஇ

MONTEUX, Pierre (1875–1964), *French conductor. He became conductor of Sergei Diaghilev's Ballets Russes (1911) and later worked with numerous orchestras in Europe and the United States.*

1 After hearing André Previn conduct the final movement of a Haydn symphony, Monteux called the younger man over to him. "Did you think the orchestra was playing well?" he asked. Previn, who had been rather pleased with the rendering, hesitated, then replied, "Yes, I thought they played very well." Monteux nodded. "So did I," he said. "Next time don't interfere with them."

2 A rehearsal of Richard Strauss's *Till Eulenspiegel* with the Philadelphia Orchestra was not going well. Monteux suspected that the trouble lay with the orchestra's overfamiliarity with the piece. Stopping the music suddenly, he said, "Gentlemen, I know that you know this piece backwards, but please do not let us play it that way."

3 Monteux was known to be fond of children. During a train journey on one of his later tours, he sat at a table in the dining car with some of his artistes. One by one, the proud parents among the group produced photographs of their offspring.

"Maestro, this is my daughter, Helen, three and a half."

"Maestro, this is my boy, David, only twelve and he wants to be an engineer."

Monteux obligingly responded to each snapshot with a word or two of praise, and finally pulled from his own wallet a rather dog-eared photograph. "My son, Claude, the flutist, forty-one," he announced.

4 In a BBC interview to mark his eighty-ninth birthday, Monteux was asked what were his remaining pleasures in life. "I still have two abiding passions," he replied. "One is my model railway, the other — women. But at the age of eighty-nine, I find I am getting just a little too old for model railways."

ॐ ॐ

MONTGOMERY, Bernard Law, 1st Viscount Montgomery of Alamein (1887–1976), *British field marshal, nicknamed "Monty". In World War II he commanded the Eighth Army in North Africa, winning a decisive victory over the Germans under General Erwin Rommel at El Alamein (1942). His autocratic ways could be a trial to his equals and superiors; Winston Churchill characterized him as "indomitable in retreat; invincible in advance; insufferable in victory."*

1 When Paris was recaptured by the Allies from the Germans in 1944 a jubilant General de Gaulle invested Monty with the Grande Croix of the Légion d'Honneur. The British Embassy was packed with a wildly excited crowd who would take no orders from anyone but Monty himself. Monty mustered his best French and said, "*Merci — et maintenant — allez-vous en.*" The crowd dispersed, but some people grumbled that Monty had said the wrong thing, been ungracious, and so on. Monty sought out A. P. Herbert. "'*Allez-vous en*' means 'go away,' doesn't it?"

"Yes, sir."

"Well," said Monty, "that's what I wanted, and that's what they did."

2 In 1944 Alan Brooke, chief of the imperial general staff and later to become first Viscount Alanbrooke, remarked to George VI that Montgomery was "a very good soldier, but I think he is after my job." Replied the king, "I thought he was after mine."

3 Climbing into a London cab one afternoon, Montgomery gave his destination as Waterloo. "Station?" quipped the driver. Monty glanced at his watch. "Certainly," he replied. "We're a bit late for the battle."

4 Montgomery carried his flair for the dramatic into civilian life. One day during a sitting of the House of Lords, he turned to the man next to him and, with his expression unruffled and voice calm, said, "Excuse me, but I'm having a coronary thrombosis." And away he went to look for medical attention.

{The doctors discovered that he had indeed suffered a heart attack.}

ॐ ॐ

MONTGOMERY, James (1771–1854), *Scottish poet and journalist.*

1 From 1792 Montgomery lived in Sheffield, where he attained a position of prominence as a writer and philanthropist. In 1812, however, his house was burgled. A treasured inkstand, presented to him by the ladies of Sheffield, was among the items stolen. There was a great public outcry, and some time later the inkstand was returned to its rightful owner with the following message: "Honored sir: When we robbed your house we did not know that you wrote such beautiful verses as you do. I remember my mother told some of them to me when I was a boy. I found what house we robbed by the writing on the inkstand. Honored sir, I send it back. It was my share of the booty, and I hope you and God will forgive me."

ॐ ॐ

MONTMORENCY, Anne, Duc de (1493–1567), *French nobleman and general.*

1 Montmorency was fatally wounded leading the Roman Catholic forces against the Huguenots at the battle of St. Denis in 1567, and was taken back to Paris to die. When a priest came to exhort him to make a good end, Montmorency said, "Father, do you believe that a man who knew how to live for nearly eighty years with honor does not know how to die for a quarter of an hour?"

ॐ ॐ

MOORE, George Augustus (1852–1933), *British author. His chief works are his autobiographical trilogy* Hail and Farewell *and the novels* A Modern Lover *(1883),* Esther Waters *(1894), and* Héloïse and Abélard *(1921).*

1 Moore was at the center of London literary life and gossip for many years. His various love affairs were well publicized — usually by the author. One woman acquaintance complained,

"Some men kiss and do not tell; some kiss and tell; but George Moore told and did not kiss."

2 Moore had trouble keeping a cook. Yeats tells how he fired six in three weeks. One of them, in protest, summoned a policeman. Moore took the officer into his dining room and demanded, "Is there a law in this country to compel me to eat that abominable omelet?" The cook left.

3 "How is it," asked a reporter of George Moore on his eightieth birthday, "that you enjoy such excellent health in your eightieth year?" Moore answered, "It's because I never smoked or drank or touched a girl — until I was eleven years old."

4 (In George Moore's *Ulick and Soracha* the old harper Tadgh dies gazing at the beautiful naked back of the young peasant woman Bridgit, whom he had married in his extreme old age. In a chapter suppressed from the published version of her *G. M.: Memories of George Moore*, Nancy Cunard, the daughter of one of George Moore's great lovers, Emerald Cunard, and herself a friend of the aged novelist, records the incident that gave rise to this scene. From time to time in the early 1920s, without any other amorous overtures, Moore had asked Nancy whether he might see her naked. She had always refused.)

"The words were as sudden as ever, said this time with a good deal of wistfulness: 'I *do* wish you would let me see you na-ked. I am an old man. . . . Oh, let me at least see your naked back.'

"Now, equally suddenly, something within me said, 'Do this!' and without more ado, facing away from him, I took off all my clothes, standing motionless a few feet from where he sat. How lightly, how easily, it came about. My clothes left me, lying in a graceful summer pool on the floor, as if they had slipped away of themselves. The night was warm and the mood serene. Without hesitation, my long, naked back and legs were at last in front of him and the silence was complete. It would be full-on he was looking at them and I did not turn my head. Of what could he be thinking? At length came a slow, murmuring sigh: 'Oh, what a beautiful back you have, Nancy! It is as long as a weasel's! What a beautiful back!'

"Then, never turning, I put my clothes on again with the same ease."

ớ ớ

MOORE, George Edward (1873–1958), *British philosopher. His main work was the* Principia Ethica *(1903), in which he tackled the problem of what we really mean by "goodness." As editor of* Mind *(1921–47) and in his own collections of papers he set a rigorous standard for philosophical inquiry.*

1 (Bertrand Russell comments on his friend's passion for truth.)

"I have never but once succeeded in making him tell a lie, and that was by a subterfuge. 'Moore,' I said, 'do you *always* speak the truth?' 'No,' he replied. I believe this to be the only lie he ever told."

ớ ớ

MORE, Hannah (1745–1833), *British moralistic writer and philanthropist. Her most famous work was* Coelebs in Search of a Wife *(1809).*

1 Mrs. More was spending a pleasant evening with a group of friends, when a late arrival to the party introduced a note of tragedy by relating a harrowing scene he had just witnessed along the road. A young mother had heroically rushed back into her blazing house to rescue her child, but in the dense smoke had mistakenly seized upon the child of another woman, leaving her own to die. The company, distressed by this tale, immediately set up a collection for the poor woman. Mrs. More played a prominent part in organizing the collection, in the course of which she approached a wealthy peer, who was not known for his generosity. "I will give you . . ." he began, as Mrs. More held out her hand expectantly, ". . . I will give you this afflicting incident for the subject of your next tragedy."

ớ ớ

MORE, Sir Thomas (1478–1535), *English statesman. He was lord chancellor (1529–32), but fell afoul of Henry VIII, was tried for high treason, and beheaded. Of More's many theological, historical, and other works, his* Utopia *(1516) remains the most famous.*

1 When young Thomas More was looking for a wife, the three daughters of a certain John Colte seemed to him eligible and attractive girls. More's inclinations led him to fix his choice first upon the second daughter, but then he thought what an affront it would be to the eldest if her younger sister was married before she was. He accordingly asked for the hand of the eldest daughter, Jane.

{She made him an excellent wife, and their very happy marriage was blessed with four children.}

2 In *Utopia* More recommends that young people should see each other naked before marriage in order to avoid disappointments and recriminations later. When Sir William Roper came early one morning to More's house at Chelsea with a request to marry one of his daughters, More led him upstairs to the room where the two young girls were sleeping. They were lying on their backs, with the sheet lightly over them. Their father whipped off the sheet. The startled girls awoke and turned quickly over onto their stomachs. "Now I have seen both sides," said Sir William, and then and there made his choice of the elder daughter, Margaret.

3 "Ascending the scaffold, [More] seemed so weak that he was ready to fall; whereupon he merrily said to the Lieutenant, 'I pray you Mr. Lieutenant see me safe up, and for my coming down let me shift for myself.' Then desired he all the people to pray for him, and to bear witness with him, that he should suffer death, in, and for the Faith of the Holy Catholic Church, a faithful servant both of God and the King. Which done, he kneeled down, and after his prayers ended, he turned to the executioner, and with a cheerful countenance, said, 'Pluck up thy spirits, man, and be not afraid to do thine office. My neck is very short, take heed therefore thou strike not awry for saving thine honesty.' Then laying his head upon the block he had the executioner stay until he had removed aside his beard, saying that that had never committed any treason. So with much cheerfulness he received the fatal blow of the axe, which at once severed his head from his body."

MOREL, Fédéric (1552–1630), *French scholar and printer.*

1 Morel was engrossed in a translation of Libanius when a messenger arrived to tell him that his wife was seriously ill. "I have only two or three passages left to translate," said Morel, without looking up from his work, "then I shall come directly." After some time, a second messenger brought the news that Mme Morel had not long to live. "Just two more words," cried the scholar, "and I shall be there." A third messenger appeared. "Your wife is dead," he announced solemnly. Morel sighed. "I am grieved indeed," he said. "She was a good woman." With that, he settled down to his translation again.

See also KARL FRIEDRICH GAUSS 2.

MORGAN, John Pierpont, Sr. (1837–1913), *US banker, financier, and benefactor of the arts. He was president of the Metropolitan Museum of Art, New York City.*

1 J. P. Morgan was as sharp an art collector as he was a banker; so the young Joseph Duveen, who in later years became one of the world's foremost art dealers, found out to his cost. Young Joseph was convinced that his uncle, Henry Duveen, was not getting as much as he should from Morgan. Accordingly, Joseph put before the great man a collection of thirty miniatures, of which six were very rare and the rest unremarkable. Morgan cast his eye briefly over the collection and then asked what the thirty pieces cost. Duveen gave him the figure, upon which Morgan pocketed the six good miniatures, divided Duveen's figure by thirty, multiplied by six, and handed over that amount. "You're only a boy, Joe," Uncle Henry told the exasperated Joseph afterward. "It takes a man to deal with Morgan."

2 Morgan once told a jeweler of his acquaintance that he was interested in buying a pearl scarfpin. Just a few weeks later, the jeweler happened upon a magnificent pearl. He had it mounted in an appropriate setting and sent it to Morgan, together with a bill for five thousand dollars. The following day the package was returned. Morgan's accompanying note read: "I like the pin, but I don't like the price. If you will accept the enclosed check for four thousand dollars, please send back the box with the seal unbroken." The enraged jeweler refused the check and dismissed the messenger in disgust. He opened up the box to reclaim the unwanted pin, only to find that it had been removed. In its place was a check for five thousand dollars.

3   The Cathedral of St. John the Divine, near Columbia University in New York City, has attached to it a Gothic château called the Cathedral House. It is an opulent structure, originally intended to be the bishop's house. At the time of its completion there were critics who felt that it was perhaps too elegant to house a humble servant of God. One of the trustees, J. P. Morgan, defended it thus: "Bishops should live like everyone else."

4   Morgan was looking for a new director for the Metropolitan Museum. Sir Caspar Purdon Clarke, director of the Victoria and Albert Museum in South Kensington, London, seemed the ideal choice. To the dismay of his English colleagues, Clarke accepted the new appointment. The secretary of the Victoria and Albert Museum was on vacation at the time; on his return he asked about some Chinese porcelains and tapestries that had come up for auction in his absence, which he had hoped to acquire for the museum. "I'm afraid J. P. Morgan bought them, sir," replied the clerk. "Good God," said the secretary, "I must tell Sir Purdon." The clerk looked a little uneasy. "Sorry, sir," he said. "Mr. Morgan bought him also."

5   A man stopped J. P. Morgan as he was leaving his Wall Street office, and asked him for a tip on what the market was going to do. "It will fluctuate," said Morgan, walking away briskly.

6   Morgan's nose was disfigured by a skin disease that made it swollen and fiery. People, while pretending politely not to notice anything extraordinary, were nonetheless mesmerized by it. There is the story of the nervous hostess at the tea table, who inquired, "Do you take nose in your tea, Mr. Morgan?"

7   Morgan disliked haggling and tended to make offers in his business dealings on a "take-it-or-leave-it" basis. The figure quoted for the purchase of Andrew Carnegie's steel interests was almost a quarter of a billion dollars. When the slip of paper bearing the figure was handed to him, he barely glanced at it before saying, "I accept." Later Carnegie met him by chance and said he regretted not having set the price 100 million dollars higher. "You'd have got it if you had," said Morgan.

8   Morgan was asked to contribute to an Ivy League medical school. Meeting representatives from the school, he said he was in a hurry and asked them quickly to show him the plans of the proposed buildings. The plans were spread out. "I'll give that, and that, and that," said Morgan, pointing to three buildings, and hurried from the room before he could even be thanked.

9   Morgan fell foul of Theodore Roosevelt over an antitrust action that the president brought in 1902 against one of his companies. When Roosevelt left office and immediately headed for Africa on a big game safari, Morgan is said to have exclaimed, "Health to the lions!"
    {On the same theme, an anonymous Wall Street wit put up the following sign on the trading floor: "WALL STREET EXPECTS EVERY LION TO DO ITS DUTY."}

ﻋﻪ ﻋﻪ

MORGAN, John Pierpont, Jr. (1867–1943), *US millionaire and head of the banking house of Morgan.*

1   A man who had been gazing enviously at J. P. Morgan's yacht said to its owner, "I'm thinking of buying a yacht myself. Can you give me an idea of the annual upkeep?" Morgan replied, "Anyone who has to ask about annual upkeep can't afford one."
    {This retort is often quoted as "If you have to ask, you can't afford it."}

2   A young employee of whom Morgan had had high hopes became involved with a chorus girl and the scandal was blazoned in the headlines and gossip columns. Morgan told the young man bluntly that he was disappointed in him. "But it's just that I'm not a hypocrite," protested the sinner. "I haven't done anything that most young men in my situation haven't done behind closed doors."
    "You may be right," said his employer, "but that's what doors are for, dammit!"

3 One of J. P. Morgan's servants availed himself of every opportunity to better and enrich himself. Eventually he decided that he had saved enough to retire in style, and so notified Morgan that he would be leaving his service. Morgan asked him to find a suitable replacement. The following day the man presented to his employer two likely candidates. Morgan interviewed them and selected one. "And I'll take the other, Mr. Morgan," said the retiring servant.

ફ્જ ➤ ✧ج

MORLEY, Christopher (1890–1957), *US writer and editor, whose best-known work is* Kitty Foyle *(1939).*

1 Christopher Morley and William Rose Benét were gazing at the window of a wig shop in which were displayed two small identical wigs on their stands. "They're alike as toupees in a pod," observed Morley.

ફ્જ ➤ ✧ج

MORLEY, Robert (1908–), *British actor. His long career as a character actor has encompassed both stage and film, and he is particularly associated with the role of the archetypical eccentric Englishman.*

1 Playwright William Douglas-Home boasted to Morley over lunch one day that actor Alfred Marks was to appear in his new play. "I've always admired Mr. Marks tremendously," said Morley enthusiastically. Then, without thinking, he continued, "Unfortunately, he always seems to choose the wrong play."

2 Morley once met an old friend, fellow-actor Llewellyn Rees, whom he had not seen for some time. "It's nice meeting old friends," said Rees warmly. "A lot of people think I'm dead."

"Not if they look closely," said Morley.

ફ્જ ➤ ✧ج

MORRIS, Clara (1847–1925), *US actress, born in Canada.*

1 (Clara Morris told the following story of her own experience:)

"Somewhere in the wide world there is an actor—and a good one—who never eats celery without thinking of me. It was years ago, when I was playing Camille. In the first scene, you will remember, the unfortunate Armand takes a rose from Camille as a token of love. We had almost reached that point, when, as I glanced down, I saw that the flower was missing from its accustomed place on my breast.

"What could I do? On the flower hung the strength of the scene. However, I continued my lines in an abstracted fashion, and began a still hunt for that rose or a substitute. My gaze wandered around the stage. On the dinner table was some celery. Moving slowly toward it, I grasped the celery and twisted the tops into a rose form. Then I began the fateful lines:

"'Take this flower. The life of a camellia is short. If held and caressed it will fade in a morning or an evening.'

"Hardly able to control his laughter, Armand spoke his lines which ran: 'It is a cold, scentless flower. It is a strange flower.' I agreed with him."

ફ્જ ➤ ✧ج

MORRIS, William (1834–96), *British poet, designer, artist, and typographer. Beginning his career as a member of the Pre-Raphaelites, he later founded a firm of decorators and designers, which heralded the Arts and Crafts movement, characterized by its respect for the work of individual craftsmen.*

1 During William Morris's last visit to Paris, he spent much of his time in the restaurant of the Eiffel Tower, either eating or writing. When a friend observed that he must be very impressed by the tower to spend so much time there, Morris snorted, "Impressed! I remain here because it's the only place in Paris where I can avoid seeing the damn thing."

{This retort has been appropriated by others.}

ફ્જ ➤ ✧ج

MORSE, Samuel Finley Breese (1791–1872), *US inventor of the telegraph. The system of dots and dashes by which telegraphic messages are conveyed is named after him.*

1 In May 1844 Morse sent the first public telegram over the specially constructed line built between Baltimore and Washington. The text of the telegram was: "WHAT HATH GOD WROUGHT."

{The honor of choosing the words was

given to Annie Ellsworth, daughter of the commissioner of patents.}

2 Morse was a successful artist as well as inventor. He once painted a picture of a man in his death agony and showed it to a friend, who happened to be a doctor. "Well, what's your opinion?" he demanded, after the doctor had studied the painting. "Malaria," said the medical man without hesitation.

৵৽ ৼৎ

MOSCARDÓ, José (1876–1956), *Spanish soldier; commander of the Nationalist forces defending the Alcázar in Toledo during its siege (1936) in the Spanish Civil War.*

1 As the defenders of the Alcázar were reduced to near-starvation rations, an officer notorious for grumbling came to see Moscardó to demand that he receive more than the usual daily allowance of food. Moscardó heard his demand through, then pulled out a 50-peseta bill and handed it to him. "Take this," he said, "and go outside and buy something if you like. It's the best I can do for you."

৵৽ ৼৎ

MOSLEY, Sir Oswald (1896–1980), *British fascist leader. A member of Parliament from 1922 to 1931, he formed the British Union of Fascists in 1932. The British fascists dressed in black shirts and black trousers during the 1930s.*

1 At a meeting of Blackshirts in 1937, Mosley was billed to speak. With elegant dignity he mounted the rostrum, dressed, as usual, in his black outfit. He acknowledged the cheers of his supporters by solemnly raising his right arm in the fascist salute. The gesture elicited still louder cheering, which encouraged the somewhat vain Mosley to keep his saluting arm raised. As the tumult died down, a voice at the back of the hall shouted, "Yes, Oswald, you can leave the room."

৵৽ ৼৎ

MOTT, Lucretia Coffin (1793–1880), *US Quaker reformer who campaigned for women's rights and the abolition of slavery.*

1 A meeting of the Anti-Slavery Society in New York was broken up by thugs, who attacked some of the speakers as they left the hall. Lucretia Mott told the gentleman accompanying her to escort some of the other ladies who were alone and frightened in the tumult. "But who will look after you?" he asked. "This gentleman," she said, turning to one of the roughest-looking members of the mob and laying her hand on his arm. "He will see me safely through." The thug was so astonished that he did as she requested and escorted her respectfully through the crowd to safety.

৵৽ ৼৎ

MOUNTBATTEN of Burma, Louis, 1st Earl (1900–79), *British naval commander, great-grandson of Queen Victoria. A flotilla commander at the beginning of World War II, he was made chief of combined operations in 1942 and subsequently supreme allied commander in southeast Asia (1943–46). After the war he served as viceroy (1947) and governor-general (1947–48) of India, First Sea Lord (1955–59), and chief of defense staff (1959–65). He was assassinated by an IRA bomb in 1979.*

1 The five-year-old Mountbatten was reluctant to go to bed alone in the dark. "It isn't the dark," he told his father confidentially. "There are wolves up there." His father smiled. "There are no wolves in this house," he said reassuringly. This was of little consolation to the rational young Mountbatten. "I daresay there aren't," he replied, "but I *think* there are."

2 During the most controversial period of the Vietnam War, Mountbatten, in Los Angeles, was Johnny Carson's guest on the *Tonight Show*. He had previously warned Carson that he would answer no questions about Vietnam. On the show, after a few minutes of conversation that went quite smoothly, Carson apparently decided to slip one over on Mountbatten. "Sir," he asked, "if you were president of the United States, what would you do about Vietnam?" Replied Mountbatten, "I'd tell the British to keep their noses out of it."

৵৽ ৼৎ

MOZART, Wolfgang Amadeus (1756–91), *Austrian composer. Mozart revealed his musical genius at an extraordinarily early age. When he was only six, his father, Leopold Mozart, took him and his gifted elder sister on a*

European tour. After an unhappy period in the service of the archbishop of Salzburg (1779–81) Mozart went to Vienna, where he failed to find adequate employment. Poverty and overwork contributed to his early death. Like Bach's, Mozart's output as a composer was astonishing: forty-nine symphonies, more than forty concertos, seven string quintets, twenty-six string quartets, and dozens of piano and violin sonatas and divertimenti, besides his great choral works. His greatest operas were all written within the last five years of his life: The Marriage of Figaro *(1786),* Don Giovanni *(1787),* Così fan tutte *(1790), and* The Magic Flute *(1791).*

1   At the age of two Mozart was taken to visit a farm, where he heard a pig squeal. "G-sharp!" he exclaimed. Someone ran to the piano. G-sharp was right.

2   On his 1762 visit to Schönbrunn, the Austrian royal palace, Mozart slipped on the polished floor while romping with the young princesses and burst into tears. He was picked up and comforted by the seven-year-old Marie Antoinette. The little boy kissed the future queen of France and told her, "You are good. I will marry you."

3   Mozart was approached by a young man, little older than a boy, who sought his advice on composing a symphony. Mozart pointed out that he was still very young and it might be better if he began by composing ballads. "But you wrote symphonies when you were only ten years old," objected the lad. "But I didn't have to ask how," Mozart retorted.
{This story is told of other composers who were child prodigies and no doubt has been adapted for early starters in other fields.}

4   At an evening party, Mozart bet Haydn a case of champagne that the older man could not play at sight a piece he had composed that afternoon. Haydn accepted the bet, the piece was placed on the spinet rack, Haydn briskly played the first few bars, then stopped short. He found it impossible to continue, for the composition prescribed playing with the two hands at the two ends of the keyboard and striking a note in the very center. Haydn

confessed himself beaten. Mozart took his place at the piano and, reaching the fatal note, bent forward and hit it with his nose. General applause.
{Authenticity is not guaranteed.}

MUGGERIDGE, Malcolm (1903–   ), *English writer, broadcaster, and journalist. He became a Roman Catholic in his late seventies.*

1   Muggeridge had little time for politicians and admitted to Jack Paar, host of US television's *Tonight Show*, that he had voted only once in his life. "On that occasion," he said, "I just had to. There was this one candidate who had been committed to an asylum and upon discharge was issued a Certificate of Sanity. Well, now, how could I resist? What other politician anywhere has an actual medical report that he is sane? I simply had to support him!"

MUGNIER, Abbé Arthur (1853–1944), *French divine. He was a friend of Proust's and much in demand in high society, being renowned for his charm and warmth of heart.*

1   The abbé was asked if he believed in hell. He replied, "Yes, because it is a dogma of the church—but I don't believe anyone is in it."

2   There are many stories about the kindliness and humanity of the Abbé Mugnier, qualities illustrated in an incident he recounted to Edith Wharton. He was administering the last sacrament to a dying parishioner when the man's pet canary flew down and started pecking at the Host. "What did you do?" asked Mrs. Wharton. "I blessed the canary," said the abbé.

3   Novelist Paul Bourget was among the Abbé Mugnier's many converts to Catholicism. After his conversion Bourget took his religious fervor to extremes and bored many listeners with his interminable theological arguments. Even the abbé found his new convert more than a little tiresome. One evening, in the middle of a particularly tedious monologue, Mugnier interrupted Bourget with the words, "I have two cassocks, Monsieur Bourget. Would you like one?"

4 A rather plump and also rather vain actress confessed to Mugnier that she sometimes looked at her naked body in the mirror. "Is it a sin?" she asked. The abbé, glancing at her ample figure, replied, "No, madame, it's an error."

5 At a social gathering, Mugnier, sitting beside an exceptionally attractive young lady, was asked by a gentleman present if he would dare to kiss her. "Certainly not!" replied the abbé. "She's not yet a relic!"

⊱ ⊰

MUHAMMAD SHAH I (fl. 14th century), *sultan of the Bahmani kingdom in southern India (1358–75). The early part of his reign was marked by wars with the rulers of neighboring territories.*

1 A ragged messenger arrived one day at the sultan's capital, bearing dreadful news. The Hindus had captured his native town; he was the sole survivor of the ensuing massacre. Muhammad Shah was so outraged at the report that he immediately sentenced the unfortunate messenger to death. "I could never bear in my presence," he said, "a wretch who could survive the sight of the slaughter of so many brave companions."

⊱ ⊰

MUIR, John (1838–1914), *US naturalist, born in Scotland. He was largely responsible for the establishment of Yosemite National Park and the shaping of national conservation policy. Muir Glacier in Alaska is named in his honor.*

1 Financial consideration played only a small part in the satisfaction John Muir derived from life. On one occasion he declared that he was richer than magnate E. H. Harriman: "I have all the money I want and he hasn't."

⊱ ⊰

MURAVIEV, Count Mikhail (?1796–1866), *Russian statesman.*

1 Although his cousin Sergei Muraviev-Apostol was one of the leaders of the Decembrist uprising in 1825 and was subsequently hanged for his part in it, Count Mikhail Muraviev attained prominence in the councils of Czar Alexander II. When Russian mismanagement in Poland led to a revolt there in 1863, he was one of those entrusted with the task of pacifying the country. The savagery with which he did this caused adverse comment, which the count brushed off by saying, "I am one of the hanging Muravievs, not one of the ones who are hanged."

⊱ ⊰

MURPHY, Charles F. (1858–1924), *US politician; head of Tammany Hall from 1902 to 1924.*

1 Charles F. Murphy was observed remaining silent during the singing of the US national anthem at a Fourth of July celebration. When a reporter asked the reason, an aide replied, "Perhaps he didn't want to commit himself."

⊱ ⊰

MURRAY, Sir George (1772–1846), *British soldier.*

1 During the expedition against the French in Egypt in 1801, Murray and his troops found themselves in the vicinity of Alexandria without water. Having had a classical education, Murray recalled that Julius Caesar had suffered the same problem in almost exactly the same spot. He lost no time in consulting the copy of Caesar's writings that he always carried with him, and was delighted to discover that the Romans had found water by digging wells in the sand to a specified depth. Murray set his men to work and before long a plentiful water supply was found.

⊱ ⊰

MURRAY, [George] Gilbert [Aimé] (1866–1957), *British classical scholar. As professor of Greek at Glasgow (1889–1908) and Oxford (1908–36), he inspired many students with the love of ancient Greek literature. He made notable translations of the Greek tragedians and of Aristophanes.*

1 Gilbert Murray's wife, Lady Mary Howard, was a teetotaler and a vegetarian. She converted her husband to her way of thinking, but when guests were present she allowed a joint of meat to be served. Murray, carving the joint, would ask the guests, "Will you have some of the corpse, or will you try the alternative?"

2 (As a student coming belatedly to Oxford after active service in World War I, poet Robert Graves was discussing Aristotle's *Poetics* with Gilbert Murray in the latter's study. Murray was pacing up and down.)

"I suddenly asked, 'Exactly what is the principle of that walk of yours? Are you trying to avoid the flowers on the rug, or are you trying to keep to the squares?' My own compulsion-neuroses made it easy for me to notice them in others. He wheeled around sharply: 'You're the first person who has caught me out,' he said. 'No, it's not the flowers or the squares; it's a habit that I have got into of doing things in sevens. I take seven steps, you see, then I change direction and go another seven steps, then I turn around. I consulted Browne, the Professor of Psychology, about it the other day, but he assured me it isn't a dangerous habit. He said, "When you find yourself getting into multiples of seven, come to me again."'"

કે❧

MURRAY, Margaret Alice (1863–1963), *British archaeologist and anthropologist. Under the guidance of Sir Flinders Petrie, she became the first woman Egyptologist. Besides excavating in Egypt and the Middle East, she wrote a number of books on ancient Egypt and was a recognized authority on folklore, especially witchcraft.*

1 Putting her knowledge of witchcraft to practical effect at the London Institute of Archaeology, Margaret Murray jestingly cast a spell upon a colleague of whose appointment she disapproved. The victim promptly fell ill and was moved to another and more suitable post.

કે❧

MUSSET, Alfred de (1810–57), *French poet, novelist, and playwright. In 1833 he began a short-lived liaison with George Sand.*

1 Alfred de Musset's affairs caused considerable scandal. A Théâtre Français actress accosted the famous poet familiarly, but in her ignorance left out the particle in his name: "Monsieur Musset, they tell me you boast of having slept with me." Musset replied, "Pardon me, but I have always boasted of the exact opposite."

કે❧

MYTTON, John (1796–1834), *British sportsman and eccentric.*

1 The impetuous Mytton once set fire to his nightshirt in order to get rid of the hiccups. He succeeded, but it should be mentioned that he happened to be inside the nightshirt at the time.

❧ N ❧

NABOKOV, Vladimir (1899–1977), *US novelist, born in Russia. He first achieved popular success with his novel* Lolita *(1955). Other outstanding titles include* Pale Fire *(1962) and* Ada *(1969).*

1 (One summer in the 1940s Nabokov and his family stayed with James Laughlin at Alta, Utah, where Nabokov took the opportunity of enlarging his collection of butterflies and moths.)

"Nabokov's fiction has never been praised for its compassion; he was single-minded if nothing else. One evening at dusk he returned from his day's excursion saying that during hot pursuit over Bear Gulch he had heard someone groaning most piteously down by the stream. 'Did you stop?' Laughlin asked him. 'No, I had to get the butterfly.' The next day the corpse of an aged prospector was discovered in what has been renamed, in Nabokov's honor, Dead Man's Gulch."

2 After the publication of *Lolita* Nabokov (who characterized himself, probably quite accurately, as a "mild old gentleman") was on occasion besieged by aspiring nymphets. In his latter years he retired from teaching and took up residence in Montreux at the Palace Hotel.

Interviewed by Alan Levy (*New York Times Magazine,* October 31, 1971), the great stylist described a post-Lolita experience that turned on a delicate question of rhetoric:

"Not long ago there was someone with an American name who kept leaving vague messages for me all over Montreux. I started leaving messages too, that I was unavailable. Then I got one more message—a slip of paper that said, 'F—— you.' Well, this was so much more explicit than the others that I asked the desk what kind of person had left this message, and the desk said, 'That wasn't a person, sir; that

was two rather wild-looking American girls.' This intrigued me even more, so I looked at the paper again. And there I found something at the end of the message which I hadn't noticed on my first reading: a question mark!"

3 (Nabokov describes a visit to the distinguished French novelist Alain Robbe-Grillet.)

"Robbe-Grillet's petite pretty wife, a young actress, had dressed herself *à la gamine* in my honor, pretending to be Lolita, and she continued the performance the next day, when we met again at a publisher's luncheon in a restaurant. After pouring wine for everyone but her, the waiter asked, '*Voulez-vous un Coca-Cola, Mademoiselle?*'"

❧ ❧

NAGURSKI, Bronko (1908–   ), *US Hall of Fame football player renowned for his strength and versatility.*

1 After making All-American on his play both as a defensive lineman and offensive back at Minnesota, Nagurski was signed by the Chicago Bears. When the Green Bay Packers played the Bears, the Packers' massive tackle, Cal Hubbard, whispered to the Bears' Red Grange, "I've heard a lot about this Nagurski. I want to test him. Your team is going to punt on the next play. Do me a favor and don't block me. I won't block the punt, but I want Nagurski to try to block me." Red laughed and agreed. When the ball was snapped, he let Hubbard through. Nagurski met him head-on and flattened him with a bone-jarring block. Hubbard got up, went to Grange, and said, "Do me a favor, Red. Don't do me any more favors."

2 Carrying the ball, Nagurski ran right over people. In one game against the New York

Giants, Benny Friedman hit him on the twelve-yard line, but did not bring him down until the one-yard line. "He hits hard enough to knock down a horse," muttered Friedman. On the next play, Nagurski did just that: he crashed through the end zone so hard, head down, that he ran into a mounted policeman and bowled over man and beast. Not quite sure what had happened, Nagurski stood up groggily, complaining, "That last man hit me awful hard."

3 Bruised and battered, the Pittsburgh Steelers were on their way home from a meeting with the Bears and Nagurski, when their train came to a jolting halt, spilling players into the aisles. "Run for your lives, men," counseled a Steeler. "Nagurski has struck again."

4 As a result of some horseplay with a teammate, Nagurski once fell out of a second-floor window. A crowd gathered. A policeman appeared. He asked, "What happened?" Replied Nagurski, "I don't know. I just got here myself."

ॐ ∾

NAMATH, Joe (1943–   ), *US football player. "Broadway Joe" was the great quarterback of the New York Jets.*

1 (Frank Howard, a former Clemson football coach, told the following story about Namath and Bear Bryan, the winningest college football coach of his period:)

"Bear had a squad meeting one time and he told his players, 'This is a class operation. I want your shoes to be shined. I want you to have a tie on, get your hair cut and keep a crease in your pants. I also want you to go to class. I don't want no dumbbells on this team. If there is a dumbbell in the room, I wish he would stand up.'

"Joe Namath rose to his feet, and Bear said, 'Joe, how come you're standing up? You ain't dumb.' Namath told him, 'Coach, I just hate like the devil for you to be standing up there by yourself.'"

ॐ ∾

NAPIER, Sir Charles James (1782–1853), *British soldier and administrator. He served in Greece in the 1820s and in India (1841–50).*

1 In August 1842 Napier annexed the province of Sind, thus giving the British control of the Indus River in what is now southeast Pakistan. Of this action Napier wrote in his journal: "We have no right to seize Sind, but we shall do so, and a very advantageous, useful, humane piece of rascality it will be." He is reputed to have dispatched news of the conquest of Sind in one Latin word: "*Peccavi*" (I have sinned).

{The historical accuracy of this pun is doubtful; *Punch* in 1856 attributed it to Lord Ellenborough, the British governor of India in 1842.}

ॐ ∾

NAPOLEON I (1769–1821), *emperor of France (1804–15). Born in Corsica, he joined the French army and first made his mark when he ordered his men to fire on a Parisian mob demonstrating against the government (1795). Appointed to lead the French forces in Italy, he scored brilliant victories against the Austrians and went on to challenge British power in Egypt. Napoleon returned to France, where he consolidated his hold on French politics; in 1799 he became first consul, in 1802 first consul for life, and in 1804 emperor. His plans to invade Britain were aborted by Lord Nelson's victories at sea, culminating in Trafalgar (1805), but Napoleon's successes at Austerlitz (1805), Jena (1806), and Friedland (1806) confirmed his supremacy on land. Napoleon's confrontation with Britain in Spain (1808–14) weakened France, but he was able to muster huge forces for his ill-fated invasion of Russia (1812), where, forced to retreat from Moscow, he lost four-fifths of his men. Defeated at Leipzig the following year, he was exiled to Elba, but returned to France in an attempt to regain his former power. He was finally crushed at Waterloo (1815) and exiled to St. Helena, where he died. He married Joséphine de Beauharnais in 1796, but divorced her in 1809 because she was childless. His second wife, Marie-Louise of Austria, presented him with a son, known in infancy as the King of Rome and subsequently as Napoleon II.*

1 (Napoleon always hated being on the losing side: when he played chess he would surreptitiously replace a forfeited piece on the board. His elder brother told a revealing story about Napoleon's schooldays.)

For an ancient history lesson the teacher brought in two huge flags, one the flag of Rome with the legend SPQR on it, and the other the flag of Carthage. With the flags set up on either side of the classroom, the children were divided into two groups to go and stand under them. Napoleon's elder brother was sent to stand under the Roman flag, Napoleon under the Carthaginian flag. When Napoleon discovered that he was standing under the flag of the defeated, he protested until the teacher allowed him to change places with his brother.

2 During Napoleon's time as first consul it was the fashion for women to wear transparent gauze dresses. Somewhat incensed at this practice, one evening Napoleon ordered the servants to build up the drawing-room fire until the room reached ovenlike temperature. As he sourly explained: "It is extremely cold and these ladies are almost naked." Joséphine understood the situation and inaugurated new fashions in dress of a somewhat more seemly nature.

3 As first consul, Napoleon often worked a sixteen-hour day. He expected that the Council of State would have stamina and zeal to match his own. One night when the councillors began to doze off, he reprimanded them, "Do let's keep awake, citizens. It's only two o'clock. We must earn our salaries." These superhuman efforts were much applauded by Napoleon's admirers, but not by royalists. One such admirer, singing the first consul's praises, remarked, "God made Bonaparte and then rested." An emigré count commented, "God should have rested a little earlier."

4 After an overnight journey Napoleon arrived at the palace of the king of Saxony and found himself in the middle of a full-scale reception. But Frederick Augustus discreetly led Napoleon into an anteroom where there was a chamber pot, saying, "I've often found that great men, like everybody else, sometimes require to be alone."

5 Receiving intelligence that seemed to link the Duc d'Enghien with royalist conspiracies against him, Napoleon authorized his agents to seize and execute him. Despite pleas for his life from Joséphine, Napoleon had the duke summarily shot. Although the matter aroused no immediate open opposition, it had the long-term effect of strengthening antagonism toward Napoleon and evoked from Comte Boulay de la Meurthe the observation: "*C'est pire qu'un crime, c'est une faute*" (It's worse than a crime, it's a blunder).

{This famous remark, in the form "*C'est plus* (more) *qu'un crime . . . ,*" has been variously attributed to Talleyrand or Fouché, and may have had its origins in something that Napoleon himself said of the Enghien affair.}

6 In a moment of vanity, Napoleon observed to his secretary, Bourrienne, "You too will be immortal."
"Why?"
"Well, are you not my secretary?"
"Name Alexander the Great's secretary," was the response.

7 Searching for a book one day in his library, Napoleon eventually located it on the topmost shelf, beyond his reach. "Permit me, sire," said the tall Marshal Moncey, stepping forward. "I am higher than Your Majesty."
"No, Marshal, you are longer," Napoleon corrected him, scowling.

8 Napoleon's conversational style was almost completely predictable. Having asked his guest's name, he would usually go on with "What part of France do you come from?" and "How old are you?" Aware of this, the deaf Duchesse de Brissac rehearsed appropriate responses. On hearing her name, however, Napoleon for once realized who she was and dispensed with his usual second and third questions. Remembering that her brother-in-law, the Duc de Brissac, had been killed as commander of Louis XVI's guard at Versailles in 1792, he asked whether she and her husband had inherited the estate. "Seine et Oise, sire," replied the duchess. Slightly surprised, Napoleon pressed on with "Have you any children?" The duchess smiled brightly. "Fifty-two, sire," she said.

9 In the path of Napoleon's advancing army, the Russians abandoned the city of Smolensk and set fire to it. Napoleon, watching the blaze with his aides, compared it to an eruption of Vesuvius, and asked his master of horse whether it was not a fine sight. "Horrible, sire," said the man. Napoleon snorted contemptuously. "Remember, gentlemen," he said, "as

one of the Roman emperors remarked, 'The corpse of an enemy always smells sweet!'"

10 A little later, Napoleon may have had a change of heart. When the French defeated the Russians at Borodino, their losses were almost as great as those of the Russians. Napoleon considered Borodino the most terrible battle he had ever fought. On the following day he and his aides rode over the battlefield in silence, reckoning up the dead. They came across a prostrate body and, hearing a cry of pain, Napoleon ordered a stretcher. "It's only a Russian, sire," said one of his aides. Napoleon retorted, "After a victory there are no enemies, only men."

11 Later still all trace of compassion—even for his own—was gone. After the French victory at Eylau over the combined Russian and Prussian forces, Napoleon walked across the battlefield, turning over with his foot the corpses of French soldiers. "Small change, small change," he said. "One Parisian night will soon adjust these losses."

12 After the Russian debacle Napoleon, fearing his position at home was precarious, left the French army in the lurch and hurried back to France almost unaccompanied. Arriving at the banks of the river Neman in his miserable sleigh, he inquired of the ferryman whether many deserters had come through that way. "No," replied the Russian, "you are the first."

13 When Napoleon made his triumphant return from Elba in March 1815, the restored Bourbon king, Louis XVIII, fled, leaving a large sum of money with the banker Jacques Laffitte. An official, thinking to curry favor with the emperor, informed Napoleon of the existence of the deposit. Napoleon, however, had it transferred to England, where Louis could have access to it. After Waterloo, when Napoleon himself was about to flee Paris, he made arrangements with Laffitte to leave a similarly large amount of money on deposit. When Laffitte sat down at his desk to write out a receipt for the deposit, Napoleon stopped him: "If I am captured and the receipt is found on me it will compromise you." And he absolutely refused to accept one.

{It is pleasing to note that Louis XVIII on his second restoration reciprocated Napoleon's honorable behavior over the money left with Laffitte and did not take the opportunity to appropriate it.}

14 The death of Napoleon on St. Helena was announced in a crowded Paris salon attended by Wellington and Talleyrand, among others. In the hush that followed the announcement, someone exclaimed "What an event!"

"It is no longer an event!" broke in the voice of Talleyrand. "It is only a piece of news."

৯৯ ৶৻

NAPOLEON III (1808–73), *emperor of France (1852–70). A nephew of Napoleon I, Napoleon won the presidential election following the 1848 revolution that overthrew the Bourbon Louis Philippe. In 1851 he dissolved the legislative assembly and a year later proclaimed himself emperor. His rule fostered domestic prosperity, but his disastrous diplomatic adventures abroad led eventually to the Franco-Prussian War (1870–71).*

1 The emperor was once implored by a lady to forbid all smoking on the grounds that it was a great vice. Laying aside his cigar, he replied, "This vice brings in one hundred million francs in taxes every year. I will certainly forbid it at once—as soon as you can name a virtue that brings in as much revenue."

2 For years Napoleon suffered agonies from stones in the bladder. The pain undermined his health and prematurely aged him. Before giving a public audience, he was seen once to hold his arm against the flame of a candle in an attempt to find some relief through a change of pain.

3 The battle of Solferino in 1859 was technically a French victory, as the Austrian forces retreated. There was appalling carnage on both sides, and Napoleon, alarmed by unrest at home, made peace three weeks later. "I don't care for war," he remarked at the time. "There's far too much luck in it for my liking."

৯৯ ৶৻

NAPOLEON, Eugène Louis Jean Joseph (1856–79), *French pretender to the imperial throne, known as the "Prince Imperial." On the* *death of his father, Napoleon III, he was pro-claimed Napoleon IV by the Bonapartists. He made no attempt to regain the throne. He was killed while serving with a British force against the Zulus in South Africa.*

1 On a holiday at Biarritz, when the Prince Imperial was little more than a toddler, he seemed afraid to enter the sea, so he was picked up and hurled in bodily. He struggled out and ran away as fast as he could, howling in terror. He was caught and soothed, and then an attempt was made to rationalize his fears. Why, he was asked, was he afraid of the sea when he had stood by while soldiers fired off their cannon and had not been frightened? The child thought this one over for a moment, then said, "Because I'm in command of the soldiers, but I'm not in command of the sea."

2 Brought up to believe that no Bonaparte ever showed pain or fear, the young Prince Imperial flinched under the hands of a doctor carrying out some trifling operation. "Did I hurt you?" the man asked. "No, but you startled me," he replied.

3 The young Prince Imperial asked his father to explain the difference between an accident and a misfortune. Napoleon III replied, "If your cousin Plon-Plon [once designated heir to the emperor] were to fall into a well, that would be an accident; if someone pulled him out, that would be a misfortune."

{This seems to be the Gallic equivalent of Disraeli's jest about Gladstone: *see* BEN-JAMIN DISRAELI 7. For more about the hapless Plon-Plon, see the following biography and anecdote.}

ॐ✦ ✦⊱

NAPOLEON, Joseph Charles Paul, Prince (1822–91), *Bonapartist heir to the French throne. He was first designated heir to Napoleon III in 1851, in case the latter should die without issue. On the death of the Prince Imperial, Napoleon III's son, in 1879, he again became heir to the Napoleonic succession. His family and close associates called him "Plon-Plon," a nickname possibly based on his childish attempts to pronounce his name.*

1 The courtesan Anna Deslion at one time shared her favors between Plon-Plon and the playwright Lambert Thiboust. Though the rivals met occasionally on the stairs of Anna's house, neither of them was inclined to make a fuss. "To be dishonored by a prince is something of an honor," said Thiboust. Plon-Plon was likewise philosophical: "To be deceived by a man of brains is no serious misfortune."

ॐ✦ ✦⊱

NARVÁEZ, Ramón María (1800–68), *Spanish general and statesman, prime minister (1844–47, 1856–57, 1864–65, 1866–68).*

1 A priest asked the dying Narváez, "Does your Excellency forgive all your enemies?"

"I do not have to forgive my enemies," retorted Narváez. "I have had them all shot."

ॐ✦ ✦⊱

NASH, Ogden (1902–71), *US writer of humorous verse. He produced over twenty volumes of verse, some for children. They include* Hard Lines *(1921) and* The Bad Parents' Garden of Verse *(1936).*

1 Radio director Tom Carlson's dog had chewed up an autographed copy of one of Nash's works. Though the book was out of print, Carlson finally managed to acquire a replacement. He sent it to Nash, explaining what had happened and asking for another autograph. The book was returned — with the dedication: "To Tom Carlson or his dog — depending on whose taste it best suits."

ॐ✦ ✦⊱

NASSER, Gamal Abdel (1918–70), *Egyptian soldier and statesman. A leader of the coup that deposed King Farouk in 1952, he became prime minister (1954–56) and president (1956–70) of Egypt. His nationalization of the Suez Canal in 1956 provoked an unsuccessful Anglo–French attack on Egypt.*

1 With emotions high on the night before the coup of 1952, one of Nasser's associates was close to tears. "Tonight there is no room for sentiment," said Nasser firmly. "We must be ready for the unexpected." Some minutes later, when the man had regained his composure, he asked Nasser, "Why did you address me in English?" Nasser laughed. "Because Arabic," he replied, "is hardly a suitable language in which to express the need for calm."

In the 1930s Guido Nazzo, an Italian tenor, sang only once in New York. The sole review read: "Guido Nazzo: nazzo guido."

— Willard R. Espy,
Another Almanac of Words at Play

NAST, Thomas (1840–1902), *US cartoonist, born in Germany. He was particularly famous for his political cartoons in* Harper's Weekly.

1 Nast's greatest campaign was his war against corruption in New York politics during the 1870s. He pilloried the Tammany Hall machine in *Harper's* until "Boss" Tweed writhed. "We gotta stop them damned pictures," Tweed told his henchmen. "I don't care so much what the papers write about me — my constituents can't read. But they can see pictures."

{It was one of "them damned pictures" that stopped Tweed. After being sentenced to jail, he escaped in 1875 and made his way to Spain. While staying incognito at Vigo he was recognized from one of Nast's caricatures, arrested, and returned to the United States.}

୫୭ ଏ୫

NECKER, Suzanne (1739–94), *Swiss society leader; wife of Jacques Necker, finance minister to Louis XVI, and mother of Mme de Staël. Born Suzanne Curchod, she was courted in her youth by the historian Edward Gibbon.*

1 The Marquis de Chastellux was once invited to one of Mme Necker's dinner parties. Having arrived early, he was left alone in the drawing-room where he found a notebook under Mme Necker's chair. Idly leafing through the pages, he discovered that the book contained detailed notes for the dinner-table conversation that evening. He carefully replaced it under the chair and later, during the course of the meal, was amused to hear Mme Necker recite word for word everything she had written down in her notebook.

୫୭ ଏ୫

NELSON, Horatio, Viscount (1758–1805), *British admiral. At the outbreak of the Napole-*onic wars, Nelson was appointed to a command in the Mediterranean. He lost the sight in his right eye at Calvi (1794) and his right arm at Tenerife (1797). He totally crushed France's fleet in the battle of the Nile (1798). During an interlude at Naples he fell in love with Lady Emma Hamilton, wife of the British envoy, an affair that caused much scandal. Victorious again at Copenhagen (1801), he was created viscount. In 1805, after an eighteen-month blockade of Toulon, the French fleet broke through and were pursued by Nelson. At the ensuing battle of Trafalgar, in which the British were victorious, Nelson was mortally wounded.

1 Shortly after the loss of his right arm, Nelson was presented to King George III, who congratulated him upon his naval victories, then added prophetically, "But your country has a claim for a bit more of you."

2 When he tried to obtain compensation for his lost eye, Nelson was told that no money could be paid without a surgeon's certificate. Annoyed by this petty bureaucracy, since his wounds were well known, Nelson nevertheless obtained the necessary documentation. As a precaution, he asked the surgeon to make out a second certificate attesting to the obvious loss of his arm. He presented the eye certificate to the clerk, who paid out the appropriate sum, commenting on the smallness of the amount. "Oh, this is only for an eye," said Nelson. "In a few days I'll come back for an arm, and probably, in a little longer, for a leg." Later that week he returned to the office and solemnly handed over the second certificate.

3 After pursuing the French fleet around the Mediterranean for some weeks, Nelson caught up with it at Alexandria. As preparations were made for the battle, Nelson sat down for dinner with his officers. "Before this time tomorrow I shall have gained a peerage, or Westminster Abbey," he said to them as they went out to their various stations.

{On this occasion — the battle of the Nile — it was the peerage.}

4 In the middle of the battle of Copenhagen, after the Danish bombardment had continued unabated for three hours, Nelson's commander, Sir Hyde Parker, sent him the signal to "discontinue action." Clapping his telescope to his blind eye, Nelson said that he did not see the signal. When the officers around him insisted it was there, he merely reiterated, "I have only one eye — I have a right to be blind sometimes — I really do not see the signal!"

{Naval historians have pointed out that this was simply a piece of pantomime, as Sir Hyde Parker had sent Nelson a private message beforehand, saying that if such a signal were hoisted, he was to use his own discretion as to whether to obey it. This does not in any way detract from Nelson's courage and accurate appraisal of the situation, which led to a splendid victory.}

5 Sir William Hamilton, husband of Nelson's Emma, behaved with perfect generosity toward his wife's lover. When he died at an advanced age in 1803, he breathed his last in Emma's arms, holding Nelson by the hand. He left Nelson a favorite portrait of Emma, done in enamel, and the codicil containing the bequest ended with the words: "God bless him, and shame fall on those who do not say, Amen."

6 Before the battle of Trafalgar, Nelson on board HMS *Victory* discussed their chances with Thomas Masterman Hardy, his captain. Hardy said that, all things considered, he would think the capture of fourteen ships a glorious outcome. "I shall not be satisfied with anything less than twenty," replied Nelson. He then ordered the sending of his last signal: "ENGLAND EXPECTS EVERY MAN WILL DO HIS DUTY."

{This is the wording in Southey's *Life of Nelson;* the words are often quoted in the form: "ENGLAND EXPECTS EVERY MAN TO DO HIS DUTY." The final outcome of the battle was another triumph of Nelson's judgment: the English fleet took twenty French vessels captive.}

7 (Mortally wounded, Nelson lingered for several hours in fearful agony, but knew before he died that the English had gained a magnificent victory. Robert Southey reports his final moments, after he had given his last orders concerning the fleet.)

"Presently, calling Hardy back, he said to him in a low voice, 'Don't throw me over-

board'; and he desired that he might be buried by his parents, unless it should please the king to order otherwise. Then reverting to private feelings: 'Take care of my dear Lady Hamilton, Hardy; take care of poor Lady Hamilton. — Kiss me, Hardy.' Hardy knelt down and kissed his cheek; and Nelson said, 'Now I am satisfied. Thank God, I have done my duty.' Hardy stood over him in silence for a moment or two, then knelt again and kissed his forehead. 'Who is that?' said Nelson; and being informed, he replied, 'God bless you, Hardy.' And Hardy then left him — for ever."

NERO (AD 37–AD 68), *Roman emperor (AD 54–AD 68). Nero succeeded his uncle and adoptive father, Claudius, by excluding and then killing his cousin Britannicus. His mother, Agrippina, and his wife, Octavia, were among subsequent victims of his crazy tyranny. The first large-scale conspiracy (65) against him failed, but in 68 the revolt of military commanders caused Nero to flee from Rome and commit suicide.*

1 Agrippina was determined to secure the imperial throne for her son despite Claudius's plans to name Britannicus as his successor. She therefore fed the elderly emperor poisonous mushrooms, and he died in agony, without have made plain his wishes concerning the succession. Nero ascended the throne, gave Claudius a splendid funeral, and later deified him. He remarked that mushrooms were indeed the food of the gods, because by eating them Claudius had become divine.

{Imperial Rome's intricacies are famous. For Agrippina sinned against instead of sinning, see the anecdotes at her name.}

2 (Suetonius tells the story of the burning of Rome.)

"Pretending to be disgusted by the drab old buildings and narrow, winding streets of Rome, he brazenly set fire to the City; and though a group of ex-consuls caught his attendants, armed with oakum and blazing torches, trespassing on their property, they dared not interfere. He also coveted the sites of several granaries, solidly built in stone, near the Golden House [Nero's palace]; having knocked down their walls with siege-engines, he set the interiors ablaze. This terror lasted for six days and seven nights, causing many people to take shelter in the tombs. . . . Nero watched the conflagration from the Tower of Maecenas, enraptured by what he called 'the beauty of the flames'; then put on his tragedian's costume and sang *The Fall of Ilium* from beginning to end."

{Hence the phrase "fiddling while Rome burns." Modern historians exonerate Nero for starting this catastrophic blaze; he himself thought the Christians were the most likely incendiaries — after all, they believed that the end of the world would come with fire — and he persecuted them with much cruelty.}

3   Fleeing from Rome with his enemies hard on his heels, Nero took refuge in a villa a few miles out of the city. The four faithful servants who attended him insisted that he should commit suicide honorably, rather than fall into the hands of those who had seized power in Rome. Still obsessed with the greatness of his own gifts as an actor, poet, and singer, Nero watched the men preparing his funeral pyre and as he watched muttered through his tears, "*Qualis artifex pereo!*" (How great an artist dies here!)

ॐ ॐ

NERVAL, Gérard de (1808–55), *French poet, translator, and playwright. His early works gained him a considerable reputation. His later writings were influenced by mysticism and the occult. Suffering all his life from bouts of insanity, he finally hanged himself.*

1   Gérard de Nerval walked in the gardens of the Palais-Royal in Paris, leading a lobster on a pale blue ribbon. Asked why he did so, he replied that he preferred lobsters to dogs or cats because they could not bark at one, and besides, they knew the secrets of the sea.

{James Joyce mentions this, perhaps the most famous of Nerval's eccentricities, in *Stephen Hero*.}

2   For some time Gérard de Nerval had carried around with him an old apron string that, he maintained, was the Queen of Sheba's garter — or a corset-string belonging to Mme de Maintenon or Marguerite de Valois. In the small hours of the morning of January 26, 1855, he knocked on the door of a dosshouse

in a poor quarter of Paris. The concierge heard the knock but decided it was too cold to open up. When daylight dawned, the poet was discovered hanged from some iron railings with the Queen of Sheba's garter. As a final macabre touch, a pet raven was hovering nearby, repeating the only words it knew: "*J'ai soif!*" (I'm thirsty!)

ॐ ॐ

NESBIT, Evelyn (1884–1967), *US model and showgirl.*

1   In 1905 Evelyn Nesbit married millionaire Harry K. Thaw. The following year the couple were dining in a smart restaurant when Harry Thaw noticed his wife's former lover, architect Stanford White, at a nearby table. He walked over, pulled out a gun, and shot his rival three times in the face. Evelyn Thaw's reaction was memorable: "My, you are in a fix, Harry!"

{Thaw was later judged insane. *See* WILSON MIZNER 10 for one reaction to White's death.}

ॐ ॐ

NEWTON, Sir Isaac (1642–1727), *English physicist and mathematician. He discovered the law of gravitation and went on to formulate the laws of motion that underlie classical mechanics. He became Lucasian Professor of Mathematics at Cambridge (1669), and in this field his major contribution was the discovery of the calculus (an honor contested by Leibniz). The reflecting telescope was a product of his work on optics. His most important publications were* Principia mathematica *(1686–87) and* Optics *(1704).*

1   In an eighteen-month period during 1665 to 1666 the plague forced Newton to leave Cambridge and live in his mother's house at Woolsthorpe in Lincolnshire (a house that can still be seen and is preserved as a museum). One day he was sitting in the orchard there, pondering the question of the forces that keep the moon in its orbit, when the fall of an apple led him to wonder whether the force that pulled the apple toward the earth might be the same kind of force that held the moon in orbit round the earth. This train of thought led him eventually to the law of gravitation and its application to the motion of the heavenly bodies.

{Voltaire, who heard the anecdote from

Newton's stepniece Mrs. Conduitt, and the antiquarian William Stukeley are early sources for this story. If not wholly apocryphal, it is probably an embroidery of the truth. It is certainly a fact that during his stay at Woolsthorpe Newton achieved the insights that led to his greatest scientific work.}

2   Newton owned a pet dog called Diamond, which one day knocked over the candle on the scientist's desk and started a blaze that destroyed records of many years' research. Newton, viewing the destruction, said only, "O Diamond, Diamond, thou little knowest the damage thou hast done."

3   A woman, hearing that Newton was a famous astrologer, visited him to ask him to find out where she had lost her purse — somewhere between London Bridge and Shooters' Hill, she thought. Newton merely shook his head. But the woman was persistent, making as many as fourteen visits. Finally, to get rid of her, Newton donned an eccentric costume, chalked a circle around himself, and intoned, "Abracadabra! Go to the façade of Greenwich Hospital, third window on the south side. On the lawn in front of it I see a dwarfish devil bending over your purse." Away went the woman — and according to the story, that is where she actually found it.
   {This story is probably apocryphal, but it neatly illustrates the popular reputation of scientists in the seventeenth-century mind.}

4   An admirer asked Newton how he had come to make discoveries in astronomy that went far beyond anything achieved by anyone before him. "By always thinking about them," replied Newton simply.

5   Newton cut a hole in the bottom of an outside door to enable his beloved cat to go freely in and out of the house. When it had kittens, Newton cut a small hole next to the original one.
   {Probably a traditional joke, foisted on Newton.}

6   Newton once lived next door to a rather inquisitive widow, who was unaware of her neighbor's identity and renown. The lady was visited one day by a Fellow of the Royal Society of London, to whom she related the strange behavior of "the poor crazy gentleman" next door. "Every morning," she said, "when the sun shines so brightly that we are obliged to draw the window-blinds, he takes his seat in front of a tub of soap-suds and occupies himself for hours blowing bubbles through a common clay pipe and intently watches them until they burst." Following his hostess to the window, the visitor saw Newton at his work. Turning to the widow, he said, "The person you suppose to be a poor lunatic is none other than the great Sir Isaac Newton, studying the refraction of light upon thin plates — a phenomenon which is beautifully exhibited upon the surface of common soap bubbles."

7   "What is your opinion of the immortality of the soul?" asked an Italian lady of Newton. "Madam, I am an experimental philosopher," Newton answered.

8   Newton, Cambridge University's representative to Parliament in 1689, was not well adapted to life as a parliamentarian. Only on one occasion did he rise to his feet, and the House of Commons hushed in expectation of hearing the great man's maiden speech. Newton observed that there was a window open, which was causing a draft, asked that it be closed, and sat down.

9   One evening during the Anglo-Dutch wars Newton came into the hall at Trinity College, Cambridge, announcing to the Fellows that there had been a naval battle that day between the Dutch and the English, and that the English had got the worst of it. As Cambridge is a considerable distance from the sea and as it was the first the Fellows had heard of any battle, they were naturally skeptical; they asked him how he knew. Newton explained that he had been in his observatory and heard a great firing of cannon, such as could only be between two great fleets. The noise had become louder and louder, which suggested that the English ships were retreating toward the English coast. The following day a full report of the battle exactly bore out Newton's summary.

10   In 1696 Jean Bernoulli and G. W. Leibniz concocted two teasing problems they sent to the leading mathematicians in Europe. After

the problems had been in circulation for about six months, a friend communicated them to Newton, who, when he had finished his day's work at the Mint, came home and solved both. The next day he submitted his solutions to the Royal Society anonymously, as he did not like to be distracted from the business of the Mint by embroilment in scientific discussions. The anonymity did not, however, deceive Bernoulli. "I recognize the lion by his paw!" he exclaimed.

11 Newton invited a friend to dinner but then forgot the engagement. When the friend arrived, he found the scientist deep in meditation, so he sat down quietly and waited. In due course dinner was brought up — for one. Newton continued to be abstracted. The friend drew up a chair and, without disturbing his host, consumed the dinner. After he had finished, Newton came out of his reverie, looked with some bewilderment at the empty dishes, and said, "If it weren't for the proof before my eyes, I could have sworn that I have not yet dined."

12 To the very end of his life Newton's scientific curiosity was unquenched. According to one authority his (somewhat improbable) last words were: "I do not know what I may appear to the world. But to myself, I seem to have been only like a boy playing on the seashore, diverting myself in now and then finding a smoother pebble or a prettier shell than ordinary, whilst the great ocean of truth lay all undiscovered before me."

NIARCHOS, Stavros (1909–), *Greek shipping magnate.*

1 Niarchos had commissioned Salvador Dali to paint his portrait for a fee of $15,000. Growing restless during the first sitting, he left as soon as the face was sketched in and told Dali to finish the picture without him. Dali promptly painted in a naked body and raised the fee to $25,000. Undeterred by Niarchos's refusal to pay, he doubled the price and sold the painting to Aristotle Onassis, his client's greatest rival. Lunching with Onassis, Niarchos found the picture displayed on the dining-room wall. "All right, how much do you want?" he sighed. "Seventy-five thousand dol-

lars," said Onassis. Niarchos paid up and took the portrait home, where it was immediately consigned to the back of a closet.

NICHOLAS I (1796–1855), *czar of Russia (1825–55). Having crushed the Decembrist uprising, Nicholas ruled autocratically, extending military discipline and a secret police network throughout the state. His ambitions in the Balkans embroiled Russia in the Crimean War.*

1 One of the Decembrist conspirators condemned to be hanged was Kondraty Ryleyev. The rope broke. Ryleyev, bruised and battered, fell to the ground, got up, and said, "In Russia they do not know how to do anything properly, not even how to make a rope." Ordinarily an accident of this sort resulted in a pardon, so a messenger was sent to the Winter Palace to know the czar's pleasure. Nicholas asked, "What did he say?"

"Sire, he said that in Russia they do not even know how to make a rope properly."

"Well, let the contrary be proved," said the czar.

NICKLAUS, Jack William (1940–), *US golfer. Between 1959 and 1981 he won the US amateur championship (twice), the US Open (four times), the British Open (three times), the US Professional Golfers' Association championship (five times), and the Masters (five times), thus winning more major championships than any other player.*

1 Nicklaus dethroned Arnold Palmer as the reigning king of golf when he came from five strokes back to tie after 72 holes in the 1962 US Open, and then won the 18-hole playoff next day. Palmer noted, "Now that the big bear's out of the cage, everybody better run for cover." Nicklaus's comment was: "I'm hungry as a bear. But I'm gonna slim down and go for the gold." Slimmed down, he became known as "the Golden Bear."

NIJINSKY, Vaslav (1890–1950), *Russian ballet dancer and choreographer. Joining Diaghilev's Ballets Russes in Paris (1909), Nijinsky quickly created a legendary reputation as a dancer in such ballets as Le Spectre de la Rose.*

In 1919 his career was brought to a premature end by mental illness.

1 When Nijinsky choreographed *Le Sacre du Printemps (The Rite of Spring)* to Stravinsky's music, most critics loathed the ballet as a disturbing departure from the themes and conventions of the classical dance to which they were accustomed. In fact, one early critic gave it a title that quickly caught on: *Le Massacre du Printemps.*

2 Nijinsky and Diaghilev, lunching with Lady Juliet Duff, one of their influential admirers in London, were asked to sign her birthday book. After his signature Diaghilev wrote, "*L'ami des dieux*" (The friend of the gods). Nijinsky, more modestly and flatteringly, wrote, "*Le Spectre à la rose*" (The Spectre *to* the rose).

৵ ৬

NILSSON, Birgit Marta (1918–), *Swedish soprano celebrated for her Wagnerian interpretations.*

1 (Miss Nilsson appeared in *Turandot* with the tenor Franco Corelli on a Metropolitan Opera tour under the management of Rudolf Bing.)
"Mr. Corelli, after having been thoroughly outshouted in 'In questa reggia,' immediately left the stage (he had no more to sing, but he was supposed to be there), sulked in his dressing room, and declared that he would not come out again. At this point, Rudolf Bing is said to have entered the dressing room with an idea wonderfully calculated to appeal to the tenor's *amour propre*. 'In America, a man cannot retreat before a woman,' Mr. Bing is reported to have said. 'Continue! And in the last act, when the time comes to kiss her, *bite* her instead.' Mr. Corelli is said to have followed instructions, and Mr. Bing, according to the story, fled to New York, where Miss Nilsson telephoned him, saying, 'I cannot go on to Cleveland. I have rabies.'"

2 "Once she was negotiating a contract with Herbert von Karajan, at the time director of the Vienna Opera, when a string of pearls she was wearing broke and scattered all over the floor. Von Karajan and several others who were present got down on their knees to search for the pearls. 'We must find every one of them,' von Karajan said. 'These are the expensive pearls that Miss Nilsson buys with her high fees from the Metropolitan.' 'No,' Miss Nilsson replied, 'These are just imitation ones, which I buy with my low fees from the Vienna Opera.'"

3 Sir Rudolf Bing, who had often engaged Miss Nilsson, was asked if the star was difficult. "Not at all," he replied. "You put enough money in and glorious sound comes out."

4 Asked what was needed for a successful Isolde, Miss Nilsson replied, "Comfortable shoes."

5 As tickets for a New York concert by Birgit Nilsson were sold out many weeks in advance, the organizers cabled Miss Nilsson to ask if she would object to their selling some extra seats on the podium. She replied by return: "Sell everything, and please don't forget the space on the piano lid."

৵ ৬

NIVEN, David (1909–83), *British movie actor. A debonair and polished performer, he made more than eighty movies, including* The Prisoner of Zenda *(1937),* The Guns of Navarone *(1961), and* Paper Tiger *(1975). His autobiography,* The Moon's a Balloon *(1972), was also extremely successful.*

1 At the Academy Awards presentations in April 1974, the proceedings were interrupted by a streaker who dashed across the stage where Niven and other celebrities were sitting. "Just think," said Niven, "probably the only laugh that man will ever get is for stripping and showing his shortcomings."

2 Niven found it hard to come to terms with the aging process and, in later life, still thought of himself as a young man. He recalled a visit to the London boat show with an attractive girl many years his junior. "Suddenly this hideous couple hove into view; a foul old creature with a crone of a wife. To my horror, the man came over and introduced himself. 'Good heavens, Niven,' he said, 'I haven't seen you since you were at school.' When they'd gone, I could sense that the girl was looking at me warily. 'Were you really at school with him?' she asked. 'Absolutely,' I told her. 'He was the music master.'"

❧ ❦

NIVERNAIS, Louis Jules Mancini Mazarin, Duc de (1716–98), *French soldier and diplomat. He was ambassador to Rome (1748–52), Berlin (1756), and London (1762–63).*

1   The widowed Duc de Nivernais was in the habit of calling on the Comtesse de Rochefort, also a widow, every morning without fail. The regularity of these visits did not escape the notice of the duke's friends, who suggested to the widower that it would be far simpler for him to marry the lady, "Oh, yes, certainly," replied the duke, "but where would I then spend my evenings?"

❧ ❦

NIXON, Richard Milhous (1913–   ), *US politician; 37th president of the United States (1969–74). Elected to Congress in 1946, he was vice president under Eisenhower from 1953 to 1961. Defeated in the presidential election of 1960 and in the 1962 contest for governor of California, Nixon staged a political comeback in the mid-1960s. As president he established diplomatic relations between the United States and China and in 1973 ended US military participation in the Vietnam conflict. However, the nation was shocked when it became plain that Nixon, despite his strenuous denials, was involved in the coverup of the notorious break-in at Democratic headquarters in the Watergate apartment complex. He was forced to resign under threat of impeachment. His successor, Gerald Ford, at once granted him a free pardon.*

1   The first major attack on Nixon's integrity came in 1952 when there were some unexplained contributions from wealthy California businessmen to a fund upon which Nixon had apparently been drawing for his own use. Eisenhower wanted to drop Nixon as his running mate on the Republican ticket, but Nixon appeared on television to defend himself in what became known as the Checkers speech. Having dwelt at length on his humble origins and his advancement in life through his own efforts,

Nixon admitted that he had accepted a gift after the nomination — namely, a spaniel puppy, which his daughter had christened Checkers. He told how his kids loved the dog and how, whatever anyone said, the family was going to keep it. Thousands of telegrams of support poured into Republican headquarters, and Nixon remained on the Republican ticket, though cynical observers described the Checkers speech as "a slick production."

2   At a Gridiron Club dinner in Washington Truman and Nixon were guests. That year the theme of the annual event was Love. When Nixon rose to give a short speech, he mentioned that during the predinner cocktail hour, he had been asked to pass a bourbon-and-water to President Truman. This he presumably did. "When Harry Truman," he said, "will accept a drink from the hand of Richard Nixon without having someone else taste it first — that's Love."

3   In one of the televised debates between presidential candidates Nixon and Kennedy in 1960, Nixon demanded that Kennedy disown the earthy language used by ex-President Truman, a vigorous Kennedy supporter, and applauded the way in which Eisenhower had restored "the dignity of the office." Kennedy just laughed. A few minutes after the ending of the debate, Nixon raged to the newsmen waiting for comments, "That fucking bastard, he wasn't supposed to be using notes!"

4   Meeting Kennedy's aide Ted Sorenson shortly after Kennedy's inaugural address, Nixon remarked that there were things in the speech that he would have liked to have said. "Do you mean the part about 'Ask not what your country can do for you . . . ?'" said Sorenson. "No," replied Nixon, "the part beginning 'I do solemnly swear. . . .'"

5   On October 28, 1970, the presidential motorcade through St. Petersburg, Florida, came to an abrupt halt when the policeman at the head of the procession was hit by a truck. Nixon rushed to the scene and offered his sympathies to the injured policeman, Don Leadbeter. By way of reply, Leadbeter apologized for holding up the motorcade. There was an awkward silence as the president searched for

something else to say. He finally blurted out, "Do you like the work?"

6   In Paris for the funeral of French president Georges Pompidou in 1974, Nixon remarked: "This is a great day for France."

7   Signing copies of his book *Six Crises,* at a local bookstore, Nixon asked each customer to what name he should address the inscription. One gentleman replied with a grin: "You've just met your seventh crisis. My name is Stanislaus Wojechzleschki."

8   "President Nixon was shaking hands and talking with members of a crowd at an airport when a little girl shouted to him, 'How is Smokey the Bear?' referring to the famous firefighting symbol who was then residing at the Washington Zoo. Nixon smiled at the girl and turned away, but she kept waving and asking her question. Unable to make out her words, Nixon sought help from his aide-de-camp, Steve Bull. Bull whispered, 'Smokey the Bear, Washington National Zoo.' Nixon walked over to the little girl, shook her hand and said, 'How do you do, Miss Bear?'"

9   Questioned by the British television interviewer David Frost about his approval of a plan of action that entailed such criminal ingredients as burglary and the opening of other people's mail, Nixon replied, "Well, when the president does it, that means it is not illegal."

ॐ ॐ

NOAILLES, Anna-Elisabeth, Comtesse de (1876–1933), *French poet and novelist.*

1   "Anna de Noailles (as Foujita puts the finishing touches to his portrait of her): 'But you haven't made my eyes big enough. My eyes have been compared to broad flowing rivers. And what have you done to my forehead? Make it broader and higher. I'm a poet — what do you suppose I do my thinking with? This portrait has got to be just right — it will be all anyone knows of how I look, after I'm dead. After all, my friend, one of these days I *will* be dead.' Foujita (between clenched teeth): 'Yes.'"

ॐ ॐ

NORBURY, John Toler, 1st Earl of (1745–1831), *Irish lawyer; chief justice of the Court of Common Pleas in Ireland (1800–27). A staunch supporter of the union of England and Ireland and of the Protestant ascendancy, Norbury was frequently accused of partiality against the Roman Catholics. He was much disliked for his sarcasm and buffoonery on the bench, although in private life he seems to have been just and kindly.*

1   Norbury was riding with another Irish lawyer, John Parsons, in Parson's carriage. Their route took them past a gibbet with a corpse still hanging on it. The melancholy sight prompted Lord Norbury to remark, "Ah, Parson, if we all had our deserts, where would you be?"
"Alone in my carriage," was the response.

2   A Dublin attorney having died in poverty, his legal colleagues set up a subscription to pay for his funeral. Lord Norbury was asked to contribute. On inquiring what sum would be appropriate, he was told that no one else had subscribed more than a shilling. "A shilling!" exclaimed the judge, reaching into his pocket. "A shilling to bury an attorney? Why, here's a guinea! Bury one and twenty of the scoundrels."
{Slight variants of this story, involving other personages, abound. *See* ALEXANDRE DUMAS *(père)* 5.}

3   Even as he lay dying, Lord Norbury could not resist a jest. Realizing that his end was imminent, he sent his valet around to another aged peer who was also on his deathbed. "James," he said, "present my compliments to Lord Erne and tell him it will be a dead heat between us."

ॐ ॐ

NORDEN, Denis (1922–), *British broadcaster and scriptwriter. In collaboration with Frank Muir, he has written scripts for numerous comedy programs on radio and television and frequently appears on panel games.*

1   During the course of conversation with Sir Peter Scott, famous ornithologist and honorary director of the Wildfowl Trust, Norden unthinkingly let slip the casual remark, ". . . doing it that way, you can kill two birds with one stone."

NORTH, Frederick, Lord (1732–92), *British statesman; prime minister (1770–82). His financial measures before becoming prime minister led to confrontation with the American colonists; hence he was held largely responsible for the outbreak of the American Revolution. British failures in the conflict were also blamed on him and forced his resignation.*

1   When North was visiting Algiers, he asked the dey if he might see the women of his harem. The dey's reaction was not at all what might have been expected of a jealous oriental potentate: "He is so ugly, let him see them all."

2   Sir Joseph Mawbey rose during a parliamentary sitting and roundly attacked Lord North for his part in the revolt of the American colonists. He asserted that it was entirely due to North's mismanagement that so much blood had been spilled and so many resources wasted in an unnecessary war. Lord North listened to the onslaught with his eyes shut. "Furthermore," continued Sir Joseph, "he is so little affected by consciousness of his misdeeds that he is even now asleep." Lord North stirred in his seat and opened his eyes. "I wish to God, Mr. Speaker, I was asleep," he remarked, and closed his eyes again.

3   After one of his frequent quarrels with his father, the Prince of Wales (later King George IV) asked Lord North to act as mediator and bring about a reconciliation. Having made the prince's peace with George III, Lord North reported his success to the prince, adding a little homily for the occasion: "Now, my dear prince, do in future conduct yourself differently — do so for God's sake, do so for your own sake, do so for your excellent father's sake, do so for the sake of that good-natured man Lord North, and don't oblige him again to tell your good father so many lies as that good-natured man has been obliged to tell him this morning."

4   In his old age Lord North became blind. He was visited by a friend who had likewise lost his sight. "Colonel, no one will suspect us of insincerity if we say we should be overjoyed to see each other," said the old man in greeting his friend.

NORTHCLIFFE, Alfred Charles William Harmsworth, Viscount (1865–1922), *British newspaper publisher and politician. He founded the* Daily Mail *(1896) and the* Daily Mirror *(1903); in 1908 he acquired* The Times.

1   Northcliffe was notorious for his arbitrary dismissal of journalists. He once singled out a certain employee and asked him if he was happy in his work. "Yes, sir," replied the journalist. "Then you're dismissed," snapped Northcliffe. "I don't want anyone here to be content on five pounds a week."

NORTHCOTE, James (1746–1831), *British artist specializing in portraits and historical paintings.*

1   Sitting for Northcote, the Duke of Clarence (afterward William IV) asked if the artist knew his brother, the Prince Regent. Northcote said he did not, and the duke was surprised: "Why, my brother says he knows you."
   "That's only his brag," replied Northcote.

NORTON, Fletcher, 1st Baron Grantley (1716–89), *British lawyer. Unscrupulous and abrasive in manner, Norton features in cartoons of the period concerning the many celebrated cases in which he appeared as "Sir Bull-Face Double-Fee."*

1   Norton was once pleading before Lord Mansfield on the subject of manorial rights. During the course of his speech, he made the unfortunate remark, "My lord, I can illustrate the point in an instant in my own person; I myself have two little manors —." Lord Mansfield, pouncing with glee upon the unintentional pun, interrupted, "We all know it, Sir Fletcher."

NOYES, John Humphrey (1811–86), *US social reformer; founder of the communistic Oneida Community in 1847.*

1   Noyes envisioned a society in which there was no money, no private property, food and shelter for all, and thus no need for competition. A visitor to the community is said to have asked her guide the nature of the fragrance that

she smelt in "the Honorable John's" house. "The odor of crushed selfishness, maybe," was the reply.

❧ ❦

NUFFIELD, William Richard Morris, 1st Viscount (1877–1963), *British car manufacturer and philanthropist. He set up the Morris car factory, which eventually became part of the nationalized motor group, British Leyland. Nuffield founded Nuffield College, Oxford, and his charitable foundation has made many important gifts.*

1   When Lord Nuffield was planning the foundation of a college at Oxford, he was invited to dine one night at Magdalen College. Leaving after dinner, he stopped to collect his hat at the porter's lodge. It was produced so rapidly that Nuffield asked doubtfully how the porter knew it was his. "I don't, my lord," answered the porter, "but it's the one you came with."

NURMI, Paavo (1897–1973), *Finnish athlete. Known as the Flying Finn, he is judged by many the greatest long-distance runner of all time.*

1   During the 1924 Olympics in Paris, Nurmi ran seven races in six days. Adrian Pavlen, former president of the IAAF and himself an Olympic long-distance runner, recalls the day in which Nurmi won the 1,500-meter event, then seventy-five minutes later won the 5,000. That night Pavlen and some friends were on a bus going from Colombes, the Olympic village, to a party in Paris. The distance was about six miles. "We looked out the window and there was Nurmi *walking* to Paris, even though he had competed in the 1,500 and 5,000 a few hours earlier."

{In his later years Nurmi suffered from thrombosis in the brain, a heart attack, partial paralysis on his left side, and blindness in his left eye. Almost to the day he died he walked eight miles a day.}

O

OATES, Lawrence Edward Grace (1880–1912), *British explorer and member of Robert Falcon Scott's ill-fated expedition to the South Pole.*

1 On their return journey from the Pole, Scott's party was beset by fearful blizzards. Oates suffered badly from frostbitten feet, which were turning gangrenous. He begged to be left behind so as not to slow up the others. His companions would not hear of it, and they struggled on for another day. The following morning the blizzard was still raging. Oates said, "I am just going outside and may be some time." He then walked out of the tent and vanished forever into the storm.

{Oates's sacrifice was in vain because Scott and the rest of the party died before reaching their base camp. The story of Oates's heroism became known only through Scott's diaries, found some months later in his tent by a search party. A cross, placed near the spot where Oates walked out into the blizzard, commemorates him as "a very gallant gentleman."}

OFFENBACH, Jacques (1819–80), *French composer born in Cologne. Born Jacob Eberst, he adopted the name Offenbach after the town in which his father lived. He wrote a number of popular operettas, such as* La Belle Hélène *(1864) and the grand opera* Tales of Hoffman *(produced posthumously 1881).*

1 Offenbach dismissed his valet, but gave the man such an excellent reference that a friend wondered why he should have let him go. "Oh, he's a good fellow," said Offenbach, "but he won't do for a composer. He beats my clothes outside my door every morning and his tempo is nonexistent."

O'HARA, John [Henry] (1905–70), *US novelist, short-story writer, and playwright. His novels include* Appointment in Samarra *(1934) and* Butterfield 8. *He had great admiration for the refined manners of the Ivy League.*

1 Pooling their money during the Spanish Civil War, Ernest Hemingway, James Lardner, and Vincent Sheean found they had some to spare. There followed a discussion as to how the surplus should be spent. Suggested Hemingway: "Let's take the bloody money and start a bloody fund to send John O'Hara to Yale."

{The anecdote was circulated in several versions.}

2 (Someone once said of O'Hara that he was master of the fancied slight.)

Robert Benchley and his daughter-in-law Marjorie, catching sight of O'Hara at the restaurant "21," called him over to their table. Marjorie said, "John, we've just been seeing *Pal Joey* again, and, do you know, I like it even better than I did the first time."

"What was the matter with it the first time?" said O'Hara.

OLDFIELD, Anne (1683–1730), *British actress.*

1 Mrs. Oldfield was a passenger on a ferry that appeared in imminent danger of capsizing. When the other passengers broke into lamentations at what seemed to be their approaching doom, Mrs. Oldfield rebuked them with great dignity. Their deaths would be merely a matter for private grief, but, she reminded them, "I am a public concern."

OLIVIER, Laurence [Kerr], **Baron** (1907–   ), *British actor, who made his name in Noël Cow-*

ard's Private Lives *(1930) and joined the Old Vic in 1937, where he played many Shakespearean roles. He played in and directed the highly successful films* Henry V *(1944),* Hamlet *(1948), and* Richard III *(1956). Regarded as one of the world's greatest character actors, he was director of the British National Theatre Company from 1961 to 1973; part of the National Theatre has been named the Olivier Theatre in his honor. He was made a life peer in 1970.*

1 At the tender age of ten, Olivier gave a highly acclaimed performance as Brutus in a school production of *Julius Caesar.* The actress Ellen Terry saw the play and declared: "The boy who plays Brutus is *already* a great actor." These words of praise were relayed to the young Olivier. "Who is Ellen Terry?" he asked.

2 On a visit to Jamaica as the guest of Noël Coward, Sir Laurence Olivier accompanied Coward to a mountaintop to see the playwright's favorite view. Looking out at the terraces of jungle sprawled beneath him, Olivier had but one comment: "It looks like rows and rows of empty seats."

৯ ৶

'OMAR *(died AD 664), Muslim caliph during whose caliphate (634–644) Arab rule was extended over what is now Syria, Iraq, Iran, and Egypt.*

1 'Omar's general 'Amr Ibn Al-as conquered Egypt in 640. In 642, when the city of Alexandria surrendered to him, 'Amr sent to 'Omar for instructions about how to deal with its great library, which contained hundreds of thousands of texts from classical antiquity. 'Omar replied, "If the writings of the Greeks agree with the Koran they are superfluous and need not be preserved; if they disagree they are pernicious, and ought not to be preserved." 'Amr therefore ordered the irreplaceable manuscripts to be used to fuel the furnaces for the public baths. It is said that they kept the furnaces going for six months.

{This story, told on the authority of the thirteenth-century Syrian churchman Bar-Hebraeus (Abulfaraj), is generally agreed to be a fabrication, but 'Omar's reported reply epitomizes the rationale of book-burners everywhere at any time.}

৯ ৶

ONASSIS, Aristotle [Socrates] *(1906–75), Greek shipping magnate. He lived on a yacht called* Christina, *where he entertained, among others, Sir Winston Churchill and Maria Callas, the opera singer, with whom he had a long and tempestuous relationship. In 1968 he married the widowed Jacqueline Kennedy. His empire included about one hundred companies and a merchant fleet of fifty-five ships, as well as numerous holdings in banks, shipyards, and hotels.*

1 On the *Christina* Onassis had installed a luxurious private bathroom adjoining his office. The door was a one-way mirror, which enabled him to observe unsuspecting visitors from the privacy of the bathroom. During a business meeting one afternoon Onassis excused himself and went to the bathroom. Comfortably enthroned, he looked up at the door and was horrified to see his own reflection staring back at him. A workman making minor repairs to the door earlier in the day had replaced the mirror the wrong way around.

৯ ৶

O'NEAL, Tatum *(1963–   ), US actress.*

1 When fourteen-year-old Tatum O'Neal was making the film *International Velvet,* a school inspector came to make sure that she was not falling behind in her studies. Noting that her math was not very good, he asked whether that did not bother her. The child star was unconcerned: "Oh, no, I'll have an accountant."

৯ ৶

O'NEILL, Eugene *(1888–1953), US dramatist. Brought up in the theater by his actor father, an attack of tuberculosis in 1913 turned him toward writing plays. His first full-length play,* Beyond the Horizon *(1920), won a Pulitzer prize.* Anna Christie *(1922) and* Mourning Becomes Electra *(1931) were further successes. In 1936 he was awarded the Nobel Prize for literature. Ill health and alcoholism dogged his later years, which nonetheless saw the creation of some of his greatest works, such as* The

Iceman Cometh *(1946) and the autobiographical* Long Day's Journey into Night *(written in 1940–41, but not performed until 1956).*

1 Working as a news reporter on the *New London Telegraph,* O'Neill sometimes found it difficult to deliver his stories in a form acceptable to his editor. One contribution came back with the following note: "This is a lovely story, but would you mind finding out the name of the gentleman who carved the lady and whether the dame is his wife or daughter or who? And phone the hospital for a hint as to whether she is dead or discharged or what? Then put the facts into a hundred and fifty words and send this literary batik to the picture framers."

2 O'Neill always strongly objected to cutting any of his plays. When director and playwright Russel Crouse asked him to shorten the script of *Ah, Wilderness!* he was very reluctant. The following day he telephoned Crouse to tell him that he had cut fifteen minutes. Surprised and pleased, Crouse said, "I'll be right over to get the changes."

"Oh, there aren't any changes to the text," O'Neill explained, "but you know we have been playing this thing in four acts. I've decided to cut out the third intermission."

ô⊷ ⊷ô

OPPENHEIMER, J. Robert (1904–67), *US physicist, director of the Institute for Advanced Studies in Princeton, New Jersey, from 1947 to 1966. He was in charge of the development of the atomic bomb at the end of World War II, and from 1945 to 1952 held a key position in US atomic policy. His misgivings about the hydrogen bomb caused him to fall foul of a McCarthyite witch-hunt (1953), and he was labeled a security risk. Thereafter he devoted himself mainly to considering the ethics of science in society.*

1 Physicist James Franck was professor of Göttingen University when the twenty-three-year-old Oppenheimer was being examined for his doctorate. On emerging from the oral examination, Franck remarked, "I got out of there just in time. He was beginning to ask *me* questions."

2 As Oppenheimer watched the first atomic bomb explode in a test at Alamogordo, New Mexico, on July 16, 1945, a passage from the Hindu scripture, the *Bhagavad Gita,* came into his mind: "If the radiance of a thousand suns were to burst into the sky, that would be like the splendor of the Mighty One." Then, as the enormous mushroom cloud darkened the sky, another sentence from the same source came to him: "I am become Death, the shatterer of worlds."

3 After his contract with the Atomic Energy Commission was canceled on security grounds, Oppenheimer continued his work at Princeton. In April 1962 he was invited to a White House dinner by President John F. Kennedy. Then in December 1963 he was awarded the Enrico Fermi Award of the Atomic Energy Commission. Accepting this sign of official forgiveness from Lyndon B. Johnson, Oppenheimer said, "I think it is just possible, Mr. President, that it may have taken some charity and some courage for you to make this award today."

ô⊷ ⊷ô

ORSAY, Alfred-Guillaume-Gabriel, Count d' (1801–52), *French dandy, who spent many years in England. He and his stepmother-in-law, Marguerite, Countess of Blessington, headed one of the most glittering of London's coteries in the 1830s and 1840s until, encumbered by debt, they had to flee to France, where they both died.*

1 After 1841 Count d'Orsay was beset by fear of arrest for debt. The curious laws of the time, however, put him in no danger of being served with a writ or arrested between sunset and sunrise. During daylight hours, visitors to his house had to establish their identity before they were allowed in, and two mastiffs prowled in the garden. Despite these precautions an enterprising bailiff, disguised as an errand boy, managed to gain admittance late one afternoon. He surprised the count in his dressing room and revealed his true identity. D'Orsay, who was halfway through his toilet, did not lose his head. He asked the officer if he might finish dressing and courteously bade him take a chair. For over an hour the man sat and watched, fascinated, oblivious to the rapidly approaching sunset. The count, however, was carefully monitoring the progress of the sun. As it slipped below the horizon, he gently reminded the officer that now his authority no longer ran and sent for a servant to show him out.

2 Seated at dinner next to the willful Lady Holland, Count d'Orsay found her ladyship determined to monopolize his attention; whenever it seemed to wander, she would reclaim it by dropping something, which, of course, the count had to retrieve for her. First her napkin fell to the floor, then a spoon, then her ladyship's fan. Finally the count lost patience and turning to the footman behind his chair, told him to place his plates and cutlery on the floor. "I shall finish my dinner there," he announced. "It will be so much more convenient for my Lady Holland."

જં ન્જ

OSCAR II (1829–1907), *king of Sweden (1872–1907) and Norway (1872–1905).*

1 Visiting a village school one day, the king asked the pupils to name the greatest kings of Sweden. The answers were unanimous: Gustavus Vasa, Gustavus Adolphus, Charles XII. Then the teacher leaned over to one little boy and whispered something in his ear. "And King Oscar," volunteered the child. "Really? And what has King Oscar done that's so remarkable?" asked the king. "I — I — I don't know," stammered the unhappy child. "That's all right, my boy," said the king. "Neither do I."

જં ન્જ

O'TOOLE, Peter (1932–), *British film actor, who rose rapidly to stardom in such films as* Lawrence of Arabia *(1962),* Becket *(1964), and* The Lion in Winter *(1968).*

1 As a little boy Peter O'Toole attended a school run by nuns. One day in a drawing class the children had been asked to draw a horse. Peter finished his and was sitting idle. A nun suggested that he make some additions — a saddle, maybe. The child got busy and after a time the nun returned. When she saw what he had drawn, she went crimson and started slapping him; he had added a penis to the horse and shown it urinating. As the nun buffeted him, the bewildered child protested, "But I was only drawing what I saw."

"Walter O'Keefe, an actor in the US in the 1930s, was once invited to address a medical convention. He found on arrival at the banquet that the convention was in fact one of chiropodists.

"O'Keefe had hardly tucked his napkin into his collar when a fanfare rang through the hall and the chiropodists leaped to attention. A spotlight roved across the heads of the multitude and picked up, on a wall bracket, Old Glory rippling in the breeze of an electric fan. After a properly patriotic salute, O'Keefe and the chiropodists again attacked their meal, an interval largely given over to a long, unhappy account by the chairman of his troubles in organizing the luncheon. Just as the ladyfingers and bombe glacée were arriving a second fanfare brought everyone up again.

"The spotlight settled on the swinging doors to the kitchen where stood a chef in a tall hat and apron. He bowed, flourished to his staff inside, and a huge foot sculptured out of ice rolled into view on a tea wagon. Amid thunderous applause, it made a slow, majestic circuit of the tables. As it drew abreast the speaker's table, the already irascible chairman turned a rich mulberry.

"'God damn it,' he snarled into O'Keefe's ear, 'they've gone and dropped the metatarsal arch!'"

—S. J. Perelman,
"Two Years down the Drain," in
'47, The Magazine of the Year

2 As a young actor Peter O'Toole landed a bit part as a Georgian peasant in a Chekhov play. All he had to do was to come on stage, announce, "Dr. Ostroff, the horses are ready," and exit. Determined to obtain what mileage he could out of this unpromising role, O'Toole conceived of the peasant as a youthful Stalin: he made himself up to look like Stalin, practiced a slight limp like Stalin's, and rehearsed his line to indicate his furious resentment against his social betters. The first-night audience was duly aroused by the entry of this ominous figure. Concentrating intensely, O'Toole

made his announcement: "Dr. Horsey, the os-troffs are ready."

❦

OTTO (1865–1900), *archduke of Austria, father of Emperor Charles I.*

1 The archduke submitted to a medical examination by a renowned Viennese physician. The latter made careful, exhaustive inquiries about his patient's symptoms, pains, and so forth. These insistent questions irritated the archduke and he was frank enough to say so. The doctor replied, "Your Highness, I suggest the next time you ask for a veterinarian. He cures without asking any questions."

❦

OUIDA [Marie Louise de la Ramée] (1839–1908), *British novelist. Her pseudonym was based on a childish mispronunciation of "Louise." The reception of her popular novels of military and fashionable society was helped by the attacks and parodies they evoked. Her most lasting success was* Under Two Flags *(1867).*

1 Ouida, who never suffered from false modesty, enjoyed the chagrin of "serious" writers whose success was a fraction of her own. Once when Oscar Wilde asked her the secret of her popularity, she confided, "I am the only woman who knows how two dukes talk when they are alone."

{She didn't, of course, and one of the pleasures readers found in her novels was spotting the ridiculous blunders she made when describing masculine conversation and pursuits. The most famous of these, "All rowed fast, but none so fast as stroke," comes, however, not from one of her books but from a parody by Desmond Coke.}

❦

OWEN, Robert (1771–1858), *Welsh manufacturer and social reformer, founder in 1825 of the New Harmony, Indiana, utopian community.*

1 There are many heart-breaking records of nineteenth-century child labor in the coal mines of England. The philanthropist Owen once talked to a twelve-year-old breaker boy, coal-black, weary from digging shale from broken coal. "Do you know God?" asked Owen. Replied the boy, "No. He must work in some other mine."

PACHMANN, Vladimir de (1848–1933), *Russian pianist. He excelled as a performer of Chopin; his eccentric and entertaining manners on the platform made him highly popular with audiences.*

1 Pachmann's eccentricities were not confined to his own stage appearances. During a concert by Leopold Godowsky, Pachmann once rushed onto the stage saying, "No, no, Leopold, you moost play it like *so.*" He then gave a demonstration to the delighted audience as Godowsky sat by, crimson-faced. He explained that he would not have bothered for just any old player. "But Godowsky is *ze zecond* greatest liffing pianist," he announced.

2 During a London recital at which he played Chopin's *Minute* Waltz Pachmann adopted a curious hunched position, crouching over the keyboard so that no one could see his hands. Feeling the audience was owed some explanation, he said, "Vy I do zis? I vill tell. I see in ze owdience *mein alte freund* Moriz Rosenthal, and I do not vish him to copy my fingering."

3 One of de Pachmann's favorite tricks before a recital was to play about with the piano stool, adjusting and readjusting it, until the audience became desperate. Then he would rush into the wings to fetch a large book, place it on the seat, and try that. He would indicate that all was still not satisfactory and would tear one page from the book and try it again. Finally, if the audience was lucky, he would begin.

❧ ❧

PADEREWSKI, Ignace Jan (1860–1941), *Polish pianist, composer, and statesman. Paderewski was renowned for the virtuosity of his playing. When World War I broke out, he dedicated himself to the service of his country, cam-paigning abroad for support for a free and united Poland. He became prime minister of Poland (1919), but, failing to bring about national unity, resigned.*

1 When Paderewski played before Queen Victoria, he won her enthusiastic approval. "Mr. Paderewski," she exclaimed, "you are a genius." Paderewski, who liked to allude to the number of hours he spent practicing every day, shook his head, "Perhaps, Your Majesty, but before that I was a drudge."

2 Paderewski's enormous reputation was not taken as seriously by fellow pianists as by the adoring public. Moriz Rosenthal went to hear Paderewski play in London and is reported to have said after the concert, "He plays well, I suppose, but he's no Paderewski."

3 A young American student visiting the Beethoven museum in Bonn was fascinated by the piano on which Beethoven had composed some of his greatest works. She asked the museum guard if she could play a few bars on it; she accompanied the request with a lavish tip, and the man agreed. The girl sat down at the piano and tinkled out the opening of the *Moonlight* Sonata. As she was leaving, she said to the guard, "I suppose all the great pianists who come here want to play on that piano." The guard shook his head; "Well, Paderewski was here a few years ago and he said he wasn't worthy to touch it."

4 Paderewski had been asked to play for the dinner guests of a certain English duchess. Somewhat taken aback by the size of the fee demanded by the pianist, the duchess decided not to invite him for the meal itself and wrote: "Dear Maestro, accept my regrets for not inviting you to dinner. As a *professional* artist you

will be more at ease in a nice room where you can rest before the concert." Paderewski promptly replied: "Dear Duchess, thank you for your letter. As you so kindly inform me that I am not obliged to be present at your dinner, I shall be satisfied with half of my fee."

See also FRITZ KREISLER 2.

5 Paderewski attended the 1919 Paris Peace Conference as the new premier of Poland. The French premier, Georges Clemenceau, was introduced to the great musician. "Are you a cousin of the famous pianist Paderewski?" he asked mischievously. "I *am* the famous pianist," replied Paderewski. "And you have become prime minister?" exclaimed Clemenceau. "What a comedown!"

6 The pianists Moriz Rosenthal and Abram Chasins attended one of Paderewski's farewell appearances. Long past his prime as a player, Paderewski turned in a dismal performance. Chasins observed sadly, "The things that man has forgotten!"

"What he forgets isn't so bad," retorted Rosenthal. "It's what he *remembers!*"

৯৶ ৶৫

PAIGE, Leroy Robert ["Satchel"] (1904–82), *US baseball player, one of the greatest of all pitchers. A prominent figure in Negro baseball in the 1920s, he later played for the Cleveland Indians (1948–51) and the St. Louis Browns.*

1 "Paige worked briefly as a coach for the now-defunct Tulsa Oilers in 1976 and every night youngsters trooped to him for autographs. He gave them a small, white business card and said, 'Look on the back. That's where my secret is.' The little leaguers turned over the card and read Satchel Paige's 'Six Rules for a Happy Life':

" '1. Avoid fried meats which angry up the blood.

" '2. If your stomach disputes you, lie down and pacify it with cool thoughts.

" '3. Keep the juices flowing by jangling around gently as you move.

" '4. Go very light on vices such as carrying on in society. The social ramble ain't restful.

" '5. Avoid running at all times.

" '6. Don't look back. Something may be gaining on you.' "

৯৶ ৶৫

"Sir William Petty, 17th-century English political economist, had a boy (that is, a young servant) that whistled incomparably well. He after wayted on a Lady, a widowe, of good fortune. Every night this boy was to whistle his Lady asleepe. At last she could hold out no longer, but bids her chamber-mayd withdraw: bids him come to bed, setts him to worke, and marries him the next day."

— *Aubrey's Brief Lives*

PAINE, Thomas (1737–1809), *British political theorist and writer. His pamphlet* Common Sense *(1776) was instrumental in justifying the American Revolution. When his* Rights of Man *(1791–92) appeared in support of the French Revolution, he was charged with treason and fled to France. He was elected to the French Convention, imprisoned by Robespierre, and escaped the guillotine only by chance. Believing that the Americans had deserted him when he was in danger in France, Paine wrote a bitter attack on General Washington. He eventually emigrated to the United States (1802), where he found himself unpopular. He died in New York.*

1 Benjamin Franklin said to Paine, "Where liberty is, there is my country." Paine answered, "Where liberty is not, there is mine."

2 When Paine was traveling through Baltimore, he was accosted by a Swedenborgian minister who had recognized him as the author of *The Age of Reason*. The deistic thesis expounded by that book had led to a large number of answers from divines of various persuasions, and the minister was clearly anxious to present the Swedenborgian viewpoint. Having introduced himself, he began, "I am minister of the New Jerusalem Church here, and we explain the true meaning of the Scripture. The key had been lost above four thousand years, but we have found it."

"It must have been very rusty," said Paine coolly.

৯৶ ৶৫

PALEWSKI, Gaston (died 1984), *French statesman, de Gaulle's chef de cabinet (Chief* *of Staff), once the lover of Nancy Mitford, in whose novels he occasionally makes a lightly disguised appearance.*

1 Noted for his amatory enterprise, Palewski, offering to drive a girl home from a party, met with the polite response, "Thank you, but I'm too tired; I think I'll walk."

ह्ल ह्ह

PALEY, William (1743–1805), *British clergyman. He wrote several books on religion, most notably* Evidences of Christianity *(1794).*

1 Appointed archdeacon of Carlisle, Paley made no secret of his feeling that his position entitled him to lord it over the lesser clergy. Feeling a draft on his back during a diocesan dinner, he summoned a footman and instructed him, "Close the window behind me and open one behind one of the curates."

ह्ल ह्ह

PALMERSTON, Henry John Temple, 3d Viscount (1784–1865), *British statesman; prime minister (1855–58, 1859–65). He entered Parliament as a Tory, but subsequently joined the Whigs. Three times foreign secretary (1830–34, 1835–41, 1846–51), he was influential in shaping Britain's strongly nationalistic policy in foreign affairs.*

1 When Palmerston was a young man, the Duke of Wellington made an appointment with him for half past seven in the morning. Someone expressed doubt that Palmerston, who kept late hours, would be able to keep the appointment. "Of course I shall," he retorted. "It's perfectly easy: I shall keep it the last thing before I go to bed."

2 Standing with Palmerston at a military review on a particularly hot day, the queen watched a company of perspiring volunteers doubling past her. Their proximity caused her to put her handkerchief to her nose. She remarked to Palmerston, "Don't you think there is rather a . . . ?"

"Oh, that's what we call *esprit de corps,* ma'am," he replied.

3 A certain Frenchman, eager to flatter the patriotic Lord Palmerston, once remarked, "If I were not a Frenchman, I should wish to be an

Englishman." Palmerston was unimpressed. "If I were not an Englishman," he replied, "I should wish to be an Englishman."

4 Palmerston's physician broke the news to the elderly statesman that he was going to die. "Die, my dear doctor?" Palmerston is said to have exclaimed. "That's the last thing I shall do!"

ह्ल ह्ह

PARK, Mungo (1771–1806), *Scottish explorer of Africa. He described his first expedition in* Travels in the Interior Districts of Africa *(1799); on his second expedition he was drowned during an attack by natives.*

1 While exploring a particularly wild and uncultivated region of Africa, Park unexpectedly came across a gibbet. "The sight of it," he later remarked, "gave me infinite pleasure, as it proved that I was in a civilized society."

ह्ल ह्ह

PARKER, Dorothy (1893–1967), *US short-story writer, theater critic, doyenne of minor light verse, and wit.*

1 While a book reviewer for *The New Yorker,* Dorothy Parker went on her honeymoon. Her editor, Harold Ross, began pressuring her for her belated copy. She replied, "Too fucking busy, and vice versa."

2 At one time Dorothy Parker had a small, dingy cubbyhole of an office in the Metropolitan Opera House building in New York. As no one ever came to see her, she became depressed and lonely. When the signwriter came to paint her name on the office door, she got him to write instead the word "GENTLEMEN."

3 A young man looking loftily around at a party said, "I'm afraid I simply cannot bear fools."

"How odd," said Dorothy Parker. "Your mother could, apparently."

4 William Randolph Hearst lived with his movie-star mistress Marion Davies in his spectacular castle, San Simeon. Hollywood personalities were frequent guests. Hearst always insisted upon the observation of certain rules. Despite his own irregular association with

Marion Davies, one of these rules was that there should be no love-making between unmarried couples. Dorothy Parker broke the rule and received a note from her host asking her to leave. In the San Simeon visitors' book she left these lines:

> Upon my honor,
> I saw a Madonna
> Standing in a niche,
> Above the door
> Of the famous whore
> Of a prominent son of a bitch.

{In a variant of this story Dorothy Parker was asked to leave San Simeon for drinking too much.}

5 After some years apart Dorothy Parker and her second husband, Alan Campbell, were remarried. At the reception following the ceremony she remarked, "People who haven't talked to each other for years are on speaking terms again today — including the bride and groom."

6 Dorothy Parker and a friend were talking about a forceful and garrulous celebrity. "She's so outspoken," remarked the friend. "By whom?" asked Dorothy.

7 Dorothy Parker wrote a report on a Yale prom at which the number and beauty of the girls present had obviously made a deep impression on her. "If all those sweet young things were laid end to end," she announced, "I wouldn't be at all surprised."

8 Dorothy Parker was told that a certain London actress had broken a leg. "How terrible," she said, "she must have done it sliding down a barrister."

9 She was asked to use the word *horticulture* in a sentence. "You can lead a horticulture, but you can't make her think," said Dorothy Parker promptly.

10 Looking at a worn-out toothbrush in their hostess's bathroom, a fellow guest said to Dorothy Parker, "Whatever do you think she does with that?"
"I think she rides it on Halloween," was the reply.

11 Attending the dress rehearsal of her play *Close Harmony,* Dorothy Parker was discouraged by the performance. The leading lady was amply endowed. At one point the producer, sitting with Dorothy, whispered, "Don't you think she ought to wear a brassiere in this scene?"
"God, no," said Dorothy. "You've got to have something in the show that moves."

12 Gossiping about an acquaintance, Dorothy Parker murmured in bogus admiration, "You know, she speaks eighteen languages. And she can't say 'No' in any of them."

13 In the hospital Dorothy Parker was visited by her secretary, to whom she wished to dictate some letters. Pressing the button marked NURSE, Dorothy observed, "That should assure us of at least forty-five minutes of undisturbed privacy."

14 Leaving her place at the Round Table one day, Dorothy said, "Excuse me, I have to go to the bathroom." She paused, then went on, "I really have to telephone, but I'm too embarrassed to say so."

15 Coming to pay her last respects to Scott Fitzgerald as he lay in an undertaker's parlor in Los Angeles, Dorothy Parker used the words spoken by the anonymous mourner at the funeral of Jay Gatsby in Fitzgerald's *The Great Gatsby:* "The poor son-of-a-bitch!"

16 Dorothy Parker once attended a party with Somerset Maugham where the guests challenged each other to complete nursery rhymes. Somerset Maugham presented Mrs. Parker with the lines: "Higgledy piggledy, my white hen/ She lays eggs for gentlemen."
Dorothy Parker added the following couplet: "You cannot persuade her with gun or lariat/ To come across for the proletariat."

17 (Lillian Hellman records an incident that took place as the body of Alan Campbell was being carried from the house where he had died.)
"Among the friends who stood with Dottie on those California steps was Mrs. Jones, a woman who had liked Alan, pretended to like Dottie, and who had always loved all forms of meddling in other people's troubles. Mrs. Jones said, 'Dottie, tell me, dear, what I can do for you.'

"Dottie said, 'Get me a new husband.'

"There was a silence, but before those who would have laughed could laugh, Mrs. Jones said, 'I think that is the most callous and disgusting remark I ever heard in my life.'

"Dottie turned to look at her, sighed, and said gently, 'So sorry. Then run down to the corner and get me a ham and cheese on rye and tell them to hold the mayo.' "

18 Dorothy Parker once collided with Clare Boothe Luce in a narrow doorway. "Age before beauty," said Mrs. Luce, stepping aside. "Pearls before swine," said Dorothy Parker, gliding through.

{This anecdote is probably apocryphal but memorable nonetheless.}

19 A friend was very upset at having to get rid of his cat. Dorothy Parker suggested, "Have you tried curiosity?"

20 There were two plays containing a character based on Dorothy Parker, one written by George Oppenheimer and the other by Ruth Gordon. Dorothy Parker grumbled that she had wanted to write her autobiography but was now afraid to do so. "If I did, George Oppenheimer and Ruth Gordon would sue me for plagiarism."

21 During her later years Dorothy Parker increasingly found refuge in alcohol. Admitted to a sanatorium, she approved the room but told the doctor she would have to go out every hour or so for a drink. He solemnly warned her that she must stop drinking or she would be dead within a month. "Promises, promises," she said with a sigh.

ॐ ৵

PARKER, Henry Taylor (1867–1934), *US music critic, known from his initials, H. T. P., as "Hell to Pay."*

1 During a symphony concert Parker had the misfortune to be seated near some persistent talkers. At last he rounded on the offenders: "Those people on the stage are making such a noise I can't hear a word you're saying."

ॐ ৵

PARKER, Quannah (late 18th–early 19th centuries), *North American Comanche Indian chief.*

1 "In his old age, after he quit the warpath, Quannah Parker . . . adopted many of the white man's ways. But in one respect he clung to the custom of his fathers. He continued to be a polygamist. He was a friend and admirer of Theodore Roosevelt and on one occasion when Roosevelt was touring Oklahoma he drove out to Parker's camp to see him. With pride Parker pointed out that he lived in a house like a white man, his children went to a white man's school, and he himself dressed like a white man. Whereupon Roosevelt was moved to preach him a sermon on the subject of morality. 'See here, chief, why don't you set your people a better example? A white man has only one wife—he's allowed only one at a time. Here you are living with five squaws. Why don't you give up four of them and remain faithful to the fifth?' Parker stood still a moment, considering the proposition. Then he answered, 'You are my great white father, and I will do as you wish—on one condition.' 'What is the condition?' asked Roosevelt. 'You pick out the one I am to live with and then you go kill the other four,' answered Parker."

ॐ ৵

PARR, Samuel (1747–1825), *English author, schoolmaster, and clergyman. Parr, greatly admired as a stylist, was closely involved, on either friendly or hostile terms, with many of the literary and political figures of his time.*

1 His contemporaries valued highly Parr's talents as a composer of Latin epitaphs. Once he said to a friend, "My lord, should you die first, I mean to write your epitaph." His friend replied, "It is a temptation to commit suicide."

2 On Easter Tuesday in 1800 Parr preached a famous sermon before the lord mayor of London. Asked his opinion, his worship replied that he heard only four things in it that he disliked—the four quarters of the hour struck by the church clock.

3 Parr rated highly his own skill at whist. He was correspondingly intolerant of lack of skill in other players. One evening he was playing with a partner who committed blunder after blunder. A lady asked Parr how the game was going. "Pretty well, madam," was the reply, "considering that I have three adversaries."

ॐ ৵

> Samuel Butler recalled with delight the reaction of the six-year-old daughter of an acquaintance of his, Edgar Paine, who, upon learning that she had acquired a little sister, exclaimed in her enthusiasm, "Does Mama know? Let's go and tell her."
>
> — Geoffrey Keynes and Brian Hill, eds., *Samuel Butler's Notebooks — Selections*

PARRISH, Maxfield (1870–1966), *US illustrator, painter, and poster designer. He also painted several outstanding murals, including one based on the theme of Old King Cole at the St. Regis Hotel in New York.*

1 Parrish specialized in painting beautiful nudes and was thus accustomed to having lovely young models in his studio. One morning, when a model arrived, Parrish suggested that they have a cup of coffee before getting down to work—a habit he had recently acquired to postpone confronting the blank canvas. They had hardly started to drink the coffee when the studio buzzer rang. Panic seized the artist. "Young lady," he cried, "for God's sake, take your clothes off—my wife's coming up to check on me."

જે ⋅ઉ

PARTRIDGE, John (1644–1715), *English cobbler turned almanac maker. His almanacs, though compounded of superstition, equivocation, and charlatanry, were nonetheless very successful commercially.*

1 In 1707 Jonathan Swift decided to laugh the fraudulent Partridge out of business. As "Isaac Bickerstaff" he published a spoof, *Predictions for the Year 1708.* "Bickerstaff" professed his concern to rescue the noble art of astrology from the hands of the quacks. In particular he would make precise predictions in place of the vague prophecies put forth by the ordinary almanac makers. Thus his very first prediction: the death of John Partridge "upon 29 March next, about 11 at night, of a raging fever."

On the morning of March 30 the London booksellers did a brisk trade in another pamphlet, hot off the presses, announcing that Bickerstaff's prediction had come true and Partridge had died the previous evening. It gave a detailed account of his deathbed, followed by an "Elegy on the Death of Mr. Partridge." Partridge hurriedly printed and distributed a denial of his death, but by then no one believed him. Other writers joined in the fun with pamphlets urging Partridge to abandon his perverse insistence that he was still alive. The Stationers' Company struck his name off their records. It was four years before Partridge recovered sufficiently from this onslaught to resume publication of his almanac, and by then "Isaac Bickerstaff" had become a household name.

2 One day Partridge, journeying to a country town, paused to rest at an inn. As he was remounting his horse to resume his journey, the ostler said, "If you take my advice you'll stay here, because if you go on you will certainly be overtaken by heavy rain."

"Nonsense!" exclaimed Partridge, and away he rode. After he had ridden a short distance, he was drenched by a heavy shower. Interested in the ostler's accuracy of prediction, he returned to the inn, admitted that the man had been quite correct, and offered him a large tip if he would divulge his secret.

Pocketing the tip, the man said, "You see, we have an almanac in the house called Partridge's almanac, and the fellow is such a notorious liar that whenever he promises fine weather we can be sure it will rain. Now today he had put down 'settled weather, fine; no rain,' so when I looked that up before I saddled your horse I was able to put you on your guard."

{Similar stories are told of other weather prophets and are no doubt equally apocryphal.}

જે ⋅ઉ

PASCAL, Blaise (1623–62), *French mathematician and writer on religion. From his youth on, Pascal did important work in mathematics and physics and in 1641 made the first calculating machine. In his early thirties he underwent a profound religious experience and became a Jansenist. Some of the fruits of his meditations on religion are contained in his Pensées (1669).*

1 Pascal's father began his son's education with a course of reading in ancient languages. When the nine-year-old Pascal inquired as to the nature of geometry, he was told that it was the study of shapes and forms. The boy immediately proceeded to discover for himself the first thirty-two theorems of Euclid—in the correct order. The elder Pascal saw that it was no use attempting to steer his son away from mathematics and allowed him to pursue his studies as he wished.

{This story comes from Pascal's sister and borders on the apocryphal.}

⋙ ⋘

PATER, Walter (1839–94), *British writer and critic. His aesthetic and philosophical theories, expounded notably in* Marius the Epicurean *(1885), were a major impulse behind the Aesthetic ("art for art's sake") movement of the 1890s, for which he also set a standard in his highly wrought prose style. His* Studies in the History of the Renaissance *(1873) was also influential, as were numerous critical essays on art and poetry.*

1 Pater taught at Oxford, where he was also a university proctor. He once asked a student, a certain Mr. Sanctuary, to see him after the lecture. The young man, wondering what misdemeanor he had committed, approached Pater's desk with some trepidation. Pater, however, appeared equally ill at ease and seemed not to know what to say. "You asked me to stay behind, sir?" prompted Sanctuary. "Oh, yes, Mr. Sanctuary," stammered Pater. "I . . . I wanted to say to you . . . what a very beautiful name you have got."

{It seems likely that this story was a happy invention by Oscar Wilde, who first put it into circulation.}

2 Pater's lectures at Oxford were notoriously inaudible, in fact virtually whispered. Max Beerbohm once asked Wilde if he had heard Pater lecture and got the response: "I overheard him."

⋙ ⋘

PATTI, Adelina (1843–1919), *Italian operatic soprano. Her coloratura singing in such roles as Lucia in* Lucia di Lammermoor *and Amina in* La Sonnambula *was famous all over Europe and the United States.*

1 Patti's successful tour of Europe brought her great acclaim from all opera-goers, including royalty. "Which crowned head do you like best?" she was once asked by a critic. Patti thought for a moment. "The Czar Alexander gives the best jewelry," she replied.

⋙ ⋘

PATTON, George S[mith], Jr. (1885–1945), *US general, nicknamed "Old Blood-and-Guts." After the Normandy landings, he led the Allied sweep across France and into Germany at the end of World War II. His unorthodox methods caused some embarrassment in military circles.*

1 In August 1943, when Patton was commanding American forces in Italy, he visited the hospital at Sant'Agata. While being shown around by the colonel in charge, he spied a man who did not seem to be wounded at all. He snapped at the colonel, "I want you to get that man out of bed right away. Get him back to the front. I won't have these men who really are wounded see that man babied so." When the soldier himself did not immediately respond, Patton struck him. It turned out that he was seriously shell-shocked. When the incident became known three months later, there was an outcry, and Patton was forced to make a public apology.

2 On August 26, 1944, one of Patton's units crossed the Seine at Melun, outflanking Paris. Patton sent Eisenhower a formal military report of the operation with the postscript: "Dear Ike, Today I spat in the Seine."

{A variant of this anecdote substitutes "pissed" for "spat."}

⋙ ⋘

PAYNE, John Howard (1791–1852), *US actor and playwright. His greatest success was* Brutus *(1818).*

1 Driven from the US stage by the jealousy of other actors, Payne led a wandering existence in Europe for the latter part of his life. Penniless, without a lodging for the night, he would hear sung in the streets and played on barrel organs a song to which he had written the lyric. It was "Home, Sweet Home."

⋙ ⋘

> The classic children's book *Make Way for Ducklings* by Robert McCloskey has a real-life analogue.
>
> One of the events in the 1928 Olympics was single-scull rowing. Henry Pearce, representing Australia, was in the lead when a family of ducks passed in front of him single file. Courteously he pulled in his oars.
>
> Yes, he won.
>
> — David Wallechinsky,
> *The Complete Book of the Olympics*

PEABODY, Elizabeth (1804–94), *US educator. She was active in the New England Transcendentalist movement, wrote for* The Dial, *and published translations by Margaret Fuller and three early works by Nathaniel Hawthorne (her brother-in-law). She was the model for Miss Birdseye in Henry James's* The Bostonians.

1　Crossing Boston Common, Miss Peabody bumped into a tree. "I saw it," she explained, "but I did not *realize* it."

ɞ∾ ⋖ʂ

PEARD, John Whitehead (1811–80), *British country squire who became the follower and friend of the Italian patriot Giuseppe Garibaldi. He played a prominent role in the battle of Milazzo (1860).*

1　Dumas *fils,* also in Garibaldi's entourage, gave a colorful account of Peard's first meeting with the Italian leader. Peard was introduced to Garibaldi on the field of battle, during a lull. They exchanged brief preliminary greetings. Then a movement in the Austrian lines attracted Peard's attention. "Pardon me, there's a devil of an Austrian over there who's catching my eye." So saying, he raised his gun and fired. The group around Garibaldi trained their field glasses on the obtrusive Austrian, who staggered forward a couple of paces and then pitched face downward and lay still. Peard nodded with satisfaction, and held out his hand to Garibaldi: "Good day, general. I hope I see you well."

PEARY, Robert Edwin (1856–1920), *US Arctic explorer. After a number of Arctic expeditions (1886–1906) he finally became the first man to reach the North Pole (1909). He wrote about his travels in* Northward over the "Great Ice" *(1898) and* The North Pole *(1910).*

1　A young lady had been questioning Peary for some time on various matters relating to his polar expeditions. "But how does anyone know when he has reached the North Pole?" she asked with a puzzled frown. "Nothing easier," replied Peary. "One step beyond the pole, you see, and the north wind becomes a south one."

ɞ∾ ⋖ʂ

PECK, Gregory (1916–　), *US film actor. He specialized in the role of the tough but romantic hero.*

1　Entering a crowded restaurant with a companion, Gregory Peck found no table available. "Tell them who you are," murmured the friend. "If you have to tell them who you are, you aren't anybody," said Peck.

ɞ∾ ⋖ʂ

PEMBROKE, Thomas Herbert, 8th Earl of (1656–1733), *British First Lord of the Admiralty (1690) and lord lieutenant of Ireland (1707). His great-uncle William Herbert, 3d Earl of Pembroke, is believed by some to be the "W. H." of Shakespeare's sonnets.*

1　Strict with his servants, Lord Pembroke would dismiss on the spot any that were found drunk. He generally turned a blind eye, however, to the misdeeds of a trusty old footman called John. But on one occasion this proved impossible, for John had appeared in full view of his master almost too drunk to stand, and the incident had been witnessed by other members of the household. Unperturbed, Lord Pembroke went straight up to the tottering footman, felt his pulse, and exclaimed, "God bless us, he is in a raging fever! Get him to bed directly and send for the apothecary." The apothecary was ordered to bleed the patient copiously and give him a strong dose of medicine every twenty-four hours, with the result that after a few days John staggered out looking weaker and paler than the most severe illness could have left him. "I am truly glad to see thee alive," cried the earl, "though you have had a wonderful escape, and ought to be thankful. Why, if I had not passed by at that time and spied the condition you were in, you would have been dead before now. But John," he added emphatically, "no more of these fevers!"

&❦ ❧

PERELMAN, S[idney] J[oseph] (1904–79), *US humorist and screenwriter. He wrote the scripts for some of the Marx Brothers' films, but is best known for the humorous short stories and sketches that he contributed to* The New Yorker *from the 1930s onward. Many collections of these pieces have been published.*

1   On a visit to Taipei, Perelman, accosted by a group of prostitutes, had some difficulty in escaping from their importunities. Having at last shaken them off he headed back to his hotel, remarking, "A case of the tail dogging the wag."

{This complex pun has been claimed by others.}

&❦ ❧

PERICLES (c. 495–429 BC), *Athenian statesman and orator. As leader of the democratic party, Pericles attained supremacy in Athenian politics in 443* BC. *He consolidated Athens's position abroad and beautified the city with public buildings, including the Parthenon. Despite the machinations of his enemies he was still guiding Athenian policy at the outbreak of the Peloponnesian War (431).*

1   During the Peloponnesian War an eclipse occurred when Pericles was about to set out to sea. As the pilot was too terrified to perform his duties, Pericles stepped forward and covered the man's head with his cloak. "Does this frighten you?" he asked. "No," said the pilot. "Then what difference is there between the two events," inquired Pericles, "except that the sun is covered by a larger object than my cloak?"

&❦ ❧

PERLMAN, Itzhak (1945–), *Israeli violinist. At the age of thirteen he won a talent competition to appear on* US *television. He went on to study in New York, subsequently touring in Israel, Europe, and the United States.*

1   In 1980 Mike Wallace interviewed the great violinist on the television program *60*

Minutes. Wallace recalled the names of masters of the instrument—Jascha Heifetz, Yehudi Menuhin, Isaac Stern, Perlman himself—and then asked why so many great violinists were Jewish. Holding up his fingers and twiddling them, Perlman replied: "You see, our fingers are circumcised, which gives it a very good dexterity, you know, particularly in the pinky."

&❦ ❧

PERÓN, Eva Duarte de (1919–52), *Argentinian actress who became the second wife of President Juan Perón. Evita, as she was known, was idolized by the poor, whose lot she campaigned to improve. After her early death from cancer, Perón's political strength was undermined.*

1   Eva rose from the obscurity of a poor working-class background through a combination of talent, beauty, and unscrupulousness. She had a series of increasingly influential lovers whom she used to further her career and then discarded. As the wife of President Juan Perón, she was sent on a tour to win friends for Argentina among the European powers. Her reception was somewhat mixed. As she drove through the streets of Milan, accompanied by a retired admiral, the crowd shouted "Whore." Angrily Eva turned to her escort, "They are calling me a whore!"

"That's all right," said the admiral soothingly. "I haven't been to sea for fifteen years, yet they still call me admiral."

{Eva's admirers circulated stories, hagiographical in character, of her goodness and charity; this story is probably an equally apocryphal fabrication of the other side.}

&❦ ❧

PEROT, H. Ross (1930–), *US computer millionaire and philanthropist.*

1   (David Frost tells this story:)
"Looking around for a suitable way of serving the community, Mr. Perot decided that he would give a Christmas present to every American prisoner-of-war in Vietnam. Accordingly, thousands of parcels were wrapped and packed, and a fleet of Boeing 707s was chartered to deliver them to Hanoi. Then the message came from the government of Vietnam—no such gesture could be considered during the course of the bloody war, which was then at its height. Perot argued. The Vietnamese replied

that any charity was impossible while American B-52s were devastating Vietnamese villages.

"'No problem,' Perot replied. He would hire an expert American construction company in order to rebuild anything the Americans had knocked down.

"The puzzled Vietnamese became inscrutable, and declined to continue this dialogue. Christmas drew closer, the parcels remained undelivered. Finally in despair Perot took off in his chartered fleet and flew to Moscow where his aides posted the parcels, one at a time, at the Moscow Central post office. They were delivered intact."

਼ ੦ੰ

PERRY, Oliver Hazard (1785–1819), *US naval commander.*

1 During the battle of Lake Erie in 1813, Perry's flagship, the *Lawrence,* was so badly damaged that he was obliged to abandon it and row to the *Niagara.* After finally forcing the British fleet to surrender, Perry made no reference to the exigencies of the battle in the dispatch announcing his victory. It read simply, "We have met the enemy, and they are ours."

{Perry's words are memorable, but have become immortal through the parody on them by Walt Kelly's inimitable cartoon character, Pogo: "We have met the enemy and he is us."}

਼ ੦ੰ

PERUGINO, Pietro [Pietro di Cristoforo Vannucci] (1446–1523), *Italian painter, born near Perugia. He was among the artists employed to paint the frescoes of the Sistine Chapel. Raphael, one of his pupils, was influenced by his graceful and balanced style.*

1 Perugino was commissioned to paint frescoes (now lost) in a convent in Florence. The niggardly prior stood over the artist while he worked, holding the little bag that contained the expensive ultramarine pigment and allowing Perugino only tiny quantities at a time. Every now and then he would wail, "How much blue that wall is eating!" Perugino said nothing, but worked steadily, occasionally cleaning his brush in a bowl of water. When he had completed his day's work, he drained the bowl and handed it back to the prior with its

sediment of pure ultramarine at the bottom. "Here you are, Father. And please learn to trust an honest man."

2 On his deathbed, Perugino refused to send for the priest. His last words were: "I am curious to see what happens in the next world to one who dies unshriven."

਼ ੦ੰ

PÉTAIN, [Henri] **Philippe** (1856–1951), *French general and statesman. The hero of the French defense of Verdun (1916), he became prime minister in 1940, just before the defeat by Germany. He signed a pact with Hitler allowing him to establish a government at Vichy for unoccupied France. At the end of the war Pétain was condemned to death as a traitor, but the sentence was commuted to life imprisonment.*

1 From February to December 1916, one of the fiercest battles of World War I was fought at Verdun-sur-Meuse in northeast France. Marshal Pétain was in command of the Allied troops; Crown Prince Frederick William commanded the Germans. At the beginning of the battle a determined Pétain said of the German troops, "They shall not pass." The resolution was upheld and the Allies ultimately triumphed, but only after one million lives had been lost.

2 In June 1940 Charles de Gaulle returned to France from England to bring Marshal Pétain an offer from Winston Churchill of "union" between the two countries to resist the German onslaught. Pétain, knowing that France's capitulation was only hours away and believing that England was doomed too, rejected the offer, saying, "What use is fusion with a corpse?"

਼ ੦ੰ

PETER I [Peter the Great] (1672–1725), *czar (1682–1721) and later emperor (1721–25) of Russia. During the 1690s Peter traveled in Europe and, influenced by the ideas he encountered there, tried to modernize his backward, feudal state by reforming the government and army and encouraging trade and industry. He also extended Russian territory to the west and southeast.*

1 In the Russian army there was a secret society whose members gained promotion by their

ability to withstand torture and who practiced inuring themselves against greater and greater degrees of pain. One of these officers was involved in a plot against Peter, and although tortured four times refused to confess. Peter, realizing that pain would not break him, went up to him and kissed him. "I know full well that you were party to the plot against me, but you have been punished enough. Now, confess freely to me on account of the love you owe to your czar, and I swear that I will grant you a complete pardon. Not only that, but as a special sign of my mercy I will make you a colonel." The man was so unnerved by Peter's tactics that he embraced him and made a full confession. Peter kept his side of the bargain and made him a colonel.

2   Peter, greatly interested in medicine, often assisted surgeons and dentists in their operations. One morning one of his valets appealed to the czar to help his wife; she was suffering dreadfully from a toothache, he said, but refused to have the offending tooth pulled and pretended to be in no pain when approached by a dentist. Peter collected his dental instruments and followed the valet to his apartments, where, ignoring the cries and protests of the struggling woman, he extracted the tooth. Some days later the czar discovered that the poor woman had never had a toothache; the painful extraction had been her husband's revenge for a domestic quarrel.

ॐ॰ ॰ॐ

PETERBOROUGH, Charles Mordaunt, 3d Earl of (1658–1735), *British diplomat, soldier, and admiral.*

1   In 1710, when the Duke of Marlborough was out of favor with the London populace, a mob attacked Peterborough in the street, mistaking him for the hated and ungenerous duke. He finally convinced them that he was not Marlborough by saying, "In the first place, I have only five guineas in my pocket; and in the second, they are very much at your service."

ॐ॰ ॰ॐ

PETRONIUS, Gaius ["Petronius Arbiter"] (fl. AD 60), *Roman writer, a favorite at the court of Emperor Nero. He is believed to have been the author of the* Satyricon, *a satirical romance.*

1   Petronius had received an invitation to a special banquet at Nero's palace. The meal was to be followed by a "licentious entertainment" featuring a hundred naked virgins. Petronius refused the invitation. "Tell the emperor," he instructed his messenger, "that one hundred naked virgins are not one hundred times as exciting as one naked virgin."

ॐ॰ ॰ॐ

PHELPS, William Lyon (1865–1943), *US scholar and critic. He taught English literature at Yale for forty-one years, holding a chair from 1901 until his retirement in 1933.*

1   Marking an examination paper written shortly before Christmas, Phelps came across the note: "God only knows the answer to this question. Merry Christmas." Phelps returned the paper with the annotation: "God gets an A. You get an F. Happy New Year."

ॐ॰ ॰ॐ

PHILIP, Prince, Duke of Edinburgh (1921–   ), *husband of Queen Elizabeth II of the United Kingdom.*

1   During a tour of Canada in the early years of their marriage, Prince Philip and Princess Elizabeth had a rather turbulent crossing to Vancouver Island on a Canadian destroyer. Tea was served in the royal suite by a young petty officer. As he entered with a large tray of cakes, the ship lurched violently and the cakes were thrown to the floor. To the officer's amazement, Prince Philip immediately went down on his hands and knees and crawled around the floor, retrieving about half of the cakes. Returning to his seat, he smiled triumphantly at Elizabeth and said, "I've got mine — yours are down there."

2   Visiting an Australian university during a royal tour in 1954, Prince Philip was introduced to a "Mr. and Dr. Robinson."

"My wife is a doctor of philosophy," explained Mr. Robinson. "She is much more important than I."

"Ah, yes," replied Prince Philip sympathetically. "We have that trouble in our family, too."

3   Prince Philip was asked by a hostile questioner what kind of work he would say that he did. "I'm self-employed," he replied.

4 An official greeted Prince Philip as he stepped from an aircraft with the words: "And how was your flight, sir?"

"Have you ever flown?" asked the prince.

"Yes, sir, often."

"Well, it was like that."

{Royalty must become very bored with both air travel and banal conversation, so it would be pleasant to think that this exchange actually happened.}

5 During a royal visit to a small English town, Prince Philip stopped to talk to two very old ladies. "I'm a hundred and four," boasted one of the women, "and my friend here is a hundred and one."

"I don't believe it," said Philip, his eyes twinkling. "Ladies always take ten years off their age."

6 Speaking at a meeting of manufacturers of man-made fibers, Philip questioned his right to be there. "I'm not very good at producing man-made fibers myself," he confessed, stroking his balding head.

❧ ❧

PHILIP II (382–336 BC), *king of Macedon (359–336 BC). His conquests and diplomacy raised Macedon to the status of a major power. After the Battle of Chaeronea (338) the hegemony of Greece passed to Philip. He was assassinated in a family plot, leaving his throne to his son, Alexander the Great.*

1 Like Alexander the Great, Philip had the reputation of being a heavy drinker. Once when drunk he gave an unjust verdict in the case of a woman who was being tried before him. "I appeal!" cried the unfortunate litigant. "To whom?" asked the monarch, who was also the highest tribunal in the land. "From Philip drunk to Philip sober," was the bold reply. The king, somewhat taken back, gave the case further consideration.

2 After Philip had subdued or formed alliances with all the major Greek city-states, Sparta still remained aloof. Finding that diplomacy had no effect on its stubborn independence, Philip sent a threat: "You are advised to submit without further delay, for if I bring my army into your land, I will destroy your farms, slay your people, and raze your city." The Spartans replied: "If." Recalling Sparta's glorious military past, Philip thought better of it and left them alone.

3 Philip was always accompanied by two men whose duty it was to say to him each morning, "Philip, remember that you are but a man." Each evening they said, "Philip, have you remembered that you are but a man?"

❧ ❧

PHILIP III (1578–1621), *king of Spain (1598–61).*

1 Politically indecisive and incompetent, Philip is said to have died of a fever. This was the consequence of overheating himself by sitting too long near a hot brazier. It did not occur to him to move away from the heat. How could he? The palace functionary whose job it was to remove the brazier could not be found. Philip's death was inevitable.

❧ ❧

PHILIP V (1683–1746), *king of Spain (1700–46). The grandson of Louis XIV of France, Philip became king under the will of Charles II of Spain.*

1 Louis XIV hesitated for nearly a week after receiving news of the death of Charles II and his bequest to Philip. He wondered whether to accept the legacy. On November 16, 1700, he made the formal announcement, after his *lever,* to the assembled court. "Gentlemen," he said, leading Philip forward, "here is the king of Spain." He then made a brief but touching speech, exhorting his grandson to be a good Spaniard and keep the peace in Europe. Overcome with emotion, the Spanish ambassador fell on his knees before Philip and kissed his hand and said, "The Pyrenees have ceased to exist."

{Voltaire attributes the famous remark about the Pyrenees to Louis himself.}

❧ ❧

PHILIP, John Woodward (1840–1900), *US naval commander.*

1 During the Spanish-American War of 1898 Captain Philip was in command of the battleship *Texas.* The entire Spanish fleet, blockaded by the Americans in the bay of Santiago de

Cuba, was destroyed when it emerged on July 3. As the *Texas* sailed past the burning Spanish cruiser *Vizcaya* in pursuit of another Spanish ship, Philip checked the natural jubilation of his crew with the words: "Don't cheer, boys; the poor devils are dying."

৵ ৶

PHILLIPS, Wendell (1811–84), *US reformer and orator. He trained as a lawyer, but devoted much of his life to the campaigns for the abolition of slavery, women's suffrage, and various other reforms.*

1 In the days before he became well known, Phillips spent a night in a hotel at Charleston, South Carolina. His breakfast was brought up by a slave, to whom Phillips began to expound his abolitionist ideals. After a time, realizing that his discourse was making little impression, Phillips gave up and told him he could go. The man stood firm. "You must excuse me," he said. "I am obliged to stay here, 'cause I'm responsible for the silverware."

2 While Wendell Phillips was on a lecture tour in the northern states, he was accosted by a minister from Kentucky who attacked him for his abolitionist views. "You want to free the slaves, don't you?" demanded the minister.

"Indeed I do."

"Then why are you preaching your doctrines up here? Why don't you try going to Kentucky?"

Phillips retorted, "You're a minister, aren't you?"

"Yes, I am."

"And you try to save souls from hell?"

"Yes, I do."

"Well, why don't you go there then?" said Phillips.

৵ ৶

PIATIGORSKY, Gregor (1903–76), *Russian cellist. Appointed principal cellist of the Bolshoi Theatre Orchestra in 1919, he emigrated to the United States in 1921, where he was acclaimed the leading cellist of his generation.*

1 Piatigorsky was having problems with one of his pupils. No matter how many times the master played a piece to show how it should sound, his student failed to make any significant progress; in fact, his playing seemed to deteriorate. It occurred to Piatigorsky that he was perhaps discouraging the young man by performing the pieces too well himself. He therefore began to introduce a few deliberate mistakes; miraculously, the pupil showed marked signs of improvement. This method of teaching continued for some weeks, with Piatigorsky taking a perverse pleasure in being free to play as badly as he pleased.

The young man went on to perform with brilliant success at his graduation. Fighting through the crowd of well-wishers to congratulate his pupil, Piatigorsky heard someone ask the new graduate what he thought of the great cellist. "As a teacher," replied the young man, "excellent. But as a cellist, lousy."

৵ ৶

PICABIA, Francis (1879–1953), *French painter of Spanish descent, one of the first exponents of Dadaism. Picabia was also a writer, much of his work appearing in his own journal 391 (1917–24).*

1 In Picabia's château the rooms were designed with different themes; the children's room was furnished with grotesque masks, instruments of torture, witchcraft trappings, and a mechanical ghost that could be animated at night to rattle chains. The painter chose this theme for the children's room because he believed in training them in fearlessness from an early age. "When they get a bit older, I shall replace the ghost with a creditor waving an unpaid bill," he said.

৵ ৶

PICASSO, Pablo (1881–1973), *Spanish artist, sculptor, and ceramist. After 1900 he worked in Paris, achieving success with pictures of stage and street life in blue (the so-called Blue Period; 1901–04) and rose (1905–08). In collaboration with Georges Braque, he developed Cubism, one of the most influential of modern painting styles, and later turned to surrealistic figure studies. Guernica (1937), his huge and controversial masterpiece, shows the destruction of the Basque capital by German planes during the Spanish Civil War. Picasso also painted some striking portraits in various styles.*

1 (Picasso recalls his mother's ambitions for him.)

"When I was a child, my mother said to me,

'If you become a soldier, you'll be a general. If you become a monk, you'll end up as Pope.' Instead I became a painter and wound up as Picasso."

2 In 1906 Gertrude Stein sat to Picasso for her portrait. At the end of many sittings he simply obliterated the picture, saying he could no longer "see" her. Later he completed the picture, in the absence of a sitter, and gave the portrait to Miss Stein. She complained that she did not look like that. Picasso said, "But you will," and this prediction was borne out as Miss Stein aged.

3 When Picasso painted his famous portrait of Gertrude Stein, he was virtually unknown. Some years later the millionaire art collector Dr. Albert Barnes, interested in the picture, asked Miss Stein straight out how much she had paid for it. "Nothing," Miss Stein replied. "Naturally, he gave it to me." Dr. Barnes was incredulous. She subsequently recounted the incident to Picasso, who smiled and said, "He doesn't understand that at that time the difference between a sale and a gift was negligible."

4 Not long after the outbreak of World War I Gertrude Stein and Picasso were standing on a street corner in Paris, watching a procession of camouflaged trucks passing, the sides of the vans disguised by blotches of gray and green paint. Picasso, in his amazement, blurted out, "*C'est nous qui avons fait ça*" (It is we who have created that).

5 During World War II Picasso suffered some harassment from the Gestapo in Nazi-occupied Paris. An inquisitive German officer, coming into his apartment, noticed a photograph of *Guernica* lying on a table. "Did you do that?" he asked Picasso. "No, you did," said Picasso.

6 Picasso fell into conversation with an American GI in Paris, who told him that he did not like modern paintings because they were not realistic. Picasso did not immediately respond, but when the soldier a few minutes later showed him a snapshot of his girlfriend, he exclaimed, "My, is she really as small as that?"

7 After World War II Picasso's pictures were changing hands for fabulous sums. An American millionairess visited the artist's studio. She paused in front of a striking example of his late style. "What does this picture represent?" she asked. "Two hundred thousand dollars," answered Picasso.

8 As the market value of Picasso's works grew, so too did the cottage industry of faking his paintings. A poor artist who owned a supposed Picasso sent it via a friend for the master to authenticate so that he could sell it. Picasso said, "It's false." From a different source the friend brought another Picasso and then a third. On each occasion Picasso disowned them. Apropos the third painting the man protested, "But I saw you paint this one with my own eyes."

"I can paint false Picassos as well as anyone," retorted Picasso. Then he bought the first painting from the impoverished artist for a sum four times as high as the owner had originally hoped it would fetch.

9 Friends lunching at Picasso's home in the south of France commented on the fact that their host had none of his own pictures on the walls. "Why is that, Pablo?" one of them asked. "Don't you like them?"

"On the contrary," replied the painter, "I like them very much. It's just that I can't afford them."

10 Picasso visited his local cabinetmaker to commission a mahogany wardrobe for his château. To illustrate the shape and dimensions he required, he drew a hasty sketch on a sheet of paper and handed it to the craftsman. "How much will it cost?" he asked. "Nothing at all," replied the cabinetmaker. "Just sign the sketch."

11 Picasso was relaxing on a beach in the south of France when he was accosted by a small boy clutching a blank sheet of paper. The child had evidently been dispatched by his parents to solicit an autographed drawing. After a moment's hesitation, Picasso tore up the paper and drew a few designs on the boy's back instead. He signed his name with a flourish and sent the child back to his parents. Relating the incident at a later date, Picasso remarked thoughtfully, "I wonder if they'll ever wash him again?"

12 Picasso was asked whether it didn't tire him to stand in front of a canvas for three or

four hours while he was painting. "No," he replied. "That is why painters live so long. While I work, I leave my body outside the door, the way Muslims take off their shoes before entering the mosque."

13 A visitor to Picasso's studio found the artist gazing disconsolately at a painting on the easel. "It's a masterpiece," said the visitor, hoping to cheer Picasso up.

"No, the nose is all wrong," Picasso said. "It throws the whole picture out of perspective."

"Then why not alter the nose?"

"Impossible," replied Picasso. "I can't find it."

{Probably an apocryphal story.}

14 A rich Dutch grocer who prided himself on his art collection managed to obtain an introduction to Picasso. He examined the works in the studio and then said, "Master, I understand every one of your productions except one."

"And that is?"

"Your dove. It seems to me so simple, so primitive that I cannot understand it."

"Sir," Picasso asked, "do you understand Chinese?"

"No."

"Six hundred million people do." And Picasso politely showed him out.

15 (The one-time surrealist Robert Desnos recounts a story that Picasso told him.)

"I had lunched at the Catalan for months," Picasso said, "and for months I looked at the sideboard without thinking more than 'it's a sideboard.' One day I decide to make a picture of it. I do so. The next day, when I arrived, the sideboard had gone, its place was empty. . . . I must have taken it away without noticing by painting it."

{Desnos comments on this anecdote, saying that it is like a fable illustrating Picasso's relationship to his subjects, that what he paints he takes possession of "as himself the creator of the object or of the being."}

16 (Picasso told the following story to André Warnod.)

"Do you remember that head of a bull I had in my last show? I'll tell you how it was conceived. One day I noticed in a corner the handle-bar and the seat of a bicycle, lying in such a way as to look like a bull's head. I picked them up and put them together so that nobody could possibly fail to realize that this seat and this handle-bar from a bike were really a bull's head. My metamorphosis was successful, and now I wish there could be another one, this time in reverse. Suppose that one day my head of a bull were to be thrown on a junk heap. Maybe a little boy would come along and notice it and say to himself, 'Now there's something I could use as a handle-bar for my bike.' If that ever happens, we will have brought off a double metamorphosis."

17 (David Douglas Duncan describes a conversation during a meal at Picasso's house.)

"During the meal I mentioned that it seemed really eerie to me to watch his gaze leap from article to article on the table and around the room, knowing perfectly well he was not seeing *anything* as I saw it, and never had. I added that it seemed incredible that one person ever dreamed of such varied images throughout a lifetime and could still be doing it today without apparently even trying. Picasso answered very simply, 'If I tried, they would all look the same.'"

18 (Ronald Penrose, Picasso's biographer, recalls a visit to the artist in his Paris apartment.)

"I happened to notice that a large Renoir hanging over the fireplace was crooked. 'It's better like that,' [Picasso] said, 'if you want to kill a picture all you have to do is to hang it beautifully on a nail and soon you will see nothing of it but the frame. When it's out of place you see it better.'"

19 In later life Picasso visited an exhibition of children's drawings. He observed, "When I was their age, I could draw like Raphael, but it took me a lifetime to learn to draw like them."

る〜 〜§

PICCARD, Auguste (1884–1962), *Swiss physicist. In 1931 and 1932 he made balloon ascents into the stratosphere in order to investigate cosmic rays and other phenomena.*

1 Auguste and his twin brother, Jean Felix, had spent the night in a strange town and were both in need of a shave. Entering the local barber's shop alone, Auguste settled down in the chair and said, "Make sure you give me a close shave. My beard grows so rapidly that two hours after I've had a shave, I need another." The barber looked at him in disbelief. "If your beard grows in two hours," he said skeptically, "I'll give you another shave free." Auguste left the shop in due course, clean-shaven and apparently satisfied. Two hours later, the barber was horrified to see his customer return with a dark growth of stubble on his chin. "Now do you believe me?" asked Jean Felix as he sat down for his free shave.

❧ ❦

PICON, Molly (1898–   ), *Yiddish–American actress.*

1 On tour with a theater company, Miss Picon overheard some of her fellow performers discussing their rather inadequate accommodations. "I never complain about such things — my grandmother brought up eleven children in four rooms," she remarked, breaking into the conversation. "How did she manage?" asked one of the other actresses. "Easy," replied Molly. "She took in boarders."

❧ ❦

PINZA, Ezio (1892–1957), *US opera singer, born in Italy. A versatile performer, he also appeared in musical comedies and a number of films.*

1 Soon after opening in the Broadway production of *South Pacific*, Pinza called at his favorite restaurant for his customary twelve-course dinner. Noticing the look of astonishment on the waiter's face as he took the order, Pinza snapped, "What's the matter with you? I may be singing musical comedy these days — but I still *eat* grand opera!"

❧ ❦

PITT, William (1759–1806), *British statesman; prime minister (1783–1801, 1804–06), known as William Pitt the Younger to distinguish him from his father, the Earl of Chatham. Pitt was the youngest British prime minister in history. At home he was chiefly concerned with reorganizing the economy, but he also faced crises over the administration of India and Ireland. He spearheaded the diplomatic offensive against revolutionary France, and from 1793, against Napoleon.*

1 A number of volunteers in London offered Pitt their services as militia. Although they were prepared to organize and equip themselves, the offer was hedged about with a number of provisos that substantially reduced its usefulness. Pitt read through their proposal until he reached a clause stating that they should never be required to leave the kingdom. At this point he picked up a pen and added in the margin, "except in the case of actual invasion."

2 Pitt had been urging Parliament to approve the immediate dispatch of the British fleet against the French. In order to secure the necessary appropriation, he had to persuade Lord Newcastle, the chancellor of the exchequer, who opposed his policy. Pitt called on the chancellor to pursue the question and found him in bed, suffering from gout. It was autumn, the room was unheated, and Pitt remarked how cold it was. Newcastle ironically replied that the weather would hinder any fleet movements and indeed hinder any comfortable discussion of the point at issue. Pitt answered that he did not so lightly relinquish his plans. Then, asking pardon, he removed his boots, climbed into the room's other bed, drew up the cover, and began a unique conference. He won his point.

3 Napoleon's victory at Austerlitz in December 1805 left him master of Europe and spelled the end of Pitt's alliance against him with Sweden, Austria, and Russia. When the news of the battle was brought to Pitt, he pointed to a large map of Europe on the wall and said, "Roll up that map; it will not be wanted these ten years."

4 Pitt died in office, worn out by overwork and crushed by the overthrow of his coalition against Napoleon. Desperately aware of the dangerous ebb of England's fortunes, he murmured as he died, "My country, oh, how I leave my country!"

{Another version is: "My country, oh, how I love my country!" Alternative last words attributed to Pitt are the far more touching "I think I could eat one of Bellamy's veal pies."}

❧ ❦

"Alferd Packer ate five prospectors whom he was guiding over a high Colorado plateau in 1874.

"The judge who sentenced Packer to hang indignantly pointed out that 'There was only six Democrats in all of Hinsdale County and you ate five of them.' "

— John Train,
True Remarkable Occurrences

(Train notes: "The Department of Agriculture startled the official community by dedicating the cafeteria in its Washington building to Alferd Packer in 1977. The General Services Administration then removed the dedicatory plaque, accusing the Department of Agriculture of 'bad taste.' ")

PLATO (c. 428–c. 348 BC), *Greek philosopher, who founded the Academy at Athens. His writings include* The Apology, Phaedo, *and* The Republic. *The great British thinker A. N. Whitehead once commented that all Western philosophy consists of footnotes to Plato.*

1 A student, struggling with the abstract concepts of Platonic mathematics, asked Plato, "What practical end do these theorems serve? What is to be gained from them?" Plato turned to his attendant slave and said, "Give this young man an obol [a small coin] that he may feel that he has gained something from my teachings, and then expel him."

2 Plato considered the abstract speculations of pure mathematics to be the highest form of thought of which the human mind was capable. He therefore had written over the entrance to the Academy "Let no one ignorant of mathematics enter here."

3 Diogenes came to Plato's house one day and was disgusted to find rich and exquisite carpets on the floor. To show his contempt he stamped and wiped his feet upon them, saying, "Thus do I trample upon the pride of Plato." "With greater pride," observed Plato mildly.

PLINY [Pliny the Younger] (c. 61–c. 133), *Roman orator, statesman, and lawyer. His letters cover a wide range of subjects, from official correspondence when he was a provincial governor to ghost stories and descriptions of boar hunts.*

1 At dinner Pliny noticed that his host distributed the food and wine according to the social standing of the diners. Rich and elegant dishes and the best wine were served to himself and his most honored guests, while cheap and paltry food and drink were set before the rest. Another guest, sensing Pliny's disapproval of these parsimonious measures, inquired how he managed in his own home. Pliny answered, "I provide each guest with the same fare, for when I invite a man to my table I have placed him on a footing of equality with me and I will therefore treat him as an equal." The other man was surprised. "Even freedmen?" he asked. "Even freedmen," replied Pliny, "because on these occasions I regard them as companions, not as freedmen." The other remarked that this must run Pliny into a great deal of expense. "Not at all," said Pliny, "for my freedmen don't drink the same wine as I do, but *I* drink what *they* do."

PLOMER, William (1903–73), *South African poet and novelist. He published* Collected Poems *in 1960, wrote libretti for Benjamin Britten's operas, and produced some memorable short stories.*

1 In Birmingham for the first time William Plomer was enthralled by the names of destinations written on the front of buses. As he and Walter Allen waited at a bus stop, he recited the names aloud. Eventually a number 12A appeared, with the legend: "WORLD'S END VIA LAKEY LANE." "Pure Auden," said Plomer.

PLOTINUS (205–270), *Greek philosopher. He settled and taught in Rome, where he founded the Neoplatonic school of philosophy. His teaching emphasized the reality of a transcendent "One" and the unreality of the material world.*

1 A friend urged Plotinus to have his portrait painted. The philosopher refused: "It is bad enough to be condemned to drag around this image in which nature has imprisoned me. Why should I consent to the perpetuation of the image of this image?"

ॐ ॐ

POE, Edgar Allan (1809–49), *US poet, short-story writer, and literary critic. He is best remembered for his masterly horror stories, contained in* Tales of the Grotesque and Arabesque *(1840), and melancholy poems, such as* The Raven *(1845).*

1   An old literary and military tradition has it that Poe was expelled from West Point in 1831 for "gross neglect of duty" because he appeared naked at a public parade. Parade dress instructions called for "white belts and gloves, under arms." Poe took this literally and appeared with rifle over his bare shoulder, wearing belt and gloves — and nothing else.

ॐ ॐ

POGGIO BRACCIOLINI, Gian Francesco (1380–1459), *Italian humanist scholar and writer. He distinguished himself in all fields of literature, but is chiefly remembered today for his rediscovery of manuscripts of classical authors believed lost.*

1   As holder of a secretarial post in the papal Curia, Poggio wore ecclesiastical dress although he was never formally ordained a priest. A cardinal reprimanded him for having children, which did not become a man wearing ecclesiastical garb, and for having a mistress, which was unbecoming even to a layman. Poggio retorted, "I have children, which is suitable for a layman, and I have a mistress, which is a time-honored custom of the clergy."

ॐ ॐ

POMPADOUR, Jeanne-Antoinette Poisson, Marquise d'Étoiles (1721–64), *French lady of the court; mistress of Louis XV. Mme de Pompadour played an important part in determining the course of French politics in the 1750s and early 1760s.*

1   (Mme de Pompadour enjoyed surrounding herself with intellectuals and supported the *Encyclopédistes* against the church. Despite her efforts, at one time the religious and antirationalist factions in the court persuaded Louis to ban the *Encyclopédie*. Soon after this a duke

wondered aloud at a royal supper party what gunpowder was made of.)

" 'It seems so funny that we spend our time killing partridges, and being killed ourselves on the frontier, and really we have no idea how it happens.' Madame de Pompadour, seeing her opportunity, quickly went on: 'Yes, and face powder? What is that made of? Now, if you had not confiscated the *Encyclopédie*, Sire, we could have found out in a moment.' The King sent to his library for a copy, and presently a footman staggered in under the heavy volumes; the party was kept amused for the rest of the evening looking up gunpowder, rouge, and so on. After this subscribers were allowed to have their copies, though it was still not on sale in the bookshops."

2   As she lay dying, Madame de Pompadour summoned her last strength and called to God, "Wait a second," as she dabbed her cheeks with rouge.

ॐ ॐ

POOLE, Oliver Brian Sanderson, 1st Baron Poole of Aldgate, (1911–   ), *British businessman. An active member of the Conservative party, he eventually became chairman (1955–57), and has been a governor of the Old Vic and a trustee of the National Gallery.*

1   During the 1970s a great many of the flashier British entrepreneurs went under. Their temporary success had been in part ascribable to the extensive loans freely made to them, often by quite conservative banks. The merchant bank Lazard Frères & Co., however, had not committed this error. Lord Cowdray, then chairman of the family business that owned Lazard Frères, once asked Lord Poole, then chairman of the firm, how he had managed to avoid making such loans. Poole replied: "Quite simple: I only lent money to people who had been to Eton."

ॐ ॐ

POPE, Alexander (1688–1744), *English poet, satirist, and translator. Crippled by illness at the age of twelve, he soon gave proof of his extraordinary talents in his* Pastorals *(1709), written when he was only sixteen. His* Essay on Criticism *(1711) ensured his entrée to the London literary world, which he dominated for nearly thirty years. He perfected the English heroic* *couplet as a satirical medium in* The Rape of the Lock *(1712; enlarged version 1714) and the* "Epistle to Dr. Arbuthnot" *(1735). The* Dunciad, *his satire on contemporary writers, came out in three versions (1728, 1729, 1743). Pope also translated Homer's* Iliad *(1720) and* Odyssey *(1725–26), and published the philosophical poems* An Essay on Man *(1733–34) and* Moral Essays *(1731–35).*

1 Statesman and financier Charles Montagu, first Earl of Halifax, prided himself upon his literary acumen. When Pope had completed the first few books of his translation of the *Iliad,* Montagu invited him to give a reading at his house. Other eminent literary figures also attended. Pope considered that the reading had gone off very well, even though Lord Halifax had interrupted, most politely, four or five times to say that there was something about that particular passage he did not think quite right and that Pope could improve it with some more thought. On the way home with physician and poet Samuel Garth, Pope confessed that he was much perplexed by Lord Halifax's rather vague objections. He went on to say that although he had been thinking about the offending passages ever since, he could not for the life of him see what should be done to make them more acceptable to his lordship. Dr. Garth reassured him; he knew Lord Halifax very well, he said, and all Pope needed to do was to leave the passages as they were, wait a couple of months, and then go back to Lord Halifax, thank him for his kind criticisms, and read him the "corrected" passages. In due course Pope had another session with Lord Halifax, reading him the passages exactly as they had been. His lordship was delighted, and congratulated Pope on getting them absolutely right.

2 Pope's translations of Homer's *Iliad* and *Odyssey* offended the classical scholar Richard Bentley. Of Pope's *Iliad* he said, "It is a pretty poem, Mr. Pope, but you must not call it Homer."

{Modern critics tend to agree with Bentley.}

3 Pope's father was a linen-draper, and, although his family was respectable, it was by no means aristocratic. George II, alert to social distinctions, advised Lord Hervey, "You ought not to write verses, 'tis beneath your rank; leave such work to little Mr. Pope; it is his trade."

4 When Pope was lying on his deathbed, the doctor assured him that his breathing was easier, his pulse steadier, and various other encouraging things. "Here am I," commented Pope to a friend, "dying of a hundred good symptoms."

෧ ෬

POPE, Arthur Upham (1881–1969), *US eccentric millionaire and authority on the art and archaeology of Iran (in his day Persia) and neighboring Arab cultures.*

1 Pope was single-minded in his intellectual interests. In 1943 he agreed to deliver the annual Lincoln's Day address at Cooper Union, New York, where Lincoln had once made an epochal speech. According to a *New Yorker* magazine account he spoke for about an hour and a half on his favorite topic, Middle Eastern cultures. At the very end, recalling his assigned subject, he discharged his obligation by stating: "Lincoln knew no Arabs, but he would have enjoyed meeting them, and they would have recognized him as a great sheik."

෧ ෬

PORSON, Richard (1759–1808), *British classical scholar renowned for his knowledge of ancient Greek and his editions of the plays of Euripides. Many stories are told of his drinking bouts.*

1 Porson had an outstanding memory, first revealed during his schooldays at Eton. A classmate, as a practical joke, had borrowed his copy of Horace's *Odes,* artfully replacing it with a different text. As the Latin lesson began, Porson was asked to read and translate one of the odes. This he did without faltering, but the master, noticing that the boy appeared to be reading from the wrong side of the page, asked which edition he was using. Porson sheepishly handed the book to his master, who was amazed to find that he had just recited the Latin ode from memory while looking at an English version of Ovid.

2 Porson was once traveling in a stagecoach with a young Oxford student who, in an attempt to impress the ladies present, let slip a

Greek quotation which he said was from Sophocles. The professor was not taken in by the young man's bluff and, pulling a pocket edition of Sophocles from the folds of his coat, challenged him to find the passage in question. Undeterred, the student said that he had made a mistake and that the quotation was in fact from Euripides. To the great amusement of the young ladies, Porson immediately produced a copy of Euripides from his pocket and issued the same challenge. In a last desperate attempt to save face, the young man announced with conviction that the passage was, of course, from Aeschylus. However, on seeing the inevitable copy of Aeschylus emerge from Porson's pocket, he finally admitted defeat. "Coachman!" he cried. "Let me out! There's a fellow here has the whole Bodleian Library in his pocket."

3   Porson arrived unexpectedly to stay with the portrait-painter John Hoppner. Hoppner told him he could not offer much in the way of hospitality as Mrs. Hoppner was away and had taken with her the key to the wine closet. In the course of the evening Porson became increasingly restless, declared that he was sure Mrs. Hoppner would keep some wine for her own private enjoyment hidden somewhere in her bedroom, and asked that he might be allowed to search for it. With some irritation Hoppner agreed, and was greatly chagrined when Porson returned from his search clutching a bottle and pronouncing it to be the best gin he had tasted for a long time.

When Mrs. Hoppner returned, her husband rather angrily told her that Porson had found and consumed her hidden drink. "Good heavens," she cried, "that was spirit of wine for the lamp!"

{This is just one of a number of stories that confirm the observation that Porson would "drink ink rather than not drink at all."}

4   Porson was once asked for his opinion of the poetical works of his younger contemporary Robert Southey. "Your works will be read," he told him, "after Shakespeare and Milton are forgotten — and not till then."

5   A junior scholar once rashly suggested to Porson that they could collaborate. Porson applauded the notion: "Put in all I know and all

you don't know, and it will make a great work."

6   Samuel Rogers, the poet and man of letters, invited Porson to dinner. "Thank you, no," was the reply, "I dined yesterday."

7   On a walk together, Porson and a Trinitarian friend were discussing the nature of the Trinity. A buggy passed them with three men in it. "There," said the friend, "that's an illustration of the Trinity."

"No," said Porson, "you must show me one man in three buggies — if you can."

ও

POUSSIN, Nicolas (1594–1665), *French classical painter who spent most of his working life in Rome. His mature works deal mainly with figures from the Old Testament or classical mythology.*

1   Exasperated by his failure to produce a satisfactory depiction of the foam around the mouth of a spirited horse, Poussin dashed his sponge against the canvas. The effect thus created was exactly what he had been striving for so laboriously.

See also FRANZ JOSEPH HAYDN 1.

ও

PREVIN, André (1929–), *German-born conductor, pianist, and composer, known especially for his televised concert performances, which have done much to widen the audience for classical music. He was conductor of the London Symphony Orchestra (1969–79) and in 1977 became music director of the Pittsburgh Symphony; he has also made many appearances as guest conductor with other major orchestras.*

1   (As a teenager Previn used to play the piano at a cinema that specialized in showing old silent movies. As he remembers, this job was short-lived.)

"One afternoon I was pounding away the appropriate music for a '20s 'Flaming Youth' movie, did not watch the screen, and was blithely unaware that the main attraction, a revival of D. W. Griffith's biblical masterpiece *Intolerance,* had begun. I was enthusiastically playing a Charleston during the scene depicting the Last Supper when the manager of the theater came storming down the aisle, and I was unemployed two minutes later."

2 After a rehearsal with the London Symphony Orchestra, Previn was sitting in the bar of the Westbury Hotel, having a drink with the soloist. He saw a young American composer whose work he had admired come into the room, and Previn beckoned him over and ordered him a drink. "I heard your orchestra a few nights ago," the composer said. "It sounded absolutely marvelous. It was the night the Beethoven Sixth was played in the first half."

"Oh, God," Previn replied, "that was the night Pollini was supposed to play the Fourth Piano Concerto in the second half, and he canceled, and we were stuck with one of those last-minute substitutions, that really appalling third-rate lady pianist. I'm really sorry you had to suffer through that." The young composer gave Previn a long and thoughtful look. "That's all right," he said coolly, "I didn't mind. The pianist is my wife."

3 To assess their suitability for adopting a Vietnamese orphan, a Miss Taylor, who had run a Saigon orphanage, stayed with the Previn family for a weekend. At breakfast on the first morning, she asked if she might have a bowl of cereal. Eager to please, Previn reached for the health-food cereal that his two small sons consumed with delight every morning and poured Miss Taylor a generous bowlful. While she ate, he held forth on the nutritional value of the cereal. Miss Taylor made no reply, however, until her bowl was empty. "To be quite honest," she admitted, "I'm not crazy about it." Previn's glance happened to fall on the jar from which he had served Miss Taylor. "I'm not surprised," he said slowly, "I've just made you eat a large dish of hamster food."

PRINGLE, Sir John (1707–82), *Scottish physician best remembered for his work to improve the facilities of military hospitals. He was president of the Royal Society from 1772 to 1778.*

1 Ill health is the cause generally given for Pringle's resignation of the presidency of the Royal Society, but there is also another explanation. Benjamin Franklin's invention of the lightning rod had given him unique status as a scientist all over the Western world. George III, however, who found Franklin's revolutionary sentiments uncongenial, was eager to discredit his scientific achievements. He therefore ordered that blunt ends should be substituted for the pointed ends on the lightning rods used on Kew Palace. Sir John Pringle is reputed to have remonstrated with the king, saying, "The laws of nature are not changeable at royal pleasure." For this undiplomatic remark he was compelled to forfeit his position in the Royal Society.

૭∾   ∾૭

PROKOFIEV, Sergei (1891–1953), *Russian composer. His many works include the* Classical Symphony *(1916–17),* Peter and the Wolf *(1936), and the opera* The Love for Three Oranges *(1919).*

1 One regular concert-goer at the Brussels Philharmonic always arrived at the concert hall armed with sketchbook and pencil. She would sketch the guest artist during the performance and have the portrait autographed afterward. When Prokofiev's turn came, however, he refused to sign the picture, considering it a poor likeness. "It looks more like Furtwängler," he said. The usher who was acting as intermediary for the lady pleaded with the composer: "Please, Mr. Prokofiev. She is such a good subscriber. Please do this little thing for the Brussels Philharmonic!" Prokofiev looked at the picture again. "All right," he sighed, picking up his pen and writing with a flourish. The usher examined the "autograph" more closely. Prokofiev had signed the picture: "Furtwängler."

૭∾   ∾૭

PULITZER, Joseph (1847–1911), *US newspaper baron, born in Hungary. He bought the* New York World *in 1883 and founded the* New York Evening World *in 1887. He also established the Pulitzer prizes, to be awarded "for the encouragement of public service, public morals, American literature, and the advancement of education."*

1 Like most great newspaper and magazine owners, Pulitzer was mildly megalomaniacal. He felt the *World* "should be more powerful than the president." He even thought it might influence the inhabitants of other planets. He once considered erecting an advertising sign in New Jersey that would be visible on Mars, and was dissuaded only when one of his assistants asked, "What language shall we print it in?"

૭∾   ∾૭

PUSHKIN, Alexander (1799–1837), *Russian poet, novelist, and playwright. His notable works include* Eugene Onegin *(1833),* Boris Godunov *(1831), and the epic* The Bronze Horseman *(1837).*

1 Pushkin once listened to Gogol reading *Dead Souls*. He laughed heartily. Then suddenly his face grew grave and he exclaimed, "Oh God, how sad our Russia is!"

❦ ❧

PUTNAM, Israel (1718–90), *US Revolutionary commander. Having served in the French and Indian War, he was appointed major general at the beginning of the Revolution and commanded at several battles.*

1 During the French and Indian War Putnam was challenged to a duel by a British major whom he had insulted. Realizing that he would stand little chance in a duel with pistols, Putnam invited the major to his tent and suggested an alternative trial of honor. The two men were sitting on small powder kegs, into each of which Putnam had inserted a slow-burning fuse. The first to squirm or move from his seat would be the loser. As the fuses burned, the major showed increasing signs of anxiety, while Putnam continued to smoke his pipe with a casual air. Seeing the spectators gradually disappear from the tent to escape the impending explosion, the major finally leaped from his keg, acknowledging Putnam as the victor. Only then did Putnam reveal that the kegs contained onions, not gunpowder.

PYLE, Ernest Taylor (1900–45), *US war correspondent. He won a Pulitzer Prize (1944) for his reporting of World War II. He was killed while covering the fighting against the Japanese in the Pacific.*

1 Reporting on the Normandy landings, Ernie Pyle always seemed to be there when the action was toughest, though without any parade of heroics. Entering Cherbourg, the correspondents found everything superficially calm, when suddenly a shell hit a tank only a few yards from them. When the men in the street stopped running and went back, they found Ernie Pyle taking down the names of those who had come out of the tank. By way of explanation he said, "They seemed to know me, so I had to stick around."

❦ ❧

PYRRHUS (319–272 BC), *king of Epirus in northwestern Greece (306–272 BC). A daring general, he was invited by the Greek cities of southern Italy to help them against the growing might of Rome. He campaigned in Italy and Sicily (280–275) without success and was killed in a skirmish in the Peloponnesian town of Argos, struck on the head by a roof tile hurled from a housetop by a woman.*

1 In 279 BC the invading Greek forces under Pyrrhus met and defeated the Romans at the battle of Asculum in Apulia. The engagement, however, cost Pyrrhus many men, some of his closest associates, and all his baggage. One of the Greeks congratulated the king on his victory, to which he replied, "Another such victory and we are ruined." Hence the phrase "Pyrrhic victory" for one that costs the victor too high a price.

❦ ❧

PYTHAGORAS (born *c.* 580 BC), *Greek philosopher born on Samos. The geometrical theorem that still bears his name and the notion of the "harmony of the spheres" were his most important contributions to science.*

1 Seeing a puppy being beaten one day, Pythagoras took pity, saying, "Stop, do not beat it; it is the soul of a friend which I recognized when I heard it crying out."

Q

QUEENSBERRY, William Douglas, 4th Duke of (1724–1810), *British nobleman known for the latter part of his life as "Old Q."*

1 Old Q was entertaining at his villa in Richmond, which had a magnificent view of the Thames River. Guest after guest admired the panorama until the duke burst out, "What is there to make so much of in the Thames? I am quite tired of it. Flow, flow, flow, always the same."

2 With advancing years Old Q became very infirm and spent much of his time at the porch or bow window of his London house, overlooking Piccadilly. In those days great households included a class of retainer called a "running footman," whose job was to run messages and errands and to clear a way through crowds for their employers. Applicants for the post of running footman in Old Q's establishment had to run a kind of trial up Piccadilly, dressed in full ducal livery, while Old Q himself watched from his vantage point.

One particular candidate ran so speedily that Old Q shouted down in delight, "You'll do very well for me."

"And your lordship's livery will do very well for me," replied the man, taking off at top speed, never to be seen again.

QUESNAY, François (1694–1774), *French economist and physician. He was leader of the Physiocrats, a group of Enlightenment theorists who believed in the paramount importance of agriculture in the economy.*

1 Louis XV once asked Quesnay, who was originally the king's physician, what he would do if he were king. "Nothing," replied Quesnay. "But then, who would govern?" asked Louis. "The laws," was the response.

QUIN, James (1693–1766), *British actor.*

1 William Warburton, bishop of Gloucester, was holding forth about royal prerogative, of which he was an ardent supporter. Quin tried to shut him up by asking him to spare his feelings, as he was a republican. "Perhaps I even think that the execution of Charles I might have been justified," he added. "Oh? By what law?" demanded Warburton. "By all the laws that he had left to the country," retorted Quin. The bishop replied that Charles would have been spared in a proper court of law, and in any case all the regicides had come to violent ends. "I would not advise your lordship to make use of *that* inference," said Quin, "for, if I am not mistaken, that was the case of the twelve apostles."

R

RABELAIS, François (?1494–1553), *French writer. By turns a Franciscan friar, a Benedictine monk, and a secular priest, Rabelais also practiced as a physician. His* Gargantua *and* Pantagruel, *published at intervals from 1532, combined obscene horseplay with satire on ecclesiastical institutions. This led to condemnation of his books by the theologians of the Sorbonne. His colorful writings doubtless encouraged the accumulation of apocryphal anecdotes about his life and death.*

1 On the way to Paris one day, Rabelais found himself stranded at a small country inn with no money to pay his bill or to continue his journey. So he made up three small packets, labeled them "Poison for the King," "Poison for Monsieur," and "Poison for the Dauphin" and left them where the landlord of the inn was sure to find them. That patriotic citizen informed the police, who promptly arrested Rabelais and hauled him off to Paris. When the packets were examined and found to be empty, Rabelais explained his subterfuge and was set free, having accomplished his journey at no expense to himself.

2 A short time before Rabelais died, he put on a domino (cloak and mask) and was seen sitting by his bed in this unusual garb. Reproached for being so frivolous at this dark and serious hour, he quipped in Latin, *"Beati qui in Domino moriuntur"* (Blessed are they who die in the Lord — or — in a domino).

3 It is said that Rabelais made the following will: "I owe much. I possess nothing. I give the rest to the poor."

RABI, Isidor Isaac (1898–   ), *US physicist, born in Austria. He taught at Columbia University from 1929, becoming professor there in 1937. He was awarded the 1944 Nobel Prize for physics.*

1 Leo Szilard, anxious to enlist other physicists in determining whether fission could produce the neutrons needed for the release of energy, sent Rabi to see the great Enrico Fermi at his home. Rabi went, saw Fermi, and reported to Szilard that Fermi had said, "Nuts!" Szilard, baffled, then accompanied Rabi to Fermi's office and asked for an explanation of "Nuts!" Fermi explained that the possibility of a chain reaction resulting from the fission of uranium was remote. "What do you mean by 'remote'?" asked Rabi. "Well, ten percent," said Fermi. Leo Szilard never forgot Rabi's quiet reply to this statement: "Ten percent is not a remote possibility if we may die of it."

RACHEL (1820–58), *French actress, born Élisa Félix, the daughter of a Jewish peddler. From 1838 she was the Comédie-Française's leading tragedienne until her early death from tuberculosis.*

1 One of Rachel's numerous lovers was François d'Orléans, Prince de Joinville, third son of Louis-Philippe. He sent her his visiting card on which he had written: *"Où? — quand? — combien?"* (Where? — when? — how much?) Rachel, equally businesslike, scrawled: *"Chez toi — ce soir — pour rien"* (Your place — tonight — free of charge) and sent the card back. Their affair lasted for seven or eight years.

2 Because of her itinerant upbringing Rachel was virtually uneducated, and to the end of her life her letters remained full of errors in spelling and grammar. Rachel was quite aware of her failings. When an admirer begged her for *"un bel autographe"* (a nice autograph), she replied, *"Un bel autographe avec ou sans orthographe?"* (A nice autograph — with or without proper spelling?)

3 Despite her lack of education, Rachel excelled at the interpretation of the classical French heroines in the tragedies of Racine and Corneille, restoring their plays to the repertoire of the Comédie-Française. Someone once pompously congratulated her on saving the French language. She answered, "Clever of me, isn't it, seeing that I never learned it."

4 Rachel was notorious for her avarice and for her guile at persuading people to give her presents. Dining at the Comte Duchâtel's, she pointedly admired the great silver centerpiece on the table. The count, completely under her spell, said he would be happy to give it to her. Rachel accepted eagerly, but was a little nervous that the count might change his mind. She mentioned that she had come to the dinner in a cab. The count offered her his carriage to take her home. "Indeed," said Rachel, "that will suit me very well, as there will then be no danger of my being robbed of your gift, which I had better take with me." The count bowed. "With pleasure," he said, "but you *will* send my carriage back, won't you?"

5 Rachel had presented Dumas *fils* with a ring. Fully aware of the actress's reputation for requesting and acquiring gifts from her friends and acquaintances, Dumas immediately slipped the ring back onto Rachel's finger: "Permit me, mademoiselle, to present it to you in my turn so as to save you the embarrassment of asking for it."

6 Boasted Rachel after a successful opening night: *"Mon dieu!* When I came out on the stage the audience simply sat there open-mouthed."
"Nonsense!" snapped a fellow actress. "They never all yawn at once."

ੲ৯ ৶৽

RACHMANINOFF, Sergei (1873–1943), *Russian composer, pianist, and conductor. After 1917 he lived mainly in the United States. He first achieved fame as a pianist performing his own compositions.*

1 Arthur Rubinstein gave a dinner party in honor of Rachmaninoff, in the course of which the composer mentioned that he thought the Grieg piano concerto the greatest ever written. Rubinstein said that he had just recorded it. Rachmaninoff insisted on hearing the recording then and there. During coffee, Rubinstein put on the proofs of the record and Rachmaninoff, closing his eyes, settled down to listen. He listened right through without saying a word. At the end of the concerto he opened his eyes and said, "Piano out of tune."

2 Rachmaninoff, taken ill in the middle of a concert tour, was admitted to a hospital in Los Angeles, where cancer was diagnosed. Knowing he was dying, the pianist looked at his hands and murmured, "My dear hands. Farewell, my poor hands."

ੲ৯ ৶৽

RACINE, Jean (1639–99), *French dramatist. His verse tragedies are considered the finest examples of the French classical drama; they include* Andromaque *(1667),* Bérénice *(1670), and* Phèdre *(1677).*

1 The actress Marie Champmêlé once asked Racine from what source he had drawn his religious drama *Athalie.* "From the Old Testament," he replied. "Really?" said the actress. "From the Old Testament? I always thought there was a new one."

ੲ৯ ৶৽

RAFT, George (1895–1980), *US film actor, famous for his sinister roles in gangster movies. He had previously been a nightclub dancer and athlete.*

1 George Raft acquired and disposed of about ten million dollars in the course of his career. "Part of the loot went for gambling," he later explained, "part for horses, and part for women. The rest I spent foolishly."

ੲ৯ ৶৽

RAGLAN, FitzRoy James Henry Somerset, 1st Baron (1788–1855), *British field marshal. He served with distinction under the Duke of Wellington during the Napoleonic Wars and was appointed commander in the Crimean War, for the conduct of which he endured much criticism. The raglan sleeve style is named for him.*

1 At the close of the battle of Waterloo Raglan was standing beside Wellington when a bullet shattered his right elbow. The arm had to be amputated, an operation Raglan bore without a murmur, but as the limb was being taken away for disposal he cried out, "Don't carry away that arm till I have taken off my ring." The arm was brought back, and Raglan retrieved a ring that his wife had given him.

ଚ୬ ଈଓ

RAINIER III [Rainier Louis Henri Maxence Bertrand de Grimaldi] (1923–   ), *prince of Monaco. The twenty-sixth ruling prince of the House of Grimaldi, in 1956 he married US film star Grace Kelly, who died following a car accident in 1982.*

1 On a tour of the Astrodome, a huge sports stadium covering some nine acres of land in Houston, Texas, Prince Rainier was asked, "How would you like to have the Astrodome in Monaco?"

"Marvelous," he replied. "Then we could be the world's only indoor country."

ଚ୬ ଈଓ

RALEIGH, Sir Walter (?1552–1618), *English soldier, explorer, and writer. A favorite of Queen Elizabeth I, he was sent by her on voyages to the New World. His vigorous anti-Spanish opinions caused his downfall under James I when the king wished to appease Spain. He was sentenced to death (1603), but the sentence was commuted to imprisonment. During his twelve years in the Tower of London he wrote some of his best-known lyrics ("The Lie," "The Pilgrimage") and began a history of the world. In 1616 he was released to search for gold in South America, but the expedition was a catastrophe and on his return the death sentence of 1603 was carried out.*

1 Although primarily a man of action, the courtly Raleigh exemplified the ideal of the Renaissance gentleman. There is an old tradition that he first caught the attention of Queen Elizabeth sometime in 1581 when she was walking along a muddy path. As she hesitated in front of a particularly large puddle, Raleigh sprang forward and, taking off his new plush cloak, laid it on the ground for his sovereign to step upon.

2 At the outset of his career as courtier Raleigh scratched with a diamond the following words on a window of the royal palace: "Fain would I climb, yet fear I to fall." The queen, as he had intended, read the line. She completed the couplet: "If thy heart fail thee, climb not at all."

3 Raleigh brought back tobacco from the New World and introduced smoking to Britain. The novelty caused much comment and considerable discussion pro and con. Raleigh was once enjoying a pipe when his servant, seeing his master enveloped in clouds of smoke, thought that he must be on fire, and quickly emptied a bowl of water over Raleigh's head.

4 (John Aubrey recounts an incident that led to Raleigh's temporary loss of favor with Queen Elizabeth.)

"He loved a wench well; and one time getting one of the Maids of Honour up against a tree in a wood ('twas his first lady) who seemed at first boarding to be something fearful of her honour, and modest, she cried, 'Sweet Sir Walter, what do you me ask? Will you undo me? Nay, sweet Sir Walter! Sweet Sir Walter! Sir Walter!' At last, as the danger and the pleasure at the same time grew higher, she cried in the ecstasy, 'Swisser Swatter, Swisser Swatter!' She proved with child, and I doubt not but this hero took care of them both, as also that the product was more than an ordinary mortal."

5 Like his father, Raleigh's eldest son and namesake was quick-tempered and a womanizer. At a dinner in great company young Walter, sitting next to his father, began to tell a discreditable anecdote, about how he had visited a whore and she had refused to lie with him because "your father lay with me but an hour ago."

Incensed and embarrassed, Raleigh hit young Walter across the face. The young man was wild, but not so wicked as to strike his father. So he turned to the man sitting on his other side and hit him, saying as he did so, "Box about; it will come to my father anon."

6 In his role as Elizabeth's favorite Raleigh was quick to seek benefits and rewards. The queen once rebuked him mildly for his rapacity, saying, "When will you cease to be a beggar?"

"When you cease to be a benefactress, ma'am," replied Raleigh.

7   The sentence of death on Raleigh was confirmed on October 28, 1618, with the execution set for the following morning. As Raleigh was led back to prison from the tribunal at Westminster, he spied an old acquaintance, Sir Hugh Beeston, whom he greeted cheerfully. "You will come tomorrow?" he asked Beeston. "But I do not know how you will manage to get a place. For my own part I am sure of one, but you will have to shift for yourself."

8   Raleigh's courage and dignity on the scaffold were part of the legend that grew up around him as a martyr to the unpopular pro-Spanish policy of James I. He tested the ax's edge, saying, "It is a sharp remedy, but a sure one for all ills." As he laid his head on the block, someone protested that it should be placed so that his head should point toward the east. "What matter how the head lie, so the heart be right?" said Raleigh.

≥∽ ⊷≤

RAMANUJAN, Srinivasa (1887–1920), *Indian mathematician. He visited England (1914–19), but fell ill and died soon after returning to India. The Cambridge mathematician G. H. Hardy edited and published after his death most of his profoundly original work.*

1   (J. E. Littlewood, a mathematician who collaborated with Hardy, recounts a conversation with Ramanujan.)

"I remember once going to see him when he was lying ill at Putney. I had ridden in taxicab number 1729, and remarked that the number seemed to me rather a dull one, and that I hoped it was not an unfavorable omen. 'No,' he replied, 'it is a very interesting number; it is the smallest number expressible as the sum of two cubes in two different ways.'"

≥∽ ⊷≤

RAMSEY, [Arthur] **Michael** (1904–), *Anglican prelate. Ordained in 1928, he was bishop of Durham (1952–56), archbishop of York (1956–61), and archbishop of Canterbury (1961–74).*

1   Even as a curate, Ramsey was renowned for his absentmindedness. His landlady was tidying up his room one day when there came a knock at the door. "Mr. Ramsey's not here," she called. "He's gone out."

"Oh, yes, yes of course," came the reply. "Thank you very much."

Recognizing the voice as that of her young lodger, the landlady opened the door in time to see Ramsey disappear around the corner.

2   In New York one day, a local photographer had been trying for some time to take a picture of Ramsey, who was there on an official visit. Unable to think of any better way to attract the archbishop's attention, he finally called out in desperation: "Archie, would you turn your head this way, please?" Turning his head, Ramsey politely corrected the American. "My name, sir, is not Archie," he said with a friendly smile. "It's Mike."

≥∽ ⊷≤

RAPHAEL [Raffaello Sanzio] (1483–1520), *Italian artist and architect. He studied in Perugia with Perugino before moving to Florence (1504) and then Rome (1508). He decorated the papal apartments in the Vatican with a celebrated series of frescoes and in 1514 was appointed to succeed Bramante as architect of St. Peter's.*

1   A couple of cardinals, watching Raphael at work on his Vatican frescoes, annoyed the artist by keeping up a stream of ill-informed criticism. "The face of the apostle Paul is far too red," complained one. "He blushes to see into whose hands the church has fallen," said Raphael.

≥∽ ⊷≤

RAYNAL, Abbé Guillaume Thomas François (1713–96), *French historian.*

1   The Abbé Raynal and the Abbé Galiani were both incessant talkers. A friend decided to amuse himself by inviting them together to a gathering at his house. Abbé Galiani seized the first opening and took over the conversation so completely that no one, not even the Abbé Raynal, could get a word in edgewise. After listening in growing frustration, Raynal turned to his host and muttered, "*S'il crache, il est perdu*" (If he spits, he's lost).

Fanny Ronalds was a nineteenth-century society beauty and singer. Leonard Jerome, a Wall Street magnate, was one of her most ardent admirers, financing her performances as a singer and being frequently seen out driving with her. At a ball she came unexpectedly face to face with Jerome's wife, Clara. As Mrs. Ronalds held out her hand, the spectators held their breath, wondering how Mrs. Jerome would react to meeting the lady with whom her husband's name was so publicly linked. Mrs. Jerome took her rival's hand and said, "I don't blame you. I know how irresistible he is."

— Anita Leslie,
The Remarkable Mr. Jerome

READING, Stella, Marchioness of (1894–1971), *British political figure, secretary to Lord Reading, whom she married in 1931.*

1 Shortly after their marriage the Readings visited Lloyd George in the hospital, where he was recovering from a prostate operation. Only Lord Reading was admitted to the patient's room, the doctor insisting that he stay no longer than ten minutes. At the end of that time the doctor reluctantly agreed to an extension. As he was about to enter the room to turn Lord Reading out, he remarked pleasantly to a woman he did not know who happened to be standing in the corridor, "I think they ought to break it off now, don't you? In any case, Lord Reading isn't very exciting, is he?" To this the woman replied, "Well, he is my husband, and I have only been married to him a fortnight." At this time she was thirty-seven, he seventy.

෧ ෧

REAGAN, Ronald (1911–), *US film actor and politician; 40th president of the United States (1981–). He won fame as a movie actor, particularly in low-budget Westerns, before moving on to politics in his later years. An ultra-conservative Republican, he was governor of California (1966–74).*

1 During a student demonstration in the 1960s Reagan's limousine was hemmed in by a crowd of chanting demonstrators waving placards. The demonstrators were chanting, "We are the future." Reagan scribbled on a piece of paper and held it up to the window so they could read the words: "I'll sell my bonds."

2 In March 1981 a would-be assassin fired several shots at the president and his party as they left a Washington hotel. Reagan was taken to the hospital with a serious chest wound that needed emergency surgery. As he was wheeled into the operating theater he smiled, looked around at the team of surgeons, and said, "Please assure me that you are all Republicans!"

3 Several other men were wounded in the assassination attempt. The president asked to be kept informed of their progress. Told that it was good, he exclaimed, "That's great news. We'll have to get four bedpans and have a reunion."

4 Even the Democrats were impressed by Reagan's first televised budget speech, in which he used a handful of small change to illustrate the current value of the dollar. "It takes an actor to do that," admitted one of his rivals. "Carter would have emphasized all the wrong words. Ford would have fumbled and dropped the cash. Nixon would have pocketed it."

5 On April 6, 1984, Reagan ended a foreign policy address at Georgetown University by recalling his entrance to a recent state dinner for François Mitterrand: "Mrs. Mitterrand and I started through the tables, the butler leading us through the people, and suddenly Mrs. Mitterrand stopped. She calmly turned her head and said something to me in French, which unfortunately I did not understand. And the butler was motioning for us to come on, and I motioned to her that we should go forward, that we were to go to the other side of the room. And again, very calmly, she made her statement to me."

An interpreter finally explained to Mr. Reagan that Madame Mitterrand was telling him he was standing on her gown.

෧ ෧

REED, Thomas Brackett (1839–1902), *US statesman. A lawyer by profession, Reed was a Republican member of the House of Representatives (1877–99) and twice served as Speaker (1889–91, 1895–99).*

1 Speaker Reed was chatting with lawyer and diplomat Joseph H. Choate and a senator of the time. Choate said pompously, "I have not drunk whiskey, played cards for money, or attended a horse race in twenty-eight years." The senator said admiringly, "I wish I could say that!" Remarked Reed: "Well, why don't you? Choate said it."

2 In the course of debate when Reed was Speaker, William M. Springer of Illinois quoted Henry Clay's famous "I had rather be right than be president." In an undertone Reed interjected, "The gentleman need not worry, for he will never be either."

❧

REGER, Max (1873–1916), *German composer and organist.*

1 After playing the piano part in Schubert's "Trout" Quintet, Max Reger received a basket of trout from an admirer. Reger wrote to thank the sender, mentioning casually that his next concert program was to include Haydn's "Minuet of the Ox."

2 After receiving a bad review from Munich critic Rudolf Louis, Reger wrote to him: "I am sitting in the smallest room of my house. I have your review before me. In a moment it will be behind me."

{This response to adverse criticism has been attributed to several people. Shall we call it *derrière-pensée?*}

❧

REHAN, Ada (1860–1916), *US actress, born in Ireland. She excelled in comic roles, and worked with Augustin Daly's company in New York from 1879 to 1899.*

1 Miss Rehan was playing opposite an inexperienced young actor in a romantic comedy. During one scene the young hero asks the heroine a vital question and she pauses to consider her answer. The hero's next line should have been: "You don't reply," but at this point the young actor lost his nerve and dried up. "You don't reply . . . you don't reply," came a hoarse whisper from the wings. "How the hell can I," retorted the young actor impatiently, "when I don't know what to say?"

❧

REINHARDT, Max (1873–1943), *Austrian theater director of Jewish parentage. He was noted for his lavish productions, of which the most famous was* The Miracle *(1911).*

1 A clever young man was instructing Reinhardt in the art of producing Shakespeare: "No lavish spectacle, no gorgeous scenery, just simple black curtains; that's how it should be done. So much more artistic." Reinhardt nodded. "Also much easier," he said.

❧

REISENAUER, Alfred (1863–1907), *German pianist, a pupil of Liszt.*

1 "Reisenauer . . . had given a concert at the palace of some German princeling. The next day, the *Hofmarschall* came to his hotel on behalf of the grand duke and offered him the choice of either one thousand marks or the Order of the Bear or the Falcon, or something like that. 'What would they charge for such a medal in shops?' asked the artist. 'Oh, I think twenty marks,' replied the courtier. 'Well,' said Reisenauer, 'I will accept the medal and nine hundred and eighty marks.'"

❧

RENOIR, Pierre Auguste (1841–1919), *French Impressionist painter. He exhibited at the first three Impressionist exhibitions and had a profound influence on the movement, though he himself more or less abandoned it after 1882. He spent the last years of his life in the south of France, where he painted many of his famous nudes.*

1 Renoir was once asked how he managed to produce such natural flesh tints and shapely forms in his nude paintings. "I just keep painting till I feel like pinching," he replied. "Then I know it's right."

2 When both were in their seventies, Renoir and sculptor Aristide Maillol exchanged views on art. Maillol said, "My ambition is to be able to sculpt a young girl between sixteen and seventeen, in accord with my ideal conception of the figure."

"And mine," said Renoir, "is to be able to paint a white napkin."

3 Renoir continued painting, magnificently, for years after he was crippled by arthritis; the brush had to be strapped to his arm. "You don't need your hand to paint," he said.

4 When Renoir became so old and crippled that he could not hold a brush, he took to modeling nudes in clay for his own entertainment. Auguste Rodin, the sculptor, asked why he did not stick to painting. Renoir replied gently, "I am too old to paint. I must do something easier."

ठ&⋅ ⋅&ठ

REPPLIER, Agnes (?1855–1950), *US essayist. Her writings include* Points of View *(1891),* Americans and Others *(1912), and* In Pursuit of Laughter *(1936).*

1 A young visitor was about to take her leave of Miss Repplier. Shifting from one foot to the other, she picked up her hat and muff, put them down again, and generally appeared to be in a state of distraction. "There was something I meant to say," she finally admitted, "but I've forgotten what it was."

"Perhaps, my dear," suggested Miss Repplier, "it was good-bye."

ठ&⋅ ⋅&ठ

REUTHER, Walter (1907–70), *US labor leader, head of the United Auto Workers, president of the Congress of Industrial Organizations.*

1 Reuther once visited an auto factory in Cleveland. A young manager talked on and on about a new process they had for automating the line. It would be, he said, highly robotized, and it would work far more efficiently and cheaply than the current line. On and on he went, describing the glory of the robots.

"And tell me," Reuther finally interrupted, "these wonderful new robots — will they go out and buy cars from your company?"

ठ&⋅ ⋅&ठ

Fanny Ronalds crowned her artistic and social triumphs by giving a grand ball to which only the cream of New York society was invited. The hostess's dress in her role as the spirit of music was one of the highlights of an evening in which no expense was spared. Some twenty years later two of Mrs. Ronalds's most devoted beaux were recalling those days. "Do you remember Fanny's celebrated ball?" Leonard Jerome asked August Belmont. "I most certainly do," Belmont replied. "After all, I paid for it." There was a slight pause. "Why, how very strange," said Jerome. "So did I."

—Anita Leslie,
The Remarkable Mr. Jerome

REYNOLDS, Sir Joshua (1723–92), *English portrait painter, first president of the Royal Academy (1768). His many portraits include those of Samuel Johnson, Edmund Burke, and David Garrick; he was also noted for his paintings of children.*

1 The Scottish painter Robert Barber was out sketching on Calton Hill, Edinburgh. He noticed a curious effect caused by the prevailing atmospheric conditions: it was as if the entire view were contained within a cylinder. Inspired with the idea of reproducing this effect artistically, he made a model of a panorama and showed it to Reynolds. The great artist was skeptical. If Barber were able to put his idea into practice, said Sir Joshua, he would get out of his bed in the middle of the night to see the outcome. Barber persevered and set up his first panorama in a house in Leicester Square, London, not far from Sir Joshua's own residence. Reynolds carried out his promise. He arrived to view the panorama wearing his dressing-gown and slippers.

ठ&⋅ ⋅&ठ

RHODES, Cecil John (1853–1902), *South African statesman and financier. Of English birth, Rhodes emigrated to South Africa for health reasons and made a vast fortune from gold and diamond mining. As prime minister of the Cape Colony (1890–96), he expanded Britain's* *colonial territories in southern Africa, but over-reached himself with the Jameson Raid (1895) against the Dutch settlers (Boers) led by Paul Kruger. The open hostility that thus resulted led to the Boer War (1899–1902). Under Rhodes's will part of his fortune was used to endow Rhodes scholarships.*

1 Rhodes was a stickler for correct dress and behavior, but not at the expense of someone else's feelings. A young man invited to dine with him in Kimberley arrived by train and had to go directly to Rhodes's house in his travel-stained clothes. Here he was appalled to find the other guests already assembled, wearing full evening dress. Feeling very uncomfortable, he waited with the rest of the company for their host to appear. After what seemed a long time, Rhodes finally appeared, in a shabby old blue suit. The young man later learned that when he arrived Rhodes had been dressed in evening clothes and was about to welcome his guests. Told of the traveler's dilemma, Rhodes had at once returned to his room and put on an old suit.

2 When asked why he had come to South Africa, Rhodes replied that there was some truth in the reasons his friends usually ascribed to him — love of adventure or on account of his health. But, he confided, "The real fact is that I could no longer stand English eternal cold mutton."

3 Rhodes died from heart disease at a low ebb in his fortunes, beset by personal scandals and discredited by the tragedy of the Boer War, which his own misjudgments and policies had helped to foment. Lewis Michell, who was at his bedside in Rhodes's cottage at Muizenberg, near Cape Town, heard the dying man murmur, "So little done, so much to do."

4 The distribution of Rhodes's vast fortune under the terms of his will, with much of the money directed toward the setting up of the Rhodes scholarships, caused some resentment in the immediate family. "Well, there it is," said his brother Arthur. "It seems to me I shall have to win a scholarship."

৵ ৵

RICE, Grantland (1880–1954), *much-loved US sportswriter, known as "Granny" to his friends.*

1 During the 1944 World Series Granny arrived at the Sportsman's Park in St. Louis to discover he had brought the wrong ticket with him. Resigning himself to missing the start of the game, the celebrated sportswriter was on the point of going back to his hotel to get the proper ticket when Frank Graham came over to him and, on learning of Granny's predicament, led him promptly toward the gateman. "This is Grantland Rice behind me," Graham declared. "He has the wrong ticket." The gateman beamed at Granny and ushered him in with great deference. When the pair reached the press box Graham made a similar introduction and the gateman there was equally welcoming. "Frankie, you are marvelous," Granny said as they took their seats. "How did you manage that?"

৵ ৵

RICH, John (1925–), *US television and film director.*

1 Working on a Western film, Rich was having difficulty with a particular outdoor shot. Each attempt was marred by extraneous noise — traffic passing, dogs barking, jets flying overhead. A passerby had stopped to watch the filming. "Why do you persist in shooting the same scene so many times?" she asked. The exasperated Rich replied: "Madam, have you stopped to consider how many cinemas there are in this country?"

৵ ৵

RICHARD I (1157–99), *king of England (1189–99), known as Richard Coeur de Lion (the Lionheart). He spent most of his reign campaigning abroad as one of the most successful leaders of the Third Crusade. Held prisoner by Emperor Henry VI in Austria on his way home, he was released only on payment of a huge ransom (1194).*

1 When Richard was captured by the Austrians, it was some time before anyone in England discovered where he was. A minstrel called Blondel searched for his master throughout Europe in vain. Returning home through Austria, however, he learned that in an ancient stronghold near Linz there was a closely guarded prisoner whose identity no one knew. Blondel, suspecting the mysterious captive was his master, went to the castle but was unable to catch a glimpse of the prisoner. He eventually located a tiny barred window, high up on the castle wall, which he thought was the prisoner's cell. Under this window he sang the first couplet of a troubadour's song, the first part of which had been composed by himself and the second by Richard. From the window a voice responded with the second part, and Blondel knew that he had found his master.

{According to one tradition Blondel then took employment at the fortress, gained access to Richard, and was the messenger through whom Richard arranged the raising of his ransom with the English nobility. There is, however, no reliable source for any part of the story.}

2 Richard I was once warned by an eminent preacher that he would be severely punished by God if he did not soon marry off his three daughters. The king protested that he had no daughters, to which the priest replied, "Your Majesty has three — ambition, avarice, and luxury. Get rid of them as fast as possible, else assuredly some great misfortune will be the consequence."

"If it must be so," replied Richard contemptuously, "then I give my ambition to the templars, my avarice to the monks, and my luxury to the prelates."

ঌ৵ ৵ঌ

RICHARDSON, Sir Ralph (1902–84), *British actor. He enjoyed considerable success in a variety of Shakespearean roles and in numerous films.*

1 In 1919 the young Richardson was an office boy for an insurance company in Brighton. To relieve the tedium of the job, he decided one day to see if he could walk around the building on a narrow ledge several stories above the street. He had meant to time this exploit to coincide with his boss's absence from the office, but unfortunately as he was edging his way past the boss's window, the man himself entered the room and froze. Richardson gave him a cheery wave and called, "I was chasing a pigeon."

2 Ralph Richardson seemed destined to have bad luck at the home of his friends, Vivien Leigh and Laurence Olivier. At a housewarming for the couple's first home in Chelsea,

Richardson brought along some fireworks to set off in the tiny backyard in celebration. He lit the first (and largest) one, but instead of soaring into the London skies, it shot straight through the open patio windows into the dining room, burned up the curtains, and set the cornice ablaze. Vivien Leigh was not amused.

Some years later, Richardson and his wife were invited to the Oliviers' new home, Notley Abbey. Recalling the disaster of the fireworks, they promised each other to be exceedingly careful. All went well at first. After dinner, Olivier mentioned that the medieval monks who had owned the abbey had left some interesting paintings on the roof beams; would anyone like to see them? The ladies declined, but Richardson and Olivier, armed with flashlights, went up to the attics. A few minutes later there came an anguished cry and a fearful crash. The women rushed upstairs to find Richardson on the bed in the main guestroom, dust and plaster everywhere, and a jagged hole in the ceiling. In his enthusiasm over the paintings, Richardson had not noticed that the attic floor was unboarded, had stepped backward from a rafter, and, like the firework through the patio door, shot straight down through the ceiling.

ঌ৵ ৵ঌ

RICHELIEU, Armand-Emmanuel du Plessis, Duc de (1766–1822), *French statesman. Taking refuge from the French Revolution in Russia, he became a successful administrator in Odessa (1803–14). He returned to join Louis XVIII in France, but after Napoleon's escape from Elba rejoined the Russian army, attempting to influence events in favor of the French monarchy during the Congress of Vienna. In 1815 he succeeded Talleyrand as prime minister and helped to relieve France of the burdens it had suffered after the defeat of Napoleon.*

1 Married at fifteen to a deformed girl three years his junior, Richelieu never had more than a formal relationship with his wife. The duchess inevitably sought her consolation elsewhere. Coming upon her in *flagrante delicto*, Richelieu rebuked her: "Madame, you must really be more careful. Suppose it had been someone else who found you like this."

2 Richelieu and his officers were planning a campaign. "We shall cross the river at this point," said one of the officers, placing his finger on the map. "Excellent, sir," remarked Richelieu, "but your finger is not a bridge."

3 When Richelieu learned an old, rich, and stupid widow of his acquaintance had died the previous day, his only comment was, "What a pity! She would have been a fine catch the day before that."

⊰◦⊱

RICHTER, Hans (1843–1916), *Hungarian conductor. He was famous for his interpretation of the works of Wagner and Brahms, and for some time led the Hallé Orchestra in England.*

1 An orchestra player who had yearned to try his hand at conducting finally realized his ambition. As he left the podium, he observed to Richter, "You know, this conducting business is really very straightforward."

"Ssh!" said Richter. "I beg you, don't give us away!"

2 Once, with Richter conducting Dvořák's Ninth Symphony, the cymbal player miscounted the bars in the finale and came in at the wrong place. The conductor fixed a furious eye upon the delinquent and glowered at him for the remainder of the piece. At the end of the concert he fired the man. A couple of days later, rehearsing the same symphony, Richter stopped the orchestra two bars before the fateful spot and muttered ominously, "Is he still alive, do you think?"

3 Richter once lost his temper (and, temporarily, his command of the English language) with an incompetent second flutist at Covent Garden. "Your damned nonsense can I stand twice or once," he roared, "but sometimes always, by God, never."

⊰◦⊱

RIGAUD, Hyacinthe (1659–1743), *French painter.*

1 A heavily made-up lady was having her portrait painted by Rigaud. She complained that his colors were much too bright. "We buy them at the same shop, madame," retorted the artist.

RILEY, James Whitcomb (1849–1916), *US versifier, known as the "Hoosier poet." His works include* Rhymes of Childhood *(1890) and* The Little Orfant Annie Book *(1908).*

1 Riley's Washington landlady told the poet one day of the sad fate of her neighbor's cook. Having worked for the family for many years, the unfortunate woman had fallen asleep over her stove and burned to death. An appropriate epitaph sprang immediately to Riley's lips: "Well done, good and faithful servant."

⊰◦⊱

RIVAROL, Antoine de (1753–1801), *French writer and wit.*

1 A bitter and merciless critic of others, who had himself produced nothing, was attacking his usual targets. Rivarol said to him, "It is a great advantage to have produced nothing, but you must not abuse it."

2 Someone asked Rivarol's opinion of a couplet produced by a mediocre poet. "Very good, but it has its *longueurs*," was the response.

⊰◦⊱

RIVERA, Antonio (died 1936), *Spanish Nationalist hero, known as "the Angel of the Alcázar."*

1 Antonio Rivera, son of a former mayor of Toledo, took refuge with other Nationalists in the Alcázar in the summer of 1936 at the start of the famous siege during the Spanish Civil War. As a pacifist, the youth refused at first to help defend the ancient stronghold, and was put on latrine duty. When the situation of the besieged became more desperate, he decided that it would not be inconsistent with his principles to aid in the defense, provided that he did not kill in hatred. He was assigned the position of loader to a heavy machine gun. It was said that he would give the signal to fire with the words: "*Tirad — pero sin odio*" (Fire — without hatred).

{Just nine days before the Alcázar was relieved, a grenade shattered Antonio's arm. The limb had to be amputated without benefit of anesthetic. When the Nationalist forces relieved the Alcázar, Antonio was carried with great honor to his father's house, but he never recovered, and died two months later.}

ૐ ❧

RIZZUTO, Phil (1918–), *US sports figure.*

1 "While broadcasting a Yankee game Rizzuto was informed that Pope Paul VI had died. He commented on the air, 'Well, that kind of puts the damper on even a Yankee win.'"

ૐ ❧

ROBERT I [Robert the Bruce] (1274–1329), *king of Scotland (1306–29). Unable at first to maintain his kingdom against the incursions of his powerful neighbor, Edward I of England, Robert eventually won a crushing victory over the English under Edward II at the battle of Bannockburn (1314). He subsequently consolidated his position, forcing the English to recognize Scottish independence in 1328.*

1 There are many popular stories and legends about Robert the Bruce and his daring deeds against the English oppressors. One, made famous by Walter Scott, concerns the period when Robert the Bruce was on the run from the troops of Edward I. Hiding in a cave, and suffering from deep despondency and uncertainty as to what he ought to do next, he watched a small spider spinning its web, trying and failing time and time again to secure it properly. The fugitive king read the spider's persistence and its eventual success as a parable for himself: he must not be discouraged by his failures, but go out and continue the struggle until he achieved the liberation of his country.

ૐ ❧

ROBERT, Léopold (1794–1835), *Swiss painter and etcher. From 1818 to 1832 he worked in Rome, where he became famous for his pictures of Italian daily life. He killed himself out of unrequited love.*

1 Léopold Robert, brought up in a pious household, was himself highly moral. In 1827, however, he painted two pictures, entitled *Two Girls Disrobing for Their Bath*, that offended by their "freedom." Robert defended himself by saying that, although ordinarily all his figures were clothed from head to foot, this

time he had wanted to choose a different subject. He went on, "But I assure you that I have placed the figures in a completely secluded spot so that they would not possibly encounter any observation from curious onlookers."

ૐ ❧

ROBINSON, Edwin Arlington (1869–1935), *US poet. He won several Pulitzer prizes for his poetry, of which he published a number of volumes. He was a protégé of Theodore Roosevelt.*

1 Robinson used to spend his summers at the MacDowell Colony near Peterborough, New Hampshire. Arriving at breakfast one morning, he found the writer Nancy Byrd Turner and a new member of the colony already seated at his table. "This is Mr. Robinson," said Nancy Byrd Turner to her companion. "Robinson! Not E. A. Robinson — not *the* Mr. Robinson?" gushed the other woman. There followed a long, uncomfortable pause, then Robinson said, "*A* Mr. Robinson."

2 In 1905 one of President Theodore Roosevelt's sons brought to his father's attention a book of poems by Robinson, *The Children of the Night*. Impressed, Roosevelt created in the New York Custom House a sinecure for the virtually destitute poet. "I expect you to think poetry first and customs second," he told Robinson when he took up the post.
{Robinson was required only to open his desk, read the morning newspaper, close his desk, and leave the newspaper on his chair as proof that he had turned up at the office. This lasted four years, during which time Robinson established himself as a poet. When Taft became president and intimated that Robinson would have to put in a full day's work, the poet resigned.}

ૐ ❧

ROBINSON, Jackie (1919–72), *US baseball player. In 1947, as the first black to play major-league baseball, he suffered vicious harassment.*

1 On the day of his first appearance with the Dodgers, Robinson kissed his wife goodbye at their hotel before setting out. "If you come down to Ebbets Field today," he said, "you won't have any trouble recognizing me." He

paused for a moment, then added, "My number's 42."

❧ ⚓

ROCHE, Sir Boyle (1743–1807), *Irish politician.*

1 Sir Boyle Roche was well known in Parliament and beyond for his extraordinary "bulls," or Irishisms, some of which are preserved in the records of parliamentary proceedings. He was an ardent advocate of the union of England and Ireland in 1800 and declared that his love for the two countries was so great that he would like to see "the two sisters embrace like one brother."

2 John Philpot Curran took the opposite view to Roche's on the union of England and Ireland, and they often clashed in parliamentary debates on the subject. Replying to some aspersion, Curran proclaimed that he needed no help from anyone but was well able to be "the guardian of my own honor." "Indeed," commented Sir Boyle Roche, "why, I always thought the right honorable member was an enemy to sinecures."

❧ ⚓

ROCHEFORT, [Victor] Henri, Marquis de Rochefort-Luçay (1830–1913), *French journalist. His tumultuous life as a radical journalist involved a series of duels and several prison sentences. In the 1890s he was a leader of the anti-Dreyfusards.*

1 On one occasion when Rochefort had been arrested, the authorities confronted him with evidence of his links with international revolutionaries. "In one of your drawers were found two photographs of Garibaldi and Mazzini with their autographs."

"That is true," said Rochefort, "for those two great patriots did send me their photos."

"But that is not all," went on the interrogator, "for there were also seized several pictures of Henri Rochefort."

Somewhat baffled, Rochefort said, "But I am Henri Rochefort."

"I am not denying that," said the interrogator, "but it is nonetheless significant that you should have so many portraits of that notorious socialist in your house."

2 Rochefort found it difficult to make ends meet by his writing. He used to observe, "My scribbling pays me zero francs per line — not including the white spaces."

❧ ⚓

ROCKEFELLER, John D[avison], Sr. (1839–1937), *US oil magnate and philanthropist. President of the Standard Oil Company, he was a dominant figure in the oil business until his retirement in 1911. He established four charitable foundations.*

1 Rockefeller found out that his family had ordered an electric car as his surprise birthday present, to enable him to get around his vast estate more easily. "If it's all the same to you," said the multimillionaire, "I'd rather have the money."

❧ ⚓

ROCKEFELLER, John D[avison], Jr. (1874–1960), *US capitalist and philanthropist, son of John D. Rockefeller, Sr. He was involved with his father's oil-trade interests and charitable foundations and planned and financed the Rockefeller Center in New York.*

1 Rockefeller once made a collect call from a coin box, which failed to refund the money he had put in. He called up the operator, who asked for his name and address so that the money could be mailed to him. Rockefeller began: "My name is John D. . . . Oh, forget it; you wouldn't believe me anyway."

❧ ⚓

ROCKEFELLER, William (1841–1922), *brother of John D. Rockefeller, Sr. William helped to run Standard Oil and to develop the company's influence upon the oil market.*

1 The growing Rockefeller empire attracted the attention of the courts owing to concern over the dangers of monopolies. When William Rockefeller was required to appear in court, he decided that his best defense would lie in the refrain, "I decline to answer on the advice of counsel," as the following exchange shows:

"On the ground that the answer will incriminate you?"

"I decline to answer on the advice of counsel."

"Or is it that the answer will subject you to some forfeiture?"

"I decline to answer on the advice of counsel."

"Do you decline on the ground that the answer will disgrace you?"

"I decline to answer on the advice of counsel."

"Did your counsel tell you to stick to that one answer?"

"I decline to answer on the advice of counsel."

At that point the whole court burst into laughter, Rockefeller included.

ॐ ✦

RODGERS, Richard Charles (1902–79), US composer. He collaborated with Lorenz Hart on The Girl Friend (1926) and Pal Joey (1940) and with Oscar Hammerstein II on Oklahoma! (1943) and The King and I (1951).

1   Dick Rodgers's collaborators Larry Hart and Oscar Hammerstein II were first-rate lyric writers. He was often asked how they differed. It should be mentioned that Hart was a very short man, about five feet three inches; Rodgers himself a few inches taller; and Hammerstein over six feet. Said Rodgers, "When I worked with Larry and people recognized us walking together, they'd say, 'The little fellow is okay but watch out for the big son-of-a-bitch.' Now, when I'm with Oscar and am recognized, people say, 'The big guy is okay, but watch out for the little son-of-a-bitch.' And that's the difference between working with Larry and working with Oscar."

2   Rodgers composed the score for the musical Chee-Chee, the story of which is based upon a novel by Charles Pettit, The Son of the Grand Eunuch. The plot hinges upon the efforts of the hero to avoid being emasculated in order to inherit his father's exalted office. At the point in the story at which the youth is taken away for the operation Rodgers inserted into the score a few bars from Tchaikovsky's Nutcracker Suite.

{Rodgers commented, "At almost every performance there were two or three individuals with ears musically sharp enough to appreciate the joke."}

RODZINSKI, Artur (1892–1958), US orchestra leader, conductor of the New York Philharmonic (1943–47).

1   On a vacation Rodzinski noticed that there was to be a radio broadcast of an open-air concert conducted by Fabien Sevitzky and that the program included one of Rodzinski's own specialties, Shostakovich's Fifth Symphony. Tuning in shortly after the concert had begun, Rodzinski listened to Sevitzky's rendering with increasing respect. "How well he sustains the line!" he murmured. "Listen to that balance! He must have studied my recording." And he ended by saying that he had done Sevitzky an injustice, that he had always thought that he had no talent but that really he was a great conductor. At the end of the performance, instead of the expected applause there was a moment of silence. Then the announcer came on, saying that the concert had been rained out and in its place the station had played a recording of Shostakovich's Fifth conducted by Artur Rodzinski.

ॐ ✦

ROGERS, Samuel (1763–1855), British writer. A banker by profession, Rogers used his considerable income and ready wit to gather around him the most select literary and artistic personalities of his day. His Table Talk, edited after his death, is particularly valued for the glimpses it gives of his celebrated contemporaries.

1   Discussing the approaching marriage of a lady whom they both knew, Lord Lansdowne observed to Rogers that she had made a good match. "I'm not so sure," replied Rogers. "Why not? All her friends approve it," said Lord Lansdowne. "Then she is able to satisfy everyone," said Rogers. "Her friends are pleased and her enemies are delighted."

2   Rogers had a considerable reputation for his biting and sarcastic wit. Once when accused of being ill-natured, he justified himself by saying, "They tell me I say ill-natured things. I have a weak voice; if I did not say ill-natured things, no one would hear what I said."

3   Rogers had a bare, polished head and a somewhat cadaverous appearance. He and

Lord Dudley once spent an hour or two exploring the catacombs in Paris. As they were leaving, the keeper caught sight of Rogers and rushed toward him with a look of horror, shouting, "No, no. You have no right to come out. Go back inside. Go back."

Lord Dudley fled from the scene in paroxysms of laughter, leaving Rogers to extricate himself from the situation as best he might. When Rogers later taxed him for his desertion, he replied, "My dear Rogers, you looked so much at home I did not like to interfere."

4 A gathering of society leaders was praising one of its absent members, a young duke who had recently come of age; they extolled his looks, his talents, his wealth, his prospects. . . . In a pause in the chorus of admiration the voice of Rogers could be heard saying malevolently, "Thank God he has bad teeth!"

ॐ ॐ

ROGERS, Will (1879–1935), *US comedian, who progressed from the vaudeville stage to become an internationally known film actor and humorist. His forte was political observations: "I don't make jokes; I just watch the government and report the facts."*

1 One of the many legends about William Randolph Hearst's fabulous weekend houseparties at San Simeon concerns Will Rogers. Throughout the weekend Hearst kept him busy amusing the rest of the company. A few days later Hearst received a large bill from Rogers for services as a professional entertainer. Hearst telephoned Rogers to protest: "I didn't engage you as an entertainer. You were invited as a guest." Rogers retorted, "When someone invites me as a guest, they invite Mrs. Rogers as well. When they ask me to come alone, I come as a professional entertainer."

2 On a visit to Paris, Rogers sent a picture postcard of the Venus de Milo to his young niece. On the back he wrote: "See what will happen to you if you don't stop biting your fingernails."

{This anecdote is told of others.}

3 Rogers had been asked by a firm of piano manufacturers to write a short testimonial for their instruments. Unwilling to endorse any product that he could not put to the test,

Rogers simply replied, "Dear Sirs, I guess your pianos are the best I ever leaned against. Yours truly, Will Rogers."

4 Rogers, having paid too much income tax one year, tried in vain to claim a rebate. His numerous letters and queries remained unanswered. Eventually the form for the next year's return arrived. In the section marked "DEDUCTIONS," Rogers listed: "Bad debt, US Government — $40,000."

ॐ ॐ

ROLAND, Jeanne Manon (1754–93), *wife of the French statesman Jean Roland (1734–93). She and her husband were outspoken protesters against royal corruption and inefficiency, but the revolutionary extremists eventually sent Mme Roland to the guillotine. At the news of his wife's death her husband committed suicide.*

1 Mme Roland's calm courage in prison and at her execution became famous. As she mounted the steps to the guillotine, she looked toward the clay statue of Liberty set up in the Place de la Révolution and exclaimed, "*O liberté! O liberté! Que de crimes on commet en ton nom!*" (Oh liberty! Oh liberty! What crimes are committed in thy name!)

ॐ ॐ

ROMANOFF, Mike [Harry F. Gerguson] (1890–1972), *US restaurateur. He was a well-known figure in Hollywood in the 1940s and 1950s, claiming to be a Russian prince.*

1 There were numerous Russian emigrés in New York in the 1920s, and someone invited the Grand Duke Dmitri of Russia to meet his "kinsman." The grand duke looked at Mike Romanoff with deep suspicion, then addressed him rapidly in Russian. The bogus prince headed for the exit, saying, "I don't think we should insult our hosts by talking in any language but theirs."

2 Another attempt to discountenance Romanoff was made by a young actor playing with Romanoff in Frank Sinatra's *Tony Rome* in 1967. The actor addressed the restaurateur in fluent Russian, but was met by a look of freezing disdain. Afterward Romanoff complained, "The vulgarity of a stranger's speaking to me in that tongue! We never spoke anything but French at court."

છે~ ~ડ

ROOSEVELT, [Anna] Eleanor (1884–1962), *US writer and lecturer, wife of Franklin Delano Roosevelt. Her writings include* It's Up to the Women *(1933) and* The Moral Basis of Democracy *(1940).*

1 In her last years Eleanor Roosevelt was probably the most easily recognized, as well as the most beloved, woman in the United States. At this period racial intolerance was still quite marked.

She was walking one day on a crowded street in Greenwich Village, New York, during a rainstorm, when a station wagon backed into her, knocking her down. She got up and without hesitation ordered the driver to make off at once without delay. Then, her ligaments torn, she hobbled off to her next speaking engagement.

The driver was black.

છે~ ~ડ

ROOSEVELT, Franklin Delano (1882–1945), *US statesman; 32d president of the United States (1933–45). Despite an attack of polio in 1921 that left him paralyzed from the waist down and threatened to end his public career, Roosevelt became governor of New York State and the only US president to be elected for four terms. The economic measures of Roosevelt's New Deal enabled the country to recover from the Depression of the 1930s. After the bombing of Pearl Harbor by the Japanese in 1941, Roosevelt took the United States into World War II. He died in office just before the end of the war.*

1 As a small boy Roosevelt was introduced to President Cleveland. Cleveland put his hand on the child's head and said, "I'm making a strange wish for you, little man, a wish I suppose no one else would make. I wish for you that you may never be president of the United States."

2 FDR appointed Frances Perkins as secretary of labor—the first woman to hold a cabinet office—over the heads of several men who had been suggested for the position by labor leaders. The trade unionists, opposed as always

to the idea of a woman's holding real power, had a stormy meeting with the president about the appointment. According to a Washington story current at the time, Mrs. Roosevelt sympathized with her husband over the confrontation. "That's all right," he replied. "I'd rather have trouble with them for an hour than trouble with you for the rest of my life."

3 The novelist Fannie Hurst wanted to surprise FDR with the change in her appearance since she had been on a diet. She managed to slip unannounced into his office. The president looked up as she entered, then gestured for her to turn around in front of him. When she completed the turn, he commented, "The Hurst may have changed, but it's the same old fanny."

4 Eleanor Roosevelt was particularly fond of sweetbreads. In one week they appeared on the White House menu no fewer than six times. The president eventually complained in a note to his wife: "I am getting to the point where my stomach rebels, and this does not help my relations with foreign powers. I bit two of them today."

5 The many details which an inaugural committee must cope with in a short time inevitably produce a few mistakes. Thus FDR, in 1937, received an invitation to his own inauguration.

Through the White House social bureau he solemnly sent word that the press of official business would keep him away. Then, relenting, he sent a further note in his own handwriting: "I have rearranged my engagements and think I may be able to go. Will know definitely January 19. F.D.R."

6 It is said that Roosevelt once made a telephone call to Joseph Stalin during the days of friendship between the United States and the Soviet Union. The call had to pass through a number of operators, but finally the connection was made. "Hello, Joe?" said Roosevelt. "It's Frank. Giants three, Dodgers nothing."

{Almost surely apocryphal—but how one wishes it weren't!}

7 Roosevelt found the polite small talk of social functions at the White House somewhat tedious. He maintained that those present on such occasions rarely paid much attention to what was said to them. To illustrate the point,

he would sometimes amuse himself by greeting guests with the words, "I murdered my grandmother this morning." The response was invariably one of polite approval. On one occasion, however, the president happened upon an attentive listener. On hearing Roosevelt's outrageous remark, the guest replied diplomatically, "I'm sure she had it coming to her."

{Maxwell Perkins, the distinguished editor, peppered his own small talk similarly at literary gatherings. Evidently writers, as well as politicians, don't listen to one another.}

છેબ જાક

ROOSEVELT, Theodore (1858–1919), *US statesman; 26th president of the United States (1901–09). A sickly boy, Roosevelt became a tough and self-sufficient man who worked as a rancher, went big-game hunting, and fought in the Spanish-American War (1898). As president, he centered his domestic policies on his Square Deal program to improve the lot of ordinary citizens and his foreign policy on the dictum "Speak softly and carry a big stick." In his administration, US influence on Latin America increased and control was established over the Panama Canal.*

1   During his time as a rancher, Roosevelt and one of his cowpunchers, riding over the range, lassoed a maverick, a two-year-old steer that had never been branded. They lit a fire then and there and prepared the branding irons. The part of the range they were on was claimed by Gregor Lang, one of Roosevelt's neighbors. According to the rule among cattlemen the steer therefore belonged to Lang, having been found on his land. As the cowboy applied the brand, Roosevelt said, "Wait, it should be Lang's brand, a thistle."

"That's all right, boss," said the cowboy, continuing to apply the brand.

"But you're putting on my brand."

"That's right," said the man, "I always put on the boss's brand."

"Drop that iron," said Roosevelt, "and get back to the ranch and get out. I don't need you anymore."

The cowboy protested, but Roosevelt was adamant. "A man who will steal *for* me will steal *from* me," he declared. So the cowboy went, and the story spread all over the Badlands.

2   When the hotel in which Vice President Roosevelt was staying caught fire, he was ordered down to the lobby with the other guests. After some time, prevented from returning to his room, he protested: "But I'm the vice president!"

"Oh, that's different," said the hotel official. Then, as Teddy started up the stairs, "Wait a minute. What are you vice president *of?*"

"Why, of the United States, of course!"

"Then get the hell back down there. I thought you were vice president of this hotel!"

3   Before retiring to bed, Roosevelt and his friend the naturalist William Beebe would go out and look at the skies, searching for a tiny patch of light near the constellation of Pegasus. "That is the Spiral Galaxy in Andromeda," they would chant. "It is as large as our Milky Way. It is one of a hundred million galaxies. It consists of one hundred billion suns, each larger than our sun." Then Roosevelt would turn to his companion and say, "Now I think we are small enough. Let's go to bed."

4   Some of Roosevelt's critics complained of his tendency to introduce moral issues in matters where none existed. Speaker of the House Thomas B. Reed once told Roosevelt, "If there is one thing more than another for which I admire you, Theodore, it is your original discovery of the Ten Commandments."

5   Shot in the chest in an assassination attempt in October 1912, Roosevelt was determined to carry on with the speech he had been about to make. "I will deliver this speech or die, one or the other," he declared.

{He gave the speech and after fifty minutes allowed himself to be taken to hospital for treatment.}

6   Shortly before he left the White House, Roosevelt, planning a big-game hunting trip to Africa, heard that a famous white hunter was visiting Washington. He invited the man to come along and give him some advice. After a two-hour tête-à-tête the hunter came out of the president's office looking dazed. "What did you tell the president?" someone asked idly. "My name," said the bemused visitor. "After that he did all the talking."

છેબ જાક

ROOSEVELT, Theodore, Jr. (1887–1944), *US soldier, explorer, and politician, the son of President Theodore Roosevelt. He served as a major and lieutenant colonel in World War I and as a brigadier general in World War II. Between the wars he led expeditions to Asia (1925, 1928–29) and was governor of Puerto Rico (1929–32) and of the Philippines (1932–33).*

1 Roosevelt had arranged to meet his wife's train. Arriving at the railroad station at the appointed time, he was dismayed to see the train speed past the platform without stopping. His wife waved anxiously from the rear car, tossing out an envelope as she passed her husband. Roosevelt retrieved the envelope with some difficulty and was amused to read the following message: "Dear Ted: This train doesn't stop here."

ह• ◆ई

ROOT, Elihu (1845–1937), *US lawyer and statesman. He became secretary of state under President Theodore Roosevelt and later was senator for New York. He won the Nobel Peace Prize in 1912.*

1 When a frail old man in his eighties, Root was frequently visited by Sol M. Linowitz, who used to read to him. One day Root asked the young man what he wanted to do in life. Linowitz replied, "I'm not sure. Maybe be a rabbi or perhaps a lawyer." Root's reply was immediate: "Be a lawyer. A lawyer needs twice as much religion as a rabbi."
  {Linowitz took Root's advice and became a distinguished lawyer and a roving ambassador in the Carter administration.}

ह• ◆ई

ROPS, Félicien (1833–98), *French painter, engraver, and lithographer; illustrator of poems by Stéphane Mallarmé.*

1 Art dealer Ambroise Vollard had occasion to visit Rops a few years before the painter's death. Rops warned him: "I'm expecting a woman. When the bell rings three times, you must leave by the other end of the studio." After some time the bell rang as predicted and Vollard took his leave. Glancing behind him as he closed the door, he saw an old housemaid

enter the room. "Come now, monsieur," she said, "it's time for your *tisane*" (herbal tea).

ह• ◆ई

ROSENBLOOM, Max (1904–76), *US light heavyweight boxer, world champion in 1930.*

1 Called Slapsie-Maxie because of his skill as a deft boxer, Rosenbloom gloried in his ability to win decisions without resorting to such crude tactics as actual knockdowns. Once one of his open gloves made contact, and his bewildered opponent collapsed on the canvas. Bellowed Maxie, "Why, you dirty double-crossing rat!"

ह• ◆ई

ROSENTHAL, Moriz (1862–1946), *Polish-born pianist. He studied with Liszt and was court pianist to the emperor of Austria and the queen of Rumania. He also played for ten seasons in the United States.*

1 One day Rosenthal was cornered into hearing a recital given by a mediocre string quartet. When the ordeal was over, the second violinist hurried over to the maestro to hear his opinion. "How did you like it?" he asked. "Excellent," lied Rosenthal. The player was still unsatisfied. "And our tempi — did they suit you?" he went on. "Brilliant," said Rosenthal, "brilliant — especially yours."

2 When Rosenthal heard that pianist Artur Schnabel had failed his physical for the army, he said, "What did you expect? No fingers!"
  {This remark is also attributed to others about others.}

3 Coerced into listening to a child prodigy, Rosenthal asked the boy how old he was. "Seven," said the child.
  "What are you going to play for me?"
  "The Tchaikovsky concerto, sir."
  "Too old!" said Rosenthal.

4 Rosenthal used to make fun of a fellow pianist much given to playing Liszt's sixth Hungarian Rhapsody at a tempo Rosenthal considered far too slow. On one occasion he invited this friend to come and see him. The man excused himself, saying that he did not have the time. "Nonsense!" retorted Rosenthal. "If you have time to play the sixth rhapsody like that, you certainly have time to pay me a visit."

ROSS, Harold (1892–1951), *US journalist, founder, and for many years editor of* The New Yorker.

1 (Ross began his journalistic career at the age of fourteen as a reporter on the *Salt Lake City Tribune.*)

"One of his assignments there was to interview the madam of a house of prostitution. Always self-conscious and usually uncomfortable in the presence of all but his closest women friends, the young reporter began by saying to the bad woman (he divided the other sex into good and bad), 'How many fallen women do you have?'"

2 Shortly after Ross had obtained his discharge from the armed forces at the end of World War I, he met the former war secretary, Newton D. Baker. He and Ross discussed the war at length, and Ross was delighted with the frankness with which Baker covered a wide range of topics. Taking leave of him, Ross remarked, "Well, Mr. Secretary, that cleans up everything except how Joe Higgins was made corporal of my squad."

3 Ross launched *The New Yorker* in 1925 on a shoestring budget. The magazine's finances continued to be very shaky for some time; its equipment and resources were therefore minimal. When Ross asked Dorothy Parker why she had not come in to do a piece she had promised him, she retorted, "Someone else was using the pencil."

4 (Ross's unavailing but persistent attempts to bring order to the offices of *The New Yorker* made life miserable for a series of assistants, who included Thurber and M. B. Levick.)

"Levick's final frantic response to the editor's demand for a method of keeping track of everything was an enormous sheet of cardboard, six feet by four, divided into at least eight hundred squares, with fine hand lettering in each of them covering all phases of the scheduling of departments and other office rigmaroles. This complicated caricature of System, this concentration of all known procedural facts, hung on a wall of the Talk meeting room until one day it fell down of its own weight. Ross had stared at it now and then without saying a word. When it crashed, he told his secretary, 'Get rid of that thing.'"

5 A promising young lad sought a place on the staff of *The New Yorker* and Ross hired him. "Don't be too pleased with yourself," he warned the new employee, "I hire any damn fool who sticks his nose in here. And don't think you'll be starting as a reporter. You'll begin as managing editor, like everyone else."

{In a variant of this story, the new member of staff is identified as James Thurber.}

6 As a practical joke Thurber once rolled a very large water bottle along the corridor past the offices of *The New Yorker*. Hearing the racket, Ross instructed the new managing editor: "Go and find out what the hell is happening. But don't tell me."

7 In a piece by S. J. Perelman, Ross noticed an allusion to "the woman taken in adultery." He wrote in the margin, "What woman? Hasn't been previously mentioned."

8 For years Harold Ross had *The New Yorker*'s cover-design character, Eustace Tilley, listed in the Manhattan telephone book. He was delighted when the city authorities eventually sent this imaginary figure a personal-property tax bill.

9 Ross's turnout was never very smart. After a winter sports holiday in Connecticut with Franklin P. Adams, someone asked Ross's host what Ross had looked like tobogganing. "Well, you know what Ross looks like *not* tobogganing," said Adams.

10 Hemingway's *Death in the Afternoon* was reviewed for *The New Yorker* by critic Robert M. Coates. After he had read the review, Ross telephoned Coates in the country and said, "Woollcott tells me there's a hell of a bad word in the book — bathroom stuff." Coates asked what the word was. "I can't tell you over the phone," said Ross.

11 (Peter De Vries tells the story of Ross at an art meeting during which sketches were selected for possible inclusion in *The New Yorker*.)

"The cover on the board showed a Model T driving along a dusty country road, and Ross turned his sharpshooting eye on it for a full two minutes. 'Take this down, Miss Terry,' he said. 'Better dust.'"

12 Many of Ross's *New Yorker* writers were lured away to Hollywood. When John McNulty headed west, Ross bade him farewell with what Thurber describes as "a memorable tagline": "Well, God bless you, McNulty, god-damn it."

See also JAMES THURBER 10.

13 A rival cartoonist once grumbled to Ross, "Why do you reject my drawings and print stuff by that fifth-rate artist, Thurber?"

"Third-rate," corrected Ross.

14 On December 11, 1936, King Edward VIII of Great Britain broadcast to the world his historic "the woman I love" abdication speech. At a cocktail party in New York, the polished Noël Coward and the unbuttoned Harold Ross listened to the broadcast. Ross burst into uncontrollable laughter. Coward, an Establishment man to his fingertips, was shocked, and reproved Ross for this unseemly exhibition. Ross would have none of it. "You mean," he said incredulously, "the king of England runs away with an old American hooker and *that* ain't funny?"

{Ross's youthful puritanism — *see* ROSS 1 — seems to have mellowed somewhat with age.}

৵৵ ৵৬

ROSSETTI, Dante Gabriel (1828–82), *British painter and poet. In 1848 Rossetti joined with John Everett Millais, William Holman Hunt, and others to found the Pre-Raphaelite Brotherhood and edited its journal,* The Germ *(1850–51), in which some of his best poems, including "The Blessed Damozel," were published. He married (1860) Elizabeth Siddal, the model for many of his paintings on medieval or religious subjects.*

1 Rossetti announced that he wanted to buy an elephant, and, when his friends asked what on earth for, he replied, "So I can teach it to wash the windows of my house." When they still seemed puzzled, he added, "Then everyone would stare and say, 'That elephant is washing the windows of the house in which lives Dante Gabriel Rossetti, the famous artist.'"

2 When Rossetti's beautiful wife, Elizabeth Siddal, killed herself with an overdose of laudanum in 1862, just two years after their marriage, Rossetti's grief was overwhelming. Most of his poems had been written for her or to her. At her burial he wrapped the little book containing the unique copies of these poems in her long golden hair and consigned them to the grave with her. As the years passed, Rossetti began to think with regret of the poems that he had lost, concluding that it was pointless to leave some of the finest works he had produced to molder in the grave with the dead. After much business to obtain permission, the grave was opened and the book retrieved. Its contents, with a few additions, were published in 1870 under the title *Poems,* and the book was immediately successful.

3 The negotiations on behalf of the Liverpool art gallery to buy Rossetti's great picture *Dante's Dream* seemed likely to be abortive when Rossetti discovered that one of the intermediaries was a critic who he considered had insulted him. A third party, called in to make peace, succeeded in convincing Rossetti that the man was "quite a good fellow at bottom." Rossetti observed afterward, "I did not mention that if he came here he had better take care that the place at which he was a good fellow did not get kicked."

৵৵ ৵৬

ROSSINI, Gioacchino Antonio (1792–1868), *Italian composer. He was an outstandingly successful composer of operas, many still in the repertoire:* Tancredi *(1813),* The Italian Girl in Algiers *(1813),* The Barber of Seville *(1816),* The Thieving Magpie *(1817), and* William Tell *(1829).* Tournedos Rossini *commemorates his inventiveness as a cook.*

1 Jacques François Halévy, another popular composer, was driven nearly to distraction by an organ-grinder who had stationed himself outside his window and was busy grinding out the hit tunes from his rival's *Barber of Seville.* Halévy went out and said to the man, "I will give you one louis d'or if you will go to Rossini's lodgings and play one of my tunes outside his window." The organ-grinder smiled. "But, monsieur, M. Rossini has paid me *two* louis d'or to play his music outside your window."

2 In a Paris music store in 1856 Rossini encountered the celebrated music theorist and scholar François-Joseph Fétis. On the counter was displayed Fétis's *Treatise on Counterpoint and Fugue.* "Must all this be learned?" inquired Rossini, gesturing toward the volume. "Not at all," replied Fétis. "You yourself are the living proof to the contrary."

3   Rossini congratulated the diva Adelina Patti on her singing. "Madame, I have cried only twice in my life," he informed her, "once when I dropped a wing of truffled chicken into Lake Como, and once when for the first time I heard you sing."

4   A singer gave a rendering of Rossini's famous aria *"Una voce,"* embellished with many showy *fioriture.* When she had finished, Rossini courteously congratulated her upon her technique. "And whose is the music?" he asked.

5   Rossini, who usually marked errors in his pupil's compositions with crosses, returned a manuscript to a mediocre student with very few crosses on it. The young man was delighted. "I'm so pleased there are so few mistakes," he said happily. "If I had marked all the blunders in the music with crosses, your score would have looked like a cemetery," said Rossini.

6   After a particularly excellent meal, Rossini's hostess turned to him and said he had done her a great honor by accepting her invitation. She hoped he would dine with her again soon. "Right away," said Rossini enthusiastically.

7   An oboist in an orchestra that Rossini was conducting played an F-sharp instead of an F. Rossini corrected him, then added consolingly, "In regard to the F-sharp, don't worry about it; we'll find some other place to fit it in."

8   Rossini attended a concert that included a set of variations on an aria from his own *Moses in Egypt,* played on musical glasses filled with water to various levels to sound the right pitch. After the tenth variation, Rossini's companion suggested that they walk out. "Not until this gentleman has finished washing Moses," replied Rossini.

9   One day a composer unknown to Rossini brought him the scores of two oratorios, seeking his opinion. Rossini tried to excuse himself, citing poor health. But the composer insisted, stating that he would return in a week for Rossini's judgment. He did so, finding Rossini in his armchair, serene and smiling, but quick to say that he had been so ill and had slept so little that he had been able to examine only one of the scores. "And what did you think of it?" was the eager question. "There are good things in it . . . but I prefer the other one."

10   When Rossini was old and eminent but still not rich, a group of his admirers raised a subscription of twenty thousand francs for a statue to their hero.
    "Give me the twenty thousand," said Rossini, "and I'll stand on the pedestal myself."

ॐ ॐ

ROTHSCHILD, Sir Nathan Meyer, 1st Baron (1840–1915), *member of the London branch of the famous family of Jewish financiers. He was a member of Parliament (1865–85) and the first Jew to be admitted to the House of Lords (1885).*

1   Alighting from a hansom cab one evening, Lord Rothschild gave the driver what he felt to be an adequate tip. "Your lordship's son always gives me a good deal more than this," said the driver, eyeing the money disdainfully. "I daresay he does," retorted Lord Rothschild. "But then, you see, he has got a rich father: I haven't."

ॐ ॐ

ROUTH, Martin (1755–1854), *British academic, president of Magdalen College, Oxford, for sixty-three years (1791–1854).*

1   The ups and downs of college life had little effect on the Venerable Dr. Routh, as he was generally called. A breathless don once stumbled into the president's room, gasping, "A Fellow of this college has killed himself!" Dr. Routh held up a calming hand. "Pray don't tell me who," he is reported to have said. "Allow me to guess."

2   An admirer asked Dr. Routh for a precept that could serve as a rule of life to an aspiring young man. The president thought for a moment and then said, "I think, sir, since you come for the advice of an old man, sir, you will find it a very good practice *always to verify your references!*"

3 Routh suffered an injury that troubled him for a long time; it was caused when he reached up for a weighty volume on a high shelf and the book fell, striking his left leg. The elderly scholar was incensed. "To be lamed by a book written by a dunce!" he cried. "A worthless volume! A worthless volume!"

ROWLAND, Henry Augustus (1848–1901), *US physicist, professor of physics at Johns Hopkins University (1875–1901). He laid the foundation for modern spectroscopy.*

1 Professor Rowland was summoned as an expert witness at a trial. During cross-examination a lawyer demanded, "What are your qualifications as an expert witness in this case?"

"I am the greatest living expert on the subject under discussion," replied the professor quietly.

Later a friend, well acquainted with the professor's modest and retiring disposition, observed that he had been amazed to hear him praise himself in this way; it was completely out of character. Rowland asked, "Well, what did you expect me to do? I was under oath."

{This anecdote is also told of others.}

RUBINSTEIN, Anton (1829–94), *Russian pianist and composer. He wrote numerous works for the piano, as well as operas and orchestral works. His concerts were acclaimed throughout Europe. In 1862 he founded the St. Petersburg Conservatoire.*

1 The telephone rang at a bad time while the maestro was practicing. His servant, François, answered the phone. It was a feminine voice tenderly asking to speak with Rubinstein. Although the sounds of the piano were clearly audible, François assured the lady that Rubinstein was not in. "But I hear him playing," she said. "You are mistaken, madame," replied François. "I'm dusting the piano keys."

2 Anton Rubinstein liked to sleep late in the mornings, often missing early appointments as

a result. Mme Rubinstein worked out a ruse to get him out of bed. She would play an unresolved chord on the piano upstairs, and her husband, who could not bear unresolved dissonances, would run up in his nightshirt to resolve it into a perfect triad. While he did this, Mme Rubinstein would sneak downstairs and remove the bedclothes to prevent him from returning to bed.

{If this is apocryphal, it is nonetheless characteristic of Rubinstein.}

RUBINSTEIN, Arthur (1886–1982), *Polish-born pianist, who became a US citizen in 1946. His interpretation of Chopin was the foundation of his international reputation.*

1 (Clifton Fadiman recalls a lunch with Rubinstein.)

"We . . . awaited him in the restaurant. He entered, his stride thirty-five years his junior, sat down at the table, ordered drinks in Italian (from the eight languages he speaks he selects one as an ordinary man would a tie), and started to apologize: 'So sorry to be late. For two hours I have been at my lawyer's, making a testament. What a nuisance, this business of a testament. One figures, one schemes, one arranges, and in the end — what? It is practically impossible to leave anything for yourself!' "

2 Rubinstein was standing in the lobby of a concert hall watching the capacity crowd streaming in to hear one of his recitals. The attendant at the box office, thinking that he had not seen the "SOLD OUT" sign, called out to him, "I'm sorry, mister, but we can't seat you."

"May I be seated at the piano?" inquired Rubinstein meekly.

3 During a radio interview with Rubinstein, the conversation took a sharp turn away from music when the interviewer suddenly asked, "Mr. Rubinstein, do you believe in God?" Rubinstein calmly replied, "No. You see, what I believe in is something much greater."

RUGGLES, Carl (1876–1971), *US composer.*

1 Henry Cowell, visiting Ruggles at his studio, found the composer at his piano playing the same chordal agglomerate over and over again. Eventually Cowell shouted, "What on earth are you doing to that chord? You've been playing it for at least an hour." Ruggles shouted back, "I'm giving it the test of time."

§~ ~§

RUSKIN, John (1819–1900), *British critic and social reformer; Slade Professor of Fine Arts at Oxford (1870–84). Ruskin's works, such as* Modern Painters *(1843–60),* Seven Lamps of Architecture *(1849), and* The Stones of Venice *(1851–53), did much to mold Victorian attitudes toward art and architecture. In the 1860s he became increasingly preoccupied with social and economic questions and instigated several practical experiments in the revival of small-scale craft industries, such as linen-weaving.*

1   In accordance with his ideas on the dignity of labor Ruskin encouraged his Oxford students to try their hand at manual work. He hit on the scheme of building a road from the nearby village of North Hinksey to Oxford to enable the villagers to reach the town by a direct route across low-lying and often muddy fields. Among the undergraduates he recruited was — of all people — Oscar Wilde. They set to work with a will under the direction of Ruskin's gardener, but somehow the charms of manual labor diminished after a while and the road was never completed. Final comment on the episode came from an anonymous resident of North Hinksey: "I don't think the young gentlemen did much harm."

{The line of the road was still visible in the mid-1960s.}

2   In the heyday of his career as art critic, Ruskin used always to maintain that it should in no way affect his friendship with an artist if he panned his work. The artists, of course, saw matters in a rather different light. "Next time I meet you I shall knock you down," one of his victims retorted, "but I trust it will make no difference to our friendship."

3   Ruskin, no lover of technological progress, was asked to comment on the completion of the British–Indian cable. "What have we to say to India?" he asked.

§~ ~§

RUSSELL, Bertrand Arthur William, 3d Earl (1872–1970), *British philosopher. His* Principia Mathematica *(1910–13), written with A. N. Whitehead, explored the relationship between pure mathematics and logic. He campaigned for numerous social, political, and moral causes, suffering imprisonment for pacifism during World War I (1918) and for civil disobedience during the Campaign for Nuclear Disarmament (1961). He won the 1950 Nobel Prize for literature.*

1   The American publisher William Jovanovich in his student days at Harvard often ate at a cafeteria that served cheap, rather bad food. Bertrand Russell also used to eat at the same place. One day Jovanovich, unable to restrain his curiosity, said to Russell, "Mr. Russell, I know why I eat here. It is because I am poor; but why do you eat here?" Russell replied, "Because I am never interrupted."

2   Russell's friend G. H. Hardy, who became Professor of pure mathematics at Cambridge in 1931, once told him that if he could find a proof that Russell would die in five minutes' time, he would naturally be sorry to lose him, but the sorrow would be quite outweighed by pleasure in the proof. Russell, wise in the ways of mathematicians, observed, "I entirely sympathized with him and was not at all offended."

3   (G. H. Hardy reports a nightmare once experienced by Bertrand Russell. In his dream he found himself on the top floor of a great library in about AD 2100.)

"A library assistant was going around the shelves carrying an enormous bucket, taking down book after book, glancing at them, restoring them to the shelves or dumping them into the bucket. At last he came to three large volumes which Russell could recognize as the last surviving copy of *Principia Mathematica*. He took down one of the volumes, turned over a few pages, seemed puzzled for a moment by the curious symbolism, closed the volume, balanced it in his hands and hesitated . . ."

4   A certain writer had compiled a book that incorporated, without acknowledgment, a good many of Russell's ideas. The plagiarist then approached Russell and asked him if he would compose an introduction for the completed text. Russell's succinct reply: "Modesty forbids."

5 When Bertrand Russell refused to grant interviews after a serious illness in China, in 1920, a resentful Japanese press carried the news he had died. Even when Russell appealed to them, they refused to retract the story. On his way home he stopped in Japan, and the press again sought to interview him. By way of reprisal he had his secretary hand out printed slips to each reporter. The slips read: "Since Mr. Russell is dead he cannot be interviewed."

{Reports of premature death are not uncommon. *See* MARK TWAIN 14.}

6 Russell was once asked whether he would be prepared to die for his beliefs. "Of course not," he replied. "After all, I may be wrong."

7 A young friend of Russell's once found the philosopher in a state of profound contemplation. "Why so meditative?" asked the young man. "Because I've made an odd discovery," replied Russell. "Every time I talk to a savant I feel quite sure that happiness is no longer a possibility. Yet when I talk with my gardener, I'm convinced of the opposite."

    ชื่อ ชื่อ

RUSSELL, Bill (1934–), *US basketball player. A great star, he led the University of San Francisco to two national collegiate titles in three seasons and the Boston Celtics to eleven national professional titles in thirteen seasons. As a coach, he guided the Celtics to two more crowns.*

1 Russell was a tall center famous for his unselfish team play. Off court he became well known for his philosophy of life. To an attractive young lady he met at a party he said, "You can get anything you want in life if you are willing to give up enough to get it."

"I want a lot of money," replied the girl, "but I come from a poor family, I have little education, and I have no special talents."

"You could become a prostitute."

"That's a terrible thing to say to someone you just met and don't know. I would never do such a thing."

"I didn't mean to insult you," said Russell. "I was just proving my point. You're a pretty lady.

You could become a high-priced prostitute if you wanted money badly enough. Apparently, you don't want it enough to give up your virtue. But, if you wanted money badly enough, and were willing to give up something that's precious to you, you could get it."

2 Russell and Wilt Chamberlain were both defensive stars in the 1960s. Russell's teams took eleven titles while Wilt's won only two. Chamberlain, however, received the first $100,000-a-year contract in basketball. When Russell was offered a similar deal, he insisted on a contract calling for $100,001. Needling his arch-rival, Russell remarked, "Poor Wilt — always a dollar short and a basket late."

    ชื่อ ชื่อ

RUSSELL, George William (1867–1935), *Irish poet who wrote under the pseudonym "AE." His play* Deirdre *(1902) was largely instrumental in the formation of the Irish National Theatre. His poetry draws on a mystical sense of the ancient wisdom in Irish folklore and history.*

1 The American dramatic critic George Jean Nathan was once at a Dublin gathering of literary figures. A dispute arose in the course of which Russell, crimson with indignation, stood up and pounded the table. Nathan remarked, "AE's Irish rose."

2 When AE was in Hamburg, he was offered a drink. "No, thank you," he said. "I was born intoxicated."

    ชื่อ ชื่อ

RUSSELL, John, 1st Earl (1792–1878), *British statesman; prime minister (1846–52, 1865–66). A lifelong Whig, Russell was instrumental in drafting the 1832 Reform Bill and in 1835, as home secretary (1835–39), was responsible for introducing the Municipal Reform Act. His character as a politician was admirably described by Sydney Smith: "He would perform the operation for the stone, build St. Peter's, or assume — with or without ten minutes' notice — the command of the Channel fleet, and no one would discover by his manner that the patient had died, the church tumbled down, and the Channel fleet had been knocked to atoms."*

1 During a fiery debate, the Tory Sir Francis Burdett objected to some sentiments from the other side that he called "the cant of patriotism." Russell immediately retorted, "There is something worse than the cant of patriotism; that is the recant of patriotism."

2 Russell was telling a friend about a party and how he had left the Duchess of Inverness and gone to talk to the Duchess of Sutherland because the Duchess of Inverness had been sitting very close to the fire and it had been intolerably hot. "I hope you told the Duchess of Inverness why you abandoned her," commented his friend. Russell reflected, then said, "No — but I did tell the Duchess of Sutherland."

3 Asked his opinion as to what would be the proper punishment for bigamy, Russell promptly answered, "Two mothers-in-law."

સ્ટ ✍

RUTH, George Herman ["Babe"] (1895–1948), *US baseball player. In 1927 he hit sixty home runs — a record unbroken until 1961.*

1 During the Depression Babe Ruth, asked to take a cut in salary, held out for his $80,000 contract. A club official protested, "But that's more money than Hoover got for being president last year."

"I know," said the Babe, "but I had a better year."

2 Babe Ruth was enormously popular, a larger-than-life-size figure in many respects, given to overeating and overdrinking. The most notorious occasion was in the course of preseason training when, on a railroad ride to New York, the Babe got off at a train stop and consumed an estimated twelve hot dogs and eight bottles of lemon-lime soda pop in a few minutes. Soon afterward he was stricken with "the stomachache heard 'round the world." (Less publicized were rumors that he had contributed to his misery with the consumption of large amounts of beer and booze.) For days ominous headlines had his fans across the country fearing for his life. Recovering, Ruth is reported to have said, "That soda pop will get you every time."

3 Babe Ruth loved kids. On one occasion when the family of a fan of the Babe's, a youngster who was seriously ill in the hospital, requested an autographed baseball for the boy, the Babe went along to the hospital himself, gave him the baseball, and promised to hit a home run for him in the game that afternoon. Sure enough, the Babe came through with the home run. The lad recovered and Babe Ruth observed, "Best medicine in the world, a home run."

4 "Grantland Rice, the prince of sportswriters, used to do a weekly radio interview with some sporting figure. Frequently, in the interest of spontaneity, he would type out questions and answers in advance. One night his guest was Babe Ruth.

"'Well, you know, Granny,' the Babe read in response to a question, 'Duke Ellington said the Battle of Waterloo was won on the playing fields of Elkton.'

"'Babe,' Granny said after the show, 'Duke Ellington for the Duke of Wellington I can understand. But how did you ever read Eton as Elkton? That's in Maryland, isn't it?'

"'I married my first wife there,' Babe said, 'and I always hated the goddamn place.'"

5 Ruth once suffered the humiliation of having the great Walter Johnson of the Washington Senators throw three straight fastballs past him. He asked the umpire if he had seen any of the pitches. "No," replied the umpire. "Neither did I," said Ruth, "but that last one sounded kinda high to me."

સ્ટ ✍

RUTHERFORD, Ernest, 1st Baron (1871–1937), *British physicist, born in New Zealand. He held professorships at Montreal (1898–1907), Manchester (1907–19), and Cambridge, where he was also director of the Cavendish Laboratory (1919–37). He received the 1908 Nobel Prize for chemistry.*

1 Rutherford's work and reputation made the Cavendish Laboratory the Mecca for experimental physicists from all over the world. As success followed success, someone observed to Rutherford that he was always at the crest of the wave. "Well, after all, I made the wave, didn't I?" said Rutherford.

❧ S ❧

SAARINEN, Eero (1910–61), *Finnish architect.*

1 Saarinen, an exceptionally slow talker, was being interviewed for a television program. The allotted time was rapidly running out, and the anxious interviewer ventured to ask Saarinen if he could speak just a little faster. "No, sir," replied the architect, casually lighting up his pipe. "But," he continued, more slowly than ever, "I could say less."

❧ ❧

SACKVILLE-WEST, Edward Charles, 5th Baron (1901–65), *British writer and critic.*

1 Sackville-West inherited the vast house and estate of Knole in Kent from his cousin, and this seems to have put him somewhat out of touch with how less fortunate mortals exist. Told that a certain person owned a dog, he exclaimed, "But how can he? He hasn't got a park to exercise it in."

❧ ❧

SAGE, Russell (1816–1906), *US financier. He left his large fortune to be distributed in benefactions by his wife, who set up the Russell Sage Foundation (1907) to improve social and living conditions in the United States.*

1 Sage's lawyer was delighted by the case his client had just laid before him. "It's an ironclad case," he exclaimed with confidence. "We can't possibly lose!"

"Then we won't sue," said Sage. "That was my opponent's side of the case I gave you."

❧ ❧

SAINTE-BEUVE, Charles Augustin (1804–69), *French critic and literary historian, whose prose style was greatly admired and emulated. His influence as a critic enabled him to promote* the careers of a number of younger writers in the French Romantic movement.

1 Although himself unpugnacious, Sainte-Beuve was once compelled to fight a duel with pistols. At the critical moment, just as the order to fire was about to be given, it started to rain. Sainte-Beuve called for a pause in the proceedings while he went to his carriage and fetched and opened a large umbrella. He then faced his opponent with the umbrella held in his left hand and the pistol in his right. The opponent protested at this derogation of the dignity of the occasion. "I don't mind being killed," Sainte-Beuve responded, "but I do mind getting wet."

{In the event neither happened.}

❧ ❧

SAINT-SAËNS, [Charles] **Camille** (1835–1921), *French composer, best known for his Third Symphony concertos in G minor and C minor, and the opera* Samson et Dalila.

1 Sir Thomas Beecham conducted a concert in London given in honor of Saint-Saëns, for which the principal piece was Saint-Saëns's Third Symphony. Beecham found the tempi in the symphony depressingly slow; so did the players, as they made clear by the way they played in rehearsal. Nor was the situation helped by Saint-Saëns's presence.

Beecham finally exaggerated the accentuation on purpose to give a semblance of life to the music without actually speeding it up. Later he asked Saint-Saëns what he thought of the interpretation. The aged composer replied, "My dear young friend, I have lived a long while, and I have known all the *chefs d'orchestre*. There are two kinds; one takes the music too fast, and the other too slow. There is no third."

In the 1930s, General Somervell was administering the WPA and was confronted with a "sit-down" strike. Union members took over space in a public building and would not leave.

The police had tried to end the strike without much success. This time Somervell simply locked all the building's bathrooms and left with the keys. The strike was over in six hours.

— Ralph L. Marquard,
*Jokes and Anecdotes
for All Occasions*

SALINGER, J. D. (1919–), *US writer who achieved almost overnight fame with his novel* The Catcher in the Rye *(1951). The hero, Holden Caulfield, epitomized the dissatisfaction of post-World War II adolescents by making a stand against what he called the "phony" adult world.*

1 When *The Catcher in the Rye* was chosen as the main selection of the Book-of-the-Month Club in 1951, the president of the club expressed anxiety over the book's somewhat ambiguous title. Asked if he would consider a change, Salinger simply replied, "Holden Caulfield wouldn't like that." The suggestion was not revived.

ह ह

SALISBURY, Robert Arthur Talbot Gascoyne-Cecil, 3d Marquess of (1830–1903), *British statesman, secretary for India (1866–67, 1874–78), Disraeli's foreign secretary (1878), and three times Conservative prime minister (1886–92, 1895–1900, 1900–02). He was the chief architect of Britain's isolationist policy at the end of the nineteenth century.*

1 In 1896, Salisbury made the undistinguished poet Alfred Austin Poet Laureate. It was widely believed that the decision was based on Austin's political leanings rather than on his talent. Asked why he had chosen a poet of such inferior ability, Salisbury simply replied, "I don't think anyone else applied for the post."

ह ह

SALK, Jonas E. (1914–), *US virologist who in 1954 developed the first effective antipolio vaccine.*

1 Salk worked hard to publicize his discovery, although he received no money from the sale of it. Someone once asked him who owned the patent. He replied, "The people — could you patent the sun?"

ह ह

SANDBURG, Carl (1878–1967), *US poet, novelist, and biographer. He is best known for his multivolume biography of Abraham Lincoln and* The People, Yes *(1936), a free-verse celebration of democracy.*

1 A young dramatist, anxious for Sandburg's opinion of his new serious play, asked the poet to attend the dress rehearsal. Sandburg slept throughout the performance. When the dramatist complained, saying that Sandburg had known how much he wanted his opinion, Sandburg replied, "Sleep *is* an opinion."

ह ह

SANDWICH, John Montagu, 4th Earl of (1718–92), *British politician. As First Lord of the Admiralty (1748–51, 1771–82), he was responsible for the unpreparedness of the British navy at the outbreak of the American Revolution. The earl gave his name to the sandwich, which he invented as a snack to sustain him through long hours of gambling.*

1 Entertaining at a dinner at which his chaplain was present, the earl brought in a large baboon dressed in clerical garb to say grace. The affronted chaplain left the room, pausing on his way out to observe, "I did not know your lordship had so near a relative in holy orders."

2 Lord Sandwich was remarkable for his ungainliness; a contemporary wit said that he could be recognized from afar by the fact that "he walked down both sides of the street at once." He liked to tell the following story: During a stay in Paris he took dancing lessons. Bidding farewell to his dancing master, he offered to recommend him to members of London society who might be visiting Paris. The man bowed and said earnestly, "I would take it as a particular favor if your lordship would

never tell anyone of whom you learned to dance."

See also TRISTAN BERNARD 7.

৯৯ ৺ঌ

SANTAYANA, George (1863–1952), *Spanish-born philosopher and poet. He spent many years at Harvard (1889–1911) and at Oxford. His philosophy is best set out in the four-volume* Realms of Being *(1927–40).*

1   Santayana inherited his simple and unostentatious habits from his father. Once he asked the senior Santayana why he always traveled third class. "Because there's no fourth class."

{This anecdote is also told of Albert Schweitzer.}

2   When Santayana came into a sizable legacy, he was able to relinquish his post on the Harvard faculty. The classroom was packed for his final appearance, and Santayana did himself proud. He was about to conclude his remarks when he caught sight of a forsythia beginning to blossom in a patch of muddy snow outside the window. He stopped abruptly, picked up his hat, gloves, and walking stick, and made for the door. There he turned. "Gentlemen," he said softly, "I shall not be able to finish that sentence. I have just discovered that I have an appointment with April."

৯৯ ৺ঌ

SARASATE [y Navascués], **Pablo de** (1844–1908), *Spanish violinist. He composed a number of works, including Spanish dances and fantasias, for the violin.*

1   By inviting Sarasate to dinner, his wealthy hostess had hoped to obtain a free violin recital for her guests after the meal. During the course of dinner she broached the subject, asking Sarasate whether he had brought his violin. "*Mais non, madame,*" replied the violinist, "*mon violon ne dine pas*" (No, madame, my violin does not dine).

See also STEPHEN COLLINS FOSTER 1.

2   In the latter part of his career, Sarasate received a visit from a famous music critic who acclaimed him as a genius. Sarasate accepted the compliment with little enthusiasm. "A

genius!" he said. "For thirty-seven years I've practiced fourteen hours a day, and now they call me a genius!"

৯৯ ৺ঌ

SARAZEN, Gene (1902–   ), *US golfer, winner of two US Opens and three Professional Golfers' Association championships.*

1   In the early years of professional golf "world championship" matches were arranged between the best two golfers each year. In 1922 Sarazen won over Walter Hagen when he defeated him over 72 holes — 36 at Oakmond in Pennsylvania one day and 36 at Westchester in New York the next day. At the end of the first day Sarazen was just two strokes behind, having been four behind at one stage after missing a five-foot putt on account of nerves. On the cross-country train ride that night Sarazen complained of stomach cramps and could not sleep, but on the following day, at the sixty-fifth hole of the match, he scored an eagle (two under par) to take a lead he held to the finish. Four hours later he underwent an emergency appendectomy. Commenting on the match later, he said, "A sick appendix is not as difficult to deal with as a five-foot putt."

৯৯ ৺ঌ

SARGENT, John Singer (1856–1925), *US portrait painter who spent much of his life in Britain and Europe. He excelled at portraits of the rich and famous, and also produced a fine series of watercolors of World War I landscapes.*

1   The commission to paint the coronation of Edward VII went to an artist named Edwin A. Abbey. This huge canvas contained about 120 portraits, and Abbey worked on it from 1902 to 1904. One important sitter was the Prince of Wales, the future George V. He surprised Abbey by asking him about Sargent's income, which apparently was much discussed among the portraitist's friends, of whom the prince was one. "Do you suppose it's ten thousand pounds?" guessed the prince. "I would say more likely twenty thousand," replied Abbey. The heir apparent was amazed: "My God! I wish I had twenty thousand pounds a year!"

2   Sargent did not take kindly to criticism of his work by his subjects. When a woman objected to his treatment of the mouth in a portrait he had done of her, his rejoinder was: "Perhaps, madam, we'd better leave it out altogether."

{Sargent suggested "A little something wrong with the mouth" should be written on his tombstone.}

3 A woman who was paying $5,000 for her portrait by Sargent said that there was something wrong with the nose. "Oh, you can easily put a little thing like that right when you get it home," said Sargent, handing her the canvas.

4 Sargent had been commissioned to do a portrait of Teddy Roosevelt. Determined to find the right setting, he and the president scoured the White House for a suitable backdrop. By the end of the second afternoon, after trying a succession of poses against various settings, Roosevelt had had enough. Pausing at the bottom of a staircase, his elbow on the newel post, he turned to the painter and said, "We're after the impossible; we'd better give it up." Sargent took in at a glance the president's pose and exclaimed, *"Don't move, Mr. President! We've got it!"*

5 Sargent once found himself sitting beside an effusive young admirer at a dinner party. "Oh, Mr. Sargent," she gushed, "I saw your latest painting and kissed it because it was so much like you."

"And did it kiss you in return?" asked the artist.

"Why, no."

"Then it was not like me," said Sargent with a smile.

❧

SARGENT, Sir Malcolm (1895–1967), *British conductor and organist who, as chief conductor at the London Promenade Concerts (1957–67), did much to bring classical music alive for younger audiences.*

1 "What do you have to know to play the cymbals?" someone once asked Sir Malcolm Sargent. "Nothing," was his reply, "just when."

2 Conducting a rehearsal of Handel's *Messiah*, Sargent was dissatisfied with the performance of the female singers in "For unto us a child is born." Asking the ladies to repeat the section, he requested: "Just a little more reverence, please, and not so much astonishment."

{For Sir Thomas Beecham's preferences as a conductor, *see* BEECHAM 7.}

3 As he was preparing to leave the Albert Hall after a concert one evening, Sir Malcolm overheard the following brief exchange between two young girls:

"How I envy Sir Malcolm."

"You mean his conducting?"

"Oh, no, not that. I mean his neat little flat behind."

4 At the age of seventy, Sargent was asked by an interviewer: "To what do you attribute your advanced age?"

"Well," replied the conductor, "I suppose I must attribute it to the fact that I haven't died yet."

5 A. P. Herbert visited Sargent in the nursing home shortly before he died and found him chuckling over the remark of an earlier visitor, Bob Boothby. Boothby had told Sir Malcolm that he had just been preparing a magnificent obituary for him, to be broadcast over the BBC: "The only thing is, I don't get anything until it's delivered."

❧

SAROYAN, William (1908–81), *US writer. His works include many short stories, the plays* The Time of Your Life *(1939) and* The Beautiful People *(1941), and a novel,* The Human Comedy *(1943).*

1 Before his death in 1981, Saroyan phoned in to the Associated Press a final Saroyanesque observation: "Everybody has got to die, but I have always believed an exception would be made in my case. Now what?"

❧

SATIE, Erik (1866–1925), *French composer of songs and piano pieces. His music is notable for its humor, its originality, and his eccentric instructions to potential performers.*

1 Satie wrote the following direction on one of his piano compositions: "To be played with both hands in the pocket."

2 Satie attended the premiere of Debussy's *La Mer,* the first part of which is entitled "From Dawn to Noon on the Sea." Asked by the composer what he thought of the work, Satie replied, "I liked the bit about quarter to eleven."

৵ ৵

SCARRON, Paul (1610–60), *French poet, playwright, and novelist. He excelled in burlesques and comedies, especially his unfinished* Roman comique *(1651–57). For twenty years he endured severe ill health and constant pain. His wife, Françoise d'Aubigné, later became Louis XIV's second wife.*

1 Scarron dedicated a collection of poems to his sister's dog: "*A Guillemette, chienne de ma soeur.*" Shortly before the publication of the poems, however, Scarron quarreled with his sister, and as a result the following notice appeared among the errata of the book: "For *chienne de ma soeur* [my sister's bitch] read *ma chienne de soeur* [my bitch of a sister]."

2 At their marriage the notary drawing up the contract asked Scarron what dowry he intended to bestow upon his beautiful but penniless young bride. "Immortality," he replied.

৵ ৵

SCHEFFEL, Josef Victor von (1826–86), *German writer. His works include the verse narrative* Der Trompeter von Säckingen *(1854) and the historical novel* Ekkehard *(1855). He was also known for his Heidelberg student songs, the most famous of which is* Gaudeamus igitur.

1 While Scheffel was a student and had already achieved some literary fame, he set out on a walking trip along the right bank of the Rhine. As the day was hot, he decided on a swim, threw off all his clothes, and plunged in. The current, however, was far stronger than he expected. After an exhausting struggle he managed to reach shore — but found himself on the *left* bank. Stark naked, he had no option but to walk to the nearest inn and appeal for help. It happened that the district military policeman had also stopped by at the inn. The latter grimly surveyed the naked, dripping Scheffel. "Where did you come from?" he demanded.

"From the opposite bank, Officer."

"And what's your name?"

"I'm the writer Josef Victor von Scheffel."

"Indeed. Show me your papers!"

৵ ৵

SCHICK, Bela (1877–1967), *Hungarian-American pediatrician and allergist; inventor of the Schick test that indicates whether someone is immune to diphtheria.*

1 "In the fall of 1923 Dr. Bela Schick assumed the directorship of the Pediatric Department at the Mount Sinai Hospital, New York. From the beginning he held his grand rounds and later his conferences on Thursdays. He started promptly at 9:30 A.M. no matter how small the gathering was. One morning during the depression years in the thirties there was an overflow attendance. Schick was delighted and commented, 'There must be an epidemic of health.'

"The following week when the attendance fell off, Schick remarked, 'Practice apparently is already better.'"

৵ ৵

SCHILLINGER, Joseph (1895–1943), *Russian-born musical theorist.*

1 One of Schillinger's favorite tricks was to play a piece on the piano and then challenge the audience to name the composer. After listeners suggested everyone from Palestrina to Bach, he would reveal, with a broad grin, that he had based the melody upon the business curve in the financial section of *The New York Times* that showed the fluctuations in wholesale prices of agricultural produce. This he had done by assigning musical values to the units of the graph, adding lines of harmony derived from the Chicago grain market, the Nebraska corn market, and the Georgia sugarcane market to create a musical composition in complete three-part counterpoint.

৵ ৵

SCHLEIERMACHER, Friedrich Daniel Ernst (1768–1834), *German philosopher and theologian.*

1 When complimented on the popularity of his sermons, which drew large audiences from many walks of life, Schleiermacher explained, "My audiences comprise mainly students, women, and officers. The students come to hear me preach, the women come to look at the students, and the officers come to look at the women."

ও৯ ৩৫

SCHLIEMANN, Heinrich (1822–90), *German archaeologist. As a merchant, he acquired knowledge of ten languages and a fortune, which enabled him to pursue his childhood vision of proving the historicity of Homer's* Iliad *and* Odyssey. *Schliemann's excavations at Hissarlik revealed a sequence of ancient cities, the second oldest of which he identified with the Homeric Troy. His later excavations brought to light the first remains of Mycenaean civilization.*

1   "I have looked upon the face of Agamemnon," exulted Schliemann when his excavations in the citadel of Mycenae unearthed a gold death mask of a warrior king. Later, doubts crept in, and his more scientifically inclined colleagues almost persuaded him that he had discovered the remains of a generation far earlier than the presumed date of Homer's Agamemnon. Schliemann resisted these suggestions hotly at first, but later came to accept them philosophically. "What," he said, "this is not Agamemnon's body and these are not his ornaments? All right, let's call him Schulze." (Schulze is the German equivalent of Smith or Jones.) After that these remains were always referred to as "Schulze."

ও৯ ৩৫

SCHNABEL, Artur (1882–1951), *Austrian pianist, renowned for his interpretation of Beethoven.*

1   A piano student came to Schnabel to ask him if he could study with him. Schnabel tested him and agreed to take him on as a pupil. "How much are your lessons?" the student asked.

"Five guineas each."

"I'm afraid I can't afford that."

"I also give lessons at three guineas — but I don't recommend them."

2   In 1940, Schnabel's son Stefan, an actor, was visited by a publicity agent. Toward the end of the interview she asked: "Are your parents in America?"

"Yes," replied Stefan.

"And your father — what does he do?"

"He is Artur Schnabel."

The lady looked bemused. "I see," she said. "But what does he do?"

"He's a pianist," replied Stefan. "He played at Carnegie Hall several times this season."

"That's nice," said the agent. "I'm always so glad to hear of a refugee getting on well."

3   An elderly lady in the front row slept right through one of Schnabel's concerts, waking with a start as the final ovation rang around the auditorium. Schnabel leaned across to apologize. "It was the applause, madame," he whispered. "I played as softly as I could."

ও৯ ৩৫

SCHÖDL, Max (1834–1921), *Austrian still-life painter.*

1   Schödl was noted for his absentmindedness. "Where to?" asked the driver of a horse-cab that the painter had hailed. Schödl reflected. "Number six," he said. "I'll tell you the street later on."

ও৯ ৩৫

SCHOLL, Aurélien (1833–1902), *notorious Belle Epoque boulevardier, journalist, and amorist.*

1   Scholl, for some reason known only to himself, on several occasions cut his friend Catulle Mendès, the novelist and playwright. Mendès decided that this kind of behavior was unacceptable. Finding Scholl sitting at a table in Tortoni's one afternoon, Mendès strode up to him and pointed an accusing finger at him, shouting, "BONJOUR!" at the top of his voice. Scholl studied the finger for a time, adjusted his monocle, then smiled and asked politely, "Where would you like me to put it, monsieur?"

2   "One challenger of Scholl's was a banker of rather shady reputation who, on certain occasions, had carried out a number of deals which had all but landed him in prison. Angered by some insinuating remarks Scholl had written about him in his newspaper, the banker burst into Tortoni's and challenged Scholl to a duel. Scholl, as always adjusting his monocle, stared coolly up at the man and asked, 'You really want to fight?'

" 'Oui, monsieur!' roared the banker.

"Scholl shrugged. '*Bon*,' he said. 'I daresay that when we arrive on the grounds they'll remove your handcuffs.' "

3   "He eventually married the daughter of a rich London brewer, a far from felicitous marriage which in no way interfered with his successful pursuit of other women. His witty approach had an individuality of its own. When one little married woman, wanting to give way yet struggling with her conscience, pleaded piteously, 'Let me be for a time, my friend! Let me retire into myself,' Scholl replied with gallant ardor: 'Allow me, madame, to accompany you.' "

ço ✑

SCHÖNBEIN, Christian Friedrich (1799–1868), *German–Swiss chemist and professor at the University of Basel. Discoverer of ozone, he was also a noted inventor.*

1   In 1845 Schönbein was carrying out an experiment with a mixture of sulfuric and nitric acid in the kitchen of his home. This was a practice expressly forbidden by his wife, who had banned the professor from her kitchen. In her absence he became so absorbed in his experiment that he spilled a little of the dangerous mixture on her kitchen table. Aware that his disobedience might be disclosed by a permanent stain on the woodwork, he grabbed the first thing at hand, his wife's cotton apron, and mopped up the offending liquid. He then hung it before the fire so that it would be dry before his wife returned. The resulting explosion, caused by the nitration of the cellulose in the cotton, eventually enabled the browbeaten chemist to invent, market, and exploit the smokeless gunpowder that became known as guncotton.

ço ✑

SCHÖNBERG, Arnold (1874–1951), *Austrian composer, pioneer of atonality, the so-called twelve-tone system. His compositions include the tone poem* Pelleas and Melisande *(1903), the song cycle* Pierrot lunaire *(1912), operas, chamber music, and other choral and orchestral works.*

1   Schönberg was strolling through the streets of his home town with a visiting friend one day, nodding graciously at the respectful greetings from the local people, many of them young boys. His friend was impressed and not a little surprised. "You really are famous," he remarked. "Even the children know you."

"That is quite true," remarked Schönberg with a smile. "You see, my son is a halfback on the high-school football team."

2   (The pianist Artur Schnabel in the course of a lecture told this story about the composers Schönberg and Stravinsky.)

"You may find this hard to believe, but Igor Stravinsky has actually published in the papers the statement, 'Music to be great must be completely cold and unemotional'! And last Sunday, I was having breakfast with Arnold Schönberg, and I said to him, 'Can you imagine that Stravinsky actually made the statement that music to be great must be cold and unemotional?' At this, Schönberg got furious and said, 'I said that first!' "

ço ✑

SCHOPENHAUER, Arthur (1788–1860), *German philosopher who developed several aspects of Kantian theory. He felt the human will to be a profoundly distorting and corrupting force, a view that underlay his deep pessimism.*

1   Visiting a greenhouse in Dresden, Schopenhauer became absorbed in contemplation of one of the plants. His eccentric gestures drew the attention of the attendant. "Who are you?" he asked. Schopenhauer looked at him for some moments, then said slowly, "If you could only answer that question for me, I'd be eternally grateful."

2   Schopenhauer, living in lodgings at Frankfurt for the last years of his life, used to take his meals at an inn frequented by English military personnel. At the start of each meal he would place a gold coin on the table in front of him. At the end of the meal he would drop the coin back in his pocket. A waiter, who had been eyeing the coin with interest, asked him why he did this. Schopenhauer explained that he had a little wager with himself every day: he would drop the coin into the poor box on the first occasion that the English officers talked of anything other than horses, dogs, or women.

ço ✑

> "Max Schling, New York florist, ran an advertisement in *The New York Times* entirely in shorthand. A lot of businessmen cut it out and, out of curiosity, asked their secretaries to translate it. The ad asked secretaries to think of Schling when the boss wanted flowers for his wife."
>
> — Jacob M. Braude,
> *Speaker's and
> Toastmaster's Handbook*

SCHUMANN-HEINK, Ernestine (1861–1936), *German contralto. She was a noted interpreter of Wagnerian roles.*

1 Schumann-Heink was an unashamed gourmand. Enrico Caruso, another lover of good food in quantity, entered the restaurant at which she was dining. Seeing her about to begin on a vast steak, he said, "Stina, surely you are not going to eat that alone?" "No, no, not alone," replied the lady, "mit potatoes."
{Told of others.}

2 When Mme Schumann-Heink appeared as the witch in *Hansel and Gretel,* her children, watching from the auditorium, were appalled at her fate at the end of the opera. "Mother! Mother!" her little boy screamed as she was pushed into the oven. A few minutes later she was back on the stage for her curtain calls. "There she is!" he cried out in relief. "There's Mother! They didn't burn her after all!"

3 Conditions were rather cramped in the Detroit concert hall where Schumann-Heink was to perform. As the portly singer struggled through the orchestra pit to make her entrance, music racks crashed to the floor. The conductor looked on in alarm. "Sideways, madam," he whispered urgently, "go sideways."
"Mein Gott!" cried the singer in reply. "I haff no sideways!"

4 In the Depression of the 1930s financial problems forced Schumann-Heink out of retirement. Despite her age and ill health, she signed a music-hall contract and took to the road. A newspaper reporter interviewing her remarked: "Things must be really bad when a great Wagnerian contralto is forced to do ten-cent shows."
"Young man," said Ernestine reprovingly, "how can times be bad when children can hear Schumann-Heink for a dime?"

ɞ ɷ

SCHWARTZ, Maurice (1890–1964), *Polish-born actor and theater director, who came to the United States in 1901 and founded the Yiddish Art Theater (1918).*

1 Schwartz was frequently accused of monopolizing all the best roles. A friend of his hotly denied the allegations. "On occasion Mr. Schwartz has been very generous with the leading parts," he said. "Take, for example, his recent production of the *Brothers Ashkenazi.* Did he play both brothers?"

ɞ ɷ

SCHWARZENBERG, Felix, Prince (1800–52), *Austrian statesman and diplomat. A ruthless reactionary, he masterminded policy in the first four years of Francis Joseph's reign (1848–52), strengthened the emperor's power through the 1849 constitution, and foiled Prussia's attempt to take advantage of Austrian weakness.*

1 Austria was forced to rely on the help of Czar Nicholas I of Russia to crush the Hungarian uprising against Austrian dominion in 1849. After this had been achieved, Schwarzenberg showed no signs in his policy of favoring Russia in any way. Asked whether he did not feel under an obligation to the czar, Schwarzenberg replied, "Austria will astound the world with the magnitude of her ingratitude."

2 After the quelling of the 1849 uprising, it was suggested to Schwarzenberg that it would be prudent to show mercy toward the captured Hungarian rebels. "Yes, indeed, a good idea," he replied, "but first we will have a little hanging."

3 Schwarzenberg's health failed quite suddenly when he was still comparatively young. A doctor called in to examine him warned him to take more rest or he would die of an apoplectic stroke. "That manner of death has my full approval," snapped back the patient.
{He had the death he approved, dropping dead as he was preparing to go to a ball.}

SCHWEITZER, Albert (1875–1965), *Alsatian-born medical missionary, theologian, and musician. Schweitzer studied theology and was principal of the theological faculty at Strasbourg before he abandoned his brilliant academic career to train as a medical missionary. He had also gained an international reputation as an interpreter and student of Bach's organ music. From 1913 he worked at the jungle hospital at Lambaréné in Gabon, Africa, which he established and for many years supported with the proceeds from his books, organ recitals, and lectures given on visits to Europe. In 1952 he was awarded the Nobel Peace Prize for his work in Africa.*

1 The phrase "reverence for life" aptly sums up Schweitzer's philosophy. On a visit to the United States he was importuned by many visitors, a group of whom interrupted his dinner to try to persuade him to explain his ethics. He talked patiently for twenty minutes. One of the visitors wanted him to give a specific example of "reverence for life." Schweitzer said, "Reverence for life means my answering your kind inquiries; it also means your reverence for my dinner hour." Schweitzer was able to return to his meal.

2 His doctrine of "reverence for life" was to be literally obeyed. It accounted for his vegetarianism, as well as for his attitude toward all animals. The American TV star Jack Paar once visited him at his hospital in Lambaréné. A dog appeared, chasing a chicken. In French Dr. Schweitzer shouted, "No! No! Remember we have won the Nobel Peace Prize!"

3 Jack Paar also recalls Schweitzer's standard attire: white pith helmet, white shirt and pants, black tie. He had worn one hat for forty years, the tie for twenty. Told that some men owned dozens of neckties, he remarked, "For one neck?"

4 (African patients leaving Schweitzer's hospital frequently stole his chamber pots to use as cooking utensils in their jungle homes.) Traveling by train in Europe, Schweitzer was asked by an inquisitive fellow passenger, "What do you do for a living?"
    "I supply Gabon with chamber pots," he replied.

5 On a train journey in the American Midwest, Schweitzer was approached by two ladies. "Have we the honor of speaking to Professor Einstein?" they asked. "No, unfortunately not," replied Schweitzer, "though I can quite understand your mistake, for he has the same kind of hair as I have." He paused to rumple his hair. "But inside, my head is altogether different. However, he is a very old friend of mine — would you like me to give you his autograph?" Taking a slip of paper from his pocket he wrote: "Albert Einstein, by way of his friend, Albert Schweitzer."

ह॰ ॰ई

SCIPIO NASICA SERAPIO, Publius Cornelius (fl. 138 BC), *Roman politician, elected consul in 138 BC. Opposed to the reforms implemented by Tiberius Gracchus, he took part in his assassination in 133 BC.*

1 Scipio Nasica called on his friend, poet Quintus Ennius, only to be told by Ennius's slave that his master was not at home. Nasica caught sight of the poet disappearing into a room at the back of the house. He did not attempt to contradict the slave, however, and left without a word. Sometime later, Ennius returned the visit. "Not at home!" cried Nasica as his friend arrived at the door. "You can't expect me to believe that — I recognize your voice," replied Ennius. "Why, you're a nice fellow," retorted Nasica. "I believed your slave, and you won't believe me."
    {The original version of an anecdote that has since been attributed to Jonathan Swift. *See also* SHIGERU YOSHIDA 1.}

ह॰ ॰ई

SCOTT, Sir Walter (1771–1832), *Scottish novelist. He first achieved fame with his poems on the feuds and loves of the medieval families living on the English–Scottish border. Waverley (1814) established him as a successful novelist and was the first in a series of historical novels.*

1 As a boy Scott was always the runner-up in his class at school. Try as he might, he could never displace the fluent, quick-witted, and studious boy who stood at the top of the class. One day Scott, watching his rival speaking in class, noticed that the lad always fumbled with a particular button on his vest while he talked. Stealthily Scott took a pair of scissors and snipped off the button. The next time the master called upon the boy to answer a question, he stood up and began to speak, feeling for the button. Failing to find it, he was so disconcerted that he stuttered and fell silent. Scott seized his opportunity, answered the question, and displaced his rival from the head of the class, a position he maintained thereafter.

2 Walking around the Abbotsford estate in spring, Sir Walter and Lady Scott passed a field full of gamboling lambs. "No wonder," said Scott, "that poets from the earliest times have made lambs the symbols of peace and innocence."

"Delightful creatures indeed," Lady Scott assented, "especially with mint sauce."

3 Scott gleaned many of the anecdotes and traditional stories used in his novels from an old Scottish lady, Mrs. Murray Keith. At the height of the speculation about the authorship of *Waverley,* Mrs. Keith challenged Scott with being "the Great Unknown" and refused to accept his customary denial. "D'ye think I dinna ken my ain groats among other folks' kail [broth]?" she exclaimed.

4 Scott's young son was ignorant of his father's fame as a novelist, but loved and admired him for reasons closer to a boy's heart. Once when he was in his teens he was in the company of some older people who were discussing Scott's genius. "Aye," put in young Scott, "it's commonly him is first to see the hare."

5 William Wordsworth once declared in the course of conversation that he had "the greatest contempt for Aristotle."

"But not, I take it," remarked Scott, "that contempt which familiarity breeds."

6 When Scott was declared bankrupt in 1826, his friends rallied around with offers of money. Scott declined their assistance, saying, "No, this right hand shall work it all off." This promise he kept, although the incessant writing ruined his health, and he dictated his last works from his deathbed while suffering great pain.

SCRIPPS, Edward Wyllis (1854–1926), *US newspaper proprietor.*

1 "[A woman] who had been his mistress in Detroit came to his office in Cincinnati where he was just getting a good start with the *Post* and tried to blackmail him. He summoned the city editor and directed him to call up the two rival papers and tell them to send over reporters. When the reporters arrived, he introduced his visitor.

"'Miss Brown,' he said, 'used to live with me as my mistress. She was paid for what she did and we parted on good terms. She has come here today threatening to revive that story and asking for money. You are at liberty to print the story. As far as I am concerned, the incident is closed.'

"The story was run with big headlines, and to the surprise of everybody, it did no harm either to the circulation of the paper or the standing of its editor."

SEBASTIANO DEL PIOMBO, Fra (?1485–1547), *Italian painter. He collaborated with Raphael in the decoration of the Farnesina, and also became a sought-after portraitist. In 1531 he was appointed keeper of the papal seals (piombi), from which he took his nickname.*

1 In later life Sebastiano ceased painting and was censured for his idleness by certain busybodies. He rebutted such criticism by pointing out, "There are now men of genius who do in two months what I used to do in two years, and I believe if I live long enough I shall find that everything has been painted. As these stalwarts can do so much, it is as well that there should also be someone who does nothing, so that they may have the more to do."

SEDGWICK, Catharine Maria (1789–1867), *US writer.*

1 Like most Sedgwicks, Catharine was very fond of her native town, Stockbridge, Massachusetts, where the burial markers of the clan are arranged in concentric circles known as the Sedgwick Pie. Someone once remarked to Miss Sedgwick that she spoke about Stockbridge as if it were heaven. "I expect no very violent transition," she replied.

> Graffiti are everywhere on the Harvard Bridge, linking Boston and Cambridge, Massachusetts, but none are as prominent as the regular "Smoot" markings along the bridge walkways.
>
> In 1958, when Oliver Reed Smoot, Jr., was a freshman pledge at the Massachusetts Institute of Technology, his fraternity, Lambda Chi Alpha, decided to use Mr. Smoot as a unit of measure to mark off the bridge. Smoot was five feet, six inches long at the time, which makes the bridge exactly 364.4 Smoots long, plus one ear.
>
> — *The Boston Globe Magazine*, November 11, 1984

SEDGWICK, John (1813–64), *US general.*

1 During the battle of the Wilderness in the Civil War, the general was inspecting his troops. At one point he came to a parapet over which he gazed out in the direction of the enemy. His officers suggested that this was unwise and perhaps he ought to duck while passing the parapet. "Nonsense," snapped the general. "They couldn't hit an elephant at this dist —"

{The reference books say that General Sedgwick was killed in action at the battle of the Wilderness.}

SEDGWICK, Theodore (1746–1813), *US judge; Speaker of the House of Representatives (1799–1801).*

1 The Sedgwicks had a black servant called Mumbet, who reared the Sedgwick children when their mother became insane. One day Mumbet heard the Declaration of Independence being read out at a town meeting. The following day she went to see Theodore Sedgwick in his office. "Sir," she said, "I heard that we are all born equal, and every one of us has the right to be free." Mr. Sedgwick promptly began a suit on Mumbet's behalf and a decree was obtained in her favor. Mumbet was so grateful she remained with the Sedgwick family for the rest of her life.

SEDLEY, Sir Charles (1639–1701), *English playwright and wit. His writings enjoyed a high reputation among his contemporaries, who also reveled in gossip about the author's scandalous personal life.*

1 Sir Charles had one daughter, Catharine, a shrewd and witty girl whom James, the Duke of York, made his mistress. When the duke ascended the throne as James II, he resolved not to see her again, but within three months their intrigue was revived. In 1686 James created Catharine Countess of Dorchester. Sir Charles, despite his own notoriety as a libertine, was sincerely upset by his daughter's situation. "I hate ingratitude," he said, "and as the king has made my daughter a countess I will endeavor to repay the civility by making his daughter a queen."

This he did by voting James II out of office in the Parliament preceding the Glorious Revolution of 1688, which brought James's daughter Mary and her husband, William of Orange, to the English throne.

SEELEY, Sir John Robert (1834–95), *British historian and essayist.*

1 In 1869 Seeley succeeded Charles Kingsley in the chair of Modern History at Cambridge, which Kingsley had resigned on grounds of ill health. Dr. William Thompson, the Master of Trinity College, observed after Seeley's inaugural lecture, "Well, well, I did not think we could so soon have had occasion to regret poor Kingsley."

SEFERIS, George [George Seferiades] (1900–71), *Greek poet and diplomat. He won the Nobel Prize for literature in 1963.*

1 (The English writer and classical scholar Peter Levi met Seferis in Athens in 1963.)

"We talked about mermaids. He said people knew he had a passion for them, and sent him presents of mermaids. There was a mermaid of bread, I think from southern Italy, hanging against the white garden wall. It had been there three years. I said she was young, for a mermaid. 'But it is old,' he said, 'for bread.' ''

❧ ☙

SELLERS, Peter (1925–80), *British comic actor. He made his name in the radio comedy series* The Goon Show, *first broadcast in the 1950s. He also appeared in many films, notably* I'm All Right, Jack *(1959),* Dr. Strangelove *(1963), and the "Pink Panther" series, in which he played the bungling detective Inspector Clouseau.*

1 In their London flat one afternoon, Sellers was busy in his study while his wife was working in the kitchen. On hearing the doorbell ring, Anne Sellers went to the door and was presented with a telegram. The message read: "Bring me a cup of coffee. Peter."

2 Sellers once received the following letter from a *Goon Show* fan: "Dear Mr. Sellers, I have been a keen follower of yours for many years now, and should be most grateful if you would kindly send me a singed photograph of yourself." Encouraged by fellow-comedian Harry Secombe, Sellers took the writer at his word. With the flame of his cigarette lighter, he carefully burned the edges of one of his publicity photographs and sent it off by return mail. A couple of weeks later, another letter arrived from the same address. "Dear Mr. Sellers," it read, "Thank you very much for the photograph, but I wonder if I could trouble you for another as this one is signed all round the edge."

3 Blake Edwards, who directed Sellers in the "Pink Panther" films, did not find him the easiest person to work with. One night, having wasted an entire day on one particular scene, Edwards was awakened by a phone call from Peter. "I just talked to God," he said excitedly, "and He told me how to do it."

The following day, Edwards set the cameras rolling to capture the results of Sellers's divine inspiration. The results were disastrous. "Peter," sighed the harassed director, "next time you talk to God, tell Him to stay out of show business."

4 In *The Mask Behind the Mask*, Peter Evans, biographer of Peter Sellers, says that Sellers played so many roles he sometimes was not sure of his own identity. Approached once by a fan who asked him, "Are you Peter Sellers?" Evans says Sellers answered briskly, "Not today," and walked on.

❧ ☙

SELWYN, George Augustus (1719–91), *British politician, eccentric, and wit. Horace Walpole said of him, "He loved nothing upon earth so well as a criminal, except the execution of him."*

1 When Henry Fox, Lord Holland, was dying, Selwyn called on him and left his card. His lordship, told that his old friend had called, instructed his footman, "If Mr. Selwyn calls again, show him up. If I am alive, I shall be glad to see him, and if I am dead, I am sure he will be delighted to see me."

2 Politician Charles Fox asked Selwyn if he had attended the execution of a highwayman, also called Charles Fox. Replied Selwyn, "I never attend rehearsals."

3 Robert Walpole once remarked in Selwyn's hearing that the British system of politics was the same under George III as it had been under his grandfather, George II, and that there was nothing new under the sun. "Nor under the grandson," put in Selwyn.

{This remark has also been used in the context of three generations — father, son, and grandson — sharing the same mistress, and is attributed to other wits.}

4 Staying at the fashionable resort of Bath out of season, Selwyn was compelled for want of better company to cultivate the acquaintance of an elderly bore. Some months later they met again by chance in a smart London thoroughfare at the height of the London season. Selwyn tried to slip past unnoticed, but the older gentleman hailed him, saying, "Don't you recollect me?"

"Perfectly," said Selwyn, "and when I next go to Bath I shall be most happy to become acquainted with you again."

5 A fashionable society beauty was showing off her new gown, which was covered with silver spangles the size of shillings. "How do you like it?" she asked George Selwyn. "You

will be change for a guinea, madam," he replied.

6 Selwyn once asserted that no woman could write a letter without adding a postscript. One of the ladies present, determined to prove him wrong, sent him a letter the following day. To Selwyn's glee, however, his triumphant correspondent had added after her signature: "P.S. Who is right now, you or I?"

᠅

SENECA, Lucius Annaeus (?4 BC–65 AD), *Roman statesman, author, and philosopher; tutor and adviser to Emperor Nero until he fell from favor and was obliged to commit suicide. Nine of his plays survive.*

1 Seneca's influence upon the vicious and mad Nero grew weaker as the years passed. Nonetheless, Seneca tried to curb his charge's cruelty, warning him on one occasion, "However many you put to death, you will never kill your successor."

᠅

SERVETUS, Michael (1511–53), *Spanish-born theologian and physician. His unorthodox views on the Trinity angered both Roman Catholics and Protestants and led to his execution as a heretic.*

1 Hiding from the Inquisition in Calvin's Geneva, Servetus was caught, tried, and condemned to be burned at the stake for his views. He said to his judges, "I will burn, but this is a mere incident. We shall continue our discussion in eternity."

᠅

SEUSS, Dr. [Theodore Seuss Geisel] (1904–), *US humorous writer and illustrator of children's books.*

1 An eight-year-old once sent him a letter saying: "Dear Dr. Seuss, you sure thunk up a lot of funny books. You sure thunk up a million funny animals . . . who thunk you up, Dr. Seuss?"

᠅

SÉVIGNÉ, Marie de Rabutin-Chantal, Marquise de (1626–96), *French writer, known for her brilliant letters.*

1 (The following anecdote is kept in the original French since it does not lend itself to translation.)

A sa fille qui lui demande:"Est-ce vrai, madame, que, dans un dîner, récemment le mot 'foutre' vous ait échappé?"

"Non," répond-elle, "j'ai dit F et j'ai passé outre."

᠅

SEWARD, William Henry (1801–72), *US statesman. Governor of New York and later a senator from that state, he was a stalwart opponent of slavery. He became secretary of state under Lincoln and in 1867 arranged the purchase of Alaska from Russia, a move branded "Seward's folly" by his enemies.*

1 After a debate in which Stephen A. Douglas had delivered a fiery diatribe against "nigger-worshipers," Seward walked home with him from the Capitol. Aware that Douglas hoped to secure the Democratic presidential nomination, Seward remarked, "Douglas, no man will ever be president of the United States who spells negro with two *g*'s."

2 Seward was in an assembly of people who were speculating about the probable destination of a secret movement of troops. A lady, noticing his silence, challenged him: "Well, Governor Seward, what do you make of it? Where do you think they are going?" Seward smiled. "Madam," he replied, "if I did not know I would tell you."

᠅

SHAFTESBURY, Anthony Ashley Cooper, 1st Earl of (1621–83), *British statesman. He began as a supporter of Charles I, then joined the Parliamentarians, and finally made his peace with Charles II. Having become lord chancellor in 1672, he was dismissed the following year. Later restored to office, he supported the Duke of Monmouth's rebellion, was charged with high treason, and fled to Holland.*

1 Shaftesbury's religious beliefs remained a mystery; very likely he was a deist. He once remarked that all wise men are of but one religion. "Which is that?" he was promptly asked. "Wise men never tell," he replied.

2 Charles II, hearing some gossip about Lord Shaftesbury, remarked to him jestingly, "I believe you're the wickedest rogue in England."

"Of a subject, sire, I believe I am," was the prompt reply.

{Benjamin Disraeli also saw the versatility in "subject." *See* DISRAELI 5.}

❦ ❦

SHAKESPEARE, William (1564–1616), *English dramatist. He came to London from his native Stratford-upon-Avon probably in the mid-1580s. By the time he joined an acting company known as the Lord Chamberlain's Men in 1594, he was already an established poet and playwright with patronage in court circles. Shakespeare's own acting abilities were not great, and he was fortunate to have other actors of stature to create such roles as Hamlet, Lear, and Richard III. Shakespeare's plays are known and performed in every country of the civilized world, and he is considered the greatest of playwrights. Yet comparatively few definite facts are known about his life, nor are the handful of anecdotes about him necessarily authentic.*

1 "Mr. William Shakespeare was born at Stratford upon Avon in the county of Warwick. His father was a butcher, and I have been told heretofore by some of the neighbors, that when he was a boy he exercised his father's trade, but when he killed a calf he would do it in a high style, and make a speech."

{It seems that "the neighbors" were pulling someone's leg; John Shakespeare, the poet's father, was a glover. This story, told by John Aubrey, would be more likely to have originated among Shakespeare's rivals on the London literary scene.}

2 At a time when Richard Burbage was playing the title role in *Richard III,* he made an assignation with a lady who lived near the playhouse. "Announce yourself as Richard III," she suggested cautiously — a suggestion Shakespeare overheard. The dramatist slipped out of the theater before the end of the play and hastened to the woman's lodgings. Here he announced himself as Richard III and was admitted to her bedroom. A short while afterward a message was brought up that "Richard III" was at the door. Shakespeare sent a message back to Burbage, saying that William the Conqueror came before Richard III.

3 Shakespeare was godfather to one of Ben Jonson's children and after the christening appeared sunk in deep thought. Jonson asked him what was the matter. Shakespeare replied that he had been pondering what to give the child as a christening present, but now he had made up his mind: "I'll give him a dozen good latten spoons and thou shalt translate them."

{The ultimate source of this witticism is a collection of "Merry Passages and Jests" in a manuscript in the British Library. Latten was a yellow metal, similar to brass in composition, which was commonly used for household utensils in the sixteenth and seventeenth centuries; the second part of the pun relies upon the alchemists' supposed practice of "translating" base metals into gold. Whether apocryphal or not, this is a pleasant illustration of the difference that their contemporaries perceived between the learned Ben and the "unLatined" Shakespeare.}

4 Once when Shakespeare was acting the role of a king, Queen Elizabeth thought she would see if she could distract him from his part and purposely let her handkerchief flutter to the stage at the actor's feet. Shakespeare did not hesitate. "Take up our sister's handkerchief," he instructed one of the stage courtiers in his train.

{There seems to be no reliable contemporary source for this pretty tale. Compare the old theatrical tradition that Shakespeare never reached any eminence as an actor greater than that of the ghost in his own *Hamlet.*}

❦ ❦

SHARIF, Omar [Michel Shalhoub] (1932–), *Egyptian actor. His films include* Lawrence of Arabia *(1962),* Dr. Zhivago *(1965), and* Funny Girl *(1968).*

1 "Tell me, Mr. Sharif," asked a journalist, "with your reputation as a ladykiller, what should one talk to women about?" "Their beauty, of course," replied the actor without hesitation. "But what if they are ugly?" "Then about other women's ugliness."

❦ ❦

SHARP, William (1855–1905) *British writer. In the 1890s his work assumed a mystical cast,* *often drawing upon Celtic myth and legend. These productions appeared under the nom de plume "Fiona Macleod," and Sharp strongly insisted on her separate existence.*

1 The English scholar W. P. Ker learned from a mutual acquaintance that Sharp always wore women's clothing to write his "Fiona Macleod" romances. "Did he? The bitch!" said Ker.

&ⷱⷱ ⷱⷱ

SHAW, George Bernard (1856–1950), *Irish playwright. Born in Dublin, he went to London at the age of twenty, where he remained for the rest of his life. After writing five unsuccessful novels he became a music and drama critic and an active socialist. He wrote more than forty plays, many of which have retained their enormous popularity. He was a witty speaker and writer of letters.*

1 When Shaw was a young man just embarking on his literary career, he met Oscar Wilde, then at the height of his fame, in the rooms of a mutual friend in London. Shaw told the company about a magazine that he intended to found, speaking with such enthusiasm that his Irish brogue became increasingly evident. Eventually Oscar Wilde interrupted to say that Shaw had not told them what the magazine would be called. "Oh, as for that, what I'd want to do would be to impress my own personality on the public — I'd call it *Shaw's Magazine*. Shaw, Shaw, Shaw," he went on, pounding the table. "And how would you spell it?" inquired Wilde.

2 Before Shaw became famous, one of his plays was consistently turned down by a certain producer. After Shaw achieved success, the producer suddenly cabled an offer to stage the rejected work. Shaw cabled in reply: "Better never than late."

3 While Shaw was still a music critic, he was dining with a friend in a restaurant that provided for entertainment an orchestra that was at best mediocre. The leader, recognizing Shaw, wrote him a note asking him what he would like the orchestra to play next. "Dominoes," replied Shaw.

4 The first performance of *Arms and the Man* (April 21, 1894) was boisterous. The author

took a curtain call and was received with cheers. While they were subsiding, before Shaw could utter a syllable, a solitary hiss was heard from the gallery. It was made by R. Goulding Bright, who later became a very successful literary agent. Bright hissed, it later appeared, under the misapprehension that Shaw's satire on florid Balkan soldiers was, in fact, a reflection on the British army. Shaw did not know this at the time, however, and as he stood on the stage he raised his hand to silence the cheers. Bowing in Bright's direction, he said, "I quite agree with you, sir, but what can two do against so many?"

5 The Theatre Guild had started rehearsals for the American premiere of Shaw's *Saint Joan*. Everything was progressing smoothly, except that the play was found to run for three and a half hours, long past the normal curtain time. Suburban playgoers would miss the last trains home. This information was cabled to Shaw, together with a request that he cut the play. Back came the reply: "Begin at eight or run later trains."

6 The success of Shaw's dramatic writings was an embarrassment to his socialistic ideals. To the play representative who had sent him a draft of money with promise of more to come, he wrote: "Rapacious Elisabeth Marbury: What do you want me to make a fortune for? Don't you know that the draft you sent me will permit me to live and preach Socialism for six months? The next time you have so large an amount to remit, please send it to me by installments, or you will put me to the inconvenience of having a bank account."

7 "George Bernard Shaw, a staunch vegetarian, refused to attend a gala testimonial because the bill of fare was a vegetarian menu. He said: 'The thought of two thousand people crunching celery at the same time horrified me.'"

8 During the rehearsals of *Pygmalion*, Shaw, dissatisfied with Mrs. Patrick Campbell's rendering of Eliza Doolittle, ticked her off for her flamboyant style. Mrs. Pat, unused to such treatment, remarked, "You are a terrible man, Mr. Shaw. One day you'll eat a beefsteak and then God help all women." The vegetarian Shaw blushed — perhaps.

9 It is said that the dancer Isadora Duncan wrote to Shaw that good eugenics indicated they should have a child together. "Think of it! With my body and your brains, what a wonder it would be," she said. Shaw replied, "Yes, but what if it had my body and your brains?"

10 "At a performance given by an Italian string quartet, Shaw's companion remarked approvingly, 'These men have been playing together for twelve years.' 'Surely,' said Shaw, 'we have been here longer than that.'"

11 At a dinner party one evening, Shaw sat next to a pompous young bore who proved to be a mine of uninteresting information. After suffering his neighbor's interminable monologue throughout the meal, Shaw observed, "You know, between the two of us we know all there is to know." His interlocutor was fascinated. "How is that?" he asked. "Well," replied Shaw, "you seem to know everything except that you're a bore. And I know that!"

12 The military theorist and historian B. H. Liddell Hart once observed to Shaw, "Do you know that 'sumac' and 'sugar' are the only two words in the English language that begin with *su* and are pronounced *shu?*"

"Sure," answered Shaw.

{Authenticity not guaranteed.}

13 Shaw was once approached by the advertising executive of a company manufacturing electric razors, in the hope that the great writer would endorse their new product by shaving off his beard. By way of reply, Shaw explained the reason why he, and his father before him, had chosen to grow a beard. "I was about five at the time," said Shaw, "and I was standing at my father's knee whilst he was shaving. I said to him, 'Daddy, why do you shave?' He looked at me in silence, for a full minute, before throwing the razor out of the window, saying, 'Why the hell do I?' He never did again."

14 An anthologist wrote to Shaw requesting permission to include one of his pieces in an anthology. He explained that he was a very young man and therefore would not be able to pay Shaw's usual fee. GBS responded, "I'll wait for you to grow up."

15 Arnold Bennett visited Shaw in his apartment and, knowing his host's love of flowers,

was surprised that there was not a single vase of flowers to be seen. He remarked on their absence to Shaw: "But I thought you were so fond of flowers."

"I am," said Shaw, "and I'm very fond of children too, but I don't chop their heads off and stand them in pots about the house."

16 Knowing that Shaw detested blood sports as much as she did, Lady Astor remarked that she hated "killing for pleasure." As Shaw said nothing, someone challenged him: "Do you hate killing for pleasure?"

"That depends on whom you kill," he said.

17 A lady notorious for courting celebrities sent Shaw an invitation reading: "Lady —— will be at home on Tuesday between four and six o'clock." Shaw returned the card annotated, "Mr. Bernard Shaw likewise."

18 "Are you enjoying yourself, Mr. Shaw?" anxiously inquired the hostess, who had noticed that her distinguished guest was standing alone in a corner. "Certainly," he replied. "There is nothing else here to enjoy."

{This is also attributed to Oscar Wilde, and probably has been told by others.}

19 Sam Goldwyn, the American movie magnate, attempted to buy from Shaw the film rights of his plays. There was a protracted haggle over what the rights should cost, which ended in Shaw's declining to sell. "The trouble is, Mr. Goldwyn," said Shaw, "you are interested only in art and I am interested only in money."

20 A country clergyman, hearing that Shaw was an expert in the brewing of coffee, wrote to ask him for the recipe. Shaw obliged, adding as an afterthought that he hoped the request was not an underhanded way of obtaining his autograph. The clergyman cut Shaw's signature from the letter, returned it with a note thanking him for the coffee recipe, and concluded: "I wrote in good faith, so allow me to return what it is obvious you infinitely prize, but which is of no value to me, your autograph."

21 Shaw once came across a copy of one of his works in a secondhand bookshop. Opening the volume, he found the name of a friend inscribed in his own hand on the flyleaf: "To

—— with esteem, George Bernard Shaw." He promptly bought the book and returned it to his friend, adding the inscription: "With renewed esteem, George Bernard Shaw."

22   In conversation with Shaw and his wife, writer Patrick Mahony asked Mrs. Shaw how she had coped with her husband's many female admirers. By way of reply, Mrs. Shaw began to recount an anecdote: "After we were married there was an actress who pursued my husband. She threatened suicide if she were not allowed to see him . . . "
  "And did she die of a broken heart?"
  "Yes, she did," interrupted Shaw. "Fifty years later."

23   Showing a friend the portrait bust sculpted for him by Rodin, Shaw remarked: "It's a funny thing about that bust. As time goes on it seems to get younger and younger."

24   Once when sitting for the photographer Yousuf Karsh, Shaw said that Karsh "might make a good picture of him — but none as good as the picture he had seen at a recent dinner party where he glimpsed, over the shoulder of his hostess, a perfect portrait of himself: 'Cruel, you understand, a diabolical caricature, but absolutely true.' He had pushed by the lady, approaching the living image, and found he was looking into a mirror!"

25   On July 26, 1946, Shaw celebrated his ninetieth birthday. Interviewed by a journalist, he commented: "I've been offered titles, but I think they get one into disreputable company."

26   Among the guests George Bernard Shaw received on his ninetieth birthday was Fabian, Scotland Yard's celebrated detective. At Fabian's suggestion Shaw agreed to have his fingerprints recorded for posterity. To the amazement of both, Shaw's fingerprints were so faint no impression could be obtained.
  "Well," announced Shaw, "had I known this sooner I should certainly have chosen another profession."

27   On a visit to GBS shortly after Shaw's ninetieth birthday, comedian Danny Kaye sought to compliment the playwright by saying, "You're a young-looking ninety." "Nonsense," came the crusty reply. "I look exactly like a man of ninety should look. Everyone else looks older because of the dissolute lives they lead."

&⸻⸻

SHAW, Irwin (1913–84), *US novelist. His books, involving contemporary political and social themes, include* The Young Lions *(1948)* The Troubled Air *(1951), and* Rich Man, Poor Man *(1970).*

1   After waiting an unacceptably long time for the waiter to take his order in a French restaurant, Irwin Shaw was finally approached by the maître d'hôtel. When the man informed Shaw that snails were the specialty of the house, the writer nodded his head. "I know," he said, "and you've got them dressed as waiters."

2   Shaw was in an airport about to go to Europe. With him was his small son, who clearly did not want to go anywhere and was causing something of an uproar. When airline officials suggested something was wrong with the child, Shaw said, "Not at all. He's just my troubled heir."

&⸻⸻

SHAW, Wilbur (1902–54), *US racing driver, first three-time winner of the Indianapolis 500. He was president of the Indianapolis Motor Speedway at the time of his death in a plane crash.*

1   Shaw was frustrated at Indianapolis until he won his first 500 at the advanced age of thirty-five. He was leading runner-up Ralph Hepburn by three miles (more than a lap on the 2½-mile course) with thirty-five laps left when an oil leak developed. Finding out from his pit crew that he was one minute and fourteen seconds ahead of Hepburn, Shaw swiftly calculated how much he could slow down to conserve his dwindling oil and still finish ahead. He cut speed drastically; Hepburn started to catch up, passed Shaw to "un-lap" himself, and now on the same lap sped around, always closing the gap. On the last turn of the last lap Hepburn came even with Shaw and nosed ahead, but Shaw took a chance, accelerated, and crossed the finish line 2.16 seconds in front. His engine quit as he pulled into "Victory Lane," but he had won the closest race in Indianapolis 500 history. "I don't wish to be immodest, but sometimes smart pays off," remarked Shaw later.

❧ ⚕

SHEARING, George [Albert] (1919–), *US jazz pianist, born in Britain. Blind from birth, he made his name in British jazz clubs before settling in the United States in 1947. His compositions include "Lullaby of Birdland" (1945).*

1 Asked by an admirer whether he had been blind all his life, Shearing replied. "Not yet."
{A variant of a traditional retort.}

2 One afternoon, at rush hour, he was waiting at a busy intersection for someone to take him across the street when another blind man tapped him on the shoulder and asked if Shearing would mind helping him to get across.
 "What could I do?" said Shearing afterward. "I took him across and it was the biggest thrill of my life."

❧ ⚕

SHEEN, Fulton J[ohn] (1895–1979), *US Roman Catholic clergyman, educator, and author, created a bishop in 1951. He broadcast regularly on the radio from 1930 and was an instructor of Catholic converts. His writings include* The Moral Universe *(1936) and* War and Guilt *(1941).*

1 Accepting a television award for spontaneity, comedian Garry Moore facetiously paid tribute to "the four guys responsible for my spontaneity—my writers." The next award went to Fulton Sheen. "I also want to pay tribute to my four writers," said the bishop. "Matthew, Mark, Luke, and John."

2 Having studied his contract for a television program in detail, the bishop came to the conclusion: "The big print giveth and the fine print taketh away."

3 In Baltimore to address an interfaith rally, Bishop Fulton J. Sheen was greeted by applause upon his appearance. He raised a hand for silence, then said:
 "When you applaud me at the start, that's faith; midway through, that's hope. But, ah, my dear friends, if you applaud me at the end, that will be charity!"

❧ ⚕

> Asked why he robbed banks, the notorious American bank robber Willie Sutton is reputed to have remarked, "Because that's where the money is."
>
> — Theodore White,
> *America in Search of Itself*

SHELBURNE, William Petty, 1st Marquis of Lansdowne (1737–1805), *British politician.*

1 In March 1780 Lord Shelburne fought a duel with a Lieutenant Colonel William Fullerton over some remarks that the former had made in the House of Lords. Shelburne was slightly wounded in the groin. As his anxious seconds bent over him, he reassured them, saying, "I don't think Lady Shelburne will be the worse for it."

❧ ⚕

SHELLEY, Mary Wollstonecraft Godwin (1797–1851), *British author. The daughter of political radicals and writers William Godwin and Mary Wollstonecraft, she eloped with Shelley, who married her in 1816 after the death of Harriet, his first wife. While living in Italy with Shelley she wrote* Frankenstein *(1818) and after Shelley's death prepared editions of his works.*

1 During the summer of 1816 Byron and Shelley were neighbors on the shores of the lake of Geneva. The two poets, together with Byron's friend Dr. John Polidori and Shelley's companions, Mary Godwin and her stepsister Claire Clairmont, spent many an evening conversing. One night Byron initiated a discussion of ghosts and the supernatural. Polidori recalled that Shelley was so distressed at the conversation that he ran from the room, maintaining that he had seen the women's breasts as eyes. Meanwhile Byron suggested that all of them write their own ghost stories. From this evening emerged an effort begun by Byron about the ruins of Ephesus, never completed; a tale by Polidori eventually published as *The Vampyre;* and, by the seventeen-year-old Mary, the tale of *Frankenstein*—a story that probably has frightened more people and led to more spin-offs than any other ghost story in the world.

2 Shelley's utter disregard for convention may have been a trial to his wife. After his death she was urged to send her surviving son, Percy Florence, to an advanced school at which the boy would be taught to think for himself. "To think for himself!" exclaimed his mother. "Oh, my God, teach him to think like other people!"

{Percy Florence Shelley was sent to Harrow.}

ಶಿ ೀ

SHELLEY, Percy Bysshe (1792–1822), *British Romantic poet. Rebellious, atheistic, mystic, Shelley was once considered as, next to Shakespeare, the greatest influence in English poetry, according to Stephen Spender. In the twentieth century his reputation suffered, but recently scholars have reinvestigated his dazzling imagery and remarkable intellectual power. The irregularity of his personal life led Shelley to Italy in 1818, where he spent his remaining years, writing most of his finest poetry.*

1 (Thomas Jefferson Hogg records an early exploit of Shelley's.)

As a young man he went on a short journey in rural Sussex. There was a full complement of passengers on the outside of the coach, but Shelley took an inside seat and for a time had the interior to himself. Then the coach stopped and picked up a large elderly woman carrying two vast panniers, one filled with apples, the other with onions. In the stuffy coach the smell of apples, onions, and sweaty old woman soon became overwhelming. Seating himself on the floor, Shelley fixed his unwanted companion with a wild glare and began to recite Richard II's lament from Shakespeare's play—"For God's sake let us sit upon the ground . . ." When he got to the words, "All murder'd," the old woman's nerve could stand it no longer and she yelled at the coach driver to stop and let her out. She duly exited, and Shelley was able to complete his journey in comfort.

2 Early in 1822 Shelley's household was joined by the young English adventurer Edward J. Trelawny, a sportsman and extrovert who greatly admired the impractical and wayward poet. Trelawny found a deep pool in the river where he liked to bathe. One day, after watching Trelawny performing various aquatic feats, Shelley said wistfully, "Why can't I swim?" Trelawny immediately offered to teach

him. Shelley stripped off his clothes and leaped in—plunging straight to the bottom of the pool, where he lay motionless. Trelawny jumped into the water and managed to haul the poet out. Shelley was not at all flustered by the narrowness of his escape. "I always find the bottom of the well and they say truth lies there. In another minute I should have found it, and you would have found an empty shell. It is an easy way to get rid of the body." Only a few months later Shelley was drowned while sailing near Leghorn in squally weather.

ಶಿ ೀ

SHERIDAN, Philip Henry (1831–88), *US army officer. His most famous feat was his victory at Cedar Creek (1864), which he brought about by a twenty-mile dash on horseback to rally his troops against the Confederates. He later became commander in chief of the US army (1883).*

1 In January 1869 Sheridan held a conference with Indian chiefs at Fort Cobb in the then Indian Territory (now part of Oklahoma). When the Comanche chief Toch-a-way was introduced, he said to Sheridan, "Me Toch-a-way, me good Indian." "The only good Indians I ever saw were dead," retorted Sheridan.

{This remark was modified later to the proverbial "The only good Indian is a dead Indian."}

2 While commanding the Military Division of the Gulf, Sheridan spent time at San Antonio, Texas. Asked by a local reporter his opinion of Texas as a country to live in, he answered, "If I owned two plantations and one was located in Texas and the other one was in hell, I'd rent out the one in Texas and live on the other one." This comment was printed with a note from the editor that read: "Well, damn a man that won't stand up for his own country."

ಶಿ ೀ

SHERIDAN, Richard Brinsley (1751–1816), *Anglo–Irish playwright. Born in Dublin, he lived in England from childhood on. His best-known comedies are* The Rivals *(1775) and* The School for Scandal *(1777). He was manager of the Drury Lane Theatre in London and a member of Parliament from 1780 to 1812. Although he never achieved political power, he* *acquired a reputation as a witty parliamentary orator.*

1 Lord Thurlow produced a bottle of particularly good Constantia wine, specially sent from the Cape of Good Hope, at a dinner at which Sheridan was a guest. Sheridan greatly appreciated the wine and tried, by praising and hinting, to persuade Lord Thurlow to bring out another bottle. The host, however, was determined not to be overgenerous with this rare treat, and Sheridan eventually saw that his efforts were vain. Turning to his next neighbor, he gestured toward the decanter of Madeira and said, "Pass the decanter. I must return to Madeira since I cannot double the Cape."

2 A lady anxious to take a walk with Sheridan observed that the weather had cleared up sufficiently for them to set out. Sheridan, equally anxious to avoid the tête-à-tête, replied, "It may have cleared up enough for one, but not enough for two."

3 Two royal dukes, meeting Sheridan in London's Piccadilly, greeted him familiarly. Said one, "I say, Sherry, we were just discussing whether you are more rogue or fool."

"Why," replied Sheridan, taking each duke by the arm, "I believe I am between both."

4 Once a servant dropped a heap of plates with a tremendous crash. Sheridan rebuked the man, saying, "I suppose you've broken all of them."

"No, sir, not one," said the man.

"Then, you mean to say you have made all that noise for nothing!"

5 Sheridan's financial affairs were constantly in disorder, and debt was a chronic state with him. "Thank God, that's settled," he is reported to have said, handing over an IOU to a creditor.

6 A long-suffering creditor importuned Sheridan to name a date for payment. "The day of judgment," cried the harassed author. "But, no — stay — that will be a busy day. Make it the day after."

7 Sheridan had borrowed five hundred pounds from a friend, who took every opportunity to remind him of the debt. On one such occasion Sheridan added insult to injury by asking for a further twenty-five pounds to pay for a journey he had to make. On receiving the inevitable refusal Sheridan complained, "My dear fellow, be reasonable; the sum you ask me for is a very considerable one, whereas I only ask you for twenty-five pounds."

8 Sheridan's tailor grew tired of asking the writer to pay off his bill. "At least you could pay me the interest on it," he reasoned. "It is not my interest to pay the principal," replied Sheridan, "nor my principle to pay the interest."

9 Edmund Burke was delivering one of his stupendous orations in the House of Commons. At the climax he underlined his point by brandishing the dagger he had brought into the chamber with him and plunging it into the desk in front of him. In the stunned hush that followed this piece of histrionics the voice of Sheridan was heard saying, "The honorable gentleman has brought his knife with him, but where's his fork?"

10 One of the nine members of Parliament controlled by the Earl of Lonsdale under the pre-Reform Bill electoral system made a highly bombastic speech in the House of Commons. Edmund Burke replied with savage and devastating sarcasm. The cheers and applause at the end of his speech were still echoing around the House when Charles Fox entered and asked Sheridan what had been going on. "Nothing of consequence," replied Sheridan, "only Burke has knocked down one of Lord Lonsdale's ninepins."

11 Sheridan had been asked to apologize for insulting a fellow member of Parliament. "Mr. Speaker," replied Sheridan, "I said the honorable member was a liar it is true and I am sorry for it. The honorable member may place the punctuation where he pleases."

12 Richard Cumberland was a dramatist specializing in a brand of sentimental comedy that was rendered unfashionable by the comedy of Goldsmith and Sheridan. Nonetheless, he agreed to take his children to see Sheridan's *School for Scandal.* The children would have enjoyed themselves hugely, but every time they laughed, Cumberland hissed, "What are you laughing at, my dear little folks? You should not laugh, my angels. There is nothing to laugh

at." Finally, in exasperation, he snapped: "Keep still, you little dunces." When this story was retailed to Sheridan sometime later, he observed, "It was very ungrateful in Cumberland to have been displeased with his poor children for laughing at my comedy; for I went the other night to see his tragedy, and laughed at it from beginning to end."

{Cumberland strongly denied the truth of this story and eventually convinced Sheridan of its falsehood, but in the meantime Sheridan had exacted a neat revenge by satirizing Cumberland in his comedy The Critic (1779) under the character of Sir Fretful Plagiary.}

13 Like his father, Sheridan's son Tom was perpetually short of money. Father and son once had a disagreement. A few days later, Sheridan told Tom that he had made his will and cut him off with a shilling. "I'm sorry to hear that, sir," said Tom. Then, after a moment's thought, he added, "You don't happen to have the shilling about you now, do you?"

14 Sheridan's son Tom was talking somewhat sanctimoniously about a prospective parliamentary career. "Many men who are called great patriots in the House of Commons are really great humbugs," said he. "For my own part, when I get into Parliament, I will pledge myself to no party, but write upon my forehead in legible characters 'To Be Let.'"

"And under it, Tom," said Sheridan, "write 'Unfurnished.'"

15 On the night of February 24, 1809, the House of Commons was suddenly illuminated by a blaze of light. It was learned that the Drury Lane Theatre, of which Sheridan was the manager at that time, was on fire. A motion was made to adjourn the House, but Sheridan, who was in the chamber, said calmly, "Whatsoever might be the extent of the private calamity, I hope it will not interfere with the public business of the country." He then left the House and walked to Drury Lane, where he watched the blazing theater with apparent calm. While he was sitting in the nearby Piazza coffeehouse, a friend approached him and remarked on the philosophic calmness with which he bore his misfortune. Sheridan answered, "A man may surely be allowed to take a glass of wine by his own fireside."

16 Sheridan was sufficiently intimate with the future George IV to make gentle fun of his idiosyncrasies, such as his habit of taking the credit for anything good that happened in England. After an unusually fine summer one year, Sheridan remarked, "What His Royal Highness most particularly prides himself upon is the excellent harvest."

17 Sheridan showed little concern when warned that his heavy drinking would destroy the coat of his stomach. "Well, then," he replied, "my stomach must just digest in its waistcoat."

SHERMAN, William Tecumseh (1820–91), US general. His strategic planning, and in particular his march to the sea (1864) from Atlanta to Savannah, were crucial to the success of the Union forces in the American Civil War.

1 After the Mexican War, Sherman was sent by President Zachary Taylor to survey the newly acquired lands of New Mexico, Arizona, and California. On his return, Taylor asked Sherman: "Well, Captain, will our new possessions pay for the blood and treasure spent in the war?" Recalling the arid lands he had just explored, Sherman replied, "Between you and me, General, I feel that we'll have to go to war again." Taylor was aghast. "What for?" he asked. "To make 'em take the darn country back!" said Sherman.

2 During one of his many engagements in Georgia in 1864, Sherman was having difficulty breaking through the enemy front. He decided to send General Cox's division to attack the opposing left. Sherman positioned himself on a high hill to watch the operations and gave Cox his final orders for the circuitous march: "See here, Cox, burn a few barns occasionally as you go along. I can't understand those signal flags, but I know what smoke means."

3 Receiving a telegram from the Republican convention asking him to be the presidential candidate in 1884, Sherman wired back: "I will not accept if nominated, and will not serve if elected."

{This is better known in the pithier version: "If nominated, I will not accept. If elected, I will not serve."}

SHI HUANGDI (late 3d century BC), *first emperor of China. He was notorious for the severity of his rule, during which he executed hundreds of opponents and burned all books that conflicted with his autocratic policies. Toward the end of his life he lived in total seclusion, governing through officials from whom he demanded instant obedience.*

1 Shi Huangdi died while on a journey to seek the elixir of life. Two of his confidants, Zhao Gao and Li Si, feared that the crown prince, who objected to his father's harsh regime, would dismiss and perhaps even execute them if he became emperor. They therefore hatched a plan to place another of Shi Huangdi's sons on the throne. The first part of this plan involved concealing the old emperor's death from the world. Enclosing the body in his traveling carriage, they gave orders to return to the capital. The weather was warm and the corpse soon began to putrefy. Zhao Gao and Li Si therefore arranged for the imperial carriage to be closely followed by a cart laden with rotting fish. The stench of fish was so overpowering that not even the emperor's bodyguard detected the smell of the putrefying body, and the conspirators succeeded in reaching the capital without the emperor's death being discovered. There they used the emperor's seal to sign a decree commanding the crown prince to commit suicide, whereupon they established their own candidate on the throne of China.

      ৡ৽ ৽ৡ

SHOR, Toots (died 1977), *New York restaurant owner.*

1 A fervent Giants fan, Shor was chatting one evening in his place with Sir Alexander Fleming, the discoverer of penicillin. A waiter told Shor that the Giants' manager, Mel Ott, had just arrived.

"Excuse me," Shor said to Fleming, "but I gotta leave you. Somebody important just came in."

2 "Toots once argued his dear friend Leo Durocher into a delicate trap that looked like it would disrupt their palship. Toots, who considered himself a master baseball strategist, had informed Durocher that he had made a colossal blunder, and Durocher told Toots he was insane.

" 'You're a slimy, creepy, crummy crumbum and also a piece of raisin cake,' Toots snarled at Leo, who had thought up to that time that they were buddies. 'You're a baseball imbecile.'

" 'Why, you walrus,' screamed Durocher, 'when we beat Cleveland in the series you said I was a genius — thanks to your help.'

" 'You bald-headed slob!' roared Toots. 'Why, if I was to name the 10 best baseball managers —'

" 'Name them; go ahead and name them!' shouted Leo. He was furious in this moment of truth. 'Who's first?' he challenged Toots. 'Stengel?'

" 'Casey Stengel?' bawled Toots. 'Why, you baseball imbecile! The No. 1 baseball manager is Leo Durocher!' "

3 "In Shor's, all men were equal, which is to say everybody was a crumb-bum. The celebrated, accustomed to obsequious bowing and scraping, encountered a different reception in the brick house. There was the night Charles Chaplin was annoyed by an invitation to wait in line for a table.

" 'It'll be about a half-hour, Charlie,' Toots bawled. 'Be funny for the folks.' "

      ৡ৽ ৽ৡ

SHUTER, Edward (1728–76), *British comic actor.*

1 Chided for having holes in his stocking, Shuter replied that he would rather have twenty holes than one darn. "A hole is the accident of a day, while a darn is premeditated poverty."

{This saying is also attributed to others.}

      ৡ৽ ৽ৡ

SIBELIUS, Jean (1865–1957), *Finnish composer. In addition to his seven symphonies and his violin concerto he wrote several tone poems based on Finnish legends, including* En Saga, The Swan of Tuonela, Finlandia, *and* Tapiola. *He ceased to compose in 1929, although an eighth symphony is thought to have been written and subsequently destroyed by the composer.*

1 Sibelius was hosting a party at which many of those invited were businessmen. "Why businessmen?" asked one of his other guests. "What do you talk about with them?"

"About music, of course," replied the composer. "I can't talk about music with musicians. All they talk about is money."
See also GEORGE BERNARD SHAW 19.

❧ ❦

SICKERT, Walter Richard (1860–1942), *British Impressionist painter. Between 1895 and 1905 he produced two fine series of paintings of Venice and Dieppe. He is also known for his music-hall scenes and depiction of domestic life.*

1 Two young men who came to have tea with Sickert at his studio rather overstayed their welcome. As they were leaving, Sickert said, quite amicably, "And do come back, when you've a little less time to spare."

2 Sickert was on vacation in Dieppe with his friend, artist Walter Taylor. The two men went out to bathe one morning, Taylor remaining close to the shore as he was not a strong swimmer. Sickert swam out for about half a mile. Turning back, he saw that Taylor was in difficulties and watched, helpless, as his friend sank below the surface. He immediately struck out for the shore, where he was amazed to find Taylor calmly sunbathing. "Good God, man!" he cried. "I saw you sinking!"
   "Yes," replied Taylor in his slow, deliberate manner, "I . . . did . . . sink, but . . . when . . . I . . . reached . . . the . . . bottom, I . . . said . . . to . . . myself, 'If . . . I . . . walk . . . uphill . . . I . . . shall . . . get . . . to . . . the . . . shore.' And so . . . I . . . walked . . . uphill . . . and . . . here . . . I . . . am!"
   The astounded Sickert could only gasp, "Why does anybody ever drown!"

3 At a dinner party Sickert was in dazzling conversational form, much to the irritation of the novelist and portrait-painter Wyndham Lewis, who himself liked to dominate the conversation. Toward the end of the meal Sickert insisted upon Lewis's accepting a cigar: "I give you this cigar because I so greatly admire your writings." Lewis's morose expression lightened but only for a moment, as Sickert went on, "If I liked your paintings, I'd give you a bigger one."

❧ ❦

SIDDONS, Sarah (1755–1831), *British tragic actress, sister of John and Charles Kemble and*
aunt of Fanny Kemble. She excelled in Shakespearean roles.

1 The daughter of the theatrical manager Roger Kemble, Sarah was brought up in the stage environment. Her father nonetheless strictly forbade his beautiful and talented daughter to marry an actor. Despite this prohibition, she bestowed her affections on William Siddons, a lowly constituent of her father's company. The exasperated Roger Kemble lectured Sarah on her choice, concluding with the statement that not only was William Siddons a member of a dubious profession but also the worst one in the troupe. "Exactly," said Sarah sweetly. "No one can call him an actor."

2 When Sir Joshua Reynolds painted his famous portrait of Sarah Siddons as the Tragic Muse, he added his name by working it into the border of her robe. Mrs. Siddons examined the picture minutely and smiled. Reynolds said, "I could not lose this opportunity of sending my name to posterity on the hem of your garment."

3 (In 1783 Sarah Siddons paid a call on Dr. Johnson, then in his seventies.)
   "When Mrs. Siddons came into the room, there happened to be no chair ready for her, which he observing, said with a smile, 'Madam, you who so often occasion a want of seats to other people, will the more easily excuse the want of one yourself.'"

4 Sarah Siddons's high dramatic style tended to spill over into her everyday life. (As Sydney Smith observed of her at the dinner table, "It was never without awe that one saw her stab the potatoes.") In Bath to play some of her favorite tragic roles, she visited a draper's shop to buy some fabric. Picking up a piece of muslin, she looked with great intensity at the shopman and said with the utmost solemnity and dramatic effect, "Did you say, sir, that this would wash?" The draper suspected that he had a lunatic in his shop. Mrs. Siddons recollected herself at the sight of his surprise, apologized, and repeated the question in a more normal tone of voice.

5 During a tour of the north of England, Mrs. Siddons was playing the role of a tragic queen who commits suicide by taking poison. At one

performance, as she raised the cup of poison to her lips, the spellbound silence of the audience was shattered by a shout of encouragement from the gallery: "That's reet, Molly. Soop it oop, ma lass, soop it oop."

৯৯ ৩৯

SIDNEY, Sir Philip (1554–86), *English writer, soldier, and courtier, whose talents and charm made him the model of Elizabethan behavior. His posthumously published writings include the love sonnets entitled* Astrophel and Stella *(1591), the prose romance* Arcadia *(1590), and the critical treatise* An Apologie for Poetrie *(1598). He died fighting the Spaniards in the Netherlands.*

1 At Zutphen Sidney was wounded in the thigh. As he was being carried along to have the wound dressed, he suffered greatly from thirst, owing to loss of blood. A water bottle was found and brought to him. Putting it to his lips, he caught sight of another wounded man, a humble soldier, looking longingly at the water. Sidney at once passed the bottle to him with the words, "Thy need is yet greater than mine."
See also ALEXANDER THE GREAT 9 and CONFUCIUS 2.

৯৯ ৩৯

SIEYÈS, Emmanuel-Joseph, Abbé de (1748–1836), *French cleric and statesman. He had considerable influence over the course of the Revolution. He later held posts under Napoleon.*

1 After the Terror, a friend inquired of the abbé what he had done during those terrible years. "*J'ai vécu* [I survived]," he said.

৯৯ ৩৯

SIGISMUND (1368–1437), *Holy Roman Emperor (1414–37).*

1 The emperor was once asked his recipe for lasting happiness in this world. "Only do always in health what you have often promised to do when you are sick," he replied.

৯৯ ৩৯

SILLS, Beverly (1929–), *US operatic soprano. She joined the New York City Opera in 1955 and in 1979 was named its director.*

1 One of Miss Sills's elder brothers was a well-known obstetrician. Someone remarked

to her that he did not attend many of her performances. "Why should he?" she replied. "I don't attend his deliveries."

৯৯ ৩৯

SILVERMAN, Fred (1937–), *US broadcaster and former president of CBS.*

1 A few days before Yom Kippur Fred Silverman was asked by a friend if he would be going home for the holiday. Silverman asked on what day the event fell. "Wednesday," the friend informed him. "Wednesday?" cried Silverman. "You mean they've scheduled Yom Kippur opposite *Charlie's Angels?*"

৯৯ ৩৯

SILVERS, Phil (1912–), *US screen and television comedian, well known to television viewers as Sergeant Bilko.*

1 A friend of Phil Silvers who saw him as the Man Who Has Everything and could think of no gift special enough, found the perfect solution when Silvers arrived for a weekend visit, driving, appropriately, a Rolls-Royce Silver Cloud.
"You won't need that bus this weekend," said the host. "Let me take it in for a checkup." Silvers not objecting, his friend arranged for the surreptitious overnight installation of a built-in bar, a high-fidelity cassette player, a color television set, and a videocassette recorder. The Rolls was delivered just before Silvers was to leave Monday morning, and his friend remarked casually, "You'd better check before you start out, Phil, just to be sure everything is in shape."
"Oh, that doesn't matter," said Silvers. "It's a rented car."

৯৯ ৩৯

SIMENON, Georges (1903–), *Belgian novelist. He is best known as the creator of Inspector Maigret, the Parisian* commissaire de police, *but the Maigret detective stories are only a small part of his prolific output.*

1 As a young man Simenon was proud of his athletic abilities. Once after a late-night discussion in a Liège bar with a stranger, he challenged the man to a hundred-yard dash. The course was marked off between lampposts in the deserted street. The race was run. Much to

Simenon's chagrin, the stranger held him to a tie. It was only afterward that he found out that the man was an Olympic runner.

2 One of the reasons for Simenon's prolific output was the speed at which he was able to produce a novel. Director Alfred Hitchcock happened to telephone him from the United States while he was working on his 158th novel. Madame Simenon took the call. "I'm sorry," she said, "Georges is writing and I would rather not disturb him."

"Let him finish his book," replied Hitchcock. "I'll hang on."

3 Strolling down a Parisian boulevard with the playwright Marcel Pagnol one afternoon, Simenon suddenly exclaimed, "Goodness, she must be very pretty!" Looking ahead, Pagnol could see only a couple of young men walking in their direction. "Who? Where?" he asked. "She's behind us," replied Simenon. "Then how can you see her?" asked Pagnol. "I can't," said Simenon. "But I can see the look in the eyes of the approaching men."

ह॰ ॰६

SIMON, John Allsebrook, 1st Viscount (1873–1954), *British politician; lord chancellor (1940–45). He was a Liberal MP for many years (1906–18, 1922–40), and held a number of cabinet offices.*

1 Simon's talent for temporizing was not appreciated by other politicians. Lloyd George is said to have complained, "John Simon has sat on the fence so long that the iron has entered his — er — soul."

ह॰ ॰६

SIMON, Richard Leo (1889–1960), *US publisher. In 1924, with Max L. Schuster (1897–1971), he founded the publishing company Simon and Schuster.*

1 Launching a new children's book, *Dr. Dan the Bandage Man*, Simon decided to include a free gift of six Band-Aids with each copy. He cabled a friend at the manufacturers, Johnson and Johnson: "Please ship half million Band-Aids immediately." Back came the reply: "Band-Aids on the way. What the hell happened to you?"

ह॰ ॰६

SINATRA, Frank (1915–   ), *US singer and film actor. He appeared in a number of successful films, including* From Here to Eternity *(1953), for which he won an Oscar,* Guys and Dolls *(1955), and* The Manchurian Candidate *(1962).*

1 In the summer of 1943, at the open-air Stadium in New York City, the New York Philharmonic Orchestra, one of the world's greatest, gave its usual distinguished performance. The guest "artist" was Frank Sinatra, who came up with "Sunday, Monday, or Always" and similar gems. At the close of his performance, acknowledging the shrieks of his young admirers, Sinatra turned with a gracious gesture to the dazed musicians behind him and said, "On behalf of myself and the boys in the band — I want to say 'thanks!' "

2 Having suffered a series of fainting fits, Sinatra consulted his doctor. "How much money do you earn, Mr. Sinatra?" asked the doctor. "Somewhere between four hundred thousand and a million dollars a year," replied Sinatra carelessly. "In that case," advised the doctor, "I suggest you go right out and buy yourself some red meat. You're suffering from malnutrition."

3 Sinatra often traveled many miles out of his way to visit hospitalized friends and sing to them. It was said that the more serious the illness, the more punctilious he was in visiting. One friend, who was suffering from a minor complaint but was afraid that the doctors were not telling him the truth, awoke suddenly in his hospital room to find Sinatra at his bedside. The singer had been in the neighborhood and had just called in. The patient was appalled. "I knew it!" he yelled. "They've been lying to me!"

ह॰ ॰६

SINGER, Isaac Bashevis (1904–   ), *US writer, born into a Jewish family in Poland. His works, written in Yiddish, often deal with traditional Jewish life in Poland; they include* Gimpel the Fool *(1957),* The Slave *(1960), and collections of short stories. Singer was awarded the 1978 Nobel Prize for literature.*

1 An interviewer asked Singer whether he was a vegetarian for religious reasons or because of his health. "It is out of consideration for the chicken," he replied.

2   Singer was asked whether he believed in free will or predestination. "We have to believe in free will," he replied. "We've got no choice."

ξ❦ ❦ξ

SITWELL, Dame Edith (1887–1964), *British poet, daughter of Sir George Sitwell. She joined her brothers Osbert and Sacheverell as rebels against bourgeois philistinism. Her most famous work is* Façade *(1922), a series of poems recited to music composed by William Walton.*

1   Miss Sitwell broke the news to her parents that she was leaving the family home. "I can write so much better when I'm alone," she explained. "And you prefer poetry to human love?" asked her father. "As a profession," replied Edith, "yes."

2   (Osbert Sitwell tells about a guest at the Sitwells' home, Renishaw Hall:)
      "A man whom we had never seen before was wished on us for luncheon one day. He was placed next to my sister, and took it into his head to enquire of her: 'Do you remember this house being built, Miss Sitwell?' Mrs. [Alice] Keppel overheard this, and said to him quickly: 'My dear man, be careful! Not even the nicest girl in the world likes to be asked if she is four hundred years old.' "

3   Edith Sitwell was accustomed to ferocious attacks on her poetry. At one gathering at which she had been reading some of her poems aloud, a woman came up to her and announced, "I just wanted to tell you, Miss Sitwell, that I *quite* enjoyed your last book of poems." She paused and then seemed about to go on when Edith Sitwell interrupted her. "Now please don't say any more," she said. "You mustn't spoil me. It isn't good for me to be spoiled."

4   In 1954 Edith Sitwell was given the title Dame of the British Empire. On a visit to the United States an American came up to her and said rather aggressively, "Why do you call yourself 'Dame'?"
      "I don't," she replied. "The queen does."

ξ❦ ❦ξ

SITWELL, Sir George Reresby (1860–1943), *British antiquarian and eccentric. His foibles are recalled by his son Sir Osbert Sitwell in his autobiography and in his book of essays,* Tales My Father Taught Me *(1962).*

1   Having in a fit of unsociability banished all visitors from his home, Renishaw Hall, Sir George was soon overcome by boredom. He confided to Osbert that he felt like taking a holiday and described the sort of hotel that he thought would suit him: a secluded country house with fine grounds, good views, and a few congenial fellow guests to whom he could talk. Osbert immediately recalled a newspaper advertisement he had seen that morning for what was clearly an expensive private institution for the mentally deranged. He described the "hotel" in glowing and inventive terms. Sir George agreed that it sounded exactly what he was looking for. Sir George's secretary was told to book a room for the month of September, and the whole Sitwell family joined in extolling the virtues of the supposed hotel. The eagerly awaited confirmation of the booking arrived. Unfortunately, the asylum director had added a postscript: "Ought a strait-waistcoat to be sent for Sir George to wear during the journey, which will be made by van? Three strong and practised male nurses will, of course, be in attendance, and prepared to quell any disturbance on the way."

2   (Sir Osbert Sitwell recalls a narrowly averted contretemps at a tea party at which one of the guests was a certain Mrs. Brooke. Sir George had begun the conversation with a spirited attack on modern art and from there he moved on to modern poetry.)
      "He was just saying: 'Then there was that young man who died in the Dardanelles—I forget his name—they try to make out he was a genius, but no good, no good, I can assure you,' when with a startling suddenness I realized *why* Mrs. Brooke's face was so familiar—from photographs in the Press of Rupert Brooke: the resemblance was very marked; she must be his mother. I gave my father a good kick under the tea-table, but he did not even pause; only the as yet undreamt-of H-bomb could have stopped him. He went on: 'His poems were grossly over-praised in the Press.' . . . I could hardly believe my ears. Could it be true that this was really happening, or was it just a nightmare

instalment of an instant in hell? Before, however, his memory could supply the missing name, the crowning horror was skilfully averted. . . . 'Sir George,' our hostess bravely intervened, 'you are sitting next to Mrs. Brooke, the mother of that wonderful young poet, Rupert Brooke. I *must* tell you, because,' she proceeded, drawing on her imagination, 'before tea you were just saying to me — but we were interrupted — how much you admired his work,' and continued, 'how different it is from the work of that other young poet — I, too, forget his name for the moment — of whom you were speaking.'

"My father looked puzzled but said no more."

୫~ ୶ई

SKELTON, John (?1460–1529), *English poet at the court of Henry VIII. He is best remembered for his lament for the death of a pet bird,* Phylyp Sparowe.

1 Enjoying the position of a licensed jester at Henry VIII's court, Skelton could satirize the great and powerful with virtual impunity. At last, however, with *Why Come Ye Not to Courte?* he went too far in his attack on Cardinal Wolsey, and the cardinal threw him into prison. In the *Merie Tales,* which contain a number of (probably fictional) anecdotes about Skelton, he is shown as kneeling before Wolsey to ask for pardon. The cardinal ranted at him for some time. At last Skelton said, "I pray Your Grace to let me lie down and wallow, for I can kneel no longer."

୫~ ୶ई

SKELTON, Red [Richard] (1913–   ), *US comedian.*

1 In 1951 Red Skelton and a party of friends flew to Europe, where Skelton was to appear at the London Palladium. As they were flying over the Swiss Alps, three of the airplane's engines failed. The situation looked very grave and the passengers began to pray. Skelton went into one of his best comic routines to distract them from the emergency as the plane lost height, coming closer and closer to the ominous-looking mountains. At the last moment the pilot spied a large field among the precipitous slopes and made a perfect landing. Skelton broke the relieved silence by saying, "Now, ladies and gentlemen, you may return

to all the evil habits you gave up twenty minutes ago."

୫~ ୶ई

SKINNER, Cornelia Otis (1901–1979), *US actress and writer.*

1 Cornelia Otis Skinner was playing the title role in a revival of George Bernard Shaw's *Candida.* Shaw cabled her: "Excellent. Greatest." The actress cabled back: "Undeserving such praise." Shaw sent another cable: "I meant the play." Miss Skinner replied: "So did I."

୫~ ୶ई

SKINNER, Otis (1858–1942), *US stage actor, father of Cornelia Otis Skinner. He starred in many plays, including* Hamlet *(1896),* Kismet *(1911–14), and* Blood and Sand *(1921–22).*

1 At the rehearsal for his daughter's wedding, Skinner asked the minister what he was supposed to say in reply to the question: "Who giveth this woman . . ."

"You don't say a thing, Mr. Skinner," replied the minister. "You just hand your daughter over."

"Nonsense," said Skinner. "I've never played a walk-on part in my life."

୫~ ୶ई

SLEZAK, Leo (1873–1946), *Czechoslovak tenor. A tall and imposing figure, he won widespread acclaim for his heroic roles, particularly in Wagnerian opera.*

1 At the end of Wagner's opera *Lohengrin* a magic swan appears, drawing a boat to take the hero back to rejoin the fellowship of the Knights of the Holy Grail. On one occasion when Slezak was singing Lohengrin, the apparatus failed to function properly and sailed off back into the wings, leaving the tenor stranded on the stage. Amid consternation among performers and stage hands Slezak muttered, "When does the next swan leave?"

{This story is also told of Lauritz Melchior and Joseph Tichatschek, but Frederick Jagel, another tenor, vouches for Slezak.}

2 Slezak had just left his residence in Vienna for a performance in Zurich when his valet discovered that the singer had left behind an important part of his costume — a magnificent crown studded with artificial jewels. He wrapped it up in a sheet of newspaper and rushed off to the station, where he just had time to thrust the package into his employer's hands as the train moved away. During the long overnight journey, a customs officer boarded the train. "Anything to declare?" he asked as he passed through Slezak's compartment. "No, nothing," replied the singer, who had been trying to catch a few hours' sleep. The customs officer glanced around the compartment. "Open that!" he snapped, pointing at the hastily wrapped package. With ill-disguised irritation, Slezak tore off the newspaper and uncovered the crown. The customs officer gasped. Then, standing to attention, he exclaimed, "Oh! Incognito! Please excuse me, Your Majesty."

ಶಿ ಆ

SMITH, Adam (1723–90), *Scottish economist and philosopher. His fame rests on his* Inquiry into the Nature and Causes of the Wealth of Nations *(1776).*

1   Smith was known for his absentmindedness. One Sunday morning he wandered into his garden wearing only a nightgown and soon became engrossed in philosophical contemplation. Totally absorbed in his train of thought, he went out into the street and began walking in the direction of Dunfermline. He had covered the twelve miles to the town before the ringing of the church bells aroused him from his reverie. Regular churchgoers arriving for the morning service were astonished to find the eminent philosopher in their midst, still clad only in his nightgown.

ಶಿ ಆ

SMITH, Alfred Emanuel (1873–1944), *US politician. Elected governor of New York State four times (1918, 1922, 1924, 1926), he carried out many reforms.*

1   Smith was in Albany for a political convention, along with James Walker, Herbert Lehman, and many others. One morning, after a night of heavy drinking, Smith and Walker, both Catholic, felt that they ought to go to early mass as it was a Roman Catholic holy day. Tiptoeing through the hotel suite, they looked wistfully at Lehman and their other Jewish colleagues, who were still peacefully sleeping off the effects of the previous night's excesses.

Turning to Walker, Smith said, "Gee, I hope we're right!"

2   Irritated by the constant interruptions of a heckler, Smith once paused in the middle of a speech. "Go ahead, Al, don't let me bother you," shouted the heckler. "Tell 'em all you know. It won't take you long." Smith was quick to respond. "If I tell 'em all we both know," he cried, "it won't take me any longer."

3   During one of his terms as governor of New York, Smith was late for a broadcast he was due to make. He hailed a taxi to take him to the radio station, but the driver, who did not recognize the governor, refused to take him. He explained that he was in a hurry himself, anxious to be home in time to hear Governor Smith talk on the radio. Smith, flattered, held out a five-dollar bill and repeated his request. The driver's eyes lit up. "Hop in, mister," he said, "and to hell with the governor."

ಶಿ ಆ

SMITH, Bessie (1894–1937), *US black jazz singer, known as the "Empress of the Blues." At the height of her fame in the 1920s she made records with Louis Armstrong and Fletcher Henderson.*

1   In September 1937 Bessie Smith, traveling with her white business manager near Clarksdale, Mississippi, was seriously injured in an auto accident. The doctor who arrived on the scene directed that the manager, who was suffering from concussion, should be sent to the nearby hospital but that the singer should go to a "blacks only" hospital many miles away. She bled to death before she got there.

ಶಿ ಆ

SMITH, F[rederick] E[dwin], 1st Earl of Birkenhead (1872–1930), *British barrister and Conservative politician. He was attorney general from 1915 until 1919, when he became lord chancellor. In this capacity he was responsible for the prosecution of the Irish nationalist Sir Roger Casement. An extremely capable lawyer with a ready wit, Smith was the subject of Margot Asquith's quip: "Very clever, but his brains go to his head."*

1   A distinguished Oxford don had a particular way of snubbing clever young undergradu-

ates. He would invite the student to accompany him on a long walk, leaving it to his companion to start the conversation. After a lengthy silence the embarrassed student would usually make some banal remark, and would immediately be crushed by the don's reply.

The undergraduate F. E. Smith, aware of the don's tactics, set off for the walk with his own plan of action carefully worked out. The two men walked in complete silence for more than an hour, and for once it was the don's turn to feel embarrassed. "They tell me," he was finally compelled to utter, "they tell me you're clever, Smith. Are you?"

"Yes," replied Smith. .

No further word was exchanged until the men returned to the college. "Goodbye, sir," said Smith, "I've so much enjoyed our talk."

2   As a young man Smith represented a tramway company in a suit brought by a boy who had been blinded. The judge directed that the boy be lifted onto a chair so that the jury could see him properly. Thinking this made an undue emotional appeal to the jury's sympathy, Smith protested: "Your Honor, why not pass the boy around the jury box?" The judge rebuked him for his improper remark. "Prompted," Smith said, "by an equally improper suggestion." Preferring not to pursue that one, the judge tried to quash the young lawyer by quoting Francis Bacon at him: "Youth and discretion are ill-wedded companions." Smith was ready with a counter-quotation: "My lord, the same Bacon also said that a much-talking judge was like an ill-tuned cymbal." The judge frowned. "Now you are being offensive, Mr. Smith," he said. "We both are," agreed Smith. "The difference is that I am trying to be, and you can't help it."

3   Smith once cross-examined a young man claiming damages for an arm injury caused by the negligence of a bus driver. "Will you please show us how high you can lift your arm now?" asked Smith. The young man gingerly raised his arm to shoulder level, his face distorted with pain. "Thank you," said Smith. "And now, please will you show us how high you could lift it before the accident?" The young man eagerly shot his arm up above his head. He lost his case.

4   Smith was cross-examining a rather nervous witness. "Have you ever been married?" he asked.

"Yes, sir," replied the witness, "once."

"Whom did you marry?"

"A — er — a woman, sir."

"Of course, of course," snapped Smith impatiently. "Did you ever hear of anyone marrying a man?"

"Er — yes, sir," ventured the witness. "My sister did."

5   Smith was conducting a lengthy and complicated case before a judge whom he regarded as slow and pedantic. As the case drew to its close, the judge intimated that some of the issues involved were no longer clear to him, upon which Smith gave the judge a short but very cogent account of all the issues and their implications. As Smith sat down, the judge thanked him courteously, but added, "I'm sorry, Mr. Smith, but I regret that I am none the wiser." Smith rose wearily to his feet again. "Possibly, my lord, but you are better informed."

6   Winston Churchill's powers of oratory became a legend; his broadcasts to the nation and his speeches in the House of Commons during World War II are world-famous. Not all his friends, however, were complimentary. In the 1920s, for example, F. E. Smith complained, "Winston has devoted the best years of his life to preparing his impromptu speeches."

7   Smith annoyed the patrons of London's Athenaeum Club, of which he was not a member, by frequently making use of their toilet facilities on his way to the House of Lords. One day a porter drew his attention to the fact that the club was for members only. "Oh," said Smith, "is it a club as well?"

8   F. E. Smith was a guest at Wilton House. His host, Lord Pembroke, was showing him the family portraits. He explained that whenever one of his ancestors had had an illegitimate child their practice had been to give it the surname Montgomery. Smith turned this over in his mind and then said, "If such an untoward event should happen to me, God forbid that I should deny my child the name of Smith."

9   Smith teased Lord Chief Justice Gordon Hewart about the size of his stomach, asking him if he was expecting a boy or a girl. "If it's a boy, I'll call him John," replied Hewart, "and if

it's a girl I'll call her Mary. But if, as I suspect, it's only wind, I'll call it F. E. Smith."

{The US version has President Taft making this retort to Senator Chauncey Depew.}

❧

SMITH, Logan Pearsall (1865–1946), *British writer and critic.*

1 Logan Pearsall Smith was asked shortly before his death whether he had found any meaning in life. "Yes," he replied, "there is a meaning; at least for me, there is one thing that matters — to set a chime of words tinkling in the minds of a few fastidious people."

❧

SMITH, Sydney (1771–1845), *British clergyman and author. He lived as a young man in Edinburgh, where he became part of a brilliant circle of politicians and philosophers and helped found the* Edinburgh Review. *His quick wit made him a favorite of London society when he moved south.*

1 In Edinburgh Smith was out walking with a friend one day when they came across two women screaming insults at each other from second-story windows on opposite sides of a narrow street. "Those two will never resolve their differences," Smith remarked to his friend. "They are speaking from separate premises."

2 At a gathering Sydney Smith met the lawyer and philosopher Sir James Mackintosh with his young Scottish cousin, an ensign in one of the Scots regiments. The young man asked Sir James in an undertone whether this was "the great Sir Sidney Smith," hero of the defense of Acre against Napoleon in 1799. Before Sir James could put the young man right, Sydney Smith had embarked on an account of the siege of Acre, complete with description of guns and attacks and counterattacks. The young ensign was entranced by this display of friendliness on the part of the famous admiral, while the rest of the party scarcely knew how to keep a straight face.

A few days later Sir James and his cousin met Sydney Smith and his wife walking in the street. Smith introduced his wife and they talked for a few minutes. As the Smiths moved on, the young Scot said in a low voice, "I didna think the great Sir Sidney was married."

"Why, er, no," said Sir James, floundering for a moment before inspiration struck, "no, not exactly married — only an Egyptian slave he brought over with him. Fatima — you know — you understand."

The nickname "Fatima" stuck to Mrs. Smith for a long time thereafter among her friends.

3 When Francis Jeffrey was lord advocate, the polar explorer John Ross tried to persuade him to get the government to finance an expedition to the North Pole. A man who agreed to act as intermediary called on Jeffrey at an unlucky moment, when he was just about to go out riding and did not want to be detained. Jeffrey became more and more impatient and eventually burst out, "Damn the North Pole!" The aggrieved intermediary complained to Sydney Smith about Jeffrey's language. "Never mind," said Smith, "never mind his damning the North Pole. *I* have heard him speak disrespectfully of the equator."

4 Sydney Smith became embroiled in an argument with a country squire who was being abusive about the Church of England. The squire concluded by saying that if he had a son who was a fool he would make him a parson. "Very probably," retorted Smith, "but I see your father was of a different mind."

5 A lady was moaning about the oppressive heat. Smith courteously agreed with her: "Heat, madam! It was so dreadful that I found there was nothing for it but to take off my flesh and sit in my bones."

6 The lady seated next to him at dinner rejected an offer of gravy. "Madam," said Sydney Smith, "I have been looking for a person who disliked gravy all my life; let us swear eternal friendship."

7 Sydney Smith was disturbed one morning at his work by a self-important little man who announced that he was compiling a history of the distinguished families of Somerset and was calling to identify the Smith arms. Sydney Smith regretted he was unable to help: "The Smiths have never had any arms, and have invariably sealed their letters with their thumbs."

8 Sydney Smith called on the newly appointed bishop of New Zealand to bid him farewell before he set sail for his diocese. Bearing in mind the reputation of the native inhabitants as cannibals, Smith advised the bishop always to keep "a smoked little boy in the baconrack and a cold clergyman on the sideboard. As for yourself," he continued, "all I can say is that when your new parishioners do eat you, I sincerely hope that you will disagree with them."

9 Smith once complained of the prosiness of some sermons, saying, "They are written as if sin were to be taken out of man like Eve out of Adam — by putting him to sleep."

10 On receiving a basket of strawberries from one of his parishioners, Smith wrote in reply, "What is real piety? What is true attachment to the Church? How are these fine feelings best evinced? The answer is plain: by sending strawberries to a clergyman. Many thanks."

11 Someone remarked that philosopher and mathematician William Whewell's forte was science. "Yes," said Smith, "and his foible is omniscience."

12 A plan was mooted to lay a wooden pavement around St. Paul's cathedral in London. "Let the dean and chapter lay their heads together and the thing will be done," said Smith.

13 Sydney Smith never attained the eminence in the church that might have been expected, mainly because the Anglican establishment disapproved of his attitude toward Roman Catholic emancipation, evinced in the *Peter Plymley Letters* (1807–08). Comparing his own career with that of his brother, Robert Percy, Sydney Smith observed, "He rose by gravity; I sank by levity."

ॐ ॐ

SMUTS, Jan Christiaan (1870–1950), *South African philosopher and statesman; prime minister of the Union of South Africa (1919–24, 1939–48), which he was instrumental in forming in 1910.*

1 Writer and journalist Wynford Vaughan-Thomas once accompanied Smuts on a "morning stroll" up Table Mountain. The year was 1947; Smuts was seventy-six and Vaughan-Thomas some thirty-eight years younger. As the writer arrived at the summit, a full ten minutes after his companion, Smuts remarked with a smile: "Young man, at my age I haven't as much time as you for loitering."

ॐ ॐ

SMYTH, Dame Ethel (1858–1944), *British composer and author. Her struggle to become a musician in the face of her father's opposition made her an ardent feminist. She composed a number of large-scale choral works.*

1 (Leonard and Virginia Woolf invited Dame Ethel, then quite elderly, to dinner at their house at Rodmell in Sussex.)
"Dame Ethel bicycled the twenty miles from the village where she lived to Rodmell, dressed in rough tweeds. About two miles from her destination she decided that perhaps she was not suitably dressed for a dinner party. She thought that possibly corsets were required to smarten up her figure. Accordingly, she went into a village shop and asked for some corsets. There were none. Distressed, she looked round the shop and her eye lighted on a bird cage, which she purchased. About twenty minutes later, Virginia went into her garden to discover Dame Ethel in a state of undress in the shrubbery struggling with the bird cage, which she was wrenching into the shape of corsets and forcing under her tweeds."

ॐ ॐ

SNEAD, Sam (1912–   ), *US golfer. He won three Masters tournaments and three Professional Golfers' Association championships, and was still playing competitively when in his sixties.*

1 Passing through Rome in 1961, Snead stopped for an audience with Pope John. The golfer had not been playing well for some time, and he confessed to one of the papal officials: "I brought along my putter, on the chance that the pope might bless it." The monsignor nodded sympathetically. "I know, Mr. Snead," he said. "My putting is absolutely hopeless too." Snead looked at him in amazement. "If you *live* here and can't putt," he exclaimed, "what chance is there for me?"

ॐ ॐ

SOBHUZA II (1899–1982), *king of Swaziland (1921–82).*

1 King Sobhuza called a meeting of his ministers and advisers to discuss recent missions to other African states. Suddenly, for no apparent reason, he asked all his officials, with the exception of Dr. Samuel Hynd, the minister of health, to leave. Turning to the doctor, Sobhuza said, "I am going." Hynd, a little surprised, asked the obvious question, "Where are you going?" By way of reply, the king simply smiled, raised his hand in a farewell gesture, and died.

ह• •ह

SOCRATES (c. 469–399 BC), *Greek philosopher. Although he wrote nothing himself, his ideas survive in the writings of Plato and Xenophon. Socrates broke with earlier philosophical traditions and laid the foundations for the development of both ethics and logic. Refusing to bow to tyranny, whether exercised by the mob or by oligarchs, Socrates was tried on the charge of corrupting the young people of Athens and sentenced to death by drinking hemlock.*

1 Knowing the frugality of Socrates' way of life, a friend was surprised to discover the philosopher studying with rapt attention some flashy wares on display in the marketplace. He inquired why Socrates came to the market, since he never bought anything. "I am always amazed to see just how many things there are that I don't need," replied Socrates.

2 Socrates' wife, Xantippe, visited him in prison and bewailed the jury's condemnation. "They are by their nature also condemned," Socrates said. "But the condemnation is unjust!" persisted Xantippe. "Would you prefer it to be just?" asked Socrates.

ह• •ह

SOLOMON (c. 973–c.933 BC), *king of Israel. He is renowned for having built the first temple at Jerusalem and for his great wisdom, which became proverbial.*

1 Two prostitutes living alone in the same house had babies within three days of each other. One baby died, and its mother stole the other while the mother slept, substituting the corpse of her own baby. Although the other woman noticed the deception, the first woman refused to relinquish the baby. So they came before King Solomon, each claiming that the living child was hers. The king commanded his officers to bring a sword and when it was brought ordered that the baby be cut in two; one half would then be given to one woman and the other half to the other. The rightful mother, stirred with love and pity for her child, said, "O my lord, give her the living child, and in no wise slay it." But the other woman said, "Let it be neither mine or thine, but divide it." The king, perceiving that the compassion of the first woman had identified her as the true mother, ordered that the baby should be given to her.

{Among the most famous judgments in Western history.}

ह• •ह

SOLON (c. 639–c. 559 BC), *Greek legislator and statesman. Coming to power in Athens in 594 BC, he remodeled the constitution, introduced new laws, reformed weights and measures and the coinage, encouraged industry, and prohibited loans on the security of the borrower's person.*

1 Solon's sweeping changes naturally came in for a good deal of criticism. Solon himself acknowledged that there were imperfections in his legal code. Challenged to say whether he had given the Athenians the best laws, he replied mildly, "No, but the best that they could receive."

2 Asked what measures could be taken to eliminate law-breaking and crime within a state, Solon replied, "Wrongdoing can only be avoided if those who are not wronged feel the same indignation at it as those who are."

ह• •ह

SOMERSET, Charles Seymour, 6th Duke of (1662–1748), *British courtier, known as "the Proud Duke."*

1 The duke's first wife was Elizabeth, heiress to the great name and fortune of the Percys, dukes of Northumberland. When she died in 1722, he married again; his second wife was Charlotte Finch, third daughter of the Earl of Nottingham. Charlotte once made the mistake of tapping playfully on her husband's arm with

her fan to attract his attention. He turned on her and said icily, "Madam, my first wife was a Percy, and *she* never took such a liberty."

❧

SOPHOCLES (496–406 BC), *Greek dramatist. He wrote about 120 plays, which won him fame and popularity among his contemporaries; only seven tragedies survive, among them* Oedipus Rex *and* Antigone.

1 At the age of eighty-nine Sophocles was brought before a court of law by his son, who, suspecting that the playwright intended to cut him out of his will, wished to have him certified as suffering from senility. Sophocles said simply, "If I am Sophocles, I am not out of my mind; if I am out of my mind, I am not Sophocles." He then proceeded to read to the court passages from the *Oedipus at Colonus,* which he had lately written but not yet staged. The judges dismissed the case.

❧

SOUTHEY, Robert (1774–1843), *British poet and prose writer; poet laureate (1813–43). His prose works include a* Life of Nelson *(1813), many letters, essays, and criticism.*

1 Southey enjoyed making a parade of the regularity of his life and the industriousness of his habits. Intending to impress a certain Quaker lady, he told her the full routine of his day; rising at 5:00 A.M., reading Spanish from 6:00 to 8:00, reading French from 8:00 to 9:00, writing poetry for two hours, writing prose ditto, and so on through to bedtime. The lady heard his recital out and then asked, "And pray, Friend, when dost thou think?"

❧

SPAAK, Paul Henri (1899–1972), *Belgian statesman; socialist prime minister (1938–39, 1947–50) and four times foreign minister (1936–38, 1939–46, 1954–57, 1961–65). He was president of the first General Assembly of the United Nations (1946) and from 1957 to 1961 was secretary general of NATO.*

1 Presiding over the first General Assembly meeting, Spaak closed it with these words: "Our agenda is now exhausted. The secretary general is exhausted. All of you are exhausted. I find it comforting that, beginning with our very first day, we find ourselves in such complete unanimity."

❧

SPEAIGHT, Robert William (1904–1976), *English actor and author. He played most of the major Shakespearean roles at the Old Vic, London, in the 1930s. He also wrote a number of biographies.*

1 Speaight once suffered a most embarrassing moment while playing the title role in a production of *Hamlet* at the Old Vic. A rather violent lunge in the fight scene caused him to rip his tights and inadvertently expose himself to the audience. Knowing Speaight to be an extremely sensitive man, the rest of the company tactfully "forgot" the incident. Later that season Speaight gave a magnificent performance as King John. Standing beside him in the gentlemen's lavatory one evening, a fellow actor struggled to think of something to say to the great man. "By the way, Bobby," he finally ventured, "may I say how much I admired your John?"

❧

SPELLMAN, Francis Joseph (1889–1967), *US Roman Catholic cardinal, nicknamed "the American pope."*

1 As a boy of eight Frank Spellman used to help out in his father's grocery store. One piece of advice that Spellman Sr. gave his son stuck in the future cardinal's mind: "Always associate with people smarter than yourself, and you'll have no difficulty finding them."

2 Receiving a generous donation for charity from the Roman Catholic organization the Knights of Columbus, Cardinal Spellman presented the newly appointed Grand Knight with a medallion of Pope John XXIII. The Grand Knight, overcome by nerves, dropped the medallion and hastily bent down to retrieve it. As he did so, he heard the cardinal murmur, "Heads!"

3 In conversation with a local businessman in a busy New York post office, Cardinal Spellman happened to remark that he was feeling rather tired. "Tell me, Your Eminence," asked the businessman, "with all the work you do, do you ever get so tired that you forget to say your prayers at night?"

"No," replied Spellman with a smile. "When I'm so tired I can't keep my eyes open, I simply say: 'Dear God, you *know* I've been working in your vineyard all day. If you don't mind, could we skip the details till morning?'"

ক্ষ৺ ৽৵

SPENCER, Herbert (1820–1903), *British philosopher and economist. He was a warm supporter of Darwinism and coined the phrase "the survival of the fittest" in his* Principles of Biology *(1864, 1867). He applied Darwinism to social and economic life in his numerous publications.*

1 Spencer was playing billiards with a subaltern who was a highly proficient player. In a game of fifty up Spencer gave a miss in balk and his opponent made a run of fifty and out in his first inning. The frustrated philosopher remarked, "A certain dexterity in games of skill argues a well-balanced mind, but such dexterity as you have shown is evidence, I fear, of a misspent youth."

{This anecdote is also ascribed to Robert Louis Stevenson.}

ক্ষ৺ ৽৵

SPENSER, Edmund (?1552–99), *English poet. After studying at Cambridge, Spenser met Philip Sidney, with whom he formed a literary club, the Areopagus. Encouraged by this literary atmosphere, he published his first major work,* The Shepheardes Calender *(1579), and began his epic-romance* The Faerie Queene *(1589, 1596). He was granted a post in Ireland (1580) and spent much of the rest of his life there. In 1598 his residence, Kilcolman castle, was destroyed in a rebellion, and the poet returned destitute to England, where he died soon afterward.*

1 Spenser presented some of his poetry to Queen Elizabeth, who received it graciously and instructed the lord treasurer, Lord Burghley, to pay the poet a hundred pounds. Burghley, a prudent keeper of the royal purse-strings, protested that it was far too generous a recompense. "Then give him what is reason," said the queen. Burghley, however, conveniently forgot to make the payment, and Spenser waited patiently for some months. Eventually he decided

that he would have to petition the queen himself, so he found an opportunity to present to her the following rhyme: "I was promised on a time/ To have reason for my rhyme;/ From that time unto this season,/ I received nor rhyme nor reason." Elizabeth scolded Lord Burghley and ordered immediate payment.

2 When Spenser first showed portions of *The Faerie Queene* to the Earl of Southampton, that great connoisseur of literature was enchanted by what he read. "Go bear Master Spenser a gift of twenty pounds," he commanded his attendants. He read on, and again the charms of the poetry encouraged him to further generosity: "Go bear Master Spenser another twenty pounds." Still he went on reading, and then cried out a third time, "Go turn that fellow out of my house, for I shall be ruined if I read further."

ক্ষ৺ ৽৵

SPILLANE, Mickey [Frank Morrison] (1918–), *US writer of detective stories featuring the character Mike Hammer.*

1 Authors become impatient with eager students of their work who find symbolism where none was intended. When the subject came up at a meeting of the Mystery Writers of America, Spillane dismissed any profound conclusions that might have been drawn from the drinking habits of his most famous character. "Mike Hammer drinks beer, not cognac, because I can't spell cognac," he declared.

ক্ষ৺ ৽৵

SPOONER, William Archibald (1844–1930), *British scholar, Warden of New College, Oxford (1903–24). He gave his name to the verbal trick, accidental or otherwise, known as a spoonerism — the transposition of the initial letters of words, especially to give a comic effect; for instance, "a half-warmed fish" for "a half-formed wish."*

1 Announcing the next hymn in a service in New College chapel, Warden Spooner said, "Kinquering congs their titles take."

{This seems to be one of the best-attested spoonerisms, but there are of course scores of likely but probably apocryphal examples: calling Victoria "our queer old dean" in a service for her Jubilee; scolding an undergraduate for "hissing his mystery lectures" and telling him to leave Oxford by "the next town drain"; etc.}

2 Meeting a stranger in the New College quadrangle, Warden Spooner could recall only that the man was a recent addition to the college Fellows. "Come to tea tomorrow," he said hospitably, "I'm giving a little party for the new mathematics Fellow."

"But, Warden," said the stranger. "*I* am the new mathematics Fellow."

"Never mind. Come all the same."

3 When Christian Socialism was first becoming a significant movement, someone asked Spooner whether there were many Christian Socialists at New College. After pondering the question, Spooner said that he thought there were just two: Dr. Rashdall (a clerical Fellow of New College) and himself. "But," Spooner continued, "I'm not very much of a socialist and Dr. Rashdall isn't very much of a Christian."

4 "Mr. Spooner was one evening found wandering disconsolately about the streets of Greenwich. 'I've been here hours,' he said. 'I had an important appointment to meet someone at "The Dull Man, Greenwich," and I can't find it anywhere; and the odd thing is no one seems to have heard of it.' Late at night he went back to Oxford. 'You idiot!' exclaimed his wife; 'why, it was the Green Man, Dulwich, you had to go to.'"

5 (Sprinkling salt over wine spilled on a linen tablecloth is said to prevent a stain.)

At dinner one day, Dr. Spooner accidentally upset the salt-cellar on the clean white linen tablecloth. Without a moment's hesitation, he reached for his wine glass and poured a few drops of claret over the spilled salt.

{Authenticity not guaranteed.}

ॐ ✦

SPURGEON, Charles Haddon (1834–92), *British Baptist minister. While still in his early twenties, Spurgeon became famous as a preacher and continued for many years to command a vast audience for his oratory and writings, which had a pronounced Calvinist character.*

1 When Spurgeon was involved in one of the many controversies that marked his career, a friend remarked jocularly, "I hear you are in hot water again."

"I'm not the one in hot water," retorted Spurgeon. "The other fellows are. I'm the man who makes the water boil."

2 "Oh, Mr. Spurgeon, that was wonderful!" cried an admirer after one of Spurgeon's sermons.

"Yes, madam — so the devil whispered into my ear as I came down the steps of the pulpit."

ॐ ✦

SQUIRE, Sir John Collings (1884–1958), *British poet, anthologist, and critic. A leader among the Georgian poets (1918–25), he edited the* London Mercury *for many years and wrote popular parodies and essays.*

1 Squire wrote an article for the London *New Statesman* about Shakespeare's *A Midsummer Night's Dream.* When the proofs were sent to him, he observed that the name "Hermia" appeared as "Hernia." He let it stand, adding an asterisk and an author's note: "I cannot bring myself to interfere with my printer's first fine careless rupture."

ॐ ✦

STAËL, Anne Louise Germaine, Baronne de (1766–1817), *French writer. The daughter of the French financier and statesman Jacques Necker, Madame de Staël was deeply involved in French political life from the Revolution to the overthrow of Napoleon. Among her many lovers she numbered Talleyrand. Once a great admirer of Napoleon, she became implacably opposed to him. He exiled her and suppressed her books.*

1 In 1797 Napoleon still seemed to Mme de Staël the epitome of the hero who would bring peace and sanity back to France. She pursued and flattered him, but he eluded her attentions whenever possible. On one occasion she called at his house, demanding to be admitted at once to Napoleon's presence. The butler explained that that was impossible since the general was in his bathtub. "No matter!" Mme de Staël cried. "Genius has no sex!"

2 In 1803 Mme de Staël published her feminist novel *Delphine,* in which she herself appears, flimsily concealed, as the heroine. The opinions and character of Talleyrand are embodied in the fictional figure of the book's villainess, Mme de Vernon. When Talleyrand next saw Mme de Staël, he greeted her with the words: "They tell me we are both of us in your novel, in the disguise of women."

3 Mme de Staël's officiousness could be a trial even to her friends. Talleyrand remarked that she was such a good friend that she would throw all her acquaintances into the water for the pleasure of fishing them out again.

4 Mme de Staël told the story of how she and the beautiful Mme Récamier were seated at dinner on either side of a young fop, who announced, "Here I am between wit and beauty."

"Quite so," said Mme de Staël, "and without possessing either."

5 Told by Napoleon that it was not fitting for a woman to take an interest in politics, Madame de Staël retorted, "In a country where women have been decapitated, it is only natural for other women to ask 'Why?'"

৯৯ ৎৎ

STAFFORD, Jean (1915–79), *US writer; Pulitzer Prize winner in 1970 for her* Collected Stories.

1 An old cowhand in Colorado, learning that Jean Stafford was a writer, observed, "That's real nice work, Jean. It's something you can do in the shade."

৯৯ ৎৎ

STALIN, Joseph [Iosif Dzhugashvili] (1879–1953), *Russian leader. He became general secretary of the Communist party (1922). On Lenin's death Stalin ruthlessly eliminated all his rivals and emerged as unchallenged dictator at the end of the 1920s. His five-year plans for collectivization in industry and agriculture led to a reign of terror in which millions died. He led the Soviet Union throughout World War II and at the peace conferences afterward established Soviet hegemony in Eastern Europe, while attacking with increasing bitterness his erstwhile allies in the noncommunist world.*

1 Lady Astor was one of a group of eminent English visitors to Russia in 1931. Never one to mince her words, she asked Stalin, "How long are you going to go on killing people?"

"As long as it's necessary," replied Stalin.

2 During the 1945 conference at Yalta in the Soviet Union, Winston Churchill and the British delegation were housed in the Alubka palace. On the grounds was a marble statue of a dozing lion, its head resting on its front paws, to which Churchill took a great liking. As he explained to Stalin, "It's so like me." He added that he understood there was a Russian tradition of presenting the best things in the country to important visitors. "Yes, indeed," responded Stalin. "The best thing we have in Russia now is socialism." The lion stayed where it was.

৯৯ ৎৎ

STANLEY, Sir Henry Morton (1841–1904), *British explorer and journalist. He was sent by the* New York Herald *to look for the explorer David Livingstone, who was missing on a journey in central Africa. After meeting at Ujiji, they explored Lake Tanganyika together.*

1 (Stanley, encouraged by rumors of a white man on the shores of Lake Tanganyika, reached Ujiji on November 10, 1871.)

"As I advanced slowly towards him, I noticed he was pale, looked wearied, had a gray beard, wore a bluish cap with a faded gold band round it, had on a red-sleeved waistcoat and a pair of gray tweed trousers. I would have run to him, only I was a coward in the presence of the mob — would have embraced him, only, he being an Englishman, I did not know how he would receive me. So I did what cowardice and false pride suggested was the best thing — walked deliberately up to him, took off my hat and said, 'Dr. Livingstone, I presume?' 'Yes,' said he with a kind smile, lifting his cap slightly. I replace my hat on my head, and he puts on his cap, and we both grasp hands, and I then say aloud — 'I thank God, Doctor, I have been permitted to see you.' He answered, 'I feel thankful that I am here to welcome you.'"

৯৯ ৎৎ

STANTON, Charles E. (1859–1933), *US colonel.*

1 On the Fourth of July 1917 the American Expeditionary Forces, newly arrived in Europe to fight in World War I, sent a contingent to visit the grave of Lafayette in Paris. General Pershing asked Colonel Stanton to make a speech on behalf of the A.E.F. Stanton made the memorably simple announcement: "Lafayette, we are here!"

{The words have also been attributed to Pershing himself, who claimed never to have said "anything so splendid."}

❧ ❧

STANTON, Elizabeth Cady (1815–1902), *US reformer and campaigner for women's rights.*

1   At a women's rights convention in Rochester, a married clergyman rebuked Mrs. Stanton for speaking in public. "The apostle Paul enjoined silence upon women," he said. "Why don't you mind him?" "The apostle Paul also enjoined celibacy upon the clergy," retorted Mrs. Stanton. "Why don't *you* mind him?"

{For Susan B. Anthony's similar retort to a sexist abolitionist, *see* ANTHONY 1.}

❧ ❧

STARK, John (1728–1822), *US general. He served in the French and Indian War and in the American Revolution, securing a notable victory at Bennington in 1777. He became a major general in 1783.*

1   On August 16, 1777, Stark's men faced two detachments of Burgoyne's troops at Bennington, Vermont. Before the battle Stark made an impassioned appeal to his men's pride and courage. "Yonder are the Hessians. They were bought for seven pounds and tenpence a man. Are you worth more? Prove it. Tonight the American flag floats from yonder hill or Molly Stark sleeps a widow!"

❧ ❧

STEELE, Sir Richard (1672–1729), *British dramatist and essay-writer. He is best remembered for his collaboration with Joseph Addison on* The Tatler *(1709–11) and* The Spectator *(1711–12). He also wrote a number of sentimental comedies.*

1   Steele was frequently in debt. A group of friends invited to dine at his house one day were therefore astonished to see the number of servants who attended them at dinner. After dinner a guest inquired how it was that Steele could afford such a lavish establishment. Steele explained that the attendants were in fact bailiffs, who were in the house on their official business. As he could not get rid of them, he had made the best of the situation by dressing them up in servants' liveries, and stationing them around his dining room. His guests were so amused that they pooled their money to pay Steele's debts and rid him of the bailiffs.

❧ ❧

STEFFENS, Lincoln (1866–1936), *US journalist, author of the famous* Autobiography *(1931).*

1   When Steffens visited Russia in 1919, he was able to observe the Bolshevik revolution at first hand. On his return he made the famous statement: "I have seen the future, and it works."

{According to William Bullitt, Steffens's traveling companion, Steffens made up the remark before he even got to Russia, and it existed in various forms until he finally polished it to this well-known sentence. Perhaps the wisest comment ever made on Steffens's famous judgment was that of journalist Max Nomad: "Well, so does the atom bomb."}

❧ ❧

STEIN, Gertrude (1874–1946), *US writer of experimental prose. After 1903 she lived mainly in Paris with her companion Alice B. Toklas. Her works include* Three Lives *(1908),* Tender Buttons *(1914), and* The Autobiography of Alice B. Toklas *(1933).*

1   In 1929 Gertrude Stein was invited to lecture at Oxford. She delivered a well-argued address in her customary style. Her lucidity and platform presence confounded those who had mainly come to jeer, although there was some laughter when she said in the course of her lecture, "Everything is the same and everything is different." At the end two hecklers jumped to their feet in different parts of the lecture hall and fired the same question at her: "Miss Stein, if everything is the same, how can everything be different?" Miss Stein replied, "Consider, the two of you, you jump up one after the other,

that is the same thing and surely you admit that the two of you are always different."

2 (Ernest Hemingway describes the probable origin of a famous phrase.)

"She had some ignition trouble with the old Model T Ford she then drove and the young man who worked in the garage and had served in the last year of the war had not been adept, or perhaps had not broken the priority of other vehicles, in repairing Miss Stein's Ford. Anyway, he had not been *sérieux* and had been corrected severely by the *patron* of the garage after Miss Stein's protest. The *patron* had said to him, 'You are all a *génération perdue.*'

"'That's what you are. That's what you all are,' Miss Stein said. 'All of you young people who served in the war. You are a lost generation.'"

3 A friend asked Gertrude Stein what it was that writers most wanted. "Praise, praise, praise," she replied, laughing.

4 Gertrude Stein had a good opinion of herself, which gave rise to a number of pronouncements recorded by her contemporaries. She told the sculptor Jacques Lipchitz that he knew very little about English literature. "Besides Shakespeare and me, who do you think there is?" she said.

5 One of the few people who refused to be overawed by Miss Stein's astounding flow of rhetoric was Mortimer Adler, the philosopher, educator, and author of *How to Read a Book*. He and Gertrude got into a violent argument one evening. Alice B. Toklas, trembling on the outskirts of the battlefield, was heard to remark, "Dear me! Gertrude is saying some things tonight that she won't understand herself for six months."

6 When Gertrude Stein was dying of cancer, she turned to Alice B. Toklas and murmured, "What is the answer?" Miss Toklas made no reply. Miss Stein nodded and went on, "In that case, what is the question?"

7 The American composer and writer Ned Rorem made his first visit to Alice B. Toklas's home after Gertrude Stein's death. He noticed on the wall two remarkable Picassos with which he was not familiar. He expressed his admiration. Miss Toklas said thoughtfully, "Yes, Gertrude always used to say: if the house were on fire and I could only take one picture, it would be those two."

{Mr. Rorem remarks that the wise Gertrude knew there is no such thing as first best.}

ॐ ◄§

STEINBECK, John (1902–68), *US novelist. His most famous novels are* The Grapes of Wrath *(1939) and* East of Eden *(1952), both of which were successfully filmed. In 1962 he won the Nobel Prize for literature.*

1 Steinbeck in his earlier days genuinely disliked personal publicity. After years of penury and unrewarded labor, he finally achieved success with *Tortilla Flat* and so could not entirely escape interviewers. He was enraged when the journalist Ella Winter, in a profile of him, did not abide by his request that he be judged by his work, not his personality. "What did I say that was so personal?" asked Miss Winter. "You mentioned that I had blue eyes," he replied.

2 Five thousand copies of Steinbeck's novel *The Wayward Bus* were destroyed by fire when the truck carrying them from the bindery was involved in a collision. The cause of the accident was a wayward bus, traveling on the wrong side of the road.

3 In 1965 Steinbeck passed through San Francisco on an automobile journey with his poodle, Charlie. He sat at a sidewalk café with advertising executive Howard Gossage and remarked, "Yesterday in Muir Woods Charlie lifted his leg on a tree that was fifty feet across, a hundred feet high, and a thousand years old. What's left in life for that dog after that supreme moment?" Gossage reflected a moment and then said, with his slight stammer, "W-w-well, he could always t-t-teach."

4 During a conversation about women, a conceited young man remarked derisively: "Women? They're a dime a dozen."

"Sure, women are a dime a dozen," agreed Steinbeck. "It's when you cut the number down to one that it gets expensive."

5 During his later years, when he was famous, his wife, Elaine, brought home a paperback book entitled *John Steinbeck,* by Frank William Watt. Steinbeck, who often felt he had been misinterpreted by many of the commentators on his life and work, read it with great interest. Finished, he remarked, "This book doesn't seem to be about me, but it's pretty interesting about somebody."

જ્જ ઢ§

STEINBERG, William (1899–1978), *US conductor, born in Germany; music director of the Boston and Pittsburgh symphony orchestras, among others.*

1 With time William Steinberg became totally bald. Relating an episode in his musical career, he once told his audience, "And there I was tearing my hair." Then he paused, gripped his bare skull, and added, "*What* am I saying?"

જ્જ ઢ§

STEINMETZ, Charles Proteus (1865–1923), *US electrical engineer, born in Germany. He made important contributions to the theory of electricity, especially on alternating-current systems, and also invented some 200 devices.*

1 When "the Electrical Wizard" was working at General Electric, he was annoyed to find in his office a sign reading "NO SMOKING." Steinmetz left a note reading "NO SMOKING — NO STEINMETZ." After that it was decided that the rule should not be applied to him.

2 After retiring, Steinmetz was recalled by General Electric to try to locate a breakdown in a complex system of machines. The cause of the breakdown baffled all GE's experts. Steinmetz spent some time walking around and testing the various parts of the machine complex. Finally, he took out of his pocket a piece of chalk and marked an X on a particular part of one machine. The GE people disassembled the machine, discovering to their amazement that the defect lay precisely where Steinmetz's chalk mark was located.

Some days later GE received a bill from Steinmetz for $10,000. They protested the amount and asked him to itemize it. He sent back an itemized bill:

Making one chalk mark . . . . $ 1
Knowing where to place it $9,999

જ્જ ઢ§

STENGEL, Casey (1890–1975), *US baseball celebrity; astute and witty manager of the champion New York Yankees for thirteen years (1949–62) and the New York Mets from 1962 until 1965.*

1 "Stengel was coaching at third one afternoon in a ding-dong contest at the Polo Grounds when a Dodger batter named Cuccinello hammered a hit to the bull pen in right field. [Mel] Ott fielded the ball brilliantly, and threw to third base. 'Slide! Slide!' screamed Stengel, but Cuccinello came in standing up, and was tagged out. 'I told you to slide,' roared Stengel. 'You'd have been safe a mile! Why didn't you do what I told you?' 'Slide?' repeated Cuccinello with some dignity, 'and bust my cigars?'"

2 Asked about the art of managing, Stengel replied, "Managing is getting paid for home runs someone else hits."

3 "Casey Stengel's eye for talent was often as keen as his wit. Early in his managerial career with the New York Mets, he was asked about the future prospects for two of his twenty-year-old players. 'In ten years, Ed Kranepool has a chance to be a star,' said Casey. 'In ten years the other guy has a chance to be thirty.'"

4 At a baseball game one day Stengel was exasperated by demands from the crowd for a player he had on the bench. He finally called for the player in question. "Am I going in?" asked the player eagerly. "No," replied Stengel, "I don't want you. Go up in the stands with your fans. *They* want you."

5 Explaining a point of strategy to young baseball star Mickey Mantle, seventy-year-old Stengel described an incident from his own days as a player. "You played?" asked Mantle, astonished. "Sure I played," said Stengel. "Did you think I was born at the age of seventy sitting in a dugout trying to manage guys like you?"

6 In his old age, Stengel was asked how he was doing. He sighed and said, "Not bad. Most people my age are dead. You could look it up."

જ્જ ઢ§

STERNE, Laurence (1713–68), *British writer and clergyman. His comic novel* Tristram

Shandy, *of which the first two volumes were published in 1759, won the obscure Yorkshire parson a* succès de scandale.

1 "Soon after *Tristram* appeared, Sterne asked a Yorkshire lady of fortune and condition whether she had read his book. 'I have not, Mr. Sterne,' was the answer; 'and to be plain with you, I am informed it is not proper for female perusal.' 'My dear good lady,' replied the author, 'do not be gulled by such stories; the book is like your young heir there' (pointing to a child of three years old, who was rolling on the carpet in his white tunic) 'he shows at times a good deal that is usually concealed, but it is all in perfect innocence!'"

ᵂ ᵂ

STEVENS, Thaddeus (1792–1868), *US politician and lawyer, congressman from Pennsylvania (1849–53, 1859–68).*

1 At the beginning of the 1861 congressional session, a woman admirer broke into Stevens's office and begged for a lock of his hair. Stevens removed his chestnut wig and invited her, "Pray, madam, select any curl that strikes your fancy."

2 In a scandal over the awarding of army contracts in the early 1860s, it was widely rumored that Simon Cameron, the secretary of war, had been less than strictly honest. Thaddeus Stevens was on record as saying that Cameron would steal anything except a red-hot stove. Cameron appealed to Lincoln, who asked Stevens to say that he had been misquoted. "Certainly I'll say I've been misquoted," said the unrepentant Stevens. "What I actually said was that Cameron would steal anything, *even* a red-hot stove."

3 A visitor who called on Stevens during his last illness remarked on the patient's appearance. "It's not my appearance that troubles me right now," Stevens replied. "It's my disappearance."

ᵂ ᵂ

STEVENSON, Adlai E[wing] (1900–65), *US statesman. He was instrumental in the founding of the United Nations and as governor of Illinois (1949–53) was able to bring about important public reforms. Twice Democratic candidate for the presidency (1952, 1956), he was defeated both times by Dwight D. Eisenhower.*

1 Harry Truman finally persuaded Stevenson to campaign for the Democratic nomination in 1952. Stevenson stayed overnight at the White House and was put in the Lincoln Room. He wandered around the room, gazing with awe at the things in it, unable to bring himself to lie in the bed. So he spent the night on the sofa. He was unaware that in Lincoln's time the bed was not there, but the sofa was.

2 It was probably during his first campaign against Eisenhower that Stevenson was approached by an enthusiastic woman supporter who said to him, "Governor, every thinking person will be voting for you." Stevenson replied, "Madam, that is not enough. I need a majority."

3 At a Labor Day rally during the 1952 presidential campaign a photographer took a famous picture of Stevenson, showing him with a hole in the bottom of one shoe. When the photographer won a Pulitzer Prize for the picture, Stevenson sent him a telegram reading: "Congratulations. I'll bet this is the first time anyone ever won a Pulitzer Prize for a hole in one."

4 Alistair Cooke, talking to Stevenson shortly after his defeat in the 1952 election, was heartened to find him able to view the situation with objective humor. "After all," he said, "who did I think I was, running against George Washington?"

Four years later Eisenhower again defeated Stevenson in the presidential election, and Cooke sent Stevenson a cable reading simply: "How now?" Back came the reply: "Who did I think I was, running against George Washington twice?"

5 Stevenson was much praised in the European press for his condemnation of the American U-2 reconnaissance flights over Europe. Stevenson read the favorable comments and said wryly, "The trouble is, I always run in the wrong continent."

6 Stevenson arrived late to address the American Society of Newspaper Editors. Apologizing, he said he had been delayed at the airport by the arrival of President de Gaulle from France. "It seems to be my fate always to be getting in the way of national heroes," he added.

7 During his 1956 election campaign Stevenson asked some children, "How many children in this audience would like to be a candidate for president of the United States?" A number of hands went up. Stevenson continued: "How many candidates for president of the United States would like to be children again?" He raised his own hand.

8 *The New York Times* reported that when Stevenson was the US delegate to the United Nations, the question was put to him: "Here's Soviet Russia pushing for votes for her satellites, even one as improbable as Outer Mongolia; how can that be counterbalanced?" Stevenson replied, "It's easy. We give Texas her independence and change her name to Outer Arkansas."

9 As President-elect John F. Kennedy tapped four of Adlai Stevenson's law partners for top government posts. Assessing the situation, Stevenson wryly quipped: "I only regret that I have but one law firm to lose for my country."

৵৽ ৵৽

STEVENSON, Robert Louis (1850–94), *Scottish writer, celebrated for novels such as* Treasure Island *(1883),* Kidnapped *(1886), and* Dr. Jekyll and Mr. Hyde *(1886), and the lyrical* A Child's Garden of Verses *(1885). He died in Samoa.*

1 A young friend of Stevenson's had complained to him about being born on Christmas Day. She received presents only once a year and felt cheated. When Stevenson drew up his will as death approached, he remembered the girl and bequeathed his own birthday to her. He subsequently added the following clause: "If, however, she fails to use this bequest properly, all rights shall pass to the President of the United States."

৵৽ ৵৽

STILLMAN, James A. (1850–1918), *US banker and friend of William Rockefeller. He was president of the National City Bank (1891–1909).*

1 After visiting the famous 1913 Armory Show, the first exhibition of the work of avant-garde European painters for the American public, Stillman remarked, "Something is wrong with the world. These men know."

৵৽ ৵৽

STIMSON, Henry Lewis (1867–1950), *US attorney and statesman. His distinguished career included terms as secretary of war (1911–13 and 1940–45) and secretary of state (1929–33).*

1 Secretary of State Stimson once tried to close down the American counterintelligence and decipherment sources (known as "the Black Chamber"). Said Stimson: "Gentlemen do not read each other's mail."

৵৽ ৵৽

STOKOWSKI, Leopold (1882–1977), *British conductor who became a US citizen in 1915. He conducted many of the leading US orchestras, among them the Philadelphia (1912–38).*

1 During a performance of Beethoven's *Leonora* Overture No. 3, the offstage trumpet call twice failed to sound on cue. The overture finished, Stokowski dashed from the rostrum in a fury to seek out the errant trumpeter. He found the player in the wings wrestling with a burly janitor. "You can't blow that damn thing here, I tell you," the janitor was insisting. "There's a concert going on."
{The same story is told about other conductors and concert halls in Europe and America.}

2 Stokowski was intensely irritated by members of the audience who coughed during a performance. At the end of a series of concerts with the Philadelphia orchestra, shortly before his departure on a six-month tour of the Far East, he turned to the audience and said, "Goodbye for a long time. I hope when I come back your colds will all be better."

৵৽ ৵৽

STOPPARD, Tom (1937–), *British playwright, born in Czechoslovakia. He made his name with the play* Rosencrantz and Guildenstern Are Dead *(1967); his later works include* Night and Day *(1978) and* The Real Thing *(1984).*

1 *Rosencrantz and Guildenstern Are Dead* became a sensational success in England, the United States, and even Tokyo and Buenos Aires. On its first production a friend, puzzled by its enigmatic character, asked, "Tom, what's it about?" Replied Stoppard, "It's about to make me a rich man."

ಶಿ ⊷ફ

STOUT, Rex (1886–1975), *US novelist, creator of the fictional detective Nero Wolfe.*

1 Stout was surrounded by books from an early age. His father had a personal library of over a thousand volumes, and his mother, Lucetta, was constantly engrossed in one book or another. Although she had nine children, her reading was rarely interrupted — thanks to a simple expedient. She kept a bowl of cold water and a washcloth beside her chair: any child who dared to disturb her would have his or her face thoroughly washed.

2 As a young man Rex Stout decided to join the navy. Examined by a medical board, he was told that he would have to have his tonsils out before he could be accepted. This was a blow; two dollars was all the money he possessed. He managed, however, to find a young doctor who agreed to perform the operation at a bargain rate. No operating theater was available, of course, but a local barber offered surgeon and patient the use of one of his chairs during a slack period. The doctor duly removed the tonsils. Stout bled profusely, and the barber, alarmed at the sight of the gore and thinking that it might deter other clients, begged Stout to leave. Stout, feeling rather groggy, remained in the chair. "I'll give you two bits to go away," said the barber in desperation. The mention of cash roused Stout; he accepted the money, crawled out of the shop, and, after lying down for a time in a vacant lot, went back to the recruiting board, which forthwith accepted him.

3 An old midwestern farmer once ponderously announced that no ear of corn ever had anything but an even number of rows in it, normally twelve. Out of sheer contrariness, Stout maintained this was not the case, although, as a midwesterner himself, he knew that what the farmer said was true. It was winter when this conversation took place, and the farmer made a $100 wager with Stout that he would not be able to produce ears of corn with odd numbers of rows come the following harvest. In the spring Stout went out to his corn field and carefully cut out a single row from no fewer than 100 young ears of corn. At harvest-time he found that he had about a dozen eleven-rowed ears on which no trace of his operations could be detected. He sent the "proof" off to the farmer, who duly mailed back a check for $100. Stout returned the check, saying that he could not win money by betting on a certainty.

ಶಿ ⊷ફ

STOWE, Harriet Beecher (1811–96), *US novelist. Her antislavery novel* Uncle Tom's Cabin *(1852) did much to enlist sympathy for the cause of abolition.*

1 *Uncle Tom's Cabin* quickly achieved fame. A woman came up to Mrs. Stowe and asked if she could clasp the hand of the woman who had written the great work. "I did not write it," said Mrs. Stowe, "God wrote it. I merely did his dictation."

{William D. Howells saw it differently: "As for the author of *Uncle Tom's Cabin,* her syntax was such a snare to her that it sometimes needed the combined skill of the proofreaders and the assistant editor to extricate her. Of course nothing was ever written into her work, but in changes of diction, in correction of solecisms, in transposition of phrases, the text was largely rewritten in the margin of her proofs. The soul of her art was present, but the form was so often absent, that when it was clothed on anew, it would have been hard to say whose cut the garment was of in many places." The practical inspiration for *Uncle Tom's Cabin* came from a reading of a pamphlet written by a runaway Maryland slave, Josiah Henson, describing the degradation of a slave's life.}

2 The feelings engendered by *Uncle Tom's Cabin* did much to polarize opinion between North and South, contributing to the outbreak of the Civil War. In 1862, when Mrs. Stowe visited President Lincoln at the White House, he greeted her (as recollected by Harriet's son, who was present) with: "So this is the little lady who wrote the book that made the big war."

STRACHEY, [Giles] Lytton (1880–1932), *British writer and a leading member of the Bloomsbury group. His* Eminent Victorians *(1918) exploded Victorian hagiography and inaugurated the modern style of biography.*

1   (Osbert Sitwell tells the following story:)
   "We might recall what he [Lytton Strachey] said to a clever, charming, rather noisy young man who had once been taken to stay with him. I do not know whether the visit could be considered a success, but when the guest next saw his former host, a whole lustrum had passed. 'Mr. Strachey, do you realize it's five years since we met?' the young man asked. He received the reply: 'Rather a nice interval, don't you think?' "

2   When military conscription became compulsory during World War I, Strachey applied for exemption as a conscientious objector. This meant that he had to appear before a tribunal that would assess the genuineness of his objections and rule accordingly. The military representative on the board boomed out questions that he usually found disconcerted the applicants. "I understand, Mr. Strachey, that you have a conscientious objection to all wars?" he began. "Oh, no, not at all," replied Strachey. "Only to this one." The military man tried again: "Tell me, Mr. Strachey, what would you do if you saw a German soldier attempting to rape your sister?" Strachey looked around at his sisters, who were sitting in the public gallery of the courtroom, and said in his piping voice, "I should try and come between them."
   {He got his exemption, but only after further examination by military doctors.}

3   The basis of Dora Carrington's devotion to the homosexual, egocentric Strachey puzzled all their friends. When Arthur Waley asked her what it was about Strachey that could possibly appeal to her, she replied ecstatically, "Oh, it's his knees!"

4   Asked what he considered the greatest thing in life, Strachey inclined his reedlike body, complete with owl eyes and spectral beard, and, in his elegant, high-pitched voice, languidly piped: "Why, passion, of course."

STRAUSS, Richard (1864–1949), *German composer and conductor. Strauss wrote a number of symphonic poems:* Till Eulenspiegels lustige Streiche *(1894–95),* Also sprach Zarathustra *(1895–96), and* Ein Heldenleben *(1898). His fifteen operas include* Salome *(1905),* Elektra *(1906–08),* Der Rosenkavalier *(1909–10), and* Ariadne auf Naxos *(1912).*

1   When *Salome* was produced, Kaiser Wilhelm II, no lover of modern music, remarked, "It will do Strauss a great deal of harm." The royal remark came to Strauss's ears; he commented, "I was able to build my villa in Garmisch, thanks to the harm."

STRAVINSKY, Igor (1882–1971), *Russian-born composer who became a US citizen in 1945. He first achieved fame with his ballet scores commissioned by impresario Sergei Diaghilev —* The Firebird *(1910),* Petrushka *(1911), and* Le Sacre du printemps *(1913). The dissonances and rhythms of these works exercised a powerful influence on subsequent twentieth-century music; Stravinsky's own later works were influenced by classical and baroque styles, adapted to modern idiom.*

1   Although the more discriminating members of the audience at the historic Paris premiere of *Le Sacre du printemps* recognized the work as a masterpiece, the fashionable and ignorant were outraged at its novelty. Sporadic interruptions swelled to a full-scale tumult. Over the noise could be heard the voice of the impresario Gabriel Astruc yelling at the hecklers, "First listen! *Then* boo."

2   (The young music critic Carl Van Vechten attended the premiere of *Le Sacre du printemps*.)
   "I was sitting in a box in which I had rented one seat. . . . Three ladies sat in front of me and a young man occupied the place behind me. The intense excitement under which he was laboring, thanks to the potent force of the music, betrayed itself presently when he began to beat rhythmically on the top of my head with his fists. My emotion was so great that I did not feel the blows for some time. They were perfectly synchronized with the beat of the music. When I did, I turned around. His apology was sincere. We had both been carried beyond ourselves."

3   When Stravinsky was fifty-seven, he settled in the United States and a year later decided to apply for American citizenship. He made an appointment to see the appropriate official. At his first interview the official asked the famous composer his name. "Stra-vin-sky," he replied, speaking each syllable distinctly. "You could change it, you know," suggested the official.

4   Drinking Scotch at the exclusive Petroleum Club in Houston, Texas, Stravinsky remarked happily, "My God, so much I like to drink Scotch that sometimes I think my name is Igor Stra-whiskey."

5   Stravinsky wrote a ballet for Billy Rose's Broadway show *The Seven Lively Arts*. After the opening one of the dancers sent a wire to the composer: "Ballet great success but if you would allow violin to play *pas de deux* instead of trumpet it would be a triumph." Stravinsky cabled back: "Satisfied with great success."

6   Stravinsky was once offered four thousand dollars to compose the music for a Hollywood film. He refused, on the grounds that the sum was too small. The producer argued that another famous composer had accepted the same fee for the score of a recent film. "He had talent," replied Stravinsky. "I have not, so for me the work is more difficult." The figure was raised accordingly, and the producer later remarked, "Now I've learned that the musical scale begins and ends with dough."
{Sibelius had a similar view of his own colleagues. *See* JEAN SIBELIUS 1.}

7   Stravinsky once had an argument with an airport official who insisted that he pay a charge for excess weight. The official, quite used to dealing with such situations, began to explain the reason for the extra charge. "I quite understand the *logic* of it," Stravinsky said impatiently. "What I am objecting to is the money."

8   In the 1950s the Venice Festival commissioned Stravinsky to write an original composition. When the piece was submitted, its length — only fifteen minutes — was found unsatisfactory. Stravinsky was unruffled. "Well, then," he said, "play it again."

9   In 1952, thirty-nine years after its tumultuous premiere, *Le Sacre du printemps* was again performed in Paris and received ecstatic applause. Pierre Monteux, the conductor on both occasions, commented, "There was just as much noise the last time, but the tonality was different."

10   A lady approached Stravinsky and told him that, of all his works, she liked *Scheherazade* best. "But, madame, I did not compose *Scheherazade*," he protested. "Oh," said his admirer, "don't be modest."

11   Stravinsky was inveighing against some critics who had treated his work rather harshly. A friend tried to reassure him: "No one can please everyone. Even God does not please everyone." Stravinsky jumped up, shouting, "Especially God!"

12   Choreographer George Balanchine tells the following story: "Stravinsky's *Circus Polka* was composed precisely for the circus — for the Ringling Brothers, Barnum and Bailey Circus in 1942. The circus impresarios wanted to do a ballet for elephants. They asked me to arrange the dance and told me I could choose the composer. Who else but Stravinsky? I telephoned him, not giving away the whole story.
"'What kind of music?' he asked.
"'A polka,' I said.
"'For whom?' he wanted to know.
"'Elephants.'
"'How old?'
"'Young!'
"'Okay, if they are very young, I'll do it.'
"What he did served its purpose very well, and our ballet . . . was done no less than 425 times."

13   Stravinsky, greatly concerned with his health, would sometimes put himself on a diet of raw vegetables. During one such period he dined on raw tomatoes and potatoes at a restaurant with composer Nicholas Nabokov. Nabokov left some of his cutlet at the side of his plate, and Stravinsky asked if he might finish it. Swallowing the morsel with a generous helping of sour cream, he declared: "I want to astonish the raw potato in my stomach."

14   Stravinsky's publisher, impatient to publish his latest composition, urged him to hurry its completion. "Hurry!" exclaimed the enraged composer. "I never hurry. I have no time to hurry."

STUART, James Ewell Brown (1833–64), *US Confederate commander. He was mortally wounded at Yellow Tavern, Virginia.*

1 In the summer of 1862 Stuart was visiting a house that was raided by Union cavalrymen, and in the confusion of his hasty departure left behind his hat and plume. A week or two later, Stuart and his men attacked the forces of General Pope and plundered the Federal camp. In the morning Stuart displayed his booty — the blue uniform coat of General Pope himself. He lost no time in sending the following proposition to Pope: "General: You have my hat and plume. I have your best coat. I have the honor to propose a cartel for a fair exchange of the prisoners."

ЖЕ ЕЖ

STUBBS, John (1543–91), *English pamphleteer.*

1 In 1579 it seemed that Queen Elizabeth was likely to marry the Duke of Anjou, much to the consternation of her Protestant subjects. Stubbs wrote an intemperate pamphlet against the marriage entitled *The Discovery of a Gaping Gulf to Swallow England.* The queen was furious; author, printer, and bookseller were apprehended and condemned to have their right hands cut off. The printer was pardoned, but the historian William Camden was an eyewitness to the execution of sentence on Stubbs and the bookseller. He records that as soon as his right hand had been struck off, Stubbs raised his hat with his left hand, waved it, and shouted, "God save the Queen!"

ЖЕ ЕЖ

STUHLDREHER, Harry (1901–65), *US football star. He was one of Notre Dame's famous "Four Horsemen" in the 1920s and later became a successful coach.*

1 In a certain Rose Bowl game, Notre Dame defeated Stanford. The great Stanford star Ernie Nevers was outstanding in defeat, but the turning point of the game came when he was stopped at the goal line on a fourth down. For years Californians insisted that he had crossed the goal line and should have been given a score. One night George Davis, a Los Angeles sportswriter, was arguing the point when a little fellow joined in. "I say he didn't score," he

said. "Where were you sitting?" Davis challenged him. "I was sitting on Nevers's neck," said the other man. "I'm Harry Stuhldreher."

ЖЕ ЕЖ

SUDERMANN, Hermann (1857–1928), *German playwright and novelist.*

1 Sudermann and fellow-dramatist Richard Voss disliked each other. When a dramatists' guild was founded, their colleagues brought them together to effect a reconciliation, as their names were of importance to the guild. After much hesitation they were persuaded to shake hands. Voss added, "Herr Sudermann, I wish for your next play the same success as you wish me." Sudermann turned to the onlookers: "Did you hear that? There he goes again!"

ЖЕ ЕЖ

SULLIVAN, Sir Arthur Seymour (1842–1900), *British composer and conductor. His greatest successes were the comic Savoy operas on which he collaborated with W. S. Gilbert.*

1 Returning home one night after a convivial party, Sullivan found he could not identify his own house in the terraced row of identical dwellings on his street. Fortunately his acute tonal sense did not desert him. He walked along the row, pausing to kick the metal shoe scrapers that stood by the sides of the front entrances. One rang a familiar note. Sullivan kicked it again. "That's it: E-flat," he muttered and walked confidently into the house.

{This or a similar tale is told of other musicians.}

ЖЕ ЕЖ

SULLIVAN, John Lawrence (1858–1918), *US heavyweight boxer. He became champion in 1882, beating Paddy Ryan at Mississippi City, and held the title for ten years.*

1 Sullivan was once accosted in a bar by a puny little drunk, who challenged the burly champion to a fight. "Listen, you," growled Sullivan. "If you hit me just once — and I find out about it . . ."

ЖЕ ЕЖ

SUMMERALL, Charles Pelot (1867–1955), *US general. He served in France during World War I, taking command of the first division in*

July 1918. Appointed chief of staff of the US army in 1926, he retired in 1930 and became president of The Citadel (1931–53).

1 Summerall's division had suffered heavy casualties at the Argonne in World War I. Asked how much longer he could continue, he replied, "As long as there are enough men for my division to be organized in depth."

"How many men will that take?"

"Two," replied Summerall. "One behind the other."

ई॰ ॰ई

SUMNER, Charles (1811–74), *US statesman. His courage and persistence greatly advanced the abolitionist cause.*

1 A possibly apocryphal story tells how Sumner in his younger days was suddenly taken dangerously ill, so ill that he could not be conveyed home. He was laid upon a couch in his office in great pain. The friend who was with him, expecting his imminent death, asked if there was anything that he would wish to do by way of spiritual preparation. "I am prepared to die," whispered Sumner, "I have read Calvin's *Institutes* through in the original."

ई॰ ॰ई

SUSANN, Jacqueline (1918–74), *US author of highly popular novels, of which* Valley of the Dolls *and* The Love Machine *were perhaps the most successful. She also excelled at the put-down wisecrack, as her husband, Irving Mansfield, recalls in his book about her. Mr. Mansfield was the producer of the successful television shows* Talent Scouts *and* This Is Show Business.

1 *The Love Machine* was competing in the best-seller lists with Philip Roth's *Portnoy's Complaint,* which dealt in part with masturbation. Asked her opinion of Roth, Jackie replied, "He's a fine writer, but I wouldn't want to shake hands with him."

2 A certain young lady, eager to appear on *Talent Scouts,* sent Mansfield a provocative photograph of herself. "I'll do anything to get on your show," she wrote, "and when I say anything, I mean anything." Unfortunately, it was Jackie who opened the letter. "I am Mrs. Mansfield," she replied, "and I do everything for my husband — and when I say everything, I mean everything."

{Also told of Dorothy Thompson and Sinclair Lewis.}

3 Jackie and her husband were dining at Maurice Chevalier's country home. The dinner was elegantly served, but the portions were extremely small. After this insubstantial meal, the party retired to Chevalier's study. "What would you like to drink, Jacqueline, *ma chère?*" asked her host. "Maurice," she replied, "I never drink on an empty stomach."

{For another response to an insubstantial meal, *see* ALFRED HITCHCOCK 1}.

ई॰ ॰ई

SUVOROV, Alexander Vasilievich (1729–1800), *Russian general.*

1 On his campaigns Suvorov lived as an ordinary soldier. Asked if he ever took off his clothes at night, he replied, "No; when I get lazy and want to have a comfortable sleep I generally take off one spur."

ई॰ ॰ई

SVYATOPOLK (11th century AD), *grand prince of Kiev and son of Saint Vladimir, who ruled for four years (1015–19) until his brother Yaroslav took control.*

1 The city-state of Novgorod liked to consider itself a free republic. Although it was under the nominal charge of an elected prince, control was really exercised by the merchant-aristocrats of the area. Thus, the suggestion forcibly put forward by Grand Prince Svyatopolk that the city accept his son as its prince was coolly received. The Novgorodvans discussed the idea and sent back their message: "Send him here if he has a spare head."

ई॰ ॰ई

SWANSON, Claude Augustus (1862–1939), *US politician. He was governor of Virginia (1906–10), senator from Virginia (1910–33), and US secretary of the navy (1933–39).*

1 Swanson made a particularly long and rambling speech at a banquet one evening. An old lady came up to him afterward to shake his hand. "How did you like the speech?" asked Swanson. "I liked it fine," she replied, "but it

seems to me you missed several excellent opportunities." Swanson looked puzzled. "Several excellent opportunities for what?" he asked. "To quit," she snapped.

৪০ ৩৶

SWEDENBORG, Emanuel (1688–1772), *Swedish mystic, scientist, and philosopher. He pioneered in the fields of crystallography and magnetic theory. In 1787 his followers in London established the sect called the Church of the New Jerusalem or simply the Swedenborgians.*

1 Swedenborg was a very practical man. In a little inn in London one day, he was eating his dinner very rapidly when he thought he saw in the corner of the room a vision of Jesus Christ. The vision uttered two words: "Eat slower." This sensible advice was the beginning of all his visionary experiences.

৪০ ৩৶

SWIFT, Jonathan (1667–1745), *Anglo-Irish clergyman, satirist, and journalist, author of the satirical masterpiece* Gulliver's Travels *(1726). He joined the household of Sir William Temple, the diplomat, in 1689 and after his ordination (1694) continued to serve as secretary there until Temple's death (1699). He then received a church appointment in Ireland, but frequently visited London. He became dean of St. Patrick's, Dublin, in 1713.*

1 When Swift first started to visit a fashionable London coffeehouse, the regular clientele, comprising some of the foremost literary men in England, were so amazed by the eccentric behavior of the unknown parson that they concluded he must be mad. Dr. John Arbuthnot, the queen's physician, was writing a letter and needed some sand, as the custom then was, to blot it. Spying the strange parson nearby and thinking to have some fun with him, he said, "Pray, sir, have you any sand about you?"

"No, sir," said Swift, "but I have the gravel, and if you will give the letter to me, I'll piss upon it." From this unlikely start, a warm friendship grew up between the doctor and the divine.

2 On his travels Swift stopped at a house where the hostess, anxious to please her eminent visitor, asked him what he would like for dinner. "Will you have an apple pie, sir? Will you have a gooseberry pie, sir? A plum pie? A currant pie? A cherry pie? A pigeon pie —"

"Any pie but a magpie, madam," interrupted Swift.

3 On a journey by foot one day Swift was caught in a heavy thunderstorm and took shelter under a large tree. Presently he was joined by a rough-looking man and a pregnant woman. Falling into conversation with them, Swift learned that they were en route to the nearby town to be married. As the woman seemed likely to give birth at any moment, Swift's offer to marry them was happily accepted and Swift performed the marriage ceremony. The pair were about to go on their way when the husband remembered that a certificate was necessary to validate the marriage. Swift obliged by writing: "Under an oak, in stormy weather,/ I joined this rogue and whore together;/ And none but he who rules the thunder/ Can put this rogue and whore asunder."

4 Dean Swift was reprimanded for preaching a charity sermon at such inordinate length that by the end the audience was very little inclined to contribute to the cause concerned. On the next occasion the dean determined to make it terse. He announced his text from Proverbs 19: "'He that hath pity upon the poor lendeth unto the Lord; and that which he hath given will he pay him again.' You have heard the terms of the loan," Swift continued, "and if you like the security, put down your money." Then he sat down. The resulting donations were generous.

5 Lady Carteret, wife of the English viceroy in Ireland, was on friendly terms with Swift. One day when she happened to remark on how good the air was in Ireland, Swift fell on his knees and besought her, "For God's sake, madam, don't say that in England, for if you do, they will surely tax it."

6 At the age of fifty Swift gazed at the withered crown of a tree and remarked to the poet Edward Young, "I shall be like that tree; I shall die from the top."
{This prediction, sadly, was fulfilled by Swift's mental decay in his last years.}

৪০ ৩৶

SWINBURNE, Algernon Charles (1837–1909), *English poet, known best for his* Poems and Ballads *(1866). His heavy drinking and defiance of conventional sexual morality made him a scandalous figure in Victorian literary circles.*

1 (Swinburne had a hard time at school; Sir Osbert Sitwell records the reminiscences of an eighty-six-year-old former schoolmate.)

"He told me how much he had enjoyed his long life. 'If a man — or a schoolboy for that matter —' he continued, 'does not get on well, it's his own fault. I well remember, when I first went to Eton, the head-boy called us together, and pointing to a little fellow with a mass of curly red hair, said, "If ever you see that boy, kick him — and if you are too far off to kick him, throw a stone." . . . He was a fellow named Swinburne,' he added. 'He used to write poetry for a time, I believe, but I don't know what became of him.'"

SZELL, George (1897–1970), *Hungarian conductor. He conducted the German Opera and Philharmonic Orchestra in Prague (1929–37), the Metropolitan Opera in New York (1942–46), and spent the remainder of his professional life with the Cleveland Orchestra.*

1 Szell, not ordinarily renowned for his sense of humor, once made the following observation in a letter to a friend: "Just now I bought a new bottle of Sheaffer's fountain pen ink (the kind you tip before opening so as to let some ink flow into a small compartment, which makes it easier to fill the pen). There's a label on the bottle with the following admonition: SCREW TIGHTLY BEFORE TIPPING. What would you think of making it obligatory to hang this sign around the necks of all hotel chambermaids?"

SZENT-GYÖRGYI, Albert von Nagyrapolt (1893–) *US biochemist, born in Hungary. In 1937 he won the Nobel Prize for medicine.*

1 Szent-Györgyi once sent a paper to the scientific journal *Nature,* describing a new sugar that he had isolated. As this sugar had to be called by a name ending in *-ose,* like all other sugars (for example, glucose), but was of unknown structure, Szent-Györgyi suggested the name "ignose." The editors of *Nature* rejected such frivolity, and the author of the paper was asked to think again. He resubmitted "Godknows."

SZILARD, Leo (1898–1964), *Hungarian-born US physicist. After leaving Hungary he worked first in England, emigrating to the United States in 1937. With his fellow-Hungarian Edward Teller he persuaded Albert Einstein to write to President Roosevelt, warning him of the possibility that Germany might make an atom bomb first.*

1 On one occasion Szilard was discussing with his colleague Enrico Fermi the possibility of the existence of other life in the cosmos. Fermi held forth on the vastness of the universe, the likelihood that stars other than the sun would have planetary systems, the aeons of time that would enable life to emerge on some of these planets, and the probability that intelligent beings not only would exist elsewhere in the universe but would be capable of traveling to our own earth. "If all this has been happening," concluded Fermi, "how is it that they have not arrived? Where are they?"

"They are already among us," replied Szilard, "but they call themselves Hungarians."

➥ T ⇜

TAFT, Horace Dutton (1890–1936), *US educator, brother of William Howard Taft. He founded the Taft School, Watertown, Connecticut, in 1890 and remained headmaster there until his death.*

1 When the son of a pompous businessman was expelled from Taft's school, his enraged father was determined to have him readmitted. He stormed into Taft's office without knocking and roared, "Mr. Taft, you think you can run this school any damned way you please, don't you?" Taft looked at him calmly. "Your manner is crude and your language vulgar," he replied, "but you have somehow got the point."

➥ ⇜

TAFT, Lorado (1860–1936), *US sculptor. His works include a number of portrait busts, the Columbus Memorial Fountain in Washington, D.C., and the Fountain of Time in Chicago.*

1 Taft was working on a classical sculpture which required the effect of windblown robes. Leaving the Art Institute of Chicago one windy day, the sculptor found himself walking on the opposite side of the street from two nuns, whose swirling robes offered a perfect model of the effect he hoped to create. Taft then realized that a man was closely following the nuns. Somewhat concerned, he crossed the street and accosted the man — only to find himself face to face with a fellow sculptor.

➥ ⇜

TAFT, William Howard (1857–1930), *27th president of the United States (1909–13) and Chief Justice of the Supreme Court (1921–30). His obesity occasioned many anecdotes.*

1 On one occasion Taft, stranded at a small country railroad station, was informed that the express train would stop only if a number of people wanted to board it. Taft wired the conductor: "Stop at Hicksville. Large party waiting to catch train." When the train stopped, Taft boarded and reassured the confused conductor: "You can go ahead. I am the large party."

2 Taft was asked to comment on his spectacular defeat in the 1912 presidential election, when he ran for reelection against Woodrow Wilson and Theodore Roosevelt. "Well, I have one consolation," remarked Taft. "No candidate was ever elected ex-president by such a large majority."

3 At Beverly Bay, Massachusetts, clad in a vast bathing suit, Taft plunged into the waves and was disporting himself in the water when one of his neighbors suggested to a friend that they also should go for a swim. "Better wait," the friend replied. "The president is using the ocean."

➥ ⇜

TALLEYRAND-PÉRIGORD, Charles **Maurice de** (1754–1838), *French statesman, twice foreign minister at critical periods in French history (1797–1807, 1814–15). He intrigued with the allies against Napoleon after 1808, and his diplomacy was crucial to obtaining a reasonable settlement for France at the Congress of Vienna (1815) after Napoleon's fall.*

1 Talleyrand had a faithful but inquisitive servant. One day, after entrusting a letter to him for delivery, he glanced out of the window and observed the man reading the letter. The following day Talleyrand sent another letter, this time with a postscript: "You may send a verbal answer by the bearer; he is perfectly acquainted with the whole business, having taken the precaution of reading this prior to its delivery."

2 Examining a draft budget prepared by Louis XVIII, Talleyrand pointed out that no provision had been made for payment of the deputies. "I think they should perform their duties without any payment," said the king. "It should be an honorary position."

"Without any payment?" exclaimed Talleyrand. "Your Majesty, that would cost us too much!"

3 During the French Revolution Talleyrand spent some time in exile in America. On his return to France he said of the United States, "I found there a country with thirty-two religions and only one sauce."

4 Pierre Roederer, charged with preparing the consular constitution, observed to Talleyrand, "A constitution should be short and —"

"Yes, short and obscure," Talleyrand interrupted, thus cutting off Roederer's intention of adding "clear."

5 Talleyrand was sitting between Mme de Staël and the famous beauty Mme Récamier, his attention very much engaged with the latter. Mme de Staël made a bid to get into the conversation. "Monsieur Talleyrand, if you and I and Madame Récamier were shipwrecked together and you could save only one of us, which would you save?" Talleyrand replied with his deepest bow, "Madame, you know everything, so clearly you know how to swim."

6 Claude Rulhières, author of a celebrated work on the Polish Revolution, *Histoire de l'anarchie de Pologne* (1807), complained in Talleyrand's hearing that people said that he was mischievous, "although I have done only one mischievous thing in my whole life."

"And when will that end?" inquired Talleyrand.

7 Talleyrand had expressed his impatience with the behavior of the chamber of peers, to which a friend replied that at least one could find consciences there. "That I don't dispute," said Talleyrand. "Take Semonville, for instance; he has at least two."

8 Talleyrand, sealing letters in a hurry, put the letter for recipient A into the envelope for recipient B and vice versa, and discovered his mistake too late to rectify it. "It is of no consequence," he said. "Neither of them will believe me."

9 During Napoleon's reign the military were at their most arrogant, referring contemptuously to civilians as *pequins* (weaklings). Talleyrand asked a certain general for an explanation of the derogatory term. "*Nous appelons pequin tout ce qui n'est pas militaire* [We call weakling anybody who is not military]," he replied. "*Ah, oui,*" said Talleyrand, "*comme nous autres appelons militaires tous ceux qui ne sont pas civiles* [Ah, yes, as we call military all those who are not civil]."

10 Talleyrand made no secret of his opposition to Napoleon's invasion of Spain and Portugal. This led to the notorious scene of January 28, 1809, when Napoleon abused Talleyrand in the grossest language in front of his other ministers, ending by shouting, "*Tenez, vous êtes de la merde dans un bas de soie*" (You're shit in a silk stocking). Talleyrand said nothing under this attack, only remarking as he left the council chamber, "What a pity such a great man should be so ill-bred!"

11 At the Congress of Vienna Alexander I of Russia inveighed against those who, like King Frederick Augustus of Saxony, had "betrayed the cause of Europe" in not joining the alliance against Napoleon. Talleyrand, mindful of the czar's own former conciliatory attitude toward the erstwhile French emperor, observed, "But that, sire, is merely a question of dates."

12 A rationalist colleague complained to Talleyrand about the difficulty of converting the French peasants. "What can one do to impress these people?" he asked. "Well," replied Talleyrand, "you might try getting crucified and rising again on the third day."

{This anecdote is often ascribed to Voltaire.}

13 Talleyrand once reprimanded a visitor for swallowing a glass of expensive brandy in a single gulp. "The first thing you should do," explained Talleyrand, "is take your glass in the palms of your hands and warm it. Then shake it gently, with a circular movement, so that the liquid's perfume is released. Then, raise the glass to the nose and breathe deeply." His visitor was fascinated. "And then, my lord?" he asked. "And then, sir," continued Talleyrand, "you replace the glass on the table and talk about it."

14 The role played by Talleyrand behind the scenes in the July Revolution of 1830, which brought Louis Philippe to the throne, remains as obscure now as it was to his contemporaries. A widely told story relates how the elderly statesman, sitting in his house in Paris during the three days of riots, heard the pealing of the bells and remarked, "Ah, the tocsin! We're winning."

"Who's we, *mon prince?*"

Talleyrand gestured for silence: "Not a word. I'll tell you who we are tomorrow."

15 The veteran statesman was unimpressed by Louis Philippe's handling of the many crises that beset his reign. "How do you think this government will end?" someone once asked.

"Accidentally," said Talleyrand.

৯৯ ৫৫

TAMAGNO, Francesco (1851–1905), *Italian tenor, renowned for his performance in the title role of Verdi's* Otello.

1 The leading tenor of an American opera company, rehearsing Tamagno's famous role in *Otello,* was puzzled by a request from the stage director. During a brief rest in the tenor part he was to walk upstage, pause, then return downstage and continue singing. The action seemed pointless and difficult to execute in the time allowed. "But it is the tradition of the role," insisted the director. "Tamagno did it." The tenor submitted with reluctance. In Italy the following year, he visited Tamagno and asked him to explain this strange "tradition." The old man's face lit up. "It is very simple," he said. "Note that in the final passage Otello must sing a high B-flat. So while the chorus was singing I went upstage to spit."

৯৯ ৫৫

TAMIRIS, Helen [Helen Becker] (1905–66), *US dancer, choreographer, and dance teacher, noted for her ability to express in dance social and political ideas. She was principal choreographer of the WPA Federal Theater Project (1937–1939).*

1 The head of the WPA dance project was Lincoln Kirstein. For his first production he convened all the dancers and choreographers and described his plan to present a cavalcade of the great dancers of history. "For example," he said, "Gluck-Sandor, you could dance the part of Nijinsky. Felicia Sorel, you might be Taglioni. And Tamiris, you could play Isadora Duncan."

"Yes," said Tamiris, "but then who will play me?"

৯৯ ৫৫

TAYLOR, Elizabeth (1932–   ), *US film actress. As a child, she starred in* National Velvet *(1944). Of her adult roles, the most acclaimed was in* Who's Afraid of Virginia Woolf? *(1966) with Richard Burton, to whom she was twice married.*

1 Miss Taylor's fabulous diamond ring drew the notice of Princess Margaret, who remarked, "That's a bit vulgar." Miss Taylor persuaded the princess to try on the ring. "There, it's not so vulgar now, is it?" she said.

৯৯ ৫৫

TAYLOR, John (1703–72), *British oculist. Nicknamed "the Chevalier," Taylor was a familiar figure at most of the courts of Europe, where he seems to have achieved a great reputation for his successful cures, despite the charlatanry of his writings.*

1 At dinner in Edinburgh, Taylor was holding forth with much impudence, boasting among other things that he could read anybody's thoughts by looking at their eyes. His hostess, the Countess of Dumfries, angered by his behavior, contemptuously inquired whether he knew what she was thinking. Taylor confidently asserted that he did. "Then," said the countess, "it's very safe, for I am sure you will not repeat it."

৯৯ ৫৫

TAYLOR, Laurette (1884–1946), *US actress, best known for her performance in Tennessee Williams's* The Glass Menagerie.

1 At a party after a poorly attended performance one evening, Miss Taylor was engaged in amiable conversation with one of her fellow guests, a complete stranger. After some time, he politely took his leave and walked over to a group of people at the opposite side of the room. Miss Taylor's smile suddenly disappeared and she turned angrily to her hostess. "That man walked out on me tonight at the theater!" she cried. "Are you sure?" asked her hostess. "Of course I'm sure. I sometimes forget a face, but I *never* forget a back!'"

ઢ૭ ◆ઽ

TAYLOR, Maxwell D[avenport] (1901–), *US army officer, military adviser to President Kennedy. He was the first US general to fight in France in World War II.*

1 At one stage of the parachute drop into Normandy on D-Day in 1944, the ratio of officers to men was 10 to 49. Commented Taylor: "Never in the history of human combat have so few been led by so many."

{This remark was, of course, a play on Winston Churchill's famous statement after the battle of Britain in 1940: "Never in the field of human conflict was so much owed by so many to so few."}

ઢ૭ ◆ઽ

TAYLOR, Paul (1930–), *US dancer and choreographer.*

1 During a modern-dance program, Paul Taylor contributed a solo in which he simply stood motionless on stage for four minutes. The reviewer for *Dance Observer* magazine responded in kind: his review consisted of just four inches of white space.

ઢ૭ ◆ઽ

TECUMSEH (c. 1768–1813), *chief of the American Shawnee Indians, who organized an Indian confederacy to resist white encroachments. General (later President) William Henry Harrison defeated him at Tippecanoe (1811). Tecumseh was killed in the battle of the Thames River (1813), fighting on the British side in the War of 1812.*

1 In 1810 Harrison, then governor of Indiana Territory, was negotiating with Tecumseh in order to try to prevent open hostilities. He ordered a chair to be brought for the Indian chief. The man who brought it said, "Your father, General Harrison, offers you a seat."

"My father!" Tecumseh exclaimed. "The

sun is my father and the earth is my mother, and on her breast will I lie." Ignoring the chair, he stretched himself out on the ground.

ઢ૭ ◆ઽ

TELFORD, Thomas (1757–1834), *British engineer. He was responsible for building many roads, canals, bridges, and aqueducts all over Britain. His best-known structure is perhaps the Menai suspension bridge, completed in 1825. Robert Southey nicknamed him "the Colossus of Roads."*

1 In his later years Telford was something of a celebrity, as well as being delightful company. In London he stayed at the Ship Inn in Charing Cross, which was always crowded with his friends. A new landlord purchased the inn without knowing that Telford was about to move into a house of his own in Abingdon Street. When he found out, he was utterly dismayed. "Not *leaving*!" he exclaimed. "I have just paid seven hundred and fifty pounds for you."

ઢ૭ ◆ઽ

TEMPLE, Frederick (1821–1902), *British clergyman, archbishop of Canterbury (1896–1902).*

1 Archbishop Temple had a reputation for intimidating his clergy, and ordinands particularly dreaded their pre-ordination interview with him. To one young man he said, "I will lie down on that couch and pretend to be ill. You leave the room, come in again, and 'sick-visit' me." The ordinand did as he was told. Coming up to the archiepiscopal couch, he gazed intently at the recumbent figure and then said reprovingly, "Why, Freddie, you're on the drink again!"

ઢ૭ ◆ઽ

TENG SHIH (6th century BC), *Chinese philosopher and administrator.*

1 A wealthy man from Teng's state had drowned in the Wei River. The corpse was recovered by a man who refused to return it to the mourning family until he had received a large payment. The relatives of the drowned man sought Teng's advice. He told them, "Wait, no other family will pay for the body." Fortified by this counsel, they waited, and in

due course the finder of the corpse grew worried and also consulted Teng. "Wait," Teng advised, "for nowhere else can they obtain the body."

{The ruler of the state eventually tired of Teng's equivocations and had him put to death.}

८ ४

TENNYSON, Alfred, 1st Baron Tennyson (1809–92), *British poet; poet laureate (1850–92). Tennyson's first important book of verse appeared in 1830. In 1832 he traveled with his Cambridge friend Arthur Hallam on the Continent. Hallam's death (1833) moved Tennyson to begin his elegiac sequence* In Memoriam, *which was not published until 1850. Some of his finest verse appeared in the collection of poetry he published in 1842, including "Morte d'Arthur" and "Ulysses." Among his later long poems are* The Princess *(1847),* Maud *(1855), and the reworkings of Arthurian legend called* The Idylls of the King *(1859–85).*

1 The Duke of Argyll and his family, on holiday near the Tennysons, were invited for dinner. When the Argylls arrived, Tennyson apologized for not having changed: "I can't dress for you, for I never dress for anyone. If I made an exception and dressed for a duke, my butler would set me down as a snob."

2 The great Shakespearean actor Henry Irving was staying with the Tennysons. One evening after dinner when they were having port, the butler filled Irving's glass, then set the decanter down by Tennyson. Tennyson was talking and continued absentmindedly to fill his own glass, failing to notice when Irving's was empty. The decanter emptied, he called for another bottle. Again the butler filled Irving's glass and left Tennyson the decanter, which he finished as before. Next morning Irving found Tennyson standing solicitously at his bedside, inquiring how he felt. "Ah, but pray, Mr. Irving, do you always drink two bottles of port after dinner?"

3 The critics' reception of Tennyson's *Maud* was predictably hostile, for the poem dealt with love, madness, murder, suicide, hysteria. One reviewer suggested that *Maud* had one vowel too many in the title, and that it would make sense no matter which was deleted.

4 One of Tennyson's admirers, a little girl called Elspeth Thompson, used to accompany the poet on his long walks around London. As he tramped through the streets, the child trotting beside him, the poet made a striking figure in his swirling Spanish cloak and great sombrero. Passersby would often turn to look at him. Tennyson grumbled to Elspeth, "Child, your mother should dress you less conspicuously; people are staring at us."

5 Tennyson was offered a baronetcy four times, as a mark of honor from the nation, and each time declined. He came around to thinking that he had made a mistake in declining and wished to accept. Accordingly, a friend, acting as intermediary between him and Gladstone, the prime minister, conveyed Tennyson's willingness. It was further suggested that Tennyson might be offered a peerage rather than a baronetcy, but Gladstone mused, "Ah! Could I be an accessory to introducing *that hat* into the House of Lords?"

6 Oscar Browning, well known as a snob, sought out Tennyson on the Isle of Wight. He marched up to him, shook him by the hand, and announced, "I am Browning." Tennyson, who knew only one Browning — the poet Robert — looked at him coolly, said, "No, you're not," and turned on his heel.

7 Tennyson was entertaining a Russian nobleman at his house on the Isle of Wight. One morning the Russian set off on a shooting expedition, returning later that day with the proud news that he had shot two peasants. Tennyson politely corrected his guest's pronunciation. "You mean 'two pheasants,'" he said. "No," replied the Russian, "two peasants. They were insolent, so I shot them."

{Authenticity not guaranteed.}

8 As a young man Tennyson was afflicted with a painful attack of piles. Accepting advice, he visited a young but well-known proctologist and was so successfully treated that for many years he had no further trouble. However, after he had become a famous poet and had been raised to the peerage, he suffered a further attack. Revisiting the proctologist, he expected to be recognized as the former patient who had become the great poet. The proctologist, however, gave no signs of recognition. It was only when the noble lord had bent over for examination that the proctologist exclaimed, "Ah, Tennyson!"

{This story is also told of others.}

9 On a holiday in 1883 Tennyson was holding forth to Sir William Harcourt on the pleasures of tobacco, telling him that the first pipe after breakfast was the best. "The earliest pipe of half-awakened bards," observed Harcourt, parodying a well-known Tennysonian line. Tennyson was not amused.

ða æð

TERESA of Ávila, Saint (1515–82), *Spanish Carmelite nun. She founded a convent at Ávila (1562) and later, with the aid of Saint John of the Cross, several other religious houses at which the reformed Carmelite rule was practiced. She wrote a number of books describing her mystical experiences.*

1 A young nun came to Saint Teresa with exaggerated tales of her spiritual trials and the fearful sins into which she had lapsed. After listening to her recitation, Saint Teresa said briskly, "We know, sister, that none of us is perfect. You must just be sure that your sins don't turn into bad habits."

ða æð

TERRY, Dame Ellen (1847–1928), *British actress. She was particularly successful in Shakespearean roles.*

1 Ellen Terry was at the height of her career when the director of a production in which she was starring turned out to be a rather opinionated and fussy young man. He told her exactly how she should play a particular scene, down to the most minute details of action and delivery. The star listened patiently and did precisely as she was told. When she had finally gone through the scene to his satisfaction, she turned to him and said, "Now, if you don't mind, I'll just do that little extra something for which I am paid my enormous fee."

2 At the turn of the century Ellen Terry was in her early fifties and, though still at the height of her powers as an actress, complained: "Now I am a grandmother, nobody will ever write a play for me." When Bernard Shaw heard this remark, he immediately wrote *Captain Brassbound's Conversion* for her. Consequently, in 1901 she enjoyed a great success in the role of Lady Cicely Waynflete. "He only did it," Ellen Terry observed of Shaw, "out of a natural desire to contradict."

ða æð

TETRAZZINI, Luisa (1871–1940), *Italian soprano. Her coloratura singing was acclaimed in America, Europe, and Russia.*

1 Tetrazzini was concerned neither about her size nor about the amount she needed to eat. She shared her predilection for Neapolitan dishes with her friend Enrico Caruso. On one occasion after a late spaghetti lunch with Caruso she had to sing Violetta in *La Traviata*. When her co-star John McCormack attempted to raise the dying Violetta in his arms, it felt, as he said later, as if he were fondling a pair of Michelin tires. He did not know that she had consumed so much spaghetti that she had had to remove her corsets. The amazement that he could not conceal started her giggling, and to the audience's astonishment both performers in this tragic death scene were soon convulsed with laughter.

ða æð

THACKERAY, William Makepeace (1811–63), *British writer. After trying his hand at the law and journalism, Thackeray became a novelist. Among his noted volumes are* Vanity Fair *(1847–48),* Pendennis *(1848),* Henry Esmond *(1852), and* The Newcomes *(1853–55). He also wrote verse, including some entertaining ballads, and was a popular lecturer.*

1 On a lecturing tour of the United States Thackeray was invited to a feast of Massachusetts oysters by his publisher James T. Fields, who knew the author's great desire to taste these delicacies. Thackeray, overcome at the sight of the six huge oysters set before him, asked in a tremulous voice how he should begin on them. Fields promptly gave a demonstration and swallowed his first oyster. Plucking up courage, Thackeray did likewise. Fields asked him how he felt. "As if I had swallowed a baby," replied Thackeray.

2 Thackeray blackballed a man named Hill, proposed for membership in London's Garrick Club. This Mr. Hill was a self-made man with a strong cockney accent. "I blackballed him because he is a liar," Thackeray explained. "He calls himself 'ill' when he isn't."

3 At his club one day Thackeray was accosted by a pompous Guards officer who exclaimed, "Ha, Thackeray, old boy, I hear you're having your portrait painted." Disliking the man's patronizing tone, Thackeray briefly assented. "Full length?" inquired the officer superciliously. "No, full-length portraits are for soldiers, so we can see their spurs," replied Thackeray. "With authors, the other end of the man is the principal thing."

ঌ৵ ৵ঌ

THALBERG, Irving J. (1899–1936), *US producer who had an important hand in the success of some of Metro-Goldwyn-Mayer's most famous films.*

1 Thalberg usually had his working hours double- or triple-booked with conferences on the many films currently in production. Important and self-important people might have to wait weeks for appointments, and when they arrived often found they had to cool their heels for hours in Thalberg's anteroom. When the Marx brothers came to talk to Thalberg about *A Night at the Opera,* they were displeased to be told they would have to wait. Lighting up two cigars apiece, they stationed themselves around the door of his sanctum and busily puffed smoke through the crack. Eventually Thalberg emerged. "Is there a fire?" he asked. "No, there's the Marx brothers," Groucho, Chico, and Harpo told him.

{The next occasion on which the Marx brothers were told that Thalberg was busy, they took reprisals by rearranging the furniture in his outer office in such a way that it was virtually impossible for him to get out of it.}

2 Another victim of the "million-dollar bench" in Thalberg's offices was George S. Kaufman. Concerning one such occasion, he remarked warily, "On a clear day you can see Thalberg."

3 In 1936, shortly before Thalberg's early death from pneumonia, his literary scout Al Lewin brought him the synopsis of a book about to be published. He was greatly excited about its potential as a film and as a vehicle for Clark Gable. The book's title was *Gone with the Wind.* Thalberg agreed to read the synopsis, but kept putting it off. Lewin went on reminding him and asking him about it until at last Thalberg said that he had read it and he agreed with everything Lewin had said about it. "But," he continued, "I have just made *Mutiny on the Bounty* and *The Good Earth.* And now you're asking me to burn Atlanta. No, absolutely not! No more epics for me now. Just give me a little drawing-room drama. I'm just too tired."

ঌ৵ ৵ঌ

THALES (?640–?546 BC), *Greek philosopher born at Miletus, on the west coast of modern Turkey. Thales, none of whose writings has survived, founded the earliest school of Greek philosophy. He held that there was a single eternal unchanging substance underlying all physical phenomena; this he identified with the element water.*

1 According to Herodotus (writing a century after Thales' death), Thales used his knowledge of Babylonian astronomy to predict an eclipse of the sun. The eclipse occurred just as the Medes and the Lydians were on the point of advancing into battle. It so terrified their armies that they packed their tents and returned home. Modern astronomical investigations have pinpointed the only eclipse in Thales' time as that occurring on May 28, 585 BC, a rare instance of establishing a precise date for an early historical event.

2 Aristotle (writing about two centuries after Thales' death) shows the philosopher as entrepreneur. People often taunted Thales, saying that all his wisdom had failed to make him rich. Thales responded by buying up all the olive presses in Miletus in a year when his knowledge of meteorology enabled him to predict a bumper crop of olives. By charging monopolistic prices for the use of his newly acquired presses, he became extremely wealthy in one season. Having proved his point, Thales then sold all the presses again and returned to philosophy.

{*See* HENRY DAVID THOREAU 5 for a similar approach to capitalism.}

3 Plato (writing about a century and a half after Thales' death) tells a more typical story of philosophical unworldliness. Thales was walking along a road with his head thrown back, studying the stars, when he stumbled into a well. In response to his cries for help a servant girl came and pulled him out, observing that while he was eager to know about things in the sky, he failed to see what lay at his own feet.

4   When Thales entertained the great Athenian lawgiver Solon at Miletus, Solon teased the philosopher about why he did not marry and have children. Thales made no reply. Shortly afterward a stranger came to his house and Thales took him aside for a few words before introducing him to Solon. The man informed Solon that he came from Athens. Solon eagerly asked for news. "No news," said the stranger, "apart from the funeral of a great man's son."

"Whose son was this?" inquired Solon.

"I cannot recollect the name," replied the stranger, "but the father is a man of great honor, who is currently traveling abroad."

Solon, whose forebodings had been growing throughout the conversation, burst out with, "Was it the son of Solon?"

"Yes, that was the name," said the stranger.

When Solon began to weep and express extreme grief, Thales took him by the hand and said gently, "These things that can strike down even a man as resolute as Solon with uncontrollable grief are the things that prevent me from marrying and raising a family. But take courage, not a word of the man's story is true."

5   Thales used to say that there was no essential difference between being alive and being dead. Someone asked why, if that was the case, he chose life instead of death. "Because there is no difference," Thales replied.

৪৯ ৫৯

THATCHER, Denis (1915–   ), *British businessman, husband of British premier Margaret Thatcher.*

1   When the Thatchers moved into 10 Downing Street, the British prime minister's official residence in London, a reporter asked Denis Thatcher, "Who wears the pants in this house?" He answered, "I do, and I also wash and iron them."

৪৯ ৫৯

THEMISTOCLES (?527–?460 BC), *Athenian statesman, responsible for the Greek victory*

over the Persian invaders at Salamis (480). Ten years later he was exiled from Athens and in disgust offered his services to the Persian king.

1   Themistocles alienated the allies of Athens by extorting money from them. Anchoring his fleet off a small island, he sent a message saying that he had two powerful deities on his side who would compel them to pay up — Persuasion and Force. The islanders sent back a message saying that they had two equally potent gods on their side — Poverty and Despair.

2   Themistocles was overheard to remark that his young son ruled all Greece. Asked to explain, he said, "Athens holds sway over all Greece; I dominate Athens; my wife dominates me; our newborn son dominates her."

Compare ELIZABETH THE QUEEN MOTHER 4.

৪৯ ৫৯

THEODORIC [Theodoric the Great] (c. 454–526), *king of the Ostrogoths and of Italy (493–526). His court at Ravenna was a center of late Roman culture.*

1   Although an Arian, Theodoric had a Catholic minister whom he trusted. This minister, thinking to ingratiate himself with the king, announced that he was renouncing his tenets to embrace Arianism. Theodoric had him beheaded, saying, "If this man is not faithful to his God, how can he be faithful to me, a mere man?"

৪৯ ৫৯

THIBAUD, Jacques (1880–1953), *French violinist. He formed a very successful trio with Alfred Cortot and Pablo Casals.*

1   Thibaud's liking for gourmet food, vintage wines, and beautiful women precluded any serious violin practice. His repertoire was consequently limited. This did not affect his brilliant success as a performer, however, and he was immensely popular. After a concert one evening, Thibaud was talking to Moriz Rosenthal in the greenroom when a young admirer came in and asked Thibaud to write a few words in his autograph book. "What shall I write?" asked Thibaud.

"Why not list your repertoire?" suggested Rosenthal.

2 Thibaud once engaged in an amorous escapade, covering his tracks with a flurry of telegrams to his wife at home: "Concert in Berlin fantastic success. Seven encores. Love, Jacques." "Rome recital sold out. Immediately re-engaged. Je t'embrasse. Jacques." "Warsaw concert unbelievable triumph. Mille baisers. Jacques."

Finally he returned home. During dinner that evening the servant brought a telegram for Madame Thibaud: "Brussels appearance sensational. Rave reviews. I miss you. Jacques."

ॐ ♥

THIERS, Louis Adolphe (1797–1877), *French statesman and historian; first president (1870–73) of the Third Republic.*

1 Someone remarked in Thiers's hearing that the great statesman's mother had been a cook. Thiers, intending to imply that she had been worthy of a higher estate in life, rushed to her defense: "She was — but I assure you that she was a very bad cook."

ॐ ♥

THOMAS, Dylan (1914–53), *Welsh poet. His talents as a reader of poetry and radio actor brought him success, but he was perpetually short of money. He died prematurely of alcoholism soon after presenting in New York his play for voices,* Under Milk Wood.

1 On one occasion when Dylan Thomas had been drinking and talking freely for some time, he suddenly stopped. "Somebody's boring me," he said. "I think it's me."

2 (Donald Hall, who later wrote about his friendship with Thomas, once had an exchange with the poet that became particularly poignant after Thomas's death.)

"I was complaining about some Sunday paper critic who used phrases like 'death-wish.' Out of brutal innocence I added, 'What a dumb idea anyway. Who wants to die?' Dylan looked up at me. 'Oh, I do,' he said. 'Why?' I demanded. 'Just for the change,' he said."

3 "There is a story of [Thomas's] friend in the funeral parlour, who looked down at the poet's painted face, loud suit, and carnation in his buttonhole, only to declare, 'He would never have been seen dead in it.'"

After a successful career on stage, Julius Tannen came upon hard times in Hollywood. Unable to get an acting job, he finally at least obtained an audition for an editor's role in a newspaper drama.

He dressed carefully and, worried about his baldness, wore a toupee. After the audition the producer shook his head and said, "I'm sorry. I don't think you will do for the part. I've always visualized a bald-headed man for the part."

Julius pulled the toupee from his head. "I think I can satisfy you on that score," he beamed.

The producer studied Tannen's polished skull but shook his head again. "I'm sorry, Mr. Tannen, I simply can't visualize you as a bald-headed man."

— Ben Hecht, *A Child of the Century*

THOMAS, [Philip] Edward (1878–1917), *British poet and critic. His early works consisted largely of miscellaneous prose; only after befriending Robert Frost in 1912 did he begin to write poetry. Many of his poems were written while he was serving in World War I. He was killed in action in 1917.*

1 Early in World War I, Thomas was asked if he knew what he was fighting for. Bending down to the ground, the poet picked up a handful of dirt and crumbled it between his fingers. "Literally, for this," he replied.

ॐ ♥

THOMAS, Norman (1884–1968), *US socialist politician and reformer.*

1 Norman Thomas campaigned regularly and unsuccessfully for the presidency from 1928 to 1948. When Franklin D. Roosevelt was president, Thomas visited him in the White House. In the course of the interview Roosevelt said, "Norman, I'm a damned sight better politician than you." Thomas replied, "Certainly, Mr. President; you're on that side of the desk, and I'm on this."

2 (In the 1960s Thomas's fears of thermonuclear war colored many of his speeches.)

"'If you cannot learn to live with Communists,' he told his audiences, 'then you might begin to think about dying with them.' . . . 'Kennedy said that if we had nuclear war we'd kill 300 million people in the first hour,' he would declare in a typical thrust. Then there would be a rhetorical pause and this clincher: 'McNamara [secretary of defense], who is a good businessman and likes to save, says it would be only 200 million.'"

3 Thomas had many distinguished supporters, but lacked mass popular backing. Complimented on the lofty character of his campaigns, he replied, "I appreciate the flowers; only I wish the funeral weren't so complete."

4 Looking back at his record of failure in his campaigns for the presidency, Thomas commented, "While I'd rather be right than president, at any time I'm ready to be both."
See also HENRY CLAY 5 and THOMAS REED 2.

&~ ~&

THOMSON, Sir George Paget (1892–1975), *British physicist who used electron diffraction experiments to confirm the suggestion of Prince de Broglie that elementary particles have a wave nature as well as a particle nature. He was the son of J. J. Thomson, the discoverer of the electron. Sir George was chairman of the Maud Committee, which advised the government in 1940 that a fission bomb could be made.*

1 The Maud Committee was given its name as a result of a telegram that Niels Bohr, the famous Danish physicist, managed to send to his friends in England shortly after the German occupation of Denmark. The telegram ended: "Please inform Cockcroft and Maud Ray, Kent," after having assured his friends that he was well. The message was mistakenly thought to be in code and skillfully decoded to mean "make uranium day and night." It was later found that Maud Ray had been Bohr's English governess.

&~ ~&

THOMSON, Joseph (1858–94), *British explorer. An expert in geology and natural history, he made important contributions to our knowledge of Africa.*

1 In 1878 Thomson made his first journey to Africa as geologist and natural historian in an expedition led by Alexander Keith Johnston. Barely six weeks after departing Zanzibar for the interior, Johnston died, leaving the twenty-one-year-old Thomson leader of the expedition. He carried on to the great lakes and brought the expedition to an almost entirely successful conclusion. On his return to London he wrote the book *To African Lakes and Back,* and became a celebrity. J. M. Barrie asked Thomson what was the most dangerous part of his travels. "Crossing Piccadilly Circus," said Thomson.

&~ ~&

THOMSON, Robert (1923–   ) *US baseball player, born in Scotland.*

1 No team in the history of American baseball has come from as far behind to win a league pennant as did the National League's New York Giants in 1951. In mid-August they trailed the Brooklyn Dodgers by 13½ games, but in the last seven weeks of the season moved up to tie for the top spot, forcing a best-of-three play-off. After each team had won one game, the Giants, in the final game, with the score 4 to 1 against them, went into the last half of the last inning, scored a run, picked up one out, and had two men on base. Dodgers pitcher Ralph Branca entered the fray to try to get the other two outs his team needed. Then Bobby Thomson came to bat and hit a three-run home run to win the game 5 to 4 and the league pennant for the Giants. Pandemonium broke out in New York's Polo Ground, and this became one of the best-remembered moments in American baseball history.

Looking back on his career, Thomson said, "I played fourteen or fifteen years in the majors. I got more than 11,700 hits and more than 100 home runs. But I'd be forgotten except for that one."

{Curiously, Ralph Branca expressed a similar sentiment about that same moment: "I pitched nine or ten years in the big leagues. I threw thousands of pitches. And no one has ever let me forget that one."}

&~ ~&

THOMSON, Roy Herbert, 1st Baron Thomson of Fleet (1894–1976), *British newspaper magnate, born in Canada. The owner of a number of Canadian and US newspapers, he became a British citizen in 1963. In 1966 he took over* The Times. *His worldwide conglomerate was estimated in the mid-1970s to be worth some 290 million pounds.*

1   Driving to the office one day, Thomson's son Kenneth, joint chairman of the Thomson Organization, took out a copy of *The Times* and began to leaf through it. "Where did you get that?" snapped Lord Thomson.

"At the shop around the corner," replied his son.

"Well, Ken," said the multimillionaire, "you take it right back and let someone else buy it. You can have mine when I've finished."

ชื่อ   เชื่อ

THOREAU, Henry David (1817–62), *US writer and transcendentalist philosopher. His best-known work,* Walden *(1854), was the fruit of two and a half years of life in a solitary hut by Walden pond. It is admired for its descriptions of natural phenomena and its exploration of man's relationship with nature.*

1   A friend asked Thoreau what he thought of the world to come. "One world at a time," said Thoreau.

2   Thoreau's *A Week on the Concord and Merrimack Rivers* did not sell. Eventually his publisher, who needed the space, wrote to ask Thoreau how he should dispose of the remaining copies. Thoreau asked that they be sent to him — 706 copies out of the edition of 1,000. When they arrived and were safely stowed away, Thoreau noted in his journal, "I now have a library of nearly nine hundred volumes, over seven hundred of which I wrote myself."

3   (Thoreau made the following entry in his journal on September 8, 1859:)

"I went to the store the other day to buy a bolt for our front door, for as I told the storekeeper, the Governor was coming here. 'Aye,' said he, 'and the Legislature too.' 'Then I will take two bolts,' said I. He said that there had been a steady demand for bolts and locks of late, for our protectors were coming."

4   Thoreau was languishing in jail after he had refused to pay the Massachusetts poll tax in

1843. Ralph Waldo Emerson came to visit him and asked him why he was there. "Waldo, why are you *not* here?" said Thoreau.

5   Thoreau, whose father had been a manufacturer of lead pencils, was confident that he could improve on the type of pencil in use at that time. His early experiments were a great success and presented him with the opportunity to make his fortune. Thoreau, however, surprised his friends by announcing that he had no intention of making any further pencils. "Why should I?" he said. "I would not do again what I have done once."

See also THALES 2.

6   Asked whether he had traveled much, Thoreau replied, "Yes — around Concord."

7   Toward the end of his life Thoreau was urged to make his peace with God. "I did not know that we had ever quarreled," he replied.

ชื่อ   เชื่อ

THORNDIKE, Dame Sybil (1882–1976), *British actress. In her long and distinguished career she played many memorable Shakespearean roles and created the title role in Bernard Shaw's* Saint Joan *(1924).*

1   Dame Sybil was the daughter of the canon of Rochester. At evensong one Sunday, she noticed that her father seemed a little distracted as he gave the blessing. She later asked him what he had been thinking about at the time. "My dear!" he exclaimed. "I was thinking how wonderful it would have been if I had been on a trapeze swinging across the aisle."

2   Sybil Thorndike was married to Sir Lewis Casson, himself a distinguished actor, and they frequently toured together, giving dramatic recitals. After his death she was asked about their long and happy marriage. "Did you ever think of divorce?" was one of the questions. "Divorce?" she said. "Never. But murder often!"

3   Dame Sybil Thorndike appeared in a play with Dame Edith Evans. The theater manager was faced with a dilemma — to which of the two distinguished actresses should the Number One dressing room be allocated? In desperation, he consulted Dame Sybil herself. "The Number Two dressing room is equally luxurious," he explained, "but it has the disadvantage of being at the top of a flight of stairs."

"There's no problem at all, my dear," replied Dame Sybil. "Let Edith have Number One. *I* can climb stairs."

ಜ್ಞ ⋅⋅⋅

THORPE, Jim (1888–1953), *US athlete of American Indian descent. He was an All-American football player at Carlisle University, later a professional. He won the decathlon and pentathlon events at the 1912 Olympics and was a major-league professional baseball player for six seasons. He was stripped of his Olympic gold medals when it was discovered that he had been playing minor-league baseball for pay in 1909 and 1910 and thus had lost his amateur status.*

1 King Gustav V of Sweden presented Thorpe with a bronze bust during the 1912 Stockholm Olympics and told him, "You, sir, are the greatest athlete in the world."

"Thanks, king," said Thorpe simply.

2 Questioned about his running ability in football, Thorpe smiled and said, "I give 'em the hip, then I take it away."

3 When word got around that the Carlisle Indians had an outstanding track team, Harold Anson Bruce, coach of the powerful Lafayette College team, invited "Pop" Warner's athletes to a dual meet on Alumni Day. Reluctantly, he agreed to pay a large guarantee. The meet was sold out. But when Bruce went to greet the visitors, he was disconcerted to find only a few young men getting off the train with Warner. "Where are your Indians?" Bruce demanded.

"I've got enough," answered Warner.

"How many?"

"Five."

"But, Pop, I've got a team of forty-six; it's an eleven-event program. This is a disaster. You haven't a chance."

"Wanna bet?" asked Warner.

Thorpe won the high jump, the broad jump, the pole vault, the shot put, and the low hurdles, and was second in the 100. Two others ran first and second in the half-mile, the mile, and the two-mile; another won the quarter-mile, and the fifth the high hurdles. Carlisle won 71–31.

ಜ್ಞ ⋅⋅⋅

> Stories involving amnesia are not rare. One of the most endearing is told about the father of the poet Alfred Tennyson. Once, visiting a new parishioner, he was politely asked by the servant admitting him to identify himself. He found he could not remember his own name, turned away, walked, lost in thought, through the village, and encountered a rustic who respectfully greeted him: "Good day to 'ee, Dr. Tennyson."
>
> "By God, my man, you're right!" exclaimed Dr. Tennyson.
>
> — Michael Innes, *The Gay Phoenix*

THRONBERRY, Marv (1933–   ), *US professional baseball player.*

1 "During their worst early years no one symbolized the hapless condition of the New York Mets better than first baseman Marv Thronberry. He was the good natured butt of many of the better (and somewhat exaggerated) Mets stories. Like the time manager Casey Stengel got a cake for his birthday and someone in the clubhouse asked why Marvelous Marv hadn't got one on *his* birthday. 'We were afraid he might drop it,' Stengel explained."

ಜ್ಞ ⋅⋅⋅

THURBER, James (1894–1961), *US cartoonist, short-story writer, and humorist. He contributed to* The New Yorker *for many years. Perhaps his finest book is the autobiographical* My Life and Hard Times *(1933).*

1 The offices of *The New Yorker* were constantly being altered on Editor Harold Ross's orders and the sound of hammering and drilling filled the air as partitions were moved around by squads of workmen. Thurber once hung up a sign outside the elevator that read: "ALTERATIONS GOING ON AS USUAL DURING BUSINESS."

2 When *The Secret Life of Walter Mitty,* with Danny Kaye in the title role, became a hit movie, Sam Goldwyn decided that he would like to have Thurber as a permanent part of his team of writers. He tried to lure Thurber to Hollywood with an offer of $500 a week.

Thurber, quite content to go on working for Harold Ross at *The New Yorker,* wrote back after a decent interval, declining Goldwyn's offer with "Mr. Ross has met the increase." Goldwyn wrote again, raising the offer to $1,000 a week, then $1,500, and finally $2,500. On each occasion the response was the same. Goldwyn decided to drop the matter for a while. Then one day he wrote again, but this time the offer had dropped to $1,500. Back came Thurber's reply: "I am sorry, but Mr. Ross has met the decrease."

3 (Some of Thurber's talent for joking may have been inherited from his mother, Mary Agnes Fisher Thurber.)

"One of her finer moments in prankishness came when she borrowed a wheelchair at a faith-healing meeting, rolled down the aisle, suddenly stood up, and proclaimed that she could walk. With hallelujahs sounding about her, she fled on foot as the owner of the wheelchair recognized his property."

4 One of Thurber's favorite stories concerned a conversation he had with a nurse while he was in the hospital. "What seven-letter word has three *u*'s in it?" he asked her. The nurse pondered and then said, "I don't know, but it must be unusual."
Compare GEORGE BERNARD SHAW 12.

5 At a party a woman lurched drunkenly up to Thurber and told him she would like to have a baby by him. "Surely you don't mean by unartificial insemination!" protested Thurber.

6 At another cocktail party a woman waxed enthusiastic over Thurber's work, saying that she found it even funnier in French than in English. "Yes, I always seem to lose something in the original," agreed Thurber.

7 Thurber and a friend attended the premiere of a Hollywood spectacular. As they were leaving the theater, Thurber inquired what his companion had thought of the movie. "Well, not to mince words, I thought it stank," was the response. "I can't say I liked it that well," murmured Thurber thoughtfully.

8 Having overdrawn his bank account, Thurber was summoned to a meeting with the bank manager. The humorist freely admitted that he kept no record of the checks he wrote. "Then how do you know how much money is in your account?" asked the manager. "I thought that was *your* business," retorted Thurber.

9 Thurber attended a friend's party after he had lost his sight. As a certain couple departed, he remarked to his host, "They're going to break up."

"That's not possible!" exclaimed his friend. "I've never seen such friendliness and smiling."

"Yes," said Thurber, "you *saw* them. I *heard* them."

Six months later, the couple separated.

10 In the fall of 1961 Thurber underwent surgery for a blood clot on the brain. He made a partial recovery but then contracted pneumonia and died on the afternoon of November 2. According to legend, his last words were: "God bless . . . God damn."
See also HAROLD ROSS 12.

THURLOW, Edward, 1st Baron (1731–1806), *British statesman, lord chancellor (1778–83, 1783–92). Thurlow's commanding presence and powers of patronage made him an important political force. Charles James Fox said of him: "No man ever was as wise as Thurlow looks."*

1 As an undergraduate at Gonville and Caius College, Cambridge, Thurlow was principally distinguished for his idleness and unruliness. His tutor summoned him and began to rebuke him: "Sir, I never come to the window but I see you idling in the court." Adopting the tutor's tone, Thurlow replied, "Sir, I never come into the court but I see you idling at the window."

2 As lord chancellor, Thurlow held the disposal of a number of church benefices and so was constantly being approached by various eminent people who wished him to confer such wealthy benefices, or livings, on their protégés. One day a poor country curate came to his office. Thurlow addressed him in his usual brusque manner: who was he? what did he want? in which lord's name did he come? and so on. The curate stammered out his name and the name of the parish for which he had come to apply. "I have no interest, my lord," he said, "and I come to you in no lord's name, but in the name of the Lord of Hosts."

"The Lord of Hosts!" said Thurlow. "The Lord of Hosts! You are the first person to apply to me in that lord's name, and I'll be damned if you don't have the living."

3 The lord chancellor and a certain bishop had the right to take turns in presenting a particular living. Thurlow got into an argument with the bishop as to whose turn it was to make the presentation. Eventually the bishop sent his secretary along to see Thurlow. The secretary said, transmitting his superior's compliments, that he believed the next turn belonged to the bishop. Thurlow replied, "Give your lord my compliments and tell him that I will see him damned before he shall present." The secretary turned pale. "My lord, this is a very unpleasant message to have to give to a bishop." Thurlow considered. Then he said, "You are right. It is indeed. Tell my lord bishop that *I* will be damned before he shall present."

4 At the adjournment of the court for the long vacation, Lord Thurlow, failing to take the customary leave of the bar, was about to depart the room in silence. "He might at least have said 'Damn you,'" said a young barrister in a stage whisper. Thurlow heard, returned, and obliged.

ཞ ‒ᦡ

TINTORETTO [Jacopo Robusti] (1518–94), *Italian painter. His nickname, which means "little dyer," refers to his father's profession of silk-dyeing. Most of his masterpieces were executed in Venice.*

1 The satirist Aretino was a highly partisan supporter of the other great Venetian painter of the High Renaissance, Titian. He lost no opportunity to jeer at the dyer's young son. When Tintoretto began to obtain commissions that Aretino considered should have been Titian's, the satirist doubled his venom, Tintoretto's poverty and pride making him an easy target. Tintoretto let it be known that he was willing to paint Aretino's portrait gratis, an offer Aretino could not resist. He went to his victim's studio, took a chair, and struck a pose. "Stand up," ordered Tintoretto. "First I must measure you." Aretino stood, and Tintoretto came toward him, drawing out a long horse-pistol, which he ran slowly over his sitter. "I find you are two and a half pistols tall," the painter concluded. "Now — go!" From that time on, Tintoretto had no further trouble with Aretino.

ཞ ‒ᦡ

TITIAN (c. 1488–1576), *Italian painter who worked mainly in Venice. He painted numerous formal portraits, mythological scenes, and religious works. Many of his female subjects have hair of "Titian red," a deep rich auburn color.*

1 The Duchess of Urbino, although ugly and advanced in years, persuaded her husband to commission Titian to paint her in the nude. As Titian was reluctant, his friend, the satirist and poet Pietro Aretino, suggested a way around the problem. They hired a prostitute, a girl with an exquisitely beautiful figure, to pose for the body, and Titian produced an idealized portrait of the duchess for the head. She was delighted, particularly as the picture was christened *The Venus of Urbino.* When it was shown to the duke, he sighed and said, "If I could have had that girl's body, even with my wife's head, I would have been a happier man." Aretino, to whom this remark was addressed, laughed so much that he suffered a stroke and died.

See PIETRO ARETINO 1.

2 When very old, Titian finished one of his masterpieces, laid down his brush, and said, "I think I am beginning to learn something about painting."

ཞ ‒ᦡ

TOLSTOY, Leo [Nikolaevich], **Count** (1828–1910), *Russian writer. After an aimless existence as a young man about town in Moscow and an officer in the Crimean War, Tolstoy returned to his family estate of Yasnaya Polyana, where he began the social experiments that were to take up much of the rest of his life. His marriage to Sonya Bers (1862) led to the creative period in which he produced* War and Peace *(1865–69) and* Anna Karenina *(1875–77). From 1880 he lived according to a doctrine compounded of pacifism and asceticism.*

1 In his last hours Tolstoy firmly resisted the efforts of those who tried to persuade him to reconcile himself with the Russian Orthodox church. "Even in the valley of the shadow of death, two and two do not make six," he said.

❧

TOOKE, John Horne (1736–1812), *British radical politician and philologist. Horne Tooke founded the Society for Constitutional Information (1771) to campaign for parliamentary reform. His support of the French Revolution occasioned his trial (1794) for high treason; he was acquitted.*

1   When Tooke was at school, a master asked him in a grammar lesson why a certain verb governed a particular case. "I don't know," answered Tooke. "That is impossible," said the master. "I know you're not ignorant, but obstinate." Tooke, however, persisted in saying that he didn't know, so the master beat him. The beating over, the master quoted the rule that covered the verb in question. "Oh, I know that," said Tooke at once, "but you asked me the *reason,* not the *rule.*"

2   Horne Tooke was advised to take a wife. "With all my heart," said he. "Whose wife shall it be?"

{Also told of Tom, son of Richard Brinsley Sheridan.}

❧

TOSCANINI, Arturo (1867–1957), *Italian conductor. He conducted at La Scala, Milan, and the Metropolitan Opera, New York, and from 1937 until his death was conductor of the NBC Symphony Orchestra.*

1   During a rehearsal Toscanini flew into a tantrum with a player and ended by ordering him from the stage. As the man reached the exit he turned around and shouted, "Nuts to you!"

"It's too late to apologize," yelled back Toscanini.

{This retort is also, wrongly, attributed to Sergei Koussevitzky.}

2   A trumpet player had attracted Toscanini's wrath during a rehearsal. "God tells me how the music should sound," shouted the exasperated conductor, "but *you* stand in the way!"

3   Just before a concert a clarinetist came up to Toscanini and said that he would be unable to play since the E-natural key on his instrument was broken. Toscanini thought deeply for a moment and then announced, "It's all right; you don't have an E natural tonight."

{There are many other tales of Toscanini's extraordinary musical memory.}

4   Every Christmas, composer Giacomo Puccini would have a cake baked for each of his friends. One year, having quarreled with Toscanini just before Christmas, he tried to cancel the order for the conductor's cake. But it was too late — the cake had already been dispatched. The following day, Toscanini received a telegram from Puccini: "Cake sent by mistake." He replied by return: "Cake eaten by mistake."

5   Puccini having died shortly before finishing his opera *Turandot,* the work was completed for performance by Franco Alfano. When Toscanini, who had a profound reverence for Puccini's music, used to conduct *Turandot,* he always laid down his baton at the point in the last act at which Puccini broke off. "Here died the maestro," he would announce to the audience, and two minutes' silence would then be kept before Toscanini launched into Alfano's finale.

6   Exasperated by the shortcomings of an orchestra, Toscanini suddenly burst out, "When I retire, I open a bordello. You know what that is? Or are you all *castrati?* I will attract the most beautiful women in the world for my bordello — it will be the La Scala of passion. But I will lock the door against *every one of you!*"

7   Toscanini used to sing with the orchestra during rehearsals. Engrossed in the music, he sometimes forgot about this habit. At Salzburg once during a dress rehearsal, his voice could be heard above the instruments. Suddenly he stopped the orchestra and exclaimed, "For the love of God, who's singing here?"

8   The orchestra's librarian was vexed by Toscanini's habit of hurling valuable scores at the orchestra if things went badly during a rehearsal. Observing him closely, he noticed that the conductor's first action when enraged was to take his baton in both hands and attempt to snap it. If the baton snapped, Toscanini usually calmed down and the rehearsal went on; if it did not, he began throwing scores.

The librarian therefore arranged for a supply of relatively flimsy batons to be available during rehearsals. If things went badly, Toscanini might break as many as six batons and the librarian would have to send for spares. "Lumber, lumber," he would shout to his assistant.

9   Arriving at a town on July 3 during a South American tour with the NBC Symphony Orchestra, Toscanini told the disgruntled players that he wished them to assemble at the theater the following morning. The players, who had been traveling for some time, were looking forward to a couple of days' rest from rehearsals. They obeyed with an ill grace. When they were assembled, Toscanini asked them to rise and led them through "The Star-Spangled Banner." "Today is the Fourth of July," he announced at the end, and dismissed them.

10   During a rehearsal of Debussy's *La Mer,* Toscanini found himself unable to describe the effect he hoped to achieve from a particular passage. After a moment's thought, he took a silk handkerchief from his pocket and tossed it high into the air. The orchestra, mesmerized, watched the slow, graceful descent of the silken square. Toscanini smiled with satisfaction as it finally settled on the floor. "There," he said, "play it like that."

ॐ ॐ

TOSTI, Francesco Paolo (1846–1916), *Italian musician and composer who became singing master to the British Royal Family. His charming drawing-room songs, notably "Good-bye!," were very popular.*

1   The young sons of Tosti's friend Mrs. Seligman used their own word, "gobinghi," to describe anything that was ordinary or mundane, and Tosti picked the word up from the little boys. Once at a dinner party at which the company promised to be rather boring, Tosti observed in Italian to Mrs. Seligman, "There're a large number of gobinghi here."

"Oh, you naughty man," said the hostess coyly, "you forget I know Italian and I understand every word you say."

"Not *every* word," said Tosti.

ॐ ॐ

TOWNSHEND, Charles (1725–67), *British politician; chancellor of the exchequer (1766–67). His premature death prevented him from seeing the catastrophic consequences of his unpopular taxes on the American colonies.*

1   A certain James Harris, author of some moralistic treatises and a once-celebrated book on a universal grammar, was elected to Parliament. After he had made his maiden speech, Townshend demanded to know who he was. "Mr. Harris of Salisbury, who has written a very ingenious book of grammar and another on virtue," someone informed him. "What the devil brings him here?" Townshend demanded. "I am sure he will find neither the one nor the other in the House of Commons."

ॐ ॐ

TRACY, Spencer (1900–67), *US film actor. His films include* Boy's Town *(1938),* Father of the Bride *(1950), and* The Old Man and the Sea *(1958). He frequently co-starred with Katharine Hepburn, notably in* Adam's Rib *(1949),* Pat and Mike *(1952), and* Guess Who's Coming to Dinner *(1967).*

1   When asked what he looked for in a script, Tracy's immediate reply was, "Days off."

2   Tracy was asked by director Garson Kanin why he always insisted on first billing when he co-starred in films with Katharine Hepburn. "Why not?" asked Tracy. "Well, after all," reasoned Kanin, "she's the lady and you're the man. Ladies first?" Retorted Tracy: "This is a movie, not a lifeboat."

3   When a young actor asked Spencer Tracy for help with his acting, Tracy gave some of the most valuable advice to date: "Just learn your lines and don't bump into the furniture."

ॐ ॐ

TRAVERS, William R. (1819–87), *US lawyer and wit.*

1   A bore who had been discoursing tediously throughout dinner turned to William Travers and inquired, "Do you think oysters have brains?"

"Y-y-yes," Travers replied in his celebrated stutter. "J-j-just enough b-b-brains to k-k-keep their mouths s-s-shut."

2 Travers was in a group of people watching the end of a yacht race at Newport. As boat after boat glided across the finish line, the names of the owners were announced — every one of them a wealthy stockbroker. Gazing at the glittering flotilla, Travers piped up, "And w-w-where are the c-c-customers' yachts?"

৯৬ ৩৬

TREE, Sir Herbert Beerbohm (1853–1917), *British actor and theater manager, known especially for his Shakespearean roles. He was Sir Max Beerbohm's half-brother.*

1 Tree was directing a rehearsal of a play in which he felt that the actresses, with their rather sophisticated appearance, had not captured the essential spirit of their roles. Stopping them, he said, "Ladies, just a little more virginity, if you don't mind."

2 Encountering a man one day in the street staggering under the weight of a grandfather clock, Tree stopped him and inquired, "My good man, why not carry a watch?"
{There are numerous versions of this story, more or less circumstantial, attributed to several people.}

3 Tree showed Max Beerbohm a letter that he had received from an admirer who had seen him act the night before. Max read it and commented, "That's very nice."
"Very," said Tree happily. "I can stand any amount of flattery so long as it's fulsome enough."

4 One of the more bizarre productions of the silent-film era was a version of *Macbeth* produced in 1916 by D. W. Griffith, who was ambitious to raise the cultural standing of the film industry. Cast in the title role, Tree did not take easily to the medium; it is said that on the first day of shooting he pointed to the camera and said, "Take that black box away. I can't act in front of it."
{Tree eventually became accustomed to the presence of the camera. He categorically refused, however, to cut any of Shakespeare's text, despite the fact that none of it would be heard. To avoid wasting expensive film, the director was obliged to tell the cameraman to pull the crank out of the camera until it was necessary to shoot some action.}

5 During the rehearsal of a scene that was not working out too well, Tree directed a young actor to step back a little. The man did so. After a while Tree stopped the rehearsal again: "A little further back, please." Again the actor did as he was bidden and the rehearsal carried on. Tree stopped it a third time: "Further back still," he requested. "But if I go any further back, I'll be right off the stage," protested the actor. "Yes, that's right," said Tree.

6 The writer Hesketh Pearson was once waiting to speak to Tree at His Majesty's Theatre in London. Another man, a stranger to Pearson, was also present on the same mission. When Tree finally arrived, he looked at the two men for a moment, then sat down between them. "Consider yourselves introduced," he said, "because I only remember one of your names, and that wouldn't be fair to the other."

7 Tree had little money sense, and his financial manager at the Haymarket Theatre was constantly warning him against being overgenerous. As an example of unnecessary expenditure, he once cited Tree's habit of taking him to lunch at the Carlton every day and paying the bill out of petty cash. Tree thanked him for his advice and promised immediate reform. At lunchtime that day, he dutifully took his manager to a nearby teashop and said to the waitress, "Madam, will you please give this gentleman a nice glass of milk and a large bun." Then, turning to his colleague, Tree said amicably, "Pick me up at the Carlton when you have had enough — but do have enough."

8 Tree once had cause to criticize a young actor for his overbearing conceit. "I assure you, sir," retorted the actor indignantly, "that I am not suffering from a swelled head."
"It isn't the swelling that causes suffering," remarked Tree. "It's the subsequent shrinkage that hurts."

৯৬ ৩৬

TRENCH, Richard Chenevix (1807–86), *British divine and biblical scholar. He was dean of Westminster (1856–64) and archbishop of Dublin (1864–84).*

1 In 1875 a fall fractured both of Trench's knees, after which he never fully recovered his health, living in fear of paralysis. A lady sitting next to him at dinner noticed that the elderly cleric was agitated and muttering to himself, "It's come at last; I can't feel a thing; I'm paralyzed." She asked Trench what was wrong. "I've been pinching my leg for the last five minutes and I can't feel a thing," he replied. "I must be paralyzed." The lady colored. "It's all right, Your Grace," she said, "it's my leg you've been pinching."

2 In 1884 Trench resigned his archbishopric on grounds of ill health. Some time later his successor invited him and Mrs. Trench back for a short stay at the bishop's palace in Dublin. Feeling comfortable and at home in the house where he had lived for so long, Trench forgot that he was not the host. At a meal at which the food was rather poor he suddenly boomed out across the table to his wife, "My dear, you must count this cook as one of your failures."

TRILLING, Lionel (1905–76), *US educator and author. Professor of English at Columbia University, he wrote many works of criticism, including* The Liberal Imagination *(1950) and* Mind in the Modern World *(1972).*

1 "The erudite Lionel Trilling and the erudite Jacques Barzun [also a Columbia proffessor] got into a punning match when a student, discussing Malthus's *Essay on Population,* cited the motto of the Order of the Garter, *Honi soit qui mal y pense*— 'Shame on him who imputes ill to it.' Barzun remarked, 'Honi soit que Malthus pense.' Trilling rejoined, 'Honi soit qui mal thus puns.'"

TROLLOPE, Anthony (1815–82), *British novelist. He worked most of his life for the Post Office, and his many novels were mainly written between 5:30 A.M. and breakfast, before he left for work. His greatest works fall into two series: the Barsetshire novels, which center on the clergymen and their families in an imaginary cathedral city, and the political novels, which deal with high-society life.*

1 Michael Sadleir describes Trollope as one "scarcely giving himself time to think, but spluttering and roaring out an instantly-formed opinion couched in the very strongest of terms." At a meeting of surveyors, Trollope suddenly fired at the speaker who preceded him, "I disagree with you entirely. What was it you said?"

2 A lady sitting next to Trollope at dinner observed that he helped himself liberally from every dish that was offered to him. "You seem to have a very good appetite, Mr. Trollope," she remarked, rather impertinently. "None at all, madam," he replied, "but, thank God, I am very greedy."

3 The character of Mrs. Proudie, the insufferable wife of the bishop of Barchester, in the Barsetshire novels is one of Trollope's greatest successes. In his *Autobiography* he owns to taking great delight in his creation of her. One morning he was sitting writing in the drawing room of his London club, the Athenaeum, when he overheard two clergymen talking about his work. They were complaining that in different books Trollope kept on introducing the same characters again and again. "If I could not invent new characters, I would not write novels at all," said one. Then the other began to complain about Mrs. Proudie. This was too much for Trollope, who approached them, confessing that he was the author of the novels they were criticizing. "As to Mrs. Proudie, I will go home and kill her before the week is over," he promised. The two clergymen, much embarrassed, begged Trollope to overlook their comments, but Trollope kept his word. The novel he was working on was *The Last Chronicle of Barset,* and in it he describes the sudden and shocking death of his old favorite, Mrs. Proudie.

4 (In 1858 the Post Office dispatched Trollope to the West Indies with the title of "missioner" to investigate and make suggestions for reorganizing the postal system in Britain's Caribbean and Central American colonies.)
"Trollope was determined to prove that a certain distance could be covered on muleback in two days. The local postal authorities declared that the journey would take three, and to support their claim purposely provided the troublesome visitor with an uncomfortable saddle. In consequence the first day's ride reduced the missioner to the extremes of raw discomfort. The morrow (if he were to carry his point) must be another, equally fatiguing day. Only one remedy was possible, and that a

drastic one. He ordered two bottles of brandy, poured them into a washbasin, and sat in it."

੭ ੭

TROLLOPE, Frances (1780–1863), *British novelist, traveler, and mother of Anthony Trollope. Forced to support her family by writing, she published some well-received novels, including* The Widow Barnaby *(1838).*

1   There was constant friction between Mrs. Trollope and the local vicar, a well-known evangelical called J. W. Cunningham. Objecting to Mrs. Trollope's allowing her daughters to act charades at parties, he asked whether she considered play-acting a suitable amusement for young ladies. "Why not?" said Mrs. Trollope. "Mrs. Cunningham has evening parties at which we are always glad to hear your daughters play the piano."

"Yes," said the vicar, "but they always keep their backs to the audience."

2   (The novelist Sabine Baring-Gould remembers meeting Mrs. Trollope at Pau one winter when she was a child and Mrs. Trollope an old lady.)

"The English residents were not a little shy of her, fearing lest she should take stock of them and use them up in one of her novels; for she had the character of delineating members of her acquaintance, and that not to their advantage. Someone asked her whether this was not her practice. 'Of course,' answered Mrs. Trollope, 'I draw from life — but I always pulp my acquaintances before serving them up. You would never recognize a pig in a sausage.'"

੭ ੭

TROTSKY, Leon [Lev Davidovich Bronstein] (1879–1940), *Russian revolutionary. With Lenin he organized the November Revolution. Elected commissar for war, he created the Red Army. He fell from favor after Lenin's death in 1924, and was finally expelled by Stalin (1929). He was assassinated in Mexico City.*

1   A Russian émigré in Vienna during World War I, Trotsky spent much of his time playing chess in the Café Central and was regarded by those who knew him as a harmless, almost pathetic figure. In March 1917, the Austrian foreign minister was informed by an excited official that revolution had broken out in Russia.

"Russia is not a land where revolutions break out," said the minister skeptically, dismissing the credulous young man. "Besides, who on earth would make a revolution in Russia? Perhaps Herr Trotsky from the Café Central?"

੭ ੭

TROY, Hugh (1906–64), *US artist and practical joker.*

1   In 1935 the Museum of Modern Art sponsored the first American exhibition of van Gogh's art. Troy suspected that many of the vast crowds of people who thronged to the show were more attracted by the sensational details of van Gogh's life than sincerely interested in his art. He made a replica of an ear out of chipped beef and had it mounted in a little blue velvet display case. Under it was a card reading: "This was the ear that Vincent van Gogh cut off and sent to his mistress, a French prostitute, 24 December 1888." The ear was placed on a table in the gallery and was immediately a prime draw for the crowd.

੭ ੭

TRUDEAU, Edward Livingston (1848–1915), *pioneer in the fight against tuberculosis.*

1   "Many patients came to Dr. Trudeau with insufficient funds. 'Doctor,' said one of them, 'before you do anything — I have very little money. . . . How much will it cost?'

"'Depends on how much you've got, and how sick you are.' He prepared to examine the

---

"James (Quick) Tillis, the young heavyweight . . . is a cowboy from Oklahoma who now fights out of Chicago. He still remembers his first day in the Windy City after his arrival from Tulsa.

"'I got off the bus with two cardboard suitcases under my arms in downtown Chicago and stopped in front of the Sears Tower,' Tillis said. 'I put the suitcases down, and I looked up at the Tower and I said to myself, I'm going to conquer Chicago.'

"'When I looked down, the suitcases were gone.'"

— *Los Angeles Times,* July 25, 1981

patient's chest. 'You see, it's this way. If you're not very sick, it will cost you quite a lot, so I can use the money on those who *are* very sick.' He proceeded to the examination. 'But if you're in a bad way, why—'

"'How bad am I, doctor?'

"'Quiet, please.' Trudeau finished the examination. And then, his face flooded with tenderness, he handed his patient a ten-dollar bill. 'It will help a bit in the days ahead.'"

৯৯ ৫৩

TRUDEAU, Pierre Elliott (1919–), *Canadian statesman; Liberal prime minister (1968–79, 1980–84). He opposed French separatism, despite his own French Canadian background, and dealt with separatist agitation in Quebec (1970) by imposing a period of martial law.*

1 Trudeau faced some criticism when opposition members learned that anonymous donors were financing a new swimming pool at the prime minister's official residence in Ottawa. "You may come over at any time to practice your diving," Trudeau told one of his opponents. "Even before the water is in."

৯৯ ৫৩

TRUMAN, Harry S. (1884–1972), *US statesman; 33d president of the United States (1945–53). Shortly after taking office upon the death of Franklin Roosevelt, he ordered the atomic bombing of two Japanese cities to end the war with Japan. In foreign policy he initiated the Truman Doctrine, sending military and economic aid to states threatened with interference from other powers. His Marshall Plan (1948) assisted Europe's postwar recovery, and he promoted the formation of the North Atlantic Treaty Organization (NATO). His Fair Deal program for domestic reform achieved improvements in old-age benefits and slum clearance.*

1 Truman had accepted the vice presidency with extreme reluctance. On April 12, 1945, he was summoned to the White House. There he was shown into Eleanor Roosevelt's sitting room and she told him gently that President Roosevelt was dead. After a moment's stunned silence, Truman asked her, "Is there anything I can do for you?"

She shook her head. "Is there anything *we* can do for *you?*" she said. "For you're the one in trouble now."

2 In December 1950 President Truman's daughter, Margaret, gave a public singing recital in Washington, which was unenthusiastically received by Paul Hume, the *Washington Post*'s music critic. He characterized her voice as having "little size and fair quality," said she sang flat much of the time, and complained that there were "few moments . . . when one can relax and feel confident that she will make her goal, which is the end of the song."

Truman penned the following letter: "I have just read your lousy review buried in the back pages. You sound like a frustrated old man who never made a success, an eight-ulcer man on a four-ulcer job, and all four ulcers working. I have never met you, but if I do you'll need a new nose and plenty of beefsteak and perhaps a supporter below. Westbrook Pegler, a guttersnipe, is a gentleman compared to you. You can take that as more of an insult than as a reflection on your ancestry."

{This letter was made public and caused a considerable furor, but most Americans seem generally to have approved Truman's fatherly readiness to leap to his daughter's defense.}

3 After Truman had referred to a certain politician's speech as "a bunch of horse manure," it was suggested to Bess Truman that she persuade her husband to tone down his language. Mrs. Truman replied, "You don't know how many years it took me to tone it down to that!"

{This is one of many variants of a probably apocryphal story.}

4 It may have been Truman who started the joke about one-handed economists. "All my economists say, 'on the one hand . . . on the other.' Give me a one-handed economist!"

5 As president, Truman kept two signs on his desk. One quoted Mark Twain: "Always do right. This will gratify some people and astonish the rest." The other read, "The buck stops here."

6 During an informal discussion with Truman, an eager young student asked, "How do I get started in politics, sir?"

"You've already started," replied the former president. "You're spending somebody else's money, aren't you?"

7 In her book *Souvenir* Margaret Truman recalls the Christmas of 1955. The president found his wife at the fireplace disposing of letters he had written to her over the years. "But think of history," he protested. "I *have*," replied Bess.

{Actually hundreds of these letters were saved; a selection is available in *Dear Bess: The Letters from Harry to Bess Truman, 1910–1959*, edited by Robert H. Ferrell.}

≈≈ ≈≈

TRUTH, Sojourner [Isabella Van Wagener] (c. 1797–1883), *US evangelist, abolitionist, feminist, and orator. During the Reconstruction period following the US Civil War she helped in the resettlement of emancipated slaves.*

1 Sojourner Truth was one of the first blacks to test the streetcar antidiscrimination law in Washington D.C. Having failed to get a trolley to stop for her when she signaled, she shouted at the top of her voice, "I want to ride! I want to ride! *I want to ride!*" A large crowd gathered, and the streetcar was unable to continue on its way. Sojourner Truth jumped aboard and was told by the angry conductor to go forward to where the horses were or he would put her out. Truth sat down quietly and informed the conductor that she was a passenger and would not be bullied: "As a citizen of the Empire State of New York, I know the law as well as you do." So saying, she rode the car to the end of the line and left it with the words, "Bless God! I have had a ride."

≈≈ ≈≈

TURNER, Joseph Mallord William (1775–1851), *British landscape painter. His later work is remarkable for its brilliant use of color, shown in such masterpieces as* The Fighting Téméraire *and his Venetian scenes.*

1 A naval officer complained to Turner that the ships in his view of Plymouth had no portholes. The painter retorted, "My business is to paint not what I know, but what I see."

2 Handed a salad at the table, Turner remarked to his neighbor, "Nice cool green, that lettuce, isn't it? and the beetroot pretty red — not quite strong enough; and the mixture, delicate tint of yellow that. Add some mustard, and then you have one of my pictures."

3 Other artists loathed being hung next to Turner at exhibitions, as the brilliance of his colors had a disastrous effect on the pictures on either side. When *Cologne* was hung between two paintings by Sir Thomas Lawrence, the great portraitist complained so bitterly that Turner good-naturedly toned down the golden sky in his painting to an overall dullness. "What have you done to your picture?" asked a friend in horror when he saw the change. "Well, poor Lawrence was so unhappy," explained Turner. "It's only lampblack. It'll all wash off after the exhibition."

4 Turner always regretted selling his paintings and would wear an expression of woe for days after a sale. "I've lost one of my children this week," he would explain.

5 The watercolorist Thomas Girtin was the exact contemporary of Turner, and their talents for evoking atmosphere by use of color were astonishingly similar. When Girtin died young in 1802, Turner observed in his characteristically generous way, "If Girtin had lived, I would have starved."

6 One of Turner's most famous and popular pictures was his painting of the fire that destroyed the old Houses of Parliament in 1834. It is remarkable for its evocation of an immensely complex scene caught at a moment of high drama. First exhibited at the British Institution, it was hung in a far from complete state. For three hours before the public were admitted, Turner worked busily on it. When he had finished, he just walked away, never turning his head to have a look at the completed picture. The historical painter Daniel Maclise, who witnessed this extraordinary scene, observed, "There, that's masterly; he does not stop to look at his work; he *knows* it is done and he is off."

≈≈ ≈≈

TWAIN, Mark [Samuel Langhorne Clemens] (1835–1910), *US humorist, writer, and lecturer. As a boy living on the banks of the Mississippi, he became enchanted with the romance of life on the great river. Although apprenticed to a printer at an early age, he never did settle down to any one profession, but made his living as a river pilot, a prospector in the Far West, a newspaper reporter. When he finally began writing in* *earnest, he took his pseudonym from the river-man's term for water just barely deep enough for safe navigation.* Tom Sawyer *(1876) and* Huckleberry Finn *(1884) are considered the masterpieces in his prolific output. As writer and lecturer Mark Twain projected an enormously popular shrewd and comic persona. Consequently, innumerable anecdotes have become attached to him.*

1   In order to apply for the post of reporter-at-large on the *Territorial Enterprise,* Samuel Clemens walked 130 miles to Virginia City in Nevada Territory. He arrived at the newspaper's offices one hot afternoon in August, a dust-covered, weary stranger in a slouch hat, with a revolver slung on his belt, and a roll of blankets on his back. He wore a blue woolen shirt and dusty trousers tucked into his boots. Dropping into a chair, he announced, "My starboard leg seems to be unshipped. I'd like about one hundred yards of line; I think I am falling to pieces." He added, "My name is Clemens, and I've come to write for the paper."

{Albert Bigelow Paine commented, "It was the master of the world's widest estate come to claim his kingdom."}

2   When Mark Twain was an impoverished young reporter in Virginia City, he was walking along the street one day with a cigar box under his arm. He encountered a wealthy lady he knew who said to him reproachfully, "You promised me that you would give up smoking."

"Madam," replied Twain, "this box does not contain cigars. I'm just moving."

3   As a cub reporter, Mark Twain was told never to state as fact anything that he could not personally verify. Following this instruction to the letter, he wrote the following account of a gala social event: "A woman giving the name of Mrs. James Jones, who is reported to be one of the society leaders of the city, is said to have given what purported to be a party yesterday to a number of alleged ladies. The hostess claims to be the wife of a reputed attorney."

4   On board ship on an expedition to the Holy Land, Clemens made the acquaintance of Charles J. Langdon, a young man from Elmira, New York, who was a great admirer of his. At some point Langdon showed him a miniature of his sister, Olivia. Clemens could not forget her face and resolved to meet her. He later maneuvered an invitation to visit the Langdon home for a week, and in that week he fell thoroughly for Livy, as the family called her. On the last day of his visit he said to Langdon, "Charley, my week is up, and I must go home." Langdon did not press him to stay longer, but said, "We'll have to stand it, I guess, but you mustn't leave before tonight."

"I ought to go by the first train," said Clemens gloomily. "I am in love."

"In what?"

"In love—with your sister, and I ought to get away from here."

Langdon was now genuinely alarmed: no one was good enough for his sister, the family's darling. "Look here, Clemens," he said, "there's a train in half an hour. I'll help you catch it. Don't wait till tonight. Go now."

{In fact, Clemens did stay until after dinner. He and Langdon were about to set off for the station when the seat of their wagon, not properly locked into place, threw them into the street. Neither was seriously hurt; Clemens was only dazed, but made sure that he did not recover too quickly. He was taken back into the house, where he remained for another two weeks. Livy did become his wife.}

5   Mark Twain's wife did her best to censor the more picturesque flights of her husband's language. One morning he cut himself shaving and cursed long and loud. When he stopped, his wife tried to shame him by repeating to him verbatim all the profanities that he had just uttered. Twain heard her out and then remarked, "You have the words, my dear, but I'm afraid you'll never master the tune."

6   A businessman notorious for his ruthlessness announced to Mark Twain, "Before I die I mean to make a pilgrimage to the Holy Land. I will climb Mount Sinai and read the Ten Commandments aloud at the top."

"I have a better idea," said Twain. "You could stay home in Boston and keep them."

7   Arriving at a small town in the course of a lecture tour, Mark Twain went to the local barbershop for a shave, and told the barber that it was his first visit to the town. "You've chosen a good time to come," said the barber. "Mark Twain is going to lecture here tonight. You'll want to go, I suppose?"

"I guess so," responded Twain.

"Have you bought your ticket yet?"

"No, not yet."

"Well, it's sold out, so you'll have to stand."

"Just my luck," said Twain with a sigh. "I always have to stand when that fellow lectures."

{Calvin Coolidge was also very much aware that he didn't get a seat at his own lectures. *See* COOLIDGE 8.}

8   There were always cats at Mark Twain's farm, and favorite cats had their own names — Blatherskite, Sour Mash, Stray Kit, Sin, Satan. His children inherited his love of them. His daughter Susy once said, "The difference between Papa and Mamma is, that Mamma loves morals and Papa loves cats."

9   As Twain and his good friend the writer William Dean Howells were leaving church one Sunday, it started to rain heavily. Howells looked up at the clouds and said, "Do you think it will stop?"

"It always has," replied Twain.

10   When the printing plates were being prepared for the illustrations to *Huckleberry Finn,* a mischievous engraver (whose identity was never discovered despite the posting of a reward) made an addition to the picture of old Silas Phelps. He drew in a male sex organ, thus altering entirely the implications of the pictured Aunt Sally's question, "Who do you think it is?" The alteration was discovered only after thousands of the books had been printed and bound, and the offending illustration had to be cut out by hand and replaced.

11   After several attempts, Mark Twain at last obtained an appointment to see General Ulysses S. Grant at home. He was elated at this prospect, but when he actually confronted Grant and looked at that square, imperturbable, unsmiling face, he found himself, for the first time, unable to think of what to say. Grant, noted for his taciturnity, nodded slightly and waited. Mark Twain hesitated, and then inspiration came. "General," he said, "I seem to be a little embarrassed, are you?" This broke the ice, and there were no further difficulties.

Twelve years later the two men met again in Chicago, at a reception for General Grant after his world tour. Twain arrived in time for the large welcoming procession. On the way to the reviewing stand, the mayor of Chicago said, "General, let me present Mr. Clemens, a man almost as great as yourself." The two men shook hands, and there was a pause. Then the general looked at Twain gravely. "Mr. Clemens," he said, "*I* am not embarrassed, are you?" They both laughed.

12   Mark Twain often did his writing in bed, regardless of the time of day. On one occasion his wife came in to tell him that a reporter had arrived to interview him. When Twain showed no sign of being ready to get up, she said, "Don't you think it will be a little embarrassing for him to find you in bed?"

"Why, if you think so, Livy," Twain responded, "we could have the other bed made up for him."

13   Henry Irving was telling Mark Twain a story. "You haven't heard this, have you?" he inquired after the preamble. Mark Twain assured him he had not. A little later Irving again paused and asked the same question. Mark Twain made the same answer. Irving then got almost to the climax of the tale before breaking off again — "Are you quite sure you haven't heard this?" The third time was too much for his listener. "I can lie once," said Twain, "I can lie twice for courtesy's sake, but I draw the line there. I can't lie the third time at any price. I not only heard the story, I invented it."

14   When Mark Twain was in London, a rumor of his death or imminent death reached the editor of the *New York Journal,* who sent its London correspondent the following cablegrams: "IF MARK TWAIN DYING IN POVERTY IN LONDON SEND 500 WORDS" and "IF MARK TWAIN HAS DIED IN POVERTY SEND 1000 WORDS." The *Journal*'s man showed the cables to Mark Twain, who suggested the substance of a reply to the effect that a cousin, James Ross Clemens, had been seriously ill in London, but had recovered. The reply ended with "REPORT OF MY DEATH GREATLY EXAGGERATED."

15   One night a group of Twain's friends and admirers in New York, remembering it was the writer's birthday, resolved to send him birthday greetings. The globe-trotting Twain was

away on his travels and none of them knew his address. So they mailed a letter superscribed "Mark Twain, God Knows Where." Some weeks later they received an acknowledgment reading simply: "He did."
Compare SIR HUMPHRY DAVY 1.

16   After attending a service conducted by Dr. Doane, later bishop of Albany, Mark Twain congratulated him on an enjoyable service. "I welcomed it as an old friend," he went on. "I have a book at home containing every word of it." Dr. Doane bristled. "I am sure you have not," he replied huffily. "Indeed I have," Twain persisted. "Well, I'd like to have a look at it then. Could you send it over to me?" The following day Twain sent him an unabridged dictionary.

17   A devotee of cigars, Mark Twain was contemptuous of those who made a great to-do about giving up smoking. He always claimed that it was easy to quit: "I've done it a hundred times!"

18   Mark Twain, careless about his dress, one day called on Harriet Beecher Stowe without his necktie. On his return Mrs. Clemens noticed the omission and scolded him. A little later a messenger turned up on Mrs. Stowe's doorstep and handed her a small package. Inside was a black necktie, and a note: "Here is a necktie. Take it out and look at it. I think I stayed half an hour this morning without this necktie. At the end of that time, will you kindly return it, as it is the only one I have. Mark Twain."

19   Mark Twain loved to brag about his hunting and fishing exploits. He once spent three weeks fishing in the Maine woods, regardless of the fact that it was the state's closed season for fishing. Relaxing in the lounge car of the train on his return journey to New York, his catch iced down in the baggage car, he looked for someone to whom he could relate the story of his successful holiday. The stranger to whom he began to boast of his sizable catch appeared at first unresponsive, then positively grim. "By the way, who are you, sir?" inquired Twain airily. "I'm the state game warden," was the unwelcome response. "Who are you?" Twain nearly swallowed his cigar. "Well, to be perfectly truthful, warden," he said hastily, "I'm the biggest damn liar in the whole United States."

20   Twain was tired of receiving photographs from men claiming to be his double. To cope with the heavy correspondence this entailed he composed the following form letter and had his printer run off a few hundred copies: "My dear Sir, I thank you very much for your letter and your photograph. In my opinion you are more like me than any other of my numerous doubles. I may even say that you resemble me more closely than I do myself. In fact, I intend to use your picture to shave by. Yours thankfully, S. Clemens."

21   "In a world without women," Twain was once asked, "what would men become?"
    "Scarce, sir," replied Twain. "Mighty scarce."

22   In later life Mark Twain suffered periodically from bronchitis and arthritis. Whenever the newspapers reported that he had had another attack, well-wishers would send him prescriptions, remedies, nostrums, and elixirs of life in the hope of bringing about his recovery. He had a standard reply for acknowledging these unsolicited items: "Dear Sir (or Madam), I try every remedy sent to me. I am now on No. 87. Yours is 2,653. I am looking forward to its beneficial results."

23   When Mark Twain was born in November 1835, Halley's comet blazed in the night sky. Twain often referred to this, and came to think of himself and the comet as "unaccountable freaks" which, having come in together, must go out together. He was right: when he died in April 1910, Halley's comet was again in the sky.

U

UCCELLO, Paolo (1397–1475), *Italian painter and craftsman who worked in Florence under the patronage of the Medicis. His paintings show his preoccupation with perspective and foreshortening.*

1 Uccello's fascination with perspective kept him up all night drawing elaborate polygons and other figures. When his wife tried to get him to come to bed, he responded, "What a delightful thing this perspective is!"

ULBRICHT, Walther (1893–1973), *East German statesman.*

1 Extolling the glories of the East German State, Ulbricht declared: "The millennium is on the horizon."

"That was a wonderful speech," an aide said to him afterward. "But is the millennium truly on the horizon?"

"Of course," said Ulbricht. "Don't you know the dictionary defines 'horizon' as 'an imaginary line which recedes as you approach it'?"

UNITAS, John (1933–), *US football player; quarterback and passing star in the National Football League (1956–63).*

1 The National Football League championship game of 1956, in which the Baltimore Colts defeated the New York Giants at New York's Yankee Stadium 23–17, was the first overtime game in league history. The Colts had entered the game favored by 3½ points: meaning that they had to win by more than 3½ points for bettors to win their bets. The teams were tied 17–17 at the end of regulation time. In overtime Unitas led the Colts within range of a three-point field goal, which would have won the game. Instead of going for the easier field goal, he went for a six-point touchdown. He completed a risky cross-field pass, then handed the ball to Alan Ameche, who ran across for the winning touchdown. Later Unitas was asked if the pass might not have been intercepted and run back for a winning touchdown the other way. "When you know what you're doing, they're not intercepted," he said. The questioner then asked why he had not called for a field goal. "I went for the touchdown," said Unitas with a grin, "because I had bet a few thousand on the game and I had given 3½ points."

UNTERMEYER, Louis (1885–1977), *US poet and writer. Besides producing many volumes of poetry and critical writings, he edited a number of poetry anthologies.*

1 Untermeyer once returned his speaker's fee to a small and impoverished group, enjoining them to put the money to good use. A little while later, happening to inquire what good use they had found for the money, he was told that they had put it into "a fund to get better speakers next year."

{This ancedote is told of others.}

2 At a New Year's Eve costume party Louis Untermeyer entered fully into the spirit of the thing, donning a funny paper hat and making an uproarious racket upon a horn. A student walked up, looked closely at him, then turned on her heel, snorting contemptuously, "And *he's* Required Reading!"

UNZELMANN, Karl Wilhelm Ferdinand (1753–1832), *German actor and singer.*

1 When Unzelmann was playing at the Berlin theater, the other actors found his ad libs so distracting that the management told him to stop. The following night, as he made his entrance on horseback, the horse committed an indiscretion. Laughter spread through the audience. "Don't you remember," said Unzelmann sternly to his steed, "that we are forbidden to improvise?"

ॐ ॐ

USTINOV, Peter (1921–), *British actor, director, playwright, and raconteur. His many film appearances include* Quo Vadis *(1951),* Spartacus *(1960), and* Death on the Nile *(1978). Among his plays are* Romanoff and Juliet *(1956), filmed in 1961, and* The Love of Four Colonels *(1951).*

1 As a father taking his very well-brought-up young daughter to the opera for the first time, Ustinov was unwise enough to choose the Baths of Caracalla in Rome. The opera was *Aida*: during one particular scene the whole stage seemed to be covered with animals — camels, elephants, horses, unwanted cats, and so on. At a climactic point, almost all the animals relieved themselves simultaneously. As he stared aghast at this incredible sight, Ustinov felt a light tapping on his shoulder, and his daughter's earnest voice —"Daddy, is it all right if I laugh?"

2 Ustinov once received an irate letter from the headmaster of his son's school. The boy persistently played the fool in lessons, making his classmates laugh, and it was felt that Ustinov should use his influence to control the child. Ustinov reminded the headmaster that the only reason he was able to afford the school's high fees was that he was paid for doing precisely the same thing.

❧ V ❧

VAN BUREN, Martin (1782–1862), *US politician, 8th president of the United States (1837–41). Though carefully groomed by his predecessor, Andrew Jackson, Van Buren was bedeviled by problems arising from Jackson's economic policies. He was glad to retire to his farm when defeated in the 1840 election.*

1 Van Buren was so obnoxious to the southern states that he received only nine popular votes there in his 1848 campaign, all from Virginia. His supporters raised a cry of fraud. "Yes, fraud," said a Virginian, "and we are still looking for the son-of-a-bitch who voted nine times."

❧ ❧

VANDERBILT, Alice (c. 1845–c. 1930), *wife of Cornelius Vanderbilt II, the financier.*

1 While having luncheon one day at the old Ambassador Hotel with her son Reggie and his new second wife, Gloria, Alice Vanderbilt enquired whether Gloria had received her pearls. When Reggie answered that he had not yet bought any because the only pearls worthy of his bride were far beyond his price, his mother calmly ordered that a pair of scissors be brought to her. When the scissors arrived, she proceeded to cut off about one-third of her own pearls, worth some $70,000, and handed them to her daughter-in-law. "There you are, Gloria," she said. "All Vanderbilt women have pearls."

❧ ❧

VANDERBILT, Cornelius (1794–1877), *US businessman. His nickname, "Commodore," derived from his ownership of a fleet of cargo schooners. He then turned to steamboats, competing in the Hudson River trade. After an adventurous decade establishing a New York-to-California line via Nicaragua, in the 1860s he developed an interest in railroad companies and by the time of his death had created a major American transportation system.*

1 After a prolonged absence from his office the commodore returned to find that Charles Morgan and C. K. Garrison, his associates in the Accessory Transit Company, had taken advantage of the power of attorney he had vested in them and had done considerable damage to his interests. Recovering from his initial rage, Vanderbilt dictated the following letter to them: "Gentlemen: You have undertaken to cheat me. I won't sue you, for the law is too slow. I'll ruin you."

{He did not quite succeed in ruining Morgan and Garrison, but he thwarted and humiliated them and regained control of his company.}

2 One of Vanderbilt's sons-in-law, needing $50,000 to set up a business, approached the commodore for the loan. The old man inquired how much he expected to make from the investment. "About five thousand a year," was the reply. "I can do better than that with fifty thousand dollars," said Vanderbilt. "Tell you what I'll do. I'll pay you five thousand a year hereafter, and you may consider yourself in my employ at that salary."

3 Cornelius Vanderbilt was an admirer of the famous and unconventional Woodhull sisters, one of whose interests was spiritualism. In his seventies he expressed a wish to get financial advice from his dead friend, Jim Fiske. Victoria Woodhull offered to contact his spirit. In the ensuing séance she managed to materialize the spirit of Vanderbilt's dead wife, Sophia. The old man was not interested. "Business before pleasure," he declared. "Let me speak to Jim."

VANDERBILT, William Henry (1821–85), *US railroad magnate, son of "Commodore" Cornelius Vanderbilt.*

1   William asked if he could buy the manure from his father's horse-car stables to enrich his land at New Dorp on Staten Island. The elder Vanderbilt agreed, and the price was settled at four dollars per load — a generous figure. A few weeks later, the commodore was surprised to learn from his son that only one load had been ferried across to the island; he had seen at least twenty wagonloads put on the scow. The younger Vanderbilt replied, "No, Father, I never let them put more than one load on at a time — one *scow* load, I mean." Cornelius was quick to realize that his son's talent could be put to better use and persuaded him to enter the world of finance.

2   A reporter cornered William Vanderbilt, head of the New York Central Railroad, declaring that the public had a right to know his mind on a particular issue. Vanderbilt pushed past him snapping, "The public be damned. I am working for my stockholders."

3   After William Vanderbilt's death his fortune was estimated at $200,000,000. Shortly before he died he said of this wealth, "I have had no real gratification or enjoyment of any sort more than my neighbor on the next block who is worth only half a million."

§

VAN DOREN, Mark (1894–1972), *US poet and literary critic. He was professor of English at Columbia University (1942–59).*

1   A bore once blundered in uninvited to a literary gathering hosted by Mark Van Doren, and immediately spread a pall of dullness over the whole party. After his departure the interloper became the topic of discussion. Someone observed that it must be heartbreaking for someone like that to see the face of everyone to whom he spoke freeze with distaste and boredom. "You forget that a person like that has never encountered any other kind of expression," said Van Doren.

2   A group of young men asked Van Doren what they should do with their lives. The professor was quite clear in his answer. "Whatever you want," he told them, "just so long as you don't miss the main thing!" When the young men asked what that was, he said simply, "Your own lives."

§

VARAH, Chad (1911–   ), *British clergyman. In 1953 he founded the Samaritans, a telephone service for the suicidal and despairing. The organization, which started with a single telephone, now has branches throughout the British Isles and the United States.*

1   When Chad Varah decided to start his telephone service for the despairing, he wanted to find a simple, easily remembered number that had something of an emergency feel about it. His center, in the crypt of the church of St. Stephen Walbrook, was in the Mansion House telephone area of London, so its telephone number would have the prefix MAN. Varah decided on MAN 9000. His next step was to find out from the Post Office whether the number was available for his use. Standing in the crypt, he noticed for the first time that there was a dusty old telephone in a corner. To his surprise, he found it was still working. He rang the Post Office telephone sales department and made his request. The Post Office clerk asked him from what number he was calling. Rubbing the center of the dial with his handkerchief, Varah was astounded to read the number — MAN 9000.

§

VATEL (?1622–71), *French chef.*

1   Louis XIV was to be the guest of honor at a dinner at Chantilly prepared by Vatel. The chef, having ordered a large quantity of fish from the nearest ports, rose early to inspect the quality of the fish as it was delivered. He found to his horror that only two hampers had been brought, not nearly enough for the royal party. "Is that all there is?" he asked. "Yes," said the fishmonger, meaning that no more would be coming from his particular fishing fleet. Vatel misunderstood; he thought that there would be no more fish coming at all. "I cannot endure this disgrace," he cried. Going to his room, he fixed his sword into the door and ran upon the point.

VEGA CARPIO, Lope Félix de (1562–1635), *Spanish playwright and poet. He wrote some eighteen hundred plays, of which fewer than a third are extant.*

1 On his deathbed in 1635, Vega asked how much time he had left. Assured that his death was at hand, he murmured, "All right, then, I'll say it: Dante makes me sick."

ॐ ॐ

VERDI, Giuseppe (1813–1901), *Italian operatic composer. He wrote a number of the works most frequently performed in the grand opera repertoire, including* Rigoletto *(1851),* La Traviata *(1853),* Il Trovatore *(1853), and* Aïda *(1871). His glorious* Requiem *(1874) was composed for Alessandro Manzoni.*

1 Though patriotic Italians cheered Verdi at every performance, the enthusiasm was not solely ascribable to their devotion to grand opera. By a fortunate chance the composer's surname was the acronym of a phrase dear to all Italian nationalists after 1861: "Vittorio Emmanuele, Re d'Italia."

2 One summer Verdi rented a large cottage in a fashionable Italian resort. A visitor was somewhat surprised to find the composer apparently occupying only one room, which served as bedroom, sitting room, and study. "Why don't you use the rest of the house?" he asked. Verdi took him into the other rooms; every one of them was packed to the ceiling with barrel-organs—ninety-five in all. "They were all churning out operas of mine," Verdi explained, "Rigoletto—Il Trovatore—and all the others. It was clearly impossible for me to work under such conditions, so I have hired the organs from their owners. It will cost me about fifteen hundred lire for the summer, but that is not too large a price to pay for peace."

ॐ ॐ

VERLAINE, Paul (1844–96), *French poet, a precursor of the Symbolist movement. Having shot the young poet Arthur Rimbaud in the wrist after an argument, Verlaine was sentenced (1873) to two years' imprisonment. While in prison he wrote* Romances sans paroles *(1874); his later works included the critical study* Les Poètes maudits *(1884).*

1 Poet and painter F. A. Cazals, a friend of Verlaine, arranged to meet the poet at a café, but was unavoidably late. When he finally did arrive, he was a trifle nervous, for Verlaine drunk was unpredictable. A mutual friend met Cazals at the door and warned him that Verlaine, hopelessly drunk, was "furious with you." Cazals entered to find Verlaine surrounded by his acolytes, but a little less drunk than he had been described. Cazals took courage: "I hear that you were abusing me just a few minutes ago."

"Who told you that?" cried the furious Verlaine.

"Somebody you don't know," replied Cazals prudently.

"Somebody I don't know!" exclaimed Verlaine. He began to weave his way through the crowded café. "I'm going outside, and the first passerby I don't know, I'll—I'll—*I'll smash his jaw!*"

ॐ ॐ

VERRALL, Arthur Woollgar (1851–1912), *British classical scholar, who taught at Cambridge for thirty-five years.*

1 A pupil of Verrall's told him that mutual friends of theirs had moved to 58 Oakley Street and remarked that he was afraid that 58 would be a difficult number to remember. "Not at all," Verrall contradicted him. "The Septuagint minus the Apostles."

ॐ ॐ

VESEY, Elizabeth (?1715–91), *British society hostess.*

1 In the late 1740s, Mrs. Vesey invited the naturalist Benjamin Stillingfleet to her salon at Bath. She countered his protest that he had no clothes suitable for such a fashionable gathering by assuring him he need not mind about dress. His arrival at the salon in blue worsted stockings caused some comment among the society leaders. Stillingfleet soon became a *habitué*, however, and so the salon gained the nickname of the "Blue Stocking Society."

{The term "bluestocking," first applied to the female members of Mrs. Vesey's salon, is still in use today.}

ॐ ॐ

VESPASIAN [Titus Flavius Sabinus Vespasianus] (AD 9–79), *Roman emperor (70–79). Vespasian rose from comparatively humble origins through his military prowess; his successes so enhanced his reputation that he was proclaimed emperor to resolve the confused situation that arose at Nero's death. As emperor he worked hard to improve the condition of the Roman people.*

1 Vespasian's avarice was one of the few faults held against him. On one occasion a favorite servant of Vespasian's asked for a stewardship for a man he claimed was his brother. Vespasian told him to wait and asked the candidate for the stewardship to come to him for a private interview. "How much commission would you have paid my servant?" he inquired. The applicant mentioned a sum. "You may pay that directly to me," said the emperor and granted him the desired post. Later the servant alluded to the matter, and Vespasian told him, "You'd better go and find yourself another brother. The one you mistook for yours turned out to be mine."

2 Vespasian imposed taxes on many commodities to restore the Roman state to solvency; he even taxed Rome's public urinals. When Vespasian's son Titus objected to this tax as beneath the dignity of the state, Vespasian took a handful of coins obtained from this source and held them to his son's nose, saying, "See, my boy, if they smell."

{In France a public urinal is still sometimes known as a *vespasienne*.}

ॐ ✦

VICTOR AMADEUS II (1666–1732), *Duke of Savoy (1675–1732). He became king of Sicily in 1713, but was forced to give up his crown in 1720 in exchange for that of Sardinia. He ruled Sardinia until his abdication in 1730.*

1 In the eighteenth century the little kingdom of Sardinia suffered severely under the burden of taxation imposed by its ambitious rulers. Once Victor Amadeus on a journey stopped to ask a laboring peasant how he was faring. "Well, master, about as well as things can go in a holy land like ours."

"Holy land?"

"Yes, surely we must be a holy land because

here the Passion of the Savior repeats itself — except in reverse."

"I don't understand."

"What's to understand? In those days One died for us all. Here all of us die for one."

ॐ ✦

VICTORIA (1819–1901), *queen of the United Kingdom (1837–1901). She came to the throne on the death of her uncle, William IV, and during her long reign built up the prestige of the British Crown. The rather stuffy rectitude of her personal life and her devotion to duty exemplified nineteenth-century Britain. She married (1840) her cousin, Prince Albert of Saxe-Coburg-Gotha (1819–61), by whom she had nine children. Her involvement with policymaking sometimes overrode the proper bounds of a constitutional monarchy, resulting in an uneasy relationship with her ministers, particularly William Gladstone.*

1 Victoria was eleven years old when she learned that she stood next in line to the throne. Her governess showed her a list of the kings and queens of England with her own name added after those of George IV and William IV. The child burst into tears as the implications sank in. Then she controlled herself and said solemnly, "I will be good."

2 As a young woman Victoria was a keen theatergoer. At a performance of *King Lear*, however, the tragedy failed to engage her attention, and for most of the early part of the play she chatted to the lord chamberlain, who was in her box. At last she began to pay more attention to the stage. After a while the lord chamberlain ventured to ask her what she thought of the play. "A strange, horrible business," she replied, "but I suppose good enough for Shakespeare's day."

3 Victoria's mother, the Duchess of Kent, totally dominated her daughter's upbringing and clearly had ambitions to be the power behind the throne once Victoria became queen. The princess slept in her mother's room and was never allowed to talk to anyone except in the presence of her German governess or the duchess. The very day that William IV died and Victoria ascended the throne, the Duchess of Kent came to Victoria after the state dignitaries

VICTORIA

had departed and inquired if there was anything she could do for her. "I wish to be left alone," replied Victoria, and the same day she gave orders for her bed to be moved from the duchess's room.

4 Stafford House, the London house of the Duke and Duchess of Sutherland, was the center of high society in the early years of Queen Victoria's reign. The duchess was a close friend of the queen. The magnificence of Stafford House led Victoria to remark to her hostess on one of her frequent visits, "I have come from my house to your palace."

5 Before she made the announcement to her councillors of her decision to marry Prince Albert, Queen Victoria was seen to be trembling. Someone asked her if she was nervous. "Yes, but I have just done a far more nervous thing," replied the queen. "I proposed to Prince Albert."

6 When Victoria was about to marry Prince Albert, she wished to have the title "King Consort" bestowed upon him by act of Parliament. Lord Melbourne, knowing the depth of opposition to such a move on behalf of an unknown German princeling, strongly advised against it. "For God's sake, ma'am, let's have no more of that. If you get the English people into the way of making kings, you'll get them into the way of *un*making them."

7 Victoria and Albert had a quarrel shortly after their marriage. Albert stalked out of the room and locked himself in his private apartments. Victoria hammered furiously upon the door. "Who's there?" called Albert. "The queen of England, and she demands to be admitted." There was no response and the door remained locked. Victoria hammered at the door again. "Who's there?" The reply was still "The queen of England," and still the door remained shut. More fruitless and furious knocking was followed by a pause. Then there was a gentle tap. "Who's there?" The queen replied, "Your wife, Albert." The prince at once opened the door.

8 After the birth of her ninth child Queen Victoria was advised by her chief physician, Sir James Clark, to have no more children. "Oh, Sir James," she replied, "can I have no more fun in bed?"

{This question was probably euphemistic, in that the queen was trying to find out as delicately as possible exactly what her chief physician implied. A more expected attitude to the sexual aspect of marriage appears in one of Victoria's letters concerning the marriage of one of her daughters: she remarks that it is doubtful whether a refined young lady could go through the wedding ceremony if she were fully aware of the physical horrors on the other side of it.}

9 In the early years of their marriage, Victoria and Albert visited Florence several times, greatly impressed by the city's architectural treasures. Of these, the Brunelleschi dome surmounting the cathedral was their personal favorite. Victoria returned to Florence some years after Albert's death to find that the dome had been magnificently restored. She ordered the carriage to stop in the piazza outside the cathedral and rolled down the window. Opening up the locket that hung around her neck, she turned the miniature of her beloved husband to face the building, so that he could share with her the splendor of the newly restored dome. Then, after a few moments' silent contemplation, she closed the locket and drove away.

10 It was well known that the queen disapproved of tobacco and had banned smoking in the royal residences. Her sons, however, smoked a great deal, and, according to a popular story, had appropriated a room in Windsor to use as a smoking room. Panic ensued when they learned that their mother intended to make an inspection of every room in the castle, until the Prince of Wales thought up a solution. The letters WC were without delay put up over the door.

11 The queen and her daughter, the Empress Frederick of Prussia, who had distinctly different literary tastes, were arguing about the merits of the popular romantic novelist Marie Corelli. The queen claimed that Marie Corelli would rank as one of the greatest writers of the time; the Empress Frederick thought her writings were trash. The empress summoned a gentleman-in-waiting, who had not heard the beginning of the discussion, and asked his opinion of Marie Corelli. He replied that he thought the secret of her popularity was that her writings appealed to the semieducated. The subject was dropped very quickly.

12   On a crossing to Ireland the ship in which Queen Victoria was traveling encountered rough weather. A gigantic wave caused such a violent lurch that the queen was almost knocked off her feet. Recovering her balance she said to an attendant, "Go up to the bridge, give the admiral my compliments, and tell him he's not to let that happen again."

13   "In order to hear how HMS *Eurydice,* a frigate sunk off Portsmouth, had been salvaged, Queen Victoria invited Admiral Foley to lunch. Having exhausted this melancholy subject, Queen Victoria inquired after her close friend, the Admiral's sister. Hard of hearing, Admiral Foley replied in his stentorian voice, 'Well, Ma'am, I am going to have her turned over, take a good look at her bottom and have it well scraped.' The Queen put down her knife and fork, hid her face in her handkerchief, and laughed until the tears ran down her cheeks."

14   On visits to the London home of Baroness Burdett-Coutts, Victoria could often be found sitting beside the window on the top floor. From there she would watch, with a childlike fascination, the traffic stream pass below her in Piccadilly. She once explained to the baroness: "Yours is the only place where I can go to see the traffic without stopping it."

15   During a visit by some of her grandchildren, the queen heard them roaring with laughter and proceeded to investigate. It appeared that one of them had made a joke of a somewhat "advanced" nature, and they were reluctant to repeat it. Eventually the queen prevailed upon one of the boys to comply with her royal command, and, hearing the joke, realized that it was not to her taste. She drew herself up and, with the dignified rebuke, "We are not amused!" left the room.
    {There are a number of stories relating to Queen Victoria's use of this phrase; this is a plausible one. What all the anecdotes have in common is that they relate to a joke, story, or piece of buffoonery that was out of place in its context as being disrespectful or too risqué for the company, especially if young unmarried women were present. The queen apparently did not object to occasional risqué stories if told in the proper company, but "We are not amused" may well have been her stock expression to cut off any train of conversation that she considered inappropriate.}

16   Victoria once received a letter from a prodigal grandson, asking for an advance on his allowance. Rather than send the money, Victoria replied with a long letter extolling the value of thrift, diligence, and initiative. The boy took the queen's advice to heart — he sold the letter for twenty-five pounds.

17   On the anniversary of Queen Victoria's death, her children would visit the mausoleum at Frogmore. One year, as they knelt piously in prayer, a dove entered the mausoleum and flew about. "It is dear Mama's spirit," they murmured. "No, I am sure it's not," contradicted Princess Louise. "It must be dear Mama's spirit," they persisted. "No, it isn't," said Princess Louise. "Dear Mama's spirit would never have ruined Beatrice's hat."
    {The original source for this story was Prince Henry, later the Duke of Gloucester.}

৯১ ৶৾

VIDAL, Gore (1925–   ), *US writer, author of* Burr, Lincoln, *and other novels and works of nonfiction.*

1   The English novelist Anthony Powell, attending an international writers' conference in Sofia, Bulgaria, found himself alongside Vidal, inspecting some pictures taken of the session. Several of these showed Vidal beside an Indian delegate. "I always sit next to a man in a turban," explained Vidal. "You get photographed more."

৯১ ৶৾

VILLA, Pancho (?1877–1923), *Mexican revolutionary.*

1   As Pancho Villa lay dying, his last words were, "Don't let it end like this. Tell them I said something."

VILLIERS de L'Isle-Adam, Auguste, Comte de (1838–89), *French writer of the Symbolist school. His works include* Premières Poésies *(1856–58), the novel* Isis *(1862), short stories, and plays.*

1 "Villiers de L'Isle-Adam, who was leaving the following day for London to be married, an expectation which was never realized, came to see Mallarmé and . . . asked to be taught English at once. 'Willingly,' replied Mallarmé, 'but I cannot begin the lessons for two days.' 'Oh,' replied Villiers, 'we can simplify matters. As it is a question of a coming marriage, you might teach me only the future tenses of the verbs.'"

৵ ৵

VIRCHOW, Rudolf (1821–1902), *German pathologist and politician. A reformer in politics, he was the outspoken opponent of Otto von Bismarck. He played a large part in modernizing Berlin, and as director of Berlin's Pathological Institute led or inspired much original research.*

1 Bismarck, enraged at Virchow's constant criticisms, had his seconds call upon the scientist to challenge him to a duel. "As the challenged party, I have the choice of weapons," said Virchow, "and I choose these." He held aloft two large and apparently identical sausages. "One of these," he went on, "is infected with deadly germs; the other is perfectly sound. Let His Excellency decide which one he wishes to eat, and I will eat the other." Almost immediately the message came back that the chancellor had decided to laugh off the duel.

2 The French ethnologist Armand de Quatrefages was incensed by the damage done to Paris's natural history museum by German shells during the Franco-Prussian War of 1870. He declared that the Prussians were by race not Nordic or Teutonic but descendants of the barbarian hordes of Huns who ravished eastern Europe during the Middle Ages. Virchow was outraged by this racial slur. As a member of the Prussian Parliament, he introduced a bill by which the physical characteristics of every schoolchild in Prussia — six million in number — could be examined and assessed. The survey was carried out, head measurements, bones, hair, and teeth were all analyzed, and Virchow proved scientifically that the Prussians were in origin Franks — cousins, in fact, of the French themselves. But the epithet, "Hun" was applied derogatorily to the Germans thereafter, especially by Germany's enemies in the two world wars.

3 Appendectomy first became widely and safely practiced in the late nineteenth century. Someone asked Virchow whether it was indeed true that human beings can survive without the appendix. "Human beings, yes," replied Virchow, "but not surgeons."

৵ ৵

VOLTAIRE [François-Marie Arouet] (1694–1778), *French philosopher, writer, and wit. His inquiring mind and skeptical views, particularly on matters of religion, epitomize the French Enlightenment. Frequently in trouble with the authorities, he was briefly imprisoned and endured a three-year exile in England (1726–29). For many years he lived with the philosopher Mme du Châtelet, author of a commentary on Newton. After her death he moved for a short time (1750–53) to the court of Frederick the Great and thereafter made his home mainly in Switzerland. His huge output included well-received verse dramas, histories, philosophical treatises, criticism, and the prose romance* Candide *(1759), satirizing the philosophy of Leibniz.*

1 In 1717 Voltaire, in consequence of a satire directed against the regent, Philippe d'Orléans, was imprisoned in the Bastille for eleven months. Liberated, Voltaire, a highly adaptable man, thanked the regent for the gracious pardon. The latter, aware of Voltaire's power, was equally anxious to effect a reconciliation and made all the appropriate apologies. Voltaire replied: "Your Highness, I am most grateful for your generosity with respect to my board but in the future you need not worry yourself about my lodging."

2 Voltaire and a select group of friends were running through Voltaire's latest play before its production. During the reading of a lengthy speech, Montesquieu fell asleep. "Wake him up," said Voltaire. "He seems to imagine that he's in the audience."

3 In 1725 Voltaire became involved in a stupid quarrel with the Chevalier de Rohan-

Chabot, a short-tempered aristocrat, possibly over Voltaire's mistress, the famous actress Adrienne Lecouvreur. There was an exchange of insults at the Opéra, in which the chevalier came out badly and left the theater threatening revenge. A few days later Voltaire was dining with a patron when he was told that someone wished to speak to him. In the street a number of ruffians hired by the chevalier fell on him and beat him up. The chevalier, who watched the whole episode from his own coach, cried out, "Be careful not to hit him on the head. Something might come out of that one day."

4   Voltaire was in exile in London at a time when popular feelings ran high against the French. One day on the street he was surrounded by an angry mob shouting, "Hang him. Hang the Frenchman!" Turning to face the mob, Voltaire said, "Men of England! You wish to kill me because I am a Frenchman. Am I not punished enough in not being born an Englishman?" This tactful speech so pleased the crowd that they cheered and escorted him safely back to his lodgings.

5   Rousseau sent a copy of his "Ode to Posterity" hot off the press to Voltaire for his opinion. Voltaire read it through and commented, "I do not think this poem will reach its destination."

6   A notoriously dissolute group of Parisians invited Voltaire to participate in an orgy. He accepted, giving such a satisfactory account of himself that the very next night he was asked to come again. "Ah, no, my friends," said Voltaire with a slight smile. "Once: a philosopher; twice: a pervert!"

7   Though it enjoyed an unprecedented success, Voltaire's *Oedipe* drew the criticism of the aged Fontenelle, who told the author that he considered some of the verses "too strong and full of fire."

"To correct myself I shall read your *Pastorales,*" Voltaire replied.

8   After a long absence a royal favorite returned to the court of Frederick the Great. Many rumors circulated as to the reason for her absence. She complained to Voltaire, "The things they say about me are incredible! They even say I retired to the country in order to give birth to twins!" Voltaire replied, "Don't let that disturb you. I believe only half of what I hear at the court."

9   At the funeral of a certain nobleman, Voltaire declared, "He was a great patriot, a humanitarian, a loyal friend — provided, of course, that he really is dead."

10   In 1759 Casanova, the author of the famous *Mémoires,* set out from Paris on a two-year journey around Europe, in the course of which he visited Voltaire in Switzerland. Voltaire had been reading some of the works of the Swiss physiologist and polymath Albrecht von Haller. He praised them to his guest. "That praise is ill returned," said Casanova, "for he has been saying that your work is nonsense." Voltaire smiled. "Perhaps we are both mistaken," he said.

11   Voltaire drank prodigious quantities of coffee throughout his life. Some killjoy warned him that he should give up the beverage because it was a slow poison. "I think it must be slow," the elderly philosopher replied, "for I have been drinking it for sixty-five years and I am not dead yet."

{This rejoinder is also attributed to Bernard Fontenelle, who died less than a month before reaching his hundredth birthday.}

12   Visitors to Voltaire's model village at Ferney near Geneva remarked on the church that the old skeptic had built there for the villagers. Over the door was the dedication: "DEO EREXIT VOLTAIRE." Voltaire liked to observe that it was the only church in Europe that was erected to God.

13   At Ferney, Voltaire once had as guests a certain Huber and also the noted mathematician Jean d'Alembert. It was proposed that each ad-lib a story involving thieves. Huber's invention was received with acclamation, as was d'Alembert's. It was now Voltaire's turn. "Gentlemen," he said, "there was once a tax collector . . . good Lord, I've forgotten the rest of the story."

14   In the last year of his life the famous invalid, domiciled at the Marquis de Villette's mansion, was visited by hordes of admirers, anx-

ious to pay their last respects. Among them were two mediocre dramatists, Antoine Lemierre and Dormont de Belloy. Voltaire remarked to them, "Gentlemen, as I take farewell of life, I am consoled by the knowledge that I leave behind me Lemierre and de Belloy." After Voltaire's death Lemierre was fond of recalling these words, never failing to add, "And poor de Belloy never suspected that Voltaire was making fun of him."

15 When Voltaire lay on his deathbed a priest arrived to shrive him. The philosopher asked: "Who sent you here, Monsieur l'Abbé?"

"God himself, Monsieur Voltaire."

"Ah, my dear sir, and where are your credentials?"

ॐ ◄§

VON NEUMANN, John (1903–1957), *US mathematician.*

1 The noted mathematician John von Neumann was an incurable practical joker. During World War II, when he constructed his famous electronic brain for the government, he identified it on delivery as a Mathematical Analyser, Numerical Integrater, and Computer.

Scientists worked with it for several days before they realized that the first letters of the name its inventor had given it spelled MANIAC.

ॐ ◄§

VUKOVICH, Bill (1918–55), *US racing driver. He won the Indianapolis 500 in 1953 and 1954, and was in the lead in the 1955 race when he crashed to his death.*

1 Asked the secret of his Indianapolis success, Vukovich said, "There's no secret. You just press the accelerator to the floor and steer left."

❧ W ❧

WADDELL, Rube (1876–1914), *US baseball player, pitcher for the Philadelphia Athletics.*

1 (Many tall stories have been told about the inimitable Rube Waddell, not all of them true. The following incident, however, really did happen to Rube while playing for the Athletics.)

"He wielded a pretty hefty bat for a pitcher, and was allowed to swing for himself one day in the eighth inning with the score 2–1 against the Athletics, two out, and tying run on second. The catcher of the opposing nine saw a chance to pick off the runner at second and heaved the ball in that general direction. It ended in center field, and the runner hot-footed for the plate. He'd have made it, too, with plenty to spare, but as the throw came into the plate, Waddell, to the amazement of everybody in the park, swung at the ball, bashed it out over the right field fence, and was promptly declared out for interference. 'Why did you do it?' wailed Manager Connie Mack. 'They'd been feeding me curves all afternoon,' explained the Rube sheepishly, 'and this was the first straight ball I'd looked at!'"

❧ ❧

WALKER, James John (1881–1946), *US politician, mayor of New York (1926–32).*

1 Henry ("Light-Horse Harry") Lee's famous toast to George Washington, "To the memory of the man, first in war, first in peace, and first in the hearts of his countrymen," was repeated at a Washington's Birthday celebratory banquet by Jimmy Walker. After a brief pause the mayor went on, "No one's ever understood how he happened to marry a widow."

❧ ❧

WALLACH, Eli (1915–   ), *US actor. After sixteen years on the stage he made his screen debut in* Baby Doll *(1956). His subsequent films include* The Moonspinners *(1964),* The Tiger Makes Out *(1967), and* The Sentinel *(1977).*

1 At the 1964 opening on Broadway of the immensely successful *Luv*, Wallach gazed contentedly at the long line of people at the box office and remarked to a fellow performer: "There's something about a crowd like that that brings a lump to my wallet."

❧ ❧

WALLER, Edmund (1606–87), *British lyric poet. In 1643, after a plot to seize London for Charles I failed, Waller barely escaped with his life and went into exile. He subsequently made his peace with the opposing Cromwell and returned to England (1651) but at the Restoration reverted to the royalist side, enjoying the favor of both Charles II and James II.*

1 One of Waller's most successful poems with a political theme is his panegyric on Oliver Cromwell. His later laudatory verses on Charles II were generally considered inferior in poetic merit. The king having commented upon this difference, Waller replied, "Poets, sire, succeed better in fiction than in truth."

❧ ❧

WALN, Nicholas (1742–1813), *US lawyer and a prominent member of the Quaker community.*

1 A Quaker meeting having detected some fault in Waln, a deputation of elders was sent to remonstrate with him. They knocked and knocked at his front door but without result. At last an upstairs window was thrown open

and Waln's head poked out. "My Friends," he called down, "you need not come in; the Master has been here before you."

჻

WALPOLE, Horace, 4th Earl of Orford (1717–97), *British writer. Walpole's house at Strawberry Hill, outside London, was a trendsetter for the Gothic architectural revival. His writings include memoirs, antiquarian studies, a vast private correspondence, and the famous gothic novel* The Castle of Otranto *(1765).*

1 Walpole had a stormy interview with an elderly uncle concerning a proposed marriage in the family. Departing unplaced, he wrote his relative a furious letter ending: "I am, sir, for the last time in my life, Your Humble Servant Horace Walpole."

჻

WALPOLE, Sir Robert, 1st Earl of Orford (1676–1745), *British statesman. He was impeached for corruption (1712) and several times lost office, but was twice First Lord of the Treasury (1715–17, 1721–42). He is regarded as the first prime minister under the political system that evolved during Hanoverian rule. Walpole's unpopular foreign policy, culminating in the War of Jenkins' Ear against Spain (1739), eventually brought about his fall.*

1 Walpole's father encouraged him to drink deep. For every time he filled his own glass he filled his son's twice. "Come, Robert," said the senior Walpole, "you shall drink twice while I drink once, for I cannot permit the son in his sober senses to witness the intoxication of his father."

2 After his arduous years in office, Walpole looked forward to retirement in his splendid mansion, Houghton Castle. Entering the library, he took down a book, perused it for a few minutes, and then returned it to the shelf. He took down another, but held that only half as long before replacing it and taking a third. This he immediately put back, and, bursting into tears, exclaimed, "I have led a life of business so long that I have lost my taste for reading, and now — what shall I do?"

჻

New college instructors often find hard challenges in coping with brash young undergraduates. At Columbia University the young Professor Raymond Weaver gave his first class in English literature their first quiz. The young men, who had been trying to make things hard for the new instructor, whistled with joy when Weaver wrote: "Which of the books read so far has interested you least?" They were silent, however, when he wrote the second, and the last, question: "To what defect in yourself do you attribute this lack of interest?"

— Jacob M. Braude, *Speaker's and Toastmaster's Handbook*

WALTER, Bruno (1876–1962), *German conductor. He directed the Vienna Court Opera (1901–12) and became renowned for his interpretations of Gustav Mahler. At the beginning of World War II, he moved to the United States.*

1 When Bruno Walter first conducted the New York Philharmonic, Alfred Wallenstein was the first cellist. Walter noticed that Wallenstein ostentatiously ignored him during both rehearsals and concerts. Rather than make a scene in public, Walter asked Wallenstein to come and speak to him privately. "What is your ambition, Mr. Wallenstein?" Walter inquired mildly. "Someday I'd like to be a conductor," replied the cellist. "Well, when you are, I hope you never have Wallenstein in front of you," said Walter.

჻

WALTON, Sir William [Turner] (1902–83), *British composer. He first attracted public notice with* Façade *(1922), a musical setting of poems by Edith Sitwell. Later works include symphonies, concertos, incidental music for Laurence Olivier's Shakespearean films, the oratorio* Belshazzar's Feast *(1931), and the opera* Troilus and Cressida *(1954).*

1 At the rehearsals for the first performance of *Façade*, the players were at first irritated, then interested, and finally delighted by the strange and difficult new sounds that the

young Walton, as composer-conductor, asked them to make. During one of the pauses in the rehearsal the clarinetist looked up from his score and asked, "Excuse me, Mr. Walton, has a clarinet player ever done you an injury?"

2 Until the success of his film score for Laurence Olivier's *Henry V* in 1942 Walton was poor, and as he himself admitted in later life, lived by scrounging off the Sitwell family. Lady Aberconway, a close friend of the Sitwells and a well-known London hostess of the 1930s, recalled that Walton was known to them by the nickname "Lincrusta." It was the trade-name for a particular kind of embossed wallpaper that was extremely difficult to detach.

WARBURTON, William (1698–1779), *British clergyman and literary scholar; bishop of Gloucester (1759–79). Besides theological polemic, Warburton brought out an edition of Shakespeare's works (1747) that was much criticized.*

1 During a debate in the House of Lords upon the Test Laws, under which those who wished to stand for public office were obliged to profess the Anglican faith, the witty and profligate Earl of Sandwich complained, "I have heard frequent use of the words 'orthodoxy' and 'heterodoxy' but I confess myself at a loss to know precisely what they mean." Bishop Warburton enlightened him in a whisper, "Orthodoxy is my doxy; heterodoxy is another man's doxy."

WARD, Artemus [Charles Farrar Browne] (1834–67), *US humorous writer.*

1 After a successful and lucrative lecture tour of the eastern states, Ward headed west in October 1863. The manager of the San Francisco opera house sent him a telegram asking what he would take for forty nights in California. Ward wired back: "Brandy and water. A. Ward."

2 Artemus Ward spent Christmas Eve 1863 with Mark Twain and some other cronies at Barnum's Restaurant in Virginia City. A great deal of liquor was consumed, and toward the end of the evening Ward proposed "a standing toast." He made several ineffectual attempts to

get to his feet, while his companions remained slumped at the table. "Well," he said, abandoning his efforts, "*consider* it standing."

WARNER, Jack (1892–1978), *US movie producer, co-founder of Warner Brothers. Warners pioneered sound movies in 1926, and in 1927 produced the first full-length talkie,* The Jazz Singer. *Some of the greatest Hollywood stars and screen successes came from the Warners' studio.*

1 The actor Pat O'Brien recalls that Jack Warner bought Sinclair Lewis's worldwide best-seller *Main Street* and changed the title to *I Married a Doctor* on the grounds that nobody "would want to see a picture about a street." The movie died.

2 In 1946, when British Field Marshal Bernard Montgomery visited California, Mr. and Mrs. Samuel Goldwyn gave a dinner for him. Goldwyn began: "It gives me great pleasure to welcome to Hollywood a very distinguished soldier. Ladies and gentlemen, I propose a toast to Marshall Field Montgomery." The silence was broken by Jack Warner's voice saying, "Montgomery Ward, you mean."

{Marshall Field is a Chicago department store; Montgomery Ward is a major US mail-order chain.}

3 Warner was in the habit of taking an afternoon nap in his office at Warner Brothers, and it was an unwritten rule of the studios that he should not be disturbed. On one occasion, however, Bette Davis burst into the office while Warner was asleep and began ranting about a script that did not meet with her approval. Without opening his eyes, Warner reached for the phone and called his secretary. "Come in and wake me up," he said. "I'm having a nightmare." Miss Davis could not help laughing, and the crisis over the script was resolved in a few minutes.

WASHINGTON, George (1732–99), *US general and statesman, first president of the United States (1789–97). As a young man Washington gained a high military reputation in the Seven Years' War (1756–63). While a member of Virginia's House of Burgesses (1759–74), he be-*

came an implacable enemy of British rule, and on the outbreak of war with Britain was appointed commander in chief of the American forces. Overcoming lack of equipment, discipline, and even food, Washington welded together his army through years of indecisive victories and costly defeats until he was able, with French aid, to force the surrender of General Cornwallis at Yorktown (1781). He presided over the Constitutional Convention (1787) and was unanimously elected president of the new Republic after the Constitution had been approved.

1   Parson Weems's *Life of Washington* (1800) contains many apocryphal stories about his hero and ranks more as hagiography than factual biography. His best-known fabrication (introduced into the 1806 edition) is the story of George Washington and the cherry tree. According to Weems, when he was about six, George Washington was given a hatchet. He went around his father's farm, testing it on all manner of things, including a fine young cherry tree. His father, discovering the damage, summoned the boy and said sternly, "Do you know who killed this beautiful little cherry tree?" The child was silent for a moment but then cried out, "I cannot tell a lie; you know I cannot tell a lie. I cut it with my hatchet." His father at once forgot his anger in his delight at the child's truthfulness.

{This story has had an enormous effect on the American people, having succeeded in making George Washington the sworn enemy of all small children.}

2   After a skirmish in the course of the Seven Years' War, Washington was reported to have said, "I heard the bullets whistle, and believe me, there is something charming in the sound." When King George II of England heard of this remark, he said, "He would not say so had he been used to hear many."

3   During the American Revolution an officer in civilian clothes rode past a group of soldiers busy repairing a small redoubt. Their commander was shouting instructions but making no attempt to help them. Asked why, he retorted with great dignity, "Sir, I am a corporal!" The stranger apologized, dismounted, and proceeded to help the exhausted soldiers himself. When the job was completed he turned to the corporal and said, "Mr. Corporal, next time you have a job like this and not enough men to do it, go to your commander in chief, and I will come and help you again." Too late, the corporal recognized General Washington.

4   During the bitterly cold winter at Valley Forge, Washington constantly went the rounds of his men, encouraging and comforting them. One day he came across Private John Brantley drinking some stolen wine with his companions. Already a little drunk, Brantley cheerily invited his commander to "drink some wine with a soldier." Replied Washington, "My boy, you have no time for drinking wine." And he turned away. "Damn your proud soul," exclaimed Brantley. "You're above drinking with soldiers." Washington turned back. "Come, I will drink with you," he said and took a pull at the jug and handed it back. "Give it to your servants," said Brantley, gesturing toward Washington's aides. The jug was duly passed around. "Now," said Brantley, when he once more had his jug, "I'll be damned if I don't spend the last drop of my heart's blood for you."

5   Early in the Revolutionary War, Washington sent one of his officers to requisition horses from the local landowners. Calling at an old country mansion, the officer was received by the elderly mistress of the house. "Madam, I have come to claim your horses in the name of the government," he began. "On whose orders?" demanded the woman sternly. "On the orders of General George Washington, commander in chief of the American army," replied the officer. The old lady smiled. "You go back and tell General George Washington that his mother says he cannot have her horses," she said.

6   As Washington was sitting at dinner one evening, the heat from the fire behind him became so intense that he said he had better move farther from the hearth. Someone in the company said jokingly that it was only right and proper for a general to be able to stand fire. "But it doesn't look good if he receives it from behind," replied Washington.

7   During the Constitutional Convention someone suggested that the size of the army be restricted to five thousand men at any one time. Washington saw the impracticality of this, but as chairman he was prevented from making a counterproposal. Instead he whispered to a delegate sitting near him that they ought to amend the proposal to provide that "no foreign army should invade the United States at any time with more than three thousand troops."

8 Walking in Philadelphia with an American acquaintance, an English visitor expressed a wish to see President Washington. A few moments later, the president happened to pass the two men on the opposite side of the street. Pointing at the solitary figure, the American said, "There he goes." The Englishman was surprised. "Is that President Washington?" he exclaimed. "Where's his guard?" The American struck his breast proudly. "Here," he declared.

9 Gilbert Stuart, who painted a famous portrait of Washington in 1795, remarked afterward to General Henry ("Light-Horse Harry") Lee on the strong passions that he could perceive beneath the president's dignified exterior. A few days later General Lee mentioned to the Washingtons that he had seen the portrait, adding, "Stuart says you have a tremendous temper." Mrs. Washington's color rose and she said sharply, "Mr. Stuart takes a great deal on himself to make such a remark." General Lee checked her: "But he added that the president has wonderful control." Washington said, almost smiling, "He's right."

10 In 1797 the French revolutionist and freethinker Constantin Volney visited the United States and asked Washington for a letter of recommendation. Not wishing to offend the Frenchman, but also anxious to avoid controversy over the man's opinions, Washington simply wrote: "C. Volney needs no recommendation from Geo. Washington."

৯ ৵

WATERTON, Charles (1782–1865), *British eccentric and naturalist. His ornithological and other studies took him to North and South America, the West Indies, and Madagascar. In 1806 he inherited Walton Hall, Yorkshire, which he turned into a bird sanctuary.*

1 While in the United States, as Edith Sitwell describes it, Waterton sprained his ankle, and

"being extremely annoyed by inquiries of other less-adventurous gentlemen, staying in the hotel, as to the progress of his 'gout,' he remembered that in the past, when his ankle had been badly sprained, a doctor had ordered him to hold it under the pump two or three times a day. It struck him therefore that it might be a kind of super-cure if he held his ankle under the Niagara Falls." Which he did.

৯ ৵

WATSON, Richard (1737–1816), *British clergyman, bishop of Llandaff (1782–1816). He had previously held the chairs of chemistry (1764–71) and divinity (1771) at Cambridge University. He wrote a famous refutation of Thomas Paine called* Apology for the Bible *(1796).*

1 The landlord of the well-known Cock Inn at Windermere in northwest England wished to compliment Dr. Watson, who had a house nearby. He changed the name of the inn to "The Bishop" and hung out a sign bearing a portrait of the eminent cleric. A rival landlord of a less popular establishment across the street thereupon changed his inn sign to "The Cock," and thus attracted a lot of the customers of the former Cock Inn. The landlord of the latter decided that he must make the identity of his inn clear to visitors to the town. When Dr. Watson next passed through Windermere, he was not at all flattered to see painted underneath his portrait on the inn sign the words: "This is the old Cock."

৯ ৵

WATT, James (1736–1819), *British engineer. He discovered how to improve the efficiency of the model of Newcomen's steam engine that he was repairing. His discovery contributed to the development of effective steam power. He coined the term "horsepower," and the metric unit of power is named after him.*

1 According to tradition, the solution to the problem of preventing the loss of energy in the Newcomen engine occurred to Watt as he observed a kettle boiling on the fire at his home. His aunt came in and rebuked him for idly fiddling about with the kettle, holding a spoon over the spout, pressing it down, and so on. She suggested that he go out and do something useful.

In *First Lady from Plains,* Rosalynn Carter gives an insight into some of the lesser-known stories about the White House:

"We learned some wonderfully odd things about the house that night; Abigail Adams hung the presidential laundry in the East Room; Thomas Jefferson used the same space for his secretary, who had to find better quarters when the ceiling literally fell in; the portrait of George Washington in the East Room is the only object known to have *always* been in the White House, except when Dolley Madison had it torn from its frame as she fled when the British were coming in 1814; Andrew Jackson once placed a fourteen-hundred-pound cheese in the Cross Hall and invited the public in to eat it. They came in droves, eating and treading crumbs into the carpets, and the smell lingered for weeks. Thomas Jefferson had a pet mockingbird that he taught to peck food from his lips and to hop up the stairs after him; the Garfield children rode large, three-wheeled velocipedes while they carried on pillow fights in the East Room; and the five children of Theodore Roosevelt slid down the staircases on trays stolen from the pantry, stalked the hall on stilts, and when one of the children had the measles, his brothers took a pony into his second-floor bedroom after riding up in the President's elevator."

WATTERSON, Henry (1840–1921), *US journalist and newspaper editor.*

1 All journalists in Watterson's time were issued with special railroad passes, which were nontransferable. Nevertheless, abuse of the system was widespread. A young man traveling on the Louisville and Nashville Railway was using the pass of a certain Mr. Smith, a correspondent on Watterson's paper. The suspicious conductor took "Smith" to see Watterson, who happened to be on the same train. The impostor trembled as the conductor asked Watterson if this young man was indeed his

employee, Mr. Smith. He was amazed and overjoyed when Watterson replied in the affirmative. After the conductor had gone, the young man thanked Watterson for saving him from a difficult situation. The other smiled. "Compose yourself, young man. I don't happen to be Colonel Watterson, but I am riding on his railroad pass."

ॐ ॐ

WAUGH, Evelyn (1903–66), *British novelist. Decline and Fall (1928) and Vile Bodies (1930) established him as a social satirist. After his conversion to Roman Catholicism in 1930 religious themes played an increasing part in such novels as Brideshead Revisited (1945). Later books include his wartime trilogy — At Arms (1952), Officers and Gentlemen (1955), and Unconditional Surrender (1961).*

1 Randolph Churchill, the journalist son of Winston Churchill and not remarkable for the sweetness of his character, went into the hospital to have a lung removed. It was announced in the press that the trouble was not cancer. Waugh commented: "A typical triumph of modern science to find the only part of Randolph that was not malignant and remove it."

2 Evelyn Waugh and Harold Acton toured southern Italy together. It turned out to be one of those vacations when everything conspires to go wrong. When they got to Naples, the British consul came to pay them a courtesy call. They were both feeling rather out of sorts, and the conversation flagged. In a desperate attempt to enliven it, the consul said to Waugh, "I have a map of Mount Ararat, which I think might interest you."

"Why should it?" said Waugh. "Has the Ark been found?"

3 In 1935, Waugh was sent to cover the Italian invasion of Ethiopia. While he was there, his editor heard a rumor that an English nurse had been killed in an Italian air raid and cabled: "Send two hundred words upblown nurse." Waugh made exhaustive enquiries, but was unable to substantiate the story. He finally cabled back: "Nurse unupblown."

4 Waugh's commanding officer was impressed by his courage during the battle of Crete in 1941. On the return journey, the writer was asked for his impression of the battle, his first experience of military action. "Like German opera," he replied, "too long and too loud."

5 (Joseph Epstein tells this story about Evelyn Waugh:)

"Once, when he had behaved with particular rudeness to a young French intellectual at a dinner party in Paris at the home of Nancy Mitford, Miss Mitford, angry at his social brutality, asked him how he could behave so meanly and yet consider himself a believing and practicing Catholic. 'You have no idea,' Waugh returned, 'how much nastier I would be if I was not a Catholic. Without supernatural aid I would hardly be a human being.'"

6 (Epstein also reports this incident:)

"Finally, from the thesaurus of Wavian anecdotes, Christopher Sykes, in his biography, reports visiting Waugh in the hospital, where he found him grumbling in great pain in the aftermath of an operation for piles. Attempting to solace his friend, Sykes remarked that he assumed the operation, painful though it might seem now, was in any case necessary.

"'No,' Waugh replied, 'the operation was not necessary, but might conceivably have become so later on.'

"'Not necessary?' said Sykes. 'Then why did you have it done?'

"'Perfectionism.'"

&ε ੬9

WAVELL, Archibald Percival, 1st Earl (1883–1950), *British field marshal; viceroy of India (1943–47). In World War II he defeated the Italians in Africa, but was less successful against Rommel. Sent to southeast Asia, he tried with inadequate forces to stem the Japanese tide and was superseded.*

1 (One of the greatest disappointments of Wavell's life came at the end of June 1941, when he was replaced by Claude Auchinleck as commander in the Middle Eastern battle zone.)

"A signal from the Prime Minister [Churchill] telling him that Auchinleck and he were to change places had arrived in the small hours of the morning, and been taken to General Arthur Smith, who had at once dressed and gone round to Wavell's house on Gezira. He found him shaving, with his face covered with lather

and his razor poised. He read out the signal. Wavell showed no emotion. He merely said: 'The Prime Minister's quite right. This job wants a new eye and a new hand'; and went on shaving."

&ε ੬9

WEBB, Sidney [James], Baron Passfield (1859–1947), *British socialist politician and economist. He was a founder of the Fabian Society (1884) and the London School of Economics (1895). His wife, Beatrice (1858–1943), collaborated with him on books that have had a lasting impact on the development of socialist thought in Britain.*

1 Asked to account for the harmonious front the Webbs presented on the important issues of the time, Beatrice explained that they had agreed early in their married life always to vote alike on great issues. "Sidney was to decide which way we voted. I was to decide which were the great issues."

&ε ੬9

WEBSTER, Daniel (1782–1852), *US lawyer and statesman. Born into a poor New Hampshire farming family, Daniel Webster showed signs of his great intellectual powers from an early age. He first became a lawyer, his remarkable skill as an orator quickly winning him a distinguished position. He then entered politics and became known for his staunch defense of the Constitution. He ran unsuccessfully for president, but achieved lasting fame with some of his speeches. His later years were darkened by political disappointments, family sorrows, and financial setbacks.*

1 Temporarily absent from home, Captain Webster left Daniel and his brother Ezekiel with specific instructions as to the work they were to do that day. On his return he found the task still unperformed, and questioned his sons severely about their idleness. "What have you been doing, Ezekiel?" he asked.

"Nothing, sir."

"Well, Daniel, what have you been doing?"

"Helping Zeke, sir."

2 As a boy, Daniel Webster worked in his father's fields. One day, told to do the mowing, he made a thoroughly bad job of it; sometimes his scythe struck the ground and sometimes it

swung too high and missed the grass entirely. He complained to his father that the scythe was not hung right. Various attempts were made to hang it better, but with no success. At last his father told him that he might hang it to suit himself, whereupon he hung it on a tree and said, "There, that's just right."

3   As a lad at school Webster committed some peccadillo for which he was called up to the teacher's desk to have the palm of his right hand caned. Aware that his hands were very dirty, he made an effort to rub off some of the dirt as he walked up to the desk. Nevertheless, the hand he held out was exceedingly grimy. The teacher looked at it sternly. "Daniel, if you can find another hand as dirty as that in this schoolroom, I'll let you off." Out from behind the boy's back came the left hand. "Here it is, sir," said young Webster. The teacher had to abide by his offer.

4   A friend advised young Webster not to attempt to enter the legal profession, which was already overcrowded and posed formidable obstacles to a man without either money or family connections to help him. "There's always room at the top," said Webster calmly.

5   Daniel Webster met Grace Fletcher, who was to become his first wife, when he was a young lawyer at Portsmouth. He was allowed to call on her, and on one of his visits was making himself useful by holding skeins of silk thread for her. Suddenly he stopped and said, "Grace, we have been engaged in untying knots; let us see if we can tie a knot which will not untie for a lifetime." Then Webster took a piece of tape and began to tie a complicated knot in it, which he gave to her to complete — this they regarded as the ceremony of their engagement.

{Grace died in 1828 and Webster remarried two years later. After his death, however, in the little box that he had marked "Precious Documents," were found the letters of his early courtship with Grace and this knot, never untied.}

6   At the beginning of his legal career, Daniel Webster was engaged as associate counsel by a lawyer acting for a gentleman from Grafton County. The lawyer made known his choice to the client, who asked if this was Daniel Webster, son of old Ebenezer of Salisbury. Receiving an affirmative reply, he cried, "What! That little black stable-boy who once brought me some horses! Then I think we might as well give up the case." It was too late to engage another associate counsel, and the case went ahead. The dejected client sat in court, not listening to the proceedings. Then he found that his attention was gradually arrested by the associate counsel's voice. He was held spellbound until the end of the speech. The lawyer turned to his client and asked, "What do you think of him now?"

"Think! Why, I think he is an angel sent down from Heaven to save me from ruin, and my wife and children from misery!"

7   The lawyer Jeremiah Mason was Webster's colleague and friend in Portsmouth. The two were often opposed in important cases, and performed impressively against each other in court. One day when a new case was called, the clerk of the court asked who was counsel on each side. "Which side are you on in this case?" Mason asked Webster. "I don't know," said Webster. "Take your choice."

8   (Webster had an immensely impressive presence, especially in court, where his magnificent voice and his dark, beetle-browed eyes were of great advantage. Van Wyck Brooks recounts the story of how Daniel Webster looked a witness out of court.)

"He had set his great eyes on the man and searched him through and through; then, as the cause went on, and this fellow's perjury was not yet called for, Webster looked round again to see if he was ready for the inquisition. The witness felt for his hat and edged toward the door. A third time Webster looked on him, and the witness could sit no longer. He seized his chance and fled from the court and was nowhere to be found."

9   A Nantucket gentleman stopped a friend in the street and told him, "I am in trouble and wish your advice."

"What's the matter?"

"Oh, I'm in a lawsuit, and Webster is against me. What shall I do?"

"My advice is that your only chance of escape is to send to Smyrna and import a young earthquake."

{Compare Sydney Smith's description of Webster: "A steam engine in trousers."}

10 Daniel Webster attended a particularly illustrious dinner party. After the ladies had retired, the host produced a bottle of Madeira for the gentlemen. This wine, he said, had been bottled by his grandfather more than seventy years before. One of the guests did some calculations on the back of a letter and remarked that if the wine was worth twenty-five cents when bottled, its present value at current interest would reach a hundred dollars. At that moment a servant announced that the carriage had arrived to take Mr. Webster to a ball given in his honor. Some of the guests escorted Webster to his carriage. As one of them was folding up the carriage step after he had climbed in, he found Webster's foot in the way, and asked whether he wished to alight. "Yes," said Webster quickly, "I want to go back and help our mathematical friend stop the interest on that damned expensive bottle of wine."

ह ई

WEBSTER, Noah (1758–1843), *US lexicographer. His* American Dictionary of the English Language *(1828) was the forerunner of a great procession of American dictionaries bearing the name Webster in their titles.*

1 Going unexpectedly into the parlor of their house one day, Mrs. Webster discovered her husband embracing their maid. "Noah, I am surprised!" she exclaimed. Webster released the maid and reassumed his professional dignity. "No, my dear," he corrected his wife, "it is *I* who am surprised; you are merely astonished."

{The authenticity of this old chestnut is doubtful.}

ह ई

WEISSMULLER, Johnny (1904–84), *US swimmer. He won five Olympic gold medals (1924, 1928) and was the first man to swim 100 meters in under a minute (1922). He later became a successful film actor, noted especially for his characterization of Tarzan.*

1 Asked if he would do a screen test for the part of Tarzan in the first sound movies of the jungle saga, Weissmuller is reported to have exclaimed, "Me? Tarzan?"

{Shorn of its question marks, this became a catchphrase of the Tarzan films.}

2 In 1959, when Fidel Castro's guerrilla troops were battling Fulgencio Batista's soldiers in Cuba, Weissmuller, part of a celebrity golf tournament, was on his way to the golf course with some friends and two bodyguards. Suddenly their car was surrounded by a band of guerrillas who disarmed the guards and pointed their rifles at Weissmuller and his party. What to do? Weissmuller drew himself up to his full height, beat his chest, and let out the famous yell. The guerrillas were stunned for a moment. Then: "Tarzan! Tarzan! *Bienvenido!* Welcome to Cuba!" An international incident had been averted. Indeed, it turned into an autographing party, followed by a triumphal procession to the golf course.

ह ई

WEIZMANN, Chaim (1874–1952), *Jewish statesman; first president of Israel (1949–52). Weizmann, trained as a chemist, in 1916 discovered a manufacturing process for the production of acetone. Because he was already prominent in the Zionist movement, his discovery gave him status in his dealings with the British government that resulted in the Balfour Declaration (1917).*

1 As a chemist at Manchester University, Weizmann came into the constituency of the Conservative politician Arthur Balfour. There was a proposal at that time to establish a Jewish "homeland" in Uganda, a suggestion hotly countered by the Zionists. A mediator arranged for Weizmann to meet Balfour to put him straight on the unacceptability of Uganda and to explain the emotional and spiritual attraction of Palestine. Trying to get this idea across to Balfour, Weizmann said, "Just suppose, Mr. Balfour, I were to offer you Paris instead of London; would you accept it?" Balfour, off guard, said somewhat crassly, "But, Dr. Weizmann, we already *have* London." Replied Weizmann: "But we had Jerusalem when London was a marsh."

ह ई

WELLES, Orson (1915–), *US film actor and director. His first film,* Citizen Kane *(1941), became a classic overnight, but earned him the hostility of William Randolph Hearst, on whom* *the principal character is based. As an actor, he has appeared in many movies, perhaps most notably in* The Third Man *(1949).*

1 Film director Vincent Korda and his son Michael once had to chase Orson Welles, who was running from contract obligations, across Europe. Landing in Venice, Naples, Capri, and Nice, they finally caught up with him in Cagnes-sur-Mer and hoisted him off to a private airplane. Michael and Welles shared the back seats with a giant basket of fruit, which Vincent had carefully selected in Nice, wedged between them. Michael eventually fell asleep. When he awoke, he eyed the basket — and realized that Welles had systematically taken a single bite out of each piece of fruit. Having thus effectively destroyed Vincent's fruit, Welles now slept soundly, his immaculate appearance marred only by a few spots of juice on his shirt front.

2 One Saturday during the production of his film *The Lady from Shanghai,* Welles decided that a certain set needed repainting for the following Monday's filming. Having been told by production manager Jack Fier that this was quite impossible, Welles gathered together a group of friends. They broke into the paint department late on Saturday evening, repainted the set themselves, and left a huge sign over the entrance to the studio: "THE ONLY THING WE HAVE TO FEAR IS FIER HIMSELF." When the official set painters arrived for work on Monday, they immediately called a strike. Fier was obliged to pay a hefty sum to each member of the crew as compensation for the work done by nonunion labor. He deducted the money from Welles's fee and had a new banner painted "ALL'S WELL THAT ENDS WELLES." Whereupon the two men, bitter enemies up to that point, called a truce and ultimately became great friends.

§◈ ◈§

WELLINGTON, Arthur Wellesley, 1st Duke of (1769–1852), *British general and statesman, nicknamed "the Iron Duke." After service in India, Wellesley led the British campaign against Napoleon in Spain and Portugal — the Peninsular War (1808–14). For this achievement he was made a duke. He and the Prussian general Blücher finally defeated Napoleon at Waterloo (1815). In 1828 he became Tory prime minister. Although a supporter of the Roman Catholic emancipation bill (1829), he opposed parliamentary reform and was eventually forced to resign (1830).*

1 On a sea voyage the vessel in which Wellington was traveling encountered a violent storm and seemed in imminent danger of sinking. The captain came to Wellington's cabin at dusk and said, "It will soon be all over with us." Wellington, about to go to bed, replied, "Very well, then I shall not take off my boots."

2 When the young Arthur Wellesley was in India, he was in charge of negotiations after the battle of Assaye with an emissary of an Indian ruler who was anxious to know what territories would be ceded to his master as a result of the treaty. Having tried various approaches and found that the general was not to be drawn on the subject, the Indian offered him five lacs of rupees (about £50,000) for the information. "Can you keep a secret?" asked Wellesley. "Yes, indeed," said the Indian eagerly. "So can I," said Wellesley.

3 Wellington's soldiers nicknamed him "Old Nosey" on account of his prominent nose. Riding up one day during his Spanish campaigns to inspect an exposed position, Wellington, about to be challenged, forgot the countersign. The sentry, an Irishman, nonetheless brought his musket to the salute and said, "God bless your crooked nose; I would rather see it than ten thousand men!"

{This remark is quoted by many of the officers who served under Wellington in the Peninsular War.}

4 During the Peninsular War a detachment of energetic but inexperienced young officers arrived to strengthen Wellington's forces. Wellington observed, "I don't know what effect they will have upon the enemy, but by God, they frighten me."

5 Although the cavalry regiments tended to get more of the limelight, Wellington was fully aware of the crucial importance of the infantry. A few weeks before the battle of Waterloo an Englishman encountered the duke in a square in Brussels and asked if he thought he could defeat Napoleon. Wellington pointed to a soldier from one of the infantry regiments, who was doing some off-duty sightseeing in the town. "It all depends upon that article there," he said. "Give me enough of it, and I am sure."

6   At one point during the battle of Waterloo an officer commanding a gun battery sent a message to Wellington saying that he could clearly discern Napoleon among the enemy troops, his guns were in position, and he requested permission to fire. Wellington forbade him. "It is not the business of generals to shoot one another."

7   At Waterloo, the Marquess of Anglesey, who was in command of the British, Hanoverian, and Belgian horse, was standing by the Duke of Wellington when a shot hit his right knee. "By God, sir," he remarked to Wellington, "I have lost my leg."

"By God, I believe you have," replied Wellington laconically.

{The leg had to be amputated, and it was buried, with an obelisk erected over its last resting place.}

8   The hero of Waterloo was sitting in his office one day when the door flew open and a man rushed in, crying, "I must kill you!" Wellington did not raise his head from his papers. He merely said, "Does it have to be today?" The intruder looked confused. "Well, they didn't tell me . . . but soon, surely," he replied. "Good," said Wellington briskly. "A little later on then, I'm busy at the moment." The man withdrew and was promptly seized by the police, who had been informed that there was an escaped lunatic on the rampage.

9   At Vienna Wellington was compelled to sit through a performance of Beethoven's *Battle of Victoria* (or, *Wellington's Victory*). Afterward a Russian envoy asked him if the music had been anything like the real thing. "By God, no," said the duke. "If it had been like that I'd have run away myself."

10   When some French officers, cut to the heart at France's defeat, turned their backs on Wellington at Vienna, an onlooker spoke sympathetically to the snubbed duke. Wellington smiled. "I have seen their backs before, madam," he said.

11   When Sir John Steell was executing the colossal equestrian statue of Wellington to be placed in Edinburgh, he was troubled by the fact that his sitter did not look particularly warlike. All his efforts to get a more animated expression, by urging the duke to recall the glorious victories of the Peninsular campaigns and Waterloo, failed to produce their effect. At last in desperation he suggested that he should model the duke as he was on the morning of the Battle of Salamanca, "as you galloped about the field inspiring your troops to deeds of valor." The duke snorted. "If you really want to model me as I was on the morning of Salamanca, you must show me crawling along a ditch on my stomach, holding a telescope."

12   Wellington once came upon a little boy sitting at the side of the road, crying as if his heart would break. "Come now, that's no way for a young gentleman to behave. What's the matter?" he asked. "I have to go away to school tomorrow," sobbed the child, "and I'm worried about my pet toad. There's no one else to care for it and I shan't know how it is." The duke reassured him, promising to attend to the matter personally.

After the boy had been at school for little more than a week, he received the following letter: "Field Marshal the Duke of Wellington presents his compliments to Master —— and has the pleasure to inform him that his toad is well."

13   Lord Douro, the duke's eldest son, was extraordinarily like him in appearance. A lady once asked the duke if the numerous caricatures of him that had been published had ever annoyed him. "Not a bit, not a bit," said Wellington, then added after a pause, "There is only one caricature that has ever caused me annoyance — Douro."

14   Sparrows invaded the newly built Crystal Palace and became trapped under the glass roof, with predictably messy results for the exhibits and visitors. Queen Victoria sought the views of her eldest statesman on how to deal with the problem. "Sparrowhawks, ma'am," was Wellington's laconic advice.

15   The French actress Mlle George boasted that she had slept with both Napoleon and

Wellington. Asked in later life who was the better lover, she replied, "*Ah, monsieur, le duc était de beaucoup le plus fort*" (Ah, sir, the duke was by far the more vigorous).

16   In his later years Wellington resented any kind of attention that implied he was decrepit. One evening, as Wellington was waiting to cross Piccadilly to reach his house, a gentleman nearly as old forcibly took the Duke's arm and made a considerable parade of escorting him across the busy thoroughfare. "I thank you, sir," said Wellington when he reached his door. The other clasped his hand and broke into effusive speech, concluding with, "I never dared to hope that I might see the day when I might render the slightest assistance to the greatest man that ever lived." Wellington surveyed him serenely. "Don't be a damn fool, sir," he said, and walked into his house.

కం ఆ

WELLS, H[erbert] G[eorge] (1866–1946), *British novelist. His novels fall into two main categories: imaginative romances or futuristic fantasies, such as* The War of the Worlds *(1898); and novels of social comedy or humor, such as* The History of Mr. Polly *(1910). His social commentaries and popularizations of knowledge were important in their time.*

1   On leaving a Cambridge party, Wells accidentally picked up a hat that did not belong to him. Discovering his mistake, he decided not to return the headgear to its rightful owner, whose label was inside the brim. The hat fit Wells comfortably; furthermore, he had grown to like it. So he wrote to the erstwhile owner: "I stole your hat; I like your hat; I shall keep your hat. Whenever I look inside it I shall think of you and your excellent sherry and of the town of Cambridge. I take off your hat to you."

2   At a dinner one evening H. G. Wells expounded his theory that mankind had failed. The dinosaur had failed because he had concentrated upon size. *Homo sapiens* had failed because he had not developed the right type of brain. So, Wells claimed, we will first destroy ourselves, then die out as a species, and revert to mud and slime. "And we shall deserve it," he added. One of the guests objected that surely it wouldn't be as bad as that. "One thousand

years more," said Wells. "That's all *Homo sapiens* has before him."

3   (C. P. Snow recounts a sobering conversation with H. G. Wells that took place well after midnight in a hotel lounge, where they were sitting under the potted palms, glasses of whiskey by their chairs. Snow comments that Wells's bursts of intimacy tended to be lugubrious.)

"Untypically for [Wells] the conversation tailed off. The silences got longer and longer. Without any introduction, he broke into the quiet. It was a simple question. He said, 'Ever thought of suicide, Snow?' I reflected. I said, 'Yes, H. G., I have.' He replied, 'So have I. But not till I was past seventy.' He was then seventy-two. We drank some more whisky and looked sombrely at the palms."

కం ఆ

WERFEL, Alma Mahler (1879–1964), *wife of composer Gustav Mahler, then architect Walter Gropius, and finally writer Franz Werfel. The lover of many Central European writers and painters, she was regarded as the femme fatale of turn-of-the-century Vienna.*

1   The German playwright Gerhart Hauptmann was a great admirer of Alma's, although he had never been her lover. He said to her, "Alma, in another life we two must be lovers. May I make my reservation now?" Frau Hauptmann was standing close enough to overhear her husband's remark. "Oh, darling," she said, "I am sure Alma will be booked up there, too."

కం ఆ

WESLEY, John (1703–91), *British religious leader. Preaching an appealing message of repentance and faith, he and his brother Charles encountered much hostility from the Anglican hierarchy, which sometimes hired ruffians to disrupt the Wesleys' meetings. The brothers had no wish to split with the Anglican Church, and the Wesleyan Methodist Church was formed only after their deaths.*

1   At a stormy meeting a ruffian raised his hand to strike John Wesley on the head, but as he brought it down he checked his blow and murmured, "What soft hair he has!"

2 Preaching one day, Wesley noticed that some of his congregation were fast asleep. "Fire! Fire!" he suddenly cried. The sleepers awoke with a start and leaped to their feet. "Where?" they asked, looking anxiously around them. "In hell," replied Wesley, "for those who sleep under the preaching of the word."

ஓ&ை ஆ&

WEST, Mae (1892–1980), *US movie star and actress; the sex symbol of the 1930s. Her best-known films were* She Done Him Wrong *(1933),* Klondyke Annie *(1936), and* My Little Chickadee *(1939).*

1 "Goodness, Mae," said a friend, on greeting her, "where did you get those beautiful pearls?"

"Never mind," said Mae West, "but you can take it from me that goodness had nothing to do with it."

{Mae West used this riposte, which may well have been apocryphal, as the title of one volume of her autobiography, *Goodness Has Nothing to Do with It,* published in 1959.}

ஓ&ை ஆ&

WEST, Dame Rebecca (1892–1983), *British novelist and political journalist. Among her books are* Black Lamb and Grey Falcon *(1942),* The Meaning of Treason *(1949), and* A Train of Powder *(1955), the latter about the Nuremberg trials.*

1 On a visit to New York Rebecca West encountered a well-known society figure and his young friend. The two men, despite the difference in their ages and heights, wore identical outfits—suits, shirts, cravats, and even hairstyles were all the same. Surveying them, Miss West remarked, "They look like a nest of tables."

2 Someone at a party remarked of Cecil Chesterton (brother of GKC) that although he had a "dingy" complexion he was in fact very clean. The speaker went on to say that when Cecil bathed at Le Touquet, "he came out of the water just as gray-blue as when he went in." Rebecca West interposed, "But did you look at the Channel?"

3 In 1945 a Nazi death list was discovered that included the names of Rebecca West and Noël Coward. When Rebecca West heard of this, she immediately wired Coward: "My dear —the people we should have been seen dead with."

ஓ&ை ஆ&

WESTINGHOUSE, George (1846–1914), *US inventor and manufacturer.*

1 In 1872 Westinghouse took out his first patent for an automatic air brake that would function far more quickly and safely than the clumsy hand brakes then in use. The railroad companies, however, were deeply suspicious of the invention. When he wrote to Cornelius Vanderbilt, president of the New York Central Railroad, pointing out the advantages of the air brake, Vanderbilt returned the letter with the words "I have no time to waste on fools," scrawled on the bottom.

Alexander J. Cassatt of the Pennsylvania Railroad, next approached, saw possibilities in the new brake, and gave Westinghouse money to continue developing his invention. The tests were successful. News of them reached Vanderbilt. He wrote Westinghouse a letter inviting him to come and see him. Back came the letter, endorsed "I have no time to waste on fools. George Westinghouse."

ஓ&ை ஆ&

WHARTON, Edith Newbold (1862–1937), *US writer; noted for* Ethan Frome *(1911) and* The Age of Innocence *(1920), which was awarded the Pulitzer Prize.*

1 At the age of eleven, Edith Wharton attempted her first novel. It began: "'Oh, how do you do, Mrs. Brown?' said Mrs. Tompkins. 'If only I had known you were going to call, I should have tidied up the drawing room.'" Her mother's sole comment, on perusing this promising effort, was a gelid "Drawing rooms are always tidy."

ஓ&ை ஆ&

WHEATCROFT, Harry (1898–), *British rose specialist. He began growing roses in 1919, on a single acre of land. By the mid-1970s his company was producing over one and a half million roses each year. He has introduced* *many commercial varieties of roses and has written several books on the subject of rose-growing.*

1 Wheatcroft was known for his flamboyant dress. One afternoon, he arrived at a flower show in his familiar brightly colored attire. Instead of the usual rosebud in his buttonhole, however, he sported a magnificent carnation. "What's this, Harry?" commented a friend. "No rose today?"

"Shh," whispered Wheatcroft. "I'm incognito!"

❧ ❧

WHEELER, Joseph (1836–1906), *US army officer and politician. At the outbreak of the Spanish–American War he was commissioned major general. He was a member of the US House of Representatives in the late nineteenth century.*

1 Wheeler had been a Confederate general in the Civil War. In the Spanish–American War he commanded six regiments in the attack on Santiago. On the road to the city his men suffered serious casualties from the superior fire power of the enemy. Nevertheless, at a certain point the Spanish abandoned their entrenchments. General Wheeler, directly behind his men, inspired them with his imperishable and unreconstructed cry, "We've got the damn Yankees on the run!"

❧ ❧

WHEWELL, William (1794–1866), *British scientist. He was Master of Trinity College, Cambridge, from 1841 and won a considerable philosophical reputation with his* History of the Inductive Sciences *(1837).*

1 During the Victorian era the River Cam in Cambridge was still used as the town sewer. On a visit to Cambridge Queen Victoria paused on one of the bridges, surrounded by college dignitaries. She remarked on the quantity of paper she could see in the stream. "All that paper, ma'am," said Whewell, "carries notices to inform visitors that the river is unfit for bathing."

2 Whewell, well read in many subjects, could speak with authority on any topic of conversation that arose in the Trinity Senior Common Room, to the infuriation of some of his colleagues. Gathering up a number of reference books, including an old encyclopedia, they selected the obscure subject of Chinese musical instruments and studied it assiduously for several days. During the after-dinner conversation the next Sunday, they introduced the topic. Those who knew nothing of the conspiracy were astounded at the unexpected erudition of their colleagues; even Whewell remained silent for a while. Then, turning to one of the conspirators, he remarked, "I gather you have been reading the encyclopedia article on Chinese musical instruments I wrote some years back."

❧ ❧

WHISTLER, James Abbott McNeill (1834–1903), *US painter who lived most of his life in London after 1860. Cantankerous and opinionated, he made many enemies in the art world — see his* The Gentle Art of Making Enemies *(1890).*

1 During a West Point examination Whistler scandalized his examiners by not knowing the date of the battle of Buena Vista. "What!" said one of them, "Suppose you went out to dinner and the company got talking about the Mexican War, and you, a West Point man, did not know the date of this battle. What would you do?" Politely but decisively Whistler replied, "I should refuse to associate with people who talked of such things at dinner."

2 Whistler's failure in his West Point chemistry examination once provoked him to remark in later life, "If silicon had been a gas, I should have been a major general."

3 A snobbish Bostonian approached Whistler at a party one evening. "And where were you born, Mr. Whistler?" she asked. "Lowell, Massachusetts," replied the painter. "Whatever possessed you to be born in a place like that?" exclaimed the lady. "The explanation is quite simple," said Whistler. "I wished to be near my mother."

4 An American self-made millionaire visited Whistler's Paris studio, intending to buy some pictures for his palatial house. He glanced around the studio with its clutter of canvases and said, "How much for the lot?"

"Four million," said Whistler.

"What!"

"My posthumous prices."

5 Whistler, priding himself on his fluency in French, insisted on doing the ordering in a fashionable Paris restaurant. His companion tried to intervene and was told, "I am quite capable of ordering a meal in France without your assistance." "Of course you are," said his friend placatingly, "but I just distinctly heard you order a flight of steps."

{Did he use *escalier* for *escalope*?}

6 Whistler had been commissioned to paint a life-size nude portrait of French actress Cléo de Mérode. With her mother sitting nearby as chaperone, Mlle de Mérode draped herself on the couch, wearing nothing but a bandeau around her head. Whistler was not totally satisfied with the effect. He stepped forward to readjust the bandeau, which completely covered the actress's ears. Her mother instantly rose to her feet. "Oh, no, no, no, monsieur!" she cried. "My daughter's ears are for her husband."

7 Whistler had dined and wined extremely well at a friend's house. He left the party and a few seconds later a loud crash announced that he had fallen down the stairs. As he was picked up, he indignantly demanded the name of his host's architect. "Norman Shaw," was the reply. "I might have known it," said Whistler. "The damned teetotaler."

8 A female admirer asked Whistler whether he thought genius hereditary. "I cannot tell you that, madam," he replied. "Heaven has granted me no offspring."

9 A notorious bore approached Whistler at a gathering and launched into conversation with "You know, Mr. Whistler, I passed your house last night—"

"Thank you," said Whistler.

10 Someone annoyed by Whistler's constant self-applause said pointedly, "It's a good thing we can't see ourselves as others see us."

"Isn't it?" responded Whistler. "I know in my case I would grow intolerably conceited."

11 Some blank canvases that Whistler had ordered had been lost in the mail. Asked whether the canvases were of any great value, Whistler replied, "Not yet, not yet."

12 "A woman said to Whistler, 'I just came up from the country this morning along the Thames, and there was an exquisite haze in the atmosphere which reminded me so much of some of your little things. It was really a perfect series of Whistlers.'

"'Yes, madam,' responded Whistler gravely, 'Nature is creeping up.'"

13 A friend of Whistler's came up to him in a London street as the artist was talking to a particularly grimy urchin selling newspapers. Whistler asked the lad how long he had been doing the work.

"Three years, sir."

"How old are you?"

"Seven, sir."

"Oh, come, you must be older than that."

"No, I ain't, sir."

Whistler turned to his friend. "I don't think he could get that dirty in seven years. Do you?"

14 A supposed conversation between Whistler and Oscar Wilde having been published in *Punch,* Wilde sent Whistler the following telegram: "*Punch* too ridiculous. When you and I are together we never talk about anything except ourselves." Back came the reply from Whistler: "No, no, Oscar, you forget. When you and I are together we never talk about anything except me."

15 Whistler was once printing etchings with the painter Walter Sickert. During the course of their work, Sickert clumsily dropped one of the copper plates. "How like you!" said Whistler derisively.

A few minutes later, however, the same accident befell Whistler himself. "How unlike me!" he exclaimed.

16 Whistler disliked Joseph Turner's work and made no secret of his opinion. Someone once asked him if he would give advice as to whether a certain picture was a genuine Turner or an imitation. "That is a fine distinction," said Whistler.

17 Whistler's presidency of the Royal Society of British Artists was short-lived. In 1888 he resigned after his autocratic ways had caused him to quarrel with most of the members. To his followers he said of this debacle, "It is very simple. The artists retired. The British remained."

18 Poet and critic Theodore Watts added the name Dunton, his mother's surname, to his own in 1896. Whistler, the deadly foe of all social pretension, signalized the event with a three-word note to his erstwhile friend: "Theodore, Watts Dunton?"

ॐ ఆశ్

WHITE, Andrew Dickson (1832–1918), *US scholar and university administrator. In 1865 he was appointed first president of Cornell University.*

1 A stickler for academic excellence, White refused permission to Cornell's football squad to travel to a game against Michigan: "I will not permit thirty men to travel four hundred miles to agitate a bag of wind."

ॐ ఆశ్

WHITE, William Allen (1868–1944), *US editor and journalist.*

1 "William Allen White once said that his happy quips just seemed to come to him from heaven. This one sounds like it; he was at the 1928 convention of the Democratic Party, and was practically forced to attend a dinner for Senator Jim Reed, of Missouri, who was an aspirant for the nomination. The lone Republican present, Mr. White hesitated, then said: 'I'd better not. I don't want God to know I'm here.'"

ॐ ఆశ్

WHITEHEAD, Alfred North (1861–1947), *British mathematician and philosopher. At Cambridge (1884–1910), he collaborated with Bertrand Russell on* Principia Mathematica *(1910–13). After ten years as professor of applied mathematics at the University of London (1914–24), he accepted a chair of philosophy at Harvard.*

1 A scholar asked Whitehead which he believed to be more important, ideas or things.

"Why, I should imagine ideas *about* things," Whitehead replied.

2 In 1933 James Bryant Conant, who had made his career in organic chemistry, was elected president of Harvard. Whitehead expressed surprise that a chemist had been chosen for this post. A colleague reminded him that the great Charles W. Eliot (president from 1869–1909) had also begun as a chemist. Said Whitehead, "Ah, but he was a *bad* chemist."

ॐ ఆశ్

WHITELAW, WILLIAM [Stephen Ian], **1st Viscount Whitelaw of Penrith** (1918–), *British Conservative politician, chairman of the Conservative party (1974–75).*

1 At a reception at the American Embassy, Whitelaw found himself chatting about one of his favorite pastimes, golf, to a man whose face seemed vaguely familiar. Sometime later, he asked a friend, "Do tell me, who is that American I was talking to? He doesn't appear to have much sense of humor."

"Bob Hope," was the reply.

ॐ ఆశ్

WHITMAN, Walt (1819–92), *US poet. He is best known for* Leaves of Grass *(1855), free-verse poems that express his democratic idealism and passionate love of life.*

1 The stir caused by Whitman's poetry was such that some people hailed him as a prophet and others abused him as a monster of depravity. One day, as Whitman was walking past the White House, he was pointed out to President Lincoln. "Well, he looks like a man" was the president's comment.

ॐ ఆశ్

WHITNEY, Stephen (c. 1850–c. 1920), *US businessman and cousin of the inventor Eli Whitney. A highly successful speculator in cotton and real estate, he left a fortune of fifteen million dollars.*

1 On hearing the news of Stephen Whitney's death, the diarist George Templeton Strong commented that he had never used any of his money for the benefit of either himself or anyone else. "His last act was characteristic and fitting," Strong observed. "He locked up his checkbook and died."

❧ ❧

WIENIAWSKI, Henri (1835–80), *Polish violinist and composer. He wrote a number of concertos and studies for the violin.*

1 Wieniawski once played to a half-empty auditorium in Boston. Despite the poor attendance, he was urged to return and perform there again. "Oh, no," replied the violinist. "I'll get out of the habit of playing in public."

❧ ❧

WILD, Jonathan (?1682–1725), *English criminal. In debtors' prison he made the acquaintance of a number of thieves. On his release he set up a complex system for the disposal of stolen goods and masterminded numerous robberies, using organized gangs of thieves and ex-convicts. He was finally arrested for theft and hanged at Tyburn.*

1 Wild remained a criminal literally to his death. As he stepped up to the gallows at Tyburn, the unrepentant rogue deftly picked the pocket of the priest administering the last rites. He died waving his trophy, a corkscrew, triumphantly at the crowd below.

❧ ❧

WILDE, Oscar (1854–1900), *British aesthete, writer, and wit. He wrote a number of brilliant comedies, including* Lady Windermere's Fan *(1892) and* The Importance of Being Earnest *(1895), as well as poetry and a novel,* The Picture of Dorian Gray *(1891). His affair with Lord Alfred Douglas resulted in a sensational court case in 1895, ending in a two-year prison sentence for Wilde. From 1897 he lived in France under an assumed name.*

1 In the nineteenth-century Oxford examinations there was a compulsory divinity section, and candidates were required to translate aloud from the Greek version of the New Testament. Wilde, assigned a passage dealing with the Passion, began to translate fluently and accurately. The examiners, satisfied, told him he could stop. Ignoring them, he continued to translate. Eventually they succeeded in halting him. "Oh, do let me go on," Wilde said. "I want to see how it ends."

2 In 1882 Wilde went on a lecture tour of the United States. A New York customs official asked if he had anything to declare. "No. I have nothing to declare"— Wilde paused —"except my genius."

3 "Wonderful man, Columbus!" exclaimed an American eager to strike up a conversation with Wilde. "Why?" asked Wilde. "He discovered America," replied the other. Wilde shook his head: "Oh no, it had often been discovered before, but it had always been hushed up."
Compare MAO ZEDONG 1.

4 Frank Harris, then editor of the *Saturday Review,* gave a dinner at the Café Royal to which some of London's most brilliant wits were invited. Harris dominated the conversation, ignoring all hints to quiet down. Oscar Wilde grew more and more restless as Harris told the company about all the great houses at which he had been a guest. Eventually he broke in with "Dear Frank, we believe you; you have dined in every house in London—*once.*"
{Sir William Rothenstein, another guest at that dinner, recalls this as the sole occasion on which he heard Oscar Wilde say an unkind thing. In another version the speaker is Whistler and the once-only diner, Wilde himself.}

5 Wilde was asked his opinion of a play that had been generally accounted a fiasco. "The play was a great success," he replied, "but the audience was a disaster."

6 Wilde and Whistler frequently exchanged insults in a feud that owed more to both parties' addiction to the limelight than to any genuine rancor. "I wish I had said that!" exclaimed Wilde after a particularly scintillating remark from Whistler. "You will, Oscar, you will," said Whistler.

7 In the course of their well-publicized feud, Whistler accused Wilde of plagiarizing his ideas on art. Wilde replied: "As for borrowing Mr. Whistler's ideas about art, the only thoroughly original ideas I have ever heard him express have had reference to his own superiority as a painter over painters greater than himself."

8 When the poet laureateship fell vacant on the death of Tennyson, the names of several

likely candidates came up frequently. Not included was that of the prolific poetaster Sir Lewis Morris. "It's a complete conspiracy of silence against me," Morris complained to Oscar Wilde. "What ought I to do, Oscar?"

"Join it," said Wilde.

9 Talking to an admirer of Dickens, Wilde moved his hearer almost to tears by the eloquence of his enthusiasm for the master's powers. And then Wilde concluded, "One would have to have a heart of stone to read the death of Little Nell without laughing."

10 After playing for some time the role of Lord Illingworth in Wilde's play *A Woman of No Importance,* Beerbohm Tree showed signs of unconsciously adopting the character's mannerisms in real life. Wilde was delighted with this phenomenon. "Ah, every day dear Herbert becomes *de plus en plus Oscarisé,*" he declared. "It is a wonderful case of nature imitating art."

11 When asked to make certain changes in one of his plays, Wilde protested: "Who am I to tamper with a masterpiece?"

12 Wilde was staying with friends at a country house, where his eccentric behavior and manner of dress startled his fellow guests. One morning he came down to breakfast looking very pale and drawn. "I'm afraid you are ill, Mr. Wilde," remarked another member of the party. "No, not ill," replied Wilde, "only tired. The fact is, I picked a primrose in the wood yesterday, and it was so ill I have been sitting up with it all night."

13 Wilde's legal battle with the Marquis of Queensberry, father of Lord Alfred Douglas, began when Wilde brought a case of criminal libel against the marquis for publicly accusing him of sodomy. Shortly after the trial began, Wilde met an actor friend, Charles Goodhart, in Piccadilly Circus, where every newspaper placard displayed his name and the newsboys were shouting it on every corner. Goodhart, feeling embarrassed, talked about the weather. Wilde, however, put him at his ease: "You've heard of my case? Don't distress yourself. All is well. The working classes are with me . . . to a boy."

14 Sentenced to two years' hard labor, Wilde stood handcuffed in driving rain waiting for transport to prison. "If this is the way Queen Victoria treats her prisoners," he remarked, "she doesn't deserve to have any."

15 Ada Leverson was a devoted friend of Oscar Wilde, who always called her "Sphinx." It was she who gave him refuge when he had nowhere to go to escape the public scandal after his first trial in 1895. When Wilde was released from prison two years later, she, her husband, and a very few others went early in the morning to the house of a mutual friend to greet him before he departed for France. It was a difficult ordeal for all concerned, but Wilde immediately put his friends at their ease. "Sphinx," he said as soon as he entered the room, "how marvelous of you to know exactly the right hat to wear at seven o'clock in the morning to meet a friend who has been away."

16 (Yeats recounts a story he was told of Wilde's visit to a brothel in Dieppe after he had been released from prison. "Dowson" is the poet Ernest Dowson.)

"Dowson pressed upon him the necessity of acquiring a 'more wholesome taste.' They emptied their pockets onto the café table, and though there was not much, there was enough, if both heaps were put into one. Meanwhile the news had spread, and they set out accompanied by a cheering crowd. Arrived at their destination, Dowson and the crowd remained outside, and presently Wilde returned. He said in a low voice to Dowson, 'The first these ten years, and it will be the last. It was like cold mutton' . . . and then aloud, so that the crowd might hear him, 'But tell it in England, for it will entirely restore my character.'"

17 Wilde died of cerebral meningitis in a hotel in Paris. He was offered and accepted a drink of champagne, remarking as he did so, "I am dying beyond my means."

{Another version of this quip is "I suppose I shall have to die beyond my means," spoken to a doctor who mentioned an exorbitant fee for an operation.}

18 Still another version of Wilde's last words has him staring at his shabby Paris bedroom. He is reputed to have said, "Either that wallpaper goes, or I do."

> A congressman was once asked about his attitude toward whiskey. "If you mean the demon drink that poisons the mind, pollutes the body, desecrates family life, and inflames sinners, then I'm against it. But if you mean the elixir of Christmas cheer, the shield against winter chill, the taxable potion that puts needed funds into public coffers to comfort little crippled children, then I'm for it. This is my position, and I will not compromise."
>
> — Mark Edward Lender and James Kirby Martin, *Drinking in America: A History*

WILDER, Billy [Samuel] (1906–), *US film director and screenwriter, born in Austria. His films include* Sunset Boulevard *(1950),* Witness for the Prosecution *(1958), and* Some Like It Hot *(1959).*

1 Wilder was sent to Berlin at the end of World War II to help reestablish the German entertainment industry. Having authorized the resumption of the Oberammergau Passion Play, he was asked if a certain actor, a known supporter of the Nazis, could reassume the role of Christ, which he had played before the war. "Certainly," replied Wilder, "if you use real nails."

2 Before their marriage, Wilder's wife lived in a rather shabby part of town, and Wilder disliked having to pick her up there for a date. "I'd worship the ground you walked on," he told her, "if only you lived in a better neighborhood."

3 Wilder was going to Europe for the opening of *Some Like It Hot.* His wife, who had recently returned from a trip to Paris, asked him to send back some Charvet ties for a friend and a bidet for herself. A couple of weeks later, Wilder cabled from France: "Charvet ties on way but impossible to obtain bidet. Suggest handstand in shower."

4 Wilder was asked by a journalist to name his personal favorite among his many films. "*Some Like It Hot,*" he replied instantly. The journalist was surprised that Wilder had not named one of his classics, such as *Sunset Boulevard.* "A nice little picture," agreed Billy, "but in those days I wasn't getting a percentage of the gross."

5 Wilder had some difficulty understanding the concept of existentialism, even when it was explained to him by Jean-Paul Sartre himself. His research into the subject, however, gave him the idea for a new film. "It's a great plot," he said enthusiastically. "This boy falls in love with his mother and marries her. They live together quite happily until one day he learns that she isn't his mother. So he commits suicide."

WILDING, Michael (1912–79), *British actor. His films include* Sailors Three *(1940),* Piccadilly Incident *(1946), and* Spring in Park Lane *(1948).*

1 Wilding was once asked whether actors had any distinguishing features that set them apart from other human beings. "Without a doubt," he replied. "You can pick out actors by the glazed look that comes into their eyes when the conversation wanders away from themselves."

WILHELMINA HELENA PAULINE MARIA (1880–1962), *queen of the Netherlands (1890–1948); mother of Queen Juliana, who came to the throne after Wilhelmina's abdication in 1948 and reigned until 1980.*

1 At a meeting with Wilhelm II during World War I, Queen Wilhelmina was not intimidated by the kaiser's exaggerated boasts. "Our guardsmen," he declared, "are seven feet tall."

"And when we open our dikes," replied the queen, "the waters are ten feet deep."

{For similar quantitative combat *see* JAMES WATSON GERARD 1.}

WILKES, John (1725–97), *British politician and journalist. He became a member of Parliament in 1757, was arrested for libel in 1763, and was outlawed the following year. Returning in 1768 from Paris, where he had lived in exile, he was twice elected MP for Middlesex, but was prevented from taking his seat until 1774. As an MP, he secured important political freedoms* *with respect to the liberty of the press and the individual and the conduct of elections.*

1 A voter once answered Wilkes's canvass with the words: "I'd sooner vote for the devil than you."

"And if your friend isn't standing?" inquired Wilkes.

2 A Roman Catholic was arguing with Wilkes about religion. "Where was your religion before Luther?" asked the Catholic. "Did you wash your face this morning?" rejoined Wilkes. When his opponent said that he had, Wilkes went on, "Then, pray, where was your face before it was washed?"

3 As the popular leader of the London mob, Wilkes was often honored by having public houses named after him and their signs painted with his picture. A lady, seeing one of these signs hanging out over the street, remarked, "Wilkes swings everywhere but where he ought."

4 After James Boswell had dined with the sheriffs and judges at a formal dinner at London's Old Bailey law courts, he complained that his pocket had been picked and his handkerchief stolen. "Pooh," said Wilkes, "this is nothing but the ostentation of a Scotsman to let the world know that he had possessed a pocket handkerchief."

5 After 1786, when Wilkes became a supporter of Pitt, and hence of the government, the Whigs liked to taunt him for his fickleness. The Prince of Wales, Wilkes's *bête noire*, one evening recited to him Sheridan's mocking verses beginning, "Johnny Wilkes, Johnny Wilkes, You greatest of bilks." Wilkes waited for revenge until a gathering at Carlton House, when the prince called for toasts. Knowing the prince's loathing for his father and his glee at the king's illness, Wilkes gave the toast: "The king; long life to him."

"Since when," sneered the prince, "have you been so anxious about my parent's health?"

"Since I had the pleasure of Your Royal Highness's acquaintance," replied Wilkes with a most courteous bow.

6 Wilkes dined one night with the Earl of Sandwich in London's Covent Garden, at the famous Beef Steak Club. After a fair amount to drink Lord Sandwich said to Wilkes, "I have often wondered what catastrophe would bring you to your end; I think you must die of the pox or the halter." "My lord," replied Wilkes instantaneously, "that will depend on whether I embrace your lordship's mistress or your lordship's principles."

{This retort has also been attributed to Samuel Foote, speaking to Lord Sandwich, and, quite improbably, to Benjamin Disraeli, speaking to Gladstone.}

WILLARD, Francis Elizabeth Caroline (1839–98), *US educator and reformer, active in the causes of temperance, women's rights, and industrial codes for women. In 1879 she became president of the national Women's Christian Temperance Union, and in 1888 president of the National Council of Women.*

1 Frances Willard, a graduate of the North Western Female College in Evanston, Illinois, spent the formative years of her career there. Although she died in New York, she always planned to return to Evanston to die. Knowing she was mortally ill, she said, "When I reach heaven, I want to register as from Evanston."
Compare RALPH WALDO EMERSON 7.

WILLES, Sir John (1685–1761), *British lawyer, lord chief justice (1737–61).*

1 Rumors of irregular conduct in the lord chief justice's household became so rife that a dissenting clergyman decided to talk with him and perhaps bring him to repentance. After approaching the matter in a roundabout way, which Willes affected not to understand, the clergyman came to the point: "They say that one of your maidservants is now with child."

"What's that to me?" said Willes.

"But they say she is with child by your lordship."

"What's that to you?"

WILLIAM I [William the Conqueror] (1027–87), *king of England (1066–87). As Duke of Normandy, William had a tenuous claim to the English throne, which he asserted on the death* *of Edward the Confessor. He defeated and killed his Anglo-Saxon rival, King Harold, at the battle of Hastings (1066) and imposed Norman rule throughout England.*

1 Leading his army of invasion ashore at Pevensey in southeast England, William stumbled and fell. The superstitious men around him exclaimed at the bad omen, but William quickly stood up and, holding out his muddied hands, cried, "By the splendor of God I have taken possession of my realm; the earth of England is in my two hands."

{A similar anecdote is told of Julius Caesar's landing in Africa.}

ಶಿ ೕ

WILLIAM I (1797–1888), *king of Prussia (1861–88) and emperor of Germany (1871–88). During his reign, guided by Bismarck, Germany was united under the leadership of Prussia.*

1 At a Berlin subscription ball, open to those of lesser rank as well as to high society, the emperor noticed his court tailor and greeted him amiably: "A lovely ball, isn't it?" The tailor bowed deeply, observing in a tone of servility, "These balls, Your Majesty, seem to draw a somewhat more mixed group of guests than formerly." The emperor smiled, then said, "True, but what can we do about it? We can't invite tailors only."

2 Daily at noon the emperor would station himself at the corner window of his Berlin palace and show himself to the thousands of subjects and visitors who came to pay homage to this embodiment of imperial power. During his later years as his health declined, his doctors were emphatic in beseeching him not to weaken himself with this daily activity. It was in fact difficult for the old emperor, but he refused to obey his doctors. "No, there's no help for it. My daily appearance is listed in Baedeker."

ಶಿ ೕ

WILLIAM II (1859–1941), *emperor of Germany (1888–1918). On his accession he made plain his determination to build Germany into a great power under Prussian hegemony. Kaiser Bill, as he was called, clashed with Britain over its colonial possessions in Africa, and his support for Austria-Hungary after the assassina-tions at Sarajevo (1914) involved Germany in World War I. After Germany's defeat he lived in exile in the Netherlands.*

1 As part of his program to build up the German navy, the kaiser himself designed a warship. When the plans were complete, he sent them to the Italian minister of the marine, Admiral Brin, who was then considered the world's leading naval architect. In due course the admiral's report was transmitted to the kaiser. The ship would easily outgun any existing battleship; its range and speed were likewise far in excess of any other vessel. Moreover, its internal arrangements were so well thought out that everyone sailing in it, from the commander to the humblest cabin boy, would find it a miracle of convenience and efficiency. The only problem, the report concluded, was that if the ship were actually put in the water it would sink like a lump of lead.

ಶಿ ೕ

WILLIAM III (1650–1702), *king of England (1689–1702) and Stadholder of the United Provinces (1672–1702). In 1677 he married James II's daughter Mary (1662–94) and in 1688 joined the opposition to his father-in-law. After the Glorious Revolution he was proclaimed joint ruler, with Mary, of England.*

1 During a journey by carriage through a village not far from Windsor, a woman who was determined to see the king pressed up close to the window to peer at the occupant. Having satisfied her curiosity, she stepped back and remarked, "Is that the king? My husband is a handsomer man than he." King William overheard her, leaned out, and said, "Good woman, do not speak so loud. Pray consider that I am a widower."

ಶಿ ೕ

WILLIAMS, TENNESSEE [Thomas Lanier Williams] (1911–83), *US dramatist. His best-known works include the partly autobiographical* The Glass Menagerie *(1945),* A Streetcar Named Desire *(1947), and* Cat on a Hot Tin Roof *(1955).*

1 Newspaper reports in 1961 announced that Williams had decided not to attend any further sessions with his psychoanalyst. Asked the reason for this decision, the playwright replied,

"He was meddling too much in my private life."

{According to his biographer, Donald Spoto, Williams was not aware of the humor in his reply.}

2 One day Williams and one of his leading ladies, Sylvia Miles, were walking through Piccadilly when Sylvia saw a very thin young girl. She whispered to Williams, "Oh, Tennessee, look—anorexia nervosa," and without the slightest hesitation he shot back, "Oh, Sylvia, you know everybody!"

{He appreciated his own joke; it appeared later in *Clothes for a Summer Hotel*.}

3 (When Williams received the gold medal for drama from the National Institute of Arts and Letters, his brief acceptance speech consisted almost entirely of an anecdote:)

"One time, Maureen Stapleton received a phone call from a friend who said that so-and-so was getting married, and the caller said, 'Why is she marrying that man, you know he is a homosexual,' and Maureen said, 'Well, what about the bride?' And the caller said, 'Well, of course we know she's a lesbian. And you know they're not even being married by a real minister, but by one who's been defrocked!' And Maureen said, 'Will you do me one favor? Will you please invite Tennessee Williams? Because he'll say, "Oh, they're just plain folks!"'"

4 The playwright once visited the fabulous thirty-nine-room Gramercy Park home of the famous publicist and art-and-celebrity collector Benjamin Sonnenberg. According to Ben Sonnenberg, Jr.'s account, Williams, after being shown through the ornate mansion, repaired to the bathroom, stayed there briefly, and was later heard to say, "It looked so shabby when I took it out, I couldn't go."

ริ๛ ๛ริ

WILSON, Charles Erwin (1890–1961), *US industrialist. He became president of General Motors Corporation in 1941 and was US secretary of defense (1953–57).*

1 Wilson, president of General Motors, was nominated by President Eisenhower to be secretary of defense. At his Senate confirmation hearing, Wilson uttered perhaps the only words for which he will be remembered: "What is good for the country is good for General Motors, and what's good for General Motors is good for the country."

ริ๛ ๛ริ

WILSON, Edmund (1895–1972), *US literary critic and essayist.*

1 Like all successful writers, Wilson was beset by people wanting his advice or help in all manner of literary and other matters. To deal with the flood of letters he had the following postcard printed: "Edmund Wilson regrets that it is impossible for him to: Read manuscripts, write articles or books to order, write forewords or introductions, make statements for publicity purposes, do any kind of editorial work, judge literary contests, give interviews, take part in writers' conferences, answer questionnaires, contribute to or take part in symposiums or 'panels' or any kind, contribute manuscripts for sales, donate copies of his books to libraries, autograph works for strangers, allow his name to be used on letterheads, supply personal information about himself, supply opinions on literary or other subjects." He was then pestered by people who wrote to him simply in order to obtain a copy of the postcard.

ริ๛ ๛ริ

WILSON, Sir Harold (1916–), *British statesman; Labour prime minister (1964–70, 1974–76). After a career as a government economist, he became a member of Parliament. In 1963 he became Labour leader and the following year prime minister. His administration was increasingly dogged by economic and industrial relations problems.*

1 At a rally in the mid-1960s, Wilson was interrupted by a cry of "Rubbish!" from a heckler at the back of the crowd. Without missing a beat, Wilson replied: "We'll take up your special interest in a moment, sir."

2 On one occasion during Harold Wilson's administration, Willie Hamilton, the vociferous member for Fife Central, harangued the prime minister for his indecisiveness on the issue of Britain's entry into the European Common Market. "First we're in, then we're out," cried the irate Labour member. "It's exactly like coitus interruptus." The House, stunned into silence, erupted with laughter when a Tory member shouted, "Withdraw."

❧ ❧

WILSON, Harriette (1786–1846), *British courtesan. She had a series of distinguished lovers and acquaintances in English high society.*

1 Around 1820 Harriette, finding herself short of money, decided to write her memoirs. The enterprise was widely publicized, Harriette making no secret of the fact that she was naming names. Some former "friends" were able to buy themselves out of the narrative by substantial cash payments. The Duke of Wellington, on being offered such a deal, is said to have responded with "Publish and be damned!" Harriette did publish; the publisher sold thirty editions of the book within a year.

❧ ❧

WILSON, Richard (1714–82), *Welsh painter. He trained as a portraitist, but after a visit to Italy in the 1750s changed his interest to landscapes. He became the first notable British landscape painter.*

1 The Italian tradition of landscape painting and the beauties of the Italian landscape were the factors that caused Wilson's change of allegiance in mid-career. On a visit to the famous waterfall at Terni, he is said to have exclaimed, "Well-done water — by God!"

❧ ❧

WILSON, [Thomas] Woodrow (1856–1924), *US statesman; president of Princeton University (1902–10); governor of New Jersey (1911–13); 28th president of the United States (1913–21). After maintaining a neutral position in the first years of World War I, Wilson eventually (1917) brought the United States into the conflict, following upon German submarine outrages. His Fourteen Points, incorporated into the Treaty of Versailles, laid the foundation for the League of Nations.*

1 As president of Princeton University, Wilson was once interrogated at length by an anxious mother who wanted to be sure that Princeton was the best place to send her son. "Madam," said Wilson, his patience exhausted, "we guarantee satisfaction or you will get your son back."

2 One afternoon during his time as governor of New Jersey, Wilson received news of the sudden death of a personal friend, a New Jersey senator. He was still recovering from the shock when the telephone rang again. It was a prominent New Jersey politician. "Governor," he said, "I would like to take the senator's place." Wilson replied, "It's perfectly agreeable to me if it's agreeable to the undertaker."

3 Shortly after the 1912 presidential election, Wilson visited an aged aunt whom he had not seen for some time. "What are you doing these days, Woodrow?" she asked. "I've just been elected president," replied Wilson. "Oh, yes? President of what?" inquired the aunt. "Of the United States." The old lady snorted impatiently. "Don't be silly!" she said.

4 President Wilson had refused to receive a deputation of Irish-American leaders headed by the agitator Daniel F. Cohalan. Wilson's private secretary, Joseph P. Tumulty, aware of Cohalan's great influence, tried to persuade the president to change his mind. "Think what a terrible impression it will make on his followers if you don't," he said. "That's just what I wanted it to do," replied Wilson, "but I think it will make a good impression on decent people."

5 During the Versailles peace negotiations, Wilson opposed the ceding of the Adriatic port of Fiume to Italy. The head of the Italian delegation, V. E. Orlando, argued eloquently that Italy's right to the city was undeniable, since its language, population, and cultural affinities were all predominantly Italian. "I hope you won't press the point in respect to New York City," countered Wilson, "or you might feel like claiming a sizable piece of Manhattan Island."

❧ ❧

WINTERS, Shelley [Shirley Schrift] (1922–), *US actress of stage, screen, and television, celebrated mainly for her comedy roles and her candor. Her many films include* A Double Life *(1948),* A Patch of Blue *(1965), and* The Poseidon Adventure *(1972).*

1 Al Horwits worked at one time for Universal Pictures in the publicity department. One of his clients was the young Shelley Winters. Scheduled to meet a certain Italian producer, she called Horwits to get some background information. Said Horwits, "He's a terrible wolf. He'll tear the clothes off your back."

"So I'll wear an old dress," said Shelley.

ॐ◆ঔ

WISE, Stephen Samuel (1874–1949), *US rabbi, born in Hungary. In 1907 he founded the Free Synagogue in New York City. He was also the founder and president of the Jewish Institute of Religion.*

1 Having accepted an invitation to address an anti-Nazi meeting in Brooklyn, Wise received a number of threatening letters. Undaunted, the rabbi attended the meeting as scheduled and opened his speech with the words: "I have been warned to stay away from this meeting under pain of being killed. If anyone is going to shoot me let him do it now. I hate to be interrupted."

ॐ◆ঔ

WODEHOUSE, Sir P[elham] **G**[renville] (1881–1975), *British humorous novelist who lived much of his life abroad, becoming a US citizen in 1955. His most famous characters include Bertie Wooster, an upper-class idiot of 1920s vintage, and his impeccable manservant Jeeves. Wodehouse's friends called him Plum.*

1 Ethel Wodehouse was a natural party giver, and on occasion her inclinations were allowed to override Plum's. Once when Ethel gave a party, some guests arrived rather late. When they rang the bell, the front door was opened not by the butler but by Plum. He surveyed them carefully and, recognizing them as friends, put out both hands in a gesture to push them away. "Don't come in," he said, "don't come in. You'll hate it!"

2 Wodehouse's terror of casual human contacts assumed almost pathological proportions. The Wodehouses were looking for an apartment in New York, and as Mrs. Wodehouse was about to go out to continue the search her husband called her back. "Get one on the ground floor," he said. "Why?" she

asked. "I never know what to say to the lift boy," was the answer.

3 On a visit to the zoo Wodehouse wandered into the monkey house and was confronted by a ferocious-looking monkey. For a while the two stared at one another. Finally the monkey turned and stalked off, revealing for the first time its scarlet, purple, and orange behind. Plum shook his head sadly. "That monkey," he declared, "is wearing its club colors in the wrong place."

ॐ◆ঔ

WOFFINGTON, Peg (c. 1714–60), *Irish actress. She excelled in Restoration comedies, often taking male roles, and was mistress of and leading lady for David Garrick.*

1 After one of her triumphs in a "breeches" part, Peg Woffington withdrew backstage, saying exultantly, "Half the pit really took me for a man."

"What's the good of that, when the other half knows precisely the opposite?" said one of her female colleagues.

ॐ◆ঔ

WOLF, Hugo (1860–1903), *Austrian composer. A disciple of Wagner, he composed more than two hundred songs, the opera* Der Corregidor *(1895), and a number of instrumental works.*

1 In 1897, Wolf went mad and was committed to an asylum. He was still sane enough, however, to be aware of his condition. "Is that clock right?" he once asked, pointing to a large clock that hung in the dining room of the asylum. "As far as I know," replied one of the attendants. "Then what's it doing here?" inquired Wolf.

ॐ◆ঔ

WOLFE, James (1727–59), *British soldier who died leading the attack on Quebec in which Britain seized the city from the French during the Seven Years' War.*

1 Wolfe's energy and self-confidence did not endear him to his fellow commanders. One of them complained to King George II that Wolfe was mad. "Mad, is he?" said the monarch.

"Then I wish he'd bite some of my other generals."

{*See* ULYSSES S. GRANT 5 for Lincoln's remark about his general.}

ઠ્ન ન્ફ

WOODBRIDGE, Frederick James Eugene (1867–1940), *US professor, born in Canada. He became professor of philosophy at Columbia University in 1902 and was also dean of the faculties of political science, philosophy, and pure science (1912–29).*

1 One of Woodbridge's former students recollects strolling on the campus with the distinguished philosopher. The dean remarked reflectively, "The Cathedral of Chartres was built by the spirit of the Virgin; the University of Virginia was built by the vision of Thomas Jefferson; Columbia was built by McKim, Mead and White."

ઠ્ન ન્ફ

WOOLLCOTT, Alexander (1887–1943), *US writer, drama critic, broadcaster, and New York wit.*

1 In his early years of service in World War I, as a sergeant in the Medical Corps, Woollcott and his outfit camped at Le Mans in appalling conditions. The tents leaked, and the men were obliged to put up their rickety beds in muddy pools of rainwater. Shortly afterward, Woollcott was transferred to the Paris office of *The Stars and Stripes,* the US army newspaper. He spent the remaining war years in luxury, frequenting the boulevard cafés and dining at the Ritz each evening. After the Armistice he happened to meet one of his former colleagues from the Medical Corps. "You made an awful mistake leaving our unit when you did," said the soldier. "The week after you went, they put wooden floors in our tents."

2 Opening an account at a New York department store, Dorothy Parker and her new husband, Alan Campbell, cited Woollcott as a reference for their financial reliability. They were soon to regret their choice. Woollcott's endorsement read: "Mr. Alan Campbell, the present husband of Dorothy Parker, has given my name as a reference in his attempt to open an account at your store. We all hope you will extend this credit to him. Surely Dorothy Parker's position in American letters is such as to make shameful the petty refusals which she and Alan have encountered at many hotels, restaurants, and department stores. What if you never get paid? Why shouldn't you stand your share of the expense?"

3 Woollcott was constantly referred to in the Broadway and literary columns. At one stage, the popular columnist Walter Winchell quoted a whole series of jokes and wisecracks he attributed to Woollcott. In fact, they had been made up by Irving Mansfield, whom Woollcott had hired for the purpose. Mansfield, who later became a well-known television producer, soon ran out of funny things to say, and Winchell's column no longer contained *bons mots* attributed to Woollcott. After a couple of weeks Woollcott sent Mansfield a telegram: "Dear Irving, whatever happened to my sense of humor?"

4 On seeing playwright Moss Hart's sumptuous country mansion and landscaped grounds, Woollcott remarked, "Just what God would have done if he had the money."

5 The writer Ludwig Lewisohn, of Jewish stock, complained to Woollcott about getting a bad review. Woollcott remarked, "Ludwig thinks he gets bad reviews because the critics are anti-Semitic. Actually it's because Ludwig has halitosis."

6 While Woollcott was a regular contributor to *The New Yorker,* he attended a dinner party in London at which the guest of honor was the Prince of Wales, the future Edward VIII. The ladies had left the room and the gentlemen had started on their port and cigars, when the prince intimated that he would like a few words in private with Mr. Woollcott. The gentlemen withdrew after the ladies, leaving Woollcott tête-à-tête with royalty, his head filled with visions of splendid commissions from the prince. "I understand, Mr. Woollcott, that you have something to do with that magazine from the States, *The New Yorker,*" began the prince. Woollcott admitted that he had. "Then why the devil don't I get it more regularly?" demanded His Highness. "Do look into it, will you?" Then they joined the rest of the party.

7 After Woollcott gave a lecture in a midwestern town, an elderly lady approached him and told him that his lecture had given her much pleasure. "And," she went on, "I was encouraged to speak to you because you said that you loved old ladies."

"Yes, I do," replied Woollcott, "but I also like them your age."

8 Childless himself, the redoubtable Alexander Woollcott was, on nineteen occasions, godparent to the children of friends. At the baptism of Mary MacArthur, daughter of Charles MacArthur and Helen Hayes, Woollcott was heard to exclaim with characteristic gusto: "Always a godfather, never a god!"

৵৽ ৵৽

WORDSWORTH, William (1770–1850), *English Romantic poet. After leaving Cambridge he went on a walking tour in Europe. While in France (1791–92), he had an affair with a French girl, Annette Vallon, by whom he had a daughter. At that time he was fired with enthusiasm for the ideals of the French Revolution. In 1795 Wordsworth, marking a new era in English poetry, met Coleridge. The Lyrical Ballads (1798) was the outcome of their collaboration. Wordsworth settled with his wife and his sister in the English Lake district, where he lived the rest of his life. Here he wrote* The Prelude, *not published until after his death.*

1 As Wordsworth's poetic arteries hardened, he became an ardent patriot and an establishment figure. At a gathering at which the youthful John Keats was present, Keats attempted to break into Wordsworth's monologue with an enthusiastic agreement with what the older poet was saying. Mrs. Wordsworth leaned over and checked him. "Mr. Wordsworth is never interrupted," she whispered.

2 Wordsworth boasted in Charles Lamb's hearing, "I could write like Shakespeare if I had a mind to."

"So it's only the mind that's lacking," murmured Lamb.

3 At the time when Wordsworth and Tom Moore were the heroes of London literary society, both were invited to a reception at which Moore promptly became the center of attraction, monopolizing the guests' attention with his wit and gaiety. The hostess noticed Wordsworth standing on the fringes of the group, looking a little sour. "Oh, Mr. Wordsworth," she said, thinking to draw him into the fun, "isn't Mr. Moore amusing? He says such entertaining things."

"Very amusing; very entertaining," said Wordsworth glumly. "You know I have only once in my life ever said anything very amusing." The hostess clapped her hands for silence and asked Wordsworth to repeat that *mot* for the guests, who all fell silent and waited expectantly. "I was walking along near Grasmere," Wordsworth began, "when I met a dalesman who appeared to be looking for something, and when he saw me the man hurried over and asked me if I had seen his wife anywhere along the road. And you know what I said? I said, 'My good man, I didn't even know that you had a wife.' That was the one time in my life that I have ever said anything very amusing."

৵৽ ৵৽

WORSLEY, "Gump" [Lorne] (1929–), *Canadian ice-hockey player.*

1 In 1963 the New York Rangers traded Worsley to the Montreal Canadiens for Jacques Plante. A television producer called both men to ask them to appear on a sports show to discuss the controversial deal. Plante asked how much he would be paid. The producer said that guests on the show were not usually paid, but he was prepared to make a payment to each man of fifty dollars. Plante then telephoned Worsley. "Are they paying you a hundred dollars too?" he demanded suspiciously. "Yeah," said Worsley. Plante then telephoned the producer again. "Why are you paying Gump a hundred bucks and me only fifty?" he asked. The producer protested that he was not, and managed to convince Plante that each man was getting only fifty dollars. Plante showed up for the program, Worsley did not. Plante then got in touch with Worsley to ask why he had not appeared. "Why should I?" exclaimed Worsley. "They were paying you a hundred dollars and me only fifty."

৵৽ ৵৽

WREN, Sir Christopher (1632–1723), *British architect, mathematician, and astronomer. He designed many new buildings, the greatest being* St. Paul's Cathedral *in London.*

1   When Wren designed the inside of Windsor Town Hall, his ceiling was supported by pillars. The building inspectors felt he had not put up enough. Wren felt differently. He put in four more pillars that did not actually touch the ceiling; they only looked as if they did. The inspectors were fooled, and the four fake pillars still stand.

❧ ❧

WRIGHT, Frank Lloyd (1869–1956), *US architect. He produced strikingly original designs for both private dwellings and public buildings, including the Imperial Hotel, Tokyo, and the Guggenheim Museum of Art, New York.*

1   In 1937, Wright built a house in Wisconsin for industrialist Hibbard Johnson and his family. One rainy evening Johnson was entertaining some distinguished guests for dinner when the roof began to leak. The water seeped through the ceiling directly above Johnson himself, dripping steadily onto the top of his bald head. Irate, he put a call through to Wright in Phoenix, Arizona. "Frank," he said, "you built this beautiful house for me and we enjoy it very much. But I have told you the roof leaks, and right now I am with some friends and distinguished guests and it is leaking right on top of my head." Wright's reply was heard by all. "Well, Hib," he said, "why don't you move your chair?"

{This anecdote is told by Samuel C. Johnson, a member of the Johnson family, famous wax manufacturers. It appears in a brochure issued by the Johnson Foundation.}

2   In 1930 novelist Rex Stout built a fourteen-room house, with his own hands, on a hilltop in Danbury, Connecticut. Later he invited Frank Lloyd Wright out to see it and waited patiently for his evaluation. Wright examined it carefully and then said, "A superb spot. Someone should build a house here."

❧ ❧

WRIGHT, Orville (1871–1948) and **Wilbur** (1867–1912), *US pioneer aviators. In December 1903 they made the first powered flight at Kitty Hawk, North Carolina.*

1   Weary of explaining the principles of their Flyer's performance to the inquisitive, the Wright brothers said simply, "The airplane stays up because it doesn't have the time to fall."

❧ ❧

WYCHERLEY, William (1640–1716), *British playwright. His scintillating comedies, such as* The Country Wife *(1673) and* The Plain Dealer *(?1674), satirized the manners and morals of Restoration society.*

1   One day when Wycherley and a friend were in a bookstore they overheard a fashionable young lady asking the bookseller if he had *The Plain Dealer*. Wycherley's friend at once pushed him across to the lady and said, "Here, madam, is the Plain Dealer himself." The lady turned out to be the widowed Countess of Drogheda. She and Wycherley exchanged compliments, and as they parted she said, "I love plain dealing best of all." Acting on this hint, Wycherley wooed her in the manner approved by the heroes of his comedies and they married in 1680.

❧ ❧

WYLIE, Elinor (1885–1928), *US poet and novelist.*

1   The novelist and short-story writer Katherine Anne Porter was roused from sleep by the doorbell at 4:00 A.M. On the step was Elinor Wylie, who announced, "I have stood the crassness of the world as long as I can and I am going to kill myself. You are the only person in the world to whom I wish to say goodbye." Since at the time Elinor Wylie was richly endowed with all the material advantages her friend lacked, Katherine Anne Porter was not disposed to be sympathetic. "Elinor," she said, "it was good of you to think of me. Goodbye."

X

XERXES (died 465 BC), *King of Persia (485–465 BC), who led the great Persian expedition against Greece in 480 BC. The Bible calls him Ahasuerus.*

1 Xerxes, surveying the great army he had assembled for the invasion of Greece, seemed at first very happy, but presently began to weep. "I am moved to pity," he said, "when I think of the brevity of human life, seeing that of all this host of men not one will still be alive in a hundred years' time."

2 On his retreat from Greece Xerxes boarded a Phoenician ship to transport him back to Asia Minor. On the way a fearful storm blew up and the ship seemed likely to founder, especially as it was overloaded with Persians who had accompanied Xerxes. The king asked the pilot if there was any hope of safety. The man replied that there was none, unless the ship's load was substantially lightened. Xerxes then turned to the Persians on deck and said, "It is on you that my safety depends. Now let some of you show your regard for your king." A number of those who heard him made obeisance to him and then threw themselves overboard. Thus lightened, the ship came safely to harbor.

After he landed Xerxes immediately ordered that a golden crown be presented to the pilot for preserving the king's life; however, he also commanded that the man's head should be cut off, as he had caused the loss of so many Persian lives.

Y

YEATS, William Butler (1865–1939), *Irish poet and playwright. His early poems reflect the decadent romantic mood of 1890s poetry, but his mature work, much of which appeared in* The Tower (1928) *and* The Winding Stair (1929), *deals powerfully with tragic themes — old age, the impermanence of human endeavor, and the bitter choices in Irish history. With Lady Gregory he founded (1904) the Abbey Theatre, Dublin, and wrote many plays for it.*

1 (Yeats had a lifelong interest in the occult. The conversation centered on this topic when Louis MacNeice and E. R. Dodds, professor of Greek at Oxford, went to tea with him in 1934.)

"He talked a great deal about the spirits to whom his wife, being a medium, had introduced him. 'Have you ever seen them?' Dodds asked (Dodds could never keep back such questions). Yeats was a little piqued. No, he said grudgingly, he had never actually seen them . . . but — with a flash of triumph — he had often *smelt* them."

2 In the 1930s a certain Dr. Steinach claimed to be able to rejuvenate aging men by implanting new sex glands. Yeats read a pamphlet about this treatment and was impressed enough to ask his physician as to the advisability of the operation. When the physician refused to commit himself, Yeats went ahead and had the operation in London in May 1934. Back in Dublin he was fully convinced of the success of the treatment. His friend Oliver St. John Gogarty, also a doctor by training, was appalled and questioned Yeats closely about it. "What was wrong with you?" Gogarty inquired. "I used to fall asleep after lunch," replied Yeats.

YOSHIDA, Shigeru (1878–1967), *Japanese politician. Having served in a number of foreign capitals before World War II, he became foreign minister in 1945 and prime minister in May 1946, as the new head of the Liberal party.*

1 Yoshida was ambassador to England in the late 1930s. Anxious to avoid a certain Japanese cabinet minister who was visiting London, he told his staff: "Whenever that man phones, tell him I'm out." The order was obeyed; the minister tried in vain on several occasions to reach the ambassador. Suspicious, he decided to call at the embassy in person. He happened to pass Yoshida in the foyer and asked him if he might speak to the ambassador. "No, sir," replied Yoshida. "The ambassador is out." The minister looked at him with a sudden flash of recognition. "But aren't *you* the ambassador?" he asked. "I am," said Yoshida. "And, sir, when you hear from Yoshida himself that Yoshida is out, you can believe it!"

See also SCIPIO NASICA SERAPIO 1.

YUSUPOV, Prince Feliks (*dates unknown*), *Russian nobleman. He was one of the chief conspirators in the murder of Rasputin in 1916.*

1 In the Metro-Goldwyn-Mayer film *Rasputin and the Empress* the studio sought to avoid trouble with Prince Yusupov by changing to Prince Chegodieff the name of the character who played his role in the story. They had reckoned without the prince's proprietary attitude to the murder. He sued the studio in a London court for depriving him of the credit for his actions. He won his case and the studio had to pay a considerable sum in damages. Then a real Prince Chegodieff came forward and sued for the libelous use of his name. He also won his case and MGM paid off once more.

Z

ZANGWILL, Israel (1864–1926), *British novelist and playwright of Jewish parentage. He depicted Jewish life in a series of novels, beginning with the highly successful* The Children of the Ghetto *(1892). He followed Theodor Herzl as leader of the Zionist movement.*

1 Zangwill was watching a tedious Sardou melodrama. Halfway through he remarked, "My leg is the only sensible part of my body; it has gone to sleep."

2 Zangwill, tired and careless of his surroundings, yawned in the face of the lady sitting next to him at dinner. "Mind your Jewish manners," said she. "I thought you were going to swallow me."

"Have no fear, madam," replied Zangwill. "My religion prohibits my doing that."

3 Andrew Lang wrote to inquire of his friend Israel Zangwill whether he planned to attend a certain event. The reply came back: "If you, Lang, will, I. Zangwill."

4 A *nouveau-riche* peer, whose accent did not match his social position, was feeling the effects of a heavy drinking session of the night before. "Oh, my 'ead! My 'ead!" he moaned. "What you need is two aspirates," recommended Zangwill.

ZENO (c. 335–c. 263 BC), *Greek philosopher, born at Citium (Cyprus). He was the founder of the Stoic school of philosophy, which he established in Athens around 300 BC.*

1 Zeno caught his slave stealing, and gave him a good beating. The slave, something of a philosopher himself, pleaded, "But it was fated that I should steal."

"And that I should beat you," retorted Zeno.

ZEUXIS (c. 424–c. 380 BC), *Greek painter.*

1 Zeuxis's painting of a boy holding a dish of grapes (*see* SIR GODFREY KNELLER 2) was executed by Zeuxis to prove that he could outdo his rival Parrhasius in trompe-l'oeil effects. When the birds attacked the grapes, it seemed certain that victory would go to Zeuxis, who then called upon Parrhasius to draw back the curtain concealing his own painting. But this supposed curtain was itself painted, and Zeuxis had to concede that while he had been able to deceive the birds, Parrhasius had been able to deceive him.

ZIEGFELD, Florenz (1867–1932), *US theatrical producer. He created the famous* Ziegfeld Follies *(1907–32) and such shows as* Sally *(1920) and* Show Boat *(1927), besides launching many stars on their careers.*

1 Ziegfeld once offered Gracie Allen $750 a week to appear in one of his London shows. She asked what he would offer if her husband and straight man, George Burns, were included. "Five hundred," was the answer.

See also GROUCHO MARX 8.

ZOG I, King of Albania (1895–1961), *king of Albania from 1928 to 1939, forced into exile by Mussolini.*

1 In 1940 Zog, accompanied by his royal retinue, arrived at the Ritz hotel in London. Some of the luggage seemed remarkably heavy, exciting the curiosity of George, the hall porter. George asked the king whether they contained anything very valuable. "Yes," replied Zog, "gold."

Nicholas Murray Butler and Professor Brander Matthews of Columbia University were having a conversation and Professor Matthews was giving his ideas as to plagiarism, from an article of his own on that subject. "In the case of the first man to use an anecdote," he said, "there is originality; in the case of the second, there is plagiarism; with the third, it is lack of originality; and with the fourth it is drawing from a common stock."

"Yes," broke in President Butler, "and in the case of the fifth, it is research."

— B. A. Botkin,
A Treasury of American Anecdotes

❧ SOURCE LIST ❧

Sources for the anecdotes are given wherever possible. Only names and titles are cited; full bibliographical information is given in the Bibliography, which follows this list. Abbreviations used in the list:

DBQ — Richard Kenin and Justin Wintle, *Dictionary of Biographical Quotation*
DNB — *Dictionary of National Biography*
EB — *Encyclopaedia Britannica*
OBALA — *Oxford Book of American Literary Anecdotes*, ed. Donald Hall
OBLA — *Oxford Book of Literary Anecdotes*, ed. John Sutherland

AARON 1: B. Uecker and M. Herskowitz, *Catcher in the Wry*

ABBOTT AND COSTELLO 1: D. Strauss and F. Worth, *Hollywood Trivia*

ABERCROMBIE 1: N. Stock, *The Life of Ezra Pound*

ABERNETHY 1: T. Pettigrew, *Medical Portrait Gallery*, in Kenin and Wintle, *DBQ*; 2: S. Smiles, *Self-Help*, in Kenin and Wintle, *DBQ*; 3. F. Winslow, *Physic and Physicians*, in D. George, *A Book of Anecdotes*; 4: G. Macilwain, *Memoirs of John Abernethy F.R.S.*, in Kenin and Wintle, *DBQ*; 5: E. Fuller, *2500 Anecdotes*; 6: W. Keddie, *Literary and Scientific Anecdote*

ACHESON 1: *Time*, Dec. 22, 1952; 2: A. Schlesinger, Jr., in K. Halle, *Randolph Churchill*

ACTON 1: P. Quennell, *The Sign of the Fish*

ADAMS, ALEXANDER 1: Oxfam, *Pass the Port*

ADAMS, ANSEL, 1: *Ansel Adams: An Autobiography*

ADAMS, F. P., 1–2: R. Drennan, *The Algonquin Wits*; 3: O. Levant, *The Unimportance of Being Oscar*; 4–5: R. Drennan, *Wit's End*

ADAMS, J., 1: Page Smith, *John Adams*, in P. Boller, ed., *Presidential Anecdotes*; 2: *Columbian Centinel*, July 12, 1826, in Boller, *Presidential Anecdotes*

ADAMS, J. Q., 1: E. Colman, *Seventy-five Years of White House Gossip*, in P. Boller, ed., *Presidential Anecdotes*; 2: E. Fuller, *2500 Anecdotes*

ADDAMS 1: E. Wagenknecht, *American Profile, 1900–1909*

ADDISON 1: R. Hendrickson, *The Literary Life*; 2: A. Bespaloff, *The Fireside Book of Wine*; 3: E. Fuller, *2500 Anecdotes*; 4: L. Hunt, *Old Court Suburb*, in C. Shriner, *Wit, Wisdom, and Foibles of the Great*

ADE 1: J. Braude, *Speaker's and Toastmaster's Handbook*

ADEE 1: '47, *The Magazine of the Year*, I

ADENAUER 1: J. Gunther, *Procession*; 3: K. Edwards, *More Things I Wish I'd Said*

ADLER 1: J. Braude, *Braude's Second Encyclopedia*

AESCHYLUS 1: *EB*

AGASSIZ 1: E. Fuller, *2500 Anecdotes*

AGRIPPINA 1–2: Tacitus, *Annals*

AIDAN 1: Bede, *History of the English Church and People*

ALBEMARLE 1: E. Guérard, *Dictionnaire Encyclopédique*

ALBERT 1: Sir S. Lee, *Queen Victoria*, in A. Hardy, *Queen Victoria Was Amused*; 2: W. Adams, *Treasury of Modern Anecdote*; 3: B. Disraeli, *Reminiscences*, in Kenin and Wintle, *DBQ*

ALBERT, D', 1: H. Hoffmeister, *Anekdotenschatz*

ALCIBIADES 1: L. Harris, *The Fine Art of Political Wit*

ALCOTT, A., 1: C. Meigs, *Invincible Louisa*

ALCOTT, L., 1: M. Worthington, *Miss Alcott of Concord*

ALEMBERT 1: I. Asimov, *Biographical Encyclopedia*

ALENÇON 1: C. Skinner, *Elegant Wits and Grand Horizontals*

ALEXANDER I 1: M. Paléologue, *The Enigmatic Czar*; 2: *Harper's Magazine*, April 1883, in C. Shriner, *Wit, Wisdom, and Foibles of the Great*

ALEXANDER III 1–7: Plutarch, *Lives*; 8: F. Paley, *Greek Wit*

ALEXANDER VI 1: O. Prescott, *Princes of the Renaissance*

ALEXANDER, GEORGE, 1: J. Aye, *Humour in the Theatre*

ALEXANDER, S., 1: Oxfam, *Pass the Port*

ALEXANDRA 1: R. Collier, *The Rainbow People*

ALFONSO X 1: I. Asimov, *Biographical Encyclopedia*

ALFONSO XIII 1: W. Churchill, *Great Contemporaries*

ALFRED 2: *Asser's Life of King Alfred*

ALI 2–3: R. Crouser, *It's Unlucky to Be Behind at the End of the Game*; 5: Letter from A. Silverman to C. Fadiman, Nov. 17, 1983

ALLAIS 1: M. Pedrazzini and J. Gris, *Autant en apporter les mots*; 2: C. Skinner, *Elegant Wits and Grand Horizontals*

ALLEN, E., 1: *Harper's Magazine*, July 1875, in C. Shriner, *Wit, Wisdom, and Foibles of the*

ALLEN (*continued*)
Great; 2: C. Fadiman and C. Van Doren, *The American Treasury;* 3: D. Fisher, *Vermont Tradition,* in B. Botkin, *A Treasury of American Anecdotes;* 4: D. Wallechinsky and I. Wallace, *The People's Almanac*

ALLEN, F., 1: Joe Bryan III, "Funny Man," *Saturday Evening Post,* Sept. 23, 1965; 2: C. Fadiman and C. Van Doren, *The American Treasury;* 3: J. Paar, *P.S. Jack Paar*

ALMA-TADEMA 1: W. Scholz, *Das Buch des Lachens*

ALTENBERG 1: S. Radecki, *Das ABC des Lachens*

ALVANLEY 1–2: W. Adams, *Treasury of Modern Anecdote*

AMBROSE 1: W. Durant, *The Story of Civilization,* IV

ANAXAGORAS 1: W. Durant, *The Story of Civilization,* II

ANAXIMENES 1: H. Hoffmeister, *Anekdotenschatz*

ANDERSEN 1–2: E. Bredsdorff, *Hans Christian Andersen;* 3: R. Godden, *Hans Christian Andersen*

ANDERSON 1: R. Nelson, *The Almanac of American Letters*

ANDREW 1: P. Bussard, *The New Catholic Treasury of Wit and Humor*

ANGOULÊME 1: W. Merwin, *Products of the Perfected Civilization*

ANTHEIL 1: S. Beach, *Musicdotes*

ANTHONY 1: W. Abbot, *Notable Women in History*

ANTISTHENES 1: W. Durant, *The Story of Civilization,* II; 2: H. Hoffmeister, *Anekdotenschatz*

APELLES 1: W. Durant, *The Story of Civilization,* II; 2: E. Fuller, *2500 Anecdotes*

AQUINAS 1: H. and D. L. Thomas, *Living Biographies of the Great Philosophers*

ARCHELAUS 1: W. Durant, *The Story of Civilization,* II

ARCHER 1: S. Behrman, *Portrait of Max*

ARCHIMEDES 1: *New Columbia Encyclopedia;* 2: W. Durant, *The Story of Civilization,* II; 3: E. Bell, *Men of Mathematics;* 4: I. Asimov, *Biographical Encyclopedia*

ARDITI 1: F. Berger, *Reminiscences, Impressions, and Anecdotes*

ARETINO 1: T. Craven, *Men of Art*

ARISTIDES 1: Plutarch, *Lives*

ARISTIPPUS 1–2: F. Callières, *Des Bons Mots et des bons contes;* 3: E. Guérard, *Dictionnaire Encyclopédique*

ARLEN 1–2: M. Arlen, *Exiles;* 3: *Book-of-the-Month Club News,* March 1944

ARMOUR 1: E. Fuller, *2500 Anecdotes*

ARMSTRONG, L., 1: J. Collier, *Louis Armstrong;* 2: C. Fadiman and C. Van Doren, *The American Treasury*

ARMSTRONG, N., 1: D. Wallechinsky and I. Wallace, *The People's Almanac*

ARNE 1: W. Cummings, *Dr. Arne and Rule, Britannia*

ARNIM 1: W. Scholz, *Das Buch des Lachens*

ARNO 1: B. Gill, *Here at The New Yorker*

ARNOLD 1: L. Trilling, *Matthew Arnold,* in J. Sutherland, ed., *OBLA;* 2: C. Sifakis, *Dictionary of Historic Nicknames*

ARNOULD 1, 3–4: L. Russell, *English Wits;* 2: E. Guérard, *Dictionnaire Encyclopédique*

ARRIA 1: *Oxford Classical Dictionary*

ASCHE 1: D. Knox, *More Quotable Anecdotes*

ASHE 1: R. Evans, *Nasty*

ASOKA 1: W. Durant, *The Story of Civilization,* I

ASQUITH, H., 1: D. Frost and M. Deakin, *David Frost's Book of Millionaires*

ASQUITH, M., 1: W. Espy, *Another Almanac of Words at Play;* 2: C. Bowra, *Memories 1898–1939;* 3: J. Abdy and C. Grere, *The Souls;* 4: E. Longford, *The Queen*

ASTAIRE 1–3: D. Niven, *Bring on the Empty Horses*

ASTOR, J. J., 1: C. Fadiman and C. Van Doren: *The American Treasury;* E. Rachlis and J. Marquese, *The Landlords*

ASTOR, M. D., 1: J. Smith, *Elsie de Wolfe*

ASTOR, N. W., 1: *Observer,* Feb. 7, 1982; 2–3: *DNB;* 5: M. Ringo, *Nobody Said It Better;* 6: W. Manchester, *The Last Lion*

ATKINSON 1: L. Missen, *Quotable Anecdotes*

ATLAS 1: D. Wallechinsky and I. Wallace, *The People's Almanac 2*

AUBER 1: L. Russell, *English Wits;* 2: E. Guérard, *Dictionnaire Encyclopédique;* 4: W. Scholz, *Das Buch des Lachens*

AUBERNON 1–3: C. Skinner, *Elegant Wits and Grand Horizontals*

AUBIGNÉ 1: L. Missen, *After-dinner Stories and Anecdotes*

AUDEN 1: H. Carpenter, *W. H. Auden;* 2, 4: W. Espy, *An Almanac of Words at Play;* 3: *Book-of-the-Month Club News,* December 1946

AUERBACH 1: *Los Angeles Times,* Nov 11, 1982

AUGUSTINE 1: *Oxford Dictionary of Quotations*

AUGUSTUS 1: Plutarch, *Lives;* 2–5: Macrobius, *Saturnalia;* 6: W. Durant, *The Story of Civilization,* III

AUMALE 1: A. Castelot, *Paris: The Turbulent City;* 2–5: C. Skinner, *Elegant Wits and Grand Horizontals*

AUSTIN, A., 1: E. Marsh, *A Number of People*

AUSTIN, W., 2: C. Fadiman and C. Van Doren, *The American Treasury*

AVEMPACE 1: W. Durant, *The Story of Civilization,* IV

AVERY 1: L. Thomas, *Late Night Thoughts*

AYMÉ 1: M. and A. Guillois, *Liberté, Egalité, Hilarité*

AZEGLIO 1: H. Morton, *A Traveller in Italy*

BABBAGE 1: R. Hendrickson, *The Literary Life;* 2: Charles Darwin, *Autobiography,* in Kenin and Wintle, *DBQ*

BACALL 1: O. Levant, *The Unimportance of Being Oscar;* 2: D. Wallechinsky and I. Wallace, *The People's Almanac 2*

BACH, C., 1: H. Schonberg, *The Great Pianists*

BACH, J., 1: S. Sadie, *New Grove's Dictionary of Music and Musicians*

BACON 1: J. Aubrey, *Brief Lives;* 2: E. Fuller, *2500 Anecdotes;* 3: L. Missen, *After-dinner Stories and Anecdotes;* 4–5: H. Hoffmeister, *Anekdotenschatz*

BADER 1: *Los Angeles Times,* Sept. 7, 1982

BAEYER 1: J. Read, *Humour and Humanism in Chemistry*

BAHR 1: W. Scholz, *Das Buch des Lachens*

BAILLY 1: H. Hoffmeister, *Anekdotenschatz*

BAKER, J., 1–2: I. Wallace et al., *Intimate Sex Lives of Famous People*

BAKER, N., 1: T. White, *America in Search of Itself*

BAKST 1: A. Dolin, *Friends and Memories*

BALANCHINE 1: B. Taper, *Balanchine: A Biography*

BALDWIN 1: *DNB;* 2: *The Times* (London), Mar. 17, 1982; 3: N. Rees, *Quote . . . Unquote*

BALFOUR 1: J. Abdy and C. Grere, *The Souls*

BALMAIN 1: R. Buckle, ed., *Self-Portrait with Friends*

BALSAN 1: C. Canfield, *Up and Down and Around*

BALZAC 1: I. Wallace et al., *Intimate Sex Lives of Famous People;* 2, 5: E. Fuller, *2500 Anecdotes;* 3: J. Timbs, *Century of Anecdote;* 4: D. George, *A Book of Anecdotes;* 6: E. de Goncourt, *Journal des Goncourts;* 7: D. Wallechinsky and I. Wallace, *The People's Almanac*

BANCROFT 1: S. Behrman, *Portrait of Max*

BANKHEAD 1: L. Hellman, *Pentimento;* 2: R. Drennan, *Wit's End;* 3: H. Teichmann, *Smart Alec;* 4: M. Ringo, *Nobody Said It Better;* 5–7: D. Herrmann, *With Malice Toward All;* 8: J. Paar, *P.S. Jack Paar;* 9: A. Faulkner and T. Hartman, *All the Best People;* 12: Celebrity Research Group, *The Bedside Book of Celebrity Gossip*

BANKS 1: C. Fadiman, *Any Number Can Play*

BARBIROLLI 1: A. Previn, ed., *Orchestra;* 2: *Book-of-the-Month Club News,* April 1947

BARHAM 1: W. Adams, *Treasury of Modern Anecdote;* 2: *DNB*

BARNES 1: *New York Times Book Review,* June 26, 1983; 2: G. Davenport, *The Geography of the Imagination*

BARNUM 1: H. Rawson, *Dictionary of Euphemisms;* 2: I. Wallace, *The Fabulous Showman;* 3: L. Lucaire, *Celebrity Trivia*

BARR 1: *Los Angeles Times,* Feb. 8, 1981

BARRIE 1–2, 4–5: C. Asquith, *Portrait of Barrie;* 3: I. Wallace, "Significa," July 24, 1983; 6:

J. Dunbar, *J. M. Barrie;* 7: R. Marquard, *Jokes and Anecdotes;* 8: E. Fuller, *2500 Anecdotes;* 9: Eve Adams, ed., *Mrs. J. Comyns Carr's Reminiscences,* in J. Sutherland, ed., *OBLA;* 10: J. Aye, *Humour in the Theatre*

BARROW 1: J. Larwood, *Anecdotes of the Clergy*

BARRYMORE, E., 1: J. Braude, *Speaker's and Toastmaster's Handbook;* 2: J. McAleer, "Globe Man's Daily Story," *Boston Globe,* 1967

BARRYMORE, J., 1, 7, 10: I. Wallace et al., *Intimate Sex Lives of Famous People;* 2: G. Lieberman, *The Greatest Laughs of All Time;* 3: B. Cerf, *Try and Stop Me;* 4: D. Niven, *Bring on the Empty Horses;* 5: E. Fuller, *2500 Anecdotes;* 6: R. Marquard, *Jokes and Anecdotes;* 8: M. Griffin, *From Where I Sit;* 9: K. Edwards, *I Wish I'd Said That Too*

BARRYMORE, M., 1–3: G. Fowler, *Good Night, Sweet Prince*

BARTÓK 1: V. Thomson, *A Virgil Thomson Reader*

BARTON 1: J. Humes, *Speakers' Treasury*

BARUCH 1: *The New Yorker,* Jan. 10, 1948; 2: B. Cerf, *Bumper Crop of Anecdotes*

BASIE 1: S. Dance, *The World of Count Basie*

BAYLIS 1: B., Forbes, *Ned's Girl;* 2: *The New Yorker,* Sept. 16, 1950

BEAN 1: B. Botkin, *Treasury of American Anecdotes*

BEATON 1–2: R. Buckle, ed., *Self-Portrait with Friends*

BEATTY 1: *DNB*

BEAUMARCHAIS 1: E. Guérard, *Dictionnaire Encyclopédique*

BEAUMONT 1: J. Boswell, *Life of Johnson*

BECKETT 1: W. Lowenfels, *The Paris Years;* 2: D. Bair, *Samuel Beckett*

BECKFORD 1: W. P. Frith, *My Autobiography and Reminiscences,* in J. Sutherland, ed., *OBLA;* 2: J. Gere and J. Sparrow, *Geoffrey Madan's Notebooks*

BEECHAM, T., 1: Kenin and Wintle, *DBQ*

BEECHAM, SIR T., 1: D. Fielding, *Those Remarkable Cunards;* 2–4, 8–13: H. Atkins and A. Newman, eds., *Beecham Stories;* 6: N. Cardus, *Sir Thomas Beecham;* 7: L. Humphrey, *The Humor of Music;* 14: S. Beach, *Musicdotes;* 15: E. Schwarzkopf, *On and Off the Record*

BEECHER 1: L. and F. Copeland, *10,000 Jokes, Toasts, and Stories;* 2: T. Masson, *The Best Stories in the World;* 3: T. Masson, ed., *Little Masterpieces of American Wit and Humor,* in R. Shenkman and K. Reiger, *One-Night Stands with American History;* 4: E. Fuller, *2500 Anecdotes*

BEERBOHM 1, 3–5: D. Cecil, *Max: A Biography;* 6: S. Behrman, *Portrait of Max*

BEETHOVEN 1: E. Forbes, ed., *Thayer's Life of*

BEETHOVEN (*continued*)
   Beethoven; 2: A. Hopkins, *Music All Around Me;* 3, 5: S. Sadie, *New Grove's Dictionary of Music and Musicians;* 4: F. Bonavia, ed., *Musicians on Music*
BEGIN 1: I. Wallace et al., *Book of Lists 2*
BEHAN 1: R. Jeffs, *Brendan Behan, Man and Showman;* 2: B. Behan, *My Life with Brendan;* 3: G. Brandreth, *Great Theatrical Disasters*
BELL, A., 1: John J. Carty, *The Smithsonian Report for 1922,* in Kenin and Wintle, *DBQ;* 2: I. Wallace et al., *Intimate Sex Lives of Famous People*
BELL, J., 1–2: I. Wallace, *The Fabulous Originals*
BELLOC 1: R. Hendrickson, *The Literary Life;* 2: L. Missen, *After-dinner Stories and Anecdotes;* 3: *New York Times Book Review,* Aug. 2, 1982; 4: A. Wilson, *Hilaire Belloc*
BELLOWS 1: Eugene Speicher, *A Personal Reminiscence,* in Kenin and Wintle, *DBQ*
BELMONT 1: D. Black, *King of Fifth Avenue*
BEMBO 1: S. Radecki, *Das ABC des Lachens*
BENCHLEY 1, 15: N. Benchley, *Robert Benchley;* 2: N. Rees, *Quote . . . Unquote;* 3: E. Fuller, *2500 Anecdotes;* 4: *Saturday Evening Post,* Sept. 23, 1965; 6: H. Teichmann, *Smart Aleck;* 7: B. Cerf, *Try and Stop Me;* 8: K. Tynan, *Show People;* 9: H. Thurber and E. Weeks, eds., *Selected Letters of James Thurber;* 10: D. Herrmann, *With Malice Toward All;* 11–13: R. Drennan, *The Algonquin Wits;* 14: R. Drennan, *Wit's End*
BENNETT, A., 1: B. Cerf, *Shake Well Before Using;* 2: R. Hendrickson, *The Literary Life;* 3: J. McAleer, "Globe Man's Daily Story," *Boston Globe,* Aug. 31, 1966; 4: E. Goossens, *Overture and Beginners*
BENNETT, J., 1: B. Morton, *Americans in Paris;* 2: P. Brendon, *The Life and Death of the Press Barons;* 3–5: D. Frost and M. Deakin, *David Frost's Book of Millionaires*
BENNY 4: I. Fein, *Jack Benny;* 6: M. L. Benny and H. Marks, *Jack Benny*
BENTON 1: E. Fuller, *2500 Anecdotes;* 2: *Harper's Magazine,* in R. Shenkman, and K. Reiger, *One-Night Stands with American History*
BERIA 1: J. Gunther, *Inside Russia Today*
BERNADOTTE 1: S. Radecki, *Das ABC des Lachens*
BERNARD 1: M. Pedrazzini and J. Gris, *Autant en apportent les mots;* 2–7, 9–12, 14: C. Skinner, *Elegant Wits and Grand Horizontals;* 8: E. Kelen, *Peace in Their Time;* 15: F. Jacob, *The Possible and the Actual*
BERNERS 1–3: E. Sitwell, *Taken Care Of;* 4: E. Salter, *Helpmann*
BERNHARDT 1–2, 4, 7: A. May, *Different Drummers;* 3: *Oxford Dictionary of Quotations;* 5: L. and M. Cowan, *The Wit of Women;* 6:

W. Abbot, *Notable Women in History;* 8: J. Aye, *Humour in the Theatre;* 9: P. Mahony, *Barbed Wit and Malicious Humor;* 10, 14–15: C. Skinner, *Elegant Wits and Grand Horizontals;* 11: E. Fuller, *2500 Anecdotes;* 12: L. Missen, *Quotable Anecdotes;* 13: P. Horgan, *Encounters with Stravinsky;* 16: J. Braude, *Speaker's and Toastmaster's Handbook*
BERNOULLI 1: E. Bell, *Men of Mathematics*
BERNSTEIN, H., 1: B. Cerf, *The Life of the Party*
BERNSTEIN, L., 1: H. Temianka, *Facing the Music*
BERNSTEIN, R., 1: P. Schwed, *Turning the Pages*
BERRA 4: L. Rosten, *People I Have Loved, Known or Admired;* 5: W. Espy, *An Almanac of Words at Play;* 6: R. Crouser, *It's Unlucky to Be Behind at the End of the Game*
BETTY 1: Anne Matthews, *Anecdotes of Action,* in F. Muir, *Irreverent Social History*
BEUNO 1: '48, *The Magazine of the Year,* vol. 2, no. 4
BEVAN 1: K. Edwards, *I Wish I'd Said That Too;* 2: M. Foot, *Aneurin Bevan*
BEVIN 2: W. Espy, *Another Almanac of Words at Play;* 3: K. Edwards, *I Wish I'd Said That Too;* 4: E. Clark, *Diplomat*
BEWICK 1: B. Conrad, *Famous Last Words*
BIALIK 1: W. Novak and M. Waldoks, *Big Book of Jewish Humor*
BING 1–8, 10: Sir R. Bing, *5000 Nights at the Opera;* 9: Sir R. Bing, *A Knight at the Opera*
BION 1: E. Fuller, *2500 Anecdotes*
BISMARCK 1, 8: E. Crankshaw, *Bismarck;* 2: C. Shriner, *Wit, Wisdom, and Foibles of the Great;* 3: W. Scholz, *Das Buch des Lachens;* 4: H. Ziegler, *Heitere Muse;* 5: C. Craig, *The Germans;* 6–7: H. Hoffmeister, *Anekdotenschatz;* 9: *Harper's Magazine,* November 1898
BLACK 1: R. Marquard, *Jokes and Anecdotes*
BLACKWELL 1: A. Powell, *London Walks*
BLAKE, E., 1–2: *The Times* (London), Feb. 15, 1983
BLAKE, W., 1: R. Hendrickson, *The Literary Life;* 2–3: J. Timbs, *English Eccentrics*
BLAND-SUTTON 1: J. Bland-Sutton, *The Story of a Surgeon*
BLECH 1: H. Hoffmeister, *Anekdotenschatz*
BLESSINGTON 1: D. Duff, *Eugénie and Napoleon III*
BLUME 1: J. Wintle and E. Fisher, *The Pied Pipers*
BLUMENTHAL 1: H. Hoffmeister, *Anekdotenschatz*
BOAS 1: J. Howard, *Margaret Mead*
BOGARDE 1: D. Bogarde, *Snakes & Ladders;* 2: D. Bogarde, *An Orderly Man*
BOGART 1: V. Thompson, *Bogie and Me*
BOILEAU 1: R. Hendrickson, *The Literary Life;* 2: W. and A. Durant, *The Story of Civilization,*

VIII; 3–4: V. Cronin, *Louis XIV*

BOLEYN 1: I. Wallace et al., *Intimate Sex Lives of Famous People;* 2: W. Abbot, *Notable Women in History*

BOLINGBROKE 1: *DNB*

BOLT 1–2: *Los Angeles Times,* Mar. 13, 1982

BONNER 1: G. Taylor, *The Great Evolution Mystery*

BOONE 1: *Book-of-the-Month Club News,* October 1972

BOOTH, J. W., 1: C. Fadiman and C. Van Doren, *The American Treasury*

BOOTH, J. B., 1, 4: W. Winter, *Other Days;* 2: E. Fuller, *2500 Anecdotes;* 3: G. Vidal, *Lincoln*

BORGE 1: P. Bussard, *The New Catholic Treasury of Wit and Humor*

BORGES 1: R. Alifano, *Twenty-four Conversations with Borges*

BORGHESE 1: Marshal Marmont, *Memoirs,* in C. Shriner, *Wit, Wisdom, and Foibles of the Great*

BORODIN 1: H. Hoffmeister, *Anekdotenschatz*

BORROMEO 1: P. Bussard, *The New Catholic Treasury of Wit and Humor*

BOSQUET 1: C. Woodham-Smith, *The Reason Why*

BOSSUET 1: W. Keddie, *Literary and Scientific Anecdote;* 2: J. Larwood, *Anecdotes of the Clergy*

BOSWELL 1: *EB;* 2: H. Pearson, *Johnson and Boswell*

BOTTICELLI 1: G. Vasari, *Lives of the Painters*

BOTTOMLEY 1: A. Sylvester, *Life with Lloyd George;* 2: A. J. P. Taylor, *English History 1914–1945,* in Kenin and Wintle, *DBQ*

BOUHOURS 1: B. Conrad, *Famous Last Words*

BOULANGER, G., 1: I. Wallace, *The Nympho & Other Maniacs*

BOULANGER, N., 1: A. Kendall, *The Tender Tyrant*

BOULT 1: A. Boyle, *Only the Wind Will Listen*

BOWEN, E., 1: H. Moss, *Whatever Is Moving*

BOWEN, L., 1: M. Cable, *Top Drawer*

BOWLES 1–2: S. C. Hall, *A Book of Memories,* in D. George, *A Book of Anecdotes*

BOWRA 1: Oxfam, *Pass the Port*

BRADFORD 1: J. Bartlett, *Familiar Quotations*

BRADLEY 1: Robert Bridges, *Three Friends,* in J. Sutherland, ed., *OBLA*

BRADY 1: B. Cerf, *Bumper Crop of Anecdotes*

BRAHMS 1, 3–4: P. Latham, *Brahms;* 5: A. Rubinstein, *My Young Years;* 6–7, 9: N. Slonimsky, *A Thing or Two about Music;* 8: P. Méras, *The Mermaids of Chenonceaux;* 11: J. Braude, *Braude's Second Encyclopedia*

BRAITHWAITE 1: G. Brandreth, *Great Theatrical Disasters;* 2: A. Faulkner and T. Hartman, *All the Best People*

BRAKHAGE 1: G. Davenport, *The Geography of the Imagination*

BRANCUSI 1: *Compton's Encyclopedia*

BRAQUE 1: R. Penrose, *Ronald Penrose Scrapbook*

BRESHKOVSKAYA 1: J. and D. L. Thomas, *Living Biographies of Famous Women*

BRIAND 1–2: E. Kelen, *Peace in Their Time*

BRIDGER 1–2: *American Scholar,* VIII (1938–39)

BRIDGES 1–2: *American Scholar,* I (1932)

BRIGHT 1: L. Missen, *Quotable Anecdotes*

BRILLAT-SAVARIN 1: D. Wallechinsky and I. Wallace, *The People's Almanac*

BRODIE, SIR B., 1: L. Cliffe, *Anecdotal Reminiscences*

BRODIE, S., 1: D. Wallechinsky and I. Wallace, *The People's Almanac*

BRODIE, W., 1: *"Daily Mirror" Old Codger's Little Black Book 4*

BRONTË, C., 1: A. Harrison and D. Stanford, *Anne Brontë;* 2: D. Frost, *Book of the World's Worst Decisions*

BROOKFIELD 1: J. Aye, *Humour in the Theatre*

BROOKS, M., 1, 3: K. Tynan, *Show People*

BROOKS, P., 1: J. Braude, *Speaker's and Toastmaster's Handbook*

BROUGHAM 1: N. McPhee, *The Book of Insults;* 2: S. Smith, *Memoir of the Rev. Sydney Smith by His Daughter;* 3: K. Arvine, *Cyclopaedia of Anecdotes;* 4: H. Pearson, *The Smith of Smiths*

BROUN 1: G. Brandreth, *Great Theatrical Disasters;* 2: H. Broun, *Whose Little Boy Are You?*

BROWN, J., 1: *The New Yorker,* Oct. 18, 1952; 2: C. Canfield, *Up and Down and Around*

BROWNE 1: A. Linkletter, *I Wish I'd Said That!*

BROWNING, E., 1: F. Winwar, *The Immortal Lovers*

BROWNING, R., 1: B. Cerf, *Laughing Stock;* 2: G. W. E. Russell, *Collections,* in J. Sutherland, ed., *OBLA;* 3: F. Winwar, *The Immortal Lovers*

BRUCE 1: John Pinkerton, *Walpoliana,* in Kenin and Wintle, *DBQ*

BRUMMELL 1–5: J. Timbs, *Century of Anecdote;* 6: D. George, *A Book of Anecdotes;* 8: E. Sitwell, *English Eccentrics*

BRUNO 1: *EB*

BRYAN 1: E. Fuller, *2500 Anecdotes;* 2: I. Stone, *They Also Ran;* 3: C. Fadiman and C. Van Doren, *The American Treasury*

BUCHANAN 1: Augustus C. Buell, *History of Andrew Jackson,* in P. Boller, ed., *Presidential Anecdotes;* 2: C. Fadiman and C. Van Doren, *The American Treasury*

BUCHWALD 1: J. Parrott, "Newsmakers," *Los Angeles Times,* Apr. 5, 1982

BUCKINGHAM 1: C. Roberts, *And So To Bath*

BUCKLAND 1: J. Morris, *The Oxford Book of Oxford;* 2: W. Keddie, *Literary and Scientific Anecdote*

BUCKLEY 1: *Los Angeles Times*, Apr. 11, 1982
BUDDHA 1: R. Tung, *A Portrait of Lost Tibet;* 2: W. Durant, *The Story of Civilization,* I
BUDÉ 1: C. Fadiman, *Any Number Can Play*
BUFFALMACCO 1: G. Vasari, *Lives of the Painters*
BULL 1: P. Phillips, *A Brief Chronicale;* 2: Anthony à Wood, *Fasti Oxonienses,* in Kenin and Wintle, *DBQ*
BULLER 1: S. Weintraub, *The London Yankees*
BÜLOW 1: H. Schonberg, *The Great Pianists;* 2–3: N. Slonimsky, *A Thing or Two about Music;* 4: H. Schonberg, *The Great Conductors*
BUNSEN 1: J. Read, *Humour and Humanism in Chemistry*
BURKE 1: Katherine C. Balderston, ed., *Thraliana,* in J. Sutherland, ed., *OBLA;* 2–3: J. Timbs, *Century of Anecdote;* 4: W. Keddie, *Literary and Scientific Anecdote;* 5: W. Adams, *Treasury of Modern Anecdote*
BURNS 1: S. Allen, *Funny People;* 2: G. Burns, *Third Time Around*
BURTON, SIR R., 1: M. Hastings, *Richard Burton;* 2: L. Blanch, *The Wilder Shores of Love*
BUSBY 1–2: E. Fuller, *2500 Anecdotes*
BUSCH 1: R. Bing, *5000 Nights at the Opera*
BUTLER, B. F., 1: D. Wallechinsky and I. Wallace, *The People's Almanac;* 2: Herbert W. Beecher, *History of the First Light Battery Connecticut Volunteers 1861–1865,* in B. Botkin, *A Civil War Treasury*
BUTLER, H. M., 1: A. Milne, *It's Too Late Now*
BUTLER, R. A., 1: N. Rees, *Quote . . . Unquote*
BUTLER, S., 1: H. Festing Jones, *Samuel Butler: A Memoir,* in J. Sutherland, ed., *OBLA;* 2: Mary MacCarthy, *A Nineteenth-Century Childhood,* in Sutherland, *OBLA;* 3–5: G. Keynes, *Samuel Butler's Notebooks*
BYNG 1: Horace Walpole, *Memoirs,* in Kenin and Wintle, *DBQ*
BYRD 1: A. Hatch, *The Byrds of Virginia*
BYRON 1: W. Keddie, *Literary and Scientific Anecdote;* 2: S. Rogers, *Table Talk;* 3–4: K. Arvine, *Cyclopaedia of Anecdotes;* 5: Albrizzi, *I Ritratto,* in D. Reiman, ed., *Shelley and his Circle*

CABELL 1: B. Cerf, *The Life of the Party*
CADBURY 1: I. and R. Poley, *Friendly Anecdotes*
CAEN 1: B. Conrad, *Fun While It Lasted*
CAESAR, JULIUS, 1–3, 5–6, 9–10: Suetonius, *The Twelve Caesars;* 4, 7–8: Plutarch, *Lives*
CAGLIOSTRO 1: W. Scholz, *Das Buch des Lachens*
CAGNEY 1: *Parade,* Aug. 5, 1984
CAINE 1: *Book-of-the-Month Club News,* 1947
CALHERN 1: *New York Times Book Review,* July 12, 1981
CALIGULA 1, 3: Suetonius, *The Twelve Caesars;* 2: W. Durant, *The Story of Civilization,* III

CALLAS 1: R. Bing, *5000 Nights at the Opera*
CALVERLEY 1: L. Missen, *After-dinner Stories and Anecdotes;* 2: J. Morris, *The Oxford Book of Oxford*
CAMBRIDGE 1: H. and D. L. Thomas, *Living Biographies of Famous Women*
CAMBRONNE 1: D. Wallechinsky and I. Wallace, *The People's Almanac*
CAMBYSES II 1: W. Durant, *The Story of Civilization,* I
CAMERON, J., 1: R. Martin, *Tennyson: The Unquiet Heart*
CAMERON OF LOCHIEL 1: T. Mason, *The Best Stories in the World*
CAMPBELL, D., 1: *"Daily Mirror" Old Codger's Little Black Book 4*
CAMPBELL, MRS. P., 1: Gabriel Fallon, *Sean O'Casey, The Man I Knew,* in J. Sutherland, ed., *OBLA;* 2: G. Kanin, *Hollywood;* 3: L. Missen, *Quotable Anecdotes;* 5, 8–9: M. Peters, *Mrs. Pat;* 6: C. Tomkins, *Living Well Is the Best Revenge;* 7: J. Braude, *Speaker's and Toastmaster's Handbook*
CAMPBELL, T., 1: G. Trevelyan, *The Life and Letters of Lord Macaulay;* 2–3: W. Keddie, *Literary and Scientific Anecdote*
CANE 1: C. Speroni, *Wit and Wisdom of the Italian Renaissance*
CANNING 1: J. Timbs, *Century of Anecdote;* 2: C. Sifakis, *Dictionary of Historic Nicknames*
CANNON 1: M. Schlesinger, *Snatched from Oblivion*
CANTOR 1: P. Mahony, *Barbed Wit and Malicious Humor;* 2: N. Rees, *Quote . . . Unquote*
CANUTE 1: Henry of Huntingdon, *Historia Anglorum*
CAPA 1: *'47, The Magazine of the Year* (October)
CAPONE 1: J. Kobler, *Capone*
CAPUS 1: C. Skinner, *Elegant Wits and Grand Horizontals*
CARDANO 1: I. Asimov, *Biographical Encyclopedia*
CARDOZO 1: R. Marquard, *Jokes and Anecdotes*
CARLETON 1: E. Fuller, *2500 Anecdotes*
CARLOS I 1: H. Prochnow, *The Public Speaker's Treasure Chest*
CARLYLE 2: Sir Thomas Henry Hall Caine, *My Story,* in J. Sutherland, ed., *OBLA;* 3: Sir Mountstuart Elphinstone Grant Duff, *Notes From a Diary,* in Sutherland, *OBLA;* 4: N. Rees, *Quote . . . Unquote;* 5: Augustus J. C. Hare, *The Story of My Life*
CARNEGIE 1: G. Fowler, *Beau James;* 2: E. Wagenknecht, *American Profile;* 3: E. Fuller, *2500 Anecdotes;* 4: *Book-of-the-Month Club News,* December 1952
CAROL II 1: J. Braude, *Speaker's and Toastmaster's Handbook*
CAROLINE, DUCHESSE DE BERRI, 1: A. Castelot,

CAROLINE OF ANSBACH 1: J. Timbs, *Century of Paris: The Turbulent City Anecdote;* 2: Hervey, *Memoirs of George the Second,* in *Oxford Dictionary of Quotations*
CAROLINE OF BRUNSWICK 1: E. Fuller, *2500 Anecdotes;* 2: M. Ringo, *Nobody Said It Better;* 3: A. Bryant, *The Age of Elegance;* 4: The Journal of Hon. Henry Edward Fox, 25 August 1821, in Kenin and Wintle, *DBQ*
CAROTO 1–2: G. Vasari: *Lives of the Painters*
CARROLL, L., 1: L. Missen, *Quotable Anecdotes;* 2: R. Green, *Diaries of Lewis Carroll*
CARSON 1–2: K. Tynan, *Show People*
CARTER 1: Bill Adler, ed., *Wit and Wisdom of Jimmy Carter,* in P. Boller, ed., *Presidential Anecdotes;* 2: J. Carter, *Keeping Faith;* 3: "He Can Catch Fire," *Time,* Jan. 5, 1981, in Boller, *Presidential Anecdotes;* 4: R. Byrne, *The 637 Best Things Anybody Ever Said*
CARTLAND 1: J. Cooper, *Class*
CARUSO 1: D. Wallechinsky and I. Wallace, *The People's Almanac;* 2: H. Greenfield, *Caruso;* 3: H. Broun, *Whose Little Boy Are You?;* 4: E. Van de Velde, *Anecdotes Musicales*
CASALS 1: A. Whitman, *Come to Judgment;* 2–3: M. Eastman, *Great Companions;* 4: Y. Karsh, *Karsh*
CASSATT 1: A. Vollard, *Recollections of a Picture Dealer*
CASTIGLIONE 1: I. Wallace et al., *Intimate Sex Lives of Famous People*
CASTLEROSSE 1: P. Ziegler, *Diana Cooper*
CASTRACANI 1: Ludovico Domenichi in C. Speroni, *Wit and Wisdom of the Italian Renaissance*
CASTRO 1–2: C. Franqui, *Family Portrait with Fidel*
CATHERINE OF ARAGON 1: W. Abbot, *Notable Women in History*
CATHERINE II 1: W. Abbot, *Notable Women in History*
CATO 1: *Oxford Companion to Classical Literature;* 2: J. Braude, *Speaker's and Toastmaster's Handbook;* 3: F. Callières, *Des Bons Mots et des bons contes*
CAVELL 1: *The Times* (London), Oct. 23, 1915, in *Oxford Dictionary of Quotations*
CECIL 1: J. Train, *True Remarkable Occurrences*
CERVANTES 1: *Compton's Encyclopedia*
CETEWAYO 1: J. Smail, *With Shield and Assegai*
CÉZANNE 1: *Compton's Encyclopedia*
CHALIAPIN 1–2: S. Beach, *Musicdotes;* 3: R. Merrill, *Between Acts*
CHALONER 1: *The New Yorker,* Nov. 26, 1955
CHAMBERLAIN, A. N., 1: *Oxford Dictionary of Quotations*
CHAMBERLAIN, J., 1: T. Masson, *The Best Stories in the World*
CHAMBERLAIN, SIR J. A., 1: Frances Stevenson

diary, Mar. 5, 1919, in Kenin and Wintle, *DBQ*
CHANEL 1–2: C. Baillén, *Chanel Solitaire;* 3: F. Steegmuller, *Cocteau*
CHANNING 1: B. Adler, *My Favorite Funny Story*
CHAPLIN 1: C. Seelig, *Albert Einstein;* 2: L. Lucaire, *Celebrity Trivia;* 3: D. Niven, *Bring on the Empty Horses;* 4: E. Fuller, *2500 Anecdotes*
CHAPMAN, JOHN, 1: Robert Price, *Johnny Appleseed, Man and Myth,* in B. Botkin, *Treasury of American Anecdotes;* 2: P. Smith, *The Nation Comes of Age*
CHAPMAN, JOHN JAY, 1: C. Canfield, *Up and Down and Around*
CHARLEMAGNE 1: Draper and Esquin sales brochure
CHARLES II 1: T. Blount, *Boscobel;* 2: J. Aubrey, *Miscellanies;* 3: Gilbert Burnet, *History of My Own Time,* in Kenin and Wintle, *DBQ;* 4: James Granger, *Biographical History of England,* in Kenin and Wintle, *DBQ;* 5: I. and R. Poley, *Friendly Anecdotes;* 6: William King, *Anecdotes,* in D. George, *A Book of Anecdotes;* 7: Jonathan Richardson, *Richardsoniana,* in J. Sutherland, ed., *OBLA;* 8: J. Bartlett, *Familiar Quotations;* 9: Gilbert Burnet, *History of My Own Time,* in B. Conrad, *Famous Last Words*
CHARLES V 1: W. Durant, *The Story of Civilization,* V; 2: H. Prochnow, *The Public Speaker's Treasure Chest*
CHARLES X 1–2: W. Adams, *Treasury of Modern Anecdote*
CHARLES FRANCIS JOSEPH 1: H. Hoffmeister, *Anekdotenschatz*
CHARLOTTE OF MECKLENBURG-STRELITZ 1: J. Timbs, *Century of Anecdote*
CHARONDAS 1: W. Durant, *The Story of Civilization,* II
CHASE, I., 1: E. Fuller, *2500 Anecdotes*
CHASE, S., 1: B. Cerf: *Bumper Crop of Anecdotes*
CHATEAUBRIAND 1: M. Ringo, *Nobody Said It Better;* 2: C. Brinton, *The Lives of Talleyrand*
CHATTERTON 1: W. Keddie, *Literary and Scientific Anecdote*
CHEKHOV 1: V. Pritchett, *The Myth Makers;* 2: A. Chekhov, *The Image of Chekhov*
CHERUBINI 1: W. Gates, *Anecdotes of Great Musicians;* 2: H. Hoffmeister, *Anekdotenschatz;* 3: J. Papesch, *Europa Lächelt Noch Immer;* 4: H. Sievers, *Musica Curiosa*
CHESTERFIELD 1, 5: E. Fuller, *2500 Anecdotes;* 2: W. and A. Durant, *The Story of Civilization,* IX; 3: J. Timbs, *Century of Anecdote;* 4: *DNB;* 6: B. Conrad, *Famous Last Words*
CHESTERTON 1, 7–8: A. Dale: *The Outline of Sanity;* 2–3, 12: G. Chesterton, *Charles Dickens* (foreword); 4: H. Hoffmeister, *Anekdoten-*

CHESTERTON (*continued*)
schatz; 6: W. Scholz, *Das Buch des Lachens;* 9: H. Pearson, *Lives of the Wits;* 10: J. Braude, *Speaker's and Toastmaster's Handbook;* 11: C. Asquith: *Portrait of Barrie;* 14: B. Cerf, *Try and Stop Me*

CHIGI 1: P. Méras, *The Mermaids of Chenonceaux*

CHOATE 1–2, 4–6: T. Strong, *Joseph Choate;* 3: M. Ringo, *Nobody Said It Better;* 7: E. Fuller, *2500 Anecdotes*

CHOPIN 1: H. Finck, *Musical Laughs;* 2: N. Slonimsky, *A Thing or Two about Music*

CHRISTIAN X 1: K. Edwards, *More Things I Wish I'd Said*

CHRISTIE, A., 1: B. Cerf, *The Life of the Party;* 2: I. Wallace, "Significa," Nov. 13, 1983

CHRISTIE, J., 1: R. Bing, *5000 Nights at the Opera*

CHRISTINA 1: W. Abbot, *Notable Women in History*

CHURCHILL, R., 1, 3: K. Halle, *Randolph Churchill;* 2: Henry Fairlie in K. Halle, *Randolph Churchill*

CHURCHILL, LORD R., 1–2: A. Leslie, *The Remarkable Mr. Jerome*

CHURCHILL, SIR W., 1: *Book-of-the-Month Club News,* April 1954; 2, 31, 45: L. Rosten, *People I Have Loved, Known or Admired;* 3–4: E. Marsh, *A Number of People;* 5: Violet Bonham Carter, *Winston Churchill, An Intimate Portrait,* in W. Manchester, *The Last Lion;* 6: A. Sylvester, *Life With Lloyd George;* 7: Elizabeth Langhorne, *Nancy Astor and Her Friends,* in Kenin and Wintle, *DBQ;* 8: K. Halle, *Randolph Churchill;* 9: W. Churchill, *Thoughts and Adventures;* 10: M. MacDonald, *Titans and Others;* 11: L. Missen, *Quotable Anecdotes;* 13: *DNB;* 14, 24: R. Collier, *The Road to Pearl Harbor;* 15: A. Herbert, *A.P.H.;* 16: K. Edwards, *I Wish I'd Said That Too;* 18, 26, 35–38, 42, 47: W. Manchester, *The Last Lion;* 20, 27, 49: O. Levant, *The Unimportance of Being Oscar;* 21: O. Bradley and C. Blair, *A General's Life;* 22: J. Green, *Morrow's Dictionary of Quotations;* 25: B. Cerf, *Shake Well Before Using;* 29, 48: N. Rees, *Quote . . . Unquote;* 30: *Penguin Dictionary of Quotations;* 32: M. and A. Guillois, *Liberté, Egalité, Hilarité;* 33: *Los Angeles Times,* Mar. 25, 1982; 34: Lord Moran, *Churchill, Taken from the Diaries of Lord Moran: The Struggle for Survival, 1940–1965,* in W. Manchester, *The Last Lion;* 39: L. Harris, *The Fine Art of Political Wit;* 41: S. Shadegg, *Clare Boothe Luce;* 46: E. Longford, *The Queen*

CHWOLSON 1: L. Rosten, *Joys of Yiddish*

CIBBER 1: Thomas Davies, *Dramatic Micellanies,* in Kenin and Wintle, *DBQ*

CICERO 1–3: Macrobius, *Saturnalia;* 4: Plutarch, *Lives*

CIMON 1: Plutarch, *Lives*

CINQUE 1: D. Wallechinsky and I. Wallace, *The People's Almanac*

CLAIRE 1: R. Lamparski, *Whatever Became Of . . .?*

CLARK, A. C., 1: C. Bowra, *Memories 1898–1939*

CLARK, G. R., 1: P. Smith, *The Shaping of America*

CLARK, M. W., 1: J. Braude, *Speaker's and Toastmaster's Handbook*

CLAY, C., 1: S. Sifakis, *Dictionary of Historic Nicknames*

CLAY, H., 1: R. Marquard, *Jokes and Anecdotes;* 2: E. Fuller, *2500 Anecdotes;* 3: H. Wright and S. Rapport, *The Great Explorers;* 4: Thomas Hart Clay, *Henry Clay,* in C. Shriner, *Wit, Wisdom, and Foibles of the Great;* 5: C. Fadiman and C. Van Doren, *The American Treasury;* 6: D. Knox, *More Quotable Anecdotes;* 7: L. Harris, *The Fine Art of Political Wit*

CLEMENCEAU 1: E. Fuller, *2500 Anecdotes;* 2: M. and A. Guillois, *Liberté, Egalité, Hilarité;* 3: J. Braude, *Speaker's and Toastmaster's Handbook;* 4: A. Sylvester, *Life with Lloyd George;* 5: H. Acton, *More Memoirs of an Asthete;* 6: B. Cerf, *Try and Stop Me;* 7: W. Churchill, *Thoughts and Adventures;* 8: D. Wallechinsky and I. Wallace, *The People's Almanac;* 9: L. Missen, *After-dinner Stories and Anecdotes;* 10: P. Smith, *America Enters the World;* 11: I. Hamilton, *Koestler*

CLEVELAND, G., 1: James Schermerhorn, *Schermerhorn Stories,* in P. Boller, ed., *Presidential Anecdotes;* 2: *American Scholar* III (1934)

CLIVE 1: Sir George Trevelyan, *Life and Letters of Lord Macauley,* in D. George, *A Book of Anecdotes;* 2: D. George, *A Book of Anecdotes*

CLURMAN 1–2: R. Lewis, *Slings and Arrows*

COBB 1: R. Marquard, *Jokes and Anecdotes;* 2: J. Humes, *Speakers' Treasury*

COCKCROFT 1: *Obituaries from the Times, 1961–70*

COCTEAU 1: H. Acton, *More Memoirs of an Asthete;* 2: H. Hoffmeister, *Anekdotenschatz;* 3: J. Braude, *Speaker's and Toastmaster's Handbook;* 4: W. Fifield, *In Search of Genius*

COHAN 1: O. Levant, *The Unimportance of Being Oscar;* 2: S. Marx and J. Clayton, *Rodgers and Hart;* 3: *Book-of-the-Month Club News,* March 1944; 4: S. Alexander, *Talking Woman*

COHN 1: M. Ringo, *Nobody Said It Better;* 2: *Los Angeles Times,* June 25, 1982; 3: G. Kanin,

Hollywood; 4: *Los Angeles Times*, Jan. 26, 1985

COKE 1: J. Aubrey, *Brief Lives*

COLE 1: *DNB*

COLERIDGE 1: W. Keddie, *Literary and Scientific Anecdote*; 2: S. T. Coleridge, *Kubla Khan*; 3: L. Russell, *English Wits*; 4: J. Braude, *Speaker's and Toastmaster's Handbook*; 5: C. R. Leslie, *Autobiographical Recollections*, in J. Sutherland, ed., *OBLA*; 6: T. Moore, *Memoirs, Journal, and Correspondence*

COLETTE 1: J. McAleer, "Globe Man's Daily Story," *Boston Globe*, Aug. 4, 1969

COLLINS, J., 1: *New York Times Book Review*, May 6, 1984

COLLINS, M., 1: W. Churchill, *Great Contemporaries*

COLUMBUS 1: S. E. Morison, ed., *Journals and Other Documents of Columbus*, in L. B. Young, *The Blue Planet*; 2: Benzoni, *Historia del Mondo Nuevo*, in D. George, *A Book of Anecdotes*; 3: I. Wallace et al., *The Book of Lists 2*

COMTE 1: B. Conrad, *Famous Last Words*

CONDORCET 1: E. Bell, *Men of Mathematics*

CONFUCIUS 1: W. Durant, *The Story of Civilization*, I; 2: H. Margolius, *Der Lächelnde Philosoph*

CONGREVE 1: Voltaire, *Letters Concerning the English Nation*, in J. Sutherland, ed., *OBLA*

CONNELLY 1: H. Teichmann, *Smart Aleck*; 2: C. Fadiman, *Any Number Can Play*; 3–4: C. Stinnett, "Travels With Marc," *Signature*, December 1981

CONNOLLY 1: *Times Literary Supplement*, Dec. 6, 1974

CONSTABLE 1: W. Adams, *Treasury of Modern Anecdote*; 2: D. Piper, *Painting in England*

CONSTANTINE THE GREAT 1: W. Durant, *The Story of Civilization*, III

CONSTANTINE, L. N., 1: J. Arlott, *Book of Cricketers*

COOK 1: F. Muir, *Irreverent Social History*

COOLIDGE 1: BBC Radio 4, Oct. 11, 1981; 2: Ishbel Ross, *Grace Coolidge and Her Era*, in Kenin and Wintle, *DBQ*; 3, 6–7, 17, 22, 26: E. Fuller, *2500 Anecdotes*; 4: J. Braude, *Braude's Second Encyclopedia*; 5: *Los Angeles Times*, Aug. 6, 1982; 8: L. Missen: *After-dinner Stories and Anecdotes*; 10: B. Cerf, *Try and Stop Me*; 11: B. Cerf, *Shake Well Before Using*; 12: Edward C. Lathem, *Meet Calvin Coolidge*, in P. Boller, ed., *Presidential Anecdotes*; 13: Boyce House, *Laugh Parade of States*, in Boller, *Presidential Anecdotes*; 14: Boller, *Presidential Anecdotes*; 15: George Allen, *Presidents Who Have Known Me*, in Boller, *Presidential Anecdotes*;

16: Edmund W. Starling, *Starling of the White House*, in Boller, *Presidential Anecdotes*; 18: *American Scholar* X (1941); 19–20: Cameron Rodgers, *The Legend of Calvin Coolidge*, in B. Botkin, *Treasury of American Anecdotes*; 21: A. Krock, *Memoirs*; 23: R. Shenkman and K. Reiger, *One-Night Stands with American History*; 24: J. Braude, *Speaker's and Toastmaster's Handbook*; 25: "The Well-Known Human Race," *Reader's Digest*, June 1933, in Boller, *Presidential Anecdotes*; 27: M. Ringo, *Nobody Said It Better*

COOPER, LADY D., 1–3: P. Ziegler, *Diana Cooper*

COOPER, G., 1: H. Smith, *The Life and Legend of Gene Fowler*; 2: G. Herman, *The Book of Hollywood Quotes*

COOPER, DAME G., 1: G. Brandreth, *Great Theatrical Disasters*; 2: R. Morley, *A Musing Morley*

COOPER, SIR W., 1: A. Lawson, *Discover Unexpected London*

COOTE 1: S. Morley, *Tales from the Hollywood Raj*

COPE 1: I. Asimov, *Biographical Encyclopedia*

COPELAND 1: E. Fuller, *2500 Anecdotes*; 2: J. McAleer, "Globe Man's Daily Story," *Boston Globe*, July 11, 1959

CORBET 1: J. Aubrey, *Brief Lives*

CORDAY 1: M. Pedrazzini and J. Gris, *Autant en apportent les mots*

COROT 1: T. Craven, *Men of Art*; 2: E. Chubb, *Sketches of Great Painters*; 3: N. Rorem, *Later Diaries*

CORRIGAN 1: R. Lamparski, *Whatever Became Of . . . ?*

CORTOT 1: D. Gill, *The Book of the Piano*

COURTELINE 1: C. Skinner, *Elegant Wits and Grand Horizontals*

COURTNEIDGE 1: C. Milne, *The Enchanted Places*; 4: R. Drennan, *Wit's End*; 5: K. Tynan, *Tynan on Theatre*; 6: R. Marquard, *Jokes and Anecdotes*; 7: R. Massey, *A Hundred Different Lives*; 8: B. Forbes, *Ned's Girl*; 9: *"Daily Mirror" Old Codger's Little Black Book 1*; 10: G. Brandreth, *Great Theatrical Disasters*; 11: S. Morley, *A Talent to Amuse*; 12: R. Buckle, *In the Wake of Diaghilev*; 13: G. Payn and S. Morley, *The Noël Coward Diaries*; 14: B. Conrad, *Fun While It Lasted*

COWELL 1: N. Slonimsky, *A Thing or Two about Music*

COWL 1: E. Fuller, *2500 Anecdotes*

CRANMER 1: J. Foxe, *Acts and Monuments*

CROCKETT 1: Daniel C. Roper and Frank Lovette, *Fifty Years of Public Life*, in B. Botkin, *Treasury of American Anecdotes*; 2: Horace Greeley, ed., *The Tribune Almanac for the Years*

CROCKETT (*continued*)
1838–1868, in R. Shenkman and K. Reiger, *One-Night Stands with American History*

CROCKFORD 1: W. Walsh, *Handy Book of Curious Information*

CROESUS 1: Herodotus, *History*, I

CROLL 1: W. Espy, *An Almanac of Words at Play*

CROMWELL 1: H. Walpole, *Anecdotes of Painting*; 2: C. Hill, *God's Englishman*; 3: C. Shriner, *Wit, Wisdom, and Foibles of the Great*; 4: J. Spence, *Anecdotes*; 5: H. Hoffmeister, *Anekdotenschatz*

CROSBY 1: C. Thompson, *Bing*

CUKOR 1: *Los Angeles Times*, July 31, 1984

CULBERTSON 1: *"Daily Mirror" Old Codger's Little Black Book 4*

CUMMINGS 1: S. Cheever, *Home Before Dark*

CUNARD 1: H. Acton, *Nancy Mitford: A Memoir*; 2. E. Marsh, *A Number of People*

CUNNINGHAME GRAHAM 1: *Book-of-the-Month Club News*, April 1950

CURIE 1: H. and D. L. Thomas, *Living Adventures in Science*

CURLEY 1: W. Manchester, *One Brief Shining Moment*

CURRAN 1–3: W. Adams, *Treasury of Modern Anecdote*; 4: D. George, *A Book of Anecdotes*

CURTIZ 1: D. Niven, *Bring on the Empty Horses*; 2: O. Levant, *The Unimportance of Being Oscar*

CUSHMAN 1: W. Winter, *Other Days*

CUVIER 1: I. Asimov, *Biographical Encyclopedia*; 2: D. Enright, *The Oxford Book of Death*

CYRUS II 1: K. Edwards, *I Wish I'd Said That*

CYRUS OF PANOPOLIS 1: T. Cornell and J. Matthews, *Atlas of the Roman World*

DAHN 1: H. Hoffmeister, *Anekdotenschatz*

DALE 1: W. Keddie, *Literary and Scientific Anecdote*

DALI 1: L. Buñuel, *My Last Breath*; 2: P. Horgan, *Encounters with Stravinsky*; 3: J. Gruen, *The Party's Over Now*

DALTON 1: I. Asimov, *Biographical Encyclopedia*

DANA 1: C. Fadiman, *Any Number Can Play*

D'ANNUNZIO 1: E. Fuller, *2500 Anecdotes*

DANTE ALIGHIERI 1–2: C. Speroni, *Wit and Wisdom of the Italian Renaissance*

DANTON 1: B. Conrad, *Famous Last Words*

DARIUS I 1: Herodotus, *History*, IV; 2: F. Paley, *Greek Wit*

DARROW 1–2: E. Fuller, *2500 Anecdotes*; 3: M. Ringo, *Nobody Said It Better*; 4: H. Prochnow, *The Public Speaker's Treasure Chest*; 5: T. Arnold, *Fair Fights and Foul*

DARWIN, C., 1: J. Chancellor, *Charles Darwin*; 2: A. Moorehead, *Darwin and the Beagle*; 3: G. Keynes and B. Hill, eds., *Samuel Butler's Notebooks*

DARWIN, E., 1: Ernst Kraus, *Erasmus Darwin*, in Kenin and Wintle, *DBQ*

DAUDET 1: E. Van de Velde, *Anecdotes Musicales*

DAVENANT 1: *DNB*; 2: B. Conrad, *Famous Last Words*

DAVIES, LADY E., 1: W. Keddie, *Literary and Scientific Anecdote*

DAVIES, M., 1: S. Marx, *Mayer and Thalberg*

DAVIS 1: I. Wallace et al., *Book of Lists 2*

DAVY 1–2: C. R. Weld, *A History of the Royal Society*, in Kenin and Wintle, *DBQ*; 3: E. Fuller, *2500 Anecdotes*

DEAN 1–2: C. Fadiman and C. Van Doren, *The American Treasury*; 3: J. Nash, *Zanies*; 4: C. Sifakis, *Dictionary of Historic Nicknames*

DEBS 1: D. Wallechinsky and I. Wallace, *The People's Almanac*

DEGAS 1: R. McMullen, *Degas: His Life, Times, and Work*; 3: J. Krantz, *Mistral's Daughter*

DE GAULLE 1: R. Buckle, *Self-Portrait With Friends*; 2: M. Ringo, *Nobody Said It Better*; 4: J. Bartlett, *Familiar Quotations*; 5, 12: P. Frederick, *Ten First Ladies of the World*; 6: *The Times* (London), Aug. 30, 1983; 7: J. Green, *Morrow's Dictionary of Quotations*; 9: L. Lucaire, *Celebrity Trivia*; 10: B. Walters, *How To Talk with Practically Anybody*; 11: R. Morley, *Book of Bricks*

DÉJAZET 1: M. Pedrazzini and J. Gris, *Autant en apporte les mots*

DE LA MARE 1: *John Bailey 1864–1931: Letters, Edited by his Wife*, in J. Sutherland, ed., *OBLA*

DE MOIVRE 1: C. Fadiman, *The Mathematical Magpie*

DEMOSTHENES 1: N. McPhee, *Second Book of Insults*; 2: Plutarch, *Lives*

DEMPSEY 1: M. Ringo, *Nobody Said It Better*; 2: B. Cerf, *Try and Stop Me*; 3: G. Perrett, *America in the Twenties*

DENHAM 1: C. Sifakis, *Dictionary of Historic Nicknames*

DENIS 1: E. Guérard, *Dictionnaire Encyclopédique*; 2: Dugas de Bois St. Just, *Paris, Versailles et les provinces*

DENNIS 1–2: R. Hendrickson, *The Literary Life*

DEPEW 1: E. Fuller, *2500 Anecdotes*; 2: I. Asimov, *Treasury of Humor*

DESCARTES 1: D. Wallechinsky and I. Wallace, *The People's Almanac 2*; 2: I. Asimov, *Biographical Encyclopedia*; 3: W. Keddie, *Literary and Scientific Anecdote*

DE SEVERSKY 1: B. Cerf, *Shake Well Before Using*

DETOURBEY 1: C. Skinner, *Elegant Wits and Grand Horizontals*

DE VALERA 1: I. Asimov, *Treasury of Humor*; 2: E. Fuller, *2500 Anecdotes*; 3–4: J. Gunther, *Procession*

DE VALOIS 1: *The New Yorker*, Sept. 16, 1950

DEVONSHIRE, DUKE OF, 1: Duchess of Devonshire, *The House*; 2: J. Pearson, *The Serpent and the Stag*

DEWEY, J., 1–3: M. Eastman, *Great Companions*

DE WOLFE 1: J. Smith, *Elsie de Wolfe*

DIAGHILEV 1: F. Steegmuller, *Cocteau*; 2: B. Taper, *Balanchine: A Biography*; 3: M. Georges-Michel, *From Renoir to Picasso*

DIANA, PRINCESS OF WALES 1: *The Times* (London), Apr. 13, 1983

DICKENS 1, 7: G. Chesterton, *Charles Dickens*; 2: R. Hendrickson, *The Literary Life*; 3: John Forster, *The Life of Charles Dickens (1872–4)*, in J. Sutherland, ed., *OBLA*; 4: Frederick Locker-Lampson, *My Confidences*, in Sutherland, *OBLA*; 5–6: E. Johnson, *Charles Dickens*

DIDEROT 1: E. Bell, *Men of Mathematics*

DIETRICH 2: Lynne Thornton, "Inside the House of Hermes," in *Connoisseur*, March 1982

DIETZ 1: *Los Angeles Times*, Mar. 30, 1983

DIGBY 1: J. Aubrey, *Brief Lives*

DIOGENES 1: Plutarch, *Lives*; 2–3: Diogenes Laertius, *Eminent Philosophers*; 4: E. Fuller, *2500 Anecdotes*; 5: H. Hoffmeister, *Anekdotenschatz*; 6: J. Braude, *Speaker's and Toastmaster's Handbook*; 7–8: H. Margolius, *Der Lächelnde Philosoph*

DIONYSIUS II 1: W. Keddie, *Literary and Scientific Anecdote*

DIRICHLET 1: H. Hoffmeister, *Anekdotenschatz*

DISNEY 1: C. Finch, *The Art of Walt Disney*

DISRAELI 1, 3: *DNB*; 2: M. Ringo, *Nobody Said It Better*; 4: Wilfred Meynell, *Benjamin Disraeli*, in C. Shriner, *Wit, Wisdom, and Foibles of the Great*; 5: W. Espy, *Another Almanac of Words at Play*; 6: B. Cerf, *Try and Stop Me*; 7: R. Marquard, *Jokes and Anecdotes*; 8: F. Muir, *Irreverent Social History*; 9: Michael MacDonagh, *Fortnightly Review*, August 1902, in Shriner, *Wit*; 10: Shriner, *Wit*; 11: Disraeli at Meeting of Society for Endowments of Small Livings in the Diocese of Oxford, Nov. 25, 1864, in *Oxford Dictionary of Quotations*; 12: H. Hoffmeister, *Anekdotenschatz*; 13: L. Harris, *The Fine Art of Political Wit*; 14: N. McPhee, *Second Book of Insults*; 15: I. Wallace et al., *Intimate Sex Lives of Famous People*; 16: H.H. Marie Louise, *My Memories of Six Reigns*, in A. Hardy, *Queen Victoria Was Amused*

DIVINE 1: D. Wallechinsky and I. Wallace, *The People's Almanac*; 2: L. Rosten, *People I Have Loved, Known or Admired*

DIX 1: P. Smith, *Trial by Fire*

DOHERTY 1: W. Adams, *Treasury of Modern Anecdote*

DONATELLO 1: A. Poliziano, *Diario*

DONNE 1: Sir James Prior, *Life of Edmond Malone*, in J. Sutherland, ed., *OBLA*; 2: Izaak Walton, *The Lives of John Donne, . . . Robert Sanderson*, in Sutherland, *OBLA*

DONOVAN 1: A. Cave Brown, *The Last Hero*

DOOLEY 1: M. Strauss, *Familiar Medical Quotations*

DOUGLASS 1: B. Botkin, *Treasury of American Anecdotes*

DOYLE 2: P. Mahony, *Barbed Wit and Malicious Humor*; 3: J. Nash, *Zanies*

DRAKE 1: J. Williamson, *The English Channel*; 2: *DNB*

DREISER 1: S. Mayfield, *The Constant Circle*

DREW 1: E. Fuller, *2500 Anecdotes*

DREYSCHOCK 1: H. Schonberg, *The Great Pianists*

DRYDEN 1: W. Keddie, *Literary and Scientific Anecdote*; 2: J. Prior, *Life of E. Malone*; 3: G. Colman, *Circle of Anecdote*

DU BARRY 1: L. and M. Cowan, *The Wit of Women*

DUCLOS 1: Dugas de Bois St. Just, *Paris, Versailles et les provinces*

DU DEFFAND 1–2: C. Pedrazzini and J. Gris, *Autant en apportent les mots*; 3: E. Guérard, *Dictionnaire Encyclopédique*

DUDLEY 1: W. Adams, *Treasury of Modern Anecdote*

DULLES 1: H. Temianka, *Facing the Music*

DUMAS, A. (PÈRE), 1: L. Russell, *English Wits*; 2: B. Cerf, *Shake Well Before Using*; 3: E. Fuller, *2500 Anecdotes*; 4–8: H. Hoffmeister, *Anekdotenschatz*; 9: L. and F. Copeland, *10,000 Jokes, Toasts and Stories*

DUMAS, A. (FILS), 1–2: C. Skinner, *Elegant Wits and Grand Horizontals*; 3: A. Castelot, *Paris: The Turbulent City*

DUNSANY 1: S. Winchester, *Their Noble Lordships*

DU PONT 1: *The New Yorker*, Dec. 13, 1952

DURANTE 1, 3: G. Fowler, *Schnozzola*; 4–5: A. Hotchner, *Choice People*

DUROCHER 1: C. Fadiman and C. Van Doren, *The American Treasury*

DUSE 1: S. Radecki, *Das ABC des Lachens*; 2: E. Fuller, *2500 Anecdotes*

DUVAL 1: C. Roberts, *And So To Bath*

DUVEEN 1: B. Cerf, *Good for a Laugh*; 2: S. Birmingham, *The Grandes Dames*; 3: M. Ringo, *Nobody Said It Better*; 4: *The New Yorker*, Sept. 29, 1951; 5: S. Holbrook, *The Age of the Moguls*

DYSON 1: Oxfam, *Pass the Port*

EDDINGTON 1: A. V. Douglas, *The Life of Arthur Stanley Eddington*, in Kenin and Wintle, *DBQ*

EDDY 1: H. and D. L. Thomas, *Living Biographies of Religious Leaders*

EDEN, A., 1: A. Cooke, *Six Men*

EDEN, SIR W., 1: C. Fadiman, *Any Number Can Play*

EDISON, C., 1: J. Braude, *Speaker's and Toastmaster's Handbook*

EDISON, T., 1: Henry Ford, *My Friend, Mr. Edison*, in Kenin and Wintle, *DBQ*; 2–6, 9: E. Fuller, *2500 Anecdotes*; 7: D. Wallechinsky and I. Wallace, *The People's Almanac*; 8: J. Braude, *Speaker's and Toastmaster's Handbook*

EDMAN 1: *Book-of-the-Month Club News*, 1947; 2: B. Cerf, *Try and Stop Me*; 3: *Book-of-the-Month Club News*, Midsummer, 1950

EDWARD I 1: E. C. Brewer, *Dictionary of Phrase and Fable*

EDWARD III 1: B. Vincent, ed., *Haydn's Dictionary of Dates*; 2: *Oxford Dictionary of Quotations*

EDWARD VII 1: *Private Life of Edward VII, by a Member of the Royal Household*, in C. Shriner, *Wit, Wisdom, and Foibles of the Great*; 2: C. Skinner, *Elegant Wits and Grand Horizontals*; 3–4, 7: R. Collier, *The Rainbow People*; 5: G. Lieberman, *The Greatest Laughs of All Time*; 6: B. Cerf, *The Life of the Party*; 8: M. Secrist, *Kenneth Clark: A Biography*; 9: H. Atkins and A. Newman, eds., *Beecham Stories*; 10: P. Mahony, *Barbed Wit and Malicious Humor*; 11: C. Aslet, *The Last Country Houses*

EDWARD VIII 1: D. Herrmann, *With Malice Toward All*; 3: A. Chambers, *Dream Resorts*

EINSTEIN 1: P. David and R. Hersh, *The Mathematical Experience*; 2: I. Rosenthal-Schneider, *Reality and Scientific Truth*; 3: P. Frank, *Einstein*; 4, 10: C. Seelig, *Albert Einstein*; 5: J. Bernstein, *Einstein*; 6: G. Whitrow, *Einstein*; 7: M. and A. Guillois, *Liberté, Egalité, Hilarité*; 8: E. Fuller, *2500 Anecdotes*; 9: A. Toynbee, *Acquaintances*; 12: W. Novak and M. Waldoks, *The Big Book of Jewish Humor*; 13, 19: S. Harris, *Pieces of Eight*; 15: *New York Times Book Review*, Sept. 26, 1982; 16: O. Levant, *The Unimportance of Being Oscar*

EISENHOWER 1: Merlo J. Pusey, *Eisenhower the President*, in P. Boller, ed., *Presidential Anecdotes*; 2: J. Gunther, *Procession*; 3: H. Donovan, *From Roosevelt to Reagan*; 4: R. Crouser, *It's Unlucky to Be Behind at the End of the Game*

ELEANOR OF AQUITAINE 1: W. Durant, *The Story of Civilization*, IV

ELIOT, C., 1: R. Marquard, *Jokes and Anecdotes*; 2: J. McAleer, "Globe Man's Daily Story," *Boston Globe*, June 27, 1963

ELIOT, J., 1: W. Keddie, *Literary and Scientific Anecdote*

ELIOT, T. S., 1: I. A. Richards, "On T. S. E.," in *T. S. Eliot: The Man and His Work*, in J. Sutherland, ed., *OBLA*; 2: L. Untermeyer, *Bygones*; 3: D. Wallechinsky and I. Wallace, *The People's Almanac 2*; 4: A. Tate, ed., *T. S. Eliot*; 5: S. Weintraub, *The London Yankees*; 6: P. Ackroyd, *T. S. Eliot*; 7–8: *Publishers Weekly*, Jan. 8, 1982

ELISABETH 1: M. and A. Guillois, *Liberté, Egalité, Hilarité*

ELIZABETH I 1: D'Israeli, *Curiosities of Literature*; 2: J. Aubrey, *Brief Lives*; 3: W. Keddie, *Literary and Scientific Anecdote*

ELIZABETH II 1: I. Wallace et al., *Significa*; 3: V. Wade, *Courting Triumph*; 4: P. Ziegler, *Diana Cooper*; 6: R. Lacey, *Majesty*

ELIZABETH THE QUEEN MOTHER 1: A. Faulkner and T. Hartman, *All the Best People*; 4: J. Bartlett, *Familiar Quotations*; 5: M. Korda, *Charmed Lives*; 6: D. Duff, *Elizabeth of Glamis*; 7: B. Cerf, *Good for a Laugh*; 8: K. Edwards, *I Wish I'd Said That*

ELLENBOROUGH 1: L. Russell, *English Wits*; 2: W. Adams, *Treasury of Modern Anecdote*

ELLIOT 1: W. Adams, *Treasury of Modern Anecdote*

ELLISTON 1: George Raymond, *Memoirs of R. W. Elliston*, in Kenin and Wintle, *DBQ*; 2: Thomas Moore, *Memoirs, Journal and Correspondence*, in Kenin and Wintle, *DBQ*

ELMAN 1: E. Fuller, *2500 Anecdotes*; 2: H. Temianka, *Facing the Music*; 3: B. Cerf, *Laughing Stock*

EMERSON 1: J. McAleer, *Ralph Waldo Emerson: Days of Encounter*; 2, 4, 10: O. Holmes, *Ralph Waldo Emerson*; 3: H. and D. L. Thomas, *Living Biographies of the Great Philosophers*; 5: *Compton's Encyclopedia*; 6: I. Wallace et al., *Book of Lists 2*; 7: Mary B. Claflin, *Personal Recollections of John Greenleaf Whittier*, in *OBALA*; 8: C. Fadiman and C. Van Doren, *The American Treasury*

EMPEDOCLES 1: *Oxford Classical Dictionary*

ENESCO 1: W. Espy, *Another Almanac of Words at Play*

ENGELS 1: G. Pijet, *Duell mit der Vergangenheit*

EPICTETUS 1: W. Durant, *The Story of Philosophy*

EPSTEIN 1: J. Braude, *Speaker's and Toastmaster's Handbook*

ERASMUS 1: E. Guérard, *Dictionnaire Encyclopédique*

ERIC THE RED 1: H. Rawson, *Dictionary of Euphemisms*

ERSKINE, J., 1: G. Lieberman, *The Greatest Laughs of All Time*

ERSKINE, T., 1: J. Timbs, *Century of Anecdote*; 2: W. Keddie, *Literary and Scientific Anecdote*

ESHKOL 1: R. Carter, *First Lady from Plains*
ESTE 1: C. Speroni, *Wit and Wisdom of the Italian Renaissance*
EUCLID 1: I. Asimov, *Treasury of Humor*
EUGÉNIE 1: D. Duff, *Eugénie and Napoleon III;* 2: F. Loliée, *Gilded Beauties of the Second Empire*
EULER 1–2: E. Bell, *Men of Mathematics*
EURIPIDES 1: W. Keddie, *Literary and Scientific Anecdote*
EVANS, SIR A., 1: C. Bowra, *Memories 1898–1939*
EVANS, DAME E., 1–2, 5: B. Forbes, *Ned's Girl;* 3: N. Rees, *Quote . . . Unquote*
EVARTS 1: R. Marquard, *Jokes and Anecdotes;* 2: E. Fuller, *2500 Anecdotes*
EVERETT 1: D. Wallechinsky and I. Wallace, *The People's Almanac*

FAGIUOLI 1: J. Papesch, *Europa Lächelt Noch Immer*
FAIRBANKS 1: B. Morton, *Americans In Paris;* 2: V. Castlerosse, *Valentine's Days*
FALLA 1: N. Slonimsky, *A Thing or Two about Music*
FALLIÈRES 1: M. and A. Guillois, *Liberté, Egalité, Hilarité*
FARADAY 1: S. Bolton, *Famous Men of Science*
FAROUK I 1: R. Byrne, *The 637 Best Things Anybody Ever Said*
FARQUHAR 1: W. Adams, *Treasury of Modern Anecdote*
FARRAGUT 1: D. Wallechinsky and I. Wallace, *The People's Almanac*
FAULKNER 1: C. Fadiman and C. Van Doren, *The American Treasury;* 2: G. Herman, *The Book of Hollywood Quotes;* 3: S. Mayfield, *The Constant Circle;* 4: G. Davenport, *The Geography of the Imagination;* 5: S. Graham, *The Garden of Allah*
FAURÉ 1: N. Rorem, *Later Diaries*
FAVRAS 1: M. Pedrazzini and J. Gris, *Autant en apportent les mots*
FAWKES 1: J. Kenyon, *Dictionary of British History*
FERDINAND I (AUSTRIA) 1: E. Crankshaw, *The Fall of the House of Hapsburg*
FERDINAND I (BULGARIA) 1: C. Skinner, *Elegant Wits and Grand Horizontals*
FERDINAND IV 1: E. Brewer, *Dictionary of Phrase and Fable*
FERGUSSON 1: *DNB*
FERMAT 1: I. Asimov, *Biographical Encyclopedia*
FERMI 1: C. Fadiman, *Enter, Conversing;* 2: P. Dunaway and G. De Kay, eds., *Turning Point*
FERNANDEL 1: P. Bussard, *The New Catholic Treasury of Wit and Humor*
FEYDEAU 1–4: C. Skinner, *Elegant Wits and Grand Horizontals*

FIELD, E., 1: G. Brandreth, *Great Theatrical Disasters;* 2: E. Fuller, *2500 Anecdotes*
FIELD, J., 1: E. Van de Velde, *Anecdotes Musicales*
FIELD, M., 1: J. Braude, *Speaker's and Toastmaster's Handbook*
FIELDING 1: J. Timbs, *Century of Anecdote;* 2: John Nichols, *Literary Anecdotes of the Eighteenth Century*, in J. Sutherland, ed., *OBLA*
FIELDS 1: G. Fowler, *Minutes of the Last Meeting;* 2: R. Lewis, *W. C. Fields;* 3: C. Fadiman and C. Van Doren, *The American Treasury;* 4: E. Fuller, *2500 Anecdotes;* 5: H. Dietz, *Dancing in the Dark;* 6: *"Daily Mirror" Old Codger's Little Black Book 1*
FILLMORE 1: James Morgan, *Our Presidents,* in P. Boller, ed., *Presidential Anecdotes*
FIRBANK 2: P. Quennell, *The Sign of the Fish*
FISKE 1: H. Prochnow, *Public Speaker's Treasure Chest*
FITZGERALD, E., 1: *Los Angeles Times,* Jan. 30, 1983
FITZGERALD, F. S., 1: A. Latham, *Crazy Sundays*
FITZGERALD, Z., 1: C. Tomkins, *Living Well Is the Best Revenge*
FITZSIMMONS 1: C. Fadiman and C. Van Doren, *The American Treasury*
FLAHERTY 1: *The New Yorker,* June 11, 1949
FLANNER 1: J. Krementz, *The Writer's Image*
FLAUBERT 1: *Book-of-the-Month Club News,* 1955
FLEETWOOD 1: J. Aubrey, *Brief Lives*
FLEMING, I., 1: Anatole Broyard's book column, *New York Times,* Apr. 9, 1983
FLETCHER 1: C. Fadiman and C. Van Doren, *The American Treasury*
FOCH 1–2, 4–5: E. Fuller, *2500 Anecdotes;* 3: J. Braude, *Speaker's and Toastmaster's Handbook*
FONDA 1: B. Adler, *My Favorite Funny Story;* 2: *Los Angeles Times,* Aug. 13, 1982
FONTANNE 1: S. Marx, *Mayer and Thalberg*
FONTENELLE 1: H. Hoffmeister, *Anekdotenschatz;* 2: W. Merwin, *Products of the Perfected Civilization;* 3, 5: M. Pedrazzini and J. Gris, *Autant en apportent les mots;* 4: E. Fuller, *2500 Anecdotes;* 6: B. Conrad, *Famous Last Words*
FONTEYN 2: M. Fonteyn, *Autobiography*
FOOTE 1: R. Hendrickson, *The Literary Life;* 2–3: E. Fuller, *2500 Anecdotes;* 4: Katherine C. Balderston, ed., *Thraliana* 1: 151, in J. Sutherland, ed., *OBLA;* 5, 8: W. Adams, *Treasury of Modern Anecdote;* 7: G. Lieberman, *The Greatest Laughs of All Time*
FORD, H., 1: C. Bowen, *Yankee from Olympus;* 2: J. Braude, *Speaker's and Toastmaster's Handbook;* 4: E. Fuller, *2500 Anecdotes*
FORD, J., 1: John Ford's son, on *The Johnny Carson Show,* July 28, 1981

FORDYCE 1: S. Rogers, *Table Talk*

FORGY 1: *Los Angeles Times,* June 3, 1982

FORREST 1: Basil W. Duke, *Reminiscences of Gen. Basil W. Duke, C.S.,* in B. Botkin, *A Civil War Treasury*

FORSTER 1: D. Knox, *Quotable Anecdotes*

FOSDICK 1: S. Harris, *Pieces of Eight*

FOSTER 1: L. Humphrey, *The Humor of Music*

FOUCHÉ 1: W. and A. Durant, *The Story of Civilization,* XI; 2: A. Duff Cooper, *Talleyrand*

FOWLER 1–3: H. Smith, *The Life and Legend of Gene Fowler*

FOX, C., 1, 5: E. Fuller, *2500 Anecdotes;* 2–3: J. Timbs, *Century of Anecdote;* 4: Lord Broughton, *Recollections of a Long Life,* in Kenin and Wintle, *DBQ;* 6: *The Gentleman's Magazine,* March 1849, in C. Shriner, *Wit, Wisdom, and Foibles of the Great*

FOX, G. 1: H. and D.L. Thomas, *Living Biographies of Religious Leaders*

FRAGUIER 1: J. Papesch, *Europa Lächelt Noch Immer*

FRANCE 1: M. Pedrazzini and J. Gris, *Autant en apportent les mots;* 2: C. Skinner, *Elegant Wits and Grand Horizontals;* 3: J. Braude, *Speaker's and Toastmaster's Handbook*

FRANCIS I 1: W. Walsh, *Handy Book of Curious Information*

FRANCIS II 1: A. Bryant, *The Age of Elegance;* 2: E. Crankshaw, *The Fall of the House of Hapsburg*

FRANCIS FERDINAND 1: E. Crankshaw, *The Fall of the House of Hapsburg*

FRANCIS JOSEPH 1: S. Radecki, *Das ABC des Lachens;* 2: P. Méras, *The Mermaids of Chenonceaux*

FRANCIS OF ASSISI 1: H. Morton, *A Traveller in Italy*

FRANCO 1: S. Bellow, *Him with His Foot in His Mouth*

FRANKLIN 1: C. Fadiman and C. Van Doren, *The American Treasury;* 2: Henry S. Randall, *The Life of Thomas Jefferson,* in P. Boller, ed., *Presidential Anecdotes;* 3: D. George, *A Book of Anecdotes;* 4–5, 13–14: P. Zall, *Ben Franklin Laughing;* 6: Arthur D. Graeff, "Anecdotes Related in Pennsylvania-German Almanacs," *The American-German Review,* VI (June 1940), in Boller, ed., *Presidential Anecdotes;* 7: C. Shriner, *Wit, Wisdom, and Foibles of the Great;* 8: Carl Van Doren, *Benjamin Franklin,* in D. Hall, ed., *OBALA;* 9: Sarah Randolph, *The Domestic Life of Thomas Jefferson,* in Hall, *OBALA;* 10: P. Smith, *A New Age Now Begins;* 11: *Harper's Magazine,* December 1873; 12: *American Jest Book,* 1789; 15: M. Strauss, *Familiar Medical Quotations*

FRANKS 1: G. Moorhouse, *The Diplomats*

FREDERICK II 1: Sholto and Reuben Percy, *The Percy Anecdotes,* in D. George, *A Book of Anecdotes;* 2: I. Asimov, *Treasury of Humor;* 3–4: W. and A. Durant, *The Story of Civilization,* X; 5–7, 11: H. Hoffmeister, *Anekdotenschatz;* 8: G. Colman, *Circle of Anecdote;* 9: H. Prochnow, *The Public Speaker's Treasure Chest;* 10: V. Nikolaev and A. Parry, *The Loves of Catherine the Great*

FREDERICK AUGUSTUS 1: W. Scholtz, *Das Buch des Lachens*

FREDERICK WILLIAM I 1: *EB;* 2: Sylvester Douglas, *Lord Glenbervie, Journals,* in D. George, *A Book of Anecdotes;* 3: B. Conrad, *Famous Last Words*

FREDERICK WILLIAM IV 1: G. Craig, *The Germans;* 2: H. Hoffmeister, *Anekdotenschatz*

FREUD 1: D. Wallechinsky and I. Wallace, *The People's Almanac;* 2: *Los Angeles Times,* July 4, 1982; 3: P. Méras, *The Mermaids of Chenonceaux*

FRICK 1: P. Smith, *The Rise of Industrial America*

FRISCO 1–2: R. Sylvester, *Notes of A Guilty Bystander*

FRITH 1: W. Walsh, *Handy Book of Curious Information*

FROHMAN 1: B. Conrad, *Famous Last Words*

FRY 1: E. Marsh, *A Number of People*

FUGGER 1: T. Robards, *The New York Times Book of Wine*

FULLER, MARGARET, 1: F. Muir, *Irreverent Social History;* 2: E. Fuller, *2500 Anecdotes*

FULLER, MELVILLE, 1: E. Fuller, *2500 Anecdotes*

FULLER, R. B., 1: B. Taper, *The Arts in Boston*

FULTON 1: M. Bishop, *The Exotics*

FURTWÄNGLER 1: H. Schonberg, *The Great Conductors*

FUSELI 1–2: P. Wescher, *Schweitzer Künstler-Anekdoten*

GABIN 1: E. Fuller, *2500 Anecdotes*

GABOR 2: K. Edwards, *I Wish I'd Said That*

GAINSBOROUGH 1: W. and A. Durant, *The Story of Civilization,* X; 2: Allan Cunningham, *Lives of the Most Eminent British Painters,* in D. George, *A Book of Anecdotes*

GAISFORD 1: J. Morris, *The Oxford Book of Oxford*

GALBRAITH 1: *Book-of-the-Month Club News,* July 1, 1981; 2–3: J. Galbraith, *A Life in Our Times*

GALEN 1: R. Calder, *Medicine and Man*

GALIANI 1: H. Sievers, *Musica Curiosa*

GALILEO 1: J. Bartlett, *Familiar Quotations*

GALOIS 1: E. Bell, *Men of Mathematics*

GALVANI 1: Wilder Penfield, *The Second Career,* in M. Strauss, *Familiar Medical Quotations*

GANDHI, I., 1: P. Frederick, *Ten First Ladies of*

the World; 2: G. Young, *Halfway Around the World*

GANDHI, M., 2: H. and D. L. Thomas, *Living Biographies of Religious Leaders;* 3: M. Ringo, *Nobody Said It Better;* 4: Jo Davidson, *Between Sittings,* in Kenin and Wintle, *DBQ;* 6: G. Brandreth, *Joy of Lex*

GARBO 1: N. Zierold, *The Moguls;* 2: D. Niven, *Bring on the Empty Horses*

GARDNER, I., 1: J. McAleer, "Globe Man's Daily Story," *Boston Globe,* Jan. 8, 1960; 2: L. Tharp, *Mrs. Jack;* 4: A. Saarinen, *The Proud Possessors*

GARLAND 1: J. Paar, *P.S. Jack Paar;* 2: A. King and M. Sheraton, *Is Salami and Eggs Better Than Sex?*

GARNER 1: J. Gunther, *Procession*

GARRICK 1: J. Boswell, *Life of Johnson;* 2: E. Fuller, *2500 Anecdotes*

GARRISON 1: E. Fuller, *2500 Anecdotes*

GARROD 1: D. Balsdon, *Oxford Now and Then*

GARTH 1: Forbes Winslow, *Physic and Physicians,* in D. George, *A Book of Anecdotes*

GATES 1: C. Sifakis, *Dictionary of Historic Nicknames*

GAUSS 1: E. Bell, *Men of Mathematics;* 2: I. Asimov, *Biographical Encyclopedia*

GEHRIG 1: E. Fuller, *2500 Anecdotes*

GELON 1: W. Durant, *The Story of Civilization,* II

GEOFFRIN 1: Dugas de Bois St. Just, *Paris, Versailles et les provinces*

GEORGE I 1: J. Spence, *Anecdotes*

GEORGE II 1: A. Isaacs and E. Martin, *Dictionary of Music;* 2: E. Guérard, *Dictionnaire Encyclopédique*

GEORGE III 2: Beckles Wilson, *George III,* in Kenin and Wintle, *DBQ;* 3: J. Timbs, *Century of Anecdote;* 4: W. Gates, *Anecdotes of Great Musicians;* 5: R. Hendrickson, *The Literary Life*

GEORGE IV 1: Benjamin Disraeli, *Lothair,* in Kenin and Wintle, *DBQ;* 2: Henry Lytton Bulwer, *Historical Characters,* in D. George, *A Book of Anecdotes*

GEORGE V 1: M. Pedrazzini and J. Gris, *Autant en apportent les mots;* 2: B. Cerf, *The Life of the Party;* 4: K. Rose, *King George V;* 5: R. Collier, *The Rainbow People;* 6, 10: N. Rees, *Quote . . . Unquote;* 7: M. Pye, *The King over the Water;* 8: W. Manchester, *The Last Lion*

GEORGE VI 1: A. Herbert, *A.P.H.;* 2: P. Berton, *The Royal Family;* 3: P. Vandyke Price, *The Penguin Book of Spirits and Liqueurs*

GERARD 1: P. Smith, *America Enters the World*

GERSHWIN 1: E. Fuller, *2500 Anecdotes;* 2–3: O. Levant, *Memoirs of an Amnesiac,* in Kenin and Wintle, *DBQ;* 4: M. Ringo, *Nobody Said*

It Better; 5: A. Rubinstein, *My Many Years;* 7: E. Fuller, *2500 Anecdotes*

GESVRES 1: L. Norton, *Saint-Simon at Versailles*

GHIBERTI 1: T. Craven, *Men of Art*

GIAMPETRO 1: H. Hoffmeister, *Anekdotenschatz*

GIBBON 1: D. George, *A Book of Anecdotes;* 2: Thomas Moore's Journal, Dec. 12, 1844, in D. George, *A Book of Anecdotes;* 3: H. Beste, *Personal and Literary Memorials*

GIBBS 1: C. Fadiman and C. Van Doren, *The American Treasury*

GIDE 1: N. Jones, *A Book of Days for the Literary Year*

GIELGUD 1: B. Forbes, *Ned's Girl;* 2: K. Edwards, *More Things I Wish I'd Said;* 3, 6: R. Morley, *Book of Bricks;* 5: *Time,* Aug. 15, 1983

GILBERT, SIR H., 1: Thomas Fuller, *The Worthies of England,* in D. George, *A Book of Anecdotes*

GILBERT, J., 1: G. Brandreth, *Great Theatrical Disasters*

GILBERT, SIR W., 1: H. Evans, *Personal Recollections;* 2: E. Fuller, *2500 Anecdotes;* 3: M. Ringo, *Nobody Said It Better;* 4: H. Pearson, *Lives of the Wits;* 5–6: N. McPhee, *Second Book of Insults;* 7–8: J. Aye, *Humour in the Theatre;* 9: G. Brandreth, *Great Theatrical Disasters*

GILES 1: *Los Angeles Times,* Dec. 15, 1981

GILOT 1: F. Gilot and C. Lake, *Life With Picasso*

GIOLITTI 1: P. Hofmann, *Rome — The Sweet, Tempestuous Life*

GIORGIONE 1: G. Vasari, *Lives of the Painters*

GIOTTO 1–2: G. Vasari, *Lives of the Painters;* 3: P. Méras, *The Mermaids of Chenonceaux*

GIPP 1: D. Wallechinsky and I. Wallace, *The People's Almanac*

GIRAUDOUX 1: H. Hoffmeister, *Anekdotenschatz*

GLADSTONE 1: C. Bowra, *Memories 1898–1939;* 2: E. Fuller, *2500 Anecdotes;* 3: J. Papesch, *Europa Lächelt Noch Immer*

GLUCK 1: E. Guérard, *Dictionnaire Encyclopédique*

GLYN 1: P. Mahony, *Barbed Wit and Malicious Humor*

GODARD 1: *Time,* Sept. 14, 1981

GODIVA 1: *EB*

GODOWSKY 1: H. Taubman, *Music on My Beat*

GOERING 1: E. Fuller, *2500 Anecdotes;* 2: I. Wallace et al., *Significa*

GOETHE 1: W. and A. Durant, *The Story of Civilization,* XI; 2: *EB;* 3: D. Enright, *The Oxford Book of Death;* 4: W. and A. Durant, *The Story of Civilization,* X; 5: *Oxford Dictionary of Quotations;* 6: S. Behrman, *Portrait of Max*

GOGARTY 1: P. Bussard, *The New Catholic Treasury of Wit and Humor;* 2: W. Yeats, *The Oxford Book of Modern Verse*

GOLDBERG 2: J. Humes, *Speakers' Treasury*

GOLDSMITH 1: C. Hibbert, *The Personal History of Samuel Johnson*

GOLDWYN 1: M. Ringo, *Nobody Said It Better;* 2: L. Hellman, *Pentimento;* 3–4: D. Niven, *Bring on the Empty Horses;* 5–6: E. Fuller, *2500 Anecdotes;* 7: R. Marquard, *Jokes and Anecdotes;* 8–9: B. Cerf, *Try and Stop Me;* 10: H. Dietz, *Dancing in the Dark;* 11: *The New Yorker,* May 24, 1952; 12–13: J. Nash, *Zanies;* 14: G. Lieberman, *The Greatest Laughs of All Time;* 15: S. Graham, *The Garden of Allah;* 16, 20: S. Birmingham, *"The Rest of Us";* 17–18, 22: N. Zierold, *The Moguls;* 19: *Life,* February 1984; 21: S. Morley, *Tales from the Hollywood Raj*

GOMEZ 1: R. Crouser, *It's Unlucky to be Behind at the End of the Game*

GOODMAN, D., 1: J. Paar, *P.S. Jack Paar*

GORDON, LORD GEORGE, 1: J. Timbs, *Century of Anecdote*

GORDON, JOHN, 1: Gen. John B. Gordon, *Reminiscences of the Civil War,* in B. Botkin, *A Civil War Treasury*

GORDON, R., 1: R. Morley, *Book of Bricks*

GORKI 1: Fuller, *2500 Anecdotes*

GOSSE 1: E. Lucas, *Reading, Writing and Remembering;* 2: C. Hassall, *Biography of Edward Marsh;* 3: A. Noyes, *Two Worlds for Memory;* 4: E. Marsh, *A Number of People*

GOULD 1: D. Wallechinsky and I. Wallace, *The People's Almanac;* 2: John Wheeler, "The Old Second Guesser," *Omaha World-Herald,* Feb. 20, 1955, in B. Botkin, *Treasury of American Anecdotes*

GRABLE 1: B. Cerf, *Laughing Stock*

GRACE 1–3: J. Arlott, *Cricket: The Great Ones*

GRAINGER 1: *The New Yorker,* Feb. 14, 1948

GRANGE 1: M. Ringo, *Nobody Said It Better*

GRANT, U.S. 1: Hamlin Garland, *McClure's Magazine,* February 1897, in C. Shriner, *Wit, Wisdom, and Foibles of the Great;* 2: *The New York Sun,* July 26, 1885, in B. Botkin, *A Civil War Treasury;* 3: E. B. Long, ed., *U.S. Grant: Personal Memoirs,* in P. Boller, ed., *Presidential Anecdotes;* 4: "Anecdotes of General Grant," *New York Daily Tribune,* Aug. 5, 1885, in B. Botkin, *A Civil War Treasury;* 5: M. Ringo, *Nobody Said It Better;* 6: Horace Porter, *Harper's Magazine,* September 1885, in Shriner, *Wit;* 7: B. Cerf, *The Life of the Party;* 8: Horace Greene, *General Grant's Last Stand* in Boller, *Presidential Anecdotes;* 9, 14: Dixon Wecter, *The Hero in America,* in Boller, *Presidential Anecdotes;* 10: Charles Tuckerman, "Personal Recollections of Notable People," *Magazine of American History,* in Shriner, *Wit;* 11: Louis Untermeyer, *A Treasury of Laughter,* in Boller, *Presidential Anecdotes;* 12: Sid Frank, *The Presidents,* in R. Shenkman and K. Reiger, *One-Night Stands with American History;* 13: *New York Review of Books,* March 1981

GRASSINI 1: J. Papesch, *Europa Lächelt Noch Immer*

GRAVES 1: M. Seymour-Smith, *Robert Graves: His Life and Work*

GRAY 1: W. Keddie, *Literary and Scientific Anecdote*

GRAZIANO 2: R. Crouser, *It's Unlucky to Be Behind at the End of the Game*

GREELEY 1: G. Fowler, *Timber Line;* 2, 4: R. Marquard, *Jokes and Anecdotes;* 3: E. Fuller, *2500 Anecdotes;* 5: Junius Henri Browne, "Horace Greeley," *Harper's New Monthly Magazine,* April 1873, in B. Botkin, *Treasury of American Anecdotes;* 6: P. Mahony, *Barbed Wit and Malicious Humor;* 7: G. Lieberman, *The Greatest Laughs of All Time*

GREEN, H., 1: I. Ross, *Charmers and Cranks;* 2: *Parade,* Oct. 17, 1982

GREEN, J., 1: B. Conrad, *Famous Last Words*

GREENE 1: *Book-of-the-Month Club News,* October 1949; 2: Clifton Fadiman

GREENWOOD 1: J. W. Robertson Scott, *The Story of the Pall Mall Gazette,* in J. Sutherland, ed., *OBLA*

GREGORY I 1: Bede, *History of the English Church and People;* 2: W. Durant, *The Story of Civilization,* IV

GREVILLE 1: B. Nichols, *The Sweet Twenties*

GREY 1: B. Tuchman, *The Guns of August;* 2: W. Churchill, *Great Contemporaries*

GRIMM 1: J. Braude, *Braude's Second Encyclopedia*

GROTE 1: J. Gere and J. Sparrow, *Geoffrey Madan's Notebooks*

GUGGENHEIM 1: P. Méras, *The Mermaids of Chenonceaux*

GUIMOND 1: F. Loliée, *Gilded Beauties of the Second Empire*

GUINES 1: S. Alsop, *Yankees at the Court*

GUINNESS 1: J. McAleer, "Globe Man's Daily Story," *Boston Globe,* June 8, 1969

GUITRY, L., 1–3: C. Skinner, *Elegant Wits and Grand Horizontals*

GUITRY, S., 1: J. Braude, *Speaker's and Toastmaster's Handbook*

GULBENKIAN 3: C. Daniel, *Lords, Ladies and Gentlemen*

GUNTHER 1: C. Fadiman, *Any Number Can Play;* 2: J. McAleer, "Globe Man's Daily Story," *Boston Globe,* Feb. 13, 1968; 3: *Book-of-the-Month Club News,* August 1947

GWYN 1: *DNB;* L. and M. Cowan, *The Wit of Women*

HADRIAN 1: W. Durant, *The Story of Civilization,* III

HAESELER 1: H. Hoffmeister, *Anekdotenschatz*

HALBE 1: H. Hoffmeister, *Anekdotenschatz*

HALDANE, R., 1: V. Castlerosse, *Valentine's Days*

HALE 1: I. Wallace and D. Wallechinsky, *The Book of Lists 2*

HALEY 1: H. Rosenberg, *Calendar, Los Angeles Times,* July 7, 1984

HALIFAX, C., 1: W. and A. Durant, *The Story of Civilization,* VIII

HALIFAX, E., 1: *Book-of-the-Month Club News,* January 1954

HALL 1: W. Walsh, *Handy Book of Curious Information*

HALSEY 1: C. Fadiman and C. Van Doren, *The American Treasury*

HAMILTON 1: C. Fadiman and C. Van Doren, *The American Treasury*

HAMMERSTEIN, II, 1: H. Fordin, *Getting to Know Him*

HAMMETT 1–3: D. Johnson, *Dashiell Hammett;* 4: L. Hellman, *An Unfinished Woman*

HAMSUN 1: H. Hoffmeister, *Anekdotenschatz*

HANDEL 1: E. Jones, *A Food Lover's Companion;* 2–4: H. C. Robbins Landon: *Handel and His World*

HANNIBAL 1: Livy, *Annals,* 39.51

HARDY 1: *New York Review of Books,* Oct. 7, 1982

HARRIMAN 1: *The New Yorker,* May 10, 1952; 2: *The New Yorker,* May 3, 1952

HARRIS, F., 1: E. Fuller, *2500 Anecdotes;* 2: D. Cecil, *Max: A Biography*

HARRIS, G., 1: J. Braude, *Braude's Second Encyclopedia*

HARRIS, J., 1: M. Gottfried, *Jed Harris: The Curse of Genius;* 2: J. Humes, *Speakers' Treasury*

HARRIMAN, BENJAMIN, 1: D. Wallechinsky and I. Wallace, *The People's Almanac*

HARRISON, PRESIDENT BENJAMIN, 1: Henry L. Stoddard, *As I Knew Them: Presidents and Politics from Grant to Coolidge,* in P. Boller, ed., *Presidential Anecdotes*

HARRISON, G., 1: D. Wallechinsky and I. Wallace, *The People's Almanac*

HART 1: O. Levant, *The Unimportance of Being Oscar*

HARTE 1: W. Scholz, *Das Buch des Lachens;* 2: H. Prochnow, *The Public Speaker's Treasure Chest*

HARTLEBEN 1: H. Hoffmeister, *Anekdotenschatz*

HARTNELL 1: R. Morley, *Book of Bricks*

HATTO 1: W. Walsh, *Handy Book of Curious Information*

HAVEMEYER 1: J. Braude, *Speaker's and Toastmaster's Handbook*

HAWTREY 1: G. Brandreth, *Great Theatrical Disasters*

HAY 1: *Quarterly Review,* no. 218, 1861, in D. George, *A Book of Anecdotes*

HAYAKAWA 1: *Los Angeles Times,* Oct. 23, 1981; 2: Clifton Fadiman

HAYDN 1: *Quarterly Review,* no. 218, 1861, in D. George, *A Book of Anecdotes;* 2: W. and A. Durant, *The Story of Civilization,* X; 3: N. Slonimsky, *A Thing or Two about Music*

HAYES, H., 1: B. Cerf, *Try and Stop Me;* 2: B. Thomas, *Thalberg: Life and Legend*

HAYES, R., 1: George F. Hoar, *Autobiography of Seventy Years,* in P. Boller, ed., *Presidential Anecdotes*

HAYWORTH 1: C. Fadiman and C. Van Doren, *The American Treasury*

HAZLITT 1: E. Fuller, *2500 Anecdotes;* 2: W. Keddie, *Literary and Scientific Anecdote*

HEARST 1: Kenin and Wintle, *DBQ;* 2: P. Kael, *The Citizen Kane Book;* 3: R. Marquard, *Jokes and Anecdotes;* 4: J. Tebbel, *The Inheritors;* 5: C. Aslet, *The Last Country Houses*

HECHT 1: *The New Yorker,* Dec. 13, 1952

HEGEL 1: B. Conrad, *Famous Last Words*

HEGGEN 1: R. Nelson, *The Almanac of American Letters*

HEIDEGGER 1: F. Muir, *Irreverent Social History*

HEIFETZ 1: O. Levant, *The Unimportance of Being Oscar;* 2, 4: H. Temianka, *Facing the Music;* 3: *Los Angeles Times,* Aug. 29, 1982

HEINE 1: M. Pedrazzini and J. Gris, *Autant en apportent les mots;* 2: D. Wallechinsky and I. Wallace, *The People's Almanac;* 3: B. Conrad, *Famous Last Words;* 4: E. Fuller, *2500 Anecdotes*

HELLMESBERGER 1: M. Jelusisch, *Geschichten aus dem Wienerwald*

HELPRIN 1: Clifton Fadiman

HEMINGWAY 1: P. Méras, *The Mermaids of Chenonceaux;* 2: B. Morton, *Americans in Paris;* 3: B. Cerf, *Try and Stop Me;* 4, 9: C. Fadiman and C. Van Doren, *The American Treasury;* 5: *Signature,* September 1983; 7: A. Hotchner, *Choice People;* 8: Y. Karsh, *Karsh*

HENRI IV 1, 5: W. and A. Durant, *The Story of Civilization,* VII; 2: *EB;* 3: E. Guérard, *Dictionnaire Encyclopédique;* 4: K. Arvine, *Cyclopaedia of Anecdotes;* 6: W. Keddie, *Literary and Scientific Anecdote*

HENRY II 1: *DNB*

HENRY IV 1: *DNB*

HENRY VIII 1: L. Copeland, *10,000 Jokes, Toasts, and Stories;* 2: *"Daily Mirror" Old Codger's Little Black Book 1*

HENRY, C., 1: J. Humes, *Speakers' Treasury*

HENRY, O., 1: O. Henry, *The Voice of the City*

HENSON 1: R. Hendrickson, *The Literary Life*

HEPBURN 1: *Parade,* Nov. 27, 1983

HERBERT 1: A. Herbert, *A.P.H.*

HERFORD 2: B. Cerf, *Try and Stop Me;* 3: J. Braude, *Speaker's and Toastmaster's Handbook;* 4–5: E. Fuller, *2500 Anecdotes;* 6: *Book-of-the-Month Club News,* February 1946

HERSCHEL 1: *DNB*

HESS 1: H. Temianka, *Facing the Music*

HIDEYOSHI 1: W. Durant, *The Story of Civilization*, I

HILBERT 1–2: George Pólya, "Some Mathematicians I Have Known," in D. Campbell and J. Higgins, eds., *Mathematics: People, Problems, Results*

HILL, J., 1: A. de Morgan, *Encyclopedia of Eccentrics*

HILL, R., 1–2: W. Adams, *Treasury of Modern Anecdote*

HILLARY 1: E. Hillary, *High Adventure*

HINDEMITH 1: R. Smullyan, *5000 B.C. and Other Philosophical Fantasies*

HITCHCOCK 1: E. Fuller, *2500 Anecdotes*; 6–7: C. Madigan and A. Elwood, *Brainstorms and Thunderbolts*; 8: D. Spoto, *The Dark Side of Genius*

HOAR 1: Clifton Fadiman

HOBBS 1: J. Arlott, *Cricket: The Great Ones*

HOBSON, L., 1: L. Hobson, *Laura Z.*

HOBSON, T., 1: *DNB*

HOCKING 1: M. Schlesinger, *Snatched from Oblivion*

HOFFMANN 1: H. Hoffmeister, *Anekdotenschatz*

HOFMANN 1: O. Levant, *The Unimportance of Being Oscar*; 2: H. Taubman, *Music on my Beat*; 3: H. Temianka, *Facing the Music*

HOGARTH 1: G. Colman, *Circle of Anecdote*

HOKUSAI 1: B. Conrad, *Famous Last Words*

HOLLAND 1: W. Walsh, *Handy Book of Curious Information*

HOLLES 1: A. Fraser, *Cromwell*

HOLLIDAY 1: G. Steinem, *Outrageous Acts and Everyday Rebellions*

HOLMES, F., 1–3: C. Bowen, *Yankee from Olympus*

HOLMES, J., 1–4: C. Bowen, *Yankee from Olympus*

HOLMES, O., SR., 1–2, 8: M. Howe, *Holmes of the Breakfast Table*; 3: L. and F. Copeland, *10,000 Jokes, Toasts, and Stories*; 5: R. Shenkman, *One-Night Stands with American History*; 6: C. Bowen, *Yankee from Olympus*; 7: C. Ticknor, *Dr. Holmes's Boston*

HOLMES, O., JR., 1–5, 7–8: C. Bowen, *Yankee from Olympus*; 6: C. Fadiman and C. Van Doren, *The American Treasury*; 9: *Chicago Sun-Times*, Aug. 8, 1982

HOME, W., 1: R. Morley, *Book of Bricks*

HOMER 1: '47, *The Magazine of the Year*, August

HOOK 1: *DNB*; 2: L. Russell, *English Wits*; 3: K. Arvine, *Cyclopaedia of Anecdotes*; 4: W. Adams, *Treasury of Modern Anecdote*; 5: D. Knox, *More Quotable Anecdotes*

HOOKER 1: John Bigelow, Jr., *Sidney V. Lovell in the Campaign at Chancellorsville*, in B. Botkin, *A Civil War Treasury*

HOOVER 1: Arthur Krock, *Memoirs*, in P. Boller, ed., *Presidential Anecdotes*; 2: Eugene Lyons, *Herbert Hoover: A Biography*, in Boller, *Presidential Anecdotes*; 3: I. and R. Poley, *Friendly Anecdotes*; 4: I. Wallace et al., *Book of Lists 2*; 5: C. Fadiman and C. Van Doren, *The American Treasury*

HORNE 1: S. Terkel, *"The Good War"*

HOROWITZ 1, 3: O. Levant, *The Unimportance of Being Oscar*; 2: J. Gaines, *Lives of the Piano*

HORTHY DE NAGYBÁNYA 1: E. Kelen, *Peace in Their Time*

HOUDINI 1: F. Oursler, *Behold This Dreamer*; 2: H. Prochnow, *The Public Speaker's Treasure Chest*

HOUSMAN 1: G. K. Chesterton, *Autobiography*, in J. Sutherland, ed., *OBLA*; 2: H. Maas, ed., *The Letters of A. E. Housman*; 3: R. Graves, *A. E. Housman*

HOWARD, C., 1: I. Wallace et al., *Intimate Sex Lives of Famous People*

HOWARD, L., 1: L. and F. Copeland, *10,000 Jokes, Toasts, and Stories*

HOWARTH 1: S. Rogers, *Table Talk*

HOWE, E., 1: J. Braude, *Speaker's and Toastmaster's Handbook*

HOWE, J., 1–2: W. Abbot, *Notable Women in History*

HOWELLS 1: M. Howe, *John Jay Chapman*; 2–3: E. Fuller, *2500 Anecdotes*

HRUSKA 1: *Congressional Quarterly*, vol. 3

HUGHES 1: L. Harris, *The Fine Art of Political Wit*

HUGO 1: R. Hendrickson, *The Literary Life*; 2: I. Wallace, *Intimate Sex Lives of Famous People*; 3: E. Samuels, *The Education of Henry Adams*; 4: R. Godden, *Hans Christian Andersen*; 5: G. Lieberman, *The Greatest Laughs of All Time*

HULL 1: J. Braude, *Braude's Second Encyclopedia*

HUMBOLDT 1: J. Train, *True Remarkable Occurrences*

HUME 1: E. Guérard, *Dictionnaire Encyclopédique*; 2: E. Fuller, *2500 Anecdotes*; 3: W. Keddie, *Literary and Scientific Anecdote*; 4: W. and A. Durant, *The Story of Civilization*, IX; 5: H. Brougham, *Men of Letters*

HUMES 1: J. Humes, *Speakers' Treasury*

HUMPHREY 1: C. Solberg, *Hubert Humphrey*

HUNTER 1: *New Scientist*, Nov. 9, 1981

HUSTON 1: D. Niven, *Bring on the Empty Horses*

HUTCHINS 1, 3: M. Adler, *Philosopher at Large*; 4: J. Braude, *Speaker's and Toastmaster's Handbook*

HUXLEY, A., 1–2, 5: D. Wallechinsky and I. Wallace, *The People's Almanac 2*; 3–4: R. Clark, *The Huxleys*

HUXLEY, SIR J., 1–2: R. Clark, *The Huxleys*

HUXLEY, T., 1: R. Moore, *Charles Darwin*; 2: E. Fuller, *2500 Anecdotes*

HUYSMANS 1: S. Radecki, *Das ABC des Lachens*

HYDE, LADY C., 1: L. and M. Cowan, *The Wit of Women*

HYDE, W., 1: E. Lucas, *A Fronded Isle*

HYDE-WHITE 1: *The Times* (London), May 12, 1983

HYLAN 1: C. Sifakis, *Dictionary of Historic Nicknames*

HYRTL 1: M. Jelusisch, *Geschichten aus dem Wienerwald*

IBN SAUD 1–2: R. Lacey, *The Kingdom*

IBRAHIM PASHA 1: R. Lacey, *The Kingdom*

IBSEN 1: Clifton Fadiman, Introduction to E. Wharton, *Ethan Frome*; 3: J. Train, *True Remarkable Occurrences*

IKKU 1: R. Hendrickson, *The Literary Life*

INCHBALD 1: Frederick Reynolds, *Life and Times of Frederick Reynolds*, in Kenin and Wintle, *DBQ*

INGE 1: Alfred Noyes, *Two Worlds for Memory*

INGERSOLL 1: L. Copeland, *10,000 Jokes, Toasts, and Stories*

INGYO 1: J. Kidder, *Ancient Japan*

IPHICRATES 1: L. Missen, *Quotable Anecdotes*

IRVING 1: Edward Heron-Allen, *We Saw Him Act*, in Kenin and Wintle, *DBQ*

ISABEY 1: J. Timbs, *Century of Anecdote*

JACKSON, A., 1–2, 6: James Parton, *Life of Andrew Jackson*, in P. Boller, ed., *Presidential Anecdotes*; 4: Leland Baldwin, *The Stream of American History*, in Boller, *Presidential Anecdotes*; 5: Benjamin Poore, *Perley's Reminiscences of Sixty Years*, in Boller, *Presidential Anecdotes*; 7: A. C. Buell, *History of Andrew Jackson*, in C. Shriner, *Wit, Wisdom, and Foibles of the Great*

JACKSON, J., 1: D. Wallechinsky and I. Wallace, *The People's Almanac 2*

JACKSON, T., 1: M. Ringo, *Nobody Said It Better*; 2: Margaret J. Preston, "Personal Reminiscences of Stonewall Jackson," *Century Magazine*, XXXII (October 1886), in B. Botkin, *A Civil War Treasury*; 3: Robert Stiles, *Four Years Under Marse Robert*, in B. Botkin, *A Civil War Treasury*; 4–5: Charles Minor Blackford, ed., *Letters from Lee's Army*, in B. Botkin, *A Civil War Treasury*; 6: Maj. Henry Kyd Douglas, *I Rode With Stonewall*, in B. Botkin, *A Civil War Treasury*; 7: B. Conrad, *Famous Last Words*

JACOBI 1: E. Bell, *Men of Mathematics*

JAMES I 1: G. Colman, *Circle of Anecdote*; 2: *"Daily Mirror" Old Codger's Little Black Book 1*; 3: W. Keddie, *Literary and Scientific Anecdote*

JAMES, H., 1–2: D. Cecil, *Max: A Biography*; 3:

D. Hall, ed., *OBALA*; 4: C. Fadiman and C. Van Doren, *The American Treasury*

JAMES, J., 1: R. Love, *The Rise and Fall of Jesse James*; 2: I. Wallace, "Significa," June 20, 1982

JAMES, W., 1: *American Scholar* I: 4 (1931); 2: L. Lucaire, *Celebrity Trivia*; 3: J. Barzun, *A Stroll with William James*; 4: *Book-of-the-Month Club News*, April 1948

JARRY 1: P. Méras, *The Mermaids of Chenonceaux*; 2: A. Vollard, *Recollections of a Picture Dealer*; 3: N. Lennon, *Alfred Jarry: The Man with the Axe*

JEFFERSON, J., 1: T. Masson, *The Best Stories in the World*

JEFFERSON, T., 1, 3, 8: Henry S. Randall, *The Life of Thomas Jefferson*, in P. Boller, ed., *Presidential Anecdotes*; 2: Edward Ellis, *Thomas Jefferson, A Character Sketch*, in Boller, *Presidential Anecdotes*; 4: Arthur D. Graeff, "Anecdotes Related in Pennsylvania-German Almanacs," *The American-German Review* VI (April 1940), in B. Botkin, *Treasury of American Anecdotes*; 6: J. Train, *True Remarkable Occurrences*; 7, 9: Margaret B. Smith, *The First Forty Years in Washington Society*, in Boller, *Presidential Anecdotes*; 10: Boller, *Presidential Anecdotes*, and C. Wiltse and H. Moser, eds., *The Papers of Daniel Webster — Correspondence*, vol. II

JEFFREYS 1: J. Braude, *Speaker's and Toastmaster's Handbook*

JÉRÔME 1: F. Loliée, *Gilded Beauties of the Second Empire*

JERROLD 1: Thomas Powell, *The Living Authors of England*, in J. Sutherland, ed., *OBLA*; 2: L. Copeland, *10,000 Jokes, Toasts, and Stories*; 3: E. Fuller, *2500 Anecdotes*; 4: W. Adams, *Treasury of Modern Anecdote*

JESSEL 2: A. Burrows, *Honest, Abe*

JOHN XXIII 4: P. Bussard, *The New Catholic Treasury of Wit and Humor*; 5: H. Arendt, *Men in Dark Times*

JOHN III SOBIESKI 1: D. George, *A Book of Anecdotes*

JOHN, A., 1: P. Mahony, *Barbed Wit and Malicious Humor*

JOHNSON, A., 1: Moncure D. Conway, "The President's Defense," *Fortnightly Review*, V (1866), in P. Boller, ed., *Presidential Anecdotes*

JOHNSON, L., 1: R. Caro, *The Years of Lyndon Johnson*, I; 2: David Halberstam, *The Best and the Brightest*, in P. Boller, ed., *Presidential Anecdotes*; 3: "Washington Wags," *Reader's Digest*, LXXV (October 1959), in Boller, *Presidential Anecdotes*; 7: Bill Adler, ed., *The Washington Wits*, in Boller, *Presidential Anecdotes*

JOHNSON, N., 1–2: N. Johnson, *Flashback*

JOHNSON, S., 1, 3, 5, 11–12, 14, 16–20, 22–23:
J. Boswell, *Life of Johnson;* 2, 7, 10, 15, 24:
C. Hibbert, *The Personal History of Samuel
Johnson;* 4: H. Beste, *Personal and Literary
Memorials;* 6: J. Timbs, *Century of Anec-
dote;* 8: W. Seward, *Anecdotes;* 9: J. Braude,
Speaker's and Toastmaster's Handbook; 13:
L. Russell, *English Wits;* 21: W. Keddie, *Lit-
erary and Scientific Anecdote*

JOHNSON, W., 1: E. Fuller, *2500 Anecdotes*

JOHNSTON 1–2: B. Johnston, *Rain Stops Play*

JOLSON 1: C. Fadiman and C. Van Doren, *The
American Treasury*

JONES, H., 1: G. Gipe, *The Last Time When*

JONES, JAMES, 1: *Book-of-the-Month Club News,*
September 1951

JONES, JOHN PAUL, 1: M. Ringo, *Nobody Said It
Better;* 2: *DNB*

JONSON 1: E. Lucaire, *Celebrity Trivia;* 2: J. Aubrey, *Brief Lives*

JOSEPH II 1: E. Guérard, *Dictionnaire Encyclopédique;* 2: C. Shriner, *Wit, Wisdom, and Foibles of the Great*

JOWETT 1: Sir Mountstuart Elphinstone Grant
Duff, *Notes from a Diary,* in J. Sutherland,
ed., *OBLA;* 2: T. Masson, *The Best Stories
in the World*

JOYCE, JAMES, 1: P. Mahony, *Barbed Wit and
Malicious Humor;* 2: unpublished ms. by
George Russell, in R. Ellmann, *James Joyce;*
3, 9: R. Ellmann, *James Joyce;* 4: S. Hud-
dleston, *Paris Salons, Cafés, Studios;* 5: R.
Ellmann, interview with Frank Budgen, in
Ellman, *James Joyce;* 7: Herbert Gorman Pa-
pers, in Ellmann, *James Joyce;* 8: R. Ellmann,
interview with Carola Giedion-Welcker, in
Ellmann, *James Joyce;* 10: R. Ellmann, in-
terview with S. Beckett, in Ellmann, *James
Joyce*

JOYCE, JOHN, 1: R. Ellmann, interview with Stanislaus Joyce, in Ellmann, *James Joyce;* 2: W.
Wiser, *The Crazy Years;* 3: unpublished notes
of Louis Gillet in Ellmann, *James Joyce*

JOYNSON-HICKS 1: Oxfam, *Pass the Port*

JUANG-ZU 1: B. Conrad, *Famous Last Words*

JULIA 1–4: Macrobius, *Saturnalia*

JULIAN 1: W. Durant, *The Story of Civilization,*
IV

JULIUS II 1: G. Vasari, *Lives of the Painters*

JULIUS III 1: C. Speroni, *Wit and Wisdom of the
Italian Renaissance*

JULLIEN 1: *Oxford Companion to Music;* 2: H.
Schonberg, *The Great Conductors*

JUSSERAND 1: William Roscoe Thayer, *Theodore
Roosevelt: An Intimate Portrait,* in P. Boller,
Presidential Anecdotes; 2: Lewis Henry, *Hu-
morous Anecdotes about Famous People,* in
Boller, *Presidential Anecdotes;* 3: *Los An-
geles Times Book Review,* Sept. 9, 1984

KAC 1: M. Kac, *Enigmas of Chance*

KAHN 1: R. Marquard, *Jokes and Anecdotes*

KALLIO 1: A. Ranjanen, *Of Finnish Ways*

KAMES 1: John Ramsay of Ochtertyre, *Scotland
and Scotsmen in the Eighteenth Century,* in
J. Sutherland, ed., *OBLA*

KANT 1: W. Durant, *The Story of Philosophy;* 2:
H. Margolius, *Der lächelnde Philosoph*

KARL ALEXANDER 1: W. Scholz, *Das Buch des
Lachens*

KARSAVINA 1: R. Buckle, *In the Wake of Diaghilev*

KASNER 1: C. Fadiman, *Any Number Can Play;*
2: C. Fadiman, *The Mathematical Magpie*

KAUFMAN 1–2: O. Levant, *The Unimportance of
Being Oscar;* 3: H. Teichman, *Smart Aleck;*
4: B. Cerf, *Try and Stop Me;* 5–6: B. Cerf,
Shake Well Before Using; 8: M. Connelly,
Voices Offstage; 9–11, 22: D. Herrmann,
With Malice Toward All; 12: J. Nash, *Zanies;*
13: J. Adamson, *Groucho, Harpo, Chico;* 14:
D. Hall, ed., *OBALA;* 15, 23: R. Drennan,
The Algonquin Wits; 16–17: R. Drennan,
Wit's End; 19: C. Fadiman and C. Van Do-
ren, *The American Treasury;* 20: C. Sifakis,
Dictionary of Historic Nicknames; 21: *Los
Angeles Times Book Review,* Aug. 7, 1983

KAUNITZ-RIETBURG 1: W. and A. Durant, *The
Story of Civilization,* X

KEATS 1–3: Charles Armitage Brown, "Life of
John Keats," in H. E. Rollins, ed., *The Keats
Circle: Letters and Papers 1816–78*

KEKULÉ VON STRADONITZ 1: J. Daintith, et al.,
Biographical Encyclopedia of Scientists

KELLAND 1: J. Braude, *Speaker's and Toastmaster's Handbook;* 2: B. Cerf: *Try and Stop Me*

KELLER 1: A. Whitman, *Come to Judgment*

KELLY, G., 1: A. Lewis, *Those Philadelphia Kellys*

KELLY, M., 1: A. Bespaloff, *The Fireside Book of
Wine*

KELVIN 1: Oxfam, *Pass the Port;* 2: S. Bolton,
Famous Men of Science; 3: A. Fleming, *Mem-
ories of a Scientific Life;* 4: E. Bell, *Men of
Mathematics*

KEMBLE, C., 1: J. Aye, *Humour in the Theatre*

KEMBLE, F., 1: Thomas B. Reed, ed., *Modern Eloquence,* X, in B. Botkin, *Treasury of American Anecdotes;* 2: J. Furnas, *Fanny Kemble*

KEMBLE, J., 1: Thomas Moore's Diary, in D.
George, *A Book of Anecdotes;* 2: J. Aye, *Humour in the Theatre*

KEMBLE, S., 1: W. Keddie, *Literary and Scientific
Anecdote*

KENNEDY, J. F., 1, 8, 14: M. Ringo, *Nobody Said
It Better;* 2: A. Whitman, *Come to Judgment;*
3–4: P. Collier and D. Horowitz, *The Ken-
nedys;* 5: R. Shenkman and K. Reiger, *One-
Night Stands With American History;* 6: I.
Wallace et al., *Intimate Sex Lives of Famous
People;* 7: R. Bing, *A Knight at the Opera;*

9: J. McAleer, "Globe Man's Daily Story," *Boston Globe,* Jan. 22, 1965; 10, 12: D. Wallechinsky and I. Wallace, *The People's Almanac;* 11: W. Manchester, *One Brief Shining Moment;* 13: H. Sidey, *John F. Kennedy, President;* 15: E. Jones, *A Food Lover's Companion;* 16: R. Martin, *A Hero for Our Times;* 17: H. Rainie and J. Quinn, *Growing Up a Kennedy*

KENNEDY, JOSEPH, 1: Cleveland Amory: *The Proper Bostonians,* in B. Botkin, *Treasury of American Anecdotes;* 2: M. Gordon, *Max Gordon Presents;* 3: P. Collier, *The Kennedys;* 4: W. Manchester, *One Brief Shining Moment*

KEPLER 1: I. Asimov, *Biographical Encyclopedia*

KEPPEL 1: G. Colman, *Circle of Anecdote*

KER 1: J. Gere, *Geoffrey Madan's Notebooks;* 2: J. MacCunn, *Recollections of W. P. Ker by Two Friends*

KEROUAC 1: R. Nelson, *The Almanac of American Letters*

KEYNES 1: C. Hession, *John Maynard Keynes;* 2: A. Cave Brown, *The Last Hero*

KHRUSHCHEV 1: M. Ringo, *Nobody Said It Better;* 2: J. Gunther, *Inside Russia Today;* 3: B. Adler, *My Favorite Funny Story;* 4: Kenneth P. O'Donnell and David E. Powers, *"Johnny, We Hardly Knew Ye";* 5: K. Edwards, *I Wish I'd Said That;* 6: D. Niven, *Bring On the Empty Horses*

KIERAN 1: B. Cerf, *Shake Well Before Using*

KINER 1: J. Humes, *Speakers' Treasury*

KINGLAKE 1: J. Gere, *Geoffrey Madan's Notebooks*

KINGSALE 1: S. Winchester, *Their Noble Lordships*

KIPLING 1: H. Hoffmeister, *Anekdotenschatz;* 2: E. Fuller, *2500 Anecdotes*

KIRCHHOFF 1: I. Asimov, *Biographical Encyclopedia*

KISSINGER 1–2: R. Valeriani, *Travels with Henry*

KITCHENER 1: A. Taylor, *English History*

KITTREDGE 1: C. Fadiman and C. Van Doren, *The American Treasury*

KLEIN 1: H. Prochnow, *The Public Speaker's Treasure Chest*

KLEMPERER 3: H. Temianka, *Facing the Music*

KLÖPFER 1: H. Hoffmeister, *Anekdotenschatz*

KNELLER 1: H. Walpole, *Anecdotes of Painting;* 2: *A Dictionary of Anecdotes* (1809), in D. George, *A Book of Anecdotes;* 3: L. Russell, *English Wits*

KNOPF 1: C. Fadiman, *Fifty Years*

KNOX, P., 1: T. Buckley, *Violent Neighbors*

KNOX, R., 1: R. Knox, *Literary Distractions;* 2–3, 6: E. Waugh, *Ronald Knox*

KNOX-JOHNSTON 1: C. Bonington, *Quest for Adventure*

KOESTLER 1: A. Koestler, *Bricks to Babel;* 2: *International Herald Tribune,* Apr. 24–25, 1982; 3: I. Hamilton, *Koestler*

KOO 1: R. Marquard, *Jokes and Anecdotes*

KOPPAY 1: S. Dryfoos, *Iphigene*

KORDA 1–5: M. Korda, *Charmed Lives*

KOUSSEVITZKY 1: O. Levant, *The Unimportance of Being Oscar;* 2–3: H. Earle Johnson, *Symphony Hall*

KREISLER 1: E. Fuller, *2500 Anecdotes;* 2: B. Cerf, *Try and Stop Me;* 3: S. Beach, *Musicdotes*

LABOUCHERE 1–2, 5: H. Pearson, *Lives of the Wits;* 3, 6: L. Russell, *English Wits;* 4: *DNB*

LAEMMLE 1: N. Zierold, *The Moguls*

LAFAYETTE 1: P. Buckman, *Lafayette;* 2: H. Prochnow, *The Public Speaker's Treasure Chest*

LA FONTAINE 1: W. Scholz, *Das Buch des Lachens*

LA GUARDIA 1: B. Cerf, *Try and Stop Me;* 2: J. Gunther, *Procession;* 3: J. Humes, *Speakers' Treasury*

LAIRD 1: H. Kissinger, *White House Years*

LAÏS 1: I. Wallace, *The Nympho & Other Maniacs*

LAMAR 1: Edward Mayes, *Life of Lucius Q. C. Lamar,* in C. Shriner, *Wit, Wisdom, and Foibles of the Great*

LAMB, LADY C., 1: *Boston Globe,* Feb. 20, 1985; 2: D. Cecil, *Melbourne*

LAMB, CHARLES, 1–2, 4–5: L. Russell, *English Wits;* 3: W. Keddie, *Literary and Scientific Anecdote;* 6–7, 9: E. Fuller, *2500 Anecdotes;* 8: *American Scholar* VI: 2 (1937)

LANDERS 1–3: M. Howard, *Eppie*

LANDIS 1: J. Braude, *Speaker's and Toastmaster's Handbook*

LANDOR 1: Richard Monckton Milnes, *Lord Houghton, Monographs,* in F. Muir, *Irreverent Social History*

LANDOWSKA 1: H. Schonberg, *The Great Pianists*

LANDRU 1: D. Wallechinsky and I. Wallace, *The People's Almanac*

LANG 1: L. Missen, *After-dinner Stories and Anecdotes*

LANGRISHE 1: A. Bespaloff, *The Fireside Book of Wine*

LANGTRY 1: I. Wallace et al., *Intimate Sex Lives of Famous People*

LAPLACE 1–2: E. Bell, *Men of Mathematics*

LARDNER 1: J. Yardley, *Ring;* 2: D. Elder, *Ring Lardner*

LARWOOD 1: Oxfam, *Pass the Port*

LATIMER 1: B. Conrad, *Famous Last Words*

LAUGHTON 2: B. Irwin, *Los Angeles Times,* May 8, 1983

LAUZUN 1: P. Smith, *A New Age Now Begins*

LAVOISIER 1: I. Asimov, *Biographical Encyclopedia*

LAW 1: A. Sylvester, *Life with Lloyd George*

LAWRENCE, D. H., 1: Edward D. McDonald, ed., *D. H. Lawrence, Phoenix: The Posthumous Papers,* in J. Sutherland, ed., *OBLA*

LAWRENCE, J., 1: D. Wallechinsky and I. Wallace, *The People's Almanac*

LAWRENCE, T. E., 1–2: R. Graves, *Goodbye to All That;* 3: E. Marsh, *A Number of People*

LAWRENCE, W., 1: J. Garland, *Boston's Gold Coast*

LAWSON 1: G. Brandreth, *Great Theatrical Disasters*

LAZAR 1: R. Anson, *Exile*

LEAHY 1: A. Hatch, *The Byrds of Virginia*

LEAR 1, 3: V. Noakes, *Edward Lear;* 2, 4: A. Davidson, *Edward Lear*

LEDERER 1: S. Marx and J. Clayton, *Rodgers and Hart*

LEDRU-ROLLIN 1: L. Harris, *The Fine Art of Political Wit*

LEE, G., 1: E. Preminger, *Gypsy & Me*

LEE, N., 1: Liber Facetiarum, in D. George, *A Book of Anecdotes*

LEE, R. E., 1: C. Fadiman and C. Van Doren, *The American Treasury;* 2: James Morris Morgan, *The Century Magazine,* LX (May 1900), in B. Botkin, *A Civil War Treasury;* 3: Gen. John B. Gordon, "Last Days of the Confederacy," *Modern Eloquence,* V, in B. Botkin, *A Civil War Treasury;* 4: George W. Bagby, *The Old Virginia Gentleman and Other Sketches,* in B. Botkin, *Treasury of American Anecdotes;* 6: M. Ringo, *Nobody Said It Better*

LE GALLIENNE 1: R. Le Gallienne, *The Romantic '90s*

LEGROS 1: P. Mahony, *Barbed Wit and Malicious Humor*

LEHMANN 1: C. Gattey, *The Elephant That Swallowed a Nightingale*

LEIGHTON 1: S. Radecki, *Das ABC des Lachens*

LENCLOS 1: J. Nash, *Zanies;* 2: G. Boissier, *Mme de Sévigné;* 3: I. Wallace, *The Nympho and Other Maniacs;* 4: I. Wallace et al., *Intimate Sex Lives of Famous People;* 5: W. and A. Durant, *The Story of Civilization,* VIII

LENYA 1: *The Times* (London), Nov. 30, 1981

LEO X 1: T. Craven, *Men of Art*

LEONIDAS 1: I. Asimov, *Biographical Encyclopedia*

LEOPOLD II 1–2: B. Kelen, *The Mistresses*

LESCHETIZKY 1: H. Schonberg, *The Great Pianists*

LESSING 1: J. Timbs, *Century of Anecdote*

LEVANT 2: B. Adler, *My Favorite Funny Story;* 3, 6–7: D. Herrmann, *With Malice Toward All;* 4: J. McAleer, "Globe Man's Daily Story," *Boston Globe,* July 10, 1964; 8: J. Paar, *P.S. Jack Paar*

LÉVIS 1: D. George, *A Book of Anecdotes*

LEWIS, C., 1: D. Balsdon, *Oxford Now and Then;* 2: R. Green, *C. S. Lewis*

LEWIS, J., 1: B. Cerf, *Bumper Crop of Anecdotes*

LEWIS, M., 1: J. Timbs, *Century of Anecdote*

LEWIS, S., 1: L. Untermeyer, *Bygones;* 2: J. McAleer, "Globe Man's Daily Story," *Boston Globe,* July 20, 1970; 3: C. Fadiman, *Party of One;* 4–5: B. Conrad, *Fun While It Lasted*

LIBERACE 1: C. Fadiman and C. Van Doren, *The American Treasury*

LI BO 1: A. Davis, ed., *Penguin Book of Chinese Verse*

LICHTENBERG 1: W. Scholz, *Das Buch des Lachens*

LIEBERMANN 1: C. Bowra, *Memories 1898–1939*

LIEBLING 1: B. Gill, *Here at the New Yorker*

LIEVEN 1: J. Griffin, ed., *Snobs*

LILIENCRON 1–2: H. Hoffmeister, *Anekdotenschatz*

LILLIE 1–3: L. and M. Cowan, *The Wit of Women;* 4–5: K. Tynan, *Tynan on Theatre;* 6, 9: *Book-of-the-Month Club News,* July 1948; 7: C. Nelson, *The Fortunate Years;* 8: C. Daniel, *Lords, Ladies and Gentlemen*

LINCOLN, A., 1–2, 12, 14: A. K. McClure, ed., *Lincoln's Own Yarns and Stories;* 3, 28: Wayne Whipple: *The Story-Life of Abraham Lincoln,* in P. Boller, ed., *Presidential Anecdotes;* 4, 11, 20, 22–24: E. Fuller, *2500 Anecdotes;* 5: I. Tarbell, *The Life of Abraham Lincoln;* 6: B. Cerf, *Shake Well Before Using;* 7: James M. Scovel, quoting Orville H. Browning in *Lippincott's Magazine,* March 1903, in C. Shriner, *Wit, Wisdom, and Foibles of the Great;* 8: P. Zall, *Abe Lincoln Laughing;* 9: K. Jennison, *The Humorous Mr. Lincoln;* 10, 19: George S. Hilton, *The Funny Side of Politics,* in P. Boller, *Presidential Anecdotes;* 13, 27: Benjamin Poore, *Perley's Reminiscences of Sixty Years,* in Boller, *Presidential Anecdotes;* 15, 29, 36: P. Smith, *Trial by Fire;* 16, 25–26: Paul Selby, ed., *Stories and Speeches of Abraham Lincoln,* in Boller, *Presidential Anecdotes;* 17: Lillie De Hegermann-Lindencrone, letter to her aunt, dated Philadelphia, July 1866; 18, 32: C. Fadiman and C. Van Doren, *The American Treasury;* 21: Tyler Dennett, ed., *Lincoln and the Civil War in the Diaries of John Hay,* in Boller, *Presidential Anecdotes;* 30: R. Marquard, *Jokes and Anecdotes;* 31: William Roscoe Thayer, *The Life of John Hay,* in Shriner, *Wit;* 33: Carl Sandburg, in D. George, *A Book of Anecdotes;* 34: Anthony Gross, *Lincoln's Own Stories,* in Boller, *Presidential Anecdotes;* 35: F. Moore, *Anecdotes, Poetry and Incidents of the War;* 37: D. Wallechinsky and I. Wallace, *The People's Almanac;*

38: Ward Hill Lamon, *Recollections of Abraham Lincoln 1847–1865,* in B. Botkin, *A Civil War Treasury*

LINCOLN, R., 1: I. Wallace, "Significa," Aug. 2, 1981

LIND 1: I. Wallace, *The Fabulous Snowman*

LINDEMANN 1: W. Manchester, *The Last Lion*

LISTER 1: H. Steinbert, *Arzt und Patient*

LISZT 1: G. Keynes and B. Hill, *Samuel Butler's Notebooks;* 2: N. Cardus, *Talking of Music*

LIVERMORE 1: M. Saxton, *Louisa May*

LLOYD, C., 1: C. Lloyd, *Chrissie*

LLOYD GEORGE 1: S. Spender, *World Within World;* 2: C. Fadiman and C. Van Doren, *The American Treasury;* 3: M. and A. Guillois, *Liberté, Egalité, Hilarité;* 4: E. Fuller, *2500 Anecdotes;* 5: P. Mahony, *Barbed Wit and Malicious Humor;* 6: I. Richards, *We, the British*

LOBENGULA 1: J. Lockhart, *Cecil Rhodes*

LOCKE 1: W. Keddie, *Literary and Scientific Anecdote*

LOMBARDI 2: M. Ringo, *Nobody Said It Better*

LONG 1: T. Harry Williams, *Huey Long,* in R. Shenkman and K. Reiger, *One-Night Stands With American History;* 2: A. Brinkley, *Voices of Protest*

LONGWORTH 1–3: D. Herrmann, *With Malice Toward All*

LONSDALE 1–2: F. Donaldson, *Freddy Lonsdale*

LOSCH 1: R. Buckle, ed., *Self-Portrait With Friends*

LOUIS XI 1: *Physic and Physicians,* in D. George, *A Book of Anecdotes*

LOUIS XIV 1: W. and A. Durant, *The Story of Civilization,* VII; 2, 7, 10: V. Cronin, *Louis XIV;* 3: E. Fuller, *2500 Anecdotes;* 4: M. Pedrazzini and J. Gries, *Autant en apportent les mots;* 5–6: E. Guérard, *Dictionnaire Encyclopédique;* 8: G. Colman, *Circle of Anecdote;* 9: L. Norton, *Saint-Simon at Versailles*

LOUIS XV 1: M. Pedrazzini and J. Gris, *Autant en apportent les mots;* 2: N. Mitford, *Madame de Pompadour;* 3: E. Fuller, *2500 Anecdotes;* 4: W. and A. Durant, *The Story of Civilization,* X; 5: T. F. Thiselton-Dyer, *Royalty in All Ages,* in C. Shriner, *Wit, Wisdom, and Foibles of the Great;* 6: A. Castelot, *Marie Antoinette*

LOUIS XVI 1: W. Merwin, *Products of the Perfected Civilization;* 2: W. and A. Durant, *The Story of Civilization,* X; 3: W. and A. Durant, *The Story of Civilization,* XI

LOUIS XVIII 1: A. Castelot, *Paris: The Turbulent City*

LOUIS, J., 1: R. Lamparski, *Whatever Became of . . . ?;* 2: B. Conn, "Unforgettable Joe Louis," *Reader's Digest,* July 1983; 5: M. Ringo, *Nobody Said It Better*

LOUIS PHILIPPE 1: A. Castelot, *Paris: The Turbulent City*

LOWE 1: C. Sifakis, *Dictionary of Historic Nicknames*

LOWELL, ABBOTT, 1: Cleveland Amory, *The Proper Bostonians,* in P. Boller, ed., *Presidential Anecdotes*

LOWELL, AMY, 1: B. Cerf, *Shake Well Before Using;* 3: L. Hillyer, "Amy Lowell — Poet," in C. Silitch, ed., *Mad and Magnificent Yankees;* 4: R. McAlmon, *Being Geniuses Together*

LOWELL, R., 1: P. Ziegler, *Diana Cooper;* 2: I. Hamilton, *Robert Lowell: a Biography*

LUBITSCH 1: S. Morley, *Tales from the Hollywood Raj*

LUCE, C., 1: W. Sheed, *Clare Boothe Luce;* 3: J. Humes, *Speakers' Treasury*

LUCE, H., 1: S. Seagrave, *The Soong Dynasty*

LUCULLUS 1: Plutarch, *Lives*

LULLY 1: *EB*

LUNT 1: I. Asimov, *Treasury of Humor;* 2: E. Fuller, *2500 Anecdotes;* 3: *Los Angeles Times,* July 31, 1983

LUTHER 1: P. Bussard, *The New Catholic Treasury of Wit and Humor;* 2: W. Durant, *The Story of Civilization,* VI

LUTYENS 1: *"Daily Mirror" Old Codger's Little Black Book 1;* 2: C. Aslet, *The Last Country Houses*

LYAUTEY 1: L. Harris, *The Fine Art of Political Wit*

LYCURGUS 1: W. Seward, *Biographiana,* V

LYNDHURST 1: Benjamin Disraeli, *Reminiscences,* in Kenin and Wintle, *DBQ*

LYTTON 1: Sir Thomas Henry Hall Caine, *My Story,* in J. Sutherland, ed., *OBLA*

MALBY 1: E. Guérard, *Dictionnaire Encyclopédique*

MACARTHUR, C., 1: S. Marx and J. Clayton, *Rodgers and Hart*

MACARTHUR, D., 2: C. Fadiman and C. Van Doren, *The American Treasury;* 3: J. Gunther, *Procession;* 4: R. Smith, *Thomas E. Dewey and His Times*

MACAULAY 1, 6: Sir George Otto Trevelyan, *The Life and Letters of Lord Macaulay;* 3: L. Russell, *English Wits;* 4: W. Adams, *Treasury of Modern Anecdote;* 5: E. Fuller, *2500 Anecdotes*

MCAULIFFE 1: H. Rawson, *Dictionary of Euphemisms*

MCCARTHY 1: S. Allen, *Funny People*

MCCORMACK 1: C. Gattey, *The Elephant That Swallowed a Nightingale*

McCORMICK 1: S. Birmingham, *The Grandes Dames*

McCOY 1: H. Smith, *The Life and Legend of Gene Fowler;* 2: B. Green, *P. G. Wodehouse*

McCULLERS 1: R. Nelson, *The Almanac of American Letters*

McKINLEY 1: R. Shenkman and K. Reiger, *One-Night Stands with American History;* 2: James Ford Rhodes, *The McKinley and Roosevelt Administrations 1897–1909,* in P. Boller, ed., *Presidential Anecdotes*

MacMAHON 1: H. Hoffmeister, *Anekdotenschatz*

MacMILLAN 1–2: L. Harris, *The Fine Art of Political Wit;* 3: K. Edwards, *I Wish I'd Said That Too*

MACREADY 1: L. and F. Copeland, *10,000 Jokes, Toasts, and Stories;* 3: G. Brandreth, *Great Theatrical Disasters*

MADISON 1: Virginia Moore, *The Madisons,* in P. Boller, ed., *Presidential Anecdotes*

MAETERLINCK 1: A. de Stoeckl and W. Edwards, *When Men Had Time to Love;* 2: P. Mahony, *Barbed Wit and Malicious Humor*

MAGRUDER 1: North Carolina Branch, Southern Historical Society, "Our Living and Our Dead, Devoted to North Carolina — Her Past, Her Present, and Her Future," in B. Botkin, *A Civil War Treasury*

MAHAFFY 1: L. Missen, *Quotable Anecdotes;* 2: F. Delaney and J. Lewinski, *James Joyce's Odyssey*

MAHLER 1: K. Bernstein, *Music Lover's Europe*

MAINTENON 1: Sebastian R. N. Chamfort, *Characters and Anecdotes,* in C. Shriner, *Wit, Wisdom, and Foibles of the Great;* 2: *The Ladies Companion,* 1853, in Shriner, *Wit*

MALHERBE 1: J. Timbs, *Century of Anecdote*

MALIBRAN 1: C. Gattey, *The Elephant That Swallowed a Nightingale*

MALLARMÉ 1: A. Vollard, *Recollections of a Picture Dealer*

MALLORY 1: D. Robertson, *George Mallory*

MANKIEWICZ 1: B. Thomas, *King Cohn;* 2–3: P. Kael, *The Citizen Kane Book*

MANN 1: E. Fuller, *2500 Anecdotes*

MANNING 1: G. Brandreth, *Great Theatrical Disasters*

MANSART 1: L. Norton, *Saint-Simon at Versailles*

MANSFIELD 1: D. George, *A Book of Anecdotes*

MAO 1: M. and A. Guillois, *Liberté, Eqalité, Hilarité*

MARCEAU 1: W. Fifield, *In Search of Genius*

MARGARET, PRINCESS, 1: B. Conrad, *Fun While It Lasted*

MARIA FËDOROVNA 1: I. Wallace et al., *The Book of Lists 3*

MARIA THERESA 1: E. Crankshaw, *Maria Theresa*

MARIE ANTOINETTE 1: *Oxford Dictionary of Quotations;* 2: Clementina Davies, *Recollections of Society in England and France,* in C. Shriner, *Wit, Wisdom, and Foibles of the Great;* 3: W. and A. Durant, *The Story of Civilization,* X; 4: B. Conrad, *Famous Last Words*

MARIE DE MÉDICIS 1: W. Keddie, *Literary and Scientific Anecdote*

MARLBOROUGH, 1ST DUKE OF, 1: J. Spence, *Anecdotes*

MARLBOROUGH, 10TH DUKE OF, 1: S. Winchester, *Their Noble Lordships*

MARQUAND 1: *The New Yorker,* October 1952; 2–3: S. Birmingham, *The Late John Marquand*

MARQUIS 1: C. Ford, *The Time of Laughter;* 2: E. Fuller, *2500 Anecdotes*

MARSHALL, J., 1: B. Botkin, *Treasury of American Anecdotes*

MARSHALL, T., 1: C. Fadiman and C. Van Doren, *The American Treasury;* 2: R. Shenkman and K. Reiger, *One-Night Stands with American History*

MARTEN 1: *The Observer,* Sept. 4, 1983

MARTIN 1: Mordecai Richler in conversation with Clifton Fadiman

MARTINELLI 1: J. Braude, *Speaker's and Toastmaster's Handbook*

MARX, C., 1: N. Rees, *Quote . . . Unquote;* 2–3: J. Adamson, *Groucho, Harpo, Chico*

MARX, G., 1: Arthur Marx, *Son of Groucho,* in Kenin and Wintle, *DBQ;* 2, 4: K. Edwards, *More Things I Wish I'd Said;* 3: L. Rosten, *Joys of Yiddish;* 5–6: J. Adamson, *Groucho, Harpo, Chico;* 7: L. Rosten, *People I Have Loved, Known or Admired;* 8: O. Levant, *The Unimportance of Being Oscar;* 9: E. Wilson, *I Am Gazing Into My 8-ball;* 10: G. Brandreth, *Joy of Lex;* 11–12: D. Herrmann, *With Malice Toward All;* 14: G. Kanin, *Hollywood*

MARX, H., 1: O. Levant, *The Unimportance of Being Oscar;* 2: O. Levant, *A Smattering of Ignorance;* 3: B. Cerf, *Bumper Crop of Anecdotes*

MARY 1: *DNB*

MARY, QUEEN CONSORT, 2: *Book-of-the-Month Club News,* April 1952

MARY, QUEEN OF SCOTS, 1: Garrett Mattingly, *The Defeat of the Spanish Armada,* in Kenin and Wintle, *DBQ*

MASARYK 1: G. Mikes, *Laughing Matter*

MASCAGNI 1: E. Fuller, *2500 Anecdotes;* 2: H. Sievers, *Musica Curiosa*

MASSENET 1: C. Skinner, *Elegant Wits and Grand Horizontals*

MATHILDE 1: A. de Stoeckl and W. Edwards, *When Men Had Time to Love;* 2: C. Skinner,

Elegant Wits and Grand Horizontals

MATISSE 1: D. Wallechinsky and I. Wallace, *The People's Almanac*

MATTHEWS 1–2: G. Brandreth, *Great Theatrical Disasters*

MATURE 2: D. Herrmann, *With Malice Toward All*

MAUGHAM 1: W. Maugham, *A Writer's Notebook;* 2: D. Fielding, *Those Remarkable Cunards;* 3: K. Edwards, *I Wish I'd Said That*

MAUREPAS 1: A. Castelot, *Marie Antoinette*

MAURY 1: *EB*, 1971; 2: M. Pedrazzini and J. Gris, *Autant en apportent les mots*

MAXWELL 1–3: R. Keyes, "Replay," in *Sports Illustrated*, December 1984

MAY 1: R. Price, *A History of Punch*

MAYER 1–2: S. Marx, *Mayer and Thalberg;* 3: N. Zierold, *The Moguls;* 4: S. Birmingham, "*The Rest of Us*"; 5: Bosley Crowther, *Hollywood Rajah*, in Kenin and Wintle, *DBQ*

MAZARIN 1: G. Lieberman, *The Greatest Laughs of All Time;* 2: G. Boissier, *Mme de Sévigné*

MEDICI 1: H. V. Morton, *A Traveller in Italy*

MEHMED II 1: W. Durant, *The Story of Civilization*, V

MEIR 2–3: R. Nixon, *Leaders*

MELBA 1: E. Fuller, *2500 Anecdotes;* 2: R. Merrill, *Between Acts*

MELBOURNE 1–3: D. Cecil, *Melbourne;* 4: J. Gere and J. Sparrow, *Geoffrey Madan's Notebooks*

MELLON 1: S. Holbrook, *The Age of the Moguls*

MELVILLE 1: J. Hawthorne, *Nathaniel Hawthorne and His Wife*

MENCKEN 1–2: S. Mayfield, *The Constant Circle;* 3: A. Cooke, *Six Men;* 4: M. Ringo, *Nobody Said It Better*

MENELIK II 1: J. Train, *True Remarkable Occurrences*

MENOTTI 1: J. Gruen, *Menotti: A Biography*

MENSHIKOV 1: D. George, *A Book of Anecdotes*

MENZIES 1: K. Edwards, *I Wish I'd Said That*

MERMAN 1: H. Pleasants, *The Great American Popular Singers*

MERRILL 1: R. Merrill, *Between Acts*

MESSIER 1: G. Murchie, *Music of the Spheres*

METAXAS 1: E. Fuller, *2500 Anecdotes*

METTERNICH, K. VON, 1: L. Missen, *Quotable Anecdotes*

METTERNICH, PRINCESS, 1: Clifton Fadiman

MEYERBEER 1: M. Ringo, *Nobody Said It Better;* 2: H. Sievers, *Musica Curiosa;* 3: E. Van de Velde, *Anecdotes Musicales*

MICHELANGELO 1, 4–6: G. Vasari, *Lives of the Painters;* 2: W. Durant, *The Story of Civilization*, V; 3: C. Speroni, *Wit and Wisdom of the Italian Renaissance;* 7: H. Morton, *A Traveller in Italy*

MICHELET 1: C. Skinner, *Elegant Wits and Grand Horizontals*

MIES VAN DER ROHE 1: A. Whitman, *Come to Judgment*

MIKES 1: *International Herald Tribune*, April 24–25, 1982

MILL 1: C. Bowen, *Yankee from Olympus*

MILLAY 1: *New York Times Book Review*, July 24, 1983

MILLER 1: W. Espy, *Another Almanac of Words at Play*

MILLIKAN 1: J. Braude, *Braude's Second Encyclopedia*

MILNE 1: C. Milne, *The Enchanted Places*

MILNES 1: B. Conrad, *Famous Last Words*

MILO 1: E. Hauser, *Italy, A Cultural Guide*

MILTON 1: *DNB;* 2: W. Keddie, *Literary and Scientific Anecdote*

MIRABEAU 1: John S. Smith, *Mirabeau*, in C. Shriner, *Wit, Wisdom, and Foibles of the Great;* 2: W. Scholz, *Das Buch des Lachens;* 3: E. Fuller, *2500 Anecdotes;* 4: J. Humes, *Speakers' Treasury*

MITCHELL 1: J. Train, *True Remarkable Occurrences*

MITFORD, N., 1: O. Levant, *The Unimportance of Being Oscar;* 2: C. Canfield, *Up and Down and Around*

MITFORD, T., 1: J. Guinness, *House of Mitford*

MIZNER, A., 1: *The New Yorker*, Nov. 22, 1952

MIZNER, W. 1, 5: D. Herrmann, *With Malice Toward All;* 2, 4, 7, 9, 12, 16: D. Wallechinsky and I. Wallace, *The People's Almanac;* 3, 10: C. Fadiman and C. Van Doren, *The American Treasury;* 6, 8: *The New Yorker*, July 29, 1950; 13: *The New Yorker*, Nov. 22, 1952; 14: A. Chambers, *Dream Resorts;* 15: G. Herman, *The Book of Hollywood Quotes*

MODIGLIANI 1: M. Georges-Michel, *From Renoir to Picasso*

MOLIÈRE 1: W. Walsh, *Handy Book of Curious Information*

MOLNÁR 1: B. Cerf, *Try and Stop Me;* 2–4, 8: *The New Yorker*, May 25, 1946; 5, 7: L. Farago, *Strictly From Hungary;* 6: G. Mikes, *Coffee Houses of Europe;* 12: J. Humes, *Speakers' Treasury*

MOMMSEN 1: H. Hoffmeister, *Anekdotenschatz*

MONROE 1: D. Johnson and E. Leventhal, eds., *Letters of Nunnally Johnson;* 2: *Los Angeles Times*, May 3, 1984

MONTAGU 1: J. Spence, *Anecdotes;* 2: F. Muir, *Irreverent Social History*

MONTAGUE 1: J. Gere and J. Sparrow, *Geoffrey Madan's Notebooks*

MONTECUCCOLI 1: S. and R. Percy, *The Percy Anecdotes*

MONTEFIORE 1: W. Novak and M. Waldoks, *Big*

MONTEFIORE (*continued*)
Book of Jewish Humor
MONTEUX 1: A. Previn, ed., *Orchestra;* 2: C. O'Connell, *The Other Side of the Record;* 3: R. Merrill, *Between Acts;* 4: Oxfam, *Pass the Port*
MONTGOMERY, B. 1: A. Herbert, *A.P.H.;* 2: R. Collier, *The Freedom Road;* 4: J. Gunther, *Procession*
MONTGOMERY, J. 1: W. Keddie, *Literary and Scientific Anecdote*
MONTMORENCY 1: M. Strauss, *Familiar Medical Quotations*
MOORE, GEORGE 1: Oliver St. John Gogarty, *As I Was Walking Down Sackville Street,* in Kenin and Wintle, *DBQ;* 2: letter from W. B. Yeats to Lady Gregory, May 1901, in *DBQ;* 3: B. Cerf, *The Life of the Party;* 4: D. Fielding, *Those Remarkable Cunards*
MOORE, G. E., 1: B. Russell, *Autobiography*
MORE, H., 1: W. Keddie, *Literary and Scientific Anecdote*
MORE, SIR T., 1: W. Roper, *Life of Sir Thomas More;* 2: J. Aubrey, *Brief Lives;* 3: W. Winstanley, *England's Worthies*
MOREL 1: M. Bishop, *A Gallery of Eccentrics*
MORGAN, J. P., SR., 1, 4: C. Tomkins, *Merchants and Masterpieces;* 3: J. Carroll, *Prince of Peace;* 6–8: E. Wagenknecht, *American Profile;* 9: Joseph L. Gardner, *Departing Glory: Theodore Roosevelt as Ex President,* in P. Boller, ed., *Presidential Anecdotes*
MORGAN, J. P., JR., 1: B. Cerf, *Laughing Stock;* 2: B. Cerf, *The Life of the Party;* 3: H. Hoffmeister, *Anekdotenschatz*
MORLEY, C., 1: C. Fadiman, *Any Number Can Play*
MORLEY, R., 1: R. Morley, *Book of Bricks;* 2: R. Morley and S. Stokes, *Robert Morley: A Reluctant Autobiography*
MORRIS, C., 1: E. Fuller, *2500 Anecdotes*
MORRIS, W., 1: L. and F. Copeland, *10,000 Jokes, Toasts and Stories*
MORSE 1: P. Smith, *The Nation Comes of Age;* 2: H. Prochnow, *The Public Speaker's Treasure Chest*
MOSCARDÓ 1: C. Eby, *The Siege of the Alcázar*
MOSLEY 1: K. Edwards, *More Things I Wish I'd Said*
MOTT 1: I. and R. Poley, *Friendly Anecdotes*
MOUNTBATTEN 1: A. Hatch, *The Mountbattens;* 2: P. Ziegler, *Mountbatten*
MOZART 1: O. Sacks, *New York Review of Books,* Feb. 28, 1985; 2: W. and A. Durant, *The Story of Civilization,* X; 3: N. McPhee, *Second Book of Insults;* 4: E. Van de Velde, *Anecdotes Musicales*
MUGGERIDGE 1: J. Paar, *P.S. Jack Paar*

MUGNIER 1: G. Painter, *Proust: The Later Years;* 2–5: C. Skinner, *Elegant Wits and Grand Horizontals*
MUHAMMAD SHAH I 1: E. Canetti, *Crowds and Power*
MUIR 1: C. Fadiman and C. Van Doren, *The American Treasury*
MURAVIEV 1: E. Crankshaw, *The Shadow of the Winter Palace*
MURPHY 1: W. Riordan, *Plunkitt of Tammany Hall*
MURRAY, SIR GEORGE, 1: W. Keddie, *Literary and Scientific Anecdote*
MURRAY, GILBERT, 1: C. Bowra, *Memories 1898–1939;* 2: R. Graves, *Goodbye to All That*
MURRAY, M., 1: *DNB*
MUSSET 1: M. Pedrazzini and J. Gris, *Autant en apportent les mots*
MYTTON 1: C. Fadiman, *Any Number Can Play*

NABOKOV 1: *New York Times Book Review,* Aug. 23, 1981; 2: J. Orgel, *Undying Passion;* 3: V. Nabokov, *Strong Opinions*
NAGURSKI 4: *Los Angeles Times,* Jan. 7, 1985
NAMATH 1: *Los Angeles Times,* Jan. 20, 1983
NAPIER 1: I. Asimov, *Treasury of Humor*
NAPOLEON I 1, 9: C. Barnett, *Bonaparte;* 2–4, 8, 10: V. Cronin, *Napoleon Bonaparte;* 5–6: W. and A. Durant, *The Story of Civilization,* XI; 7: L. and F. Copeland, *10,000 Jokes, Toasts, and Stories;* 11: D. Duff, *Eugénie and Napoleon III;* 12: H. Hoffmeister, *Anekdotenschatz;* 13: A. Castelot, *Paris: The Turbulent City;* 14: A. Duff Cooper, *Talleyrand*
NAPOLEON III 1: H. Hoffmeister, *Anekdotenschatz;* 2: D. Duff, *Eugénie and Napoleon III;* 3: E. Crankshaw, *The Fall of the House of Hapsburg*
NAPOLEON, E., 1–2: D. Duff, *Eugénie and Napoleon III;* 3: F. Markham, *The Bonapartes*
NAPOLEON, J., 1: F. Loliée, *Gilded Beauties of the Second Empire*
NARVÁEZ 1: B. Conrad, *Famous Last Words*
NAST 1: *American Scholar* X (1941)
NECKER 1: W. Keddie, *Literary and Scientific Anecdote*
NELSON 1: A. Lincoln and R. McEwan, eds., *Lord Eldon's Anecdote Book;* 2–3, 5–7: R. Southey, *Life of Nelson;* 4: *DNB*
NERO 1: W. Durant, *The Story of Civilization,* III; 2–3: Suetonius, *The Twelve Caesars*
NERVAL 1–2: G. Wagner, *Selected Writing of Gérard de Nerval*
NEWTON 1, 12: *DNB;* 2: R. Hendrickson, *The Literary Life;* 3: S. Radecki, *Das ABC des Lachens;* 4, 10: E. Bell, *Men of Mathematics;* 6: W. Keddie, *Literary and Scientific Anecdote;* 7: J. Spence, *Anecdotes;* 8: I. Asimov,

Biographical Encyclopedia; 9: S. Waterlow, *In Praise of Cambridge;* 11: T. Moore, *Memoirs, Journal and Correspondence*

NIARCHOS 1: W. Espy, *Another Almanac of Words at Play*

NICHOLAS I 1: E. Guérard, *Dictionnaire Encyclopédique*

NIJINSKY 1–2: R. Buckle, *Nijinsky*

NILSSON 1–2: W. Sargeant, *Divas;* 3: R. Bing, *A Knight at the Opera*

NIVEN 1: F. Worth, *Complete Unabridged Super Trivia Encyclopedia;* 2: *Los Angeles Times,* Aug. 8, 1983

NIVERNAIS 1: J. Braude, *Speaker's and Toastmaster's Handbook*

NIXON 1: Earl Mayo and Stephen Hess, *President Nixon: A Political Portrait,* in P. Boller, ed., *Presidential Anecdotes;* 2: C. Daniel, *Lords, Ladies and Gentlemen;* 3: D. Wallechinsky and I. Wallace, *The People's Almanac;* 4: Bill Adler, ed., *The Washington Wits,* in Boller, *Presidential Anecdotes;* 5–6, 8: A. Wallace et al., *The Book of Lists 3;* 9: D. Frost, *"I Gave Them a Sword"*

NOAILLES 1: A. Lanoux, *Paris in the Twenties*

NORBURY 1: W. Adams, *Treasury of Modern Anecdote;* 2: A. Lincoln and R. McEwan, eds., *Lord Eldon's Anecdote Book;* 3: *DNB*

NORDEN 1: R. Morley, *Book of Bricks*

NORTH 1: Broughton, *Recollections of a Long Life;* 2–3: A. Lincoln and R. McEwan, eds., *Lord Eldon's Anecdote Book;* 4: W. Adams, *Treasury of Modern Anecdote*

NORTHCLIFFE 1: P. Brendon, *The Life and Death of the Press Barons*

NORTHCOTE 1: K. Arvine, *Cyclopaedia of Anecdotes*

NORTON 1: W. Keddie, *Literary and Scientific Anecdote*

NOYES 1: M. Bishop, *The Exotics*

NUFFIELD 1: N. Rees, *Quote . . . Unquote*

NURMI 1: *Los Angeles Times,* Aug. 12, 1983

OATES 1: *DNB*

OFFENBACH 1: S. Beach, *Musicdotes*

O'HARA 1: Matthew J. Bruccoli, *The O'Hara Concern,* in J. Sutherland, ed., *OBLA;* 2: B. Gill, *Here at the New Yorker*

OLDFIELD 1: T. Davies, *Dramatic Micellanies*

OLIVIER 1: J. Lasky, *Love Scene;* 2: J. McAleer, "Globe Man's Daily Story," *Boston Globe,* Jan. 1, 1963

'OMAR 1: W. Walsh, *Handy Book of Curious Information*

ONASSIS 1: F. Brady, *Onassis*

O'NEILL 1: *The New Yorker,* Feb. 28, 1948; 2: R. Hendrickson, *The Literary Life*

OPPENHEIMER 2–3: A. Whitman, *Come to Judgment*

ORSAY 1: C. Roberts, *And So To Bath;* 2: W. Adams, *Treasury of Modern Anecdote*

OSCAR II 1: H. Hoffmeister, *Anekdotenschatz*

O'TOOLE 1–2: G. Talese, *Fame and Obscurity*

OTTO 1: H. Hoffmeister, *Anekdotenschatz*

OUIDA 1: W. Abbot, *Notable Women in History*

OWEN 1: J. Sanford, *Winters of That Country*

PACHMANN 1–3: H. Schonberg, *The Great Pianists*

PADEREWSKI 1, 3: E. Fuller, *2500 Anecdotes;* 2: H. Schonberg, *The Great Pianists;* 4–5: A. Zamoyski, *Paderewski;* 6: B. Cerf, *Try and Stop Me*

PAIGE 1: *Los Angeles Times,* June 12, 1982

PAINE 1: A. Outram Sherman, address before the Huguenot Society of America, New Rochelle, NY, July 1910, in C. Shriner, *Wit, Wisdom, and Foibles of the Great;* 2: Hesketh Pearson, *Tom Paine: Friend of Mankind,* in J. Sutherland, ed., *OBLA*

PALEWSKI 1: *New York Times Book Review,* Oct. 14, 1984

PALEY 1: W. Adams, *Treasury of Modern Anecdote*

PALMERSTON 1: R. B. Brett, *The Yoke of Empire,* in C. Shriner, *Wit, Wisdom, and Foibles of the Great;* 2: Arthur Ponsonby, *Henry Ponsonby: His Life and Letters,* in A. Hardy, *Queen Victoria Was Amused;* 4: B. Conrad, *Famous Last Words*

PARK 1: E. Fuller, *2500 Anecdotes*

PARKER, D., 1, 19, 21: O. Levant, *The Unimportance of Being Oscar;* 2–3: E. Fuller, *2500 Anecdotes;* 5, 18: R. Drennan, *Wit's End;* 6: R. Marquard, *Jokes and Anecdotes;* 7: B. Cerf, *Try and Stop Me;* 8–9: D. Wallechinsky and I. Wallace, *The People's Almanac;* 10–11: D. Herrmann, *With Malice Toward All;* 12, 20: John Keats, *You Might as Well Live,* in D. Hall, ed., *OBALA;* 13–14, 16: R. Drennan, *The Algonquin Wits;* 15: B. Thomas, *Thalberg: Life and Legend,* An Unfinished Woman;* 17: L. Hellman, *An Unfinished Woman*

PARKER, H., 1: L. Humphrey, *The Humor of Music*

PARKER, Q., 1: J. Humes, *Speakers' Treasury*

PARR 1: R. Hendrickson, *The Literary Life;* 2: *DNB;* 3: J. Timbs, *English Eccentrics*

PARRISH 1: J. Humes, *Speakers' Treasury*

PARTRIDGE 1: *DNB;* 2: W. Walsh, *Handy Book of Curious Information*

PASCAL 1: I. Asimov, *Biographical Encyclopedia*

PATER 1: H. Pearson, *The Life of Oscar Wilde;* 2: S. Behrman, *Portrait of Max*

PATTI 1: C. Gattey, *The Elephant That Swallowed a Nightingale*

PATTON 1–2: C. Fadiman and C. Van Doren, *The American Treasury*

PAYNE 1: I. Wallace et al., *Book of Lists 2*

PEABODY 1: L. Tharp, *The Peabody Sisters of Salem*

PEARD 1: *Country Life*, May 20, 1982

PECK 1: S. Harris, *Pieces of Eight*

PEMBROKE 1: W. Keddie, *Literary and Scientific Anecdote*

PERELMAN 1: W. Espy, *Another Almanac of Words at Play*

PERICLES 1: Plutarch, *Lives*

PERLMAN 1: M. Wallace and G. Gates, *Close Encounters*

PERÓN 1: I. Wallace et al., *Intimate Sex Lives of Famous People*

PEROT 1: D. Frost, *Book of Millionaires*

PERRY 1: J. Bartlett, *Familiar Quotations*

PERUGINO 1: G. Vasari, *Lives of the Painters*

PÉTAIN 1: P. Méras, *The Mermaids of Chenonceaux*; 2: P. Frederick, *Ten First Ladies of the World*

PETER I 1: R. Massie, *Peter the Great*; 2: W. Keddie, *Literary and Scientific Anecdote*

PETERBOROUGH 1: *DNB*

PETRONIUS 1: F. Seymour Smith, *A Treasury of Wit and Wisdom*

PHELPS 1: E. Fuller, *2500 Anecdotes*

PHILIP, Prince 3: L. Lucaire, *Celebrity Trivia*; 4: N. McPhee, *Second Book of Insults*

PHILIP II 1: Valerius Maximus, *Facta et Dicta Memorabilia*; 2: I. Asimov, *Treasury of Humor*; 3: E. Guérard, *Dictionnaire Encyclopédique*

PHILIP III 1: B. Tuchman, *The March of Folly*

PHILIP V 1: V. Cronin, *Louis XIV*

PHILIP, J., 1: C. Fadiman and C. Van Doren, *The American Treasury*

PHILLIPS 1–2: B. Botkin, *Treasury of Modern Anecdotes*

PIATIGORSKY 1: H. Temianka, *Facing the Music*

PICABIA 1: M. Georges-Michel, *From Renoir to Picasso*

PICASSO 1: F. Gilot and C. Lake, *Life with Picasso*; 2, 8: A. Whitman, *Come to Judgment*; 3: Edward Burns, ed., *Gertrude Stein on Picasso*, in J. Mellow, *Charmed Circle*; 4: J. Mellow, *Charmed Circle*; 5, 15, 18–19: R. Penrose, *Picasso*; 6: B. Adler, *My Favorite Funny Story*; 7: A. Rubinstein, *My Many Years*; 13: B. Cerf, *Bumper Crop of Anecdotes*; 14: F. Weiskopf, *Gesammelte Werke*; 16: A. Lanoux, *Paris in the Twenties*; 17: D. Duncan, *Picasso's Picasso*

PITT 1: Lord Stanhope, *Conversations with Lord Wellington*, in C. Shriner, *Wit, Wisdom, and Foibles of the Great*; 2: H. Hoffmeister, *Anekdotenschatz*; 3: W. and A. Durant, *The Story of Civilization*, XI; 4: *Stanhope's Life of the Rt. Hon. William Pitt*, in *Oxford Dictionary of Quotations*

PLATO 1–2: I. Asimov, *Treasury of Humor*; 3: E. Fuller, *2500 Anecdotes*

PLINY 1: Pliny, *Letters*

PLOMER 1: W. Allen, *As I Walked Down New Grub Street*

PLOTINUS 1: E. Monegal and A. Reid, *Borges: A Reader*

POE 1: R. Hendrickson, *The Literary Life*

POGGIO 1: W. Durant, *The Story of Civilization*, V

POMPADOUR 1: N. Mitford, *Madame de Pompadour*

POPE, Alexander 1, 4: J. Spence, *Anecdotes*; 2–3: S. Johnson, *Lives of the English Poets*

POPE, Arthur 1: J. Howard, *Margaret Mead*

PORSON 1–2: W. Keddie, *Literary and Scientific Anecdote*; 3: J. Timbs, *Century of Anecdote*; 4–5: L. Missen, *Quotable Anecdotes*; 6: C. Fadiman, *Any Number Can Play*; 7: E. Barker, *Literary Recollections*

POUSSIN 1: *Quarterly Review*, no. 218, April 1861, in D. George, *A Book of Anecdotes*

PREVIN 1: A. Previn, ed., *Orchestra*; 2: R. Morley, *Book of Bricks*; 3: R. Morley, *Second Book of Bricks*

PRINGLE 1: W. Walsh, *Handy Book of Curious Information*

PROKOFIEV 1: *Book-of-the-Month Club News*, February 1940

PULITZER 1: P. Brendon, *The Life and Death of the Press Barons*

PUSHKIN 1: C. Fadiman, Foreword to N. Gogol, *Chichikov's Journeys*

PUTNAM 1: B. Botkin, *Treasury of American Anecdotes*

PYLE 1: *'47, The Magazine of the Year*

PYRRHUS 1: Plutarch, *Lives*

PYTHAGORAS 1: Diogenes Laertius, *Eminent Philosophers*, vol. 8

QUEENSBERRY 1: J. Timbs, *Century of Anecdote*; 2: W. Walsh, *Handy Book of Curious Information*

QUESNAY 1: W. and A. Durant, *The Story of Civilization*, X

QUIN 1: *DNB*

RABELAIS 1: R. Hendrickson, *The Literary Life*; 2: F. Winslow, *Physic and Physicians*, in D. George, *A Book of Anecdotes*; 3: K. Arvine, *Cyclopaedia of Anecdotes*

RABI 1: P. Wyden, *Day One*

RACHEL 1–3: J. Agate, *Rachel*; 4–6: E. Fuller, *2500 Anecdotes*

RACHMANINOFF 1: A. Rubinstein, *My Many Years;* 2: H. Schonberg, The Great Pianists

RACINE 1: E. Guérard, *Dictionnaire Encyclopédique*

RAFT 1: *Santa Barbara News Press,* Nov. 25, 1980

RAGLAN 1: *DNB*

RALEIGH 1–2: T. Fuller, ed., *Worthies of England;* 3: W. Walsh, *Handy Book of Curious Information;* 4–5: J. Aubrey, *Brief Lives;* 6: J. A. St. John, *Life of Sir Walter Raleigh,* in D. Wallechinsky and I. Wallace, *The People's Almanac 2;* 7: I. A. Taylor, *Sir Walter Raleigh,* in C. Shriner, *Wit, Wisdom, and Foibles of the Great;* 8: *DNB*

RAMANUJAN 1: C. Fadiman, *Any Number Can Play*

RAPHAEL 1: E. Fuller, *2500 Anecdotes*

RAYNAL 1: J. Larwood, *Anecdotes of the Clergy*

READING 1: A. Sylvester, *Life with Lloyd George*

REAGAN 1: B. Adler and B. Adler, Jr., *The Reagan Wit;* 2–3: "Reagan Out of Surgery," *Fort Worth Star Telegram,* Mar. 31, 1981; 4: D. McClellan, *Ear on Washington;* 5: *Los Angeles Times,* Apr. 7, 1984

REED 1: E. Fuller, *2500 Anecdotes;* 2: *McClure's Magazine,* June 1911, in C. Shriner, *Wit, Wisdom, and Foibles of the Great*

REGER 1: N. Slonimsky, *A Thing or Two about Music;* 2: N. Slonimsky, *Lexicon of Musical Invective*

REHAN 1: G. Brandreth, *Great Theatrical Disasters*

REINHARDT 1: A. Milne, *It's Too Late Now*

REISENAUER 1: A. Rubinstein, *My Young Years*

RENOIR 2: H. Hoffmeister, *Anekdotenschatz;* 3: M. Cowley, *The View From 80;* 4: T. Craven, *Men of Art*

REPPLIER 1: J. Braude, *Speaker's and Toastmaster's Handbook*

REUTHER 1: *Parade,* Apr. 10, 1983

REYNOLDS 1: E. Lucas, *A Fronded Isle*

RHODES 1, 3: J. Lockhart, *Rhodes;* 2: G. le Sueur, *Cecil Rhodes;* 4: V. Castlerosse, *Valentine's Days*

RICE 1: R. Smith, *To Absent Friends from Red Smith*

RICHARD I 1: 13th-century chronicle, *Recits d'un menestral de Reims,* in D. George, *A Book of Anecdotes;* 2: W. Keddie, *Literary and Scientific Anecdote*

RICHARDSON 1–2: K. Tynan, *Show People*

RICHELIEU 1: D. Wallechinsky, et al., *The Book of Lists;* 2: H. Hoffmeister, *Anekdotenschatz*

RICHTER 1: S. Beach, *Musicdotes;* 2: E. Goossens, *Overture and Beginners;* 3: L. Harris, *The Fine Art of Political Wit*

RIGAUD 1: W. Seward, *Biographiana,* vol. 1

RILEY 1: B. Cerf, *Treasury of Atrocious Puns*

RIVAROL 1: E. Guérard, *Dictionnaire Encyclopédique;* 2: W. Scholz, *Das Buch des Lachens*

RIVERA 1: C. Eby, *The Siege of the Alcázar*

RIZZUTO 1: E. Lucaire, *Celebrity Trivia*

ROBERT I 1: W. Scott, *Tales of a Grandfather*

ROBERT, L., 1: P. Wescher, *Schweizer Künstler-Anekdoten*

ROBINSON, E., 1: Chard Powers Smith, *Where the Light Falls,* in D. Hall, ed., *OBALA;* 2: I. Wallace, et al., *Book of Lists 2*

ROBINSON, J., 1: B. Adler, *My Favorite Funny Story*

ROCHE 1: *DNB;* 2: W. Adams, *Treasury of Modern Anecdote*

ROCHEFORT 1: Henri Rochefort, *The Adventures of My Life,* in C. Shriner, *Wit, Wisdom, and Foibles of the Great;* 2: M. Pedrazzini and J. Gris, *Autant en apportent les mots*

ROCKEFELLER, W., 1: R. Shenkman and K. Reiger, *One-Night Stands with American History*

RODGERS 1: H. Fordin, *Getting to Know Him;* 2: S. Beach, *Musicdotes*

RODZINSKI 1: H. Rodzinski, *Our Two Lives*

ROGERS, S., 1: E. Fuller, *2500 Anecdotes;* 2: Henry Taylor, *The Autobiography of Henry Taylor,* in D. Sutherland, ed., *OBALA;* 3–4: W. Adams, *Treasury of Modern Anecdote*

ROGERS, W., 1: E. Fuller, *2500 Anecdotes;* 2: B. Cerf, *Shake Well Before Using*

ROLAND 1: *EB*

ROMANOFF 1: D. Niven, *Bring On the Empty Horses;* 2: R. Lamparski, *Whatever Became Of . . . ?*

ROOSEVELT, E., 1: J. Lash, *Eleanor*

ROOSEVELT, F. D., 1: "Next Week," *Colliers,* LXXXIX, June 18, 1932, in P. Boller, ed., *Presidential Anecdotes;* 2: J. Lash, *Eleanor and Franklin;* 3: "Fanny Hurst," *New York Times,* Feb. 24, 1968, in Boller, *Presidential Anecdotes;* 4: D. Wallechinsky and I. Wallace, *The People's Almanac;* 5: J. McAleer, "Globe Man's Daily Story," *Boston Globe,* Mar. 29, 1961; 6: B. Botkin, *Treasury of American Anecdotes;* 7: D. McClellan, *Ear on Washington*

ROOSEVELT, T., Sr., 1: H. Hagedorn, *Roosevelt in the Bad Lands;* 2: *Publishers Weekly,* Aug. 5, 1983; 3: William Beebe, *The Book of Naturalists,* in P. Boller, ed., *Presidential Anecdotes;* 4: E. Wagenknecht, *American Profile, 1900–1909;* 5: L. Lucaire, *Celebrity Trivia;* 6: Emily Bax, *Miss Bax of the Embassy,* in Boller, *Presidential Anecdotes*

ROOSEVELT, T., Jr., 1: E. Fuller, *2500 Anecdotes*

ROOT 1: J. Baer, *The Self-Chosen*

ROPS 1: A. Vollard, *Recollections of a Picture Dealer*

ROSENBLOOM 1: O. Levant, *A Smattering of Ignorance*

ROSENTHAL 1: B. Cerf, *Try and Stop Me;* 2–3: H. Schonberg, *The Great Pianists;* 4: H. Finck, *Musical Laughs*

ROSS 1, 4, 10–12: J. Thurber, *The Years with Ross;* 2, 8: *'48, The Magazine of the Year,* March; 3, 6–7, 13: C. Holmes, *The Clocks of Columbus;* 5: B. Cerf, *Good for a Laugh;* 9: B. Gill, *Here at the New Yorker;* 14: R. Collier, *The Rainbow People*

ROSSETTI 1: C. Roberts, *And So To Bath;* 2: Hall Caine, *My Story,* in J. Sutherland, ed., *OBLA;* 3: H. Caine, *Recollections of Dante Gabriel Rossetti*

ROSSINI 1, 10: S. Beach, *Musicdotes;* 2, 5–8: N. Slonimsky, *A Thing or Two about Music;* 3: T. FitzGibbon, comp., *The Pleasures of the Table;* 4: W. Adams, *Treasury of Modern Anecdote;* 9: E. Van de Velde, *Anecdotes Musicales*

ROTHSCHILD 1: A. Faulkner and T. Hartman, *All the Best People*

ROUTH 1–2: J. Morris, *Oxford;* 3: J. Burgon, *Twelve Good Men*

ROWLAND 1: I. Asimov, *Treasury of Humor*

RUBINSTEIN, Anton, 1: H. Hoffmeister, *Anekdotenschatz;* 2: N. Slonimsky, *A Thing or Two about Music*

RUBINSTEIN, Arthur, 1: C. Fadiman, *Enter, Conversing;* 2: B. Adler, *My Favorite Funny Story;* 3: R. Smullyan, *5000 B.C. and Other Philosophical Fantasies*

RUGGLES 1: V. Thomson, *A Virgil Thomson Reader*

RUSKIN 1: J. Morris, *Oxford;* 2: *DNB*

RUSSELL, Bertrand, 1: A. Whitman, *Come to Judgment;* 2: C. Fadiman, *Any Number Can Play;* 3: G. Hardy, *A Mathematician's Apology*

RUSSELL, G., 1: C. Fadiman, *Any Number Can Play;* 2: L. and F. Copeland, *10,000 Jokes, Toasts and Stories*

RUSSELL, J., 1: *DNB;* 2: D. Cecil, *Melbourne;* 3: H. Hoffmeister, *Anekdotenschatz*

RUTH 1: B. Cerf, *Good for a Laugh;* 4: D. Anderson, *The Red Smith Reader;* 5: L. Green, *Sportswit*

RUTHERFORD 1: C. Snow, *Variety of Men*

SACKVILLE-WEST 1: W. Allen, *As I Walked Down New Grub Street*

SAGE 1: J. Braude, *Speaker's and Toastmaster's Handbook*

SAINT-SAËNS 1: T. Beecham, *A Mingled Chime*

SALINGER 1: A. Silverman, "The Fragile Pleasure"

SALISBURY 1: M. Seymour-Smith, *Robert Graves*

SALK 1: S. Bolton, *Famous Men of Science*

SANDBURG 1: B. Cerf, *Good for a Laugh*

SANDWICH 1: W. Walsh, *Handy Book of Curious Information;* 2: J. Timbs, *Century of Anecdote*

SANTAYANA 1: H. and D. L. Thomas, *Living Biographies of the Great Philosophers*

SARASATE 1: J. Wechsberg, *Red Plush and Black Velvet;* 2: E. Fuller, *2500 Anecdotes*

SARGENT, J., 1: S. Weintraub, *The London Yankees;* 2–3: B. Conrad, *Fun While It Lasted;* 4: P. Boller, ed., *Presidential Anecdotes;* 5: D. Knox, *Quotable Anecdotes*

SARGENT, M., 1: Leslie Ayre, *The Wit of Music,* in Kenin and Wintle, *DBQ;* 2: E. Fuller, *2500 Anecdotes;* 4: K. Edwards, *I Wish I'd Said That;* 5: A. Herbert, *A.P.H.*

SAROYAN 1: *Time,* Jan. 16, 1984

SATIE 1: O. Levant, *The Unimportance of Being Oscar;* 2: J. Williams, *The Magpie's Bagpipe*

SCARRON 1: W. Keddie, *Literary and Scientific Anecdote;* 2: H. and D. L. Thomas, *Living Biographies of Famous Women*

SCHEFFEL 1: H. Ziegler, *Heitere Muse*

SCHICK 1: L. Wolf, *Aphorisms and Facetiae of Bela Schick*

SCHILLINGER 1: N. Slonimsky, *A Thing or Two about Music*

SCHLEIERMACHER 1: H. Hoffmeister, *Anekdotenschatz*

SCHLIEMANN 1: W. Durant, *The Story of Civilization,* II

SCHNABEL 1: *Sunday Telegraph,* Apr. 11, 1982; 2: A. Faulkner and T. Hartman, *All the Best People*

SCHÖDL 1: M. Jelusisch, *Geschichten aus dem Wienerwald*

SCHÖLL 1–3: C. Skinner, *Elegant Wits and Grand Horizontals*

SCHÖNBEIN 1: J. Daintith et al., *Biographical Encyclopedia of Scientists*

SCHONBERG 2: R. Smullyan, *5000 B.C. and Other Philosophical Fantasies*

SCHOPENHAUER 1: W. Scholz, *Das Buch des Lachens;* 2: W. Durant, *The Story of Philosophy*

SCHUMANN-HEINK 1: L. Humphrey, *The Humor of Music;* 2: A. May, *Different Drummers;* 3: G. Lieberman, *The Greatest Laughs of All Time*

SCHWARTZ 1: B. Botkin, *Treasury of American Anecdotes*

SCHWARZENBERG 1–3: E. Crankshaw, *The Fall of the House of Hapsburg*

SCHWEITZER 1: A. Whitman, *Come to Judgment;* 2–3: J. Paar, *P.S. Jack Paar*

SCIPIO NASICA 1: E. Brewer, *Dictionary of Phrase and Fable*

SCOTT 1, 6: J. Timbs, *Century of Anecdote;* 2: D. George, *Book of Anecdotes;* 3: W. Keddie, *Literary and Scientific Anecdote;* 4: G. Davenport, *The Geography of the Imagination;*

5: P. Mahony, *Barbed Wit and Malicious Humor*

SCRIPPS 1: M. Eastman, *Great Companions*

SEBASTIANO 1: G. Vasari, *Lives of the Painters*

SEDGWICK, C., 1: J. Stein, *Edie*

SEDGWICK, J., 1: D. Frost, *Book of the World's Worst Decisions*

SEDGWICK, T., 1: J. Stein, *Edie*

SEDLEY 1: Kenin and Wintle, *DBQ*

SEELEY 1: J. Sutherland, ed., *OBLA*

SEFERIS 1: P. Levi, *The Hill of Kronos*

SELLERS 3: *Life*, August 1983; 4: J. McAleer, "Globe Man's Daily Story," *Boston Globe*, June 17, 1961

SELWYN 1, 3: *DNB*; 2: R. Hendrickson, *The Literary Life*; 4: J. Timbs, *Century of Anecdote*; 5: J. Jesse, *George Selwyn and his Contemporaries*; 6: W. Keddie, *Literary and Scientific Anecdote*

SENECA 1: V. Cronin, *The View from Planet Earth*

SERVETUS 1: E. Monegal and A. Reid, *Borges*

SÉVIGNÉ 1: M. Pedrazzini and J. Gris, *Autant en apportent les mots*

SEWARD 1: John Bigelow, *Retrospections of an Active Life*, in C. Shriner, *Wit, Wisdom, and Foibles of the Great*; 2: Frederic Bancroft, *Life of William H. Seward*, in Shriner, *Wit*

SHAFTESBURY 1: W. and A. Durant, *The Story of Civilization*, VIII; 2: *DNB*

SHAKESPEARE 1: J. Aubrey, *Brief Lives*; 2: J. Manningham, *Diary*; 3: E. K. Chambers, *William Shakespeare: A Study of Facts and Problems*, in J. Sutherland, ed., *OBLA*; 4: K. Arvine, *Cyclopaedia of Anecdotes*

SHARP 1: E. V. Lucas, *Reading, Writing and Remembering*, in J. Sutherland, ed., *OBLA*

SHAW, G., 1: Hesketh Pearson, *The Life of Oscar Wilde*, in J. Sutherland, ed., *OBLA*; 2: O. Levant, *The Unimportance of Being Oscar*; 3, 23: K. Edwards, *More Things I Wish I'd Said*; 4: St. John Ervine, *Bernard Shaw: His Life, Work, and Friends*; 5: H. Teichmann, *Smart Aleck*; 6: J. Smith, *Elsie de Wolfe*; 7: G. Lieberman, *The Greatest Laughs of All Time*; 8: *The Journals of Arnold Bennett, 1911–1921*, in J. Sutherland, ed., *OBLA*; 10: L. Russell, *English Wits*; 11, 13, 21: J. Braude, *Speaker's and Toastmaster's Handbook*; 12: B. Cerf, *Try and Stop Me*; 14: B. Cerf, *Shake Well Before Using*; 15: B. Cerf, *The Life of the Party*; 16: H. Pearson, *Lives of the Wits*; 17: N. McPhee, *Second Book of Insults*; 18: Oxfam, *Pass the Port*; 19: N. Rees, *Quote . . . Unquote*; 20: I. Wallace et al., *The Book of Lists 2*; 22: P. Mahony, *Barbed Wit and Malicious Humor*; 24: Y. Karsh, *Karsh*; 25: A. Barrow, *Gossip*; 27: J. McAleer, "Globe Man's Daily Story," *Boston Globe*, Aug. 3, 1963

SHAW, I., 1: B. Cerf, *The Life of the Party*

SHEARING 1: P. Bussard, *The New Catholic Treasury of Wit and Humor*; 2: J. McAleer, "Globe Man's Daily Story," *Boston Globe*, Aug. 23, 1962

SHEEN 1: J. Braude, *Speaker's and Toastmaster's Handbook*

SHELBURNE 1: W. and A. Durant, *The Story of Civilization, X*

SHELLEY, M., 2: I. Wallace, *The Square Pegs*

SHELLEY, P., 1: Thomas Jefferson Hogg, *The Life of Percy Bysshe Shelley*, in D. George, *A Book of Anecdotes*; 2: E. Trelawny, *Recollections of the Last Days of Shelley and Byron*

SHERIDAN, P., 1: D. Wallechinsky and I. Wallace, *The People's Almanac 2*; 2: Adapted from Maj. Alson B. Ostrander, *An Army Boy of the Sixties*, in B. Botkin, *Treasury of American Anecdotes*

SHERIDAN, R., 1: J. Timbs, *Century of Anecdote*; 2–3: L. Russell, *English Wits*; 4: H. Pearson, *Lives of the Wits*; 5–6: Walter Sichel, *Sheridan*, in C. Shriner, *Wit, Wisdom, and Foibles of the Great*; 7, 15: T. Moore, *Memoirs of the Life of the Rt. Hon. Richard Sheridan*; 8: E. Fuller, *2500 Anecdotes*; 9: R. Hendrickson, *The Literary Life*; 10: W. Keddie, *Literary and Scientific Anecdote*; 12: *Sheridaniana*, in J. Sutherland, ed., *OBLA*; 13, 16–17: L. Harris, *The Fine Art of Political Wit*; 14: N. McPhee, *Second Book of Insults*

SHERMAN 1: Melville D. Landon, *Eli Perkins: Thirty Years of Wit*, in R. Shenkman and K. Reiger, *One-Night Stands with American History*; 2: Washington Davis, *Campfire Chats of the Civil War*, in B. Botkin, *A Civil War Treasury*; 3: M. Ringo, *Nobody Said It Better*

SHI HUANGDI 1: P. Fitzgerald, *Ancient China*

SHOR 1: J. McCarthy, *Days and Nights at Costello's*; 2: E. Wilson, *Hot Times*; 3: R. Smith, *To Absent Friends From Red Smith*

SHUTER 1: *DNB*

SICKERT 1–2: O. Sitwell, *Noble Essences*

SIDDONS 1: J. Timbs, *Century of Anecdote*; 2: A. Cunningham, *Lives of the Most Eminent British Painters*; 3: J. Boswell, *Life of Johnson*; 4: K. Arvine, *Cyclopaedia of Anecdotes*; 5: J. Aye, *Humour in the Theatre*

SIDNEY 1: Fulke Greville (Lord Brooke) in D. George, *A Book of Anecdotes*

SIEYÈS 1: E. Guérard, *Dictionnaire Encyclopédique*

SIGISMUND 1: W. Seward, *Biographiana*, vol. 1

SILLS 1: W. Sargeant, *Divas*

SILVERMAN 1: *Los Angeles Times*, Aug. 25, 1981

SILVERS 1: W. Espy, *Another Almanac of Words at Play*

SIMON, J., 1: John Gunther, *Inside Europe*, in E. Kelen, *Peace in Their Time*

SIMON, R., 1: B. Cerf, *Good for a Laugh*

SINGER 1: D. Straus, *Under the Canopy;* 2: *The Times* (London), June 21, 1982

SITWELL, E., 1: C. Hassall, *Biography of Edward Marsh;* 2: O. Sitwell, *Tales My Father Taught Me;* 3: S. Spender, *World Within World;* 4: L. and M. Cowan, *The Wit of Women*

SITWELL, SIR G., 1–2: O. Sitwell, *Tales My Father Taught Me*

SKELTON, J., 1: J. Skelton, *Poems*

SKELTON, R., 1: H. Smith, *The Life and Legend of Gene Fowler*

SKINNER, C., 1: R. Hendrickson, *The Literary Life*

SLEZAK 1: L. Humphrey, *The Humor of Music*

SMITH, ADAM, 1: W. Keddie, *Literary and Scientific Anecdote*

SMITH, AL, 1: B. Botkin, *Treasury of American Anecdotes;* 2: L. Harris, *The Fine Art of Political Wit;* 3: J. Braude, *Speaker's and Toastmaster's Handbook*

SMITH, B., 1: D. Frost, *Book of the World's Worst Decisions*

SMITH, F. E., 1: J. Morris, *The Oxford Book of Oxford;* 2: *The Times* (London), January 8, 1982; 4: S. McCann, *The Wit of the Irish;* 5: K. Edwards, *I Wish I'd Said That;* 6, 9: N. Rees, *Quote . . . Unquote;* 8: H. Pearson, *Lives of the Wits*

SMITH, L., 1: J. Bartlett, *Familiar Quotations*

SMITH, S., 1: W. Espy, *Another Almanac of Words at Play;* 2: J. Timbs, *Century of Anecdote;* 3: Harriet Martineau, *Autobiography,* in J. Sutherland, ed., *OBLA;* 4–5, 12: H. Pearson, *Live of the Wits;* 6: *Oxford Dictionary of Quotations;* 7: *A Memoir of the Rev. Sydney Smith by his Daughter, Lady Holland,* in Sutherland, *OBLA;* 8: W. Adams, *Treasury of Modern Anecdote;* 9: J. Larwood, *Anecdotes of the Clergy;* 10: N. McPhee, *Second Book of Insults;* 11: Kenin and Wintle, *DBQ;* 13: M. Ringo, *Nobody Said It Better*

SMUTS 1: W. Vaughan-Thomas, *Madly in All Directions*

SMYTH 1: S. Spender, *World Within World*

SNEAD 1: S. Snead and A. Stump, *The Education of a Golfer*

SOBHUZA II 1: *The Times* (London), Aug. 25, 1982

SOCRATES 2: E. Guérard, *Dictionnaire Encyclopédique*

SOLOMON 1: Bible

SOLON 1: W. Durant, *The Story of Civilization,* II; 2: F. Paley, *Greek Wit*

SOMERSET 1: C. Roberts, *And So To Bath*

SOPHOCLES 1: *EB*

SOUTHEY 1: Thomas Jefferson Hogg, *The Life of*

Percy Bysshe Shelley, in J. Sutherland, ed., *OBLA*

SPAAK 1: M. and A. Guillois, *Liberté, Egalité, Hilarité*

SPEAIGHT 1: R. Morley, *Second Book of Bricks*

SPELLMAN 1: A. Whitman, *Come to Judgment*

SPENCER 1: W. Walsh, *Handy Book of Curious Information*

SPENSER 1: T. Fuller, ed., *Worthies of England;* 2: G. Colman, *Circle of Anecdote*

SPILLANE 1: *New York Times Book Review,* Dec. 27, 1981

SPOONER 1: J. Morris, *Oxford;* 3: Ronald Knox, *Literary Distractions,* in J. Sutherland, ed., *OBLA;* 4: A. Hare, *The Story of My Life*

SPURGEON 1: J. Ellis, *Spurgeon Anecdotes;* 2: J. Gere and J. Sparrow, *Geoffrey Madan's Notebooks*

SQUIRE 1: I. Brown, *A Charm of Names*

STAËL 1: J. Herold, *Mistress to an Age;* 2: J. Timbs, *Century of Anecdote;* 3: C. Fadiman, *Party of One;* 4: E. Guérard, *Dictionnaire Encyclopédique*

STAFFORD 1: *Publishers Weekly,* Jan. 8, 1982

STALIN 1: *Harper's Magazine,* December 1935, in J. Gunther, *Procession*

STANLEY 1: H. Stanley, *How I Found Livingstone*

STANTON, C., 1: J. Bartlett, *Familiar Quotations*

STANTON, E., 1: H. and D. L. Thomas, *Living Biographies of Famous Women*

STARK 1: C. Fadiman and C. Van Doren, *The American Treasury*

STEELE 1: G. Birkbeck Hill, ed., *Samuel Johnson — Lives of the English Poets,* in J. Sutherland, ed., *OBLA*

STEFFENS 1: Justin Kaplan, *Lincoln Steffens,* in D. Hall, ed., *OBALA*

STEIN 1: J. Mellow, *Charmed Circle;* 2: E. Hemingway, *A Moveable Feast;* 3: '47, *The Magazine of the Year* (October); 4: Jacques Lipchitz and H. H. Arnason, *My Life in Sculpture,* in Mellow, *Charmed Circle;* 5: B. Cerf, *Try and Stop Me;* 6: I. Wallace et al., *Intimate Sex Lives of Famous People;* 7: N. Rorem, *Late Diaries*

STEINBECK 1, 5: J. Benson, *True Adventures of John Steinbeck, Writer;* 2: *Book-of-the-Month Club News,* May 1947; 3: B. Conrad, *Fun While It Lasted*

STEINBERG 1: L. Humphrey, *The Humor of Music*

STEINMETZ 1: C. Fadiman, *Party of One*

STENGEL 1: B. Cerf, *Shake Well Before Using;* 3: R. Crouser, *It's Unlucky to Be Behind at the End of the Game*

STERNE 1: W. Scott, *Laurence Sterne*

STEVENS 1: G. Vidal, *Lincoln;* 2: R. Marquard, *Jokes and Anecdotes;* 3: T. W. Lloyd, *The Green Bag,* July 1904, in C. Shriner, *Wit,*

Wisdom, and Foibles of the Great

STEVENSON, A., 1, 4–5: A. Cooke, *Six Men;* 2: *Los Angeles Times,* Nov. 25, 1983; 3, 6–7: B. Adler, *The Stevenson Wit;* 8: M. and A. Guillois, *Liberté, Egalité, Hilarité*

STEVENSON, R., 1: J. Braude, *Speaker's and Toastmaster's Handbook*

STILLMAN 1: C. Fadiman and C. Van Doren, *The American Treasury*

STOKOWSKI 1: B. Cerf, *Try and Stop Me;* 2: H. Kupferberg, *Those Fabulous Philadelphians*

STOUT 2–3: *The New Yorker,* July 16, 1949

STOWE 1: D. Wallechinsky and I. Wallace, *The People's Almanac;* 2: C. Madigan and A. Elwood, *Brainstorms and Thunderbolts*

STRACHEY 1: O. Sitwell, *Noble Essences;* 2–3: M. Holroyd, *Lytton Strachey;* 4: C. Fadiman, *Any Number Can Play*

STRAUSS 1: B. Grun, *Gold and Silver*

STRAVINSKY 1: Gabriel Astruc, *Le Pavillon des Fantômes,* in F. Steegmuller, *Cocteau;* 2, 4, 10–11: P. Horgan, *Encounters with Stravinsky;* 3: BBC Radio 4, July 5, 1982; 5, 8: O. Levant, *The Unimportance of Being Oscar;* 6: C. Gattey, *The Elephant That Swallowed a Nightingale;* 9: N. Slonimsky, *Lexicon of Musical Invective;* 12: G. Balanchine and F. Mason, *Balanchine's Complete Stories of the Great Ballets;* 13: W. Wiser, *The Crazy Years;* 14: J. Braude, *Speaker's and Toastmaster's Handbook*

STUART 1: Maj. Henry Kyd Douglas, *I Rode with Stonewall,* in B. Botkin, *A Civil War Treasury*

STUBBS 1: William Camden, *Annales,* in J. Sutherland, ed., *OBLA*

SUDERMANN 1: H. Hoffmeister, *Anekdotenschatz*

SULLIVAN, SIR A., 1: E. Fuller, *2500 Anecdotes*

SUMNER 1: George F. Hoar, *The North American Review,* January 1878, in C. Shriner, *Wit, Wisdom, and Foibles of the Great*

SUSANN 1–3: I. Mansfield, *Life with Jackie*

SUVOROV 1: *Harper's Magazine,* February 1852, in C. Shriner, *Wit, Wisdom, and Foibles of the Great*

SVYATOPOLK 1: W. Durant, *The Story of Civilization,* IV

SWANSON 1: J. Humes, *Speakers' Treasury*

SWEDENBORG 1: Caroline Fox, *Journal,* June 6, 1842, in D. George, *A Book of Anecdotes*

SWIFT 1: Thomas Sheridan, *The Life of the Rev. Dr. Jonathan Swift,* in J. Sutherland, ed., *OBLA;* 2: E. Fuller, *2500 Anecdotes;* 3–4: G. Colman, *Circle of Anecdote;* 5–6: H. Pearson, *Lives of the Wits*

SWINBURNE 1: O. Sitwell, *Noble Essences*

SZELL 1: H. Temianka, *Facing the Music*

SZENT-GYÖRGYI 1: C. Fadiman, *Any Number Can Play*

SZILARD 1: F. Crick, *Life Itself*

TAFT, L., 1: J. Braude, *Speaker's and Toastmaster's Handbook*

TAFT, W., 3: Lewis Henry, *Humorous Anecdotes about Famous People,* in P. Boller, ed., *Presidential Anecdotes*

TALLEYRAND-PÉRIGORD 1, 6: J. Timbs, *Century of Anecdote;* 2: J. Humes, *Speakers' Treasury;* 3–4: M. Pedrazzini and J. Gris, *Autant en apportent les mots;* 5: Oxfam, *Pass the Port;* 7: E. Fuller, *2500 Anecdotes;* 8: W. Adams, *Treasury of Modern Anecdote;* 9: W. Keddie, *Literary and Scientific Anecdote;* 10, 14: C. Brinton, *The Lives of Talleyrand;* 11: A. Duff Cooper, *Talleyrand;* 12: K. Edwards, *I Wish I'd Said That;* 15: F. Mitterrand, *The Wheat and the Chaff*

TAMAGNO 1: E. Fuller, *2500 Anecdotes*

TAMIRIS 1: R. Lewis, *Slings and Arrows*

TAYLOR, E., 1: K. Kelley, *Elizabeth Taylor: The Last Star*

TAYLOR, J., 1: *Boswelliana,* in D. George, *A Book of Anecdotes*

TAYLOR, M., 1: J. Keegan, *Six Armies in Normandy*

TECUMSEH 1: Arthur Wallace Dunn, *From Harrison to McKinley,* in P. Boller, ed., *Presidential Anecdotes*

TELFORD 1: E. Lucas, *A Fronded Isle*

TEMPLE 1: Oxfam, *Pass the Port*

TENG SHIH 1: W. Durant, *The Story of Civilization,* I

TENNYSON 1, 3: W. R. Nicoll and T. J. Wise, eds., *Literary Anecdotes of the Nineteenth Century,* in R. Martin, *Tennyson: The Unquiet Heart;* 2: G. W. Smalley, *Studies of Man,* in Martin, *Tennyson;* 4, 9: Sir Charles Tennyson, *Alfred Tennyson,* in J. Sutherland, ed., *OBLA;* 5: *The Gladstone Papers,* in Martin, *Tennyson;* 6: E. F. Benson, *As We Were: A Victorian Peep Show,* in Martin, *Tennyson;* 7: J. Train, *True Remarkable Occurrences*

TERESA OF AVILA 1: P. Bussard, *The New Catholic Treasury of Wit and Humor*

TERRY 1: D. Gill, *The Book of the Piano;* 2: *The Times* (London), June 12, 1982

TETRAZZINI 1: C. Gattey, *The Elephant That Swallowed a Nightingale*

THACKERAY 1: E. Fuller, *2500 Anecdotes;* 2: P. Porzelt, *The Metropolitan Club of New York;* 3: H. Prochnow, *The Public Speaker's Treasure Chest*

THALBERG 1: J. Adamson, *Groucho, Harpo, Chico;* 2–3: B. Thomas, *Thalberg: Life and Legend*

THALES 1–2: *EB;* 3: Plato, *Theaetetus;* 4: Plutarch, *Lives;* 5: W. Durant, *The Story of Civilization,* II

THATCHER 1: *Los Angeles Times,* Apr. 21, 1981

THEMISTOCLES 1: Plutarch, *Lives;* 2: R. Marquard, *Jokes and Anecdotes*

THEODORIC 1: E. Guérard, *Dictionnaire Encyclopédique*

THIBAUD 1–2: H. Temianka, *Facing the Music*

THIERS 1: J. Timbs, *Century of Anecdote*

THOMAS, D., 1: A. Bespaloff, *The Fireside Book of Wine;* 2: D. Hall, *Remembering Poets;* 3: A. Sinclair, *Dylan Thomas*

THOMAS, E., 1: *New Criterion,* December 1982

THOMAS, N., 1–4: A. Whitman, *Come to Judgment*

THOMSON, SIR G., 1: J. Daintith et al., *Biographical Encyclopedia of Scientists*

THOMSON, J., 1: J. Dunbar, *J. M. Barrie*

THOREAU 1, 7: M. Saxton, *Louisa May;* 2: H. Thoreau, *Journal,* October 27, 1853; 3: Thoreau, *Journal,* September 8, 1859; 4: C. Fadiman and C. Van Doren, *The American Treasury;* 5: article by Ralph Waldo Emerson in *The Atlantic Monthly,* 1862, in D. Hall, ed., *OBALA;* 6: E. Chubb, *Sketches of Great Painters*

THURBER 1, 10: C. Holmes, *The Clocks of Columbus;* 2: B. Cerf, *Good for a Laugh;* 3–4: B. Bernstein, *Thurber, A Biography;* 5: N. Johnson, letter to Groucho Marx; 7: E. Fuller, *2500 Anecdotes*

THURLOW 1, 4: W. Adams, *Treasury of Modern Anecdote;* 2–3: L. Missen, *After-dinner Stories and Anecdotes*

TINTORETTO 1: H. Morton, *A Traveller in Italy*

TITIAN 1: D. Wallechinsky and I. Wallace, *The People's Almanac*

TOLSTOY 1: *"Daily Mirror" Old Codger's Little Black Book 4*

TOOKE 1: K. Arvine, *Cyclopaedia of Anecdotes;* 2: Lord Broughton, *Recollections of a Long Life,* in Kenin and Wintle, *DBQ*

TOSCANINI 1: L. Humphrey, *The Humor of Music;* 2: C. Fadiman and C. Van Doren, *The American Treasury;* 3: S. Beach, *Musicdotes;* 5: BBC Radio (Desert Island Discs, March 5, 1982); 6: H. Taubman, *The Maestro;* 7–9: H. Taubman, *Music on My Beat;* 10: J. Braude, *Speaker's and Toastmaster's Handbook*

TOSTI 1: V. Seligman, *Puccini among Friends*

TOWNSHEND 1: Sir James Prior, *Life of Edmond Malone . . . with Selections from his MSS ANECDOTES,* in J. Sutherland, ed., *OBLA*

TRACY 1: R. Byrne, *The 637 Best Things Anybody Ever Said;* 3: *People,* July 1978

TRAVERS 1–2: A. Leslie, *The Remarkable Mr. Jerome*

TREE 1: H. Teichmann, *Smart Aleck;* 2: D. Cecil, *Max;* 4: K. Brownlow, *Hollywood: The Pioneers;* 5: E. Fuller, *2500 Anecdotes;* 6, 8: J. Braude, *Speaker's and Toastmaster's Handbook;* 7: J. Aye, *Humour in the Theatre*

TRENCH 1–2: L. Missen, *Quotable Anecdotes*

TRILLING 1: W. Espy, *Another Almanac of Words at Play*

TROLLOPE, A., 1–2, 4: M. Sadleir, *Trollope: A Commentary;* 3: A. Trollope, *Autobiography*

TROLLOPE, F., 1: M. Sadleir, *Trollope: A Commentary;* 2: *Outlook,* July 21, 1923

TROTSKY 1: G. Mikes, *Coffee Houses of Europe*

TROY 1: D. Wallechinsky and I. Wallace, *The People's Almanac*

TRUDEAU, E., 1: H. and D. L. Thomas, *Living Adventures In Science*

TRUMAN 1: J. Lash, *Eleanor and Franklin;* 2: F. Muir, *Irreverent Social History;* 3: J. B. West, *Upstairs at the White House,* in P. Boller, ed., *Presidential Anecdotes;* 4: "Free to Choose," *The New Republic,* CLXXX, March 22, 1980, in Boller, *Presidential Anecdotes;* 5: Merle Miller, *Plain Speaking,* in Boller, *Presidential Anecdotes;* 7: *Los Angeles Times,* Aug. 14, 1983

TRUTH 1: P. Smith, *Trial By Fire*

TURNER 1: G. Painter, *Proust: The Early Years;* 2: W. Frith, *My Autobiography;* 3–4: E. Chubb, *Sketches of Great Painters;* 5–6: D. Piper, *Painting in England*

TWAIN 1, 4, 8, 11, 22: A. Paine, *Mark Twain;* 2: B. Cerf, *Good For a Laugh;* 3: R. Hendrickson, *The Literary Life;* 5: B. Cerf, *Try and Stop Me;* 6: B. Cerf, *Shake Well Before Using;* 7: L. Copeland, *10,000 Jokes, Toasts, and Stories;* 9, 13, 15–16, 20: E. Fuller, *2500 Anecdotes;* 10, 23: J. Kaplan, *Mr. Clemens, and Mark Twain;* 12: C. Clemens, *My Father Mark Twain;* 14: Stanley Weintraub, *The London Yankees,* in D. Hall, ed., *OBALA;* 17: D. Wallechinsky, I. and A. Wallace, *The Book of Lists;* 18: H. Prochnow, *Public Speaker's Treasure Chest;* 19: J. Nash, *Zanies*

UCCELLO 1: T. Craven, *Men of Art*

UNTERMEYER 1: R. Hendrickson, *The Literary Life;* 2: S. Harris, *Pieces of Eight*

UNZELMANN 1: W. Durant, *The Story of Philosophy*

USTINOV 1: H. Vickers, *Great Operatic Disasters*

VAN BUREN 1: Holmes Alexander, *The American Talleyrand: The Career and Contemporaries of Martin Van Buren,* in P. Boller, ed., *Presidential Anecdotes*

VANDERBILT, A., 1: D. Wallechinsky and I. Wallace, *The People's Almanac*

VANDERBILT, C., 1, 3: S. Holbrook, *The Age of the Moguls;* 2: A. May, *Different Drummers*

VANDERBILT, W., 1: Frank Crowninshield, "The House of Vanderbilt," in *Vogue's First Reader,* in B. Botkin, *Treasury of American Anecdotes;* 2: M. Ringo, *Nobody Said It Better;* 3: B. Conrad, *Famous Last Words*

VAN DOREN 1: B. Cerf, *Shake Well Before Using;* 2: J. Humes, *Speakers' Treasury*

VARAH 1: C. Varah, *Samaritans in the 70s*

VATEL 1: D. Wallechinsky and I. Wallace, *The People's Almanac*

VEGA CARPIO 1: R. Byrne, *The 637 Best Things Anybody Ever Said*

VERDI 1: V. Seligman, *Puccini Among Friends;* 2: N. Slonimksy, *A Thing or Two about Music*

VERLAINE 1: J. Bayard, *The Latin Quarter Past and Present*

VERRALL 1: E. Marsh, *A Number of People*

VESEY 1: *DNB*

VESPASIAN 1: Suetonius, *The Twelve Caesars;* 2: W. Durant, *The Story of Civilization,* III

VICTOR AMADEUS II 1: J. Papesch, *Europa Lächelt Noch Immer*

VICTORIA 1, 5: J. Adair, *The Royal Palaces of Great Britain;* 2, 7: H. and D. L. Thomas, *Living Biographies of Famous Rulers;* 3, 6: D. Cecil, *Melbourne;* 4: Lord Gower, *Records and Reminiscences;* in C. Shriner, *Wit, Wisdom, and Foibles of the Great;* 8: D. Duff, *Albert and Victoria;* 9: J. Paar, *P.S. Jack Paar;* 10: A. R. Mills, *Two Victorian Ladies,* in A. Hardy, *Queen Victoria Was Amused;* 11: Frederick Ponsonby, *Recollections of Three Reigns,* in Hardy, *Queen Victoria;* 12: B. Cerf, *The Life of the Party;* 13: V. Cowles, *The Kaiser;* 14: J. Bone, *The London Perambulator;* 15: Arthur H. Bevan, *Popular Royalty,* in Hardy, *Queen Victoria;* 16: E. Fuller, *2500 Anecdotes;* 17: P. Ziegler, *Diana Cooper*

VIDAL 1: A. Powell, *The Strangers Are All Gone*

VILLA 1: R. Byrne, *The 637 Best Things Anybody Ever Said*

VILLIERS DE L'ISLE-ADAM 1: J. Bayard, *The Latin Quarter Past and Present*

VIRCHOW 1: E. Fuller, *2500 Anecdotes;* 2: R. Calder, *Medicine and Man;* 3: H. Hoffmeister, *Anekdotenschatz*

VOLTAIRE 1: J. Papesch, *Europa Lächelt Noch Immer;* 2: L. Russell, *English Wits;* 3: N. Mitford, *Voltaire in Love;* 4, 10: E. Fuller, *2500 Anecdotes;* 5–6: B. Cerf, *Try and Stop Me;* 7: W. and A. Durant, *The Story of Civilization,* IX; 8: W. Scholz, *Das Buch des Lachens;* 9: E. Kelen, *Peace in Their Time;* 11: W. Ukers, *All About Coffee;* 12: W. Durant, *The Story of Philosophy;* 13–14: Dugas de Bois St. Just, *Paris, Versailles et les pro-*

vinces; 15: H. and D. L. Thomas, *Living Biographies of the Great Philosophers*

WADDELL 1: B. Cerf, *Bumper Crop of Anecdotes*

WALKER 1: C. Fadiman and C. Van Doren, *The American Treasury*

WALLER 1: L. Missen, *Quotable Anecdotes*

WALN 1: I. and R. Poley, *Friendly Anecdotes*

WALPOLE, H., 1: R. Ketton-Cremer, *Horace Walpole*

WALPOLE, SIR R., 1: *Blackwood's Edinburgh Magazine,* April 1868, in C. Shriner, *Wit, Wisdom, and Foibles of the Great;* 2: K. Balderston, ed., *Thraliana*

WALTER 1: E. Fuller, *2500 Anecdotes*

WALTON 1: O. Sitwell, *Laughter in the Next Room;* 2: *The Observer,* Feb. 7, 1982

WARBURTON 1: J. Bartlett, *Familiar Quotations*

WARD 1: *The Complete Works of Artemus Ward,* in B. Botkin, *Treasury of American Anecdotes;* 2: J. Kaplan, *Mark Twain and His World*

WARNER 1: L. Cannon, *Reagan;* 2: D. Niven, *Bring on the Empty Horses*

WASHINGTON 1: M. Weems, *Life of Washington;* 2: William Gordon, *History of the Independence of the United States,* in P. Boller, ed., *Presidential Anecdotes;* 3: P. Hood, *World of Anecdote;* 4: P. Smith, *A New Age Now Begins;* 5: E. Fuller, *2500 Anecdotes;* 6: Paul Wilstach, *Patriots Off Their Pedestals,* in Boller, *Presidential Anecdotes;* 7: Freeman Hunt, *American Anecdotes,* in Boller, *Presidential Anecdotes;* 8: B. Botkin, *Treasury of American Anecdotes;* 9: Francis R. Bellamy, *The Private Life of George Washington,* in Boller, *Presidential Anecdotes;* 10: Paul L. Ford, *The True George Washington,* in Boller, *Presidential Anecdotes*

WATERTON 1: E. Sitwell, *English Eccentrics*

WATSON 1: L. Missen, *After-dinner Stories and Anecdotes*

WATT 1: W. and A. Durant, *The Story of Civilization,* X

WATTERSON 1: B. Botkin, *Treasury of American Anecdotes*

WAUGH 1: N. Rees, *Quote . . . Unquote;* 2: H. Acton, *More Memoirs of an Aesthete;* 3: R. Claiborne, *Our Marvelous Native Tongue;* 5–6: J. Epstein, "Evelyn Waugh," *New Criterion,* 3, April 1985

WAVELL 1: B. Fergusson, *Wavell*

WEBB 1: L. Missen, *Quotable Anecdotes*

WEBSTER, D., 1–2: C. Lanman, *The Private Life of Daniel Webster;* 3: B. Botkin, *Treasury of American Anecdotes;* 4: *Oxford Dictionary of Quotations;* 5, 7; P. Harvey, *Reminiscences of Daniel Webster;* 6, 9: C. Fuess,

WEBSTER (*continued*)
  Daniel Webster; 8: V. Brooks, *Life of Emerson;* 10: Richard Lathers, *Reminiscences,* in C. Shriner, *Wit, Wisdom, and Foibles of the Great*
WEBSTER, N., 1: R. Marquard, *Jokes and Anecdotes*
WEISSMULLER 1: M. Ringo, *Nobody Said It Better;* 2: D. Wallechinsky, *The Complete Book of the Olympics*
WEIZMANN 1: R. St. John, *They Came From Everywhere*
WELLES 1: M. Korda, *Charmed Lives*
WELLINGTON 1: J. Timbs, *Century of Anecdote;* 2: *Records of the Conferences between Wellington and Scindiak after the Battle of Assaye,* in D. George, *A Book of Anecdotes;* 3, 5: A. Bryant, *The Age of Elegance;* 4: N. McPhee, *Second Book of Insults;* 6: George, *Anecdotes;* 7: D. Duff, *Albert and Victoria;* 8: H. Hoffmeister, *Anekdotenschatz;* 9–10: N. McPhee, *Second Book of Insults;* 11: E. Fuller, *2500 Anecdotes;* 12: M. Garland, *The Changing Face of Childhood;* 13, 16: William Fraser, *Words of Wellington,* in C. Shriner, *Wit, Wisdom, and Foibles of the Great;* 14: *The New Yorker,* Mar. 10, 1951
WELLS 1: E. Fuller, *2500 Anecdotes;* 2: H. Nicolson, *Diaries;* 3: C. Snow, *Variety of Men*
WERFEL 1: I. Wallace et al., *Intimate Sex Lives of Famous People*
WESLEY 1: H. and D. L. Thomas, *Living Biographies of Religious Leaders;* 2: E. Fuller, *2500 Anecdotes*
WEST, M., 1: K. Edwards, *I Wish I'd Said That Too*
WEST, R., 1: B. Cerf, *Shake Well Before Using;* 2: G. P. Wells, *H. G. Wells in Love;* 3: *Times Literary Supplement,* Oct. 1, 1982
WESTINGHOUSE 1: W. Walsh, *Handy Book of Curious Information*
WHARTON 1: E. Wharton, *A Backward Glance*
WHEELER 1: P. Smith, *The Rise of Industrial America*
WHEWELL 1: L. Missen, *Quotable Anecdotes;* 2: W. Keddie, *Literary and Scientific Anecdote*
WHISTLER 1–2: L. Russell, *English Wits;* 3: K. Edwards, *I Wish I'd Said That Too;* 4, 7–8, 12–13, 17: D. Seitz, *Whistler Stories;* 5: B. Cerf, *The Life of the Party;* 6: P. Mahony, *Barbed Wit and Malicious Humor;* 9: L. and F. Copeland, *10,000 Jokes, Toasts and Stories;* 10: H. Pearson, *The Man Whistler;* 11: H. Gerwig, *Fifty Famous Painters;* 14: J. Whistler, *On the Gentle Art of Making Enemies;* 15: J. Braude, *Speaker's and Toastmaster's Handbook;* 16: E. Fuller, *2500 Anecdotes;* 18: D. Wallechinsky, I. and A. Wallace, *The Book of Lists 2*

WHITE, A., 1: D. Wallechinsky and I. Wallace, *The People's Almanac*
WHITE, W., 1: *Book-of-the-Month Club News,* April 1944
WHITEHEAD 1: *American Scholar,* XVI, no. 1 (1946–47)
WHITELAW 1: R. Morley, *Second Book of Bricks*
WHITMAN 1: C. Fadiman and C. Van Doren, *The American Treasury*
WHITNEY 1: P. Smith, *The Nation Comes of Age*
WIENIAWSKI 1: N. Slonimsky, *A Thing or Two about Music*
WILD 1: H. Bagust, *London Through the Ages*
WILDE 1: Miss Joyce Hawkins, in J. Sutherland, ed., *OBLA;* 2: Hesketh Pearson, *The Life of Oscar Wilde,* in Sutherland, *OBLA;* 3, 9, 13; H. Pearson, *Lives of the Wits;* 4: Sir William Rothenstein, *Men and Memories,* in Sutherland, *OBLA;* 5: R. Marquard, *Jokes and Anecdotes;* 6: B. Cerf, *Shake Well Before Using;* 7: J. Bartlett, *Familiar Quotations;* 8: Walter Jerrold, *A Book of Famous Wits,* in Sutherland, *OBLA;* 10: G. Brandreth, *Great Theatrical Disasters;* 11: G. Mikes, *Laughing Matter;* 12: A. Hare, *The Story of My Life;* 14: N. McPhee, *Book of Insults;* 16: W. Yeats, *Autobiograhies;* 17: D. Wallechinsky and I. Wallace, *The People's Almanac;* 18: *Time,* Jan. 16, 1984
WILDER 1–5: T. Wood, *The Bright Side of Billy Wilder, Primarily*
WILKES 1: L. Russell, *English Wits;* 2: E. Fuller, *2500 Anecdotes;* 3–4: J. Timbs, *Century of Anecdote;* 5: R. Postgate, *That Devil Wilkes;* 6: P. Stockdale, *Memoirs of the Life and Writings of P. Stockdale*
WILLARD 1: H. and D. L. Thomas, *Living Biographies of Famous Women*
WILLES 1: Lord Campbell, *Lives of the Chief Justices,* in D. George, *A Book of Anecdotes*
WILLIAM I (ENGLAND) 1: *DNB*
WILLIAM I (PRUSSIA) 1: W. Scholz, *Das Buch des Lachens;* 2: F. Syben, *Preussische Anekdoten*
WILLIAM II (GERMANY) 1: E. Benson, *The Kaiser and English Relations*
WILLIAM III (ENGLAND) 1: J. H. Jesse, *England under the House of Hanover,* in C. Shriner, *Wit, Wisdom, and Foibles of the Great*
WILLIAMS 1: J. Rosner, *A Hater's Handbook;* 2–3: D. Spoto, *The Kindness of Strangers;* 4: I. Barmash, *Life and Times of Benjamin Sonnenberg*
WILSON, C., 1: P. Smith, *The Rise of Industrial America*
WILSON, E., 1: A. Whitman, *Come to Judgment*
WILSON, SIR H., 2: BBC Radio 4, Oct. 23, 1984
WILSON, H., 1: *Harriette Wilson's Memoirs of Herself and Others,* in J. Sutherland, ed., *OBLA*

WILSON, R., 1: D. Piper, *Painting in England*

WILSON, W., 1: J. Humes, *Speakers' Treasury;* 2: Bill Adler, ed., *Presidential Wit from Washington to Johnson,* in P. Boller, ed., *Presidential Anecdotes;* 4–5: E. Fuller, *2500 Anecdotes*

WINTERS 1: *Los Angeles Times,* March 24, 1984

WISE 1: J. Braude, *Braude's Second Encyclopedia*

WODEHOUSE 1: F. Donaldson, *Freddy Lonsdale;* 2: F. Donaldson, *P. G. Wodehouse;* 3: B. Nichols, *The Sweet Twenties*

WOFFINGTON 1: E. Guérard, *Dictionnaire Encyclopédique*

WOLF 1: P. Mahony, *Barbed Wit and Malicious Humor*

WOLFE 1: M. Ringo, *Nobody Said It Better*

WOODBRIDGE 1: *The Observer,* March 5, 1972

WOOLLCOTT 2: J. Nash, *The Innovators;* 3: I. Mansfield, *Life With Jackie;* 4: M. Hart, *Act One;* 5: O. Levant, *The Unimportance of Being Oscar;* 6: H. Teichmann, *Smart Aleck,* 7: J. Braude, *Braude's Second Encyclopedia;* 8: J. McAleer, "Globe Man's Daily Story," *Boston Globe,* Dec. 16, 1962

WORDSWORTH 1: F. Muir, *Irreverent Social History;* 2: L. Missen, *Quotable Anecdotes;* 3: E. Marsh, *A Number of People*

WREN 1: N. Lo Bello, *European Detours*

WRIGHT, F., 1: The Johnson Foundation

WRIGHT, O., 1: H. Thomas, *Living Adventures in Science*

WYCHERLEY 1: J. Spence, *Anecdotes*

WYLIE 1: Virginia Spencer Carr, *The Lonely Hunter: A Biography of Carson McCullers,* in D. Hall, ed., *OBALA*

XERXES 1: E. Fuller, *2500 Anecdotes;* 2: D. George, *A Book of Anecdotes*

YEATS 1: L. MacNeice, *The Strings Are False;* 2: M. Cowley, *The View from 80*

YUSUPOV 1: S. Marx, *Mayer and Thalberg*

ZANGWILL 1: A. Thwaite, *Waiting for the Party;* 2: W. Novak and M. Waldoks, *Big Book of Jewish Humor;* 4: P. Mahony, *Barbed Wit and Malicious Humor*

ZENO 1: W. Durant, *The Story of Civilization,* II

ZEUXIS 1: T. Fuller, *The Holy State*

ZIEGFELD 1: S. Allen, *Funny People*

❧ BIBLIOGRAPHY ❧

This bibliography is divided into two sections: Books; and Periodicals, Radio Programs, and Television Shows. In many instances old or classical references do not have specific publication data.

BOOKS

ABBOT, WILLIS J. *Notable Women in History*. Philadelphia: Winston, 1913.

ABDY, JANE, AND CHARLOTTE GRERE. *The Souls*. London: Sidgwick & Jackson, 1984.

ACE, GOODMAN. *The Book of Little Knowledge: More Than You Want to Know about Television*. New York: Simon & Schuster, 1955.

ACKROYD, PETER. *T. S. Eliot*. New York: Simon & Schuster, 1984.

ACTON, HAROLD. *Memoirs of an Aesthete, 1939–1969*. London: Methuen, 1948.

ACTON, HAROLD. *More Memoirs of an Aesthete*. London: Methuen, 1970.

ACTON, HAROLD. *Nancy Mitford: A Memoir*. New York: Harper & Row, 1975.

ADAIR, JOHN. *The Royal Palaces of Great Britain*. London: Thames & Hudson, 1981.

ADAMS, ANSEL. *Ansel Adams: An Autobiography*. Boston: New York Graphic Society/Little, Brown, 1985.

ADAMS, W. DAVENPORT. *Treasury of Modern Anecdote*. London: Thomas D. Morison, 1886.

ADAMSON, JOE. *Groucho, Harpo, Chico and Sometimes Zeppo: A History of the Marx Brothers and a Satire on the Rest of the World*. New York: Simon & Schuster, 1984.

ADLER, BILL. *My Favorite Funny Story, by Billy Graham . . . and Others*. New York: Four Winds Press, 1967.

ADLER, BILL. *The Stevenson Wit*. New York: Doubleday, 1966.

ADLER, BILL. *The Wit and Wisdom of Billy Graham*. Tadworth, England: World's Work, 1968.

ADLER, BILL, AND BILL ADLER, JR. *The Reagan Wit*. Aurora, IL: Caroline House, 1981.

ADLER, MORTIMER J. *Philosopher at Large: An Intellectual Biography*. New York: Macmillan, 1977.

AGATE, JAMES. *Rachel*. New York: Viking, 1928.

ALEXANDER, SHANA. *Talking Woman*. New York: Delacorte, 1976.

ALIFANO, ROBERTO. *Twenty-four Conversations with Borges*. New York: Grove Press, 1984.

ALLEN, STEVE. *Funny People*. New York: Stein & Day, 1981.

ALLEN, WALTER E. *As I Walked Down New Grub Street: Memories of a Writing Life*. Chicago: University of Chicago Press, 1981.

ALSOP, EM BOWLES, ed. *The Greatness of Woodrow Wilson, 1856–1956*. New York: Rinehart, 1956.

ALSOP, SUSAN MARY. *Yankees at the Court: The First Americans in Paris*. New York: Doubleday, 1982.

American Jest Book, 1789.

ANDERSON, DAVE. *The Red Smith Reader*. New York: Random House, 1982.

ANSON, ROBERT SAM. *Exile: The Unquiet Oblivion of Richard M. Nixon*. New York: Simon & Schuster, 1984.

ARDOIN, JOHN LOUIS, AND GERALD FITZGERALD. *Callas*. New York: Holt, Rinehart & Winston, 1974.

ARENDT, HANNAH. *Men in Dark Times*. New York: Harcourt, Brace, & World, 1968.

ARLEN, MICHAEL J. *Exiles*. New York: Farrar, Straus & Giroux, 1970.

ARLOTT, JOHN. *Cricket: The Great Ones*. London: Pelham Books, 1967.

ARLOTT, JOHN. *John Arlott's Book of Cricketers*. London: Sphere, 1982.

ARNOLD, THURMAN. *Fair Fights and Foul: A Dissenting Lawyer's Life*. New York: Harcourt, Brace & World, 1965.

ARVINE, KAZLITT. *Cyclopaedia of Anecdotes of Literature and the Fine Arts*. Boston: Gould and Lincoln, 1851. Rpt., Gale Research Co., Detroit, 1967.

ASIMOV, ISAAC. *Asimov's Biographical Encyclopedia of Science and Technology*. New York: Doubleday, 1964.

ASIMOV, ISAAC. *Isaac Asimov's Treasury of Humor.* Boston: Houghton Mifflin, 1971.

ASLET, CLIVE. *The Last Country Houses.* New Haven: Yale University Press, 1982.

ASQUITH, CYNTHIA. *Diaries 1915–1918,* ed. E. M. Horsley. New York: Knopf, 1969.

ASQUITH, CYNTHIA. *Portrait of Barrie.* New York: Dutton, 1955.

Asser's Life of King Alfred, ed. W. H. Stevenson. London: Oxford University Press, 1959.

ATHERTON, GERTRUDE FRANKLIN. *Adventures of a Novelist.* New York: Liveright, 1932.

ATKINS, HAROLD, AND ARCHIE NEWMAN, eds. *Beecham Stories: Anecdotes, Sayings and Impressions of Sir Thomas Beecham.* New York: St. Martin's, 1979.

AUBREY, JOHN. *Brief Lives and Other Selected Writings.* Rpt., New York: Scribner, 1949.

AUBREY, JOHN. *Miscellanies,* ed. John Buchanan-Brown. Rpt., Arundel, England: Centaur Press, 1972.

AYE, JOHN. *Humour in the Theatre.* London: Universal Publications Ltd., 1932.

BAER, JEAN. *The Self-Chosen: "Our Crowd" Is Dead — Long Live "Our Crowd!"* New York: Priam/Arbor House, 1984.

BAGUST, HAROLD. *London Through the Ages.* Cheltenham, England: Thornhill Press, 1982.

BAILLÉN, CLAUDE. *Chanel Solitaire.* New York: Quadrangle/New York Times Books, 1974.

BAIR, DEIRDRE. *Samuel Beckett: A Biography.* London: Jonathan Cape, 1978.

BAKER, RICHARD. *Richard Baker's Music Guide.* North Pomfret, VT: David & Charles, 1979.

BALDERSTON, KATHERINE C., ed. *Thraliana: The Diary of Mrs. Hester Lynch Thrale (Later Mrs. Piozzi) 1776–1809.* Oxford: Clarendon Press, 1942.

BALANCHINE, GEORGE, AND FRANCIS MASON. *Balanchine's Complete Stories of the Great Ballets.* Revised and enlarged ed., New York: Doubleday, 1977.

BALSDON, DACRE. *Oxford Now and Then.* New York: St. Martin's, 1970.

BARKER, EDMUND HENRY. *Literary Recollections and Contemporary Reminiscences of Professor Porson and Others.* London: J. R. Smith, 1852.

BARMASH, ISADORE. *"Always Live Better Than Your Clients": The Fabulous Life and Times of Benjamin Sonnenberg, America's Great Publicist.* New York: Dodd, Mead, 1983.

BARNETT, CORRELLI. *Bonaparte.* London: Allen & Unwin, 1978.

BARROW, ANDREW. *Gossip.* London: Hamish Hamilton, 1978.

BARTLETT, JOHN. *Familiar Quotations.* 14th, 15th eds., Boston: Little, Brown, 1968, 1980.

BARZUN, JACQUES. *A Stroll with William James.* New York: Harper & Row, 1983.

BAYARD, JEAN EMILE. *The Latin Quarter, Past and Present,* trans. Percy Mitchell. New York: Brentano's, 1927.

BEACH, SCOTT. *Musicdotes.* Berkeley, CA: Ten Speed Press, 1977.

BEDE. *History of the English Church and People.* Rpt., Harmondsworth, England: Penguin, 1968.

BEEBE, WILLIAM. *The Book of Naturalists.* New York: Knopf, 1944.

BEECHAM, SIR THOMAS. *A Mingled Chime.* New York: Putnam, 1943.

BEHAN, BEATRICE, WITH DES HICKEY AND GUS SMITH. *My Life with Brendan.* Los Angeles; Nash, 1974.

BEHRMAN, SAMUEL NATHANIEL. *Portrait of Max: An Intimate Memoir of Sir Max Beerbohm.* New York: Random House, 1960.

BELL, ERIC TEMPLE. *Men of Mathematics.* New York: Simon & Schuster, 1937.

BELLOW, SAUL. *Him With His Foot in His Mouth and Other Stories.* New York: Harper & Row, 1984.

BENCHLEY, NATHANIEL. *Robert Benchley.* New York: McGraw-Hill, 1955.

BENNY, MARY LIVINGSTONE, AND HILLIARD MARKS, WITH MARCIA BORIE. *Jack Benny.* New York: Doubleday, 1978.

BENSON, E. F. *The Kaiser and English Relations.* London and New York: Longmans, Green, 1936.

BENSON, IVAN. *Mark Twain's Western Years.* Palo Alto, CA: Stanford University Press, 1938.

BENSON, JACKSON J. *The True Adventures of John Steinbeck, Writer.* New York: Viking, 1984.

BERGER, FRANCESCO. *Reminiscences, Impressions, and Anecdotes.* London: S. Low, Marston, 1913.

BERNSTEIN, BURTON. *Thurber: A Biography.* New York: Dodd, Mead, 1975.

BERNSTEIN, JEREMY. *Einstein.* New York: Penguin, 1973.

BERNSTEIN, KENNETH. *Music Lover's Europe: A Guidebook and Companion.* New York: Scribner, 1983.

BERTON, PIERRE. *The Royal Family: The Story of British Monarchy from Victoria to Elizabeth.* New York: Knopf, 1953.

BESPALOFF, ALEXIS. *The Fireside Book of Wine.* New York: World, 1971.

BESTE, HENRY DIGBY. *Personal and Literary Memorials.* London: H. Colburn, 1829.

BING, SIR RUDOLF. *5000 Nights at the Opera.* New York: Doubleday, 1972.

BING, SIR RUDOLF. *A Knight at the Opera.* New York: Putnam, 1981.

BINGHAM, J. *Courage to Change: An Introduction to the Life and Thought of Reinhold Niebuhr.* New York: Scribner, 1972.

BIRMINGHAM, STEPHEN. *The Grandes Dames.* New York: Simon & Schuster, 1982.

BIRMINGHAM, STEPHEN. *The Late John Marquand: A Biography.* Philadelphia: Lippincott, 1972.

BIRMINGHAM, STEPHEN. *"The Rest of Us": The Rise of America's Eastern European Jews.* Boston: Little, Brown, 1984.

BISHOP, MORRIS. *The Exotics; Being a Collection of Unique Personalities and Remarkable Characters.* New York: American Heritage, 1969.

BISHOP, MORRIS. *A Gallery of Eccentrics.* New York: Minton, Balch, 1928.

BLACK, DAVID. *King of Fifth Avenue: The Fortunes of August Belmont.* New York: Dial, 1981.

BLAND-SUTTON, SIR JOHN. *The Story of a Surgeon.* Boston: Houghton Mifflin, 1930.

BLOUNT, THOMAS. *Boscobel.* London: for H. Seile, 1662.

BOGARDE, DIRK. *An Orderly Man.* New York: Knopf, 1983.

BOGARDE, DIRK. *Snakes & Ladders.* New York: Holt, Rinehart & Winston, 1979.

BOISSIER, GASTON. *Mme de Sévigné,* trans. Arthur Stanley. Paris, 1887–1919.

BOLLER, PAUL, ed. *Presidential Anecdotes.* New York: Oxford University Press, 1981.

BOLTON, SARAH K. *Famous Men of Science.* New York: T. Y. Crowell, 1889.

BONAVIA, FERRUCCIO, ed. *Musicians on Music.* New York: McBride, 1956.

BONE, JAMES. *The London Perambulator.* New York: Knopf, 1925.

BONINGTON, CHRISTIAN. *Quest for Adventure.* New York: C. N. Potter, 1982.

BOORSTIN, DANIEL J. *The Discoverers.* New York: Random House, 1983.

BOSWELL, J. *Life of Johnson.* London: Oxford University Press, 1934 (first published in 1791).

BOTKIN, B. A. *A Civil War Treasury.* New York: Random House, 1960.

BOTKIN, B. A. *A Treasury of American Anecdotes.* New York: Random House, 1957.

BOUHIER, JEAN. *Souvenirs de Jean Bouhier.* Paris: Emile Voitelain, 1866.

BOURRIENNE, LOUIS. *Memoirs of Napoleon Bonaparte.* New York: P. F. Collier, 1891.

BOWEN, CATHERINE DRINKER. *Yankee from Olympus.* Boston: Atlantic–Little, Brown, 1944.

BOWRA, CECIL MAURICE. *Memories 1898–1939.* London: Weidenfeld and Nicolson, 1966.

BOYD-CARPENTER, JOHN. *Way of Life: The Memoirs of John Boyd-Carpenter.* London: Sidgwick & Jackson, 1980.

BOYDELL, THOMAS. *My Luck Was In: With Spotlights on General Smuts.* Capetown: Stewart, 1947.

BOYLE, ANDREW. *Only the Wind Will Listen: Reith of the BBC.* London: Hutchinson, 1972.

BRADLEY, OMAR NELSON, AND CLAY BLAIR. *A General's Life: An Autobiography.* New York: Simon & Schuster, 1983.

BRADY, FRANK. *Onassis: An Extravagant Life.* Englewood Cliffs, NJ: Prentice-Hall, 1977.

BRANDRETH, GYLES. *Great Theatrical Disasters.* New York: St. Martin's, 1982.

BRANDRETH, GYLES. *The Joy of Lex: How to Have Fun with 860,341,500 Words.* New York: Morrow, 1980.

BRAUDE, JACOB M. *Braude's Second Encyclopedia of Stories, Quotations and Anecdotes.* Englewood Cliffs, NJ: Prentice-Hall, 1957.

BRAUDE, JACOB M. *Speaker's and Toastmaster's Handbook of Anecdotes by and about Famous Personalities.* Englewood Cliffs, NJ: Prentice-Hall, 1971.

BREDSDORFF, ELIAS. *Hans Christian Anderson: The Story of His Life and Work 1805–75.* New York: Scribner, 1975.

BRENDON, PIERS. *The Life and Death of the Press Barons.* New York: Atheneum, 1983.

BREWER, EBENEZER CORHAM. *Brewer's Dictionary of Phrase and Fable* (1870). London: Cassell, 1923; Centenary Ed., ed. Ivor H. Evans. New York: Harper & Row, 1981.

BRIDGES, ROBERT SEYMOUR. *Three Friends: Memoirs of Digby Mackworth Dolben, Richard Watson Dixon, Henry Bradley.* London: Oxford University Press, 1932.

BRINKLEY, ALAN. *Voices of Protest: Huey Long, Father Coughlin, and the Great Depression.* New York: Knopf, 1982.

BRINTON, CRANE. *The Lives of Talleyrand.* New York: Norton, 1936.

BROOKS, VAN WYCK. *The Life of Emerson.* New York: Dutton, 1932.

BROUGHAM, HENRY, LORD. *Men of Letters and Science Who Flourished in the Time of George III.* Paris: Baudry's European Library, 1845.

BROUGHTON, LORD. *Recollections of a Long Life.* London: J. Murray, 1909.

BROUN, HEYWOOD HALE. *Whose Little Boy Are You?: A Memoir of the Broun Family.* New York: St. Martin's, 1983.

BROWN, ANTHONY CAVE. *The Last Hero: Wild Bill Donovan.* New York: Times Books, 1982.

BROWN, IVOR. *A Charm of Names.* London: The Bodley Head, 1972.

BROWNLOW, KEVIN. *Hollywood: The Pioneers.* New York: Knopf, 1979.

BRYANT, ARTHUR. *The Age of Elegance, 1812–22.* New York: Harper, 1951.

BUCKLE, RICHARD. *In the Wake of Diaghilev.* New York: Holt, Rinehart & Winston, 1983.

BUCKLE, RICHARD. *Nijinsky.* New York: Simon & Schuster, 1971.

BUCKLE, RICHARD, ed. *Self-Portrait with Friends: The Selected Diaries of Cecil Beaton, 1926–1974.* New York: Times Books, 1979.

BUCKLEY, TOM. *Violent Neighbors.* New York: Times Books, 1983.

BUCKMAN, PETER. *Lafayette.* New York: Paddington Press, 1977.

BUÑUEL, LUIS. *My Last Breath.* New York: Knopf, 1983.

BURGON, JOHN. *Lives of Twelve Good Men.* New York: Scribner & Welford, 1888.

BURNEY, CHARLES. *A General History of Music from the Earliest Ages to the Present Period (1789), with Critical and Historical Notes by Frank Mercer.* Rpt., New York: Dover, 1937.

BURNS, GEORGE. *The Third Time Around.* New York: Putnam, 1980.

BURROWS, ABE. *Honest, Abe.* Boston: Little, Brown, 1980.

BUSSARD, PAUL. *The New Catholic Treasury of Wit and Humor.* New York: Meredith, 1968.

BUTLER, PETER, ed. *The Wit of Prince Philip.* New York: Hawthorne, 1966.

BYRNE, ROBERT. *The 637 Best Things Anybody Ever Said.* New York: Atheneum, 1982.

BYRON, GEORGE GORDON, LORD. *Byron's Letters and Journals,* ed. Leslie A. Marchand. Cambridge, MA: Harvard University Press, 1973–1982.

CABLE, MARY. *Top Drawer.* New York: Atheneum, 1984.

CAINE, T. HALL. *Recollections of Dante Gabriel Rossetti.* Boston: Roberts Bros., 1883.

CALDER, RITCHIE. *Medicine and Man: The Story of the Art of Science and Healing.* New York: New American Library, 1958.

CALLIÈRES, FRANÇOIS DE. *Des Bons Mots et des bons contes.* Geneva: Slatkine Reprints, 1971.

CAMERON, KENNETH NEILL. *Shelley: The Golden Years.* Cambridge, MA: Harvard University Press, 1974.

CAMPBELL, DOUGLAS, AND JOHN HIGGINS. *Mathematics: People, Problems, Results.* Vol. I. Belmont, CA: Wadsworth, 1984.

CANETTI, ELIAS. *Crowds and Power.* London: Gollancz, 1962; New York: Viking Press, 1962.

CANFIELD, CASS. *Up and Down and Around: A Publisher Recollects the Times of His Life.* New York: Harper's Magazine Press, 1971.

CANNON, LOU. *Reagan.* New York: Putnam, 1982.

CANTOR, N. F., AND M. S. WERTHMAN, eds. *The History of Popular Culture.* New York: Macmillan, 1968.

CARDUS, NEVILLE. *Sir Thomas Beecham: A Memoir.* London: Collins, 1961.

CARDUS, NEVILLE. *Talking of Music.* New York: Macmillan, 1957.

CARO, ROBERT A. *The Years of Lyndon Johnson.* Vol. I: *The Path to Power.* New York: Knopf, 1982.

CARPENTER, HUMPHREY. *W. H. Auden: A Biography.* Boston: Houghton Mifflin, 1981.

CARROLL, JAMES. *Prince of Peace.* Boston: Little, Brown, 1984.

CARTER, HARRY. *A History of the Oxford University Press.* Vol. I. London: Oxford University Press, 1975.

CARTER, JIMMY. *Keeping Faith: Memoirs of a President.* New York: Bantam, 1982.

CARTER, ROSALYNN. *First Lady from Plains.* Boston: Houghton Mifflin, 1984.

CASTELOT, ANDRÉ. *Marie Antoinette d'après des documents inédits.* Paris: Amiot-Dumont, 1953.

CASTELOT, ANDRÉ. *Paris: The Turbulent City 1783–1871,* trans. Denise Folliot. New York: Harper & Row, 1962.

CASTELOT, ANDRÉ. *Philippe Egalité: le Prince rouge.* Paris: SFELT, 1950.

CASTLEROSSE, VALENTINE, VISCOUNT. *Valentine's Days.*

CAVETT, DICK, AND CHRISTOPHER PORTERFIELD. *Eye on Cavett.* New York: Arbor House, 1983.

CECIL, LORD DAVID. *Max: A Biography.* Boston: Houghton Mifflin, 1965.

CECIL, LORD DAVID. *Melbourne.* New York: Grosset & Dunlap, 1954.

CELEBRITY RESEARCH GROUP. *The Bedside Book of Celebrity Gossip.* New York: Crown Publishers, 1984.

CERF, BENNETT A. *Bumper Crop of Anecdotes and Stories.* New York: Garden City Books, 1959.

CERF, BENNETT A. *Good for a Laugh.* New York: Hanover House, 1952.

CERF, BENNETT A. *Laughing Stock.* New York: Grosset & Dunlap, 1945.

CERF, BENNETT A. *The Life of the Party.* New York: Hanover House, 1956.

CERF, BENNETT A. *Shake Well Before Using.* New York: Simon & Schuster, 1948.

CERF, BENNETT A. *Treasury of Atrocious Puns.* New York: Harper and Row, 1968.

CERF, BENNETT A. *Try and Stop Me.* New York: Simon & Schuster, 1944.

CHAMBERS, ANDREA. *Dream Resorts.* New York: C. N. Potter, 1983.

CHANCELLOR, JOHN. *Charles Darwin*. New York: Taplinger, 1976.

CHARTERIS, E. *Life and Letters of Sir Edmund Gosse*. New York: Haskell House, 1982.

CHEEVER, SUSAN. *Home before Dark*. Boston: Houghton Mifflin, 1984.

CHEKHOV, ANTON. *The Image of Chekhov: Forty Stories in the Order in Which They Were Written*, trans. Robert Payn. New York: Vintage, 1963.

CHESTERTON, G. K. *Charles Dickens: The Last of the Great Men*. New York: The Press of the Reader's Club, 1942.

CHUBB, EDWIN W. *Sketches of Great Painters*. Cincinnati: Stewart & Kidd, 1915.

CHURCHILL, WINSTON S. *Great Contemporaries*. New York: Putnam, 1937.

CHURCHILL, WINSTON S. *Thoughts and Adventures*. London: T. Butterworth, 1932.

CLAIBORNE, ROBERT. *Our Marvelous Native Tongue: The Life and Times of the English Language*. New York: New York Times Books, 1983.

CLARK, ERIC. *Diplomat: The World of International Diplomacy*. New York: Taplinger, 1974.

CLARK, RONALD W. *The Huxleys*. New York: McGraw-Hill, 1968.

CLARK, RONALD W. *The Life of Bertrand Russell*. New York: Knopf, 1976.

CLEMENS, CLARA. *My Father Mark Twain*. New York: Harper & Bros., 1931.

CLIFFE, LEIGH. *Anecdotal Reminiscences.*

COLERIDGE, SAMUEL T. *Kubla Khan*. Boston: Wells and Lilly, 1816.

COLERIDGE, SAMUEL T. *Table Talk*. 3rd ed., London: J. Murray, 1851.

COLLIER, JAMES L. *Louis Armstrong: An American Genius*. New York: Oxford University Press, 1983.

COLLIER, PETER, AND DAVID HOROWITZ. *The Kennedys: An American Drama*. New York: Summit Books, 1984.

COLLIER, RICHARD. *The Freedom Road: 1944–1945*. New York: Atheneum, 1984.

COLLIER, RICHARD. *The Rainbow People*. New York: Dodd, Mead, 1984.

COLLIER, RICHARD. *The Road to Pearl Harbor 1941*. New York: Atheneum, 1981.

COLMAN, GEORGE. *Circle of Anecdote and Wit*. London: J. Williams, 1826.

Compton's Picture Encyclopedia. Chicago: F. E. Compton, 1968 ed.

CONNELLY, MARCUS. *Voices Offstage: A Book of Memoirs*. New York: Holt, Rinehart & Winston, 1968.

CONRAD, BARNABY. *Famous Last Words*. New York: Doubleday, 1961.

CONRAD, BARNABY. *Fun While It Lasted*. New York: Random House, 1969.

CONSIDINE, BOB. *It's All News to Me: A Reporter's Deposition*. New York: Meredith, 1967.

COOKE, ALISTAIR. *Six Men*. New York: Knopf, 1977.

COOPER, A. DUFF. *Talleyrand*. London: Jonathan Cape, 1932.

COOPER, JILLY. *Class*. New York: Knopf, 1981.

COPELAND, LEWIS, AND FAYE COPELAND. *10,000 Jokes, Toasts and Stories*. New York: Halcyon House, 1939.

CORNELL, TIM, AND JOHN MATTHEWS. *Atlas of the Roman World*. New York: Facts on File, 1982.

COUGHLIN, ROBERT. *The Private World of William Faulkner*. New York: Harper, 1954.

COWAN, LORE, AND MAURICE COWAN. *The Wit of Women*. London: Leslie Frewin, 1969.

COWLES, VIRGINIA. *The Kaiser*. New York: Harper & Row, 1963.

COWLEY, MALCOLM. *The View from 80*. New York: Viking, 1980.

CRAIG, GORDON. *The Germans*. New York: Putnam, 1982.

CRANKSHAW, EDWARD. *Bismarck*. New York: Viking, 1981.

CRANKSHAW, EDWARD. *The Fall of the House of Hapsburg*. New York: Viking, 1963.

CRANKSHAW, EDWARD. *Maria Theresa*. New York: Viking, 1970.

CRANKSHAW, EDWARD. *The Shadow of the Winter Palace: Russia's Drift to Revolution*. New York: Viking, 1976.

CRANKSHAW, EDWARD. *Tolstoy: The Making of a Novelist*. New York: Viking, 1974.

CRANKSHAW, EDWARD. *Vienna: The Image of a Culture in Decline*. New York: Macmillan, 1938.

CRAVEN, THOMAS. *Men of Art*. Garden City, NY: Halcyon House, 1931.

CRICK, FRANCIS. *Life Itself: Its Origins and Nature*. New York: Simon & Schuster, 1981.

CRONIN, VINCENT. *Louis XIV*. Boston: Houghton Mifflin, 1965.

CRONIN, VINCENT. *Napoleon Bonaparte: An Intimate Biography*. New York: Morrow, 1972.

CRONIN, VINCENT. *The View from Planet Earth: Man Looks at the Cosmos*. New York: Morrow, 1981.

CROUSER, RICHARD L. *It's Unlucky to Be Behind at the End of the Game and Other Sports Retorts*. New York: Morrow, 1983.

CUMMINGS, W. H. *Dr. Arne and Rule, Britannia.*

CUNNINGHAM, ALLAN. *Lives of the Most Eminent British Painters and Sculptors*. New York: J. Harper, 1831.

CURTIS, GEORGE TICKNOR. *Life of Daniel Webster.* New York: D. Appleton and Co., 1870.

DAICHES, DAVID. *James Boswell and His World.* New York: Scribner, 1976.

"Daily Mirror" Old Codger's Little Black Book, The. London: Mirror Books, 1977.

DAINTITH, JOHN, SARAH MITCHELL, AND ELIZABETH TOOTILL. *Biographical Encyclopedia of Scientists.* New York: Facts on File, 1981.

DALE, ALZINA STONE. *The Outline of Sanity: A Biography of G. K. Chesterton.* Grand Rapids, MI: Eerdman's, 1982.

DANCE, STANLEY. *The World of Count Basie.* New York: Scribner, 1980.

DANIEL, CLIFTON. *Lords, Ladies and Gentlemen: A Memoir.* New York: Arbor House, 1984.

DARWIN, CHARLES. *Autobiography.* Rpt., New York, Norton, 1969.

DAVENPORT, GUY. *The Geography of the Imagination: Forty Essays.* San Francisco: North Point Press, 1981.

DAVID, PHILIP, AND REUBEN HERSH. *The Mathematical Experience.* Boston: Houghton Mifflin, 1981.

DAVIDSON, ANGUS. *Edward Lear: Landscape Painter and Nonsense Poet (1812–1888).* New York: Dutton, 1939.

DAVIN, DAN. *Closing Times.* London and New York: Oxford University Press, 1975.

DAVIES, THOMAS. *Dramatic Micellanies.* London, 1783–84.

DAVIS, A. R., ed. *The Penguin Book of Chinese Verse,* trans. Robert Kotewall and Norman L. Smith. Baltimore: Penguin, 1962.

DEIGHTON, LEN. *Action Cook Book: Len Deighton's Guide to Eating.* London: Jonathan Cape, 1965.

DELANEY, FRANK, AND JORGE LEWINSKI. *James Joyce's Odyssey: A Guide to the Dublin of Ulysses.* New York: Holt, Rinehart & Winston, 1983.

DE MORGAN, AUGUSTUS. *The Encyclopedia of Eccentrics.* LaSalle, IL: Open Court, 1974.

DE STOECKL, AGNES, AND WILFRED S. EDWARDS. *When Men Had Time to Love.* London: J. Murray, 1953.

DEVONSHIRE, DEBORAH VIVIEN FREEMAN-MITFORD CAVENDISH, DUCHESS OF. *The House: A Portrait of Chatsworth.* London: Macmillan, 1982.

Dictionary of National Biography. Sir Leslie Stephen and Sir Sidney Lee, eds. 63 vols., supplements. London: Oxford University Press, 1885–1900, 1921–1927, 1960.

DIEHL, DIGBY. *Supertalk.* New York: Doubleday, 1974.

DIETZ, HOWARD. *Dancing in the Dark.* New York: Quadrangle, 1974.

DIOGENES LAERTIUS. *Lives of Eminent Philosophers.* Cambridge, MA: Harvard University Press, 1929.

D'ISRAELI, ISAAC. *Curiosities of Literature.* Boston: Lilly, Wait, Colman & Holden, 1833.

D'ISRAELI, ISAAC. *Miscellanies of Literature.* New York: J. and H. G. Langley, 1841.

DOLIN, ANTON. *Friends and Memories,* ed. Andrew Wheatcroft. London: Routledge & Kegan Paul, 1982.

DONALDSON, FRANCES. *Freddy Lonsdale.* Philadelphia: Lippincott, 1957.

DONALDSON, FRANCES. *P. G. Wodehouse: A Biography.* New York: Knopf, 1982.

DONOVAN, HEDLEY. *From Roosevelt to Reagan.* New York: Harper & Row, 1983.

DRAPER & ESQUIN (SAN FRANCISCO WINE MERCHANTS). Sales brochure.

DRENNAN, ROBERT E. *The Algonquin Wits.* New York: Citadel Press, 1968.

DRENNAN, ROBERT E. *Wit's End.* London: Leslie Frewin, 1973.

DRYFOOS, SUSAN W. *Iphigene: Memoirs of Iphigene Ochs Sulzberger of the New York Times Family as Told to Her Granddaughter.* New York: Dodd, Mead, 1981.

DUFF, DAVID. *Albert and Victoria.* London: Muller, 1972.

DUFF, DAVID. *Elizabeth of Glamis.* London: Muller, 1973.

DUFF, DAVID. *Eugénie and Napoleon III.* New York: Morrow, 1978.

DUGAS DE BOIS ST. JUST, JEAN LOUIS MARIE. *Paris, Versailles et les provinces au dix-huitième siècle.* Paris: H. Nicole, 1811.

DUNAWAY, PHILIP, AND GEORGE DE KAY, eds. *Turning Points: Fateful Moments that Revealed Men and Made History.* New York: Random House, 1958.

DUNBAR, JANET. *J. M. Barrie, The Man Behind the Image.* Boston: Houghton Mifflin, 1970.

DUNCAN, DAVID DOUGLAS. *Picasso's Picasso.* New York: Harper, 1961.

DURANT, WILL. *The Story of Philosophy: The Lives and Opinions of the Greater Philosophers.* New York: Simon & Schuster, 1926.

DURANT, WILL, AND ARIEL DURANT. *The Story of Civilization.* 11 vols. New York: Simon & Schuster, 1935–1965.

EASTMAN, MAX. *Great Companions.* New York: Farrar, Straus & Cudahy, 1959.

EBY, CECIL. *The Seige of the Alcázar.* New York: Random House, 1965.

EDWARDS, KENNETH. *I Wish I'd Said That: An Anthology of Witty Replies.* London: Abelard-Schuman, 1976.

EDWARDS, KENNETH. *I Wish I'd Said That Too.* London: Abelard-Schuman, 1977.

EDWARDS, KENNETH. *More Things I Wish I'd Said, and Some I Wish I Hadn't*. London: Abelard-Schuman, 1978.

EISENHOWER, DWIGHT D. *At Ease: Stories I Tell to Friends*. New York: Doubleday, 1957.

ELDER, DONALD. *Ring Lardner: A Biography*. New York: Doubleday, 1956.

ELLIOT, JOHN HAROLD. *Berlioz*. London: Dent, 1938; reissued 1967.

ELLIS, JAMES J. *Spurgeon Anecdotes: Being Authentic Anecdotes*. London: J. E. Hawkins, 1892.

ELLMANN, RICHARD. *James Joyce*. Oxford: Oxford University Press, 1959; *New and Revised Edition*, 1982.

Encyclopaedia Britannica. Chicago: Encyclopaedia Britannica, 1960, 1961, 1967, 1969, 1971.

ENRIGHT, D. J. *The Oxford Book of Death*. New York: Oxford University Press, 1983.

ERSKINE, DAVID, ed. *Augustus Hervey's Journal*. London: Kimber, 1953.

ERVINE, ST. JOHN GREER. *Bernard Shaw: His Life, Work, and Friends*. New York: Morrow, 1956.

ESPY, WILLARD R. *An Almanac of Words at Play*. New York: C. N. Potter, 1975.

ESPY, WILLARD R. *Another Almanac of Words at Play*. New York: C. N. Potter, 1980.

EVANS, CHRISTOPHER. *The Micro Millennium*. New York: Washington Square Press, 1979.

EVANS, H. SUTHERLAND. *Personal Recollections*.

EVANS, RICHARD. *Nasty: Ilie Nastase vs. Tennis*. New York: Stein & Day, 1979.

FADIMAN, CLIFTON. *Any Number Can Play*. Cleveland: World Publishing, 1957.

FADIMAN, CLIFTON. *Enter, Conversing*. Cleveland: World Publishing, 1962.

FADIMAN, CLIFTON. *Fifty Years*. New York: Knopf, 1965.

FADIMAN, CLIFTON. *The Mathematical Magpie*. New York: Simon & Schuster, 1962.

FADIMAN, CLIFTON. *Party of One: The Selected Writings of Clifton Fadiman*. Cleveland: World Publishing, 1955.

FADIMAN, CLIFTON, AND CHARLES VAN DOREN. *The American Treasury 1455–1955*. New York: Harper & Row, 1955.

FARAGO, LADISLAS. *Strictly from Hungary*. New York: Walker, 1962.

FAULKNER, ALEX, AND TOM HARTMAN. *All the Best People . . . The Pick of Peterborough, 1929–1945*. Boston: Allen & Unwin, 1981.

FEIN, IRVING A. *Jack Benny: An Intimate Biography*. Boston: G. K. Hall, 1976.

FERGUSSON, BERNARD. *Wavell: Portrait of a Soldier*. London: Collins, 1961.

FIELDING, DAPHNE. *Those Remarkable Cunards: Emerald and Nancy*. New York: Atheneum, 1968.

FIFIELD, WILLIAM. *In Search of Genius*. New York: Morrow, 1982.

FINCH, CHRISTOPHER. *The Art of Walt Disney: From Mickey Mouse to the Magic Kingdoms*. New York: H. N. Abrams, 1973.

FINCK, HENRY. *Musical Laughs*. New York and London: Funk & Wagnalls, 1924.

FITZGERALD, PATRICK. *Ancient China*. Oxford: Elsevier-Phaidon, 1978.

FITZGIBBON, THEODORA, comp. *The Pleasures of the Table*. New York: Oxford University Press, 1981.

FLEMING, SIR AMBROSE. *Memories of a Scientific Life*. London: Marshall, Morgan & Scott, 1934.

FONTEYN, MARGOT. *Margot Fonteyn: An Autobiography*. New York: Knopf, 1976.

FOOT, MICHAEL. *Aneurin Bevan: A Biography*. New York: Atheneum, 1963.

FORBES, BRYAN. *Ned's Girl*. Boston: Little, Brown, 1977.

FORBES, ELLIOT, ed. *Thayer's Life of Beethoven*. Princeton, NJ: Princeton University Press, 1964.

FORD, COREY. *The Time of Laughter*. Boston: Little, Brown, 1967.

FORD, FORD MADOX. *Ancient Lights* (1911).

FORDIN, HUGH. *Getting to Know Him: A Biography of Oscar Hammerstein II*. New York: Random House, 1967.

FORKNER, BEN, ed. *Modern Irish Short Stories*. Preface by Anthony Burgess. New York: Penguin, 1980.

FOWLER, GENE. *Beau James: The Life and Times of Jimmy Walker*. New York: Viking, 1949.

FOWLER, GENE. *Good Night, Sweet Prince*. New York: Viking, 1944.

FOWLER, GENE. *Minutes of the Last Meeting*. New York: Viking, 1954.

FOWLER, GENE. *Schnozzola: The Story of Jimmy Durante*. New York: Viking, 1951.

FOWLER, GENE. *Timber Line: A Story of Bonfils and Fammen*. Garden City, NY: Halcyon House, 1933.

FOXE, JOHN. *Acts and Monuments*, ed. H. M. Seymour. New York, 1855.

FRANÇOIS, JACOB. *The Possible and the Actual*. New York: Pantheon, 1982.

FRANK, PHILIPP. *Einstein, His Life and Times*. New York: Knopf, 1947.

FRANQUI, CARLOS. *Family Portrait with Fidel*, trans. Alfred MacAdam. New York: Random House, 1983.

FRASER, ANTONIA. *Cromwell, The Lord Protector*. New York: Knopf, 1973.

FRASER, SIR WILLIAM. *Disraeli and His Day*. London: K. Paul, Trench, Trubner, 1891.

FREDERICK, PAULINE. *Ten First Ladies of the World*. New York: Meredith, 1967.

FREUD, SIGMUND, *Wit and Its Relation to the Unconscious* (1916).

FRITH, WILLIAM POWELL. *My Autobiography and Reminiscences*. New York: Harper, 1888.

FROST, DAVID. *Book of the World's Worst Decisions*. New York: Crown, 1983.

FROST, DAVID. *"I Gave Them a Sword": Behind the Scenes of the Nixon Interviews*. New York: Morrow, 1978.

FROST, DAVID, AND MICHAEL DEAKIN. *David Frost's Book of Millionaires, Multimillionaires, and Really Rich People*. New York: Crown, 1984.

FUESS, CLAUDE MOORE. *Daniel Webster*. Boston: Little, Brown, 1930.

FULLER, EDMUND. *2500 Anecdotes for All Occasions*. New York: Crown, 1943.

FULLER, THOMAS. *Fuller's The Holy State and the Profane State*, ed. Maximilian Graff Walten. New York: Columbia University Press, 1938.

FULLER, THOMAS, ed. *The Worthies of England*, intro. and notes by John Freeman. New York: Barnes & Noble, 1952.

FURNAS, J. C. *Fanny Kemble: Leading Lady of the Nineteenth-Century Stage*. New York: Dial, 1982.

GAINES, JAMES R., ed. *The Lives of the Piano*. New York: Holt, Rinehart & Winston, 1981.

GALBRAITH, JOHN KENNETH. *A Life in Our Times*. Boston: Houghton Mifflin, 1981.

GARLAND, H. *Ulysses S. Grant: His Life and Character*. New York: Doubleday & McClure, 1898.

GARLAND, JOSEPH. *Boston's Gold Coast*. Boston: Little, Brown, 1981.

GARLAND, MADGE. *The Changing Face of Childhood*. New York: October House, 1965.

GATES, W. FRANCIS. *Anecdotes of Great Musicians: Three Hundred Anecdotes and Biographical Sketches of Famous Composers and Performers*. Philadelphia: T. Presser, 1898.

GATTEY, CHARLES NEILSON. *The Elephant That Swallowed a Nightingale and Other Operatic Wonders*. London: Hutchinson, 1981.

GEORGE, DANIEL, ed. *A Book of Anecdotes: Illustrating Varieties of Experience in the Lives of the Eminent and the Lives of the Obscure*. Secaucus, NJ: Citadel, 1958.

GEORGES-MICHEL, MICHEL. *From Renoir to Picasso: Artists in Action*, trans. Dorothy and Randolph Weaver. Boston: Houghton Mifflin, 1957.

GERE, J. A., AND JOHN SPARROW. *Geoffrey Madan's Notebooks: A Selection*. New York: Oxford University Press, 1984.

GERIN, W. *Anne Thackeray Ritchie; A Biography*. New York: Oxford University Press, 1981.

GERWIG, HENRIETTA. *Fifty Famous Painters*. New York: T. Y. Crowell, 1926.

GIBBON, EDWARD. *The History of the Decline and Fall of the Roman Empire*. 3rd ed., London: W. S. Strahan & T. Cadell, 1777. Rpt., New York: Modern Library, 1983.

GILCHRIST, ALEXANDER. *The Life of William Blake*. New York: Dodd, Mead, [1906?].

GILL, BRENDAN. *Here at the New Yorker*. New York: Random House, 1975.

GILL, DOMINIC, ed. *The Book of the Piano*. Ithaca, NY: Cornell University Press, 1981.

GILOT, FRANÇOISE, AND CARLTON LAKE. *Life with Picasso*. New York: McGraw-Hill, 1964.

GIPE, GEORGE. *The Last Time When*. New York: Newspaper Enterprise Assn., 1980.

GODDEN, RUMER. *Hans Christian Andersen: A Great Life in Brief*. New York: Knopf, 1954.

GOGARTY, OLIVER ST. JOHN. *It Isn't This Time of Year at All! An Unpremeditated Autobiography*. New York: Doubleday, 1954.

GOGOL, NIKOLAI V. *Chichikov's Journeys: Home Life in Old Russia*, trans. Bernard Guilbert Guerney. New York: The Readers Club, 1942.

GONCOURT, EDMOND DE. *Journal des Goncourt: Mémoires de la vie littéraire*. Paris: E. Fasguelle, 1891–1907.

GOOSSENS, EUGENE. *Overture and Beginners: A Musical Autobiography*. Westport, CT: Greenwood Press, 1972.

GORDON, MAX, WITH LEWIS FUNKE. *Max Gordon Presents*. New York: Geis, 1963.

GOTTFRIED, MARTIN. *Jed Harris: The Curse of Genius*. Boston: Little, Brown, 1984.

GRAHAM, SHEILAH. *The Garden of Allah*. New York: Crown, 1970.

GRAVES, ROBERT. *Goodbye to All That*. New ed., rev., New York: Doubleday, 1957.

GRAVES, R. P. *A. E. Housman: The Scholar Poet*. New York: Scribner, 1980.

GREEN, BENNY, comp. *London*. New York: Oxford University Press, 1984.

GREEN, BENNY. *P. G. Wodehouse: A Literary Biography*. New York: Rutledge, 1981.

GREEN, HORACE. *General Grant's Last Stand*. New York: Scribner, 1936.

GREEN, JONATHAN. *Morrow's International Dictionary of Contemporary Quotations*. New York: Morrow, 1982.

GREEN, LEE. *Sportswit*. New York: Harper & Row, 1982.

GREEN, ROGER LANCELYN. *C. S. Lewis: A Biography*. New York: H. Z. Walck, 1963.

GREEN, ROGER LANCELYN, ed. *The Diaries of Lewis Carroll*. New York: Oxford University Press, 1954.

GREENFIELD, HOWARD. *Caruso*. New York: Putnam, 1983.

GRIFFIN, JASPER, ed. *Snobs*. New York: Oxford University Press, 1982.

GRIFFIN, MERV, WITH PETER BARSOCCHINI. *From Where I Sit: Merv Griffin's Book of People*. New York: Arbor, 1982.

GRUEN, JOHN. *Menotti: A Biography*. New York: Macmillan, 1978.

GRUEN, JOHN. *The Party's Over Now: Reminiscences of the Fifties — New York's Artists, Writers, Musicians, and Their Friends*. New York: Viking, 1972.

GRUN, BERNARD. *Gold and Silver: The Life and Times of Franz Lehár*. New York: D. McKay Co., 1970.

GUEDALLA, PHILIP. *The Liberators*. London: Hodder & Stoughton, 1942.

GUEDALLA, PHILIP. *Supers and Supermen: Studies in Politics, History and Letters*. New York: Knopf, 1921.

GUÉRARD, E. *Dictionnaire Encyclopédique d'anecdotes modernes, anciennes, françaises et étrangères par Edmond Guérard*. Paris: Firmin-Didot, 1879.

GUILLOIS, MINA, AND ANDRÉ GUILLOIS. *Liberté, Egalité, Hilarité*. Paris; Fayard, 1972.

GUINNESS, JONATHAN, WITH CATHERINE GUINNESS. *House of Mitford*. New York: Viking, 1985.

GUNTHER, JOHN. *Inside Russia Today*. New York: Harper, 1958.

GUNTHER, JOHN. *Inside South America*. New York: Harper & Row, 1967.

GUNTHER, JOHN. *Procession*. New York: Harper & Row, 1965.

HAGEDORN, HERMAN. *Roosevelt in the Bad Lands*. Boston: Houghton Mifflin, 1921.

HALL, DONALD. *Remembering Poets*. New York: Harper & Row, 1978.

HALLE, KAY. *Randolph Churchill, The Young Unpretender: Essays by His Friends*. London: Heinemann, 1971.

HAMBURGER, MICHAEL, ed. *Beethoven: Letters, Journals and Conversations*. New York: Pantheon, 1952.

HAMILTON, IAN. *Koestler: A Biography*. New York: Macmillan, 1982.

HAMILTON, IAN. *Robert Lowell: A Biography*. New York: Random House, 1982.

HAMMOND, JOHN WINTHROP. *Men and Volts: The Story of General Electric*. Philadelphia: Lippincott, 1941.

HANCOCK, W. K. *Smuts*. London: Cambridge University Press, 1962–1968.

HARDY, ALAN. *Queen Victoria Was Amused*. New York: Taplinger, 1977.

HARDY, G. H. *A Mathematician's Apology*. London: Cambridge University Press, 1940.

HARE, AUGUSTUS JOHN CUTHBERT. *The Story of My Life*. New York: Dodd, Mead, 1896.

HARRIS, LEON A. *The Fine Art of Political Wit*. New York: Dutton, 1966.

HARRIS, SYDNEY J. *Pieces of Eight*. Boston: Houghton Mifflin, 1982.

HARRISON, ADA, AND DEREK STANFORD. *Anne Brontë: Her Life and Work*. New York: J. Day, 1959.

HART, MOSS. *Act One: An Autobiography*. New York: Random House, 1959.

HARVEY, PETER. *Reminiscences and Anecdotes of Daniel Webster*. Boston: Little, Brown, 1887.

HASSALL, CHRISTOPHER VERNON. *Biography of Edward Marsh*. New York: Harcourt, Brace, 1959.

HASTINGS, MICHAEL. *Sir Richard Burton: A Biography*. New York: Coward, McCann & Geoghegan, 1978.

HATCH, ALDEN. *The Byrds of Virginia*. New York: Holt, Rinehart & Winston, 1969.

HATCH, ALDEN. *The Mountbattens: The Last Royal Success Story*. New York: Random House, 1965.

HAUSER, ERNEST O. *Italy, A Cultural Guide*. New York: Atheneum, 1981.

HAWTHORNE, JULIAN. *Nathaniel Hawthorne and His Wife*. Boston: James R. Osgood, 1884.

HECHT, BEN. *A Child of the Century*. New York: Simon & Schuster, 1954.

HEINE, HEINRICH. *Confessions*, trans. Peter Heinegg. Malibu, CA: J. Simon, 1981.

HELLMAN, LILLIAN. *Pentimento*. Boston: Little, Brown, 1973.

HELLMAN, LILLIAN. *An Unfinished Woman*. Boston: Little, Brown, 1969.

HEMINGWAY, ERNEST. *A Moveable Feast*. New York: Scribner, 1964.

HENDRICKSON, ROBERT. *The Literary Life and Other Curiosities*. New York: Viking, 1981.

HENRY, O. *The Voice of the City and Other Stories*. New York: Limited Editions Club, 1935.

HENRY OF HUNTINGDON. *Historia Anglorum*.

HERBERT, ALAN PATRICK. *A.P.H.: His Life and Times*. London: Heinemann, 1978.

HERMAN, GARY. *The Book of Hollywood Quotes*. London and New York: Omnibus, 1979.

HERODOTUS. *History*, trans. H. Carter. Oxford: Oxford University Press, 1962.

HEROLD, J. CHRISTOPHER. *Mistress to an Age: A Life of Madame de Staël*. Indianapolis: Bobbs-Merrill, 1958.

HERRMANN, DOROTHY. *With Malice Toward All*. New York: Putnam, 1982.

HESSION, CHARLES H. *John Maynard Keynes*. New York: Macmillan, 1984.

HIBBERT, CHRISTOPHER. *The Personal History of*

HIBBERT *(continued)*
Samuel Johnson. London: Longman Group, Ltd., 1971.

HILL, CHRISTOPHER. *God's Englishman: Oliver Cromwell and the English Revolution.* New York: Dial, 1970.

HILLARY, EDMUND. *High Adventure.* New York: Dutton, 1955.

HOBSON, LAURA Z. *Laura Z.: A Life.* New York: Arbor House, 1983.

HOFFMEISTER, HERBERT. *Anekdotenschatz, von der Antike bis auf unsere Tage.* Berlin: Verlag Praktisches Wissen, 1957.

HOFMANN, P. *Rome — The Sweet, Tempestuous Life.* New York: Congdon & Lattès, 1982.

HOLBROOK, STEWART H. *The Age of the Moguls.* New York: Doubleday, 1953.

HOLLAND, VYVYAN. *Time Remembered after Père Lachaise.* London: Gollancz, 1966.

HOLMES, CHARLES S. *The Clocks of Columbus: The Literary Career of James Thurber.* New York: Atheneum, 1972.

HOLMES, OLIVER WENDELL. *Ralph Waldo Emerson.* Boston: Houghton Mifflin, 1884.

HOLROYD, MICHAEL. *Lytton Strachey: A Biography.* New York: Holt, Rinehart & Winston, 1967.

HOOD, PAXTON. *World of Anecdote.* Philadelphia: Lippincott, 1874.

HOPKINS, ANTONY. *Music All Around Me: A Personal Choice from the Literature of Music.* London: Frewin, 1967.

HORGAN, PAUL. *Encounters with Stravinsky.* New York: Farrar, Straus & Giroux, 1972.

HOTCHNER, A. E. *Choice People: The Greats, Near-Greats, and Ingrates I Have Known.* New York: Morrow, 1984.

HOWARD, JANE. *Margaret Mead: A Life.* New York: Simon & Schuster, 1984.

HOWARD, MARGO. *Eppie: The Story of Ann Landers.* New York: Putnam, 1982.

HOWE, MARK A. DE WOLFE. *Holmes of the Breakfast Table.* New York: Oxford University Press, 1939.

HOWE, MARK A. DE WOLFE. *John Jay Chapman and His Letters.* Boston: Houghton Mifflin, 1937.

HOWELLS, WILLIAM DEAN. *My Mark Twain: Reminiscences and Criticisms.* New York: Harper & Brothers, 1910.

HUDDLESTON, SISLEY. *Paris Salons, Cafés, Studios.* Philadelphia: Lippincott, 1928.

HUMES, JAMES C. *Speakers' Treasury of Anecdotes about the Famous.* New York: Harper & Row, 1978.

HUMPHREY, LANING. *The Humor of Music and Other Oddities in the Art.* Boston: Crescendo, 1971.

INNES, MICHAEL. *The Gay Phoenix.* New York: Penguin, 1981.

ISAACS, ALAN, AND ELIZABETH MARTIN. *Dictionary of Music.* New York: Hamlyn, 1982.

JACOB, FRANÇOIS. *The Possible and the Actual.* New York: Pantheon, 1982.

JAMES, ROBERT RHODES, ed. *Chips: The Diaries of Sir Henry Channon.* New York: Penguin, 1970.

JASEN, DAVID A. *P. G. Wodehouse: A Portrait of a Master.* New York: Mason & Lipscomb, 1974.

JEFFS, RAE. *Brendan Behan, Man and Showman.* Cleveland: World Publishing, 1968.

JELUSISCH, MIRKO. *Geschichten aus dem Wienerwald.* Vienna: Tieck Verlag, 1937.

JENNISON, KEITH W. *The Humorous Mr. Lincoln.* New York: Crowell, 1965.

JEROME, JEROME A. *My Life and Times.* London: J. Murray, 1983.

JESSE, JOHN HENEAGE. *George Selwyn and His Contemporaries.* Boston: C. F. Rice, 1843.

JOHNSON, DIANE. *Dashiell Hammett.* New York: Random House, 1983.

JOHNSON, DORIS, AND ELLEN LEVENTHAL, eds. *The Letters of Nunnally Johnson.* New York: Knopf, 1981.

JOHNSON, EDGAR. *Charles Dickens: His Tragedy and Triumph.* Boston: Little, Brown, 1952.

JOHNSON, H. EARLE. *Symphony Hall.* Boston: Little, Brown, 1950.

JOHNSON, NORA. *Flashback: Nora Johnson on Nunnally Johnson.* New York: Doubleday, 1979.

JOHNSON, SAMUEL. *Lives of the English Poets,* ed. John Wain. New York: Dutton, 1975.

JOHNSTON, BRIAN. *Rain Stops Play.* London: W. H. Allen, 1979.

JONES, EVAN. *A Food Lover's Companion.* New York: Harper & Row, 1979.

JONES, NEAL T. *A Book of Days for the Literary Year.* London: Thames & Hudson, 1984.

JONSON, BEN. *Timber; or Discoveries,* ed. G. B. Harrison. New York: Dutton, 1966.

KAC, MARK. *Enigmas of Chance.* New York: Harper & Row, 1985.

KAEL, PAULINE. *The Citizen Kane Book.* Boston: Little, Brown, 1971.

KANIN, GARSON. *Hollywood.* New York: Viking Press, 1974.

KAPLAN, JUSTIN. *Mark Twain and His World.* New York: Simon & Schuster, 1974.

KAPLAN, JUSTIN. *Mr. Clemens and Mark Twain.* New York: Simon & Schuster, 1966.

KARSH, YOUSUF. *Karsh: A Fifty-Year Retrospective.* Boston: NYGS/Little, Brown, 1983.

KEDDIE, WILLIAM. *Cyclopedia of Literary and Scientific Anecdote: Illustrative of the Characters, Habits, and Conversation of Men of Letters and Science.* London: Columbus, Follett, Foster, 1859. Rpt., Ann Arbor, MI: Gryphon Books, 1971.

KEEGAN, JOHN. *Six Armies in Normandy: From D-Day to the Liberation of Paris, June 6th–August 25th, 1944.* New York: Viking Press, 1982.

KELEN, BETTY. *The Mistresses.* New York: Random House, 1966.

KELEN, EMERY. *Peace in Their Time: Men Who Led Us In and Out of War, 1914–1945.* New York: Knopf, 1963.

KELLEY, KITTY. *Elizabeth Taylor: The Last Star.* New York: Simon & Schuster, 1981.

KENDALL, ALAN. *The Tender Tyrant, Nadia Boulanger: A Life Devoted to Music: A Biography.* London: MacDonald & Jane's, 1976.

KENIN, RICHARD, AND JUSTIN WINTLE. *Dictionary of Biographical Quotation of British and American Subjects.* New York: Knopf, 1978.

KENYON, JOHN PHILLIPS. *A Dictionary of British History.* New York: Stein & Day, 1983.

KETTON-CREMER, ROBERT WYNDHAM. *Horace Walpole.* New York: Longman's, 1964.

KEYNES, GEOFFREY, AND BRIAN HILL, eds. *Samuel Butler's Notebooks — Selections.* New York: Dutton, 1951.

KIDDER, JONATHAN EDWARD. *Ancient Japan.* New York: John Day, 1965.

KING, ALAN, AND MIMI SHERATON. *Is Salami and Eggs Better Than Sex?* Boston: Little, Brown, 1985.

KISSINGER, HENRY. *White House Years.* Boston: Little, Brown, 1979.

KNOX, D. B. *More Quotable Anecdotes.* London: T. F. Unwin, 1926.

KNOW, D. B. *Quotable Anecdotes for Various Occasions.* New York: Dutton, 1924.

KNOX, RONALD ARBUTHNOTT. *Literary Distractions.* New York: Sheed & Ward, 1958.

KOBLER, JOHN. *Capone.* New York: Putnam, 1971.

KOESTLER, ARTHUR. *Bricks to Babel.* New York: Random House, 1980.

KORDA, MICHAEL. *Charmed Lives: A Family Romance.* New York: Random House, 1979.

KRANTZ, JUDITH. *Mistral's Daughter.* New York: Crown, 1983.

KREMENTZ, JILL. *The Writer's Image.* Boston: David R. Godine, 1980.

KROCK, ARTHUR. *Memoirs.* New York: Popular Library, 1968.

KUPFERBERG, HERBERT. *Those Fabulous Philadelphians: The Life and Times of a Great Orchestra.* New York: Scribner, 1969.

LACEY, ROBERT. *The Aristocrats.* London: Hutchinson, 1983.

LACEY, ROBERT. *The Kingdom: Arabia and the House of Sa'ud.* New York: Harcourt Brace Jovanovich, 1982.

LACEY, ROBERT. *Majesty: Elizabeth II and the House of Windsor.* New York: Harcourt Brace Jovanovich, 1977.

LAMPARSKI, RICHARD. *Whatever Became Of . . . ?* New York: Crown, 1966.

LANDON, H. C. ROBBINS. *Handel and His World: A Documentary Biography.* Boston: Little, Brown, 1984.

LANE, MARGARET. *Purely for Pleasure.* New York: Knopf, 1967.

LANG, GEORGE. *The Cuisine of Hungary.* New York: Atheneum, 1971.

LANMAN, CHARLES. *The Private Life of Daniel Webster.* New York: Harper and Bros., 1852.

LANOUX, ARMAND. *Paris in the Twenties.* New York: Arts, Inc., 1960.

LAROUSSE, PIERRE. *Grand Dictionnaire universel du 19ième siècle.* Paris: Union Générale d'Editions, 1975.

LARWOOD, J. *Anecdotes of the Clergy.* London: Chatto & Windus, 1881.

LASH, JOSEPH P. *Eleanor: An Appreciation.* New York: Norton, 1984.

LASH, JOSEPH P. *Eleanor and Franklin: The Story of Their Relationship.* New York: Norton, 1971.

LASKY, JESSE L., AND PAT SILVER. *Love Scene.* New York: Berkley, 1981.

LATHAM, AARON. *Crazy Sundays: F. Scott Fitzgerald in Hollywood.* New York: Viking, 1971.

LATHAM, PETER. *Brahms.* New York: Pellegrini & Cudahy, 1949.

LAWSON, ANDREW. *Discover Unexpected London.* Oxford: Elsevier-Phaidon, 1977.

LE GALLIENNE, RICHARD. *The Romantic '90s.* New York: Doubleday, Page, 1925.

LEGOUIS, PIERRE, ed. *André Marvell, Poète, Puritain, Patriote, 1621–1678.* New York: Russell & Russell, 1965.

LENDER, MARK EDWARD, AND JAMES KIRBY MARTIN. *Drinking in America: A History.* New York: The Free Press, 1982.

LENNON, NIGEY. *Alfred Jarry: The Man with the Axe.* Los Angeles: Panjandrum, 1984.

LESLIE, ANITA. *The Remarkable Mr. Jerome.* New York: Holt, Rinehart & Winston, 1954.

LE SUEUR, GORDON. *Cecil Rhodes: The Man and His Work; By One of His Private and Confidential Secretaries, Gordon le Sueur.* New York: McBride, Nast, 1914.

LEVANT, OSCAR. *A Smattering of Ignorance.* New York: Doubleday, Doran, 1940.

LEVANT, OSCAR. *The Unimportance of Being Oscar*. New York: Putnam, 1968.

LEVI, PETER. *The Hill of Kronos*. New York: Dutton, 1981.

LEWIS, ARTHUR H. *Those Philadelphia Kellys, with a Touch of Grace*. New York: Morrow, 1977.

LEWIS, ROBERT. *Slings and Arrows: Theatre in My Life*. New York: Stein & Day, 1984.

LEWIS, ROBERT. *W. C. Fields: His Follies and Fortunes*. New York: New American Library, 1967.

LIDDELL HART, B. A. *Reputations, Ten Years After*. Boston: Little, Brown, 1928.

LIEBERMAN, GERALD F. *The Greatest Laughs of All Time*. New York: Doubleday, 1961.

LINCOLN, ANTHONY L. J., AND ROBERT LINDLEY MCEWAN, eds. *Lord Eldon's Anecdote Book*. London: Stevens & Sons, 1960.

LINKLETTER, ART. *I Wish I'd Said That! My Favorite Ad-libs of All Time*. New York: Doubleday, 1968.

LIVY (TITUS LIVIUS). *Annals of the Roman People*.

LLOYD, CHRIS EVERT. *Chrissie: My Own Story*. New York: Simon and Schuster, 1982.

LO BELLO, NINO. *European Detours: A Travel Guide to Unusual Sites*. Maplewood, NJ: Hammond, 1981.

LOCKHART, JOHN GIBSON. *Life of Sir Walter Scott*. New York: Dutton, 1906.

LOCKHART, JOHN GILBERT. *Cecil Rhodes*. New York: Macmillan, 1933.

LOLIÉE, FRÉDÉRIC AUGUSTE. *Gilded Beauties of the Second Empire*, adapted by Bryan O'Donnell. New York: Brentano's, 1910.

LONGFORD, ELIZABETH. *The Queen: The Life of Elizabeth II*. New York: Knopf, 1983.

LOVE, ROBERTUS. *The Rise and Fall of Jesse James*. New York: Putnam, 1926.

LOWENFELS, WALTER. *The Paris Years*.

LUCAS, EDWARD VERALL. *A Fronded Isle, and Other Essays*. New York: Doubleday, Doran, 1928.

LUCAS, EDWARD VERALL. *Reading, Writing and Remembering: A Literary Record*. New York: Harper & Bros., 1932.

LYSONS, DANIEL. *Environs of London*. London: Cadell, 1795–1811.

MAAS, HENRY, ed. *The Letters of A. E. Housman*. Cambridge, MA: Harvard University Press, 1971.

MCALEER, JOHN. *Ralph Waldo Emerson: Days of Encounter*. Boston: Little, Brown, 1984.

MCALMON, ROBERT. *Being Geniuses Together 1920–1930*. New York: Doubleday, 1968.

MCCANN, SEAN. *The Wit of the Irish*. London: Frewin, 1968.

MCCARTHY, JOE. *Days and Nights at Costello's*. Boston: Little, Brown, 1980.

MCCLURE, ALEXANDER KELLY. *Lincoln's Own Yarns and Stories*. Chicago, Philadelphia: Winston, 1900.

MACCUNN, J. *Recollections of W. P. Ker by Two Friends*.

MACDONALD, MALCOLM. *Titans and Others*. London: Collins, 1972.

MCMULLEN, ROY. *Degas: His Life, Times, and Work*. Boston: Houghton Mifflin, 1984.

MACNEICE, LOUIS. *The Strings Are False: An Unfinished Biography*, ed. E. R. Dodds. New York: Oxford University Press, 1966.

MCPHEE, NANCY. *The Book of Insults*. New York: St. Martin's, 1978.

MCPHEE, NANCY. *The Second Book of Insults*. New York: Penguin, 1983.

MACROBIUS AMBROSIUS AURELIUS THEODOSIUS. *Saturnalia*.

MADIGAN, CAROL ORSAG, AND ANN ELWOOD. *Brainstorms and Thunderbolts: How Creative Genius Worked*. New York: Macmillan, 1984.

MAHONY, PATRICK. *Barbed Wit and Malicious Humor*. New York: Citadel Press, 1956.

MALTBY, WILLIAM. *Recollections of the Table Talk of Samuel Rogers. To Which is Added Porsoniana*. New York: Appleton, 1856.

MANCHESTER, WILLIAM. *The Last Lion: Winston Spencer Churchill: Visions of Glory: 1874–1932*. Boston: Little, Brown, 1983.

MANCHESTER, WILLIAM. *One Brief Shining Moment: Remembering Kennedy*. Boston: Little, Brown, 1983.

MANNINGHAM, JOHN. *Diary*.

MANSFIELD, IRVING. *Life with Jackie*. New York: Bantam Books, 1983.

MARGOLIUS, HANS. *Der lächelnde Philosoph*. Munich: Bechtle Verlag, 1963.

MARKHAM, FELIX. *The Bonapartes*. New York: Taplinger, 1975.

MARQUARD, RALPH L. *Jokes and Anecdotes for All Occasions*. New York: Hart Publishing, 1977.

MARSH, EDWARD. *A Number of People*. New York: Harper & Bros., 1939.

MARTIN, RALPH. *A Hero for Our Time: An Intimate Story of the Kennedy Years*. New York: Macmillan, 1983.

MARTIN, ROBERT BERNARD. *Tennyson: The Unquiet Heart*. London: Oxford University Press, 1980.

MARX, HARPO. *Harpo Speaks!* New York: Geis Associates, 1961.

MARX, SAMUEL. *Mayer and Thalberg: The Make-Believe Saints*. New York: Random House, 1975.

MARX, SAMUEL, AND JAN CLAYTON. *Rodgers and Hart, Bewitched, Bothered, and Bedeviled;*

An Anecdotal Account. New York: Putnam, 1976.

MASSEY, RAYMOND. *A Hundred Different Lives: An Autobiography.* Boston: Little, Brown, 1979.

MASSIE, ROBERT K. *Peter the Great: His Life and World.* New York: Knopf, 1980.

MASSON, THOMAS L. *The Best Stories in the World.* New York: Doubleday, 1913.

MAUGHAM, W. SOMERSET. *A Writer's Notebook.* New York: Doubleday, Doran, 1949.

MAY, ANTOINETTE. *Different Drummers: They Did What They Wanted.* Millbrae, CA: Les Femmes, 1976.

MAYFIELD, SARA. *The Constant Circle: H. L. Mencken and His Friends.* New York: Dell, 1969.

MEIGS, CORNELIA LYNDE. *Invincible Louisa.* Boston: Little, Brown, 1933.

MELLOW, JAMES R. *Charmed Circle: Gertrude Stein & Company.* New York: Praeger, 1974.

MÉRAS, PHYLLIS. *The Mermaids of Chenonceaux.* New York: Congdon & Weed, 1983.

MERRILL, ROBERT. *Between Acts: An Irreverent Look at Opera and Other Madness.* New York: McGraw-Hill, 1976.

MERWIN, W. S., trans. *Products of the Perfected Civilization: Selected Writings of Chamfort.* New York: Macmillan, 1969.

METROPOLITAN OPERA. Program notes: *The Barber of Seville.* March 1982.

MIGNET, FRANÇOIS. *Notices historiques* 2nd ed., Paris: Paulin, L'Heureux et cie, 1853.

MIKES, GEORGE. *Coffee Houses of Europe.* New York: Thames and Hudson, 1983.

MIKES, GEORGE. *Laughing Matter: Towards a Personal Philosophy of Wit and Humor.* New York: Library Press, 1971.

MILLS, JOHN. *Up in the Clouds, Gentlemen Please.* New Haven: Ticknor & Fields, 1981.

MILNE, ALAN ALEXANDER. *It's Too Late Now: The Autobiography of a Writer.* London: Methuen, 1939.

MILNE, CHRISTOPHER. *The Enchanted Places.* New York: Dutton, 1975.

MISSEN, LESLIE ROBERT. *After-dinner Stories and Anecdotes.* London: Allen & Unwin, 1968.

MISSEN, LESLIE ROBERT. *Quotable Anecdotes.* London: Allen & Unwin, 1966.

MITFORD, NANCY. *Madame de Pompadour.* New York: Harper & Row, 1968.

MITFORD, NANCY. *Voltaire in Love.* New York: Harper & Row, 1957.

MITTERRAND, FRANÇOIS. *The Wheat and the Chaff.* New York: Seaver Books/Lattès, 1982.

MONEGAL, EMIR R., AND ALASTAIR REID. *Borges, A Reader: A Selection from the Writings of Jorge Luis Borges.* New York: Dutton, 1981.

MONTGOMERY-MASSINGBERD, HUGH. *Royal Palaces of Europe.* New York: Vendome, 1983.

MOORE, FRANK. *Anecdotes, Poetry and Incidents of the War: North and South, 1860–1865.* New York: Arundel, 1882.

MOORE, RUTH. *Charles Darwin: A Great Life in Brief.* New York: Knopf, 1973.

MOORE, THOMAS. *Memoir of the Life of the Right Honourable Richard Brinsley Sheridan.* London: Longman, Rees, Orme, Brown and Green, 1825.

MOORE, THOMAS. *Memoirs, Journal, and Correspondence of Thomas Moore,* ed. by the Right Honourable Lord John Russell, MP. Boston: Little, Brown, 1853.

MOOREHEAD, ALAN. *Darwin and The Beagle.* New York: Harper & Row, 1969.

MOORHOUSE, GEOFFREY. *The Diplomats.* Atlantic Highlands, NJ: Humanities, 1977.

MORLEY, ROBERT. *A Musing Morley: The Selected Writings of Robert Morley,* ed. Sheridan Morley. London: Robson Books, 1974.

MORLEY, ROBERT. *Robert Morley's Book of Bricks.* New York: Putnam, 1978.

MORLEY, ROBERT. *A Second Book of Bricks.* London: Weidenfeld & Nicolson, 1981.

MORLEY, ROBERT, AND SEWELL STOKES. *Robert Morley: A Reluctant Autobiography.* New York: Simon & Schuster, 1967.

MORLEY, SHERIDAN. *A Talent to Amuse: A Biography of Noel Coward.* New York: Doubleday, 1969.

MORLEY, SHERIDAN. *Tales from the Hollywood Raj: The British, the Movies, and Tinseltown.* New York: Viking, 1984.

MORTON, BRIAN N. *Americans in Paris.* Ann Arbor, MI: Olivia & Hill, 1984.

MORTON, H. V. *A Traveller in Italy.*

MORRIS, JAMES. *Oxford.* New York: Harcourt, Brace & World, 1965.

MORRIS, JAN. *Destinations.* Oxford: Oxford University Press, 1980.

MORRIS, JAN. *The Oxford Book of Oxford.* Oxford: Oxford University Press, 1979.

MOSS, HOWARD. *Whatever Is Moving.* Boston: Little, Brown, 1981.

MUIR, FRANK. *An Irreverent and Thoroughly Incomplete Social History of Almost Everything.* New York: Stein & Day, 1976.

MURCHIE, GUY. *Music of the Spheres.* Boston: Houghton Mifflin, 1961.

MURRAY, WILLIAM. *Italy: The Fatal Gift.* New York: Dodd, Mead, 1982.

NABOKOV, VLADIMIR. *Strong Opinions.* New York: McGraw-Hill, 1973.

NASH, JAY ROBERT. *The Innovators: 16 Portraits of the Famous and the Infamous.* Chicago: Regnery/Gateway, 1982.

NASH, JAY ROBERT. *Zanies: The World's Greatest Eccentrics.* Piscataway, NJ: New Century, 1982.

NELSON, C. M. *The Fortunate Years.* New York: Vantage, 1983.

NELSON, RANDY F. *The Almanac of American Letters.* Los Altos, CA: William Kaufmann, 1981.

New Columbia Encyclopedia, The, William H. Harris and Judith S. Levey, eds. New York and London: Columbia University Press, 1975.

NICHOLS, BEVERLEY. *The Sweet Twenties.* New York: British Book Centre, 1958.

NICOLSON, HAROLD. *Harold Nicolson: Diaries and Letters.* New York: Atheneum, 1967.

NIKOLAEV, VSEVOLD A., AND ALBERT PARRY. *The Loves of Catherine the Great.* New York: Coward, McCann & Geoghegan, 1982.

NIVEN, DAVID. *Bring on the Empty Horses.* New York: Putnam 1975.

NIXON, RICHARD. *Leaders.* New York: Warner Books, 1981.

NOAKES, VIVIEN. *Edward Lear: The Life of a Wanderer.* Boston: Houghton Mifflin, 1969.

NORTON, LUCY, ed., trans. *Saint-Simon at Versailles.* New York: Harmony Books, 1980.

NOVAK, WILLIAM, AND MOSHE WALDOKS. *Big Book of Jewish Humor.* New York: Harper & Row, 1981.

NOYES, ALFRED. *Two Worlds for Memory.* New York: Sheed & Ward, 1953.

Obituaries from the Times [London], *1951–60, 1961–70, 1971–75.* Frank C. Roberts, comp. Reading, England: Newspaper Archives Developments, Ltd., 1975, 1978, 1979.

O'CONNELL, CHARLES. *The Other Side of the Record.* New York: Knopf, 1947.

O'DONNELL, KENNETH, AND DAVID F. POWERS. *"Johnny, We Hardly Knew Ye."* Boston: Little, Brown, 1972.

ORGEL, JOSEPH R. *Undying Passion.* New York: Morrow, 1985.

OURSLER, FULTON. *Behold This Dreamer.* New York: Macaulay, 1924.

OXFAM. *Pass the Port.* Cirencester, England: Christian Brann, 1976.

Oxford Book of American Literary Anecdotes, ed. Donald A. Hall, New York: Oxford University Press, 1981.

Oxford Book of Literary Anecdotes, ed. John Sutherland. Oxford: Clarendon Press; Oxford University Press, 1975.

Oxford Classical Dictionary, ed. M. Cary et al. Oxford: Clarendon Press, 1940.

Oxford Companion to Classical Literature, ed. Sir Paul Harvey. Oxford: Clarendon Press, 1966.

Oxford Companion to Music, ed. Percy Alfred Scholes. London and New York: Oxford University Press, 1970.

Oxford Dictionary of Quotations. 2nd ed., London and New York: Oxford University Press, 1953.

PAAR, JACK. *P.S. Jack Paar: An Entertainment.* New York: Doubleday, 1982.

PAINE, ALBERT BIGELOW. *The Adventures of Mark Twain.* New York: Harper & Bros., 1916.

PAINE, ALBERT BIGELOW. *Mark Twain: A Biography.* New York: Harper & Bros., 1912.

PAINTER, GEORGE D. *Proust: The Early Years.* Boston: Little, Brown, 1959.

PAINTER, GEORGE D. *Proust: The Later Years.* Boston: Little, Brown, 1959.

PAIS, ABRAHAM. *"Subtle Is the Lord . . .": The Science and Life of Albert Einstein.* Oxford and New York: Oxford University Press, 1982.

PALÉOLOGUE, MAURICE. *The Enigmatic Czar: The Life of Alexander I of Russia,* trans. Edwin and Willa Muir. New York: Harper & Bros., 1938.

PALEY, F. A. *Greek Wit: A Collection of Smart Sayings and Anecdotes.* London: George Bell & Sons, 1881.

PALMER, GEORGE HERBERT. *The Life of Alice Freeman Palmer.* Boston: Houghton Mifflin, 1908.

PAPESCH, JOSEPH FRIEDRICH. *Europa Lächelt Noch Immer.* Graz: Laykam-Verlag, 1952.

PARKINSON, NORMAN. *Fifty Years of Style and Fashion.* New York: Vendome, 1983.

PARMELIN, HÉLÈNE. *Picasso Says,* trans. C. Trollope. South Brunswick, NJ: A. S. Barnes, 1969.

PAYN, GRAHAM, AND SHERIDAN MORLEY. *The Noël Coward Diaries.* Boston: Little, Brown, 1982.

PEARSON, HESKETH. *Johnson and Boswell.* New York: Harper & Row, 1958.

PEARSON, HESKETH. *The Life of Oscar Wilde* (1947). Rpt., Westport, CT: Greenwod, 1978.

PEARSON, HESKETH. *Lives of the Wits.* New York: Harper & Row, 1962.

PEARSON, HESKETH. *The Man Whistler.* New York: Harper & Row, 1952.

PEARSON, HESKETH. *The Smith of Smiths: Being the Life, Wit and Humor of Sydney Smith.* New York: Harper & Row, 1934.

PEARSON, JOHN. *The Serpent and the Stag.* New York: Holt, Rinehart & Winston, 1984.

PEDRAZZINI, MARIE-CHARLOTTE, AND JEANNETTE GRIS. *Autant en apportent les mots.* Paris: Robert Laffont, 1969.

Penguin Dictionary of Quotations, ed. J. M. Cohen and M. J. Cohen. New York: Penguin, 1982.

PENROSE, ROLAND. *Picasso: His Life and Work.* New York: Harper & Row, 1959.

PENROSE, ROLAND. *Roland Penrose Scrapbook.* London: Thames & Hudson, 1981.

PEPYS, SAMUEL. *The Diary of Samuel Pepys,* ed. R. Latham and W. Matthews. London: Bell & Hyman, 1983.

PERCY, SHOLTO, AND REUBEN PERCY. *The Percy Anecdotes: Original and Selected.* New York: W. B. Gilley, 1821.

PERRETT, GEOFFREY. *America in the Twenties: A History.* New York: Simon & Schuster, 1982.

PETERS, MARGOT. *Mrs. Pat: The Life of Mrs. Patrick Campbell.* New York: Knopf, 1984.

PHILLIPS, PETER. *A Brief Chronicale.*

PIJET, GEORG W. *Duell mit der Vergangenheit.* Halle (Saale): Mittel Deutscher Verlag, 1976.

PIPER, DAVID. *Painting in England 1500–1870.* Harmondsworth: Penguin, 1965.

PLATO. *Phaedo,* ed. David Gallop. London: Oxford University Press, 1975.

PLATO. *Theaetetus and Sophist.* trans. Harold North Fowler. New York: Putnam, 1928.

PLEASANTS, HENRY. *The Great American Popular Singers.* New York: Simon & Schuster, 1985.

PLINY (Caius Plinius Caecilius Secundus). *Letters,* trans. William Melmoth, Cambridge, MA: Harvard University Press, 1940.

PLUTARCH. *Plutarch's Lives,* trans. B. Perrin. London: Heinemann, 1914–1926.

POLEY, IRVIN, AND RUTH POLEY. *Friendly Anecdotes.* New York: Harper & Bros., 1950.

POLIZIANO, ANGELO. *Diario odeporico-bibliografico inedito del Poliziano: c memoria del Giovanni Pesenti.* Milan: U. Hoepli, 1916.

PORZELT, PAUL. *The Metropolitan Club of New York.* New York: Rizzoli, 1982.

POSTGATE, RAYMOND. *That Devil Wilkes.* New York: Vanguard, 1929.

POWELL, ANTHONY. *London Walks.* New York: Holt, Rinehart & Winston, 1982.

POWELL, ANTHONY. *The Memoirs of Anthony Powell.* Vol. 3: *Faces in My Time.* New York: Holt, Rinehart & Winston, 1976.

POWELL, ANTHONY. *Memoirs.* Vol. 4: *The Strangers Are All Gone.* New York: Holt, Rinehart & Winston, 1982.

PREMINGER, ERIK LEE. *Gypsy & Me: At Home and on the Road with Gypsy Rose Lee.* Boston: Little, Brown, 1984.

PRESCOTT, ORVILLE. *Princes of the Renaissance.* New York: Random House, 1969.

PREVIN, ANDRÉ, ed. *Orchestra.* New York: Doubleday, 1979.

PRICE, R. G. G. *A History of Punch.* London: Oxford University Press, 1984.

PRIESTLEY, JOSEPH. *Memoirs of Dr. Joseph Priestley to the Year 1795.* Rpt., Bath: Adams & Dart, 1978.

PRIOR, SIR JAMES. *Life of Edmond Malone, Editor of Shakespeare.* London: Smith, Elder, 1860.

PRITCHETT, V. S. *Balzac.* New York: Knopf, 1973.

PRITCHETT, V. S. *The Myth Makers: Literary Essays.* New York: Random House, 1979.

PROCHNOW, HERBERT V. *The Public Speaker's Treasure Chest.* New York: Harper & Bros., 1942.

PROCOPIUS. *Secret History.* Rpt., Ann Arbor, MI: University of Michigan Press, 1961.

PYE, M. *The King over the Water.* New York: Holt, Rinehart & Winston, 1981.

QUENNELL, PETER. *Samuel Johnson: His Friends and Enemies.* New York: American Heritage Press, 1972.

QUENNELL, PETER. *The Sign of the Fish.* New York: Viking Press, 1960.

RACHLIS, EUGENE, AND JOHN E. MARQUESE. *The Landlords.* New York: Random House, 1963.

RADECKI, SIGISMUND VON. *Das ABC des Lachens: Ein Anekdotenbuch zur Unterhaltung und Belehrung.* Hamburg: Rowohlt, 1953.

RAINIE, HARRISON, AND JOHN QUINN. *Growing Up a Kennedy: The Third Wave Comes of Age.* New York: Putnam, 1983.

RAJANEN, AINI. *Of Finnish Ways.* Minneapolis: Dillon, 1981.

RAWSON, HUGH. *A Dictionary of Euphemisms and Other Doubletalk.* New York: Crown Publishers, 1981.

RAYMOND, G. *Memoirs of Robert William Elliston.* New York: B. Blom, 1969.

READ, JOHN. *Humour and Humanism in Chemistry.* London: G. Bell, 1947.

REES, NIGEL. *Quote . . . Unquote.* Boston: Allen & Unwin, 1978.

REIMAN, DONALD H., ed. *Shelley and his Circle,* vols. VII, VIII. Cambridge: Harvard University Press, 1985.

RÉMUSAT, CLAIRE ELIZABETH JEANNE GRAVIER DE VERGENNES, COMTESSE DE, *Mémoires de Madame de Rémusat.* Paris: C. Levy, 1880.

RICHARD, IVOR. *We, the British.* New York: Doubleday, 1983.

RIDLEY, JASPER. *Lord Palmerston.* New York: Dutton, 1971.

RINGO, MIRIAM. *Nobody Said It Better.* Chicago: Rand McNally, 1980.

RIORDAN, WILLIAM L. *Plunkitt of Tammany Hall.* New York: Dutton, 1969.

ROBARDS, TERRY. *The New York Times Book of Wine.* New York: Quadrangle, 1976.

ROBERTS, CECIL. *And So To Bath*. New York: Macmillan, 1940.

ROBERTSON, DAVID. *George Mallory*. London: Faber & Faber, 1969.

RODZINSKI, HALINA. *Our Two Lives*. New York: Scribner, 1976.

ROGERS, SAMUEL. *Table Talk*.

ROLLINS, HYDER E., ed., *The Keats Circle: Letters and Papers 1816–78*. 2nd ed., Cambridge: Harvard University Press, 1965.

ROOSEVELT, THEODORE. *An Autobiography*. New York: Macmillan, 1914.

ROPER, WILLIAM. *The Life of Sir Thomas More*. Rpt., New Haven: Yale University Press, 1962.

ROREM, NED. *The Later Diaries of Ned Rorem*. San Francisco: North Print Press, 1983.

ROSENTHAL-SCHNEIDER, ILSE. *Reality and Scientific Truth: Discussions with Einstein, von Laue and Others*, ed. Thomas Braun. Detroit: Wayne State University Press, 1980.

ROSE, KENNETH. *King George V*. New York: Knopf, 1984.

ROSNER, JOSEPH. *A Hater's Handbook*. New York: Delacorte, 1965.

ROSS, ISHBEL. *Charmers and Cranks*. New York: Harper and Row, 1965.

ROSTEN, LEO. *The Joys of Yiddish*. New York: McGraw-Hill, 1968.

ROSTEN, LEO. *People I Have Loved, Known or Admired*. New York: McGraw-Hill, 1970.

RUBINSTEIN, ARTHUR. *My Many Years*. New York: Knopf, 1980.

RUBINSTEIN, ARTHUR. *My Young Years*. New York: Knopf, 1973.

RUNCIMAN, S. *The Fall of Constantinople*. Cambridge: Cambridge University Press, 1969.

RUSKIN, JOHN. *Deucalion: King of the Golden River and The Eagle's Nest*. Boston: Dana Estes, 1865.

RUSSELL, BERTRAND. *The Autobiography of Bertrand Russell*. Boston: Little, Brown, 1967.

RUSSELL, JOHN. *Paris*. New York: Viking Press, 1960.

RUSSELL, LEONARD. *English Wits*. Port Washington: Kennikat Press [first pub. 1940].

SAARINEN, ALINE B. *The Proud Possessors*. New York: Random House, 1958.

SADIE, STANLEY. *The New Grove Dictionary of Music and Musicians, in 20 Volumes*. Washington, D.C.: Grove's Dictionaries of Music, 1980.

SADLEIR, MICHAEL. *Trollope: A Commentary*. New York: Farrar, Straus, 1947.

SAINT-FOIS [GERMAIN FRANÇOIS POULLAIN]. *Essais sur Paris de Monsieur de Saint-Fois*. Paris: Veuve Duchesne, 1776–1777.

ST. JOHN, ROBERT. *They Came From Everywhere: Twelve Who Helped Mold Modern Israel*. New York: Coward, McCann, 1962.

SALTER, ELIZABETH. *Helomann: The Authorised Biography of Sir Robert Helpmann*. New York: Universe, 1978.

SAMUELS, ERNEST. *The Education of Henry Adams*. Boston: Houghton Mifflin, 1918.

SANDBURG, CARL. *Abraham Lincoln: The War Years*. New York: Harcourt, Brace, 1939.

SANFORD, JOHN. *Winters of That Country*. Santa Barabara, CA: Black Sparrow Press, 1984.

SARGEANT, WINTHROP. *Divas*. New York: Coward, McCann & Geoghegan, 1973.

SAXTON, MARTHA. *Louisa May: A Modern Biography of Louisa May Alcott*. Boston: Houghton Mifflin, 1977.

SCAMMEL, MICHAEL. *Alexander Solzhenitsyn: A Biography*. New York: Norton, 1984.

SCHLESINGER, MARIAN CANNON. *Snatched from Oblivion: A Cambridge Memoir*. Boston: Little, Brown, 1979.

SCHOLZ, WILHELM VON. *Das Buch des Lachens: Schnurren, Schwanke und Anekdoten*. Stuttgart: Verlag Deutsche Volksbücher, 1953.

SCHONBERG, HAROLD C. *The Great Conductors*. New York: Simon & Schuster, 1967.

SCHONBERG, HAROLD C. *The Great Pianists*. New York: Simon & Schuster, 1963.

SCHWARZKOPF, ELISABETH. *On and Off the Record: A Memoir of Walter Legge*. New York: Scribner, 1982.

SCHWED, PETER. *Turning the Pages: An Insider's Story of Simon & Schuster 1924–1984*. New York: Macmillan, 1984.

SCOTT, WALTER. *Lawrence Sterne*.

SCOTT, SIR WALTER. *The Tales of a Grandfather*.

SEAGRAVE, STERLING. *The Soong Dynasty*. New York: Harper & Row, 1984.

SECRIST, MERYLE. *Kenneth Clark: A Biography*. London: Weidenfeld & Nicolson, 1983.

SEELIG, CARL. *Albert Einstein: A Documentary Biography*. London: Staples, 1956.

SEITZ, DON C. *Whistler Stories*. New York: Harper & Brothers, 1913.

SELIGMAN, VINCENT. *Puccini Among Friends*. New York: Macmillan, 1938.

SEWARD, WILLIAM. *Anecdotes of Distinguished Persons, Chiefly of the Last and Two Preceding Centuries*. 5th ed., London: T. Cadell and W. Davies, 1804.

SEWARD, WILLIAM, *Biographiana*. New York: Garland, 1970.

SEYMOUR SMITH, FRANK. *A Treasury of Wit & Wisdom*. London: J. Baker, 1966.

SEYMOUR-SMITH, MARTIN. *Robert Graves: His Life and Work*. New York: Holt, Rinehart & Winston, 1983.

SHADEGG, STEPHEN. *Clare Boothe Luce: A Biog-*

raphy. New York: Simon & Schuster, 1970.

SHAW, GEORGE BERNARD. *Collected Letters*. New York: Dodd, Mead, 1965.

SHEED, WILFRID. *Clare Boothe Luce*. New York: Dutton, 1982.

SHENKMAN, RICHARD, AND KURT REIGER. *One-Night Stands with American History*. New York: Morrow, 1980.

SHRINER, CHARLES A. *Wit, Wisdom, and Foibles of the Great*. New York: Funk & Wagnalls, 1918.

SIDEY, HUGH. *John F. Kennedy, President*. New York: Atheneum, 1963.

SIEVERS, H. *Musica Curiosa*. 2nd ed., Tutzing, Germany: Hans Schneider, 1971.

SIFAKIS, CARL. *Dictionary of Historic Nicknames*. New York: Facts on File, 1984.

SILITCH, CLARISSA M., ed. *Mad and Magnificent Yankees*. Dublin, NH: Yankee, Inc., 1973.

SILVERMAN, AL. "The Fragile Pleasure," *Daedalus*.

SIMPSON, EILEEN. *Poets in Their Youth: A Memoir*. New York: Random House, 1982.

SINCLAIR, ANDREW. *Dylan Thomas: No Man More Magical*. New York: Holt, Rinehart & Winston, 1975.

SITWELL, DAME EDITH. *English Eccentrics*. New York: Vanguard Press, 1957.

SITWELL, DAME EDITH. *Taken Care of*. New York: Atheneum, 1965.

SITWELL, OSBERT. *Laughter in the Next Room*. Boston: Little, Brown, 1948.

SITWELL, OSBERT. *Noble Essences*. Boston: Little, Brown, 1950.

SITWELL, OSBERT. *Tales My Father Taught Me*. Boston: Little, Brown, 1962.

SITWELL, SACHEVERELL. *Liszt*. Boston: Houghton Mifflin, 1934.

SKELTON, JOHN. *John Skelton: The Complete English Poems*, ed. John Scattergood. New Haven: Yale University Press, 1983.

SKELTON, JOHN. *Poems of John Skelton*. Oxford: Clarendon Press, 1969.

SKINNER, CORNELIA OTIS. *Elegant Wits and Grand Horizontals*. Boston: Houghton Mifflin, 1962.

SLONIMSKY, NICHOLAS. *Lexicon of Musical Invective*. New York: Coleman-Ross, 1953.

SLONIMSKY, NICHOLAS. *A Thing or Two about Music*. New York: Allen, Towne & Heath, 1948.

SMAIL, J. L. *With Shield and Assegai*. Cape Town: H. Timmins, 1969.

SMITH, CHARD POWERS. *Where the Light Falls*. New York: Macmillan, 1965.

SMITH, H. ALLEN. *The Life and Legend of Gene Fowler*. New York: Morrow, 1977.

SMITH, JANE S. *Elsie de Wolfe: A Life in the High Style*. New York: Atheneum, 1982.

SMITH, LOGAN PEARSALL. *Unforgotten Years*. Bos-

ton: Little, Brown, 1939.

SMITH, PAGE. *America Enters the World*. New York: McGraw-Hill, 1984.

SMITH, PAGE. *The Nation Comes of Age: A People's History of the Ante-Bellum Years*. New York: McGraw-Hill, 1981.

SMITH, PAGE. *A New Age Now Begins: A People's History of the American Revolution*. New York: McGraw-Hill, 1976.

SMITH, PAGE. *The Rise of Industrial America: A People's History of the Post-Reconstruction Era*. New York: McGraw-Hill, 1984.

SMITH, PAGE. *The Shaping of America: A People's History of the Young Republic*. New York: McGraw-Hill, 1980.

SMITH, PAGE. *Trial by Fire: A People's History of the Civil War and Reconstruction*. New York: McGraw-Hill, 1982.

SMITH, RED. *To Absent Friends from Red Smith*. New York: Atheneum, 1982.

SMITH, RICHARD NORTON. *Thomas E. Dewey and His Times*. New York: Simon & Schuster, 1982.

SMITH, SYDNEY. *A Memoir of the Rev. Sydney Smith by His Daughter, Lady Holland*. New York: Harper, 1855.

SMITH, SIR WILLIAM. *Everyman's Smaller Classical Dictionary*, rev. E. H. Blakeney and J. Warrington. New York: Dutton, 1952.

SMULLYAN, RAYMOND. *5000 B.C. and Other Philosophical Fantasies*. New York: St. Martin's, 1983.

SNEAD, SAM, AND AL STUMP. *The Education of a Golfer*. New York: Simon & Schuster, 1962.

SNOW, CHARLES PERCY. *Variety of Men*. New York: Scribner, 1967.

SOLBERG, CARL. *Hubert Humphrey: A Biography*. New York: Norton, 1984.

SOUTHEY, ROBERT. *Life of Nelson*. New York: Eastburn, Kirk; Boston: William Wells, 1813. Rpt., New York: Dutton, 1962.

SPENCE, JOSEPH. *Anecdotes, Observations and Characters of Books and Men*. London: W. H. Carpenter, 1820. Rpt., Carbondale, IL: Southern Illinois University Press, 1964.

SPENDER, STEPHEN. *World Within World: The Autobiography of Stephen Spender*. Berkeley, CA: University of California Press, 1966.

SPERONI, CHARLES. *Wit and Wisdom of the Italian Renaissance*. Berkeley, CA: University of California Press, 1964.

SPOTO, DONALD. *The Dark Side of Genius: The Life of Alfred Hitchcock*. Boston: Little, Brown, 1983.

SPOTO, DONALD. *The Kindness of Strangers: The Biography of Tennessee Williams*. Boston: Little, Brown, 1985.

STANLEY, HENRY MORTON. *How I Found Livingstone*. New York: Scribner, 1872.

STEEGMULLER, FRANCIS. *Cocteau.* Boston: Atlantic–Little, Brown, 1970.

STEIN, JEAN, WITH GEORGE PLIMPTON. *Edie: An American Biography.* New York: Knopf, 1982.

STEINBERG, ALFRED. *The Man from Missouri.* New York: Putnam, 1962.

STEINBERT, HILTRUD. *Arzt und Patient.*

STEINEM, GLORIA. *Outrageous Acts and Everyday Rebellions.* New York: Holt, Rinehart & Winston, 1983.

STEVENS, STEWART. *The Poles.* New York: Macmillan, 1982.

STINNETT, CASKIE. "Travels with Marc," *Signature,* December 1981.

STOCK, NOEL. *The Life of Ezra Pound.* New York: Pantheon Books, 1970.

STOCKDALE, PERCIVAL. *Memoirs of the Life and Writings of Percival Stockdale.* London: Longman, Hurst, Rees & Orme, 1809.

STONE, IRVING. *They Also Ran.* New York: Doubleday, 1966.

STRAUS, DOROTHEA. *Under the Canopy.* New York: G. Braziller, 1982.

STRAUSS, DAVID, AND FRED WORTH. *Hollywood Trivia.* New York: Warner, 1981.

STRAUSS, MAURICE B. *Familiar Medical Quotations.* Boston: Little, Brown, 1968.

STRONG, THERON G. *Joseph H. Choate.* New York: Dodd, Mead, 1917.

SUETONIUS (GAIUS SUETONIUS TRANQUILLUS). *The Twelve Caesars,* trans. Robert Graves. Baltimore: Penguin, 1957.

SYBEN, FRIEDRICH. *Preussische Anekdoten: nach Memoiren und Biographien erzählt.* Berlin: Bernard & Graefe, 1939.

SYLVESTER, ALBERT J. *Life with Lloyd George: The Diary of A. J. Sylvester,* ed. Colin Cross. London: Macmillan, 1975.

SYLVESTER, ROBERT. *Notes of a Guilty Bystander.* Englewood Cliffs, NJ: Prentice Hall, 1970.

TACITUS, GAIUS CORNELIUS. *Annals,* ed. C. D. Fisher. London: Oxford University Press, 1906.

TALESE, GAY. *Fame and Obscurity.* New York: World Publishing, 1970.

TAPER, BERNARD. *Balanchine: A Biography.* New York: Times Books, 1984.

TARBELL, IDA M. *The Life of Abraham Lincoln.* New York: Doubleday & McClure, 1900.

TATE, ALLEN, ed. *T. S. Eliot, The Man and His Work: A Critical Evaluation by Twenty-Six Distinguished Writers.* New York: Delacorte Press, 1966.

TAUBMAN, HOWARD. *The Maestro: The Life of Arturo Toscanini.* New York: Simon & Schuster, 1951.

TAUBMAN, HOWARD. *Music on My Beat.* New York: Simon & Schuster, 1943.

TAYLOR, ALAN JOHN PERCIVALE. *Bismarck: The Man and the Statesman.* New York: Vintage Books, 1967.

TAYLOR, ALAN JOHN PERCIVALE. *English History: 1914–1945,* Oxford History of England, Vol. 15. New York: Oxford University Press, 1965.

TAYLOR, BAYARD. *Critical Essays and Literary Notes.* New York: Putnam, 1880.

TAYLOR, GORDON RATTRAY. *The Great Evolution Mystery.* New York: Harper & Row, 1983.

TEBBEL, JOHN. *The Inheritors: A Study of America's Great Fortunes and What Happened to Them.* New York: Putnam, 1962.

TEICHMANN, HOWARD. *Smart Aleck: The Wit, World, and Life of Alexander Woollcott.* New York: Morrow, 1976.

TEMIANKA, HENRI. *Facing the Music: An Irreverent Close-Up of the Real Concert World.* New York: D. McKay, 1973.

TERKEL, STUDS. *"The Good War": An Oral History of World War Two.* New York: Pantheon, 1984.

THARP, LOUISE HALL. *Mrs. Jack.* Boston: Little, Brown, 1965.

THARP, LOUISE HALL. *The Peabody Sisters of Salem.* Boston: Little, Brown, 1950.

THOMAS, BOB. *King Cohn: The Life and Times of Harry Cohn.* New York: Putnam, 1967.

THOMAS, BOB. *Thalberg: Life and Legend.* New York: Doubleday, 1969.

THOMAS, HENRY, AND DANA LEE THOMAS. *Living Adventures in Science.* Garden City, NY: Hanover House, 1954.

THOMAS, HENRY, AND DANA LEE THOMAS. *Living Biographies of Famous Rulers.* Garden City, NY: Garden City Publishing, 1940.

THOMAS, HENRY, AND DANA LEE THOMAS. *Living Biographies of Famous Women.* Garden City, NY: Garden City Publishing, 1942.

THOMAS, HENRY, AND DANA LEE THOMAS. *Living Biographies of Religious Leaders.* Garden City, NY: Garden City Publishing, 1942.

THOMAS, HENRY, AND DANA LEE THOMAS. *Living Biographies of the Great Philosophers.* Garden City, NY: Garden City Publishing, 1941.

THOMAS, LEWIS. *Late Night Thoughts on Listening to Mahler's Ninth Symphony.* New York: Bantam, 1983.

THOMPSON, CHARLES. *Bing: The Authorized Biography.* New York: McKay, 1975, 1976.

THOMPSON, VERITA, AND DONALD SHEPHERD. *Bogie and Me.* Los Angeles: Pinnacle, 1984.

THOMSON, SIR BASIL. *The Scene Changes.* New York: Doubleday, Doran, 1937.

THOMSON, VIRGIL. *A Virgil Thomson Reader.* Boston: Houghton Mifflin, 1981.

THOREAU, HENRY DAVID. *The Journal of Henry D. Thoreau,* ed. Bradford Torrey and Francis H. Allen. Boston: Houghton Mifflin, 1906.

THURBER, HELEN, AND EDWARD WEEKS, eds. *Selected Letters of James Thurber.* Boston: Atlantic–Little, Brown, 1981.

THURBER, JAMES. *The Years with Ross.* Boston: Atlantic–Little, Brown, 1959.

THWAITE, ANN. *Waiting for the Party: The Life of Frances Hodgson Burnett, 1849–1924.* New York: Scribner's, 1974.

TICKNOR, C. *Dr. Holmes's Boston.* Boston: Houghton Mifflin, 1915.

TIMBS, J. *Century of Anecdote from 1760 to 1860.* London; R. Bentley, 1864.

TIMBS, J. *English Eccentrics and Eccentricities.* London: Chatto & Windus, 1890. Rpt., Detroit: Singing Tree Press, 1969.

TOMKINS, CALVIN. *Living Well Is the Best Revenge.* New York: Dutton, 1982.

TOMKINS, CALVIN. *Merchants and Masterpieces: The Story of the Metropolitan Museum of Art.* New York: Dutton, 1970.

TOYNBEE, ARNOLD. *Acquaintances.* London: Oxford University Press. 1967.

TRAIN, JOHN. *True Remarkable Occurrences.* New York: C. N. Potter, 1978.

TRELAWNY, E. J. *Recollections of the Last Days of Shelley and Byron.* Boston: Ticknor & Fields, 1858.

TREVELYAN, G. M. *Trinity College.* London: Cambridge University Press, 1943.

TREVELYAN, G. O. *The Life and Letters of Lord Macaulay.* Rpt., London: Oxford University Press, 1961.

TRILLING, LIONEL. *Matthew Arnold.* New York: Norton, 1939.

TROLLOPE, ANTHONY. *Autobiography,* ed. Michael Sadleir and Frederick Page. London: Oxford University Press, 1980.

TUCHMAN, BARBARA. *The Guns of August.* New York: Macmillan, 1962.

TUCHMAN, BARBARA. *The March of Folly.* New York: Knopf, 1984.

TUGGLE, ROBERT. *The Golden Age of Opera.* New York: Holt, Rinehart & Winston, 1983.

TULLY, GRACE. *F.D.R., My Boss.* New York: Scribner, 1949.

TUNG, ROSEMARY J. *A Portrait of Lost Tibet.* New York: Holt, Rinehart & Winston, 1980.

TYNAN, KENNETH. *Show People.* New York: Simon & Schuster, 1979.

TYNAN, KENNETH. *Tynan on Theatre.* Harmondsworth, England: Penguin, 1964.

TYNDALL, JOHN. *New Fragments.* New York: Appleton, 1892.

UECKER, BOB, AND MICKEY HERSKOWITZ. *Catcher in the Wry.* New York: Putnam, 1982.

UKERS, WILLIAM HARRISON. *All About Coffee.* New York: The Tea and Coffee Trade Journal Co., 1922.

UNTERMEYER, LOUIS. *Bygones: The Recollections of Louis Untermeyer.* New York: Harcourt, Brace & World, 1965.

UNTERMEYER, LOUIS. *A Treasury of Laughter.* New York: Simon & Schuster, 1946.

VALERANI, RICHARD. *Travels with Henry.* Boston: Houghton Mifflin, 1979.

VALERIUS MAXIMUS. *Facta et dicta memorabilia.*

VAN DE VELDE, ERNEST. *Anecdotes Musicales.* Tours, France: Editions van de Velde, 1926.

VANDYKE PRICE, PAMELA. *The Penguin Book of Spirits and Liqueurs.* New York: Penguin, 1980.

VARAH, CHAD. *Samaritans in the 70s: To Befriend the Suicidal and Despairing.* London: Constable, [1980].

VASARI, G. *Lives of the Painters,* trans. A. B. Hinds. London: J. H. Dart, 1983.

VAUGHAN-THOMAS, WYNFORD. *Madly in All Directions.* London: Longmans, 1967.

VICKERS, HUGH. *Great Operatic Disasters.* New York: St. Martins, 1979.

VIDAL, GORE. *Lincoln.* New York: Random House, 1984.

VINCENT, BENJAMIN, ed. *Haydn's Dictionary of Dates.* New York: Harper, 1870.

VOLLARD, AMBROISE. *Recollections of a Picture Dealer,* trans. Violet MacDonald. Boston: Little, Brown, 1936.

WADE, VIRGINIA. *Courting Triumph.* New York: Mayflower, 1978.

WAGENKNECHT, EDWARD. *American Profile, 1900–1909.* Amherst, MA: University of Massachusetts Press, 1982.

WAGNER, G., trans. *Selected Writings of Gérard de Nerval.* London: Panther, 1968.

WALKER, STELLA A. *Horses of Renown.* London: Country Life, 1954.

WALLACE, AMY, DAVID WALLECHINSKY, AND IRVING WALLACE. *The People's Almanac Presents the Book of Lists 3.* New York: Morrow, 1983.

WALLACE, IRVING. *The Fabulous Originals: Lives of Extraordinary People Who Inspired Memorable Characters in Fiction.* New York: Knopf, 1955.

WALLACE IRVING. *The Fabulous Showman: The Life and Times of P. T. Barnum.* New York: Knopf, 1959.

WALLACE, IRVING. *The Nympho & Other Maniacs.* New York: Simon & Schuster, 1971.

WALLACE, IRVING. *The Square Pegs: Some Americans Who Dared to Be Different.* New York: Knopf, 1957.

WALLACE, IRVING, DAVID WALLECHINSKY, AND AMY WALLACE. *Significa*. New York: Dutton, 1983.

WALLACE, IRVING, DAVID WALLECHINSKY, AMY WALLACE, AND SYLVIA WALLACE. *Intimate Sex Lives of Famous People*. New York: Delacorte, 1981.

WALLACE, IRVING, DAVID WALLECHINSKY, AMY WALLACE, AND SYLVIA WALLACE. *The People's Almanac Presents the Book of Lists 2*. New York: Morrow, 1980.

WALLACE, MIKE, AND GARY GATES. *Close Encounters*. New York: Morrow, 1984.

WALLECHINSKY, DAVID. *The Complete Book of the Olympics*. Harmondsworth, England, and New York: Penguin, 1984.

WALLECHINSKY, DAVID, AND IRVING WALLACE. *The People's Almanac*. New York: Doubleday, 1975.

WALLECHINSKY, DAVID, AND IRVING WALLACE. *The People's Almanac 2*. New York: Morrow, 1978.

WALLECHINSKY, DAVID, AND IRVING WALLACE. *The People's Almanac 3*. New York: Morrow, 1981.

WALLECHINSKY, DAVID, IRVING WALLACE, AND AMY WALLACE. *The People's Almanac Presents the Book of Lists*. New York: Morrow, 1977.

WALPOLE, HORACE. *Anecdotes of Painting*. Rpt., New York: Arno Press, 1969.

WALSH, WILLIAM S. *Handy Book of Curious Information*. Philadelphia: Lippincott, 1913.

WALTERS, BARBARA. *How to Talk with Practically Anybody about Practically Anything*. New York: Doubleday, 1970.

WATERLOW, SYDNEY. *In Praise of Cambridge: An Anthology in Prose and Verse*. London: Constable, 1912.

WAUGH, EVELYN. *The Life of the Right Reverend Ronald Knox*. London: Collins, 1962.

WECHSBERG, JOSEPH. *Red Plush and Black Velvet: The Story of Melba and Her Times*. Boston: Little, Brown, 1961.

WECTER, DIXON. *The Hero in America: A Chronicle of Hero-Worship*. New York: Scribner Sons, 1941.

WEEMS, M. L. *Life of Washington*. Marcus Cunliffe, ed. Cambridge, Mass.: Harvard University Press, 1962.

WEINTRAUB, STANLEY. *The London Yankees: Portrait of American Writers and Artists in England, 1894–1919*. New York: Harcourt Brace Jovanovich, 1979.

WEISKOPF, FRANZ CARL. *Gesammelte Werke*. Berlin: Dietz, 1960.

WELD, C. R. *A History of the Royal Society*. New York: Arno Press, 1848.

WELLS, G. P. *H. G. Wells in Love: Postscript to an Experiment in Autobiography*. Boston: Little, Brown, 1984.

WELLS, H. G. *Experiment in Autobiography: Discoveries and Conclusions of a Very Ordinary Brain*. New York: Macmillan, 1934.

WESCHER, PAUL. *Schweitzer Künstler-Anekdoten aus zwei Jahrhunderten*. Berlin: Holbein, 1942.

WEST, GEOFFREY. *H. G. Wells: A Sketch for a Portrait*. Folcroft, PA: Folcroft Library Editions, 1972.

WHARTON, EDITH. *A Backward Glance*. New York: Appleton-Century, 1934.

WHARTON, EDITH. *Ethan Frome*. New York: Limited Editions Club, 1939.

WHISTLER, JAMES MCNEILL. *On the Gentle Art of Making Enemies*. New York: Putnam, 1890.

WHITE, THEODORE. *America in Search of Itself: The Making of a President 1956–1980*. New York: Harper & Row, 1982.

WHITMAN, ALDEN. *Come to Judgment*. New York: Viking, 1980.

WHITROW, G. J. *Einstein: The Man and His Achievement*. New York: Dover, 1973.

WILLIAMS, JONATHAN. *The Magpie's Bagpipe: Selected Essays of Jonathan Williams*. San Francisco: North Point Press, 1982.

WILLIAMSON, JAMES ALEXANDER. *The English Channel*. London: Collins, 1959.

WILSON, A. N. *Hilaire Belloc*. New York: Atheneum, 1984.

WILSON, EARL. *Hot Times: True Tales of Hollywood and Broadway*. Chicago: Contemporary Books, 1984.

WILSON, EARL. *I Am Gazing into My 8-Ball*. New York: Doubleday, Doran, 1945.

WILSON, EDITH BOLLING GALT. *My Memoir*. Rpt., New York: Arno, 1980.

WILTSE, CHARLES, AND HAROLD D. MOSER, eds. *The Papers of Daniel Webster: Correspondence*, vol. 2. Hanover, NH: University Press of New England, 1976.

WINCHESTER, SIMON. *Their Noble Lordships: The Hereditary Peerage Today*. Boston: Faber & Faber, 1978.

WINSTANLEY, WILLIAM. *England's Worthies*. London: University Microfilms International, 1983.

WINTER, WILLIAM. *Other Days: Being Chronicles and Memories of the Stage*. New York: Moffat, Yard, 1908.

WINTLE, JUSTIN, AND EMMA FISHER. *The Pied Pipers: Interviews with the Influential Creators of Children's Literature*. New York: Paddington Press, 1975.

WINWAR, FRANCES. *The Immortal Lovers: Elizabeth Barrett and Robert Browning*. New York: Harper, 1950.

WISER, WILLIAM. *The Crazy Years: Paris in the Twenties*. New York: Atheneum, 1983.

WOLF, I. J. *Aphorisms and Facetiae of Bela Schick*.

Baltimore: Waverly Press, 1965.

WOOD, ANTHONY À. *Athenae Oxonienses, with Fasti Oxonienses.* Rpt., London: Lackington, Allen, 1976.

WOOD, TOM. *The Bright Side of Billy Wilder, Primarily.* New York: Doubleday, 1969.

WOODHAM-SMITH, CECIL. *The Reason Why.* New York: McGraw-Hill, 1954

WOODWARD, LLEWELLYN. *The Age of Reform.* 2nd ed., Oxford: Clarendon Press, 1962.

WORTH, F. L. *Complete Unabridged Super Trivia Encyclopedia.* Los Angeles: Brook House, 1979.

WORTHINGTON, MARJORIE. *Miss Alcott of Concord: A Biography.* New York: Doubleday, 1958.

WRIGHT, HELEN, AND SAMUEL RAPPORT. *The Great Explorers.* New York: Harper's, 1957.

WYDAN, PETER. *Day One; Before Hiroshima & After.* New York: Simon and Schuster, 1984.

YARDLEY, JONATHAN. *Ring: A Biography of Ring Lardner.* New York: Random House, 1977.

YEATS, W. B. *Autobiographies.* London: Macmillan, 1955.

YEATS, W. B. *Letters,* ed. Allan Wade. New York: Macmillan, 1955.

YEATS, W. B., ed. *The Oxford Book of Modern Verse.* Oxford: Clarendon Press, 1936.

YOUNG, GAVIN. *Halfway Around the World: An Improbable Journey.* New York: Random House, 1981.

YOUNG, G. M. *Victorian England.* New York: Oxford University Press, 1953.

YOUNG, LOUISE B. *The Blue Planet.* Boston: Little, Brown, 1983.

ZALL, P.M., ed. *Abe Lincoln Laughing: Humorous Anecdotes from Original Sources by and about Abraham Lincoln.* Berkeley, CA: University of California Press, 1982.

ZALL, P.M. *Ben Franklin Laughing.* Los Angeles: University of California Press, 1980.

ZAMOYSKI, ADAM. *Paderewski.* New York: Atheneum, 1982.

ZIEGLER, HANS SEVERUS. *Heitere Muse: Anekdoten aus Kultur und Geschichte.* Munich: Türmer-Verlag, 1974.

ZIEGLER, PHILIP. *Diana Cooper: A Biography.* New York: Knopf, 1981.

ZIEGLER, PHILIP. *Mountbatten: A Biography.* New York: Knopf, 1985.

ZIEROLD, NORMAN. *Moguls.* New York: Coward, McCann, 1969.

PERIODICALS, RADIO PROGRAMS, AND TELEVISION SHOWS

The American Scholar
The Atlantic Monthly
BBC Radio
Bookman
Book-of-the-Month Club News
The Boston Globe
The Boston Globe Magazine
The Century Magazine
The Chicago Sun-Times
Colliers
Connoisseur
Columbian Centinel
Congressional Quarterly
Country Life
Daedalus
Daily Telegraph
Edinburgh Journal
Fortnightly Review
Fort Worth Star Telegram
'47, The Magazine of the Year
'48, The Magazine of the Year
Harper's Magazine
Holiday
International Herald Tribune
The Johnny Carson Show
Ladies Literary Cabinet
Life
Lippincott's Magazine
The Los Angeles Times

The Los Angeles Times Book Review
McClure's Magazine
New Criterion
The New Republic
New Scientist
New York Daily Tribune
The New Yorker
The New York Review of Books
The New York Times Book Review
North American Review
The Observer
Outlook
Parade
People
Publishers Weekly
Quarterly Review
Reader's Digest
Santa Barbara News Press
The Saturday Evening Post
Signature
"Significa"
Sports Illustrated
The Sunday Telegraph
The Sunday Times (London)
Time
The Times (London)
The Times Literary Supplement
Truth
Verbatim

❧ INDEX OF NAMES ❧

This index lists the name of every person appearing in the book (except for those in the boxed anecdotes). Boldface indicates those persons who have biographies and anecdotes of their own. These people may be mentioned as well in other persons' anecdotes, as indicated by any indented names. Persons whose names are set in lightface type appear only in other persons' anecdotes or biographies (denoted as *bio*). Numbers are those of anecdotes, not pages. Thus:

Albert, Prince
 Coward 5
 Disraeli 16
 Victoria *bio*, 5–7, 9

means that Prince Albert has anecdotes and a biography of his own, and is mentioned in anecdote 5 for Noël Coward, anecdote 16 for Benjamin Disraeli, and the biography and anecdotes 5–7 and 9 for Queen Victoria.

᪥ INDEX OF SUBJECTS ᪥

The publisher is grateful to the following publishers and individuals for permission to quote from material as noted.

Richard Boehm Literary Agency for excerpts from *5000 Nights at the Opera* by Sir Rudolf Bing.

Christian Brann Limited for excerpts from *Pass the Port* compiled by Oxfam (distributed in the United States by Sterling Publishers under the title *After-Dinner Laughter*). Reprinted by permission.

Cass Canfield, Sr., for excerpts from his book *Up and Down and Around: A Publisher Recollects the Times of His Life*.

Don Congdon Associates, Inc., for excerpts from *Fun While It Lasted* by Barnaby Conrad. Copyright © 1967 by Barnaby Conrad. Reprinted by permission.

Dodd, Mead & Company, Inc., for excerpts from *Joseph H. Choate* by Theron Strong.

Doubleday & Company, Inc., for excerpts from *P.S. Jack Paar: An Entertainment* by Jack Paar. Copyright © 1983 by Jack Paar. Reprinted by permission.

Doubleday & Company, Inc., for excerpts from *The Bright Side of Billy Wilder, Primarily* by Tom Wood. Copyright © 1969 by Tom Wood. Reprinted by permission.

Farrar, Straus and Giroux, Inc., for excerpts adapted by permission of the publisher from *Encounters with Stravinsky* by Paul Horgan. Copyright © 1972 by Paul Horgan.

Hamish Hamilton Ltd. for excerpts from *A Number of People* by Sir Edward Marsh. Reprinted by permission.

Holt, Rinehart and Winston for excerpts from *The Remarkable Mr. Jerome* by Anita Leslie. Copyright 1954 by Henry Holt and Company, Inc. Reprinted by permission.

David Higham Associates Limited for excerpts from *Noble Essences* by Osbert Sitwell, copyright 1950 by Sir Osbert Sitwell; and for excerpts from *Tales My Father Taught Me* by Osbert Sitwell, copyright © 1962 by Osbert Sitwell. Reprinted by permission.

Alfred A. Knopf, Inc., for excerpts from *Peace in Their Time: Men Who Led Us In and Out of War, 1914–1945* by Emery Kelen, copyright © 1963 by Emery Kelen. Also for excerpts from *Diana Cooper: A Biography* by Philip Ziegler, copyright © 1981 by Philip Ziegler. Both excerpts are reprinted by permission.

Robert Merrill for excerpts from his book *Between Acts: An Irreverent Look at Opera and Other Madness*.

William Morrow & Company, Inc., and Howard Miles Teichmann for excerpts from *Smart Aleck: The Wit, World, and Life of Alexander Woollcott* by Howard Teichmann, copyright © 1976 by Howard Teichmann and Evelyn Teichmann. Reprinted by permission.

Oxford University Press for excerpts from *James Joyce, New and Revised Edition* by Richard Ellmann, copyright © 1959, 1982 by Richard Ellmann. Reprinted by permission.

Putnam Publishing Group and International Creative Management for excerpts from *Eppie: The Story of Ann Landers* by Margo Howard, copyright © 1982 by Margo Howard. Reprinted by permission.

Putnam Publishing Group and the Estate of Oscar Levant for excerpts from *The Unimportance of Being Oscar* by Oscar Levant, copyright © 1968 by Oscar Levant. Reprinted by permission.

Putnam Publishing Group and Weidenfeld & Nicolson Limited for excerpts from *Robert Morley's Book of Bricks* by Robert Morley, copyright © 1978 by Robert Morley and Weidenfeld and Nicolson. Reprinted by permission.

Putnam Publishing Group and John Farquharson Ltd. for excerpts from *Bring on the Empty Horses* by David Niven, copyright © 1975 by David Niven. Reprinted by permission.

Random House, Inc., and Weidenfeld & Nicolson Limited for excerpts from *Self-Portrait With Friends: The Selected Diaries of Cecil Beaton, 1926–1974*, edited by Richard Buckle copyright © 1979 by Richard Buckle. Reprinted by permission of Times Books, a division of Random House, Inc., and Weidenfeld & Nicolson Limited.

Random House, Inc., for excerpts from *Charmed Lives: A Family Romance* by Michael Korda, copyright © 1979 by Success Research Corporation. Reprinted by permission.

Robson Books Ltd. for excerpts from *Beecham Stories: Anecdotes, Sayings and Impressions of Sir Thomas Beecham*, edited by Harold Atkins and Archie Newman.

Patrick Searle for excerpts from *Life With Lloyd George: The Diary of A. J. Sylvester*, edited by Colin Cross.

Simon & Schuster, Inc., for excerpts from *Music on My Beat* by Howard Taubman, copyright © 1943 by Howard Taubman, renewed © 1970 by Howard Taubman. Reprinted by permission.

Mrs. Helen Thurber for excerpts from *The Years With Ross* by James Thurber.

Viking Penguin, Inc., and Penguin Books Ltd. for excerpts from *Come to Judgment* by Alden Whitman, copyright © 1980 by Alden Whitman. Reprinted by permission.

Weidenfeld & Nicolson Limited for excerpts from *Memories 1898–1939* by C. M. Bowra. Reprinted by permission.